A
CATHOLIC DICTIONARY
OF
THEOLOGY

Volume One

Abandonment — Casuistry

A
CATHOLIC DICTIONARY
OF
THEOLOGY

A WORK PROJECTED WITH THE APPROVAL OF THE CATHOLIC HIERARCHY

OF ENGLAND AND WALES

Volume One

Abandonment — Casuistry

THOMAS NELSON AND SONS LTD

LONDON   EDINBURGH   PARIS   MELBOURNE   JOHANNESBURG   TORONTO AND NEW YORK

THOMAS NELSON AND SONS LTD
Parkside Works Edinburgh 9
36 Park Street London W1
117 Latrobe Street Melbourne C1

302-304 Barclays Bank Building
Commissioner and Kruis Streets
Johannesburg

THOMAS NELSON AND SONS (CANADA) LTD
91-93 Wellington Street West Toronto 1

THOMAS NELSON AND SONS
18 East 41st Street New York 17, N.Y.

SOCIÉTÉ FRANÇAISE D'ÉDITIONS NELSON
97 rue Monge Paris 5

———

Nihil obstat:

AIDANUS WILLIAMS, ABBAS O.S.B., S.T.D.
JOSEPH HUGO CREHAN, S.J.
HENRICUS FRANCISCUS DAVIS, D.D.
IVO THOMAS, O.P., S.T.M.
Censores Deputati

Imprimatur:

E. MORROGH BERNARD
Vic. Gen.
Westmonasterii, die 14 Octobris 1961

Printed in Great Britain by
Thomas Nelson and Sons Ltd, Edinburgh

Editorial Board

Foreword

Those who are familiar with *A Catholic Commentary on Holy Scripture*, published in 1953, and who have appreciated its contribution to scholarship, will welcome this companion work : *A Catholic Dictionary of Theology*.

With the approach of the Second Vatican Council interest in theological questions will no doubt grow considerably. An up-to-date authoritative statement of Catholic faith and morals should help to dissipate doubts and misinterpretations in these days when brilliant material scientific achievement may have somewhat obscured the things of the spirit.

It is now over fifty years since the *Catholic Encyclopedia* was published (1907–14). New needs have arisen, and the Editors of this Dictionary have worked for several years to meet them. The English language is very widely used and it is confidently hoped that the *Catholic Dictionary of Theology* will attract readers in many lands. We hope and pray that this may be so, and that the painstaking work of the Editors and Contributors may be blessed and rewarded by leading the readers to the knowledge of the faith professed by many millions of Christians.

We congratulate all who have had part in the production of this volume, and our heartfelt blessing goes out to them all. We warmly commend this important work.

✠ William Cardinal Godfrey
Archbishop of Westminster

Editors' Preface

The growing interest of the English-speaking world in Catholic theology is a sign of the times. A century ago Cardinal Newman remarked upon the spread of the English language throughout the world (and now some 250,000,000 use it as their first language), but not even his wildest dreams would have made him aware of the present-day demand for the accurate presentation of Catholic theological ideas that has followed upon this expansion. The great success of the *Catholic Commentary on Holy Scripture* encouraged the present Editors to undertake a companion work on Catholic doctrine which they plan to complete in four volumes. The present volume may not seem to take them far on their way, but it should be borne in mind that the Patristic Greek Lexicon, in the first of its five fascicules recently published, goes but a little way beyond the first letter of the alphabet ; the great number of theological terms to be found under the letter A can take the blame for this.

Our work aims at presenting Catholic doctrines with the sources from which they are drawn in Scripture and Tradition, since the study of these sources is leading to a rejuvenation of theology in many parts of the Catholic world today. It has not been thought necessary to enter into matters of Catholic discipline, or of the Canon Law which governs them, except where these have doctrinal importance. Bibliographies have been added to each article, and, while every effort has been made to include recent contributions of importance, it is not possible in a corporate work of this kind to cite the very latest material in the theological reviews which may have appeared while this volume was going through the press. In accord with the temper of modern theology considerable attention has been given in the volume to the liturgical sources of theology. These may be well known to the liturgical scholar but are often impenetrable to the theologian because of their manifold difficulties. On many historical questions the last word has by no means been said, and the Editors have to contemplate with what equanimity they can muster the fact that revision of their work will have to start soon after publication has taken place. They wish to express their thanks to the printing staff of Messrs Nelson at Parkside Works in Edinburgh who have nursed this volume through its various stages with much patient attention.

There are times when men avoid theological discussion and times when they seek it. St Thomas More wrote : ' This is a thing well known unto every man that in every session of peace, every session of gaol delivery, every leet throughout the realm, the first thing that the jury have given them in charge is heresy. And for all this,

through the whole realm, how many presentments be there made in the whole year ?
I ween, in some seven year not one.' So could he write on the eve of the Reformation,
but what a change ensued. At other times also in the history of England theological
stagnation has given way to theological tumult. The present is a time of intense
theological discussion and exploration. To help on that exploration the Editors have
undertaken their task.

List of Contributors to Volume One

A. B.   BAER, Rev. Dom Alban, OSB
J. M. T. B.   BARTON, Right Rev. Mgr J. M. T.
J. B.   BLIGH, Rev. John, SJ
L. B.   BOASE, Rev. L., SJ
V. A. B.   BYRON, Rev. V. Alban, SJ
D. A. C.   CALLUS, Rev. D. A., OP
F. C. C.   COPLESTON, Rev. F. C., SJ
T. C.   CORBISHLEY, Rev. Thomas, SJ
J. H. C.   CREHAN, Rev. Joseph H., SJ
J. D. C.   CRICHTON, Rev. J. D.
G. C.   CULKIN, Rev. Gerard
H. F. D.   DAVIS, Very Rev. Mgr H. F.
G. D.   DOLAN, Rev. G., SJ
P. D.   DONNELLY, Rev. Philip, SJ
M. D.   DOUGLAS, Mrs Margaret
D. E.   EGAN, Rev. Denis
G. E.   ELLARD, Rev. G., SJ
E. E. E.-P.   EVANS-PRITCHARD, Professor E. E.
D. F.   FOGARTY, Rev. Dr Dermot
H. G.   GRAEF, Miss H.
E. H.   HARDWICK, Rev. Dr E.
J. H.   HENNIG, Dr John
D. H.   HURST, Rev. Dom David, OSB
† H. J. T. J.   JOHNSON, Rt. Rev. Mgr Humphrey J. T.
L. J.   JOHNSTON, Rev. Leonard
W. J. J.   JORET, Rev. W. J.
F. K.   KEEGAN, Rev. F., SJ
A. K.   KERRIGAN, Rev. Alexander, OFM
K.   KILLIAN, Rev., OFM Cap.
H. P. C. L.   LYONS, Rev. H. P. C., SJ
† J. McC.   McCANN, Right Rev. Abbot J., OSB

J. McD.   McDONALD, Rev. Dr Joseph
F. McS.   McSHANE, Rev. F., SJ
G. M.   MATHEW, Rev. G., OP
L. M.-P.   MINIO-PALUELLO, Professor L.
P. M.   MOLINARI, Rev. P., SJ
F. X. M.   MURPHY, Rev. F. X., C.SS.R
J. M.   MURRAY, Rev. John, SJ
R. M.   MURRAY, Rev. R., SJ
K. O'C.   O'CALLAGHAN, Rev. K., SJ
W. A. O.   ODDIE, Rev. W. A.
S. O'R.   O'RIORDAN, Rev. S., C.SS.R
D. O'S.   O'SHEA, Rev. Denis
T. T. P.   PAINE, Rev. T. T., SJ
R. P.   PILKINGTON, Rev. Prebendary Ronald
J. Q.   QUINN, Rev. James, SJ
H. R.   RIEDMATTEN, Rev. H. de, OP
P. R.   ROBINSON, Rev. Peter, SJ
R. R.   RUSSELL, Rev. Dom Ralph, OSB
T. R.   RYAN, Rev. T., C.PP.S
B. S.-J.   SCOTT-JAMES, Rev. Bruno
D. S.   SHANAHAN, Right Rev. Mgr Daniel
E. A. S.   SILLEM, Rev. Dr Edward A.
F. G. S.   SITWELL, Rev. Dom Francis Gerard, OSB
R. F. S.   SMITH, Rev. R. F., SJ
E. F. S.   SUTCLIFFE, Rev. E. F., SJ
I. T.   THOMAS, Very Rev. Ivo, OP
J. M. C. T.   TOYNBEE, Miss J. M. C.
D. T.   TRAPP, Rev. D., OESA
C. V.   VELECKY, Rev. C., OP
M. E. W.   WILLIAMS, Rev. Dr M. E.

Abbreviations

(1) THE BOOKS OF THE BIBLE

Old Testament (OT)

Gen	Deut	1 Kg	1 Par	Neh	Job	Cant	Jer	Dan	Abd	Hab	Mal
Ex	Jos	2 Kg	2 Par	Tob	Ps	Wis	Lam	Os	Jon	Soph	1 Mac
Lev	Jg	3 Kg	1 Esd	Jdt	Prov	Ecclus	Bar	Jl	Mic	Agg	2 Mac
Num	Ru	4 Kg	2 Esd	Est	Eccl	Is	Ez	Am	Nah	Zach	

New Testament (NT)

Mt	Lk	Ac	1 Cor	Gal	Col	1 Tim	Phm	Jas	2 Pet	2 Jn	Jude
Mk	Jn	Rom	2 Cor	Eph	1 Thess	2 Tim	Heb	1 Pet	1 Jn	3 Jn	Apoc
				Phil	2 Thess	Tit					

(2) PATRISTIC QUOTATIONS

Note : Works which do not appear in the following list are given in full the first time they are quoted, and an abbreviated title is given thereafter.

Ambrose	*De Sacramentis*	de. sac.
Clement of Alexandria	*Protrepticus*	Protrep.
	Paedagogus	Paed.
	Stromata	Strom.
Clement of Rome	*epistula prima*	I Clem.
ps-Clement	*epistula secunda*	II Clem.
Epiphanius	*Panarion haeresium*	Haer.
Eusebius	*Historia ecclesiastica*	HE
Hippolytus	*Refutatio haeresium*	Ref. haer.
	Traditio apostolica	Trad. apost.
Ignatius	*epistula ad Ephesios*	Eph.
	— — *Magnesios*	Magn.
	— — *Philadelphenos*	Phil.
	— — *Polycarpum*	Pol.
	— — *Romanos*	Rom.
	— — *Smyrnaeos*	Smyrn.
	— — *Trallenses*	Trall.
Irenaeus	*adversus haereses* (Harvey)	adv. haer. H
Justin	*apologia prima*	apol.
	apologia secunda	append.
	dialogus cum Tryphone	dial.
Origen	*contra Celsum*	c. Cels.
	de principiis	princ.
Tertullian	*adversus Marcionem*	adv. Marc.
	apologeticus	apol.
	de anima	de an.
	de baptismo	de bapt.

Common titles such as *epistula, homilia, sermo, tractatus* may be abbreviated as *ep., hom., serm., tr.*

ABBREVIATIONS

(3) STANDARD WORKS OF REFERENCE

AAS	*Acta Apostolicae Sedis*		ICC	*International Critical Commentary*
AA.SS	*Acta Sanctorum*		IER	*Irish Ecclesiastical Record*
AB	*Analecta Bollandiana*		ITQ	*Irish Theological Quarterly*
AER	*American Ecclesiastical Review*			
ASS	*Acta Sanctae Sedis*		JBL	*Journal of Biblical Literature*
AV	*Authorised Version*		JE	*Jewish Encyclopedia*
			JEH	*Journal of Ecclesiastical History*
Bfr	*Blackfriars*		JRB	*Bulletin of John Rylands Library*
Bi	*Biblica*		JTS	*Journal of Theological Studies*
BS	*Biblische Studien*			
BZ	*Biblische Zeitschrift*		Kn	Knox, *New Testament*
			KTW	Kittel, *Theologisches Wörterbuch*
CAP	Charles, *Apocrypha and Pseudepigrapha*			
CBQ	*Catholic Bible Quarterly*		LTK	*Lexicon für Theologie und Kirche*
CCL	*Corpus christianorum latinorum*		MGH	*Monumenta Germaniae Historica*
CCS	*Catholic Commentary on Holy Scripture*		MN	*The Month*
CE	*Catholic Encyclopedia*		Med St	*Medieval Studies* (Toronto)
CIC	*Codex Iuris canonici*			
CR	*Clergy Review*		NRT	*Nouvelle Revue théologique*
CSEL	*Corpus Scriptorum Ecclesiasticorum Latinorum*			
			OCA	*Orientalia Christiana Analecta*
			OCP	*Orientalia Christiana Periodica*
D	Denzinger-Bannwart, *Encheiridion Symbolorum*			
			PG	*Patrologia Graeca*, Migne
DAC	*Dictionnaire d'Archéologie chrétienne*		PL	*Patrologia Latina*, Migne
DAFC	*Dictionnaire Apologétique de la Foi catholique*		PO	*Patrologia Orientalis*, Graffin-Nau
DbR	*Dublin Review*		PW	Pauly Wissowa, *Real-encyclopädie*
DBV(S)	*Dictionnaire de la Bible* (Vigouroux) *Supplement*			
			RAM	*Revue d'Ascétique et de Mystique*
DCB	*Dictionary of Christian Biography*		RB	*Revue Biblique*
DR	*Downside Review*		RBn	*Revue Bénédictine*
DSp	*Dictionnaire de Spiritualité* (1935–)		RHE	*Revue d'Histoire ecclésiastique*
DTC	*Dictionnaire de Théologie catholique*		RSPT	*Revue des Sciences phil. et theol.*
DV	*Douay Version*		RSR	*Recherches de Science religieuse*
			RevSR	*Revue des Sciences religieuses*
EB	*Encyclopedia Biblica*		RT	*Revue thomiste*
EHR	*English Historical Review*			
ER	*Études religieuses*		Std	*Studies*, Dublin
ERE	*Encyclopedia of Religion and Ethics*			
ET	*Expository Times*		TQ	*Theologische Quartalschrift*
ETL	*Ephemerides theologicae Lovanienses*		TS	*Theological Studies*
			T&S	*Texts and Studies*
GCS	*Griechischen Christlichen Schriftsteller*		TU	*Texte und Untersuchungen*
HDB	Hastings' *Dictionary of the Bible*		WV	*Westminster Version*
HJ	*Hibbert Journal*			
HL	Hefele-Leclerq, *Histoire des Conciles*		ZKT	*Zeitschrift für katholische Theol.*
HPR	*Homiletic and Pastoral Review*		ZKG	*Zeitschrift für Kirchengeschichte*
HTR	*Harvard Theological Review*		ZNTW	*Zeitschrift für neutestamentliche Wissenschaft*
HUCA	*Hebrew Union College Annual*			

The *Summa Theologica* of St Thomas is referred to by Arabic numerals for part, question and article ; the body of the article being referred to by c, and the answers to objections by @1, @2, @3, e.g. 3a:69:9c ; 1–2æ:73:5@2

List of Articles in Volume One

A
CATHOLIC DICTIONARY
OF
THEOLOGY

A

ABANDONMENT The subject-matter of this article is Abandonment of oneself to Divine Providence. The best Latin equivalent for the term Abandonment is *resignatio*, as used for example in the *Imitation of Christ*. The modern French equivalent is *abandon*. The subject will be discussed under two heads: I True Abandonment, II False Abandonment.

In current English the word abandonment denotes a dereliction or casting off. It could be applied to the experience of Christ on the Cross when He cried ' Eli, Eli, lama sabacthani ? ' He experienced abandonment by His Father. In the present context the word is used in a different sense, a sense which it would not carry in current English, apart from this context.

I True Abandonment. Abandonment here signifies a good disposition of mind and will in relation to God. It may therefore be classed as a virtue. It is the disposition to will what God wills, motivated by love of Him, and carried to a high degree.

Abandonment presupposes obedience. The disposition to obey the express commands of God is obedience ; it may be motivated by fear of punishment, by hope of reward, or by disinterested love of God.

As obedience is constituted of active and of passive elements, so is abandonment. The passive element in obedience is the assent of the will to the divine will ; the active element is the carrying out of what the divine will enjoins. This active element may be negative in character, as it may consist in restraining impulses. Leo XIII, in his Encyclical *Testem Benevolentiae*, 22 Jan. 1899, stated that ' there does not exist, and there cannot exist, any virtue that is really passive '. Even the passive element in obedience is in itself an active choice of the will, and is passive only in the sense that the choice is dictated by the divine will.

When obedience is complete, and is motivated by charity, or supernaturalized love of God for His own sake, the disposition of mind and will is closely approximate to abandonment.

Beyond the scope of the express commandments of God there lies a wide field of free choice. Within this field divine providence indicates preferences of the divine will, without imposing the choice of these under pain of sin. Such are, for example, the evangelical counsels. These divine preferences are presented to individual souls as invitations, or vocations, by impulses of grace. Abandonment is a disposition of mind and will which makes the soul readily responsive to such impulses. Abandonment is to obedience as in general the Gifts of the Holy Ghost are to the virtues. Under a very special and persisting impulse of grace abandonment may be extended to the disposition always to choose the more perfect thing, or the better alternative between choices that are all good. It is, however, in the responsiveness to the impulses of grace that the disposition of abandonment consists, and it can be attained in perfection without carrying out the evangelical counsels by entering the religious state, and still more without binding oneself to do the more perfect thing ; for the impulses of grace do not prompt all persons to these special vocations.

Besides being distinguished into express command and free invitation, the will of God for an individual is also distinguished in another way. It sets before the individual certain alternatives of conduct, between which the created will must choose, exercising initiative ; but it also imposes upon the individual circumstances and conditions which afford no opportunity of exercising initiative ; the alternative is only between submissive acceptance and rebellious discontent. Here lies the most characteristic field for the practice of abandonment to Divine Providence. The abandonment consists in the submissive acceptance, motivated by charity, of the action of Divine Providence upon oneself, whether the secondary causes through which that divine action is exerted be responsible agents or not, and if they are responsible agents, then irrespective of whether they are acting in accordance with God's will of good pleasure or only by His permissive will.

It is because this characteristic field of operation of abandonment does not call for action other than adjustment to circumstances that abandonment appears to be predominantly a passive disposition. But in fact much interior action, bearing on one's subjective state, is required. Moreover, the pressure of circumstances often entails a duty of reacting to the circumstances by positive action, and such action is far from being incompatible with abandonment. If, for instance, a fire starts in the house of a person practising abandonment, that person's immediate duty is to put it out. If an abandoned soul falls sick in body, true abandonment dictates the application of such remedies as are reasonably within reach.

Between abandonment to Divine Providence and indifference, or detachment, there is at least a close connection. St Francis de Sales said that abandonment was perfect indifference. If indifference is conceived as a poise or balance of will, which eliminates all inclination towards created things anterior to the choice of obeying the will of God, abandonment can only be distinguished from it as being a more positive desire to will what God wills. Such a subtle distinction accords with St Francis de Sales' assertion, for the more positive desire would add perfection to a simple refraining from making a choice.

Detachment from creatures, including self, cannot be really distinguished from indifference, and consequently the same can be said of its relation to abandonment as has been said concerning indifference.

Abandonment to Divine Providence is a disposition of mind and will which is evoked by the divine attributes of wisdom and love. It is called abandonment to the providence of God because it is evoked by the conviction that God knows all things and by His infinite wisdom controls all things, even the outcome of the free acts of His creatures. This conviction is associated with the further conviction that God is infinitely loving towards His creatures and by His divine providence directs all things to the ultimate good of those that love Him.

In order to arrive at this twofold conviction in a manner apt to inspire the response of abandonment, it is necessary to have supernatural faith. It is a practical necessity that this faith should be a living faith, informed by charity. Hence there is required at least that degree of indifference which precludes attachment to sin. Faith in the wisdom and good-will of God would not evoke the response of abandonment unless there were present the further conviction that this wisdom and goodwill are directed to one's own good ; but such a conviction constitutes confidence or hope. Finally, as already stated, the response of abandonment must be motivated by charity, if it is to be what is properly called abandonment.

This analysis sets out what some writers call the foundations of abandonment and others the constituent elements.

It is evident that abandonment, like faith and hope and charity to which it is so intimately linked, is a practical form of adoration of God.

II False Abandonment. The virtue of abandonment can be distorted into false abandonment. For while the perfection of this virtue consists in complete conformity of the creature's will with the Creator's, the distortions of false abandonment spring from wrong ideas of the relation of the created will to God's will. They tend towards annihilation of the created will, either by negation of the reality of human freedom, or by an illicit abdication of that freedom.

A first, cruder form of false abandonment is concerned not so much with the wills of Creator and creature as with their activities in the temporal sphere. False abandonment in this sphere is the disposition of mind which draws from the premise that everything depends on God the conclusion that man need do nothing. It may fallaciously claim to be justified by the Sermon on the Mount (Mt. 6:25–34), ignoring the fact that Christ was only denouncing inordinate attachment to temporal things, and the anxieties that arise therefrom. This crude form of false abandonment, the nurse of thriftlessness and sloth, is based on a misconception of the relation between the activity of the Creator and that of creatures, and reality provides a corrective : if man does not act, he suffers from starvation or some other effect of his idleness. Experience lends force to the adage which is here appropriate : God helps those who help themselves (Aide-toi : le Ciel t'aidera).

An example of abandonment so indiscreet that it verges on being false abandonment would be the religious superior, or founder, who should forbid all means of subsistence, even those held in common, for his subjects (D 494, 577). This example emphasizes the truth that abandonment is a delicate balance between initiative and the spirit of dependence. 'Do not provide gold or silver or copper to fill your purses, nor a wallet for the journey, nor second coat, nor spare shoes or staff,' said Jesus to His apostles (Mt 10:9–10) ; but He counterbalanced this when He said : ' Now it is time for a man to take his purse with him if he has one, and his wallet too ; and to sell his cloak and buy a sword, if he has none.' (Lk 22:36.)

Indiscreet or even false abandonment is shown by the subject who fails to inform his superior that the work allotted to him is beyond his capacity. So, too, false abandonment is the fault of one who will not use normal and available means of curing sickness.

The subtler and more pernicious forms of false abandonment are in the spiritual sphere. The core of the error is the idea that the created will is so to be absorbed into the divine will as to be annihilated. True abandonment, on the contrary, is a conformity of the created will to the divine, which does not annihilate the created will, but brings it to full existence.

The root of the error may be pantheistic. If so, the created will is deemed never to have had existence, except as an illusion, and spiritual growth is conceived not as annihilation of the will but as realization of its non-existence.

Through contact with Islam, and the infiltration of Arabian thought, error of this kind seeped into Christendom. But Islam is professedly theistic, not pantheistic, and its influence should be sought rather in a fatalism which undermines belief not in the existence but in the freedom of the created will.

The Brothers and Sisters of the Free Spirit, in the 14th cent., notably in Germany, afford a dreadful example of false abandonment which was in fact an illicit abdication of freedom. On the pretext that their will was wholly abandoned to God, they declared that they were no longer bound by the Commandments, and could without guilt indulge in what for others would have been vice. A like aberration was found among the Béghards of Catalonia.

Luther, before he excogitated the doctrine of justification by faith alone, assuaged his conscience by a similar device. Since corrupt man had no power of avoiding sin, it was a more perfect abandonment to God, he declared, if one submitted to the hopeless situation and sinned vigorously.

Molinos later resuscitated the evil, asserting that there was no sin in yielding to temptation, since in so doing one was abandoning oneself more fully to the divine will which permitted the temptation.

Very frequently the point of insertion for the error of false abandonment is prayer. As the action of the Holy Spirit becomes more marked in prayer, the soul's own activity appears to be diminished. It is difficult, even for an impartial director, to maintain a true balance in the soul, or to distinguish commendable passivity from culpable inertia. The error of false abandonment in this matter consists in declaring complete, deliberate inertia to be the duty of the soul in prayer. The Alumbrados of Spain in the 16th and 18th cents. went so far as to declare themselves exempt from all activity in prayer, especially vocal prayer, including even the obligation of attending Sunday Mass and using the Sacraments.

This is the essence of Quietism. From absolute inertia in prayer it is an easy step to the abdication of moral responsibility. The error lies in confusing a paralysis and consequent atrophy of the will with the possession of the will by the Spirit of God. True abandonment is life; false abandonment is death.

The idea that the human will is absorbed by the divine will in the state of abandonment—falsely conceived—led sometimes to the illusion that the soul was confirmed in grace. Furthermore, divine authority was arrogated to all the person's actions, on the ground that no action was performed by that person except under the direct impulse of the divine will.

False abandonment is a deliberately suicidal idea, aiming at the annihilation of the created will. It issued in the idea that even the desire of one's own perfection and salvation must be suppressed. Similarly it precluded prayer for any particular intention, or the performing of any act of virtue, unless and until a perceptible pressure of grace from within compelled such actions.

The development of false abandonment can be studied in the history of Quietism, notably in the *Moyen Court* of Madame de Guyon. Earlier influences can be traced. As the German mystics of the 14th cent. such as Eckhart, Tauler and Suso, and the Flemish van Ruysbroeck, though not themselves to be charged with false abandonment, did increase the danger of it by their insistence on passivity in prayer, so others later fostered tendencies towards it while avoiding it themselves. Recent study has shown this concerning Benet Canfield, and concerning 'The Lady of Milan', Isabella Berinzaga, with whom the Jesuit Fr Gagliardi was somewhat perilously associated. Within living memory the prohibition of a practice known as *annihilation* has shown that the dangers of false abandonment spring from the heart of man and will be always with us.

Bibliography. J. P. de Caussade SJ, *Abandonment to Divine Providence* (1861) (Eng. tr. E. Strickland (1921) and A. Thorold (1933)) ; the same, *Spiritual Letters* on the practice of self-abandonment, books I–III, tr. A. Thorold (1934) ; books IV–V (*Ordeals of Souls*) (1936) ; books VI–VII (*Comfort in Ordeals*) (1937) ; the same *On Prayer*, tr. by A. Thorold (1931) ; M. Viller SJ, *Abandon* (D Sp 1:2–25) ; P. Pourrat,

Le Faux Abandon (D Sp 1:26–49) ; V. Lehodey, *Le Saint Abandon* (1919) ; A. Poulain SJ, *The Graces of Interior Prayer* (1950 ⁵) ; R. Knox, *Enthusiasm* (1950) ; St Francis de Sales, *Treatise on the Love of God* (Eng. tr. T. Car (1630) and many later).

On the *Breve Compendio* of Isabella Berinzaga (The Lady of Milan) who influenced Bérulle and Canfield, two articles by P. Pirri SJ, in *Archivum Historicum* SJ 14 (1946) 1–72 : 20 (1951) 231–53.

On Benet Canfield, O. Van Veghel OFM Cap., *Benoît de Canfield* (1949).

On the prohibited devotion of 'annihilation', J. Crehan SJ, 'Two forbidden devotions', CR (1940) 407–19.   L. B.

ABBOT, ORDINATION BY Whether a simple priest can, by papal indult, confer the diaconate and the priesthood is a disputed question. Most theologians used to deny that the Pope could grant any such privilege ; but several weighty authorities, among them Innocent III, Vasquez, Gerson, Durandus and Aureolus, held the contrary opinion (cf. Baisi). The Council of Trent declared that the ' powers of the bishops to confirm and ordain are not held in common with priests' (D 967). But since there is certainly an extraordinary minister of confirmation, the Council cannot be held to exclude an extraordinary minister of orders. (For the distinction between bishop and priest *see* BISHOP).

The publication of two papal Bulls in the last thirty years has led to a marked change of opinion. Until these documents were discovered the only alleged case of such an indult was a Bull of Innocent VIII issued in 1489 which granted to the General of the Cistercians and four other abbots and their successors for ever the right to confer the diaconate on their subjects. Yet for a variety of historical accidents, the force of this document could be evaded. (For the authenticity of this Bull, cf. Baisi, 16–24, where he also shows that the powers were in use in Rome in 1662 with the knowledge and approval of the Pope.)

The first of these newly published Bulls was issued in 1400 by Boniface IX and gave the Abbot of St Osyth's in the London diocese the right to confer both the diaconate and the priesthood on his subjects. The terms are beyond dispute : there are two copies in the Lateran Register and the terms are recapitulated in a further Bull of 1403 withdrawing the privilege on the grounds that it infringed the patronage of the Bishop of London (Lennerz, 145–7).

The second document is a Bull of Martin V, dated 1427, giving the Cistercian Abbot of Altzelle in the diocese of Meissen the right to confer on his subjects ' omnes etiam sacros ordines', the standard curial formula for all three major orders (Lennerz, 148). The fact would appear to be established : the Popes have issued these indults. Theologians who have to assume the episcopal character of these abbots and, even (in the case of Innocent's Bull), of their successors for ever, are making a last desperate stand against facts.

Writing before the publication of the latest documents, C. Pesch maintained that, even if established, one act of the Pope would not constitute a law or make a dogma. And Hocedez maintains that the Bulls are merely disciplinary decrees based on a false view of papal powers. But Santi (*Praelectiones Iuris Canonici* I, 133, 4th ed.) and Gasparri (*De Sacra Ordinatione* II, n. 798), both writing before the discovery of the Bulls of Boniface and Martin, held that, were the fact established, the question would be settled. An ever-increasing number of theologians is drawing this conclusion from the facts. Their reason is that if the Pope erred in granting these privileges, then, in his official capacity as Pope, he imposed material idolatry on those of the faithful who sought the ministry of men ordained in virtue of these Bulls.

Bibliography. C. Baisi, *Il ministro straordinario degli ordini sacramentali* (1935); H. Lennerz, *De Sacramento Ordinis* (1953); C. Journet, *The Church of the Word Incarnate* I (1955) 113–15.   A. B.

ABDICATION, PAPAL The fact of abdication by a reigning Pontiff, such as that of Celestine V in 1294, is of importance theologically since it shows, as it were in a limiting case, something of the nature of papal authority. Though other instances are somewhat controversial matters of history, the act of Celestine is perfectly clear. According to the contemporary annalist, Eberhard, 'whereas there was an opinion of the experts that a Pope could not resign, he issued a Constitution (Potthast, 24019) saying that popes could resign, both now and in the future, and declared that he was able by the plenitude of his power to issue such a Constitution. When this was done, he at once resigned.' His successor, Boniface VIII, informing Edward I of England about this event, wrote that 'the Roman church had become vacant by the free and voluntary retirement of our beloved son, fra Peter of Murrone, formerly Pope'. He added that 'the acts of former Popes and their Constitutions show clearly that this can lawfully be done, and there was also the express agreement of the Cardinals to its being done'. None the less, Boniface issued a Constitution of his own, 'lest this statute should in course of time be forgotten, or doubt on the matter be prolonged and recur over and over again'; and the present canon law (in canon 221) is drawn from this, laying down that, if the Pope resigns, his resignation takes effect at once and is not dependent for its validity on its acceptance by the Cardinals or by anyone else.

The first theological conclusion that emerges from this fact of abdication is that, as the end of papal power is decided by the will of the Pope, so is its beginning, and that the Pope is capable of exercising his papal authority from the moment when by his own free act he accepts the election of himself by the Cardinals assembled in conclave. On a hasty reading this might look like fallacious reasoning, but abdication is not being adduced merely as one of the conditions or part-causes why a man ceases to be Pope; rather it is the only cause, not being dependent on the consent of the Cardinals. If, then, free choice brings a Pontificate to an end, it must also have a great deal to do with its beginning, and must certainly exclude the idea that before a Pope can enter on his authority he needs confirmation by anyone else. Had Pope Celestine been regarded as a 'retired Pope' with a papacy 'in partibus infidelium', there might be a case for saying that his own free choice did not entirely undo his papacy, but in fact he was described by his successor as simple Fra Peter of Murrone, even though he had been consecrated and crowned after his election. At the conclave the Cardinals are to give the newly-elected Pope a period for deliberation, and then, when he gives his consent to the election, he *straightway* (even if not yet a priest) becomes possessed of full and absolute jurisdiction over the whole Church and can use it. See AAS 38:97. In theory any Catholic man can be elected Pope, though the last non-Cardinal to be elected was Urban VI in 1378. As long ago as 769 a Council of Rome limited the electors' choice to Cardinal priests or deacons (MGH, *Concilia aevi carolini* I, 86), but this and other such limitations are not regarded as having force by modern canonists. The fact of abdication made clear to the theologians that the charisma of papal infallibility was not something imposed on the individual without his cooperation at any point (as on most views the inspiration of the biblical writers was), and hence it was argued that the moment for the start of this power was the free act of acceptance of election by the new Pope. This further conclusion led to a difference being established between the status of a Pope and that of a bishop, where episcopal consecration might be held to confer a character on the soul which cannot be effaced (*see* BISHOP). Some canonists in the past tried to assimilate papal acceptance of election to episcopal consecration, saying that it set up an indissoluble spiritual marriage between the Pope and the Church, but their view—which would forbid abdication in any proper sense—seems to be ruled out by the facts. The furthest modern canonists will go in this direction is to say (e.g. as Wernz-Vidal say *Ius canonicum* II, 436) that for a Pope to resign without good reason (as Benedict IX may have done in 1045) would be sinful, while the act of resignation would still be valid.

A second conclusion from all this is that if the start of papal jurisdiction is to be reckoned from the moment of acceptance of election, it cannot be claimed that the Pope is invested with authority by the Cardinals—who might in that case claim to be superior to him—but simply designated by them, receiving authority directly from Christ, with whose offer he freely cooperated. In a similar way, the emphasis placed on free choice in the act of abdication by a Pope serves to support those theories which are put forward by Bellarmine (*de romano Pontifice* 2:30) and Billot to show how a Pope who in his private capacity might have taught heresy could be regarded as having made a voluntary abdication of his authority, the stubborn maintenance of an heretical opinion, even though uttered in a private way, being regarded as equivalent to a refusal to cooperate further with the gift from Christ and a separating of himself from the mystical Body. (*See* INFALLIBILITY OF POPE.)

Conditional abdication has been resorted to in the past. When Pius VII in 1804 set out from Rome to crown Napoleon in Paris, he left an act of abdication in the hands of Cardinal Pignatelli, Archbishop of Palermo, to take effect should he be made prisoner by the French and not allowed to return to Italy. This expedient would obviously safeguard the papacy as an institution against the modern techniques for breaking down the human will. In ancient times a similar expedient seems to have been used, for when Pontian (pope from 231 to 235) was carried off to the Sardinian mines, a successor, Anteros, was elected before Pontian's death, and the records say that before Pontian departed *discinctus est*, i.e. he got himself divested of office.

Bibliography. The canonists discuss abdication when treating of canon 221, and among earlier canonists Schmalzgruber vol. I, titulus 9, section 13, deals with it ; a treatise of Olivi *de renuntiatione Pontificis* was printed in *Archivum Franciscanum historicum* 11 (1918) ; J. Leclercq, in *Revue de l'histoire de l'église de France* 25 (1939) 183–92, *La Rénonciation de Célestin V et l'opinion théologique en France* ; C. Journet, *The Church of the Word Incarnate* (1955), excursus IX ; M. D'Herbigny SJ, *De ecclesia* II (1921).   J. H. C.

ABEL IN THE LITURGY In the present-day liturgy Abel is referred to as a saint only in the beginning of the litany of the *Commendatio animae*, where he appears as the leader of the *chorus Iustorum*. Early parallels to this invocation are the *Apostolic Constitutions* (Book 8) and the *Oratio S. Gregorii Papae*. Cyprian (*ep.* 56 ; PL 4:353) speaks of ' Abel the just, who began the line of martyrs ', and Tharasius (PG 87 3:3241) lists him with other OT saints. While the invocations of Abel and Abraham (*see* ABRAHAM IN LITURGY) are not found in other medieval litanies of the *Commendatio animae*, there is a strong Irish tradition of devotion to Abel, represented by a note on St Columba's hymn *Altus Prosator*, the *Commemoratio pro defunctis* in the *Stowe Missal*, the hymn Sen Dé by St Colman moccu Cluasaig, the *Martyrology of Tallaght*, the *Félire* of Marianus Gorman and several litanies in Latin and Irish (Plummer, *Irish Litanies*, 4 and 32), describing Abel as the first martyr or listing him among the leaders of ' those who had intelligence of the law of nature '—an impressive illustration of the prominent part played by Ireland in introducing devotion to OT saints to the West.

The oldest Latin source for the reference to *Abel iustus* in the Canon of the Mass (*see* CANON) is Ambrose *de sacramentis* ; but in earlier Eastern records such as the Jacobite Syrian liturgy, the Anaphora of the Nestorians, the liturgy of St Cyril of Alexandria and *Apostolic Constitutions* there are striking parallels. The Ambrosian liturgy still retains the preface first found in the *Leonine sacramentary* (Feltoe, 161) speaking of the ' host, of which Abel the just one began the prefiguring types '.[1] Reference to the sacrifices of Abel, Abraham and Melchisedec in the post-consecration prayer asking for acceptance of the sacrifice is almost universal. The reference to Abel in the (Gelasian) *Secreta* for the 7th Sunday after Pentecost was derived from this prayer.

Gen 4 is read in the office for Thursday after Septuagesima, but a reference to *Abel iustus* with whom the Church began has already been made on Septuagesima, from St Gregory's homily on the gospel of that day, and here is found the phrase *ecclesia . . . ab Abel*, which St Thomas (*de Veritate* 29:4:@i9) would uphold as orthodox.

In several medieval martyrologies the death of Abel is listed among the main events of the history of our redemption collectively commemorated on 25 March. The preface for the consecration of an altar speaks of ' Abel, the forerunner in his passion of the mystery of salvation ',[2] by whose blood the altar was consecrated—an interesting illustration of the freedom with which the liturgy uses Scripture, for Gen 4:8 says that Abel was slain ' in the field, outside '.

Mt 23:35, where Christ speaks of *Abel iustus*, is read on the feast of St Stephen, the first martyrs of the OT and the NT thus being linked. The most recent liturgical reference to Abel is in the Secret for the feast of Precious Blood, where Heb 12:24 is glanced at.

The tradition of liturgical references to Abel from the 4th to the 19th cents. is a significant link between the Eastern and the Western churches and an important reminder of medieval devotion to OT saints, a subject worthy of more detailed study from both the historical and the theological standpoints.

Bibliography. DAC (iconographical) ; DBV ; DTC ; CE ; J. Hennig, ' Abel's place in the liturgy ', TS 7 (1946) 126–41 ; Y. Congar, ' Ecclesia ab Abel ', *Abhandlungen über Theologie und Kirche* (Karl Adam Festschrift) (1952) 79–108.   J. H.

The theology of the sacrifice of Abel is largely governed by the comment of Augustine on 1 Jn 3:12 (PL 35:2017) : ' God did not look at the offering but scrutinized the heart within, The one whom He saw sacrificing with charity, his sacrifice He regarded. The one whom He saw make the offering with envy, from his sacrifice did He turn away His gaze. The good works of Abel are charity ; the evil works of Cain are hatred of one's brother.'[3] Heb 11:4 does not make clear whether the sacrifice of Abel was considered ' greater ' in quantity or in quality, but according to Oecumenius and Theophylact (PG 119:404 ; 125:341) it is his sacrifice

---

[1] hostia cuius figuram Abel iustus instituit

[2] Abel salutaris mysterii in passione praecursor

[3] Non intendit Deus ad munus ; sed in corde vidit : et quem vidit cum caritate offerre, ipsius sacrificium respexit ; quem vidit cum invidia offerre, ab ipsius sacrificio oculos avertit. Opera ergo bona Abel non dicit nisi caritatem ; opera mala Cain non dicit nisi odium fraternum.

rather than his faith which is here declared to have led to his being called just by Christ (Mt 23:35). The Jewish legend of the fire from heaven which consumed his sacrifice is given by Jerome (PL 23:944) and was accepted by St Thomas (on Heb 11:4), though he qualifies his acceptance by the word 'perhaps' and inclines rather to the view of Augustine that God 'regarded Abel' (Gen 4:4) by scrutinizing his heart rather than by any external act. St Thomas is careful to point out that, whereas a sacrament is not affected by the malice of the minister thereof, this offering being non-sacramental was certainly affected in that way. Theologians also discuss whether Abel was urged to do sacrifice by the natural law or by a special revelation (La Taille, *Mysterium fidei* 7 n. 1), Chrysostom being in favour of both (PG 53:155, *hom. in Gen.* 18:5). The use of the figure of Abel as a type of Christ in His passion is frequent among the Fathers, from Melito of Sardis (*hom. in passione* 59 and 69) and Irenaeus (*adv. haer.* 4:39 H) onwards.   J. H. C.

ABELARD, PETER This article gives (I) some biographical notes, (II) an account of his works together with critical editions, (III) some of the more important points of his theology.

I Life. The main sources are *Historia Calamitatum* (Abelard's own account which has been translated by J. T. Muckle, *The Story of Abelard's Adversities* (1954)); *Letters of St Bernard*; Geoffrey of Auxerre, *Life of St Bernard*; Otto of Freising, *De Rebus Gestis Imp. Frid. I* Book I, ch. 47; also HL Tome V part I, 610, 616.

Abelard was born *c.* 1079 in Brittany and studied under the leading figures of the day. He reacted against Roscelin on the Trinity, disagreed with William of Champeaux on the question of universals, and was dissatisfied with the conservative exegesis of Anselm of Laon. He set up his own school in Paris and secured a large following by the brilliance of his lectures. The Héloïse incident caused him to flee and he eventually became a monk at St Denis. In 1121 he was condemned at Soissons and his *Summi Boni* ordered to be destroyed. Between this date and 1136 he wrote many important works. He returned to Paris in 1136 and resumed teaching. In 1140 he was opposed by St Bernard and William of St Thierry and condemned at Sens. Propositions of his can be found D 368, some of which he retracted. The verdict of Sens was confirmed by the Pope and his works were publicly burnt in Rome where they had been popular with the Cardinals in Curia. He retired to Cluny and died 1142.

II Works. Migne PL 178 is a useful starting-point but for any serious study it is essential to consult modern critical editions. The best account of the works of Abelard and his school is found in A. M. Landgraf, *Einführung in die Geschichte der theologischen Literatur der Frühscholastik* (1948) 62ss. Information on MSS needs to be supplemented by Stegmüller, *Repertorium Biblicum Medii Aevii* IV (Petrus Abaelardus) 1954. It is now established

that Abelard was continually revising his work and developing his thought; he never completed any treatise and did not arrive at a definitive exposition of doctrine. J. Cottiaux, *La Conception de la théologie chez Abélard* RHE 28 (1932) 247–95, 533–51, 788–828 and H. Ostlender in his introduction to the critical edition of *Summi Boni, Beiträge zur Geschichte der Philosophie und Theologie* XXXV deal with the nature of these changes.

The more important of his works are: (*a*) *Summi Boni* (or *De Unitate et Trinitate Divina*. Critical edition: Ostlender, *Beiträge* 35). Composed after 1118. A reply to Roscelin. Ordered to be burnt at Soissons. (*b*) *Theologia Christiana*. Written after Soissons. Same arrangement of subject matter as in *Summi Boni*, but greater use is made of Fathers. (*c*) Theologia, '*Scholarium*' (or *Introductio in Theologiam*. Critical edition: Ostlender, *Geisteswelt des M.A.; Studien und Texte* (1935)). Written before Sens. This is the most important of the three works, and is often known simply as the *Theologia*. It is best to consider these three works not as separate entities, but as three attempts at a *Summa* of theology, the *Scholarium* being the last and the one that was to have the most influence on theological method. Theology was to be considered under three heads, Faith, Charity, Sacraments. Under Faith would be included Hope and Mysteries, under Charity all moral theology, under Sacraments the Incarnation. This ordering of sacred science was to be followed by several later theologians notably the *Sententiae* of Roland Bandinelli, the *Summa* '*Omnebene*', the *Epitome Theologiae* (of Herman, not of Abelard as formerly thought). See Landgraf, *Einführung* 65.

For its influence on the codification of theology consult J. De Ghellinck, *Le Mouvement théologique du XIIe siècle* (1948²) 157s. The *Scholarium* as we now possess it contains only the first section, dealing with *De Deo Uno et Trino*. All these works are incomplete in their present form; the division into books and chapters is of later date and numerous passages are almost identical in the three tracts. (*d*) *Sic et Non*. An ordered collection of biblical, patristic and conciliar texts for and against 158 theses. For a long time one of the outstanding problems had been the reconciliation of apparently contradictory texts. Abelard was not the first to attempt a solution, but his prologue is an important contribution to the right use of sources and the development of positive theology. Many of the principles he laid down there were adopted by later theologians and canonists like Peter Lombard and Gratian. Abelard shows here his keen critical mind. (*e*) *Commentary on Romans* contains much of his teaching on Original Sin and is one of the works mentioned by St Bernard as containing error. (*f*) *Ethics* (or *Scito te ipsum*. Eng. tr. *J. R. McCallum, *Abelard's Ethics* (1935)). Important for teaching on Morals and the Sacrament of Penance. (*g*) The first edition of Abelard's philosophical writings was V. Cousin, *Œuvres inédites d'Abélard* (1836). Critical edition, B. Geyer, *Beiträge* 21. They include literal glosses on texts of Aristotle and Porphyry, a coordinated exposition of the whole of logic, and the *Dialectica*, edited (1956) by L. M. de Rijk. (h) Other works are *Apologia, Dialogue between a Jew, a Philosopher and a Christian, Problemata Heloissae* (answers to scripture difficulties), Commentaries on *Hexameron, The Lord's Prayer*, and the *Quicumque*, Sermons, and Letters (Eng. trs. of letters in Med St 15 (1953), 17 (1955), 18 (1956)).

III Teaching. Today Abelard's place in the history of theology is better recognized. This is due to a more methodical chronology of his works which takes into account the continual revision, a clearer recognition of the logical principles he applies to dogma, and a better knowledge of MSS which show the development of his thought and the existence of an important school. This rehabilitation does not deny his errors nor his temerity, nor the excesses of many of his followers. Not only is he important in the history of method but he is the first to pose many of the questions which exercise the minds of the scholastics : (*a*) Faith and Reason. In theory Abelard recognized the subordination of reason to faith. The motive of faith is divine revelation alone. In practice a difficulty arises about his attitude to mysteries. He certainly taught the existence of some truths which cannot be proved from reason. He understood the limits of the human mind more than some of his contemporaries and he is particularly scathing towards the ' dialecticians '. The Incarnation, mysteries of salvation and the life of grace cannot be known apart from revelation. But his attempt to show that the Trinity was reasonable led him into difficulties, probably because in his day there was a certain amount of confusion between credibility and accessibility to human reason, knowledge of an object and demonstration of it. (*b*) The Blessed Trinity. St Bernard accused Abelard of Sabellianism and there is still a certain amount of discussion as to whether Abelard did admit the distinction between the three divine persons. In setting out the catholic teaching on the Trinity Abelard is orthodox. Difficulties arise when he begins to explain the doctrine. The condemnation of his former master Roscelin for tritheism causes him to stress that the plurality of persons does not destroy the unity of the divine substance. He is also at pains to show that the central truth of the Christian religion, far from being repugnant to reason, can be known to some extent by non-Christians. All can know that God is powerful, wise and good, yet the Christian understands something more by these terms, viz. the three persons. That there are three persons who are really distinct can only be known by revelation, but this truth is based on the three attributes of power, wisdom and goodness which can be known by reason. This mistaking of appropriations for personal properties led him into serious difficulty and he minimized the distinction of the persons, Father, Son and Holy Ghost designating essential attributes only. (*c*) *The Incarnation.* Abelard sincerely anathematized the errors of Eutyches and Nestorius, but his dialectical

analysis of ' the Word was made flesh ' led him to a position very near to Nestorius. Basing himself on Phil. 2:7, some passages from the Fathers, and Boethius's definition of person, he argued : Every rational substance is a person, therefore since the Body and Soul of Christ is not a human person, it cannot be a substantial reality. The fear of admitting a created element in God led him to say that Christ as man is not a substantial reality. This is not a denial of the reality of His manhood, but of its substantial reality. In this way the humanity becomes an accident, something with which the Word is clothed. In the school of Abelard there arose the thesis *Christus ut homo non est aliquid*. This was finally condemned by Pope Alexander III in 1179. (*d*) *The Redemption.* Abelard took his stand against the prevailing view of his day, typified in Anselm of Laon, that by the Fall the devil had certain rights over man. Anselm of Canterbury had already argued against this view, but Abelard did not pursue Anselm's theory of satisfaction, neither did he attempt to expound the whole mystery of the Redemption, but concentrated on the subjective and psychological aspect. The death of Christ on the Cross is an appeal to our love. Abelard did not sufficiently stress the objective value of the redemption. Interest in the psychology of salvation became a characteristic of his school. (*e*) *The Sacrament of Penance.* Contrition immediately reconciles the sinner with God and obtains remission of eternal punishment Only by positive precept is confession necessary. It is needed in order that the priest may know what satisfaction to impose so that temporal punishment may be remitted. It also excites humility. In this Abelard is very much in line with his predecessors. His originality is in his insistence on contrition. Unlike the Laon school he holds that the important element in contrition is not fear but love of God and hatred of sin. From his time a distinction is drawn between the origins of contrition, which can be fear, and the motive, which is always love of God. His view of the rôle of the priest in the sacrament led him to deny that Christ gave the power to remit sins to the successors of the Apostles. He makes the power of the keys dependent on the sentence being confirmed by God. Later he retracted and admitted that the power of binding and loosing was given to all the successors of the Apostles, even the unworthy, as long as the Church tolerates them. (*f*) *Moral Questions.* There is a development in Abelard's teaching on the nature of sin. In his *Commentary on Romans*, owing to a confusion of deliberate will with involuntary desire, he held that concupiscence is sin ; later in the *Ethics* he is explicit that concupiscence and involuntary desire is not sin. This is connected with his teaching that the whole morality of acts depends on intention. His reaction to the prevalent objectivism in morals goes to the extreme of denying any objectivity, and although others did not follow him on this, it did serve as a corrective and helped to underline the importance of the subjective element. He makes a valuable contribution when he says that the whole value of intention comes from simplicity of heart and purity of soul.

Bibliography. Besides the works quoted in the text one can note : E. Portalié, *Abélard* DTC ; C. Otta-viano, *Pietro Abelardo, la vita, le opere, il pensiero* (1931) ; G. Delagneau, Le Concile de Sens de 1140 in *Revue Apologétique* 52 (1931) 385ss ; *J. G. Sikes, *Peter Abailard* (1932) ; J. Rivière, Les 'Capitula' d'Abélard condamnés au Concile de Sens in *Recherches de Théologie Ancienne et Médiévale* 5 (1933) 5ss ; J. Rivière, *Le Dogme de la Rédemption au début du moyen-âge* (1934) 134–53, 170–94, 363–409 ; Paré-Brunet-Tremblay, *La Renaissance du XIIe siècle. Les Écoles et l'enseignement* (1934) 275–312 ; I. Rozycki, *Doctrina Petri Abaelardi de Trinitate* (2 vols) 1938–9 ; J. Rohmer, *La Finalité morale chez les théologiens de S. Augustin à Duns Scot* (1939) 31–51 ; J. Rivière, Le Dogme de la Rédemption au XIIe siècle d'après les dernières publications in *Revue du Moyen-Age Latin* 2 (1946) 101–12 ; *J. R. McCallum, *Abelard's Christian Theology* (1948) ; P. Anciaux, *La Théologie du sacrement de pénitence au XIIe siècle* (1949) 64–70, 165–86, 275–95, 312–22 ; O. Lottin, *Psychologie et morale au XIIe siècle* (1942–54) II 421, III 19,103, IV 27–9, 310–15 ; E. Gilson, *Héloïse and Abelard* (1953) ; A. M. Landgraf, *Dogmengeschichte der Frühscholastik* (1952–56) I/1 69–74, I/2 212–16, II/1 372–4, II/2 50–62, III/2 307–10, IV/1 18–20, 77–80, 373–375 ; G. Truc, *Abélard avec et sans Héloïse* (1956) ; R. Blomme, A propos de la définition du péché chez Pierre Abélard in ETL 33 (1957) 319–47 ; L. Nicolau d'Olwer, 'Sur la date de la *Dialectica* d'Abélard', in *Revue du Moyen-Age Latin* 1 (1945) 375–80 ; *Petrus Abaelardus : Dialectica*, edited by De Rijk (1956) ; *Pietro Abelardo, scritti filosofici* (1954) ; and such general works as E. Gilson, *History of Christian Philosophy* (1955) 153 ff. ; F. Copleston, *History of Philosophy* II (1950) 136–55 ; Helen Waddell, *Peter Abelard* (1934).   M. E. W.

ABLUTIONS AND THE LAITY When the practice of giving Holy Communion under both kinds was going out of use in the Western Church (during the 12th and 13th cents.) it became the custom to give the laity wine to drink from a chalice immediately after they had received the sacred Host, in order to help them to swallow the morsel and to prevent irreverence to the sacrament through spitting. This is made clear by the decree of the Council of Lambeth (1281) presided over by John Pecham : ' Let priests be careful, when they communicate the simple, at Easter or at any other time, diligently to instruct them that the Body and Blood of Our Lord are given to them together under the species of bread, nay, the whole living and true Christ, who is entire under the species of the sacrament. Let them further instruct them that what is at the same time given them to drink in the chalice is not the sacrament but simply wine, given them to help them to swallow the sacred Body they have received. For only to those who celebrate is it granted in smaller churches of the kind to receive the Blood under the species of consecrated

wine.' [1]   (Mansi, 24, 406.) The practice of the smaller churches, which is here dealt with, soon became the norm for all churches. The decree of Peter Quivil's Synod of Exeter in 1287 (Mansi, 24, 789), ordering that the people be instructed that what they receive in the chalice is blood shed by the body of Christ, does not show opposition to the Lambeth decree of six years earlier but rather that the custom of communicating in both kinds was not yet given up in Cornwall and Devon, which never marched with the rest of the country in the pace of their liturgical developments. Pecham had visited the diocese of Exeter in 1282, as was his canonical right. The phrase used by Quivil is borrowed from an earlier treatise on the sacraments by Richard Marsh. Other parts of Quivil's decrees are borrowed from Pecham's *Ignorantia sacerdotum*. It is true that personal relations between Pecham and Quivil were not very good, but this was due to matters other than doctrinal, as has been shown by Miss Douie in her *Archbishop Pecham* (1952) 136–9. The rubric that still stands in the Roman missal (*Ritus celebrandi missam* 10:6) directs that the server, after communion, is to take a vessel of wine and water and offer it to each of the communicants, though this rubric is generally disregarded. The late Fr Thurston was able to show (MN 118 (1911) 337–52) that the use had been maintained in Eng-land until 1688 or later, for the Doway Catechism of that year still directed the server to observe it. In Portugal the practice went on until 1890, while in the parishes of Heppenheim and Dieburg of the diocese of Mainz (Rhineland) it was still kept up in 1914. The English Brigittine nuns of Chudleigh had preserved the practice of drinking water from a chalice immediately after communion throughout the centuries of persecution until the practice was suppressed by a visiting prelate in 1867.

The utilitarian basis of the practice, as declared by the Lambeth council, is not to be wondered at, since much earlier in the *Regula magistri* (PL 88:992) there is a direction that the reader who is to read to the monks at their refection after mass should have a drink of wine before starting, lest he do irreverence to the sacrament by spitting,[2] and in the Rule of St Benedict the same thing is allowed *propter com-munionem sanctam*. In the *Blickling Homilies* (written in 971, but using Latin exemplars of much earlier times) there is a description of the chapel of St Michael at Monte Gargano which contained a spring. ' By this piece of water was a glass vessel hung on a silver chain which received the pleasant

[1] Attendant insuper sacerdotes quod cum sacram com-munionem porrigunt simplicibus, paschali tempore vel alio, sollicite eos instruant sub panis specie simul eis dari corpus et sanguinem Domini, immo Christum integrum, vivum et verum, qui totus est sub specie sacramenti. Doceant etiam eos, illud quod ipsis eisdem temporibus in calice propinatur sacrum non esse, sed vinum purum eis hauriendum, traditum ut facilius sacrum corpus glutiant quod perceperunt. Solis enim celebrantibus sanguinem sub specie vini consecrati sumere in huiusmodi minoribus ecclesiis est concessum.

[2] Ipse suum merum propter sputum sacramenti accipiat et tunc incipiat legere.

fluid. And it was the custom of this people when they had gone to the sacraments that they by steps should ascend to the glass vessel and there take and taste the heavenly fluid.' (Early English Text Society, vol. 58, 208 ; for the Latin see MGH *Scriptores rerum Longobardicarum* 543.) The Cistercian Customary (of *c.* 1180) shows that the monks were given the draught of wine even though they had received the sacrament under both kinds (Guignard, *Monuments primitifs* 148). Spitting in church was deprecated by the Rule of St Columbanus (SHL 2:162), but still more the endangering of the sacrifice. This motive of reverence for the minutest crumb of the eucharistic bread is shown by the *Catecheses* of Cyril (PG 33:1125) and by the *Canon* of Rabbulas of Edessa (*c.* 420) which directed : ' Let any crumb of the holy Body which falls to the ground be searched for, and if it be found, let the place be scraped should it be of earth, and the dust therefrom mixed with water and given to the faithful as a draught of blessing' (Nau, *Canons et résolutions canoniques*, 91).

In the very early days (Hippolytus, *Trad. apost.* 23:7) three cups of milk and honey, water and wine were given to the newly-baptized after they had been given the Body of Christ, and the custom was kept up in the time of Jerome (Crehan, *Early Christian Baptism* 171–3), and the symbolic reasons for the practice do not clearly exclude the utilitarian. The curious variation in usage at ordinations (J. Bligh, *Ordination to the Priesthood* (1956) 154) in the 13th cent., whereby if the Pope was the ordaining prelate the ordinands received communion under both kinds, while if he was not they received under one kind and then were given to drink of a chalice of unconsecrated wine, may be parallel to the variation recorded by Pecham's decree of 1281 which was limited to ' smaller churches', and which thus implied that in a cathedral all would communicate under both kinds still. The gradual abandonment of reception under both kinds in the West was due to its inconveniences, but the step could not have been taken had it not been clearly understood to be unessential, and this fact was taught by the liturgies of the Dark Ages, for in all the main *Ordines* (Andrieu, *Ordines Romani* (1948 and 1954) 1:108–22 ; 4:71–2 ; 5:85–8 ; 6:70 ; 9:44–5) it is the practice to describe the reception of the Blood of Christ as a *confirmatio*, while the term *communio* means the reception of the Body. *Diaconus confirmat omnes sanguine dominico quos communicaverit pontifex corpore dominico* is a typical rubric (ibid. 6:70). What was not essential could be dropped, and the inconvenience of spilling the wine of the ablutions would not make for the same irreverence to the sacrament as if the consecrated wine was itself being drunk.

Bibliography. H. Thurston SJ, ' The Laity and the unconsecrated chalice', MN 118 (1911) 337–52 ; ' The early Ritual of Holy Communion', MN 124 (1914) 159–68 ; J. A. Jungmann SJ, *Missarum Sollemnia* (1954³) ; P. Browe SJ, ' Mittelalterliche Kommunionriten', *Jahrbuch der Liturgiewissenschaft* 15 (1941) 26–57 ; E. Dublanchy, ' Communion sous les deux espèces', DTC 3, 552–72.   J. H. C.

ABORTION The practice of abortion seems to have been known to every race and civilization in the recorded history of man. After (I) defining what is meant by abortion, this article will treat the subject under (II) its moral aspect and will then outline (III) the legislation concerning abortion in English law and in (IV) ecclesiastical law. Section IV will also deal with the question of mediate and immediate animation of the foetus, as this has a bearing on both ecclesiastical law and the practice of foetal baptism.

I Definition. Abortion is the expulsion of the living foetus from the womb before viability. The term foetus includes every stage of development from the fertilization of the ovum until birth. The foetus is viable when it can exist apart from its mother, and it is taken to have reached viability after twenty-eight weeks of pregnancy. However, it is possible that, by means of modern equipment and technique, the foetus could be kept alive even if expelled before this time. When the expulsion of the foetus is caused by accident or disease, it is called spontaneous abortion. An expulsion brought about by intentional human interference is voluntary or induced abortion. This intentional interference can be direct or indirect. It is direct when means are employed for the specific purpose of ejecting the foetus. If the expulsion of the foetus is a secondary and incidental effect of treatment designed principally for some other purpose, the abortion is indirect. The name therapeutic abortion, which may be found in medical writings and in civil law, is given to direct abortion when it is performed to safeguard the life or health of the mother. The expulsion of a viable foetus before it has reached full term is not abortion. It is performed to obviate difficulties which may arise at full term and it is referred to as the induction of premature labour.

II The Morality of Abortion. The Church condemns voluntary direct abortion because it is the direct killing of an innocent human being. The child in the womb is a human being with an inalienable right to its life. To remove the foetus from the womb into an environment in which it cannot live, is directly to kill it. The child is innocent because it occupies the place designed for it by nature, nor, by its presence in the womb, does it infringe the right of another. To remove the inviable foetus from the womb is, therefore, the killing of the innocent. No human authority, neither State nor private individual, has the right to order the direct killing of an innocent person. Nor can it be argued that the child is an unjust aggressor on the life of the mother. Mere occupation of one's rightful place does not constitute aggression. It has been objected that the Church's teaching on abortion, especially in cases where there is serious danger both to the life of the mother and of the child, is unrealistic and cruel. For, when faced with the choice of two evils, the death of both or the death of one, the lesser evil should be chosen and steps should be taken accordingly to terminate the pregnancy. This solution, however, cannot be maintained. The choice does not lie between evils of the same category. The death of the mother and child, though distressing in the extreme, is a physical evil. The direct taking of the child's life is a moral evil. No one may do that which is morally evil, even for a good end. Nor, in these circumstances, would the death of the mother and child be imputable to a person who refused to take such immoral means. The objection that, if the death of the child is certain, merely to hasten the inevitable in order to save the mother's life cannot be immoral, is again fallacious. The killing of the innocent cannot be justified simply because the intended victim is already moribund. The Church's teaching on abortion is, therefore, human and realistic. It is a most realistic evaluation of the sacredness of the innocent person's right to life.

To these answers the following observations may be added. (a) The number of maternity cases in which there is a possibility of both the mother and the child dying is very small indeed. There are non-Catholic medical experts, in Britain and the United States of America, who state that, in consideration of the recent advances made in obstetrics, therapeutic abortion is rarely, if ever, necessary. (b) Many cases which formerly would have been solved by terminating pregnancy may be avoided by pre-natal care and observation. (c) Certain dangerous or difficult pregnancies could be obviated by careful pre-nuptial examination.

In direct abortion, then, the life or health of the mother is preserved by means of a direct attack on the life of the foetus. This is never permissible. If, however, certain treatment is given to the mother in order to preserve her health or life, and this treatment not only has the primary effect of curing her, but also a secondary and incidental effect which produces an abortion, the abortion is indirect. For such treatment to be morally permissible, several conditions are necessary. (a) The treatment itself, e.g. the drugs or operation, must be morally allowable. (b) The two effects of the treatment, the curing of the mother and the abortion, must be independent of each other. That is to say, that the abortion is not the means by which the mother's life is saved. (c) The abortion must not be willed or intended, but merely tolerated. (d) The last condition for the application of the principle (the principle of double effect), which underlies the above statement, is that the good effect produced must be of as serious a nature as the evil effect. Since the good effect is the saving of a life, and the evil effect the losing of a life in the case being discussed, this proportion will be maintained. These four conditions must all be satisfied in any one case, for the treatment to be morally permissible.

In a case of rape it is morally allowable to endeavour to eject the semen before conception takes place. The reason for this is that the semen is injected by unjust aggression. Once conception has taken place, a new human being is brought into existence with an inalienable right to its life. No action, therefore, can be taken against the foetus.

The induction of premature labour is permissible for a serious reason. In this case there is no question of abortion, since the foetus is viable.

III English Civil Law. The legislation concerning abortion in English law is set down in the Offences Against the Person Act, 1861, in sections 58 and 59. This Act states that any woman who, whether pregnant or not, by unlawfully taking poison or other noxious thing or by unlawfully using an instrument or other means whatsoever, endeavours to procure her own miscarriage, shall be guilty of felony and, on conviction, shall be liable to imprisonment. Similar punishment is enacted for others who endeavour to procure the miscarriage. Those who supply the means for these endeavours, with knowledge of their purpose, are guilty of a misdemeanour. It should be noted that, unlike the legislation in Canon Law, the Act does not require that the abortion should actually take place. The London Central Criminal Court (Rex v. Bourne, 1938) decided that an abortion is lawful if deemed necessary for the mental health of the mother.

IV Ecclesiastical Law. Although the Church has always condemned voluntary direct abortion and punished the perpetrators with canonical penalties, there have been variations in these penalties dependent on whether or not the foetus was judged to have been animated. This distinction between an animated and non-animated foetus is based on the theory that a foetus does not receive a human soul until some time after the fertilisation of the ovum. Aristotle put forward this view in his De partibus animalium and De generatione animalium. He states that there are two kinds of semen, male and female. In consequence of the motion imparted by the male semen to the female semen in coition, the product of the union begins to move, grow and undergo certain changes. The first stage reached is that which characterizes vegetative life and at this stage the embryo is animated by a vegetative soul. Further development leads to the appearance of sensitive life and finally, when the embryo reaches a specifically human stage of organization, the human soul comes into existence. The time when this takes place is on the fortieth day for the male and on the eightieth day for the female. Other theories were advanced later which supported the idea that the soul came into existence at the time of fertilization, but the fear of Traducianism strengthened the position of the Aristotelian or mediate animation theory. The Traducianists held that the soul came from the substance of the parents and was transmitted with the semen. This was condemned in 498 by Pope Anastasius II (D 170). The Greek Fathers were quoted by the supporters of both the immediate and mediate animation theories in their own favour. The revival of Aristotelian philosophy gave a new impetus to the mediate animation theory which continued to be held until modern times. The last great supporter of the theory in this country was Dr E. C. Messenger in his *Theology and Evolution*. Nowadays immediate animation is accepted by theologians and scientists alike, but there has been no official pronouncement on the point by the Church. The influence of the mediate animation theory can be seen in the following legislation. In A.D. 314, the Council of Ancyra mitigated the punishment to be imposed on a woman who voluntarily underwent abortion. The sentence was reduced from that of life exclusion from the Church to ten years' penance. There was no mention in the canon of whether the foetus was animated or not. In the same year the Council of Neo-Caesarea held that the baptism of a pregnant woman did not avail for her child as well, i.e. the child *in utero* was already a person. A particular decision of Innocent III (A.D. 1211) declared the abortion of the animated foetus to be homicide but not the abortion of the non-animated foetus. In 1588, Sixtus V in the Bull ' *Effraenatam* ' imposed excommunication on all abortions irrespective of whether the foetus was animated or not. Gregory XIV, however, in 1591, in the Bull ' *Sedes Apostolica* ' renewed the penalties, but again distinguished between an animated and non-animated foetus. Pius IX, in his Constitution ' *Apostolicae Sedis* ' published in 1869, makes no mention of the distinction. Finally, in the Code of Canon Law, promulgated in 1917 and effective from 19 May 1918, canon 2350, §1 states . 'All who effectively procure abortion, the mother included, thereby incur excommunication reserved to the Ordinary.' There is no distinction made here between animated and non-animated foetuses and, indeed, canon 747 explicitly makes no distinction. It states that care must be had that all aborted foetuses, at whatever stage of pregnancy they are born, are to be baptized. If they are certainly alive, they are to be baptized absolutely ; if it is doubtful whether they are alive, they are to be baptized conditionally. From these canons it is certain that, for all practical purposes, the Church favours the immediate animation theory. This is supported by the fact that the Church declares the Blessed Virgin Mary to have been free from sin from the first moment of conception, and has fixed the feast day of the Immaculate Conception nine months before the feast of her Nativity. The spacing of the two feasts (8 Dec. and 8 Sept.) goes back to Byzantine times, as does the other cycle of feasts of John the Baptist, the Conception on 23 Sept. and the Nativity on 24 June.

Besides these enactments enjoining canonical sanctions for those who procure abortion, the Church has condemned abortion in particular or general terms over the centuries. A decree of the Holy Office in 1895 condemned therapeutic abortion, while another decree of the same Congregation, published in 1898, allowed the acceleration of the birth of a viable foetus, but condemned abortion, when the mother's life was in danger. Pope Pius XI in his Encyclical ' *Casti Connubii* ', 31 Dec. 1930, explicitly states the Church's teaching on abortion.

Bibliography. J. Antonelli, *Medicina Pastoralis*

(1909) ; Wernz-Vidal, *Jus Canonicum* Vol. 7 (1937) ; A. Bonnar, *The Catholic Doctor* (1951) ; C. McFadden, *Medical Ethics* (1953) ; E. C. Messenger, *Theology and Evolution* (1949).   G. D.

ABRAHAM IN TRADITION AND LITURGY It is the purpose of this note to supply an account of the use made by the Church of the figure of the patriarch Abraham. First of all, in time as in importance, he is looked upon as the Father of the faithful, a prototype in the exercise of faith. Clement of Rome (*I Clem.* 31:2) says that he was blessed because he wrought justice and truth by means of faith. The almost contemporary Epistle of Barnabas (9:7) claims that in his practice of circumcision he looked forward to Jesus, and it finds an allegory for the name Jesus in the (Greek) numerals that designated the total number of those whom he circumcised. This reads like an attempt to expand the cryptic saying of Christ (Jn 8:56) that Abraham saw His day. Ambrose similarly claims (*de Abraham* 1:3:21) that Abraham foresaw that Christ would be his heir by taking a body that was descended from him. It is in the spirit of these declarations that the Church prays, in the collect which follows the reading of the story of Abraham and Isaac in the Easter vigil, ' O God, great Father of the faithful, . . . thou dost make by this Easter sacrament thy servant Abraham the father of all nations.' [1] In the Magnificat-Antiphon for the First Vespers of Quinquagesima, when the reading of Gen has reached the beginning of the story of Abraham, he is saluted as ' the father of our faith '. The praise of the faith of Abraham in Heb 11:8–19 culminates in the episode of his readiness to sacrifice Isaac. This made Abraham appear to be a type of God the Father, and he was so understood by Melito of Sardis (*hom. in Passionem*, 59 69 and 83 and *fragmenta* 9–12). He thus became the figure of a sacrificing priest. Hippolytus (*Trad. apost.* 3) in the prayer of consecration for a bishop has this idea, ' Thou gavest an ordinance to the Church by the word of Thy grace. Thou who foreordainedst originally a family of righteous men ; from Abraham Thou ordainedst judges and priests and Thou didst not leave Thy sanctuary without ministers.' [2] The parallel was not perfect, for God cannot sacrifice to any higher being, but the sacrifice of Abraham became established as one of the chief forerunners of that of Christ. In a famous Preface the Leonine sacramentary (Feltoe, 161) speaks of the sacrifice of praise which the just Abel began in figure, Abraham made better known, Melchisedech showed forth and Christ the eternal priest fulfilled.[3]

[1] Deus fidelium pater summe, . . . per paschale sacramentum Abraham puerum tuum universarum sicut iurasti gentium efficis patrem. . . .

[2] Tu qui dedisti terminos in ecclesia per verbum gratiae tuae, praedestinans ex principio genus iustorum (ab) Abraham principes et sacerdotes constituens et sanctum tuum sine ministerio non derelinquens. . . .

[3] Hostiam laudis . . . cuius figuram Abel iustus instituit . . ., celebravit Abraham, Melchisedech sacerdos exhibuit, sed verus agnus et aeternus pontifex hodie natus Christus implevit.

This Preface was adopted by the Gelasian sacramentary for the third mass of Christmas, by the Ambrosian rite for the octave day of Christmas and by the Mozarabic missal for the first Sunday after Pentecost. The Armenian lectionary (Conybeare, *Rituale Armenorum* 519) which gives the scripture readings of the church of Jerusalem in the 5th cent. has the story of the sacrifice of Isaac not only for the Paschal vigil but also on the Thursday preceding. The Preface for the Consecration of an altar in the *Roman Pontifical* compares the altar that is being blessed to that one on which Abraham placed his son Isaac.[1] The anonymous pilgrim from Piacenza, who seems to have visited Palestine in the 6th cent., reports the existence then of an altar of Abraham near the rock of the crucifixion, claiming also that this was the site of the offering by Melchisedech of the bread and wine (PL 72:906). The naming of the sacrifice of Abraham in the Canon of the Mass goes back to the days of Ambrose, for he quotes it in *De Sacramentis* 4:27.

The mention of 'the light which was promised to Abraham and to his seed' is first found in the burial service given in the third part of the old Gelasian sacramentary (Wilson, 297), whence it must have passed into the Offertory of Requiem masses, both documents being probably from Celtic sources. A similar prayer is found in the additions made by Alcuin to the Gregorian sacramentary (Wilson, 211), this time coupling the idea of a place of light for the dead with that of Abraham's bosom. Lk 16:22 supplied the cue for this introduction of Abraham's bosom into the liturgy of the dying, and it is now found in the prayers at the expiry and also in the hymn *In Paradisum* at the burial. The promise of light to Abraham is not recorded in scripture, but the Jewish traditions which may be seen in *Testament of Abraham* 7 and *Apocalypse of Abraham* 17 clearly suppose it.

Abraham is also connected with the idea of liberation, for the Church prays (in the *Ordo Commendationis Animae*) that the soul may be set free as Abraham was set free from Ur of the Chaldees.[2] The *Itinerarium* has a collect referring to this liberation of Abraham, and in Ac 7:2–3 St Stephen shows knowledge of the Jewish tradition which is not found in Gen. Here again the background of the prayer is Jewish tradition which had a long saga of how Abraham escaped death by fire after disputing with Nimrod. The *Epistle of Barnabas* (8:4) gives another ground for seeing Abraham as a sign of liberation. At the sacrifice of the red heifer the Jews (*Mishna, Parah* 3:2) had three boys to carry the water that was mixed with its ashes. Who are these boys? asks the Christian writer. They tell us of our liberation from sin, and they stand for Abraham, Isaac and Jacob.

Bibliography J. Daniélou, 'Abraham dans la tradition chrétienne', and B. Botte, 'Abraham dans la

---

liturgie', in *Cahiers Sioniens* 5 (1951) 69–95 ; T. Klauser, 'Abraham, Christliche Kult', in *Reallexicon für Antike und Christentum* 1:22–5.   J. H. C.

ABSOLUTION is here understood of remission of sins by a priest in the sacrament of PENANCE. This power of absolution is considered (I) in Scripture, (II) in the Fathers of the West (with brief reference to the Eastern Church), (III) in the Scholastics up to the Reform, and (IV) in the Catholic teaching of Trent. An added section (V) considers the form of absolution.

I Absolution in Scripture. Christ's kingdom is to convert from sin (Mt 4:17) and to destroy Satan (Lk 11:20) and Christ claims for Himself a power to absolve (Mt 9:2–6). His parables show there will be sinners within the kingdom and Christ envisages forgiveness of the sins of the children by the Father (Mt 6:11, 14–15). The existence of rituals of forgiveness in the OT suggests a similar possibility in the NT. Three major texts are held to contain a power for that purpose, a power promised and then given.

The promise is contained in Mt 16:19 and Mt 18:18. The former shows Peter the Rock being promised the keys so that what he binds or looses on earth will be bound or loosed in heaven, a phrase applied to all the Apostles in the second text. The general authority signified by the Keys is specified and clarified by the power to bind and to loose, and is seen to include a power to impose or dissolve obligations in conscience (cf. CCS 657k). The context of Mt 18 would convey to Jewish minds that the Church authorities like those of the synagogue can impose or dissolve obligations on the sinner even in regard to exclusion from the Church. Now, however, the binding is also in heaven, so the conclusion must be that they are using divine power over sinners, a power that ought to include true absolution.

This conclusion is confirmed by Jn 20:23, which uses the word *aphienai* for 'forgive', a word used of God and of Christ (Mt 6:12, 14 ; 9:2–6). The giving of the Spirit emphasizes that the absolution is true absolution of guilt and not just a declaration of God's forgiveness. This last interpretation, given by some scholastics and by the Reformers, would make the power to bind meaningless.

It follows that the power is hierarchical, to be used by the heads of the community, corresponding to the heads of the synagogue. Thus it is given to the apostles, is intended to be exercised judicially (as the twofold or disjunctive power, and also the nature of the matter, demands) and they are told of the power to bind in terms of synagogue practice which was hierarchical. Furthermore, the power to absolve extends to sins after Baptism, for it is concerned with brethren, those within the Church, and the effects and the judicial procedure are clearly not those of Baptism. Finally it is a universal power, for all time and all sins, since the terms are all quite unrestricted. Some seek to find restrictions, unforgivable sins, in the Sin against the Holy Ghost (Mt

---

[1] sicut illud super quod Abraham seminarium fidei nostrae Isaac filium suum . . . toto corde imposuit.

[2] Libera Domine animam servi tui sicut liberasti Abraham de Ur Chaldaeorum.

12:32), the Sin to Death (1 Jn 5:16), and in some passages from Hebrews (6:4–8; 10:26; 12:17–17). But it is clear that the restrictions are not in the power given but are due to the defective dispositions of the sinners concerned (cf. CCS 654c and Galtier, *De Poenitentia* (1950²) 166–76).

Some traces of the use of this power of the keys are found in the rest of the NT. Authority over sinners is exercised and the power to bind seems clearly used (cf. 2 Thess 3:14–15; 1 Cor 5:5; 2 Tim 2:16, 24–6; 3:6). The only example of absolution is found in 2 Cor 2:5 ff. (cf. 12:20 to 13:10), and some interpret the imposition of hands in 1 Tim 5:22 as an act of absolution rather than as a ceremony of ordination. No clear picture seems possible from such fragmentary evidence (cf. P. Galtier, *Aux origines du sacrament de pénitence* (1951) 57–107).

II Absolution in the Fathers. Much development takes place in this period (*see* PENANCE), and the material can only be treated summarily.

(1) The **Subject** of absolution is the sinful Christian, and the critical hypothesis of a church of the saints neither needing nor envisaging absolution is against the evidence both apostolic and patristic (cf. Galtier, *De Poenit.* 110–13).

(2) On the **Matter** of absolution practice varied. The principal question is whether the Church ever considered any sinner or any sin as beyond her competence to absolve. By Nicaea in 325, Innocent I in 405 and Celestine in 428 (D 57, 95, 111) it is clear that she teaches her universal power, though an early restrictive severity is mentioned. This severity seems absent at the beginning of the 2nd cent. as it is shown to us by Clement of Rome (*1 Clem.* 57:1), Ignatius (*Phil.* 3.2, 8.1), and even later by Polycarp (6:1–2) and Justin (*dial.* 47). Then Hermas preaches universality of forgiveness but restricts it to a single occasion (*Mand.* IV) and mentions some rigorist doctors who say there is no forgiveness. These rigorists seem to have existed but to have been opposed to the normal teaching (cf. P. Batiffol, *Études d'histoire* (1st series, 1926) 47–68). Yet the restriction of canonical penance to one occasion must have arisen in this century, providing only one absolution of the capital sins, murder, apostasy and fornication or adultery.

Tertullian as a Catholic at the beginning of the 3rd cent. speaks of universal forgiveness (*De Poenitentia* 4:4); but as a Montanist he clearly denies that the Church may forgive the capital sins (*De Pudicitia* 21:7 ff.). It is clear, however, that Tertullian has changed his doctrine (cf. ibid. 1:10–13). The Church had some considerable rigorism in regard to capital sins while not denying that they could be forgiven, and even this rigorism is progressively mitigated. Some evidences of restrictive teaching taken from Hippolytus, Cyprian and Origen are found on examination to concern only the need for proper dispositions. Ultimately it must be confessed that there are many obscurities as to both the theory and the practice of these centuries.

The position is somewhat clearer as to restrictions concerning particular sinners. Absolution was sometimes denied to sinners seeking penance only in danger of death, for their dispositions were judged doubtful (cf. e.g. Council of Arles, canon 22). It was also denied to those who relapsed, that is to those who after undergoing public penance and receiving absolution fell again into similar sins. Such people were helped to repent and to seek forgiveness from God; but they were not allowed to enter the ranks of public penitents a second time (cf. Augustine, *ep.* CLIII). This restriction continued, though gradually diminishing for several centuries (*see* PENANCE).

(3) The **Minister** of absolution is the bishop and, in due course, the presbyter. The scarcity of early evidence led critics to argue that initially charismatics absolved since no established hierarchy was available. This, they continue, left traces in later texts and practices (cf. Galtier, *De Poenit.* 134 ff.). Assuming the original existence of a hierarchy (*see* HIERARCHY IN THE EARLY CHURCH) we may have traces of their activity in 1 Tim 5:20–22; *1 Clem.* 57:1; Ignatius, *Phil.* 8:1. St Polycarp (6:1–2) speaks of presbyters as judges of sinners.

In the 3rd cent. more evidence is available and it shows us a communal activity in the reconciliation of sinners (cf. Tertullian, *De Poenit.* 9:4; Cyprian, *ep.* 17:1; 19:2) which continues even up to St Augustine (Serm. 296:11–12). Yet Tertullian as a Montanist states explicitly that lesser sins are forgiven by the bishop (*De Pudicitia* 18:18), and his denial of the bishop's power to forgive the capital sins clearly shows us the Catholic teaching and practice that it is the bishop who absolves (ibid. 1:6; 21:17).

The current practice and some doubtful texts then fall more into place (cf. Galtier, *op. cit.* 140 ff.). The whole Church (faithful, martyrs, confessors, deacons and presbyters) works with the bishop by intercession, satisfaction and even by seeking to influence the judgment (cf. Cyprian, *ep.* 17:1; 59:15). But the ultimate judgment is that of the bishop who has the discretion of fitting the cure to the crime and to the penitent, as Cyprian shows us (*ep.* 55:11, 13–15; 59:15–16; 64:1). Thus also the *Didascalia Apostolorum* stresses the often-used medical metaphor (2:20:10–11; 2:41:3–9; cf. Basil, PG, 32:671). We see the same discretion in the forgiveness of non-capital sins without public penance, in the varying treatment of those who fell. Examples also occur where circumstances lead to the exemption of capital sinners from public penance itself (cf. Galtier, *op. cit.* 245 ff.). These indications not only show us the basis of the solution to the 'private penance' dispute, but tell us that it is the bishop who has the final judgment and who strictly reconciles or absolves. Deacons who are said to give Peace and Communion in emergency will then only be giving external reconciliation. Monks (apart from some abuses that are reproved) act only as directors of souls unless they are priests, as do others of the laity (cf. Teetaert, *La Confession aux laïques* (1926)).

Eventually the function of absolution is seen to

devolve upon the presbyter as a normal penitentiary testified to by the *Liber Pontificalis* (i, 249), by Socrates (HE v, 19) and by Sozomenos (HE vii, 16) for the 4th and 5th cents. Yet it seems that when required the presbyter had administered penance and absolved from the earliest days (cf. *I Clem.* lvii:1 ; Cyprian, *ep.* xvi:2 ; xviii:1 ; xix:2 ; Denis Alex., PG 20:630 ff. ; Jerome, PL 26:118). (Galtier, *op. cit.* 463–4 ; Batiffol, *op. cit.* 145 ff.)

(4) The **Time and Efficacy** of absolution. The time of absolution varied for capital sins and for other sins. Sins other than capital sins were absolved without delay and repeatedly if need be (Tertullian, *De Pudicitia*, xviii:18 ; Origen, *In Levit.*, *hom.* xv:2). The capital sins which called for public penance present an unresolved difficulty. Confession was followed by imposition of a satisfactory penance to be carried out for varying periods. This ended with an imposition of hands restoring peace and the right to communion, especially to the Eucharist.

A controversy still exists whether absolution was given at the beginning so that final reconciliation was only ecclesiastical and non-sacramental. Many Catholics defend an early and private sacramental absolution, for while a deacon could sometimes give the Pax, the priest is said to absolve *Confitentes*, i.e. those who confessed. Further, some texts make Penance and Absolution seem to be equivalents, and Viaticum was made available to the dying without recourse to the longer process of public penance. Many other Catholics (Vacandard, D'Alès, Galtier) consider on historical grounds that the final reconciliation was the sacramental absolution. They argue that in general reconciliation with the Church was reconciliation with God ; that the Montanists and Novatians denied absolution by refusing Pax, that Callistus (or Agrippinus) stated explicitly that he would absolve those who had completed their penance (Tertullian, *De Pudicitia*, 1:6). These points make this the more acceptable position.

Many non-Catholic critics and, with reservations, K. Adam and B. Poschmann (*Die abendlaendische Kirchenbusse im Ausgang des christl. Altertums*, 1928) go further. They argue that priestly absolution cannot be proved until private penance prevails in the 7th and 8th cents. Previously there was only ecclesiastical reconciliation. This theory seems unacceptable both historically and dogmatically (cf. K. Adam, *Die geheime Kirchenbusse nach dem heiligen Augustin* (1921) ; TQ (1929) 1–66). In answer to such theories cf. Galtier, *L'Église et la rémission des péchés aux premiers siècles* (1932). For a belief in the efficacy of the Church's absolution can be shown by a number of considerations in this period. First the Montanists argue that the Church could not forgive the capital sins, for this is '. . . the right and judgment of the Lord and not of the servant, of God himself and not of the priest' (Tertullian, *De Pudicitia*, 21:17). This aptly pinpoints the opposing Catholic belief and claim that their Pax was a divine forgiveness, true absolution (cf. ibid. 18:18 ; 2:13). Secondly the paralleling of Penance with

Baptism is fairly frequent and includes necessarily a belief that its reconciliation is true absolution. Such parallels can be found in Hermas (*Vis.* 3:5 ; *Mand.* 4:3), in the Catholic Tertullian's famous ' second plank of salvation' (*De Poenitentia*, 12:9 ; cf. 3:2–3), and in the *Didascalia Apostolorum* (2:41:1–2) : 'The imposition of hands will be for him [the sinner] in place of Baptism ; for men receive the sharing of the Spirit either by the imposition of hands or by Baptism' (cf. Cyprian, *ep.* 57:4).

Such evidences seem clear, though we must not neglect the obvious emphasis on previous satisfaction, which in practice would mean that penitents were very normally reconciled to God by charity before actually receiving absolution. We shall see later how this causes difficulty to the Scholastics. Nor should we be misled by a group of texts that censure imprudent absolution without regard to dispositions. These texts only stress the dependent position of the minister upon God without denying his true absolving power (cf. Galtier, *De Poenit.* 122 ff.).

III Absolution in the Scholastics. The major question here is concerned with the efficacy of the absolution given by the priest and we shall say a little of the minister also, and of his Jurisdiction.

(i) **The Efficacy of Absolution.** Between the 5th and 11th cents. little change is noted. True absolving power is affirmed and used more frequently by priests, with a growth in private penance. But theological precision is still lacking, so that some texts obscure the idea of the priest's absolution removing not only the penalty but also the guilt of sin. Hence the questionings of the early scholastics find difficulty in this matter. Yet their achievement is remarkable, for they had to use a mass of uncoordinated texts dealing with a subject that included many aspects of a complicated and developing practice. Hence interpretation alone was a difficult matter. (For the most confusing texts cf. Galtier, *De Poenit.* 158 ; Debil in RHE, 15 (1920) 256–73, 442–5.) In addition they had to work out a sacramental theory both in general and for Penance in particular. Finally they had to come to an agreed terminology through a maze of undefined terms (cf. P. Anciaux, *La Théologie du sacrement de pénitence au XIIe siècle*).

Abelard set the direction of development. He asserted the efficacy of CONTRITION understood as Perfect Contrition or charity. Then he began to seek what was left for the priest's absolution to do. In this he reacted against some abusive uses of the power by denying the keys (in the sense of forgiving sins) to any except to the Apostles. This error, which he retracted, was condemned (D 379). Yet those who followed found it hard to explain that same efficacy, for they rightly agreed with Abelard as to the necessity for contrition and as to the efficacy of perfect contrition to remit sins.

The Victorines asserted the priest's power to forgive the eternal penalty of sin but only at the expense of leaving perfect contrition with a suspended effect, making God's forgiveness conditional (Anciaux, *op. cit.* 295 ff.). Peter Lombard sought a solution by teaching that the priest's absolution is declarative of God's forgiveness and remits also some temporal punishment (*IV Sent.* dist. 18 ; Anciaux, *op. cit.* 328 ff.). This became the most general theory with numerous small adaptations such as that of Robert Pulleyn that the act of the priest is the sacramental sign of repentance. A few others point to the inseparability of the act of God, the principal, and of His minister or instrument (Anciaux, *op. cit.* 611).

The 13th-cent. writers were able to build upon these patient efforts and finally harmonized the notions of contrition and attrition, the desire of the sacrament, its principal cause and minister, its eternal and temporal punishment, and the constituent parts of the sacrament. St Thomas rounded off the development of thought by teaching that the acts of the penitent and the act of the priest are two parts of the one process, the quasi-material of the sacrament and its form (3a:84:1–3). Both have efficacy in the remission of sins but they must be taken together even if only joined by the *votum*, the will desiring the sacrament (3a:90:2:@1). Thus priestly absolution signifies and effects God's giving of grace to the contrite sinner (remitting sin or increasing grace according to the state of the penitent) and so is truly though instrumentally efficacious of grace (3a:84:3). The relation of attrition and contrition needed much further development as also did the nature of the causality involved, but the major problem was resolved. No sin is forgiven without true dispositions and yet a real efficacy over sins and for grace is seen in absolution, even when it follows contrition and is given to a soul already in grace.

This solution was generally accepted until Trent taught it (D 896 ff.) with little variation. One variant was the theory of Scotus, followed by Occam and some Nominalists. He took to the limit the real efficacy of the absolution, going so far as to make it the whole sacrament (*In IV Sent.* D 14:Q 2). Thus the penitent's dispositions can be reduced to a minimum, contrition being required outside the sacrament and attrition (even at the lowest level of desire to receive the sacrament and to retain no attachment to sin) being enough in the sacrament. A second variant was that Biel (d. 1495) put forward again the absolute necessity of contrition in the sense of charity and so revived the position of Lombard as to the efficacy of absolution, which was regarded as merely declarative of forgiveness and remissive of temporal punishment He added that it can increase sanctifying grace in those already justified (*In IV Sent.* Dist. 14 & 18).

These centuries of development explain some of the Protestant reaction and provided materials which they would adopt and build into theories with their own special background of justifying faith (*see* ATTRITION).

(ii) **The Minister of Absolution.** By this time it is agreed that bishop and priest are the ministers of the sacrament and absolve. The only difficulty felt arises from the practice of confession to lesser clerics and to laymen (cf. Teetaert, *La Confession aux laïques*). Evidenced by Origen and recommended by many after Bede, this practice never appealed, in its own justification, to the layman's having the power of the keys. Even in the 13th cent., when the sacramental nature of such confession was explicitly debated, only St Albert (*IV Sent.* dist. 17:art. 59 ; also art. 39 @3 and art. 58) is said to have defended it as sacramental, and he denies the layman to have the power of the keys. Its real value, as St Thomas explains it, lies in the fact that, like charity, it contains the desire of priestly absolution, and so can be said to have a kind of sacramental value (*Supplementum 3 partis*:8:3).

(iii) **The Need for Jurisdiction.** The idea of jurisdiction being required for the use of the keys and so for absolution is seen in the early centuries in the dependence of all ministries, including that of reconciliation, upon the bishop. Then, with priest-penitentiaries and the growth of the parish, there developed a body of practices concerned with confession, excommunication and reconciliation, all basically containing this idea, though their origin and full explanation seems to have been eventually forgotten. Thus when the Scholastics in the 12th cent. began to discuss Penance and the power of the keys the idea of such jurisdiction lay for them hidden behind a number of statements and practices. They saw the power to bind and loose connected with the parish or the other cure of souls given by the bishop, and therefore limited, as in the rule that the penitent should confess to his own priest and the priest should not absolve any but those entrusted to him by his superior. The consideration of practical cases of heretics, schismatics, excommunicates and bad priests made the theologians work out the implications of the need for approval or toleration by the Church, for union with the Church, for authorization or establishment by the bishop, if the power of the keys given in ordination is to be used. Thus they were able to see how the common teaching that ordination gives the keys can be reconciled with the idea that the ability to use them can come later and be restricted or removed. Finally the word 'jurisdiction' is used in its present sense by Stephen Langton and the way was open for a full solution of the question (cf. Anciaux, *op. cit.* 523, 539 ff.).

The Council of the Lateran (1215) laid down the precept of annual confession to one's own priest and the need to seek permission (under pain of invalidity) to confess to another (D 437). St Thomas (*IV Sent.* dist. 18:q. 1:art. 1:sol. II:@2) and St Bonaventure (*IV Sent.* dist. 19:art. 2:q. 2) then distinguished clearly between the power of the keys given in ordination and the later jurisdiction which enables the priest to use them (cf. D 474a, and 699). Denied by the Wycliffites along with the power of orders, the need of jurisdiction was taught by Trent (D 903, cf. 921) as the constant belief of the Church. A later denial by the schismatic Synod of Pistoia reducing the need for jurisdiction to an administrative convenience was condemned by Pius VI in

1794 (D 1537). Trent taught also the absence of reservations (and so the possession of jurisdiction by any priest) in danger of death, a practice and teaching long established (D 903).

Whether jurisdiction is needed for absolution of venial sins is less clear. It ought to be, for it also implies a judgment of the sinner, but St Thomas quite inconsequentially denied it (ibid. q. 2:art. 3:sol. I:@3) and others agreed. In practice the question is settled by the decree of Innocent XI, 'Cum ad aures' (1679), forbidding bishops to allow a priest without jurisdiction to hear confessions even of venial sins.

IV The Form of Absolution. Our insufficient knowledge of the earliest ritual of reconciliation makes it impossible to be certain of the formula used. The imposition of hands is mentioned in Origen (*In Levit.*, *hom.* 2:4) and by Cyprian (*ep.* 16:2), and then frequently in the West (cf. Coppens, *L'Imposition des mains* (1925) 374 ff.). We hear of an accompanying invocation of the Spirit, or prayer, from the 5th cent. (e.g. Leo, *ep.* 108): 'The forgiveness of God cannot be obtained except by the prayers of the priests.'

It seems that all such forms in East and West were deprecative, in prayer form, a position that still continues in most Eastern rites unless they have undergone Western influence. In the West (cf. J. Jungmann, *Die lateinischen Bussriten in ihrer geschichtlichen Entwickelung*) a mixed indicative and deprecative form appears in the 12th cent. A few authors, like William of Auvergne (*De Sacra Penitentia*, 19), contended that the deprecative form alone was valid. St Thomas, however, (3a:84:3) argued that the deprecative 'Misereatur tui . . .' was only a prayer, and asserted the indicative *Ego te absolvo* . . . to be the true form. This was universally accepted in the West, being stated by Florence (D 699) and by Trent (D 896), which regarded any other words as not necessary for validity. Yet the deprecative form in various renderings continues to be regarded as valid, as in the Instruction of Clement VIII (1595), the Bull of Benedict XIV, 'Etsi pastoralis' (1742), and the Decree of the Holy Office, 6 Sept. 1865. All these concern its use by the Greeks, the last saying they should use it even when absolving Westerns.

Some problems arise from all this, and the first is, how such varied forms can all be valid. The best solution seems to be that used in other sacraments, namely that many forms are possible if they all have the same significance (cf. SACRAMENTS IN GENERAL). The significance here must be of a judicial absolution which is clearly found in the indicative form and can be seen in others either from the words themselves or from the circumstances in which they are used.

A further problem concerns the validity of the deprecative form in the West today. Billot (*De Penitentia*, Thesis 3) denies its validity because the Church has fixed the form as indicative and so indicates that she deprives of jurisdiction a priest who uses the deprecative. Most theologians reject this view, for despite the rule of the Church it still remains that the deprecative form can be equivalent in significance to the indicative. Furthermore, the Church does not seem to intend to withdraw jurisdiction from the Greeks, as her attitude to them suggests; she also forbids other indicative forms, which nobody would deny to be valid. So it remains that to vary the form would be unlawful but could not necessarily make the form invalid.

A final problem concerns the precise meaning of the form: I absolve thee . . . For cases can arise when sin is not actually there and then absolved (e.g. because of bad dispositions or because the penitent has no sin except those already forgiven) so that the form would seem to be falsified. St Thomas (3a:84:3:@5) suggests: 'Sacramentum absolutionis tibi impendo' (I give thee the sacrament of absolution). This, with varying precisions, is commonly accepted, for the sacrament of absolution can always be given even in such difficult cases.

V Catholic Teaching at Trent. Trent lays down the main points of Catholic teaching as against various Protestant positions (which will not be here detailed, but can be gathered from the statements of Trent). First it is taught that the power of absolution is derived from Jn 20:30; Mt 16:19 and 18:18 (canon 3, D 913 (cf. D 894, 899, 902): and canon 10, D 920). Then it is taught that this power is not just to preach the Gospel of remission or to declare that sins are forgiven by God (canon 3, D 913; canon 9, D 919: cf. D 894, 902), but that its purpose is true remission (cf. D 894, 895, 896, 899, 902) by a judicial process (canon 9, D 919, and *passim*). Finally it is taught that this power was given by Christ to the apostles and their successors, bishops and priests, and not to all the faithful (canon 10, D 920, cf. 902), and that these priests need jurisdiction to use the power they have received in ordination (D 903).

Bibliography. A. D'Alès, *L'Édit de Calliste* (1914); E. Amann and A. Michel, 'Pénitence', DTC 12,722–948 & 948–1127; P. Anciaux, *La Théologie du sacrement de pénitence au XIIe siècle* (1949); E. Doronzo, *De Poenitentia*, 4 vols (1949); E. Göller, *Studien über das gallische Busswesen* (1929); the same, *Papsttum und Bussgewalt in spätrömischer Zeit* (1933); P. Galtier SJ, *L'Église et la rémission des péchés aux premiers siècles* (1932), *De Poenitentia* (1950) and *Aux origines du sacrement de pénitence* (1951); J. Jungmann SJ, *Die lateinischen Bussriten* (1932); *R. Mortimer, *The Origins of Private Penance* (1939); B. Poschmann, *Poenitentia secunda* (1940) and *Busse und letzte Ölung* (1951); A. Teetaert, *La Confession aux laïques* (1926); *O. Watkins, *A History of Penance* (1920); J. Crehan SJ, *Private Penance in the Early Church*, MN 175 (1940) 190–99.   J. McD.

ABSTINENCE Quite apart from being an ascetical practice (for which *see* ASCETICISM), abstinence from food, in the sense of a restraint upon quality rather than quantity, involves one or two theological questions which can be dealt with briefly: (I) the status in the early Church of the food-laws of Ac 15, (II) the purpose of the *statio*, described by Tertullian as *semiieiunium*, and (III) abstinence as a form of supplication.

I The Food-laws of the Council of Jerusalem were enacted for the churches of Syria and Cilicia, i.e. Antioch, Tarsus, Damascus, Anazarba and such towns. It is now generally admitted that the form of text in codex Bezae and its allies, which reduces the legislation to a series of ethical precepts concerned with idolatry, murder and fornication, is secondary, and that the primary form of text deals with restrictions on the kind of food Gentile Christians could take if they wished to live in harmonious social relations with the Jewish Christians who would be numerous in the regions mentioned. Meat that had been offered to idols and was then sold in the meat-market was not in itself evil, as Paul pointed out (1 Cor 8:8–9), but fear of contamination by idolatry was stronger among Jews than it could ever have become among Gentiles. The other prohibition, of meat with the blood in it, was peculiarly Jewish and no one could expect that it would be much appreciated by Gentiles. None the less, the Council was ready to impose these restraints upon parts of the Church for the sake of harmony. It does not seem that they were extended to the new Gentile churches of Greece and Italy, for in 1 Cor Paul writes (from Ephesus) as if no such law weighed upon those who were to hear his epistle. The 'Western' text of Ac, wherever it may have originated, seems to have been revised in such a way as to transform this food-law into one of general ethical conduct, and thus to set free the countries which had that text from the need for observing this kind of abstinence. Ac 16:4 makes clear that the legislation was imposed by Paul on the church of S. Galatia, and the same thing may have been done elsewhere, but there is really no clear evidence until late in the 2nd cent., when the words of one of the martyrs of Lyons imply that the prohibition was in force there (Eusebius, HE 5.1.26), and Minucius Felix (*Octavius*, 30) also appeals to it. Justin a little earlier (*Dial.* 47.2) bears witness rather to a state of confusion about this observance. What seems to have happened generally is that the prohibition of idol-offerings endured, while that of meat not killed in the Jewish way did not. Thus Novatian, writing his *de cibis iudaicis*, considers that idol-meat serves only to strengthen that which is diabolical in a man, while he makes no observations about the other prohibition. He embarks on a theology of meat-eating which cannot be traced earlier and which may have influenced the Church at large (e.g. Jerome, PL 23:237). He claims [1] that man before the Fall lived on fruit and vegetables and that meat-eating was brought in when the duty of earning his bread by hard labour was put upon man. Augustine (*contra Faustum* 32:13 ; PL 42:504) considers the law about ' blood ' abrogated.

II The purpose of the statio is not easily deter-

mined. It was a voluntary practice among Catholics, according to Tertullian's sneer (in a work written when he had joined the Montanists, *De Ieiunio*, 10 and 13:CSEL 20:286 and 291), and it could be called a half-fast (*semiieiunium*). This meant that a man when ' doing sentry for Christ ' (for that is what the military term *statio* implied) went without food until the ninth hour, i.e. until after 3 p.m. or 4 p.m. The connection of this practice with *xerophagia* (or eating of dry, i.e. non-animal, food) is not clear. The word *statio* (transliterated into Greek) is first used in a Christian context in the *Shepherd* of Hermas (GCS 48:52 and 55), where it is a fast on bread and water, the purpose being to give to the poor the equivalent of what has been saved by avoiding normal meals. There is no sign here of the duration of the fast, though it probably lasted for the whole day. The ' half-fast ' of Tertullian will then be a limiting of the duration rather than of the quality of the fast, making it end about 3 p.m. But Tertullian did not distinguish very clearly between fasting by reduction of quantity and abstinence by change of quality of food. He speaks (*De Ieiunio*, 9:CSEL 20:284) of Daniel's living on vegetables (Dan 1:10) as a ' limited fast ' (*portionale ieiunium*), praising it as a means of winning visions from God, and then goes on to cite another and more severe fast of Daniel (10:3), calling it a *statio*, and saying that it too won a vision from God. It seems that the rigorist heretics were trying to bring in their practice of abstaining from meat and wine (i.e. of confining themselves to vegetables) as a stational practice for those who did not wish to fast. Irenaeus says that Tatian was the first to devise this form of blasphemy of the Creator, despising His gifts of meat and wine (*adv. haer.* I:xxvi:1 H). The orthodox rejected it, as we see from Tertullian (*De Ieiunio*, 16:CSEL 20:296), saying that it was what the priests of Isis did. Tertullian's reply was that the devil and his priests always ape the ways of God, but that supposed the Christians were the pioneers of the practice.

The heretics were the pioneers of this xerophagy, but in time it was adopted by orthodox Christian ascetics, and Athanasius cites with approval (*De Virginibus*, 8:TU 14:2a:43) the adage that ' all food is holy that is without a soul '. The same thing happened again with the Manichees. Augustine (*De Moribus Ecclesiae*, 2:14:PL 32:135) says they do not eat eggs nor support their strength with milk.[2] This same abstinence, rejected at the time, afterwards found a place in Christian practice and lasted until recent times. In the same passage Augustine lays down three motives for abstinence, to mortify one's appetite, to avoid being led into idolatry oneself (by taking food or drink that would lead to it), and to avoid giving scandal to others who might think there was idolatry where there was none. As the danger of idolatry waned, the motive of self-denial became paramount. But meanwhile the Church had to take action against those who refused to eat meat. The Council of Ancyra (canon 14,

[1] quia iam non paradisus custodiendus sed mundus totus fuerat excolendus, robustior cibus carnis offertur. Novatian, *de cibis iudaicis*, 2.

[2] nec ova sumunt . . . nec alimonia lactis utuntur.

in Turner's edition 8 and 86), held in 314, ruled that clerics must be degraded for this. 'Those who are priests or deacons, and who abstain from meat, should by the decree of the great and holy synod taste it first, and then, if they wish, they can abstain ; but if they refuse it altogether or will not eat vegetables that have been cooked with the meat, . . . then they must withdraw from the ranks of the clergy.' [1] This tasting would be a reasonable way of weeding out the Manichees. The Apostolic canons, which are 4th-cent. material, order degradation for those who will not eat meat on feast-days (canons 48 and 57 ; Turner, 32z and 32aa). An attempt is made here to enforce once more the prohibition of meat with blood in it, and this is repeated in the Council of Gangra (canon 2 : Turner, 184-6), but in both cases the law seems to be no more than a literal-minded revival of legislation that was in abeyance.

III Abstinence as a form of supplication is suggested as early as the letter of Polycarp to the Philippians (7:2), where ' sobriety with a view to prayer ' is advised. Given the common belief in antiquity that such plants as lettuce, mint, purslane and hemlock led to a cooling of the passions, it can be seen that St Paul's advice (Rom 14:2, in the Western text) to eat vegetables could easily be construed as a hint that the Church linked together diet and contemplation. Quite apart from Tertullian's claim that abstinence helped towards visions, there is the fact that Origen (HE 6:3:9 and c. Cels. 8:30) practised abstinence from wine and from all but the simplest food. Asterius of Amasea at the end of the 4th cent. rails against those who grumble at vegetables and who despise lentils (PG 40:380), adding that they seek to comfort themselves with counterfeit preparations while abstaining from wine. Augustine in a Lenten sermon (PL 38:1043) notices the same thing : ' Some seek to replace their customary wine by unwonted liquors and by the distilling of other fruits they make up to themselves, and that more sweetly, what they deny themselves from the grape.' He goes on to say that with true abstinence prayer is lifted up on wings. Thus not only was abstinence regarded as a meritorious deed which God might be expected to reward with some gift of contemplation but it was also seen as a physical preparation for prayer. Novatian (de cibis, 6), recalling that a Christian must pray at night as well as by day, describes how the mind is numbed by a heavy banquet and not left free to pray.[2] This view passes into the common inheritance of the ascetic writers of the days of early monasticism.

Bibliography. J. Schuemmer, *Die altchristliche Fastenpraxis* (1933) ; V. Ermoni in DAC I:207-13 ; and *see also* FASTING. J. H. C.

ACACIAN SCHISM A schism between the Eastern and Western Churches, lasting from 484 to 519, which originated under Acacius, Patriarch of Constantinople from 471 to 489, during the Monophysite controversy. It was caused by the so-called *Henoticon* of the Emperor Zeno, propounded in 482 as a Christological formula of compromise designed to reconcile the Monophysites with the orthodox, but which practically abandoned the definition of Chalcedon on the two natures in Christ. Its principal author was most probably Acacius. The formula, far from restoring peace between the two parties, only increased the tension. The uncompromising Monophysite Peter Mongus was made Patriarch of Alexandria with the help of Acacius and Zeno, in opposition to the orthodox choice of John Talaia. The latter complained to the Pope, Felix III, who sent two legates, bishops Vitalis and Misenus, to Constantinople to summon Acacius to Rome to defend himself against the accusations before a synod. Instead, the two legates let themselves be persuaded by Acacius to communicate with him and Peter Mongus. The Pope thereupon excommunicated them at a synod held in Rome in 484, together with Acacius himself, who was deposed, excommunicated and anathematized. Felix III notified Acacius of the decree in a letter of 28 July 484, carried to Constantinople by another envoy named Tutus. Acacius refused to accept the condemnation ; he even won over Tutus to his cause and erased the name of the Pope from the diptychs, thus formally expressing the separation of Constantinople from the Roman see. The Eastern Churches followed the lead of Acacius and enforced the acceptance of the Henoticon by persecuting the Catholics, especially the Acoemetae monks who faithfully defended the doctrine of Chalcedon. The schism continued even after the death of Acacius, being finally ended in 519 when the Emperor Justin submitted to Pope Hormisdas.

Bibliography. E. Schwartz, *Publizistische Sammlungen zum acacianischen Schisma* (Abhandlungen der bayrischen Akademie der Wissenschaften (1934), n. 10) ; also DHGE s.v. and DTC s.v. Acace de Constantinople. H. G.

ACCIDENTS The following plan forms the framework of this treatment of accidents : (I) The real things of this world which we experience are totalities which are structures of substance and accidents. Since accidents are real, we try to discover what they are—(II) the essence of accidents. A grasp of what an accident is should lead to a clear idea of the type of (III) existence accidents have. Finally there is (IV) the division of accidents, in which the categories and other divisions are mentioned.

I We experience structures of substance and accidents. It is quite impossible to grasp the meaning of accident as understood by the scholastics without relating it to their doctrine of substance and the real distinction of the latter from accident. This distinction of substance and accident is intimately

---

[1] Qui presbyteri aut diaconi sunt et abstinent se a carne, placuit sancto et magno synodo ut gustent primum et sic, si voluerint, abstineant se ; si autem spernunt, vel olera quae cum ipsa carne coquntur non manducant, . . . conpescant se ab ordine clericorum.

[2] molem pectori inpositam mens cibo vinoque sopita non valuerit excutere.

connected with the theory of knowledge, and error here may lead to the reduction of all reality to substance or, and this is equally disastrous, to the conviction that reality is phenomena (cf. Descartes, *The Principles of Philosophy*, part I, ch. 53 ; Hume, *A Treatise of Human Nature*, bk. 1, I, §vi and bk. 1, IV, §vi). One might also claim that a false theory of knowledge is closely linked to a false psychology, and the search for a true understanding of accidents might well begin in this field of thought.

In psychology it is unsound to sever man's senses from his intellect though the operation has been performed and at times without any clear idea of intellect. Sense experience is sometimes considered to be clear if not entirely objective, and impressions are supposed to form the content of our knowledge. An approach such as this cannot but destroy all hope of discovering the true nature of accidents and their division.

The Thomist approach is adequately expressed in the phrase 'non proprie loquendo sensus aut intellectus cognoscit, sed homo per utrumque'. Our consciousness is one, at the same time sensitive and intellective, and it is the consciousness of the man. We cannot claim a sense experience divorced from intellectual experience, for the activity of our faculties of sense entails the activity of our intellect and *we* are conscious. We experience, and the objects of our experience are particular real entities, realities, either living or inanimate. In our common grasp of reality we are conscious of our possession of determined things, of totalities, which totalities, subjected to philosophical scrutiny, disclose themselves as structures of substance and accidents. (Non-technically we may speak of an underlying reality and its appearances.) These total realities which form the objective content of our experience may be things other than ourselves or we may ourselves become objects of our experience and consideration. An external object, an other thing, is a totality whole and distinct from the remainder of reality. In our experience of it, it changes in appearance while retaining its identity, and so it allows us to distinguish between a subject which suffers change whilst remaining intact in itself and its changed state. The distinction between substance and accident is made.

Our experience of self is still more lucid, and a consideration of self through various states of joy, sickness or activity discloses a persistent and stable subject which remains such though undergoing various changes. There is a permanent and fundamental subject which is not merely of the order of consciousness but is also material and extended, and this persistent reality is variously modified at different times whilst remaining fundamentally the same. We are discovering a structure of substance and accidents in the total reality of experience and it is these accidents we must examine.

II The essence of accidents. The relationship of accidents to substance is such that we must unavoidably refer to the latter. Indeed a first approach to the understanding of accidents might be gained by realising that they do *accede* to a substance. They are not a part of that substance though together with it they constitute the total reality of experience. This should not be understood to mean that accidents are separate but minor totalities in some way affixed to another and more important totality. They are not like labels on a jar or paint on a door but do intrinsically affect that subject in which they inhere. They affect it, determine it, modify it, while leaving it basically the same. In a sense they are surface changes though they really are changes and not merely additions. They are not added as existing things to existing substances. Indeed they cannot be called 'things' in the full sense of the word. They are not so much things which exist as those by which a particular thing which is of some basic type is determined in a further way, a way conformable with the type it is. Even this is not exact, for though it may appear that accidents exist in substances which exist in themselves, modifying those remaining substances, such inherence is not entirely necessary. If it were of the nature of an accident to inhere in a substance it would be impossible for accidents to exist otherwise. To exist otherwise would be equivalent to an alteration of the essence of the accident. It would be the destruction of accident. Moreover, one should not attempt to state the essence of an accident by including its existence in the definition. Accidental existence is in no way part or the whole of accidental essence. At least this is true in Thomism where there is a real distinction between essence and existence. The Thomist therefore defines an accident as that to which belongs existence in another as in its subject (cf. St Thomas, *IV Sent.* 12:1:1: *solutio* 1 : @2). He means that the essence of an accident is such that it demands to exist in another, and that naturally it cannot exist without being in another as in its subject. And the subject in which it inheres is a constituted substance which provides support for the accident, is actualized by it in a secondary fashion, and regards accidents as a material and sometimes as an efficient cause (cf. St Thomas, *Quaestio de Virtutibus in communi*, 3).

Since an accident is not to be defined by including its existence in the definition, for an accident is that which has an aptitude to exist by inherence in something else as in its subject, there would appear to be no reason why an accident should not by God's power be separated from substances. The aptitudinal inherence of an accident need not be actualized, yet the accident could exist if the basic inability for existence in itself were supplemented by some effective support which itself did not become a subject for the accident. This is the case in the Eucharist, where God supports the accidents of the bread and wine without these accidents inhering in and modifying Him (cf. *Summa*, 3a:77:1:c).

This description of accidents in general would not be complete without mention of the fact that some accidents do not inhere in their substance immediately. Their immediate subject is another and more basic accident. Such is the case of the qualities of bodies. Though inhering mediately in substance, their immediate subject is quantity (cf. *Summa*, 3a:77:2 @1).

III The existence of accidents. Up to the present, the emphasis has been on the essence of accidents, on what they are, and this refers them to their subject. The existence or entitative act of accidents forms a point of controversy. It is the common and more likely view amongst Thomists that accidents do have their own existence and do not exist with the existence of the substance they modify. A full treatment of this controversy is out of place here, but the basic argument of the majority of Thomists might be mentioned briefly. It is based on the ideas that existence regards essence as act does potency, and that there is a proportion between act and potency (*see* ACT AND POTENCY). The existence of an accident ought therefore to be proportioned to its essence, which would not be the case if the accident existed with the existence of the substance (St Thomas, *IV Sent.* 12:1:1:*solutio* 3: @5). The problem does not arise for Suarezians or Scotists who do not admit a real distinction between essence and existence. It must, however, be borne in mind that to attribute its own existence to an accident is not to elevate it to the status of substance. The conservation of the accidental essence demands that it be related to its subject. Any view of accidents which distinguishes them from substances as from equals, any view which implicitly assumes that accidents require to exist in themselves, is quite false and destructive of the essence of accidents.

IV Divisions of accidents. We have seen that accidents form part of our experience of reality. We have tried to discover their essence and the type of existence which actualizes that essence. The next point for consideration is the division of accidents. There are various divisions of accidents, and again some controversy concerning the number of ways in which a substance may be accidentally modified. But leaving controversy aside for the moment we can turn first of all to the metaphysical predicaments or categories. As there is classification of object in zoology, so in metaphysics there is a classification of being, the object of metaphysics. The supreme groupings of being, which groupings are mutually exclusive, are known as the categories or predicaments. In origin these categories are Aristotelian, in number they are ten. They are, substance, quantity, quality, relation, action, sufferance, whenness, whereness, posture, and state. Substance is not our concern here, so we may say there are nine fundamental classes or groups of modifications of a substance. They are the ultimate groupings of the determinants which can alter a substance whilst leaving it fundamentally the same. Not all scholastics are prepared to admit these ten categories are really distinct one from another. To admit less than ten that are so distinct is to affirm there are not ten supreme classes of being. One can only admit as many categories as supreme classes of being, and to decide the question each category should be examined in itself and should be retained only if the evidence for it as a really distinct class of being is adequate. (To deny that the categories are really distinct one from another and at the same time to insist on ten categories is to consider the categories not as supreme classes of being but simply as predicates.) The Thomists in general admit the ten traditional categories. Those scholastics who are not prepared to accept a real distinction between all ten find no difficulty with the first three categories. The controversy is restricted to 'relation' and the following six predicaments, and those who maintain the traditional view do allow the dependence of these last six categories on something extrinsic to the modified reality. They insist, however, on some resulting intrinsic determination in the substance. It is hardly the place in this article to treat the question at any length since the defence of some of the categories belongs to other parts of philosophy.

Omitting substance, and taking the traditional view of the remaining categories (for convenience, since one can discard any of the last seven which cannot be proved) the categories are defined or described in the following manner :

Quantity is an accident giving substance parts outside parts, *or* it is that by which a body is said to be of this or that size. *Quality* is an accident which determines and perfects a substance in itself by reason of form (e.g. warmth, texture or will). *Relation* is an accident whose essence it is to refer to something else (e.g. fatherhood). *Action* is an accident which belongs to an agent in so far as the agent is the source of movement in another. *Sufferance* is an accident which belongs to a subject in so far as the subject is the recipient of motion from another. *Whenness* is an accident resulting in a subject from the time by which it is measured. *Whereness* is an accident resulting in a subject from its being surrounded by place. *Posture* is an accident resulting in a body from the arrangement of the parts of that body in place. *State* is an accident resulting in a body due to its being clothed, armed, or ornamented.

On the assumption that these categories are really distinct one from another it is evident they are not all of equal interest. Nevertheless, they all merit some philosophical consideration if they are supreme classes of determinations of substances.

The division into nine supreme *genera* is not the only division of accidents in scholasticism. Accidents are divided into absolute and modal. Absolute accidents modify the substance immediately, e.g. quantity, and at least by divine power can exist separate from a substance. This is the case of quantity and qualities in the Eucharist. Modal accidents affect absolute accidents immediately and only through the absolute accidents do they affect the substance. They cannot exist alone even by divine power. So, for example, the curvature of a line could not exist alone.

A further division of accidents is into proper and common. Proper accidents are said to be those which flow from the specific essence of the subject so that they belong solely to the individuals of that species. In this sense it is true that reason is a proper accident of man. Common accidents are said to proceed from the generic essence and in this way they are common to the individuals of the various species included in that genus. As an example one might take quantity which is common to all bodies.

Finally one may discover in scholasticism a division of accidents into intrinsic and extrinsic. An intrinsic accident is one which inheres in a subject which it intrinsically modifies. An accident is said to be extrinsic if it merely extrinsically denotes the subject though it does not inhere in that subject. So knowledge is an intrinsic accident of the knower. The thing which is known is a known thing, and knowledge is said to be an extrinsic accident of that thing.

It might be well to point out that throughout this article when accident has been referred to substance it has been to finite substance that reference has been made. Infinite substance, being pure actuality, is beyond any accidental modification.

Bibliography. The sources, of course, are Aristotle and St Thomas Aquinas. Aristotle's *Categories* and his *Metaphysics*, VII, 4–5, should be consulted. In addition to the references in the text, see St Thomas Aquinas, *De Ente et Essentia*, VII. A useful selection of modern authors is : P. Coffey, *Ontology* (1938) ; F. Van Steenberghen, *Ontology* (1952) ; L. De Raeymaeker, *Philosophie de l'être, essai de synthèse métaphysique* (Éditions de l'institut supérieur de philosophie (1947)) ; and P. Dezza, *Metaphysica Generalis* (1948²). Some treatment of accidents will be found in any textbook of scholastic philosophy. One might mention here just a few authors, such as Boyer, Gredt, Hugon, and Maquart.

For a discussion whether some predicaments are really distinct intrinsic determinations of substance, confer P. Hoenen, *Cosmologia* (1945³) 67 ff., 218 ff., 249, and 449 ff. W. A. O.

ACCLAMATIONS One of the methods for electing a Pope, still held lawful by the present legislation of the Church (in the Constitution *Vacante sede* of Pius X), is the way of acclamation in which, as it were by inspiration, the whole body of Cardinals shout the word *Eligo* when one of their number has put forward the name of a candidate. This usage is a survival of the method followed in the early Church at all elections of priests and bishops. The Church seems (as Jerome noted, *epist.* 146) to have taken over a secular practice here, for the army often nominated an emperor in this way, e.g. Antoninus Diadumenos, who, according to his Life in the *Scriptores Historiae Augustae*, was presented to them as a boy and was greeted with the cry, *Puer Antoninus dignus imperio* (the boy Antoninus is worthy of imperial power). Hippolytus (*Trad. apost.* 6, Ethiopic and *Testamentum Domini*, I, 21) lays it down that after the prayer of ordination of a priest the people are to cry out, ' Amen and Amen ; he is worthy '. When Fabian was present in the meeting (traditionally dated to 10 Jan. 236) held to elect a successor to Pope Anteros, a dove settled on his head and the whole assembly cried out with one accord, ' Worthy is he ' (Eusebius H.E. 6, 29, 4). The election of St Ambrose was equally unrehearsed, as his Life by Paulinus (PL 14, 31) shows and as Theodoret relates (HE 4, 7, 3 ; GCS 44, 219).

Origen has an outspoken criticism of such elections. ' Let the rulers of the Church learn not to designate in testamentary fashion as their successors men joined to them by ties of blood and relationship and not to treat positions of authority in the Church as legacies, but let them fall back on the judgment of God, not choosing the one whom human affection recommends but leaving the whole matter of the choice of a successor to the decision of God.' He does not refer to the choice of Matthias by lot, but cites Num 27:18–20 on the choice of Josue to follow Moses (where Josue is described as ' a man in whom is the Spirit '), and he adds, ' No popular acclamation here, no regard of kindred, no thought of nearness in blood ' (*hom. in Num.* 22, 4 ; GCS 30, 208). The effect of such strictures seems to have been to defer the acclamation until after the descent of the Spirit at the laying-on of hands, as shown by Hippolytus's ordering of the ceremony. But this delay in letting the people have their say about the candidate until he was actually ordained did not seem logical to all the Fathers. Theophilus of Alexandria (canon 6 ; PG 65, 40) lays down that the body of priests is to choose the new priest, the bishop is to test him, and then the election is to take place in the presence of the whole people, the bishop calling to them in the hope that they will bear witness to the candidate's worthiness. In similar fashion the ordaining bishop makes a pause in the ceremony even today, and the question is put to the people about the worthiness of the candidate, although the answer of the Archdeacon is now part of the ceremonial. On one occasion at least (Synesius, *epist.* 67 ; PG 66, 1413) the people did not wait for the *interrogatio* but shouted that they would not have the candidate proposed to them as bishop. It would not be fair to conclude from all this that the Church had a democratic constitution based on universal adult suffrage, for she had borrowed the institution from an empire in which only the merest outward forms of democracy survived, but at the same time the institution did enable the faithful to fulfil their rôle of passive guardians of the Tradition, for when a candidate was presented whose teachings were heretical, he might be rejected by acclamation, in the same way as when the Lector gave a newly-improvized twist to a familiar passage of Scripture he might be shouted down.

The classic instance of acclamations in the choice of a bishop is St Augustine's putting forward (26 Sept. 426) of Eraclius as his own coadjutor with right of succession (*epist.* 213 ; PL 33, 966). Two bishops are present with seven priests, many clerics and the people, and the whole transaction was taken down by notaries. Here the acclamations (*Fiat, fiat,* and the like) are actually counted and we are told that, for example, the people shouted, ' We thank you for your decision ' sixteen times. Along with these 'official' shouts, there were many that expressed simple goodwill, and here perhaps for the first time the *laudes* are met with, in the form of the cry *Exaudi, Christe; Augustino vita* (Hear us, Christ; long life to Augustine). At the end of the same century (*Collectio Avellana* 103; CSEL 35, 478, and 487) Pope Gelasius is greeted with the same cry (13 May 495), and now the addition of what was to become a litany has been made: *Domine Petre, tu illum serva* (Lord Peter, do thou preserve him). From such small beginnings came the whole liturgical development of litany-prayers, of the *Christus vincit*, and also of the *laudes regiae* which were begun by the emperors after Charlemagne who did not want to be outdone by Pope or bishops. Even the *deprecatio Gelasi*, with its refrain of *Kyrie eleison*, may have come from a similar canalization of popular emotion, and the Visigothic practice of having no service on Good Friday but of resorting to the church and shouting the word *Indulgentia* some 500 times is due to the same (PL 85, 428–9).

When a newly-consecrated bishop has to approach his consecrator at the end of the service and chant his *Ad multos annos* three times with rising pitch, he is doing what the Latin *Pontificals* have prescribed since the 13th cent., but he is also preserving a tradition of acclamation which has elsewhere almost died out in the Church. It is hardly true that acclamation had, as Kantorowicz claims, constitutive power, but it was certainly used to designate or to elect for an office one who had been previously selected by the body of priests. By the way in which Byzantine usages have taken root in Russia it may even be possible that the Soviet idea of an election, with no rival candidates and a unanimous vote, owes something to this early Christian usage. It merits the attention of theologians, not for this reason but for its importance in giving sharper definition to the concept of the Church in an age when so little was formulated about the nature of the Church, and its influence on the liturgy was immense.

Bibliography. E. Peterson, *Heis Theos* (1926); *E. Kantorowicz, *Laudes Regiae* (1946); F. Dölger, *Sol salutis* (1925); *H. J. Tillyard, 'Byzantine Acclamations', in *Annals of British School at Athens*, 18 (1911) 239–60; T. Klauser, RAC I, 217–33; F. Cabrol, OSB in DAC I, 240–65.   J. H. C.

ACCOMMODATED SENSE, THE This is not a sense of Scripture, but a sense attributed to the words of Scripture by their application to some person or thing not contemplated by the sacred writer. Such an application may be made in two different ways. It may retain the meaning of the biblical words while substituting a new application. Thus a person after succumbing to temptation might say 'The serpent deceived me', Gen 3:13. Such usage of Scripture is called accommodation by extension. And secondly an application of a scriptural text may retain its words but with a meaning different from that intended in the Bible. Thus

a zealous missionary might use the words of the king of Sodom in the Vulgate translation ' *Da mihi animas*', Gen 14:21 (lit. 'Give me souls'; DV 'Give me the persons'). Such application is called accommodation by allusion.

I Names. Theodore of Mopsuestia, who erroneously thought that the Evangelists cited passages of the OT not as predictions but merely as applicable also to events of the NT, spoke of them as applied κατ' ἔκβασιν, i.e. in accordance with (the similarity of) the event. (This opinion was anathematized by Pope Vigilius in the fifth Council of Constantinople in 553 (Mansi, 9:212, 229, 386). Cardinal Cajetan, who wrote a short treatise, 1519, defending the Holy See against the charge of having made an illegitimate use of Scripture in the decretals, speaks of using texts *transumptive* when their meaning is 'transferred' to something not intended by the inspired writer. But it was only later in the 16th cent. that this question of altering the application or meaning of Scripture texts came to receive formal treatment; and the modern terminology has its roots in this time. Vasquez, 1598, speaks of texts used *per accommodationem*. Nicolaus Serarius, 1612, and Jacobus Bonfrerius, 1625, use the term *sensus accommodatitius*, but this was finally denounced by Francis Xavier Patrizi, 1844, as rather barbarous, and *sensus accommodatus* was substituted in its place.

II Legitimacy. There can be no question of the legitimacy of this applied use of Scripture texts as it is found in the Scriptures themselves. Thus St John in Apoc 11:4 writes, 'These are the two olive trees and the two lamps which stand before the Lord of the earth' (WV) and he is speaking of the two witnesses. But in Zach 4:3, 14, whence the figure is taken, the two persons intended are Jesus (Joshua), the high-priest, and Zorobabel. This is an example of accommodation by extension. Then our Lord Himself said that 'in that day' He would use the words 'Depart from me, you that work iniquity', Mt 7:23. Now these words are from Ps 6:9, where they are the expression of the psalmist's own wish, whereas in the Gospel they are the words of the Judge of the world and express a very different kind of departure. This is an example of accommodation by allusion.

It is not surprising, therefore, that the Church should also make use of accommodation in her liturgy. Thus the praise of Aaron in Ecclus 45:8, ' He made an everlasting covenant with him, and gave him the priesthood of the nation, and made him blessed in glory', is applied to canonized bishops. This is accommodation by extension. Then of the Saints in general the Church makes use of Ps 66:36, ' *Mirabilis Deus in sanctis suis*', understood in the sense that 'God is wonderful in his saints', whereas the meaning originally intended refers to God in His heavenly sanctuary. This is accommodation by allusion. The Fathers too make frequent applications of biblical texts to thoughts of their own, and what they term a spiritual sense is often this accommodated sense. In many passages St Bernard's writings are almost a mosaic of Scripture terms and phrases, and his skill in their use shows what unction this method can achieve.

III Abuses. Pope Pius XII in his Encyclical *Divino afflante Spiritu* (*Enchiridion Biblicum* (1954²) §553) warns writers and preachers against ever using transferred meanings as if they were the true sense of Scripture. And the Council of Trent, Sessio 5, cap. I *de reformatione*, severely condemns all unworthy and irreverential use of Scripture and orders the due punishment of offenders (*Enchiridion Biblicum*, (1954²) §64). Finally, the accommodated sense should never be used in the proof of sacred truths, as its use would add nothing to the validity of the argument and would at least appear to be making an unwarranted appeal to the authority of the Bible.

Bibliography. Thomae de Vio Caietani Cardinalis, *Opuscula Omnia* (1588), Tom. I Tract. 30 ; G. Vazquez SJ, *Opera* (1631, 1st ed. 1598) I Disput. XIV ; N. Serarius SJ, *Prolegomena Biblica* (1612) 152–4 ; J. Bonfrerius SJ, *Pentateuchus Moysis . . . praemissis . . . Praeloquiis* (1625) cap. xx, §vii ; F. X. Patritius SJ, *De Interpretatione Scripturarum* (1844) 284–91 ; R. Cornely SJ, *Introductio in V.T. Libros Sacros* (1885) I, 543–9.   E. F. S.

ACOLYTES. *See* ORDERS

ACT AND POTENCY The doctrine of act and potency is primarily an explanation of (I) change and among its many applications (II) supernatural change is included. Secondly it is used as (III) an interpretation of all Being.

I Change, as Aristotle and the Scholastics show, involves not only a cause outside the thing changed but also two factors within it. There must be not only an external cause with the *active potency* or power to change something else and produce something new, e.g. to heat a body and produce a new state of heat ; but also there must be in the thing changed both passive potency and act. *Passive potency*, a capacity to be changed, to receive some new state or determination, cannot exist by itself ; it must be in a subject or substance which is what it is because of its act. This technical term ' act ' can apply not only to action or operation but also to what is effected by an action, and even to any positive determination or perfection. Thus a state of heat can be regarded as an act, and a man's soul, which makes him the sort of thing he is, is an act. All finite substances have some positive perfection or act, but they are changeable, at least as regards accidental states or conditions, and can become to some extent other than what they are. As possessing positive perfection they have or are act ; as changeable they are potential, possess potency for an additional act. Hence an act which does not inhere in or intrinsically modify another act is called a *first* or primary act, e.g. a soul. A real accident is something which of its nature can exist only by inhering in its substance ; it is a *second(ary)* act with regard to its substance. If, however, the accident is an active potency, e.g. an acquired skill, it is itself first act with regard to its operation. A substance, then, is first act as regards both its real accidents and its operations. Properly so called potency belongs to an existing substance or subject and is therefore called *subjective* potency to distinguish it from objective potency or mere possibility.

A material substance, moreover, can be changed substantially. It can, that is, lose its individual identity and be changed into a thing of another kind. So, e.g. food is transformed into living tissue and an egg when fertilized becomes a new animal. The passive potency for this deeper change is called *Matter* or *Prime Matter*, and the act which determines the essence of a thing, making it the kind of thing it is, is called *substantial form*. Matter and form do not exist only at the moment of change but by their union a material substance is constituted and they remain as long as it does. A finite immaterial substance, too, has both act and potency though it has not the potency of substantial change which is called matter.

The notions of act and potency and the principles concerning them are applied in many ways by Scholastics. Especially noteworthy are the explanations of the operations of man's intellect and will. By his intellect man knows reality but neither all of it at once nor at every moment. He is changed in coming to know and his intellect must first of all be actuated and determined in order to know this particular thing rather than that. That is why the human intellect is sometimes called a passive power :[1] though active, it is not purely active. Now sense-elements or states, being affected by material conditions, are unable by themselves to act directly on the immaterial, spiritual intellect. God, of course, can act on it directly and St Augustine sought to explain human knowledge by divine illumination. St Thomas on the other hand wishing to safeguard man's secondary causality without any trace of or excuse for OCCASIONALISM adopted from Aristotle the theory of the active intellect (*intellectus agens*). The only function of this wholly active power in man is to determine its correlative power, the passive intellect (*intellectus possibilis*), and thus enable it to produce its particular act of knowing. The active intellect is not changed by acting, it is always ' in act ' ; it is thus a good example of the truth that a cause as such is not changed by causing (*agens qua agens non mutatur*), but its effects on the passive intellect are conditioned by the sense-presentations or ' phantasms ' which it ' illumines ' and makes ' actually intelligible '.

The human will likewise, though an active potency is not always in operation and in order to will a particular object it has to be actuated by a final cause, some good, that is, known by the intellect, which attracts the will. When, however, several goods are presented, the will can sometimes itself freely decide which of the goods attracting it shall prevail. Scholastic theories designed to reconcile both God's natural cooperation in created activity

---

[1] *potentia passiva, virtus passiva.* (See St Thomas, 1a:79:2 ; ibid. 3@1 ; *De Veritate* 16:1@13 ; *In Boethium de Trinitate* 1:1c.)

and the supernatural movements of grace with the freedom of man's will do not all apply the principles of act and potency in the same way. *See* FREE WILL; GRACE. While almost all admit the necessity of God's immediate cooperation (*concursus immediatus*), some maintain further that any created activity, human free will included, must receive from God an additional power (*complementum virtutis*) before it can produce its second act, its operation, and be constituted *in actu secundo*, and this even though it is not only remotely (*in actu primo remoto*) but even proximately (*in actu primo proximo*) ready or equipped for action. Others deny the necessity of this physical premotion by God and this divergence of views seems ultimately to entail a difference in ideas of created active potency.

The most important use of the theory is in proving the existence of God (*see* GOD, EXISTENCE OF). Metaphysical proofs of the existence of God involve inferences from potency to pure act, from the dependent to the wholly independent and from the relative to the Absolute, God. Some, besides using other proofs, argue from any real change, that is from any actuation of passive potency to its first and wholly independent cause, which is God. Others consider this proof insufficient by itself to prove a transcendent first cause and prefer another line of proof which is accepted by all Scholastics and is more fundamental. This proof starts from a substance's dependence on something else not merely for the acquisition of a second, accidental act, but even for its first act and for its whole being. Any substance which begins to be is clearly contingent in the sense of being dependent on something else for its being. Any substance, too, which is in any way changeable, i.e. which possesses any passive potency, can be shown to be contingent in this way. Now such dependence involves a first necessary being on which every contingent thing depends, at least ultimately. So whatever is potential is contingent and God, the first cause and necessarily existing being, is distinct from all other beings and is transcendent. God is pure act, while all other things are composed of act and potency in varying degrees, this variation giving rise to the metaphysical scale or hierarchy of being, things being of greater or less perfection as they have more act or less, less passive potency or more, and with the increase in perfection goes their greater likeness to God.

II Supernatural change. While the philosopher explains change and that which is of its nature changeable the theologian deals with the supernatural change called justification and with that supernatural state of union with God which intellectual creatures can enjoy though God's free gift. In philosophical terms sanctifying grace is the act in a creature by which it is supernaturalized and the passive potency corresponding to it is called *obediential potency*, the name, drawn from St Augustine (*De Genesi ad litteram* 9.17.32, PL 34:406; *De Praedestinatione Sanctorum* 5:10, PL 44:968), indicating the creature's 'obedience' or subjection to the supernatural action of God. About the exact nature of obediential potency in this sense (a full tabulation and explanation of the different senses of this word are given by Garrigou-Lagrange, *De Revelatione* (1929³) I, 376-8), opinions vary with the positions adopted concerning the exact nature of the SUPERNATURAL and the possibility of a natural desire of the BEATIFIC VISION, but it seems best to say that obediential potency for the supernatural life is simply an existing intellectual creature's real capacity of being raised to a supernatural state by God. A dog cannot be so raised, for it has no intellect and it is only the possession of an intellect that makes it possible for a creature to be supernaturally united to God in knowledge and love. This potency, then, is not mere possibility, objective potency, but is an existing reality bound up with the nature of an existing intellectual being. Nor on the other hand is it a special preparation for or disposition to the supernatural. It is not something added to the existing thing nor can it be taken away from it. In that respect it is natural, indeed necessary, to its subject, as Scotus rightly insisted. Its actuation or fulfilment, however, is supernatural and in this respect the potency looks towards the supernatural. The term 'obediential potency' has the merit of including both these aspects. Lastly some have held that a power of action can be supernaturally increased or stepped up by God so as to share instrumentally in the production of a supernatural effect. This theory of an active obediential potency seems quite consistent with the presuppositions of those who hold it, notably Suarez (*Disputationes Metaphysicae*, Disp. 43.4.6; *In tertiam partem S. Thomae*, Disp. 31, §5, nn. 8-9, and §6), but will not fit in with some other Scholastic systems.

III Interpretation of Being. All who admit that God is not bound to create must agree that there is some distinction between the creature's essence and its existence, for if creation is not necessary the creature's essence does not, as God's essence does, entail existence (*see* PANTHEISM). Again in every being which is not unique in its kind there is certainly some distinction between its specific essence, by which it is similar to other members of its species, and its haecceity or individuality, by which it is this particular individual distinct from other members of its species. But about the exact nature of these distinctions there is disagreement among Scholastics. According to the view most commonly accepted today, that of the Thomistic school, the first of these distinctions, that between created essence and its existence, is a real distinction, one, that is, which in no way depends on our thought, for in all existing creatures essence and existence are two elements or principles, essence being subjective passive potency with respect to existence, its act. This follows from the still more fundamental thesis of this school that act being of itself without limit can be limited only by the passive potency which receives it. So the act of existence is limited by the essence which it actuates. There is a further distinction in a material thing for its essence is

made up of form and matter, the form, the act of
the essence, being both limited and multiplied in
different individuals by matter, its receptive potency.
An angel on the other hand being a pure spirit has
no matter to limit or individuate its act or form,
and therefore contains the whole perfection of its
species and is unique in its species. All being is thus
comprehended under act and potency, the most
fundamental distinction possible being that between
God, pure act, who alone is absolutely simple, and
creatures, composed at least of potency and the act
of existence. Lastly, among the theologians who
defend a real essence-existence distinction only
some, e.g. Capreolus, Billot (*De Verbo Incarnato*
(1927³), thesis 7, §3 136–46), use it in their explanation of the HYPOSTATIC UNION. Making the act of
existence the ultimate constituent of a person they
explain the fact that Christ's human nature has no
human personality but is supernaturally united with
the Second Person of the Trinity, by its being a
created essence which is actuated only by his divine
existence.

Though the Thomistic synthesis just outlined has
some difficulties—few systems are perfect and not
all are properly understood—it reaches a high degree
of consistency, especially now that some exaggerations have disappeared. Still there are some minor
differences over, for example, the exact meaning of
the terms ' real distinction ' or ' limit '.

Other Scholastics either deny the Thomistic theses
on the limitation of act and on the distinction
between created essence and its existence, like Scotus
and Suarez (Suarez may well have known only a
more exaggerated Thomistic theory about essence
and existence and not the more refined one current
today. See, e.g. *Disp. Metaphysicae*, Disp. 31:1, nos.
3, 7, 13), or else regard them as not proved. For
these other Scholastics the most radical distinction is
that between the necessary being, God, and contingent being. They accept in common with all
Scholastics the fundamental Aristotelian teaching on
act and potency as the explanation of change and
they admit that all finite things must have some
passive potency, at least accidental, but they regard
the Thomistic theory of act being of itself unlimited
and its corollary, a real distinction between created
essence and its existence, as an excessively Platonist
development. This divergence seems to come
finally from different views about knowledge by
universal ideas, for the Thomistic school tends to
emphasise the universal and to descend to individual
things while other Scholastics claim that they start
with individual things and build up their interpretation thereon. Of course if too much stress is laid
on the individual there is danger of NOMINALISM,
for if the individual alone is real then the universal
is only a general term, a common noun.

Bibliography. I. Aristotle treats of Act and
Potency in *Metaphysics*, book 5, ch. 12 and book 9.
St Thomas does so in his *Commentary on Aristotle's
Metaphysics*, L.4 lect. 14 and L.9 and he frequently
refers to these notions, e.g. 1a:25:1 ; *De Potentia*, 1:1.
Besides Scholastic manuals see Maritain, *Introduction
to Philosophy*, 239–52 ; D'Arcy, *Thomas Aquinas*,
104–10, 114–18.

II. For treatment of obediential potency outside
theological manuals see A. M. Pirotta, *Disputatio de
' Potentia Obedientiali ' iuxta thomisticam doctrinam* in
Divus Thomas (Piacenza) 32 (1929) 574–85 ; 33
(1930) 129–48, 360–85, 560–75 ; G. Laporta,
Appétit naturel et puissance obédientielle, in ETL 5
(1928) 257–77 ; L. Charlier, *Puissance passive et
désir naturel selon saint Thomas* ibid. 7 (1930) 5–28,
639–62 ; and a historical note, *Aux origines de la
' puissance obédientielle '*, in RT 47 (1947) 304–10.
Among the older theologians Ripalda, *De Ente
Supernaturali* (1634, reprinted 1871), vol. 2, Disp.
25–8. Suarez's theory is exposed by P. Dumont in
DTC 14:2665–70.

III. The Thomistic synthesis is defended in many
works. Among the more recent are G. Manser,
Das Wesen des Thomismus (1949³) (Spanish tr. 1952)
and R. Garrigou-Lagrange, ' Thomisme ' in DTC
15:831–47 ; Eng. tr. with additions, entitled *Reality*
(1950) 37–57, 357–67. Among rejections of the
Thomistic theses see P. Descoqs, *Hylémorphisme*,
(1924) 124–65 ; Fuetscher, *Akt und Potenz* (1933)
(Spanish tr. 1948) ; Martinez del Campo, *Doctrina
Sancti Thomae de Actu et Potentia* (1945). E. Gilson
treats of the history of the essence-existence distinction in two very similar books : *Being and Some
Philosophers* (1952²) and *L'Être et l'essence* (1949).

T. T. P.

ACTS, HUMAN ' Acts which are freely exercised
by man are called human acts, because free acts are
peculiar to man, who differs from irrational creatures
in as much as he is master of his own acts ' (Davis,
Moral and Pastoral Theology i, II). This article deals
with (I) the nature, (II) the field, (III) formation and
measure, (IV) finality of the human act, and (V) its
place in theology.

I The nature of the human act. Human act
(*actus humanus*) is a technical expression signifying
the dominion man has over his actions ; the correlative expression, used where that dominion is
absent, is act of man (*actus hominis*).

This dominion over action can be considered from
two angles, that revealed by nature, and that manifested by the agent. The hierarchic organisation of
the natural powers of man results in a certain form
of dominion over action. The higher powers have
dominion over the lower ; the mind is able to
command, the will is able to move, the actions of
other faculties. This form of dominion over action
is expressed by the terms commanded (*actus
imperatus*) and elicited (*actus elicitus*) acts. In the
human act, man uses this natural organisation of his
powers, his free will, but the dominion supposed by
the human act is something more than this. It is a
dominion manifested by the agent : man is master
of his own actions because he makes them. The
problem of the human act is to see in what sense it
can be said that man makes his actions.

Excluding causal activity, which is not here in
question, an action can originate from the agent in

three positive modes : natural, voluntary, and deliberate. The negative correlatives are unnatural, involuntary and not deliberate. In the first mode, natural, the agent determines its movement ; the principle of movement is intrinsic ; the action begins precisely in order to end. In the second mode, voluntary, there is added to the intrinsic principle of movement the perception of the end : the action begins in order to end because of this perception of the end. In neither of these modes of producing an action can it be said that the agent makes the action. There is not the flexibility in the mode of acting which would permit a making of the action. It is with the third mode, deliberate, where the knowledge of the end passes beyond perception to conception, that this flexibility is found. In this context it becomes significant to speak of making the action.

In the natural mode of activity, the sphere of *Bios*, action is structured on function. Situation structures action in the voluntary mode of acting, the sphere of *Pathos*. In the deliberate mode of activity, the sphere of *Logos*, action is structured on rationalization. Because specifically human activity supposes this rationalization, man can make his actions, and by this title claim dominion over them.

II Field of the human act. Applying the theory of stratification to the spheres in which the activity of man is manifested and to the types of action, PHENOMENOLOGY enables the question of the field of the human act to be stated in more satisfactory terms.

Although rationalized action is seen most clearly in the intentional act proper to the sphere of *Logos*, this is not to say that it is only here that the human act appears. Expressivity is the proleptic presence of the human act in the sphere of *Bios*. The human act, in the sphere of *Pathos*, appears as enjoyment. In the pre-intentional act, pleasure in function is a manifestation of the human act ; in the supra-intentional act, happiness. Even at the depth of mood, where man moves as one with his world, the presence of the human act can be seen : pure feeling is rationalized to become heart (Strasser, *Das Gemuet*, 126).

Because of the fundamental unity of man, the field of the human act is co-extensive with human activity. When the distinction is made between the *Eidos* of the human act and the appearances that *Eidos* takes, it becomes possible to discuss the problem of the human act in primitive civilizations and in all the phases of man's life. There is place for a typology of the human act ranging from heart to beatitudes. ('Beatitudes are none but perfect works', St Thomas, 1-2ae:70:2c.)

There are, however, certain limits to the field of the human act. Besides the accidental limits, the obstacles which stand in the way of the action proceeding from the agent as voluntary and deliberate (violence, fear, concupiscence and ignorance), there are necessary limits to the field of the human act. Theologians point out that beatific vision is not a human act in the technical sense of the word.

It is not by rationalization that the Blessed see God ; that vision is a gift. Again, in the line of intention, the first response of the will to beatitude is not a human act. Man does not make the one action in virtue of which all his making is possible ; the desire of happiness is the gift of nature.

III Formation and measure of the human act. When finally accomplished, the human action is the result of many factors : faculties used, habits and influences, circumstances of time and place, etc. But at the head of this, the external act (*actus externus*), there stands, as the mobilizing force, the internal act (*actus internus*). The question of the formation of the human act is basically the question of this internal act.

Given the unrestricted nature of the object of the will, which is the good or end as such, it follows that the will has to be orientated to a particular end. This is the function of the internal act. The formation of this act is the result of the interplay of reason and will. Reason judges that an end is desirable ; to this the will responds by giving its approval to that end. This consent (*voluntas*) of the will is an uncommitted one, a kind of Platonic love. Moved by this consent, reason goes on to judge that the end is one that can be attained. The response of the will to this judgment is to commit its consent (*intentio*). The will being thus engaged, reason goes on to judge the ways by which the end is to be reached. Here the approval of the will means that its consent is now deliberate (*electio*). This progression in judgment and approval of the end issues in the formation of the internal act ; its form is provided by reason, its force, by the will.

The rationalization which the human act implies is the making of the internal act. It also extends to the making of the external act, this being the incarnation of the internal act.

Since human action is this process of rationalization, it can be seen that reason is the measure or rule according to which man acts. ' Now there are two rules of the human will : one which is proximate and homogeneous, viz. the human reason ; the other is the first rule, viz. the eternal law, which is God's reason, so to speak' (St Thomas, 1-2ae:71:6c). When the action, both in its cause (internal act) and in its effect (external act), conforms to its measure, it is said to be morally good. As man's knowing is measured by the object, so his doing is measured by reason (*see* CONSCIENCE). Morality, the relation of conformity to measure, is a property of the human act.

IV Finality of the human act. The formation of the human act reveals its finality. Man's doing is not simply a matter of satisfying particular needs, of confronting the various situations in which he finds himself. He uses action to manifest himself, to demonstrate his own standing in the order of being ('Die Zweckdienlichkeit der lebenden Natur ist lediglich die notwendige Vorbedingung fuer die Entfaltung des demonstrativen Seinswertes'. F. Buytendijk, *Die Frau*, 96).

Himself the incarnated spirit, man's action is an

incarnation. As he spiritualizes the objects he knows by incarnating them in the idea, so he spiritualizes his action by making it the incarnation of the idea. He has the mission of transforming his world by inserting significance into activity. Since, as spirit, he transcends the material world, man is master of his actions. The human act is the sign of the incarnated spirit. Man is *homo faber* because he is *homo cogitans*. It is here that the dialogue with philosophical Marxism has its place.

By giving significance to his action man makes what he does the image of himself. There is a true analogy of being (*see* ANALOGY) between man and his work and the Creator and creation. The world is a sign which embodies the meaning given to it by God ; analogously the human act carries within it the significance given to it by man. The finality of the human act is to reveal man the creator.

St Thomas (1–2ae:1:2c) points out that, in the work of moving creation to its end, God uses the dynamism of the irrational creature as an instrument, whereas man He uses as a true agent. In the human act man's activity has an authenticity and value which is unique. The created creator has his place in the movement of creation towards its perfection. In this context, the human act is at once a liberty and a fidelity.

V Place in theology. There is a theology, a knowledge of God, to be derived from creation (Rom 1:19–20) ; irrational creatures are the vestigia, the image of God is man (Gen 1:26–7). St Thomas devotes the long second part of the *Summa Theologica* to this knowledge of God as He is seen in the medium of the human act.[1]

It is of the nature of man's knowing that it leads on to action. The idea gives man a certain possession (*assimilatio*) of what he knows. This limited possession creates the tension, desire, which moves man to seek, in real union, the total possession of what he knows ; his action is the consummation of his knowing, a form of knowing. From his knowledge of God man is able to pass on to the desire to see God. This raises the problem of the natural desire to see God and the further problem of the relation between nature and grace (*see* SUPER-NATURAL). The human act, the medium in which man manifests himself as the incarnated spirit, is the place where he awaits God, the mentality able to receive the event of God's free call to the supernatural. The supreme mastery which the human act gives to man in the natural order lies in this awaiting God. What the medieval theologians called the *potentia obedientialis*, the capacity to be taken up into the supernatural order, is a property of the human act.

1 . . . postquam praedictum est de exemplari, scilicet de Deo, . . ; restat ut consideremus de eius imagine, id est, de homine, secundum quod et ipse est suorum operum principium, quasi liberum arbitrium habens, et suorum operum potestatem. 1–2ae : Prologus. (After God, the exemplar, has been spoken of, it remains that we should consider man, His image, according as he is the source of his own acts, as one who has free choice and dominion over his own activity.)

Given the fact of the elevation of man to the supernatural order, the human act is perfected to become the sign that man is the image of God, not only as associated with the work of creation, but in so far as, in Christ, he is the adopted son of God with the mission of making the Kingdom of God. The theology of the sacraments and of grace reveals the messianic and theological dimensions of the human act, while moral theology defines its exalted measure.

Bibliography. Besides St Thomas, *Summa Theologica*, 1–2ae and commentators, the following are important : S. Strasser, *Das Gemuet* (1956) ; O. Lottin, *Morale fondamentale* (1954) ; A. Marc, *Dialectique de l'agir*. For the practical applications of the doctrine of the human act *see* H. Davis, *Moral and Pastoral Theology*, i (1935). E. H.

ACTS OF THE HOLY SEE, VARIETY OF

The divinely instituted universal jurisdiction of the Roman Pontiff comprises the power, not only of governing the Catholic Church in all parts of the world (*see* POPE, PRIMACY OF THE), but also the duty of instructing the faithful in matters of faith and morals (*see* MAGISTERIUM). In doing this the Pope in certain circumstances enjoys the special assistance of the Holy Spirit, who preserves him from all danger of leading his flock into error (*see* INFALLIBILITY OF THE POPE). At present the official organ for the promulgation of the Acts of the Holy See is the *Acta Apostolicae Sedis : Commentarium Officiale*, published normally every month. The more important Acts are also published in the Vatican daily newspaper, the *Osservatore Romano*. This is an 'officious' organ, not an official one, and the Holy See is not responsible for all its contents.

Papal Acts take a number of different forms. The most solemn are the ratification and promulgation of the decrees and canons of Ecumenical Councils. Then there are the solemn definitions *ex cathedra* made by the Sovereign Pontiff. These are binding on the faith of all Christians under pain of falling into heresy. There are also *Apostolic Letters* of various kinds, including Encyclicals directed to the bishops of the whole world, by which the Pope elucidates Christian doctrine. These are not guaranteed infallible, but may be considered as being ' morally certain ', so that it would be rash to doubt them and in any case they must be obeyed. ' It must not be thought,' said Pius XII in *Humani Generis* (AAS 42, 568), ' that the teachings of encyclical letters do not require assent of themselves, since the supreme teaching authority of the Pope is not exercised in them. Yet it is by the ordinary teaching authority of the Pope that their teachings are proposed, and to it extends the saying : He who hears you, hears Me. For the most part also the teachings they contain are already on other grounds matters that pertain to Catholic doctrine. Further, if in a matter hitherto open to controversy the Popes of set purpose in their Letters pronounce a verdict, it is clear to all that the matter cannot, according to the mind and intention of the Popes, be still considered to be a subject for free disputation among theologians.' (For the dogmatic questions involved here, *see* INFALLIBILITY OF THE POPE.)

Less solemn are the *Allocutions*, which the Pope addresses to groups of individuals. Papal *Constitutions* may concern not only doctrine, but also the discipline of the Church. The most imposing ones are called *Litterae patentes* or Bulls from the leaden seal or *bulla* attached to them. They are written on parchment and begin with the words *N. Episcopus servus servorum Dei*. Briefs are simpler in form and are sealed with the Fisherman's ring on red wax. They begin with the Pope's name and number, e.g. Joannes PP. XXIII. *A Motu proprio* is issued on the Pope's own initiative. The seal is simply in ink. It is in the form of a Decree rather than of a Letter.

The Decrees, Instructions and Rescripts, including Decretals, of the various Roman Congregations and other Offices are Acts of the Holy See and as such binding on the conscience of Catholics in a greater or less degree and, according to their nature, concern the Church in general or particular bodies, or individuals. It should be noted that the doctrinal decrees of the Holy Office may be approved by the Sovereign Pontiff either *in forma communi* or *in forma specifica*. In the first case they remain pronouncements of the Congregation only, and they must be received almost with the same submission as that due to non-infallible pronouncements. If they are approved *in forma specifica*, they become declarations of the Pope himself, though most theologians would not regard them as infallible or irreformable.

Bibliography. L. Choupin, *Valeur des décisions doctrinales et disciplinaires du Saint-Siège* (1929³) ; P. Maroto, *Institutiones Iuris Canonici*, tom. I (1918) ; Anne Fremantle, *Papal Encyclicals* (1957) ; on the special question of the value of Encyclicals, see the debate between J. Salaverri SJ (' Valor de las Encíclicas ') in *Miscellanea Comillas* 17 (1952) 135–71 (where an infallible *ordinary* magisterium of the Pope is defended) and J. B. Beumer SJ, ' Sind päpstliche Enzykliken unfehlbar ? ' in *Theologie und Glaube* 42 (1952) 262–9 (which is opposed to Salaverri) ; and a summing up by B. Brinkmann SJ, ' Gibt es unfehlbar Äusserungen des Magisterium ordinarium des Papstes ', in *Scholastik* 28 (1953) 202–221 (which is in favour of Beumer).   R. P.

ADAM The divisions of this article will be (I) a discussion of the Scriptural account of Adam, (II) the theology of his gifts, (III) the problems connected with his body and its formation, (IV) a theological account of his sin, as far as that was personal to himself (for its further effects *see* ORIGINAL SIN), (V) a brief account of his possibility of salvation (though the full theology of the Second Adam will be treated under ATONEMENT), and finally (VI) a section on the legend of his burial at the site of Calvary.

I The scriptural account in Gen. 1:26–2:3 and 2:4–2:25 falls naturally into two parts of which the first is poetical in style and elevated (as Gen 9:26–7 or 27:27–9), giving the bare fact that Adam was made by God in His image and likeness, while the second account is much more prosaic and detailed, describing how God took the dust of the earth and breathed into it a living soul and set Adam in Paradise (see CCS 141a–3m). It has been the fashion among critics to assign these two accounts to different authors and to make the second account (J) the earlier in time, while assigning the first account (P) to the priestly editors of post-exilic times, but the Wellhausen hypothesis (from which these critical views come) was made at a time when very little was known of the transmission of religious traditions in primitive times and there was not yet available the material for making a comparison here between the Jews and other races of the Near East. Recently Heidel has argued that the ' Babylonian Genesis ' (a creation-story with many killings of gods and the making of man out of the blood of a god and the dust of the earth) was put together at some time between 1900 and 1600 B.C. and that it is quite wrong to suppose the Hebrews had to wait until the exile of the 6th cent. to become acquainted with this material. There are points of resemblance and of difference between the story of Adam and the Babylonian tale of Enuma elish, and the evidence does not go so far as to compel anyone to believe that Jews copied Babylonians, Babylonians Jews, or both a common source. Between the J narrative and the Babylonian stories a point of contact has been sought in Gen 2:5–6, which has been held to imply a Babylonian setting (where irrigation from rivers, and not rain from the sky, is the source of fertility), but others think that the words ' Yahwe did not rain upon the earth ' demand a Palestinian outlook in the author of them, who looked for such rain, as no Mesopotamian would have done. Where such conflict of interpreters reigns, all one can do is to say that the present state of research does not permit an exact judgment about the literary origin of the J passage, save that it is, while being a popular narrative adapted to the mentality of a primitive people, immensely superior in dignity and simplicity to what one reads in the Babylonian story of Marduk : ' Marduk's heart prompts him to create ingenious things. He conveys his idea to Ea : "Blood will I form and cause bone to be ; then will I set up *lullû* ; Man shall be his name. Yes, I will create *lullû*. . . . Upon him shall the services of the gods be imposed that they may be at rest".'

The religious truths which are enshrined in the Genesis account are that Adam is created as the crown of the material world, that he is somehow like unto God, that he consists of body and soul, that (Gen 2:19) he has understanding of the natures of things, being able to name them as they should be named, and that he has a mate like unto himself, Eve. (For questions connected with this last point, *see* EVE.) The purpose of Adam's creation is not, as in Babylonian legend, to set free the lesser gods from their uty of worship, but (Gen 2:15) ' to work and keep the garden '. His continuance in this state is made by God to depend upon a test of his self-restraint, in which Adam fails.

The absolute form of the command in Gen 2:17 which simply declares : Thou shalt not . . ., and is not in the casuistical form of a hypothesis (If thou shouldst . . .), is held to denote a likeness with the Mosaic legislation and a difference from the Babylonian. The geographical passage (Gen 2:10–14) is thought by many to be a later addition (for it differs in style), and thus there is no need to suppose any particular location of the Paradise of Adam. It is enough to say, with Chrysostom, that the narrative teaches that Paradise was on earth and not in some heavenly region. The allegorizers cannot be allowed to think it away altogether.

The poetical style of the earlier P passage is perhaps responsible for a minor confusion, for Adam is not named in it with his personal name, the account (Gen 1:26) simply speaking of *man* (collectively) and going on to use the plural ' male and female did He create them '. The name Adam cannot be given an entirely acceptable derivation ; some think of *adamah* (the red earth) or the common noun *adam* meaning man. This common noun, with the article, is used throughout the J account, and it is not until Gen 4:25 that the word is used as a proper name for Adam. It has been thought that the collective in 1:26 implies the creation of several men together, but in view of the elevated style of the piece it is more reasonable to take it as describing in general terms the creation of the first parents of the human race (*see further* POLYGENISM). It is according to the nature of the repetitions in Hebrew narrative that the later account(s) add details that are necessary to give full clarity to the primary one. In this first account God is always Elohim, while in the second one He is Yahwe Elohim. The reason for the double name is not apparent ; it is, however, to be remarked that this double use (which is not found again after Gen 2 and 3 except in Ex 9:30) upsets the neat division of this early material into Yahwe passages and Elohim passages.

The religious truths enumerated above are certainly enshrined in a popular narrative which itself is dependent on the world-picture of its first hearers, but the truths themselves are not dependent on that picture. The task of deciding what detail is really part of the trappings and what is part of the essential message has been made much easier since the discovery of Babylonian and Sumerian stories of creation, but the Church as the guardian of the Scripture insists that she should be the final judge in such a delicate matter. The Sumerian material is older than the Babylonian by about five centuries and is, by contrast with the Hebrew, marred by childish fancies, but it may give a clue here and there. Yet if there is to be any ' bleaching-out ' of the mythological colouring from the picture in Genesis, it is in the last resort the Church that must take this in hand, not the private judgment of the individual. It has, for instance, been proposed that one character in the Sumerian story, Nin-Ti (whose name means both ' the lady of the rib ' and ' the lady who makes alive ') supplies a clue to the name of Eve as ' mother of the living ' in Gen 3:20 (literally, from

the Hebrew *hawwah* ' she who makes alive ') and to the detailed account of Eve's creation, but the Sumerian material is still fragmentary and awaits further elucidation. In other parts the Sumerian story is clearly inferior. It makes Enki, the lord of wisdom, resolve to create men at the request of his mother Nammu, to help the other gods who have trouble in getting bread for themselves. At a feast Enki and Ninmah (the earth-goddess ?) drink wine and he then allows her to fashion six human beings from the clay which is over the abyss ; the account of the making of four of these is missing but the fifth and sixth are ' a woman who cannot give birth ' and a natural eunuch. Presumably the others were : normal man and woman, a double-sexed being, and one other. All six were regarded as so many different creatures not yet united in the one species of man, whereas from the start the OT account makes mankind one stock.

II The gifts of Adam are traditionally described by theology as sanctifying grace, integrity, and immortality. These are linked by St Thomas (after Augustine) as being three subjections, of the soul to God, of the lower powers of the soul to reason (integrity or the freedom from concupiscence), and finally the subjection of the body to the soul (or freedom from death). He can thus make the effect of Adam's sin to be as it were a chain-reaction, the loss of God's friendship or grace leading to the upsetting of the other two subjections. The difficulty that might arise in this explanation, namely that death, or the separation of the soul from the body, is natural, and that therefore its suppression in Adam would be somehow a violence to nature, is faced by St Thomas in *Compendium theologiae* 152 (*see also* 186 and 192), where he argues that death is both natural and unnatural, natural if one looks at the body, which is always on the way to corruption, but unnatural if one looks at the soul, which by its purely spiritual or contemplative activity is shown to be more than a mere activating principle for the body. The human soul has an overlap, a surplusage of being on this account, and, for it most suitably to become the form or animating principle of the body, the body had to be given by God a supernatural disposition to prepare it for the soul's inhabitation, and this was what is called by the technical name of immortality. Thus Adam's condition after creation was not unnatural (nor will that of the blessed be when they are reunited with their bodies) but our own condition since the Fall (when this gift was lost) is to some extent unnatural. Our soul is naturally meant to dwell in a body, but it is not meant only for that, and the existence of that overlap leaves us in a state of tension and disease while we live in this world. If we had the disposition that was given to Adam, we should find our body was completely subject to the soul. Not only would a runner or an oarsman by ' thinking about it ' get more out of his muscles and sinews, but the body would answer to the swiftest thought of the mind and what the advocates of mind-cures now dream about would then be true.

The existence of these gifts in Adam is taught by the Church in the decree of Trent on Original Sin (D 788) which said that Adam had been established [1] by God in holiness and justice. This teaching was soon afterwards enforced against Baius (D 1024). Integrity and immortality were declared to have been given to Adam as gifts, against the view of the semi-Pelagians, by the second Council of Orange in 529 (D 175, 192). Earlier still (D 101) a Council of Carthage in 418 had condemned the view of Pelagius that Adam would have died, sin or no sin. Death had to be understood as the wages of Adam's sin. That the Council did not go on to say the same about integrity as it had about immortality shows that the theology of the two gifts is not quite parallel (see CONCUPISCENCE). Ultimately the evidence for Adam's gifts can be found in Ecclus 17:5–12 with 15:14. Here the vaguer idea of the Genesis account that Adam is set in Paradise as a friend of God is made more explicit.

> He created in them the knowledge of the Spirit ;
>   He filled their heart with understanding,
>   And evil and good He shewed them.
> He set His eye upon their hearts to shew them
>   the great things of His works ;
>   That they might praise the name of sanctifica-
>   tion,
>   And glory in His marvellous works. . . .
> He added discipline unto them,
>   And made them inherit the law of life.

There is no word yet of the gift of immortality, for to the Hebrew mind this truth had not yet come by revelation (cf. Fr Sutcliffe, *The OT and the Future Life*). It was to be made clear to them by Christ that eternity for body and soul was to be the reward (or punishment) of men from the God of the living, and hence (by what was called *recirculatio* among the early Fathers) it was argued that such also has been Adam's gift.

On the extent of Adam's knowledge the medieval theologians let themselves go, and speculation ran riot. A neo-Platonic principle which was at the base of much of this was the idea expressed by St Thomas (*quaestiones de veritate* 18:4) that nature always starts with the perfect specimen and that subsequent specimens of a kind are declensions from that. Bonaventure (*II Sent.* 23, 2, 1) was willing to admit that, though Adam could have had no lethargy from the clogging encumbrance of the body, yet he would have been slowed down in his natural understanding by the vegetative processes of the body. All concede that Adam did not know the future, and when contrasting his knowledge of God with that of the blessed in heaven Bonaventure says that he had an intellectual vision not of God Himself but of some grace or influence from God,

such as the mystics also experience at times. The narrative in Gen 2:20 of Adam's naming of all other creatures implies a wide natural knowledge (for to the Hebrew mind the name was a comprehensive definition of the thing) but it is an exaggeration to suppose that Adam had great linguistic ability or that—as some theologians claimed—he was the pioneer of the Hebrew language. It was exaggerations such as these which led to the heresy of TRADITIONALISM. If God made Adam the guardian of a primitive revelation, it cannot have been one that went beyond a very few points of doctrine, and it is supposed (by those who still defend this idea) that it was given rather after the Fall than before it, since the content of such a revelation seems to them to have borne upon that event and to have enshrined memories of it in humankind that would eventually provide the anthropologist with his Golden Age mythology so often found. Lagrange urged the idolatry of Abraham's ancestors (Jos 24:2) against the possibility of any such transmitted revelation.

Though the theology of man as the image and likeness of God will be treated under IMAGO DEI, it must here be said in brief that the words of Gen 1:26 were very soon taken by the Fathers to describe the gifts which Adam had received from God. According to Irenaeus (*adv. haer.* V:vi:1 H) if the Spirit of God be lacking to a man, such a one is indeed in the image of God in his fashioning but is imperfect, in that he has not received the likeness of God through the Spirit. Son and Spirit are in the language of Irenaeus the two hands of God and thus he says in another place (V:xvi:1 H) that man is made precious in the sight of the Father by that likeness which he has to the Son of God. In this view there is a distinction between natural image and supernatural likeness, and Irenaeus is quite consistent in holding to this distinction in the other passages where he touches on the question (III:xviii:1, IV:lxiii:2, and V:xxviii:3 H). It passes into the work of such men as Cyril of Alexandria (PG 75:1013), but in the Clement and Origen stream of thought the words of Gen 1:26 are taken in a different way, the likeness being generally reserved for the blessed in heaven (Origen, *princ.* 3:6:1). Gregory of Nyssa seems to use the two terms as synonyms, as Philo did.

Since the discovery of the *Epideixis* of Irenaeus his thought on the likeness of God in Adam has become clearer. From *Epideixis* 11 and 97 it is clear that he considered Adam to have been made in the bodily image of God ; not that he was inclined to the heresy of anthropomorphism, but that he considered the Incarnate Son of God, as the first-born before all creatures, to have supplied in His human nature the bodily pattern for Adam as well as the life of grace. ' God gave Adam's frame the outline of His own form, that the visible appearance too should be godlike—for it was as an image of God that man was fashioned and set on earth. . . .' ' The Son of God received from the Father dominion over our life . . . joining and uniting the Spirit of God with the creature formed by God so that man

---

[1] This word was chosen to avoid settling a debate between theologians whether Adam was created by God with these superadded gifts or was given them immediately after his creation. The words ' holiness and justice ' come from Eph 4:24, where they apply to the ' new man in Christ ' what was originally given to the first Adam (cf. Col 3:10).

should be according to the image and likeness of God.'

III The body of Adam did not give much trouble to the Fathers or to medieval theologians ; it is only since the coming of evolutionary theories that it has been subject to so much discussion. The picturesque language of Gen 2 does not really give any help in such a debate, and attempts to torture the word *haphar* (dust) serve no purpose. Chrysostom, for instance, says, 'When you read that God fashioned man and breathed into his face the breath of life, think of the power that declared : " Let it be done ", and consider how it was God's good pleasure, after He had created angels, to bestow a rational soul upon this body that was from earth, a soul that would make use of the limbs of that body' (hom 13:2 on Gen PG 53:107). Elsewhere he asks, What was this body before it received a soul ? His answer is that it was a lifeless image, incapable of movement (εἰκὼν ἄψυχος καὶ ἀνενέργητος). Such language does not suggest that he was an evolutionist before his time. He emphasizes that in the account of creation the divine Author of the Scripture is making use of condescension (συγκατάβασις) by having things expressed in a way that the simple mind can follow. He says that the words of Scripture are like precious spices ; the more one runs them through the hands, the greater fragrance they yield. He points out how in spite of the popular and pictorial style it is made clear that the manner of the creation of man is different from that of the beasts : for them it is enough that a command be given for the water to bring forth reptiles, but for man there has to be a more intricate operation.

The principal teaching of the Church on the matter came from Pius XII, first in an address to the Papal Academy of Science in 1941 (D 2285) and then in the encyclical *Humani Generis* (D 2327) of 1950. The first was an interim statement that the manifold researches of the scientists on the origin of man had not produced anything positive that was clear and certain. The second was a more important declaration, 'The teaching authority of the Church does not forbid (to Catholics) the examination of the theory of evolution in so far as it seeks for the origin of the human body out of pre-existing living matter, by means of research and discussion among scientists and theologians who are learned in both fields ; the Catholic faith, however, bids us hold that souls are immediately created by God. The arguments on either side, pro and con, should be weighed and judged with due seriousness, moderation and restraint, provided always that all are prepared to submit to the judgment of the Church, which is appointed by Christ as the proper interpreter of the Scripture and the guardian of religious truth.'[1]

[1] Ecclesiae magisterium non prohibet quominus evolutionismi doctrina, quatenus nempe de humani corporis origine inquirit ex iam existente ac vivente materia oriundi—animas enim a Deo immediate creari catholica fides nos retinere iubet—pro hodierno humanarum disciplinarum et sacrae theologiae statu, investigationibus ac disputationibus peritorum in utroque campo hominum pertractetur ; ita

In the nature of things the proofs of the evolutionary hypothesis when and if completed will be in the form of an argument from the convergence of probabilities. In that case it becomes vital to establish when the convergence has reached a degree which can justly command assent. It is therefore of importance to note that the papal pronouncement calls for *experts in both fields* to undertake the discussions (and not simply those in one field, for the text has *utroque campo* and not *alterutro*) for only they will be able to judge about the convergence, and in particular of the evidence which God the author of revelation has given us to supplement that evidence which we gather from the works of God in nature. It is a pity that these operative words have been completely missed by the French version of the encyclical and perhaps by others.

Earlier Catholic pronouncements were local in character. In 1860, two years after Darwin published his work, a local council at Cologne (not infallible in character) said that ' the opinion which held that men, so far as his body was concerned, came from a spontaneous process of change from lower to higher which finally reached the human level was opposed to the Scripture and to the faith '. No other region followed the lead of the German bishops, but it may have been due to this decree that first of all Mivart in 1871, and later Père Leroy O.P. in 1891, and Dr Zahm of Washington in 1899, were all privately taken to task for their views on the evolution of man's body. In these earlier debates there was at times some lack of that *moderatio atque temperantia* which the papal encyclical calls for, and as with most new theories both welcome and disapproval tended to be too emphatic. That stage ended by the time of Pius XI, when such works as those of Dorlodot, Dr Messenger, and Père de Sinéty were left in peaceful possession.

Advocates of the evolution of Adam's body from the animal condition have shown much ingenuity in suggesting how this could be achieved. It is not necessary here to enter into their explanations, but the difficulties are grave. As Père Lagrange pertinently asked, how did the body of an animal which had had perhaps twenty years in which to form animal habits, suddenly come to cast them off when a human soul was superinduced to it by the miraculous intervention of God ? Some have been driven by this argument to propose that the human soul took charge of the animal material at the very earliest stages of embryonic life, so that Adam was born a man, though from an animal parent. This would run counter to what some of the Fathers say about Adam having been created in adult age, though others in patristic times thought of Adam and Eve as children before the Fall. Scripture gives no

quidem ut rationes utriusque opinionis, faventium nempe vel obstantium, debita cum gravitate moderatione ac temperantia perpendantur ac diiudicentur ; dummodo omnes parati sint ad ecclesiae iudicio obtemperandum cui a Christo munus demandatum est et sacras Scripturas authentice interpretandi et fidei dogmata tuendi. AAS 42 (1950) 576.

guidance about this. For further discussion of the problems involved *see* EVOLUTION.

The theory that there were pre-Adamites, other human beings who lived before Adam, was first put forward by Isaac de la Peyrère in 1655. He seems to have been moved by the thought that the newly worked-out chronology of Ussher, with its date of creation in 4004 B.C., did not allow enough time between Adam and Abraham (1948 years). He took Gen 1:26 as announcing the creation of men in general and 2:7 that of Adam himself. He proposed that Gen 6:1–4 should be taken as showing that the two races, the earlier one and Adam's, eventually linked up. He used Rom 5:13 'until the law' as if it meant 'a law given by God to Adam'. In the midst of the stir his work had caused he abandoned Calvinism and became a Catholic, and afterwards he renounced his theory in the presence of Pope Alexander VII. But theological opinion has generally seen no harm in the supposition that there could have been men before Adam, as long as it is always held that they had died out before the creation of Adam. (The condemnation in 1459 of Zanino di Solcia, a canon of Bergamo, who taught that all Christians were saved, that the law of Christ would pass away as the law of Moses had done and that Adam was not the first man (D 717c), was an indiscriminate affair, as he seemed to be challenging, in the spirit of the early Renaissance, all that was previously accepted, and no theologian has made use of this affair in modern times. In any case, what Zanino denied was that Adam was the first of *our* human race.) Some invoke such an hypothesis to account for the remains of Neanderthal man and to exclude him and his like from the pedigree of Adam. *This* human race fell in Adam and was then redeemed ; theology is not concerned directly with any prior race, any more than it is with the creatures if any on other planets.

Already in Augustine (*de genesi ad litteram* 3:22 ; CSEL 28:89) there is a rejection of the theory that Adam's body when created was bi-sexual and that the formation of Eve was a simple process of division after the pattern of the Platonic myth in the *Phaedrus*. Augustine points to the wording of Gen 1:26–7, where the plural implies that *two* were created. It would have been hard for God to bless *them*, if there was only one. Jewish legend was very busy with such 'harmonizations' of the biblical story with classical mythology (cf. Strack-Billerbeck, I, 802 ; IV, 405). For the formation of the body of Eve from Adam *see* EVE ; it must here suffice to note with Augustine that one good reason for the deep sleep that was cast over Adam during the making of Eve was to hide from man's scrutiny the wonderful work of God. He goes on to draw a parallel between the creation of Eve and the Virgin Birth : ' Are we to say that a man could come of a woman without sexual conjunction and that from a man a woman could not ?'[1] The implication of such a comparison

is certainly that the formation of Eve was miraculous, and it may be that a diligent search through the Fathers would show that they were unanimous in holding that the doctrine of *recirculatio* (or point-counterpoint between Eve and Mary) demanded such a parallel ; but so far no-one has undertaken the task of searching.

People are sometimes surprised that the Church shows such interest in this detail of the creation of Eve from Adam, but there is really no choice about the matter. In 1 Tim 2:11–15 (cf. 1 Cor 11:9) St Paul uses the fact as the basis of a somewhat Rabbinical argument about the relation of the sexes in marriage. Adam had as it were a right of primogeniture, and so he has founded an overlordship for the husband in marriage, an overlordship which yet does not destroy a true equality of the partners (D 2233). True to the doctrine of his speech in Athens (Ac 17:26) St Paul holds that Adam must be regarded as the head and origin of the human race, and therefore that Eve is somehow secondary. When St Thomas came to enlarge upon this idea, he was misled by the mistaken biology of the time (which went back to what Galen had written in *de usu partium* about the passive rôle of the female in generation) and thought that, when Gen 2:18 spoke of Eve being created as a helper to Adam, the sense was that she was to be his helper only in generation, playing therein a passive rôle (1a:92:1c and @2). There was a twofold subjection of woman to man, one the result of sin (Gen 3:16) and one that was prior to the Fall. He based this latter not on Scripture or biology but on the principle that ' by nature there is a more abundant and wiser use of reason in man than in woman '.[2] There might be disagreement about this inductive principle, and if the point of view be taken that (as Irenaeus said) what God did in Adam and Eve was done with a view to what was to come in Christ and the Church, then one would have reason for saying, not indeed that God *had to* make the man before the woman, but that since He had in fact done so, there must be some reason for it and for the later reservation of priesthood to men, to the exclusion of women. But that would be to take the Scotist point of view about Christ as the pattern of all creation.

IV The sin of Adam followed upon the sin of Eve. Both are punished by God (Gen 3:9–19) but not without trial, whereas the tempter is given his penalty without being questioned. If the story were meant simply to explain to people of the author's own time why men sweat when they dig, why their gardens produce weeds that are stronger and more abundant than crops or flowers and why men and women wear clothes, then it would not imply any more than that at a given moment in the past and in spite of the initial goodness of God's creation, some dislocation had taken place, the historical nature of which was not (by the story) more fully determined, save that it must have been the work of a human will and must have been

---

[1] An vero sine cuiusquam concubitu vir ex femina fieri potuit, femina ex viro non potuit ? *de genesi ad litteram* 9:17 ; CSEL 28:290.

[2] Naturaliter in homine magis abundat discretio rationis.

inherited somehow by posterity. But is this all that the story involves for a Catholic?

There are in fact more 'explanations of present realities' to be found in the narrative of the Fall than those mentioned. The reason why animals are wild, why serpents are to be avoided (or trodden on?), why women suffer the pains of childbirth, why we die, and so on. It is not very easy to see why a writer of the 9th or 8th cent. B.C. should set forth a narrative in which was the one event that started off all these various troubles; it would have been equally possible for him, had he been reflecting unaided by any divine communication, to ascribe some of these to one event and others to one or several later events in the course of an extended history. For a Catholic there is always the problem how far such aetiological writing is consonant with the fact of divine veracity in the inspiration of the Scriptures. If the human writer did not know what had taken place in the past, but merely postulated his X as the hypothetical cause of what he saw in his own time, how could his work be regarded as history in *any* sense? A few Catholics have taken this view of the Fall narrative, following a work by J. Guitton in 1947, but it seems more reasonable to repeat here what Canon van Hoonacker wrote on the question in 1918: 'What was as a matter of history lying beyond the natural ken of the author of our narrative may have been in some way or other conveyed to him by means of that same divine interference which made the early chapters of Genesis convey divine teaching to us' (*The Expositor* 16 (1918) 373–400).

The partisans of mythology in the OT have had a happy time with the narrative of the Fall, but it does not seem that they are quite consistent with themselves. There is now the greatest uncertainty what is meant by a myth. In classical mythology it might be claimed that the religious idea of satiety leading to insolence and to chastisement was given a mythological dress by the tragedy of Prometheus or of Heracles; but did that make either of them an unhistorical character? He might be real and the idea his life was made to illustrate in the tragedy might yet be untrue of anyone, himself or another. Thus there are two levels of mythology possible, and some Christians seem to want to accept as true certain religious ideas—such as that of man's fallen state—without having them anchored to any historical personages; from what has been said it will be seen that this does not commend itself to Catholics. Parable-making may be a mythopoeic activity, but parables can be built round real people; the story of Archelaus and its connection with Lk 19:12 (the parable of the pounds) is an instance. That some of the details of the Fall story—such as the cherubim, set like Babylonian winged bulls at the entrance to the garden, and the apparatus of serpent and tree of life—should be (as in Ezech 28:12–19) picturesque adornments of an essentially truthful story need not be denied.

The kind of sin Adam and Eve committed is held by St Thomas (2-2ae:163:2c), following Augustine, to have been pride, shown in his desiring to gain a

likeness to God, not in being (which he had), but in knowledge (which he had not save in potency), and this against the positive command of God. He remarks that it was not so grave a sin as blasphemy, but none the less was mortal. He thought that Eve sinned more grievously than Adam, for she went against a known command of God, while Adam 'did not think it was true that God had forbidden the eating of the fruit lest the pair should attain the divine likeness in knowledge, but wanted to gain this likeness by his own efforts' (ibid. 4c). In Jewish legend the sin was made out to be one of anticipating a divine permission to practise sexual intercourse. The Apocalypse of Moses (19) makes Eve say: 'He [the serpent] went and poured upon the fruit the poison of his wickedness which is lust, the root and beginning of every sin, and he bent the branch to the earth and I took.'

This idea is repeated with some hesitation by Clement (*strom.* 3:14:94; GCS 15:239) and by Zeno of Verona and others (cf. CCS 145b). It is to be noted that 'knowledge of good and evil' means no more than a knowledge 'of all things whatsoever', as in Jer 42:6, Gen 24:50, etc. Thus there is no suggestion that the tempter made offer of an initiation into adult life to a pair who had so far been of childish mentality. Adam's shame at being naked (Gen 3:10) is not due to a sudden onset of lust, but in the mentality of the time is a matter of self-reproach simply because nakedness was the lot of the slave, the captive in war, the criminal (Nah 3:5; Is 20:4). The possession of clothes was a mark of dignity (Is 3:6), and Adam feared to appear before God without them now that he had come to see what in his former carefree state he had not heeded. If one reads the narrative with the mind of Goethe (from whom, as from Schiller, flowed all the ideas about the mythology of Genesis which Wellhausen propagated) one can see in Adam a Faust-figure, who with his descendants is doomed to sin as he advances in culture and enlightenment, but this is far from the Hebrew mind. It is also necessary for those who accept the sexual theory of Adam's sin to treat Gen 2:23–24 as an interpolation, for this realization could not on their view have been Adam's before he ate.

That death was a penalty for the sin, while yet being natural for Adam (as Gen 3:19 says), is not a contradiction as some critics have supposed, for the other penalties are on the same footing. There would have been child-bearing if the Fall had not taken place; but now there is the pain of childbirth. There was before the Fall the keeping of the garden (as a leisure occupation); now there is toil with sweat. So too, Adam had a body that was naturally corruptible (even though God, as Gen 3:22–3 implies, had provided a means to overcome this) and now he is punished by not having access to that remedy. The dilemma offered, that death must either be natural or a penalty, is eluded by the fact that it is both. Ecclus 25:24 is sufficient guide here.

The Babylonian myth of Adapu is sometimes

adduced as a parallel to the Fall narrative, but the differences are extreme, as may be seen from this citation. Adapu, son of Ea has broken the wing of the south wind and Anu, the father of the gods has summoned him : ' Anu saw him. He called out : " Come here. Adapu. Why hast thou broken the wing of the south wind ? " Adapu answered : " My lord, I was catching fish on the sea ; the sea was like a mirror ; the south wind came blowing and submerged me. I was plunged into the realm of my lord. In the wrath of my heart I cursed the south wind. . . ." Anu's heart became calm, he fell silent : " Why has Ea revealed to an impure man the heart of heaven and earth ? . . . Bring him the food of life that he may eat ".' The dramatization which this myth displays is quite lacking in Genesis, the only trace of human emotion there ascribed to God being the apparent sarcasm of Gen 3:22. What might have been done in this direction can be seen from the extensive Jewish legends which grew up round the narrative. The Talmud (TB *Sanhedrin* 38b) cites Johanan ben Hanina as saying that Adam was but twelve hours in his elevated state ; in the first hour the dust was gathered ; in the second it was kneaded ; in the third limbs were shaped ; in the fourth the soul was added ; in the fifth he stood upright ; in the sixth he named the beasts ; in the seventh Eve was made while he slept ; in the eighth he ' knew his wife ' ; in the ninth he was given the command not to eat of the tree ; in the tenth the sin was committed ; in the eleventh came his trial, and last of all his expulsion. In contrast with all this is the simplicity of the teaching of the Catholic faith (D 788) that by his sin Adam lost his grace and gifts, and ' was wholly changed for the worse, both body and soul, and set in captivity to the devil who has power over death ' (Heb 2:14). The idea that the devil tempted Adam through the serpent is not due to legend but is from the Scriptures (Wis 2:24 ; Apoc 12:9 ; 20:2).

V The possibility of Adam's personal salvation is implied by Wis 10:1-2 ; ' She kept him that was first made of God father of the world, when he was created alone, and she brought him out of his sin, and gave him power to govern all things.' Gen 4:1 and 4:25 indicate that Eve was somehow aware that God was still with them after the Fall, and the same may be understood of Adam. Augustine says (*ep.* 164:3 ; CSEL 44:526) that when Christ went down to Limbo, He liberated Adam, and that this is the view of practically the whole Church (*ecclesia fere tota consensit*). It was the heretics, Tatian, Marcion, Valentinus, and others, who, according to Epiphanius (*haer.* 46 ; GCS 31:206), thought Adam was damned. Tertullian (*De Poenitentia* PL 1:1248) says that by penance Adam was restored to his paradise,[1] but this seems to be one of his usual exaggerations. None the less, the early Church seems to have taken the expulsion of the penitents on Ash Wednesday to be an imitation of the driving of Adam from Paradise. The old enemy would

[1] Adam exomologesi restitutus in paradisum suum.

not be vanquished if he were allowed to keep his spoil, wrote Irenaeus (*adv. haer.* III:xxxiii:1 H). Adam was not cursed, but the earth was and the serpent.

The Byzantine liturgy knew a feast of Adam on 19 December, and the widespread belief that Adam was buried at the foot of the cross on Calvary (§VI) was obviously an aid to thinking that he had been saved. One discordant voice was heard in the Middle Ages, that of Rupert of Deutz (PL 167:318), who held that God could not have given back to Adam the dominion of the beasts (' the power to govern all things ') as Wisdom said, and he urged that the book was apocryphal. The usual answer to this was that God had not restored such a complete dominion as had been proper to Adam before the Fall. Ultimately, all such theological speculation goes back to the Pauline doctrine of Christ as the second Adam, whose task it is to undo the work of the first (Rom 5:12-21 ; 1 Cor 15:22, 45). Both Mark and Luke in their gospels are thought to show some trace of this doctrine, for Luke (3:38) takes back the genealogy of Christ to Adam (whereas Matthew had ended it with Abraham, being concerned with the Jewish problem alone), while Mark (1:13) adds to the description of Christ in the desert the note that He was with the beasts, a note which is by some held to indicate that he is pointing the likeness to the state of Adam when he too was tempted. Paul's use of the term ' the one man ' for Christ in Rom 5:15 (and, according to the text used by many of the Fathers, at 5:19 also) implies that he is interpreting Christ's title of Son of Man as meaning ' the man, par excellence ', ' the man who is counterpart to the first man ' (so J. Jeremias in Kittel, s.v. Adam). 1 Cor 15:21, Eph 5:31 and 1 Tim 2:5 show further use of this line of thought. It provides a link between the ' Son of Man preaching ' of Christ Himself and the developed doctrine of the second Adam in Paul which obviates the need for an appeal to direct revelation to Paul as the source of the latter. By his changing the text of 1 Cor 15:47 and by denying that Adam was saved, Marcion did his best to destroy this doctrine of the two Adams and with it a most powerful typological link between OT and NT, but it is hardly necessary to show from the Fathers that he failed completely. His failure naturally gave a great impetus to the idea of *recirculatio* in Irenaeus, and in later writers even the smallest details of the correspondence were used. Thus one might see in the plural of Gen 1:26 (Let *us* make man) a plenary sense, ascribing to the Trinity this act, and by correspondence derive the idea that the Incarnation also was the work of the whole Trinity, though only one Person became man.

What is today known as the heresy of the *homo assumptus*—that Christ took to Himself a general and not a particular humanity—was early noticed and seems to have come from Jewish-Christian sources. In the 4th cent. Marius Victorinus (on Gal 1:19 ; PL 8:1155) says that the followers of Symmachus (the translator of the LXX) said that Christ was

Adam himself, and that He assumed a general human soul.[1] The same idea, that Christ was Adam returned to earth, is found in the *Symposium* of Methodius (3:3 ; GCS 27:30) where it is said that Christ was more than the antitype of Adam, being the very same. ' For it was fitting that the First-begotten of God . . . should mingle with human nature and become man in the first-created and first-begotten of men.' ' God once took virgin earth and made a man from it without human seed, and so He did again (at the Incarnation).' Philo may be to blame for the origin of this idea, since his Logos is prior to all creation, and yet entered into some relation with mankind, though not that of hypostatic union. *See further* under INCARNATION.

VI The burial of Adam at the site of Calvary was a Jewish tradition noticed by Origen (on Mt 27:33 ; GCS 38:265), who says : ' It has come to my notice that the Jews have a tradition that the body of Adam is buried there.' Jerome (on Eph 5:14) was inclined to take Paul's words calling on the sleeper to awake and be enlightened by Christ as a call to Adam from the Cross, but elsewhere he favoured the idea that Hebron was the place of Adam's burial. Ambrose (*in Lucam* 10:114 ; CSEL 32:498) also knew the story as Jewish, and the anti-Marcionite poem (lines 196–201; PL 2:1067) recorded it as something received : ' We are told that the first man's body rested here, so that his dust, joined with the blood of Christ, might by trickling drops of water be raised up.' [2]

The *quaestiones ad Antiochum* of the pseudo-Athanasius (PG 28:628) show the same ideas prevalent in the Eastern Church. Perhaps the derivation of Adam's name from the points of the compass (*Anatole*, *Dysis*, *Arctos* and *Mesembria* in the Greek language) coupled with the idea that Jerusalem was the centre of the world (as it still is on the medieval map in Hereford Cathedral) led to the acceptance of this legend that Adam had been buried at the point from which all these directions were to be measured. It so far prevailed in art as to have produced the skull and cross-bones which are found on many crucifixes. In the same way the silver ampullae, such as some of those at Monza from *c.* 600, which bear the legend : ' Holy oil from the tree of life of the holy places ', had on the side a representation of a bare cross with a man and woman kneeling on either side, said to be not John and Our Lady but Adam and Eve.

It has to be remembered that the first evidence of this tradition comes from a time prior to the identification of the site of the crucifixion in the days of Constantine. Before that time the opinion seems to have been that (as an early Syrian commentary on Genesis says) ' that mountain of the Amorites (where Isaac was sacrificed) as some say is the mountain of Zion, and the same is Golgotha '.

---

[1] Symmachiani dicunt : Eum Ipsum (Christum) Adam esse, et esse animam generalem, et alia huiusmodi blasphema.

[2] Hic hominem primum suscepimus esse sepultum ; . . . pulvis Adae ut possit veteris cum sanguine Christi commixtus stillantis aquae virtute levari. . . .

Traces of this belief can be found in the book of *Jubilees*, but the location of Isaac's sacrifice, Adam's burial and the redemption of the Cross in one spot seems like an attempt to make typology dictate to geography.

Bibliography. Apart from works cited in CSS one may mention these : C. Hauret, *Origines* (Genèse I-III) (1953) ; F. Ceuppens OP, *Genèse* I-III (1946) ; H. J. Johnson, *Catholics and Evolution*, in DR 67 (1949) 375–94 ; A. Vitti SJ, ' Christus-Adam ', in *Biblica* 7 (1926) 121–45, 270–85, 384–401 ; H. Cazelles, s.v. ' Mythes ', in DBS ; the same ' À propos du Pentateuque ', in *Biblica* 35 (1954) 279–298 ; A. Dubarle OP, ' Le Péché originel dans la Genèse ', in RB 64 (1957) 1–34 ; a series of articles by various hands in Gregorianum 29.4 (1948) ; *A. Levene, ' The early Syrian Fathers on Genesis ' (1951) ; *Darwell Stone, material for the article on ' Adam ', in the lexicon of patristic Greek, in JTS 24 (1923) 473–5 ; A. van Hoonacker, ' The literary origin of the narrative of the Fall ', in *The Expositor* 8 (1914) 481–98 ; the same, ' Is the narrative of the Fall a myth ? ', in *Expositor* 16 (1918) 373–400 ; *J. Jeremias s.v. ' Adam ', in Kittel's *Wörterbuch* ; H. F. Davis, ' Organic Evolution ', in CR 37 (1952) 478–88 ; H. J. Johnson, ' The formation of Eve ', in DR 69 (1950) 16–30 ; *A. Heidel, *The Babylonian Genesis* (1950) ; *S. N. Kramer, *Sumerian Mythology* (1945) ; B. Vawter CM, *A Path through Genesis* (1957) ; J. L. MacKenzie SJ, *The two-edged Sword* (1957) ; an Eng. tr. of the article by Père Dubarle OP was published in DR 76 (1958) 223–50.

J. H. C.

ADDAI AND MARI, LITURGY OF The theological importance of this East Syrian liturgy is that it is sometimes adduced as an early example of an anaphora which is addressed to Christ, and not to the Father, and that it lacks all trace of the words of institution of the eucharist. To examine these points something must be premised about the transmission of this anaphora to us. It is found in modern times still in use among the Assyrian Christians formerly resident in Kurdistan and also—in a somewhat Latinized form—among the Malabar Christians of St Thomas in South India. It is supposed to be the liturgy of Edessa and ultimately of the apostle Thaddeus (or Addai), who evangelized that part of Syria. Modern editions of it have worked upon MSS which do not go back earlier than the 16th cent., and there is large scope for purifying the text from the accretions of time. Professor Ratcliff began critical research on the liturgy by suggesting that all the whispered prayers (Kushapa) should be omitted, as this practice of whispering could be proved to be of late introduction. When this was done, and the scripture-reading part of the liturgy was ignored, one was left with the nucleus of an anaphora which, as he claimed, must then be freed from an interpolated *Sanctus* and epiclesis, thus leaving a prayer addressed to Christ. What remained would simply be a prayer of thanksgiving for creation and redemption, along with a solemn declaration that : ' We . . . who are gathered together in Thy name, stand before Thee and have received by tradition the type that is from Thee. . . .'

In criticism of this simplification it can be said that it would not be natural for early Syrians to attribute the creation to the Son of God, and that the dialogue (of the *Sursum corda* type) which opens the anaphora and which must on any view be primitive, speaks thus :

' Raise up your minds : To Thee, God of Abraham, Isaac and Israel, king of glory : Offering is made to God the lord of all : It is right and just.' The name *Qurbana*, or offering, is commonly used in Syriac (as Greek ἀναφορά and Gaelic aifreann) for what we call the ' mass ' and it does not seem likely that this dialogue—which is neglected by Professor Ratcliff—has been altered in its general drift. If it has not, then the case for addressing the whole anaphora to the Son must fail. The condemnations by councils at Hippo (393) and Carthage (397) of prayers addressed to the Son (Mansi, iii:884) cannot be claimed to throw much light on possible aberrations in Syria, whereas the habit of turning in prayer from Father to Son is not unknown there.

The omission of the words of institution is clear from the (late) MSS. It has been argued by some that the omission was due to reverence, and that the words were recited by heart. Fr Raes has suggested that the words were omitted as long ago as the 5th cent. in favour of a Nestorian epiclesis of the Spirit which would take away the action from the humanity of Christ. It is certain that the liturgy of Addai and Mari was abbreviated by the Nestorian patriarch of Adiabene, Isho'yabh III, about 650, and it is possible that he may have made such a change. There is a citation of the liturgy in the Homilies of Narsai (T&S 8:i:20) which testifies to the presence in it, in the later 5th cent., of the *anamnesis* : ' We typify and commemorate Thy passion, death and resurrection'. In all other early anaphoras this is the sequel to the words of institution, even in those of Theodore and Nestorius. There are some short anaphoras, such as that of Xystus, whose MSS. date from the 13th cent., in which the institution of the eucharist is narrated but the actual words of Christ are not given. This abbreviation of the matter, made at a time and place when the words of institution were not thought to be vital, may have led to a similar but more drastic revision of the anaphora of Addai and Mari. It would at all events be most unsafe to take this liturgy in its present state as a witness to primitive usages at the eucharist, seeing that so much revision of it has already taken place. To reconstruct the original is hardly a safe proceeding until far more evidence is available in the shape of early citations to check the modern guesswork. The large agreement of Malabar and Assyrian forms of the liturgy is not really the independent witness of disparate traditions to an early form of service ; at best it points to certain common characters of Nestorian worship.

Bibliography. *E. C. Ratcliff. The original form of the liturgy of Addai and Mari (JTS 30 (1929) 23–32). A. Raes sj, ' Les Paroles de consécration dans les anaphores syriennes', in OCP 3 (1937) 486–504 ; the same, ' Le Récit de l'institution eucharistique dans l'anaphore chaldéenne', in OCP 10 (1944) 216–226 ; B. Botte, ' L'Anaphore chaldéenne des apôtres', in OCP 15 (1949) 259–76 ; P. Placid, ' The present Syro-Malabar liturgy', in OCP 23 (1957) 313–31.

J. H. C.

ADOPTION OF SONS Adoption is the free act of taking into the family, as child and heir, of a person who is not of the stock. The fact that the just are God's adopted children is part of the Christian faith. It is certain that this adoption is effected by sanctifying grace : but its precise relation to sanctifying grace and the exact determination of its principles are matters of theological speculation. We shall examine (I) the fact of adoptive sonship and (II) its nature, discuss (III) its principles and conclude with a (IV) summary of the theological situation.

I The fact of adoptive sonship. St Paul alone uses the word ' adoption ' (Rom 8:14 ff. ; Gal 4:4 ff. ; Eph 1:3 ff.). The term has plainly a far deeper content than when applied to Israel (Rom 9:4) : Christian adoption implies an intrinsic physical reality. While we await its glorious fulfilment (Rom 8:19 ff. ; cf. 1 Jn 3:2), we are already in real fact made God's children and joint heirs with Christ, this reality attested not only by the supernatural filial instincts of our own spirit but by the Spirit of God (Rom 8:16 f. ; Gal 4:6 f.). This Spirit of God's Son sent into our hearts empowers us from within to live in accord with our new nature (Rom 8:14 ff. ; Gal 4:7). It is indeed a new nature we are given and not just a juridic title ; for we are ' predestined to bear a nature in the image of his Son's, that he should be first-born among many brethren ' (Rom 8:29 WV) : this is confirmed by the doctrine of regeneration (e.g. Tit 3:5). Nevertheless neither our sonship nor our title to inheritance is of natural right ; for we are ransomed by God's Son, born of a woman, to enter upon our adoption as sons and are heirs by act of God (Gal 4:4–7) : our sonship is due to the free liberality of God's loving will (Eph 1:5–7). St John does not use the word ' adoption ' but declares the revelation with equal insistence. We are born of God (Jn 1:13 ; 1 Jn 2:29 ; 3:1, 9 ; 4:7 ; 5:1, 4, 18). Spirit communicates spirit in this new generation (Jn 3:6–8) ; and God's seed abides as a permanent principle in God's adopted child (1 Jn 3:9). Yet, clearly, we are not children of God by nature : this has been bestowed on us of God's gracious love (cf. Jn 1:12 ; 1 Jn 3:1). St Peter speaks of the Christian as having been begotten anew by God in the abundance of His mercy not from perishable but from imperishable seed (1 Pet 1:3, 23) ; and it is reasonable to see our ' partaking of the divine nature ' (2 Pet 1:4) as the communication made to us in our regeneration. St James says that God has given birth to us of His own free will (Jas 1:18). Both declare the Christian to be heir to eternal life (1 Pet 1:4 ; 3:9, 22 ; Jas 2:5). This clear revelation of sonship is naturally taken up by the Fathers. The Greek Fathers in particular see adoptive sonship as real participation in, assimilation to, union with the incarnate Son through the Holy Spirit : the doctrine is developed dogmatically in the context of grace and used apologetically in the Arian and Macedonian controversies (cf. Irenaeus, *adv. haer.* III, 20, 1 H. ; Athanasius, *Contra Arianos*, orat. 2, 59: PG 26, 271 f. ; Cyril of Alexandria, *In Joannem commentarius*, 1, 9: PG 73, 153 ff.). Adoptive sonship is no less clearly taught by the Latin Fathers ; but even St Augustine does not seem to grasp the richness of its implications nor does he integrate it into his teaching on grace (cf. Cyprian, *de dominica oratione*, 9 ff.: PL 4, 541 ff. ; Augustine, *In Joannem tr*. II, c.1, n. 13 ff.: PL. 35, 1394 f. ; *Sermo* 166: PL 38, 907 ff.). There was never need for explicit definition of a truth so manifestly and fundamentally part of Christian revelation and so living in the Church's prayer and preaching. It is, however, repeatedly declared, e.g., by the Council of Trent in its decrees on original sin and justification (D 792, 794, 796).

II Nature of adoptive sonship. It is plain that divine adoption differs greatly from human adoption. In human adoption the person adopted is already of the same specific nature as the adopting parent : in divine adoption the created person is clearly not of the same nature but is given a share, analogically but ontologically, in the divine nature. Human adoption is simply a legal declaration producing no intrinsic physical change but only a status in the juridic order : divine adoption, effected by a real regeneration, changes the physical constitution of the adopted creature through communicated participation in the divine nature and through real assimilation to and union with the incarnate Son : it makes the Christian really a member of God's family. And as heir the Christian enters into, not the partial estate of a deceased parent, but the glory of the eternal life of the living God. Yet there are essential differences between the Christian's adoptive sonship and Christ's natural Sonship. Christ is Son by natural right through necessary, eternal, uncreated generation from the Father ; uniquely the second person of the Trinity, He can in no sense be an adopted son, although His humanity is elevated by sanctifying grace ; for filiation is an attribute of the person. Adoptive sonship is through regeneration, through the gratuitous communication of created principles of grace, whose efficient cause is the blessed Trinity.

III Principles of adoptive sonship. The sources indicated have shown us that Christian sonship is effected through the rebirth of supernatural regeneration. It is this that makes theologians almost unanimous in the assertion that adoptive sonship is the formal effect of sanctifying grace. Man is made God's adopted child, lifted to the plane of the love of true friendship, given title to the divine inheritance, by the communication of the divine nature through supernatural regeneration : but this com-

munication of divine nature is the formal effect of habitual grace given in the regeneration of justification. Scotus, however, and many Nominalists denied that adoption was a necessary, intrinsic effect of sanctifying grace : they required a further extrinsic, positive ordinance of God's for man, having received grace, to be constituted an adopted son and heir. In this they withdrew from the common teaching, whose main principles were set out by St Albert, St Thomas, and St Bonaventure. For St Thomas, as for scholastics generally, adoption is through grace and charity, which effect an intrinsic change in the creature, giving it a participation in the divine nature and an assimilation to the Son. This communication of grace is, however, a creative work directed outwards from the Trinity : adoption must, therefore, be referred to the Trinity as to its efficient cause and the Christian regarded as a son of the Trinity (cf. chiefly 3a:23:1-3). While St Thomas's teaching has in the main been generally accepted by post-Tridentine theologians, there has been, from the time of Lessius, a slowly growing tendency to associate adoption with the indwelling of the divine persons (*see* INDWELLING OF THE TRINITY), particularly of the Holy Spirit, and regard it as not simply an outward work of the Trinity. Lessius's modified view was that we were formally constituted sons of God by habitual grace as the intrinsic form uniting us to the person of the indwelling Holy Spirit (*De perfectionibus moribusque divinis*, Antwerp edition, 1626). His view, commonly rejected, was taken up by Petavius, who taught that the formal principle of adoptive sonship was the substantial presence of the Holy Spirit, to whom the adopted had a personal relation (*Opus de theologicis dogmatibus*, De Trinitate, Liber VIII). Strongly attacked by most theologians, his opinion has been revised and developed, e.g., by Scheeben (cf. bibliography) and Mgr Waffelaert (*Collationes Brugenses*, 15 (1909) 441, 513, 625, 673 ; 16 (1910) 5). According to Mgr Waffelaert sanctifying grace disposes the human person for union with the person of the Holy Spirit : this union, immediately and properly with the third divine person, gives the human person the new moral dignity of sonship. More recently, elaborating St Thomas's teaching, Fr S. I. Dockx (cf. bibliography) has linked the grace of adoption with the missions of the Son and the Holy Spirit : the intrinsic formal principles of our elevation are sanctifying grace, charity, and wisdom ; the divine persons, immanent in our souls, are the extrinsic formal principle which terminate our supernatural activity. He distinguishes a triple filiation : a supernatural filiation by sanctifying grace, which assimilates and refers us, not to the divine persons, but to the divine nature common to the divine persons ; a spiritual filiation deriving from charity, which assimilates and specially relates us to the person of the Holy Spirit ; a mystic filiation dependent on the real presence of the Holy Spirit, who, acting as soul, forms of Christians a mystical body and one mystical person with the incarnate Word and enables them, analogously, to share, in the Holy Spirit, a ' filial ' love for the eternal Father. This notion of a really filial relation properly to the first person of the blessed Trinity has been developed by no one more vividly than by Fr E. Mersch (cf. bibliography). The sacred humanity of Christ, he wrote, created by the Trinity, subsists in the Son alone ; and the entire human, supernatural perfection of Christ is the consequence of this humanity's assumption by and subsistence in the Son : it is therefore properly related to the first divine person and is strictly filial in character. The grace of the Christian derives from and is the immediate outcome of real union with the incarnate Son : it, too, therefore, is filial in character ; and, sons in the Son, Christians are related properly to the eternal Father. A development of this view has been tentatively proposed in the ETL (H. P. C. Lyons SJ, *The Grace of Sonship*, 27 (1951) 438–66). In the case of Christ we attribute to the Trinity as efficient cause the production of His humanity's natural and supernatural perfection in the order of essence, while ascribing its existential actuation properly to the divine act of existence as personal to the Son : in the case of the Christian we may make a similar distinction between the two orders of essence and existence. In the supernatural regeneration of justification the production of the essence of the supernatural perfection is the effect of the efficient causality of the Trinity : but the Christian is simultaneously actuated to a supernatural corporate existence by Christ's act of existence. The Christian is not hypostatically united to the Son by this actuation, because this supernatural, corporate existence supervenes on, without destroying, his natural, individual existence : he is only an adopted son, because his supernatural perfection, essential and existential, is wholly gratuitous. But this existential actuation bestows on the Christian a strictly ontological unity with the incarnate Son and makes him properly a son, with and in the Son, of the eternal Father.

IV Summary. It will be readily recognized from this brief review that theologians generally have retained the basic principles of St Thomas : our adoption is effected fundamentally by the communication of sanctifying grace, which makes the just sharers in the divine nature, united and assimilated to the incarnate Son. Speculation has proved the increasing realisation of the importance of the doctrine and has led to a deeper consideration especially of two closely linked mysteries, the connection of created habitual grace with the uncreated presence of the divine persons and the relation of the adopted son, through and with and in the incarnate Son, to the Father in the unity of the Holy Spirit.

Bibliography. J. Anger (tr. J. J. Burke), *The Doctrine of the Mystical Body of Christ* (1932) ; S. I. Dockx OP, *Fils de Dieu par grâce* (1948) ; P. A. Dorsaz, *Notre Parenté avec les personnes divines* (1923) ; E. Mersch SJ (tr. C. Vollert) *The Theology of the Mystical Body* ; J. Scheeben (tr. C. Vollert), *The Mysteries of Christianity* (1946) ; *Nature and Grace* (1954) ; J. B. Terrien SJ, *La Grâce et la gloire* (revised edition 1901) ; Mgr Waffelaert, *L'Union de l'âme aimante avec Dieu* (1916.)　　　H. P. C. L.

ADORATION The English word adoration is derived from the Latin *adorare* which in its turn is most probably derived from *manum ad os mittere*, to bring one's hand to one's mouth and throw a kiss to a person and particularly to the statue of a god whom one wishes to honour. The Greek Christian distinguished carefully between *latreia*, the worship of God and *proskunesis*, the veneration given to other sacred persons or objects. Both Greek words were translated into Latin by one word, *adoratio*, and as a result the distinction of concepts was at times obscured. In this article the term adoration is constantly used in the modern, strictly religious sense, as designating an act of honour paid exclusively to God. This article will examine the **philosophical** idea of adoration, (I) its essence and (II) function, and then go on to consider **theologically** (I) its object and (II) function, (III) its relation to Christ, and (IV) to the Church, with finally (V and VI) some special types of adoration.

A Philosophy
I Essence of adoration. Solid philosophical reflections occasioned by man's innate desire for speculative truth and by his craving for a final solution to the deepest moral problems of his personality, establish the existence of a supreme, infinitely perfect, absolutely transcendent and personal Being, who in His omnipotent and completely unselfish goodness has freely created man and all other finite beings, preserves them in existence and through His providence directs them towards an ever fuller realization of his creative design : which is His external glory in the communication of His goodness to personal beings capable of finding happiness in loving God and being loved by Him (*see* GOD ; CREATION). Guided by this intellectual insight man understands that he cannot ultimately exercise his personal freedom in accordance with his metaphysical condition unless he acknowledges God as his creator and in doing so completely surrenders himself and his whole activity to the law of God's loving will : the act by which man humbly accepts his condition as a creature and explicitly manifests to God his decision to recognize Him as his Lord and Master is technically called adoration (*see* HUMILITY). The act of adoration contains therefore in its most complete form the following essential psychological elements :

(i) intellectual appreciation of the existence of God and of, at least, the most important divine attributes (*see* ATTRIBUTES OF GOD) ;
(ii) understanding of one's own contingency and utter dependence on God ;
(iii) reverential awe, admiration of God's majesty and rejoicing in His goodness ;
(iv) firm decision to efface oneself completely and to surrender oneself unconditionally to God's holy will ;

(v) manifestation to God of this basic attitude in a special act of personal homage or prayer of adoration.

Though principally an act of man's spiritual faculties, adoration requires, by its very nature, participation of and extension to the various strata of man's whole existence. Hence (a) the necessity of expressing adoration by way of bodily attitude, signs, gestures, words or ceremonies. As is always the case with material expressions of mental attitudes, the outward manifestation of adoration may vary greatly according to the different types of persons, races, countries or times, but it should, in a particularly dignified manner, express the exclusiveness of man's surrender to God. Hence (b) the necessity of acknowledging God's supremacy not only by way of private and individual adoration but also by way of public and common acts of adoration in family, tribe, nation or even wider social communities. Here again the exact particular forms cannot be laid down philosophically, but there should, for instance, be at least some public homage to God in the most solemn acts of the public and political life.

II Function of adoration. The function of adoration in man's moral and religious life may be gathered from the following considerations :

(i) Properly understood the moral act is not an act of obeying or disobeying of impersonal laws and precepts but a personal reply of man to the personal claims of the personal God (*see* ACTS, HUMAN).

(ii) As soon as a man capable of moral acts has acquired a sufficient knowledge of the existence of God and of His personal claims on man's personality, he must therefore give a personal reply to God. This first personal reply is, in fact, the so-called fundamental (though not irrevocable) election by which man either surrenders himself unconditionally to God or else rejects Him and in doing so commits a sin in the most formal sense of the word (*see* SIN).

(iii) Precisely because this fundamental election is a personal reply to the personal claims of the personal God, it cannot stop short at a decision about God but must needs take the form of a personal Yes or No said to God : it is either the sinful ' I will not serve Thee ' or the adoring ' Who is as the Lord ? ' Adoration is, therefore, most intimately and essentially connected with the morally sound basic election in as far as this is an act of love and as such requires a personal manifestation of the loving acknowledgment to the Divine Majesty.

(iv) Owing to his being subjected to material conditions, man cannot in this life exhaust his moral activity in one single act. The above consideration must hence be extended to the variety of subsequent moral acts, even though the same degree of awareness and imputability and the same need for explicit adoration are, of course, not always necessarily implied. But since on the other hand man's moral activity is not a mere succession of isolated acts, but on the contrary, rather a vital and organic development of a fundamental attitude, the basic orientation of man's moral life (as decided on in the fundamental good election and as necessarily manifested to God in adoration) exercises its influence even on these less perfect acts by conferring on them the dignity of man's personal dealings with God. With a view to this extremely important function of adoration in every sound moral activity of man, it becomes understandable that man is frequently, though in a somewhat wider sense of the word, said to adore God by his very life and by every good moral act.

(v) The preceding reflections reveal the intimate union between man's moral and religious activities and the important function of adoration in the process of finalization and synthesis of all man's good acts. Simultaneously they also enable us to understand why adoration as being man's highest religious act is at the root of every religious activity itself. In fact, all prayers, sacrifices, rites, etc., are either acts of adoration or else logically presuppose it, contain it, lead up towards its more conscious and perfect forms (*see* PRAYER; RELIGIOUS LIFE; MASS) and in this way prepare man for the final adoration in the world to come which while being the fulfilment of God's creative design is at the same time man's highest perfection and ultimate happiness.

III Practical application. It is obvious then that acts of adoration should be frequently repeated and that their motivation should keep pace with the actual conditions of religious knowledge and the maturity of each person individually.

B Theology

Both the OT and NT frequently speak of and insist on the eminence, importance and necessity of adoration : Gen 24:26-8, 48 ; 47:31. Ex 20:3-6. Deut 5:6-10 ; 6-13. Jos 23:7. 1 Kg 1:3. 3 Kg 1:47-8. 4 Kg 17:36. Jdt 13:17. Est 13:16. Job 42:1-6. Ps 8 ; 18 ; 32 ; 33 ; 46 ; 47 ; 62 ; 64 ; 72 ; 74 ; 77 ; 80 ; 85 ; 94 ; 97 ; 103-5 ; 110 ; 112 ; 116 ; 133 ; 138 ; 145-50. Ecclus 42:15 ; 43:37 ; 50:13-27. Is 25:1-6 ; 27:13 ; 45:15-26. Bar 6:5. Dan 3:5-6, 18. 1 Mac 4:55.—Mt 4:10 ; 26:39 ; 28:9, 17. Mk 14:35. Lk 4:8 ; 10:21 ; 11:1-3 ; 24:52. Jn 4:21-5 ; 17. Ac 10:25. 1 Cor 14:25. Phil 2:6-12. Heb 1:6. Apoc 4:10-11 ; 5:14 ; 7:11-12 ; 22:9 etc. (For Commentary on these texts, see CCS.)

Christian tradition has hence in practice and theory constantly considered adoration to be the very heart of Christian perfection. Doctrinally the above findings of philosophy are confirmed and supernaturally deepened by revelation and theology.

I Object of Adoration. The dogma of the Trinity implies the adorability of the one godhead in three distinct persons : God the Father, God the Son, God the Holy Ghost (*see* TRINITY). We may note that the early Christian practice of adoring the Second and Third Person has helped theologians to come to a clearer understanding of the divinity of the Eternal Word and of the Holy Spirit (*see* J. Lebreton, *Histoire du dogme de la Trinité*, II (1928) 175-247). The dogma of the Incarnation implies the adorability of the humanity of Christ in as far as this is hypostatically united to the divinity of the Word (see D. Index systematicus VIII e ; INCARNATION ; HYPOSTATIC UNION), whereas the dogma of transubstantiation reveals the adorability of the Eucharistic Christ (see EUCHARIST ; TRANSUBSTANTIATION). In principle, whatever is hypostatically united to the Divine Word is by this very union adorable ; in practice, however, the adoration of parts of Christ's humanity remains subject to the approbation of the Church ; she alone judges their fitness to symbolize the whole reality of the Incarnate Word as well as the origin of such special devotions. Thus the Church encourages the adoration of the Sacred Heart (see HEART, SACRED) but disapproves of the adoration of some other parts of Christ's humanity. Mary and the Saints are not adorable since they are neither divine nor hypostatically united to the divinity. They enjoy veneration (*hyperdulia, dulia*) because of the sanctity which they have acquired (see MARY ; SAINTS). As we know from the constant teaching of the Church, relics, images and other religious objects receive no adoration whatever but only indirect veneration (see ICONOCLASTS).

II Function of revelation and grace in Christian adoration. Revelation manifests in a highly superior way the majesty, beauty and goodness of God whereas internal grace enables man to circumstantiate his adoration by supernatural faith, hope and charity (see REVELATION ; FAITH ; HOPE ; CHARITY). Christian adoration reaches its perfection through the infused virtue of charity which supernaturally informs and unifies man's whole life to a life of perfect adoration ; a life or basic ontological attitude that expresses itself necessarily in conscious acts of adoration and is simultaneously strengthened by them (see HABITS, SUPERNATURAL ; CHARITY).

III Christological and trinitarian aspects of adoration. Precisely in the light of the Catholic doctrine of grace in general and of the theological virtues in particular, it becomes clear further in what sense the adoration of the Christian is christological and trinitarian. For since the function of grace and these virtues consists precisely in incorporating man into the humanity of Christ, it is obvious that man's adoration becomes thus a participation in the adoration of Christ Himself. From this it seems to follow that the most typical form of Christian adoration is the adoration of the Father in the Spirit through, with, and in Christ (see K. Adam, *Christ our Brother*, 1933, 38–76).

IV Ecclesiological aspect of Christian adoration ; its social elements ; its highest objective forms. As Christian adoration is a participation in the adoration of Christ Himself it requires not only grace (see GRACE ; PELAGIUS), but also communication of grace through the Church, Mystical Body of Christ and as such source of all graces and Christian activities (see BODY, MYSTICAL ; GRACE). This fundamental Catholic doctrine makes clear :

(i) that the adoration of the individual Christian is through its union with the adoration of Christ simultaneously vitally united to and intercommunicating with the adoration of the Angels (see ANGELS) and of all actual and virtual members of the Mystical Body and in this way participating in the one great adoration of the Universe offered to God by Christ in His Church (see SOLIDARITY ; COMMUNION OF SAINTS ; PURGATORY ; PRAYER) ;

(ii) that the objectively most perfect and complete adoration of the Christian is found in his active participation in the highest and most solemn act of adoration practised by the Church, the Holy Mass, Christ's perfect sacrifice of adoration, with its many explicit acts of adoration such as the Gloria, Sanctus, Benedictus, the doxologies and the many prayers of adoration found in the changeable texts of the Mass (see MASS ; DOXOLOGIES) ; in the official counterpart of the Mass, the Breviary with its constantly repeated doxologies, its psalms of adoration (particularly the daily repeated opening psalm 94), its canticles and hymns of adoration such as the Benedictus, Magnificat, Te Deum laudamus, etc. (see BREVIARY) ; and finally in the other liturgical prayers of adoration proposed by the Church ;

(iii) that the public and non-public adoration of the Christian should under all its aspects be in harmony with the teaching of the Church, which alone guarantees its conformity with the mind of Christ's adoration.

V Non-public adoration. In accordance with the fact that different gifts and graces are bestowed upon the individual members of the Mystical Body, there exists a great variety of legitimate forms and types of non-public personal adoration. The great schools of Catholic spirituality may even be classified by this criterion. Useful information hereon can be found in DSp, Adoration, 220–2 (see also BERULLIAN SPIRITUALITY), whereas the article MYSTICISM explains how at the very height of mystical experience, the awareness of God's presence causes mystics to adore God in a way which may rightly be called the closest anticipation of heavenly adoration in the blissfulness of the BEATIFIC VISION.

VI Perpetual adoration. In modern times various religious congregations have been founded whose members oblige themselves to procure in their communities an uninterrupted adoration, particularly of the Eucharistic Christ, and to guarantee in this way the continuity of visible adoration in the Church. A similar practice of perpetual adoration is today more and more frequently organized in parishes and convents all over the world, usually in connection with the 40-Hours adoration of the Blessed Sacrament.

Bibliography. CE, ' Adoration ' (W. L. Sullivan); DTC, ' Adoration ' (E. Beurlier) ; LTK, 1958², *Anbetung* (O. Karrer) ; DSp, Adoration (A. Molien) ; W. Brugger, *Philosophisches Wörterbuch* (1948) Religion (J. Lotz) ; *Enciclopedia Filosofica* (1957) Culto (G. di Napoli), Religione (G. Graneris) ; DB, Adoration (S. Many) ; *Catholic Biblical Encyclopedia* (J. Steinmueller-K. Sullivan) OT (1956) ' Prayer ', NT (1949) ' Adoration ' ; *Bibel-Lexikon* (1951) ' Gebet ' (W. Grossouw) ; DAC, ' Adoration ' (H. Leclercq) ; F. Cabrol, *La Prière des* *premiers chrétiens* (1929) ; M. Rouët de Journel-J. Dutilleul, *Enchiridion Asceticum* (1930) Index s.v. *Oratio* ; St. Thomas, 2-2ae : 84, 103 ; Suarez, *De virtute religionis*, tr. 2, bk 1, ch 1–3 in *Opera Omnia* XIII, 77–90, De Incarnatione, disp. 51–6, *Opera Omnia* XVIII, 540–663 ; Billuart, diss. III, a 1 ; B. Häring, *Das Gesetz Christi* (1956) 629–50 ; O. Lottin, *L'Ame du culte* (1920) ; F. Heiler, *Das Gebet* (1925) ; J. de Guibert, *Theologia Spiritualis ascetica et mystica* (1939²) and the specialized literature quoted in these works. Concerning the modern Magisterium of the Church, see the Encyclical Letters of Pope Pius XII : *Mystici Corporis*, AAS 35 (1943) 193 ff. ; *Mediator Dei*, AAS 39 (1947) 551 ff. ; *Haurietis Aquas*, AAS 48 (1956) 309 ff.   P. M.

ADVENT There are five sections of this article, (I) the origin of Advent, (II) the Keltic liturgy, (III) Rome and Ravenna, (IV) Advent as a parallel to Lent, and finally (V) the theology of Advent.

I Origins. The two comings of Christ, the one in the lowliness of human nature and the second in the royal majesty of His Father, are associated in the (2nd cent.) Muratori fragment and frequently in the Fathers (e.g. in Hilary, PL 9:1054), and the association is admirably expressed in the prayer of the *Mozarabic Sacramentary* for Advent (in Férotin's edition, 33) in the words : *Qui iam venit humilis et adhuc venturus est in maiestate terribilis* (who came once in lowly wise and is still to come terrible in majesty). The first sign that the Church has begun to set apart a season for the contemplation of these mysteries is in the fragment of Hilary of Poitiers (*de mysteriis* 1:9 ; CSEL 65:16), where, commenting on the parable of the gardener and the fig-tree, he says, ' Holy Mother Church magnifies for herself the coming of the Saviour by setting aside annually a period of three weeks '.[1] He died in 367 and soon after that the Council of Saragossa is found enacting in 380 (Mansi III, 624) that, ' For twenty-one days from 17 December until the Epiphany which is 6 January, day by day, it shall not be allowed that any-one be absent from the church, skulking at home or sitting in his villa or going up the mountains, nor must they go about barefoot, but all assemble at church '.[2] The Roman Saturnalia began on 17 December, and although the official feast lasted only seven days, the licence of the times made it in practice longer (e.g. a whole month, according to the *Acts* of St Dasius). Going barefoot at the feast was a practice of the slaves, as implied by Statius (*Silvae* I, 6:4), and the account given by Macrobius (who is a contemporary of this Council) shows that there was every reason to rally the faithful daily at church during that time ; Romans who were plea-sure-bent took their daily bath in the morning

(instead of in the late afternoon) in order to start celebrating early.

II The Keltic liturgy. A three weeks' Advent is catered for in the *Bobbio Missal*, the Trier lectionary and the *Missale Gallicanum vetus*, and all agree in making Advent the start of their liturgical year. It is also of some significance that in the *Leonine Sacramentary* there are signs of its adaptation to a place where a three weeks' Advent was kept. It is usual to deny that the *Leonine* has any trace of Advent, but Mohlberg's careful edition shows that alongside three Prefaces, 1260, 1262 and 1322, Tironian notes (of an Irish type) have been added (*hic requirendum de adventum*, ' this will be needed for Advent ' or the like). One of the collects in *Bobbio* (39) is found in the *Gelasian Sacramentary* in a changed form (though eleven others stand un-changed in both books), and the *clausula* of the Bobbio collect (*purificati Tibi servire mereamur*) is more correct and therefore earlier, than the Gelasian form (*purificatis Tibi servire mentibus mereamur*). This fact would suggest that the *Bobbio Missal* and its com-panions have an earlier version of Advent than the *Gelasian Sacramentary*, however they came by it.

There can be no doubt that the Keltic liturgy made of Advent a time for pondering the Second Coming. In *Bobbio* the first mass has a lesson from Jas 5:7 : ' Let us be patient until the advent of the Lord . . .', and there are frequent references in the col-lects to the need for vigilance and to the ' terrible advent '. The keynote may be found in the third *contestatio* or Preface : ' that as we have believed in Thy coming long ago for the release of captives, so we may deserve to be on the watch and to see Thee when Thou comest again in majesty '.[3] The pre-occupation with John the Baptist in the scripture-readings (Mt 11:2–15 and 3:1–12) is explained when one sees that in the old-Irish *Martyrology of Oengus* the Advent fast is called ' the fast of Elias ', for in any meditation on the Second Coming there has to be place for ' Elias who is to come first '. The place of the preaching of John the Baptist in the events prior to the birth of Christ is not at all so appropriate as his rôle in the Second Coming, and it would seem that the somewhat disconcerting presence in the modern Roman missal of two gospels for Advent that deal with John is due to this Elias motif. The very ancient Introit (*Ecce advenit*) for the Epiphany, taken from Malachy's prophecy of the coming Ruler and Judge, is also reminiscent of some of these ideas. Three sermons of St Columbanus (VIII to X, in the SLH edition, pp. 94–106) deal with the end of life, but while the first of these is more personal, the second and third (which seem to have been delivered on successive days) recall the prophecies about the end of the world and Second Coming. They harmonize with the collects of the *Bobbio Missal* in striking fashion.

III Rome and Ravenna. In Rome the keeping of ·

---

[1] Sancta mater ecclesia Salvatoris adventum annuo recursu per trium septimanarum secretum spatium sibi incitavit.

[2] Viginti et uno die, quo a XVI Kal. Ianuarii usque in diem Epiphaniae, quae est VIII Idus Ianuarii, continuis diebus nulli liceat de ecclesia se absentare—nec latere in domibus nec sedere ad villam nec montes petere—nec nudis pedibus incedere sed concurrere ad ecclesiam.

[3] Ut Te quem dudum venisse credimus pro remedio captivorum, in secundo adventu Tuo Te cum maiestate venturum sustinentes videre mereamur cum indulgentia peccatorum.

Advent was unknown at the time when St Benedict compiled his Rule, and it is likewise ignored in the *Sermons* of St Leo. At Ravenna, however, under Byzantine influence the season seems to have been honoured at least since the time of St Peter Chrysologus (archbishop *c.* 430–50). Some of his sermons (91 and 92 on John the Baptist and 140 with 142 on the Annunciation) seem to have been preached just before the feast of the birth of Christ was kept. The *Rotulus* of Ravenna is a collection of prayers for Advent, ending with one that is rubricated for the vigil of Christmas. One of the prayers refers to the *ineffabile decretum magni consilii*, which from the context must be the decree of Ephesus (D 111 a) and thus the whole collection must belong to the same period as the works of Peter Chrysologus. In these prayers the idea is everywhere manifest that the coming of Christ which is being prepared for is His *first* coming, now in some mystical fashion to be renewed. The earth 'desires the presence of its Redeemer' (collect 1342 in Mohlberg's edition); we look for a coming in which the Virgin will bring forth for us the divine Christ (1351); we see the birth of Christ according to the flesh coming nigh (1355); the Saviour is about to come forth from the body of the Virgin (1368). Only once (1349) is there mention of the Second Coming, and then it is brought in only by way of contrast with the First. This 5th-cent. belief and practice of Ravenna is what gives us the present-day understanding of what Advent is about, but how did it come to supplant or to join up with the other stream of tradition about the Second Coming? Theologically, the question is of some importance.

The practice of Ravenna seems to be a direct importation from Constantinople, for at that city the custom was to keep the Sunday before Christmas as a feast of Our Lady and the Sunday preceding that as sacred to John the Baptist. Proclus preached a sermon for the former feast on 23 December 428, and his practice is followed by Peter Chrysologus at Ravenna. The tenth Council of Toledo (in 656) enacted in its first canon that 18 December was to be kept as a feast of Our Lady, and appealed to the custom of 'many churches remote from us in distance and location' as justification; [1] in view of the large extent of Byzantine influence in Visigothic Spain, it is safe to say that Constantinople is one of the places meant. The Georgian *Kanonarion* (which represents the 7th-cent. usage of Jerusalem) has a similar feast and there is some trace of it in the 6th-cent. Syriac Lectionary printed by Burkitt (*Proceedings of British Academy* (1921) 333). The earlier Armenian lectionary which gives the Jerusalem practice of the days of Cyril has no trace of such a December feast. The Fathers of Toledo asked rhetorically, 'What other feast of the Mother is there save the Incarnation of the Word?' They say that Lent is not a suitable time for such a feast nor yet the time after Easter, when the Resurrection is being commemorated, and thus they opt for

[1] In multis ecclesiis a nobis et spatio remotis et terris hic mos agnoscitur retineri.

December. This mixture of theological argument and Eastern custom seems to have been especially potent in the West after 700. One can only surmise how astonished the compiler of the Mozarabic *Libellus Orationum* (of which the 7th-cent. MS. is at Verona, published by Bianchini in 1741) would have been by it all, for his Advent keeps the idea of the Second Coming to the fore, e.g. in the prayer for the First Sunday: 'Thou camest first to free the condemned, and mayest Thou come again to free from punishment the liberated'.

IV Advent as a parallel to Lent. There is evidence from Armenia going back to Gregory Asharuni (of 690, cf. Conybeare *Rituale Armenorum*, 515) that a forty-day period of fasting was kept before Epiphany, just as before Easter, and was regarded as another Lent. Not merely two but three Lents a year was the Irish custom, witnessed by many *Penitentials* and adopted according to Bede (HE. 3:27) by the Saxon, Egbert, who died in 729 aged 90. These were the Lent of Elias before Christmas, that of Jesus in the spring before Easter, and that of Moses in the summer at Pentecost. What seems to be the first mention of these three Lents is in the *Penitential* of Gildas, which was used in the British church of the 6th cent. For a theft the penitent is ordered 'to do penance for one year, and especially at the three Lents' (Hadden and Stubbs, *Councils of Britain* I, 114). The only possible link between Britain and Armenia at that time seems to be Jerusalem, whither Pelagius had gone in the preceding century and to which St David is said to have gone with SS Teilo and Padarn about this time. Now it is obvious that a forty days' fast prior to the Epiphany must begin just at the time when Advent is now held to begin (about 27 November), whereas, if the fast is made to precede Christmas and is not shortened, it will have to start about 15 November. Thus one finds that the Mozarabic rite took the feast of St Acisclus (17 November) as *initium Adventus*, while the *Martyrology of Oengus* starts it on 18 November and some Gallican and Ambrosian texts call it the *quadragesima Martini* and make it begin on 11 November.[2] The gradual emergence of Christmas as the greater feast and the abandonment of baptisms on the Epiphany may thus account for the choice of an earlier start to Advent, though Epiphany baptisms are the custom at Carthage as late as 480–90 (Victor Vitensis *historia persecutionum* 2:17; CSEL 7:42) and are allowed for by the *Sacramentary of Gellone*, *c.* 750-775. Leo the Great (as Siricius before him) had discouraged the use of the Epiphany for baptisms (PL 54:701 and 13:1134), and this fact, along with the difficulty of the climate in northern countries, must have caused the day gradually to lose its baptismal character, though it seems that the great baptism of five thousand Anglo-Saxons by Augustine on the banks of the Swale in Kent took place at Epiphany. The prohibition of the solemnizing of

[2] Perpetuus of Tours (*c.* 490) ordered [Gregory of Tours, *Historia Francorum* 10:31 *de depositione Martini usque Natale Domini terna in septimana ieiunia*] 'three days of fasting a week from St Martin's day till Christmas'.

marriages from the beginning of Advent to the Epiphany is found in the *Decretum* of Burchard (PL 140:816), from which it was copied by Gratian and by the Council of Trent (session 24:10).

The curious 4th-cent. Spanish document which was published by Dom Morin in 1928 (*Revue Bénédictine* 40:296–302) has knowledge of a three weeks' fast towards the end of December, and connects the time with preparation for the Second Coming.[1] It has also a passing reference to the Saturnalia. It also mentions John the Baptist as the one who is the herald of His advent (*adventus Illius praedicator est*). Similarly, there is Byzantine evidence, though of a much later date, for a 'Lent of St Saba' kept for three weeks from the feast of the saint (6 December) to Christmas (AA. SS. July, III:559 and 581). St Stephen Thaumaturgus is there represented as keeping such a Lent at Jerusalem in 762. By that time in the West, as Bede shows (*de ratione temporum* 48), rationalization had been at work: the start of the year had been moved to 24 September, to copy the Jewish practice, and a feast of the Conception of John the Baptist on that day was meant to measure the nine months' interval before the feast of his Nativity on 24 June, this event being chosen as the beginning of the whole cycle of salvation.

V The theology of Advent.

The use of Isaias in Advent is witnessed by the *Gallican Antiphonary* from Fleury (RBn 22 [1905] 336–43), and the *Mozarabic Antiphonary* (Eph. Lit. 49 [1935] 126–45) for Advent is largely drawn from Isaias. Now it seems clear that, while some part of the content of the passages chosen can be referred to the First Coming, there is much which can find fulfilment only in the Second. It seems then safe to say that when and where the Church is committed to using Isaias for this season (and the evidence points to Ireland, Gaul and Spain) she is also committed to the idea of an Advent which will honour both Comings. Books of the Keltic-Gallican tradition, such as the *Comes of Würzburg*, the *Freising Benedictional* and the *Lanalet Pontifical*, which have an Advent (of five Sundays) inserted at the end of their liturgical year, may just as well have put it there because that place seemed most fitting for a commemoration of the Second Coming as through a desire to find a place for something which did not belong to their original scheme of feasts and seasons.

The five Sundays of Advent (found in the *Gelasian Sacramentary*, the *Liber Comitis*, the *Lectionary of Naples*, the *Sacramentary of Gellone* and in many older works known to Amalarius) were reduced to four in the 'Gregorian' reform of the Sacramentary, and there was an attempt to remove from its prayers those which gave special attention to the Second Coming. Thus it was that the group of *aliae*

---

[1] Nos in coniunctione decimi et undecimi mensis orationem ieiunio copulemus, ut . . . per adnuntiationem angeli, id est revelationem Spiritus, futurorum nobis arcana pandantur. . . . Sicut Israelitici milites tribus ebdomadis in ieiuniis et orationibus servientes. . . . (300–1). The Saturnalia are alluded to in the wish that the mob which has gathered for sinful pleasure would die away (*omnis quae se ad luxuriam collegerit turba moriatur*).

orationes de Adventu was set down after the liturgy for the four Sundays had been made up, as if the reformers did not feel they could omit them entirely but did not want them to be in regular use. The proper Prefaces which survive in the *Leofric Missal* and in *codex Ottobonianus* of the Gregorian, with such telling phrases as : *Iustificet in secundo adventu qui nos redemit in primo*, and *sicut venit ad nos redimendum occultus, ita iustificet cum ad iudicandum venerit manifestus*, have disappeared from the reformed missals, and today there is no proper Preface for Advent. It is the more surprising then to find that Gregory the Great himself gave a homily (PL 76:1077–81) on the gospel of the First Sunday of Advent in which he dealt largely with the Second Coming ; even if the gospel of the day was Lk 21:25–32, one would think that he could have altered that, but it has kept its place until now. Gradually the Middle Ages (with Rupert of Deutz and Bernard leading) evolved a theory of the spiritual Advent of Christ to the individual soul, which turned the make-believe of the Ravenna prayers into substantial theology and provided a more acceptable alternative to the Keltic preoccupation with the Second Coming.

Bibliography. J. Jungmann SJ, *Advent und Voradvent* in ZKT 61 (1937) 341–90 ; W. Croce SJ, *Die Adventsliturgie* in ZKT 76 (1954) 257–96 ; A. Chavasse, *L'Avent romain au vi–viii siècle* in Eph. Lit. 67 (1953) 297–358 ; A. Baumstark ' Die Kirchenjahr in Antiochien ', in *Römische Quartalschrift* 11 (1897) 31–66 ; the same s.v. ' Advent ' in *Reallexicon für Antike und Christentum* ; F. Cabrol, s.v. ' Avent ' in DAC I ; and the standard editions of the early liturgical texts cited in the course of writing this article. There are still many unsolved problems connected with the theology of Advent. Why, for instance, did the users of the Trier gospel-lectionary (RBn 33 [1921] 47) want to read during Advent the Palm Sunday gospels, Mk 11:1–10 ; Lk 19:29–38 and Mt 20:29–21:17 ?   J. H. C.

AETIUS was the most radical of the Arians, holding that God the Father was *in no way like* to Christ (from which belief came the name of *Anomoians* that was given to his followers) ; for his attempt to apply the philosophy of Aristotle to Christian theology he is deserving of some notice. He was born about 300, a Cilician slave, who became a goldworker and a doctor and was therefore of some education. He learnt Arianism from Paulinus, the Arian bishop of Tyre and Antioch (*c.* 323), but was banished to Anazarba by Eulalius in 324. Here he was welcomed by the Arian bishop who read the gospels with him. He went back to Antioch only to be banished again, and then made his way to Alexandria where he won fame by vanquishing in argument the Manichee, Aphthonius. Here he acquired his Aristotelianism, which he made into a most potent instrument for the upsetting of traditional beliefs. His syllogisms and dilemmas, of which some 47 have been preserved by Epiphanius (*Haer.* 76:11 ; GCS 37:340–414), made it hard at first for the orthodox to defend their faith. Athanasius placed his confidence in the use of Scripture, but many were content to say that they believed ' like fishermen, not like Aristotelians '. The reply of Aetius to this seems to have been to compare what he called their blind faith to the state of a maiden who, being deaf, dumb and blind, cannot say who has violated her, did not see her assailant and does not even hear the questions of those who want to help her. Epiphanius replies to this by comparing Aetius, with his ' like and unlike ' and his science of predicates, to a blind man who sets himself up to judge what is black and white or purple or green. The effect of Aetius on the Cappadocians was to make them sharpen their own dialectic to answer his puzzles, while it is notable that Didymus of Alexandria (de Trinitate III, 2; PG 39:785) has a series of 55 syllogisms which sum up his first two books about the Trinity.

Many of the arguments of Aetius turned on the unguarded application of human concepts to the Godhead ; he asked, for instance, how, if there was no causality between the divine Persons, one of these could be born of the other. This attack on the credal statement genitum non factum (begotten, not made) is met by Epiphanius with the answer that if birth implies inequality then it must be denied of God, but there can be a begetting with equality. He did not generalize his reply to state that before any human perfection is predicated of God it must have its limitations ' thought away '. A theory of analogy was needed to meet Aetius with, but that was not provided until the Cappadocians had done their work (see ANALOGY). Another way in which Aetius came up against traditional teaching was in his choice of Aristotle as a philosophical guide rather than Plato, who had so far been the choice of the more speculative among the Fathers. Aristotle, with his denial of human immortality and his ultimate pantheism, was in need of considerable expurgation, as St Thomas was later to find, before he could be made suitable for Christian theology.

Aetius returned to Antioch in 358, and the bishop Eudoxius favoured him, but his teaching, which ran contrary both to the acceptance of homoousia and of homoiousia between Father and Son, soon caused his condemnation at the third Synod of Sirmium ; both parties could at least agree that this new radicalism was what neither of them wanted, and so he was banished to Pepuza. He turned up the next year at the Synod of Seleuceia in Isauria and went thence to Constantinople, where in 360 he was deposed from the diaconate and then banished by the emperor Constantius to Mopsuestia. When Julian the Apostate succeeded in 361, Aetius, who had at one time been his tutor, was recalled, and consecrated bishop (but without a diocese) at Constantinople ; the emperor gave him a farm in Lesbos. He died in Constantinople about 367. It is told of him by Epiphanius (who had a journalistic flair for such details) that he used to rebaptize those who had been orthodox or Arian, holding them upside down (to emphasize the unlikeness of God to man) and using

a formula which invoked, ' the name of the uncreated God, and of the created Son, and of the Spirit, the sanctifier, who was created by the created Son '. He made them at the same time take an oath not to desert his teachings (Haer. 76:54 ; GCS 37:414). The conclusion of one of his letters is preserved (ibid. 409) where he says : ' May the God that is self-begotten, the only one truly called God, by the One He sent, Jesus Christ, that was before all ages and is truly of begotten substance, keep you all from all impiety, in Christ Jesus our Saviour, through whom be all glory to our God and Father now and for ever '. To Epiphanius this doxology seemed wrong because it lacked the title of Lord at the two mentions of Christ, but one could find other dogmatic faults with it too. According to a fragment (PG 89:1181) preserved by Anastasius of Sinai, Aetius prepared the way for the Monothelite heresy by saying that, if we agree that the Son is two-willed, as Athanasius claims, then we fall into the Manichaean heresy of saying that the will of the flesh goes against the will of God. ' Every separation makes a dyad ' was one of his maxims, which he applied to the problems of Christology, and as Christ could not be two, it must be allowed, he claimed, that there is only one nature in Christ, and that one entirely different from the Father. Aetius would thus seem to have provided the bridge for heresy to pass from Trinitarian problems to the later disputes about the two natures in Christ. None the less, it was his pupil, Eunomius, who was to extend the great Trinitarian theologian, Gregory of Nyssa, and to set the pace of discussion for years to come.

Bibliography. The primary source is Epiphanius (Haer. 76) and the relevant entries in the Church historians, one of whom, Philostorgius, made Aetius one of his heroes. Among modern studies, one may mention : G. Bardy, L'Héritage littéraire d'Aétius, in RHE 24 (1928) 809–26 ; V. Grumel, ' Les Textes monothélites d'Aétius ', in Échos d'Orient 28 (1929) 159–66 ; J. de Ghellinck SJ, La Dialectique d'Aristote et les conflits trinitaires, in RHE 26 (1930) 5–42. The notice of his life in DCB is probably still the best available.   J. H. C.

AFFECTIVE PRAYER   Affective prayer is essentially a prayer of acts or aspirations, and as such is the natural and spontaneous expression of our sentiments towards God. In this sense anyone who has ever prayed spontaneously has used affective prayer. But as the term is used today it describes a particular method or kind of prayer, and it implies then a habit of using acts, not just occasionally, but regularly and for relatively long periods. It is possible to develop such a habit by the use of ' forced ' acts, perhaps taken from the psalms or a book, which may at times become spontaneous, and the prayer is then approaching what is sometimes called acquired contemplation. Affective prayer has only been known in this way as a special kind of prayer since the Counter-Reformation, and it has come to be contrasted with meditation. This, in the modern sense, is a special technique of private prayer in which the methodical consideration of points of doctrine or of Our Lord's life is used to excite the will to make acts, in which the prayer properly consists. An over-rigid distinction between the two kinds of prayer, which has sometimes been made, is harmful. It is a question of emphasis. Too strict adherence to set schemes of considerations may be enforced to the detriment of real prayer, but the work of the intellect is never entirely eliminated in affective prayer, and when the will is sluggish it may be employed on the acts in a manner which is in effect meditation.

In the Middle Ages precise methods of prayer had not been elaborated, but instructions on the spiritual life, which were always addressed to those leading what we should now call a contemplative form of life, always demanded reading, meditation and prayer as the ingredients. The reading was evidently spiritual, and the meditation was a devout consideration of some of the truths of religion. We have examples of the sort of thing it was in the 14th-cent. *Speculum Inclusorum* (Part II, chap. 2), or in the works of the 12th-cent. abbot, Pierre de Celle. It was discursive, often more or less ' affective ' in form. What the form of prayer was which accompanied these exercises we can only surmise, for detailed instructions on methods of prayer were unknown, but many examples of what we call affective prayer have come down to us. The great exemplar seems to have been found in the *Confessions* of St Augustine, where from a full heart he breaks forth frequently and at length into prayer. Examples of this kind of thing can be found in the writings of the 11th-cent. abbot, Jean de Fécamp, or in the 14th-cent. English treatise *A Talkyng of the Love of God*. To minds fed on extensive spiritual reading and meditation this kind of thing would come easily, and it is evident that such prayer was practised. Much has come down to us in manuscripts, and obviously most of it was never written down.

The affective approach to theology, as exemplified in writers like St Bernard and St Bonaventure, is something different from affective prayer properly so called.

Bibliography. *Speculum Inclusorum*, ed. L. Oliger (1938) ; J. Leclercq, *La Spiritualité de Pierre de Celle* (1946) ; Leclercq, J. and J.-P. Bonnes, *Un Maître de la vie spirituelle, Jean de Fécamp* (1946) ; *A Talkyng of the Love of God*, ed. C. M. Westra (1950) ; Baker, Augustine, *Sancta Sophia* (1657).　　　　F. G. S.

AFRICAN LITURGY The liturgy of the African church is of interest to the theologian owing to the fact that this church was the first to use Latin for its official language. Some of the concepts of theology thus found refuge in the ' fortresses of thought ' provided by a Latin technical vocabulary which was that of African Christians. It has even been argued that the first Latin liturgy used (*c.* 380) at Rome came from the Africans domiciled at Rome, who were using Latin there while all the other Christian

groups there used Greek. The evidence available can be divided historically into two periods, that of Tertullian and Cyprian (I), and that of Augustine and Optatus (II). The brief initial period during which the African church is presumed to have used the Greek liturgy of the unknown pioneers who brought it Christianity has left no trace.

I Tertullian and Cyprian afford a considerable amount of information about the liturgy, even though this is given incidentally in their writings. The term ' dominicum ' used for the celebration of the Eucharist is the earliest Latin name for the Mass, and must have been given at a time when Sunday was the only day to have a liturgy. It is used by Cyprian while Tertullian seems to have had only makeshift terms such as *oratio* and sometimes *oratio sacrificii* (*de oratione* 19 ; CSEL 20:192). None the less, he can speak of the eucharist as a sacrifice : ' A victim belonging to God and acceptable to God, which He indeed sought for and which He planned for Himself, this victim, dedicated with our whole heart, fed upon faith, guarded by truth . . . we must escort to God's altar in a procession of good works, to the accompaniment of psalms and hymns, and it will obtain all things for us from God ' (*de oratione* 28 ; CSEL 20:198). This gives a picture of the liturgy as it must have been carried out in Tertullian's day and shows that in spite of persecution some degree of solemnity had already been attained.

Cyprian (*ep.* 65:4) is sometimes cited for an epiclesis in the Mass, but his words : ' The offering cannot be sanctified in that place whence the Holy Spirit has departed ', really mean no more than that the bishop Fortunatianus had lapsed and was therefore in a state of sin, his liturgy being thereby, according to Cyprian's exaggerated view, not only unlawful but even invalid. This view he has put (*ep.* 63:9) in a form that could command acceptance but from which exaggerations could easily follow. ' The sacrifice of the Mass is not attended with lawful hallowing unless our offering and sacrifice answer to His passion.' [1] The distinction between what was lawful and what was valid would only come to the fore after the rebaptism controversy had been fought to a finish. The ends of the Mass are set forth in *ep.* 61:4 : ' In our sacrifices . . . we do not cease to give thanks to God through Christ, to pray and to beseech ', while *ep.* 1:2 speaks of the refusal of a Mass for a departed layman who has caused a cleric to engage in secular affairs.[2] It is also clear from the letters that on occasion—as when some of the faithful were in prison and could be visited—Mass was said by a priest alone, without the presence of the bishop (*ep.* 5:2). In his treatise on the Our Father (*de oratione dominica*, 31) he speaks of the Preface (*praefatio*) of the Mass, quotes the words ' *Sursum corda ; habemus ad Dominum* ', and shows (ibid. 24) that the kiss of peace was probably given before the

---

[1] Nec sacrificium dominicum legitima sanctificatione celebrari nisi oblatio et sacrificium nostrum responderit passioni.

[2] Non est quod pro dormitione eius apud vos oblatio aut deprecatio aliqua nomine eius in ecclesia frequentetur.

offertory procession took place. Intercession at Mass for all classes of men, known from Tertullian (*de oratione* 29), is urged by Cyprian (*ep.* 62:4) in a phrase which is very near to the formula found in the Mozarabic liturgy : *Ecclesiam sanctam catholicam in orationibus in mente habeamus . . . . Omnes lapsos, captivos, infirmos atque peregrinos in mente habeamus . . .'.* The mention of *lapsi* here points to a time before A.D. 300 for the origin of this litany.

Abel and Melchisedech (*de oratione dominica*, 24 and *ep.* 63:4) are cited as foreshadowing the Eucharist, and in spite of his use of words such as *imitatio* and *commemoratio* for the Mass, no one can doubt the meaning of Cyprian when he says (*ep.* 63:17) : 'The passion of Christ is the sacrifice which we offer.' Christ, he says, was 'like Melchisedech in offering bread and wine ; the bread and wine is His body and blood'. Here, as in a similar passage of Tertullian (*adv. Marc.* 4:40 ; CSEL 47:559), the manner of the change from bread to body is not discussed but the fact is asserted. ' Saying that He had desired to eat the Pasch as something that belonged to Himself, He took the bread, distributed it to His disciples and made it His body, saying This is My body (i.e. a type of His body [is, or becomes, His body]), for it would not have been a type, unless the body were there in truth.' [1] As Ambrose (*de sacramentis* 4:5:21 ; CSEL 73:55) has the words *quod figura est corporis Domini* in his mass-canon, it is probable that Tertullian already knew them from a similar source, *figura* being the accepted word for the Greek τύπος and having no reference to ' appearances ' in our sense. Tertullian was preoccupied (*adv. Marc.* 3:19 ; CSEL 47:408) with the prophecy of Jeremias (11:19), which he saw as a foreshadowing of the eucharistic sacrifice, the ' wood upon the bread' being taken to show the future bread (i.e. body of Christ) upon the wood of the cross.

II Augustine has a more developed liturgy. The custom of holding the first part of the Mass (the readings and psalms) in one place and then going in procession to the church for the rest is noted (*serm.* 325 ; PL 38:1449). The lessons were sometimes three (*serm.* 45:1 ; PL 38:262), sometimes two with a psalm between (*serm.* 176:1 ; PL 38:950). Choice of lessons was made by the bishop (*serm.* 362:1 ; PL 39:1611), but there was a programme of continuous readings for some seasons, e.g. of Acts after Easter (*serm.* 315:1 ; PL 38:1426). No rule was fixed for the frequency of Mass : ' In some places no day is allowed to pass without offering, elsewhere it is held on Saturdays and Sundays, elsewhere on Sundays only ' (*ep.* 54:2 ; CSEL 34:2:160). Christ desired it to be daily (*Civitas Dei* 10:20).

After the sermon and dismissal, there were *precationes* for unbelievers, for catechumens and for the faithful (*ep.* 217:1 ; CSEL 57:4:404). During the procession of gifts, Augustine caused psalms to be sung, and this roused the conservative laity to oppose him (*Retractationes* 2:37 ; CSEL 36:2:144). The kiss of peace seems still (*serm.* 82:3 ; PL 38:508) to have preceded this procession of gifts though *serm.* 227 puts it later. The recital of names from a *tabula* with a prayer *post nomina* may have come just before or just after the offertory-procession (*ep.* 149:16 ; CSEL 44:3:362 ; *contra epistulam Parmeniani* 3:6 ; CSEL 51:1:140 ; *serm.* 273:7 ; PL 38:1251 ; *ep.* 78:4 ; CSEL 34:2:337). Augustine has no trace of a Sanctus. He speaks of the consecration as operative of the change in the elements : ' Take away a word, there is bread and wine ; add a word and the mystery is enacted ' (*serm.* 6, Denis).[2] In spite of this he can say (*de Trin.* 3:4:10 ; PL 42:874) that the sanctification can only take place by the invisible work of the Spirit of God ; but here he is not speaking with technical precision, and it is the former passage that gives his theology of the matter. He gives us no clue to what prayers his canon had after the consecration concerning the heavenly altar and the consummation of the sacrifice (*see* EPIKLESIS). He says (*ep.* 149:16 ; CSEL 44:3:362) that the term *orationes* is used of the prayers recited when the elements are blessed and hallowed and are broken for distribution, as distinct from the *precationes* which come earlier, and that all these are rounded off by the Lord's Prayer. Immediately before communion came the *benedictiones* (as the nuptial blessing still does and as the blessing of fruit, etc., did in Hippolytus). These are called *interpellationes* wherein by imposition of hands the bishop commends his charges to the merciful power of God. Imposition of hands was the Jewish manner of blessing (used by Christ at the Ascension) and it may be that this, rather than the present sign of the cross, was familiar to Augustine. After the communion came *gratiarum actio* and dismissal.

Augustine's evidence is supported by an African decree, later ascribed to the council of Milevis (A.D. 402), that mass-prayers, whether those of the canon or those of the blessing (*sive praefationes sive commendationes*), were not to be used unless they had been approved by the council or else composed by the *prudentiores* (Mansi, IV, 330). The large number of blessings in the Mozarabic and Gothic missals indicates what the council may have had in view. Optatus (*contra Parmenianum* 6:1 ; CSEL 26:142) speaks of the altar, ' to which the offerings of the people and the members of Christ are brought, where God almighty is invoked and where the Holy Ghost comes down at our request '.[3] This is evidence for some kind of epiclesis, but for what purpose, consecratory, or merely for the union of the faithful in the one Bread ? The 4th-cent. mosaic of Thabarca seems to indicate in its picture of a church a stone altar with three candles near it. According

---

[1] Professus itaque se . . . concupisse edere Pascha ut suum, . . . acceptum panem et distributum discipulis, corpus illum suum fecit, Hoc est corpus Meum dicendo ; id est ' figura corporis Mei '. Figura autem non fuisset, nisi veritatis esset corpus.

[2] Tolle verbum, panis est et vinum ; adde verbum et fiet sacramentum.
[3] Altaria Dei . . . in quibus vota populi et membra Christi portata sunt, quo Deus omnipotens invocatus sit, quo postulatus descenderit Spiritus sanctus.

to Augustine (PL 37:1484) altars were consecrated by use, i.e. by having Mass said upon them. For a general sketch of the setting of the liturgy, one can turn to his letter to Maximinus (*ep.* 23 ; CSEL 39:1:66). Reservation of the eucharist at home still continued (PL 45:1315) as in the days of Tertullian. It was the custom to admit *some* sinners to the whole of the Mass, even though they were not allowed to communicate (*serm.* 351:4 ; PL 39:1546). What he wrote on the frequency of communion (*ep.* 54 ; CSEL 34:2:162) was used by St Pius X. Of later writers only Fulgentius gives much information about the liturgy. He seems (PL 65:789) to paraphrase part of an epiclesis-prayer, arguing that the purpose of it is to produce an effusion of charity in the congregation rather than a change in the elements of the sacrifice : ' Renewing the memory of His death we suppliants beseech that by that charity which won Christ for His passion we also may be crucified to the world and the world to us.' [1]

Bibliography. W. Roetzer OSB, *Des heiligen Augustinus Schriften als liturgie-geschichtliche Quelle* (1930) ; *W. C. Bishop, *The African Rite*, in JTS 13 (1912) 250–70 ; *J. H. Srawley, *The Early History of the Liturgy* (1949) ; F. Cabrol, *Afrique, liturgie*, in DAC I, 591–657 ; *E. C. Ratcliff, *The Institution narrative of the Roman Canon*, in TU 64, ii (1957) 64–82 ; L. Brou OSB, *The Psalter Collects* (1949) where the African series of these collects is published ; a further study on the African series is in *Sacris Erudiri* 6 (1954) 73–95, showing that they were composed between 450 and 500.   J. H. C.

AGAPE Meals in common, where rich gave of their abundance to poor, were not unknown among the Jews (e.g. in the Qumran community, *Manual of Discipline* 6 ; 1), and the rule for the Passover was that something should be set aside for the poor (TB *Pesachim* 99b ; cf. Jn 13:29). That the early Christians should have such a meal in connection with the Eucharist is therefore not surprising. Much controversy went on in the early years of this century about the precedence of Agape or Eucharist, but as much of the argument depended on the interpretation of the *Didache*—which is not a safe guide to anything orthodox in the 1st cent.—it was doomed to sterility. New evidence shows that in the 2nd cent. the Agape was held after the Eucharist, as one would expect from Paul's protest (1 Cor 11: 20–2) at the abuses caused by having the Agape first. The *Acts of Paul* (new portion (1936) 6: 33) relate that Paul at a night-vigil, before setting out for Rome, held the Eucharist and that an Agape followed. The *Epistle of the Apostles* (15) retells and dramatizes Peter's escape from prison : ' One of you will be sorrowful because he keepeth not Easter with you. And I will send my angel . . . and the doors of the prison shall open, and he shall . . . come to you and keep the night-watch with you until the

cock-crow. And when ye have accomplished the memorial which is made of Me and the Agape, he shall again be cast into prison.' This evidence from Asia Minor is not contradicted by what Pliny reported (*ep.* 10, 96) about Christian meetings, for under stress of persecution a change in habits may have been made in Bithynia at that time (A.D. 110).

Denis of Alexandria (*ep. ad Basiliden*, edited by Feltoe 94) says that in Rome they wait till cock-crow to have their meal after the Easter-vigil, while in Egypt they start sooner, and others (unspecified) have the meal in the evening. His own principle is that it is to be held at the time when the resurrection may be thought to have taken place. He does not say it is an Agape, but in view of the evidence already given, this is most probable.

The name Agape is used in Jude 12, and almost certainly in 2 Pet 2:13, as a technical term for these gatherings, but these texts tell us nothing about the usage save that it was open to abuse. Ignatius (*Smyrn.* 8:2) put the Agape under the control of the bishop, and (*Phil.* 6:2) urges that it should be kept up with generosity. The famous prescript to his letter to the Romans, where the church at Rome is probably described as ' presiding at the Agape ' (i.e. at the united family of churches), would imply that already the Agape has become subject to the regulation that it has in the days of Hippolytus (*Trad. apost.* 16), who lays it down that those present shall recite psalms after the bishop has said the prayer for the lighting of the lamp and that they shall take a little bread from the hand of the bishop before partaking of their own food, and when the bishop speaks everyone is to be silent and no one is to talk across the room but all are to wait until the bishop speaks to them. Such minute regulation may not go back in its entirety to the time of Ignatius but he clearly envisaged something of the kind by putting the holding of an Agape under the control of the bishop. There is no evidence about the frequency of the Agape in the 2nd cent. ; Socrates (HE 5:22 ; PG 67:636) knows of a weekly Agape in Egypt and the later *Canons of Hippolytus* (canon 164) seem to expect it every Sunday : ' If an Agape is taking place on the Lord's Day at the time of the lighting of the lamp, let the deacon rise up . . . ' The *Testamentum Domini* (2:11–13, 19–20) seems to allow for only one Agape in the year on the night of Maundy Thursday. Private enterprise was the mainspring of the Agape, for the Council of Gangra (canon 11) in the 4th cent. ordered that no one was to bring in contempt those who out of faith and zeal for the honour of God called together the brethren for an Agape. The prayer in the *Gelasian Sacramentary* (Wilson, 261) ' for those who hold an Agape ' implies the same conclusion. Family funeral feasts and *refrigeria* at the tombs of martyrs gradually took away interest from the charitable supper that was to aid the poor and the widows. Chrysostom (on 1 Cor 11:22 ; PG 61:223) still knew of it, but Ishodad of Merv on the same passage (in spite of his having the work of Theodore of Mopsuestia to consult) can only say, ' It was a custom among the

---

[1] Commemorationem mortis Eius facientes, hoc supplices exoramus ut per ipsam caritatem, qua pro nobis Christus crucifigi dignatus est, nos quoque mundum crucifixum habere et mundo crucifigi possimus. . . .

Corinthians, and perhaps with others also, that on the first day of the week after the communion of the mysteries everyone brought equally in his hands to the church something sufficient, and rich and poor ate that they might be bound together in love . . .' This was the essential of the matter ; the Eucharist symbolized the unity of the faithful with one another in Christ, while the Agape carried this unity into practice (as Heb 13:10 and 13:16 imply). It was not a command of Christ, nor meant for all time, but it expressed the doctrine of the Mystical Body with a directness that a latter-day communion-breakfast cannot hope to recapture. The 4th-cent. Council of Laodicea (canon 27) had to forbid the carrying away of food from the Agape by clergy or laity and even the holding of an Agape in church. That local abuses and the exaggerated importance given to the custom of *apoforeta* could give rise to such legislation need cause no surprise when it is considered how prone is human nature to misuse traditional practices that have to do with eating and drinking, and the history of the Agape affords a significant commentary, by contrast, upon the divinely-protected institution of the Eucharist.

Bibliography. ★J. Keating, *The Agape and the Eucharist* (1901) ; ★Bo Reicke, *Diakonie, Festfreude und Zelos in Verbindung mit der altchristlichen Agapenfeier* (1951) ; H. Leclercq, in DAC I, 775–848 ; P. Batiffol, *Études de théologie positive* (1926) ; ★K. Volker, *Mysterium und Agape* (1927) ; W. Goosens, *Les Origines de l'eucharistie* (1931) ; ★G. Dix, *Shape of the Liturgy* (1949). Dix mistakenly supposed that the Agape was called the Lord's Supper in antiquity ; the only evidence for this is an ambiguous word in the 6th-cent. Arabic version of the *Canons of Hippolytus*. J. H. C.

AGAPETAE Also called *subintroductae* or *syneisaktai*, women, mostly consecrated virgins, living together with clerics or lay ascetics, though a distinction is often made between *agapetae*, who lived together with laymen, and *subintroductae* living together with priests. The custom of having *agapetae* was fairly widespread in the first Christian centuries, not only among the Gnostic sects (cf. Tertullian, *De exhort. cast.* 12), but also among the orthodox, as is evidenced by the frequent condemnations of bishops and the legislation of the councils. Consecrated virgins would often receive a man, also bound by a vow of chastity, into their house to see to their secular affairs, a practice that seems to have prevailed especially among wealthy ladies in Constantinople, while priests lived together with women who would look after their household. Paul of Samosata, for example, bishop of Antioch from c. 260–8, was denounced, together with his presbyters and deacons, by a council held in that city in 268, not only for heresy, but also for living and travelling about with young maidens. The pseudo-Clementine Letter on Virginity and the *Epistola Titi, discipuli Pauli, de dispositione sanctimonii*, opposed the practice ; Cyprian's (d. 258) letter to Pomponius (n. 4) deals with a case in which virgins who had

shared house with men, among whom was also a deacon, had declared themselves ready to be physically examined but refused to part from the men to whom they were attached. Cyprian decided that they must separate whatever their relations, or marry if they absolutely refused to part. If they continued in their present state they were to be excommunicated. Nevertheless, the custom persisted, and St Jerome (c. 342–420) could still speak of the *pestis agapetarum* (ep. 22 *ad Eustochium*). Basil of Caesarea (ep. 55) severely reprimanded an old priest who insisted on using the services of a young virgin ; Gregory of Nazianzus (epigrams 10–20) and Gregory of Nyssa (*De virginitate* 23) also inveighed against the custom. Very little later Chrysostom (d. 407) wrote two treatises on the subject (*Adversus eos qui apud se habent virgines subintroductas* and *Quod regulares feminae viris cohabitare non debent*, PG 47:495–532). There are also two spurious treatises ascribed to Cyprian and another of Pseudo-Jerome, *Ad Oceanum*, combating the abuse.

Conciliar legislation was equally opposed to the custom. Canon 19 of the Council of Ancyra (314) forbade consecrated virgins to live together with men, and canon 3 of the Council of Nicaea (325) forbade all clerics to have *subintroductae*, allowing only close relatives such as mothers, sisters or aunts to live together with them. Canon 17 of the Synod of Carthage (397) defined the degrees of kinship between the clergy and their housekeepers more exactly than Nicaea, and other councils followed suit. The custom gradually died out, though Gregory the Great had still to deal with the case of a Sardinian archdeacon in 597.

Bibliography. H. Achelis, *Virgines Subintroductae* (1902) ; H. Koch, *Virgines Christi* (TU xxxi, 1907) ; P. de Labriolle, ' Le " Mariage spirituel " dans l'antiquité chrétienne ', in *Revue historique* 137 (1921) 204–25. *See also* articles s.v. in DDC and EC. H. G.

AGATHO, ST Pope from 678 to 681. According to the *Liber Pontificalis* he was a native of Sicily. During his reign he held two councils in Rome, one in 679, when he restored St Wilfred of York to his see from which he had been unjustly deposed by Theodore of Canterbury ; the other, in 680, in which he prepared the decrees of the Sixth Oecumenical Council held at Constantinople in the same year. In the Acts of this Council are incorporated two doctrinal letters of the Pope dealing with the Monothelite heresy, addressed to the Emperor Constantine Pogonatus. The first of these was composed by the Pope himself ; apart from expounding the doctrine of the two wills in Christ it is particularly important because it solemnly affirms the principle of Papal infallibility, based on the NT (Lk 22:32) and defies the heretics to prove that the Church of Peter has ever strayed from the path of apostolic tradition. Agatho probably stressed this infallibility of the Church of Rome on account of the case of Pope Honorius, who had himself expressed Monothelite views. Honorius was condemned by the Council without protest from the Papal legates ; on the other hand, the letter of Pope Agatho was accepted without contradiction by the Council, which declared that St Peter had spoken by the mouth of Agatho. These two letters ended the Monothelite heresy and were accepted as authoritative both in the East and in the West. Feast day 10 Jan., in the Greek Church, 20 Feb.

Bibliography. Articles s.v. in DTC, DHGE and EC.   H. G.

AGNOETAE The Agnoetae denied that Christ as man had anything like complete knowledge. His question (Jn 11:34) to the friends of Lazarus : 'Where have you laid him ?', and his words about the day of judgment (Mk 13:32) were cited as examples of this ignorance. The first use of this argument is found among the followers of Eunomius in the later days of Arianism (Sozomenus, HE 7:17 ; PG 67:1465). Eutychius, one of these, thought of using Jn 16:15 ('All things whatsoever the Father hath are Mine') to counter the force of the texts which seemed to show ignorance in Christ, and he claimed that Eunomius himself had accepted this in his last days before his death in exile, but the rest would not accept either his argument or his claim, and the sect became still more divided. The importance of such an argument to those who wanted to say (with the Arians) that Christ was less than the Father will be obvious.

The name was revived in the 6th cent. for Themistius and his supporters. According to the deacon of Carthage, Liberatus, in his *Breviarium*, the Monophysite, Timothy of Alexandria (III, died 535), had taught that Christ's body was corruptible. From this Themistius later inferred that therefore Christ must have been ignorant in some things. His view was not accepted and he formed a sect of his own, called the Agnoetae (PL 68:1034). At the end of the 6th cent. Eulogius, patriarch of Alexandria and friend of Gregory the Great, wrote against the Agnoetae. There are some citations of his work in Photius (PG 103:1081). He uses Jn 16:15 as a general basis of his argument ; he replies to the difficulty about Jn 11:34 by saying that Christ's question was meant to arouse the attention of the crowd and was not a request for information, while Mk 13:32 was a case of *anaphora* (a 'carrying back' or substitution of whole for part) whereby the ignorance of the day of judgment that belongs to the Body of Christ, which is His Church, is attributed to Christ, head and members. Not being entirely satisfied with this he suggests that the words could have been spoken 'by economy', i.e. for a special purpose, to make the disciples watchful, just as Christ asked for the name of the demon at Gadara, to show the disciples how very serious the case was, or as God in the OT asked Cain where his brother Abel was, to excite remorse. Gregory the Great wrote two letters to Eulogius on the matter (*ep.* 10:35 and 39 ; PL 77:1091 and 1096), saying that there was complete agreement between the Fathers of the East and of the West on the question (an interesting use of the argument from Tradition), and adding that it was absurd to argue from Mk 11:13 (the question about the fig tree) that the Creator of all things was in ignorance of the time of figs. He then gave the same explanation (of *anaphora*) for Mk 13:32 as Eulogius, but added a distinction, that Christ knew the day of judgment *in* human nature though not *from* human nature. Clearly the dispute was advancing towards a discussion of the unity of consciousness in Christ. It is known that Themistius held that Christ's knowledge was *one*, just as His power of acting was (PG 91:172, where Maximus cites him for this view and thus makes him a forerunner of the Monothelites). It was time for some Platonist among the Fathers to bring in from Plato's *Theaetetus* the distinction between having and using knowledge.

In the West, Augustine had been troubled by the argument that Christ had assumed all human infirmities, ignorance included. He clung to the text (Heb 4:15) that Christ was like to us in all things, sin alone excepted, and proceeded to argue that ignorance came from sin (and led to it), so that it could not be in Christ (*de peccatorum meritis* 2:29 ; PL 44:180 ; *de civ. Dei* 22:22 ; CSEL 40:636 ; *de Trin.* 13:19 ; PL 42:1034).

Bibliography. Apart from the sources cited in the text of the article, the only modern works to mention are the articles in DCB (s.v. Agnoetai) ; DTC (s.v. Science de Jésus-Christ) ; and LTK (s.v. Agnoeten). A brief account of the 6th-cent. heresy will be found in *Christian Egypt : Church and People* by E. R. Hardy (1952).   J. H. C.

AGNOSTICISM This article gives the occasion (I) from which Agnosticism took its rise, and (II) a statement of its position. Its essential opposition to religious belief (III) is next considered and finally (IV) its real causes.

Although the word *Agnosticism* did not come into existence until it was invented by T. H. Huxley, in the year 1869, the philosophical attitude which it represents is as ancient as the history of philosophical speculation. Thus Protagoras (in the 5th cent. B.C.), who identified knowledge and sense-perception, and Heraclitus before him, who denied any stability or permanence to reality, were true agnostics, whilst in modern times, with the break from the *philosophia perennis* which is one of the consequences of the Reformation, the movement of thought amongst Western philosophers has tended more and more in the direction of agnosticism and scepticism. English Agnosticism is but one branch of this development.

I A violent debate between scientists and theologians marked the middle years of the 19th cent. Biology, under the impulse of Darwin's *Origin of Species* (1859), was beginning to assume that exaggerated importance which it has since held in modern thinking. Certain theologians, perhaps foolishly, read into the doctrine of Natural Selection an attack on the fundamentals of Christianity, whilst their protests seemed to men like Huxley to be sheer obscurantism and a wholly unwarranted persecution of those whose sole interest was the advancement of truth. The result was that these latter were driven into an attitude of mind towards religious opinions which was possibly more destructive than it might otherwise have been. 'The cause of scientific discovery was paramount to all else ; and whatever even appeared to impede it, he assailed ruthlessly ', writes Wilfrid Ward of Huxley. 'His anti-Christian rhetoric was calculated . . . to destroy religious belief wholesale, including positions which the writer himself, to say the least, considered quite tenable. He said to me once, in 1894, "Faulty and incorrect as is the Christian definition of Theism, it is nearer the truth than the creeds of some agnostics who conceive of no unifying principle in the world".' (Wilfrid Ward, *Problems and Personalities, T. H. Huxley* (1903) 241.)

But whatever personal motives lay behind the attack, the outcome was a whole-hearted rejection of the Christian teaching with regard to the supernatural, and indeed of any real meaning in the term, God. Strictly speaking, it is necessary to distinguish between the position of the 'atheist' and that of the 'agnostic', however closely in practice their views on religious matters coincide. It is not irrelevant here to quote a passage from R. H. Hutton. He tells us that, at a meeting of the Metaphysical Society, 'Huxley said that far from being an atheist, his faith could not be expressed better than by the inscription on the Athenian altar, that St Paul took as the text of his sermon at the Areopagus : ἀγνώστῳ θεῷ [to the Unknown God]. He could not pretend to say what the ultimate power was like, he regarded it as an enigma he would not venture to characterize, but far from denying its existence, he recognized it, though he held its nature to be unknown and perhaps inscrutable. He wished to call himself an agnostic. . . .' (Maisie Ward, *The Wilfrid Wards and the Transition* (1935) I, 128.)

It is true that even the most orthodox Catholic theologians use language about the unknowableness of the divine nature (e.g. St Thomas : *De Veritate* 5:2@11) which may seem to parallel Huxley's attitude, but the important difference is to be found in their positive insistence on the fact that the existence of God can be known by reason, strengthened by faith, and that the inscrutability of God is due to the very fullness and completeness of His Being, so far transcending the objects of which we have empirical knowledge (*see* ANALOGY). God is completely knowable in Himself (*in se*) ; it is only with respect to us human beings (*quoad nos*) that He is incomprehensible. The typical agnostic implies, if he does not openly state, that the truly real is the empirically observable.

II The most lucid and convenient **statement of the agnostic position** is to be found in Herbert Spencer's *First Principles* (Popular Edition, 1911), Part I of which is headed 'The Unknowable'. In this part of his work he sets out with the avowed object of arriving at some position by means of which it may be possible to effect a reconciliation between Religion and Science, between which, as he asserts, there

exists an antagonism of belief which is 'the oldest, the widest, the most profound and the most important'. Whilst Science is 'simply a higher development of common knowledge ', this is how he speaks of Religion : 'In that nescience which must ever remain the antithesis to science, there is a sphere for the exercise of (the religious) sentiment'. In the foregoing sentence, the word 'nescience' gives the clue to Spencer's line of thought, a line of thought developed in the chapter entitled 'Ultimate Religious Ideas'. Starting from a discussion of the difficulty we find in 'conceiving' the earth as a whole, although 'the piece of rock on which we stand can be represented with something like clearness, [since] we are able to think of its top, its sides and its under surface at the same time, or so nearly at the same time that they seem present in consciousness together ; and so we can form what we call a conception of a rock ', he has no qualms in asserting that 'great magnitudes, great durations, great numbers are none of them actually conceived, but all of them are conceived more or less symbolically . . .' (18–19). If Spencer's argument were valid, it would mean that mathematical calculation would become more precarious the larger the sum involved. It is, of course, untrue that in order to be able to think correctly or possess any real knowledge of any object, it is necessary to be able to *picture* or *imagine* it in the mind. What is true is that the sense of familiarity with which imagination clothes an object, sometimes, and indeed commonly *simulates* knowledge, making us feel that we know more about it than about certain other objects of thought which cannot be put into a picture.

The same confusion of thought is revealed in the following important passage (25) : 'The non-existence of space cannot by any mental effort be *imagined*. And if the non-existence of space is absolutely *inconceivable*, then necessarily its creation is absolutely inconceivable.' (The relevant words have been italicized to bring out the confusion in Spencer's thought.) In the same way, he argues that 'self-existence necessarily means existence without a beginning : and to form a conception of self-existence is to form a conception of existence without a beginning. Now by no mental effort can we do this ' (23).

It is fair to suggest that the failure to grasp the distinction between reasoning and imagining is due to the scientific bias of the mind. Physical science is based on measurement of material objects, on observation of material things, on the use of the balance and the microscope. To a mind unversed in philosophical speculation it might well seem that the marvellous advance made by the physical sciences in the last century was due to its strict limitation to the field of the material, to observation, measurement and the like. The whole agnostic mentality is indeed an outcome of the positivist attitude which refuses to recognize the validity of any statement referring to a reality other than that observable by the senses.

We have another example of the same approach

in the 20th-cent. philosophical school which, for a time, went under the name of LOGICAL POSITIVISM. The basic tenet of this school was the ' principle of verification ', according to which no statement could have meaning unless it was capable of verification by experience. This manifest begging of a whole series of questions was, in theory, abandoned by later disciples of the first promoters of it, but it continued to colour much of their attitude to metaphysical problems. As the principle stands, of course, it is inevitably agnostic, in that it refuses to admit that any statement about God can have meaning, since God cannot be the subject of experimentation or sense-awareness. Although philosophers of the mid century called themselves linguistic analysts rather than logical positivists, and concerned themselves mostly with the dissection of words, phrases and propositions, reducing philosophy sometimes to the level of philology, they inherited a distrust of metaphysical speculation.

III Agnosticism and religious belief. It is true that some philosophers who did not hesitate to describe themselves as positivists, nevertheless denied that their attitude of mind was necessarily destructive of religious belief. Thus it has been said : ' Positivistic philosophers have certainly not thought of themselves as supporters of religion. But that could be because they have mistaken what is important about religion. Theologians have thought of positivistic philosophers as the enemies of religion. But that could be because theologians have mistakenly thought that what the positivists very properly pointed out strikes at what is most important in religion, whereas what it strikes at is what is least important, something concentration on which has led to a mistaken emphasis in accounts of what religion is. Perhaps positivistic philosophy has done a service to religion. By showing, in their own way, the absurdity of what theologians try to utter, positivists have helped to suggest that religion belongs to the sphere of the unutterable. And this may be true. . . . Positivists may be the enemies of theology, but the friends of religion.' (McPherson : ' Religion as the Inexpressible ', pp. 140–1 in *New Essays in Philosophical Theology*, ed. Flew & Macintyre (1956).)

But this is merely to attempt to safeguard religion by taking up a Barthian position (*see* PROTESTANT-ISM : Modern Protestant Theology) which in turn is a return to the Kantian appeal to the Practical Reason to restore what the Critique of Pure Reason had dissolved away (*see* KANT AND THEOLOGY). Plato, on the other hand, equated the reality of a thing to its knowableness, so that any attack on the knowableness of an entity is bound to undermine our belief in its reality. True as it may be that religion is much more than theology, just as literature is much more than grammar, it is nevertheless idle to claim that the enemies of theology can be the friends of religion. It is significant that the great ages of religious belief and practice have been the great ages of theological growth, whilst the professing agnostic is not markedly religious in outlook.

The great Christian tradition which incorporated so much of the wisdom of the greatest Greek thinkers, has always maintained that where the frontiers of reason were reached, there began the whole realm of truths, revealed to reason and defended by reason but not discoverable by reason in the way in which what Spencer called ' common knowledge ' is discoverable.

IV The real causes of Agnosticism. The fact is, of course, that agnosticism, for all its parade of logic and scientific objectivity, is no more a sheerly intellectual position than is religious belief. Various factors are at work to produce the agnostic mentality. In the first place, whilst it is true that the existence of God can be shown to be a reasonable belief, the conclusion of any process of argumentation leading to the admission of God's existence takes us beyond the sphere of ordinary life into a region that does not carry with it the immediacy of appeal which this everyday world possesses. Moreover, the existence of that ' Beyond ' makes upon us certain demands which we do not wholly relish. This is not to suggest that the agnostic is necessarily vicious ; many an agnostic is indeed high-minded enough. But it is true that the intellectual appeal of agnosticism is not the most powerful motive for accepting the agnostic position. Indeed, had not the movement of philosophical thought in Western Europe coincided with a general decline in the spirit of religion, it is probable that its sceptical tendency would have been no more successful than were the earliest agnostics amongst the Greeks to whom reference has already been made.

Agnosticism is, in fact, more of a mood than an intellectual decision. Until the 17th cent. it was never more than a minority movement. The rationalism of the 18th cent., the Kantian critique, the aggressive scientism of the 19th cent. and the materialism of modern industrial and technical civilization have conspired to produce a malaise, a kind of neurosis which enfeebles man's vision of the reality to which the changing scene of this sense world points. Valuable as are the great contributions which scientific investigation has made to the sum of human knowledge, the words of Wilfrid Ward remain true : ' It is perhaps worth while to remind ourselves that truths may be lost as well as gained ; that there are old truths to preserve as well as new truths to learn ; that scientific discovery is concerned only with new truth ; that though all truth is intrinsically consistent, it may not always appear so in the course of its attainment ; and that at a given stage a too exclusive concentration on steps towards new truth may obscure for the individual mind its perception of truths already possessed.' (*Witnesses to the Unseen* (1893) 68). This is a valid commentary on 19th-cent. scientific agnosticism ; it is not without relevance to 20th-cent. philosophizings.

Bibliography. *Herbert Spencer, *First Principles* (1862) ; *A. J. Balfour, *Foundations of Belief* (1895) ; *Papers of the Synthetic Society* (1909) this Society having been founded in 1896 to discuss the problems raised by Balfour's book and to find a working philosophy of religious belief; *James Ward, *Naturalism and Agnosticism* (1899) 2 vols.; *R. Flint, *Agnosticism* (1903); F. von Hügel, *Religion and Agnosticism* (posthumously published for him by E. Gardner, along with *The Reality of God* in 1931); Wilfrid Ward, *Witnesses to the Unseen* (1893); *A. Flew and A. Macintyre, *New Essays in Philosophical Theology* (1956); *M. Foster, *Mystery and Philosophy* (1957).   T. C.

AGONY The word 'Agony', derived from the Greek noun ἀγωνία (=anxiety) in Lk 22:43, signifies the events after the Last Supper when in Gethsemani (=oil press) and in the presence of the three witness Apostles (Peter, James, John) Christ underwent an experience of intense shock and fear at the approach of His messianic 'hour'—an experience which led Him to pray that the cup of His suffering be removed from Him, if that were the Father's will. An angel appeared to strengthen Him and thereafter His interior struggle reached its climax when His sweat became as drops of blood. The events are described by the synoptics (Mt 26:36–46; Mk 14:32–42; Lk 22:40–6), harmonize with the Johannine Passion chronology (Jn 18:1–2), and are referred to in Heb 5:7–10 and possibly in Phil 2:8. Consideration of Christ's Agony may be limited to three points: (I) the historicity of the accounts; (II) the possibility of a bloody sweat; (III) the theological implications of the Agony.

I The Agony narrative as a whole is accepted as factual by Catholic and non-Catholic exegetes with the exception of Bultmann and Goguel; cf. Vincent Taylor, *The Gospel according to St Mark* (1952), p. 551. This unanimity does not, however, extend to Lk 22:43–44; these verses are not found in many manuscripts of Lk and the information they contain about the comforting angel and the bloody sweat is not found in Mt and Mk. The weight of critical opinion, however, admits the Lucan authorship of these verses; cf. Josef Schmid, *Das Evangelium nach Lukas* (Regensburg, 1955³), p. 336; and even when Lucan authorship is denied them, the verses are nevertheless attributed to a primitive tradition; cf. Alfred Plummer, *The Gospel according to St Luke* (1922⁵), p. 509. From the Catholic viewpoint these two verses of Lk are certainly inspired, as Trent has declared (Session IV, April 1546) and as the Biblical Commission has more recently reiterated (26 June, 1912); cf. Simon-Dorado, *Novum Testamentum*, 1 (1951⁷), p. 938.

II There can be no doubt today of the possibility of a bloody sweat, since cases of bloody sweat (hematidrosis) stemming from intense emotional experiences have been clinically observed; cf. R. L. Sutton and R. L. Sutton Jr, *Diseases of the Skin* (1943¹⁰), p. 1154. The bloody sweat of Christ accordingly need not be regarded as miraculous, but is nevertheless an accurate index of the intensity of Christ's interior sufferings.

III The prayer of Christ during the Agony (Mt 26:39; Mk 14:36; Lk 22:42) is the classical text for the existence of a human will in Christ, for the prayer clearly expresses Christ's possession of a will distinct from and subordinate to the Father's will with which the divine will of Christ is identified; cf. St Thomas, *In Matt.*, c. 26, lect. 5. The prayer likewise furnishes evidence for the double act found in Christ's human will—the instinctive will-act (*voluntas ut natura*) and the reasoned will-act (*voluntas ut ratio*). Christ's repugnance for the Passion was an instinctive act of His human will, while His acceptance of the Father's will was a reasoned act of the same will; cf. *S.T.* 3a:8:5; *Compendium theologiae*, c. 233. The experience of Christ in Gethsemani also brings out the mystery of Christ's psychological state during the Passion when the highest joy and the deepest sorrow co-existed in Him. Christ's human intellect always enjoyed the beatific vision; ordinarily the joy of the beatific vision radiates a proportioned joy to all the faculties, but by a special providence this natural consequence of the beatific vision was prevented from taking place, thus permitting the simultaneous presence of joy and sorrow in the soul of Christ; cf. *S.T.* 3a:46:7 and 8; *Compendium theologiae*, c. 231–32. Finally the Agony of Christ implies an attitude toward trials and suffering. Christ opposes any stoic repression or denial of sensibility, does not hesitate to seek human consolation and to petition the Father for the removal of suffering, but withal remains steadfastly obedient to the will of God.

Bibliography. G. Filograssi, ' Agonia di Gesù Cristo ', *Enciclopedia cattolica* 1, 497–9; J. Lebreton, ' Jésus Christ ', DBV(S) 4, 1045–9; B. Pascal, ' The Mystery of Jesus ', in *Great Shorter Works of Pascal* (Philadelphia, 1948) 133–6; L. Picchini, *La sudorazione di sangue in Cristo* (Turin, 1953); G. Rabeau, ' Agonie du Christ ', in *Catholicisme* 1, 226–8.

R. F. S.

ALBERT THE GREAT, ST There are four sections to this article: (I) his life, (II) his writings, (III) his influence and (IV) the Albertist school.

I His Life. Born of a Swabian knightly family in Lauingen before 1200, Albert entered the Dominican Order in 1223, while an undergraduate in the Faculty of Arts at Padua, ' where the study of letters flourished for a long time ' (Albertus Magnus, *De Natura Locorum*, III. ch. 2, ed. Borgnet, ix. 570b). In 1228 he lectured on theology at Cologne, and then successively at Hildesheim, Freiburg, Regensburg and Strassburg. About 1240 he went to Paris, ' the city of philosophers ', as Albert styles it (ibid. 571a), first as *cursor biblicus*, then as *baccalaureus sententiarius*, gaining his mastership in theology c. 1245. Here he wrote his commentary on the *Sentences* (completed in 1249), and contemporaneously his first *Summa Theologiae* in five parts: *De Quatuor Coaequevis*; *De Homine*; *De Bono sive de Virtutibus*; *De Incarnatione*; and *De Sacramentis et De Resurrectione*. In 1248 he was entrusted with the organization and direction of the newly-erected *Studium Generale* at Cologne, where he lectured on pseudo-Denis and the *Nicomachean Ethics*, the first to our knowledge to use the complete translation of the

Ethics and of the Greek commentators made by Robert Grosseteste (1245-6). These lectures are preserved in the *reportatio*, or notes taken down in class by his pupil, St Thomas Aquinas (1248-52). St Thomas's autograph of the Dionysian corpus is extant in the Biblioteca Nazionale of Naples (MS. B.I. 54). From 1254 to 1257 he was Provincial of the German Province. In October 1256 we find him at the Papal Curia in Anagni, where he strenuously defended the Mendicant Orders against the attack of William of St Amour and wrote the treatise *De Unitate intellectus contra Averroem*. In 1260 he was appointed Bishop of Regensburg, but resigned his see two years later. He took part in 1274 in the Council of Lyons and, according to a venerable tradition, in 1277 undertook in his old age the long journey to Paris to defend St Thomas's teaching. In a newly-discovered work of St Albert, the *De XLIII Problematibus ad Magistrum Ordinis*, written in 1271, he states that, almost blind through old age (*fere caecutiens prae senectute*), he would rather prefer to apply himself to prayer than to discuss subtle questions. And indeed he devoted the last years of his life to writing ascetic and devotional treatises, such as *De Sacrificio Missae* and *De Eucharistiae Sacramento*. He died at Cologne on 15 November 1280.

II His writings are manifold, and embrace every branch of learning. Although it seems a paradox, it is doubtless true that St Albert's influence was felt more in the fields of philosophy and the natural sciences than in theology. It seems a paradox, since St Albert was first and foremost a theologian, and his theological works outnumber by far those on philosophical and scientific subjects. Yet his theological writings, apart from the commentaries on pseudo-Denis (of which we shall treat later), did not obtain the same ascendancy as his philosophical and scientific corpus. His commentary on the *Sentences*, for example, did not rank with those of his younger contemporaries St Thomas and St Bonaventure, nor even with those of Peter of Tarentaise and Giles of Rome. Nevertheless, there can be no doubt that St Albert was one of the greatest 13th-cent. theologians. The anonymous author of the *Summa Philosophiae* (published by L. Baur among the works of Robert Grosseteste), a strict contemporary, praised him as 'the most famous of modern theologians' (*modernorum theologorum famosissimus*, XII, xvii, 505). Albert's reasoning, in fact, is faultless, his considerations are profound, his views are often original. Admittedly, the many digressions which he was fond of inserting in season and out of season, his exuberant erudition, his eagerness to impart to others whatever he had learnt, often obscure the main issue and hinder the flow of his argument; but the treatment of the problem is always systematic and well ordered; it reveals him as a great architect who has planned his edifice in every detail. It is easy to be misled by facile generalizations. A superficial reading may obviously give the impression that Albert is a mere compiler borrowing from others a large part of his material. But a close examination of his doctrine in all its funda-

mental points, a patient, if sometimes laborious, analysis of his theological thought enables a keen investigator to discover, under a somewhat traditional terminology, a deeper meaning, an insight, a penetration, a never suspected independence. His innovations are sometimes delineated rather than fully expressed; more often, however, they are elaborated almost to perfection. But whether Albert borrows from others or follows a new line of approach, he goes always his own way, even if the path has been trodden by others before him, and whatever he has to give, it is his own doctrine. In the interpretation of Scripture he was a pioneer in stressing the literal sense and one of the very first to rise against the abuse in exegesis of the allegoric interpretation; particularly in his later works he was impatient with those who would detect multiple symbolism in every phrase or word of the Bible or in the ceremonies of the Mass. In our days the attention of scholars is turning more and more to St Albert's theology; we now have valuable monographs on several aspects of his theological teaching, but a comprehensive study is still wanting. This neglect is the more inexcusable since he himself has warned us that, in order to understand fully his own personal views on such or such a problem, we should turn not to his philosophical but more truly to his theological writings, *in theologicis magis quam in physicis* (*In De Somno et Vigilia*, III. tr. i, c. 12, ed. Borgnet, ix. 195ᵇ).

III Yet his influence was more deeply felt in the domain of mystical theology. Convinced that a perfect knowledge of philosophy can only be achieved through the study of Aristotle and Plato (*In Metaphys.*, I. v. 15, Borgnet, vi. 113ᵃ), he brought into his works both streams of thought, which often run together, sometimes mingled, not infrequently simply juxtaposed, lacking that unity which an austere and adequate synthesis alone can give. The Platonic, or rather neo-Platonist, inspiration was drawn from St Augustine, Boethius, the *Liber de Causis*, Avicenna and, above all, from pseudo-Denis. It was this inspiration that exerted a profound and wide influence on the German Dominicans, Ulrich of Strassburg, Dietrich von Freiberg (Theodoricus Teutonicus), Berthold von Mossburg, and many others. Assuredly, it would be an exaggeration to claim that St Albert was the creator of the German mystic school and of the *devotio moderna*, but there cannot be two opinions that the neo-Platonist element in the Rhineland mystics derives to a large extent from St Albert, particularly through his commentaries on pseudo-Denis, and above all from the *De Divinis Nominibus*, still unprinted. How far Meister Eckhart depends on Albert has not yet been thoroughly investigated; but there seems to be direct influence on John Tauler and other German mystics. E. Vansteenberghe and Mgr M. Grabmann have shown the influence exerted by Albert on Nicholas of Cusa and Dionysius Ryckel the Carthusian, 'one of the last representatives of the German neo-Platonist school originated by St Albert'.

But St Albert's highest reputation among his contemporaries lies in the philosophical and scientific fields. The true significance of his achievement consists in this, that he was the *first* to expound Aristotelian learning systematically and to make it manifest to the Western world in its entirety, and with it the complete philosophy of the Arabs, particularly the natural sciences. His is not a commentary on Aristotle in the strict sense of the word, analysing the text and explaining it pericope by pericope, but an exposition of Aristotle's doctrine in separate treatises bearing the name of the Aristotelian books, blended with his own and others' thought. Thus his teaching has that mark of unity and completeness which no commentary can give. It appears as a well-organized system of philosophy, a synthesis of Aristotle, its perfect and complete achievement. Thus Aristotelian learning appeared for the first time under a new light; Albert 'did indeed make it intelligible to the Latins'. He was acclaimed in the schools as 'an authority', just like Aristotle, or Avicenna or Averroes. In Roger Bacon's words, 'never a man on earth had in his lifetime such an authority in his teaching' (*Opus Tertium*, c. ix, ed. Brewer, R.S., p. 30). His influence was unequalled, not only in Paris, but all over Christendom, and in his own days he was regarded as 'a wonder and miracle of his time' (Ulrich of Strassburg). He became known to posterity under the name 'The Great', *Albertus Magnus*; the Schools bestowed upon him, and the Church confirmed, the title of *Doctor Universalis*. He was canonized and declared Doctor of the Church by Pope Pius XI on 16 December 1931. Ten years later, on 16 December 1941, Pope Pius XII proclaimed St Albert the Great Patron of Scientists.

IV The Schola Albertistarum. To counter Nominalism more efficaciously a new movement issued in the 15th cent., under the patronage of Albert the Great, the *Schola Albertistarum*. It owed its origin to John de Nova Domo, a leading champion of the Realists in the Faculty of Arts at Paris. From Paris it spread to Cologne through the agency of one of John's disciples, Heymeric de Campo (1390–1460). John de Nova Domo, leaning towards the neo-Platonist elements in Albert's teaching, stressed unduly the divergence between his doctrine and that of St Thomas. When Heymeric in 1423 began to expound at Cologne the doctrines he had learnt in Paris, representing the two Doctors as mutually opposed, the *Antiqui* in the Faculty of Arts divided themselves into two rival parties, and, while some with Henry of Gorkum, the founder of the Thomist College, and Gerard de Monte (from whom the College became known as *De Montana*), remained faithful to Thomism, others supported Heymeric and formed the Albertist School. It was unfortunate that such disputes between Albertists and Thomists should arise at Cologne, where Albert had always been held in honour side by side with, not in contrast to, Aquinas. The conflict weakened the Realist resistance and created a new situation between Nominalism and Realism. But from the 15th down to the close of the 17th cent. the movement grew, and from Paris and Cologne spread to Louvain, Cracow, Prague, Copenhagen, Uppsala, Prague, Basle, Heidelberg, Ingolstadt, Tübingen, and other German universities. There were in its ranks over a hundred writers, and some left works of outstanding importance.

Bibliography. *Editions.* *Opera Omnia*, ed. P. Jammy, Lyon (1651) 21 vols; *Opera Omnia*, ed. A. Borgnet (Paris, 1890–9) 38 vols; *Opera Omnia*, critical edition by B. Geyer and others, Münster i. W. (1955–) (in progress, 4 vols publ.).

Full bibliography in Ueberweg-Geyer, *Die Patristische- und Scholastischezeit*, II (1928) 400–16, 739–43; M. H. Laurent and M. J. Congar, Essai de bibliographie albertinienne, *Revue Thomiste*, 14 (1931) 422–68; Serta Albertina, *Angelicum*, 21 (1944); A. Walz, *Enciclopedia cattolica*, i (1948), 698–705; S. Brounts, Albertus Magnus-Literatuur, *Tijdschrift voor Philos.* 14 (1952) 87–96. Later publications are listed and analysed in the *Bulletins* of *Revue des Sciences Philosophiques et Théologiques* (Paris) and in the *Bulletin de Théologie ancienne et médiévale* (Louvain).

Select bibliography : G. Meersseman, *Introductio in Opera Omnia B. Alberti Magni, O.P.* (1931); idem, *Geschichte des Albertismus*. I. Der Pariser Anfänge des Kölner Albertismus. II. Die ersten Kölner Kontroversen. (*Dissertationes Historicae Instituti Historici O.P.*, Romae ad S. Sabinae, iii et v) (1933–5); *Decisionum S. Thomae, quae ad invicem oppositae a quibusdam dicuntur, concordantiae editae per Gerardum de Monte*, ed. G. Meersseman (1934); A. Pelzer, 'Le Cours inédit d'Albert le Grand sur la Morale à Nicomaque recueilli et rédigé par saint Thomas d'Aquin', RNS, 24 (1922) 333–61; 479–520; M. Grabmann, 'Die Lehre des heiligen Albertus Magnus vom Grunde der Vielheit der Dinge und der lateinische Averroismus', *Mittelalterliches Geistesleben*, ii (1936) 287–312; 'Der Einfluss Alberts des Grossen auf das mittelalterliche Geistesleben', ibid. 324–412; 'Die Aristoteleskommentare des Heinrich von Brüssel und der Einfluss Alberts des Grossen auf die mittelalterliche Aristoteleserklärung', Sitzungsber. Bayer. Akad. Wissens. Philos.-hist. Abt. (1943). H. 10. München, (1944); B. Geyer, 'Die handschriftliche Verbreitung der Werke Alberts des Grossen als Maszstab seines Einflusses', in *Studia Mediaevalia, R. J. Martin* (1948) 221–8; *Studia Albertina* : 'Festschrift für Bernhard Geyer zum 70. Geburtstage, herausgegeben von H. Ostlender' (*Beiträge zur Geschichte der Philos. u. Theol. des Mittelalters*. Supplementband 4) (1952). B. Geyer, 'Zur neuen Gesamtausgabe der Werke des Albertus Magnus', in *Gregorianum*, 36 (1955) 272–83; D. A. Callus, 'Une œuvre récemment découverte de S. Albert le Grand : *De XLIII problematibus ad Magistrum Ordinis* (1271)', in RSPT, 44 (1960) 243–61.   D. A. C.

ALBIGENSES This sect troubled the Church in southern France in the 12th and 13th cents. and was once described by Innocent III as a greater menace

than the Saracens themselves. Their neo-Mani-
cheanism was not merely a heterodox interpretation
of certain dogmas, but a complete religious system,
not only anti-Catholic or anti-Christian but a danger
to the whole social order. This article has five
divisions : I origin, II doctrine, III morality, IV
organization, V the action of the Church.

I The Origin of this revival of Manicheanism in
Europe is obscure, but it would seem to have begun
with the establishment of the Paulician sect in
Bulgaria in the 9th cent. (*see* BOGOMILS). It spread
right across Central Europe from the Black Sea to
the Pyrenees and from North Italy to Flanders.
Colour is given to this theory of its origin by two
of the names given to members of the sect in France,
Bougres and *Publicani*. By the end of the 12th cent.
they had become so firmly established in Languedoc
that they are said to have constituted the majority of
the population. Albi was for long an important
centre of the sect, whence they were given the name
of *Albigenses* (a name first used officially by the
Church in 1179). They normally called themselves
Catharists (i.e. ' the pure ', from the Greek *katharoi*),
but were given various other names which tend to
confuse them with other contemporary movements
such as the *humiliati* (*see* WALDENSES).

II The Doctrine of the sect is a dualism; the
material element is created by the evil god (or devil),
who is styled ' the prince of this world ', while the
spiritual element comes from the good god. Man's
body comes from the devil, and his soul from God,
who created celestial men with immaterial bodies
and unisexual, all being created at once in a world of
light. The bad god, whom they identified with
Jehovah of the OT in contrast with the good God
of the NT, being jealous of the world of light,
entered it by assuming the form of an angel. By
promising great happiness on earth, he induced the
celestial men to leave their heavenly home. Then
they had to abandon their ethereal bodies for those
that were terrestrial and of the devil's creation, and
the good God permitted them to be thus imprisoned
as a punishment.

Salvation comes through the soul's emancipation
from the body. Death should thus be sought as a
deliverance. All that causes bodily life or hinders
this deliverance is evil, and the supreme act of virtue
is suicide. Short of this, the ideal is a state akin to
that of the Hindu Nirvana, in which man loses
consciousness of his corporeal existence through the
intensity of his contemplation and the cessation of
all bodily activity. The good Catharist's soul will
return to heaven, there to be reunited with his
celestial body. There will, of course, be no resurrection of the flesh. There is eternal damnation only
for demons. If man dies without the necessary rites,
he will have to complete his purification by re-
incarnation, perhaps in an animal body.

Having left the celestial souls in the power of
Lucifer for a thousand years, the good God sent His
Son, the highest angel, who had only an apparent
material body (for otherwise it would be necessary
for Him to have sinned). There was no true

Incarnation ; He descended into the ear of Mary
(who was likewise an angel with a celestial and
asexual body) and thus was born of her. Christ
could not suffer, die nor rise again, save only in
appearance. His purpose in coming was to draw
souls away from adoring Jehovah and from the
tyranny of matter. Men are redeemed by His
teaching, not by His apparent death. (Some
Catharists posited no more than an ideal Christ,
speaking through St Paul.) Only the names of the
Trinity are kept ; the Son is a creature, and the Holy
Ghost too, who is the greatest of the guardian angels
and subordinate to the Son. The Church was the
incorrupt guardian of the teaching of Christ until the
time of Pope Sylvester I, who accepted the Donation
of Constantine. This pope was anti-Christ and he
turned the Church into the synagogue again ; since
his time the Cathari had been the true church and
outside their body there was no salvation. They used
as Scripture a vernacular version of the NT and
several apocryphal works such as the *Visio Isaiae* and
the *Interrogatio Iohannis*. Their teaching on the evil
of matter led to a complete rejection of sacraments
(save for a form of confession and a blessing of
bread) and also of images, crucifixes, and even of
church buildings.

III Their morality being based on the evil character
of matter, they set high value on an extreme asceticism in external things. This was expected of the
Perfect, and even of the others in a lesser degree.
Since original sin was an involvement with matter
and actual sin was derived from it, material contacts
were to be reduced as much as possible. Fasting,
especially from animal food, was urged ; the use of
material wealth and of marital relations were to be
avoided. Abortion (which would avoid the im-
prisoning of another soul in matter), unnatural vice
and concubinage were all better than marriage.

The Perfect were forbidden all relations with the
infidel except that they could attempt their conversion ; ordinary believers were advised to do the
same, and to confess any other such relations as sinful. They refused oaths, forbade killing in self-
defence and denied the right of the State to inflict
capital punishment. The Catholic hierarchy were
to be regarded as an institution of the devil ; they
had no right to privileges or temporalities. Churches
were to be burned and pillaged and the clergy
assaulted. In some regions this resulted in a reign of
terror. The full rigorist teaching was for the Perfect
only, but the ordinary believers won support when
their open asceticism was seen to contrast with the
worldliness of many of the clergy.

IV The organization of the sect was headed in each
area by a bishop, who had two assistant vicars
(*filius maior* and *filius minor*), while deacons were in
charge of parishes. The Perfect were those who had
received the *consolamentum*, about which presently,
and these were bound to renounce property, marriage and the eating of flesh. They wore black
cloaks, with a leather pouch that contained the NT.
They lived as solitaries, or else in communities
devoted to manual work (such as weaving), to

education or to the care of the sick. Some acted as tutors in noble families. The men travelled around in pairs administering the *consolamentum*, and were held in veneration in consequence. Ordinary believers, while not bound to the strict observance, made a promise (*convenientia*) that they would receive the *consolamentum* before death and thus finally accept the obligations of the Perfect.

The *consolamentum* was normally conferred after penitential exercises and an absolute fast of three days. It was considered to be a true spiritual baptism, uniting the soul to the Holy Spirit in the person of its guardian angel. Baptism by water was held to be an institution of the devil. The Catharist rite consisted in a laying on of hands, the recipient being naked save for a symbolic belt of linen or wool (*vestitus*) which he had to wear for ever after.

The *apparellamentum* or *servitium* consisted in a public monthly confession, practised probably by all, save great sinners, who were allowed to confess in private. The sinners knelt before a cleric who after their avowal put the NT upon each head in turn. The Perfect who were present touched the book with the right hand and, after the recital of the Our Father, pronounced the absolution. The *melioramentum* was a rite preliminary to the *consolamentum*. Should the Perfect themselves fall into sin, they could receive a *reconsolatio animae*. In order to ensure salvation, some seem to have received the *consolamentum* many times, and even (at a later period) to have submitted to the *endura*, an attempted suicide, by starvation or by asphyxiation, after which they could be called confessors or martyrs respectively. Döllinger asserted that more of them died in this way than at the hands of the Inquisition, but they may have chosen it to avoid the stake. It seems that the *endura* was more of an ideal than a practice, even among the Perfect, but there are cases of adults and even children being forced to undergo it, while others opened veins or took poison.

The chief act of liturgical worship was conducted with the utmost simplicity. On a table covered with a white cloth they set the NT, open at Jn 1. The ceremony began with a scripture reading followed by a commentary. The believers then made a triple genuflection before the Perfect, who recited the Our Father (completed by doxology), and the blessing was then given. At some of their meetings the Perfect would bless bread (but never wine) and hand it to each one to eat, in the manner of an Agape (*see* AGAPE). This *benedictio panis* was not a eucharist, but the blessed bread was called the ' bread of God ' and was kept at home in special vases. The chief Christian feasts were kept, but with a Catharist meaning.

V The action of the Church can be seen in the decrees of the 2nd, 3rd and 4th Lateran Councils (D 367, 401, 428), the first of these being repeated verbatim from the local council of Toulouse in 1119. The sending of preachers (first the Cistercians under Pierre de Castelnau and then the Dominicans under St Dominic) was preferred to more violent measures, though the Council of Verona in 1184 called for an episcopal Inquisition to be set up (*see* INQUISITION). After the murder of a papal legate, in 1208, the struggle against the Albigenses (who had become a counter-church in much of Gascony and Provence) was turned into a crusade and entrusted to Simon de Montfort The war between him and Raymond of Toulouse was made more complex by Simon's secular ambitions. After its close, in 1229, a papal Inquisition was for the first time set up and entrusted to the Dominicans and Franciscans by Gregory IX. Many of the Catharists fled from France to Italy and Spain, and their territorial domination was thus broken. The fact that they took refuge in the towns of Lombardy meant that the Cathars now became a middle-class movement, instead of one that depended on nobles with a following of peasants.

Bibliography. J. Döllinger, *Beiträge zur Sektengeschichte des Mittelalters* (1890) ; *C. Schmidt, *Histoire et doctrine de la secte des Cathares ou Albigeois* (1849) ; F. Vernet in DTC II, 1987–99 and I, 677–87 ; J. Guiraud, *Cartulaire de N.D. de Prouille* (1907) ; B. Jarrett OP, *Life of St Dominic* (1924) ; P. Hughes, *History of the Church* (1948) II, 340–52 ; A. Fliche, *Innocent III et la réforme de l'Église*, in RHE 44 (1949) 87–152 ; A. C. Shannon, *The Popes and Heresy in the 13th Century* (1949) ; A. Luchaire, *Innocent III* (1905). In recent years there have been discovered several original texts about the Cathari which go to confirm those collected by Schmidt a century ago : Peter Martyr, *Summa contra Patarenos* edited by T. Kaeppeli OP in *Archivum fratrum Praedicatorum* 17 (1947) 295–335 ; *De haeresi Catharorum in Lombardia*, edited by A. Dondaine OP, ibid. 19 (1949) 280–312 ; *Tractatus de haereticis* of Anselm of Alexandria, ibid. 20 (1950) 234–324 ; *Acts of the Council of St Felix*, edited by the same in *Studi e Testi*, 125 (1946) 324–55, but above all the *Liber de duobus principiis*, edited by the same in 1939, along with a fragment of a Catharist ritual. In the recent past there has appeared in France a periodical *Cahiers d'Études cathares* (1949 onwards), which is chiefly supported by admirers of the late Simone Weil. The work by A. Borst, *Die Katharer* (1953) surveys the historians who have written on the Cathari, with or without prepossessing ideas, in the last century and provides a very full bibliography.

D. O'S.

ALCUIN, INFLUENCE OF Alcuin (AS Ealhwine, Lat. Albinus), Northumbrian nobleman, born *c.* 730, York(?) ; died, Tours, 19 May 804. Educated at York, under Egbert and Aelbert, he served as the latter's associate as teacher and librarian. In 778 he became headmaster and librarian. In hierarchy he was a deacon. On Continental trips he had strongly impressed Charlemagne, who (781) invited him to Francia as ' " civilizer " in that empire ', in Gilson's fine expression. He came in 782, and, save 790–3, spent the remainder of his life in Charlemagne's circle, teaching, writing, etc. The king, queen, royal children, courtiers, select youth from everywhere, were his pupils. He wanted to enter Fulda as a monk, 796, but the king made him abbot of St Martin's, Tours, where his last years were spent.

'The ubiquity of his activities', says Wallach (*Speculum* 24 (1949) 587), 'as theologian, educator, statesman, administrator, poet and writer, is not paralleled by any of his gifted friends of the palace school fellowship, although the Spanish Goth, Theodulph of Orléans, undoubtedly was a finer poet, the Italian, Paul the Deacon, the better historian, and the Patriarch Paulinus of Aquileia a more original theologian.'

'Alcuin purified the [Bible] text, as well as standardizing it', says Miss Smalley. His chief doctrinal treatise, *De Fide . . . Trinitatis* (PL 101: 9–64), based on Augustine, was written as a *Summa* for priests. Vacandard ascribed to him a decisive influence in the history of confession. His many anti-Adoptionist writings show a growing skill in framing theological argument.

The royal policy, *De Litteris Colendis*, educators are agreed, and the allied Carolingian Renaissance, are owing mostly to him. Paleographers praise his perfecting and spreading everywhere the newly developed Carolingian Minuscule (Lowe). More and more, historians are convinced that Alcuin's was the guiding hand in the imperial coronation (Ganshof). The Roman Rite being then made obligatory, Alcuin revised the Missal, in ways which Rome took over, as his most lasting monument.

His other writings cover a wide range : Scripture commentaries, moral exhortation, *Lives*, poems, 300 letters, etc. Froben Forster's 1777 edition is reprinted in PI 100, 101. Spurious : *Albini Confessio Fidei* (101:1027–98) ; *De Divinis Officiis* (101:1174–1286) ; *De Processione S. Sancti* (100: 63–83) ; *De Psalmorum Usu* (except last two chapters (PL 10:1493–509)). Also MGH Ep. IV (1895), MGH Poet. lat. I (1881), MGH SS. rer Merov. (1885 sq.). Vita Alcuini (anon), in MGH SS. XV I, 184.

Bibliography. E. A. Duckett, *Alcuin, Friend of Charlemagne* (1951) ; A Kleinclausz, *Alcuin* (1948) ; E Amann, *Histoire de l'Église* (1947)

BIBLE. F. L. Ganshof, 'La Révision de la Bible par Alcuin', *Bibliothèque d'Humanisme et Renaissance* 9 (1947) 7–20 ; E. K. Rand, ' Preliminary Study of Alcuin's Bible', HTR 24 (1931) 381–5 ; B. Smalley, *The Study of the Bible in the Middle Ages* (1952²) 37

DOGMA. E F. Araujo, 'La institución de la Iglesia según Alcuino', *Revista española de Teología* 8 (1948) 231–74 ; B. Poschmann, *Busse und letzte Ölung* (1951) ; E. Vacandard, 'Confession . .', DTC III, 885.

EDUCATION. C. Dawson, *The Making of Europe* (1932) ; J. de Ghellinck, *Littérature latine . . renaissance carolingienne* (1930) ; E. Gilson, 'L'Humanisme médiéval', *Les Idées et les lettres* (1932) 177 ; M Grabmann, *Die Geschichte der katholischen Theologie* (1933) ; W. Levison, *England and the Continent in the Eighth Century* (1946) ; E. A. Lowe, 'Handwriting', *The Legacy of the Middle Ages* (1926); M. Manitius, *Geschichte der lat. Literatur des MA* I (1911).

POLITICS. F. L. Ganshof, *The Imperial Coronation of Charlemagne : Theories and Facts* (1949) ; L. Halphen, *Charlemagne et l'empire carolingien* (1947) ; *Libri Carolini*, cf. L. Wallach, 'Charlemagne and Alcuin', *Traditio* 9 (1953) 129–54.

LITURGY. N. J. Abercrombie, 'Alcuin and . . . Gregorianum', *Archiv für Liturgiewissenschaft* 3 (1953) 99–103 ; R. Amiet, 'Alcuin, Le Prologue *Hucusque*', *Scriptorium* 7 (1953) 177–209 ; 9 (1955) 76–84 ; E. Bishop, *Liturgica Historica* (1918) ; B. Capelle, 'L'Introduction du Symbole à la Messe', *Mélanges . . . de Ghellinck*, II (1951) 1003–27 ; G. Ellard, *Master Alcuin, Liturgist* (1956) ; A. Wilmart, 'Le Lectionnaire d'Alcuin' *Ephemerides Liturgicae*, 51 (1937) 136–97.

G. E.

ALEXANDRIA, THE SCHOOL OF

This, understood *strictly* as a regularly organized institution, dates from the time of Pantaenus (d. *c.* 190) and Clement (*c* 150–215), who seem to have acted on their private initiative both in opening the school and teaching their lessons. Of Pantaenus's achievements as a teacher we really know nothing. Clement's teaching, to judge from his literary output, must have been brilliant but it was reserved for pupils who were rich and already acquainted with philosophy. A catechetical school under direct ecclesiastical control was founded *c.* 200 for the purpose of providing candidates for baptism with the elements of Christian doctrine. Origen (*c* 185–*c.* 254) was its first director and fulfilled his humble duties there with success for fifteen years. In 215 he divided the original school : to his helper, Heraclas, he entrusted the catechetical instruction, reserving for himself the teaching of profane and sacred sciences at university level. Thanks to Origen's brilliant teaching this school, in spite of opposition, became one of the most celebrated in Christendom. Forced to break with his bishop, Origen left Alexandria for Caesarea in 230. On his departure the fortunes of the Catholic university began to decline, though the catechetical school continued its useful work for many years.

The school of Alexandria in the broad sense of the term denotes the biblical interpretation (*see* CCS 3e, 5a, 39i) as well as the theological ideas and habits of thought found in the writings of teachers, most of whom actually lived at Alexandria. Thus understood, the school of Alexandria is invariably contrasted with that of Antioch (*see* SPIRITUAL SENSE). Two distinct, though related, trends can be distinguished in Alexandrine theology : the older, apologetical, trend (I) is represented by Clement and Origen ; the later trend (II), which is a very self-conscious orthodoxy, is chiefly represented by leading churchmen such as St Athanasius (*c.* 296–373), Apollinaris of Laodicea (*c.* 310–*c.* 390) and ST CYRIL (d. 444).

I The Older Tradition. As an apologist CLEMENT set himself a dual task : to ensure that Christians exercise the right of studying Greek philosophy and to prove that this study does not involve them in the contaminations of Gnosticism. Recent studies on

Clement show that, far from being a pure intellectual, he was a spiritual Christian in the true sense of the word. All his spirituality rests on faith and its goal is charity, namely, perfect resemblance with God. For him, Gnosis, which is a grace as well as a form of asceticism, fills the interval between faith and charity. Spiritual growth takes place within the bosom of the Church. Baptism inaugurates it ; it is sustained by the Eucharist and it flowers into mystical union with Christ. Clement presents this spirituality to his contemporaries in language which he sometimes wishes to be understood in the sense of Greek philosophy, but to which, on other occasions, he gives an entirely new Christian meaning. This creates ambiguities and explains why Clement can be interpreted in ways that are diametrically opposed. The salient traits of Clement's spiritual doctrine are expounded with greater cogency and warmth by ORIGEN, who should be considered primarily as a mystic, although his fame rests chiefly on his biblical, apologetical and speculative writings. Thanks to him both biblical interpretation and biblical theology were established for all time at the centre of the activities of the Church. His treatise, *De Principiis*, in which he presents a Christian view of the world to his contemporaries, entitles him to be regarded as the father of systematic theology. His thought was not free from errors : he believed in the pre-existence of the human soul and he taught that the Devil would be eventually redeemed ; in relating the Logos to God he did not successfully maintain their co-equality. It should be remembered, however, that he was a pioneer and that his mistakes for the most part concerned matters on which the Church had not yet said the final word.

II The Later Tradition. Circumstances led the later Alexandrine theology to take a particular interest in Christology. Carrying forward the tradition represented by Athanasius and Apollinaris (without his peculiar error of course) it found its definitive expression in the writings of Cyril. Closely woven into this tradition is the *Logos-Flesh* idea, an explanation of the union of the divine and human natures in Christ that was directly influenced by Jn 1:14.

In the Trinitarian controversies, ATHANASIUS revealed his theological greatness by furnishing a satisfactory explanation of Christian monotheism : there is no difference between the three Persons save the different aspect with which each presents the whole reality of God ; God exists as Father, as Son and as Spirit, but He is always one and the same God. On the other hand Athanasius devoted less attention to Christology. Even then he seems to be chiefly interested in the soteriological aspects of problems : Jesus Christ is the Logos Himself, who has become man in order to redeem fallen humanity. Athanasius insists that only God Himself could achieve this redemption. Although he holds that Christ is *totus homo*, he does not work out the implications of this truth. Nor in his scriptural exegesis does he ever allude to the activities of Christ's human soul.

For APOLLINARIS the Logos, while remaining what

He was, took to Himself a human nature making it His very own and altogether inseparable from Himself. Though Christ can be said to be man, He is so only titularly : He possesses a human body and an animal soul but has not a human mind. Apollinaris taught that the essence of mind was constituted by the power of self-determination. That being so, he argued that, if there were two minds in Christ, there would be two self-determining subjects and that consequently the basic principle of the unity of His Person would be undermined. Here precisely lay Apollinaris's great error : in Christ the divine Spirit of God the Son takes the place of the human soul. The flesh or body is united to the Logos, Whose energies and powers flow into it in physical fashion. Indeed it is this vital influence that constitutes the bond of union in Christ. In this explanation there can be no doubt about the oneness of Christ's Person, for in the circumstances there can be but one will and one activity in Him. In addition, the reality of redemption is assured, because the absence of the human mind, the source of changeableness, ensures Christ's absolute sinlessness. Apollinaris's Christological ideas are summed up in the formula coined by him : μία φύσις τοῦ Θεοῦ Λόγου σεσαρκωμένη. To the expression φύσις Apollinaris gave the very restricted meaning of a being which is self-determining ; and since there is but one self-determining being in Christ, consequently there is only one φύσις in Him. It was unfortunate that Apollinaris was involved in an error destructive of the Truth that, for our salvation, the Logos became man in the real sense of the word. Of all the writers of this period his thought was the sharpest and his style the most concise (*see* APOLLINARIS). On the positive side he achieved considerable success in clarifying the meaning of Athanasius's teaching and in revealing the dynamism of the dogma that was defined at the Council of Nicea (325). Subsequent events, however, were to show that the reality of Christ's human soul and activity formed an essential part of Alexandrine teaching.

Before the outbreak of the Nestorian controversy (428) CYRIL's Christology was little more than a restatement of that of Athanasius. He was then chiefly concerned with maintaining Christ's perfect Godhead against the Arians. Though he seems to have admitted its reality, Christ's human soul had no theological significance for him in his early writings. Nor did he pay attention to the errors concerning it which were defended by the Arians and the Apollinarian party. When NESTORIUS (d. c. 451) began his sermon warfare against the title of *Theotokos* or Mother of God, Cyril protested on behalf of orthodoxy. At the Council of Ephesus (431) it was he who made the Fathers attentive to the relevant formula of the Nicene Creed which contained an implicit condemnation of Nestorius : ' one and the same is the Eternal Son of the Father and the Son of the Virgin Mary . . .' who, therefore, may be correctly styled Mother of God. The controversy with Nestorius obliged Cyril to undertake profound studies which eventually led him to modify his ideas. His position was midway between Apollinaris and Nestorius. Against the latter he constantly harped on the fact that the 'nature' ($\phi\acute{v}\sigma\iota s$) of Christ is one. Against the former he was constrained by the Antiochenes to confess that the human nature of Christ is also a 'nature' ($\phi\acute{v}\sigma\iota s$). His terminology implied a contradiction, which his opponents were not slow to exploit. In order to grasp Cyril's peculiar position it is imperative never to forget that after 429 he was literally haunted by the horror of 'dividing' Christ. His whole thought became more and more concentrated on the unity of Christ, though he did not neglect the distinction between His Godhead and His manhood. The controversy itself showed that the main problem at stake was to determine in what respect Christ is 'one' and in what respect His natures are 'different'. An important subsidiary problem was to find a single terminology to express these respects. Cyril's real difficulty lay in his attachment to the formula $\mu\acute{\iota}a$ $\phi\acute{v}\sigma\iota s$ $\tau o\hat{v}$ $\Theta\epsilon o\hat{v}$ $\Lambda\acute{o}\gamma ov$ $\sigma\epsilon\sigma a\rho\kappa\omega\mu\acute{\epsilon}\nu\eta$ (or $\sigma\epsilon\sigma a\rho-\kappa\omega\mu\acute{\epsilon}\nu ov$) which he found in a document purporting to have been written by Athanasius but which was composed in reality by one of the Apollinarian party. For Cyril the expressions $\phi\acute{v}\sigma\iota s$ and $\acute{v}\pi\acute{o}\sigma\tau a\sigma\iota s$ were practically synonymous : he used them to designate a real concrete substance that subsists individually. The $\mu\acute{\iota}a$ $\phi\acute{v}\sigma\iota s$ formula as used by him lays stress on the fact that the $\phi\acute{v}\sigma\iota s$ or $\acute{v}\pi\acute{o}\sigma\tau a\sigma\iota s$ of the Logos, which is now an incarnate $\phi\acute{v}\sigma\iota s$ or $\acute{v}\pi\acute{o}\sigma\tau a\sigma\iota s$, is one. The formula expresses Christ's unity admirably but its reference to the distinction of the natures is less clear. It supposes the idea of personality, although Cyril does not sufficiently emphasize the personal element, nor does he distinguish it conceptually and terminologically from the concept of nature. It was the Apollinarian associations of this formula which aroused the suspicions of Cyril's adversaries. Unlike Apollinaris, Cyril admitted that Christ had a human soul. Under the pressure of criticism he was compelled to make this admission tally with the meaning which he gave to the expression $\phi\acute{v}\sigma\iota s$. Actually his opponents wrung the following avowals from him : the human element in Christ has the power of self-determination and is therefore a $\phi\acute{v}\sigma\iota s$; Christ has a human soul which is a real principle of suffering ; Christ's human acts of obedience and oblation were of paramount importance (PG 77:245). These admissions were equivalent to abandoning the *Logos-Flesh* scheme. If Cyril had been really logical, he would have abandoned the $\mu\acute{\iota}a$ $\phi\acute{v}\sigma\iota s$ formula as well. But, thinking that it had the sanction of authority, he continued to use it, exposing himself thereby to the criticism of employing a double-meaning terminology. Withal he was a great theologian, whose titles to fame were his clear vision of the reality of Christ's substantial unity, and the tenacious efforts which he made to have this truth accepted by Christendom : the Godhead and the human nature have been so 'compounded' into the Person of the Logos that the subject of attribution of the actions and sayings of Christ recorded in the Gospels is one

Person, namely, the God Who has become man. Cyril retained the closeness of the link forged by Apollinaris between the Logos and the human element, though he explicitly disavows the latter's error. He also upheld the principle of 'recognizing the natures'. Scholars differ as to how this principle should be interpreted. As explained by one of Cyril's most faithful disciples, Severus of Antioch (*c.* 465-538), it concedes that the two 'natures' can be seen with 'the eyes of the soul' as existing side by side with their respective attributes and qualities. But this 'vision' does not 'divide into two', for when the mind refrains from considering this imaginary duality, the object to which it immediately turns is the *one Person* of the incarnate Logos. Despite the fact that some of Cyril's opponents were of the opinion that his doctrine was unilateral, its more moderate form was given official approval at the Councils of Ephesus (431) and Chalcedon (451). The Monophysites came to regard him as their Doctor *per excellentiam*. He was the last great authoritative exponent of the school of Alexandria whose prestige rapidly declined with the advent of Monophysitism.

III Conclusion. Reared in the Platonic tradition the Alexandrines tended to emphasize the abstract rather than the concrete. When considering Christ's dual nature their vision centred itself instinctively on the Logos, of Whose life and activity the Incarnation was but an episode. Passing from the Logos to Christ, they never forgot that the immediate and direct object of their vision was the Logos. They experienced little difficulty in admitting that in becoming incarnate the Logos never ceased to be God. Their real difficulty consisted in genuinely convincing themselves that He was really man. The *Logos-Flesh* Christology reflected this outlook. Its chief defect was that it tended to overlook the completeness of Christ's manhood and the rôle played by His human psychology in the work of redemption. This defect can be ascribed to the presence of a Stoic idea in the Alexandrine system ever since the times of Clement and Origen : the role played by the $\acute{\eta}\gamma\epsilon\mu o\nu\iota\kappa\acute{o}\nu$, that is to say, the principle of organic life, thought and will, in ordinary men, devolves on the divine $\acute{\eta}\gamma\epsilon\mu\acute{\omega}\nu$ in Christ's case ; in such circumstances Christ's manhood cannot but be incomplete and His activities are not authentically human. Apart from this shortcoming, which they corrected when pressed by their adversaries, the Alexandrines emphasized certain truths of paramount importance : in Christ it is the Logos Who is the bearer of the human nature and His two natures are so closely bound together that they form a single substantial and indivisible unity. Thanks to the exertions of the Alexandrines these truths became accepted as integral parts of revelation by Christendom.

Bibliography. G. Bardy, RSR 27 (1937) 65-90; idem, Vivre et Penser 2 (1942) 80-109 ; A. Grillmeier-H. Bacht, *Das Konzil von Chalkedon* (1951) I, 60 ff., 160 ff. ; J. Quasten, *Patrology*, II (1953) 1 ff. ; ★G. L. Prestige, *Fathers and Heretics* (1954) ;

*R. V. Sellers, *Two Ancient Christologies* (1953) ;
*W. Völker, *Das Vollkommenheitsideal des Origenes*
(1931) ; idem, *Der wahre Gnostiker nach Clemens
Alexandrinus, TU,* 57 (1952). A. K.

ALOGI This name was apparently coined by St
Epiphanius (d. 403) in *Haer.*, 51:3 (GCS 31:250), to
designate a group who opposed the doctrine of the
Logos or Word of God; hence ἄ-Λογος. He says
they rejected both the Fourth Gospel and the Apocalypse and ascribed them to Cerinthus, though the
latter had denied the divinity of Christ which these
books clearly teach. (In fact this judaizing Docetist
was a troublesome opponent of St John.) Epiphanius proceeds at some length to disprove that the
Fourth Gospel clashes with the others, showing how
they have different purposes and are complementary.
He defends the Apocalypse against the charges of
silliness (showing how it all has a spiritual sense),
and of falsehood, for the Alogi had said there was no
church at Thyatira for St John to write to. But there
was later, says Epiphanius, so John is proved a true
prophet, for it turned Montanist (and expelled the
Alogi). Later (54:1) Epiphanius says Theodotus was
an 'offshoot' of the Alogi. He denied Christ's
divinity and was active against the Trinitarians.

Long before, St Irenaeus (2nd cent.) had mentioned unnamed heretics who, because they denied
the manifestation of the Holy Spirit, rejected St.
John's Gospel. (*adv. haer.*, 3, 11, 12 H). These look
like Epiphanius' anti-Montanist 'Alogi'. St Philas-
trius of Brescia (*d.* before 397) also mentions those
who ascribed the Fourth Gospel and the Apocalypse
to Cerinthus. Harnack tried to discredit these accounts and see behind the Alogi a group of tradition-
alists on the NT canon, who had long since been
blackened by the supporters of 'St John'. But the
tradition has been both confirmed and further
illuminated by the discovery of fragments of the
Chapters against Gaius of St Hippolytus of Rome
(d. 235) in a Syriac commentary by Dionysius Bar-
Salibi (12th cent.). The most important reads,
'Hippolytus of Rome said : " A man named Gaius
appeared, who said that the Gospel was not John's,
nor the Apocalypse, but that they were the work
of the heretic Cerinthus." ' Hippolytus then sum-
marizes the reasons why this is impossible. Gaius
had also said that the Marriage at Cana clashed with
the other Gospels (a charge which St Epiphanius
answers against the Alogi), and his quoted attacks
on the Apocalypse show an anti-millenarian tendency. Eusebius mentions Gaius as a cleric at Rome
who wrote a dialogue against the Montanist Proclus ;
he does not call him a heretic, nor mention the
Alogi. Doubtless these were connected with Gaius,
but not organized as a counter-church like the
Montanists.

Thus we can form a picture of a sect arising in the
later 2nd cent., probably in Asia Minor, in opposition to the Montanists. Against the latter's exaggerated *mystique* of the Holy Spirit and their
millenarianism, respectively, the Alogi rejected the
Fourth Gospel and the Apocalypse, at a time when,

as the Muratorian fragment shows, the Roman
Church received both as by St John and canonical
They also denied the eternal generation of Christ
and bred the Adoptianist Theodotus.

Bibliography. G. Bareille in DTC I, 898, 'Aloges';
A. Bludau, ' Die ersten Gegner der Johannes
Schriften ', *Biblische Studien* 22 (1925) The newer
evidence from Hippolytus is most easily found in a
note on Gaius in Lawlor and Oulton's translation of
Eusebius (1928) II, 208. R. M.

ALPHONSUS, ST This article will treat of the
(I) life, (II) character, (III) works, and mainly of (IV)
the influence of St Alphonsus.
I Life. St Alphonsus Maria de' Liguori was born
at Naples in 1696. At first a barrister, he was ordained priest in 1726 and worked mainly for the poor
of Naples, the surrounding countryside, and the
wild, mountainous country farther inland. With
the foundation of his Congregation of the Most
Holy Redeemer (Redemptorists) in 1732, he became
the father of a religious and missionary family. In
1762 he was made bishop of Sant' Agata dei Goti.
He retired in 1775 and died on 1 August 1787.
Canonized in 1839, he was declared a Doctor of the
Church by Pius IX in 1871 and Patron of Confessors
and Moral Theologians by Pius XII in 1950.
II Character. St Alphonsus had the ardent tem-
perament of the Mediterranean. An understanding
of it is vital to a just appreciation of his character.
Temperamental antipathy accounts for much of the
animus displayed against him, especially against his
Mariology, by Döllinger-Reusch (*Geschichte der
Moralstreitigkeiten . . .*, 1889) and Heiler (*Der
Katholizismus*, 1923) The same is true of Pusey's
charge of 'Mariolatry' (*Eirenicon*, 1865), to which
Newman wisely replied: ' St Alfonso wrote for
Neapolitans, whom he knew, and whom we do not
know' (*Letter to Pusey on the Eirenicon* (1866) 103 ff.;
cf. also *History of My Religious Opinions* (1865) 373 ff.
and 348 ff.). Manning was a strong admirer of St
Alphonsus' personality (cf. his *Mission of St Alphonsus* (1864)). In modern times Benedetto Croce—
himself a Neapolitan—shows an instinctive understanding of it in the pages he devotes to St Alphonsus
in *Uomini e cose della vecchia Italia* (1956). For him
Alphonsus was a true representative of the Gospel
spirit of ' *moderazione e indulgenza* '.
III Works. St Alphonsus was a prolific writer.
The first of his one hundred and eleven works, large
and small, appeared in 1728, the last in 1778:
(*a*) *Ascetical writings.* Most of St Alphonsus'
writings are ascetical in character: *Visits to the
Blessed Sacrament* (1745), *How to Converse Continually
and Familiarly with God* (1754), *The Practice of Loving
Jesus Christ* (1768). He considered this ' the most
devotional, the most useful of my works '), *Reflections on the Passion of Jesus Christ* (1773), and many
more. *The Glories of Mary* (1750) is partly devotional
and partly theological (on it in particular see Dillenschneider, *La Mariologie de s. Alphonse de Liguori:*
Hitz, *Maria und unser Heil*).
(*b*) *Dogmatic writings.* St Alphonsus' dogmatic

works, Italian and Latin, are not strictly dogmatic: in writing them he had, as in all his works, immediate, practical ends in view. He combats the errors of the day: deism, materialism, 'regalism' (the Neapolitan equivalent of Gallicanism), and above all Jansenism. (For his resistance to Jansenism on the issue of frequent communion, see *Praxis Confessarii*, ed. crit. IX, 148 ff.) Regalism prevented him from publishing his Latin *Defence of the Supreme Power of the Roman Pontiff* (1768). For Tanucci, the Neapolitan Prime Minister, it was an 'article of faith' that the Pope was *not* infallible (Croce, *op. cit.* 50).

The most important of the dogmatic works is *Concerning the Great Means of Prayer* (1759). Prayer is the supreme 'practice' of the Christian life: on it salvation itself depends, for 'we have nothing, but if we ask we shall have everything' (I, ii, 8). St Alphonsus multiplies texts of Scripture and quotations from the Fathers and saints to prove his point. With the possibility and necessity of prayer for all men as a starting-point, he works out a theory of actual grace (*see* GRACE). All men receive sufficient grace to pray. If they do pray, they will receive all further graces necessary for salvation and sanctification (cf. *op. cit.* II, iv, and especially *Concerning the Way in which Grace Operates in the Justification of the Sinner*, 1769). Different 'systematic' interpretations of St Alphonsus' theory have been proposed. For some (e.g. J. Herrmann CSSR, *De Divina Gratia* (1904), 259–501) he is Molinist in the first part of his theory and Augustinian in the second. More recently he has been regarded as a modified Thomist (*see* M. Schmaus, *Katholische Dogmatik*, III, ii (1951⁴) 341–2). In fact, however, St Alphonsus' doctrine of grace and prayer is primarily 'personalist', not systematic. Man *encounters* God in prayer, and out of this encounter his personal salvation must come. A full study of St Alphonsus' thought on this subject remains to be made: for a preliminary survey see Cacciatore, *S. Alfonso de' Liguori e il giansenismo*, 223–300.

(*c*) *Pastoral writings.* St Alphonsus wrote much on directly pastoral matters, especially with a view to rescuing the preaching of his day from the empty rhetoric that bedevilled it. The Word of God, he insists, should be preached as Christ and the Apostles preached it, simply, clearly, effectively, in language that all can understand (cf. his letter on *How to Preach Apostolically*, 1761: Tellería, 'Renovador de la elocuencia sagrada', *San Alfonso María de Ligorio*, I, 727 ff.).

(*d*) *Moral theology.* Over a third of all St Alphonsus' works are concerned with moral theology, understood as the science of the confessional. Nine editions of the largest and most elaborate of all his works, the *Theologia Moralis*, appeared during his lifetime, the last in 1785; but the substance of the final work is already present in the second edition (1753–5), apart from his theory of equiprobabilism (*see* PROBABILISM) which, in its definitive form, dates from 1762. (On St Alphonsus' method of composition, and on the general history of the growth of the *Theologia Moralis*, see Gaudé, ed. crit. Preface.)

Annexed to the *Theologia Moralis* from the second edition onward was the *Praxis Confessarii*. Without it, St Alphonsus said, the *Theologia* would be 'incomplete and imperfect' (ed. crit. IV, 524). It contains a great wealth of counsels on the actual hearing of confessions and a special chapter on spiritual direction. Against others who regarded it as 'a waste of time' Alphonsus insists on the duty of the confessor to foster the positive life of grace in the souls of his penitents (*Praxis* VIII, 120 and IX *passim*). Thus moral theology in the restricted sense is only part of a wider practical theology, the object of which is to lead all men to intimate union with God. Moral theology, in other words, merges into ascetical theology.

A third major work of moral theology by St Alphonsus is the *Homo Apostolicus* (in Italian 1757, in Latin 1759). It is his idea of what a handbook of moral theology should be. Here again the ultimate viewpoint is ascetical (cf. Appendix I, a reproduction of chapter IX of the *Praxis Confessarii*).

IV Influence. This can be considered (*a*) in general and (*b*) in particular.

(*a*) *In general.* 'Practice' (*pratica* in his Italian writings, *praxis* in the Latin) was everything to St Alphonsus. He was a totally 'committed', *engagé* man, both in his personal life and in his apostolate, and theology was for him a weapon of spiritual combat. He saw everything in relation to the practice of the Christian life as it must be lived here and now. 'Practice' is, in fact, as central a word in his vocabulary as *praxis* or practical activity is, from a diametrically opposite point of view, in the vocabulary of Marx. Thus all his writing is designed for the communication of *practical* truth: he aims directly at *results*. This gives him a characteristic *immediatezza* or directness, both as a man and as a writer: but it necessarily involved a corresponding limitation in his approach to theology. His concepts are on the psychological rather than on the speculative level. (cf. Cacciatore, 'Alfonso Maria de' Liguori', EC 866.)

Moreover, as 'a man of practice and of life' (P. Lippert SJ, ZKT, 51 (1927) 97), St Alphonsus wrote firmly within his own historical setting, that of 18th-cent. Naples. He wrote of eternal things, but he wrote of them for men and women *as he knew them*. The Neapolitan world of his time colours all his writings—just as other historical settings colour the writings of the Fathers and Scripture itself. Allowing for this 'time-bound' element in St Alphonsus' writings, the discerning and understanding reader will find in them immense and enduring treasures of practical teaching in a wide variety of fields.

(*b*) *In particular.* St Alphonsus did much to renew the pastoral spirit of the Church, and his ascetical writings have exercised a direct influence on the lives of countless men and women. During his lifetime 90 translations of writings by him were published outside of Italy (the *Visits* appeared in German as early as 1757); in all he has been translated into over 60 languages. No Doctor of the

Church has been such a popular writer as he, both in the range and depth of his influence (cf. Lippert, *art. cit.* 95–7).

He played a decisive part in the overcoming of Jansenism as a corrosive force within the Church (cf. Pius IX, Decree of March 23, 1871, *ap.* Gaudé, *Theol. Mor.* ed. crit. xlvii). He prepared the way for the definition of the Immaculate Conception in 1854 and for that of Papal Infallibility in 1870 (cf. Pius IX, ibid.) He is largely responsible for the now general acceptance of the doctrine of Mary's universal mediation of intercession (*see* MARY, and cf. E. Dublanchy SM, 'Marie Médiatrice', DTC, 2402–03), and is indeed one of the chief founders of the modern Mariological movement in the Church.

In moral theology he worked within the methodological framework that came in after the Council of Trent with the *Institutiones Morales* of Azor (cf. L. Vereecke, *ap.* Häring, *La Loi du Christ* I, 71 ff.). In recent times the deficiences of this method have been investigated from the Scriptural, Patristic and especially Thomist points of view (cf. Vereecke, ibid.: Th. Deman OP, 'Probabilisme', DTC 417 ff. and *La Prudence* (1949²): Labourdette, 'Théorie de la vie morale', RT 50 (1950) 206 ff.: Bérubé, 'Saint Alphonse moraliste actuel ?', *Revue de l'Université d'Ottawa* 12 (1957) 65 98). Conscience is the axis of the *Institutiones Morales*; but charity and Christian discernment (St Thomas's *prudentia*) are the axes of evangelical, Patristic and Thomist moral theology. Prudence *uses* conscience, but it far transcends it. In actual fact, however, St Alphonsus always transcends, while using, the categories of the *Institutiones Morales* (cf. Labourdette, *art. cit.* 224). Charity is his ultimate category (cf. *Praxis*, IX–XI). He has no treatise on prudence in the *Theologia Moralis*, but he dwells on the necessity of both charity and prudence for the confessor (*Praxis*, Introduction and *passim*). Charity and prudence were his own greatest gifts in dealing with his fellow-men, and they permeate the whole of the *Theologia Moralis*. Repeatedly his great prudence, his discernment, his intuitive capacity for tracing a true middle way between the extremes of harshness and laxity, have been singled out for praise in official Papal documents (*see* C. Damen CSSR, 'Doctor Prudentiae', *Rassegna di Morale e Diritto*, 5 (1939) 220–9, 6 (1940) 43–55) and have had a major influence in winning for him the title of patron of confessors and moral theologians. (*See* AAS 17 (1950) 595–7.)

St Alphonsus gave much time and thought to the elaboration of his theory of equiprobabilism as a middle way between probabiliorism and pure probabilism. Still, its importance in his moral theology as a whole must not be exaggerated. It was a fixed principle with him 'always to put reason before authority', '*semper rationem auctoritati praeponere*' (*Theol. Mor.* Preface). Truth comes first: when it is clear, the opinions of theologians one way or the other cease to count: but when it is not clear, it is important (because *prudent*) to have sound principles for choosing between the various opinions advanced by theologians on the matter under discussion. Out of 300 cases discussed by St Alphonsus and investigated by Damen only about 40 are solved by the equiprobabilist system: the rest are all solved directly, in terms of inherent truth alone (cf. Damen, *art. cit.* 47). The results of his casuistic labours are of permanent service to moral theology. He bequeathed to it ' a body of really sure moral opinions, as far removed from one extreme as from the other, carefully weighed by the conscience of a saint. To have done this was to have rendered an outstanding service to the Church' (Labourdette, *art. cit.* 230). St Alphonsus is a moral theologian of ' exceptional greatness' (ibid. 224).

Bibliography. St Alphonsus, *Opere ascetiche, dogmatiche e morali* (1887): *Lettere* (1887): *Opera Dogmatica*, tr. into Latin and ed. A. Walter (1903): *Theologia Moralis, Praxis Confessarii*, 4 vols, ed. crit. L. Gaudé and G. Blanc (1905–21, reprinted 1953): *Opere ascetiche*, ed. crit. (1933–); M. de Meulemeester CSSR, *Bibliographie de s. Alphonse-M. de Liguori* (1933); R. Tellería CSSR, *San Alfonso María de Ligorio*, 2 vols (1950–1); *B. Croce, *Uomini e cose della vecchia Italia* II (1956³) 121 ff.; H. Castle CSSR, 'Alphonsus Liguori', CE 334–41; H. Thurston SJ, 'Liguori', ERE 8:66–9; *'Alphonsus Liguori', *Oxford Dictionary of the Christian Church* (1957); G. Cacciatore CSSR, 'Alfonso Maria de' Liguori', EC 864–73: *S. Alfonso de' Liguori e il giansenismo* (1944); B. Häring CSSR, *Das Gesetz Christi* (1957⁴) (*La Loi du Christ* I, 1957³); 'Alfons von Liguori als Patron der Beichtväter und Moraltheologen', *Geist und Leben*, XXIII (1950) 376–9; B. Häring and E. Zettl CSSR, 'Alfonso Maria di Liguori', LTK² 330–2; *E. B. Pusey, *Eirenicon* (1865); J. H. Newman, *Letter to Pusey on the Eirenicon* (1866); C. Dillenschneider CSSR, *La Mariologie de s. Alphonse de Liguori*, 2 vols (1931–4); P. Hitz CSSR, *Maria und unser Heil* (1951); R. Culhane CSSR, ' St Alphonsus on the Immaculate Conception ', IER 82 (1954) 391–401; G. Bérubé CSSR, 'Saint Alphonse moraliste actuel ?', *Revue de l'Université d'Ottawa*, 12 (1957) 65–98; J. A. Cleary CSSR, 'The Return to St Alphonsus', ITQ 18 (1951) 161–76; M. Labourdette OP, 'Théorie de la vie morale', RT 50 (1950) 206–30.   S. O'R.

ALTAR The theology of the altar, a topic much neglected in the past, was a very early development in the growth of Catholic doctrine. The ' heavenly altar ' (to which the Canon of the Mass refers, *in sublime altare Tuum*) was by Irenaeus (IV:xxxi:5, H) declared to be ' the place whither our prayers and offerings ascend ', and he cited Apoc 11:19 and 21:3 in evidence. A little later Victorinus of Pettau (CSEL 49:72) commented on the saying of Apoc 6:9 that the souls of the martyrs were under the altar by bringing in the OT with its golden and brazen altars; here the golden altar is that of heaven, and the brazen that of earth; Mt 5:23 should be understood, he claimed, of the heavenly altar, ' for certainly our prayers—which are our gifts—ascend to heaven; the high priest went in to the golden altar once in the year, . . . signifying that the Holy

Spirit was to do this for us '.[1] The poem ADVERSUS MARCIONEM of about the same time has (IV 182–5) the same idea of a golden altar in heaven whither our prayers ascend, and to which Christ referred in Mt 5:23.[2] See also Hermas 42:2; GCS 48:39. It is important thus to insist on the clear acceptance in the primitive Western Church of the idea of a heavenly altar, as it is mainly in the East that the development of the idea can be followed in later times. The incessant praise of God which the angels render at the heavenly altar had much to do with Western attempts to make the praise of God continual in its monasteries, but the theology of sacrifice which could have grown out of the idea of the heavenly altar did not mature, owing to what looked like a simple assertion by Ambrose (de sac. 4:2:7 and 5:2:7; CSEL 73:49, 61) that the altar was forma corporis Christi. The word forma here seems to be used to mean a shape or mould, which gives its character to the body of Christ which is the Church, all the faithful being grouped round it to form the Church, but it was easy for later readers to think that Ambrose meant that the stone altar (which they were familiar with but which had hardly been adopted in his day) was somehow a type of Christ, in the sense intended by 1 Cor 10:4. No one could find a likeness to Christ in the wooden table-altars which were still used in the days of Optatus (de schismate 6:1; CSEL 26:143) and of the mosaics of S. Vitale in Ravenna.

The early Church had much ado to prevent pagan superstitions infiltrating through the ritual that concerned the altar. The taking of an oath while touching the altar (Chrysostom homil. in Ac 9:6; PG 60:84) was a practice of the pagans which the Church had to accept perforce, as also was the right of sanctuary for those who touched the altar. Gregory of Nyssa says that no pagan should touch a Christian altar (PG 46:581), and this veto may have been an attempt to keep separate the Christian practice from the pagan. An imperial constitution of the year 397 (Cod. Theodos. IX:45:2) allowed the right of sanctuary to Christian churches, but it had been exercised as a matter of custom for at least 50 years before that. It may even have been this right of sanctuary which led to the use of a permanent stone altar in place of the wooden table that was set up and taken down on the occasion of each Mass. One of the earliest indications of the use of a stone altar is the report of the lady Egeria (4:2; CSEL 39:41) that she visited the cave of Elias on Horeb, that there was a stone altar there which was used by the pilgrims for Mass (Ostenditur etiam ibi altare lapideum, quem posuit . . . Elias ad offerendum Deo. . . . Fecimus ergo et ibi oblationem.)

With a stone altar two things can be done that are

not possible with a wooden table; it can be consecrated in OT fashion (Gn 28:18) by the pouring of oil upon it, and it can be compared to the tomb of Our Lord, the cloth spread upon it then being likened to the Shroud or Sindon in which Christ was wrapped. Both developments had taken place by the 6th cent. The Gallican council of Albon (Epaona) in 517 decreed[3] that none but stone altars were to be hallowed with chrism (HL II:1031). In the East, Isidore of Pelusium (ep. 1:123; PG 78:264) writes that, ' the pure sindon which is spread for the service of the heavenly gifts is the deed done by Joseph of Arimathea. Thus we, hallowing the bread of proposition upon a sindon, find without cease the Body of Christ.' The apocryphal Acts of Thomas (49) have an episode where, ' the apostle bade his deacon to set forth a table, and he set out a stool which they found there and spread a sindon upon it and put thereon the bread of blessing . . .' The Greek version of these Acts was probably made from the Syriac about the 4th cent., and the use of the word sindon here would be borrowed from current practice rather than from an earlier tradition.

The placing of the altar over the grave of a martyr is attributed by the Liber pontificalis to the action of Pope Felix I (269–74), and it can be proved for the time of Ambrose, who thus (ep. 22:13; PL 16:1023) describes his placing of the bodies of Gervase and Protase beneath the altar: ' Let the triumphant victims come to the place where Christ is the sacrifice. He is upon the altar who suffered for all; they beneath it who are redeemed by His passion.' One cannot be sure how long before this the literal carrying out of Apoc 6:9 had occurred to the piety of Christians. Its further elaboration in the imagination of the hagiographer is responsible for the story of Lucian of Antioch (PG 114:409) who, when dying in prison after being tortured, bids his disciples bring in the bread and wine, and as they cannot smuggle an altar into the prison he says that he himself will be the altar. He celebrates Mass then upon his own breast, and communicates himself and them, before he dies. Such pious liberties, if not regulated, can lead on to the enormous blasphemy of the satanic black mass.

There are three ways in which an altar was deemed to be consecrated. Either it was hallowed by the descent of the Spirit in the course of the celebration of the Eucharist upon that altar, or it was anointed, or relics were placed in it or beneath it. Origen (in the Latin version of Rufinus) seems to favour the first view when he speaks of the altar (hom. in Josue 2:1; GCS 30:296) as ' consecrated by the precious blood of Christ ', and the Roman usage down to the 10th cent. was to consecrate altars by saying Mass upon them. But once the idea is abroad that the altar is a type of Christ, then the anointing of it before it is put to use becomes proper. The OT practice of Jacob can then be invoked and a ritual elaborated. Such a practice is witnessed by Caesarius of Arles (in his sermo 228, of Morin's edition) and wherever

---

[1] Utique ad caelum ascendunt orationes, utique munera nostra orationes sunt quas efficere debemus . . . nam et sacerdos semel introibat in templum . . . ad aram auream: significabat Spiritum sanctum hoc esse facturum. . . .

[2] Ara nitens auro caelum declarat in alto,
   Quo sacrae subiere preces sine crimine missae.
   Hanc aram Dominus dixit, qua munera si quis
   Offert, ut primum pacem cum fratre retractet.

[3] Altaria nisi lapidea chrismatis unctione non sacrentur.

the Church underwent a recrudescence of OT ideas it was generally adopted. It is in Anglo-Saxon circles that the practice of placing relics in the altar is first looked upon as the act of consecration, as in the *Egbert Pontifical* (26 and 46) and the *Benedictional of Archbishop Robert* (96). In the latter work (85), as in the *Lanalet Pontifical* (12) there is a prayer which asks that ' this altar may be worthy that the elements chosen for the sacrifice and placed upon it may by a secret power be converted into the Body and Blood of the Redeemer ', a sufficient indication of a realist theology about the Eucharist.[1]

It cannot be denied that in the symbolism which was followed by the Eastern churches (where the altar was the tomb of Christ and the bread and wine like the embalmed and buried body of the Lord), the remembrance of the Resurrection was clearer, while in the Western symbolism there was better pre-served the remembrance of the Passion. In the homilies of Narsai (T&S VIII:i:21) it is claimed that at Mass ' the Spirit which raised Him from the dead comes down and celebrates the mysteries of the Resurrection of His Body ', and holy communion is compared to the apparitions of the risen Christ (*see* EPIKLESIS). In the West, however, the tradition which comes down from Bede to Amalarius and to St Thomas (3a:83:1:@2) is that the altar is a mem-orial of the cross of Christ (*altare est representativum crucis Christi*). Bede says (PL 93:155) that Christ offered Himself on the altar of the cross. If the cross was an altar, then truly the present altar can be com-pared with the cross. In commenting on Heb 13:10 St Thomas says that the altar there spoken of is either the cross or Christ Himself, who is the golden altar in heaven (as Cyril of Alexandria held: PG 68:620). This text, which seems to modern Catholics a plain hint that the early Church knew of an altar of sacrifice on earth, was not much used in antiquity (see CCS 944 f.) Rupert of Deutz (PL 168:366) draws in two other texts (Amos 9:1 and Jn 12:32) to illustrate this idea of Christ being *on* the altar as He was on the cross, but it is clear that such an interpretation could only have arisen after the practice of reservation had begun.

The adornment of the altar—an endless topic, but hardly theological save in one or two points—began very early. Origen knows of it (*hom. in Josue* 10:3; GCS 30:360), while the 4th-cent. Arian material in the *Paschal Chronicle* (PG 92:737) tells how Con-stantius, the emperor, gave for the altar cloths that were woven with gold and jewels. In Augustine (*serm.* 35 of Mai's edition) there is authority for flowers being used to decorate an altar (not placed on it but set round about) for he speaks of the newly-baptized decorating the altar like lilies. This prac-tice the Church had to approve against Jansenist prohibitions (D 1532). Candles were hung from the ciborium above the altar or else placed near it on the ground. This is the sense of Paulinus of Nola's

line, ' the altar is brightly crowned with a thicket of candles '.[2]

Bibliography. F. J. Dölger, ' Die Heiligkeit des Altars ', in *Antike und Christentum* 2 (1930) 161–83; T. Klauser, ' Altar, christlich ', in RAC I; E. Bishop, ' The History of the Christian Altar ', in *Liturgica Historica* (1918); H. Lucas SJ, ' The early Fathers and the Christian Altar ', in MN 72 (1891) 39–51 (a reply to Westcott's treatment of Heb 13:10 and to his thesis, taken up again by Wieland in *Mensa und Con-fessio*, that no altar of sacrifice is known in Christian-ity until Irenaeus); J. Brinktrine, *Der Messopferbe-griff in den ersten zwei Jahrhundert* (1918); J. Braun SJ, *Der christliche Altar* (1924); the same, *Das christ-liche Altargerät* (1932).   J. H. C.

ALTRUISM A term coined by the French posi-tivist Auguste Comte from the Italian adj. *altrui*, was used in a general sense (esp. through adoption by Spencer) of regard for others as a principle of action. Psychologically it denotes an attitude or disposition of love for another. In ethics it describes the theory according to which the moral end of conduct is the good of others, however conceived. It involves discussion of the problems of love of others, including God, in the natural order, for current misconceptions of the subject are notoriously misleading. By unselfishness (a substitute for char-ity) a woman chiefly means taking trouble for others; a man means not giving trouble to others. Thus each sex, as C. S. Lewis put it ' without any obvious unreason, can and does regard the other as radically selfish ' (*Screwtape Letters*). Though it is impossible to sunder human love from sexuality without yield-ing to an angelic illusion, love is not a euphemism for sexual desire, nor is it an obsession (like Hazlitt's love for his landlady's daughter) which is a subjective imitation of the reciprocated ideal. Love is the strongest and highest act of the will whereby we deliberately choose God as the supreme value and wish others as much good as we wish ourselves. Unselfish human love may well be a specific talent which some possess. The article proceeds historic-ally, from Comte (I) to the Utilitarians (II) and to the modern followers of Kant (III). Aristotle (IV) is next considered as the foundation for the medieval theology of love (V), and there is (VI) a note on modern psychological theories of love.

I For Comte social happiness is man's ultimate end and morality becomes identical with extreme universal altruism. ' The object of morals ', he wrote, ' is to make our sympathetic instincts pre-ponderate as far as possible over the selfish instincts, social feeling over personal feelings ', and on the basis of a modified form of Gall's theory of cerebral physiology he distinguished three sympathetic in-stincts: attachment, veneration and benevolence (*Positive Polity* 1, 73, 566). But, except for a touch-ing faith in the effect of ' the Social State ', the mental dynamics by which personal selfishness is to be trans-formed into universal love are obscure, nor does he

---

[1] Dignumque sit supra quod electas ad sacrificium creaturas in corpus et sanguinem redemptoris virtus secreta convertat . . .

[2] Clara coronantur densis altaria lychnis (*carmina* 14:99; CSEL 30:49).

give any moral ground why altruism *ought* to prevail. Christianity, in his view, fostered selfishness, and a disinterested worship of humanity as a whole should take its place. This extravagant positivist religion appears to have sprung from the private ritual by which he commemorated the death of the undistinguished Madame Clotilde de Vaux (*op. cit.* Preface).

In the Preface to his *Data of Ethics* (1894) Herbert Spencer expresses horror at 'the absolute subjection of the ego in convents and monasteries', and devotes four chapters (XI–XIV) to the opposition between egoism and altruism.

In his evolutionary theory of ethics both are considered essential to the preservation of the species, and we must, for the present, be content with a compromise (which 'seems to imply permanent antagonism') between the two. A complete reconciliation is deferred to a future ideal social state where (by the forces of natural evolution) a transfigured egoism will no longer oppose the ultimate form of altruism—'a sympathetic gratification which costs the receiver nothing'. No wonder charity became associated with philanthropy and help to the poor.

II Hedonists and Utilitarians create a problem for themselves in their endeavour to bridge the gap separating their two systems. In modern ethics Hedonism (from Greek ἡδονή, pleasure) includes a variety of theories from the crude egoism of Hobbes' *Leviathan* to Butler's more refined theory of longsighted selfishness. Some (psychological Hedonists) hold that pleasure is the sole *possible* object of desire; others (ethical Hedonists) maintain that it is the only thing which *ought* to be desired. Both identify happiness with pleasure. The universalistic (as distinct from the egoistic) form of ethical Hedonism, best described as Utilitarianism, holds that each man ought to desire the general happiness. Utilitarianism, peculiarly characteristic of English ethics, was given final shape by Bentham, John Stuart Mill and Sidgwick. Utility is to be understood as 'happiness', 'enlightened benevolence' or, more completely (after Bentham), 'the greatest happiness of the greatest number'. Its foundation is stated by Bentham in the opening sentences of his *Introduction to the Principles of Morals and Legislation* (1789). It belongs to pain and pleasure alone 'to point out what we ought to do, as well as to determine what we shall do'. This is taken up and re-stated by Mill in *Utilitarianism* (1863). The greatest happiness principle is the foundation of morals, and actions are right in proportion as they tend to promote it. By happiness 'is intended pleasure and the absence of pain' (ch. 2). For his calculus of pleasures Bentham had assumed that all pleasure is qualitatively the same ('push-pin is as good as poetry'). To save the system from an obvious criticism, Mill admitted a qualitative distinction ('better to be Socrates dissatisfied than a fool satisfied'). But for all his modification of Benthamism Mill could not show why one *ought* to seek the general happiness, or *how* in seeking it, the individual is also promoting his own. His well-known attempt to do so on grounds of pure

logic consisted in the sophistic argument that if each man's happiness is the end of each, then all men's happiness is the end of all, and, therefore, all men's happiness is the end of each. What he attempted (as is clear from the rest of ch. 4) was to argue from the so-called *psychological fact* that pleasure was the sole object of desire to the *ethical conclusion* that each individual *ought* to desire the general happiness. The initial psychological assumption, as simple as it is unwarrantable, really implies that there is no point in drawing the conclusion. If egoism is the sole motive of action, it is idle to speak of obligation. The theory at its worst, was not unreasonably construed as the corrupting of one's neighbour as oneself in the pursuit of pleasure. At its best it proposes disinterested public spirit as the best motive for socially useful work. When Sidgwick realized that Mill had not resolved the conflict between Interest (private happiness) and Duty (general happiness) he re-read Kant and Butler, abandoned psychological Hedonism, and as a rational ground for the subordination of self-interest to duty, appealed to the axiom of rational Benevolence ('the clearest and most certain of moral intuitions'). To reconcile this with his self-evident axiom of rational Self-Love ('one ought to aim at one's own good on the whole') was for him the most profound problem of ethics (see *Methods of Ethics* (1907[7]), especially Preface to 6th edition). His last word is that their ultimate harmony is to be regarded 'as a hypothesis' which is 'logically necessary' if we are to avoid 'a fundamental contradiction' in ethics (508). An insoluble conflict between self-love and benevolence is inevitable in a system that identifies happiness with pleasure, or chooses an agreeable psychological state as its criterion of morality. The problems of the Utilitarian are real only if we grant the basic premise that social well-being is the ultimate end of man.

III Happiness and Duty. In modern English ethics and in Kant the word 'happiness' has a narrower and a more 'selfish' meaning than it had for the Greeks. The conventional translation of εὐδαιμονία as 'happiness' is the most convenient one, although the Aristotelian idea would be more correctly rendered by 'well-being'. For Aristotle it is an activity, not a state of feeling, though pleasure naturally accompanies it. Human happiness consists primarily in the activity by which man exercises his highest faculty on its highest object (*Nic. Eth.* X, 7). In St Thomas's reconstruction we get away from the self-perfectionism of natural ethics for he transcends the merely human and transforms the Aristotelian ethic. In discussing man's supreme good or final end (1–2ae:1:5) he begins with Aristotle's conception of happiness but ends with the doctrine of the BEATIFIC VISION (q.v.). Aristotle's happy philosopher has become a saint. In all this St Thomas distinguishes man's natural desire for an all-satisfying good, i.e. for happiness (*beatitudo*); the objective good itself (God); and the possession of it (subjective end), which is the vision of God. Man necessarily desires the happiness which *de facto* can only be found in the vision of God. Pleasure or delight (*delectatio*) is not happiness, but an effect or concomitant of the happiness which is itself consequent on the attainment of our objective final end. Charity, therefore, does not seek the loved good for the sake of the pleasure to be derived from it, nor is altruism, as the misinformed suppose, a sublimated egoism in the sense of a belief that well-doing will lead to well-being. Those who despair of any objective goal to strive for acquire a contempt of self and others which may be so strong as to be a prevailing tendency, as in Ibsen's Hedda Gabler.

Kant wrought a major revolution in ethics by making duty rather than goodness or end the fundamental conception. To have moral value, he argues (*Metaphysic of Ethics*) an action must not only accord with duty but must be done for the sake of duty (I must do what I ought precisely because I ought) and in determining our duty we must take no account of our inclinations or even of our happiness. Though it is best to be a cheerful giver, the cheerfulness has nothing to do with the moral worth of the action. With some of his successors (e.g. the Oxford School of Neo-Intuitionists) duty became completely dissociated from happiness, and altruism came to mean ' doing good to others for duty's sake '. It is variously assumed that desire and inclination spring from sub-rational levels and that any action not done from a sense of duty is selfish and is done from inclination or self-interest, and whenever apparently altruistic it is really disguised selfishness. But to accuse a man who acts generously because he wants to do so, of covert egoism is to construe the object of rational desire (to do good to another) as a kind of sub-rational craving or desire to satisfy a benevolent inclination. This would reduce generosity to a trick of self-love and prayer to a sublimation of the libido. The Kantian divorce of duty from interest and of morality from happiness is based on a mistake about the nature of both desire and happiness. Self-love is only a vice if it means undue regard for self or indifference to the welfare of others; unselfishness is a virtue only if it is balanced by self-regard. Kant's theory is largely a rationalization of the Christian doctrine of perfection *as he understood it*, just as the Utilitarian's duty is an importation into natural ethics of an ideal that belongs to Christianity and finds its logical setting only in a doctrine of love.

IV The basis of benevolence for Aristotle is the love the good man has for himself. Of the three types of *philia* or friendship, based on utility, pleasure and goodness, only that for the sake of the good is said to realize the true ideal wherein a man wishes well to his friend for his friend's sake, not as a means to his own happiness; and which consists ' in loving rather than in being loved ' (*Eth*. VIII, 3:7:8). A reasonable self-love, totally different and distinguishable from selfishness, he considers as the source of a real love for others. The good man should have a right regard for his real (i.e. thinking) self, and this same regard he will have towards his friend, as towards ' another self '. The difficulty about deciding whether we love ourselves or others most arises from not distinguishing between proper

and improper self-love (IX, 4:7–9). Though Aristotle's use of the term ' good ' as applied to what he may, or may not, have meant by the self is not always clear, he cannot lightly be accused of a doctrine of enlightened selfishness or of the self-deification which leads to an egoism *à deux*. He often returns to the case of a mother's love. What Aristotle meant by friendships founded on utility or pleasure is part of what St Thomas includes under love of desire, which is love only in a restricted sense. *Amor amicitiae*, love of friendship or (more conveniently) direct love, is concerned not with qualities but persons, loved absolutely and for themselves (1–2ae: 24:4; 28:3). Its basis is discussed when St Thomas treats of charity as a kind of friendship, *quaedam amicitia*. Self-love is the principle and root (*forma et radix*) of benevolence; for direct love consists in bearing for others the regard which we bear for ourselves (ibid. 25:4). A man is said to love himself when he loves his spiritual nature and in this way he ought to love himself, after God, more than any other (26:4). But he goes beyond Aristotle in introducing the principle of similitude as the metaphysical foundation for deriving love of others from love of self. Benevolence is founded on something shared in common, and it is only because the good which I love in myself is somehow shared by my friend that I can love him as directly as myself. The priority of self-love, which holds universally for Aristotelians, has to be restricted in a metaphysic of creation. It is not true of the relation of creature to God. The creature's love for God as absolute value is what is primary, and is the basis of its love for itself. We love ourselves and others as images of Him whom we love more directly (*see* IMAGO DEI, THEORY OF). The basis of this communion in love is a subsistent likeness to God present in all and loved in and above all. Thus the reconciling of love of self and love of God has none of the radical difficulty which it would present to an Aristotelian. What I love in myself is a value which is the source of my being. It is the natural love of God above all things (as first principle and last end of the universe) that is perfected by CHARITY (q.v.). For in the fallen state of man charity is needed if the love of God is to prevail (1–2ae:109:3); cf. Johann, *The Meaning of Love*, for the precise nature and function of similitude in St Thomas's theory of love and its ultimate foundation in a metaphysic of participation.

V In Medieval theology the disinterestedness of love was a central question. The compatibility of self-love with love of our neighbour and of God was then a problem of the relation between *philia* and *caritas*. Apart from St Augustine's incomplete synthesis of EROS (q.v.) and AGAPE, the main influence (until Aristotle's *Ethics* was re-discovered in the 13th cent.) was Cicero's *De Amicitia*. Cicero's view of disinterested friendship may be summed up in the identification of friendship with *benevolentia* or goodwill (ch. v), the note of disinterestedness (ch. ix), and the reciprocal character of love (' *redamare* ') based on likeness in virtue (ch. xiv) whereby a friend is regarded as ' another self ' (ch. xxi).

The Ciceronian theme is easily traceable in Abelard and the Cistercians and was not unknown to the courtly poets of the day. It is the foundation of the dialogue *De Spirituali Amicitia* (1164–5) of Ailred of Rievaulx (see introduction to Engl. trans. by C. H. Talbot).

The exaltation of disinterested love by Abelard is the ideal of a love prepared to sacrifice its object (PL 178:891–3). Gilson, who shrewdly infers an influence other than Cicero's, sums it up as stating that God is not to be loved as Abelard loved Heloïse but as Heloïse loved Abelard. The implied assumption is that love of God could be described in the same terms as the human love which has to envisage the frustration of its joy in its object—not unlike the alleged disinterested love of the troubadour who loved without recompense when there was nothing else to be done. In his *De Diligendo Deo*, St Bernard develops a doctrine of love which seeks for no recompense but does not go unrewarded. Love is the desire to possess God, but pure love is the possession of God (PL 182:984–5)—a doctrine which has nothing to do with the spiritual life of Mme Guyon. This pure love of God is reconciled with self-love in his doctrine of the image of God in man (see esp. *Sermo* 82, PL 183:1180–81). To empty oneself of the false ego of unlikeness (an illusory personality of self-will) is not to lose but to find oneself once more, and to restore the true self whose nature it is to have been made to the likeness of God. The self at this limit loves itself only as a likeness to God and the famous antinomy disappears (cf. Gilson, *The Mystical Theology of St Bernard*, 127–152 and Appendix on Abelard).

Rousselot, *Pour l'histoire du problème de l'amour au moyen âge* (1908), claimed that the Schoolmen were divided between two irreducible conceptions of love: the physical or 'Graeco-Thomist' conception, based upon the natural inclination of man to seek his own proper good; the ecstatic conception, characteristic of those who wished to empty love of all self-reference. (Nygren was to come later, but that is another question; *see* CHARITY.) Gilson, among others, denies any such clear-cut distinction, and gives good reasons why St Bernard was not embarrassed by a choice (*loc. cit.* and especially Notes 179 and 181). The early Scholastic writers, he contends, constantly change over and cannot be divided into two opposing camps, nor did St Thomas solve the difficulty by the theory attributed to him by Rousselot, viz. the notion of unity and the analogy of the relation of a part to a whole. Gilson argues convincingly that the central point of the solution of St Thomas is the traditional description of man as the image of God. Since man is an image of God, in loving the image truly, he loves the original. Hence, those who would say that if man of necessity loves himself he cannot love God with disinterested love, forget that to love God with disinterested love is man's true way of loving himself. (*Spirit of Mediaeval Philosophy*, ch. xiv.) Without a true self-love there would be no proper basis for the 'as thyself' which is commanded as the measure of our love for others.

VI Psychology and self-giving. By empirical methods depth-psychology has shed much light on the psychological foundation of love for our neighbour. For psychotherapy the maturity of affective life is above all a problem of relationship with oneself and others. Hence its valuable study of the psychological evolution which leads from the self-regarding, dependent love of the child (where the object is loved for the function it fulfils) to the self-sacrificing, disinterested love of which the mature adult should be capable (where someone is loved for his own sake and not for the function he may fulfil). If the symptoms of neurosis reveal a serious disturbance in human relationship, a duality in the very structure of consciousness, represented by the mental images of self and others, becomes acutely actualized in psychopathological states. The normal man faced with the same existential problems harmonizes the two images in a co-existence of which the sign of balance is the love of his neighbour. In *Psychoanalysis and Personality* (1954) Nuttin gives a dynamic theory of normal personality in terms of egoistic and altruistic contact (love). Though he admits that man's erotic and self-assertive tendencies are very powerful needs (and in this asceticism agrees with the systems of dynamic and depth-psychology) he denies that either the sexual libido (Freud) or the power instinct (Adler) dominate human behaviour. A double complex tendency—towards self-development and towards contact with others—is, he argues, what is most fundamental in man's psychic dynamism. Hence the ultimate fusion of these two basic drives or needs in the fact that it is in and through contact with others that man maintains and develops himself—especially by what he calls the moral as distinct from the psychological 'gift of oneself'. Guitton uses psychoanalytic studies of the phenomena of projection to clarify the question of marital love. Love is 'a projection of the self upon another' and the 'reception in oneself of the projection of another self', and the lover 'substitutes the other's image of him for his own image of himself and, in that act, is cured of the self-hatred which self-love engenders'. (*Essay on Human Love*, 71, 177). Sympathy, which involves a projection of self into the situation of another, is an affective rather than a reciprocal sharing, and can be indifferent to moral value.

Bibliography. Apart from works mentioned, see Part III of *Love of our Neighbour* (1955), a symposium ed. by A. Plé OP; *J. Burnaby, *Amor Dei* (1938), mainly a study of St Augustine; J. Crehan SJ, *Ethics* (*Mediaeval*), Ency. Brit. (1958); J. Coventry SJ, *Morals and Independence* (1949); M. D'Arcy SJ, *The Mind and Heart of Love* (1954²); G. Zilboorg, *Love in Freudian Psychoanalysis*, in *Selection* II (1954); and for a good account of recent literature R. Johann SJ, *The Meaning of Love* (1955).   D. E.

AMBROSIAN RITE The theory of the Eastern origin of the Ambrosian rite, of which the chief upholder was Duchesne, is now universally rejected. It was never accepted by Ambrosian scholars like

Ceriani and Magistretti and modern scholars like Borella may be said to have finally disposed of it. It may be, as Gregory Dix said, that the exposure by Wilmart of the letters of pseudo-Germanus of Paris and the attribution of the *De Sacramentis* to St Ambrose by Morin, Faller, Connolly and now Dom B. Botte, have brought about a complete change of outlook and removed ' the greatest single obstacle to a clear understanding of the development of the eucharistic liturgy in the West' (*The Shape of the Liturgy*, 459–60).

Yet all this does not solve the problem of the origin of the Ambrosian rite. On the one hand we have the Canon of the Mass in *De Sacramentis* (4:5:21–5; 6:26–8, and cf. *De Mysteriis*, 8:43–9; 9:50–4, PL 16:443–5 and 403–07) and on the other the first Ambrosian books of which the earliest is most probably an *Expositio Missae* dating from the 8th or 9th cent. (ed. by Wilmart and then by Dold; cf. Righetti, III 510). What happened between these two dates?

There is first the question of the provenance of the Canon in *De Sacramentis*, about which there is a considerable diversity of opinion among scholars. That this text is the oldest example we have of the Roman Canon is accepted by all. The question is whether Milan received it from Rome or Rome from Milan. The balance of probabilities seems to indicate a Roman origin. Twice St Ambrose says that he follows the Roman church in all things: ' We are not unaware that the Roman Church lacks this custom, and it is the model and the law of that Church which we follow in all things ';[1] and later: ' *In omnibus cupio sequi ecclesiam romanam* ' (*De Sacr.* 3:1:5), though this does not prevent him from vigorously defending the Milanese custom of washing the feet after Baptism. The expression ' *summus sacerdos*' applied to Melchisedech is found both in the *De Sacramentis* Canon and in that of Rome about the year 375 (cf. ' Ambrosiaster ', *Quaestiones Veteris et Novi Testamenti*, 109; PL 35:2329 and the discussion of it in *Eucharistie*, by N. Maurice-Denis et R. Boulet (1953), 339–40). This as yet unindentified writer was familiar with both Rome and Milan (cf. Morin, in Righetti, III:552–3). Finally, a comparison between the passage of the Ambrosian Canon from ' *Ergo et memores* ' down to ' *et petimus* ' inclusively (*De Sacr.* 4:6:26) and the Latin version of the Verona MS of the *Apostolic Tradition* of Hippolytus (ed. Botte, *La Tradition apostolique*, 32–3, 1946) would seem to indicate a family likeness to it. That this latter is a Roman text, though written originally in Greek, is almost beyond dispute and it may be that in spite of successive translations, editings and additions, a common pattern of the Canon was found throughout the 3rd and 4th cents. in Rome. Of this the Ambrosian Canon may be one version, yet still Roman. This argument is strengthened if we may accept Dix's view that the *anamnesis* and the offertory prayer, *et petimus*, that immediately follows it, is

' an old pre-Nicene peculiarity ' which the Ambrose Canon has retained (cf. *Shape of Liturgy*, 556–7).

Yet the differences between the Ambrosian and Roman Canons remain. At this point it may be necessary to say that we must not look for too great a fixity in the prayers of the liturgy at this time. The late Dom G. Morin said with some vehemence that it was *simpliste* to look for a single uniform Ambrosian liturgy having the force of law throughout the diocese of Milan; there was no doubt, he says, an underlying common type but this would not prevent the existence here and there of notable differences (RB 20 (1903) 385 sq.; cf. Righetti, III, 509). The same may be said of the Roman Canon, which Cabrol, for instance, regards as ' a text corrected from the *De Sacramentis* (The *Mass of the Western Rites*, Eng. trans., 41, 1934). If we may take this view, that seems very plausible, it enables us to accept the attractive plea of Canon Borella that the *De Sacramentis* text owes something to St Ambrose (e.g. the use of ' *rationabilis* ', the mention of Abel, Abraham and Melchisedech, favourite themes in the writings of the saint, and the use of several phrases that occur frequently in his works, cf. Righetti, III: 553–4). In any case, this was a period of formation and it is significant that the Alexandrian ' *de tuis donis et datis* ' is found in the Roman Canon as soon as we know it, while it is lacking in Ambrose's text.

Certain other features of the Ambrosian rite that are regarded by many as primitive, and which are undoubtedly very early, demand a brief notice. There is the announcement after the Gospel on Sundays of the ensuing feasts and the invitation to those who wish to be baptized to give in their names. There is the position of the *Pax* at the beginning of the offertory that is more primitive than its position in the Roman rite. The *oratio super sindonem* is most probably the conclusion of the prayers for all classes of people, of which St Ambrose speaks in *De Sacramentis* (4:4:14). The multiplicity of Prefaces represents a pre-Gregorian use (see Righetti, III:550, summarizing the important work of Paredi who attributes them to Eusebius (fl. 5th cent.)). The position of the *Pater noster* after the fraction is likewise pre-Gregorian, though St Ambrose seems to say that it came immediately after the Canon: *quae postea sequitur* (cf. *De Sacr.* 5:4:24 Dom B. Botte translates this: ' qui suit immédiatement ').

The difficulty of filling the gap between the 5th and the 9th cents. remains. There is a complete lack of documents. All one can do is to follow the excellent Milanese scholars and say that it was during this period that the Ambrosian rite was ' Gallicanized' and acquired several Greek features. Of the first group the most important are the texts *Mandans quoque* and *Haec facimus* after the consecration of Maundy Thursday and the *Vere sanctus* before it in the Resurrection Mass of Holy Saturday. Borella describes this latter as Gallican in style, and Coebergh, who speaks of the ancient character of their *epicleses*, thinks they should most probably be attributed to the 6th or 7th cents. (Righetti, II:442–3).

[1] Non ignoramus quod ecclesia romana hanc consuetudinem (feet-washing at Baptism) non habeat cuius typum in omnibus sequimur et formam.

It is suggested that the 'Gallican' features of the rite came in at the time of the exile of Milanese bishops at Genoa during the 6th and 7th cents. (cf. Archdale A. King, *Liturgies of the Primatial Sees*, 301–2 and 297). Of the second group we may mention the Lenten litany *Divinae pacis* (or *Dicamus omnes*) that replaces the *Gloria* and the texts and chants of the *Confractorium* and the *Transitorium*. These all derive from Greek liturgies, and the latter may very well have been brought in by refugee Greek monks in the 7th and 8th cents. (cf. Archdale A. King, *op. cit.* 304) 'Numerous texts in the Ambrosian rite are derived directly from Byzantine troparies and canons sometimes with their original Greek melodies'.

Like so many rites the Ambrosian is a composite one but with a marked Roman or 'Italian' character. Its primitive features are of high interest and we may endorse Callewaert's view that in years to come Milan will play an important part in the historical study of the Roman Mass (Letter to Canon Borella in Righetti, III:552).

Bibliography. Ambrose, St, *De Sacramentis, De Mysteriis*, ed. B. Botte, Sources Chrétiennes, 25, Paris, 1950. Critical text (twelve MSS collated), introduction, translation and notes. For authenticity of *De Sacr.* see pp. 7–32. The text is also found in PL 16:405–82; Righetti, M., *Storia Liturgica*, III:508–63, Excursus: La Messa ambrosiana, by Pietro Borella (1949); the same II (2nd ed. 1955) Excursus II, L' anno liturgico Ambrosiano, by P. Borella, 442–3, for *Vere sanctus* and *Haec facimus* texts and discussion; the same, IV (1953), Excursus on Baptism, by P. Borella, 427 sq.; King, Archdale A., *Liturgies of the Primatial Sees*, Rite of Milan, pp. 286–456 (1957); Dix, G., *The Shape of the Liturgy*, pp. 459–62, 556–7, 563–5 (1944); Sources of the Ambrosian Rite are fully given in Righetti and King.   J. D. C.

AMERICA, THEOLOGICAL SIGNIFICANCE OF

The discovery of America and its subsequent colonization in the 16th and 17th cents. brought theologians once again to the perplexing problem of the infidel and the possibility of his justification. In the case of the millions who remained in lifelong ignorance of Christian revelation, how is the sincere and universal salvific will of God to be verified? The question demanded an answer not only to clarify further a theological dogma, but more immediately to provide a procedure and practice for the missionaries and apologetes who would face the pagans of the New World. The solution of Thomas Aquinas was most widely accepted at this time, according to which a faith in Christ as mediator was demanded from infidels who lived before the Redemption, but this faith could be found implicit in a pagan's faith in God and His remunerating providence (*Commentary on Heb.* 11, *lectio* 2). After the time of the Gospel, however, an explicit faith in the Trinity and the Incarnation was required, but it must be recalled that this Thomistic thesis and the other medieval expressions were conditioned by the belief that the Gospel had reached out through the world. Only rarely had a theorizer appeared such as Vergilius of Salzburg, who was censured by Pope Zachary I in 848 for holding the possibility of the earth's rotundity and the existence of antipodes. Boniface, who had cited him to Rome, rejected his teaching on the grounds that it implied a race of men not descended from Adam, a situation that would conflict with the universality of Redemption.

But once the conquistadores and missionaries of the 16th cent. returned from the New World with evidence of vast unknown continents and countless souls unreached by revelation, the restrictions of the medieval theological claim could not be maintained without dooming millions, perhaps milliards through no fault of their own. The Tridentine fathers when faced with this crisis wisely refrained from incorporating any particular theory into conciliar decrees, but asserted with firmness that 'faith is the beginning of human salvation, the foundation and root of all justification' (D 801). This granted Renaissance theologians opportunity for speculation, and their arguments progressed more or less along three paths.

I An adult limbo. Claudius Seyssell, archbishop of Turin, proposed that pagans who remained ignorant of the faith required for salvation were thereby deprived of a supernatural end, but if they lived according to their conscience they could achieve a natural happiness in Limbo, a theory that was to be reintroduced with modifications four centuries later by Cardinal Billot who relegated heathens to an adult Limbo because they were equivalently infants incapable of moral, responsible acts.

II Possibility of revelation. The histories of Hispano-America that appeared at this time described religious customs suggesting traces of some primitive revelation or perhaps even Christian revelation. José Acosta, for example, a Jesuit official in Peru for seventeen years, published his *Historia natural y moral de las Indias* in 1590, which recorded many Aztec rites, such as the eating of the god Vitzilipuztli, that in some details seemed familiarly Christian. And in his *Origin de los Indios del mundo*, Gregorio de García OP, a missionary for twelve years, concluded that the American Indians had their origins in Asia or the Old World. We remark here that some of the leaders of the Protestant revolt, notably Calvin, increased the guilt of the infidels by judging that they had rejected some previous revelation. In fact Zwingli and Theodore Beza seemed convinced that the pagans had been evangelized somehow by the Apostles.

III Implicit faith. But the greater number of theologians spent their efforts to establish the minimum requisites of the faith declared indispensable by the Council. The opinions of Andrew Vega OFM and Dominic Soto OP were among the more liberal to appear. Vega, in the supposition of invincible ignorance, taught that it was enough for the infidel to do what was in his power, in which event either supernatural faith was not required *in casu* or he possessed it *in voto*; Soto held that an infidel could have his natural knowledge so elevated that his faith while remaining objectively natural became at the same time subjectively supernatural. Suarez introduced a distinction according to which the only explicit faith necessary *in re* for justification is faith in God the rewarder ; explicit faith in Christ and the Trinity, obligatory by a positive law, may be had *in voto*. Thus the tendency was to admit for the infidels the type of faith that Thomas Aquinas allowed to those who lived before the promulgation of the Gospel, and to insist that God will employ extraordinary means to bring the conscientious pagan to justification, according to the axiom, *Facienti quod in se est, Deus non denegat gratiam* : (God does not refuse grace to one who does his best).

Bibliography. L. Billot, ' La Providence divine et le nombre infini d'hommes hors de la voie normale du salut ', ER 161–76 (1919–23) ; L. Capéran, *Le Problème du salut des infidèles* (Toulouse, 1934) ; S. Harent, ' Salut des infidèles ', DTC 7, 1726–1930 ; A. Liège, ' Le Salut des autres ', *Lumière et vie* 18 (1954) 13–41 ; R. Lombardi sj, *The Salvation of the Unbeliever* (1956) ; F. S. Shea, ' Principles of Extra-Sacramental Justification ', in *Proceedings of the Catholic Theological Society of America* (1955) 125–51 ; P. Soullard op, 'Les Infidèles peuvent-ils être sauvés?', *Lumière et vie*, 18 (1954) 779–800.   F. McS.

ANALOGY OF BEING The article on this difficult and important subject begins with (I) a description and definition of analogy, and then (II) traces the origins of analogy among the Greeks. The metaphysical presuppositions (III) of the theory are next discussed, and an attempt is made (IV) to estimate its value as a help to the knowledge of God. The various divisions according to which analogy has been classified (V) are examined, and a long section is devoted (VI) to analogy in the works of St Thomas. Thereafter the later Scholastics (VII) are considered and finally (VIII) something is added about the modern developments in the theory of analogy.

I Description and definition of analogy. Analogy is a Greek term meaning proportion and is in a general way used to designate the resemblance that exists, or which may be fancied to exist, between things or between the relations of things to one another. Some analogies are obviously fanciful, as Hamlet found when he tried to get Polonius to see the likeness of the whale in the cloudy sky, and by what is termed the pathetic fallacy many human qualities are by analogy transferred to inanimate or unreasoning things where they do not properly belong. But if all likenesses in nature are to be denied, there would be an end of general ideas, and this is a condition that no philosopher can contemplate with calmness unless he is an extreme Nominalist (*see* NOMINALISM), and even then he would have some trouble in eliminating all general ideas from his system. A modern Nominalist has asserted that ' we achieve communication by means of language ', which means in effect that men cause other men to have ideas by means of words, and in that case the general notions of man, cause, ideas, words, and otherness are all presupposed in a No-

minalist system that undertakes to exclude all general notions.

It is necessary to add to this explanation of analogy a note about being. The rise of the existentialist philosophies has led to a widespread desire to show that St Thomas by his notion of the activity of being (*actus essendi*) had anticipated their leading idea. For the relation of essence to existence in his philosophy, *see* ACT AND POTENCY and ATTRIBUTES OF GOD. Here it may suffice to note that the most abstract notion of being—about which one is concerned when dealing with analogy—is prior to, or prescinds from, such a discrimination between essence and existence.

There has been much discussion since 1945 of the existentialist interpretation of St Thomas, and this is not the place to go into its technicalities. It must, however, be noted that the most complete attempt to work out a Thomist existentialism (in M. Gilson's *Being and some Philosophers*, 1952[2]) led to very searching criticism by L. M. Regis op, with the result that in an appendix to his second edition M. Gilson withdrew many of his ideas. He had tried to fit into Thomism the idea of Kant (*see* KANT AND THEOLOGY) that existence is not a predicate (and that therefore existence is not known by a concept). This he withdrew under criticism, but made a distinction between concept and conception (in order to keep to the idea that the concept of existence was unique and not like other concepts) which did not seem to have much justification. It might be that if care was taken to analyse what is involved in the human mind having an intuition of its own activity, there would be some ground for saying that the view of the mind-while-acting and the view of the mind-as-having-acted, as in the process of reflection, provided a foundation for distinguishing between two kinds of mental attitude which could be compared with each other in the same way as essence and existence are compared ; but here one is dealing with intuitions rather than with abstract concepts.

Analogy of being is a relation of similarity (which carries with it dissimilarity as its counterpart) between created and uncreated being which cannot be broken down into more simple terms. Being is not a genus to which a *differentia* can be added, or from which it may be withheld, so as to give two varieties of being, created and uncreated. Thus ' being-like ' is not being *plus* likeness, for likeness is itself being—if it is real at all—and one cannot subtract the notion of created and uncreated and then rest content with what is just being, for then being would be more primitive than the uncreated being which is God. Hence the very being of man is a being-like-God, and this unique relationship is discovered only after the existence of God has been ascertained (*see* GOD, EXISTENCE OF). Arising from the discovery of that existence, as a natural consequence comes the realization that nothing in the world can afterwards be the same again, for all things have now to be thought of as somehow, in greater or less proximity, standing in a relation of likeness to God. Scholastic theologians quickly set up the two broad divisions of this likeness, saying that creatures possessed of reason had the image of God upon them (*see* IMAGO DEI), while lesser creatures bore only His trace or vestige.

The importance of analogy can be seen from the central place it occupies in Scholasticism. If a theory of real participation of the godhead by created being is allowed to prevail, then one will have fallen over into Pantheism, while if there is no true relation of likeness between created and uncreated being, then there is no basis for man's knowledge of God, for all that man has to work with is what is delivered to him by his scrutiny of created being; no man can scan God.

Before the growth of the idea is traced from its origin in Greek speculation, it is important to make one essential distinction between two types of analogy, which may be called downcast and upcast. Man is essentially dependent upon God and the relationship between them is in this upward direction —from man to God—a real one ; but to God even the whole of creation is in no way essential, and from His side—in a downward direction—the relationship is unreal ; it puts no new reality in God. The distinction of downcast and upcast analogies is thus founded on the asymmetry or non-mutual character of the relationship between creatures and God. The Greek terms *proodos* and *epistrophe* were used by the neo-Platonists to distinguish between the movement out from God and the return to Him, and some Christians gave too much attention to the *proodos* and not enough to the *epistrophe*. When God adds creatures to Himself, there are more beings, but there is not more being ; God is not enriched by the accretion. God is not somehow working out a great process of evolution, for there is no process in God's nature. This is what is meant by the saying of Scripture that God dwells in light inaccessible. If all creatures ceased to be, His being would not suffer any change thereby.

Historically it was the analogical state of human knowledge that was first mapped out, and the scrutiny of being itself came later, but this does not mean that the analogy of being is simply a projection from certain phenomena of the knowledge-process. As Averroes showed (*Epitome in libros metaphys.* (1552) 172a), analogy of being itself is required by the elimination of the two logical alternatives to it, univocal being on the one hand, and a set of entirely disparate beings on the other. Even so, it is not right for the human mind to grow optimistic from its discovery of the analogy of being, for as the Fourth Lateran Council remarked (D 431) : ' Between creator and creature there cannot be discovered so great a likeness but that with it there is to be noted an even greater difference.' [1]

II The origins of analogy among the Greeks. Analogy came into use when the Greek mathematicians were working out for the first time a theory of proportions, arithmetic, geometric and harmonic. When there were three terms in the proportion, it was called continuous by the Greeks, and when there were four it was called discrete. This distinction was made by Eudoxus and can be

found in Aristotle (*Eth. Nicom.* 1131 a 31), where distributive justice is said to be a four-term proportion, on the view that as a king is to a thane, so should be the share that the king receives from the state to that received by the thane. This application of mathematical theory to ethics and to metaphysics was begun by Plato, and even before his time there are signs that Greek thought was using mathematical helps to precision. Anaxagoras (fragment 12) has the view that mind alone, and no lesser thing, has a relation of likeness with other minds, this relation of likeness being the basis on which the later theory of analogy was to rest. In the myth of Plato's *Phaedo* (111 A) an illustration is used to convey the idea that human knowledge can be transcended by that of minds disengaged from bodies just as the vision of creatures that live in water is by that of those which walk in the air of this world, this illustration being a statement of an analogy in four terms. Likewise in the *Republic* (508 C) Plato uses the analogy of the sun with the form of the Good to convey what would otherwise not be easily expressed in human language (*see* LIGHT, METAPHYSIC OF). Immediately afterwards (509 B) he puts forward the simile of the divided line—which is a primitive attempt to make a theory of analogy and to apply it to the evaluation of human knowledge. A more elaborate application of the theory, this time to reality as much as to our knowledge of it, is to be found in *Symposium* (210 A–211 C), where the approach to beauty-in-itself is outlined, along with many statements about the negative knowledge of this absolute beauty.

Plato was obviously anxious to control the use of analogy in reasoning. Before his time the Hippocratic school made free use of analogy in their medical reasoning, comparing, for instance, the rising of the milk in the breasts to that of oil in the wick of a lamp. Herodotus, following the geographers, drew conclusions from the analogy between the Nile and the Danube, holding that the two rivers were equal in length and that the Nile bisected Africa just as the Danube did Europe (*Histories* 2:33), but some control of this kind of reasoning was necessary. Plato suggested that only the lover of truth could use analogical reasoning with profit (*Republic* 475 C–476 A). To him the difficulty in using it was not insurmountable, for by conforming the ' orbits of reason in the soul ' to those of the heavens, some order could be introduced into human thinking (*Timaeus* 47 B). This cosmological fancy was borrowed by Cicero in his *Somnium Scipionis* and thus passed to the Christian West. In particular, Plato thought that the three-term, or continuous, analogy was the best (*Timaeus* 31 C), since it made its terms one in a way that the four-term did not. (Obviously when the word ' sweet ' is used of sounds by analogy with tastes agreeable to the palate, there is no real sweetness in the sound ; only the relationships are similar.) It is from this point that the dispute among Scholastic theologians takes its rise, some preferring a four-term analogy to state the position between man and God, and others requiring a three-term analogy.

[1] Inter creatorem et creaturam non potest tanta similitudo notari quin inter eos maior sit dissimilitudo notanda.

III The metaphysical presuppositions. A theory of analogy requires a view of the universe as an ordered hierarchy of beings. This Plato set out to establish, though without the express intention of building upon it a theory of analogy (*Timaeus* 30 B). When he says that, ' of all things by nature visible no work that is without reason will ever be more beautiful than what has reason ', he was setting up the major division in the orders of being. In the *Republic* (book 2) he had already made some use of the classification of lives according to the level at which they were lived, whether it was that of instinct, passion or reason ; it was natural to go on from this to build up an ordered picture of the universe. But he looked on it as more than a picture. In *Timaeus* (31 C) he speaks of the need of inserting two middle terms (air and water) between the extremes of fire and earth, since the extremes are three-dimensional, and between cubes (a^3 and b^3) one has to have two terms (a^2b and a^2b) to keep the proportion continuous. This intrusion of mathematics into the theory of the elements may seem fanciful now, but to him it was a peremptory argument, for mathematical objects were intermediaries between ideas and sense-objects.

To a modern philosopher this idea of degrees of being may seem strange, but it was part of the mental furniture of Scholasticism, gaining entry there by way of Plotinus, who made it the key to his system. Modern Scholastics have sometimes tried to defend it (e.g. Romeyer, ' S. Thomas et notre connaissance de l'esprit humain ', *Archives de Philosophie* VI, ii, 10) on the ground that it is an intuition or an immediate experience, but it seems sounder to regard it as due to a *reductio ad absurdum*. If reasoning beings are not essentially higher than unreasoning, then there is an end of all philosophy, and the thought-process is only a prolongation of the evolutionary life-process that arose by random mutation (*see* EVOLUTION). St Thomas, after Aristotle, used as an illustration of the degrees of being the variation in the heat of the sun according to one's proximity ; the sun was a maximum of heat and it seemed easy to argue to a maximum of being. But the argument of degrees was not simply a piece of picture-thinking. He did not say that because the sun was a maximum, therefore there must be an absolute of truth, goodness and beauty ; but while using the sun as an illustration he rested the argument on the ascertained fact, familiar from Augustine (*Civitas Dei* 8:6), that there was an inner beauty in the mind of the beholder which it would be absurd not to call higher than the external sight or sound from which it arose. The argument of degrees owes more to the Platonic dialectic than to the syllogising of Aristotle, as the more modern critics of it have noted, especially L. Geiger (*La Participation*, 357) and G. Ducoin (' S. Thomas, commentateur d'Aristote ', *Archives de Philosophie* XX (1957) 256–7). It may be that to appreciate the argument one needs certain preliminary *exercitationes animi*, as Augustine suggested, in order to enter into an understanding of exemplar causality,

but one cannot for all that say that the argument is simply an intuition in slow motion.

In a baffling passage of the *Epinomis* (990 D) Plato claims that geometry is able by a marvel of divine origin to make like or to assimilate numbers that are not like to one another by nature. He does not make clear what exactly he is thinking about, but goes on to infer that the whole of nature, genus and species, is sketched out. He may be thinking of a geometrical construction by which the geometric mean between two lines can be found by using them as the diameter of a circle and then drawing the perpendicular from the point where they meet to the circumference. This would make a surd number geometrically comparable with the natural numbers, and it was a method known to the Greeks. Plato goes on to claim that (991 E) there is one harmony of numbers, music and the heavenly motions, thus extending the scope of analogy almost to the borders of metaphysics. When the Christian Platonist, Athenagoras, used language about the persons of the Trinity that implied a comparison of their relationship to that existing between two friendly numbers, he was but extending the practice of Plato himself and taking a step forward on the way to the full theory of analogy that was worked out by the Scholastics. Plato had declared a preference (*Timaeus* 31 B) for the three-term proportion over the four-term, and this was to have its consequences too in Scholasticism.

IV Analogy and the knowledge of God. Aristotle was familiar, from his Platonic training, with the uses of analogy, but he did not let it interfere with his metaphysics. He looked to it for help in classifying our ways of knowing, but he does not seem to connect it with being. Thus (in *Eth. Nicom.* 1096 b 28) he is considering why we call wisdom, pleasure and honour good when there is no one fixed sense of the word good that will apply to all three. He dismisses the problem as fit for another time—which in his idiom means for ever—and says laconically that perhaps all three have a common element by being from one source or directed to one end, or else they are all ' somehow analogous. For as sight is in the body, so is understanding in the soul, while each is in fact disparate '. This sentence was fraught with consequence for Scholasticism, for it seemed to differentiate between relations of dependence, whether of efficient or exemplar causality, and the relation of two analogates (i.e. the two terms related by analogy). The fact that Aristotle indicated a preference for the latter explanation in this passage made St Thomas, and still more his later disciples, turn to the four-term analogy. St Thomas comments on the place (in *Eth. Nicom.* 1:7), ' One term can be applied to different objects where their difference is not complete but allows of some point in common. Sometimes this will be when they are referred to one beginning . . . or else when they are referred to one end . . . but sometimes it will be according as they have different relations to the same subject, as quantity and quality are both said to have being . . . or according to their having the same relation to different subjects, for sight has the same relation to the body as understanding has to the soul. . . . Thus Aristotle says that good is predicated of many things . . . by analogy, i.e. according to the same relation, in so far as all good things depend upon the one first cause of goodness, or are directed to the one end. Aristotle did not wish this goodness to be a separate idea and form of all good things but their beginning and end. Again all good things are called good rather according to this analogy, that as sight is the good of the body, so is understanding the good of the soul ; and therefore he prefers this third relation, since it is drawn from the goodness that is inherent in things, whereas the two former relations exist according to a separate goodness, which is not so proper a source of analogous predication.'

In this Aristotelian context St Thomas is anxious not to disagree with his master, but elsewhere he will be more ready to accept something of the Platonic notion of participation of being, a notion which carried with it a theory of analogy in embryo. The Platonic theory was not in agreement with the Aristotelian, and the variation between the two theories, or rather their combination in various ways, is the factor which has led to the endless debates of the Scholastics about the meaning of what St Thomas held about analogy.

If Plato had worked out his theory of analogy, it would certainly have extended to reality and not stopped short at the human ways of knowing. He held that there was a close connection between the two, and his ' divided line ' was meant to show this. Aristotle, however, uses (*Eth. Nicom.* 1132 a 25) analogy merely as a way to illustrate how the judge in administering justice has to fix a proportion between crime and penalty, the person wronged and the offender (as Plato used it in Laws 757 D 5), and he is not in the least anxious to extend analogy to being as such. He guards (*Metaph.* 1003 a 33) against saying that being is analogous, while admitting that it is from one source and directed upon one end. Participation is not an idea that he welcomed. Analogy can be used (*Phys.* 191 a 8) to gain knowledge of prime matter or of general ideas, but it does not extend to reality itself, being but a modification of the human way of knowing things. The nearest he comes to such an extension is in *Metaph.* 1093 b 18, but all that he is there concerned to say is that in every category of being there can be found instances of analogy. The examples he gives—straightness in lines compared with smoothness in surfaces, and oddness in numbers compared with the colour white—verge on the metaphorical and show that to him analogy is really to be found on our side of the line and not on the side of things. Once (*De partibus anim.* 645 b 6) he says that where analogy is found, the natures of the analogates are somewhat alike. He did not probe into that ' somewhat ' any further.

The mixing of the streams, Platonic and Aristotelian, took place in the Middle Platonism of Albinus and others in the 2nd cent. A.D., and in him can be found the three ways of coming to know God, by negation, by causality and by analogy or extrapolation (R. Witt, *Albinus* (1937) 132). The same triple classification was taken over by the Christian philosopher Athenagoras, and he is the first Christian to have a statement of doctrine which approximates to the analogy of being (*de resurrectione* 12). Albinus also used the idea (from *Theaetetus* 176 B) that the end of life for man is to become as like to God as possible, and this text (which later became the favourite quotation of Clement of Alexandria) implies that there exists some basic likeness between God and man and that it is for man to develop this and to make progress along a line on which God has already started him. The Early Fathers such as Irenaeus found a home for this idea in Scripture by distinguishing between the image and the likeness of God ; man was created in the one, but he did not receive the other except by grace. Once this idea was launched (*see* IMAGO DEI), it was inevitable that a theory of analogy of being should be developed in Christian thought and not merely a theory of analogous knowledge.

Among the three ways of knowing God, it is clear that analogy is the most important. The negative knowledge sees that human knowledge does not trespass beyond its foundation, which is the relation of likeness, and prevents it indulging in the vain supposal that likeness means real kinship, while the knowledge gained by way of causality is simply the result of certain projections from our nature to His, as when it is said that the beauty of the created universe is a faint trace of the beauty of God who made it so beautiful. At times it has occurred to some thinkers to exaggerate the negative character of this knowledge and to deny that God as cause is in any way like His effects. The Scholastics had two maxims : an effect does not exhaust the power of its cause, and like agent produces like effect. The two maxims have to be held in balance, for one can easily fall into the illusion that the malignancy which can sometimes be observed in created nature is somehow a reflection of God (*see* EVIL), whereas it is due to the effects falling short of their cause in a notable way. The two maxims were axiomatic in neo-Platonism and were taken over into the Scholastic theology ; their justification can be found in the priority of being to action (*see* ACT AND POTENCY) and in the hierarchic structure of the universe as already discussed.

V Divisions of analogy. Analogy can be divided into extrinsic and intrinsic, according as there is absent or present a foundation for the analogy in the reality it is being used to describe. Thus to discern a connection between left-handedness and injustice (as the Latin language did) is to do little more than to produce a picturesque metaphor. When the scientist draws out an elaborate analogy between the solar system and the ultimate particles within the atom, he is setting up a hypothesis which he then sets out to verify. He has projected into an unknown realm a relationship which is known to exist between planets and satellites, and he has to establish experiments which will test his hypothesis. Yet to use a four-term analogy to describe the nature of God from relationships which are known to exist between created beings or their parts is a projection which it is hard to verify by experiment.

The four-term analogy where it is only the relation of A to B that is declared to be identical with that between C and D, and A and C or B and D are otherwise dissimilar (Pitt is to Addington as London is to Paddington), is called the analogy of proportionality, while the analogy of attribution is that which exists between two subjects in respect of a quality which both possess in different ways, or in respect of an end to which both are somehow directed by different paths, or the like ; but in every case the nature of things, and not merely the human apparatus of knowing, is affected by the analogy. This analogy needs no more than three terms. Thus existence is predicated of God and of creatures, and it belongs to both. The difference in the manner of this belonging appears as soon as one considers that God is, by identity, His own existence, while every creature is somehow in receipt of its existence from another. If one is thus inclined to prefer the Platonic strain in Scholasticism to the Aristotelian, and to set the three-term analogy of attribution before the four-term analogy of proportionality, it has to be acknowledged that not all theologians are content to do the same, and that a vigorous championship of the analogy of proportionality is still maintained by many.

Bonaventure (2 Sent. d. 16 : art. 1 : qu. 1) made a fourfold classification of analogies : (a) analogy by complete agreement, as between the persons of the Trinity ; (b) analogy by participation of one and the same generic nature, as that of man and donkey in the nature of animal ; (c) analogy of proportionality, where there is agreement of two relationships such as those of charioteer and helmsman in respect of what they guide ; (d) analogy by *convenientia ordinis* (or orderly agreement), as when a copy depends upon its exemplar. In this grouping it is clear that the analogy of attribution has been split up, now forming classes b and d, the one requiring a theory of participation of being and the other one of exemplar causality, both of which are thoroughly Platonic. Bonaventure rejected type b as not being a proper statement of the analogy between God and creatures, since the participation of being is there not so absolute as to require Pantheism and being is not a genus. He looked on type c as being an analogy of action rather than one of being, but allowed that both c and d were valid for application to the problem of God and creatures. Today, when the Barthians will admit an analogy of action but deny one of being, it is of interest to consider the distinction which Bonaventure laid down, and it may be that in his work there could be found the means of satisfying the Barthians.

VI Analogy in St Thomas. St Thomas did not take over the classification of Bonaventure nor did he anywhere elaborate a theory of analogy, but here and there in his writings at various times he made statements about analogy out of which his followers have constructed more or less tidy theories of analogy for themselves. The difficulty here is that only in the very recent past has it been possible to put the works of St Thomas into anything like an accurate time-series, and so in most of the theories no account has been taken of the possibility that he may have changed his mind as he grew older. A *locus classicus* from the early works of St Thomas is found in *Quaestiones de veritate* 2:11 (from *c.* 1257). Here St Thomas does seem to reject all analogy of attribution and to confine himself to proportionality alone. He is examining the relationship between God's knowledge and ours. 'No creature has such a definite relationship to God as by it a divine perfection can be defined.' Thus analogy of attribution is rejected in favour of proportionality. But even here, not every four-term relationship is calculated to inform us about God. When it is said that God is the sun of the universe (as He was for the Platonist) in that He stands to the universe as the sun to material creation, there is a flaw in the statement, for matter is of the essence of the sun's relationship and cannot be essential to God. As appears from the reply here (@6) St Thomas is concerned to deny a real definability of God in terms of creatures, but he is not elaborating in a positive way how he thinks that a four-term analogy can deliver to us knowledge of God that is better than mere equivocation. It is true that in the four-term proportion of the mathematician the relationship of the one side to the other remains the same however great are the ratios on either side. Does this mean that he would have us construct such a four-term proportion for God and creatures, so that God would be said to be related to His existence as creatures are to theirs ? From the time of Cajetan many have accepted such an implication in the statement ; but the difficulty that arises for them then is that the relationship between the two sides of the proportion is by no means the same, for God is His existence by absolute identity, while creatures have to receive theirs from another. The more real the composition is in creatures, the less true does the relationship become. A clue to the mind of St Thomas at this period is provided by a cancellation in the autograph of his commentary on Boethius, *de Trinitate* (*c.* 1257-8) (Decker's edition 223), where he dealt with our knowledge of spiritual substances and wrote these words : *Habemus de eis aliquam confusam cognitionem quid est*, and then cancelled the last five words, substituting for them *loco cognitionis quid est, cognitionem per negationem, per causalitatem et per excessum.* Thus he wavered from the idea that we know something of the essence of these realities to the idea that we have to approach them by the threefold path of negation, causality and extrapolation.

St Thomas did not entirely expel from his system the idea of participation, as the work of Geiger, Fabro, de Finance and Little has shown. Thus in this early period (in *Quaestiones de Veritate* 18:2:@5, from *c.* 1259) he still hankers after it. 'Created being is darkness, he says, in so far as it comes from nothing, but in so far as it comes from God, it shares in His likeness and so leads us towards assimilation to Him.' Later, in the period of the *Summa* (from 1266 onwards), he will admit (*Summa* 1:13:5c and 1:16:6c) that where two realities are causally linked, predicates that belong to both (as healthy does to medicine and to the animal that is cured by it and to the urine that is a sign of health) denote that there is something present in both cause and sign in virtue of which one is justified in applying the predicate to them as well as to the reality to which it primarily belongs. It is more a question here of some analogy of attribution than of a system of relations with four terms in which the only likeness to be found would be that between the relations and the terms would be unlike. An internal linkage of dependence in being seems here to be required rather than what is called an extrinsic denomination. At the end of *Summa contra Gentiles* 1:33 (which belongs to 1261) he explains how creaturely predicates can belong to God : ' If by such predicates we know of God only what He is not, e.g. if He is called living only because He does not belong to the inanimate order, then it will be necessary at least to say that the predicate living when used of God and creatures has a common meaning in its being a denial to both subjects of what is inanimate, and thus it will not be an equivocal term.' If this reasoning were extended to the predicate ' being ', it would then have to be said that God and creatures share the one predicate of being in so far as by it they are both opposed to not-being or to nothingness, and this common element in predication saves the term from pure equivocation. This was, in fact, the conclusion drawn by Suarez out of St Thomas, but he was helped thereto by what he learnt from Fonseca and the Aristotelians of Coimbra of the difficulties they found with the explanations of Cajetan.

The reason why St Thomas in his middle period (1258–64) seems to deny that we have any knowledge at all of God's essence may be found in his reading of the pseudo-Denis *On the Divine Names*, a work which he commented on *c.* 1260. He begins by noting that in this work its use of Platonic phrases causes difficulty. He does his best to interpret it in a thoroughly Christian fashion, but he still leaves intact (e.g. ch. 7, lectio 4) the purely Plotinian idea that the highest knowledge of God to which men can attain is by some manner of contact with the divine which is quite beyond the range of mind in its ordinary working.[1] For the ordinary knowledge of God (by the three ways) he has a careful regard, but even here the negative way is emphasized. ' We can attach predicates to God in virtue of the remote likeness there is between creatures and God, but we can deny them of God and predicate their opposites by reason of His super-excellence '[2] (ch. 1, lectio 1). Again (in ch. 7, lectio 4) he says

that we deny wisdom of God because He exceeds all our wisdom. Yet even so St Thomas does not call God a super-cause. He says that whatever exists in creatures proceeds from God as from a cause, and that God by His very being is the efficient and final cause of all that is, in that all things flow out from and are drawn to Him.[3]

This leaning on Denis was a mark of his earlier and less mature thought. Thus in the very early commentary on the Sentences (1 Sent. 8:1:1:@4, from before 1257) he has borrowed a detailed account of how the soul enters the cloud of unknowing by stages. First the corporeal predicates and metaphors must be done away, next the intellectual attributes must be denied of Him, as when He is said to be without wisdom and goodness because of His excess thereof. Being alone remains, then, and the mind grows confused. Finally being is itself removed and the groping mind enters into its learned nescience. Commenting on Boethius, *de Trinitate* (1:2:@1, from 1257–8), he maintains the same idea : ' The mind is then most perfect in its knowledge of God when it ascertains that His essence is above all that can be apprehended in this earthly condition, and thus while what God is remains unknown, the knowledge that He is can be achieved.'[4]

To say that God's essence is totally unknown did not seem to St Thomas to be dangerous, as he had something like this in John Damascene (PG 94:798), whom he quotes in *Quaestiones de Potentia* (7:5:@1, from 1265). He adds the comment that God's being is unknown but we know the fact of His existence when we frame the proposition ' God exists ', making use of His effects to do so. He still depends on the pseudo-Denis, who is quoted (PG 3:142) in the same context as saying that only negative attributes are true of God, His positive attributes being incomprehensible (*incompacta*). St Thomas takes the sting out of this statement by saying at once that we deny of God the *modus significandi* when we predicate positive attributes of Him while the *res significata* is true of Him all the time. The term *incompacta* is then taken to mean ' not quite properly connected ' (*non omnino convenienter coniuncta*) and further passages from Denis are adduced (PG 3:594, 635, 979–82) where wisdom is said to be in God since there is in Him some pattern of the wisdom that flows to us from Him, though He may be called not-wise in that He has not wisdom after our fashion ; or better, He can be styled super-wise, for the negation is not meant to remove all wisdom from Him but only to indicate His non-creaturely wisdom. Created wisdom must then be said to represent divine wisdom *aliqualiter et deficienter*, in a poor sort of way, and the final solution is that there cannot be a perfect definition of God, even though

[1] Est alia perfectissima cognitio . . . per unitionem quamdam ad divina, supra naturam mentis.
[2] Secundum quod aliqualis similitudo creaturarum est ad Deum . . . ; secundum quod creaturae deficiunt a repraesentatione Dei, nomina a nobis imposita a Deo removeri possunt et opposita eorum praedicari.

[3] Propterea removemus ab Eo sapientiam quia omnem sapientiam excedit. . . . Quidquid est in creaturis procedit a Deo sicut a causa.
[4] Mens in Dei cognitione tunc perfectissime invenitur quando cognoscitur Eius essentiam esse supra omne id quod apprehendere potest in statu huius viae ; et sic, quamvis maneat ignotum quid est, scitur tamen quia est.

the attributes which the human mind predicates of Him are true of Him.[1]

In the following *Quaestio* (*de Potentia* 7:6) he considers the simplicity of God's essence alongside the multiplicity of these attributes. Can it be, he asks, that when we say that God is good we mean no more than that He exists and causes goodness? This would be very strange, he replies. What we mean is that God has goodness or wisdom, besides being the cause of them in us. If this were not true, we could say that God is the sky, since He causes that too, but we do not. The power God has of producing good or wise creatures is not totally alien, but is a superlative likeness of the effects themselves (in virtue of the principle that like produces like). But is there an exact correspondence of attribute in God and created perfection in man? No, the relation is that of one to many, as each attribute conveys to us only an imperfect likeness of God. Perfect understanding would do away with this multiplicity. Bringing in revelation at the last, St Thomas adds: 'The Word of God is one and not many, for the Word is the perfect likeness of God.

In the next question (*de Potentia* 7:7) he explains that the likeness of God cannot be produced univocally in creatures because of the infinite distance between the two. He denies that exemplarity gives ground for such a predication, instancing the fact that the design of a house in the mind of its planner and that design worked out in bricks and mortar do not warrant univocal predication about the house as such. But on the other hand he will not accept that the names of God are applied by pure equivocation to creatures, as Maimonides held, for that would be pure agnosticism and would deny that cause and effect are somehow sharers in a relation of likeness. Between univocal and equivocal predication he then considers it right to insert analogical. But what type of analogy does he appeal to? Penido has taken this text as the final choice by Aquinas of the analogy of proportionality, appealing to the words: 'A different relationship to being makes impossible the univocal predication of being; now God is differently related to being (*esse*) than is any creature, for He is His own being, a property that belongs to no creature.' Lyttkens, however, points out that the object of the passage is 'to reject a complete likeness, not to prove an analogy. We therefore maintain that the causal relation is not stated of God extrinsically but is in fact the fundamental reason why our names of God indicate His essence' (*op. cit.* 300). It is true that St Thomas here seems to deny the value of exemplarity as a basis for his analogy, but if he did so, he would not then be consistent in harking back thereafter to the likeness of effect to cause. As so often, one must find from elsewhere in his work the qualifications that are to be introduced into his apparently categoric and unguarded statements. It is also clear that the argumentation is somewhat artificial here, since it is assumed that

[1] Quodlibet istorum nominum significat divinam substantiam, non tamen quasi comprehendens ipsam sed imperfecte.

agnosticism is ruled out, and the analogy that is being considered is rather the downcast analogy than the upcast, whereas it is on this last that we depend in our attempts to find God.

St Thomas never quite absorbed the theory of Avicenna that God had no essence, but he went some way to admitting that, if He had, it was unknowable. In his later development he moved away from this position and made room for a more positive knowledge of God. He can be seen towards the end of *contra Gentiles* (3:41-6, from *c.* 1264) rejecting Arabian attempts to show that the soul of man had direct knowledge in this life of angels and separate substances, but he was ready then to allow that the soul had some awareness of its own acts, so that its attribution of intellect and will to these substances, after some kind of analogy with its own, was not unfounded. But in the *Summa* (1a:13:3: @1-2, from 1266) he will allow that predicates, such as good, living and being are properly applied to God. In the next *quaestio* he elaborates this (1a:14:1c and @1) by pointing out that freedom from matter is the root of the power of knowing, and that God, as supremely free from matter, is therefore the most fully possessed of this power. The manner of knowing is different in God and in creatures (so that one cannot now maintain a four-term proportion stating that God is to His knowledge as man is to his), for in God knowledge is not a quality nor a disposition but the very substance of His being and pure act. Plato comes back (in 1a:16:6c) now, for it is laid down that all things have ontological truth according as they derive from the one primary truth which is God. The Platonic ideas, now located in the divine mind, are made use of to help out the analogy of truth.

A difficulty had troubled St Thomas from his early days, since the sense-bound character of human knowledge seems to debar us from all valid predication of spiritual attributes about God (4 Sent. 49:2:7: @12, from *c.* 1254-6), and it is not solved until his latest period, when (*c.* 1270) he is dealing with the *Ethics* of Aristotle. The best life for man is there said to be the life of contemplation, lived according to the divine in man (1177a 13-17). In 1177b 26-33 this life is said to be more than human, being in some way divine, and man is encouraged by Aristotle to play the immortal as far as he may. In his comment St Thomas (in *Eth. Nicom.* lib. 10, lectio 11) says that life on the intellectual level is compared to the moral life as divine is to human. On that level man lives not as man but according as his intellect participates in the divine likeness. God-like reason is thus not a sense-bound calculating machine; it has a life of its own on a higher plane. It was the novelty of St Thomas that he made the divine illumination of the human intellect a natural operation and not the work of grace (*see* LIGHT, METAPHYSIC OF). He could therefore claim that this divine illumination made possible a knowledge of God that was hardly proper for a sense-bound human soul, but which was none the less strictly natural. No wonder after this that Roger Marston and other

Oxford contemporaries of St Thomas began the cry that Friar Thomas was a Pelagian.

In one of his latest works, the *Compendium theologiae* (ch. 27), that was unfinished at his death, St Thomas gives a final glimpse of the way in which he views analogy. Predicates are taken from created things and are attributed to God, and these are neither equivocal nor univocal. 'They are attributed to God according as He has a certain order towards these things. . . . They are predicated by analogy, that is according to their relation to one thing.' Narcissus sees in the pool not himself but the Face that is looking over his shoulder. There is no question here of the likeness of two relations, and so none of proportionality, but of the order of the several things possessing the predicate to the one original possessor of it. The signs are that St Thomas was becoming more confident as he grew older that he could discern some natural likeness between the being of man and of God. In *Summa* (1a:93:2c) he speaks more firmly about the image of God in man than he did in the days when he was more swayed by the pseudo-Denis. His commentary on the *Metaphysics* of Aristotle (from 1271-2) shows that, while accepting that being is not a genus (bk. 3, lectio 8), he makes it clear that he regards the identity that is asserted in the act of predication as resting upon some agreement of subject and predicate (bk. 5, lectio 9). Now where predication is concerned with absolute identity (as in the proposition : God is), the mind throws this identity into the form of a relation in order to give it expression, even though there is no relation there in reality. He finds the justification for this procedure in the fact that while there cannot be an infinite regress in real relations (for if the relation by which a thing was identical with itself was a real relation, then there could be a relation between this first relation and the thing itself, and so on *ad inf.*), there is no difficulty in allowing such a regress in the operation of the mind, for the mind can reflect upon its own act, and then upon this act of reflection, and so on, without any viciousness in the regress. Thus St Thomas has based the truth of the existential judgment that God exists upon the ordinary operation of the mind in its acts of predicating unities about created and composite things, but he does not seem to have gone into the question of the connection between the two activities. Had he done so, his theory of analogy of being would have been made much more definite than it ever became in his works.

VII. The later Scholastics. The attempts made after the death of St Thomas to fill the gaps he had left in the theory are perhaps the best proof of its incompleteness at his death. Duns Scotus accepted the great innovation of St Thomas about the illumination of the human intellect, but he made of being an univocal concept, though allowing that the modalities of finitude and infinity made God and creatures at once unlike (*primo diversa*) and broke up the unity that the concept had precariously established. This would mean (according to a modern Scotist, E. Bettoni, in *International Congress*

of Philosophy 3 (1953) 121-3) that there was no analogy in things but only in concepts, and that what was *in actu primo* an univocal concept of being becomes *in actu secundo* a multiple concept. Scotus is a pioneer in thus calling in psychology to help out metaphysics, and his change from confused univocal concept to clear but disseveral concepts goes down to Henry of Harclay and many more in the sequel. Scotus says in one place (*Collationes* 3) that being is univocal but not a genus, and again that things equivocal as realities are modally univocal,[1] but what he meant by that is not clear ; even his greatest disciple, Maurice O'Fihely, was not sure whether he denied analogy or not, and some of his followers were able to discern in his writings as many as four distinct kinds of univocal predication. His introspective turn of mind made him take more kindly to the conceptual side of the theory of analogy, to the depreciation of the metaphysical, and he made things harder by his refusal to present a tidy theory where he was not convinced that the reality to be presented in the theory was itself tidy.

Henry of Harclay (d. 1317) did not follow Scotus the whole way, but was ready to argue that when philosophers prove that God exists the word 'exists' either stood for a concept common to God and creatures or it did not ; if it did, then there was an univocal concept of existence or being ; if it did not, then existence cannot belong to creatures alone (for then it could not be applied to God) or to God alone (for then the proposition becomes, God is God, and this does not need saying), and so there is no solution that way either. The way out for Harclay was to say that, as Scotus asserted, there was a confused univocal concept, and that a progress from confused to distinct took place in the use of this concept, so that there was a link between God and creatures in the realm of knowing if not in that of being. He denied that there was any bond of being (*communitas in re*) for God and creatures, but allowed that there was likeness, so that when one thought of God as being, this real relation of likeness was there to substantiate the thought. He held too that the relation was mutual and so that it was real on both sides. Ockham (whose commentary on the *Sentences* appeared in 1318) was somewhat to the left of Harclay, being still a conceptualist rather than a nominalist in his theory of knowledge. Nothing, he said, that is really existing in created being (i.e. outside the mind) except perhaps a spoken word, can by any manner of abstraction or stripping-down be attributed to God ; all that can be predicated of Him and of creatures in common is a concept, which exists in neither of them.[2] The image of God in man then becomes no more than this, that if *per impossibile* wisdom, love and such attributes were accidents in God, the human soul would have accidents of the

---

[1] Aequivoca ut quid sunt univoca ut modus.
[2] Nihil quod est realiter in creatura (extra animam) nisi forte vox per nullam separationem vel ablationem potest Deo attribui sed tantum attribuitur sibi et creaturae unus conceptus qui nec est in Deo nec in creatura (extra) quamvis de utroque praedicatur. (Ordinatio 2:9.)

same genus. But as God is wisdom in a much higher way, man can *somehow* be called wise or loving. This is not very encouraging to one who is looking for the image of God in man, but Ockham will still admit (3 *Sent.* 9) a difference between calling God a rock and calling Him wise ; one is a metaphor, the other is not. His distinction of intentional equivocation (as in analogical predication) from chance equivocation (*Quodlibet* 4:16) shows how far he had moved from the view of analogy taken by his predecessors.

Cajetan, in opposition to the prevailing Scotist system which he had encountered at Padua in the teaching of O'Fihely and Trombetta, went back to what he understood to be the Thomist theory of analogy. He classified analogies according as they were in thought, in reality, or in both. Every genus was predicated analogically of its inferiors, and this was an analogy in being, but one of inequality, since not all the inferiors shared the genus equally. Analogy of attribution was in thought alone, for here the predication was of some character that belonged to one subject alone but which was secondarily predicable of another subject by reason of its relation to the first. A medicine might properly be called healthy, but the colour of the patient after he had taken it might also be called healthy in a secondary way, by attribution. Finally there was the analogy of proportionality, with two varieties, one a metaphor and the other the real analogy. The smile on the face of the tiger was metaphorical, but corporeal and intellectual vision were linked by a real analogy of proportionality, since just as sight presented an object to a sensitive being, so did understanding present an object to the perceiving mind. Metaphors belong to the mind alone, but true proportionality belongs to reality and to mind at the same time. Some modern Thomists, such as Manser, follow the system of Cajetan. The one deviation that Cajetan permitted himself from the Thomist position as he understood it was to say that the relations on either side of the proportion were not identical but similar. This change may have been due to the influence of Averroes (Averroes *metaph.* 12, textus 28), for the revived Aristotelianism which Cajetan had met at Padua had much of Averroes in it. The chief modern objection to this system is that only God could use such an analogy and He does not need it. Some Thomists answer that the analogy is one of being not of knowing, but this is to depart from Cajetan himself.

Francis Sylvester of Ferrara started another line of interpretation, claiming that (*contra Gentiles* 1:34) St Thomas had combined analogy of attribution with that of proportionality in order to strengthen man's endeavour to know God. There was, he said, a quasi-analogy of attribution at the heart of the analogy of proportionality, and thus, however infinitely remote from us God's essence might be, it remained true that there was a relation between essence and existence on both sides of the proportion. By attribution we knew *that* being is in God, but *what* that being was we did not know at all, simply conceiving that in the Great Other there was being. The objection put by Bochenski and others to an unsupported analogy of proportionality is that in it the common element in both relations is purely formal, consisting in the isomorphy of those relations, and this gives no new knowledge. Thus we might know that essence and existence in creatures was related in a certain way, but all that we could know about the other side of the proportion would be that God's essence and existence, if there were such entities, were related in God's way, whatever that might be. But if from attribution it can be ascertained that every essence is somehow united with an existence, then the parallelism of relations can be of more use to us. It is essential to this view that man has no real knowledge of the essence of God. This was certainly the view taken by St Thomas in what has been called above his middle period (and it is a work from this period, the *contra Gentiles*, that Sylvester was commenting upon), but the later period of St Thomas showed him moving away from such a position. He even (in *Summa* 1a:14:3:@2) uses proportionality to argue that God is finite to Himself, and that as created being does not go beyond the capacity of created intellect, so the divine being does not go beyond the capacity of the mind of God. Here was a statement about the essence of God which, though reached by negative and analogical ways, did convey some information about God. Again (in *Quaestiones de Potentia* 7:5c) he says quite clearly, and at a date that is later than the *contra Gentiles*, that attributes drawn from creatures such as wisdom and goodness really do denote the nature of God, even though imperfectly, while the name ' He who is ' belongs most properly to God as it does not denote any particular attribute but signifies being in general.[1]

The Suarezian analogy was that of attribution alone, and this was, against Cajetan, claimed to be intrinsic, in the sense that there was a real similarity in being between God and creatures, not just a fancied similarity that would be ground for no more than metaphorical predication. Yet this similarity did not lead to a Pantheist view of reality as if it was founded every way upon internal relations (*disputationes metaphysicae* 2:6). He revived the notion of confused and clear concepts of being, from Scotus, agreeing also that God and creatures are *primo diversa*, but going on to say that the similarity between them is real. In *Disp. metaph.* 28:3:14 he analyses the idea of attribution, distinguishing a proper sense of intrinsic attribution from all merely extrinsic denomination. The reason for saying that creatures and God are connected by an analogy of intrinsic attribution is that they are beings by participation of that reality which is God's by essence. Every creature is a being by virtue of some participation or imitation of the being of God, depending for its

---

[1] Quodlibet istorum nominum significat divinam substantiam, non tamen quasi comprehendens ipsam sed imperfecte ; et propter hoc, nomen Qui est maxime Deo competit, quia non determinat aliquam formam Deo sed significat esse indeterminate.

being upon God much more than accidents depend upon substance. Accidents are not ultimately defined in terms of substance as to their being, though they may be so defined at first view. Thus Plato is brought in to save Aristotle, and the strictly Aristotelian theories of Fonseca and the men of Coimbra were modified to meet the difficulties of Cajetan.

VIII The modern debate about analogy. This may be said to have begun with a work by Sertillanges in 1906–8. In controversy with M. Gardair he wished to stress the freedom of Scholastic thought from anthropomorphic concepts of the godhead (*see* ANTHROPOMORPHISM) and said that there was a healthy agnosticism about the Thomist theory of analogy. In the analogy of proportionality—which he upheld as the one proper to the case—there was a similarity between the two relations, of essence and existence in man and in God, even though God's essence was strictly identical with His existence and man's was not, and even though we knew only the existence of God and nothing of His essence. This position was thought by some to go too far in the direction of agnosticism, and many Thomists were moved to take part in the ensuing debate, restating the original theory of analogy to meet the new difficulties. The view of Sylvester has many followers, e.g. abroad, Blanche and van Leeuwen, and in England, Fr Columba Ryan and E. Mascall. Descoqs is the best-known modern Suarezian, and he has influenced Patterson and Lyttkens along with a number of German writers. Cajetan has comparatively few followers now, though Gredt and Phillips follow Cajetan as explained by John of St Thomas. As so often, there are two questions inextricably involved. What did St Thomas think, and what is the true analogy to be called? No one hitherto has tried to put the opinion of St Thomas in its historical sequence of development, nor was this until recently possible, and it may be hoped that the attempt so to present it here will help towards the solution of the other question, by enabling other thinkers to carry on the lines of development from the position which St Thomas had reached at the end of his life.

Man does not need to enter a cloud of unknowing in order to know something of God. What he has by nature may be only a bat's eye-view, but it is his by nature and not something supplied to him by the grace of God; it is not the product of a divine *Seelenfunklein* within him, as Eckhart dreamed (D 510, 527), but the groping of his very own reason towards the God whose image it bears. The human mind, since the days of Leibniz, has elaborated a whole science of the order of small quantities in mathematics; with no less right does it elaborate its science of God, and by the use of procedures which bear some comparison with those of the Leibnizian calculus.

What may perhaps be of no small moment in attempting to bring back into English thought the theory of analogy is the fact that there was in the past an extensive discussion of its problems by English writers from Archbishop King and Bishop Browne in the 18th cent. to the debate between Copleston and Grinfield (1821–2). Berkeley was a defender of analogy and wrote : ' This doctrine of analogical perfection in God, or our knowing God by analogy, seems very much misunderstood and misapplied by those who would infer from thence that we cannot frame any direct or proper notion, though never so inadequate, of knowledge or wisdom as they are in the Deity, or understand any more of them than one born blind can of light or colour.' (*Alciphron* dialogue 4, ch. 21.)

Bibliography. The traditional sources are sufficiently set forth in the text of the article. Here the modern writers will be given.

P. Grenet, *Les Origines de l'analogie philosophique dans les dialogues de Platon* (1948) ; *A. R. Lacey, ' A passage in Epinomis 990 D ', *Phronesis* I (1956) 81–104 ; C. Baeumker, *Der Platonismus im Mittelalter* (1916) ; G. Söhngen, ' Die neuplatonische Scholastik und Mystik der Teilhabe bei Plotin ', in *Philosophisches Jahrbuch* 49 (1936) 98–120 ; *M. Horten, *Des Averroes Metaphysik* (1912) ; G. M. Manser OP, *Das Wesen des Thomismus* (1949) ; T. L. Penido, *Le Rôle de l'analogie dans la théologie dogmatique* (1931) ; J. Habbel, *Die Analogie zwischen Gott und Welt nach Thomas von Aquin* (1928) ; B. Landry, *La Notion d'analogie chez s. Bonaventure et s. Thomas* (1922) ; L. Geiger OP, *La Participation dans la philosophie de S. Thomas* (1942) ; *H. Lyttkens, *The analogy between God and the world* (1952) ; G. B. Phelan, *St Thomas and Analogy* (1948) ; *D. Emmet, *The nature of metaphysical thinking* (1946) ; *R. L. Patterson, *The Conception of God in the Philosophy of Aquinas* (1933) ; E. Przywara SJ, *Analogia Entis* (1932) ; A. Breuer, *Der Gottesbeweis bei Thomas und Suarez* (1929) ; F. A. Blanche OP, ' La Notion d'analogie dans la philosophie de S. Thomas ', RSPT 10 (1921) 169–93 ; A. Gardeil OP, ' La Structure analogique de l'intellect ', RT 32 (1927), 3–19 ; A. Marc SJ, ' L'Idée thomiste de l'être ', RNS 35 (1933) 158–64 ; A. van Leeuwen SJ, ' L'Analogie de l'être ', RNS 39 (1936) 293–320 ; 469–96 ; C. de Moré-Pontgibaud SJ, ' Sur l'analogie des noms divins ', RSR 19 (1929) 481–512 ; J. Santeler SJ, ' Die Lehre von der Analogie des Seins ', ZKT 55 (1931) 1–43 ; M. Grabmann, ' Die Schrift *de ente et essentia* und die Seinsmetaphysik des hl. Thomas ', in *Mittelalterliches Geistesleben* I, 314–31 ; K. Feckes, ' Das Opusculum *de ente et essentia* ', in *Grabmann Festschrift* (1935) ; I. M. Bochenski OP, ' On Analogy ', in *The Thomist* 11 (1948) 442–50 ; J. Le Rohellec, ' De fundamento metaphysico analogiae ', in *Divus Thomas* (Piacenza) 29 (1926) 77–101 ; H. MacDonagh OFM, ' La Notion d'être dans la métaphysique de Duns Scot ', RNS 30 (1928) 400–17 ; 31 (1929) 81–96, 148–81 ; T. Barth OFM, ' De fundamento univocationis apud Scotum ', *Antonianum* 14 (1939) 181–206, 277–98, 375–92 ; A. Maurer, ' Henry of Harclay on Univocity of Being ', *Med. St.* 16 (1954) 1–18 ; F. Pelster SJ, ' Heinrich von Harclay und seine Quaestionen ', in *Miscellanea F. Ehrle* (1924) 1:307–56 ; C. Shircel, *Univocity of*

Being in Scotus (1942) ; M. C. Menges, *Univocity in Ockham* (1952) ; J. F. Anderson, *The Bond of Being* (1949) ; *E. Mascall, *Existence and Analogy* (1949) ; C. Ryan OP, 'God and Analogy', Blackfriars 25 (1944) 137–43 ; P. Descoqs SJ, *Institutiones Metaphysicae generalis* (1926) ; A. Goergen, *Cajetans Lehre von der Analogie* (1938) ; J. Lappe, *Nicolaus de Autricuria* (1908) ; E. Gilson, *Being and some Philosophers* (1952²) ; J. Moreau, 'L'Etre et l'essence chez Aristote', in *Autour d'Aristote* (1955) 180–204 ; G. Klubertanz SJ, 'The Problem of the Analogy of Being', in *Review of Metaphysics* 10 (1957) 553–79 ; R. Bauer, *Gotteserkenntnis bei Kajetan* (1955) ; B. Gundersen, *Cardinal Newman and Apologetics* (1952) ; R. P. Phillips, *Modern Thomistic Philosophy* (1935) ; J. Gredt OSB, *Elementa Philosophiae Scholasticae* (1953).

J. H. C.

ANAPHORA The Greek term meaning ' offering ' was early used (Origen in *Ioan.* 6:13 ; GCS 161) for what is now called the Mass. It was taken over into Syriac (*annaphūra*, synonymous with *kurbōno* and *kurōbho*), into Coptic (*anafora*) and Ethiopic ('*enfora*, parallel with *keddase* = the holy thing). In Latin *illatio* was used as an equivalent (as in Isidore, *de officiis* 1:15, and the Mozarabic liturgies) and in Irish the word was *aifrenn*. The name implies an elementary theology of what happens at the Mass and also shows what was considered the essence of the Mass. The epistle of James of Edessa (cited by Brightman, *Eastern liturgies* 492) says that the priest ' supplicates for the descent of the Holy Ghost and afterwards he also makes the commemorations, and thus concludes the *kurōbho* '. What followed (the *pax*, the *Pater noster*, the *sancta sanctis* and the communion) was considered to be outside the *anaphora*. Amalarius supplies the other limit of the *anaphora* with the remark that the canon begins at *sursum corda*. The *Apostolic Constitutions* (2:59:4) also exclude the communion from the *anaphora*. Thus the views of modern moral theologians about the limits of the obligation of hearing Mass could be supported —or weakened—by reference to the tradition of early times.

The Byzantine liturgy has kept two anaphoras for use, the Coptic and Chaldaic three, the Armenian one (though fourteen were known at an earlier time), the Ethiopic twenty and the Syriac eighty. The uniform Canon of the Latin Mass, with its variable *Preface* and *Hanc igitur*, represents a compromise of a different kind between fixity and variety. The Council of Ancyra (canon 2) of 314 forbade to deacons the act described as *anapherein*. Nicaea (canon 18) and Laodicea (canon 58) use the term *prosphora*, which is also used in Serapion's prayer-book.

The word *illatio* in the sense of ' offering a sacrifice ' seems to have been a distinctive Christian-Latin usage, for the ordinary meaning of the word was that of ' burial ' or ' bringing in a contribution ' to a tax or to a court, or else the ' tendering ' of an oath. It would therefore seem to have been consciously chosen (in Spain, Gaul and Ireland) to express what

the Mass was about. Argument made by the Reformers and later adopted by the Jansenists (D 1528) to show that communicants other than the minister himself were essential to the eucharistic liturgy passed over this early evidence.

Bibliography. RAC s.v. *anaphora*; *F. Brightman, *Liturgies Eastern and Western* I (1896) ; A. Raes SJ, *Anaphorae Syriacae* (1939–61) ; *W. Frere, *The Anaphora* (1938). J. H. C.

ANATHEMA. *See* NOTES, THEOLOGICAL

ANCESTOR WORSHIP Some kind of belief in survival after death is very general, but the attitudes of the living to the dead vary widely. Ancestor cults are usually distinguished from other cults of the dead in so far as each line of descendants of a given ancestor forms a distinct ritual community. The religious congregation is recruited by birth, defined by descent and set apart from other similar congregations derived from other ancestors.

The beliefs and cult practices vary considerably. Often, as in China, the cult is an extension of filial piety : the dead are thought to be dependent on the living for support, and the living hope for providential care from the ancestors. In many parts of the world, in addition to the belief in their benevolent powers, there is fear of incurring their displeasure. Each dead man is commonly supposed to be concerned in the welfare of his own descendants. To some extent his interests are bound up with theirs, since the continuation of his cult depends on their numbers increasing, and on their solidarity not being broken by strife and separation. He is expected to confer fertility, to withhold it if his cult is neglected and to punish with misfortune such faults as quarrelsomeness between his descendants. He is not likely to punish offences they may commit against members of other descent-groups.

Generally the ancestors' powers of conferring and withdrawing health and prosperity are derived from a superior or supreme spiritual being to whom the dead have access. Ancestors mediate between living human beings and gods. Therefore the cult of ancestors, even in its most developed forms, is misnamed ' worship ' : ancestors are not gods so long as they are thought to retain their own identity after death ; if their identity is thought to be lost in that of a divine being, the cult associated with that being is not ancestor worship.

Ancestor cults are most likely to be highly developed among people whose social life is organised on the basis of lineal descent, so that the ritual community which unites to honour its ancestor is also a unit for other kinds of co-operation. The number of generations of ancestors honoured varies, partly according to the genealogical depth of lineages which is normal in the society in question, and partly according to the existence of aids to memory, such as written records, or an institution of professional historians. Royal dynasties tend to honour a longer list of individually named ancestors than do their subjects. If there is little development of lineage organization, only the most recently dead ancestors may be given individual recognition in ritual, as is the case among the Manus islanders of the Admiralty Group, who have a one-generation ancestor cult. On the other hand, the religion does not necessarily include an ancestor cult wherever lineal descent prevails.

In other cults of the dead the spirits of the dead are not thought of as the founders of distinct lines of descent, but as an undifferentiated collectivity of the dead of the whole community. For example, the sparsely scattered peoples of Central Africa pay respectful cult to the collective dead of each village whom they consult by oracles before any important undertaking ; the Trobriand Islanders of Melanesia believe in the annual friendly visitation of their dead in the course of their harvest festivals.

Finally, there are attitudes to the bad dead which are distinct from, and may exist side by side with, ancestral cults. These bad dead, who may have been marked out by the immorality of their lives, or by the unusual manner of their deaths, are thought not to have been admitted to the company of the ancestors. Such persons, anti-social in their life, are often thought to aid sorcerers or others wishing to use necromancy against their neighbours.

It should be said that ancestor cults may form a prominent or a quite minor part of the religious behaviour of the people who practise them. It is rare for them to comprise the whole religion, and more usual for them to be supplemented by other cults.

Ancestor cults are highly developed in Asia, especially in China and Japan, and also in South and West Africa. They are also found in Peru and among the Pueblo Indians of S.W. of North America. They are not characteristic of the aboriginal Indians of North America, nor of the Australian aborigines, and are very rare in Melanesia.

Bibliography. H. Callaway, *Religious System of the Amazulu* (1870) ; R. Fortune, *Manus Religion*, American Philosophical Society (1935) ; M. Freedman, *Lineage Organisation in South Eastern China*, L.S.E. Monographs in Social Anthropology, No. 18 (1958) ; M. Granet, *La Religion des Chinois* 2nd ed. (1953) ; J. J. M. de Groot, *The Religious System of China*, 6 vols (1892–1910) ; Denise Paulme, *Les Gens du Riz, Kissi de Haute-Guinée Française* (1954) ; P. Van Wing, *Études Bakongo*, II, 'Religion et magie', I.R.C.B., Bruxelles (1938) ; M. Fortes, *Oedipus and Job in West African Religion* (1959) ; M. Wilson, *Rituals of Kinship among the Nyakyusa* (1956).   M. D.

ANGELS This article gives (I) a synthesis of the Scripture theology of the Angels. (II) A description of the development in the Scripture witness and doctrine. (III) A discussion of the question of Angels and the Liturgy, with special relation to early tradition on the subject. (IV) A summary of Patristic theology concerning the Angels. (V) The present teaching of the Church concerning the Angels.

I A Synthesis of the Scripture Theology concerning Angels.

(i) *Their Name.* Most frequently they are referred to by the word ' angel ', which corresponds to the Greek and Hebrew words for ' messenger '. Only rarely is it used in Scripture for earthly messengers. Angels are, either explicitly or implicitly, ' angels (or messengers) of God ', or ' of the Lord '. At times they are angels of the Father, or Jesus, or of the Son of Man. In one place angels of the devil are mentioned (Mt 25:41). On one occasion the expression ' angel of light ' is used. The word ' spirit ' is occasionally used both for good angels (Heb 12:9 ; 1:14 ; Apoc 1:4 ; cf. 3:1 ; 4:5 ; 5:6), and for evil ones (Mt 12:43 ; Mk 1:23 ff.; 3:11 ff., and parallels; Ac 5:16 ; 8:7 ; etc.). Occasionally they are called ' sons of God ' (e.g. Job 1:6 ; 2:1 ; 38:7 ; Wis 5:5) ; ' holy ones ' (Job 5:1 ; 15:15 ; Ps 89:6 ; Dan 4:10, 14, 20 ; 8:13 ; Zach 14:5 ; Eccl 42:17 ; Wis 5:5). Individuals and groups are occasionally called by some other name, as ' prince ' (Dan 10:13, 20, 21 ; 12:1) ; the ' heavenly army ' or ' hosts ' (3 Kg 19:10 ; Jos 5:15 ; 2 Esd 9:6) ; ' principalities, powers, dominations ' (Eph 1:21 ; Col 1:16) ; ' virtues ' (Eph 1:2) ; ' thrones ' (Col 1:6) ; ' archangels ' (1 Thess 4:15) ; ' watchers ' (Dan 4:10, 14, 20). To these should be added the ' cherubim ' (Gen 3:24) and ' seraphim ' (Is 6:2) and ' living creatures ' (Ez 1 and Apoc 4, 5).

(ii) *The Existence and real Personality of the Angels.* The existence of a multitude of beings, superior to, and nearer to God than men, usually referred to as angels, is an essential part of the revelation which has come down to us through Jesus Christ and the prophets, and recorded in the Scriptures. They are spoken of as having heaven for their home (cf. Mt 18:10 ; 22:30 ; 28:2 ; Mk 12:25 ; 13:32 ; Lk 12:15 ; 22:43 ; Jn 1:51). Because the word ' angel ' connotes the privilege of being sent by God, St Augustine thinks this is their most glorious title.

Belief in angels is universal in the OT and NT. It is found in the oldest as well as the latest book of the Bible, and is reflected in every type of scripture literature. Angels are indeed regarded as inseparably bound up with each phase of God's actual plan for the salvation of mankind.

It is, moreover, not possible to dismiss this belief as conscious mythologizing or symbolizing of natural forces. The angels are given undeniable personal characteristics ; and their mission is frequently to individual persons or peoples.

(iii) *The Angel of the Lord.* There is, however, one group of passages, referring to the ' angel of the Lord ' or the ' angel of God ' in which the term appears, from the context, to apply to God Himself. This angel of the Lord, for instance, will in one place say, ' I am the God of Bethel ' (Gen 31:13) ; or ' I am the God of your fathers ' (Ex 3:2). People who have found themselves to have been visited by the ' angel of the Lord ' have considered that they have been in God's presence (Jg 6:22).

(iv) *The existence of angels not discoverable by*

natural means. Whatever is the true interpretation of the ' angel of the Lord ', other angels are superior beings who praise God in heaven, and are used by Him as messengers on earth. They are part of that world of faith, which is no less real to the Christian for all that it is invisible to our senses and undiscoverable by our reason. The initial unwillingness of many people outside the Church to accept the reality of the angelic world is due to this natural unverifiability, joined to preconceived notions as to their supposed unimportance for our salvation. Acceptance of their existence and importance will be in proportion to our readiness to prefer the facts of God's written word to any preconceived notions of Christianity.

(v) *The Nature of the Angels in Scripture.* In God's written word the vocation and functions of angels are given far more prominence than their nature. Of the latter we are told little beyond their superior gifts and their nearness to God. It is always high praise to say that a man is ' like an angel ' (cf. Gen 33:10 ; Heb 2:7). They have greater knowledge than human beings (cf. Mt 24:36 ; Apoc 4:6 ff., the living creatures full of eyes in front and behind). David is praised for having wisdom ' like the wisdom of an angel of God to know all things that are on the earth ' (2 Kg 14:20). Yet they do not know the hour of the judgment (Mk 13:32).

Angels are described as ' greater in strength and power ' than men (2 Pet 2:11 ; cf. Ps 103:20). They live in God's presence and form his court (Mt 18:10 ; Lk 12:8 ; Job 1:6 ; Tob 12:15). This is especially true of seven angels or spirits before God's throne (Apoc 1:4 ; 3:1 ; 4:5 ; 5:6 ; 8:2 ; Tob 12:15). Daniel sees thousands of them before God's throne (Dan 7:10 ; cf. Heb 12:22 ; Apoc 5:11 ; Gen 32:2). They form a heavenly army, with many legions (Lk 2:13 ; Mt 26:53).

The good angels' nearness to God is reflected in the reverence with which they are treated by those aware of their presence (Num 22:31 ; Jos 5:14, 15). Tobias and his family fell on the ground and worshipped God for several hours when they realized they had been in an angel's presence (Tob 12:10 ff.). Holiness is attributed to these good angels in a special way (Ps 89:7 ; Job 5:1 ; Dan 4:10, 14, 20 ; 8:13 ; Mk 8:38 ; Lk 9:26). Yet it is not forgotten that, as creatures, they must not be adored (Apoc 22:8 ff. ; Col 2:18). They, like ourselves, have the duty of worshipping God (Apoc 7:11 ; Is 6:3 ; Apoc 5:11, 12), and of praising and blessing Him (Ps 29:1 ; 103:20 ; 148:2 ; Is 6:3).

Their superior and invisible nature is sometimes expressed in the word ' spirit ' used both for good angels (Heb 12:9 ; 1:14 ; Apoc 1:4 ; cf. 3:1 ; 4:5 ; 5:6), and evil (Mt 12:43 ; Mk 5:2 ff. ; 9:16 ff., and parallels). Their spiritual nature is expressed negatively in a popular way in that they do not eat (Jg 13:16), neither marry nor are given in marriage (Mt 22:30 ; Mk 12:25), have no flesh and bones (Lk 24:39), and are not naturally visible as angels (Num 22:31).

They have free will, and have made their decision for or against God (cf Mt 25:41 ; 2 Pet 2:4 ; Jude 6 ; Apoc 12:7 ; 20:10).

(vi) *The Missions and Functions of the Angels, especially their relationship to Christ.* Angels are not introduced for their own sake but for their missions in regard to human beings. Certain angels watch over individual human beings either on special occasions (cf. Tob 5:5 ff. ; 12:14 ; Ac 12:15), or when God's children specially need them (Ps 91:11), or as special guardians through life to individual human beings (Mt 18:10).

Angels are frequently recorded as being sent as messengers of God's will or as announcers of specific acts of His salvific providence (cf. Gen 16:9 (Agar) ; 19:5 (Lot) ; Jg 6:14 (Gedeon) ; 4 Kg 1:3 (Elias) ; Lk 1:11 (Zachary) ; 1:26, 30, 35 (Mary) ; Mt 1:20 ; 2:13, 19 (Joseph) ; Ac 10:3 (Cornelius.)) They assist the apostles in their evangelic work (Ac 5:19 ; 8:16 (Philip) ; 12:7 ff. (Peter) ; 27:23 (Paul)).

They are assumed to have certain functions as intermediaries between God and man. It appears to have been angels that interpreted Daniel's dreams (Dan 7:16 ; 8:16 ; 9:21 ff.), and the vision of Zecharias (Zech 1:19 ff. ; 2:3 ff. ; 6:4 ff.). God spoke to the prophet Ezechiel through ' a man, whose appearance was like bronze ' (Ez 40:3 ff. ; 43:6 ff. ; 47:3 ff.). Angels are spoken of by Our Lord as carrying the poor man Lazarus to Abraham's bosom (Lk 16:22). They offer our prayers before God's throne (Tob 12:12). They rejoice over the conversion of the sinner (Lk 15:10). They are all ministering spirits sent to serve for the benefit of the redeemed (Heb 1:14).

Undoubtedly the noblest office given to the angels is their part in ministering to Jesus Christ. An angel had the privilege of announcing His coming (Lk 1:30 ff.). An angel gave the good news of His birth to the shepherds, and a multitude of angels was seen and heard singing the first hymn to Christ (Lk 2:9 ff.). An angel saved the divine infant from Herod (Mt 2:13), and told Joseph when it was safe to return to Nazareth (Mt 2:19). Angels ministered to Christ after His temptation in the desert (Mt 4:11). An angel came to strengthen Him during His agony (Lk 22:43). Angels came as Our Lord's messengers after the Resurrection and Ascension (Mt 28:2 ff. ; Mk 16:5 ff. ; Lk 24:5 ff. ; Ac 1:10 ff.). He could have had legions of angels, but preferred to act alone (Mt 26:53), since He was to redeem the world by the ' failure ' of the Cross rather than by a display of power.

In the OT angels are recorded as being God's ministers in punishing or protecting or in other ways applying the powers of nature for God's purposes. The angels who visited Lot protected the latter by striking with blindness his attackers, and afterwards declared that they would destroy the cities of Sodom and Gomorrah (Gen 19:11-12). An angel brought pestilence upon Jerusalem in punishment of David, and was about to destroy the city (2 Kg 24:15, 16). An angel slew 185,000 in the camp of the Assyrians (4 Kg 19:35). Newman thought that the thunders and lightnings and the sound of a trumpet on Mt

Sinai were brought about by angels, though the Scripture text does not say so (Ex 19:16 ff.).

Below, it is explained that NT teaching seems to take away from the angels these powers over nature as a result of the dominion given to Christ after His victorious Resurrection and Ascension. However, it would appear from the Apocalypse that angels (unless these are mere personifications) will again be ministers of God to produce natural portents at the end of the world. Four angels are seen by St John as holding back the four winds (Apoc 7:1), and these four angels will have power to harm after the sealing of the servants of God (Apoc 7:3). Angels will bring down hail and fire mixed with blood (Apoc 8). Angels have many other powers as ministers of God's justice (Apoc, chs 10 ff. and 14 ff.).

There is also recorded in the Apoc the great battle in heaven between Michael and the good angels, on the one side, and the great dragon, the ancient serpent, who is called the Devil and Satan, on the other (Apoc 12).

Examples of angelic activity not expressly connected with God's redemptive work are the cures at Bethsaida (Jn 5:4) and the striking of Herod (Ac 12:23).

Apart from this, angels are depicted as being concerned over our salvation (cf. the conversion of sinners, Lk 15:10). St Paul says that he is a spectacle to the world, angels and men (1 Cor 4:9).

At the Second Coming, angels will be closely associated with the Son of Man (Mt 25:31 ; 13:41 ; Mk 8:38 ; Lk 9:26). They will be associated with the judgment (Mt 25:31 ; Lk 12:8 ff. ; Apoc 14:6 ff.). Yet St Paul speaks of the saints judging angels (1 Cor 6:3). Other functions of the angels at the end of the world are mentioned in the Apoc 7 ff.).

The Apoc appears to give the angels a liturgical function in the praise of God in heaven (cf. Erik Peterson, Le Livre des anges, Préface de Jean Daniélou (1954)). For this see especially Apoc 4, 5 ; Is 6:2 ff. ; Heb 1:14.

There is evidence in the NT of a tradition that the angels had some part in the giving and in the maintaining of the Jewish Law (cf. St Stephen's speech in Ac 7:38, 53 ; also Gal 3:19 ; Heb 2:2 ; the LXX version of Dt 33:2 and Ps 68:18 ; cf. also Philo, De Somniis 1:141 [Cohn-Wendland 3:235] ; Josephus, Ant. 15:5, 3 ; Midrash on Exod ; Jubilees 1). The destroying angel (1 Cor 10:10) seems to have been one of those whose office it was to enforce the Law. It has been suggested that the covering of women's heads in church because of the angels (1 Cor 11:10) refers to the same office. It is clearly a part of St Paul's doctrine that Christ, in abolishing the Law, displaced the angels in their office as intermediaries.

But there is also evidence in St Paul that, before Christ, angels may have had certain cosmic powers. Some have thought to see such a doctrine as underlying our Lord's reference to the 'Prince of this World' (Jn 12:31 ; 14:30 ; 16:11), who is already judged and will be cast out. According to this view,

the devil would have had these cosmic powers before he fell, and began to abuse these powers after his fall. Christ's coming has taken away any angelic power that might be used against Him (Col 2:15 ; cf. Eph 2:2). Mgr Cerfaux thinks that some such view may underlie the thought of the Captivity Epistles : ' We could perhaps come near to Saint Paul's way of thinking by imagining that the Powers, undivided, jointly possess the world, good or bad. From among the Powers some are bound up with this erring world which is marked out for destruction : Christ's victory has forced them into submission. Others, who have a title in the world to come, have been faithful to their office of governing creation, and have the task of leading it to God by submitting themselves fully and freely to the kingdom of Christ.' (L. Cerfaux, Christ in the Theology of St Paul (1959) 106 ; cf. the whole section on ' The Kingdom of Christ and the Powers ', 98 ff. ; cf. also L. Cerfaux, The Church in the Theology of St Paul (1959) 338 ff.). The good angels, of course, rejoice to see Christ's triumph (1 Pet 1:12 ; 1 Tim 3:16). All of them are now subject to Christ (1 Pet 3:22 ff.).

The mystery of Christ's Body and of our salvation has only recently been made known to the angels (Eph 3:10 ; cf. Rom 11:33 ff.). Christ has been raised above all creation, including the angels (Phil 2:10 ff.), for He it was in whom they were created (Col 1:15 ff.). It is not clear whether the principalities and powers He disarmed and made a public example of (Col 2:15) embrace both good and evil angels, i.e. all who had dominion over this world, or only the evil angels who had tried to destroy His saving work.

Mgr Cerfaux thinks that it is certain that the angels are not now included in either the pleroma or the body of Christ. They are not then part of the Church. ' The Church always remains the new people of the elect, "the Christians", those who, whether Jews or pagans, are the heirs of Abraham, privileged recipients of the promise, forming the same "body" (σύσσωμα), Eph 3:6.' (L. Cerfaux, The Church in the Theology of St Paul (1959) 339.) But the same author recognizes that many exegetes, (including E.-B. Allo, ' L'Évolution de l'Évangile de Paul' in Vivre et penser, 1st series, 116 ff., cf. L. Cerfaux, op. cit. 340-1), have thought differently.

Incidentally, angels in the Scriptures, with the exception of the cherubim and seraphim and the living creatures of Ezechiel 1, are not represented with wings. Often they appear as men of exceptional appearance. The angels ascending and descending Jacob's ladder do not use wings. There is a common tradition to represent them as clothed in bright or white garments (Ac 10:30 ; Mt 28:3 ; Ac 1:10 ; Mk 16:5 ; cf. Apoc 4:4 ; 15:6 ; 19:14).

II Development in the Scripture Witness and Doctrine about the Angels. While it is true that the angels appear clearly in every part of the Bible as creatures, nearer to God than men, used by God in the natural and supernatural government of the world, there is without doubt a development in the revelation. In the pre-exilic period the doctrine appears in its simplest form. Angels are in great numbers, live in heaven, near to God, and are sent as messengers to men. They are sometimes called 'angels' or messengers, sometimes simply referred to as men. The principal development of this doctrine comes with the post-exilic period. The manner in which angels are described is influenced, on the one hand by popular Jewish religion, on the other hand by the religion of the neighbouring peoples. Together with a greater emphasis on God's transcendence comes a tendency to underline the angelic office of intermediary.

It is during the post-exilic period that the various names of the angels develop, such as princes, archangels, thrones, dominations and powers. In Job, Daniel, Tobias and the pseudepigraphical writings we already find the personal names of Michael, Gabriel, Raphael and Uriel. Regarding their nature, the pseudepigraphical writings declare the angels to be incorporeal, or even of the nature of fire.

The NT accepts the post-exilic background, but the language and form of doctrine are severely restrained. Angels are God's messengers in His more important salvific actions. They are accepted as being a mighty host, dwelling in God's presence. They are given an important eschatological mission, both for individual souls after death, and as escorts to Christ at the end of the world. The most distinctive NT feature is the relationship of the angels with Christ.

III The Angels and the Liturgy. Erik Peterson, *Le Livre des anges* (1954) and P. Odilo Heiming, *Der Engel in der Liturgie und die Engel in der Welt von Heute* (1957) argue that the early Church saw an important link between the Christian liturgy and the heavenly liturgy of the Angels before the throne of God in the heavenly Jerusalem, as depicted in the Apoc. The first-mentioned of these writers has argued that this heavenly worship of God by the angels is the source and centre of all divine worship. Our earthly worship, in Erik Peterson's understanding of the early Fathers and Liturgies, is a uniting of ourselves and our cult to that of the heavenly choirs. This is the reason for the presence of the triple *Sanctus* in all Eucharistic anaphoras. Monastic worship, he argued, was conscious of this, and understood thus the Vulgate translation of Ps 137, '*In conspectu angelorum psallam tibi*'. Is 6 and the Apoc, together with some passages in Heb, are the Scripture references that seem to recognize this. In all other parts of Scripture, however, angels' functions are given as missions to Christ or the rest of mankind.

E. Peterson has undoubtedly been able to discover many references to the angels in connection with the early liturgy. He has concluded that early liturgical worship was conscious of this union between our cult and angelic worship. In close relation to this he sees the early patristic idea of God's use of the angels in sacramental activity, as well as the patristic conviction of angelic participation in our liturgy. The strength of this theory is its unifi-

cation of all created worship of God. Its weakness is an appearance of subordinating the worship in Christ's Mystical Body (under Christ's priestly headship) to the worship of the angels who are now subordinate to Christ.

There is certainly much evidence for a consciousness in liturgical prayer of close association with the angels. In the Great Entry of the Byzantine Liturgy we read in the *Cherubicon* accompanying the bringing in of the offerings : 'We present mystically the Cherubim, and sing the triple *Sanctus* hymn to the life-giving Trinity. We wish to put aside all the cares of life, in order to receive the King of All, who will be invisibly escorted by the Hosts of Angels.' This prayer accompanies the offerings which are the symbol of Christ and occurs long before the consecration, though its thought is of the angels attending upon Christ sacramentally present.

It is well known that angels have an important place in the Roman liturgy. St Michael has a place of honour in the *Confiteor*. The Higher angels have a special mention in the Preface, just before the angelic *Sanctus* is recited. In the Canon we ask God to 'bid these things be carried by the hands of thy holy angel up to thy altar on high'. (For a vindication of the meaning of these words as really applying to an angel, and not to Christ, see P. Odilo Heiming, *op. cit.*) At High Mass we ask God to bless the incense 'at the intercession of blessed Michael the archangel, who stands at the right hand of the altar of incense'. The liturgy for the faithful departed recalls the tradition that angels carry the soul into paradise. Finally, the prayer at the end of Compline and in the blessing of houses refers to the dwelling of angels in our homes.

There are many references among early Christian writers to a similar liturgy. St Ambrose asks God to receive this oblation by the hands of angels (*De Sac.* 4:6:27), and Tertullian speaks of an *angelus orationis* (*De Oratione* 16 ; CSEL 20:190). St Ambrose (on Lk 1:11 ; CSEL 32:25) and St John Chrysostom (*De Sacerdotio*, 6:4) both speak of the participation by angels in the eucharistic sacrifice. Some of the Fathers speak of an angel cleansing the waters of baptism (cf. Tertullian, *De Bapt.* 4:5 ; 5:6 ; 6). Hermas speaks of an angel of repentance (*Visio* 5:7 ; GCS 48:23). Erik Peterson also quotes passages from St Gregory Nazianzen (*Oratio* 40:4 ; PG 36:364) and St Cyril (*Contra Iulianum* 4 ; PG 76:688), where these authors speak of angels being present rejoicing at each baptism.

Erik Peterson's conclusion is that early Christian liturgy justifies us in saying that 'the Church's worship . . . is never a merely human affair. The angels, together with the whole universe, take part in it. Ecclesiastical chant reflects heavenly chant, and the interior life of the Church varies according to the manner in which one takes part in the heavenly song. The angels, in the Church's worship, express that worship's official nature as an offering to God. Since angels have a relationship with the religious commonwealth of heaven, the Church's worship likewise acquires a necessary relationship with social life. . . . They (angels) also awaken in the Church the mystical life, which reaches its created nature'. (Erik Peterson, *op. cit.*, 101-2, our translation.)

IV The Doctrine of the Angels in the Patristic Period. There was no treatise on the Angels until that of the Pseudo-Denis, unless Clement ever wrote a work he announced (*Strom.* 6:3:32 ; GCS 15:446), not now known, with the object of distinguishing between the ' angels ' of Scripture and the ' demons ' of Greek popular belief. On the other hand, all the Fathers and ecclesiastical writers are convinced of the existence of a world of beings, called in Scripture angels, superior in their power and gifts to mankind. On essentials, the patristic view remained in strict harmony with that of Scripture. Yet occasionally their views of angelic nature or powers or numbers may have been affected by the predominant part played by angels in the apocryphal literature of the centuries immediately preceding and following Christ.

None of the Fathers succumbed to the Gnostic heresy of angelic creators. St Irenaeus and Clement of Alexandria insisted that all the powers and spirits are themselves God's creatures. There is a difficult passage in St Justin (*apol.* 1:6), which superficially might seem to put the angels on a par with the Trinity. It is, however, so isolated, and so inconsistent with St Justin's monotheism, that it must be susceptible of some other interpretation (cf. Justin, *apol.* 60, 61, 65, 67). The Fathers also saw the angels as capable of either good or evil. St Ignatius (*Smyrn.* 6, ACW trans.) says that they ' must either believe in the Blood of Christ, or else face damnation '.

There is no unanimity about the time of their creation. Hermas is content to say they were created first, and then placed in charge of God's creatures (*Visio* 3:4:1 ; GCS 48:11). The later Fathers are divided mainly as between the school of Origen and that of St Epiphanius. Origen held that all souls or spirits were created before the material world (*princ.* 1:8 ; GCS 22:94). His reason for this view appears to have been his theory that all differences between rational beings must have come about on the basis of merit. Spirits dwelling in human bodies are fallen spirits, who have deserved to be enclosed in a body as a punishment. Origen had at least two arguments for this position. On the one hand, it would be unworthy of God's goodness to create rational beings unequal ; on the other, Origen thought that the original sin of new-born children must be a sin those children committed before their birth. Those Fathers who followed Origen's view of the pre-existence and therefore pre-creation of angels did not, for the most part, accept his explanation of human souls as fallen spirits. These fathers included St Basil (*Hom. in Hexaemeron* 1:5 ; PG 29:13), St Gregory Nazianzen (*Oratio* 38:9 ; PG 36:320), St Ambrose (*Hexaemeron* 1:5:19 ; CSEL 32:15) and St Hilary (in *Ps.* 135, 8 ; CSEL 22:79). Cassian (*Collationes* 8:7 ; CSEL 13:222) even goes so far as to say that none of the faithful doubts that the angels were created before visible matter.

In spite of Cassian's statement, there was another view, defended by St Epiphanius (*Haer.* 65, 5 ; GCS 37:7), according to which it is God's word that the angels were created after the stars and after the heavens and the earth. Several later Greek Fathers (e.g. Theodore of Mopsuestia and Theodoret) appear to have favoured St Epiphanius's view (cf. G. Bareille, *Angélologie d'après les pères*, DTC, I, 1194).

St Augustine long hesitated, but finally settled for a compromise view, according to which ' the heavens and the earth ' in Gen 1:1, was meant to include the angels. The angels would thus precede the creation of the heavenly luminaries. St Augustine could not decide whether ' in the beginning ' meant ' before everything else ' or ' in the Word '. The Pseudo-Denis tried to settle the question by distinguishing three kinds of duration. God was above eternity, the angels in a lower kind of eternity, and the creatures of this material world in *time*. St Thomas was later to call God's duration *eternity*, as contrasted with that of the angels, which he called *aevum*.

In general, the Fathers were all concerned to show the inferiority and subordination of the angels to Jesus Christ. Those passages which seem to attribute divine powers to the ' Angel of the Lord ' were regarded by the Fathers as proofs that the latter Angel was no other than the Word and Son of God. (cf. St Athanasius, *Contra Arianos*, III:12 ; PG 26:345.) In general the Fathers agreed with the view expressed by St Athanasius that Heb 1:14 must apply to the whole angelic hierarchy. ' The Angels are all ministering spirits ; they are always ready to obey the commands of God.' (St Athanasius, *loc. cit.*) The Pseudo-Denis is out of harmony with the general tradition in his view that the highest angels are occupied exclusively before the throne of God, and are not sent forth as messengers (cf. Denis, *Hierarchia Caelestis*, vii, 1). The Fathers are anxious to show how this ministering function of the angels is especially either preparation for, or in the service of Christ. For their mission to individuals and nations, *see* GUARDIAN ANGELS.

About the nature of the angels, the Fathers are indefinite. The angelic appearances recorded in the Scriptures seemed to preclude complete incorporeity. They agree that the angels are spirits, but this word had not yet a clearly defined technical meaning. As among most ancient peoples, spirit seems to have been accepted as a thin, ethereal substance, like air or breath. This notion was helped by the passage from the psalm (Ps 104:4, LXX) which they tended to take in its more obvious verbal meaning : ' Who makest thy angels spirits : and thy ministers a burning fire '. In line with this psalm, they attributed to the angels the invisibility of wind, the subtlety of fire, and the intelligence of God's chosen messengers and ministers. Only gradually, from the 4th cent. onwards, did they come to understand ' spirit ' in the philosophical sense of ' immaterial '. Usually they would say that the angels had no bodies in the normal sense of the term. Some

Fathers do say, however, that they had some sort of body, for God alone, they would declare, is completely spiritual and immaterial.

Tertullian thought that all creatures must have bodies. Yet certainly, he said, they have no flesh, and, 'if they have bodies, the latter are special ones proper to a spiritual nature' (*De Carne Christi*, 6). St Gregory Nazianzen said that they were without bodies, or 'as near as possible to that' (*Oratio* 28:31 ; PG 36:72). St John of Damascus declared that they were indeed 'incorporeal and immaterial', but, like everything outside of God, were 'dense and material' as contrasted with God (*de Fide Orthodoxa*, 2:3 ; PG 94:865). The latter view is even repeated by St Gregory the Great (*Moralia*, 2:3:3), in spite of his defence of angels' incorporeity.

St Hilary, St Basil and St Gregory Nazianzen all thought that the angelic nature could be described as a kind of spirit or fire (Hilary, *De Trinitate*, 5:11 ; PL 10:136 ; St Gregory Nazianzen, *loc. cit.* ; St Basil, *De Spiritu Sancto*, 16:38 ; PG 32:137). Cassian said that neither angels nor the human soul were completely without bodies. Nothing indeed, he thought, can be completely bodiless except God (*Collationes*, 7:13 ; PL 49:684). St Fulgentius suggested that the good angels had bodies of fire, the evil angels of air.

The Pseudo-Denis summarized and purified the earlier views by saying that the angels were intelligent, intelligible, simple and without figure, having nothing material in their nature (*De Caelesti Hierarchia* 15).

Another aspect of patristic tradition concerns the accepted angelic hierarchy. This is not, of course, directly and expressly found in Scripture. There is, however, a suggestion of it in St Paul's lists of angelic spiritual forces, as well as in the fact that various names are used in different contexts in the books of the Bible. St Cyril of Jerusalem, St John Chrysostom, St Gregory Nazianzen, the *Apostolic Constitutions* and the anonymous author of the life of Peter the Iberian, all give lists of about nine choirs of angels. The order and number vary slightly from one list to another. It is eventually the Pseudo-Denis who fixed both the number and the order, who attempted to assign different functions and gave the higher angels a mediatorial ministry in relation to the lower one (cf. Pseudo-Denis, *Caelestis Hierarchia*, 7:9).

All the Fathers assume that the angels are of an intellectual nature, and are endowed with free will. All agree that some angels abused their freedom, and became evil spirits, while others obeyed God, and became good angels. There is no final and universal teaching about the length of the angelic period of trial (*see* DEVIL).

V The Present Teaching of the Church concerning the Angels. Very little has been actually defined. Clearly the Scripture doctrine of angels as God's special messengers to mankind, with its implications of their superior nature, is part of the Church's tradition guaranteed by her ordinary *magisterium*. That they form part of the wider communion of saints, able and willing to intercede for us, and entitled to our honour, is implicit in the Church's liturgical life.

The 4th Lateran Council (1215), followed by the Vatican Council (1870), defined that God, at the beginning of time, had created out of nothing all beings, both spiritual and corporeal. In these documents the Church assumed the existence and defined the created nature of the angels. Are we to understand the phrase '*simul ab initio temporis*', given as the time of all creation, to imply a conciliar definition that angels and the material world were all created at the same time ? Though some theologians have thought this, it seems extremely unlikely. A more natural understanding of such words would be that none of God's creatures was eternal, and that all of them, angels and men and matter, had a beginning in time.

The Church has never defined the pure spirituality of the angels. Most theologians accept the theology of St Thomas on this point, that the angels are immaterial and incorporeal. In St Thomas's language, they are pure forms or separated substances. There was a rival school in the Middle Ages, represented by St Bonaventure and Scotus. These latter attributed to the angels a special 'spiritual matter'. The two schools took up a different position on many questions of angelology, following the logic of their several principles. The Thomist doctrine of individuality led to the view that each angel must form a distinct species, since there could be in their nature no principle of individuality within a species. Scotus, on the other hand, with his doctrine that the 'this-ness' of a being is its principle of individuality, found it possible to conceive of many individual angels within a species, as in the case of human beings. These schools also held varying views regarding the angelic period of trial. St Thomas thought that their angelic perfection and pure spirituality made them capable of an instantaneous and decisive life-choice for or against God. Such a decisive choice is not possible for man because of the weakness and materiality of his nature. The dual nature of man makes all his acts less fully conscious and responsible than those of a pure spirit. Scotus, on the other hand, saw no reason why angels could not have a period of trial as we have, and he saw no reason why they could not be offered a grace of repentance after a fall. For him, in harmony with Scotist voluntarism, the end of the period of trial, whether for angels or men, would depend purely on a free act of God's will. For St Thomas, angels and men would have sufficient grace during their period of trial, but this period would end, for man on the separation of body and soul, for angels as a result of their fully conscious first deliberate act. The two schools also differed regarding the angelic power of reasoning. In all such matters, the Scotist understood angelic psychology as much nearer to that of man.

The encyclical *Humani Generis* (1950), though it defined nothing about angels, indicated the generally accepted tradition where it warned us in general terms against those who question the personal nature of angels or denied the essential distinction between matter and spirit.

Some questions discussed by St Thomas reflected the cosmological views of his time rather than the teaching of the Church. Among these was his view of the angelic function of controlling the stars and planets (see ASTROLOGY AND THEOLOGY). It is interesting to note that Newman in his Anglican days still inclined to such a view (cf. *Parochial and Plain sermons*, ii, pp. 359 ff., *Apologia*, p. 28). While opinion would today be regarded as open regarding such natural ministry of angels, no theologian would doubt their capacity to act upon matter, if God so willed. Traditional and Scriptural teaching would accept that God does occasionally send angels on a mission which involves the use of such powers. Within certain limits it has been generally assumed that evil spirits can use the powers of nature for their purposes (cf. DEVIL).

That angels come within the supernatural order is universally accepted. They were offered supernatural grace, and the good angels enjoy the beatific vision (cf. Mt 18:10).

Newman, following logically on the thought that all spiritual being is intellectual, spoke of the very temples and palaces of heaven being made up of angels, and thus :

> The smallest portions of this edifice,
> Cornice, or frieze, or balustrade, or stair,
> The very pavement is made up of life—
> Of holy, blessed, and immortal beings,
> Who hymn their Maker's praise continually.
>
> (*Dream of Gerontius* in *Verses*, p. 354)

Angels then, together with human souls, will form, in the presence of God, Father, Son and Holy Spirit, the whole reality of heaven as it now exists until the resurrection of the human body and the renovation of the material universe. If this is so, Christian teaching cannot regard the angels as of no importance in relation to man's salvation.

Bibliography. The classical treatise on Angels is that of St Thomas (the Angelic doctor) in *Summa* 1a, 50–64 and 106–14. This was commented on by Suarez (amongst others), who devotes a whole volume (tome II of the general edition of his works) to the Angels. Petavius, *Theologica dogmata* III, 1–116 (in the edition of 1700), gathers much patristic teaching together ; but in general the treatise on the Angels has been crowded out of much theological work of more recent times. There are the following monographs : F. Andres, *Die Engellehre der griechischen Apologeten des II. Jahrhunderts* (1914) ; the same, *Die Engellehre des Klemens von Alexandrien* in *Römische Quartalschrift* 34 (1926) 13–27 ; K. Pelz, *Die Engellehre des heiligen Augustinus* (1913) ; J. B. Frey, *L'Angélologie juive au temps de Jésus-Christ*, in RSPT 5 (1911) 75–110 ; H. Lemonnyer, *Angélologie chrétienne*, in DBS I, 255–62 ; E. Peterson, *Le Livre des anges* (tr. from the German) (1954). For the angels in art, see DAC I, 2080–161, and for devotion to the angels, D Sp. I, 598–619. There are two

sermons of Newman on the angels, *Parochial and Plain Sermons* II, sermon 13 and IV, sermon 29.

H. F. D.

ANGLICANISM Since the doctrines of Anglicanism cannot be understood unless they are put each time into their historical context, this article will treat of (I) the genesis of Anglicanism, (II) its early struggle with Puritanism and (III) the gradual formation of the Latitudinarian and Evangelical parties in the church. The High Church revival (IV) of the 19th cent. was a doctrinal movement before it became a ritualist crusade, and (V) the Broad Church movement was in many ways a reaction to both of these ; the opposition continued into (VI) the present century, with the contrast between ritualists and modernists being maintained. The spread of Anglicanism overseas (VII) brought in new factors to alter the alignment of opposing doctrinal tendencies, and a final estimate (VIII) of the present position of Anglicanism has to take account of all these legacies from the past.

For the question of ANGLICAN ORDERS, see the article ORDINATION.

I The Genesis of Anglicanism. This term is used to cover the established Church of England and the English-speaking churches throughout the world whose worship is based on the Book of Common Prayer. Anglicanism, therefore, came into existence in 1549, the year which saw the first edition of this book. The statement is frequently made that Henry VIII was the founder of the Church of England. This is not strictly true. Henry's religious policy paved the way for the Protestant Prayer Book ; but its coming was delayed till that monarch was dead. Its imposition was the work of those who ruled the kingdom in the name of Edward VI. The first version of the Prayer Book appeared in 1549 and is known as the 'first Prayer Book of Edward VI'. It is a drastic simplification of the old offices. The Psalter is recited once a month instead of weekly, as was formerly the case. The Psalms are recited without the antiphons. Mattins and Lauds are replaced by Morning Prayer, which is indeed a greatly-abridged form of them ; Vespers and Compline are replaced by Evening Prayer ; all the lessons are from Scripture ; the Communion Office is still called the Mass and in its structure closely follows it. We have the same sequence of Introit, Kyrie, Gloria, Collects, Epistle, Gospel, Creed, Offertory and Canon. There is no last Gospel and people leave after being dismissed with a blessing ; they communicate under both kinds. In the Litany all invocation of Our Lady and the Saints is omitted ; some traces of prayers for the dead survive in the Occasional Offices ; many ceremonies of Catholic origin are retained.

Provision is made for the Unction of the sick. After Baptism the child is clothed with a white vestment and is anointed. At Confirmation each candidate is signed with a cross on the forehead ; on the other hand, very ancient rites disappeared. This was the case with the blessing of the ashes, the blessing of palms and the creeping to the Cross. In the following year, 1550, there was published as a supplement to the Prayer Book the first Anglican Ordinal. (*See* ORDINATION.) The preface asserts the desire of the reformers to perpetuate the threefold ministry of Bishops, Priests and Deacons ; provision is made for two ceremonies which later disappeared, handing of the chalice and bread to the Ministers of the Second Order, styled Priests, while the Pastoral Staff is given to Bishops. The Act of Uniformity of January 1549 was the logical complement of the Henrician reforms. It closed an important stage in the history of the English Reformation. Why did it display so little permanence ? It had the backing of only a small minority of the people. It was too revolutionary to make an appeal to the conservative-minded majority, even to that part of it which cared little about the Pope. It smacked too much of the old order to be acceptable to the extreme Protestant party which was hourly gaining strength.

The attacks on the Prayer Book multiplied, the 'second Prayer Book' of Edward VI which was promulgated in 1552, represents the high-water-mark of Prayer Book Protestantism and sets forth the views of the foreign reformers Peter Martyr and Martin Bucer. A comparison of the two books will speedily indicate the standpoint of those responsible for them. The book of 1549 is what we should now call High Church, that of 1552 Low Church. As might be anticipated, the most striking differences are to be met with in the Communion Office. In this latter the changes are sweeping. The outward resemblance to the Mass contained so clearly in the former almost disappears ; there is no canon ; Mass vestments, prescribed in 1549, are prohibited in 1552 ; the officiating Minister was to wear a surplice only. The book was attached to an Act of Parliament and, so far as is known, never received the sanction of Convocation (i.e. of the organized Spirituality of the realm). A few weeks after it had been authorized the young king died and the Mass was restored under the rule of his elder sister.

When Mary in her turn died after a reign of five years, four alternatives presented themselves, they were (1) the retention of the Mass with acceptance of Papal supremacy, (2) the retention of the Mass without the acceptance of Papal authority, (3) the restoration of the first Prayer Book of Edward VI, (4) the restoration of the second Prayer Book of Edward VI. It may be that a majority in the nation would still have preferred the Mass to the Prayer Book, even if it had little enthusiasm for the Pope. But Elizabeth with her adviser Cecil, for reasons which must be left to our conjectures, decided once more to abolish the Mass. They would have preferred the book of 1549 to that of 1552. But the men responsible for the former were dead or had returned to the allegiance of Rome and the authors of the latter, active as they were, yet professed a shade of Protestantism for which the bulk of the nation was as yet unprepared. The Queen and her advisers executed a master-stroke. While they made the second book the foundation of their policy, they

introduced some significant amendments into it. Mass vestments were again prescribed so as to make the new Service as like the old as possible. The so-called 'black rubric', printed at the end of the Communion Service and directed against the real presence, was deleted. The words of administration of the elements were taken from the Communion Office of 1549 and joined to those of 1552. A loophole was left, or intended to be left, for reconciliation with Rome by the excision from the Litany of the petition 'from the tyranny of the Bishop of Rome and all his detestable enormities, Good Lord deliver us'.

Of scarcely less importance for the student of Anglicanism are the Articles of Religion promulgated originally just before Mary's accession, being then in number 42. The new edition in which they were reduced to 39 was agreed to by Convocation in 1562 and finally ratified in 1571. Some of the articles are uncompromising, such as those touching faith in the Blessed Trinity, the Incarnation and Resurrection of Christ. They are drawn up so as to range the Church of England among the Trinitarian bodies, others show clearly the spirit of compromise designed to include as many persons as possible in the new Church. Belief in the Blessed Sacrament had for so many centuries formed the central part of the devotional life of the people that the advisers of Elizabeth I, unlike those of Edward VI, did not deem it prudent to attack it directly. Accordingly, there was deleted from Article 28 the words ' the faithful man ought not either to believe or openly to confess the real and bodily presence, as they call it, of Christ's Body and Blood in the Sacrament of the Lord's Supper'. The promulgation of the Articles of 1562 was the coping-stone of the English Reformation but it was far from giving unity of faith to the English people.

II The Struggle with Puritanism. Two substantial bodies of Englishmen repudiated the Elizabethan settlement of religion as embodied in the Act of 1559. The Catholics carried on for generations a heroic though losing struggle against it ; yet were so far successful as to prevent the total absorption of the Catholic remnant into the Protestant mass. At the other extreme those adherents of what is called the 'Reformed Religion', for whom the settlement was too conservative, refused to accept it and ultimately separated from the established Church which already in 1592 they found dissonant from Christ's institution. The Puritans found popery in the surplice, in the sign of the cross in baptism and the ring in marriage, but their chief objection to the Elizabethan settlement lay in its episcopal character. Some of the Puritans sought to reform the Church of England from within, others, such as the Brownists, set up organizations of their own which became the parents of English nonconformity, though Robert Brown himself, from whom they were named, when an old man, accepted ordination in the Church of England. The Puritans denounced the established Church for retention of Bishops, though they were willing to retain them provided that their powers were curtailed by the creation of Colleges or *Classes* of Presbyters whose approval they needed for certain episcopal acts.

It need hardly be said that the use of vestments as ordered by the Prayer Book of 1549 was completely disregarded by the Puritans. Even the surplice was too popish for them, and when in 1566 Archbishop Parker, despairing of getting the rubric of 1559 obeyed, issued ' advertisements ', trying to secure a minimum of order, and enjoined the use of the surplice as a compromise, he was completely unsuccessful. Cotton Mather, a name famous in the annals of New England Protestantism, confessed to not having worn a surplice for fifteen years, when visitors sent by Archbishop Williams of York arrived at his door. Kneeling at Communion was an even bigger stumbling block. The Hampton Court Conference, summoned by James I the year after his accession, in which the King himself took a leading part, revealed an incompatibility between Puritanism and the religion of the Prayer Book which precluded the possibility of a national Church which should comprise both Puritans and Anglicans. For an opposition to Puritanism had developed tendencies in the Church of England which if not going so far as to teach the doctrine of the Apostolic Succession yet set great store by episcopacy as a form of Church government and by orderliness and decency in divine worship. The best-remembered names in the anti-Puritan party are those of Lancelot Andrews, Bishop of Winchester in the reign of James I, William Laud, Bishop of London and later Archbishop of Canterbury in that of Charles I, and the Jacobite Bishop of Bath and Wells, Thomas Ken, at the end of the century.

Under Charles I the Puritans showed increasing aggressiveness ; even the Communion Table was put to profane uses. In 1642 the Civil War began, ending in 1646 in a Puritan victory, which resulted not only in the suppression of the religious forms of the Prayer Book but in their substitution by a religion according to the views of its opponents. Anglican worship was, however, carried on surreptitiously. This was possible by memorizing the contents of the Prayer Book or at least considerable parts of it. Anglican worship was also carried on by English exiles in France. When the nation grew tired of the Puritan overlord and the King returned, the religion of the Prayer Book came back with him.

An attempt to find common ground between Anglicans and Presbyterians which would have admitted of the formation of a single national Church comprising both broke down after the Savoy conference which sat between April and July 1661, and from the non-Anglican Protestants originated the Dissenters or Nonconformists. The Ministers intruded into Anglican livings during the years of Puritan ascendancy were required by a new Act of Uniformity to suffer ejection or accept the Prayer Book. Plans for reforming it in the Protestant direction continued to be aired, the most important being the projected abolition of the necessity of kneeling for Communion. The revolution of 1688 gave comprehensiveness a new opportunity. In the autumn of the following year a meeting took place in the Jerusalem Chamber of Westminster Abbey between Anglican and Dissenting divines. A scheme of reunion was worked out which included the following points : the custom of chanting the divine service in Cathedrals was to be discontinued on the ground that it made it unintelligible to the people ; the omission of Deutero-canonical lessons from the lectionary ; permission for those who objected to receive Communion kneeling to receive it in their pews, and leave for those who so desired to dispense with godparents. The use of the surplice was still a cause of trouble. The Commission agreed that if a Minister should refuse to wear one, the Bishop might at the request of the congregation substitute for him a Minister who *was* willing. The whole matter was to be left to the discretion of the Ordinary. With regard to Ministers ordained in Protestant Churches abroad, it was decided that reordination should be unnecessary in order to qualify them to hold Anglican livings. But Episcopal ordination was to be required in the case of those who had received only non-Episcopal ordination. This reordination was, however, to be merely conditional. But High Church influences in the lower House of Convocation were powerful enough to wreck the scheme of comprehension. The Dissenters broke with the national Church and came to occupy a position of isolation, a position which they still retain to some extent. Though tolerated, it was not until 1829 that they acquired full civil rights. At an even later period they were discriminated against in certain respects.

III Latitudinarianism and Evangelicalism.

The names High Church, or High-flying Church, and Low Church go back to the 17th cent. and were applied by their opponents to those Anglicans who set much store on Episcopacy and were noted for what would now be termed their ' Ecclesiasticism ', though in this direction few and perhaps none went to the lengths of the Tractarians. We now apply the term Low Church to the Evangelicals, but originally it was given to those whom we now term Latitudinarians. The origins of the Latitudinarian party go back to the first half of the 17th cent. If anybody should be regarded as their founder it should probably be Edward Hales, Fellow of Eton and later Canon of Windsor, who, in his capacity of Chaplain to Sir Dudley Carlton, went on his embassy to the Synod of Dort. This was taking place as a result of the rise of a powerful Arminian party which took a milder view of predestination than did the official Calvinism. Hales sided with the Arminian party and tersely summed up his rejection of Calvinism in the words : ' I bid John Calvin goodnight '. Hales had been a follower of Laud but later broke away from him. In England Calvinism was associated with the Parliament and Arminianism with the Crown.

After the revolution of 1688 the majority of the bishops were Whigs and Latitudinarians while the High Church party was overwhelmingly Tory in its sympathies and enjoyed a majority in the Lower House of Convocation. Shortly after the accession of the House of Hanover, Convocation was suppressed for censuring a sermon by Bishop Hoadley on the 'Kingdom of Christ'. The Latitudinarians were opposed to the Athanasian Creed and tended to Arianism and even Socinianism in their theology. An Arian movement developed during the reign of Queen Anne. Those mainly responsible for it were Samuel Clarke, one of Anne's Chaplains in Ordinary, and William Whiston, who succeeded Sir Isaac Newton as Professor of Mathematics at Cambridge. At St James's, Piccadilly, of which he was the incumbent, Clarke changed the doxology into a form which Arians could have used, 'To God through Christ his Son our Lord all glory be'. The Bishop of London was displeased but took no effective measures. Whiston was expelled from Cambridge in 1710 for his Arian opinions, though the Arian movement enjoyed sympathy in high quarters. Latitudinarianism began to decline in the latter half of the 18th cent., especially after the 'Feathers Tavern petition', presented to Parliament in 1772. The petition, signed by about 200 clergy and a number of civil lawyers, asked that the signatories be relieved of the obligation of subscription to the Thirty-nine Articles at the Universities. The House of Commons, however, rejected the measure. The Latitudinarian bishops had not been pastors noted for their zeal, and non-residence was a scandal amongst them. Thus, Watson, Bishop of Llandaff, lived far from his see and devoted himself to agriculture in the Lake District. He was a staunch opponent of the Athanasian Creed and he introduced into the House of Lords the Bill providing for the discontinuance of its recitation. But soon came the French Revolution and anti-Trinitarian views were no longer regarded with the same fervour.

Latitudinarianism had also had its effect beyond the Atlantic and showed itself in the Revised Prayer Book and new Constitution of the Protestant Episcopal Church of the United States when the insurgent colonies gained their independence. One congregation, that of the King's Chapel in Boston, deleted all Trinitarian formulae from its prayer book. The majority did not, of course, go so far but adopted a service book which omitted the Athanasian Creed. The reaction against Latitudinarianism took the form of the Evangelical revival. It has been said and with truth that the Anglican Church in the early Hanoverian period had, to a large extent, sunk to the position of a branch of the Civil Service. From this condition the High Church party was too weak to rescue it; for it had suffered as a consequence of its associations with Jacobitism. The Evangelicals had no such embarrassing connections; so far as they had a spiritual ancestry it was to be found in men of the school of John Bunyan. It was from the Evangelicals therefore that the religious revival spread. The two chief names associated with its beginnings and indeed its first leaders were John Wesley, son of a Lincolnshire clergyman and himself an Oxford Fellow, leader of the Arminian

wing, and George Whitefield, son of the keeper of the Bell Inn at Gloucester and himself a poor servitor of Pembroke College, Oxford. Whitefield led the Calvinist wing. The movement started in Oxford itself where Wesley and a group of friends formed what its critics called the 'Holy Club'—a group of pious Fellows who offered a challenge to the religious tone which then predominated at the university. Like the Oxford Movement, it eventually spread beyond its original bounds. In 1738 at a meeting in Aldersgate Street when Luther's Preface to the Epistle to the Romans was being read, Wesley's heart 'strangely warmed' and he said that he 'did trust in Christ and Christ alone for salvation'. From that moment the religious revival with which he was associated became a nation-wide one.

The Methodist preachers, as they were called, met with strong opposition not only from the rougher elements of the community but from the official Anglican hierarchy and many of the parochial clergy. Bishop Lavington of Exeter said that Methodism was as dangerous as Popery, while the apologist, Warburton, said that Satan was 'man-midwife at the new birth of which the Methodists made so much'. The great religious revival of the 18th cent. profoundly transformed the face of English society; it did so to a much greater extent than did the Oxford Movement of the following century and without it England in the 19th cent. would have been something very different from what it was. It undoubtedly helped to bring about a great revival of personal religion, yet against this must be set its tendency to condemn innocent forms of amusement, thus paving the way to antinomianism. This fault was inherited from it by the later Evangelicals and, it is said, apparently with truth, that the sons of clergymen belonging to this party often turned out badly. Owing to the opposition to the movement in official circles it was not easy for clergymen of Methodist leanings to obtain livings; but Lady Huntingdon, the Calvinistic supporter of the movement, was able to exercise her rights as a Peeress to appoint a private chaplain and thus broke down the barrier which kept them from possibility of preferment. Eventually the official opposition wore away and Lord Liverpool appointed an avowed Evangelical to the See of Gloucester in 1815.

The Methodist movement broke into two currents, one, the more moderate of the two, remained in the Church of England and formed the Evangelical party. The other, after long hesitation, seceded from the Church of England and constituted itself into a variety of Methodist sects. In the 19th cent., the Evangelical party, though it had many worthy men in its ranks, tended to be less austere and self-sacrificing than in the previous one. Characters like 'Dinah Morris' may have occasionally been met with but were very rare, and Evangelicalism had its strength in watering-places and the residential suburbs of large towns. It was not strong intellectually and Newman said of it that it was 'at no time conspicuous as a party for talent or learning'. Its influence probably began to decline about 1860 and though it retains a certain strength it has shown no signs of returning to its former degree of influence.

IV The High Church Revival. The 18th cent. was for the High Church party a period of little influence. This was largely due to its association with the exiled Stuart dynasty. After the revolution of 1688 Archbishop Sancroft and five of his colleagues, together with about four hundred clergymen, refused to take the oath to William and Mary. The recalcitrant Bishops were deprived of their sees and in company with the Jacobite clergy formed a non-juring sect. They remained Anglicans, however, as they continued to use the Prayer Book. They were strengthened a few years later by the accession to their ranks of a number of clergymen who refused to take the oath of allegiance to the House of Hanover ; the most famous of these was William Law. The non-juring movement failed to secure the adhesion of more than a very small number of laymen, but it was large enough to be frowned upon by the Government. It was not, however, persecuted, not being sufficiently numerous. The chief result of the non-juring movement was its weakening effect on the High Church party. At the beginning of the 19th cent. there were to be found a certain number of old-fashioned High Churchmen, such as the elder Keble, but the Evangelicals and Latitudinarians far outstripped them in numbers and influence.

The party, known satirically as 'high and dry', which disliked Rome but disliked also the Dissenters, was numerous and influential. There were no ritualists, properly so called. The use of the cope survived till the end of the 18th cent., but chasubles had not been seen since the reign of Elizabeth I, though there is one possible exception in the case of Theophilus Leigh, an Oxonian Jacobite, who in his country living at Huntspill in Somersetshire used a 'distinctive vesture for Holy Communion'. Probably, however, this was a cope and not a chasuble. The eccentric poet, Robert Hawker of Morwenstowe in Cornwall, officiated in a cope and a 'magnificent purple velvet robe'. The High Church revival in the Church of England in the last century was not primarily a ritualistic movement, though to outsiders it appeared to be so. The first generation of High Church leaders was not addicted to ritualism ; E. B. Pusey even disliked it. Men such as he were content with the traditional methods of conducting the services ; they feared no doubt that if new and unaccustomed ritual was introduced the import of the teaching which they were introducing would become overlooked and that ritualism would thus obtain a more important position than dogmatic teaching. Newman's position would not have differed very greatly from this. Before the end of the 1840s, however, ritualism, some of it Roman in origin, some of it claiming to rest on Anglican tradition, was beginning to make its appearance. Eucharistic vestments were worn at St Thomas's, Oxford, as far back as 1849 and a few London churches followed soon after. In their general position the Tractarian leaders began where the

Non-jurors left off. They had no real precursors in the Anglicans of the Caroline period. The 17th-cent. High Churchmen were much more Protestant than the Tractarians seemed to imagine. The fear of Rome was in their day something so potent that a movement such as the Oxford one could not have taken place, at least in the form in which it actually did.

The elder Pitt said that the Church of England possessed 'a Popish Liturgy, Calvinist Articles and an Arminian Clergy'. The High Churchmen based themselves on the Popery to be discovered in parts of the Prayer Book, some of which may have been almost forgotten when Newman, Pusey and Keble called attention to it. Put briefly, the position of the Oxford High Churchmen in its most evolved form was that the Church of England was not to be classed among the sects which originated at the Reformation but could claim sisterhood with the venerable churches of the East and the West. Along with the older High Churchmen they proclaimed belief in baptismal regeneration and based themselves on the doctrine of the Apostolic Succession. Their Eucharistic doctrine is not always quite easy to understand but all would have claimed to have held the real presence in one form or another. They opposed Erastianism, believing the Church to be a divinely-appointed institution, one with whose constitution the State had no right to interfere.

The Oxford Movement is spoken of as the Tractarian Movement because its inception took the form of the publication of a series of tracts expounding the doctrinal and ecclesiastical basis of the movement. The year 1833, which saw the publication of the first tracts, is counted as the beginning of the movement because it saw also the delivery of the so-called Assize Sermon. The success of the tracts was remarkable and for a few years it seemed as though the position of their authors was going to become the dominant one in the Anglican Church. The hopes of those who believed this were frustrated. In 1845 John Henry Newman, who had been for some years the unquestioned leader of the movement, pushed the tractarian doctrines to lengths to which his colleagues would not venture to go and himself left the Church of England to seek refuge in that of Rome. This brought the tractarian movement to an end but did not stop the High Church revival ; from now onwards those who accepted the new doctrines either did as the leader had done or sought to promote the High Church revival inside the Church of England. The official Anglican hierarchy and the bulk of the lower clergy remained incurably hostile and High Churchmen had to face angry mobs as well as controversialists. The High Church movement, though it never succeeded in dominating the Anglican Church as a whole, after a long struggle won an established position within it.

From 1850 onwards ritualism rather than doctrinal teaching excited Protestant fury and futile attempts were made by enraged Protestants to crush the ritualist movement. What its opponents did not, however, grasp was that they were fighting not merely a ritualist movement, nor an ecclesiastical one, but an aesthetic movement as well. In 1874 Archbishop Tait, with the support of the Prime Minister, Mr Disraeli, introduced into the House of Lords the Bill which became the Public Worship Regulation Act. After angry scenes, it became law and under its provisions some half-dozen Anglo-Catholic clergymen went to prison. This did the authors of the measure but little good and after the last prosecution under it, that of Mr Bell Cox, a Liverpool clergyman, in 1887, this unhappy measure was discarded by the Protestants as a useless weapon. Since that time, ritualist practices have continued unabated, vestments have been worn in an increasing number of churches, the use of incense has increased and Roman ritual has in a large number of churches illegally superseded that of the Prayer Book.

V The Broad Church Movement. It was not only against the Evangelicals that the Tractarians had to contend. They met with antagonists in some ways more formidable in the young Broad Church Movement. This, through Archbishop Whateley, could claim a link with the Latitudinarians. The movement arose contemporaneously with the Tractarian one. It had no-one who could be described as its actual founder but A. H. Clough attributes its foundation primarily to Jowett. The main position for which it contended was that of an undogmatic Christianity. It disliked Ecclesiasticism, which it regarded as inseparable from Tractarianism. It preached manliness and showed an interest in social reform. It never took any hold over the masses. Its conquests were in academic circles and numerically it could not contend with either Tractarians or Evangelicals. At first it showed little interest in the higher criticism of the Bible and it was only at a later date that it ventured to put forward a claim to discard belief in the miraculous. In its turn the Broad Church Party was to be a parent of the one whose members are now spoken of as Modernists.

VI The Twentieth Century; Ritualism and Modernism. The conflicts which were shaking the Church of England in the 19th cent. continued in an even more exacerbated form into the 20th. The very beginning of the century coincided with the outbreak of lawlessness and violence which marked the so-called Kensitite campaign against ritualism. John Kensit, a London bookseller, was convinced that the bishops were too weak to make an effective stand against ritualism and himself inaugurated a campaign of violence against the ritualist practices to be met with in so many churches. This was not something new : forty years before when Tait became Bishop of London a similar outbreak had occurred. Now the same thing threatened to develop on a larger scale. The bishops were not agreed as to what should be done ; eventually, however, the Prime Minister, Mr Arthur Balfour, appointed a Royal Commission under the presidency of Sir Michael Hicks Beach to inquire into the extent of the alleged illegal practices. It sat from 1904 to 1906 and when it produced its report the Conservatives were no longer in office and the

Liberal government under Sir Henry Campbell-Bannerman had taken its place. Chief of the recommendations which it made was an amendment to the rubrics of the Prayer Book and this in its turn raised the whole question of Prayer Book reform. Up till then the only change in the Prayer Book which had been seriously considered was that of a deletion of the Rubric requiring the recitation of the Athanasian Creed ; but once the question of Prayer Book revision was under consideration a long and acrimonious series of discussions was under way. Convocation discussed the revision of the Prayer Book from 1909 till 1927, a period lengthened by four years of war. Eventually it produced a plan. It offered a Prayer Book revised on the one hand in an Anglo-Catholic direction and on the other hand in a Modernist one. It is impossible here to do more than indicate its work on the briefest possible lines. Its most important provisions were the making of Eucharist vestments unconditionally and unambiguously valid. Against this can be set the omission of any injunction requiring the recitation of the Athanasian Creed. A new Communion Service was offered resembling the Scottish one and concessions were made to the Modernists in the shape of some changes in the Baptismal Service.

During the First World War prejudice against prayers for the dead completely broke down, and this showed itself in the new book. Parliament had to be consulted as well as Convocation and it proved to be under the influence of Protestant intimidation. Sponsored by the then Archbishop of Canterbury, Dr Davidson, the book passed the House of Lords but was rejected by the Commons in 1927. With some slight alterations it was again submitted to Parliament in the following year and again rejected. Portions of it are now used with Episcopal permission, though this is technically illegal. The Communion Service has not received Episcopal sanction. The Ritualist controversy plays a smaller part in Anglican life than formerly, for Ritualism is an aesthetic movement as well as a religious one. The ceremonial developments and Church decoration, formerly the monopoly of Anglo-Catholics, are now to be met with in churches officiated in by clergymen belonging to other parties. More important than the Ritualist controversy during the last generation has been the Modernist one, arising out of the claim of extreme Broad Churchmen to remain Ministers of the Church of England, while rejecting belief in the miraculous. At the beginning of the century the bishops were almost unanimous in rejecting that claim. In 1905 the Convocation of Canterbury passed a resolution adhering to the doctrinal statements of the Nicene and Athanasian Creeds. They shrank, however, from initiating penal measures against those who implicitly fell under their condemnation and the Episcopal declaration was repeated by the Fifth Lambeth Conference in 1908. The adherence to the Modernist group of Dr William Sanday, Lady Margaret Professor of Divinity at Oxford, the foremost NT scholar in the country, greatly strengthened the position of the Modernists.

This was in 1914. The next Lambeth Conference was due to take place in 1918 ; owing to the war it did not meet until 1920. Feeling still ran high on the Modernist issue but in part it had been weakened by the emotions generated by the war. Davidson was able to use this situation and his influence prevented a discussion on the Creeds by the Sixth Lambeth Conference which took place under his aegis in 1920. The Modernist issue began gradually to lose its fierceness, but the last had not yet been heard of it. In 1922 the two Archbishops appointed a commission to ascertain how much doctrinal unity existed among the parties in the Church of England. The Commission did not issue its report till 1938 and the report tolerated scepticism with regard to the miraculous. Once more the tide of opinion began to run high. Davidson was by this time dead and his successor was his colleague, Archbishop Lang of York, that see being now filled by Archbishop William Temple, son of Archbishop Frederick Temple and for many years Bishop of Manchester. The two Primates handled the situation with an adroitness which would have been worthy of Archbishop Davidson. They declared their personal belief in the doctrines of the Virginal Birth and the Resurrection, and clergymen who did not feel able to subscribe to them were urged to abstain from publicly giving expression to their scepticism but would not be required to make any retractation ; while the Bishop of Gloucester, Dr Headlam, one of the foremost theologians in the Church of England, maintained that while to deny the divinity of Christ would be heresy, the denial of the miracles of His virgin birth and bodily resurrection was not so. In any case there were to be no more trials for heresy in this controversy. The Archbishops' pronouncement was made in 1939 and the ensuing two decades were relatively quiescent ones. Demands for punitive measures when these issues were to the fore almost faded away and few could anticipate the possible disruption of the Church of England on this question, which indeed was thrown into the shade by another one, namely that of inter-communion with bodies lacking in episcopal organization.

VII The Anglican Communion overseas. The careful student of Anglicanism will not forget to bear in mind that Anglicanism is not limited to the Church of England, that is to say the Established Church of the Provinces of Canterbury and York, but includes also the Anglican Communities overseas. We shall understand this if we visualize four concentric circles, all centred on Canterbury. The first embraces the Church of England as established in these two provinces ; the second covers, in addition to these, the disestablished Anglican churches in Ireland and Wales and the Episcopal Church in Scotland; the third will embrace the Anglican communities of the English-speaking countries overseas; the last will include all Anglicans, whether of English-speaking parentage or not.

The Archbishop of Canterbury remains the honor-

ary President of the loose federation which embraces all these communities, and when a new province is founded he assists at it, if not personally, at least by delegation. A new province can be founded when there are as many as five dioceses requiring it and once it has been canonically set up no other body, nor the Primate himself, has any direct jurisdiction over it. The provinces of the Anglican Communion are a species of loose federation which holds together in spite of jolts, in spite of bitter controversies such as those we have seen threatening the Church of England.

Anglicanism made its first venture overseas when a Chaplain was appointed to the little group of colonists who settled on the fever-ridden swamps on the banks of the James River. Virginia was an Anglican colony as the New England ones were Puritan, and the clergymen who went overseas on colonizing expeditions continued for long to be under the jurisdiction of the Bishop of London ; but as early as the reign of Queen Anne demands were being made by the Society for the Propagation of the Gospel for the appointment of Anglican bishops in the New World. The government would not concede such a request and Anglicanism remained without bishops in the American colonies ; after the American Revolution this situation could not continue and bishops were provided for the Anglican Church in the new American republic by consecration of their bishops by Anglican ones at home ; a suggestion that orders might be obtained from Denmark was narrowly averted. Had such consecration been really given to the American bishops and accepted by them as sufficient, the Church of England at home could hardly have remained in communion with its American daughter. When an episcopal organization had been provided for the Anglicans of the United States the Government changed its policy and made its first overseas appointment in Bishop Inglis of Nova Scotia in 1787. Other appointments followed, of which perhaps the most notable was that of Bishop Heber, the first Anglican Bishop in India, who was made Bishop of Calcutta in 1815. The Anglican Church in Australia began life as an Archdeaconry of the Diocese of Calcutta. Today the Anglican Church at home is far inferior in the number of its bishops to the Anglican Church abroad and this remains the case even if those from Scotland, Ireland and Wales are added in. The growth of dioceses has, however, relatively outstripped the numbers of communicants in England and so far as numbers are concerned the 20th cent. has tended to register a decline. It does not seem that this is likely to be arrested in any foreseeable future and should this be the case, the Established Church of England will become a sect, even if a large one—a sect among a score of others.

VIII The Future. The present (1957) state of the Church of England is more quiescent than that of half a century ago. Disruption did not come over the Modernist issue, nor did it come over the Ritualist one. It now seems less likely that it will come over the question of reunion, and when the admission of women to the ministry becomes a live issue, it is not unlikely that a judicious compromise may prevent the situation from developing into a critical one. The main issue which confronts Anglicans today is that of reunion with the non-episcopal Protestant churches. Looked at from the Anglican point of view the battle for reunion, as it is called, is a struggle being waged on three fronts. First, there is what Lord Halifax called ' Reunion with Rome '. This name is not strictly accurate, for at no time has the Anglican Church as we know it been in communion with Rome. From the Catholic point of view all that this can mean is that the Anglican communion, or some portion of it, great or small, should accept the supremacy of the Holy See and the doctrinal definitions of 1854, 1870 and 1950, together with those of the Council of Trent, and then be corporately admitted to Catholic fellowship. This admission might imply widespread concessions in the matter of discipline, in matters such as a vernacular liturgy, and perhaps also in that of clerical celibacy, whose partial abrogation might be conceded. This idea has attracted many Catholics, but it does not seem likely at present that it will reach fruition even on a small scale. Such amalgamation either with the Church of England strictly so-called or with the Anglican communion as a whole is, as anyone with the smallest knowledge of these matters knows to be the case, inconceivable.

It is inconceivable also, with the High Church party as a whole, for this party not only has had, but still has, a strongly anti-papal wing. Something less than this, union with a section of the High Church party, that is to say, the pro-papal one, at one time appeared to be within the sphere of practical politics, but now that we have seen the hesitations and uncertainties shown by the Anglo-Catholic clergy, even in such a matter as their attitude towards the South India scheme, we may question whether more than isolated conversions from Anglicanism to Rome can be expected. Of such conversions there has been a steady stream since the days of the Oxford Movement. The signs of the times seem to indicate that this stream will continue and become even more considerably broadened, but anything which could be spoken of as corporate union seems as far off as it has ever been. The Anglican Church has been in a measure catholicized, that is to say that in a large measure it has adopted Catholic ceremonial, and in a smaller measure many Anglicans have accepted Catholic dogma. Yet the essential character of the Church of England remains unchanged. It is still what it was when the Reformation was complete, the Church embodying Catholic and Protestant elements, in a way which argues remarkable skill on the part of those who framed the Anglican settlement.

We may then assume with some security that the break-up of the Church of England, should it occur, will be brought about by some developments which we cannot as yet visualize. Let us now consider the possibilities that the Anglican Church may break down the barriers which at present separate her from the non-Roman churches both Episcopal and non-

Episcopal. First, there are to be considered the possibilities that some kind of union or even of inter-communion will one day come about. The anti-papal confession of the Eastern Churches has strongly commended them to Protestants. On the other hand, the ' Mariolatry ' of the Orthodox Eastern Church is as shocking to the Protestants as is commendable their denunciations of the Papal claims. As far back as the 17th cent. attempts were made to build a bridge between the Anglican and Orthodox Churches. Charles I had some friendly relations with Cyril Locar, Orthodox patriarch of Alexandria, and in the following century some of the Nonjuring bishops attempted to establish friendly relations with the Metropolitan of St Petersburg. Again, in the 19th cent., some of the Tractarians embarked on a similar venture. The strong pro-Turkish inclinations of successive British Governments did not improve relations between the two Churches, though an attempt to improve Anglo-Russian relations was made when one of Victoria's sons married the daughter of the Emperor of Russia.

Nevertheless, a small body of enthusiasts, chief of whom was Mr W. J. Birkbeck, worked tirelessly to bring about the desired improvement in Anglo-Orthodox Church relations. In this campaign they received very little sympathy from the great bulk of their fellow Anglicans and in their approaches to the Orthodox they were compelled to lay as little stress as possible on the elements in Anglicanism such as are the least agreeable to members of the Orthodox Church. Some half-hearted overtures by the Eastern Church have, however, been made. The Oecumenical Patriarch of Constantinople had provisionally recognized Anglican Orders in 1922, shortly before the Turkish reoccupation of the City. The Patriarch of Jerusalem followed suit during the next year and a third Patriarch, that of Alexandria, did so in 1930. The Church of Cyprus recognized Anglican Orders in 1928. In 1925 the Patriarch of Alexandria attended a celebration on the sixteenth centenary of the Council of Nicaea. Anglican ordinations were recognized by the Roumanian Patriarch in 1936. The provisional character, however, of so many of these actions considerably lessens their value in promoting permanent inter-communion between Canterbury and Moscow. A somewhat different story is to be met with when we come to the study of relations between the Church of England and other Protestant Churches, though here we must remember that Anglicans draw a broad distinction between Episcopal and non-Episcopal forms of Church government. Many—perhaps most—Anglicans would indeed be prepared for and would perhaps even welcome a scheme of reunion by which the Church of England was swept without further ado into a great pan-Protestant movement but others will insist on the retention by the non-Episcopal Churches of some shreds of Episcopal rule, though they will not press too closely for a clear definition of the precise meaning of Episcopacy. Anglicans can claim that inter-communion has been reached with a little body of Old Catholics, and something near to it has been established with the Lutheran Church of Sweden. A considerable measure of inter-communion has been achieved with the Churches of Finland and Latvia. With the Churches of Norway, Denmark and Iceland an attempt to reach inter-communion has been made. This proved unsuccessful. Not much more hopeful negotiations were entered into after the Lambeth Conferences of 1920 and 1930 with the non-Episcopal Churches of the British Isles. Discussions with this end in view have more than once taken place between representatives of the Churches of England and Scotland and definite proposals for limited inter-communion have been put forward (1957). But past experience has shown, after they have taken place, that while they have led to a deeper understanding of each other's positions, the gulf between Anglicanism and Presbyterianism has remained wide. With the Free Churches little or no advance towards inter-communion has yet been registered. Yet more recently discussions between Anglicans and Wesleyans, the last body to secede from the Church of England, have been taken up. There seems to be some sort of idea on the Anglican side that the Noncomformists should take their place in a fully National Church in the manner in which the different religious Orders hold their place in the Catholic Church. There is, however, no real parallel between the two cases. In what is considered the most important pronouncement in this connection from the Anglican side, namely, the sermon preached by Dr Fisher, Archbishop of Canterbury, in the University Church in Cambridge, on 3 November 1946, the Primate urged Free Churchmen to take Episcopacy into their own system and experiment with it to see whether it is really something alien from their ideals. From the many failures which have resulted from Anglican gestures in this matter we must not, however, conclude that nothing will come of the Anglican approaches to the Protestant Churches of the British Isles. Unable to secure recognition by Rome, and receiving only ambiguous pronouncements from the Orthodox Eastern Church, Anglicans have returned inevitably to the Protestant Churches of Western Europe and have been offered by them terms of inter-communion such as would be at present rejected. One thing, however, seems clear that ' the splendid isolation ', once characteristic of the Anglican Church, will be discarded in favour of reunion with the non-Episcopal Protestant bodies at no very remote date.

At one time the status of the Church of England as an established Church militated strongly against cordial relations between the established and non-established Protestant Churches but the Church of England has been disestablished piecemeal and only a shadow remains of the former prestige attaching to the establishment. It is still a prerogative of the Archbishop of Canterbury to anoint and crown the Sovereign, and the Archbishop, who bears the title of the Primate of All England, takes precedence immediately after Princes of the blood royal and before all the great Officers of State. The Arch-

bishop of York ranks immediately after the Lord Chancellor and before the Prime Minister. The other bishops rank before barons, and 24 of them have seats in the House of Lords. The Crown appoints the bishops and nominates to a very large number of benefices. The Anglican Church is not, however, paid by the State, as so many English Catholics and a good many foreigners believe to be the case. In the Universities of Oxford and Cambridge the Church of England enjoys a limited establishment owing to the fact that certain professorships are limited to members of that Church. A beneficed clergyman also enjoys certain privileges not shared by members of other denominations. Anglican clergymen are not permitted, if elected, to take their seats in the House of Commons. In the case of nonconformist bodies, opposition to the idea of an Established Church has now largely been overcome, and they would not reject entering into cordial relations or even inter-communion with the Anglican Church on account of the relics of Ecclesiastical Establishment. The political influence moreover of the Nonconformists who were closely attached to the great Liberal Party has been sensibly lessened by the decline of that party. Moreover, the political prestige of the nonconformists, or Free Churchmen, as they are now more often called, has been weakened by the circumstance that Free Churchmen are now largely divided in their political affinities between Liberalism and Labour. On the other hand, the Free Churchmen do not experience the same degree of spiritual isolation as do the Anglicans for they are in communion with the Protestant Churches on the Continent, both established and non-established, in a way that Anglicans are not. There is, therefore, a stronger desire on the part of the Anglicans for some kind of fellowship with the German, Dutch and Scandinavian Protestants than there is for inter-communion with the Church of England on the part of the Protestant bodies, both English and foreign. Opposition to closer relations with the Nonconformists is still strong on the part of the great bulk of the Anglo-Catholic party as was witnessed in 1955 when the question of the recognition of the Church of South India was under consideration. And even some of the Anglo-Catholics were attracted by such an idea, and their one-time rigidity showed signs of an approaching modification. To anyone old enough to remember the crisis over the Kikuyu Conference in 1913 and the fierce passions which it aroused, the present situation seems not far removed from tranquillity. It is no longer impossible to envisage a united Protestant Church in which Anglo-Catholics will with almost universal consent have agreed to a less rigorous train of pronouncements while Nonconformists on their part will have accepted an order of worship embodying traces of the Anglican order of Public Worship and will have become reconciled to a limited standard of ritual, reflecting that to be met with in moderate Anglican Churches. Abroad, in the English-speaking communities overseas, there is no establishment of religion even though there is felt the need for a limited and informal 'establishment' of English-speaking Christianity over against non-Christian religions. In this climate schemes of inter-communion may reach fruition more rapidly than in the more formal atmosphere of Anglicanism at home.

Bibliography. Sources: *Gee and Hardy, *Documents illustrative of English Church History* (1896); *R. Hooker, *Ecclesiastical Polity* (1841); *Strype, *Annals of the Reformation* (1822) and *Ecclesiastical Memorials* (1824); Cardwell, *History of Conferences, etc.* (1841); *C. Hardwick, *History of the XXXIX Articles* (1884); *G. K. Bell, *Documents on Christian Unity* (1924–58); *A. G. Matthews, *Calamy Revised* (1934).

Collective doctrinal works that mark the stages of evolution of modern Anglican thought: *Essays and Reviews* (1865); *Lux Mundi* (1889); *Foundations* (1912); *Essays Catholic and Critical* (1926); *Report of Commission on Doctrine* (1938); *The Apostolic Ministry* (1946).

Lives of leading men: *Archbishop Laud*, by *C. Le Bas (1836); *Thomas Tenison*, by *E. F. Carpenter (1948); *Kenneth White*, by *G. V. Bennett (1957); *Life of A. C. Tait*, by *R. Davidson and W. Benham (1891); *Life of Pusey*, by *H. Liddon (1893–7); *Archbishop Benson*, by *A. C. Benson (1899–1900); *Life of Father Dolling*, by *C. G. Osborne (1903); *Life of Charles Gore*, by *G. L. Prestige (1935); *Randall Davidson*, by *G. K. Bell (1935); *Life of Lord Halifax*, by *J. G. Lockhart (1936); *Cosmo Gordon Lang*, by *J. G. Lockhart (1949); *Retrospect of an unimportant life*, by *Hensley Henson (1942, 1943 and 1950); *Life of William Temple*, by *F. Iremonger (1948); *Edward Stuart Talbot*, by *Lady G. Stephenson (1936).

General works: H. J. T. Johnson, *Anglicanism in Transition* (1938); *N. Sykes, *Old Presbyter and new Priest* (1956) and *Church and State in the Eighteenth Century* (1934); *L. Wickham Legg, *English Church Life from the Restoration to the Tractarian Movement* (1914); *Sir L. Dibdin, *Establishment in England* (1932); *W. J. Birkbeck, *Russia and the English Church* (1895); *R. W. Church, *The Oxford Movement* (1892); *E. A. Knox, *The Tractarian Movement* (1933); *R. W. Dixon, *History of the Church of England* (1878–92); *Ollard, Crosse and Bond, *Dictionary of English Church History* (1948); *C. Garbett, *Church & State in England* (1950).

H. J. T. J.

ANGLICAN ORDERS. *See* ORDINATION

ANIMALS IN THEOLOGY This article comprises five sections: (I) animals in religion, Jewish and pagan, (II) animals in sacred art, (III) the Christian philosophy of animals, (IV) the treatment of animals according to principles derived from this doctrine, and finally (V) two special cases, vivisection and bull-fighting. Animals are living creatures enjoying some measure of sentient life, differentiated from plants at the lower level and man at the higher. The word, often restricted in practice to mammals, also embraces birds, fish and reptiles. It derives from the Latin, *anima*, originally air, wind or breath and indicated a breathing creature.

I Animals in Religion. The OT makes it clear that man is master of the animal kingdom, that animals are subordinated to man and man's purposes. 'Let us make man to our image and likeness; and let him have dominion over the fishes of the sea, and the fowls of the air, and the beasts, and the whole earth' (Gen 1:26). Man's food was to be vegetarian, consisting of herbs and the fruits of trees (Gen 1:29–30): destruction of animal life was out of harmony with the balance and peace of Eden. Animals were drawn into the consequence of original sin and many of them became rebellious against and hostile to man. But man's dominion over the animals was re-affirmed after the flood. 'Let the fear and dread of you be upon all the beasts of the earth . . . all the fishes of the sea are delivered into your hand' (Gen 9:2). Man might now use animals for his food. 'Every thing that moveth and liveth shall be meat for you: even as the green herbs have I delivered them all to you.' (Gen 9:3), with the exception that they are forbidden to eat 'flesh with blood', blood being looked upon as the carrier of life. Subsequently, the Law excluded large numbers and categories of animals from consumption by the Jews (Lev 11:1–31).

Both among Jews and pagans, animals were offered in sacrifice (q.v.). They were the chief object of sacrifice. Carefully selected, they were presented to God for the various ends of sacrifice and then immolated. Man relinquishes his ownership of this particular animal that it may be consecrated, that is, made sacred or holy, for God. The OT shows a gradual purification of the notion of sacrifice; the sacrifices of the Old Law are to culminate in the supreme sacrifice of Christ. This is the paramount theme of Hebrews.

There is evidence of pagan cults of animals, possibly, the actual worship of an animal or, more commonly, the association of some animal with a god or goddess. This primitive attitude towards animals is complicated by the belief that animals incorporated spirits or the souls of men in temporary captivity. Positivist sociology (Durkheim, Lévy-Bruhl) attempted to explain religion as the development of primitive man's relation to society, and in this animals played a significant part. They were treated as totems, representing the spirit of the community or tribe, and a rigid set of tabus was connected with them. Animals are important in Hinduism. Siva is held to be incarnate in Hanuman, the monkey-god, and Durga in the jackal. Garuda, the king of birds, is related to Vishnu. Perhaps the most widespread object of animal cult was the serpent; traces of the serpent cult can be discovered in ancient Greece and Rome, SE Asia and the Americas.

II Animals in Sacred Art. Animals provide a natural form of artistic decoration, and this came to be emphasized by Christians in contrast with the sterile forms and arabesques of Islam, in which neither man nor animals were allowed to be portrayed. Early Christian art used them as a *décor* and symbol. His lamb accompanies the Good Shepherd; the dove recalls in the catacombs the soul released after death while the peacock symbolizes the soul's immortality (*see* ART AND THE CHURCH). Most familiar of all symbols is that of the fish for Christ Himself, the five letters of the Greek word, *Ichthus*, providing initial letters for a simple profession of faith in His Divinity. The four animals came later to denote the evangelists.

Byzantine artists (*see* BYZANTINE ART) employed a rich variety of animal forms, including fantastic creatures like the dragon with a human head and the winged lion. But it was the Gothic era that was richest and wildest in these decorative motifs, witness the cathedrals of Northern France, Paris, Rheims and Laon. There, domesticated sheep and oxen mingle with lions, stags and bears on capitals and cornices as also with legendary beasts like unicorns, basilisks and griffins. The saints, too, were painted with their favourite and distinguishing animals : Roch with a dog, Hubert with his stag, Jerome with the lion, Paul the hermit with a raven.

III The Christian philosophy of Animals. Animals are not highly-intricate machines, as Descartes asserted. Yet we have to avoid the 'pathetic fallacy' by which, especially in countries of the English language, animal behaviour is interpreted in human terms. They have senses even though not all animals enjoy their full range. This is evident from their elaborate sensory systems and from the fact that the higher animals can be trained. Yet their capacity for learning is very limited. Their behaviour is for the most part innate. Animals reared in isolation will perform all the complicated activities of nest-building, mating, guarding eggs, fighting with rivals, in the same way as those brought up more normally. The animal reaction is called forth by sensory stimuli. Sometimes, there is a series of reactions, a rhythm of action and response, the response evoking each time a further action. Animal behaviour is most satisfactorily explained through *instinct*—a complex and delicately adjusted series of unconscious responses to stimuli for the preservation of individual or species. There is purpose there—the whole process is highly purposive—but the purpose is with the creator of Nature, not with the animals themselves. The animal does not act purposively, with recognition of a certain objective ; he does so, in accordance with his nature, in reaction to a stimulus.

What might appear like organized social behaviour in animals is instinctive. Acts are performed which elicit responses in other members of the species, for instance, alarm calls, mating ceremonies, threat- and fight-devices.

Scholastic writers explained animal behaviour by means of a *vis aestimativa*, which was included among the internal senses. In their eyes, instinct was a natural capacity guiding animals in the unreflecting performance of complicated actions useful

in preserving the species or the individual. The *vis aestimativa* belonged to the *anima sensitiva*.

In animals as in man, the *anima sensitiva* and the vegetative principle were regarded as identical. But this animal 'soul' is not a spiritual principle. It is not a substantial form intrinsically independent of, and separable from, matter as is the soul of man. All animal actions remain intrinsically dependent upon a material organism. And their principle is also intrinsically dependent and cannot exist after the break up of the organism. In Scholastic terms the 'soul' of animals is a substantial form wholly immersed in the subject that it animates. It does not therefore require a special divine creative act. But it is none the less simple, since sensitive activity is a simple immanent operation.

IV Treatment of Animals. Since man is master of the animal realm he may use animals for his proper purposes ; such purposes certainly include food, service, the advantage of the human race, and, it would seem, entertainment. St Thomas makes this explicit (*contra Gentiles*, 3:112:7) :[1] 'Thus is excluded the error of those who make it a sin for man to kill animals. By divine providence in the natural order of things they are meant for man's use, and so he may use them, by killing them or in any other way, without doing wrong.'

Some pagan writers encouraged kindness to animals, e.g. Pythagoras, who, accepting the doctrine of *metempsychosis*, thought it likely that human souls were reincarnated in animal bodies. There are traces of this attitude in some Roman legislation, and Cicero (*De Finibus*, 3:20) comments upon the error of attributing human rights to animals. The OT also recommended a proper treatment of animals. Jews were forbidden to muzzle the ox that trod out the corn (Deut 25:4) or to yoke ox with ass (Deut 22:10).

Christian authors rarely treat of this theme, though with the Franciscan movement there was an awakening love of Nature and the sense of close kinship with all God's natural creation (*see* BONAVENTURE). St Thomas encourages kindness towards animals by insisting that pity arises from the sufferings of others and, since animals may feel pain, men may therefore feel pity for them (1–2ae:102:6: @8). Referring in *contra Gentiles*, 2:112 to prohibitions of the OT favouring animals he states that they were issued, 'lest anyone by exercising cruelty towards animals, might become cruel also towards men' or because an injury to animals involved its owner in loss. The human reference is clear throughout. Proper treatment of animals is thought of as a training ground for the proper attitude towards human beings. Cruelty to animals was reprobated largely because of its evil effect upon man.

This has led critics to accuse Catholic teaching of an insensitiveness, a callousness even, towards

---

[1] Per hoc excluditur error ponentium homini esse peccatum, si animalia bruta occidat ; ex divina enim providentia naturali ordine in usum hominis ordinantur, unde absque injuria homo eis utitur occidendo vel quolibet alio modo.

animals. The charge is more usually levelled in Anglo-Saxon countries where, in the matter of domesticated animals, sensibility has far outrun sense, and where, as in Britain today, animals are sometimes better protected against ill-treatment than are children. The question is made more nebulous by an appeal to the 'rights' of animals. If that term be used correctly, animals have no 'rights', for these can belong only to persons, endowed with reason and responsibility. Cruelty to animals is certainly wrong : not because it outrages animal 'rights' which are non-existent, but because cruelty in a human being is an unworthy and wicked disposition and, objectively, because ill-treatment of animals is an abuse and perversion of God's design. Man has been given dominion over the animal kingdom, and it is to be exercised in conformity with human reason and God's Will.

It should be observed that the English Common Law never took cognizance of acts of cruelty to animals. Direct legislation dates from the 19th cent. and was due to public opinion, encouraged by the Royal Society for the Prevention of Cruelty to Animals. Various measures were passed in 1822, 1835, 1837, 1849 and 1854. The law relating to domestic and captive animals is now incorporated in the Protection of Animals Act of 1911 and the amending act of the following year.

V Animals: Special Cases. Two cases of particular controversy should be mentioned. The first is *vivisection* of animals for medical research purposes. Though it has been opposed by a number of doctors and of Christian leaders, the ethics of the question appear straightforward. Provided it is carried out under suitable conditions, avoiding unnecessary pain—and British law is stringent on this point—it is a proper, even a commendable exercise of man's dominion, since its end is the cure of human diseases and generally human welfare.

The second is the question of *bull-fighting*, particularly in Spain. It is a Spanish phenomenon and to the critics the Spaniards answer that the skill and bravery it calls for place it in a far higher category than fox-hunting or even heavy-weight boxing. Church authorities have never approved and on occasions have severely censured bull-fighting, e.g. St Pius V (Constitutio, *De Salute,* 1 November 1567) who condemned it everywhere, threatening princes and participants with dire penalties. Gregory XIII (*Exponi,* 23 August 1575) moderated this for Spanish laymen and Clement VIII (*Suscepti Muneris,* 12 January 1597) reduced it to the *jus commune.* The general opinion of Spanish moralists is that bull-fighting is not against the natural law since the craft and dexterity of the *toreros* make the danger of death a remote one. The spectacles are forbidden to the clergy and the Church certainly does not encourage them.

Bibliography. There is little that deals with this precise topic in modern times. An English adaptation of *L'Église et la pitié envers les animaux* by the Marquise de Rambures was published anonymously in 1906 ; a handbook on the Churches and animal welfare has been issued (1952) by the Universities Federation for animal welfare ; patristic ideas on animals can be found in the work called *Physiologus,* which was compiled about the 3rd cent. and which circulated in many vernacular versions soon after the Greek original appeared. A critical edition by F. Sbordone (with Italian apparatus) was published in 1937 ; *Beasts and Saints* (1934) by H. Waddell will give further light on the Fathers ; on Scriptural ideas about animals there are numerous passages in CCS indexed s.v. *Animals* and a paper by the late Hugh Pope OP entitled 'St Jerome at the Zoo' is printed in the memoir of him by K. Mulvey.

J. M.

ANIMISM The word 'animism' has often been used for those religions of the world that are not classed among what are termed the higher religions, e.g. those who in India are not Hindus, Muslims, Christians, Parsees, etc. are said to be animists. The word was given a more precise meaning and wide currency in anthropological writings by E. B. Tylor (*Primitive Culture* (1871)). As he used it, it had a double sense : (1) the attribution by primitive peoples of a soul to human beings and hence to other living creatures and to inanimate objects ; (2) a theory held by Tylor, that (*a*) the idea of the human soul was the product of faulty reasoning about certain psychic experiences, especially dreams, and (*b*) the notion of spiritual beings was derived from this idea of the human soul and belongs therefore to a later stage of cultural development.

This theory, after holding the field for a long time, was challenged from several sides. Among its critics, R. R. Marett (*The Threshold of Religion* (1909)) pointed out that animistic conceptions are not the simplest elements in primitive religions, and, therefore, if the most primitive conceptually is to be regarded as the most primitive chronologically, as Tylor's theory implied, animism belongs to a later stage than that of the simpler elements, a stage Marett called 'Pre-animistic religion'. Andrew Lang (*The Making of Religion* (1898)) raised the objection that the Australian aborigines, considered to be some of the most primitive hunters and collectors known to science, undoubtedly believe in gods and are far from being animists pure and simple ; an objection also most cogently raised, with an enormous wealth of ethnographic detail, by P. W. Schmidt (*Der Ursprung der Gottesidee* (1926–1955); *The Origin and Growth of Religion* (1931)). Emile Durkheim, who argued that in Australia totemism must be regarded as more primitive than animism, brought other criticisms to bear on Tylor's theory, holding that it was little less than absurd to contend that religion, out of which have sprung law, science and the arts, could mer ely be the product of illusion, hallucinations without any objective foundation. In general, we may say that there is no evidence to support Tylor's rationalist, or intellectualist, theory of the origin of the idea of soul or his contention that this idea is prior, logically and chronologically, to belief in spirits and gods.

Tylor's error was doubtless due in part to the inadequacy of the information at his disposal. In the light of present-day knowledge, insufficient though it is, it is questionable whether any people are animistic in the sense that the word generally used to convey. The attribution of soul to human beings need not be discussed, because belief in the human soul is also found in higher religions and cannot therefore be a distinguishing characteristic of the religions of so-called animists. The distinguishing mark would be the attribution of soul to inanimate objects. But when it has been stated that peoples are animists in that sense, the statement must be received with much caution, for in a matter of this kind a foreign observer may easily misunderstand a primitive people, especially if he is not thoroughly conversant with their language and ways of thinking. When a people are said to attribute soul to inanimate objects it is probable that in many cases what they wish to convey to the inquirer is that the objects are associated with spirits, which are thought of as being in, or behind, them, but also as being in other objects as well as being independent of all of them. In other cases it is probable that objects which appear to be treated as though they were persons are so treated because they have virtue which is in no way intrinsic but is inculcated by ritual acts, in which, rather than in the materials themselves, the virtue resides. Even when words are used which seem to imply that soul, or personality, is attributed to material objects it has to be recognized that the words the European observer translates by 'soul' and 'person' may have a very different meaning to the natives from what 'soul' and 'person' mean to him. Moreover, allowance is often not made for metaphor, symbolism and poetic usage ; and it is not always appreciated that a word and a concept are not the same. Consequently, when we are told that a people's religion is animistic we are really told little about it ; and if the word 'animism' is to be retained, much more detailed research will have to be done into the ideas and practices to which it is applied before a satisfactory definition of it can be formulated.

Bibliography. W. Schmidt s.v.d., *Der Ursprung der Gottesidee*, 12 vols (1926–55) ; English summary *The Origin and Growth of Religion* (1931) ; F. König and others, *Christus und die Religionen der Erde* (1951) ; *E. O. James, *Prehistoric Religion* (1957) ; W. Koppers, *Primitive Man* (1952).   E. E. E-P.

ANSELM, ST This article will treat of the (I) life, (II) character, (III) works, and mainly of (IV) the influence of St Anselm.

I Life. St Anselm was born at or near Aosta in Piedmont in 1033 or 1034. He received his earliest education from his mother and probably from the Benedictines at Aosta. When his mother died he left Italy in order to escape from the harsh treatment he suffered from his father and went to France, settling first at Avranches, and later at Bec, whither he was drawn by the renown of Lanfranc, Prior of the recently founded monastery, under whom

young Anselm wished to pursue his studies. In 1060 Anselm became a monk at Bec and for the next three years worked under the direction of Lanfranc, who trained him as a monk and did much to foster the great love he had for learning. When in 1063 Lanfranc left Bec to found a new monastery at Caen, Anselm succeeded him as Prior. On the death of Herluin, founder and first abbot of Bec, Anselm was elected abbot in 1078. After fifteen years as abbot, he was chosen to succeed Lanfranc as Archbishop of Canterbury in 1093. The see had been vacant for four years on account of the disputes that had been going on between the king, William Rufus, and the Church. Anselm continued to resist the king, especially over his abuses of the privilege of lay investiture, and eventually he appealed to the Pope, Urban II. He left England for Rome in 1097 ; he assisted at the Council of Bari in 1098, playing an important part in explaining to the Greeks the teaching of the Latin Church about the processions in the Blessed Trinity and the need of the *Filioque* in the Creed. He had to remain in exile until king Rufus died in 1100, in which year he returned to Canterbury. He went into exile again from 1103 to 1106 as the old quarrels over lay investiture broke out once more with Henry I. He died at Canterbury on 21 April 1109, aged 76. He was canonized by Alexander VI in 1494.

II Character. No matter how one considers him, as a theologian, a monk or an Archbishop, St Anselm is always one and the same—a man of intense and splendid piety, of great strength of mind and character, and at the same time of remarkable personal charm. In Fr Bainvel's words, ' the theologian is inseparable from the man and the monk' (DTC, 'Anselme', 1327–50). His theological works are radiant with his noble love of God, of Jesus Christ and his saints (cf. for example *Proslogion* 1 : 26). His letters, many of which treat of matters of theology, give a vivid idea of the extent of the influence he had on other people. His own distinctive personal charm is reflected in the care, grace and artistry with which he writes, in the delight he often takes in thoughts and arguments he cherishes as beautiful (cf. *Cur Deus Homo* 1 : 2 and 2 : 8), and in the pleasing way in which he illustrates his ideas (cf. *Cur Deus Homo* 1 : 15 ; 1 : 19 ; 1 : 24 ; *De Incarnatione Verbi* 13). As Fr Bainvel said, ' There is a kind of aestheticism pervading his most abstruse meditations' (*op. cit.* 1342). The outstanding vigour of his mind is as evident to those who study his writings as the strength of his character is evident to those who study his life. Fr de Ghellinck considered that between the epoch of St Augustine and that of St Thomas there was no theologian in the West to equal him (J. de Ghellinck sj, *Le Mouvement théologique du XIIe siècle* (Paris 1948) 79). Aimé Forest considers that if one wishes to see Christian thought at its best before it met with Aristotelianism, ' preference should be given to its presentation by St Anselm' (A. Forest, *Histoire de l'Église*, ed. by Fliche and Martin (Paris 1951) xiii:64).

III Works. In giving a survey of his most important writings it will be helpful to divide them into three groups : (a) those which he published while he was at Bec between 1063 and 1093, (b) those which he published later as Archbishop, and (c) private works never intended for publication.

(a) The *Monologion* was probably the first work that he ever published. It is a series of closely reasoned meditations on the existence and nature of God (1–29), followed by a similar series of meditations on the Trinity (30–76) showing how we can know and love the three Divine Persons. Fr Cayré, with every reason, considers that this is ' one of the most closely reasoned works on God that have ever been written '. This was followed by the *Proslogion*, or Address to God, written as the meditation or theological prayer of one striving to raise his mind to the contemplation of God and seeking to understand what he believes (cf. *Prooemium*). In place of the three lengthy arguments for the existence of God he had given in the *Monologion*, Anselm now offers one short and concise argument which he regarded as self-sufficient and as capable of bringing conviction to all men, even the fool of Psalm 13. This is the famous *a priori* or Ontological argument, based on the idea we have of the greatest conceivable being, the existence of which we cannot deny, it is argued, without contradicting ourselves. In reply to Gaunilo, who objected to the argument in the name of the fool of the Psalmist, St Anselm wrote the *Liber Apologeticus contra Gaunilonem Respondentem pro Insipiente*.

While he was at Bec St Anselm wrote the *De Veritate*, *De Libertate Arbitrii* and the *De Casu Diaboli* ; although these were written at different times he eventually grouped all three together in the order given, explaining in the *Praefatio* which he wrote when publishing them together that he had decided to group them together because they are alike in being in the form of a dialogue between a master and his disciple, and in having a certain continuity of theme and treatment. To these, we must add an elementary treatise on logic, the *De Grammatico*, which is an introduction to Aristotle's *Categories*, of special interest considering the use St Anselm made of reason in theology. All these works are to be found in Volume I of Dom Francis Schmitt's edition of the *Omnia Opera*.

(b) The *Epistola (de Trinitate et) de Incarnatione Verbi*, addressed to Urban II, was commenced and all but finished at Bec, but St Anselm actually completed it when he was Archbishop either in 1093 or 1094. It was written against the Trinitarian errors of Roscelin, and, despite its title, it deals more with the theology of the Trinity than with that of the Incarnation. It contains some very important passages giving his ideas on the relations between faith and reason, about the use of the words ' nature ' and ' person ', and of absolute and relative terms in thinking of the Blessed Trinity, all of which were matters elaborated later in the medieval schools.

The *Cur Deus Homo*, which is often considered to be St Anselm's masterpiece, was commenced in England in great tribulation of mind while he was on the verge of his first exile, and finished in Italy (cf. *Praefatio*). It is one of Anselm's most original and carefully prepared works, written in the form of a dialogue between himself and a friend, Boso. It gives for the first time in history the theory of the Redemption which became classical amongst the great Scholastics. Anselm showed that Christ came on earth to make satisfaction for the sins of men to God alone, and he disposed once and for all of an old theory that Christ died to strip the devil of rights which he had acquired over sinful men and which he misused in bringing about his crucifixion.

The *De Conceptu Virginali et de Originali Peccato* is complementary to the *Cur Deus Homo* ; in fact St Anselm wished that the two should be sent together in one volume to Pope Pascal II. The *De Processione Spiritus Sancti* was also written while he was an exile in Italy after the Council of Bari ; it is an exposition of the arguments which the saint had presented at the Council in defending the insertion of the *Filioque* in the Creed. His last work, *De Concordia Praescientiae et Praedestinationis et Gratiae Dei cum Libero Arbitrio*, is of interest as an early treatise, on Augustinian lines, devoted to the study of a perennial problem which came into its own later in the development of theology. All these works are to be found in Volume II of Dom Schmitt's edition of the *Omnia Opera*.

(c) Apart from these published works St Anselm left a considerable correspondence of about 450 letters. Volume III of Dom Schmitt's edition gives 147 letters belonging to the years he was at Bec ; Volume IV gives 162, and Volume V another 163 letters he wrote as Archbishop of Canterbury. Many of these letters are concerned with matters of theology. He also left a number of prayers and meditations which can be found in Volume III of Dom Schmitt's edition. These are the most widely and popularly known of all his writings.

IV Influence. We can consider this (a) in general and (b) in particular.

(a) *In general.* St Anselm is often called the father of scholasticism (M. Grabmann, *Geschichte der scholastischen Methode*, i:259–339) ; it is as the father of scholastic theology that his influence has been at its greatest. Something new appeared in theology with his writings, this being his *method* of working, based as it is on an invigorating conception of the relations between faith and reason which later became fundamental in the structure of scholastic theology. For St Anselm theology is divine faith impelling the believer to seek an understanding of the truths he believes, and hence to call in the aid of reason which he must use if he is to profit spiritually from what he believes. Theology is *fides quaerens intellectum*, the effort of the human mind to work its way, to the best of its powers, into the truths of faith. Reason can enter into the truths of faith to a certain extent because they are in accord with the basic principles of all thinking. St Anselm was not the inventor of this manner of thinking in theology ; he derived it from St Augustine whose disciple he professed to

46130

be. In the Prologue to the *Monologion* he says that he cannot find anything in his work ' which does not agree with the writings of the Fathers and especially with those of Augustine '. He seems to have visualized his theological method as Augustinian, as doubtless it is in principle. But he uses the method of scrutinizing the truths of faith in order to draw from them all that they logically contain or imply so much more thoroughly, systematically and purposefully than St Augustine ever did, that the work of St Anselm is much more scholastic in method and outlook than that of St Augustine (cf. E. Gilson, *Reason and Revelation in the Middle Ages* (New York 1950) 22–7). Unlike St Augustine, St Anselm is prepared to reason about the truths of faith, ' leaving out Christ, as if there had never been a word of Him ', or ' as if we knew nothing of Him ', to quote his own bold expressions in the *Praefatio* to the *Cur Deus Homo*, i.e. he tries to show that the Christian faith is intrinsically reasonable and intelligible even to the non-believer.[1] The theology of St Anselm is thus a dialogue between divine revelation and human reason or logic (E. Gilson, *La Philosophie au Moyen-Age* (Paris 1945) 250). It is this advance), effected by bringing together divine revelation and the full armoury of human reasoning within the organic unity of one science, which makes St Anselm, monk as he was, the founder of the theology which flourished later in the schools and universities of Europe.

St Anselm has, as we might expect, been charged with being a rationalist. He is certainly not a rationalist if this is understood to mean that he so exalted the rights of reason as to impair in any way the supremacy of divine revelation. He has not a rationalist's conception of reason. He does not, for example, make our ability to understand the intrinsic necessity of the contents of revelation the criterion of their truth. He does not begin with reason and work his way into theology as best he can ; he is not a philosopher who becomes a theologian to the extent of his ability to justify theology by philosophical reasoning. Anselm is first and foremost a theologian of the Augustinian school. His theology begins and ends in faith, reason being only the tool the believer uses to make the best he can as a thinking man of his faith. ' I seek not, Lord, to scan Thy majesty, for I set not my mind in comparison with Thee, but I desire somehow to grasp Thy truth which my heart believes and loves. I seek not to understand that I may believe, but I believe that I may understand, for I accept that word : Unless ye believe, ye shall not understand.'[2] St Anselm is not interested in the genesis of the act of faith but in the contents of divine faith, and the believer's attitude towards its contents. Before reasoning at all about God a man needs to believe in Him and all He has taught us, to love what he believes, and to live humbly according to the truths he believes and loves : ' First cleanse the heart by faith, first enlighten the eyes by keeping the Lord's commandments, first let us become little children by waiting upon the Lord's testimonies, first let us set aside the things of the flesh and live according to the spirit before we discuss and determine the mysteries of faith.'[3] For St Anselm divine faith affects not merely the mind, but the whole soul, and the believer needs to speculate humanly about God in order to seek God with his entire self. Speculation about the truths of faith is not necessary because of the demands of human reason, but rather because it is called for by the truths themselves as a mark of our appreciation of them : ' Just as right order requires that we believe the mysteries of Christian faith before we presume to scrutinize them, so it seems to me there would be neglect if, after we are well established in faith, we did not try to understand what we believe.'[4] St Anselm thus established the importance of the place reason ought to have in theology. There is no question of his holding that our consent to the truths of faith ought to be conditional on our ability to show that they meet the absolute demands of human reason ; he always regards faith as absolute and supreme over reason, which never has any sort of jurisdiction over divine faith, but has rather to be raised up to adjust itself to the supreme demands of faith : ' No Christian should argue that what the Catholic Church believes inwardly and confesses outwardly does not exist, but while he ever holds firmly that faith, loves it and lives up to it, he should seek humbly as best he can reasons why it should be so. If he can understand, let him thank God ; if he cannot, he should not lower his horns to start tossing, but bow his head in adoration.'[5] Those who accuse him of rationalism forget that St Anselm opposed both the conservative theologians of the time who wished to keep revelation and reason apart in two watertight compartments, and the dialectical theologians of the time (such as Peter Abélard and Berengarius of Tours) who were for subordinating revelation to reason in a rationalist spirit.

[1] *remoto Christo, quasi numquam aliquid fuerit de illo*, and again, *quasi nihil sciatur de Christo* (cf. also i:10 and ii: 10). cf. J. McIntyre, chapter 1, which gives a careful study of Anselm's methodology.

[2] *Proslogion* 1 : Non tento, domine, penetrare altitudinem tuam, quia nullatenus comparo illi intellectum meum ; sed desidero aliquatenus intelligere veritatem tuam, quam credit et amat cor meum. Neque enim quaero intelligere ut credam, sed credo ut intelligam. Nam et hoc credo, quia ' nisi credidero, non intelligam '.

[3] *De Incarnatione Verbi* 1 : Prius ergo fide mundandum est cor, . . . prius per praeceptorum domini custodiam illuminandi sunt oculi, . . . et prius per humilem obedientiam testimoniorum dei debemus fieri parvuli, . . . prius inquam ea quae carnis sunt postponentes, secundum spiritum vivamus quam profunda fidei diiudicando discutiamus.

[4] *Cur Deus Homo* 1 : Sicut rectus ordo exigit ut profunda Christianae fidei prius credamus quam ea praesumamus ratione discutere, ita negligentia mihi videtur si, postquam confirmati sumus in fide, non studemus quod credimus intelligere.

[5] *De Incarnatione Verbi* 1 : Nullus Christianus debet disputare quomodo quod catholica ecclesia corde credit et ore confitetur non sit ; sed semper eandem fidem indubitanter tenendo, amando, et secundum illam vivendo, humiliter quantum potest quaerere rationem quomodo sit. Si potest intelligere, deo gratias agat ; si non potest, non immittat cornua ad ventilandum, sed submittat caput ad venerandum.

St Anselm did not progress as far as the scholastics of the 13th cent. to distinguish clearly between what belongs to theology and what to philosophy. None the less his basic ideas about the relations between the two are so sound that he is never guilty of seriously confusing them, even though he does at times make exaggerated claims for reason in theology. It was because his method of combining faith and reason is fundamentally sound that he provided the foundations on which the scholastics could build a theology in which the relations between the two are minutely determined. He considered that reason has a twofold function to perform in theology, (*a*) to meet the objections of unbelievers and heretics (cf. *De Incarnatione Verbi* 2) who reject the Catholic faith because they consider it to be repugnant to reason, and (*b*) to prove the truth of the articles of faith by cogent reasoning (*rationibus necessariis*) (cf. Prologue to the *Monologion* ; *Cur Deus Homo, Praefatio* and i:25 ; and *De Incarnatione Verbi* 6). Some hold that St Anselm erred by excess in supposing that the reasons he gives for the Incarnation and for the existence of the three Persons in God are ' necessary ', i.e. that his arguments from reason are by themselves alone, ' *et remoto Christo* ', sufficient to prove the truth of the divine mysteries. It seems doubtful that St Anselm did mean that we can prove the truth of these mysteries by reason alone.[1] It is true that he failed to distinguish clearly, as the scholastics did, between arguments which are ' necessary ' in the strict sense of the term in that they lead inevitably to their conclusions, and those which are merely very fitting, or most apt, leading to a conclusion which is feasible but not inevitable. But it is an exaggeration to say that this imprecision in his use of the word ' necessary ' led him to think that the arguments he advanced really prove, apart from revelation, that there must be processions in God, and that Christ's coming could be seen by pure reason as inevitable. It has to be remembered that St Anselm always reasoned from within the faith ; he sought reasons for the truths he believed. He did not conceive his arguments from reason as inevitably leading an unbeliever to the faith, nor as inevitably keeping a reasonable believer in the faith by force of logic, but only as enabling a believer to explain his faith to an unbeliever and as helping to keep a believer in his faith (cf. E. Gilson, *History of Christian Philosophy in the Middle Ages* (London 1955) 130). Even if he claims too much, at least verbally, for the powers of reason by talking of ' necessary reasons ' to be found for divine mysteries, he never treats divine mysteries as purely philosophical questions. There is no suggestion that the arguments given for the divine processions or for Christ's coming are so necessary that denial of them would involve a denial of the principle of contra-

diction : St Anselm always had in mind his, ' I seek not to scan Thy majesty ' (cf., for example, *Cur Deus Homo* i:19). Whereas he claims to be able to prove the existence of God by an argument, rejection of which leads inevitably to self-contradiction, he never makes such a claim for the ' necessary reasons ' he gives to prove supernatural mysteries (cf. *Cur Deus Homo* i:18, p. 82 of Schmitt). The great scholastic theologians never censured St Anselm for his *rationes necessariae* : on the contrary, as Fr Chenu says, ' the Schoolmen were haunted by Anselm's *rationes necessariae* (M. D. Chenu OP, *Introduction à l'étude de s. Thomas d'Aquin* (Paris 1950) 158) ; the Schoolmen did, however, make the requisite distinctions in the use of the word ' necessary '.

St Anselm was, then, the first of the philosopher-theologians of the Middle Ages ; he had the makings of a pure philosopher, and the elements of a system of metaphysics and of a rational psychology. He was, however, essentially a theologian, but one who theologized as a metaphysician and a logician would. Thus Fr de Ghellinck called him ' the great metaphysician of dogma ' (*op. cit.* 80).

(*b*) *In particular.* St Anselm's influence was great and predominantly general in nature, but it is also recognisable in many particular domains of theology. He was the founder of natural theology as it has been known for centuries in the Church, in the treatise *De Deo Uno*. He was a pioneer in studying the proofs for the existence of God, the metaphysical essence of God, and in deducing the divine attributes one by one from the divine essence. As we have said, he thought out the classical theory of the Redemption so that the *Cur Deus Homo* is indeed ' the first real treatise on the Atonement ' (J. Rivière, ii:14-45, 199-202). After St Augustine, St Anselm is perhaps the deepest thinker in the West on the theology of the Trinity and Incarnation prior to the 13th cent. ; his metaphysical reflections on the Trinity and Incarnation, the key mysteries of the faith, prepared the way for the use of the scholastic method in all domains of theology. He has the credit of having composed the formula which the Council of Florence used in the *Decretum pro Jacobitis* (D703), and which soon became a key formula in Trinitarian theology, that in God all is one ' where there does not enter in a contrast of relations ' (*De Processione Spiritus Sancti* 1).[2] The influence of St Anselm in Mariology, though unquestionable, is difficult to determine (Le Bachelet, DTC, 995-1004, ' Immaculée Conception ').

Finally there is the intangible influence St Anselm has had on thousands of readers as a spiritual writer. His influence has not merely been that of a great thinker, a purely speculative theologian, but first and foremost that of a person who lives in his works, and for whom living and thinking, praying and writing are merely so many different ways of doing one and the same thing—loving and serving God. His prayers and meditations have a fascination which

---

[1] cf. J. McIntyre, 51-5. P. H. Wicksteed held that in St Anselm's view we can prove the necessity of divine mysteries not before but after God has revealed them to us (cf. *The Reactions between Dogma and Philosophy* (London 1926), 50-5).

[2] The Council defined that in God ' *omnia sunt unum, ubi non obviat relationis oppositio* '.

is almost irresistible. They contain all that is most typical of his spirit, as we can see, for example, in the famous prayer at the end of the third Meditation: ' Grant, I beseech Thee, Lord, that I may lovingly appreciate what I knowingly perceive, that I may be aware in my heart of what I am aware with my mind. I owe Thee more than my entire self, but I have no more, and even this I cannot of myself give back in full. Take Thou, Lord, into Thy love even the whole of this self. All that I am is Thine by creation ; make it all Thine in love.' [1]

Bibliography *Sancti Anselmi Opera Omnia*, 6 vols, critical edition by Dom F. S. Schmitt (1946-61). This supersedes the edition which is in PL 158-9 ; *Un Inédit de saint Anselme. Le Traité* De Unitate divinae essentiae et pluralitate creaturarum, *d'après Jean de Ripa*, par André Combes (Paris 1944) ; Eadmer, *Vita Sancti Anselmi* (PL 158: 49-118) ; Charles de Rémusat, *Saint Anselme de Cantorbéry* (Paris 1868) ; R. W. Church, *St Anselm* (1905); ★J. M. Rigg, *St Anselm of Canterbury* (1896) ; ★Dictionary of National Biography i, 482-503 ; J. Bainvel SJ, ' Anselme ', DTC, 1327-50 ; P. Richard, ' Anselme de Cantorbéry ', DHGE, 464-85 ; M. Mähler, ' Anselme de Cantorbéry ', DSp, 690-6 ; E. Gilson, ' Sens et nature de l'argument de s. Anselme ', *Archives d'hist. doctrinale et litt. du M.A.* ix (1934) 5-51 ; J. Bainvel SJ, ' Argument de saint Anselme ', DTC, 1350-60 ; A. Koyré, *L'Idée de Dieu dans la philosophie de s. Anselme* (Paris 1923) ; C. Filliatre, *La Philosophie de s. Anselme* (Paris 1920) ; ★K. Barth, *Fides quaerens intellectum, Anselms Beweis der Existenz Gottes im Zusammenhang seines theologischen Programms* (Munich 1931, English translation 1960) ; J. Fischer, *Die Erkenntnislehre Anselms von Canterbury* (Münster 1911, Beiträge 10, 3) ; ★J. McIntyre, *St Anselm and his Critics: A Re-interpretation of the ' Cur Deus Homo '* (1954) ; M. Jacquin, *Les ' rationes necessariae ' de S. Anselme*, in the *Mélanges Mandonnet* ii, 67-78 (Paris 1930) ; J. Rivière, *The Doctrine of the Atonement*, translated from the French by L. Cappadelta (1909), ii, 14-45, 199-202 ; A. Wilmart OSB, ' La Tradition des prières de s. Anselme ', in RBn 36 (1924) 52-71 ; F. Copleston SJ, *A History of Philosophy* (1950), ii ; F. Cayré AA, *Patrologie et histoire de la théologie* (Paris 1955), ii 334-53 ; A. M. Landgraf, *Einführung in die Geschichte der theologischen Literatur der Frühscholastik* (Regensburg 1948) ; M. Grabmann, *Geschichte der scholastischen Methode* (Freiburg 1909) 1, 258-339 ; ★ R. W. Southern, ' St Anselm and his English pupils ', in *Medieval and Renaissance Studies* 1 (1944) 3-34. E. A. S.

ANTHROPOMORPHISM is the erroneous ascription to God of human features, characteristics, activities or emotions. From the articles on ANALOGY

[1] Fac precor, domine, me gustare per amorem quod gusto per cognitionem. Sentiam per affectum quod sentio per intellectum. Plus debeo quam me ipsum totum, sed nec plus habeo nec hoc ipsum possum per me reddere totum ; trahe tu, domine, in amorem tuum vel hoc ipsum totum. Totum quod sum tuum est conditione ; fac totum tuum dilectione. (Schmitt's edition, iii:91)

and ATTRIBUTES OF GOD it will be clear that pure perfections (i.e. those free from material conditions) in man may legitimately be attributed to God, if but in an analogical sense, while mixed perfections cannot be ascribed to Him until stripped of their imperfections. If pure perfections thus belong to analogical predication about God, what remains is fit for metaphor alone. The danger here, as with all use of metaphor, is that the metaphors become atrophied, and it is then forgotten that they are metaphors.

It is Catholic teaching that man left to himself and without the aid of revelation could only with difficulty and after a long time conceive an idea of the one God, and even then he would not fail to disfigure his idea by adding errors to the truth he had seen. The pre-history of religion bears this out. Apart from the Jews, who show in the OT a gradual purification of their idea of God under divine tutelage, the ancient world generally shows a process of gradual but erratic declension towards magic and superstition, and what is whispered in Homer about the pliability of the gods is the common assumption of all the dabblers in magic of the time of the Roman Empire. Sometimes, as with the *Birds* of Aristophanes, a piece of mockery may suggest nobler ideas, for to say that the men of Athens might punish the gods by cutting off from them the sweet savour of the sacrifices on earth does but recall to mind the fact that the very idea of the gods savouring earthly sacrifices must be a metaphor, and thus the declension might be arrested for a time.

The Jews, though not given to philosophical speculation, managed to preserve a belief in one God whose nature was spiritual, and to avoid contamination from the star-god religions of the East and from the animal-worship of Egypt (CCS 109c-d ; 137a ; 591e-h). They did not secure this by analysis of the operations of the spiritual faculties in man (intellect and will) but rather by an all-pervading notion of the holiness of God. This led the makers of the LXX often to substitute circumlocutions for the more crudely anthropomorphic passages of the Hebrew text and to ascribe to an almost personalized concept of the wisdom of God or to the Shekinah many of the divine activities that seemed to bring down to human level the majesty of God. This preoccupation with the holiness and majesty of God led them sometimes to attribute to God mundane events where the operation of any number of secondary causes could have been discerned by a more philosophic view. Nor were they free from the error of ascribing human signs of anger to God, the strength of their own passions disabling them from a calmer notion.

After the coming of Christianity one heretical sect alone championed the error of anthropomorphism. Audius, head deacon of Edessa in Syria (*c.* 325), broke with the Church on matters of discipline (Epiphanius, *Haer.* 70 ; GCS 37:232-49) then took up this error, arguing from Gen 1:26-7 that it was the material part of man, the slime of the earth, that was in the likeness of God, and that God had therefore full human characteristics.

Epiphanius used against him the evidence of Jn 1:18 that no man has seen God, and suggested that there was a difference between seeing and scrutinizing, as one might be said to see the sea from afar off on a mountain-top without being able to describe it. Audius was eventually banished by Constantine to Scythia, where he preached his new doctrine to the Goths and set up monasteries, only to be turned out again by Athanarich. The Audians died out before 500, yet not before they had managed to absorb some elements of Manichean doctrine. Theodoret (PG 83:428) made the most damaging point against their exegesis by saying that God speaks to man in the Scriptures according as man has capacity to understand. There is a divine condescension which accommodates the language to human thought of the time, making it not too high but just so far above what man is used to that the effort to understand can seem worth while. The essentials of the message are not falsified but the wrappings are arranged to suit the audience. Chrysostom (PG 54:589) went another way about the difficulty, calling in 1 Cor 11:7 to show that the likeness between God and man is not the same in male and female and that therefore it cannot be a bodily likeness. Cyril of Alexandria in his polemic against the sect (PG 76:1066) followed the same line as Theodoret.

In modern times Barth (*Dogmatik* II, i, 250–60) has claimed that *all* predication about God is anthropomorphic; he quotes Marius Victorinus (PL 8:1033) for the fact that 'we describe the actions of God from our own',[1] though he does not mention the opening words of the sentence, where Victorinus shows that he is comparing our predication about God with a perfect description of Him. No human predicate or sum of predicates is ever going to be adequate to express the nature of God, but there is a clear distinction, here as in so many spheres, between metaphorical and analogical predication, and it is quite arbitrary to assume, as Barth does, that God must be quite alien from such predicates as beauty and goodness or understanding and will, or to say that analogy may hold good from God downwards to ourselves but not in the reverse direction.

The old evolutionary idea that man had to progress from animal gods to man-like gods is now generally given up. The late Fr W. Schmidt SVD came in 1935 to accept as the most likely explanation of the correspondence in patterns of worship and belief in so many widely separated primitive tribes the existence of a primitive revelation filtered down to them by oral tradition. He was not moved thereto by dogmatic considerations, but solely by the evidence, which he and his disciples had done so much to collect. As late as 1930 he admitted that he was quite uncertain to what result the gathering of the evidence would lead. That he should after so wide a survey eventually come to the conclusion he reached is of some importance, even though his

[1] Quoniam non est invenire nomen dignum Deo . . . a nostris actionibus nominamus actiones Dei.

methodology has been attacked in more recent times.
Bibliography. W. Schmidt SVD, *Ursprung der Gottesidee* VI (1935); *J. Hempel, *Die Grenzen des Anthropomorphismus Jahwes im Alten Testament*, ZAW 57 (1939) 75–85; *K. Barth, *Kirchliche Dogmatik* II, i (1946); W. Koppers SVD, 'Pater Wilhelm Schmidt', an obituary in *Zeitschrift für Ethnologie* 79 (1954) 243–53; *L. Köhler, *Theologie des Alten Testamentes* (1936); P. Heinisch, *Theologie des Alten Testamentes* (1940); *E. O. James, *Prehistoric Religion* (1957); Archbishop F. König (ed.) *Christus und die Religionen der Erde*, 3 vols (1951); W. Koppers, *Primitive Man* (1952).

J. H. C.

ANTI-CHRIST As the Church has made no definition about the nature or the future activity of anti-Christ, this article will be confined to considering the scriptural teaching about him in (I) John and (II) Paul, with some attention to possible Jewish antecedents of their ideas, and will then (III) go on to the patristic difference of opinion about the plurality of anti-Christs and (IV) the later perversions—ideas of a 'mystical body of the devil' as a counterpart of the mystical body of Christ.

I John. In the I Epistle of John (I Jn 2:18–22; 4:1–3) there is a statement of who this anti-Christ is; it does not give a very clear answer, for while the definite article is used with the title (2:22 and perhaps 2:18) it is also said (2:18) that there are many anti-Christs already in the world. It is said of these that they are apostates—'they went out from us but they were not of us'. John asks who is *the* liar, if not he who denies that Jesus is the Christ; such a man is the anti-Christ. Here John seems to be alluding to a figure who is met with in the Dead Sea Scrolls, 'the man of sin'. Jewish apocalyptic had made use of such a figure for some time before the coming of Christ, since Pompey is styled 'the sinner' or perhaps 'the man of sin' in the so-called *Psalms of Solomon* (2 and 17) for what he did to Jerusalem in 63 B.C. It would seem that John took this well-known Jewish figure, with its contours as uncertain as the 'great Leviathan' of the political writers of a later age, and made use of it to illustrate what he had to say about another figure, anti-Christ, about whom his audience had already heard something (4:3). John says that this anti-Christ is already in the world, and his words led to much speculation among Jewish-Christian groups towards the end of the 1st cent. about the *Nero redivivus* who was then expected to return from Parthia and persecute the Church, as originally he had done in A.D. 64.

In the Apocalypse (16:13; 19:20; 20:10) John describes 'the false prophet' who is associated with 'the beast'; to him are ascribed miracles and he is credited with leading men astray just as the anti-Christ does in 1 Jn. The two are not formally identified, but, given the elevated literary style of the Apocalypse in contrast with the plainer speech of the epistle, it is not unreasonable to suppose that John did identify them. The 'many seducers' of 2 Jn 7, who are said to have come into the world and who are then identified with ' *the* seducer and *the* anti-Christ', seem to be meant for historical characters such as Simon Magus (who is shown by the now extensive dossier of the 2nd cent. Gnostics to have been one of their pioneers), and, if this is true, then John may be taken throughout to be using anti-Christ as a type (such as Harlequin, the Green Man or the *Miles gloriosus*) whose features fit various historical personages. This is the readiest way of reconciling his singular/plural antithesis. The common feature of the early heretics was a denial that Jesus was the Christ (for the first creeds were Christ-creeds, confined to articles about Him) and this denial is what John (1 Jn 2:22) ascribes to anti-Christ, adding also that this denial involves a denial of the Father (and the first expansion of the creed is the addition of a first article concerning the Father). The curious ascription of Parthia as the place to which John's epistle was sent (an ascription accepted by Augustine and Cassiodorus and probably by Clement of Alexandria) may owe something to the belief that the restored Nero was to appear among the Parthians.

II In St Paul (2 Cor 6:15) we are introduced to another Jewish figure, Beliar, who is adduced as the counterpart of Christ. Beliar appears in the *Sibylline Oracles* (3:63–92) and the *Testament of Levi* (18:12) says that the new priest shall bind Beliar. The *Ascension of Isaiah* (4:2–18), in a passage that has suffered Christian interpolation, elaborates his story. This adversary or counterpart of Christ is described in 2 Thess 2:3–12; Paul had preached about him in Thessalonica and wrote to clarify some of the things he had said. There was a time for him to appear, when he would sit in the Temple and give himself out for God, but he would be slain by Christ at the second coming; meanwhile there was 'a stopper' to delay his appearance, and Paul had told them all about this, but does not tell us. Hence the difficulty of his words. He uses another Jewish title, ' man of sin ', for this figure, but he is less easy to interpret than John in the sense that a whole series of men will reproduce the common features of such a type of iniquity. In his treatise on anti-Christ (6; GCS 1:8) Hippolytus took Paul quite literally: anti-Christ would be a Jew; he would have apostles and would rally the Jews; he would restore the Temple (in this counterfeiting the act of Christ who rose again and restored the temple of His body) and his death would come from Christ. This line of thought continues throughout Christian theology, until a man like Suarez (*de mysteriis Christi* 54:1:7) can say that the unique and personal character of anti-Christ is an assured truth of the faith (*res certissima et de fide*), though all the while there is another stream of tradition which is seen in Tertullian (*adv. Marc.* 3:8; CSEL 47:388) basing itself on John and seeing in the many whom John called anti-Christ for their denials of the Messiahship of Jesus so many immature and abortive Marcionites.[1]

[1] Praecoces et abortivos quodammodo Marcionitas . . . apostolus Ioannes antichristos pronuntiabit, negantes Christum in carne venisse.

When the ' suffering servant ' of Isaias can be taken as at once a single person and a collectivity, foreshadowing at once Christ and His mystical body, it does not seem difficult to take Paul's anti-Christ as also one and many, though he nowhere puts forward the idea that there could be a mystical body for the devil (*see* BODY, MYSTICAL).

III Patristic theories of the plurality of anti-Christs start from Tertullian, who has just been cited above, and from Origen. Commenting on Mt 7:24 Origen declares that the downpour, the rivers and the winds mentioned in that parable are the devil, the anti-Christs and the spirits of wickedness respectively (fragment 151; GCS 41:75). Jerome followed him in this interpretation. Later in the same commentary he says of Mt 27:35 (fragment 552; GCS 41:226) that Christ stretched out His hands on the cross in order that by the majesty of the cross He might bring to naught the powers that lay over against Him. On the other hand Victorinus of Pettau, who is elsewhere indebted to the writings of Papias and the school of Ephesus, says in commenting on Apoc 12:3–5 that the Gentiles are all destined to be under the motion of anti-Christ against the saints, that the seven heads of the beast are seven Roman emperors as he will show later (in a part of the commentary now lost).[2] He seems to have no doubt that anti-Christ will be one man, and his own death in the Diocletian persecution might well have inclined others to the same view. Irenaeus seems to have believed (*adv. haer.* V: xxx:2 H), that anti-Christ would be a Jew of the tribe of Dan, and therefore not a Roman emperor. On the slaying of anti-Christ as described in 2 Thess 2:8, Victorinus (CSEL 49:24) cites Apoc 1:16 as confirmation, the two-edged sword there attributed by John to Christ being taken as the instrument of the slaying and as an explanation of Paul's words in the text. Later (on Apoc 8:1; CSEL 49:82) Victorinus has a very enigmatic passage[3] about anti-Christ: ' The prayers of the Church are sent down (?) from heaven by an angel and they are received; and as we read in the gospel there is poured forth by the holy angels wrath and the kingdom of the vertiginous anti-Christ.'

Commodianus, whose century and native land are uncertain, shows a lively interest in anti-Christ. One of his *Instructiones* (I, 41:CSEL 15:53) deals with the times of anti-Christ. Apparently three rulers, later defined as Caesars, are to advance against him and to be defeated by him; Nero ruined the city of Rome but this anti-Christ will ruin the whole world (*carmen apologeticum* 911 and 933: CSEL 15:175). Some of the Christians will ' gain stout martyrdom ' from him (*Instructiones* II, 3: CSEL 15:63). By contrast, there were times at which no interest was taken in the coming of anti-Christ. The sermons of Caesarius of Arles, which

[2] Omnes enim gentes sub machina antichristi contra sanctos staturae sunt. Septem capita septem reges romanos, ex quibus et antichristus in priore dicemus. (CSEL 49:118.)

[3] Mitti de caelo orationes ecclesiae ab angelo, et suscipi eas et contra effundi iram et scotomari regnum antichristi per angelos sanctos et in evangelio legimus.

survive *in extenso*, carry no mention of him. Leo the Great, with his phrase (in *serm.* 70 ; PL 54:383) about the passion of Christ going on till the end of time, does, however, provide the theoretical basis for the notion that the successive persecutors of the Church are in fact a series of anti-Christs who attack Christ in His members.

In patristic times the Church underwent from time to time waves of what can only be described as excessive attention to its Jewish origins. At such times the interest in anti-Christ quickened, for the Jewish apocryphal writings have much to say about ' Beliar, prince of this world, who is to come down in the shape of a man.' Qumrân has shown how easily the ' sons of darkness' could be identified as the army of Belial, and in one of the hymns (16:15) is the prayer : ' Suffer not Belial to arise and immerse himself in Thy servant's spirit.' In view of this close parallel, it does not seem unlikely that Rigaux may be right when he claims that the ' stopper' (ὁ κατέχων) who is holding back anti-Christ, according to what Paul wrote to the Thessalonians, is not the apostolic preaching, nor Paul himself, but some factor which was already made clear by Jewish tradition. If one can think that Paul is simply conjecturing and not speaking from knowledge that had been revealed to him, then this way out seems perhaps the best. One might even conjecture that the restraining factor had some connection in the mind of Paul with the conversion of the Jews, or at least of the ' remnant' which was to be brought into the Church before the Parousia.

From the time of Tertullian (*de resurrectione carnis* 24 ; CSEL 47:60), who asked briefly what was the restraining factor and answered : ' What, save the Roman state', down to Jerome (*ep.* 121:11 ; CSEL 56:53) there was a school of thought, chiefly Western, which saw the Roman Empire as the one bulwark against the powers of evil. Should this fall, then the reign of anti-Christ could begin and the end would not be far away. Jerome took the *discessio* of 2 Thess 2:3 quite literally as the breakaway of the subject peoples from the Empire. This philosophy of history found its way into the liturgy and survived at least until the 10th cent., when Adso, abbot of Montier, wrote his *libellus de antichristo* for Queen Gerberga in 954 (PL 101:1289). Adso says, ' One of the kings of the Franks will rule the whole Roman empire . . . and after he has faithfully governed his kingdom he will come to Jerusalem finally and lay down his crown and sceptre on the mount of Olives. . . . This will be the final consummation of the Christian and Roman empire . . . and then the man of sin will be disclosed.'[1] The influence of this idea on the later enterprise of the Crusades does not seem to have been noticed by historians.

IV Later perversions of the idea of anti-Christ

[1] Unus e regibus Francorum Romanum imperium ex integro tenebit . . . qui postquam regnum suum fideliter gubernaverit ad ultimum Hierosolymam veniet et in monte Oliveti sceptrum et coronam suam deponet ; hic erit finis et consummatio Romanorum et Christianorum imperii . . . et tunc revelabitur ille homo peccati.

begin with Joachim of Flora, who was the first to suggest that the Pope was anti-Christ. John XXII in 1318 condemned the idea that there were two churches, one carnal and corrupt, the other pure and holy (D 485). From this to the assertion that there was a mystical body for the devil was but a step, and the step was taken by some of the Reformation controversialists, as may be seen from Newman's essay (among his *Essays Critical* II) on the Protestant idea of anti-Christ. Love of self even to the contempt of God (as Augustine defined the principle of the city of evil) does not make for cohesion or for the unity of even a ' moral body' ; but if it is true that anti-Christ is a collectivity, then it may be allowed that the successive instances of his manifestation have some continuity one with another. Modern exegetes have tried to argue that the endurance of the ' restraining factor' requires a collective anti-Christ, while others have countered with the assertion that Paul clearly thinks of a single man, for he distinguishes between the general power of evil or the devil and anti-Christ himself, who is to have his manifestation and the proofs of his credibility just as Christ had. Much of this argumentation is as unsound as that of the 17th-cent. High Anglican who claimed that the Pope must be anti-Christ because he protected the Jews in Rome. In these modern arguments, until very recently, no account was taken of the ambivalent treatment (as between singular and collective) of the Servant of Jahweh, which should imply by contrast a similar and opposite ambivalence in the idea of anti-Christ, nor was much regard paid to the Jewish way of indicating uncertainty by straddling the future event with positive and negative descriptions. Thus it was quite in order for Paul to say that anti-Christ would be one man, and also that he would be a series, if he really meant that he did not know which. (*See* CCS 38c for this Jewish practice.) Paul knew from Mt 24:24 there would be false Christs and also that Daniel 11 spoke of one man of wickedness. He accepted both.

Bibliography. B. Rigaux, *L'Anté-christ* (1932) and *Les Épîtres aux Thessaloniens* (1956) ; P. H. Furfey, ' The mystery of lawlessness', in CBQ 8 (1946) 179–191 ; *H. Rowley, *The Relevance of Apocalyptic* (1944) ; D. Buzy, in DBS I s.v. and ' L'Adversaire et l'obstacle', in RSR 24 (1934) 402–31 ; *T. F. Torrance, *Kingdom and Church* (1956) ; M. Schmaus, *Von den letzten Dingen* (1948) and again in *Dogmatik* IV, 2 (1953) ; J. Schmid, ' Der Antichrist und die hemmende Macht', in TQ 129 (1949) 323–43 ; J. P. Arendzen, ' The Conversion of the Jews' (dealing with the connection of this event with the coming of anti-Christ), in CR 27 (1947) 379–86 ; J. B. Orchard OSB, ' St Paul and the Book of Daniel', in Bi 20 (1939) 172–79.   J. H. C.

ANTINOMIANISM The troubles caused by this aberration—which consisted in denying the value of the Jewish law, or of any law at all, as a help towards salvation—came chiefly from certain followers of Luther, who did not lack encouragement from their leader. In England they were seen principally in the doings of the Anabaptists and of the Brownists in the 16th cent. Luther had taken the Pauline polemic against the Law (Gal 3 and Rom 7) as being an attack not so much on the ceremonial practice of the Jews as on the ethical principles enshrined in the ten commandments. In modern times there has taken place a certain de-Lutherizing of St Paul and the question of Antinomianism has lost significance save as a matter for those who have to interpret Luther's doctrinal system and to indicate how far Melanchthon and Calvin moved away from him. This matter is still subject to lively controversy in Germany, but elsewhere the question is in abeyance. It will be dealt with briefly here.

In 1527 the Lutheran, Agricola, denied that Christians were bound by any part of the Law, even the ten commandments. Christ frees us from the curse of the Law ; the *theological* usage of the Law is simply to allow it to be an accuser of sin, while faith sets us free. Melanchthon, while holding that the Decalogue was abrogated, thought that there was a *political* usage of the Law possible, whereby it served to keep libertines within bounds by its threats. Much dispute arose over this usage and over a third usage, which may loosely be called *pedagogic*, whereby the Law is conceived as leading men to Christ even while not being able to justify them. This third usage is central to Calvin's position, as he shows in his commentary on Gal 3:19, 24 ; for him the Law not only shows forth the sanctity of God and thereby gives a mirror for men's souls, but all the ceremonies of the Law are like so many sacraments leading men to Christ in the days before He had come. It is ironical to see after all this that the stiff Calvinists of Cromwell's day (including his chaplain, Saltmarsh, and the author of the first English work on devotion to the Heart of Christ, Thomas Goodwin) fell back into complete Antinomianism. As they put it : if a man was of the number of the elect, no power of heaven or earth could prevent his salvation, sin how he might. The mercy of the Heart of Christ to sinners is for them mercy of a predestinarian kind.

The Antinomianism met with in the early Church does not seem to have come from any misunderstanding of St Paul. The story about Nicolaus (told by Clement of Alexandria, and cited by Eusebius *HE* 3:29) is not very coherent, but seems based on some facts or other about the errors he taught, for Irenaeus (1:xxiii, H) and Hippolytus (*Ref. haer.* 7:36 ; GCS 26:223) say that he regarded fornication and the eating of sacrificial meats as indifferent acts (cf. also Justin, *dial.* 45–6). They may be jumping to conclusions from Apoc 2:6, 14, but they were in a position to verify them. It needed but the briefest consideration of this attitude of the early Church to warrant the Council of Trent deciding, against the followers of Luther (D 830 and 804), that no man, however justified he might be by grace, was exempt from observing the commandments of God.

Bibliography. *H. J. Schoeps, *Theologie und Geschichte des Judenchristentums* (1949) and *Paulus* (1959) ; *W. Joest, *Gesetz und Freiheit* (1951) ; *W. Elert, *Zwischen Gnade und Ungnade* (1948) ; R. A. Knox, *Enthusiasm* (1950).   J. H. C.

ANTIOCH, CHALICE OF This chalice, of which details were published to the world by G. A. Eisen in 1916 (*American Journal of Archaeology* 20:426–437), is of interest to theology for the claim, made for it by Eisen, that it is the very cup used at the Last Supper. It stands $7\frac{1}{2}$ ins. high, is of silver with two golden figures of Christ and several of the apostles, set in a decorative scheme of vine-branches, doves, an eagle, baskets and rosettes. The most extravagant claims were made for the chalice. It was alleged to have been made up from the Grail cup in A.D. 64 (from the number of rosettes), to give the earliest portrait of Christ, to show the *four* evangelists, to indicate by the attitudes of the apostles that they were proclaiming His divinity, and so on. Much discussion took place, especially between 1924 and 1926, but the work is now almost forgotten. The critics had the best of it, and such studies as that by Père de Jerphanion SJ, of the Oriental Institute, Rome, did much to weaken the enthusiasm of its early supporters. The critics argued for a date about A.D. 500, and their arguments were not answered with any real success. The recent finding of other chalices in Syria (cf. L. Bréhier in *Syria* 28 (1951) 256–64) which can be dated to before 430 and which bear images of Christ, Peter, Paul and the Church (in the figure of a woman with breasts displayed) have served to put the Antioch chalice into its proper perspective. The negative decision—that nothing can be concluded from its decoration for the state of theology in the 1st cent.—is valuable, and some of the articles written in the first heat of discovery are worth reading as cautionary examples for those who have to deal with any new discovery. The Antioch chalice is simply one among many instances of artistic portrayal of Christ as the teacher of the apostles and of the *traditio legis*.

Bibliography. G. de Jerphanion SJ, ' Le Calice d'Antioche ', in *Orientalia Christiana* 7 (1926) 1–175 ; *G. A. Eisen, *The Great Chalice of Antioch* (1923) 2 vols ; *M. Conway, ' The Antioch Chalice ', in *Burlington Magazine* 45 (1924) 106–10 ; *J. A. Montgomery in *American Journal of Archaeology* 21 (1917) 80–1 ; *A. B. Cook, in *Cambridge Review* 45 (1924) 213–16 ; a final review by G. de Jerphanion SJ, in *La Voix des monuments* (1938), Vol. II, 27–34, where he compares it to the 6th-cent. chair of Maximian at Ravenna.   J. H. C.

ANTIOCH, LITURGY OF There are some 80 anaphoras or Mass-texts in Syriac, and these are being published from the Oriental Institute, Rome (*Anaphorae Syriacae*, ed. A. Raes SJ (1939–61)). Not all of these are Antiochene by origin, but as critical texts of them gradually appear, it will eventually be possible to sketch some kind of picture of their relationships ; that time has not yet come.[1] For the present the safest guide is still the collection of citations of the liturgy of Antioch in the works of St John Chrysostom, a collection made by Brightman (*Liturgies Eastern and Western*, I, 470–81). This collection will be used for the first section of this article and to it will be added a section (II) giving a broad outline of the later development of the Antiochene liturgy throughout the East.

It must first be noted that, since Brightman wrote, it has become necessary to discard the idea (which he and all his predecessors had held) that the so-called *Apostolic Constitutions* VII and VIII give the substance of the Antiochene liturgy of the 4th cent. C. H. Turner showed (JTS (1929) 128–41) that this was an Arian compilation, and, when one calls to mind how far the depreciation of the Son of God could go among the Arians, it will at once be seen that it would be most unsafe to take what the *Apostolic Constitutions* contain as representing the orthodox practice of Syria in the days of Chrysostom. Reconstructions which have been made by attempting to harmonize Chrysostom with this document are therefore misleading.

I The Liturgy in Chrysostom. Just before the catechumens were dismissed, this prayer was said over them ; it is preserved in Chrysostom's second homily on 2 Cor, where he goes through it phrase by phrase, adding his own commentary to it : ' Let us pray for the catechumens : that the merciful and all-pitying God would hear their prayers : that He would open the ears of their hearts and instruct them in the word of truth : that He would sow His fear amongst them and strengthen His faith in their understandings : that He would unfold to them the gospel of justification : that He would grant them a mind filled with God, a judgment that is sober and a way of life that is virtuous, so that their thoughts are ever of Him, their reflections of Him and their plans of Him, that they be established in His law, day and night. Let us make invocation yet more intensively for them : that He withdraw them from all wicked and improper deeds, from all devilish sin and from all infestation of the adversary : that at the fitting time He may find them worthy of the laver of regeneration, the forgiveness of sins and the robe of immortality : that He may bless their comings in and goings out, their whole life, their houses and homes : that He may bless their children as they grow up and bring them to fullness of years in wisdom : that He may direct all their projects towards what is good. Invoke the angel of peace, ye catechumens. May all your projects be in peace. Pray that this present day may be in peace and all the days of your lives. Your goal is with Christ, to commit yourselves to the living God and to His Christ. Amen.'

From the same set of homilies (18:3 ; PG 61:527)

[1] Fr Raes (OCP 24 (1958) 5–16) argued that the Syriac anaphora of the XII Apostles and the so-called Byzantine Liturgy of John Chrysostom are practically identical. He appeals to Leontius of Byzantium (PG 86, 1:1368) where the only two liturgies envisaged as being in use are that of the XII Apostles and that of Basil.

it appears that a similar prayer was said over the *energumeni* and over the penitents, both of these groups probably being dismissed after the catechumens (*hom.* 71 in Mt ; PG 57:666). After these dismissals came the kiss of peace, which those alone who were entitled to partake of the mysteries exchanged. The intercessions for bishops and priests, emperors and magistrates, for sea and land (i.e. for quiet passage and good harvests) and for the weather, were made in the presence of the faithful alone (ibid. *hom.* 2:8). In his 9th homily on Penance Chrysostom speaks of the worthy participation in the Mass : ' When the priest said, " Let us raise up our hearts and minds " (*Sursum corda*), you said, " We have them raised to the Lord." Do you not blush to be found a liar at this solemn hour ? When the mystic table is set for you, when the Lamb of God is slain for you, when the priest is engaged in contest for your sake, when the spiritual fire wells up from the holy table, and Cherubim and Seraphim hover nearby..., when the spiritual fire comes down from heaven, when the Blood is poured into the chalice from the holy side of Christ for your cleansing, are you not struck with fear and confusion at being found a liar at that hour ? ' The double mention of the spiritual fire (coming from the altar and from heaven) is quite in accord with Chrysostom's view elsewhere (*see* EPIKLESIS) that the words of consecration and the invocation of the Holy Spirit are both operative in this sacrament. That the fire is here said to come down before the chalice is filled with blood might indicate that the epiklesis at Antioch came before the recital of the words of institution, but the order of the phrases cannot be pressed. Evidence of the *Sanctus* is found in *hom.* 14 on Eph 4 (PG 62:105). ' How can you exclaim with Cherubim and Seraphim, " Holy, holy, holy", when you use your lips for reviling ? '

An important declaration on the force of the words of institution is found in *hom.* 2 on 2 Tim (PG 61:612) : ' The sacrifice is the same, whoever offer it, whether Peter or Paul or anyone else ; it is the same that Christ gave to His disciples and that is now carried out by the priests . . . The words which God spoke then are the same as the priest uses now . . . That was His Body, and this is now. Anyone who thinks that this is less than that fails to realise that Christ is even now present and *even now is working.*' This idea of the activity of Christ in each Mass is of great theological importance. (It recurs in *hom.* 1:5 de proditione Iudae, PG 49–50:380). The epiklesis is described (*hom.* de coemeterio et cruce 3 ; PG 49–50:398) as a request that the Spirit should come and touch the oblations, but in *de sacerdotio* (3:4 ; PG 48:642) Chrysostom says, ' The priest speaks it at some length, not that some torch kindled in heaven should consume the oblations but that grace, coming upon the sacrifice, should by its means kindle the hearts of all and make them brighter than fire-tried silver.' Here the emphasis is upon the fruit of the sacrifice in the hearts of the faithful, and it does not seem unfair to suppose that the epiklesis at Antioch had words which asked for this effect.

The Our Father was 'tacked on' to the eucharistic prayer, according to *hom.* 27:8 in Gen (PG 53:251), where Chrysostom says that if we forgive our enemies we can come to the liturgy and say with a good conscience 'those words which are yoked with the prayer' (συνεζευγμένα τῇ εὐχῇ) ; his language he excuses on the ground that the faithful know what secrets he is talking of. At the Communion it was the Antioch custom to have the 144th Psalm (*Exaltabo Te, Deus meus, rex*) sung, with the people answering each verse by the refrain contained in the 15th verse, 'The eyes of all hope in Thee, O Lord : and Thou givest them meat . . . .' Chrysostom notes this in his exposition of the psalm, just as he does in dealing with the 41st Psalm (which was presumably used at baptism). In the history of Socrates (HE 6:8 ; PG 67:689) it is stated that Ignatius of Antioch had a vision of angels singing antiphonally in honour of the Trinity and passed on this method to his church ; at least a considerable antiquity must have belonged to the custom when Socrates wrote. Theodoret (HE 2:24 ; GCS 44:154) credits Diodore of Tarsus and Flavian with the introduction of this manner of singing, but he must be speaking of its revival.

The fraction is mentioned in *hom.* 24 on 1 Cor (PG 61:200), where Chrysostom asks why Paul spoke of the bread *which we break*. 'This', he says, 'one can see at the eucharist. It did not happen on the cross, but Christ endures this at the oblation for your sake and He submits to the fraction that He may replenish all.' The scene is described in *hom.* 3 on Eph (PG 62:29). 'The curtain is drawn aside and the broken sacrifice, the Lamb as it were slain, is brought forth, and then the deacon cries out, "Let us make intercession for all", and again, "For all those who have slept in Christ and for those who carry out (or pay for) their commemoration"' (cf. also *hom.* 41 in 1 Cor ; PG 61:361). The idea seems to have been that the proper moment for these intercessions was that immediately preceding the communion when all the faithful became one by receiving the one bread ; communion was not just participation but *koinonia* or 'oneing with Christ' (PG 61:200) and it was most fitting that the one body should then be mindful of its absent members. The *sancta sanctis* was said about this time (*hom.* 7 on Mt ; PG 57:80) as the allusion suggests. There is no trace of an extended diaconal litany at the time of the fraction ; while some were breaking the consecrated bread within the veil, others would be leading off the various intercessions, and the longer litany may have been devised to fill this gap when the intercessions were moved to an earlier point in the liturgy.

Chrysostom does not talk about the offertory-procession, the *anamnesis* or the fraction-prayer. A specimen of this last has come down to us (PO 28:285) which, though it may not be contemporary with Chrysostom, reflects the ideas of his time : ' May they (the consecrated elements) not be for us

a judgment of condemnation, but rather may they be a remedy for our soul and spirit. Yea, Lord, grant us thus to flee all thoughts displeasing to Thee by Thy holy Name. Grant us to put far from us all counsel of death by that Name that is within the veil of Thy sanctuary . . . Grant us, Lord, Thy holy Spirit that we may dare to say with full freedom : Our Father . . .' The similarity of this prayer to one in the *Stowe Missal* which, while being a thanksgiving for Communion, asks that the sacrament may not be a judgment but rather a remedy for the soul, seems to show yet another of those links between Syriac and Celtic Christian antiquity which are now generally admitted.

Chrysostom in describing the fraction (*hom.* 3 in Eph, cited above) alludes to the popular belief about the parts of the church and their symbolism which is explicitly stated much later on. The apse stood for heaven, the altar was the throne of God. Between the sanctuary and the nave was the *qestrôma* (from κατάστρωμα) or diaconical raised walk, which symbolized Paradise. Below was the nave which stood for the earth, while in the centre of the nave was a semi-circular raised platform or *exedra* (symbolizing Jerusalem) on which the bishop sat facing towards the altar. This platform was also called *bema* and from it the sermon was delivered in Chrysostom's day (cf. Sozomenus HE 8:5 ; PG 67:1528) ; the preacher was like a player who adopts the theatre-in-the-round technique. Remains of such a *bema* have been found in Syrian churches of the 5th cent., but the full account of the symbols comes from the *Explicatio officii* of 'George of Arbela'. Chrysostom says : 'When you see the curtain drawn aside, think then that heaven above is opened and that the angels come down.' This fits in with the idea of the deacons as angels from Paradise bringing down the Eucharist to the communicants of earth. The Western custom of having the bishop in the apse facing the people across the altar seems quite different from what is found in Chrysostom. The *bema* was used by the Manichaeans and must be a very early feature of the Syrian liturgy.

II Liturgical influence of Antioch.

The Antiochene liturgy had a very wide influence. A Syrian mission to Ethiopia soon after 520 introduced there the Syriac text of the gospels and the Syriac anaphora of James, thus transforming the original Ethiopic traditions, which were Alexandrian. From about 410 the Chaldean Christians in Persia were cut off from all influence of Christianity in the Roman empire, and thus there passed to the churches of the farther East a liturgy that owed much to Antioch. The Armenian churches began to make a vernacular liturgy in the 5th cent., and as there are Syriac *graffiti* in the Armenian church of Tekot, which was probably built about 485, and Syriac influence in the ornamentation of these early churches, it is likely that the liturgy too was indebted to Antioch. Theodore of Mopsuestia was an Antiochene by birth and education, and he was ordained there in 383 ; the anaphora which goes by his name may therefore contain some Antiochene features, but as he was so original a mind, it may be that he had reshaped the patterns he had received. The anamnesis in that anaphora (Renaudot, *Liturgia orientalis* II, 619) is a simple statement that ' as Thou didst command us, so we are gathered together to celebrate this great mystery.' There is no explicit mention of Passion or Resurrection. The anaphora of Severus of Antioch (Renaudot, II, 324) has an anamnesis which recalls only the Second Coming : ' Completing this bloodless sacrifice, we ask, Lord, for Thy love towards men ; we are mindful also of Thy second coming in glory. . . .' From this variety it would seem that the Antiochenes were not tied to any particular form of anamnesis.

Waves of Byzantine influence upon the local liturgies of Antioch can be seen to fall in the 6th and the 10th cents. and the service books of later date are not free from contamination. The Melkites at least went on using Greek for the liturgy until the 9th cent.

The Malabar Christians use only the anaphora of the XII Apostles, in Syriac, thus perpetuating their connection with Antioch long ago. The great puzzle about this Antiochene influence is to settle why it led to such a variety of anaphoras, when the tendency of Antioch was to a liturgical conservatism and when for instance Theodore is so severely blamed by Leontius of Byzantium (*loc. cit.*) for ' improvizing an anaphora of his own, contrary to *the one* which had from ancient times been handed down in the churches'. Jerusalem was the one place which in early times exerted any liturgical influence upon Antioch. This is clear from the fact that the Syrian bishop's throne in the *exedra* was held to symbolize Jerusalem and to represent the gathering of the apostles in the Cenacle at Pentecost, the bishop and his circle of presbyters standing for the primitive preachers of the gospel, and the path by which they advanced to the altar being called *Seqaqone* or ' the way of truth', recalling the very early description of Christianity as ' this way ', at a time before the name of Christians had been conferred in Antioch. That the Syrian church failed to spread its type of church-arrangement to other lands may in part explain why the Syriac liturgy, when applied to unfamiliar surroundings, underwent so many changes.

Bibliography. A. Raes SJ, *Anaphorae Syriacae* (1939–60) and 'La Liturgie byzantine de s. Chryso-stome', in OCP 24 (1958) 5–16 ; J. Lassus, ' Ambons syriens', in *Cahiers archéologiques* 5 (1951) 75–122 ; H. Engberding, ' Die syrische Anaphora der XII Aposteln', in *Oriens Christianus* 3rd series, 12 (1938) 213–47.   J. H. C.

ANTIOCH, THE SCHOOL OF will be con-sidered historically in its chief representatives, (I) Eustathius and Diodore of Tarsus, (II) Theodore of Mopsuestia, (III) Nestorius with Theodoret of Cyrrhus. Antioch, the capital of Syria, never had an institute comparable with the catechetical school of Alexandria. The school of Antioch, therefore,

denotes the method of literal exegesis of Scripture (*see* CCS §§3e, 5bc) and the theological traditions which prevailed at Antioch, opposition of some kind to the school of Alexandria being usually implied. As at Alexandria so at Antioch theology from the middle of the 3rd cent. onwards was chiefly interested in Christology. Actually two different doctrinal trends developed there, the one Greek, the other Syrian. The former, largely influenced by Origen, was represented by Malchion (3rd cent.) and Lucian (d. 312) ; towards 373 Apollinaris of Laodicea (*c.* 310–*c.* 390) lectured at Antioch and must have initiated his listeners into the typically Alexandrine doctrine concerning the unity of Christ. Of the more important Syrian trend the chief exponents were Paul of Samosata (3rd cent.), Eustathius (d. *c.* 337), Diodore of Tarsus (d. *c.* 390), Theodore of Mopsuestia (*c.* 350–*c.* 428), Nestorius (d. *c.* 451), Andrew of Samosata (d. *c.* 451) and Theodoret of Cyrrhus (*c.* 393–*c.* 458). St John Chrysostom (*c.* 347–*c.* 407), whose exegetical writings warrant his being considered the greatest of Christian expositors, made no conspicuous contribu-tion to Christology. The mentality of most of the last mentioned teachers can be partly explained by the direct influence which the celebrated rhetorician, Libanius, exercised on them. The factor, however, which best accounts for the traits peculiar to both the Greek and the Syrian traditions seems to have been a type of Greek culture with strong Aristotelian leanings which was widespread in the East. To its influence must be ascribed not only the importance that Lucian attached to the argument of reason in theology but also the attraction felt by the Syrians for empirical and ethical problems as well as their unbounded interest in man as a free agent.

The Christology of the Antiochenes has been styled the *Logos-Man* scheme because its starting point is *Phil.* 2:5 *ff.* Their system can be summarized as follows : in order to redeem mankind, the Logos, without ceasing to be God, underwent a voluntary humiliation in that He united a real and complete human nature (' the man ') to Himself ; the result of this union is one Jesus Christ, Who is divine and human. Their favourite word to designate the union was ' conjunction ' (συνάφεια) and in their writings they were wont to refer to the Logos as ' dwelling in the man '. The Alexandrines instance these and similar expressions as proof positive that the Antiochenes taught that the Logos and the human nature were united only morally and accidentally, the result of such a union being not one but rather ' two Sons '. The Antiochenes invariably rejected this interpretation as untrue ; there is no doubt that the doctrine which they *wished* to defend was fundamentally that of their opponents, though they nearly always failed to convince the latter that it was.

I Eustathius, Bishop of Antioch from 324 to 330, was the first to expound a typically Antiochene Christology. He emphasized not a few doctrinal aspects destined to become characteristic of the Antiochene system : (1) the sole purpose of the

Incarnation was the redemption of the human race ; (2) the Logos assumed a complete manhood consisting of soul and body ; (3) Christ's perfect obedience contributed effectually to the redemption. Eustathius taught that Christ's manhood, since it has its own individuality, can be practically regarded as a person. In this last respect he foreshadowed what was particularly vulnerable in the system of Nestorius.

Another Antiochene, Diodore of Tarsus, a brilliant exegete, played an important rôle in securing the condemnation of Apollinaris of Laodicea at the Council of Constantinople (381). Strange to say, there is no reference to Apollinaris's erroneous teaching on Christ's human soul in any of the extant fragments of Diodore's works. Such an omission in an Antiochene certainly causes surprise. Diodore's Christology can scarcely be called a *Logos-Man* pattern at all. It is really a *Logos-Flesh* scheme which lays stress on the duality of the natures rather than on their union : wishing to avoid 'mixing' the natures at all costs, Diodore avails himself of every opportunity to 'divide' them. He strongly opposed those features of Apollinarianism which tended to diminish the divinity of the Logos. To Apollinaris's formula, μία ὑπόστασις, he was particularly hostile, on the ground that it made a single 'natural' unity of the Logos and the flesh. This aversion was Diodore's chief contribution to the Christological controversy.

II Between the Councils of Constantinople (381) and Ephesus (431) no one contributed more conspicuously to Christology than **Theodore of Mopsuestia.** He subjected not only Apollinarianism but also the *Logos-Flesh* scheme itself to a most penetrating criticism, showing how the latter's fundamental weakness—one which infallibly led to the exclusion of Christ's human soul—lay in the Stoic idea of the λόγος ἡγεμών which had been incorporated by the Alexandrines into their Christology. Theodore argued correctly that, if, on account of the vital union which binds Him closely to the flesh, the Logos were to fulfil all the functions exercised normally by the human soul, He would necessarily play the rôle of the body as well. On the contrary, he insisted, the Logos must have assumed both a body and a soul, because redemption would be utterly incomplete unless man's body be freed from death and his soul be cleansed from sins. Before death could be vanquished, sins had first to be removed, for they were the cause of death. Now sins take place in the soul. Accordingly, Christ must have first assumed a soul and then, on account of it, have assumed a body. Indeed the body could not be saved at all except by means of a spiritual soul. Salvation became an accomplished fact, Theodore continued, because the Logos when 'taking' a human soul endowed it with the grace that enabled it to control the passions of the body. It was thus that He freed it from sinful movements and made it immutable. In this *Logos-Man* pattern, which, previous to Theodore, had never been presented with such clarity, Christ lived a genuinely human

life, the real principle of which was His created soul. His human life made a decisive contribution to the redemption of the human race. Nor could the redemption have been brought about at all, if He had not had the opportunity of conquering sin Himself by mastering victoriously the passions of His soul and body.

The *Logos-Man* system had a congenital weakness which showed itself no less in Theodore than in other Antiochenes : in order to exclude the danger of 'mixing' the natures he harped on the principle of 'dividing' them, using terminology, however, which suggested that the union between the Logos and the human nature was only of the moral order. On the other hand he frequently protested that he really wished to maintain the unity of Christ. What he really lacked was the conviction so deeply rooted in the Alexandrines that in Christ the 'I' and the ultimate subject of attribution is the Logos— that the human nature is completely subordinated to this single 'I'. For him the 'I' of Christ does not seem to have been the Logos but rather a kind of common unity-personality resulting from the union of the two natures but distinct from them. In keeping with the Antiochenes Theodore usually styled it a πρόσωπον ; on occasion he called it an ὑπόστασις (this term belonged to the terminology of the Apollinarians but he ascribed a new meaning to it).

Despite its shortcomings, Theodore's Christology had undoubted advantages. Of all the Greek theologians of the 4th cent. he gave the profoundest explanation of the theological significance of Christ's human soul. And he threw much light on an aspect of Christ's inner life concerning which the *Logos-Flesh* scheme was utterly silent : created grace and its rôle in the work of redemption. It was lamentable that the passionate quarrels of the Apollinarians and the Monophysites injured his reputation and led to the condemnation of his writings (553). His brilliant exegetical works themselves alone entitled him to a better fate.

III Nestorius and Theodoret. The points of doctrine on which Theodore laid stress were emphasized with much greater disproportion by Nestorius, who was condemned at the Council of Ephesus (431) thanks chiefly to the influence of St Cyril of Alexandria (d. 444) and his party. At first the Antiochenes refused to recognize the decisions of Ephesus. In 433, however, after laborious negotiations, each party recognized the other's fundamental orthodoxy. The Antiochenes, however, admitted Cyril to communion only when he had explained to their satisfaction certain passages of his *Twelve Anathematisms* (a treatise against Nestorius written in 430) which, as they alleged, savoured of Apollinarianism, and had agreed to a formulary of reunion submitted to him by them. In this phase of the controversy the chief representatives of the school of Antioch were Theodoret of Cyrrhus and Andrew of Samosata. Their doctrine represented a compromise between the older Antiochene Christology and the formulary signed by Cyril in 433. As regards terminology, they tended more and more to reserve the terms οὐσία and φύσις to designate Christ's natures and to equate the word ὑπόστασις with πρόσωπον as a designation of the person. From their writings it is clear that the Antiochenes were anything but unprepared for the distinction which the Council of Chalcedon (451) was destined to make between the one ὑπόστασις (or πρόσωπον) of Christ and His two φύσεις. At Chalcedon, Theodoret was reinstated in the see of Cyrrhus from which he had been unjustly deposed in 448 by Dioscorus of Alexandria and his supporters. After the Council, Theodoret wrote a scriptural justification of the term ὑπόστασις as applied by Chalcedon to Christ ; he also instituted a parallel between the doctrine of the Council and the concepts and terminology of Trinitarian doctrine. These were his principal contributions to Christology. Earlier in his career he had strongly opposed Cyril's ' natural union ' (ἔνωσις φυσική, a term which he completely misunderstood), on the ground that ' nature ' (φύσις) conjures up the idea of compulsion and involuntariness ; this objection was inspired by the characteristically Antiochene preoccupation to uphold at all costs the absolute freedom of the Logos in assuming human nature. Although his terminology resembled that of Chalcedon, he really used the expression πρόσωπον in its primitive meaning of countenance or appearance. He never fully disentangled himself from the idea dear to his school that the Logos ' dwells ' in the human nature. Of itself that idea tended to loosen the bond of union between the two natures. To balance such an impression Theodoret recurred frequently to the expedient of emphasizing that the divinity and the humanity of Christ are united in one πρόσωπον, that is to say, in one individual figure as presented to perception. The divinity, he said, is visible in the humanity of Christ and so illumines His countenance. In a word, Theodoret tried to describe Christ by means of comparisons and illustrations rather than by means of rigorous metaphysical concepts. In addition to his dogmatic writings, Theodoret wrote valuable scriptural commentaries, not a few of which have been preserved. The Council of Constantinople (553) proscribed those works of his which criticized Cyril and the decisions of Ephesus together with some of his letters and sermons. He was the last great representative of the school of Antioch, whose reputation, which was in decline as a result of Ephesus, was almost completely ruined by the high-handed action of Dioscorus of Alexandria (d. 454) and his minions.

Conclusion. It has been said that the critical and literal exegesis of the Antiochenes influenced them to pay more attention in their scriptural studies to the human lineaments of Christ than to His divinity. This tendency in exegesis was wedded to an outlook, derived from Aristotelianism, that urged them to be more interested in concrete and ethical problems than in metaphysical investigations. In the last resort it was this outlook which distinguished them from the Alexandrines and which inspired them to

emphasize to a greater extent than the latter the distinction between the two natures that are united in Christ and the truth that Christ is a perfect human being whose constant obedience to the divine will effectually brought about man's redemption. Although their doctrine was fundamentally that of the Alexandrines, their emphasis lacked proportion and would have endangered the purity of revealed truth, had it not been balanced by the points of doctrine on which the Alexandrines laid stress. The terminology of the Antiochenes on occasion was clearer than that of their opponents, but the latter's metaphysical concepts were altogether more profound.

Bibliography. A. Grillmeier, H. Bacht, *Das Konzil von Chalkedon*, I (1951) 120–59, 182–93 ; O. Bardenhewer, *Geschichte der altkirchlichen Literatur* III (1923) 230 ff. ; *G. L. Prestige, *Fathers and Heretics* (1954) ; *R. V. Sellers, *Two Ancient Christologies* (1953). A. K.

APOLLINARIS, surnamed the younger, of Laodicea, lived in Syria in the 4th cent. He was probably younger than Athanasius and must have died about the end of the century. His importance for the history of Christian doctrine is twofold : he turned the current of theological thought in the direction of Christology, and in the course of his writings he provided a large number of the dogmatic statements which were used by Alexandrian Christology and later by the Monophysites. He was a man of extremely high intellectual quality (a fact which caused him in his youth some misunderstandings with his bishop) and published, perhaps along with his father, quite a number of Christian works at a time when Julian the Apostate had forbidden Christians to use the ancient classics. He was a theologian of distinction and was of great assistance to Athanasius in the second phase of the Arian crisis ; quite probably he was the bishop of a small community at Laodicea that held to the faith of Nicaea, just as Paulinus was at Antioch. It was in Antioch that Apollinaris gave the lectures on exegesis which Jerome attended in 374. The reputation he enjoyed is quite well shown by the way in which Epiphanius and Basil speak of him ; with the latter he exchanged letters at the time that Basil was having his dispute with Eustathius of Sebaste. This correspondence— which I consider to be beyond all doubt authentic— shows the subtle thought of Apollinaris in action, his powerful dialectic and a certain weakness for formulas that are well-turned even though they may be paradoxical or obscure. The story of the Apollinarist crisis shows that this weakness was allied to a lack of candour and a taste for equivocation.

His works must have been extensive in all departments, but of them there remain but fragments that are preserved in *florilegia* and some pieces that passed under the names of substitute authors (Gregory Thaumaturgus, Julius of Rome, Athanasius) and thus were adopted as authorities by Cyril of Alexandria. This ' Apollinarist fraud ' is an episode that has not yet been properly unravelled in the story of the

Christological controversies; it would probably be wrong to see in it a pious act of the partisans of Apollinaris anxious to preserve the literary heritage of their master. One must rather look to a certain lack of scruple on the part of some of the adversaries of Nestorius who deceived the unsuspecting Cyril of Alexandria by providing him thus with material that was admirably suited to his purpose. All this material has been edited, with some approach to finality, by H. Lietzmann (*Apollinaris von Laodicea und seine Schule* (1904)), a work which is the natural foundation of any research about Apollinaris. Some additional material has been dealt with by the writer (JTS 7 (1956) 199–210 and *Das Konzil von Chalkedon* I, 203–12). The exegetical fragments are for the most part still not edited; a summary list of them can be found in an article by the writer (RSR 44 (1956) 560–6).

It was between 370 and 380 that the Christology of Apollinaris came into the full light of day, though there is every possibility that the celebrated *Tomus ad Antiochenos*, produced by the Synod of Alexandria in 363, may touch upon controversies provoked by his teaching. At Antioch, Vitalis, a disciple of Apollinaris, set up a church that was independent of that of Paulinus, and the efforts of Vitalis to secure recognition, especially by Rome, brought Apollinarism out into the open and led eventually to the condemnation by Pope Damasus (D 65).

Apollinaris taught a Christology which, grounded upon a doctrine of salvation that was firmly attached to the divinity of Christ, turns upon the idea of the unique character of the humanity of Christ; here the Word takes the place of a spiritual principle, soul, mind or νοῦς, so that divinity and humanity combine in a single nature (μία φύσις). In this way the body shares in the properties of the Word (*see* COMMUNICATIO IDIOMATUM) without making it necessary to admit a divinization of the flesh or to deny that His flesh is kin to our own. The theory is developed in a field where Apollinaris is able to employ all his subtlety and learning in psychological and anthropological questions, while at the same time pursuing a literal exegesis of the Scriptures to the point of distorting their spirit. As a philosopher he draws inspiration much more from the Stoics than, as is sometimes claimed, from Plato or Aristotle. He accepts a threefold structure of man and a traducian theory of the origin of the human soul, but like all his contemporaries he puts forward a system that is a syncretism and he cannot without distortion be made subject to a classification.

Bibliography. For general works, see G. Voisin, *L'Apollinarisme* (1901); *H. Lietzmann, *Apollinaris von Laodicea* (1904); *G. L. Prestige, *Fathers and Heretics* (1940); H. de Riedmatten, 'La Christologie d'Apollinaire de Laodicée', in *Studia Patristica* (TU 64 (1957) 208–34). H. de R.

APOLOGETICS The attempt to provide a rational justification of the Christian faith begins with (I) the early Christian preaching, and is developed by (II) St John, passages from whose gospel

had great influence (III) on the thought of Aquinas. The Apologists of the early centuries (IV) gradually elaborate the two main arguments, from miracle and prophecy, (V) Origen and (VI) Eusebius being particularly influential. (VII) A basis for the argument is found in the Platonic teaching that the end of life is an ever greater assimilation to God. (VIII) The advent of Islam calls for further clarification of the criteria by which one is to judge between religions that claim to be revealed. (IX) Aquinas deepens and clarifies the traditional argument, and with the coming of the Renaissance, (X) More and (XI) Vives prepare to deal with men who have no revealed religion. (XII) The Reformers add little, but with the Counter-Reformation (XIII) Gregory of Valentia separates the rational judgment of credibility from the grace-inspired act of faith. (XIV) Grotius and (XV) Butler improve the argument, while (XVI) Kant would have marred it. (XVII) Hermes in his reaction to Kant goes into a blind alley, but with (XVIII) Newman a way is once more opened for the justification of the judgment of credibility. In modern times (XIX) Rousselot leads a reaction against the severance between judgment of credibility and act of faith, leading to (XX) a general attack on the usefulness of Apologetics. (XXI) The rejection of Rousselot's theory and the papal teaching of (XXII) *Humani Generis* have led to a further clarification of (XXIII) the purpose of Apologetics. The details of the apologetic argument are treated under REVELATION, MIRACLES, PROPHECY, CHRIST (MISSION OF, RESURRECTION OF, etc.). It consists of an examination of the capabilities and duties of both God and man in regard to a possible revelation, establishing therefrom that if God made a revelation He would authenticate it by signs or tokens of its credibility. For those who receive the revelation of God in Christ, the principal tokens authenticating it are the miracles and resurrection of Christ, the prophecies made or fulfilled by Christ, and the coherence of His character with His message, all of which are evidenced by writings of historical worth such as the four gospels and are not left without some support in pagan documents.

I The early Christian preaching was addressed to Jews and had to justify itself by an appeal to the Old Testament; 'without Scripture we make no assertions', wrote the Jewish Christian author of the apocryphal *Preaching of Peter* (cited by Origen in *In Ioannem* 6:15, 128) somewhat after the beginning of the 2nd cent. The manner in which large tracts of Isaias, Zacharias and other OT works were expounded by the Apostles and their successors for gospel-preaching or 'kerygmatic' ends has been reconstructed in recent times, notably by Professor Dodd. This free exposition of Scripture is better understood now, owing to the example set before us by the *Habacuc Commentary* among the Desert Scrolls. The Christian approach to the pagan is less easy to recapture. The two pictures of Paul, at Lystra and in the Areopagus, given to us by St Luke, are almost the only material we have until we come to the *Epistle to Diognetus*, for in the epistles of Paul one never entirely escapes the Jewish overtones. But the substance of the apologetic argument is already there, in Heb 2:3, where salvation is said to have taken its rise from the Lord's preaching and to have been handed down to us securely by His hearers, God also bearing witness to it by signs and wonders and manifold deeds of power and impartings of the Holy Spirit according to His will. This echoes the words of Paul (Rom 15:18–19) and the ending of Mark's gospel. Thus by A.D. 70 the elements of the apologetic argument (or of kerygmatic theology) are present in the Church (CSS934d).

II St John before his death added his own contribution (Jn 14:11) by recording the word of Our Lord to the Apostles : ' Believe Me that I am in the Father and the Father in Me. If you cannot do that, believe for My works' sake.' This ordering of the motives of belief among themselves shows that, while the immediate attraction of Christ's person and doctrine are normally to be experienced by the hearers of His message, it is recognized that this will not always be adequate, and a last line of defence is supplied by the miracles. Jn 14:12 gives a promise that the works are to continue after the Ascension and even to increase in splendour. Elsewhere in Jn (5:36 ; 10:25 ; 10:37 ; 15:24) the same idea is expressed (CSS803g).

III In treating of these passages in John the great patristic commentators, Augustine and Chrysostom, do not give more than a cursory glance at the problems of Apologetics involved in them, but St Thomas in his *Expositio in evangelium Ioannis* (lectio 6, cap. 5) is more anxious to elaborate an orderly explanation of the way one comes to the faith : ' In three ways did God bear witness to Christ, by works, by Himself and by the Scriptures. . . . It is natural for a man to learn the qualities and nature of things from their activity, and so Christ Our Lord rightly claims that His true quality may be ascertained from the works He does. Since therefore He wrought divine works by His own power, it must be believed that the power of God was in Him. Later on He says (15:24) : " If I had not done among them works which no one else has done, they would not have the sin ", that is, of infidelity, and thus He points the way to knowledge of Himself by means of His works, saying, " The works which the Father has given Me to do [giving to Me, the Word, by eternal generation power equal to His own, or granting Me at my human conception to be a single Person, human and divine], He has given them to Me to do by My own power, not as others, who work miracles by intercession with God and not by their own power ".' Apart from the testimony of the works, St Thomas considers that God gave testimony to Christ by the Scriptures, in the numerous prophecies about Him, and by Himself, in the voice from heaven twice heard in the gospels ; the works, however, afford the principal and natural argument for the truth of His claims. St Thomas later in the same work (lectio 6, cap. 15)

elaborates the argument from miracles, showing that the miracles of Christ were greater than those of others in three ways, by their nature (for no one else had cured a man born blind or raised from death one who had been four days in the tomb), by their number (as instanced in Mt 14:35), and by their manner (for whereas others besought God to work the miracle and made it clear that they were not acting by their own power, Christ worked His miracles by a word of command). St Thomas comments thus on the statement that if Christ had not done His miracles the Jews would have been excused their infidelity : ' Christ draws men by words, by signs visible and by signs invisible. These last are interior warnings and promptings of the heart. . . . What Christ says is therefore to be understood not only of visible signs but also of the interior prompting and the attraction of the doctrine, and if Christ had not provided all these, they would have been excused.' On Jn 12:39 his comment is : ' The Lord leads a man to the faith in two ways, by miracles and by doctrine. When the Jews did not pay heed to the miracles of Christ with due attention, He declares that the eyes of their hearts are blind. . . . Secondly, the words of Christ are like fire or like a hammer cracking stones (Jer 23:29), like fire in that they kindle the fire of charity, and like a hammer in that they terrify by their threats and grind to powder by their manifest truth.' The relative importance and the interdependence of miracles and doctrine are matters not settled by a passage like this, but remain as problems for later theologians.

IV The Christian apologists of the early centuries were hardly concerned with Apologetics in the modern sense save incidentally ; their business was to refute the three or four gross calumnies against the Christians which were finding general acceptance among educated pagans, and then to carry the war into enemy territory by attacking pagan worship and all its attendant obscenities. When writing for Jewish readers the Fathers naturally made full use of the argument from OT prophecy, which thus received from them far more elaboration than the argument from miracles, while the argument from the truth of the prophecies made by Christ Himself was hardly used at all. The *Epideixis* of Irenaeus is full of argumentation from the OT, yet there is no proof, and no agreement among its editors, that its recipient, one brother Marcianus, was a Jew ; he may even have been a Christian bishop. In his larger work (*adv. haer.* H 2:48:2) Irenaeus appeals to the miracles of Christ against the pseudo-Christian Gnostics who used various tricks to deceive their followers, putting sherbert in their eucharistic wine and engaging in faith-healing, but in the end (2:49:3) he falls back on the argument from prophecy. He says in effect : If the Gnostic replies that Christ's miracles were a sham, or were due to natural powers of faith-healing, we must then bring them to the argument from prophecy and to the reality of the exorcisms performed by Christians. Some men, he adds, have been raised from the dead and have lived until our own time, but he clearly regards this evidence as of less importance than that, ' all those things were actually prophesied about Him and were most surely fulfilled'.

V Origen in his younger days uses the same line of argument, but with a certain intellectual snobbery. He says (*In Ioannem* 2:204) : ' The deeds of marvellous power were able to invite men to the faith in the time of the Saviour, but did not keep all their force in later times, coming to be looked upon by some as mere legends. But the argument from prophecy now worked out has more force to persuade men than the miracles of former days, and it is able to keep inquirers from disbelieving in the miracles.' In his more mature work *contra Celsum*, written about 248, he puts things with a different emphasis. Now (*c. Cels.* 2:51) he says that one should examine the moral character of those who profess to do miracles and watch what has resulted from the miracles in order to be able to distinguish between divine works and diabolical trickery. The existence and growth of the Church then becomes the guarantee for the miracles of Christ, assuring the inquirer that he is face to face with one sent by God and not with a deceiver. Origen is quite emphatic, however, that ' even to this day those whom God wills are cured in the name of Jesus '. (*c. Cels.* 1:46 and 2:33.)

VI Eusebius. One cannot find in patristic writing an attempt to bring a man step by step through the logical arguments for the existence of God, for a Providence and for a man's need of a religion finally to face his duty of being on the look-out for what help God may have given him to perfect his religion. In a world where some belief in God was common, Christians were content to proclaim themselves a third race, neither Jew nor Greek, but with a creed better than either of these. By the time of Eusebius's *Demonstratio evangelica* pagans have produced a reply to this to the effect that Christians are traitors to Hellenism, since they forsake the gods of the city, and they are not good Jews either, since they do not keep the Jewish law. Eusebius in his answer to this attack makes out that Christians are like to those great figures, Enoch, Noah and the rest, who lived before Abraham, believers in one God and virtuous men, but neither Jew nor Greek. Elaborating Origen's defence of the argument from miracles, Eusebius (*Demonstratio evangelica* 3:4: GCS23:119–21) dramatizes the situation. He imagines the Apostles discussing how they are to succeed with a gigantic fraud, and puts a speech into the mouth of one of them in which he harangues the rest to adhere to the same story about the Resurrection and miracles of Christ, even though they may have known none of these things to have happened. Eusebius then asks how such a bluff could have succeeded when they all separate and travel so far, meeting death for their story in so many different lands. A generation that has seen the breaking-down of the Stalin myth knows how to appreciate such an argument better than the untroubled Victorians did.

VII The basis for the argument. The Greek Fathers, principally Clement of Alexandria (fl. 190–210), provided for the apologetic argument a sound philosophical base, grounding it on the Platonic dictum that the end of life for men is to become like unto God as far as possible. Fifteen times in the *Stromata* (*Strom.* 6:17:150:3 and often) and four times elsewhere Clement uses this idea, citing Plato's *Theaetetus* (176 B ; see also *Republic* 500 B and 613 A ; *Timaeus* 90 B) as an argument *ad hominem* against the pagans, but going on to use what Christ said (Mt 5:48) about being perfect as a means of showing that Christianity would fulfil their best aspirations. This Platonic foundation for Apologetics was accepted with enthusiasm by the men of the Renaissance when they came to re-think the traditional arguments.

VIII After the coming of Mahomet another chapter in Christian Apologetics had to be written alongside the answer to the Jews, and the fact that Moslem thinkers based their work on a neo-Platonic or an Aristotelian philosophy meant that the Christian apologist could claim certain positions as held in common by his adversary and himself. For details of the early attempts at an answer to the Moslems, *see* SYRIAN THEOLOGIANS. Here it must suffice to notice the treatise of Theodore Abu Qurra (bishop of Harran in Mesopotamia 740–820) on God and the true religion (Graf, *Des Theodore Abu Kurra Traktat über … die wahre Religion* (1913)). After some discussion of natural theology he runs through various religions—Zoroastrian, Samaritan, Jewish, Christian, Manichee, and followers of Marcion, Bardesanes and Mahomet. The common characteristics of all these, he claims, are a description, dependent on revelation, of the nature of God, and the rules of good and bad conduct, and a theology of rewards and punishments. To explain how one is to choose among so many rivals, he tells an elaborate parable. A wise king who led a retired life sent his young son, whom he had never seen, into a distant province accompanied by a doctor. He there falls seriously ill. News is brought to the king, but before he can send instructions for the care of the boy, his enemies in the court send many false remedies harmful to the boy. How is the boy to find out the genuine message from the king ? With the doctor's aid he examines what each message says about his father's nature, judging this nature by the likeness he bears in himself, about the nature of the illness and about the methods of curing it. The one that seems most reasonable on all three grounds is accepted as true. God is the father in the parable, Adam his son and the doctor is reason personified. The meaning is that the criterion of the true religion is the harmony between its revealed teaching about the nature of God, right and wrong, and rewards and punishments and what reason would expect. The argument from miracles and from the spread of Christianity is then offered as ' another way in which our reason can prove that the Christian religion is from God '. This elaborate treatment shows that Eastern Christians were at this time far ahead of the West in the depth and range of their Apologetics. Theodore was no isolated teacher, but one of a long line, going back through John Damascene to the great Armenian theologian, Eznik of Kolb (fl. 430). John Damascene (PG 94:765 and 96:1335-48) had written against Mahomet, regarding his doctrine as a Christian heresy and stressing that he had picked up many of his ideas from an Arian monk.

IX Aquinas. It is not until the 13th cent. that Western handbooks of Apologetics, such as Raymond Martin's *Pugio fidei* (1278) equal or surpass those produced so much earlier in the East. Raymond devotes his first book to those who deny all revelation, for gradually the spread of the neo-Platonic philosophy in its purer form had made the Arabians familiar with the idea of Plotinus that while man can hope for contact with God in moments of ecstasy, no intelligible communication from God to man is possible (*see* REVELATION). The handbook produced by St Thomas (the *Summa contra Gentiles*) has had various estimates made of its purpose in recent times, but the soundest seems to be that of his contemporary. William of Tocco : 'He shows clearly to those races not subject to the Christian faith the greatness of that faith ; for even though it pass the bounds of human reason and cannot for its very height above us be made the object of proof, yet can it by natural reason be most plausibly commended. Unbelievers, then, may from this book gain some acquaintance with the faith and may not disdain to regard the book as worthy of their intelligence, when they realise that there is no argument they can bring against the faith to which its defenders have not a reply' (AA.SS. *Martii* 1:665). Aquinas then conceives that the apologist is not principally one who lays a rational foundation of ethics and natural theology and then proceeds to build upon it an argument for the truth of revelation, but rather that he presupposes the faith all the time but uses common ground where he can find it in the (neo-Platonic) positions of his adversaries in order to provide a retrospective justification of the faith. He does, however, keep some of the traditional treatment where (*contra Gentiles* 1:6) he contrasts the miracles of Christ with the credentials of Mahomet and where he uses the reply of Augustine (*Civitas Dei* 22:5) to one who objected to the gospel-miracles : 'Very well ; if you say that they did not happen, you must then admit that it is a much bigger miracle that the disciples of Christ should have converted the world without miracles than with them'.

At the same time (1257-8) St Thomas was feeling his way towards a much deeper justification of the faith. He was much influenced by a passage from Hilary (*De Trinitate* 2:10 ; PL 10:59) where man is said to be at an infinite distance from God and yet to be bound to seek an ever-increasing knowledge of God, for though he will never arrive at his goal, yet will he benefit by the progress he makes. This text is cited in *contra Gentiles* 1:8 ;

Quaestiones disputatae de Veritate 5:2:@11 ; *Expositio super Boethium de Trinitate* 2:1:@7. Towards the end of his life he elaborated (in his lectures on the *Ethics* of Aristotle) this idea of an unattainable goal of natural happiness, which is really no more than the Platonic notion (used by Clement) of becoming like to God as far as nature will permit, an idea which Shakespeare gives to Cressida in the words (*Troilus and Cressida* 1, ii) : ' Things won are done ; joy's soul lies in the doing.' Man will find happiness in increasing his knowledge of God, even though there will naturally be no end to that process. If then man is performing this duty he will always be on the look-out for whatever divine revelation may come his way. If the goal of this natural happiness were ever to be attained, one would then have to say that man had covered the infinite distance from himself to God and had from a creature become himself divine. In his purely philosophical speculations on the *Ethics* St Thomas concludes that it is reasonable to conjecture that God will find a way out of this impasse, but in pure philosophy such a way is not manifest (lectio 14, on *Ethics* 1099 b 13), ' If there is to be anything given to men by the gods, that is by the spiritual substances which the Ancients called gods, then it is fitting to expect that happiness will be given to man by the highest of these.' At the very end of his life St Thomas came to know the work now called *Theologia Aristotelis* which his brethren were busy translating from the Arabic. This was in reality the work of an 8th-cent. Christian in Syria who had borrowed most of his matter from Plotinus and had adapted it in his own fashion. The work was accepted by St Thomas as containing the secret doctrine of Aristotle (*De Unitate Intellectus* 46) and he was happy to think that his Christianizing interpretation of Aristotle was thus justified by the Philosopher himself, but had he known the true character of the work, he might have been tempted to throw aside as worthless his recent speculations about natural happiness (Crehan, *Acta III Congressus Thomistici* (1950), 134-8).

X With the coming of the Renaissance there emerged a new creature, the complete agnostic, for whom there was no revelation at all. More than any Averroist of the Middle Ages he was prepared to call in question or to reject the very idea of revelation, and it became necessary to make use of the foundations that had been laid by Aquinas long before. In his *Utopia* St Thomas More showed the way. He there portrayed a state that was governed by natural reason alone, with no idea of Christianity and with a natural religion. This religion was not a closed system sufficient unto itself and able to satisfy all the godward stirrings of the human mind, but it was ready to welcome any help that God might give. The Utopian prayed thus : ' If there be any other [religion or form of government] better than either of them is [in Utopia], being more acceptable to God, he desireth Him that He will of His goodness let him have knowledge thereof, as one that is ready to follow what way soever He will lead him'. In accordance with this attitude the Utopians welcome the arrival of Christian travellers and accept what they say about God. It is quite misguided of E. Cassirer to write (*Platonic Renaissance in England* 108) that, 'More in his *Utopia* attempts to oppose to the system of dogmatic theology an entirely new form of religion. He outlines here the ideal of religion without dogma as the purest and best worship of the divine being.'

XI Luis Vives, the friend of More, left at his death the first modern treatise of Apologetics *De veritate fidei Christianae*, which was published in 1543. An English version appeared in 1639. His commentary on Augustine's *Civitas Dei* (1522) had caused him to ponder the arguments from miracles and prophecy when he dealt with Books 19 and 22 of that work, but in his manual he establishes the pattern for all modern works, starting with the end of man, going on to some consideration of primitive religion, the suitability of the mission of Christ, His Messiahship, the finality of Christ's mission (this against the Moslems, who accepted Christ as a forerunner), and ending with an account of the excellence of Christianity. Those who decry Apologetics as the invention of the Protestants Grotius and Wolf have no inkling of its nobler pedigree. Vives in a capital passage (2:3) uses the Platonic foundation which was familiar to Clement and to St Thomas : 'Plato appears to have told his followers that his own instructions were to be followed and his laws obeyed until some man more approved by heaven should come on earth and disclose the real fountain of truth, and him all should follow'. In the last paragraph of his work he recurs to the principle Clement took from Plato, saying : The more Christian a man is, the more he is like to God.

XII The new churches of Luther and Calvin did not at first think it needful to produce credentials of their own, being content to proclaim themselves reformers of that Catholic Church which had its own commission from Christ. But with the lapse of time they had to give their own independent lines of apologetic, and the work of the 'Huguenot Pope', Plessis Mornay (1581), is typical of the Calvinist approach. In place of the claim to have miracles that showed continuity with those of Christ, one is offered the moral miracle of Calvinism, an offer which provoked the Catholic exile, William Reynolds, to compile in 1597 his *Calvino-Turcismus*, wherein (4:11–13) he compares them with the Moslems to their disadvantage. Another weakness of the Reformers' position was their inability to show any great expansion of their creed among backward peoples, whereas Catholicism was in those regions calling into being just then a new world to redress the balance of the old.

XIII Gregory of Valentia, one of the chief theologians of the Counter-reformation (he was a Spaniard and contemporary of Suarez who spent his life teaching at Ingoldstadt), was one of the first to bring clarity into the question of the logical value of apologetic arguments. In his *Commentarii* (3:1:1:@4) he lays it down that the mind holds the conclusions of Apologetics with a prudential (or 'moral') certainty which excludes the possibility not of every doubt but of all prudent doubt. He thus separates evident credibility from evident truth, and his distinction has by now passed into the accepted teaching of the Church, being admitted by the Council of Cologne (*Collectio Lacensis* 5:279) and at the Vatican Council (*Mansi, Concilia* 51:235). By thus giving recognition to a judgment of credibility distinct from the act of faith, he was committed to the position that one could have faith and knowledge about the same proposition, faith from the act of believing in the revelation of Christ and knowledge as the conclusion of the (credible) apologetic argument. He was here going back from St Thomas (2–2æ:1:5c and 2–2æ:2:4:@2) and Scotus to the view of Albert and Bonaventure. After he had thus introduced some order into the subject by his distinctions, he proceeded to give some nineteen arguments for the evident credibility of the fact of Christian revelation, that from miracles being the chief. One of his reasons for allowing faith and knowledge about the same truth to be possible is that otherwise there would be no point in a man being educated to understand the arguments for such a truth as the existence of God. He might believe it when a child with a supernatural act of faith, and then this would seem to make all attempts to master the proofs in later life quite vain and idle. Gregory's treatment of the judgment of credibility was to be taken up and elaborated by his contemporaries, Bellarmine and Suarez and by De Lugo in his celebrated work *De Fide* (1646), also by the English Jesuit, Compton Carleton, in his *Cursus theologicus* (vol. 2, disputatio 7–8, Liège 1664) where the connection between the motives of credibility (or the arguments of Apologetics) and the subsequent judgment of credibility is discussed in all its aspects.

XIV Hugo Grotius, whose manual *De veritate religionis Christianae* (1622) is commonly held to be the pioneer work in modern Apologetics, is thus in fact at the end of a long process of Renaissance development. The only addition he made to the scheme of Vives was to include a chapter on the authenticity of the gospels by way of replying to an objection which might be made after the claims of Christ, resting on His miracles and the prophecies, had been presented. The link between the ethical foundation of the end for man and the superstructure of the apologetic dialectic is again provided by an appeal to the proposition that it is man's good to become as like God as possible, and that if anything presents itself as a God-given way of achieving this, it should be accepted as most true and assured. Grotius used the argument from prophecy simply as an *ad hominem* to the Jews, showing them who their Messias really was, and this led Bossuet to censure him as one who came near to the position of the Socinians (*Œuvres* (1743) tome 2:519–41). In reply Bossuet pointed to the fact that Paul spent a whole day (Ac 28:23) arguing about the prophets in Rome, that Peter used the figure of David to prove the Resurrection and that (2 Pet 1:15–19) he regarded the word of prophecy as being the more reliable argument. It may be that in his desire for the reunion of the churches Grotius had gone somewhat too far in the direction of Socinus, as if striving to present a lowest common multiple of Christianity, but on the other hand there is Bossuet's own statement (ibid. 535 and 540) that he was more than half-way to becoming a Catholic, yet 'sans avoir enfanté l'esprit du salut qu'il avait conçu'. An English version of Grotius was made by F. Coventry in 1632 (*True religion explained and defended*) and the timeliness of this work against the Deist propaganda of Lord Herbert of Cherbury is quite plain. Jacques Abbadie, a follower of Grotius, whom a grateful Anglican church made Dean of Killaloe, produced his own manual in 1684. It was put into English in 1694 but was considered not to be Protestant enough, and in 1717 he produced another work in which the apologetic argument was made to terminate more clearly in the Anglican church.

XV Butler. *The Analogy of Religion* (1736), by Bishop Joseph Butler, is the principal work of Apologetics to appear in Europe in the 18th cent. Its influence on Newman, to give but one instance, was enormous. Butler was that rarity, an English metaphysician, having as a schoolboy tested Samuel Clarke with his philosophical questions, and he was, as his biographer said, 'wafted into his see of Durham on a cloud of metaphysics'. Against the Deists of his time he urges : 'The benefit arising from this supernatural assistance which Christianity affords to natural religion is what some persons are very slow in apprehending. And yet it is a thing distinct in itself, and a very plain obvious one. For will any in good earnest really say that the bulk of mankind in the heathen world were in as advantageous a situation with regard to natural religion as they are now amongst us' (Part 2, ch. 1). But he does not look at the other side of the picture to see how man's nature, deeply penetrated by its supreme law of assimilation to God as far as possible, is all the time calling out for some such supplement and completion as Christianity offers.

Butler was the source of a confusion that is still with us. He regarded (ibid.) the miracles and prophecies of Scripture as an authoritative publication of natural religion, and thus he is the cause of the confusion in the mind of the scientist of today that somehow the fact of miracle is needed for the proof of the existence of God. But Butler would have saved us trouble if he had been careful to say that evidence of miracles is logically subsequent to an acceptance of the existence of God, but that they often in fact help a man to accept God (as when a man should say that if the miracle-working Christ was not God he cannot believe in God). He did, however, find the complete answer to Hume's allegation against miracles from the presumption resting upon our experience of uniformity in nature. 'There is a presumption', he wrote, 'of millions to one against the story of Caesar or of any other man.'

For some years Butler assisted the vicar of East Hendred, one of the few villages in England where the Mass never ceased in penal times, and he must have had some acquaintance with Catholics. There were accusations against him during his life of Romish practices and after his death rumours that he died a Papist, but in his scheme of Apologetics the Church has a very diminished rôle ; he seemed to regard man as provided with the book of nature as his guide to natural truths and the book of Scripture as his guide to revealed truths in exactly parallel fashion. He once (Part 2, ch. 6) speaks of Catholics as having had, 'the system of Christianity so corrupted, the evidence so blended with false miracles, as to leave the mind in the utmost doubtfulness', and he must have been far from being an *anima naturaliter catholica*, yet from his work Newman was to derive his chief inspiration for the *Grammar of Assent*. His whole view of Christian evidences as engulfed in difficulties in order to provide men with a fitting probation on earth drove Newman forward to elaborate his views on certainty and belief. Butler was in reaction from men like Wolf, who with an optimism he had caught from Leibnitz boasted : 'My method always keeps to a geometrical strictness of proof'. If men sickened with despair of ever being able to achieve this geometric rigidity in Apologetics, Butler would not have them abandon hope of making reason *somehow* a help to revelation and would not let them fall back helpless into Deism. Butler (Part 2, ch. 6, *n.*) appeals to Grotius for this idea of God deliberately making the evidences of Christianity harder to discern, but ultimately, like so much else in theology, it goes back to Augustine who uses this as an explanation of the obscurity of the Scriptures. Some twenty years before Butler an obscure work had appeared at Paris that presented *The Truth of Christianity demonstrated geometrically* ; it was time for a reaction to set in.

The Irish theologian, Luke Joseph Hooke (1716-1796), who taught at the Sorbonne, produced in 1754 his *Religionis naturalis et revelatae Principia* which became almost the standard Catholic manual for a century, being reprinted in the *Cursus theologicus* of the Abbé Migne. Hooke used Butler freely and at critical points, so that he seems at times to be doing no more than put Butler into Latin. He also used the long discussion of miracles to be found in Benedict XIV's work on Canonization, and was thus enabled to bring some order into the problem of eliminating the pseudo-miracles of diabolical agency. His Jacobite ancestry made him the more ready to devote himself to refuting the Whig philosophers and Deists, and he survived long enough to reply in later editions of his work to the theories of Rousseau's *Émile*.

XVI Kant. The essence of the Liberal Christianity of the 19th cent. is to be found in Kant's principal work on the philosophy of religion : *Die Religion innerhalb der Grenzen der blossen Vernunft* (1794), (*Works* 6:139-353). Taking natural religion to be the recognition as God's commands of what we already know to be our moral duties, while supernatural religion becomes the recognition as moral duties of what we already know to be God's commands, Kant finds it congenial to argue that all religions claiming to be revealed are really degenerate cases of true natural religion, to which in the limit they approximate. Asserting that a man must be content to be God's servant and not indulge foolish hopes of becoming His favourite, he claims that it is unnecessary to prove that whatever a man does to please God, over and above his leading a moral life, is mere delusion and superstition. A distinction of the life of the counsels from that of strict moral obligation is alien to his mind. He works out a transcendental deduction of the liturgy by reducing the worship of God to four duties : private prayer, in which a man strengthens his resolve to lead a moral life ; public worship on fixed days, when he communicates that resolve to others ; an initiation service, in which men secure the continuation of their efforts by the next generation ; and a common meal from time to time where they celebrate the union on terms of equality of all those who are striving towards a morally good life. This sets forth the pattern of what has come to be known as public-school religion. What Kant omitted from his scheme was the religion which is not simply natural, nor yet superstitiously inclined against nature, but simply beyond nature. Had he considered how natural godward striving calls out in its apparently endless frustration for some heavenly completion that will prolong, sustain and round off its efforts, he would not have assumed as axiomatic (ibid. 320) that there were only the two possibilities, natural religion and fetish-worship. Ever since Descartes men had been keeping natural and supernatural in two hermetically sealed compartments (definitions near to Kant's can be found in the *Demonstratio evangelica* of B. Stattler (1770), a Catholic work) and this was the view Kant inherited. He also took over Hume's view (ibid. 345) that belief in miracles can be ruled out by identifying experience of uniformity with uniformity of experience, and in general he regarded historical experience as incapable of producing universally valid conclusions. Here again he was the victim of the geometrician's mirage, that the argument of Apologetics must move forward with the smoothness of Euclid. Had he attended to the non-Euclidean geometries which were beginning to be formulated in his time, he might have found that not even Euclid was an ideal, and thus have come to be content with arguments for Christianity that were no more than morally certain.

XVII Hermes. When the Catholic theologian, Georg Hermes, died in 1831 it is said that there were thirty of his disciples holding chairs of theology in Germany, and it is owing to his theories that Apologetics went into a blind-alley in the first half of the 19th cent. He took his cue from a passage in the *Kritik* of Kant (*Works* 3:555) in which the problem of the relation of belief to knowledge is glanced at. The system Hermes evolved is now summarized for us in the condemnations of the Vatican Council (D1811-15), but the Council's analysis does not make clear the connection between these various propositions in the mind of their author. Hermes began with a more-than-methodic doubt (D1815) of all his beliefs. From this process there emerged what he thought to be two kinds of inevitable conclusion ; those that were given to him in his inner experience (such as the awareness of his own existence and of the principle of sufficient reason) and those which were necessary presuppositions of his living a moral life. Not surprisingly these two types answer to what Kant called *Fürwahrhalten* and *Fürwahrnehmen*. The proof of the credibility of Christianity, resting upon the historical evidence of miracles, cannot for Hermes be vindicated by reduction to the first type of conclusion, and so a way must be found somehow to show that it is a necessary presupposition of moral conduct. Here Hermes surpassed himself in ingenuity, though a spark of humour would have saved himself and us from much trouble. The practical reason, he said, tells us that we cannot carry out our highest moral duty—which is that of preserving our human dignity—without using every means that is available. Now, if once it is believed that Christ walked on the water by natural means, others will try to do it and be drowned ; if they believe He fed the five thousand naturally, there will be others who will die of hunger in the desert ; and bodies will be left unburied in the expectation of a natural restoration to life, if men think that Lazarus was raised by natural means. It is therefore necessary for the moral good of mankind to accept the miraculous character of all these events. Delusion can scarcely go further than this (D1813). When pressed by Catholic critics to say at what point in the process grace could find an entrance, he fell back on the words of the Council of Orange (D179) that grace was needed for one to believe in a fitting manner (*sicut oportet*), implying that it was not needed for the simple act. Grace-aided faith, he said, was belief animated by charity and issuing at once in action ; his faith was a necessary act of the practical reason, being an earlier stage in the process altogether and one in which there was no choice (D1814 and 1811).

XVIII Newman. Hermes had succeeded in telescoping the judgment of credibility (which is, or may be, a natural act) and the act of faith itself, to which a man is moved by grace, while reserving for the preliminary stage his pitiful parody of Kant's practical reason. In spite of the popularity of this analysis among German Catholics at the time, there gradually grew up a more sober method of reckoning with Kant, as a result of the work of Kleutgen and Scheeben, while in Rome Fr Perrone, who had been concerned in the first condemnation of Hermes, produced in the mind of Newman that clarity of principles which was later to issue in the *Grammar of Assent*. In his *Apologia* (Part 3) Newman tells how Butler's *Analogy* had influenced his mind at an early stage and directed him on to the problem of the logical cogency of faith. At Rome he formulated several propositions on the matter which he submitted to Fr Perrone (these have been published in *Gregorianum* 18 (1937), 227–60). But it was quite suddenly, while he was on holiday at Glion, above the Lake of Geneva in 1866, that the thought came into his head which provided him with the clue to the whole problem. Four years later the *Grammar* was published, and this clue, that certitude was a form of assent and was sharply to be distinguished from the inference that might precede it, had been elaborated fully. In the days of Modernism Brémond was to make out that for Newman a miracle was rather an object of faith than a motive of belief, but this was a perversion of his work. He did not fit easily into any of the recognized schools of thought among the professional theologians and to Frenchmen there seemed to be a strange opacity about his thought, so that these misunderstandings persisted and were not dispelled until about the middle of the present century, chiefly by the work of Mgr P. Flanagan.

In the *Essays on Miracles* (93–4) Newman had shown how there is a convergence of independent probabilities, all pointing to the truth of the facts, so that the inquirer was justified in accepting them as true ; in the *Grammar* he came to examine the machinery of this process of assent to a convergent manifold of signs, urging after the example of Butler that ' an event is proved if its antecedents could not *in reason* be supposed to have happened unless it were true' (321). This was to rest the argument upon the principle of sufficient reason, a principle which sufficed to lift the conclusion of such an argument above the level of its probable premisses and made it differ essentially from a mere heaping together of probabilities or congeries which was rightly condemned (D 2025) in Modernist days as a travesty of truth. Newman's work, on the other hand, was accepted and carried on by Harent in his article on Faith (DTC 6:195–8) and by Pinard de la Boullaye (*L'Étude comparée des religions* (1929), 2:405–24), while *The Nature of Belief*, by Fr M. D'Arcy, aims at rounding off the argument of Newman in an important particular.

XIX The theory of P. Rousselot, expounded in two articles on *Les Yeux de le foi* (RSR 1 (1910) 241–59 ; 444–75 ; also 4 (1913) 1–36) though it owed much to the work of M. Blondel, also made appeal to Newman. Rousselot said in effect : ' Newman shows that an antecedent spiritual sympathy makes a person ready to accept the arguments of credibility, but he was wrong in not saying that this sympathy is the work of grace '. The essence of the new theory was to describe the process of belief as a single act with two objects, one known *ut quod*, the other *ut quo*, or, as we might say, differing as principal and accessory. To see a sign (or miracle) is to see its significance (or the doctrine it attests), according to Rousselot, and this was his reason for putting back the judgment of credibility into the act of faith, with the result that even this judgment has to be produced by the action of grace. Cajetan was a forerunner here (*In* 2–2æ:

1 :4:@3) for the view that the light of faith is designed to produce in us evidence of the credibility of our faith. Within the act of faith, on this view, there is a reciprocal causality, the rational judgment being logically, but not chronologically, prior to the supernatural assent of faith, and each aiding in the formation of the other. He was at once asked how on this view the sin of infidelity could occur, and said (RSR 5 (1914) 69) not very convincingly that a man might have made both the judgment of credibility and the assent of faith and thrust both aside through viciousness of will, or he might have both presented to him and accept neither. On no account could the theory say that he had the one without the other. Here one could see a need for an appeal to the psychology of conversion, evidence about which was not so abundant at the time when Rousselot wrote. He had also been misled by the false interpretation of Newman put out by Brémond, for Newman did not make the judgment of credibility depend upon a secret spiritual sympathy but on the appeal, more or less consciously made, to a logical *reductio ad absurdum* (i.e. to the principle of sufficient reason) which gave cogency to the observed convergence of probabilities. Newman's work was put in a true light by F. Bacchus (MN 139 (1922) 1–12 ; 143 (1923) 106–15) and by E. Przywara (*Stimmen der Zeit* 105 (1923) 218–26), this last being of great importance for setting the rising school of Newmanists in Germany on the right lines.

More serious were the questions raised about the orthodoxy of the theory of Rousselot. During his lifetime he was able to brush aside the accusation that he was reviving the errors of Bautain (RSR 5 (1914) 453–58) by pointing out that the proposition signed by Bautain in proof of his orthodoxy read in its French original (D 1626 *n.*) : ' L'usage de la raison précède la foi, et y conduit l'homme par la révélation et la grâce ', though the last six words, so vital for his own theory, do not appear in the Latin text afterwards issued from Rome. But this subtlety does not really suffice, for another undertaking made by Bautain (ibid.) was not to teach that reason cannot acquire a genuine and full certitude of the motives of credibility. In 1924 the Holy Office issued a list of condemned propositions (published 27 Feb 1925, in the *Semaine religieuse de Quimper* and reprinted in *Periodica* 14 (1926), 17–19, one of which ran : ' The apologetic argument cannot be historically convincing, at least not completely so, unless it be accepted with the assent of faith'. Another said that the value of the arguments for the credibility of the Christian religion does not depend on their evidence but on the subjective needs of the individual in his life and conduct. These condemnations do not mention Rousselot by name but they touch his theory.

XX The attack upon Apologetics. Still Rousselot's theory was made the subject of much discussion, being defended by H. Lang OSB in *Die Lehre des hl. Thomas von der Gewissheit des übernatürlichen Glaubens* (1929) and attacked by A. Stolz OSB in *Glaubensgnade und Glaubenslicht* (1933) and

by M. J. Congar OP (*Bulletin thomiste* 7 (1930), 40–6),
while K. Eschweiler in *Die zwei Wege der neueren
Theologie* (1925) drew a moral from it, claiming
that theology had gone astray with Molina and
Lugo, and should give up its separation of Apologetics from dogmatic theology, uniting once more
both in the one track, just as the act of faith and
judgment of credibility had been united in the
view of Rousselot and in the medieval synthesis of
Aquinas. When it was pointed out that Pius XI had
just (AAS 15 (1923) 318) been praising St Thomas for
having put Apologetics on its true foundation and
having clearly marked off the spheres of reason and
faith, and that the double action of believing (by
judgment of credibility and act of faith), though not
found literally in St Thomas, does come out of his
thought and does represent a progress of theological
thought, the onslaught on Apologetics began to abate,
but not before some had been carried away by it.

XXI The rejection of Rousselot. The mind of
St Thomas, which Rousselot claimed to be interpreting, was further explored by J. de Wolf (*La
Justification de la foi chez s. Thomas*, 1946), who
followed up a clue given by Stolz and worked out
how for St Thomas *opinio* gives only a probable
conclusion while *opinio fortificata rationibus* (or
opinion which is supported by an appeal to the
principle of sufficient reason) gives a certain conclusion. This second category had been entirely
neglected by Rousselot, whose theory could therefore not claim to descend from St Thomas but must
be based on a false dilemma between opinion and
knowledge. Examples of the use of this 'convergence' argument in St Thomas, though they are
not elaborated with all the fullness of Newman,
can be found at 3a:55:6:@1 ; 2–2æ:70:2c ; *Quaestiones de Veritate* 14:2c. J. Huby SJ did attempt to
reply (RSR 34 (1947) 462–80) to De Wolf, but the
passages he brought up from St Thomas (*Quaestiones
de Potentia* 6:2:@9 and *In* 1 Cor 2:lectio 3) to show
that St Thomas was really in favour of Rousselot
are not convincing and are quite general assertions
that grace finds a place somewhere in the approach
to the faith, which no one wanted to deny. More
useful was the research of J. Chéné (RSR 35 (1948)
566–88) on the meaning of *initium fidei*, a term
used by the Council of Orange (D 178) to denote
the first act of faith, rather than the first step taken
towards faith, and with this clarification the last
support of the Rousselot theory seemed to have been
pulled away. All theological schools of thought
would hold that divine grace is aiding the inquirer
in his approach to the faith, but they part company
when it comes to deciding what exactly he can do
unaided. Rousselot would deny that any purely
natural movement is made. Newman, seeing very
clearly the force of prejudice that moves fallen
human nature towards disbelief, would call in grace
to enable a man to be honest with himself in casting
off those prejudices and in preserving a watchful
attention to God. Others would allow a man to
make the judgment of credibility (*credibile est*)
unaided, provided that this judgment does in fact

precede—as is not always the case—the judgment
that belief is a good thing (*credendum est*). *See*
FAITH for further elaboration of this point.

XXII The encyclical *Humani Generis* (AAS 42
(1950) 562) was emphatic in asserting that the divine
origin of the Christian religion can be proved with
certainty even by the merely natural light of reason.
But (ibid. 574) it made a notable concession to the
Rousselot theory by the place it allowed to 'connatural knowledge' in the approach to the faith.
Citing St Thomas for this (2–2æ:1:4:@3 and
45:2c), it claimed that the mind can sometimes
experience, whether by nature or by grace, an
emotional sympathy with the higher ideals presented
to it and that this sympathy can assist the mind in
its search to determine the nature of those ideals.
At the same time such assistance was not to be
mistaken for a power of intuition which the emotions
somehow conferred upon the mind. With this
concession the element of truth in the theory of
Rousselot has been assimilated into Catholic
theology. Souls of great natural rectitude may find
that they are urged by a strong desire to say to
themselves : 'I must believe that God has spoken
through Christ, and this desire may be God-given';
but no-one can deny that a man may listen to the
exposition of the traditional apologetic arguments
—as happens when a non-Catholic youth mechanically attends the religious instruction given in a
Catholic school—and not think any more about
them than if they were so many arguments about
Caesar or Nero, and then after the lapse of years
he may by some secret desire be urged on a sudden
to turn to the faith. Such cases are not unreal, and
they go to show that the experience of converts
does not belie the theoretical position taken up by
Catholic theology.

When Pius XII in *Humani Generis* (*loc. cit.*)
repeated the words of the Vatican Council (D 1794)
about the many marvels that were set forth by
Providence to produce the evident credibility of the
Christian faith, he made the wording more precise
by saying that these marvels were *external signs*, and
that they were sufficient to produce certainty. This
emphasis on the rôle of miracles in the apologetic
argument was not without significance, for K. Adam
had appealed to the same passage of the Vatican
Council (where it says that the Church 'makes her
children sure' that their faith is well-founded, the
Latin being *certiores faciat*) as if it showed that the
fact of the Church, in the full splendour and vitality
of her existence, had to be brought in to make the
argument from miracles sure. This was to press
the dead comparison in *certiores* beyond what it
would bear and what the Fathers of the Council
intended. Other attempts to depreciate the argument from miracles had been made more recently,
and St Thomas was brought in, with his repeated
statement about the interior 'touch' of God, which
together with the external signs, draws a man to
the faith. St Thomas looked upon the Apostles as
being drawn chiefly by this interior 'touch', since
in some cases they followed Christ before He had

shown them His miracles. But for ordinary mortals St Thomas insists firmly (2-2æ:10:1:@1) that there must be external preaching as well as the interior drawing, and the external preaching he considers to include an appeal to the performance of miracles in confirmation of what is said, whether these be present or past. In 2-2æ:6:1:c he explains that miracles and preaching are an insufficient cause of the assent of faith, but this is not to say that they are incapable of motivating a judgment of credibility, a judgment which is here (@2) described as a *persuasio ad credendum* or a preliminary to the act of faith. One has only to consider Lk 1:36, 45 to see that even for Our Lady there was some process of presentation of credentials by the angel and of the verification of these in the visit to Elizabeth before the sublime act of faith pronounced in the *Magnificat*. The *Fiat* of Lk 1:38 may well have been due to an interior urging, but it is not presented by Luke as the whole cause of the act of faith in 1:46-7. The discussion of the other limiting case, the faith of demons (2-2æ:5:2:c), shows that superior sharpness of intellect can bring its possessor to an unavoidable assent to the evidence of credibility, but the clouded intellect of man is never in that favoured state of clarity, and his assent remains free.

XXIII The purpose of Apologetics.

In recent years discussion has turned upon the question of the purpose of Apologetics : is it addressed to an inquirer into the faith or is it merely to remove those fluttering doubts that assail the mind of one who has already come to accept the faith ? In the supposition that conversion is a momentary flash or crash, and never a lingering, slow, sweet skill, there can be only one answer to this question, and this answer is the one preferred by R. Aubert, who has exhaustively examined so much of recent controversy on belief. Other assumptions of his are questionable, quite apart from this one supposition. He considers (750-4) that the traditional division of the process into the three moments, judgment of credibility, practical judgment that belief is desirable or even necessary, and act of faith, is *simpliste* (779), and that things never happen like that, though theoretically they could. At the same time he admits that there is a shortage of good psychological accounts of conversion, an admission which detracts from his own previous pronouncement. He also makes out that the condemnation of Sanchez (D 1154), for having taught that a non-believer will be excused from his sin of unbelief if he is led by a less probable opinion, was no more than the equivalent of an assertion that it is wrong to use probable opinions in a matter of faith. It is never easy to settle exactly what positive teaching is involved in a negative condemnation of this kind, but it is at least possible that the Holy Office meant to urge just the one point, that the unbeliever sins if he neglects to go on with his search into the faith when he knows that he has weightier reasons for belief than for unbelief. If one tells him that certainty is to be expected in a sudden flash, by some Barthian inrush of grace, and that the patient building-up of a

judgment of credibility is not worth while, then it would seem that the preaching of the Christian evidences should come to an end and nothing else be done than to kneel down and pray for the grace. Some holy men have held to this policy, but their example has not been universally followed. The three stages in the way to faith are not only distinct in a theoretical analysis, and even if the first and the second are often interchanged in order of time, they can yet be recognised in very many narratives of conversion, a type of literature which is more abundant in the English tongue than in the languages of the theological discussions of the past.

Bibliography. The argument of Apologetics is best studied in the primary sources such as L. Vives, *De Veritate fidei christianae*, Basel 1543 ; *H. Grotius, *De Veritate religionis christianae* (Paris 1622) ; *J. Butler, *The Analogy of Religion* (London 1736) ; J. H. Newman, *The Grammar of Assent* (London 1870) ; M. D'Arcy, *The Nature of Belief* (London 1934) ; W. R. O'Connor, *The Eternal Quest* (New York 1947) ; while of the manuals of Apologetics the most useful at present is A. C. Cotter, *Theologia Fundamentalis*.

On points of detail the following can be consulted : N. Balthasar and A. Simonet, ' Le Plan de la Somme contre les Gentils ', *Revue Néoscolastique de Philosophie* 6 (1930) 189-210 ; G. Graf, *Des Theodor Abu Kurra Traktat über den Schöpfer und die wahre Religion* (Beiträge XIV.1) (Münster 1913); *A. Guillaume, ' A Debate between Christian and Moslem Doctors ', *Journal of Royal Asiatic Society*, supplement (1924) 233-44 ; J. H. Crehan, *Quid senserit S. Thomas de naturali beatitudine*, Acta III Congressi Thomistici (Rome 1950) 134-8 ; P. Charles, *Le Concile du Vatican et l'acte de foi*, NRT 52 (1925) ; 513-36 ; P. Rousselot, *Les Yeux de la foi*, RSR 1 (1910) 241-259, 444-75 ; J. de Wolf, *La Justification de la foi chez s. Thomas* (Louvain 1946) ; R. Aubert, *Le Problème de l'Acte de Foi* (Louvain 2, 1950) ; M. Brillant and M. Nédoncelle, *Apologétique* (Paris 1937) ; M. Nédoncelle, *L'Influence de Newman sur Rousselot*, RevSR 27 (1953) 321-32 ; P. Flanagan, *Newman, Faith and the believer* (London 1946) ; J. H. Newman, ' Theses de Fide ', *Gregorianum* 18 (1937) 219-60 ; J. Walgrave OP, *Newman, le développement du dogme* (Paris 1957) ; A. J. Boekraad, *The Personal conquest of truth* (Louvain 1956). J. H. C.

APOSTASY

There are three questions to answer about this subject; (I) what it is exactly, (II) how it can be thought to come about, and (III) whether it can be cured or made good by the Church.

I The notion of apostasy is that of a total falling away from the revelation which Christ has committed to His Church, as somehow distinct from the partial defection of one who denies a particular doctrine and thus makes himself a heretic. An apostate turns away, not simply from the law of Christ which he will no longer obey, but from that adhesion of mind to Christ and His revelation in the Church which is generally described as faith (see FAITH). Abandonment of belief in God is treated under ATHEISM.

The Church (by canon 942) gives a sinner the benefit of every possible doubt, decreeing that the Last Anointing is to be refused to a Catholic only when he is impenitent and is openly continuing in a mortal sin with contumacy. If any one of these details is doubtful, he may receive the sacrament conditionally and is not regarded as finally fallen away. This attitude of the Church goes back to early times, for Hermas (*Visio* 3:7:2; GCS 48:13) speaks of 'those who have completely apostatized and do not admit into their minds the thought of repentance, for they love their wantonness and the evil things they have done'. Thus in matters of faith the most tenuous adhesion to Christ's revelation as set forth by the Church keeps a man from being an apostate.

Apostasy from Moses was known and spoken of by the Jews (Ac 21:21) and a notorious instance of it was Tiberius Julius Alexander, a contemporary of St Paul. Paul gives warning (1 Tim 4:1) of similar defections among Christians; men will have made their hearts proof against grace by cauterizing them, thus becoming finally impenitent. John (1 Jn 2:19) tells of some 'who have gone out from us but who were not of us'. (These words are sometimes used by theologians to argue that the faith can sometimes be abandoned because it was never properly received. John, however, is not laying down a rule here but simply describing certain unknown people; he may have been thinking of Simon Magus and Helena, but he does not give any clue. The 'not being of us' is not so much the reason for their defection as a reflection on what was true all the time but not realized till later, a use of the philosophical imperfect tense which is not unknown in John's writing.)

The law of the Church (canon 1325) lays down the distinction of apostate from heretic as given above, but there is a difficulty about the theoretical explanation of this distinction if one follows St Thomas in holding (*Summa*, 2–2ae:5:3) that a heretic who denies one revealed truth thereby removes from himself the possibility of holding the other truths of revelation with a true assent of faith. This would seem to make all heretics ultimately apostates. It is therefore necessary to examine how apostasy by its origins may still be thought to differ from heresy.

II The root-cause of apostasy is a refusal to have any link with the revelation of Christ as transmitted by the Church, whereas the heretic *chooses* (as the Greek word for heresy implies) the kind of link he will have, or very often the kind of Church he will have to transmit to him what God has revealed. He will eat his own bread and be clothed with his own garments, but would still desire the name of Christ to be invoked upon him (Is 4:1). To hold some truths of Christ's revelation (as the heretic does) not on divine faith but because they commend themselves to his private judgment is to have some link left with the revelation of Christ, though it must be tenuous and it does not leave much scope for an idea of the Church. God does not abandon a man unless He has been abandoned first, as the Vatican Council said (D 1794), and the tenuous link which the heretic keeps, the apostate willingly lets go. He comes

near to the condition of one who sins against the Holy Ghost.

If the apostate is sinning against the light, it would seem to follow that he cannot be pardoned by the Church while he is in that condition. This inference seems to have been drawn by early writers such as Hermas (*Similitudes* 9:26:7; GCS 48:95), but this matter will be discussed below. What must here be attempted is to lay bare, if that is at all possible, something of the way in which, in the case of the apostate, the normal working of the machinery of belief goes into reverse. The distinction of judgment of credibility from act of faith is helpful here (*see* APOLOGETICS (XIII)). One who has already by heresy wiped out his act of faith may still have intact his rational judgment of credibility and also what is technically called the *pius credulitatis affectus*, or the moral judgment that faith would be a good thing for him. Of these two remaining assets, the first is often the product of unaided reason, while the second is fostered by the transient actual graces God may give to the man. If now he comes by reasoning (however erroneously) upon his world to the conclusion that it is a closed system which does not admit of a supernatural revelation at all, he at once sets up a tension between this, his latest reasoned judgment (one of *incredibility* now), and the desire to believe or the grace-aided judgment that belief is a good thing. The tension may be resolved in various ways, but it is clear that one way out will be to jettison the wish to believe in deference to the supposed claims of reason. A man of austere, dry intellectuality may fall into this way of resolving his tension, content with a formal Deism and spurning the desire for belief as if it were a 'soft option'. Another man, who has a stronger yearning for belief, will go over his supposed proof that the world is a closed system until he finds a flaw in it and then the process of coming-to-believe will once more be open to him. It is over cases like these that modern theologians have joined in a debate about the culpability of such apostasy: must it be supposed in all such men?

The Vatican Council (D 1794) taught that no one can ever have a just cause for changing or calling in question the faith they have once received from the teaching Church. This proposition would seem to make all apostates culpable in some way or other, but various attempts have been made to modify the absoluteness of the proposition. A. Stolz OSB, in 1930 tried to limit the Vatican condemnation to those who followed the heretical system of the German theologian Hermes, who was certainly aimed at by the Council and whose methodic doubt in theology was certainly the excitatory cause of the decree. But, as in so many cases, an occasion may be mistaken for a *vera causa*, and Dom Stolz did not find many who were ready to follow him in his interpretation of the Council.

One might argue that even on the natural plane a man ought to follow out as a supreme law of his being that assimilation to God which pagan philosophy already recognized as the end of life (*see* APOLOGETICS (XI)), and that in doing so he is bound to judge that belief is good for him and to be maintained or fostered as much as in him lies. Failure in this moral duty will then be culpable, quite apart from the rejection of grace that may be involved.

The passage from a state of the habitual exercise of the act of faith to one of apostasy is easier to evaluate, for where no heresy intervenes it is obviously much harder to exculpate one who makes such a wholesale rejection of grace. Even if reason build up the contrary of his original judgment of credibility and prick him with the idea that he is living on an illusion, the implanted dispositions which theologians call the infused virtues (see FAITH) will make it easier for him to hold on, and in the same measure harder for him to jettison his faith without culpability.

It was also taught by the Vatican Council (D 1799) that faith sets reason free from error and comes in to supplement the wavering mastery that reason may have of a given subject-matter. Now when this subject-matter happens to be the moral law, it is plain that the Church may urge certain conclusions (e.g. about divorce) as supported by revelation which reason can but feebly discern. When a man through weakness or through passion is making for himself repeatedly the practical judgment that the faith is not worth while if it stops him from putting his own interpretation on the moral law, the parallel speculative judgment that revelation is entirely credible becomes very soon undermined, and thus both presuppositions of his act of faith are lost through what was in origin a moral weakness. A man in this state may go on believing for a time, in spite of his warped judgment that faith is not worth while and that the motives of credibility he once accepted are not now worth considering, but it will not be easy for him to believe. Should he lose his faith, the loss would be put down by theologians to a voluntary act (and therefore culpable) that is free in its cause even if not in itself. There was a time when he could have halted the process and he failed to do so.

Debate went on after the Vatican Council whether its teaching that no-one could have just cause for abandoning the faith, meant a cause that was just for himself alone (or subjectively) taking into account a possible confusion of his mind, or simply a cause that was just when viewed by itself (or objectively) in contrast with the splendour of revelation and the abundance of its credentials. The act of faith should be a human act though one that is divinely aided (see ACTS, HUMAN), and there may sometimes be an external acceptance of the faith which does not fulfil the conditions of a human act; an adult pagan may accept baptism during a famine if what he really wants is the bag of rice that might go with it, but all that he would be thinking about would be the rice. He would be ready to go through any process of instruction to secure that his hunger was kept at bay, but he would not make an internal act of faith, whatever words he said. When such cases as this are set aside, it cannot be said that the distinction of objectively and subjectively just causes of apostasy

has much to commend it. From *Collectio Lacensis* VII. 182 it appears that a similar distinction was rejected at the Council. On the way into the Church a convert will have had such ' moral certainty ' about the credibility of revelation (see APOLOGETICS) that all prudent doubts about it will have gone, leaving only what are imprudent fears and scruples. These may so work upon him that they destroy his former certainty, but only if he allows them to do so by sinful neglect of the graces and dispositions he received at baptism, or if he becomes so unbalanced that his final withdrawal from the Church cannot be called a human act. Between these alternatives it does not seem easy to find room for an apostasy that would be subjectively in good faith, though some theologians such as Aubert have tried to find it.

Others have tried to find a loophole in the words of the Council that those ' who have received the faith through the teaching of the Church ' can have no just cause for apostasy (*qui fidem susceperunt sub ecclesiae magisterio*), arguing that a defective Catholic education would then be an excuse. Fr Lombardi, in his *Salvation of the Unbeliever* (320–4), sets out their case with some diffidence, but the determining factor should be what the Council meant by the phrase. It was distinguishing between those who give their adherence to other religions, led by human reasoning, and those who through the heavenly gift of faith have adhered to Catholic truth. There is no thought of education in the context, and in fact one of the alternative wordings in the draft spoke of ' receiving the faith at baptism '. Trent (D 870) had already ruled out the idea of children ratifying their baptism when they grew up.

III The forgiveness of apostasy by the Church was early called in question. Cyprian (*ep.* 67:6; CSEL 3:741) in the height of the persecution referred to a decretal of Pope Cornelius which allowed that those who had apostatized through fear might be admitted to do penance but were not to be ordained as clerics or consecrated as bishops.[1] Some 50 years later the Spanish council of Elvira (canon 1; HL I:221) laid it down that those who reverted to idolatry after baptism were not to be admitted to ' communion ' even at the end of their lives.[2] There has been much debate about the meaning of this word *communio*, for it came to have two senses for the Christians; it could signify the reception of the Eucharist, or, at a lower level, the right to be present at the Eucharist and not to be dismissed with the various groups, catechumens, penitents and possessed, who were not allowed to stay for the offertory and the beginning of the sacrifice. Hefele and Leclercq take opposite sides in interpreting the meaning of this Canon. One might argue that the act of Cornelius was notorious throughout the West and that Elvira could not have intended to go back on

[1] Nobiscum et cum omnibus omnino episcopis in toto mundo constitutis etiam Cornelius collega noster, sacerdos pacificus et iustus et martyrio quoque dignatione Domini honoratus, decreverit eiusmodi homines ad poenitentiam quidem agendam posse admitti, ab ordinatione autem cleri adque sacerdotali honore prohiberi.

[2] Placuit nec in finem eum communionem accipere.

that. Prosper in his *Chronicon* (MGH *Auctores* IX, 439, under the year 253) attributes to Cornelius's willingness to admit apostates to penance[1] the rise of Novatianism, and Elvira was not a Novatian council.

In the East the tradition which finds expression in the *Didascalia* seems to have prevailed. Here (2:23, in Connolly's edition, 75) bishops are instructed to follow the example of what the Lord did with Manasseh: 'You have heard, beloved children, how Manasseh served idols with evil and bitterness, and slew righteous men; yet when he repented God forgave him, albeit there is no sin worse than idolatry'. This Eastern tradition found its way from Egypt through Visigothic Spain to Ireland, along with so much else, and thus came to be at the base of the Celtic penitential practice which spread all over Western Europe.

As early as 357 the Christian emperors began the process of imposing civil sanctions on apostates, it being decreed in that year that if a Christian passed over to Judaism his goods were to be confiscated by the imperial treasury. Justinian reinforced these sanctions and extended them, thus preparing the ground for many a Church-State conflict of future ages. If at baptism there is a pact between God and the baptized, then the renouncing of such a pact might be said to give bad example to all makers of pacts in civil society and therefore to be an offence within the cognizance of the civil law, but the external renunciation is only a very small part of apostasy which is so largely a lapse in the mind (cf. *Summa*, 2–2ae:12:1:@2).

Bibliography. Suarez *de fide* disputation 16; R. Aubert, *Le Problème de l'acte de foi* (1950[2]); A. Stolz OSB, 'Was definiert das Vatikan Konzil über den Glaubenszweifel?', in TQ 113 (1930) 519–60; H. Lennerz SJ, *De obligatione Catholicorum perseverandi in fide* (1932); R. Lombardi SJ, *The Salvation of the Unbeliever* (1956); G. Guzzetti, *La perdita della fede nei cattolici* (1940); A. Michel, s.v. Apostats in the index to DTC (1950).   J. H. C.

APOSTLES The general sense of the word in the Bible will first be examined (I), then (II) its technical restricted sense, and the persons of whom it is so used. There follows naturally (III) a study of the mission of the Apostles, of the duties and concomitant powers of the Apostolic office. (IV) The Apostolate of Matthias, Paul and Barnabas is next discussed, which leads to the question of (V) the apostolic succession, which is fully treated, however, in a separate article. There follows (VI) the necessary distinction between the essential powers of the office and the personal prerogatives of the Twelve, and finally (VII) a brief survey of non-Catholic theories about the Apostolate.

I The general sense of the word in the Bible. The word is derived from ἀποστέλλειν, to send. Although the Aramaic equivalent to the NT ἀπόστολος cannot be established with absolute certainty, the intimate connection between ἀποστέλλειν

---

[1] . . . eo quod Cornelius poenitentes apostatas recepisset. . . .

and the OT šālaḥ has been proved (Hatch, Concordance to the LXX; cf. CCS 657d). Examples of the divine sending of men on missions in the OT are Gen 45:5 (Joseph); Ex 3:10, 12 (Moses); Jg 6:14 (Gideon); 1 Kg 15:1 (Samuel), 15:8 (Saul); 2 Kg 12:1 (Nathan); Is 6:8 (Isaias); Jer 7:25, 19:14, 25:4 (prophets); cf. Jer 14:14–15 (false prophets not so commissioned), Ez 2:3–4, 3:5–6 (Ezechiel), Abd 1 (an ambassador). Regularly the OT šālaḥ is translated in the LXX by the verb ἀποστέλλειν or a compound of it. Such divine commission involves authority and the necessary power for its fulfilment, and success is often guaranteed by the divine assurance: 'I am with you' (cf. U. Holzmeister, 'Dominus tecum', in *Verbum Domini* 23 (1943) 232–7, 257–62). An appreciation of this total notion of divine mission, so strong in the Hebrew mind, gives added force to the NT accounts of the sending of his chosen ones by the Son of God. In the NT the word is used in both a general sense, and a restricted technical sense. The general sense is seen in Lk 1:26 (Gabriel); Mt 23:34 (cf. Lk 11:49, 'I will send to them prophets and apostles' DV); Jn 13:16 ('neither is the apostle greater than he that sent him' DV); Ac 14:4, 14 (Barnabas and Paul—Gk); 2 Cor 8:23 (Paul's fellow-labourers, 'the apostles of the churches' DV); Phil 2:25 (Epaphroditus 'your apostle' DV), Apoc 2:2 (of false apostles—cf. 2 Cor 11:13); Heb 3:1 ('Jesus, the apostle and high priest of our confession' DV). In Rom 16:7, 1 Thess 2:7, 1 Cor 4:9 the force of the word is disputed. In 1 Cor 12:28 and Eph 4:11 it is perhaps used of the charismatic gifts. For full treatment, cf. H. Dieckmann, *De Ecclesia* I (1925), nn. 249–311.

It is claimed (e.g. by H. Riesenfeld in *Religion in Geschichte und Gegenwart*, s.v. Apostolos) that Paul's use of 'the Twelve' and 'all the Apostles' in the list of those to whom Christ appeared (1 Cor. 15:7, 9) proves that there was a category of Christian officials called Apostles outside the narrow group of the Twelve. But Paul's change of term in his list implies no more than that the Twelve, when they were all assembled at the Ascension of Christ, were then actually commissioned as Apostles and should therefore be styled as such. Andronicus and Junias (Rom 16:7), who are alleged as members of this wider group, are no other than Andrew and John. with their names given in a Westernized form (cf. J. Donovan, *The Authorship of St John's Gospel*, 1935). Timothy and Apollos are never called Apostles in any sense by the NT or by the early Christian writers. That Clement of Rome is called an Apostle by his namesake of Alexandria (*Strom.* 4:17, GCS 15:273) may be a slip, as he names him in three other passages without the title, or he may have written ἰσαπόστολος meaning that Clement was a contemporary of Apostles.

II The technical restricted sense. The classical text is Lk 6:13, 'He called unto him his disciples: and he chose twelve of them (*whom also he named apostles*') DV. (Cf. minimizing view of this text, Dom J. Dupont, 'Le Nom d'apôtres a-t-il été donné aux Douze par Jésus ?' (1956).) Many had attached themselves to Christ since the beginning of the public ministry. From among them, after a night spent in prayer, he makes a significant choice of twelve. The number suited his purpose, and it further symbolized that they are the twelve patriarchs of the New Israel (CCS 752 f., cf. 692c, Mt 19:28, Ac 13:17, Gal 6:16, Apoc 21:14). Mark records the occasion with less solemnity ('and he made that twelve should be with him' DV, 3:14) and Mt 10:1 gives it in a compressed form. All three synoptics then give lists of the twelve chosen, which are best set out in table form, together with the list from Ac 1:13. All are given with the DV spelling.

Mt 10:2-4	Mk 3:16-19
Simon Peter	Simon named Peter
Andrew his brother	James of Zebedee
James of Zebedee	John his brother
John his brother	Andrew
Philip	Philip
Bartholomew	Bartholomew
Thomas	Matthew
Matthew—publican	Thomas
James of Alpheus	James of Alpheus
Thaddeus	Thaddeus
Simon the Cananean	Simon the Cananean
Judas Iscariot	Judas Iscariot

Lk 6:14-16	Ac 1:13
Simon named Peter	Peter
Andrew his brother	John
James	James
John	Andrew
Philip	Philip
Bartholomew	Thomas
Matthew	Bartholomew
Thomas	Matthew
James of Alpheus	James of Alpheus
Simon Zelotes	Simon Zelotes
Jude, br of James	Jude, br of James
Judas Iscariot	

The names fall into groups of four. The first named in each group is the same, otherwise the order in the groups varies, save that the Iscariot is always last. Peter always heads the list, one of the many signs of the extraordinary prominence accorded to him in the NT. Mt emphasizes this by calling him 'the first', a phrase unnecessary at the head of a list unless it indicates pre-eminence of dignity (CCS 692d). If order of time were the only consideration, Andrew or John would have been placed first, Jn 1:40. Bartholomew is commonly identified with Nathanael, Jn 1:45, James of Alpheus (possibly 'of Cleophas', Jn 19:25) with James the Less, Mk 15:41, 'brother' of the Lord, first bishop of Jerusalem, Gal 1:19, Ac 15:13. Simon the Cananean's title derives from an Aramaic root meaning 'the zealous one', which Lk is careful to translate for his non-Jewish readers. It is uncertain whether the title describes his personal zeal for the Law, or his membership of the fanatical party of the Zealots (contrast CCS 692e with 728i). There is some textual support for Lebbeus instead of, or in addition

to, Thaddeus in Mt and Mk. It is not difficult to identify him with Lk's Jude, the brother of James: the unfortunate possession of the traitor's name calls for the qualification 'of James', or the use of a second name (CCS 752 f). Mt supplies the identification of himself with Levi the publican. Mk alone retains the nickname 'Boanerges' for James and John. Jn 11:16, 20:24 tells us that Thomas means the 'twin', Didymus. Iscariot probably means the man of Qeriyôth, an unidentified village of Judah, Jos 15:25.

This definitive call of the twelve as a distinct group had been preceded by the first call of Andrew, John, Simon, Philip and Nathanael, Jn 1:35-51, and by the second call of the first four of these, which involved their leaving their secular occupations to be with Christ, Mt 4:18-22, Mk 1:16-20, Lk 5:1-11; later, a similar call is given to Matthew, Mt 9:9-13, Mk 2:13-17, Lk 5:27-32.

III The nature of the Apostolic office. Christ now sets the twelve aside as a distinct group, a unit for which he has definite plans. He begins to instruct and form them with special care; they are to share in his work, for they are destined to be its chief continuators; they are his envoys to the world, to whom He entrusts his own mission from the Father (Jn 20:21; 17:6, 8, 14, 18), and with whom he identifies himself: 'he that receiveth you, receiveth me, and he that receiveth me, receiveth him that sent me' (Mt 10:40, DV). To them he commits that revelation of divine truth which is one of the chief purposes of his coming into the world: 'neither doth anyone know the Father, but the Son, and he to whom it shall please the Son to reveal . . . to you it is given to know the mysteries of the kingdom of heaven, but to them it is not given' (Mt 11:27, 13:11, DV; cf. Mt 13:51-2). Their mission is, first, one of teaching (Mt 28:19-20) the whole of Christ's revelation, supported by the power of miracles (Mk 16:17-18, 20). The apostles will be enlightened by the spirit of truth (Jn 14:16-17, 26) and assisted by the invisible support of Christ himself (Mt 28:20). But their mission implies more than teaching; they are, secondly, to govern Christ's followers, who are bound to submit to them (Lk 10:16), for their judgments will be ratified in heaven (Mt 18:18), and their power extends even to that of excommunication (Mt 18:17). Thirdly, they are to sanctify Christ's followers not only with the life-giving word of the Gospel, but by baptism (Mt 28:19), remission of sins (Jn 20:22-3) and the Eucharist (Lk 22:19; 1 Cor 11:24-5). This threefold mission corresponds to the threefold office of Christ in the world, for He is Prophet, King and Priest. That His work in the world should be continued by mere men, divine power is needed, and all necessary power and authority is given them (Mt 28:18-20; cf. Jn 15:16). Their mission among men in the name and in the power of Christ is guaranteed success through the effective word of Christ (Jn 17:20-1). The frequent expressions 'the twelve', 'one of the twelve', show how clearly the distinct unity of the Apostolic college was recognized. They are still 'the twelve' after Judas' defection and death (Jn 20:24 ; 1 Cor 15:5, in the best Gk MSS.).

Their special call is mentioned by the *Epistle of Barnabas*, 5:9, and either of the titles of the *Didache* bears witness to the recognition of their corporate unity. Their commission, authority and powers are given to them as a body. After the Ascension, the defection of Judas from their number must be made good, the college must be completed.

IV Matthias, Paul and Barnabas. Although not called by Christ himself, Matthias clearly ranks as an Apostle. After his choice, in the making of which room is left for the divine guidance (Ac 1:24–25), he is 'numbered with the eleven apostles' (Ac 1:26). Their mission in itself is universal and enduring, and it must be safeguarded. Yet they themselves are clearly mortal men (Jn 16:2 ; 21:18–19, 23), and it is noteworthy that the martyrdom of James (Ac 12:2) does not call for an identical completion of the 'twelve'. They have been chosen as eye-witnesses of the Lord, and that personal testimony will sooner or later be ended by death in the case of all But their witness can endure, and must endure ; their mission, with its necessary authority, is to the end of time, to all men. Even in their lifetime the same essential Apostolic office is entrusted by God certainly to Paul (Ac 9:15 and 22:21) and most probably to Barnabas (Ac 13:2 ; 1 Cor 9:5–6). Certainly Paul always claimed the fullness of the Apostolic office, and constantly exercised its threefold power ; he was recognized as one of themselves by the other apostles (Gal 2:9) ; his Apostolate was equally successful (2 Cor 3:1–3), and it was confirmed by numerous miracles (Ac 13:10–11, 14:3, 7–9, 16:18, 25–6, 19:11–12, 20:9–12, 28:8–9 ; 2 Cor 12:12). It is interesting that the litany of the saints names Matthias and Barnabas at the end of the list of Apostles, before the Evangelists Luke and Mark, while the 'Communicantes' in the Canon of the Mass, using the same order, omits Matthias and Barnabas ; but they appear in the 'Nobis quoque' with John. Especially in Galatians Paul vindicates his claim to the Apostleship, and the whole strength of his argument rests on the assumption that there is this universally accepted special calling, which he has received in full measure. The others were Apostles before him (1:17), but they are no more fully Apostles than he is, for their teaching is at one with his (2:2–9), and his call has come directly from God (1:1, 12 ; cf. the first verse of Rom, 1 and 2 Cor, Eph, Col, 1 and 2 Tim, Tit).

V Apostolic succession. The personal witness of the Apostles must cease with their deaths. But their mission is enduring, to all nations for all time ; their work is Christ's work, which is of universal benefit, and on this essential framework he builds his Church, through which all men are to profit by the Redemption. In their own lifetime God directly extends the call to Paul, Barnabas and perhaps others. But this is not to be the normal method of the communication of the Apostolic commission, authority and powers. The Apostles are seen giving a minor share in their powers to the seven deacons (Ac 6:1–6) ; even this lesser authority is passed on by the laying on of hands and prayer (Ac 6:6). And Paul appoints full successors to himself in Timothy and Titus. Timothy in Ephesus and Titus in Crete take Paul's place : they are commissioned to teach (1 Tim 4:6 ; Tit 2:1), to rule (1 Tim 5:17–20 ; Tit 1:10–14) and to sanctify (1 Tim 2:1–10 ; Tit 2). Their powers have come to them through the laying on of hands (1 Tim 4:14, cf. 5:22 for an extension of the principle ; 2 Tim 1:6 ; Tit 1:5, where both principles are expressed). In these three epistles and in Galatians there is constant stress against innovation ; the Apostle's mission is to hand on (*tradere*) in all its fullness and all its purity what he has in his turn received, the saving truth of Jesus. Thus the Apostle's work in the world is to be a minister of Christ, a faithful transmitter of God's truth and God's grace. That is the Apostle's divinely appointed function, to extend in place and time the power of Christ. The Apostles, in their essential functions, must have successors, and similarly Peter, the head of the whole hierarchical structure, must have a successor in his primatial office. These points are dealt with in separate articles ; *see* APOSTOLIC SUCCESSION, BISHOP, MAGISTERIUM, PETER, TRADITION, ORDINATION. St Ignatius of Antioch voices the belief of tradition in the divine functions of the Apostles and their successors, e.g. *Trall.* 2, and *passim* in his epistles.

VI Personal prerogatives of the Apostles. The essential functions of the Apostolic office must be handed on. They are to teach, to rule and to sanctify in the name and the power of Christ. But Catholic theology also recognizes that the Apostles possessed personal privileges, not essential to the office as such. Not all of them are asserted by theologians with equal unanimity, and here we merely enumerate them : (a) immediate election, instruction and mission by Christ ; (b) universal jurisdiction ; (c) the gift of miracles ; (d) personal infallibility (cf. 1 Thess 2:13) ; (e) possession of the charismatic gifts ; (f) immediate revelation and/or inspiration for establishing (i) the totality of the deposit of faith, (ii) the means of sanctification, (iii) the essential framework of church government ; (g) infused knowledge ; (h) confirmation in grace ; (i) the grace of martyrdom. The article in the *Dictionnaire de droit canonique* (s.v. apôtre) suggests that each apostle had an indefinite, rather than a universal, jurisdiction during the period when the Church was being founded. Argument on such topics is largely *a priori*, for the texts (e.g. 1 Thess 2:7) are capable of being used for either view.

VII Non-Catholic theories. There is place for only summary treatment. Radical critics who reject in whole or in great part the authenticity of the NT explain the origin of the Apostolate either without reference to Christ, e.g. Eschatologists, or admit that He made special choice of certain of His followers, but deny that He intended to found a Church, to give them an enduring mission, or to commit to their ministry a definite body of doctrine. For some the Apostolate was invented by Paul to strengthen his own position against the Judaizers. Others would admit only a ministry of the word, with no further authority. All who deny the divinity of Christ necessarily explain the Apostolate on purely human grounds. Such as hold Scripture to be the sole rule of faith can give no essential function to the Apostles in the divine scheme. Others deny the whole hierarchical nature of the Church. For others, the Apostolate is a charismatical gift which does not necessarily endure, and in any case cannot be transmitted. Some would admit many of our contentions about the Apostles themselves, but would deny that Christ intended the office to be handed on. The answer to these and kindred notions is indicated in a general way in the body of the article.

Bibliography. Ch. Journet, *L'Église du Verbe Incarné* (1955) esp. vol. 1, and *Primauté de Pierre* (1953) ; P. Batiffol, *L'Église naissante* (1927) ; DAFC I (1911) col. 251–61 ; DTC I (1909) col. 1647–60 ; J. Salaverri SJ, 'De Ecclesia' in *Sacrae Theologiae Summa* I (1955) ; A. M. Javierre, *La sucesión primacial y apostólica en el evangelio de Mateo* (1958) ; CCS, esp. 655a–9 f. ; *O. Linton, *Das Problem der Urkirche* (1932) pp. 68–100 ; *J. B. Lightfoot, *St Paul's Epistle to the Galatians* (1890) ; *Jenkins and MacKenzie, *Episcopacy Ancient and Modern* (1930) ; *K. E. Kirk (ed.), *The Apostolic Ministry* (1946) ; *H. Monnier ,*La Notion de l'apostolat* (1903) ; *A. Harnack, *Die Mission und Ausbreitung des Christentums* (1924) ; *Das Wesen des Christentums* (1920) ; F. M. Braun OP, *Aspects nouveaux du problème de l'Église* (1942) ; *J. A. Robinson, *The Christian Ministry* (1921) ; *K. Barth, *L'Église, congrégation vivante de Jésus-Christ* (1949) ; *O. Cullmann, *Peter : Disciple, Apostle, Martyr* (1953).   W. J. J.

APOSTLES' CREED The Creed which is now known as the Apostles' Creed was the product of a gradual historical evolution. Apart from minor changes it had reached its present form by the end of the 4th cent. This article will therefore deal (I) with this 4th-cent. Roman creed, going on (II) to explain the additions made in later times, and finally (III) giving some account of the theories advanced about its origin.

I The Roman creed of the 4th cent. was commented on line by line in the work of Rufinus of Aquileia, written about 404 ; it is also found in the 7th cent. *codex Laudianus* of the NT, a MS. which may have been used in Sardinia, giving, therefore, the form of creed in use there since the 4th cent. It runs as shown on p. 129.

It will be seen that there are only eleven articles, though Rufinus (PL 21:337) has the legend that each of the apostles contributed his portion to the creed before they separated to preach the faith. Ambrose (PL 17:1193) has the same idea in his *Explanatio symboli* and it is found in the Orient also (*Apostolic Constitutions* 6:4). The Greek form of the above creed is found quoted by Marcellus of Ancyra when in 340 he wrote to Pope Julius I and sought to establish his orthodoxy by professing a creed which

was identical with that used by the Pope himself (Epiphanius, *Haer.* 72:3 ; GCS 37:258). Marcellus ends his creed with the phrase 'Life everlasting', and these words are also found in the creed that was used by Nicetas, bishop of the remote diocese of Remesiana in old Serbia, towards the end of the 4th cent. Perhaps they were added to bring up the number of articles to twelve in accordance with the legend. The evidence then points to the use throughout the West of this Roman creed from the early years of the 4th cent. at the latest. It was a baptismal creed, as the context in which it appears is generally that of pre-baptismal instruction. It was not written down but learned by heart (owing to the rule of secrecy, for which *see* CATECHUMENATE). Hence local variations in wording could arise with the lapse of time.

The structure of the Roman creed is Trinitarian with a long expansion of the second article about Christ into a series of statements of the 'facts about Christ' as they are given in the primitive preaching of the apostles (*see* the sermons of Peter and Paul in Ac chs. 2, 10, 13). After the mention of the Holy Ghost there is no unity in what follows, save that the articles deal rather with man than with God. There is no mention of sacraments other than (by implication) baptism, which is covered by the words 'forgiveness of sins', as in the Nicene creed.

II The additions made to the Roman creed are seven : the words 'creator of heaven and earth' in the first article, 'conceived' in the third, 'died' in the fourth, 'He descended into hell' in the fifth, the word 'almighty' in the sixth, the word 'Catholic' in the ninth and 'communion of saints.' Of these some are matters of drafting, i.e. the second and the fifth additions ; if the Father is called almighty in the first article, it is natural to put the word in the sixth article also, and if it is desired to indicate more precisely the manner of the Virgin Birth the word 'conceived' has to be introduced. The word 'died' in the fourth article may be due to the need of making clear that crucifixion involved death, to a generation and a land where the punishment of crucifixion was unknown, or there may have been some influence of the Greek creeds here with their three participles : 'suffered, crucified, buried.' The major additions are the descent into hell and the communion of saints. Rufinus in his *Commentary* said that the Roman creed and most Eastern creeds lacked the mention of the descent but he knew of it as an article of belief. It was not known to Peter Chrysologus at Ravenna nor to Nicetas ; Ildephonsus of Toledo has it but not the Mozarabic liturgy. It is in the *Gallican Sacramentary* but not in the creeds of Faustus of Riez or of Cyprian of Toulon. Of the longer Eastern creeds that of the Arians at Sirmium in 359 has it and it is found in the so-called Athanasian creed. Sirmium has quite an elaborate statement : 'He went down to the lower world and established order there ; the wardens of Hades saw Him and were struck with fear.' The idea that the pains of Hell ceased for a moment at the resurrection

Credo in Deum patrem omnipotentem,	I believe in God the Father almighty,
et in Christum Iesum filium Eius	and in Jesus Christ, His only Son, our Lord,
unicum, Dominum nostrum,	who was born of the Holy Ghost
qui natus est de Spiritu sancto	and of the Virgin Mary,
et Maria virgine,	who was crucified under Pontius Pilate
qui sub Pontio Pilato crucifixus	and buried,
est et sepultus ;	the third day He rose again from the dead,
tertia die resurrexit a mortuis,	He ascended into heaven, sitteth at the right hand of
ascendit in coelos, sedet ad dexteram	the Father,
Patris,	from thence He shall come to judge the living and
unde venturus est iudicare vivos et mortuos ;	the dead ;
et in Spiritum sanctum,	and in the Holy Ghost,
sanctam ecclesiam,	the holy Church,
remissionem peccatorum,	the forgiveness of sins,
carnis resurrectionem.	the resurrection of the body.

of Christ is found in some Western liturgies and in Celtic tradition (*see* HELL).

Nicetas has the addition 'communion of saints' in his creed. It occurs again in Faustus of Riez and in the creed of Arles and may have come to Gaul from Illyricum with St Martin who was a native of what is now Jugoslavia. For the meaning of the article *see* COMMUNION OF SAINTS. It is included in the creed of the Mozarabic liturgy and thence goes into the Irish creeds.

The addition of the words 'creator of heaven and earth' is characteristic of the African creeds, being found in Augustine (*serm.* 215 ; PL 38:1072) and Fulgentius. It is in the creed of Arles but not in that of Toulon nor in the Mozarabic liturgy. It is finally established in the Irish creeds. Africa had plenty of trouble with Manicheans, and the denial by these that the world could have been made by God must have called for watchfulness on the part of Catholics. Greek influence is not likely in this addition, as the usual word in Latin for the Greek ποιητής is *factor*, not *creator*.

The word 'Catholic' was first applied to the Church by Ignatius (*Smyrn* 8:2) who says that, while the bishop is head of the local church, Christ is head of the Church as a whole. By the time of Pope Cornelius (who uses the word in a letter preserved by Eusebius, HE 6:43:11) the word means 'that which is established throughout the world'; he argues that there cannot be two bishops in one place both belonging to this world-wide Church. It is first found in the creed of Nicetas, who explains it in the sense used by Cornelius and contrasts it with the pseudo-churches of Manicheans, Montanists and Marcionites.

The African creed (from the time of Cyprian *ep.* 70:2) had the ending differently worded : 'forgiveness of sins, resurrection of the body, life everlasting through the holy, Catholic Church.' This gave a greater unity to these final articles but took away the close relation of holy Spirit and holy Church which in some creeds (e.g. the Irish) is made into a causal relation, the Church being declared holy in or by the Holy Ghost. How these various additions came to be gathered into one formula in

Visigothic Spain, Northern France and Ireland is a complicated story, depending upon that of the *Bobbio Missal* and the much-travelled St Pirminius ; it must suffice here to note that the expanded creed went back to Rome, probably through the tribute of liturgical books which was exacted by the Popes from the abbey of Reichenau in the 10th and 11th cents.

III The theories which have been formed about the origin of the Roman creed are endless. Some of the chief will be noticed here. K. Holl in 1919 thought that the second article, with its two attributes of Christ, that He was Son and Lord, had provided the cue for the expansion of these two ideas of Sonship and Lordship into the third and fourth to seventh articles respectively ; but this supposed too logical a development and took no account of the apostolic preaching which had all the facts about Christ displayed from the beginning in the order they are found in the creed. Lietzmann made many valuable detailed suggestions but overvalued as a source the form of creed found in the liturgical papyrus from Der-Balyzeh, which was then thought to give an early 2nd cent. Roman tradition, whereas it is really no more than a witness to Egypt in the 6th. Much was also made of the so-called *Epistle of the Apostles*, an apocryphal work of *c.* 160–180 which has a five-member creed expressing belief in, 'the Father, the Lord almighty, in Jesus Christ our Redeemer, in the Holy Ghost the comforter, in the holy church and the remission of sins'. The work is extant only in an Ethiopic version for this part of its length and should not be trusted too far ; the singular use of 'comforter' as attribute of the Holy Ghost (found only in the Jerusalem creed of 350 apart from this case) raises doubts. Lietzmann also thought that the baptismal creed was originally a simple Trinitarian confession—whether by affirmation or by replies to interrogations—and that the expanded Christological articles came from the Eucharist. This view is not now held by many.

The *Traditio apostolica* ascribed to Hippolytus is held by some to give a baptismal creed that is practically identical with the Roman creed of the early 4th cent. and thus to take us back to a point near 200 when the catechumenate can have been in existence for but a short time. There are, however, many reasons for suspecting such a simplification. The CATECHUMENATE (q.v.) must have begun much earlier; there is grave reason for thinking the Latin version of Hippolytus (as well as the Ethiopic, and perhaps more so) has been interpolated or brought up to date by those who made the version from the original Greek. In this Latin version, for instance, the creed has the phrase in article 6 *vivus ex mortuis* (living from the dead), a phrase found only in the creeds of Visigothic Spain and in that of Nicetas, all three coming from localities where Arianism was strong. It is not a doctrinal addition but it would be very hard to explain how, if the Roman creed had the word in the time of Hippolytus, it ever came to lose it.

The present writer has argued at length elsewhere (*Early Christian Baptism and the Creed*, 1950) that the Christological part of the creed was the primitive baptismal profession made by the candidate. To this was added an article about the Father, to meet Marcionite attacks on the God of the OT who was said to be at war with Christ, the God of the NT. Perhaps also the difficulty experienced with pagans (who could not so readily as converts from Jewry accept the Father) led to the inclusion of this article. The mention of the Holy Ghost, along with certain facts about His work, would most naturally come when Montanism was claiming to give the Spirit more fully, who was now incarnate in Montanus. Alongside this expanding creed (which was the candidate's affair) went the use of a Trinitarian formula for baptizing, which Justin (*apol.* 61) claimed as having been received from the apostles (*see* BAPTISM), and also the use of Trinitarian doxologies in Christian worship. It seems quite likely that when Roman legal ideas began to influence the practice of the Church (in the latter part of the 2nd cent.) the notion that baptism involved a contract or *stipulatio* led to the adoption of formal interrogations at baptism, this being required for a *stipulatio*. If, however, the use of ἐπερώτημα in 1 Pet 3:21 can be pressed, as implying that contractual ideas were already at work, then some would conclude that interrogations were introduced much earlier. There seems to be no early evidence that creeds were used at the Eucharist or for exorcism; baptism provides the sole occasion for their being drawn up. The Jews had no formal creed. Islam had the *shahada* (the two phrases) expressing belief in God and in His prophet, sometimes with the addition that Jesus was the apostle of God and a denial of the Trinity.

Bibliography. The earlier literature on this subject is surveyed in J. de Ghellinck SJ, *Patristique et Moyen Age*, I (1949²); *O. Cullmann, *The earliest Christian Confessions* (1949); J. Crehan SJ, *Early Christian Baptism and the Creed* (1950); *J. N. Kelly, *Early Christian Creeds* (1950); *H. Lietzmann's *Symbolstudien*, published in article-form in ZNTW are summarized in his *Geschichte der alten Kirche*, II, iv.

J. H. C.

APOSTOLIC FATHERS This term was first used towards the end of the 17th cent., when the writings of Clement of Rome, Ignatius of Antioch and Polycarp were collected in one volume. The epistle of the pseudo-Barnabas was sometimes included. The first idea was to gather together the non-scriptural writers who belonged to the *time* of the Apostles. The *Shepherd* of Hermas was included owing to the idea that Hermas was the man mentioned in Rom 16:14, and the fragments of Papias, owing to his link with John the apostle. The *Didache*, when it was discovered, was admitted to the group, and also the *Epistle to Diognetus*, which (in ch. xi) purports to be by one who was taught by the apostles. Modern critical opinion would place the dates of composition of these works on an extended scale between the years 70 and 180, a period far too long for the life-time of a sub-apostolic generation. Hence it is now quite uncertain what exactly makes a writing eligible for this designation.

Lightfoot suggested that it could be confined to 'those who were historically connected with the Apostles'. This would exclude Hermas, Diognetus and probably the *Didache*, while it might be necessary to add to the list certain other writings which have come to light in more recent times, such as the (apocryphal) *Epistle of the Apostles* and the *Odes of Solomon*, if any evidence of their authorship could be found. Other attempts have been made to isolate the Jewish-Christian document which is at the base of the Clementine writings, but without much success. If this document were restored to us, it would also have to be counted as apostolic in this sense. There is not much likelihood that the so-called *Traditio apostolica* of Hippolytus represents the liturgy of the apostolic age; much rather it gives what Hippolytus—and some of his followers—wanted people to think was apostolic.

Tertullian used the Latin term *apostolicus* to denote one who was a disciple of the apostles (he uses it for Mark and Luke in *adv. Marc.* 4:2; CSEL 47:426) while in Irenaeus and Clement of Alexandria the same term in Greek can be found in use. The preoccupation here is with those who were alive while the deposit of revelation was still open to augmentation. On any sane view of Tradition these men are of great importance, and the words of the prologue which Papias wrote for his book of *Expositions* give expression to this: 'If perchance at any time there came my way someone who had actually travelled about with the Ancients, I would make enquiry about the sayings of the Ancients—what did Andrew say? or Peter? what did Philip or Thomas or James say? what said John or Mathew, or some other of the Lord's disciples?—and about what Aristion and the Ancient, John, disciples of the Lord, were still saying. For I took it for granted that excerpts from the Books were not so helpful to me as the utterances of the living voice of a survivor.'

Thus while it may remain difficult always to determine the extent of the class of writings called Apostolic Fathers, the existence of such a class is theologically important as a witness that revelation was complete at the death of the last apostle and that in consequence the writings of those who were in contact with the apostles are to be given the more consideration.

Bibliography. J. Bligh SJ, 'The Prologue of Papias', in TS 13 (1952) 234–40 ; *J. B. Lightfoot, *Apostolic Fathers*, Part I : *Clement of Rome*, vol I, 1–13 ; J. Quasten, *Patrology* (1950) vol. I ; G. Jouassard, 'Le Groupement des pères dits apostoliques', in *Mélanges de Science religieuse* 14 (1957) 129–34.

J. H. C.

APOSTOLIC SUCCESSION The apostolicity of the Catholic Church is proclaimed in the Nicene creed. This article will begin (I) with a brief statement of the Catholic doctrine and the origins of the modern interest in the succession from the apostles ; (II) the notion of a succession will be examined in its historical context of pagan society of the first centuries, along with (III) the Jewish idea of rabbinical succession. (IV) The origin of the Christian succession from Christ will next be shown ; (V) the peculiar position of James, brother of the Lord, athwart the Petrine line, will be considered, and also (VI) the distinction made in modern times between doctrinal and sacramental succession. Finally (VII) some modern objections to the succession will be considered.

I The Catholic doctrine of the apostolic succession can be found in the Bull *Unam sanctam* of Boniface VIII (D 468) which declared that : 'There is one head of the Church, Christ, and his vicar Peter, and the successor of Peter, the Lord having said to Peter : Feed my sheep ; "mine" quite generally, and not in especial these or those, by which words He is to be thought to have entrusted to him all of them. If, then, the Greeks or others say that they have not been entrusted to Peter and his successors, they must admit that they are not of the sheep of Christ, for He said in John's gospel that there was one fold and one shepherd.'

In the council of Trent (D 960) it was taught that, 'bishops, who were by succession in the place of the Apostles, hold the principal degree in the ecclesiastical hierarchy, being set by the Holy Ghost to rule the Church of God'. Much earlier, in the letters of Pelagius II (D 247) to the schismatic bishops of Istria (c. 585) Augustine is quoted for the sentence that, 'upon those is the Church of God established who are known to hold authority in apostolic sees by a succession of rulers, and whoever withdraws himself from communion with, and the authority of, those same sees is shown to be in schism'.

It was this notion of apostolic succession which Newman in the first of the *Tracts* (in 1833) brought back into the field of discussion with the words, 'Christ gave His spirit to His apostles ; they in their turn laid their hands on those who should succeed them ; and these again on others, and so the sacred gift has been handed down to our present bishops . . .'. It was his realization that the line had been broken at the Reformation that led to his conversion.

A modern Anglican in the Tractarian way of thought, C. H. Turner (*Early History of the Church and Ministry*, 107), requires two conditions for a bishop to belong to the succession, (i) that he should have been lawfully chosen by the community to occupy the vacant cathedra of its church, and (ii) that he should have been lawfully entrusted with the charisma of the episcopate by the ministry of those who lawfully possess it. The manner of election of a bishop is dealt with elsewhere (*see* BISHOP) ; but it is the sacramental succession (outlined in Turner's second condition) which is the main stumbling-block to modern non-Catholic theologians. There is quite a ready acceptance of some kind of doctrinal succession, it being accepted that in early times there was anxiety that any new appointee should have the traditional doctrine of the apostles. This doctrinal succession, it is agreed, can be traced back to Irenaeus, but the sacramental succession, by laying on of hands in a continuous series, is said by these non-Catholics to become important only from the time of Augustine. It is clear therefore that the history of the idea must be investigated.

II The notion of διαδοχή **or succession** as first taken up by Christians is sometimes said to have found expression first of all in the anti-Montanist treatise (of A.D. 192) cited by Eusebius (*HE* 5:16:7), where it is claimed that Montanus made prophecies contrary to the practice which was according to the tradition and succession of the Church from earlier times. Slightly earlier than this passage is the Letter of Ptolemy to Flora (cited by Epiphanius, *Haer.* 33:7:9) in which the Gnostic author laid claim to a tradition 'which we *also* have received by succession'. The word *also* should have made it clear that Ptolemy was admitting that Catholics already had some kind of 'succession' that they appealed to, but instead this passage has been taken by recent Protestants to show that the Catholic notion of succession came from the Gnostics.

Prior to these writers of the late 2nd cent. there is the much-debated passage of Hegesippus, cited by Eusebius (*HE* 4:22:3) in which he tells of his visit to Rome in the time of Pope Anicetus (c. 154–165) and of how 'I made for myself a succession-list as far as Anicetus, whose deacon was Eleutherus. After Anicetus there succeeded Soter, and after him Eleutherus.' This passage was emended by Sir Henry Savile so as to lose its reference to the compiling of a list, and subsequent historians so mauled the passage that Harnack gave it up as hopelessly corrupt. But in more recent times there has been a reaction, and now it is quite generally accepted as saying what has been reported above, even by such an opponent of Catholicism as von Campenhausen. What has not been observed is that behind Hegesippus stands the notable precedent of the Epicurean school at Athens, who petitioned the emperor Hadrian through his mother Plotina (as the Christians did through Silvanus Granianus) asking that they might be allowed to record their business about the appointment of a *diadoch* in the Greek language and to choose a provincial who was not a Roman citizen as successor. This reveals that in 121 one of the chief schools of philosophy was freed from its previous limitations of having to keep its succession within the citizen-body and to keep the records of that succession in Latin. If such matters were so clearly regulated for philosophers, can it not be argued that the Christian church, which put itself forward in these times as a way of life and a school of doctrine, would show some signs of trying to keep its affairs in order by establishing succession-lists for the principal churches, lists which were then available for copying to a traveller such as Hegesippus ?

III The Jewish idea of succession. If the pagan precedents are clear, even more could be said of the Jewish. Rabbinical succession was a closed system. Jewish tradition told of one rabbi who suffered death at the hands of the Romans for his act in handing on the succession at a time when the last revolt (A.D. 132-4) had failed. This succession was a matter of laying on of hands (*see* ORDINATION). Polycrates of Ephesus, who was born *c.* 126 (Eusebius, *HE* 5:24), speaks of his having succeeded to some of his own kinsfolk, seven of whom were bishops, and of his having inherited their traditions. This, combined with the facts about the Jerusalem bishopric and the tenancy of that position by descendants of the Brethren of the Lord, suggests that the early Church was not unfamiliar with the Jewish practice of having family-priesthoods, though there is no case of a Christian being designated in childhood, as some Jewish boys were, as 'future-ruler', or μελλάρχων. Jewish practice, as it can be observed in the synagogues of Rome, was to separate ruler-ship from priesthood and, after the destruction of the Temple, membership of a priestly family was all that the word 'priest' could denote. A similar separation of 'overseers' from priests can be found in the Qumran community ; the overseer has to teach, to shepherd, to loose from bonds, to interpret the law, and even to imprison a feeble-minded priest (*Manual of Discipline* 6:11 and *Zadokite Work* 13:6). The Jewish precedents therefore suggest that the succession which was so carefully guarded in the Christian Church would be one of teaching authority, if of nothing else. Should the Christian diadochs be found to combine with this a priestly office, then one would have in embryo the two powers, called technically the power of Jurisdiction and the power of Order, from the very beginning of the Church.

IV The origin of the succession in Christ. Law-giving and atonement were the work of Christ and He committed to His apostles a share in each of these (*see* APOSTLES). The crucial statement about what the apostles did in their turn to hand on these functions is found in the *Epistle of Clement to the Corinthians* (*I Clem* 44) : 'For this reason (i.e. the likelihood of contention) the apostles exercised proper forethought and appointed (as bishops) the aforesaid (i.e. their first-fruits), and afterwards they imposed an additional law, that if these should go to their rest, other tested men should have the

succession to their ministry'. The discovery of an Old Latin version of this letter in 1893 (after Light-foot's careful analysis of it had been published) helped to elucidate the meaning of some of the terms used. There can be no doubt that Clement is speaking of a law established by the apostles (*legem dare* in the version is the technical phrase for 'to enact a law'), and the reference to 'first-fruits' points to such men as Timothy and Titus, also possibly Gaius, whom Origen (PG 14:1289) declared to have been according to tradition the first bishop of Thessalonica. Linus at Rome, Polycarp at Smyrna and Mark at Alexandria could be other examples of such first-fruits.

Christ is called an apostle once in the NT (Heb 3:1) and elsewhere in that work the idea that Christ is the first apostle is accepted as a familiar part of the preaching (Ac 3:20, 26 ; 7:35 ; 26:23 ; Jn 5:36) ; from the very manner of the commissioning of the Twelve (Jn 20:21) it is clear that a certain continuity is contemplated. Since the relation between Christ and the Church was no transient one (for the glori-fied Christ continues in His Church the work He performed by word and deed during His life on earth), it is natural to look for some continuance of the 'sending' which first created and then sent abroad the original Twelve. If, then, Clement of Rome bears witness that this is in fact what the Twelve did take care to continue, there can be no reason to refuse his evidence.

V The position of James in the succession : One difficulty has been raised, over the position of James the first bishop of Jerusalem, who seems to some not to fit into any orderly picture of the succession but to upset the whole idea of it. Eusebius (*HE* 2:23:3) cites a passage from Hegesippus to the effect that 'James, the brother of the Lord, succeeded to the church along with the apostles'. Oddly enough, he describes Hegesippus in this place as one 'who was born in the time of the first succession from the apostles', i.e. during the lifetime of the second generation of Christians (*c.* 50-120), and thus, what-ever Hegesippus may himself have thought, Euse-bius does not seem to doubt that there was an orderly succession. The citation begins abruptly and we do not know if Hegesippus was speaking about the whole Church or simply, as the context suggests, about the church of Jerusalem. Moreover, there was among Jewish Christians of his time, as we learn from the new portions of the Gospel of Thomas, an unabashed exaltation of James. 'James is our leader', says one of the new extracts of that work, while the Clementine apocrypha are full of phrases that raise James above the rest. Clement of Alexandria who (*Quis dives salvetur* 21:4=GCS 17:198) had no doubts about the pre-eminence of Peter, says that after the Ascension Peter, James and John did not indulge in litigation to gain glory but elected James as bishop of Jerusalem. Clement else-where (*Strom* 6:5:43=GCS 15:453) shows his acquaintance with the tradition of a twelve-year residence of the apostles at Jerusalem followed by their departure to various parts of the world. In default of other reliable evidence he is not to be presumed to mean that this election of James as bishop of the holy city came immediately after the Ascension, but rather at the end of the period when all were together. In fact the twelve-year period answers very well to the rough chronology of what is narrated in Acts about the events between the Resurrection and the departure of Peter ' to another place' (c. A.D. 33–45). As James did not preside at the Jerusalem assembly of c. 49 (see PETER), there can be no ground for supposing that he had prior to this been put in charge of the whole Church. If Peter, John and James the Greater were not anxious for glory, that need not mean any more than that they allowed James, brother of the Lord, to remain in possession of the holy city and all its prestige while Peter went Romewards and John to Asia Minor, their relative positions of authority being unchanged. But even with Clement, as with Hegesippus before him (and cf. Epiphanius, *Haer.* 78:7), one is never certain that he is not seeing the past through the eyes of the makers of a Jewish-Christian tradition which can only be described as deviationary.

VI Doctrinal and sacramental succession cannot be opposed as if there was one line of teachers and another line of sacred ministers. Clement of Alexandria (*Strom.* 7:16:105 ; GCS 17:75) says that the teaching-office of Christ began under Augustus and Tiberius, and that of the Apostles went on till the time of Nero. The teaching of the Apostles was one, like their tradition (ibid. 107), and the Church is a διδασκαλεῖον or teaching-corporation (*Paed.* 3:12:98 ; GCS 1:289). Justin (*apol.* 67) ascribes to the one who presides at the eucharist a teaching function, and we now have in the contemporary homily of Melito (on the Passion) an example of the way in which that function was exercised. Justin (*dial.* 80:3 and *append.* 2:13) has also a clear idea of a continuity of doctrine that began with Christ. Polycarp, bishop of Smyrna, was described by the crowd at his martyrdom as ' the teacher of Asia' (*Martyrium Polycarpi* 12:2 ; 16:2 ; and 19:1), and by the author as an apostolic teacher. This word ' apostolic' is not used elsewhere in NT or the Apostolic Fathers save for the place (*Trall.* 1) where Ignatius claims to address the Trallians with words of an apostolic stamp. Peter's own activity is described by the Presbyter in Papias (Eusebius, *HE* 3:39) as διδασκαλία and Paul coined a new word in Greek (1 Tim 1:3 and 6:3) meaning to go to a wrong teacher. At the end of the 2nd cent. Hippolytus (*Ref. haer.* preface) claims to have the charisma of teaching by succession from the apostles ; whatever his position was in regard to the Roman church, this claim makes clear the conditions which must have prevailed in that church. Thus the early Church did not adopt the separation of sacerdotal and didactic powers which after the destruction of the Temple became familiar to the Jews and which was already the practice of the Qumran sect. Rather did they go back to the example of Moses and the elders, a type to which appeal was made in the ordination service from the earliest times and which

seems to be known to Ignatius (*Trall.* 3:1) who calls the presbyters ' the Sanhedrin of God'. About the middle of the 2nd cent. the Jews gave up the practice of ordaining a rabbi by laying on of hands, largely (according to the *Jewish Encyclopedia*, s.v. ' Ordination') owing to the use of this rite by Christians. The Jewish belief always was that the laying on of hands by Moses gave to the candidate a share of the spirit of Moses (Deut 34:9). Thus by analogy the Christians can have meant no less in their rites of succession (see also CHARISMATA).

VII Modern objections against the idea of apostolic succession are principally directed towards showing that there was nothing for the Apostles to hand on ; the Church as the Body of Christ was not the residuary legatee of a dead man's property or rights which it had at all costs to hand on. Even if it is further admitted that the Apostles were plenipotentiaries of Christ, after the manner of the Jewish *sheluchim*, there was no Jewish precedent for the idea that they could themselves sub-delegate those functions to other men after them. The Church once launched in the Apostolic age had to make its own way. To meet this attack it is vital to consider the behaviour of the Church in the course of the 2nd cent. The contemporary *Acts of John* (14) picture him as ' consolidating the whole *didaskaleion* of Asia', a clear instance of the exercise of teaching authority and of the Church as a school. The fact that the heretics, Marcion (Eusebius, *HE* 5:13) and Valentinus (Irenaeus, *adv. haer.* I. v. 1 H ; cf. I, xiv. 4 ; I, xxvi. 1), both set up schools in Rome to propagate their views makes it clear that the Church in rejecting them was claiming to teach a received doctrine (Irenaeus IV, xl. 2 H). The assumption, too, that the Church is not to be an articulated Body of Christ is quite contrary to the doctrine of Col 2:19 and Eph 4:15 (see BODY, MYSTICAL). That the Apostles did make delegation of their commission from Christ is what Clement of Rome says (see above, IV), though they could obviously not delegate their own quality of eye-witnesses of the risen Christ. The Christians of the 2nd cent. had an exclusive idiom in Greek for describing the making of a disciple, a use that first appears in Mt 28:19 (see BAPTISM II), and this by itself would show that they understood the apostolic function to persist in the men who were in charge of the reception of catechumens, i.e. the bishops. At the end of the cent. when Pope Victor was on the point of accepting the prophecies of Montanus (Tertullian, *adversus Praxean* 1) he was dissuaded by Praxeas who ' defended the authoritative acts of his [Victor's] predecessors and forced him to recall the letters of peace that were already on their way [to the Montanists] '. Though this account comes from a Montanist, it can be trusted for what it shows of the practical working-out of the apostolic succession, Victor being bound by the acts of his predecessors. In the 3rd cent. the succession is taken for granted by Origen (on Isaias, *hom.* 6:4 ; GCS 33:274), by Cyprian (*epp.* 3:3 and 45:3) and by Clarus of Mascula (*Sententiae episcoporum* 79) who spoke of ' the apostles whose successors we are, governing the Church with the same power as they'.[1] For the older difficulty that a supposed expectation, in apostolic times, of an imminent Second Coming, which might have precluded care about the succession, see CHRIST, MISSION OF.

Bibliography. *C. H. Turner, 'Apostolic Succession', in *Essays on the Early History of the Church and Ministry* (1918) ; C. Journet, *The Church of the Word Incarnate* I (1955) ; J. Donovan SJ, on Hegesippus IER 27 (1926) 449–67 ; R. Hull SJ (on the same) AER 88 (1933) 426–32 ; Mn 159 (1932) 255–7 ; *E. Caspar, *Die älteste römische Bischofsliste* (1926) ; D. van den Eynde OFM, *Les Normes de l'enseignement chrétienne* (1933) ; G. Bardy, *Les Écoles romaines au 2ᵉ siècle*, RHE 28 (1932) 501–32 ; *G. La Piana *The Roman Church at the end of the 2nd century*, HTR 18 (1925) 201–77 ; *K. E. Kirk and others, *The Apostolic Ministry* (1946) ; *T. W. Manson, *The Church's Ministry* (1948) ; *E. Molland, *Irenaeus and the Apostolic Succession*, JEH 1 (1950) ; *H. von Campenhausen, *Kirchliches Amt und Geistliche Vollmacht* (1953) ; *A. Ehrhardt, *The Apostolic Succession* (1953).   J. H. C.

APPROPRIATIONS. *See* TRINITY

ARABIAN THEOLOGIANS. *See* SYRIAC and ARABIAN THEOLOGIANS

ARIANISM This article treats the heresy of Arius historically, starting with (I) his personal heresy, where an analysis of the main points of the system is given. (II) The political Arianism of Eusebius of Nicomedia is next treated, without which the heresy would not have had a long life. (III) The councils of Antioch and of (IV) Nicaea, in which it was defeated, are considered ; (V) the counter-attack by the Arians and (VI) the rise of semi-Arianism after the death of Arius are dealt with. (VII) The council of Sardica and (VIII) the long period of wrangling ending in the apparent but short-lived triumph of the Arians come next, while the long survival of Arianism in the West is considered in some detail, in view of its importance for the ecclesiastical history of Spain, Ireland and England.

In the 18th cent. it was the fashion to use the term 'Arian' for those who favoured the Deists. They are treated under a separate heading, and the modern Arians (Jehovah Witnesses and the like) are so changing in their beliefs that it would not be possible to give them any systematic theological examination.
I The personal heresy of Arius seems to have begun almost by accident. He was a Libyan, tall and handsome, and the parish priest of the important church of Baucalis in Alexandria, down by the docks where the Egyptian grain harvest was shipped to the hungry cities of the Roman Empire and where a day's rioting could cause a panic in Rome or in Constantinople. He had a great following among the ladies, seven hundred virgins taking his side

when the dispute broke out (according to Epiphanius, *haer.* 69:3 ; GCS 37:154) but only seven priests and twelve deacons. Dark-skinned, and wearing a sleeveless tunic with a short mantle, he must have been a striking figure as he preached in his church where the body of St Mark was preserved. It was from one of these sermons that the trouble began. He had undertaken to expound the Scriptures on Wednesdays and Fridays and in one of these expositions he dealt with Prov 8:22 : ' The Lord established me in the beginning of His ways, before He made anything from the beginning.' This he took to be a statement that, ' the Son of God, the Lord Christ, has been created before all other creatures' (PO 7:544 ff.). To say this was to make the Son of God a mediator between the Father and mankind and to declare, ' that there was a time when He (the Son of God) was not '. He preached the same ideas on a second occasion, criticizing also his bishop for what he called a Sabellian utterance (confusing the three Persons in one), and thereupon the bishop forbade priests to preach in his diocese.

Arius had not a good record. He had joined for a time the schismatic Meletian church of Upper Egypt, but had left them and at the age of fifty had come to Peter of Alexandria in 306 who made him a deacon. He had been excommunicated once again but had come round and the present bishop, Alexander, had ordained him priest. It was now 318 and he was about sixty years old. To place the Son in a subordinate position to the Father was not a shocking thing to suggest to one who followed the fashion of the new philosophy of Plotinus, where the whole universe was ranged in a series of descending hypostases. It was a more spiritual way of looking at the mystery than all the talk of the sun and its rays, the spring and the stream, and other materializations beloved of the popular mind. There was a passage in another great African writer which said practically the same as Arius was saying, and it was far more ancient than Plotinus, for Tertullian had said : ' God could not be a Father before He had a Son, nor a judge before there was sin ; and there was a time when neither sin nor Son existed.'[2] Going back still further, Arius could have cited the way in which Justin (*dial.* 61:1) interpreted Prov 8:22, where the begetting of the Son is said to be due to the will of the Father (θελήματι) and not to the eternal nature of God. The axiom of a later time which said : *Voluntate, non natura, fit creator creatura* (By will and not by nature does the Creator become a creature), and which meant to refer to the Incarnation of the Son of God, was by Arian thinkers applied to the generation of the Son of God. It was a clash between philosophy and tradition and it had to come sooner or later, but Arius seems to have been a very surprised man that the storm should have broken on his head. There had been trouble before, in the days when Denis was bishop and his namesake of Rome had pointed out with

[1] Apostolos, quibus nos successimus . . ., eadem potestate ecclesiam Dei gubernantes. . . .

[2] Nec pater potuit esse ante filium, nec iudex ante delictum ; fuit autem tempus cum et delictum et filius non fuit (*adversus Hermogenem* 3 ; CSEL 47:129).

some warmth that, 'it is no common blasphemy, but a very great one, to say that the Lord is in any sense a creature. If the Son has come to be, there was a time when He was not ; but we know from His own words that He is from eternity, seeing that He said, "I am in the Father", and the Scriptures show that Christ is the Logos and the wisdom and power of God.' (*Letters* of Denis, edited by Feltoe, 179.)

When his clergy made representations against Arius (not without some denunciations of Arius being added by the Meletians) Alexander called both sides together, and finding Arius stubborn, called a synod of a hundred bishops, where Arius was asked for a profession of faith, and on this proving unsatisfactory, he was excommunicated, and bidden to leave the city. On the contrary, he remained, with some popular support, and set up a schismatic church of his own, having two Libyan bishops to support him (Secundus of Pentapolis and Theonas). In giving word of the trouble to the rest of the church Alexander is able to name five priests and six deacons who sided with Arius, and to set down (Socrates, *HE* 1:6) a brief profession of Arian faith which sums up the heresy. In this the Father is said to be a mystery even to the Son, who is Wisdom and Word of God only by a misuse of language, 'for the Son of God is of a changeable nature like all other rational beings'. This was argued from Phil 2:9 ; for, if God exalted the Lord Christ, then He must have been giving him the reward of his freely-chosen goodness. To Alexander it seemed mere atheism to transfer all that was held about the incarnate God-man to the eternal Son of God, and it was about this time that the faithful changed their manner of reading Jn 1:3, 4 so as to say that without the Word was made nothing *that was made*, thus making it impossible for the Arians to argue that the verse meant that nothing, not even the Word Himself, was unmade. The Arian second Person could not be worshipped in quite the same way, and the doxology was changed by the Arians, so that now glory was given to the Father *by* the Son *in* the Holy Ghost, and not, as always previously, to the Three equally (so Theodoret, PG 83:414).

Arius now began writing letters to secure support from Christians in other lands. Envoys were sent with these in the hope that letters of communion would not be refused to them by distant churches. One of these letters, to Eusebius of Nicomedia, has survived. In it, Arius, who appeals to Eusebius as a fellow-pupil of Lucian of Antioch, claims to have been turned out of the city by Alexander. He cites various slogans which have been used by his opponents, and he was not backward in making up such himself. 'God from eternity, the Son from eternity', said the orthodox, and Arius used against them his cry : 'Time was when the Son was not.' The *Thalia* of Arius, which was his only considerable writing and of which some fragments survive, was composed about this time, in Sotadean verse.

II The political Arianism of Eusebius of Nicomedia was more dangerous to the faith than the tumultous disputes of Alexandria. This Eusebius had been bishop of Beirut, but having gained somehow the confidence of the wife of Licinius (who was sister to Constantine) he contrived to have himself translated to Nicomedia, where in the close proximity of the royal palace he was able to wield an influence far beyond that due to the position he held. Ammianus (*historia* 22:9) credits him with having been the tutor of the future emperor Julian the Apostate, whose distant relative he was.[1] Thus Eusebius was able to call a synod of the bishops of Bithynia where it was resolved that all the other churches (including that of Alexander) should be asked to receive back the Arians to communion as men of right faith (Sozomenus, *HE* 1:15). Eusebius wrote also to Paulinus of Tyre, Eusebius of Caesarea and Patrophilus of Scythopolis, defending the views of Arius as scriptural. 'We know not of two Unbegotten beings. . . . The Son came to be not from the substance of the Father and not having any part in the unbegotten nature.' Here there was the provocation that led to the use of the term *Homoousios* ('of the same substance') by the orthodox. Licinius helped on the cause of Eusebius by decreeing that in his dominions there should be no further synodal assemblies of bishops, thus giving the new heresy time to germinate unchecked by rigorous episcopal examination. The Palestinian bishops whom he had canvassed declared themselves for the acceptance of Arius but urged him to come to an understanding with Alexander. A modified Arian profession of faith was circulated to this end, in which the main position was upheld but some change had been made in the statement of the changeable nature of the Son of God, who was now said to be ἄτρεπτος (not subject to change) in fact though He might be in theory.

III The Synod of Antioch was not mentioned by the ancient historians of Arianism and has been rescued from oblivion by Schwartz who published at the beginning of this cent. the one Syriac document which tells of it. Constantine had beaten Licinius at Adrianople (3 July 324) and at Chrysopolis (18 Sept 324), and the close season for councils was at an end. It is almost certain that Osius of Cordova presided at the Antioch meeting, where a strongly anti-Arian creed was drawn up declaring that the Son was begotten not from nothing but from the Father, that His begetting was mysterious and indescribable, and that He was the image not of the will of the Father or of anything else but of the very substance of the Father. More surprising (and this has been concealed by Eusebius and the other historians who depend upon him) the synod excommunicated Eusebius of Caesarea, Theodotus of Laodicaea and Narcissus of Neronias, who were given time for repentance until the great synod of Nicaea—which had already been convoked—should meet. Anathema was pronounced upon those who said that the Son was unchangeable by His own will and not by His very nature.

[1] Nicomediae ab Eusebio episcopo educatus, quem genere longius contingebat.

This preliminary round of the contest makes the assembly at Nicaea much more intelligible, and while one can understand the motives Eusebius had for concealing his own part in it, the fact that he did keep silent about this synod does make his whole history of these times much less trustworthy than had hitherto been supposed. Fifty-six bishops signed the Antioch decree of whom forty-nine went on to Nicaea some four months later, and so the old view (e.g. of Gwatkin) that Nicaea was 'rather a surprise than a solid conquest, a revolution which a minority forced through', falls to the ground. When Nicaea met, there were no more than seventeen supporters of Arius present, though the lobbying had been strenuous. All during 324 Alexander of Alexandria had been writing to the bishops of other parts (one letter going to Pope Sylvester to tell of the expulsion of eleven priests and deacons for Arianism) and the other side had not been inactive. After his victories the Emperor Constantine took the Christians in hand; they were wasting his time and their own over a foolish question of philosophy (the letter was addressed to Alexander and to Arius alike) ; they should embrace as brothers and thank God for the peace that had been given to them (Eusebius, *Vita Constantini* 2:64–77 ; GCS 7:67).

Osius was sent to deliver this letter, but his mission was a failure. On his return the emperor seems to have realized that nothing short of a full-dress debate would succeed in ending the controversy and his first idea was to have the assembly meet at Ancyra. The change to Nicaea was made out of deference to the Western bishops (who would find it more accessible and more congenial in climate) and it was hither that the excommunicated three had to come to make their apology.

IV The Council of Nicaea was the end of primitive Arianism. The meeting lasted from about 20 May to 27 July in 325 ; the decrees are dated to 19 June. For the rest of the decrees, *see* NICAEA I AND II. Here attention will be given simply to the Arian question at the council. The emperor, without whose *cursus publicus* (or official system of post-horses) the bishops would not have been able to assemble at all, made them a solemn address, which is described by Eusebius of Caesarea as a philosophizing about the way of conceiving the divine, about bodiless natures and about the *Homoousios*. It was this last point that irked him. Who had suggested it ? Athanasius (*historia Arianorum* 42) gave the credit to Osius, and the Arian Philostorgius (*HE* 1:7 ; GCS 21:9) thought that Osius and Alexander were to blame for it. Ambrose, on the other hand (*de fide*, 3:15 ; PL 16:614) says that Eusebius of Nicomedia had used the term in a letter which was read out at the council and that the assembly took it from there. ' "If we say that the Son of God is truly uncreated, then we are beginning to admit that He is of one substance with the Father." When this letter was read in the council of Nicaea, the Fathers put this word in their declaration of the faith, as they saw it caused dismay to their adver-

saries.'[1] Hilary in his historical fragments (2:33 ; CSEL 65:154) says that Athanasius was the one who most insisted on the term,[2] while Basil (*epp.* 81, 244 and 263) says that it was Hermogenes of Caesarea who read it out. It is quite wrong to think of the term as a surprise sprung on the bishops by the emperor ; it was used by Pope Denis in his letter to Denis of Alexandria some seventy years before (cf. *Letters* of Denis, Feltoe 188). The Latin phrase *consubstantialis Patri Filius* may have been familiar at Rome for some time.

The new evidence about the position of Eusebius of Caesarea, who was present at Nicaea as a penitent seeking absolution, has done much to destroy the theories of Hort, Harnack and Burn, who held that the creed of Nicaea was the one submitted by Eusebius as being the traditional one of his own church, plus certain additions made in view of the heresy of Arius. It can no longer be maintained that Eusebius's creed was the base on which the council worked. He had to clear himself and in doing so cited a compound of his baptismal creed, and that used at ordination, as he tells in the letter he wrote to his diocese after the council to explain his own acceptance of it and the desertion of his former pro-Arian position. Whether the presentation of this creed by Eusebius took place before the debate on the Arian position is not certain, but the emperor's remark to Eusebius that his profession would satisfy, save for the fact that he had left out the *Homoousion*, points to the conclusion that the main debate and the acceptance of the *Homoousion* was already over. Apart from Eusebius's letter there are three accounts of what took place at the council, one by Eustathius of Antioch (in Theodoret *HE* 1:8 ; GCS 44:33–4), one by Athanasius (*de decretis* 19–20 ; PG 25:449–52), and another by the same (in his *epistula ad Afros episcopos* 5–6 ; PG 26:1036–40) written twenty years after the former. Eustathius says, ' When there was debate about the manner of the creed (*pistis*), the writing of Eusebius, full of blasphemy, (probably E. of Nicomedia) was brought forward, a manifest self-refutation, and, when everyone heard it read, straightway it caused unmeasured consternation in the audience by its being so far out of the true path, and the one who wrote it was shamed for ever. Since the workshop of the Eusebian gang was now laid bare, the wicked writing being torn to shreds in the sight of all, a group, acting in concert and putting forward the pretext of maintaining peace, put to silence those who were normally wont to speak to most advantage. Those enamoured of Arius, fearing ostracism . . . rushed forward and anathematized the forbidden profession, and wrote their condemnation with their own hands.' It would seem from this that the anathemas preceded the formulation of a creed.

[1] Si verum, inquit, Dei filium et increatum dicimus, homoousion cum Patre incipimus confiteri. Haec cum lecta esset epistola in concilio Nicaeno, hoc verbum in tractatu fidei posuerunt patres, quia id viderunt adversarii s esse formidini.
[2] Huius intimandae cunctis fidei Athanasius vehemens auctor extiterat.

The council condemned ' those who say, " Time was when He was not ", or " He was not before He was begotten ", or " He came to be out of nothing, or from another substance or being ", or that " The Son of God is created or subject to change or alteration "'. To insert these condemnations into a pre-existing creed would be a matter of drafting. The model creed used may have been that of Jerusalem, but there is no real proof of this. It might even be that the model offered by Eusebius of Nicomedia was reformed by having these clauses, lethal to his heresy, inserted in it. One can be sure that, if the council did take a baptismal creed from any centre, it neglected the final sentences and confined its attention to the Trinitarian part. It cast its final formula in the plural (not in the singular as would have been proper with a baptismal creed) and this was no doubt meant to express the united sense of the council : ' We believe in one God, the Father Almighty, creator of all things visible and invisible : and in one Lord Jesus Christ, the son of God, *begotten of the Father as His only-begotten*, i.e. *from the substance of the Father* : God of God, light of light, *true God of true God, begotten not made* : *homoousion with the Father*, through whom all things came into being, in heaven and on earth : who for us men and for our salvation came down and took flesh, *was made man*, suffered and rose the third day and went up to heaven, and will come to judge living and dead : and in the Holy Ghost.'

The creed was not perfect ; it might have been improved by the insertion of ' before all ages ' in the clause ' begotten of the Father '. The anti-Arian clauses, underlined above, cover most of the points raised in the anathemas. As Jn 17:3 was used by the Arians to argue that, if Christ calls the Father the only true God, He cannot have shared that dignity Himself, it was necessary to assert that Christ was true God in the same sense as the Father. The assertion that the Son of God *was made man* is due to a belief of Arius that the Incarnation was quite literally a taking of flesh and did not mean that He had a human soul (*see* INCARNATION). Athanasius tells how the council tried to keep to scriptural terms ; if they had said that the Son was ' from the Father ', the Arians would have appealed to 1 Cor 8:6 as an excuse for holding that even so He was a creature. Hence the Fathers had to use plainer terms, and one can see in Ambrose (*de fide* 3:15 cited above) the remains of an argument for the justification of the term *Homoousion* ; it might not be in Scripture, but there were in Scripture two other substance-words ἐπιούσιος and περιούσιος. It was not thought necessary to add that the ' substance ' intended was not the Stoic notion of a *material* substrate, as the Arians professed to fear when they said that ' of one substance ' would imply that the generation of the Son involved a division of the Father's being. When Heb 1:3 was cited in the council and other phrases of Scripture which called the Son wisdom and power of the Father, the Arian group with winks and nods signalled to each other : ' Let us agree to this, for we too (1 Cor

11:7) are the image and glory of God, and in Him we live and move.' Even when they detected this Arian trick, the Fathers were not deliberately innovating in their language, for the phrase ' from the substance of God ' had been used of the Son by Theognostus (cited, Athanasius *de decretis* 25 ; PG 25:460), who wrote *c*. 250-80.

Eusebius of Caesarea accepted the creed and the anathemas, and in his apology to his diocese he said that when the *Homoousion* was explained as not implying that the Son was a part of the Father, he accepted the term for peace sake, indicating that he took it in the sense that the Son was in all things made *like* to the Father (κατὰ πάντα τρόπον ἀφομοιῶσθαι τῷ πατρί), thus giving a cue to the later group of *Homoiousians*. The anathemas he defended, saying neatly that they forbade the use of unscriptural terms about the Son. Even the condemnation of ' Time was when He was not ' Eusebius could stomach, for he said that the Son before His generation was *potentially* in the Father (δυνάμει ἦν ἐν τῷ πατρὶ ἀγεννήτως). Clearly this should have been held against Eusebius as insufficient, but if he spoke his mind on the matter at the council he was not pressed further, and thus the seeds were sown of a longer and more intricate dispute.

Marcellus of Ancyra seems to have been firm in holding at the council that the Homoousion meant *identity* of substance between Father and Son, and not merely that they were two instances of the same genus (for in that case it would be polytheism to worship them both), and his later quarrel with Eusebius of Caesarea began here (cf. his fragments 66-7 cited in Eusebius *theologia ecclesiastica* ; GCS 14:197). Eusebius had to admit two kinds of eternity (ἀίδιον and τὰ διὰ παντός) since he had got himself into a position where he was saying that the Son's generation was eternal but *before that* He was only in potency. Athanasius also glosses the *Homoousion* as meaning *sameness* of substance (*de decretis* 23 ; PG 25:456), and as one-ness of substance (*orat. contra Arianos* 3:3 ; PG 25:328) ; he made it clear that likeness was not enough : ' Bronze is not the true offspring of gold, nor the cushat from the common dove.'

The traditional number of bishops present at the council is 318, as may be seen in Jerome's *Chronicle* or in Athanasius, *ad Afros* 2 (if the text there is genuine), but the lists give no more than about 220 names. Eustathius (in Theodoret *HE* 1:8 ; GCS 44:34) says they were 270 in number and Constantine says ' about 300 '. Of these, seventeen at first showed dissent with the creed formulated, but soon this group was reduced to five, Eusebius of Nicomedia, Theognis of Nicaea, Maris of Chalcedon, and the two Africans, Theonas and Secundus. Only the Africans held out to the end and were forbidden by the council to set foot in Alexandria, whereupon the emperor banished them, with Arius, to Illyricum (where they were able to spread their ideas among Western Christians and where in the next generation Ursacius and Valens would be a peril to the orthodox). Not many Western bishops took part in the council; the Pope sent his two *directi* Vincentius and Vito, and Domnus (the primate of Pannonia) with Caecilianus of Carthage and Nicasius of Die in Gaul, provided the only Latin colouring, along with Osius of Cordova, whose rôle in the presidency of the council must be discussed elsewhere (*see* PRIMACY), for there is some possibility that he also was acting for the Pope.

V The counter-attack of the Arian party was not long in coming. Eusebius of Nicomedia was banished to Gaul (with Theognis) soon after the council, probably for having tried to support the Melitians (who were now receiving the emperor's attention) in return for their support of Arius, but he was back in Asia after two years. Some historians hold that there was a minor 'recall' of the council of Nicaea late in 327, when Arius was admitted back to communion, but the facts are not certain. The letter of the emperor to Arius of 27 Nov 327, in which he is blamed for stubbornness and bidden get on the *cursus publicus* and come to court at once, is genuine (Socrates, *HE* 1:25), but what is not clear is how the bishops came to accept what the emperor had himself accepted from Arius in the shape of a profession of faith. If the bishops were again summoned to Nicaea, not many can have assembled there.

The three leaders of the orthodox were now to be struck at one by one. Eustathius of Antioch was accused of being a Sabellian, of having had an illegitimate child and of having called Helena, the emperor's mother, a *stabularia*. This last accusation could be made into the *crimen laesae maiestatis* and may have weighed more than the theological point with the emperor; anyhow Eustathius was banished to Illyricum with many priests and deacons (Athanasius, *historia Arianorum* 4; PG 25:700), after which the Arians got many of their supporters into bishoprics of Syria. Marcellus of Ancyra, whose views were quite orthodox about Arianism but who had other eccentric ideas of his own about the kingdom of the Son coming to an end (after 1 Cor 15:24) with the end of time, was condemned at a synod in Constantinople in 336, where Eusebius of Nicomedia presided and the rôles of Nicaea were reversed. Marcellus went to Rome and waited for his accusers to turn up there and repeat to the Pope what they had brought up in the synod, but after a year and more they still did not appear, and Marcellus, leaving his profession of faith with Pope Julius (Epiphanius, *haer* 72:2; GCS 37:257), returned to Galatia. He has left his mark on our creed, for the clause 'of whose kingdom there is no end' was devised to meet his aberration and is first met with in Cyril of Jerusalem (cf. *Cat.* 15) and Epiphanius, but by that time both Arius (17 April 336) and Constantine (22 May 337) were dead.

Athanasius had succeeded Alexander as bishop of Alexandria (8 June 328) and was soon marked down for attack. The Arians were able to use the Meletian schismatics against him, and charges were brought to the emperor that he was imposing taxes, using violence and financing rebellion (Theodoret, *HE*

1:25; GCS 44:81), but these charges he met by going in person to Constantinople and refuting them. The emperor took a fancy to him and sent a strong letter to Alexandria in his support (Theodoret, *HE* 1:27; GCS 44:82). Arius was still waiting for re-admission to communion in Alexandria and further charges were made against Athanasius. This time he was said to have murdered the bishop Arsenius, but when in 333 Athanasius was able to show that Arsenius was hiding in a monastery, very much alive, the emperor wrote still more strongly (Gelasius, *HE* 2:36; GCS 28:128) that the Arians were to be called Porphyrians, their writings burnt and those keeping secret copies put to death. Although Arius went to court and with the help of the royal ladies Constantia and Basilina gained some immunity for himself, it would seem to be due to this edict that his *Thalia* is now lost and that the collections of official letters and decrees, which were used by the Arians for propaganda purposes, were in large part destroyed; few theological papyri of the Arian period have come from Egypt. One or two private letters (such as Pap. Lond. 1914) tell how 'Athanasius (by reason of the writings that come to him from abroad) causes us distress . . . and has imprisoned a bishop in the meat-market . . .', but the controversial literature has perished, save where it was early quoted by the church historians. In 335 the emperor wanted to have a synod of reconciliation at Tyre, before holding Jubilee celebrations at Jerusalem. Athanasius left Egypt on 11 July, but under the guidance of Eusebius at Caesarea the meeting turned into a trial of Athanasius, who walked out and went to see the emperor (*apologia contra Arianos* 9 and 82; PG 25:264 and 396). He called for the bishops to appear before him, but they sent a delegation of six, who now changed the accusation against Athanasius and said that he had threatened to cut off the corn-supply of the empire; without waiting to hear Athanasius, the emperor banished him to Trier, where he began to learn Latin.

VI Semi-Arianism begins soon after the death of Arius (a death which, as it took place in a public lavatory at Constantinople, was compared in the tradition to that of Judas), and the Dedication Council of 341, when some hundred bishops met at Antioch, brings the first formulae of this now mitigated belief. Four creeds came of this meeting, the first being affixed to the letter sent from Antioch to Pope Julius, who had recently sent out a long vindication of Athanasius (Athanasius, *apologia* 21–35; PG 25:281–308). The creed drops the *Homoousion*, perhaps because the following of Eusebius of Nicomedia now included Anhomoians such as Aetius (*see* AETIUS), and although it states that 'the Son of God was with the Father that begot Him and was in existence before all ages', this might be an attempt to bring in the distinction of two eternities which was made by Eusebius of Caesarea. An assertion in the part dealing with the Incarnation that 'Christ carried out to the full the whole of the Father's will' looks like an honest endeavour to clear up the imbroglio about the eternal generation being due to the will and not to the nature of the Father ; if the will was emphasized here, in the matter of the Incarnation where it really belonged, then people would not be tempted to bring it in where it did not belong. A clause was added about Christ remaining king and God to all ages, and thus Marcellus of Ancyra was given his quietus.

The second creed from this Dedication council is ascribed by Sozomenus (*HE* 3:5) to Lucian of Antioch, who had been the master of so many of the Arians and who had suffered martyrdom in 312. In the eyes of the bishops of 341 it had the merit of being prior to the Homoousian dispute. It defined the Son as ' image without parallax of the godhead, substance, will, power and glory of the Father, and first-begotten of (or before) all creatures '. These ambiguities may indeed have come from a pre-Arian time, though the assertion that the Son was unchangeable, if really due to Lucian, cannot have been a part of his teaching which Arius adopted. This creed the assembly, in presence of the eastern emperor, Constantius, accepted, adding an anathema for those who would not likewise accept it. With its placing the unity of the godhead in a συμφωνία or harmony, it could hardly be found acceptable by Julius or by Athanasius. The third creed of this council is a private effort by one Theophronius of Tyana, and the fourth is of uncertain purpose, Socrates saying (*HE* 2:18) that the four bishops sent to deliver the second creed of Antioch to the western emperor, Constans, at Trier, wavered in their mission and handed him this one instead. Maris of Chalcedon, one of the original partners of Arius at Nicaea, was one of the four and has not a good record for sticking to his views ; it may be that as the mission travelled westwards, it became clearer that they could never hope to pass off the rambling and old-fashioned Lucianic creed as one that would now rally all the theologians of the West.

This fourth formula was long sponsored in the East, being used by the eastern council of Sardica and at Sirmium in 351. This fourth creed differs from all the rest in admitting some acquaintance with the decisions of Nicaea. It has the anathema on those who say the Son was from nothing or of another substance and not from God or that Time was when He was not. It adds the words ' before all the ages ' to the clause about the begetting of the Son, an improvement which lasted. On the other hand it omits ' true God of true God ' and the qualification ' not made ' which Nicaea had put after the word ' begotten '. Indeed, with Oriental guile by calling the Father κτίστης of all, it might be said to hint at the Arian view of Prov 8:22. It also omits the Nicaean anathema on those who say that the Son is κτιστόν (a created thing) or of another substance than the Father. Pope Julius had written to the Orientals that at Nicaea it was agreed that the judgments made at the present meeting should be subject to revision at a meeting in the future (PG 25:284, perhaps following the practice which had

been observed at the preceding synod of Antioch in the case of Eusebius of Caesarea and his suspension for heresy) and it seems that this Dedication synod now wanted to have a revision not only in disciplinary matters but also in the doctrine of Nicaea.

Eusebius of Caesarea died 30 May 339 and Eusebius of Nicomedia at the end of 341, but now a third Eusebius, of Emesa, came to the fore in the same group, and the recent vindication for him of some sermons that are extant in a Latin version (cf. E. Buytaert, *Eusèbe d'Émèse* (1949)) helps us to see what his opinions were. His fourth sermon was preached at Caesarea in commemoration of its dead bishop and perhaps at his funeral. He is defended from a charge of having made profession otherwise than he believed, and the dangers of Sabellianism are very much emphasized. The Father is said to be *singularis natura* (unique in nature), Jn 17:3 is explained as meaning ' not that the only-begotten Son is not truly God, but that He is not so by and of Himself, if it is right to call Him so ' (in Buytaert's edition (1953) 112 and 113). No predicate should be admitted if it is not scriptural : ' If it is not written, let it not be spoken ; if it is written, let it not be blotted out.' [1] This Emesene was put up as the one to succeed Athanasius when he was turned out of his see for the second time in 339, but he prudently declined the position and was given to Emesa instead by the Antioch council. His *floruit* is put by the *Chronicle* of Jerome at 347, and his writings bridge the gap in the evidence about this time.

VII The council of Sardica was intended to end the sorry dispute, now as much political as theological, but, as this council broke in two, it only helped to perpetuate it. The semi-Arians went off and formed their own council across the mountains at Philippolis, while the orthodox (usually called the Western council, though the majority of its bishops came from the East) passed disciplinary decrees to regulate the troubles arising out of the heresy by strict control of the movement of bishops. An exceptionary clause in these canons was quite clearly meant to favour Athanasius, who, as the victim of persecution, was allowed to reside in another diocese than his own. No formulary creed was issued by this council ; the doctrinal epistle given in Theodoret (*HE* 2:8:37–52 ; GCS 44:112–18) reads more like a catechesis.

Constantius now became preoccupied by the Persian wars (which had the effect of stirring up persecution for the Christians who lived in the Persian empire) and when his brother Constans threatened to put back Athanasius in Alexandria by himself (Theodoret, *HE* 2:8:54 ; GCS 44:118) he consented to his return. Athanasius went back on 21 October 346 and remained until 9 February 356. In these so-called ' golden years ' of his episcopate religious fervour was renewed, monasticism spread apace and the conversion of Ethiopia was begun by Frumentius. Apart from the affair of Photinus

[1] Si quid scriptum non est, ne quidem dicatur; si quid autem scriptum est, ne deleatur (ibid. 110).

(bishop at Sirmium, but an Oriental by origin) there was little danger from heresy. Photinus had been the disciple of Marcellus of Ancyra and went far beyond the Sabellian leanings of his master ; according to him the Son of God came into being at the Incarnation ; there was not an eternal generation for him (and thus the whole dispute of Arian and orthodox was to be by-passed—a likely way out for an unscrupulous young man) ; the term $\pi\lambda\alpha\tau\upsilon\sigma\mu\acute{o}s$ (amplification) was used to describe the production of the Son from the Father, a term used by Tertullian, which implied that Father and Son together were in being more than the Father alone. Photinus had been condemned at Rome in 345, but none the less the Arians used him as a whipping-boy and got themselves back into favour for sound theology. They added 27 anathemas to the creed (Antioch IV) of Sirmium in 351 and in some of these they contrived to intrude semi-Arian points of doctrine (e.g. they protect the Eusebian distinction of two eternities when they condemn those ' who say that there was a time or an age ($\alpha\iota\acute{\omega}\nu$) when He was not ' ; cf. Hilary, de synodis, PL 10:513).

Constantius had married an Arian, Eusebia, and he had the company of Eusebius of Emesa during some part of his Persian campaigns ; it is thus more from personal motives than from a desire to see the Christians of the empire united in one belief that he supported Arianism. When approached by Pope Liberius with a request to facilitate the meeting of a council in Northern Italy to confirm the faith of Nicaea (Hilary, fragmenta historica ; CSEL 65:93) he agreed, but saw to it that Milan (where the council met in 355) should be full of semi-Arian bishops. When Eusebius of Vercelli was asked to subscribe the decree condemning Athanasius, he said that there should first be a check on the credentials of the bishops (prius de sacerdotali fide constare debere) and producing a copy of the creed of Nicaea he said that, if they would all sign this, he would be ready to do whatever they asked. Denis of Milan came forward to sign the creed, but the pen was snatched from his hand by the bishop Valens, and the people in the church below hearing the clamour began to cry out ' The bishops have attacked the creed ' ; the bishops withdrew into the imperial palace where they carried through the condemnation and sent Denis, Eusebius and Lucifer of Cagliari into exile. (Hilary, ad Constantium I ; CSEL 65:187). Soon Liberius was himself exiled, and after two years wrote the letters that have caused so much controversy about his position (see PRIMACY). Athanasius too was forced to take refuge with the monks in upper Egypt (after 9 February 356) but did not leave the country.

VIII With the triumph of Arianism there came, as in the crisis of some Greek tragedy, a sudden reversal of fortune, for the heretics split among themselves, AETIUS leading the left wing and holding out for the unlikeness of Son to Father, Acacius (see ACACIAN SCHISM) leading the Homoians (who confined themselves to asserting a simple likeness of the two Persons), while a great number were no more than semi-Arian, holding with Basil of Ancyra that the likeness was one of substance, and thus receiving the name of Homoiousians. To a philosophic mind every degree of likeness implies a degree of difference, and thus it was possible for Anhomoians and Homoians sometimes to agree in credal statements which the followers of Basil found unacceptable. In particular the assertion that the Son was in all things like the Father ($\kappa\alpha\tau\grave{a}\ \pi\acute{a}\nu\tau\alpha$) was abominable to the first two parties, while in the minds of the Homoiousians it often came to mean almost the same thing as the faith of Nicaea. In what is called the Dated Creed, drawn up at Sirmium in 359 by Mark of Arethusa and used by the emperor to promote unity among Arians at the synods of Rimini and Seleucia in that year, these words are introduced, and when Ursacius and Valens, those old converts of Arius, came to sign, they tried to cut out those three words, whereas Basil of Ancyra added his own gloss to them, saying, ' not just in will but in hypostasis, existence and substance ' (Epiphanius, haer. 73:22 ; GCS 37:295). At Constantinople in 360 the three words were omitted, and this creed became standard for the Arians everywhere.

The death of Constantius and the accession of Julian the apostate, brought a respite to the orthodox, at least from the pressure of heresy. Athanasius was back in his see from 21 February 362 until October 362. In this interval he was able to hold a council of Alexandria from which issued the Tomus ad Antiochenos in which Athanasius finally laid to rest the doubts about the use of the Greek term $\upsilon\pi\acute{o}\sigma\tau\alpha\sigma\iota s$ for the Persons in the Trinity. Three hypostases was not the same as three gods, though many in the West thought this when they heard the expression on the lips of Easterners, and the one hypostasis which Nicaea spoke of did not mean a single person, as Arius made believe it did. It had taken all the wanderings of Athanasius and many years of dispute to thrash out this question of terms (PG 26:785-810). In October 362 Athanasius had to go on the run again, until the Christian emperor Jovian allowed him to return on 14 February 364. Julian had been at first indifferent to the struggle of orthodox and Arian, and when he seized full power in Gaul in 360 he allowed Hilary to come back from exile and lead a council at Paris which rallied the bishops of Gaul and produced a letter to the Eastern bishops in which silence about the homoousion was blamed and the likeness of Son to Father was stated not to be unacceptable, as long as it was a likeness worthy of God ; ' it is not the uniqueness of the divinity that should be held but the unity, for uniqueness would make a single Person, whereas unity expresses the true generation and fullness of the Son '.[1] (Hilary, fragmenta ; CSEL 65:44.) The coming and going of bishops to and from exile served providentially to build up a much greater sense of solidarity among the orthodox and a better

[1] Ita ut non unio divinitatis sed unitas intelligatur quia unio sit singularis, unitas vero secundum nativitatis veritatem plenitudo nascentis sit.

comprehension of their own doctrine ; Hilary wrote (*de synodis* 91 ; PL 10:545) that he had not heard the Nicene creed till after he had been a bishop for some time and was about to go into exile (he was consecrated about 353 and exiled in 356). The importance of Illyricum as a bridge between East and West, at a time when the two halves of the empire tended to draw further apart, may be seen in the fact that it was a native of Illyricum, Martin, who visited Hilary in 355 and most probably brought him the Nicene document. In a similar way Ambrose of Milan was to have his contacts with the great Cappadocians later on who liquidated the Arianism of the East so effectively in the decade 370–80.

The emperor Valentinian (364–75) was himself orthodox though his wife Justina was Arian ; having to avoid religious controversy at home he was not anxious to spread it abroad and his policy was to leave well alone. In 365 Liberius was able to readmit to communion sixty-four Eastern bishops whose deputies, Eustathius of Sebaste, Silvanus of Tarsus and Theophilus of Castabala, came to Rome and accepted the Nicene creed. Valens, the Eastern emperor, was Arian in his sympathies, but his failure to dislodge Athanasius from Egypt (save for sending him on a temporary rustication, 5 October 365 to 1 February 366) and his preoccupation with frontier wars made him less of a danger to the orthodox in the East than Constantius had been. Gradually, under the influence of men like Epiphanius, Cyril of Jerusalem, and the great Cappadocians, the Homoiousians came to accept Nicaea again, while the Homoians and the Anhomoians fought among themselves, the division of opinions now being complicated by the question of the likeness of the Holy Spirit to the Son, on which the followers of Macedonius had derogatory views of their own (*see* HOLY GHOST). From 370 onwards APOLLINARIS also distracted the attention of many from Trinitarian to Christological issues, which in the Arian system had taken a second place. With the death of Athanasius in 373 the real Arian struggle is practically over (*see* CONSTANTINOPLE) ; Basil succeeds to the rôle of champion of Nicaea, but the challengers are not equal to him.

IX Arianism lingered in the West long after it had been thrown off by the churches of the East. The Goths took to it eagerly, their first evangelists having been Arian, and when the East was preoccupied with the great controversies about the two natures of Christ, the West went on insisting that candidates at baptism should confess to the Trinity ' *una manente substantia* ' (where the one substance abides), as is said in the *Missale Gallicanum vetus* or ' *unam habente substantiam* ', as the *Bobbio Missal* says. It seems that more Arian writings survive from the Latin West than from the East. An Arian fragment from Verona (published (1902) by Mercati, *Studi e Testi* 7) attacks the orthodox for making the Three Persons equal in their writings while denying this equality in their liturgy ; an Arian sermon (JTS 13 (1912) 22–8) argues that if the placing of Christ

on the right of the Father means that He is not inferior to the Father, then the Church, which is on the right of Christ according to Ps 44, is not inferior to Christ ; the lengthy *Opus imperfectum in Matthaeum*, which has survived only in Latin, though it had a Greek original, in many places shows its Arian (and Anhomoian) faith, taking the Lord of the vineyard to be Christ and His steward to be the Holy Ghost, ' who cannot therefore be of the same substance or of equal dignity ' (PG 56:820). The spirited account of the debate between the Arian bishop Germinius of Sirmium on 13 January 366 and an orthodox layman is without parallel in the Greek works of the time (published by C. P. Caspari, *Kirchenhistorische Anecdota* 1883). There is some chance that the Latin versions of the *Apostolic Constitutions* and of Hippolytus, *Traditio apostolica* were made for an Arian community in North Italy *c.* 500.

When the Arian emperor Valens and two-thirds of his army perished in battle against the Goths at Adrianople (9 August 378), another reversal of fortune took place. Arianism was finished in the Roman world, but the victorious Goths would carry it on as their own religion wherever they went. The Spanish pope, Damasus, with his *tomus* of 382 (cf. D 61:68–70) and the Spanish emperor, Theodosius, joint-ruler with Gratian, and author of the law *Cunctos populos* (*Codex Theodosianus* 16:5:5), would proclaim the faith of Nicaea, and Theodosius in his law would even call upon ' all the nations which are ruled by our clemency to adhere to the religion which was taught by St Peter to the Romans ', but at the same time beyond the sway of imperial Rome, Auxentius of Dorostorum was writing his *de fide vita et obitu Wulfilae* (edited by F. Kauffmann, 1899) which shows how the barbarian was quite happy with the diminished Christianity of the Arians. More than half the trouble that was caused for the Celtic churchmen by the mission of Augustine to Britain was due to this idea that Roman and Catholic meant the same thing and that to be outside the one meant to be outside the other. The saying of St Patrick : ' Church of the Irish, nay rather of the Romans ; may you be Christians, truly, may you be Romans ',[1] is probably an echo of the law of Theodosius rather than of any worry about hair styles or Easter. Already in the last years of the 4th cent. Pope Anastasius (D 93) was congratulating his brother bishop of Milan on the freedom of Italy from Arianism and the whole heresy was to him but an episode. Visigoths, Celts and Armenians would have a different tale to tell. The influence of Martin of Tours (a firm Nicaean) on Irish Christianity (shown in the similarity of his creed with St Patrick's) and the strongly Trinitarian features in the Irish liturgy (such as the prayer *Remittit Pater, indulget Filius, miseretur Spiritus sanctus* at the pouring of the wine into the chalice) give the impression that Arianism remained a danger in the West for centuries. Columbanus (*sermo* I in

[1] Ecclesia Scotorum, immo Romanorum ; ut Christiani, ita, ut Romani sitis.

his *Opera* ; SHL 2:60–4) preached against Arianism, and his foundation of Bobbio, which gathered most of the surviving Arian Latin MSS., was meant as an anti-Arian centre.

Bibliography. The texts for the earlier part of the story of Arianism are collected in H. Opitz, *Athanasius* III, i (' Urkunden zur Geschichte des arianischen Streits ') 1934 and II, i (' Apologien ') 1935–40 ; owing to the death of the editor Opitz there seems little prospect that this edition of Athanasius will be continued. Other texts have to be sought in the church historians and in Epiphanius. Eusebius of Emcsa has been edited by E. Buytaert (2 vols, 1953 and 1957). The best general study is perhaps Norman Baynes, ' Constantine and the Christian Church ', in *Proceedings of the British Academy* 15 (1929) 341–442. Other studies are : *A Burn, *The Council of Nicaea* (1925) ; V. de Clercq, *Ossius of Cordova* (1955) ; *J. N. Kelly, *Early Christian Creeds* (1950) ; G. Bardy, *Études sur Lucien d'Antioche* (1936), 'L'Occident et les documents de la controverse arienne ', in RevSR 20 (1940) 28–63, and ' La Politique religieuse de Constantin après le concile ', in RevSR 8 (1928) 516–51 ; R. Arnou SJ, ' Arius et les relations trinitaires ', in *Gregorianum* 14 (1933) 269–72, and ' Unité numérique et unité de nature ', ibid. 15 (1934) 242–54 ; J. Jungmann SJ, ' Die Abwehr des germanischen Arianismus ', in ZKT 69 (1947) 32–99 ; *H. Berkhof, *Die Theologie des Eusebius von Caesarea* (1939) ; I. Ortiz de Urbina SJ, *El símbolo niceno* (1947) ; *G. Prestige, *God in Patristic Thought* (1952) ; *W. Telfer, ' When did the Arian controversy begin ', in JTS 47 (1946) 129–42 ; *H. Chadwick, ' Ossius of Cordova and the Presidency of the Council of Antioch ', in JTS 9 (1958) 292–304 ; *K. Aland, ' Die religiöse Haltung Kaiser Constantins ', in TU 63 i : 549–600 ; *E. Schwartz, ' Zur Kirchengeschichte des vierten Jahrhunderts ', in ZNTW 34 (1935) 129–213 gives a useful chronicle of events during the Arian crisis but is dominated by his conception of a State-church, a conception which was shown by Norman Baynes to be unsound. J. H. C.

ARISTOTLE, PLACE OF This article will be mainly concerned with the reception of Aristotle into the Latin Middle Ages (for the place of Aristotle in earlier and non-Latin theology cf. Aetius, Boethius, Monophysites, etc.). This will be considered thus : (I) the reception of individual works in earlier times, (II) in the 13th cent., (III) the reception of some of the leading ideas of Aristotle, and (IV) the ecclesiastical reaction to this reception.

I In earlier times. All the works of Aristotle which we still possess in Greek—with the exception of the *Constitution of the Athenians*, nearly the whole of the *Eudemian Ethics*, and most minor fragments—were translated into Latin between the second half of the 4th cent. and the third quarter of the 13th. From the beginning, this diffusion of Aristotle's works into the Latin centres of study was one aspect of a wider phenomenon : the spreading of the works from the Greek schools of Athens, Alex-

andria, etc., to other quarters, and the self-assertion of languages other than the Greek as appropriate means of communication for philosophical and theological disciplines. Translations of Aristotle into Armenian and Syriac—perhaps Persian and Georgian—and later on into Arabic, Hebrew and the European vernaculars are part of the same movement.

Marius Victorinus's lost translation of the *Categories*, and that—partly preserved—of Porphyry's introduction to Aristotle's logic (*Isagoge*) reflected the Latin world's interest in the aristotelizing neo-Platonism of Plotinus's pupil and friend. At the same time, or shortly after, the school of Themistius left its mark in Rome through the translations or adaptations by the pagan intellectual leader Agorius Praetextatus of paraphrases of the *Analytics*, now lost, and, by an unknown scholar of the same circle, of a paraphrase of the *Categories* which was later ascribed to St Augustine and became one of the three main texts of logic in the schools of the 8th to the 10th cent. Again, towards A.D. 400, Martianus Capella summarized, probably from Latin sources, the *Categories* and *De Interpretatione* (*De Nuptiis*, book iv). One century later, *c*. A.D. 500, Boethius formulated his plan of rendering into Latin as much as he could find of Aristotle's and Plato's works, of commenting upon them, and of showing the fundamental agreement between the two philosophies. This Porphyrian ideal, which probably came to Boethius from the Athenian, not Alexandrian, tradition of Proclus, was never achieved. Boethius seems to have been able to obtain only one volume of Aristotle's works, what was later called the *Organum*, or to have been prevented by death from carrying on his task. His translation of the *De Interpretatione* (*Peri ermenias*), accompanied by two full commentaries, became the standard text of this work from the end of the 8th cent. onwards ; from the end of the 10th, his *Categories*, with a commentary, displaced effectively the pseudo-Augustinian paraphrase ; his versions of the *Prior Analytics*, *Topics* and *Sophistical Arguments* were properly rediscovered in the second quarter of the 12th cent. without commentaries (with the possible exception of the *Prior Analytics*). Boethius's translations were almost unchallenged until the end of the 15th cent. But his rendering of the *Posterior Analytics* does not seem ever to have been used ; it was already lost, at least in parts, by the middle of the 12th cent.

The two provinces where the tradition of the late Greek (Aristotelian and neo-Platonic) schools was still or newly alive, the Byzantine Empire in the East and the Mohammedan world of the West, contributed material and inspiration for the new impulse towards Aristotelian studies in Latin centres of culture near the middle of the 12th cent. James of Venice (Iacobus Veneticus), probably a lawyer who gave advice to the archbishop of Ravenna and may have been in touch with the schools of Bologna, was in Constantinople in 1136. Apart from translating anew the *Posterior Analytics*, and perhaps the *Prior Analytics*, *Topics* and *Sophistical Arguments*, he was the first—as it seems—to render into Latin the *Physics*, *De Anima*, parts of the *Parva Naturalia* and at least part of the *Metaphysics*. He also translated an introduction to the *Physics* and scholia to the *Metaphysics*, and commented upon, in the Greek fashion, the *Sophistical Arguments* and possibly other logical works. Some of his translations remained fundamentally the authoritative texts of those works for over three hundred years. Henry ' Aristippus ', a Sicilian archdeacon and court dignitary, with scientific leanings, probably of Norman extraction, ambassador to Constantinople in 1158, translated, side by side with two dialogues of Plato and perhaps some works of Gregory Nazianzen and Diogenes Laertius, Aristotle's chemical treatise (*Meteorologics*, book iv). About the same time, other scholars, whose names are not known, translated from the Greek the *De Sensu et Sensato*, the *De Generatione et Corruptione*, the *Nicomachean Ethics*, and again the *Posterior Analytics*, the *Physics* and most of the *Metaphysics*.

About one generation after James of Venice, the mathematician and astronomer Gerard of Cremona translated in Toledo from the Arabic the *Meteorologics* and *De Caelo* as well as the *Posterior Analytics*, *Physics* and *De Generatione et Corruptione*. At the same time, Alfred of Sareshel was translating from the Arabic the pseudo-Aristotelian *De Plantis*, whose Greek original by Nicolas of Damascus (1st cent. B.C.) is lost.

II The 13th century. The Aristotelian or pseudo-Aristotelian works which had not yet been translated from the Greek in or before the 12th cent., or whose translations had been lost, were put into Latin in the 13th cent. ; and the available Graeco-Latin translations were revised and corrected on the basis of Greek manuscripts. This was done partly in England and France by Robert Grosseteste and his collaborators from Southern Italy, Sicily and Greece (*Nicomachean Ethics*, *De Caelo*, *De Mundo*) shortly before the middle of the century, partly immediately after the middle of the century by Bartholomew of Messina at the court of King Manfred (*Magna Moralia*, *Problems*, *Physiognomics*, and again *De Mundo*), but mainly in Greece and probably Italy by the Flemish Dominican philosopher, William of Moerbeke, whose extensive learning, exact scholarship, varied philosophical and scientific interests, and flair for important works of the past led him to enrich and renew the Greek literature available to Latin readers in the third quarter of the century. He translated for the first time the *Politics*, and *Poetic*, and probably for the first time the *Rhetoric* and book xi of the *Metaphysics* ; for the first time from the Greek books i-iii of the *Meterologics*, and the many books *On the Animals* ; he translated anew the *Categories*, *De Interpretatione*, *De Caelo*, *Meteorologics* iv ; he corrected the older Graeco-Latin translations of the *Posterior Analytics*, *Sophistical Arguments*, *Physics*, *De Generatione et Corruptione*, *De Anima*, *Parva Naturalia*, *Metaphysics* and probably *Nicomachean Ethics*.

In the meantime, in the second quarter of the 13th cent., the books *On the Animals* had been translated from the Arabic by Michael Scot, to whom we probably owe the translations from the Arabic of the full texts of the *Physics*, *De Caelo*, *De Anima* and most of the *Metaphysics*, which accompany the Latin versions of Averroes' large commentaries.

Aristotelian doctrines also reached the medieval philosopher and theologian through the elaborations by Greek-writing philosophers of the 2nd to 12th cents., and by Arabic-writing authors of the 9th to the 12th. Gerard of Cremona translated from the Arabic Themistius's paraphrase of the *Posterior Analytics* ; Grosseteste, from the Greek, Simplicius's commentary on the *De Caelo* and a group of commentaries on the *Nicomachean Ethics* ; William of Moerbeke, Simplicius's commentary on the *Categories* and again, that on the *De Caelo* ; Alexander of Aphrodisias on the *Meteorologics* and *De Sensu et Sensato* ; Themistius on the *De Anima* ; Ammonius on the *De Interpretatione* ; and part of Philoponus's commentary on the *De Anima*. But it was through Avicenna's, Alfarabi's and Avicebron's works that a number of Aristotelian doctrines or concepts first became known to some students of the 12th and 13th cents. : they were translated in Spain in the middle of the 12th. The commentaries and expositions of Aristotelian works by Averroes, translated in the second quarter of the 13th cent. in Spain and Italy (apart from the large commentaries mentioned above, the expositions of the *Organon*, *De Generatione et Corruptione*, *Nicomachean Ethics*, *Rhetoric* and *Poetic*, etc.) exercised a much greater influence than the Greek commentaries ; they provided a vast exegetical material, a thorough and often exact analysis of Aristotle's writings, and a model for their systematic interpretation.

III The reception of Aristotelian ideas. No extensive inquiries have been carried out so far with the purpose of assessing the part effectively played by Aristotelian doctrines in theology during the Middle Ages. It is particularly difficult to determine through which texts individual doctrines became the basis of theological elaborations. Such concepts as substance and accident, form and matter, potency and act, contingency and necessity, efficient and final cause, all of which owe to Aristotle much of their philosophical and technical value, had already acquired a wide circulation before the relevant Aristotelian texts were properly studied. The doctrine of the ten categories became inextricably involved with the formulation and solution of trinitarian problems through the wide popularity enjoyed from the 9th cent. onwards by Boethius's *De Trinitate*, which was possibly the best example for the Middle Ages of how basic texts of philosophy or dialectic (Porphyry's *Isagoge* and Aristotle's *Categories*) could be used for the rationalization of faith. Aristotle's aporetic attitude, formulated in the often quoted sentence of the *Categories* : ' Perhaps it would be difficult to make confident assertions about such matters without considering them repeatedly, but it will not be without profit if we doubt them one by one',[1] (*Categ.* 7, 8 b 23–4) added discipline to the intellectual expectations based on the text '*pulsate et aperietur vobis*,' and contributed powerfully to the methods of inquiry and exposition exemplified by Abelard's *Sic et Non* and by the *quaestiones* of the 12th and 13th cents. The Aristotelian origin of the various forms and levels of logical argumentation (demonstrative, probable, sophistical syllogisms ; *argumentum a causa, ab effectu, ab oppositis*, etc. ,eventually *a priori, a posteriori*) is only blurred by the fact that the authoritative texts on which this art was studied were for a long time those of Boethius (*De Categoricis Syllogismis, De Hypotheticis Syllogismis, De Differentiis Topicis*). But it is a simplified and crystallized set of Aristotelian rules that provided the formal structure of much theological argument and systematization in the Middle Ages.

The interpretations of the doctrine of form and matter were often the channels through which fundamentally different views on the nature of created things—living and not-living, earthly and celestial—and on the technique of creation were expressed. The refusal to accept the possibility of a totally neuter prime matter, without even incipient native forms, was countered by the refusal to accept the possibility of purely potential forms in matter ; on the other hand, form, on the one side, was strictly considered as a counterpart and complement of matter in all created things in such a way that even angels must have matter, while, on the other side, created form was considered as a full substance in its own right : the rather unhistorical label of 'Augustinianism' was often applied to the doctrines centred on the two first alternatives. The most serious difficulties in the handling of the Aristotelian concept of form concern the definition of the soul as form of the body. A strictly literal interpretation of this formula would imply the mortality of the soul. On the other hand, an interpretation which would allow for the form having a substantial independence from the matter of which it is, temporarily, a form, might lead to the consequence that, for example, nothing of the 'form' of Christ would have remained in His body at His death, and that the form of the dead body—as far as it had an organized nature, a shape, etc.—would have been totally different from that of the body of Christ, viz. that the dead body would not have been that of Christ (in Aristotelian terms, 'man' is only equivocally, not univocally, predicated of the dead man). A way out would lie in the doctrine of plurality of forms, which might be supported by some Aristotelian texts : the form of 'corporeity' would remain in the dead body, and each of the other 'forms' (vegetative soul, sensitive soul, rational soul) would have its own destiny.

Aristotle's cosmological physics, based on the mutability of sub-lunar and non-circular motion—which allows of coming-to-be and passing away—as against the immutability of circular, supra-lunar motion, led to the impossibility of conceiving creation *ex nihilo* and, even more, final destruction or reshaping of the world as a whole. The eternity of this world seems to be inescapable, and to be sealed by the teleological doctrine of beings : every being is what it is when it actually and actively realizes its possibilities, and *this* is its *end*.

The obscurity of some passages in the *De Anima* may encourage the view that knowledge possessed by the individual, at the highest level, is sharing in truth in such a way that the minds of all individuals would be one and the same mind in this act of contemplation ; and that only at this level is man really immortal. The unity or uniqueness of the intellect realizing its possibilities (*intellectus possibilis*), and the negation of individual immortality would be two of the inevitable consequences of this view.

IV The ecclesiastical reaction. It is around such doctrines that many of the theological fights of the 13th cent. were fought. The doctrines of the eternity of the world and unity of the possible intellect were considered characteristic of the extreme Aristotelians who followed Averroes's analyses and, to a certain extent, interpretations (the term 'Averroism' had acquired much wider application in modern times, until recent reactions). The doctrine of the plurality of forms has been considered characteristic of the Franciscans and of a dissentient wing of the Dominicans.

The impact of Aristotelianism on theology may be exemplified by reference to the attitude taken by some Church authorities at two critical moments in two critical places : at the beginning of the time when the '*Libri naturales*' and the *Metaphysics* were being assimilated (1210–30), and when the spreading of the study of the whole Aristotelian corpus was in full swing (1270–85) ; in Paris and in Oxford.

In 1210, at a council of the Sens province, it was decided that : 'Neither the books of Aristotle on natural philosophy nor commentaries upon them should be read at Paris, publicly or privately'.[1] This prohibition was renewed—again for Paris only—and extended to the *Metaphysics* by the papal legate, Robert de Courçon, in 1215. The condemnation of Amaury of Bène, David of Dinant and of the '*Summae*' of those works (perhaps Avicenna's *Shifa*) which accompanies the prohibition, seems to point to the dangerous influence, in the direction of pantheism and materialism, which those works might have on unprepared minds. In 1231, Gregory IX entrusted William of Auxerre and two other Theologians with the task of examining and correcting the prohibited works. This was never done ; and by 1255 those texts—which had already found readers and teachers in other places—had become part of the syllabus in Paris University.

In 1270 a decree of Stephen Tempier, bishop of Paris, condemned a series of propositions, many of which represented directly, or indirectly, doctrines originating in Aristotle's works : 'The intellect of all men is numerically one and the same ; all that

---

[1] fortasse difficile sit de huiusmodi rebus confidenter declarare nisi saepe pertractata sint, dubitare autem de singulis non erit inutile.

[1] nec libri Aristotelis de naturali philosophia nec commenta legantur Parisiis publice vel secreto.

happens here in the lower world is subject to the necessitating action of the heavenly bodies ; the world is eternal ; the soul, man's proper form, is dissolved with the body ; God does not know individual things.'[1] In 1277 the same bishop, following John XXI's invitation, submitted a long list of false and dangerous propositions, which he then condemned ; these included some propositions by Aquinas. Immediately after, the Dominican archbishop of Canterbury, Robert Kilwardby, condemned in his turn a number of propositions, including those which summarized Aquinas's doctrine of the unity of form in man : ' The sensitive and vegetative souls are dissolved when the intellectual soul is induced ; a body both living and dead is only equivocally a body ; a dead body is, as such, a body only in an applied sense.'[2] This condemnation was renewed in 1284 and 1286 ; the Thomistic doctrine of the unity of form was finally and officially rehabilitated only in 1914. (The canonization of St Thomas in 1323 meant that his writings were given ' droit de cité ' in the Church (cf. DTC 15:693) ; Vitoria and the Council of Trent carried this process further, and the Thomist revival under Leo XIII culminated in the drawing up of the XXIV theses of 1914.—*Editorial Note.*)

In the sphere of political philosophy, the doctrine of the natural character of the state (' *homo naturaliter politicus* ') led to a re-appraisal of, and opposition to, the doctrine that the state was a consequence of, and partial remedy for, the fall of man. The Aristotelian point of view, enlarged to embrace the whole of human kind, combined with a vestige of the doctrine of the unity of the possible intellect, and with an interpretation of human happiness as achieved, in one of its aspects, on earth itself, was used by Dante for his theory of the independent supreme power of the Emperor as against the claims of the Pope : Dante's *Monarchia* was soon condemned. Much less opposition was aroused by doctrines connected with Aristotle's ethical theories. The theory of virtue as a habit, or as the proper fulfilment of the potentialities inherent in man and, above all, the ethico-metaphysical doctrine of the final cause considered as the good motive of action, and its counterpart, that every action aims at some good, had a big share in shaping moral theology (*see* ACTS, HUMAN).

Bibliography. Apart from the standard histories of philosophy (F. Überweg, K. Prächter, B. Geyer, *Grundriss der Geschichte der Philosophie*, I–II (1926)[12], (1928)[11] ; M. De Wulf, *Histoire de la philosophie médiévale* (1934–47)[6] (Eng. trans. 1935–56) ; É. Gilson, *History of Christian Philosophy in the Middle*

___

[1] quod intellectus omnium hominum est unus et idem numero ; quod omnia quae hic in inferioribus aguntur, subsunt necessitati corporum caelestium ; quod mundus est aeternus ; quod anima, quae est forma hominis secundum quod homo, corrumpitur corrupto corpore ; quod Deus non cognoscit singularia.

[2] quod, intellectiva introducta, corrumpitur sensitiva et vegetativa ; quod corpus vivum et mortuum est aequivoce corpus, et corpus mortuum, secundum quod corpus mortuum, sit corpus secundum quid.

Ages (1955)), the following works may be consulted : (*a*) *for the reception of Aristotle* : G. Lacombe, etc., *Aristoteles Latinus, Codices* (1939–55) ; L. Minio-Paluello, *Iacobus Veneticus Grecus, Canonist and Translator of Aristotle*, in *Traditio* 8 (1952) 265–304 ; E. Franceschini, *Roberto Grossatesta, vescovo di Lincoln, e le sue traduzioni latine*, in ' Atti del Reale Istituto Veneto ' xciii. 2 (1933–4) 1–138 ; M. Grabmann, *Guglielmo di Moerbeke O.P., il traduttore delle opere di Aristotle* (1946) ; (*b*) *on Aristotle and theology* : F. van Steenberghen, *Siger dans l'histoire de l'aristotélisme* (1942) ; D. A. Callus, *Introduction of Aristotelian Learning at Oxford*, in ' Proceedings of the British Academy ' 29 (1943, but published 1946), and *The Condemnation of St Thomas at Oxford* (1946) ; M. Grabmann, *Mittelalterliches Geistesleben* (1926 and 1957), *I divieti ecclesiastici di Aristotele sotto Innocenzo III e Gregorio IV* (1941) and *Die Geschichte der scholastischen Methode* (1909–11) ; O. Lottin, *Psychologie et morale aux xiie et xiiie siècles* (1942–58).   L. M.-P.

ARK OF THE COVENANT The Ark of the Covenant was a rectangular box (dimensions, roughly $4' \times 3' \times 3'$) made of acacia wood, covered with gold, and carried by means of bars passed through rings near the top of the box.

It was the central object in Israel's cult ; the Tabernacle and, later, the Temple were made to house it ; and in both, it stood in the heart of the sanctuary in a little room known as the Holy of Holies. According to the Bible it dates from the earliest days of Israel's existence after the Exodus, accompanied them in their wanderings and wars, and when conditions became more settled it found a fixed home in the Temple at Jerusalem. It was presumably destroyed in the sack of the Temple in 587. (2 Mac 2:4–8 records the tradition that it was hidden away by Jeremias.)

The gods that men naturally worship are gods accessible to the mind and imagination and experience ; gods, therefore, that can be represented visibly. To Israel it was revealed that God is transcendent, He is not on the same plane as the objects of man's normal experience. He cannot be called by any name such as the pagan gods had— Bel, Moloch, Hadad or Ra : His name is ineffable. And in the same way, His person is not to be identified with any object of visible experience. Indeed, the non-representation of God is the best way of conceiving Him—He is utterly unlike anything that we know. However, human nature does need some visible object as a focus of its worship ; and to satisfy this need without endangering the principle of ' non-representation ', Israel has the Ark. It is the symbol of His presence ; it is His footstool (Ps 98:5) ; between the Cherubim, the winged figures which surmount it, He sits enthroned.

The Egyptians carried in procession images of their gods enshrined in little coffers ; the secret inner shrine of the Babylonian ziggurat probably contained a statue of the god. In this box in the heart of Israel's sanctuary, there was a copy of the

Law. For the Law is the expression of the Covenant by which God comes close to His people : ' There is no other nation so great as to have its gods so close to them as our God is to us when we call on Him. Which other nation has laws like this law which I make known to you today ? ' (cf. Dt 4:7 f.).

The Ark, then, is the seat and symbol of the covenant by which God becomes present with His people, becomes ' God with them '. For this reason the Tabernacle which houses the Ark is known as the Tent of Meeting ; there the children of Israel could meet God, could ' stand before the face of God '. It was from the Ark that God spoke and made known His will (cf. Ex 25:22). That, too, is why the Ark went before them when they crossed the Jordan (Jos 3:3), and led them into battle (cf. I Kg 4:3 ff.). It shared something of the awful holiness of God, so that to touch it brought death (cf. 2 Kg 6:7).

Aaron's rod and a pot of manna were also placed in the inner sanctuary near the Ark (according to Heb 9:4, actually in the Ark).

The inner sanctuary was entered only once in the year, on the Day of Atonement, when the priest sprinkled the Ark with blood (Lev 16:1-17) in expiation for the sins of the whole people. The word used for the lid of the Ark, therefore (*kapporet*), came to have a double meaning : the covering of the Ark, or the place where sins were covered. This latter meaning is the one selected in the Greek and Latin translations (ἱλαστήριον, *propitiatorium*) : the throne of God is also the Mercy Seat.

In the NT, the idea of propitiation naturally connected our Lord with the Ark : God makes Him a propitiation, through His blood (Rom 3:25 ; cf. I Jn 4:10). Heb 9:1-14 suggests the same comparison. The Fathers continue the same line of symbolism : the Ark signified God's presence in the midst of His people—and Christ is really Emmanuel, ' God with us '. There may even be a reference to this in Jn 1:14 : the Hebrew word for this invisible presence of God was šekinah, in Greek σκήνωσις : as John says, ἐσκήνωσεν ἐν ἡμῖν. Again, Ps 46:6 refers to the Ark being carried in procession : ' *Ascendit Deus in jubilo, et Dominus in voce tubae* ' ; and this is applied to our Lord's Ascension. The secret, hidden presence of God enthroned on the Ark in the Holy of Holies indicates to the Fathers (especially with the association of the manna in the Ark) the Eucharistic presence of Christ. The symbolism then becomes more detailed : the Ark signifies Christ, containing the pot of manna, which is the divinity, the rod of Aaron, which is his priestly power, and the tables of the Law, of which he is the author ; the Ark is made of incorruptible wood, just as Christ's sinless body is free from corruption ; the Ark is lined inside and out with gold, just as Christ has the outward nature of sinless man and the inner nature of God.

The next natural step is the extension of the symbolism to our Lady. If Christ's sinless body is incorruptible, she is the source from which that body came, and she too is free from corruption.

Our Lord is the mediator of the new covenant ; and she is the Ark, containing that covenant. She bore in her womb Christ, the food of our souls ; just as the Ark contained the manna. Ps 131:8— ' Rise, thou and the ark of thy holiness '—is applied to her being taken up into heaven.

In the Apocalypse, just as the Woman of ch. 12 is sometimes seen as our Lady, sometimes as the church, so also the Ark mentioned just before this (Apoc 11:19) is sometimes referred to her and sometimes to the Church.

Bibliography. The subject is seldom treated. The article *Arche* in DAC is entirely given up to the Ark of Noe. C. Spicq OP, in his *L'Épître aux Hébreux* I (1952) 72 and 298, has some helpful passages. Other commentaries on the texts cited in the article can be consulted. For the use of Ark-typology in Mariology, see J. Crehan SJ, *The Ark of the Covenant*, in CR 35 (1951) 301-10. L. J.

ARK OF NOE IN LITURGY AND TRADITION

The application of the OT story of Noe (Gen 6:8 to 10:1) to the Christian dispensation is one of the clearest cases of the use of the spiritual sense of Scripture (*see* SPIRITUAL SENSE) by the Church.

Apart from the reference to Noe in Christ's own discourse (Mt 24:37-8) there is the plain teaching of St Peter (1 Pet 3:20 and 2 Pet 2:5 and 3:5-9) that Noe's escape from the deluge was somehow a type of the salvation that was to be found in the Church. Heb 11:7 stressed the faith of Noe, and the term used for him in 2 Pet is one which recurs as a title in the Dead Sea Scrolls, ' teacher of justice '. There can be no doubt that some part of the revelation communicated to the apostles was concerned with the understanding of this patriarchal figure. In Jewish speculation Noe was beginning to be a figure of interest in the 1st cent. In the OT he had been quite neglected after his appearance in Genesis ; he was not included in the great prayer of Nehemias and only in Wisdom (10:4 and 14:6), Isaias 54:9 and Ecclus 44:17 are there allusions to his fate. Later on the interest in him quickened ; in 4 Macc 15:31 his ark is taken as a type of ' the mother of the race that did weather the storms ', and in Philo the ark full of animals is compared to the human body and its passions (*de plantatione Noe* 43). In the Talmud (*Sanhedrin* 108b) there is a curious enlargement on the tale, making out that the black colour of the Negro is a curse due to the incontinence of Cham with his wife while they were in the ark, the other human beings having all observed strict continence during that period. The Zadokite work makes the presence of four human couples in the ark an argument for monogamy. In the face of all this speculation it was only to be expected that the apostles should receive some guidance.

Noe as a type broods over the pages of Acts ; Peter's vision (Ac 10:11-13) of the ' great vessel ' with its ' beasts, creeping things and fowls ' and his being told to ' do sacrifice and eat ' are all reminders of Noe, and Paul's preaching at Lystra alludes to the covenant with Noe. It is not surprising that early in the 2nd cent. the decree of the council of Jerusalem was taken to mean that Gentiles, when converted, had to observe the Noachic laws. 1 Clement (7:6 and 9:4) makes Noe a preacher of penance and regeneration and says that he ' was found faithful by reason of his liturgy', indicating that Noe was already being associated in the Christian mind with baptism and the eucharist, his sacrifice to God after coming out of the ark gaining him a mention among the patriarchs who were later to be called upon by name during the Mass, as in the *Stowe Missal*.

Pope Callistus (as reported by Hippolytus *ref. haer.* 9:12 ; GCS 26:250) used the presence of clean and unclean animals in the ark as a justification for allowing sinners to remain in the Church, while with Cyprian (*de unitate* 6) the parallel of ark and Church has become a reason for asserting the exclusiveness of the latter (*see* SALVATION OF NON-CATHOLICS). Jerome also asserts this exclusiveness with emphasis (*ep.* 15:2 ; CSEL 54:64), ' He who is not in this ark will perish while the flood is raging'.[1] Augustine (*civ. Dei* 15:26 ; CSEL 40:116) has a remarkable parallel between the ark and the body of Christ on the cross ; the measurements of the ark correspond to those of the human body, where the height is six times the breadth from shoulder to shoulder and ten times the thickness from chest to spine, thus giving proportions of 300, 50 and 30. Further, a door was opened in the side and this ' is that wound inflicted when the side of the Crucified was pierced by a lance'. A special tractate was devoted to the meaning of the ark for Christians by Gregory of Elvira ; it was written before 362 and was recovered in modern times by Dom Wilmart (published in RBn 26 (1909), 1–12). It pictures the Holy Spirit as the dove, going out from the ark and not finding rest among the nations who did not yet believe in Christ but returning into ' the ark that is the Church of the apostles'.

In Gregory of Elvira can be seen the same preoccupation with the seven churches and the one Church that is found in the Muratori fragment, but here the interpretation given is that the seven others in the ark with Noe represent the seven gifts of the Spirit ; Noe ' carried the image of Christ, and these seven stand for the sevenfold Church'. It is not hard to see after this where the Celtic idea comes from of having seven churches built in a group for the use of a single monastery. Gregory has also the eschatological ideas that are common to Spain and Ireland (*see* ADVENT), since for him the parallel is to be found between the escape of the eight souls from the cataclysm of the flood and the need to be in the ark of the Church at the final conflagration of the world.

Origen (*hom.* 2 *in Gen.* ; GCS 29:28–30) does not fail to call Christ ' our Noe' and has much to say, as one might expect, about the inner structure of the ark, making it appear that the fewness of those who live on the top storey indicates that only

[1] Si quis in Noe arca non fuerit, periet regnante diluvio.

few, out of the great number of the baptized, ever attain to the spiritual sense of the Scripture. More daring is Cyprian, who takes the drunkenness of Noe as a type of the Passion of Christ ; this is surprising, as he is usually quite restrained in his appeal to the spiritual sense, and he must here (*ep.* 63:3 ; CSEL 3:702) be drawing upon earlier and bolder writers. ' In the book of Genesis we find a type of the Lord's Passion in the mystery of Noe. He drank wine, he was inebriated, he was stripped of his garments in his own house . . . .' Christ drank wine at the Last Supper, He loved His own to the end, being carried away by His love ; He was exposed naked on the cross (and this is emphasized in the homily of Melito on the Passion) ; He was reverently taken down and covered by Joseph and Nicodemus. The parallel is quite in the spirit of the early Church but would be strange to a modern Catholic. Clement of Alexandria comments on the passage from Genesis, but simply to say that Noe's drunkenness is a warning to us, and he does not attempt to find a spiritual sense here. Cyprian may have derived his idea from Syria. Apelles, the disciple of Marcion, had attacked this part of Genesis as being immoral, and the Christian defence, as so often, was to turn to the spiritual sense. Thus it is not difficult to make a distinction between those typological features in the story of Noe which are ' given' as coming from revelation, and those which are artificial, being started in a time when revelation was finally complete.

In the Sarum calendar 17 March was kept as the day when Noe went into the ark (*Ingressio Noe in arcam*) and 29 April as the day when he came out ; no other Use seems to have kept these feasts.

Bibliography. J. Fink, *Noe der Gerechte in der frühchristlichen Kunst* (1955) ; RAC s.v. *Arche* ; A. Wilmart, ' Arca Noe', in RBn 26 (1909) 1–12 ; *E. G. Selwyn, *Commentary on 1 Peter* (1946) in the appendix ; apart from the patristic authors cited in the article, there are some later sermons, such as those of Basil of Seleucia (PG 85:76–101), devoted to Noe.   J. H. C.

ARMENIAN DECREE The Armenian Decree of the Council of Florence, 1439, by means of which reunion was effected between the Armenian Church and the Holy See, contains a section which is of considerable importance in the theology of the Sacraments. (I) The historical background of the Decree is sketched. (II) An account is given of its contents, with special attention to the Instruction on the Sacraments. (III) The dogmatic value of the Instruction is assessed ; and the two most important theological problems to which the Decree is relevant are investigated : (IV) the power of the Church to determine the matter and form of the Sacraments, and (V) the teaching of the Decree on the matter and form of Orders.

I The historical background is well summarized by J. de Guibert, ' Le Décret du Concile de Florence, sa valeur dogmatique', *Bulletin de Littérature ecclésiastique*, 10 (1920) 157–62. The founding of the

Armenian Church is ascribed by the Armenians to St Gregory the Illuminator, a contemporary of the Emperor Constantine the Great. In the 6th cent. it broke away from both Rome and Constantinople by embracing the monophysite heresy at the Synod of Tvin (c. 527). Various attempts at reunion were made during the period of the Crusades, and an uneasy union was achieved under Innocent III in 1198 with the Patriarch, or more correctly the 'Catholicos', Gregory. In 1293, when the Catholicos transferred his residence westwards from Greater Armenia to Sis in Little Armenia (Cilicia), communications with Rome became easier and relations improved. Friars Minor and Dominicans opened convents in Armenia and acted as intermediaries with the Holy See. The Council of Sis in 1307, completed by that of Adana in 1316, attempted to consolidate dogmatic unity with Rome and to enforce several Roman liturgical uses ; but there remained considerable resistance groups. In 1330 a Dominican called Bartholomew the Small and an Armenian, John of Kerna, founded an Order of 'Brothers of Unity' to promote closer union with Rome. At the Genoese colony of Caffa in the Crimea, this Order, which within thirty years was seven hundred strong, established a house of studies, where various works of St Thomas were put into Armenian, including the *Tertia Pars* of the *Summa* which contains St Thomas's treatment of the Sacraments. A few years later, two of the Brothers of Unity, by name Nerses of Ourmiah and Simeon of Garin, sent to Pope Benedict XII a list of 117 errors which the Armenians were supposed to hold. In 1341, on receipt of a request for military aid from the King of Armenia, Benedict replied that he could not furnish help so long as the Armenians persisted in holding these errors. Not satisfied with a reply sent by one Daniel of the Friars Minor, the Pope insisted that a Synod be called to condemn the errors. A Synod accordingly met at Sis in 1344 or 1345, and replied to the charges point by point. When the acts of the Synod were brought to Rome, they did not entirely satisfy the new Pope, Clement VI ; but after further negotiations complete agreement and union was established in 1355. However, about twenty years later, when Lesser Armenia fell to the Turks, the union was again interrupted.

The Armenian Church remained more or less explicitly separated from Rome until the time of Eugenius IV. When negotiations were opened for the reunion of the Greek Church with Rome, the Papal envoys were instructed to invite the Armenians as well to send delegates to the Council of Reunion, which was held eventually at Florence. When the Catholicos, Constantine VI, received the invitation at Sis, he was evidently in favour of reunion, because he dispatched four delegates to the Council with instructions to accept 'whatever the Holy Ghost should inspire that holy Synod' to enjoin. Arriving at Constantinople after the Greek delegates had set sail, the Armenians were held up for months on end by bad weather and lack of shipping, and did not arrive in Florence until 13 August 1439, when the

main business of the Council was already over—the reunion of the Greek and Roman Churches had been solemnly proclaimed a few days earlier.

Eugenius at once set up a special commission to hold discussions with the Armenians. It included three Cardinals and a number of theologians, the chief among whom seems to have been the Dominican, John of Montenegro—the Doge of Genoa later described him as the 'architect' of the union with the Greeks and Armenians (cf. G. Hofman, 'Die Einigung der armenischen Kirche mit der katholischen Kirche auf dem Konzil von Florenz', OCP, 5 (1939), 160–1). After a month of discussions, the Armenian Decree of Union was drawn up. It was ratified in a solemn session of the Council on 22 November 1439, and signed by Pope Eugenius IV, eight Cardinals, two Patriarchs, five Archbishops, thirty-five Bishops, and the Armenian envoys (cf. G. Hofmann, 'Documenta Conc. Florentini de Unione Orientalium, II, De Unione Armenorum', in *Textus et Documenta*, Ser. Theol., 19 (1935), 44 f.).

II Contents of the Decree. The Decree consisted of the following parts : (1) the Nicene Creed with the addition of the *Filioque*—the Armenians are not to sing the Creed without this addition ; (2) the definitions of Chalcedon (on the two natures in Christ) and of Constantinople III (on the two wills and operations in Christ), which are simply renewed ; (3) a dogmatic declaration on the orthodoxy of the Council of Chalcedon and of St Leo, with an injunction to honour St Leo among the saints ; (4) a brief formula of dogmatic instruction on the seven Sacraments, together with an injunction to mix a little water in the wine for consecration at Mass ; (5) the Athanasian Creed and the Decree of Union with the Greeks, both simply renewed ; (6) a disciplinary decree about the dates of Feasts.

The Instruction on the Sacraments (D 695–702) follows closely the wording of St Thomas's treatise *In Articulos Fidei et Sacramenta Ecclesiae Expositio* (ed. Parma (1864), XVI, Opusc. IV, 120 ff.), but there are various omissions and additions, the additions being largely taken from St Thomas's fuller treatment of the Sacraments in the *Pars Tertia* (the texts of the Conciliar Decree and of St Thomas's *Opusculum* are printed out in parallel columns with comments by J. de Guibert, art. cit., 196–207). First, the Instruction has a section on the Sacraments in general, enumerating the seven and distinguishing their different purposes and effects. Then it is explained that in every Sacrament three elements can be discerned : 'things as matter, words as form, and the person of the minister conferring the sacrament with the intention of doing what the Church does'.[1] St Thomas's *Opusculum*, written in 1261–2, appears to be the first attempt that was ever made to apply the terminology of matter and form to all

---

[1] Haec omnia sacramenta tribus perficiuntur, videlicet rebus tanquam materia, verbis tanquam forma, et persona ministri conferentis sacramentum cum intentione faciendi quod facit Ecclesia.

seven Sacraments. The attempt does not entirely succeed—for the Sacrament of Penance St Thomas and the Council following him find only a *quasimateria* (the acts of the penitent), and for the Sacrament of Matrimony none at all.

After the general introduction, the Sacraments are taken one by one, and an account is given of the matter, the form, the ordinary minister (and extraordinary, where applicable) and the effects. The Decree's most considerable departure from the text of the *Opusculum* has to do with the matter of the Holy Eucharist, where arguments of some length are adduced from *Summa*, 3a:74:6c in justification of the mixing of a little water with the wine at Mass. This section ends with a practical decree : ' We decree, therefore, that the Armenians too should conform themselves with the whole Christian world, and that their priests should mix a little water in the offering of the chalice ' (D 698).

III The Dogmatic Value of the Instruction on the Sacraments. The digression on the mixing of water with wine should not lead one to the conclusion that the Instruction as a whole is a purely practical document. In its opening sentence the Instruction clearly announces itself as doctrinal : ' To facilitate the instruction of Armenians both now and in the future, we bring together the truth about the Sacraments of the Church in this brief formula ' [1]—i.e. its main purpose is to show not how the sacramental rites are to be administered, but how they are to be explained to the people. Since the Pope and Council are not here teaching the whole Church, but only the Armenians, the Decree does not fulfil the definition of an infallible *ex-cathedra* pronouncement according to the terms of the Vatican Council (*see* INFALLIBILITY and D 1896). Nevertheless, since it is a solemn declaration of doctrine by the ecclesiastical *magisterium*, one should be very slow to follow the view of Cardinal van Rossum (*De Essentia Sacramenti Ordinis*, 1914) that its teaching on the matter and form of Order is erroneous. What the Council is doing in this Instruction is to set forth for the benefit of the Armenians an authoritative interpretation of the sacramental rites *as then practised in the Armenian Church*.

IV The Church's power to determine the matter and form of the Sacraments. A disadvantage of the official adoption of the terminology of ' matter ' and ' form ' in sacramental theology was that it led some theologians (e.g. van Rossum) to think that the matter and form of every Sacrament must be unchangeable—in Aristotelian physics, a change of substantial form in a physical body means the production of a new and different body ; hence, by parity of reasoning, a change in the form of a Sacrament would seem to mean the introduction of a new sacrament, other than the Sacraments instituted by Christ ! Hence it was concluded that the Church has no power to alter the matter and form of

any of the Sacraments. This view is historically indefensible (*see esp.* EXTREME UNCTION), and was certainly not held by the Council of Florence. On the contrary, the Council, though it did not explicitly pronounce on the point, clearly held that the Church has power, within certain limits, to determine and alter the matter and form of some of the Sacraments. As regards matter, in treating of the Sacrament of Confirmation, after mentioning that in Ac 8:14 ff. the Apostles impart the Holy Ghost by the laying-on of hands, it continues : ' in place of that laying-on of hands there is given in the Church Confirmation '—i.e. the anointing with chrism. As regards form, after saying that in Baptism the form is : ' I baptize thee in the name of the Father and of the Son and of the Holy Ghost ', it adds : ' But we do not deny that true baptism is given by the words " The servant of Christ, N., is baptized in the name of the Father and of the Son and of the Holy Ghost " or " N. is baptized by my hands in the name of, etc." '. For the Sacrament of Matrimony no set form is specified. The Council gave no explicit teaching on the extent of the Church's power to alter the matter and form of the Sacraments, but in justifying the variant forms of Baptism it clearly assumes that all permissible forms will be substantially identical in meaning. The Council of Trent affirmed the Church's power to determine and alter the administration of the Sacraments *salva illorum substantia* (D 931).

V The Matter and Form of Orders. Of the Sacrament of Orders the Decree says : ' its matter is that by the giving of which the Order is conferred ; thus the priesthood is conferred by the giving of a chalice with wine and of a paten with bread. . . . The form of the priesthood is as follows : " Receive power to offer sacrifice in the Church for the living and the dead, in the name of the Father and of the Son and of the Holy Ghost " ' (D 701).[2] Cardinal van Rossum felt compelled to condemn this as erroneous because he knew that the ' tradition of instruments ' (i.e. delivery of chalice and paten) and the accompanying words were introduced into the rite of ordination as late as the 10th cent. Supposing that the matter and form of the Sacrament of Orders is unchangeable and has therefore remained unchanged from the beginning, he concluded that the laying-on of hands must be the matter of the Sacrament, since it can be shown to have been part of the rite from the very beginning, and that therefore Eugenius IV and the Ecumenical Council of Florence were in error on this point of doctrine. However, as was shown above, the initial supposition (fixity of matter and form) is unsound, and was not accepted by the Council. The theologians of the Council knew very well that the Greek Bishops, with whom they had just been holding discussions, ordained their priests

---

[1] Quinto, ecclesiasticorum Sacramentorum veritatem pro ipsorum Armenorum tam praesentium quam futurorum faciliore doctrina sub hac brevissima redigimus formula.

[2] Sextum sacramentum est ordinis, cuius materia est illud per cuius traditionem confertur ordo : sicut presbyteratus traditur per calicis cum vino et patenae cum pane porrectionem. . . . Forma sacerdotii talis est : *Accipe potestatem offerendi sacrificium in ecclesia pro vivis et mortuis, in nomine Patris et Filii et Spiritus Sancti.*

without the tradition of instruments, and yet they never questioned the validity of the Greek ordinations. Plainly, in the Instruction on the Sacraments, the Council understood itself to be determining, consistently with its views on the variability of matter and form, what was the essential matter and form in the Armenian rite of ordination.

In 1344, the Synod of Sis had sent to Rome a copy of its rite of ordination to prove that, contrary to the allegations of certain critics, it did contain the tradition of instruments—in accordance with instructions received from Rome two hundred years earlier (cf. de Guibert, *art. cit.*, 207, n. 4, and D 547). Hence it seems that the Armenian rite which the Council is interpreting will have corresponded, at least in its general structure, to the rite of ordination as practised at Rome two hundred years before, i.e. *c.* 1150. This is a point of considerable importance for the understanding of the Decree. In the intervening centuries the Roman rite had received various accretions, most important of which was a second laying-on of hands inserted after the Communion with explicit mention of the power to absolve. These liturgical developments had had their repercussions in the theological schools : many theologians, perhaps the majority, followed Scotus's interpretation of the developed Latin rite, viz. that ' in regard to the priesthood it seems probable that there are two partial forms, in the first of which is conferred power to consecrate the Eucharist, and in the second, power to give absolution, and with these two partial forms are conjoined two matters ' (*In IV Sent.*, d. 24:q. 1:3).[1] The reason why the Council was able to propose the doctrine of St Thomas to the Armenians with every appearance of certainty and without any allusion to the Scotist opinion, is that St Thomas was interpreting the earlier and simpler Latin rite (cf. St Thomas, *In IV Sent.*, d. 24:q. 2: a. 3) with which the Armenian rite corresponded, whereas Scotus was interpreting the later and more complicated Latin rite, which contains ceremonies unknown to the Armenian Church.

It is incorrect, therefore, to imagine that the Council of Florence by its teaching in the Decree for the Armenians was at the same time defining the essential matter and form of the contemporary Roman rite of ordination. The European controversy was left quite untouched by the Instruction. The first theologian who invoked the Decree for the Armenians in the European controversy was Ruard Tapper in 1559. In the intervening hundred and twenty years the debate had continued in the theological schools as before, and the Holy See had never suggested that the question had been closed by the Council of Florence.

Uncertainty about the essentials of the Roman rite of ordination continued until 1947, when Pope Pius XII, in order to put an end to the scruples of priests who felt that in their case some possibly

essential part of the long and complicated rite had not been properly performed, defined, in the Constitution *Sacramentum Ordinis*, that thenceforth (from 1947) ' in ordination to the priesthood the matter is the first imposition of the Bishop's hands which takes place in silence. The form consists of the words of the Preface, of which the following are essential and required for validity : Bestow, we beseech Thee, almighty Father, on this Thy servant the dignity of the priesthood. . . .' (*See* ORDINATION ; also AAS 40 (1948) 7.) This Constitution refrained from saying what had been the matter and form in the period before 1947. From all that has been said above it will be clear that there is no contradiction between the doctrine of Eugenius IV and Pius XII. Eugenius IV was giving an authoritative interpretation of the Armenian Rite for the Armenian Church ; Pius XII was giving an authoritative interpretation of the Latin Rite for the Latin Church.

Bibliography. A. Balgy, *Historia Doctrinae Catholicae inter Armenos Unionisque Eorum cum Ecclesia Romana in Concilio Florentino* (1878) ; H. Lennerz, *De Sacramentis Novae Legis in genere* (1939) and *De Sacramento Ordinis* (1953)[2] ; G. M. Parella, ' Il decreto di Eugenio IV pro Armenis relativo al sacramento dell' ordine ', *Divus Thomas*, Ser. 3a, XIII (1936) 448–83 ; J. Gill, ' The Sources of the *Acta* of the Council of Florence ', OCP, 14 (1948) 43–79 and *The Council of Florence* (1959) ; J. Bligh, *Ordination to the Priesthood* (1956). J. B.

ART AND THE CHURCH TO *c.* 500 is a subject
that belongs not less to the story of the ancient Graeco-Roman world in its latest phase than it does to Christian history. It covers the stage in which pagan types of buildings, both religious and secular, and the styles, techniques and even motifs of the pagan plastic arts were adapted and ' baptized' for Christian use. Some notable survivals from this stage are found throughout the 6th cent. and occasionally later ; but after *c.* 500 the Church rapidly evolved an architecture and an art that, to a large extent, broke with the classical tradition and bore a more specifically Christian stamp. These form part of the Byzantine and medieval chapters of the history of Christian art.

I Architecture.

(i) House-Churches. As is well known from
the Acts of the Apostles (1:13–14 ; 2:46 ; 20:6–12), the earliest Christians met for prayer and the offering of the Eucharistic Sacrifice in the homes of members of their community ; and the primitive Christian church building, prior to the Peace of the Church under Constantine, would appear to have remained a house in all its essential characteristics. Optatus of Milevis (*De Schismate Donati* 2:4) and Eusebius (*HE* 8, 1) suggest that by the beginning of the 4th cent. Christian places of assembly were numerous in Rome and that some of these places, in Rome and elsewhere, were thronged with crowded congregations. Optatus (*loc. cit.*) writes of forty ' basilicas ' in Rome ; and Eusebius (*loc. cit.*) also indicates that

---

[1] Sed in sacerdotio videtur probabile quod ibi sunt duae formae partiales, in quarum altera confertur potestas conficiendi Eucharistiam, in reliqua potestas absolvendi in poenitentia. Et istis coniunguntur duae materiae.

there was a movement at this time to 'erect from the foundations churches of spacious dimensions in all cities', since the Christian communities were no longer content with 'buildings of the old style' (τὰ παλαιὰ οἰκοδομήματα), i.e. house-churches. But it would be a mistake to deduce from this that before the 4th cent. there was a general Christian habit of meeting for worship, no longer in private houses but in large buildings specially constructed for the purpose, i.e. in independent basilicas. Neither literary nor archaeological evidence supports any such idea. Optatus was, anyhow, writing in the second half of the 4th cent. ; it is clear that in the 3rd and early 4th cents., the term 'basilica' was widely and loosely used, both in pagan and Christian circles, for any large halls that served for a great variety of purposes ; and when a 3rd-cent. author (Pseudo-Clement, *Recognitiones* x, 71) tells us of how a certain Theophilus, a leading citizen of Antioch-on-the-Orontes, 'consecrated as a church the large basilica of his house' (*ita ut Theophilus, qui erat cunctis potentibus in civitate sublimior, domus suae ingentem basilicam ecclesiae nomine consecraret*), he is simply alluding to a house-church, a private residence, the largest room in which was given over to Christian assembly. Again, there is no reason to suppose that the Christian buildings confiscated by Valerian in 258 and restored by Gallienus in 259 or 260 to their rightful owners, the bishops and priests, were anything more than house-churches ; and we have a text describing the seizure by a Roman magistrate at Cirta (Constantine) in North Africa in 303, during Diocletian's persecution, of books, holy vessels, vestments and other goods from what was clearly a typical house-church (DAC, s.v. 'Constantine', cols. 2717–20). Finally, the *tituli*, the titular or parish churches of Rome, owed their origin to house-churches existing on their sites in pre-Constantinian times. The most complete remains of such a Roman house-church are those excavated beneath the Church of St John and St Paul on the Caelian Hill. There is, indeed, nothing to show that before the reign of Constantine the Christian Church had evolved a monumental architecture that might have served as a model for the Constantinian and post-Constantinian large-scale, independent basilica.

House-churches fall into two main types. Type A covers those in which the *ecclesia* proper, the assembly-place of the Christians, was one room in a pre-existing private house, a room set apart and adapted for Christian worship, but not specifically and originally designed for it. The clearest archaeological evidence for a Type A house-church that we possess is the example that was excavated in 1931–2 in the Roman frontier-city of Dura-Europos on the Euphrates, a city which fell to the Sassanian Persians in 256. A full description of this building and of the circumstances of its discovery is to be found in ed. M. I. Rostovtzeff, *The Excavations at Dura-Europos. Preliminary Report on the Fifth Season of Work, October 1931–March 1932* (1934), 238–88. The house is a typical Duran private residence, with a central courtyard surrounded by rooms. (*See* Plate 1a.) When it was adapted, *c.* 230, for Christian use, two rooms on the south side were thrown together to form one large one, the place of assembly proper, with a platform for a portable altar (?) or for the chair of the presiding bishop or priest (?), while a baptistery was installed in the room that occupied the western half of the northern side. Into the west end of this room a rectangular basin was built up above the level of the floor and covered by a canopy resting on four supports. On the walls of this baptistery eight Christian paintings survived. These include the Good Shepherd, the Healing of the Paralytic Man, the Walking on the Water and the Holy Women at the Holy Sepulchre ; all are suggestive of the neophyte's salvation ; and they contain what are probably the earliest known representations of Our Lord.

The Type A house-church did not wholly disappear after the Peace of the Church. It survived in country districts ; and an interesting example of what is most probably, if not quite certainly, a rural house-church came to light in 1949 in the Romano-British villa at Lullingstone in Kent, situated in the Darent valley, half-way between Sevenoaks and Dartford. It seems that here, about the middle of the 4th cent., three, possibly four, intercommunicating rooms at the northern end of the house were set apart for Christian use. A door leading from one of them into the rest of the villa was blocked up and a new door opened up through which this set of rooms could be entered directly from the outside world. These rooms were on the ground floor ; and below the largest and easternmost of the series was a basement room, into which the former's painted walls collapsed when the house met its end by fire. From among the many thousands of fragments of the painted plaster that have been collected, the whole design of the west wall has been reconstructed. It showed within a colonnaded building six richly-robed human figures, three of whom were standing with extended arms, in the *Orans* attitude. From the south and east walls of the same room came large-scale renderings of the Chi-Rho monogram, each within a wreath of leaves and flowers ; while portions of a similar Chi-Rho, flanked by Alpha and Omega, were found in the adjoining room, which, if the large room were a chapel, may have been a sacristy. No evidence of actual liturgical worship has so far been unearthed, but the size and elaboration of the Christian paintings, the presence of the three Chi-Rhos, the isolation of these rooms from the rest of the house, and their continued use for roughly twenty years after the kitchens and baths of the villa had ceased to function, all combine to create a very strong presumption that this was indeed a house-church. For further details, see G. W. Meates, *Lullingstone Roman Villa* (1955), 135–55.

In the house-church of Type B the church-building was not a pre-existing room adapted, but a new installation in a pre-existing house. Two examples occur in Spain, an urban one at Mérida

(Augusta Emerita) (R. Menéndez Pidal, *Historia de España ii : España Romana* (1935) 722-7, figs. 562-7 ; J. de C. Serra Rafols, *La vida en España en la época romana* (1944) 98, with fig.) and a rural one in the villa of Fortunatus at Fraga (Serra Rafols, *op. cit.*, 181, with fig.). In both of these buildings the Christian additions, in the first case a pair of rectangular apsed chambers, in the second a rectangular building containing a square apsed chamber, dated from the 4th cent. The Type B house-church was the normal type of church in Syria during the 4th cent. Two examples only can be cited here, those of the apsed basilical building in the large Julianos church at Umm-al-Jamal in southern Syria (DAC, s.v. ' Syrie ', cols. 1893-4, fig. 11020) and of the rectangular room with platform (*bema*) in the small church at Qirk Bezzé in northern Syria (ibid. col. 1866, fig. 11001).

(ii) **Small rectangular structures without internal colonnades** represent the simplest form of independent church-building erected in the 4th cent. The earliest 4th-cent. church at Parenzo in Istria consisted of two adjacent halls, of which the northern one was the church proper, with the remains of four altar-posts at its eastern end : the southern hall was probably a sacristy or place for instructing catechumens (A. W. Clapham, *English Romanesque Architecture before the Conquest* (1930) 3, fig. 1). But the majority of these small early churches had an apse at one end, as had, for instance, the small cemetery-church discovered beneath the present Church of St Severin at Cologne, situated outside the south gate of the Roman city and dating from early in the 4th cent. (F. Fremersdorf, *Ältestes Christentum, mit Berücksichtigung der Grabungsergebnisse unter Severinskirche in Köln* (1956)). For the study of early Christian cemetery-churches of the Roman imperial period no source of material is richer than the ruins of Salona, the early Christian metropolis on the Dalmatian coast near Spalato. These ruins have been intensively studied and published by the Norwegian archaeologist E. Dyggve in his *History of Salonitan Christianity* (1951) and his work has thrown a flood of light on Christian sepulchral cult and architecture during the 4th and 5th cents. Here Christian and pagan seem to have drawn very closely together, in external appearances at least, for not only were the local Christian martyrs buried in the midst of pagan cemeteries but their shrines were derived architecturally from pagan models ; and there is abundant archaeological evidence to show that Salonitan Christians of this period held at their martyrs' tombs funerary feasts (*refrigeria*) with customs that differed very little from their pagan counterparts (cf. the *refrigeria* celebrated at the 3rd-cent. cult-centre of St Peter and St Paul by the Via Appia, south of Rome—a phenomenon for which no parallel exists elsewhere in Rome and Italy ; see also J. Toynbee and J. Ward Perkins, *The Shrine of St Peter and the Vatican Excavations* (1956) 171-2, 189-90). At Salona the shrines (*memoriae*), whether of ordinary dead persons or of martyrs, were simple, apsed, rectangular structures

(Dyggve, *op. cit.*, fig., iv, 13-16). In the Marusinac cemetery there was a group of small *memoriae* dating from the 4th cent. which in the 5th cent. were incorporated in a building-complex containing as its main feature two large sepulchral structures, one a court open to the sky, apsed at one end, and surrounded by columned porticoes, the other a colonnaded hall with gabled roof and clerestory, in fact a basilica proper (see below) (Dyggve, *op. cit.*, fig. iv, 22-5).

Two other examples of small, rectangular, apsed churches, both non-sepulchral in function, may be mentioned. At Zurzach, the Roman Tenedo, in northern Switzerland, a small building of this type, with baptistery attached and dating from *c.* 400, nestled within the walls of the late-Roman fort erected on high ground above the Rhine (*Ur-Schweiz* xix, 4 (1955)). The second example, the tiny structure excavated in the Romano-British tribal capital of Calleva Atrebatum (Silchester) in Hampshire, is more complicated in design and more problematic (*Archaeologia* liii (1893)). It is almost unanimously accepted as a church and is, indeed, decidedly churchlike in plan, with its apse at the western end, its narthex at the eastern end, its low walls dividing the building into nave and aisles, but yielding no evidence that columns ever stood upon them, and its quasi-transepts projecting slightly beyond the aisle-walls. Again, the black-and-white chequered mosaic pavement, set in front of the apse, looks as if it were designed for an altar-emplacement. On the other hand, no Christian object, no scrap of clinching evidence of Christian worship, was found in this building ; and the very similar lay-out of the shrine of the Syrian Goddess on the Janiculum in Rome (É. Mâle, *La Fin du paganisme en Gaule* (1950) fig. opp. p. 116) warns us that the Silchester structure cannot be proved on ground-plan alone to be a Christian church.

(iii) **Basilicas proper, with internal colonnades, apse and clerestory-lighting.** The origins of the word ' basilica ' as an architectural term, and the various types of buildings to which the Graeco-Roman world applied it, have been fully discussed by J. B. Ward Perkins in the *Papers of the British School at Rome* xxii (1954) 69-90. This Greek word meaning ' royal ' is in essence an adjective, with which some such noun as ' hall ' must have been understood. The pagan buildings described as ' basilicas ' were overwhelmingly secular. But in Greek lands the word was never used for secular buildings. We have, indeed, no *direct* evidence that it was used in those lands at all until the 6th cent. A.D., when it denoted a Christian church. It is in the West, in Italy, and in the 2nd cent. B.C. that the term first appears in Latin form to indicate a type of building. Yet it seems unlikely that the Romans would have borrowed this Greek word in such a context had they not already found it so used east of the Adriatic ; and when Constantine issued his plans for the Church of the Holy Sepulchre, he instructed Macarius, the bishop of Jerusalem, to erect the finest βασιλική yet seen (Eusebius, *Vita*

Constantini iii, 31, 1), which implies that Macarius would have understood completely the type of building that the Emperor had in mind. Nevertheless, the origins remain a puzzle, since no Hellenistic buildings, from which the Roman republican basilica could have been derived, have so far come to light. If we emphasized the 'columned hall' aspect of basilicas, we might connect them with the Hellenistic *stoai*, so many of which, in Athens and elsewhere, were royal foundations, and believe that the use of the word 'royal' took its rise from that fact. But the Athenian and other *stoai* were very different from the western basilicas in architectural type. Another theory assumes the existence of columned audience-halls built by the Ptolemaic kings in Hellenistic Egypt and would derive from them the word 'basilica'. But for such Ptolemaic audience-halls no evidence, either literary or archaeological, has survived to us.

Of the various Roman types of basilical buildings two, the religious and the urban civic, would appear to have chiefly influenced the Constantinian architects. To the list of four pagan cult-basilicas given by Ward Perkins (*loc. cit.*, 75) three more may be added—the London Mithraeum found in Walbrook, 1954 (ed. R. L. S. Bruce Mitford, *Recent Archaeological Excavations in Britain* (1956) pls. 26, 27); the Mithraeum at Lambaesis in North Africa (*Académie des Inscriptions et Belles-Lettres : Comptes Rendus* (1954) 270, fig. 1); and the so-called 'Sacello delle Tre Navate' at Ostia, probably also a Mithraeum (G. Becatti, *Scavi di Ostia ii : I mitrei* (1954) figs. 15, 16, pl. 14, 1). These shrines are, as Ward Perkins puts it, 'good evidence of what was felt to be suitable for a place of worship'; they were, in fact, the type of place in which many converts to Christianity had already been accustomed to worship; and the early-Christian basilica, besides being excellently adapted to Christian liturgical purposes, was also well calculated to make the great masses of pagans now entering the Church feel at home in the architectural setting provided for their new faith.

Nevertheless, all these pagan cult-basilicas were comparatively small, designed for relatively select religious communities; whereas the monumental Christian basilica that was evolved after the Peace of the Church was intended to accommodate very large congregations. For this purpose the Constantinian architects must have been, to a very large extent, inspired by the great civic basilicas of republican Rome and Italy and of all the cities of western Europe and North Africa during imperial times—basilicas that were attached to the fora and used mainly for commercial and judicial business. Accounts of these great structures, with internal colonnades, clerestorys and, in many cases, apses, will be found in Ward Perkins's paper, cited above, and in any handbook of Roman architecture. It is interesting to note the instances of the conversion of these civil basilicas into Christian churches, such as those conversions effected under Justinian at Lepcis Magna and Sabratha in Tripolitania (*Archaeologia* 95 (1953) 23, fig. 8 ; 8, 9, figs. 2, 3).

It should also be remembered that in Palestine, from the middle of the 2nd cent. A.D. onwards, Jewish synagogues took the form of basilical buildings, some of them apsed (E. R. Goodenough, *Jewish Symbols in the Graeco-Roman Period* iii (1953) figs. 484, 503-7, 519, 520, 532, 535, 626, 631). But we have no evidence that such synagogues directly influenced 4th-cent. western Christian architecture. It is much more likely that churches and synagogues represent parallel, but not interrelated, developments from pagan models.

The most recent discussion in English of Constantine's great basilical church-foundations, two in Rome and two in Palestine, is that by Ward Perkins (*op. cit.* 81-7). St John Lateran, the Cathedral Church of Rome (*omnium urbis et orbis ecclesiarum mater et caput*), now dedicated to the Baptist, but originally dedicated to Our Saviour, has been proved by recent research to have been a basilical building without a continuous transept, the existing continuous transept being an addition of the Middle Ages (but for its 4th-cent. quasi-transepts, see *Rivista di Archeologia Cristiana* (1958) 59–72). The three other churches, those of St Peter's in Rome, of the Holy Sepulchre in Jerusalem, and of the Nativity in Bethlehem, share in common the fact that they were built, not only for liturgical purposes and to accommodate large concourses of faithful, but primarily to house a holy place. The original Church of the Holy Sepulchre consisted of a colonnaded narthex, an apsed assembly-hall with double colonnade, and an open, colonnaded courtyard, rounded at one end, which enclosed Our Lord's tomb. At Bethlehem is found the same triple arrangement—a colonnaded forecourt or atrium, a colonnaded assembly-hall, and, (in place of an apse) the octagonal structure that sheltered the cave of the Nativity. The three elements appear again in Old St Peter's (for which see also Toynbee and Ward Perkins, *op. cit.*, 195–211)—a large colonnaded atrium, an assembly-hall with double colonnades, and an apse, on the chord of which stood the original shrine of St Peter. In this church there was an additional feature—a great transept, with projecting ends, perhaps designed to hold large numbers of the clergy on great occasions or to assist the circulation of pilgrims to the shrine.

For one more illustration of early monumental basilicas we return to Salona, to what may be described as the 'episcopal complex', the headquarters of the city's Catholic (as opposed to its Arian) community. The complex included two early-4th-cent. oratories, a baptistery, a waiting-room and instruction-room for neophytes and two basilicas, one of the 4th, the other of the 5th, cent. Attached was the bishop's residence, a large house built in two storeys, in the upper one of which the bishop lived, while the lower one comprised kitchen, storerooms and oil- and wine-presses, used for the service and work of the Church (Dyggve, *op. cit.* fig. ii, 13, 14).

(iv) Centralized types of churches. Of early-Christian circular buildings, Santa Costanza on the

Via Nomentana, just outside Rome, generally believed to have been built *de novo* as the tomb-shrine of Constantine's daughter, Constantina, has now been demonstrated to have been a pagan mausoleum, adorned with vault-and floor-mosaics—both those existing *in situ* and those known only from Renaissance drawings and descriptions—that were unequivocally pagan (see K. Lehmann, *Art Bulletin*, 1955). The round Church of St George at Salonika was a 3rd-cent. pagan structure, converted into a church and decorated with Christian mosaics on its cupola (see below) probably during the 5th cent. (J. G. Davies, *The Origin and Development of Early Christian Church Architecture* (1952) 53, fig. 15 and pl. 9). The polygonal baptisteries, that of the Lateran (313–33) and those of the Catholics and of the Arians at Ravenna (5th cent.), were modelled architecturally on pagan sepulchral structures.

Meanwhile, in the East and in northern Italy, under eastern influence, a new and more specifically Christian type of centralized church-building was evolved during the 4th and 5th cents. This was the cruciform church, of which an early example was the church erected by St Ambrose at Milan in 383 : it seems to have assumed the form of a free-standing cross. Another western instance of the free-standing cross is the mausoleum of Galla Placidia at Ravenna (450) : there the vaulted arms are connected at the centre by a dome (Davies, *op. cit.* 76, fig. 29). An eastern instance, dating from the end of the 5th cent., is the Church of St Simeon Stylites at Kal'at Sim'an in northern Syria : this consists of four colonnaded basilicas converging on a central octagon (M. Laurent, *L'Art chrétien des origines à Justinien* (1956) pl. 36). A variant of this type is the cross-in-square lay-out, well illustrated by the Church of the Prophets, Apostles and Martyrs built in 464 at Gerasa (Jerash) in Transjordania (Davies, *op. cit.* 77, fig. 30). The more complex, 6th-cent. centralized church structures, such as San Vitale at Ravenna and Santa Sophia in Constantinople, belong to the Byzantine chapter of this story.

II The Plastic Arts. Nowhere was the early Church's acceptance of her classical environment more patent and more inevitable than in the sphere of the plastic arts. The Church had received from her Founder no manuals of Christian carving and painting, no directions for the invention and use of artistic style, symbolism and imagery. If she were to have an art as part of her equipment for her mission, if she were to speak through it a language that the world could understand, these could not but be firmly rooted in the traditions of pagan civilization ; and during the earliest period of Christian art, during the late 2nd, the 3rd, 4th and possibly well on into the 5th cent., the Church must have employed artists who were either pagans or Christians trained in their skills and crafts in pagan workshops. Even assuming the existence in this age of workshops owned and staffed by Christians and turning out works that were distinctively Christian or 'neutral' in their content, these evolved no revolutionary, specifically Christian

artistic conceptions. In style and technique the Christian and pagan works of this period are indistinguishable.

Most pagan converts under the Roman Empire had led, before accepting Christ, a very intense and elaborate religious life. They had probably already hoped for individual, personal survival after death ; and had believed, up to a point, that their conduct in this life had some bearing on their destiny hereafter. They had doubtless looked forward to their souls' admittance to some paradise of bliss ; and many would have cultivated more than one of the saviour-deities who promised to deliver them from death and evil and win for them eternal happiness. They had also been accustomed to accept the stories, figures and motifs of traditional polytheistic mythology, not in their literal sense, but as allegories and symbols of higher and more spiritual religious doctrines ; and they had been in the habit of seeing this interpretation of mythology expressed all around them in art, and, in particular, in tomb-art. Such converts, while appreciating the complete newness of the cardinal Christian doctrines, may well have regarded some, at least, of their old beliefs as types or figures of the new reality ; and it is easy to imagine their readiness to carry over to the service of their Christian faith the styles of carving and of painting and not a little of the picture-language and imagery that had externalized such of their pagan hopes, ideas and aspirations as had pre-disposed them to the acceptance of Christianity.

We almost certainly possess examples of the art of some of the numerous syncretistic sects, the adherents of which consciously distorted the Christian revelation in order to bring it into line with various semi-mystical, semi-philosophical pagan systems of thought. The biblical iconography of these sectarian productions stands markedly apart from that of the Catholic painting of the official catacombs and of orthodox Christian sculpture ; and they contain a very strong admixture of pagan borrowings (see below). But it would be a mistake always to scent ignorance or half-hearted profession of the faith, and even formal heresy, wherever pagan, Graeco-Roman decorative motifs, symbols and allegorical themes appear in Christian contexts.

(i) Sculpture in the round. The notable rarity of early Christian sculptures in the round, as contrasted with the great abundance of carvings in relief, calls for an explanation. This is doubtless to be sought in the Church's fear that independent statues and statuettes of Christ and His Saints might savour too strongly of the cult- and votive-images of pagan shrines ; whereas figures in relief (however high) on carved sarcophagi, which the pagans themselves never placed in temples, were less likely to be construed as idols, as objects of worship in the strict sense.

Such literary allusions as we have to Christian representations in the round are mainly concerned with works that were unorthodox in context. Irenaeus, writing in the latter part of the 2nd cent.

(*adv. haer.* I, xx, 4H) and Epiphanius (*Haer.* 27, 6) mention *imagines* (εἰκόνες) of Christ venerated by Gnostics along with those of St Paul, Homer and several Greek philosophers. Some of these images were painted, but others were of gold, silver and other materials used for working in the round. The figure of Christ that Alexander Severus (222–235) is stated by the 4th-cent. writer of the *Historia Augusta* to have placed in his *lararium* or private chapel, along with figures of Apollonius of Tyana, Abraham and Orpheus (*Vita Alex. Sev.* 29, 2), is likely to have been a statue or a statuette. The bronze group that Eusebius saw at Caesarea Philippi is very unlikely to have represented Christ and the Woman with the Issue of Blood, as the local Christian inhabitants alleged (*HE* 7:18).

A recent attempt has been made (M. Laurent, *op. cit.* 92–3) to assign to 2nd-cent. Gnostic circles the delightful marble statuette, now in the Museo Nazionale Romano delle Terme and unfortunately of unknown provenience, presenting Christ in the guise of a seated, youthful teacher (O. Thulin, ' Die Christus-Statuette im Museo Nazionale Romano ', *Mitteilungen des Deutschen Archaeologischen Instituts : Roemische Abteilung* xliv (1929) 201–59, pls. 53–6). But the ' Antonine ' appearance of this piece is superficial. The drilling of the wig-like hair, that frames the face and reaches to the shoulders, is much more summary and less naturalistic in effect than that found on 2nd-cent. sculptures ; the softness and roundness of the face and forms of the body are those of works of the ' Constantinian renaissance ' ; while the markedly large eyes gazing into the distance from beneath the arched, schematic brows, the parted lips and the general atmosphere of intense interior spirituality are those of mid-4th-cent. Christian art, the context to which Thulin correctly attributes the figure. (*See* Plate 1b.)

Apart from the ' Hippolytus ' statue in the Lateran Christian Museum, which would appear to be less an original Christian work than a copy of a classical type of seated philosopher (*Bulletino del Museo dell' Impero Romano* lxviii (1941) pl. facing p. 128), the remaining free-standing Christian figures that survive all depict the Good Shepherd, the favourite guise in which Our Lord was represented throughout our period—in catacomb and other (e.g. Dura house-church) paintings and on sarcophagi. The reasons for its popularity are obvious. In the first place, the type was ' neutral '. Its essential feature, an animal carried across the shoulders of its bearer, had long been familiar in pagan art from archaic Greek to Roman imperial times, in divine figures (*Hermes Kriophoros*), in *genre* groups (*Moschophoros*), and in personifications of the seasons of spring and winter. To the list of examples cited by Toynbee and Ward Perkins (*op. cit.* 122–3) may now be added a 4th-cent. B.C. terra-cotta statuette of a *Kriophoros* recently discovered at Gela in Sicily (*American Journal of Archaeology* lxi (1957) pl. 113, fig. 32 ; *Fasti Archaeologici* 10 (1957) 147, fig. 41). Thus the figure not only had the non-committal character that could be a convenience in persecution

times, but was also one with which the pagan convert would have felt at ease. In the second place, its clear reminiscence of St Luke 15:5 and St John 10:11–16 had important doctrinal implications. It promised, in an age in which fidelity to Christian faith and morals was often sorely tried, forgiveness of post-baptismal sins (hence Tertullian's antagonism towards it and his resentment at its rendering on a cup : *De Pudicitia* 10) and the soul's salvation in the sheepfolds of the Church here and now and of Paradise hereafter. The best and most familiar of these Good Shepherd figures is the marble statuette in the Lateran Museum, of which most of the Shepherd's legs, part of His tunic, His arms and the legs of the lamb held in His hands and part of the lamb's nozzle are modern restorations (Laurent, *op. cit.* pl. 19 ; Thulin, *op. cit.* 238, fig. 12). Christ has long, curly hair, large eyes and slightly parted lips, and He wears a short, slipped tunic (*exomis*) girded at the hips and a leather scrip slung at His left side. This is a *genre* piece carried out in the full Hellenistic tradition. The dress and the treatment of the hair place it in the second half of the 3rd cent.

(ii) Sarcophagi. (1) CHRISTIAN USE OF PAGAN SARCOPHAGI. This practice is well illustrated by a 3rd-cent. piece discovered in the recent excavations beneath St Peter's (M. Guarducci, *San Pietro in uno documento precostantiniano della necropoli vaticana* (1953) 23, fig. 9). It is a typical pagan hunt-sarcophagus, on which the portrait-like equestrian figure of the dead man, supported by *Virtus* (the personification of prowess), is spearing a lion that bounds towards him. To the pagan client, for whom most probably this piece was carved in the first instance, this scene was an allegory of the soul's victory over death and evil—an allegory readily adapted to a Christian context by the Christian woman, Valeria Florentia, who, as the secondary inscription on the lid informs us, caused the bones of her husband, Valerius Vasatulus, to be placed in it. The use of the word *depositio*, an exclusively Christian burial-formula, reveals the creed that the pair professed. The lion, symbol of the ravening powers of death, would personify the dangers that, according to contemporary Christian thought, beset the soul on its way to God at, and immediately after, the moment of death—'*Domine Jesu Christe . . libera eas* (sc. *animas defunctorum*) *de ore leonis*'. For a particularly vivid visual illustration of this prayer, see the funerary plaque of Beratius Niketoras in the Lateran Museum (*Mitteilungen des Deutschen Archaeologischen Instituts : Roemische Abteilung* liii (1938) 50–69, with fig.).

(2) 3RD-CENTURY CHRISTIAN SARCOPHAGI. It is with the carved sarcophagi of the late pre-Constantinian period, of the middle and second half of the 3rd cent., that Christian sculpture first emerges in any considerable bulk ; and nowhere in early Christian art is the mingling of the old and new, the expression of a new idiom in the old vocabulary, displayed more vividly than here. Some specifically Christian scenes, drawn from both Testaments, appear. But taken all in all the main emphasis is on allusive and

symbolical, perhaps designedly 'neutral', themes. The central thought is salvation—the rescuing from evil and death of the instructed and baptized Christian soul through the redeeming act of Christ as Saviour, and the soul's safe enfolding by the *Pastor Bonus* in the celestial pastures. The pastoral-paradise was, indeed, a not uncommon motif of pagan after-life imagery, as on a 3rd-cent. sarcophagus in the Museo Nazionale Romano bearing the name of a high-up civil servant, Julius Achilleus (*Archaeologischer Anzeiger*: (*Jahrbuch des Deutschen Archaeologischen Instituts* lv) (1940) cols. 447–52, figs. 21, 22). There, between two great lions devouring antelopes, symbols of the greed of death, on the curved ends, is a rustic scene depicting the herding of horses, cattle, sheep and goats, and the monumental gateway of the farm. A very similar farm-scene, again with monumental gateway, occurs on a Christian piece in the Lateran Museum (F. Gerke, *Die christlichen Sarkophage der vorkonstantinischen Zeit* (1940) pl. 3, fig. 1); but there it is terminated on the left by a Good Shepherd group and on the right by a veiled *Orans* standing before a curtain. The meaning of the *Orans* figure in the Christian art of this period has been lengthily debated; but there can be no doubt that here, as also on the pastoral-paradise Christian piece in the Villa Medici in Rome (ibid. pl. 4, fig. 1), the *Orans* represents the soul of the departed Christian in Paradise, offering prayers of praise and thanksgiving for deliverance and perhaps interceding for its friends on earth. The same applies to the Lateran Museum piece with rams on its rounded ends, where an *Orans* stands beside the *Pastor Bonus* and the trees and sheep of Paradise (ibid. pl. 51, fig. 1), and to the piece (almost certainly, if not quite conclusively, Christian) from La Gayolle in Provence, where the *Orans* stands in the same idyllic pastoral context (ibid. pl. 52, fig. 1). There is, indeed, no reason why the *Orans* in any scene of cure or deliverance should symbolize the Christian soul anxiously praying, in some subterranean Hades, for an improvement in its lot (see E. Stommel, *Beiträge zur Ikonographie der konstantinischen Sarkophagplastik* (1954); A. Stuiber, *Refrigerium Interim: die Vorstellungen von Zwischenstand und die frühchristiche Grabkunst* (1957)). These souls have escaped the dangers attendant on death and have already attained to that intermediate state of beatitude (*refrigerium*) which they can possess before the General Resurrection. In their case the petition in the Canon of the Mass—*omnibus in Christo quiescentibus locum refrigerii, lucis, et pacis ut indulgeas deprecamur*—has already been answered.

A good illustration of the narrative and more biblical aspects of pre-Constantinian sarcophagus carving is the Jonah piece in the Lateran Museum (Gerke, *op. cit.*, pl. 1, fig. 1), on the front of which the prophet's swallowing and vomiting by the whale (in the guise of the sea-dragon of classical tradition) and his rest beneath the gourd-tree form the principal themes and occupy most of the space (*see* Plate 2a). In the two lower corners are idyllic sea-scenes, of which the angler in the right-hand

corner (also shown on the La Gayolle piece) is a well-known allegory of baptism. Into the right-hand upper corner is packed the group of a shepherd tending two sheep in a temple-like sheepfold; while three more scenes—the Raising of Lazarus, Moses-Christ-Peter bringing Water from the Rock and the Arrest of Peter (?)—are crammed on to a ledge that cuts horizontally across two-thirds of the upper surface. A minute Noah in his Ark is squeezed in between the second and third Jonah episodes. If, as has been suggested (*Journal of Jewish Studies* vii (1956)), some Jewish composition depicting the Jonah story lay behind the leading elements in this design, it would probably have been pictorial (cf. the famous painted Synagogue of Dura-Europos), not sculptural, since no examples of Jewish narrative sculpture are known (F. Saxl, *Lectures* i (1957) 47), and the composition has been adapted to the needs of Christian teaching on death, on the promise of bodily resurrection, and, in the gourd-tree scene, which is not strictly biblical, on the naked soul's rest in the *refrigerium*. All the diminutive 'interpolated' scenes are expressive of deliverance from death and of the attainment of eternal life in Paradise.

(3) 4TH-CENTURY CHRISTIAN SARCOPHAGI. With the Peace of the Church under Constantine, Christian sarcophagus-carvers largely abandoned the method of allegory and adopted themes that were almost exclusively biblical. But the primary purpose of this novel content was not to narrate the episodes of Bible-history: it was instructive and dogmatic, the subjects being chosen to convey, in varied ways, those Christian truths that were more or less directly linked with the great central topic of salvation. OT scenes were selected for their suitability as types and illustrations of NT events and doctrines. The objections to the commonly accepted theory that the choice of these themes (and of those of catacomb paintings) was determined by the prayers for the dying, the *Ordo Commendationis Animae* (based on Jewish prayers), have been set out by Stuiber (*op. cit.*), who connects them rather with those 'summaries' or pithy narratives presenting figures and events from sacred history which the early Church inherited from the OT and from late Jewish tradition and enriched with some NT examples. It should be noted that in all the 4th-cent. pieces classified below it is the youthful, beardless type of Christ that appears.

The earliest 4th-cent. category may be described as that of the 'Latin frieze-sarcophagi'. On these the main face of the coffin is decorated either with a single frieze, or with two superimposed friezes, of scenes of very small figures, crammed together, regardless of aesthetic principles, in order to enforce as many theological lessons as possible on a single monument. Often a shell or a circular medallion, containing the portrait of the dead person, or the portraits of a pair of dead persons, on a much larger scale, forms the central, focal point of the design; and a couple of small figure-scenes adorn the lid. The frieze-sarcophagi present us with the sculptural counterpart of many of the Roman catacomb-paintings ; and the workshops in which they were carved are likely to have been located in Rome itself or in the immediate neighbourhood. The cycle of salvation begins with man's creation by the Blessed Trinity, portrayed as three identical bearded male figures (Lateran Museum 'Husband-and-Wife' sarcophagus : Laurent, *op. cit.* pl. 22) and ends with the arrests of St Peter and St Paul, symbolic of the passion and eventual deliverance of Christ's Church on earth (ibid.). Among the most popular scenes are those of the Sacrifice of Isaac, which, as Stommel (*op. cit.*) demonstrates, combines in a single group the ideas of death and resurrection, of Good Friday and Easter morning, and was therefore felt to be more complete in content than a straightforward Crucifixion-scene ; the Deliverance of Daniel *ex ore leonis* ; Moses-Christ-Peter bringing Living Water from the Rock ; the Adoration of the Magi, sometimes with the bearded figure of the Holy Ghost standing behind Our Lady's chair (Lateran Museum 'Husband-and-Wife' sarcophagus), a scene more favoured than that of the Adoration of the Shepherds (shown on the lid of the Adelfia and Balerius sarcophagus in the Syracuse Museum : G. Wilpert, *I sarcofagi cristiani antichi* I (1929) pl. 92, fig. 2) in that it covers the Conception, the Nativity and the Epiphany all at once, besides denoting the salvation of Gentile converts ; the Raising of Lazarus. Another favourite group is that of Christ, St Peter and the cock, convincingly interpreted by Stommel (*op. cit.*) as primarily depicting the threefold conferment by Christ on St Peter of the latter's pastoral office : the cock is to remind us of the threefold denial, to which Christ's threefold questioning of Peter corresponded. The fact that the cock scene sometimes occupies the centre of a whole composition indicates its importance as expressing faith in Peter's primacy as *Vicarius Christi*, while it is on the Christian's membership of the Church founded by Christ on Peter that hope of help in the hour of his death depends (Stommel, *op. cit.*).

A slightly later class of 4th-cent. sarcophagi comprises the columnar pieces, on the front of which appears a series of single figures, or small groups of figures, each within a colonnette-flanked niche (see M. Lawrence, *Art Bulletin*, 1932). This scheme ultimately derives from that of the pagan columnar sarcophagi that were produced in large quantities in 2nd- and 3rd-cent. Asiatic workshops and often exported to the West. The chief centre of the production of the Christian columnar pieces has been variously assigned to southern Gaul (M. Lawrence) and Rome (F. Gerke), the arguments for southern Gaul being by no means conclusive. The niches, which are sometimes five sometimes seven in number and are surmounted by an architrave, contain either Christ, seated or standing, in the centre, and Apostles and Prophets at His sides, or Christ or an *Orans* in the centre, with a series of biblical scenes on either side. On an exceptional piece at Arles, trees arching overhead take the place of columns and

architrave. To the columned class also belong the Passion and Resurrection sarcophagi, of which the focal feature in the central niche is the Chi-Rho monogram within a wreath surmounting a cross-like motif, while two Roman soldiers are keeping guard below. The monogram-in-wreath is Christ Himself rising triumphant from the tomb on Easter morning with Good Friday's Cross as His emblem of victory. The lateral niches contain either figures of the Twelve Apostles or scenes from the Passion—Christ before Pilate, the Crowning with Thorns and the Carrying of the Cross, as on a Lateran Museum sarcophagus (Wilpert, *op. cit.* i (1929) pl. 146, fig. 3) (*see* Plate 2b). On the front of another piece in the Lateran Museum (ibid. pl. 121, fig. 4) the central theme is the *Traditio Legis*—Christ enthroned above the heavens, which are personified by the traditional pagan sky-god, and handing the scroll of the New Law to St Peter, while St Paul stands on His other side. Biblical scenes occupy the lateral niches ; and on the short sides of the piece are depicted the cock scene, in one case, Moses-Christ-Peter striking the Rock and the Healing of the Woman with the Issue of Blood, in the other. It is noteworthy that on these sarcophagi the *Traditio Legis* is made exclusively to Peter in his capacity as *Vicarius Christi*. This theme again appears in the centre of the upper frieze of the well-known two-tiered columnar sarcophagus of Junius Bassus, dated 359 by its inscription and now in the museum below St Peter's (F. Gerke, *Der Sarkophag des Iunius Bassus*, 1936). The four other niches of the upper frieze and all five niches of the lower frieze are filled with biblical scenes, while the short sides show purely pagan compositions of vintaging and harvesting Cupids, to convey, presumably, the notions of the Vintage and the Harvest of the Lord.

To the last decades of the 4th cent. must be attributed the so-called 'city-gate sarcophagi', on which biblical and other Christian scenes are enacted in front of an architectural background that imitates the walls and gates of a city (see M. Lawrence, *Art Bulletin*, 1927). The favourite theme is the *Traditio Legis* by Christ to St Peter in the presence of the other Apostles ; and to this class also belongs the familiar Crossing-of-the-Red-Sea group of pieces. M. Lawrence suggested that these sarcophagi were mainly carved in northern Italy and southern Gaul by visiting Asiatic craftsmen ; while F. Gerke has noted their close relationship with the Roman 'frieze-sarcophagi'.

(4) MISCELLANEOUS CHRISTIAN SARCOPHAGI. There are a number of interesting Christian pieces of the 3rd and 4th cents. that cannot be fitted into any of the above categories. First, there are the Christian counterparts of the pagan 'strigilated' sarcophagi, especially characteristic of the 3rd cent., on which large portions of the front are occupied by two areas of vertical or S-curved flutings, generally with a figured panel in the centre, between the strigilated areas, and a figured panel at each of the two extremities. From Ostia comes such a piece, probably of 3rd-cent. date, with the figure of a dead Christian at

either end and, between the strigilated areas, Christus-Orpheus accompanied by sheep and a dove in a tree, in place of the wild beasts that surround His pagan prototype (Wilpert, *op. cit.* ii (1923) pl. 256, fig. 6). A 4th-cent. strigilated piece, which was placed beneath the floor of Old St Peter's and came to light during the recent Vatican excavations, shows an *Orans*, flanked by palm-trees, in the central panel and on the lid eight portly dolphins rolling along in double file through waves from which emerge two tridents, emblems of Neptune (Toynbee and Ward Perkins, *op. cit.* pl. 29). This is a Christian version of the pagan theme of the journey of the souls of the departed on the backs of marine creatures across the ocean to the Blessed Isles (ibid. pl. 28). In the Lateran collection is a notable example of the pagan inhabited vine-scroll adapted to a Christian context (Wilpert, *op. cit.* i (1929) pl. 117, fig. 4). On the front of this sarcophagus minute Cupids and Psyches are harvesting grapes, milking goats, etc., while three large-scale Good Shepherds, a bearded one in the centre, and a beardless one at either end, of the design, stand on pedestals that are adorned in low relief with pagan motifs (Bacchic masks, griffins, tripod). The Good Shepherds' and the Cupids' hair-styles, and the type of drilling used in the rendering of the vine, suggest for this piece, despite the wholly symbolic nature of its subject-matter, a date in the early 4th rather than in the 3rd cent. Here it should be noted that when the Good Shepherd appears in duplicate or triplicate on one and the same monument, these figures must represent, not Christ Himself, but His followers and imitators. Lastly, mention must be made of another Vatican find, the lid of what was probably, although not certainly, a Roman ' frieze-sarcophagus ', on which are represented the story of Joseph, a theme otherwise unknown in the early-Christian sarcophagus-repertory, and the Adoration of the Magi, where the most noteworthy feature is a large plain cross behind Our Lady's chair, perhaps the earliest direct representation of the Cross in orthodox Christian pictorial art that is so far known (*Rivista di Archaeologia Cristiana* xxi (1944-5) 249 ff.). This lid is in the crypt of St Peter's.

(5) 5TH-CENTURY CHRISTIAN SARCOPHAGI. A well-known Ravenna group of carved sarcophagi illustrates the persistence, in the Christian art of the 5th cent., of the naturalistic, representational, Graeco-Roman style. The commonest themes are the Apostles offering their crowns to Christ, the *Traditio Legis* (sometimes to St Paul, instead of to St Peter) in the presence of the other Apostles, and Christ with St Peter and St Paul only. Two of the pieces with biblical scenes may be specially noted. There is a spirited and vivid Adoration of the Magi on the front, and a Daniel among the Lions and a Raising of Lazarus on the short sides, of the sarcophagus of the Exarch Isaac in the Church of San Vitale (M. Lawrence, *The Sarcophagi of Ravenna* (1945) fig. 12). On the short sides of a piece in the ' Sepolcreto di Braccioforte' are a charming Visitation and a no less delightful Annunciation, in which Our Lady

sits spinning, distaff in hand and wool-basket beside her, while Gabriel bows respectfully towards her as he makes his salutation—*Ave Maria, gratia plena* (ibid. figs. 33, 34). On other Ravenna sarcophagi it is symbolic figures—lambs, stags, peacocks—that dominate the decoration.

III Mosaics.

(i) **Floor-mosaics.** Of the Christian floor-mosaics of our period the earliest, dating from the first half of the 4th cent., and the most interesting, are those arranged in two fields on the floor of the first basilica at Aquileia. In the one field are compartments of various shapes, framed by guilloche borders and containing naturalistic figures of birds and animals, including Pegasus, a borrowed pagan symbol of resurrection, and a cock-and-tortoise-combat, an allegory of the fight between the Christian faith and paganism (*see* Plate 3a). In the other field are figure-scenes, including a Victory holding wreath and palm above a vase and a receptacle containing loaves—probably a Eucharistic allusion (Laurent, *op. cit.*, 172-3 ; G. Brusin, *Aquileia* (1924) 267, fig. 262).

(ii) **Wall and vault mosaics.** Until the excavation during the 1940s of the Vatican necropolis, the earliest known Christian wall- or vault-mosaic was that in the apse of Old St Peter's, executed under Constans and destroyed when Constantine's church was demolished, but recorded in the careful copy that was made of it, at the request of Clement VIII, in 1592 (J. Wilpert, *Die römischen Mosaiken und Malereien* (1917) i, fig. 114 and pp. 361-7). Its principal theme was Our Lord enthroned between St Peter and St Paul. But among the mausolea on the Vatican that Constantine obliterated, by packing them with earth to form a level platform for his church, was the tiny family-tomb of the Julii, originally built in the 2nd cent. for the burial of a pagan infant and completely redecorated in the mid-3rd cent., when its owners embraced the Christian faith and caused its low vault and three of its walls to be adorned with polychrome figured mosaics worked in *tesserae* of opaque glass paste. The scenes on the walls are unequivocally Christian—the angler-scene, allegory of Baptism, on the north wall, Jonah falling into the whale's maw, allegory of death and resurrection, on the east wall, and the Good Shepherd on the west wall. There can, then, be no doubt but that the charioteer, with rayed nimbus, holding a globe in his left hand, and raising his right hand in greeting, who, surrounded by a great spreading vine, occupies the centre of the vault, is Christus-Helios, Our Lord in the guise of the ' baptized ' pagan sun-god as *Sol Salutis* and *Sol Iustitiae*. For a commentary on these mosaics in the light of contemporary Christian writings, see O. Perler, *Die Mosaiken der Juliergruft im Vatikan* (1953). The other surviving wall mosaics of our period in Rome are, first, the much restored, but still impressive, scenes of Our Lord enthroned between Apostles in the apses of Santa Pudenziana, *c.* 400 (Laurent, *op. cit.* 179-81, pl. 50) and of St Paul's-without-the-Walls, *c.* 440-60 (ibid. 183-4, pl. 51) ; secondly, those that cover the triumphal arch (NT scenes) and the spaces between the clerestory windows and the columns of the nave (OT scenes) of St Mary Major. The date of the St Mary Major's mosaics has been lengthily debated ; but it is very likely that we have in them examples of 5th-cent. Christian monumental art. For their literature, see Laurent, *op. cit.*, 184–9, 207 and C. Cecchelli, *I mosaici della basilica di Santa Maria Maggiore* (1956). Despite the Byzantine rigidity which has begun to invade some of the figures, these mosaics, seen as a whole, carry on the naturalistic, pictorial tradition of the ancient Graeco-Roman world. Only one detail can be mentioned here. In the uppermost scene on the right-hand side of the triumphal arch, that of the Presentation in the Temple, the temple is not that of Jerusalem, but of Eternal Rome, whose image is unmistakably depicted in the pediment (Laurent, *op. cit.* pl. 52).

Of the Ravenna mosaics, those in the Mausoleum of Galla Placidia and in the Catholic and Arian Baptisteries fall within the 5th cent. (Laurent, *op. cit.* 196–200, pls. 38, 56–60 ; C. O. Nordström, *Ravennastudien* (1953) pls. 1, 2, 3, 4, fig. a, 7, 8, 9, I, II ; G Bovini, ' La decorazione musiva del cosidetto mausoleo di Galla Placidia ' (*Bull. Economico della Camera di Commercio di Roma* (1954)). In the Galla Placidia monument it is the Good Shepherd scene, in one of the lunettes, that is most noticeably classical in style. Our Lord is young and beardless and is seated in an informal attitude, affectionately tickling the chin of one of His flock, in the midst of a Hellenistic landscape. In the cupola of each baptistery the Baptism-scene shows naturalistic water and landscape features and the Jordan personified as a river-god in the full pagan manner. In the Catholic baptistery Our Lord is bearded ; in the Arian, He is beardless. In the former building, in a circle outside the central picture, is a lively procession of Apostles offering their crowns to Christ ; and outside that again is another circular zone containing porticoed *exedrae*, in each of which is seen, alternately, an empty throne for Christ and an altar supporting a Gospel-book. In the Arian Baptistery, encircling the central picture, is a single zone, in which Apostles in procession converge on an empty throne.

The mosaic zone at the base of the cupola of the Church of St George at Salonika is generally assigned to the 5th cent. (Laurent, *op. cit.* 195–6, pl. 55). It displays a fantastic architectural drop-scene, almost Pompeian in appearance, composed of two-storeyed palaces, *exedrae*, and porticoes, with columns, cupolas, hanging lamps, curtains and perching birds, while frontal praying figures occupy the foreground. H. Torp has recently attempted to date these mosaics to the closing decades of the 4th cent. (*Proceedings, ixth. Byzantine Congress at Salonika* (1955) 491)

IV Roman catacomb-painting. The Christians of the first two centuries possessed no communal cemeteries. The poor were buried either in pagan graveyards (e.g the Vatican necropolis) or in the family tombs of their wealthier co-religionists. It

was not until the beginning of the 3rd cent. that the first specifically Christian subterranean cemetery was founded and organized in Rome by St Calixtus. This was known as τὸ κοιμητήριον, and it is represented today by the oldest part of the catacomb beside the Via Appia that bears St Calixtus's name. We may therefore take it that catacomb-painting as a Christian art did not develop on any scale until after c. 200, although a few paintings in the privately-owned hypogea may go back to the latter part of the 2nd cent. In view of the extremely popular and often highly eclectic character of painting of this kind, it is useless to attempt to arrange the pictures in the Roman catacombs in any chronological sequence on stylistic grounds alone. Differences of style are to be explained less by date than by varying degrees of artistic skill on the part of the craftsmen or by varying tastes or by conscious harking back to earlier formularies. On the other hand, the costumes, hair-styles and general content of some paintings clearly proclaim them to be later than the rest. No underground pictures are likely to have been executed after c. 410.

The repertory of painted themes is restricted—in some ways more restricted, in others less so, than that of the carved sarcophagi. But here, as there, the keynote is salvation, the story of man's redemption, beginning with the Fall, continued through the OT and the history of Our Saviour's Life and Passion, worked out in the sacramental life of the Church on earth, and culminating in the Christian soul's beatitude in Paradise.

The OT themes may be listed under four headings. (i) the Fall : Adam and Eve ; (ii) Patriarchs : Noah (a favourite), the Sacrifice of Isaac (fairly common), Jacob's Dream (once), Moses striking the Rock (the first favourite), the Burning Bush, the Rain of Manna, the Threatening of Moses and Aaron ; (iii) Kings and Prophets : David and Goliath, Balaam and the Star, Micheas, Elias going up to Heaven, Jonah (the second favourite) ; (iv) Others : Job, Tobias, Daniel among the Lions (the third favourite), Susanna, the Three Children refusing to adore the Image and in the Fiery Furnace.

The scenes from the NT fall into seven groups. (i) the Infancy of Christ : the Annunciation (twice), the Crib (once), the Magi and the Star (twice), the Magi and Herod (three times), the Adoration of the Magi, the Virgin and Child with Balaam and the Star (once), a late Virgin and Child with the Chi-Rho Monogram ; (ii) the Baptism of Christ ; (iii) Cures : of the Blind Man, of the Leper or of the Man Possessed, of the Bent Woman (once), of the Paralytic Man ; (v) other Miracles : the Raising of Lazarus, the Raising of Jairus's Daughter (once), the Multiplication of Bread, Cana ; (vi) other Events : the Samaritan Woman at the Well ; (vii) the Passion : St Peter's Denial, the Mocking of Christ (once).

The symbolic representations of Our Lord are of six types. (i) the Good Shepherd, in many variants ; (ii) Christus-Orpheus ; (iii) Christus-Helios ; (iv) Christ as Lawgiver ; (v) Christ seated with Apostles ;

(vi) the bearded Christus Pantocrator (a late type).

Among specific Saints, St Peter and St Paul are represented.

Under the heading of Sacraments come a scene of Baptism, Eucharistic symbols, the Eucharistic Consecration—in one case at a small three-legged table (*see* Plate 3b), in another, at a semicircular table (*sigma*) at which seven persons are seated, while the celebrant spreads his hands over a plate of loaves ; the consecration or ' clothing ' of a virgin.

The next world is represented by a Judgment-scene, and by dead persons, described as being *in pace*, praying as *Orantes* amid the trees, flowers and birds of Paradise.

Among the ' neutral ' decorative motifs may be noted a spreading vine ; the flowers, corn-ears, vines and olives of the four seasons ; and the numerous soul-birds (peacocks, parrots, etc.) that are familiar also in pagan funerary art. Purely pagan motifs are a Cupid ; Cupid and Psyche ; a Bacchic head ; an Oceanus head ; and personifications of the seasons—all used symbolically. Reminiscent again of pagan funerary art are the daily-life and professional scenes. These include representations of catacomb-diggers (who also formed a kind of ' minor order ' of the early Church) ; olive-gatherers ; a baker ; a green-grocer ; coopers with their barrels ; a shopping-scene ; scenes from the *annona* (the corn-supply of Rome) ; and the transport of *amphorae*. We should probably classify as episodes from daily life the two rollicking banquet-scenes with inscriptions in which orders are being given to two serving-maids named Irene and Agape. These are hardly decorous enough to be intended to represent even funerary feasts (*refrigeria*) on the pagan model, still less the Eucharist or the *Cena Caelestis*.

On the paintings of the Roman catacombs J. Wilpert's monumental work, *Die Malereien der Katakomben Roms* (1903) is still fundamental.

V Syncretistic painting in Rome. In addition to the public and officially-sponsored Catholic catacombs there are six important subterranean sites, located either in or near Rome, and all, with one exception, sepulchral in purpose, which appear to have been of a more or less private or unofficial character. All of them, to judge by the paintings that adorn their walls and vaults, were syncretistic, that is to say, owned by persons whose religious creed was compounded of Christian and pagan elements fused together in varying proportions. To what extent such persons were formal heretics, it is sometimes hard to say. But their Christian iconographic repertory differs notably from, and is, as a matter of fact, considerably richer in its range than, the repertory of the Catholic catacombs ; and their choice of themes for these paintings reveals a far more thorough-going acceptance of specifically pagan images and myths than that displayed by any other group of Christian monuments that we have so far considered. The principal work in which these sites (with the exception of the last on the list)

are collected together is C. Cecchelli's *Monumenti cristiano-eretici di Roma* (1944).

(i) The Via Livenza hypogeum (Via Salaria). This dates from the 4th cent. and was almost certainly not sepulchral. Its chief feature is a niche flanked by purely pagan paintings, Diana hunting on the one side and a Nymph on the other. At the foot of the niche is a basin for water. On one of the walls beside the niche is figure-decoration in two tiers, below, a pagan painting of boating, fishing, and swimming Cupids, above, a mosaic that depicts Moses striking the Rock. Since Diana and the Nymphs had aquatic associations the hypogeum is likely to have been the scene of a pagan water-cult, with the Moses episode borrowed from Christian iconography.

(ii) The hypogeum of Trebius Justus (Via Latina). This sepulchral monument derives its title from the name of the deceased, which appears in inscriptions accompanying the principal paintings. Here we see three scenes in which the dead youth is (*a*) seated in the midst of writing-materials of every description, (*b*) accompanied by his parents, who hold up between them a cloth containing funerary offerings, (*c*) standing in the centre of a quartette of gardeners with tubs of plants. Other paintings show building-operations and the transport of garden-produce. So far nothing has been cited from this tomb that might not fit a pagan family, the members of which had made reputations as men of letters and as managers of building and market-gardening businesses. But a painting of the Good Shepherd on the vault of one of the chambers gives the place a Christian flavour. We seem, in fact, to be dealing here with a Christian family whose outlook was still strongly coloured by its pagan past.

(iii) The hypogeum of Vincentius and Vibia (Via Appia). In the paintings of this monument the pagan elements are even more explicitly stressed than they are in (i) and (ii) ; and there is not a single scene among them that is specifically Christian. Indeed, it is only in virtue of their superficially Christian colouring that these works merit a place in our series ; and it would seem that the owners were pagans who borrowed certain art-forms and some religious phraseology from their Christian neighbours. The main inscription on the paintings tells us that the place was Vincentius's ' gate of peace ' (*ostium quietis*), a phrase with a Christian flavour, and that he was priest of the oriental mystery-god, Sabazios. One scene shows Vincentius reclining at a banquet with six other priests ; another depicts Vibia's death and descent into Hades under the guise of the Rape of Persephone (*abreptio Vibies et descensio*) ; a third scene shows her judgment before the thrones of Pluto and Persephone ; and a fourth presents her *introductio* into paradise by an *angelus bonus* and her feasting there in the company of persons labelled *bonorum iudicio iudicati*. Death, Judgment, Heaven and Hell—here we have the pagan counterparts of the ' four last things ' of Christianity.

(iv) The tomb of M. Clodius Hermes under

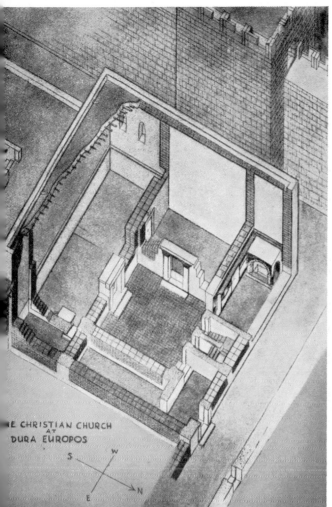

Plate 1a

Drawing of 3rd century house-church
at Dura Europos
(*Yale University Art Gallery*)

Plate 1b
4th century marble statuette
of the youthful Christ
(*Museo Nazionale delle Terme*)
Photo : Anderson

Plate 2a   Pre-Constantinian sarcophagus, showing the story of Jonah   (Lateran Christian Museum, Rome)   Photo : Anderson

Plate 2b   4th century columnar sarcophagus showing scenes from the Passion   (Lateran Christian Museum, Rome)   Photo : The Vatican

Plate 3a   Early 4th century mosaic from earliest church at Aquileia, north Italy
(*Atteliu Brisighelli di Udine*)

Plate 3b   Painting depicting the Eucharistic consecration   (*Catacomb of St Calixtus, Rome*)
Photo : Alinari

Plate 4a
3rd century syncretistic painting
of St Paul   (*Hypogeum of the Aurelli,
Viale Manzoni, Rome*)
Photo : Alinari

Plate 4b
Engraved glass bowl of the 4th century
depicting the sacrifice of Isaac
(*Landesmuseum, Trier*)

the Church of San Sebastiano (Via Appia). On the exterior of the ' attic ' that surmounts this house-tomb are a series of Christian paintings very different from any yet discovered in the official catacombs. They are an idyllic *Pastor Bonus* scene ; a banqueting scene, that has been variously interpreted as the Miracle of Cana, the Feeding of the Multitude, an *Agape*, or a *Cena Caelestis* ; and the story of the Gadarene Swine, which is unique in early-Christian iconography. Inside this tomb are three more quasi-Christian paintings—what appears to be a ' camouflaged ' Ascension, mourners surrounding a corpse, and figures grouped round a seated person-age, who might be a Christian bishop performing a ceremony. The owners of this tomb were probably Christian sectaries of some kind.

(v) **The hypogeum of the Aurelii**, situated in the modern Viale Manzoni, inside the circuit of the Aurelian Walls, and dating from the first half, or middle, of the 3rd cent., probably belonged to Gnostics. That the owners were Christians of a sort is clear from the Latin cross (not displayed in Catholic art until a hundred years later) painted on a staircase wall and from the striking figures, in the principal chamber, of the Twelve Apostles, among whom the familiar types of St Peter and St Paul (see Plate 4a) can be recognized, although here the primacy seems to be accorded to St James, from whom the Naassenian Gnostics claimed to have received the true doctrine. All the most important pictures in the tomb are concentrated in this cham-ber. The bearded shepherd, seated with an open scroll upon a flowery hill, on the slopes of which sheep and goats are feeding, is more likely to be some Gnostic ' pastor ' than Christ Himself, Who is always beardless in this early phase of Christian art. An impressive *ovatio*-scene of a Roman general riding into Rome, followed, and received, by crowds, may well be a disguised rendering, in view of the ass in stall featured in one corner, of the Triumphal Entry into Jerusalem. A bird's-eye prospect of a walled and porticoed ' forum ' and one of a walled park, the gates of both being guarded by the Gnostic Sophia, represent the Celestial City and the gardens of Paradise. In a banquet-scene, perhaps a conflation of the Last Supper and the *Cena Caelestis*, the Chalice, which the Naassenian Gnostics exalted above the Host, is noticeably prominent. But the most intriguing scene of all depicts the return of Odysseus to Penelope who stands between him and her loom—an episode adapted to a Chris-tian context as an allegory of the soul's return to its celestial home ; while there is literary proof that, to the Naassenian Gnostics, Penelope's suitors, here seen in the guise of three naked men, stood for the ' saved ' en route for Paradise, which is delineated in this painting as an idyllic ' Ithacan ' landscape in the background. This is not the only episode from the Odyssey that found a place in early-Christian thought and art. For instance, on two sarco-phagus-lids (G. Wilpert, *I sarcofagi cristiani antichi* i (1929) pls. 25, fig. 3 ; 24, fig. 7) Odysseus, bound to the mast and delivering his companions from the

Sirens' wiles, is a type of Christ Who, once bound to the Cross, saves His people in the ship of His Church from the perils and allurements of the world (cf. H. Rahner, ' Antenna Crucis i : Odysseus am Mastbaum ' (*Zeitschrift f. Kathol. Theologie* lxv (1941)). The best modern illustrated discussion of the hypogeum of the Aurelii is Part ii of J. Carco-pino's *De Pythagore aux apôtres* (1956), where will be found references to the earlier literature of the monument.

(vi) **The private catacomb on the Via Latina.** The paintings in this burial-place not only introduce us to many scenes from both Testaments never found in the official catacombs, but they also illus-trate the furthest lengths to which, so far as we know, Christians, or quasi-Christians, ever went in the matter of borrowing and adapting pagan other-world allegories and imagery. The pictures fall into four main categories. (1) OT scenes : the themes that are new to early-Christian painting are Cain and Abel, Noah Drunk, the Flood, Jacob and Esau, Joseph with Ephraim and Manasses, the Crossing of the Red Sea, Balaam and his Ass, Abraham enter-taining the Three Angels, Samson and the Lion and others. (2) Among the novel (so far as painting goes) NT episodes are the Massacre of the Innocents, the Sermon on the Mount and the Roman soldiers casting lots into a vase for Christ's garment at the Crucifixion ; and there is a new variant of the Raising of Lazarus, in which the miracle is wit-nessed by a vast crowd of Jews. (3) Of the daily-life scenes the most remarkable is that of a medical class, in which a doctor lectures to a group of pupils in the course of treating a prostrate patient. (4) The purely pagan paintings include six from the Hercules-cycle—a selection of his Labours and the hero grouped with his patroness, Minerva. There is ample evidence to show that Hercules, in his capacity of conqueror of death and evil and as the friend and ' saviour ' of mankind, was regarded in certain Christian circles as a kind of type of Christ (see M. Simon, *Hercule et le christianisme* (1935)). For photographs of a selection of these paintings, see *La Civiltà Cattolica* (April, 1956) ; *Römische Quartalschrift für christliche Altertumskunde und Kir-chengeschichte* li (1956) ; *American Journal of Archae-ology* lxi (1957).

VI The Christian minor arts. The works of minor art with Christian content can be but summarily treated here. They comprise (i) vessels of engraved and gold-leaf glass, mostly of 4th-cent. date, with portraits or biblical scenes that follow closely the iconography of monumental works (see Plate 4b) ; (ii) the 5th-cent. ivory diptychs and caskets (e.g. the well-known Brescia casket) and the prob-ably 5th-cent. ivory throne of Maximianus at Ravenna ; (iii) silver-work (e.g. the Proiecta casket in the British Museum and (if it be accepted as authentic) the Antioch chalice in New York) ; and (iv) wood-work, of which the 5th-cent. carved doors in the Church of Santa Sabina on the Aventine constitute the most outstanding example. One of the panels of these doors depicts a relatively realistic

Crucifixion; and the iconography of categories (ii), (iii) and (iv) includes many themes, both biblical and non-biblical, that are wholly unknown to 3rd- and 4th-cent. Christian painting and sculpture. A general account of these objects, with good illustrations, will be found in chapters xx, xxi and xxiv of Laurent's book. To the bibliography there cited should be added R. Delbrueck's *Probleme der Lipsanothek in Brescia* (1952), and his 'Notes on the Wooden Doors of Santa Sabina' (*Art Bulletin* (1952)).

Bibliography. The works relevant to each particular category of objects have been cited in the course of this article, but a brief résumé of the chief works cited may be made here : M. Laurent, *L'Art chrétien des origines à Justinien* (1956) ; *J. G. Davies, *The Original Development of Early Christian Architecture* (1952) ; G. Wilpert, *Die Malereien der Katakomben Roms* (1903) ; *I sarcofagi cristiani antichi* i (1929) ii (1933) ; E. Stommel, *Beiträge zur Ikonographie der konstantinischen Sarkophagplastik* (1954) ; J. M. C. Toynbee and J. B. Ward Perkins, *The Shrine of St Peter* (1956) ; *E. Dyggve, *History of Salonitan Christianity* (1951) ; O. Perler, *Die Mosaiken der Juliergruft im Vatikan* (1953) ; C. Cecchelli, *Monumenti cristiano-eretici di Roma* (1944) ; J. Carcopino, *De Pythagore aux apôtres* (1956).

J. M. C. T.

ASCENSION OF CHRIST, THE The fact of the Ascension as it is narrated in Luke and Acts will first be examined (I), and the various traditional interpretations put upon these texts will be briefly discussed (II). These lead naturally to the question (III) of the feast and of its separation from Pentecost. A section (IV) will be devoted to the relation of this mystery to theories of space, and its place in the scheme of salvation will finally be considered (V).

I The fact of the Ascension is most simply expressed in the Apostles' Creed : ' He ascended into heaven'. (For the clause : 'Sitteth at the right hand of God', *see* HEAVEN.) Additions to this brief phrase were made in later formularies of the faith. Epiphanius (D 13) insisted on the reality of Christ's body in the Ascension, and he was followed in this by Leo IX (D 344) and Innocent III (D 429). The Toledo creed of A.D. 400 is the first to include the statement that the Ascension was on the fortieth day (D 20). This Spanish formula seems to have influenced the whole Western Church, for in the profession of faith of Leo IX (D 344) for Peter of Antioch in A.D. 1053 the fortieth day is again mentioned, as also in the formula of the Council of Lyons (D 462) from A.D. 1274. The Council of Florence did not repeat the words, and they are not found in the formula of Pius IV, but it would be temerarious now to deny that the Ascension took place forty days after the Resurrection, even though some of the Fathers have strange views about the meaning of the term ' forty days' in Acts 1:3. Eusebius in his *Demonstratio evangelica* (8:2:110 ; GCS 6:387) goes so far as to say that it is equivalent to the three and a half years of the public life of

Christ. This general belief about the date of the event did not at first affect the liturgy, for not all the early feasts of Christ are anniversaries.

The fact itself of the Ascension is chiefly established by Lk 24:51 and Ac 1:2-11 but it was prophesied by Christ according to Jn 1:51 ; 6:62 ; 14:2 ; 16:28 and 20:17. It was preached by Peter (Ac 3:21), and Paul has already situated it in a scheme of salvation familiar to the Jewish mind (Eph 4:8-10), while in Heb 7:26 and 9:14 the approach of Christ to the Father is compared to the entry of the High Priest into the Holy of Holies. Peter adds further witness (1 Pet 3:22), remarking on the presence of angels at the event. In 1 Tim 3:16 the Ascension figures as one of the principal facts about Christ to be commemorated in an early Christian hymn which is there quoted ; Luke's word ἀνελήφθη is repeated here for the first time in the NT, but the popular character of the hymn suggests that this word was well-established in the vocabulary of the early preaching. It is used by Justin (*dial.* 32:3, and probably in *apol.* 26:1), and Plummer is justified in his note (on Lk 9:51) that claims this as ' the usual biblical expression for ascending to heaven'. The brief statement of the fact in the ending of Mk (16:19) may have been meant to suggest the parallel with Elias (4 Kg 2:11) but, as Chrysostom noticed (PG 50:450), the account there (LXX) speaks of Elias being taken up *as it were* into heaven, while here no such qualification is added.

The search for OT precedents did not lead the Fathers to see much that reminded them of Enoch, Elias or even of the legends of Moses and Isaias, but the vision of Isaias (19:1), where he saw the Lord seated on a light cloud, was brought by Chrysostom into relation with the cloud which Luke describes as taking away from the disciples the further sight of Christ. The words of the angels to the apostles gave warrant for seeing in the cloud a sign of the majesty Christ was now assuming, to hold it till He come again. What is perhaps of more significance is the vision of Ezechiel (11:22-3), in which he saw the Shekinah departing from Jerusalem on the winged chariot of the Cherubim, and this chariot resting on the mountain that is to the east of the city. Theodoret (PG 81:901), who is the only patristic author to have written a full commentary on Ezechiel that still survives, claims the vision as a type of the Ascension.

Luke gives a brief notice of the Ascension in his gospel, and then, in the manner familiar to Jewish historians in the OT, he returns over his account, adding many details in Acts which he had not cared to tell in the gospel. Modern critics, not seeing that Luke is following a practice he had learned from his beloved Septuagint, have argued that the two accounts are so disparate as to be by different authors or to come from different periods of Luke's work. That the gospel account should make the event seem to follow immediately on the Easter apparition while the Acts place some forty days in between is not a sign of Luke having changed his mind or of someone else having corrected him, but of the gradualness of Hebrew historical style. The readings of D and the Old Latin, with their omission both times of the words that describe the actual taking up and with a substitution of a word meaning 'taken away', seem to represent a second century editorial attempt to bring out the naturalness of the happening. This may be due to fear of Docetic misuse of the Ascension as an argument for their view that Christ was abandoned by the Godhead. Tatian seems to have had the words 'he ascended into heaven' from Lk 24:51 in his *Diatessaron*, but the scribes of the Codex Sinaiticus hesitated before including them.

II The interpretation of the Texts. Another cause of uncertainty in the second century, leading probably to emendation of the texts, was the rise of rival views about the time of the Ascension. Jn 13:32, with its emphasis on the immediacy of the glorification that was to come to Christ, seems to have set going among less orthodox Christians a view that Christ went up to heaven straight from the cross at Calvary. The *Gospel of Peter* makes this happen even before He dies ; the *Acts of John* (97-102) have it happen on Olivet during the darkness of the crucifixion, John having fled from Calvary and Christ having followed him, appearing to him in a cave on Olivet and thence being taken up to heaven. Origen himself is troubled about this immediate glorification, not on account of these Docetic fancies but by reason of the promise to the Good Thief (Lk 23:43), which he thinks may have been kept literally (*in Jn*, GCS 4:479). The *Catecheses* of Cyril (PG 33:809) and Chrysostom (PG 49:40) follow this idea, and Cassian reports some strange juggling with the text by heretics to avoid it (*Conlationes* 1:14 ; CSEL 23:8). Tertullian (*de anima* 55) is clear that Christ went down to Limbo before going to heaven, and there are some writers, such as Titus of Bostra (TU 21:245), who take up Origen's suggestion that 'today' in the promise to the Thief meant 'in the new Messianic age'. The principle which will serve for the resolution of these perplexities was already present in the saying of Ignatius (*Smyrn.* 3:3) that after the resurrection Christ was able to eat and drink with His disciples in the flesh though according to the spirit He was already united with the Father. Thus Origen in his newly discovered *Dialektos* (ch. 8) can say, when explaining the meaning of Christ's word to Magdalen : 'Touch Me not', that Christ ascended to the Father and then went to His disciples, as if it made no difference how many times Christ in His risen state left this world and returned to it. Something of the same idea is implied in Jerome's remark in a sermon on Easter (*Anecdota Maredsolana* 3:418) that Sunday is called the day of the Lord because on that day Christ ascended victorious to the Father (*Dominica dicitur quia Dominus in ea victor ascendit ad Patrem*).[1]

<hr>

[1] The statement in the *Ascension of Isaias* (Ethiopic version 9:16) that the Messias was to remain on earth 545 days after rising from the dead implies a belief on the

The opinion that the Ascension happened on the day of Pentecost can be found in the statement of Eusebius (*De solemnitate paschali*, PG 24:700) : 'The number of the fifty-days (Pentecost) is not established by the seven weeks, but, overshooting these, it sets the great feast-day of the Ascension of Christ as a seal upon the one final day that comes after the seven weeks.' The *Doctrine of Addai* (Pratten *Syriac Documents*, p. 36) is even more explicit : 'The first day of the week and the completion of Pentecost, . . . on this same day the disciples came from Nazareth . . . to the mountain which is called Baith Zaithe, Our Lord being with them but not being visible to them. And at the time of the early dawn Our Lord lifted up His hands and laid them upon the heads of the eleven disciples, and gave to them the gift of the priesthood ; and suddenly a bright cloud received Him and they beheld Him as He went up to heaven. . . .' It is possible that the *Epistle of Barnabas* (15:9) which places the Ascension on a Sunday is to be understood in this sense too. The opinion must have been widespread,[2] for it seems to have led to the emendation of the text of Ac 1:2, where by the transposition of a phrase Luke is made to say that Christ chose His apostles by means of the Holy Ghost, as if the visible descent of the Spirit upon those whom He had that moment blessed made it certain that they were set apart from the rest of the hundred and twenty gathered in the room. At the beginning of his commentary on Matthew, Jerome tells us (PL 26:57) that the Montanists began to fast after Pentecost because then the Bridegroom was taken away, and though this evidence would not be of much value by itself it counts when added to the total. But the most strange piece of evidence is that provided by the pilgrim lady Etheria that in her visit to Jerusalem she found the Ascension being commemorated on the day of Pentecost.

III The rise of the feast of the Ascension cannot be exactly dated, for the account in Etheria has received widely different datings between 380 and 450, but there is one firm statement in Filastrius (*haereses* 121, from about the year 384, and valid for North Italy) that the Ascension was kept on the fortieth day after Easter. Etheria herself (*Itinerarium*, 43) is quite definite that after the descent of the Holy Spirit had been commemorated on the morning of Pentecost the faithful assembled again in the afternoon at the Mount of Olives and the NT accounts

<hr>

part of its Gnostic or Jewish-Christian authors that this was the time that elapsed after Christ's resurrection. The period of eighteen months seems to have been arrived at artificially by taking half the length of the public life or else from the numerical significance of Jesus' name IH. This view is called heretical by Ephrem in his *Commentary on Acts* (1:2). He seems to have found it in a work called *The Childhood of Christ*. Irenaeus (1:1:5 and 1:28:7 H) attributes such a view to the Ophites and to some of the Valentinians.

[2] Augustine (*contra Felicem* 1:4) reads : *in die quo apostolos elegit per Spiritum sanctum et praecepit praedicare*. . . . The author of the *contra Varimadum* (late fourth century, in Spain) has almost the same, and Ephrem and the Syriac of Thomas of Harkel (text and margin) support this reading.

of the Ascension were read ; then a procession was formed and went slowly back to the city, ending with mass late at night at the church of Sion. The old Armenian lectionary which gives the readings for the feasts kept at Jerusalem about the middle of the 5th cent. (Conybeare, *Rituale Armenorum*, pp. 509, 525) has no trace of an Ascension feast, though the later lectionary-commentary of Asharuni (from *c.* 690) says that the account of the Ascension was read at Pentecost. On the other hand the Arian document which is known as the *Apostolic Constitutions*, and which dates from about 380, has (5:20:2) the feast of the Ascension on the fifth day of the week, forty days from Easter. The earliest homilies for the feast are those of Gregory of Nyssa and of Chrysostom (PG 46:689, preached before 394 ; and PG 50:441, before 400). Augustine (*ep.* 54:1 *ad Januarium*) asserts that the feast was kept universally according to apostolic tradition, but he does not say it had a day to itself ; he cannot have had in Africa a clear picture of what was happening at Jerusalem. The general impression one receives from the evidence is that a separate feast of the Ascension was coming into use gradually from 375 to 450, though the earlier idea of commemorating the triumphal departure of Christ on Pentecost Day itself was not everywhere displaced even by 450. An account of the celebration of the feast at Constantinople in 426, when Sisinnius became bishop, is given by Socrates (*hist. eccl.* 7:26 ; PG 67:800). The importance of this gradual evolution for the dogmatic theologian who is trying to investigate the rise of the feast of the Assumption of Our Lady will be obvious.

The liturgical books of the Church carry evidence of the Ascension in the Canon of the Mass where the words *sed et in caelos gloriosae ascensionis* occur in the Anamnesis ; they are found in the Gelasian canon as given in the Stowe missal and in the Vatican MS. (Wilson, *The Gelasian Sacramentary*, 235), but are missing in earlier forms of the canon in Hippolytus' *Traditio apostolica*, in the Der-Balyzeh papyrus, the Ethiopic anaphora of the Apostles (Brightman, *Eastern Liturgies*, 233) and the *Sacramentary* of Serapion (JTS 1 (1900), 105). One curious feature occurs in the *Missale Gothicum*, where the *Immolatio* (or Preface) for the Mass of Ascension Day is practically the same as our present Preface for Pentecost : *Ascendit super omnes caelos ; sedetque ad dexteram tuam ; promissum spiritum sanctum in filios adoptionis effudit.*[1] This would seem to be a survival from the time when both mysteries were commemorated on one day. The Rogations which in most Western liturgies precede Ascension day are generally ascribed to Mamertus, bishop of Vienne (*c.* 468), and they clearly suppose that a fully established feast of the Ascension had been in existence for some time. The mention of the Ascension in the *Suscipe sancta Trinitas* is hardly earlier than A.D. 1000.

IV The Ascension and theories of space is a subject which considerably exercised medieval theologians. On the assumption that the outermost sphere (of the Ptolemaic world-picture) was made of impenetrable material there had to be a special miracle postulated for Christ to pass bodily through this. This outside shell of the universe was also looked upon (e.g. by St Thomas 3a:57:4: @2) as the limit beyond which there could be nothing worthy of the name of locality but where a complete vacuum reigned. The Leonine edition of St Thomas omits this difficulty and solution, but the editors, in the Preface to that volume (11:xviii), admit that the textual problem is far from clear. The MSS. which have the paragraph may have derived it from *Quodlibet*, 6:3@:2, where St Thomas made a change in his earlier opinions about the empyrean. The idea that Christ in glory existed bodily in that void led to Durandus and others making the objection that sensation would be impossible to Him, as no sense-impressions could be transmitted where there was no medium to take them. Suarez enlarged upon the difficulty of this conception, saying (*Opera*, 19:960) that this supposed that all the blessed would have fixed places in such a heaven, all arranged according to their merit, as in a Fra Angelico picture. Suarez (ibid. 970) goes on to assert that the continuous motion of Christ through the heavens lasted only so long as the eyes of the disciples could follow Him. What happened after that can only be conjectured by more or less probable arguments. This theological opinion of Suarez, given in the days when the Copernican theories had not yet been fully discussed, is of greater significance at the present time, when many popular difficulties are brought against the doctrine. A common misconception is to regard place as a physical substance into which, as into a bucket, bodies have to be put. To restrict oneself to a mathematical system of co-ordinates is not much help, as the illusion of containment by a place is still there. The reticence of Suarez is to be commended, especially in his remark (ibid. 970) that while there is no controversy among Catholics about Christ's upward motion while He was within sight of the Apostles, there is disagreement about what happened afterwards.[2] The attitude of post-Copernican theologians may be summed up in the judgment of Scheeben (*Dogmatik* [1882], 3:307) that with the falling away of the Ptolemaic theory there falls away too its theological application, since nothing forces us to admit that the ideally perfect and most excellent point of the universe is also at its uttermost zenith ; it might equally well be at its centre. If heaven be defined as the system of conditions in which redeemed human beings while still remaining human can enjoy the vision of God for ever, it is easy to see that Christ in His humanity must be part of those conditions, while it is no less difficult to penetrate the mystery of how these conditions are related to our present knowledge of the world

---

[1] It is the Preface of the Mass for the Vigil of Pentecost in the *Leonine Sacramentary* (Feltoe 24).

[2] Durasse motum ascendentis donec nubes suscepit eum . . . nulla est controversia ; de reliqua parte motus dissentiunt catholici.

geographically and astronomically. Lutheran literal-mindedness took Eph. 4:10 to mean that Christ's body in heaven somehow filled the universe, whereas the traditional interpretation understood either that Christ by ascending had *fulfilled* the last prophecy, or that the gifts He sent from heaven reached to the farthest corners of the world.

V The place of the Ascension in the scheme of salvation is worked out by St Thomas (3a:57:6) ; from the point of view of the Christian there is to be found in the Ascension a motive for increased faith, hope and charity, and for a greater reverence towards the humanity of Christ, while from Christ's own point of view the Ascension is a glorification (Phil 2:9 and CCS 907d) and a preparation of the way for Christians to follow ; it is an entry within the heavenly sanctuary, there to make intercession for us, and it is an essential preliminary to the beginning of that shower of gifts from heaven which He promised to His disciples. For the heavenly consummation of Christ's sacrifice, *see* EUCHARIST. Thus while the passion of Christ merited our salvation, the Ascension sets going the machinery that is to bring it about. In one of the verse-inscriptions attributed to Pope Damasus (PL 13:377) this same idea is expressed for the fourth century :

> Christ vanquished death; of right He goeth home,
> To show His followers their life to come.[1]

If the Ascension thus had a didactic purpose, it may be asked, as it was asked by St Thomas (3a:57:6@3), whether Christ has descended to earth in full human nature since that time. The appearance to St Paul on the way to Damascus is an obvious case in point. St Thomas and Suarez (*loc. cit.*) are emphatic in saying that Paul saw Christ bodily present before him in the same way as the other apostles. The fact is that Paul, while claiming to have seen the Lord, does make a slight distinction between his own vision and theirs (1 Cor 15:8) by calling himself the *abortivus* (literally, the one child that was born by caesarean section). He may be taken to mean that Christ had in some way to do violence to the ordered scheme of salvation to bring about Paul's vocation to the apostleship, while the others were made apostles in a natural way. The comparison may have been suggested by the story of the birth of Benjamin. Paul was likened to Benjamin in very early times (cf. Hippolytus on Gen 49:27) owing to his having been a ravening wolf ; it may be that the circumstances of Benjamin's birth, when he was saved 'from the ruins of his mother', put Paul in mind of such a comparison. This interpretation would justify the conclusion that Christ is not likely to grant a similar favour to other saints, and that their visions of Him are no more than the effect of spiritual communications to mind and imagination. This certainly seems to be the idea of the prayer in the Mozarabic liturgy for the Ascension (PL 85:607) that 'we may love

Thee in spirit who are now not able to look on Thee in the flesh' (*ut Te spiritu diligamus quem in carne nunc videre nequimus*).

The idea that Christ at the Ascension consecrated the Apostles as bishops is found in Isidore (*de ecclesiasticis officiis*, 2:5 ; PL 83:782) and in the pseudo-Augustine *Quaestiones VT et NT* (PL 35:2296). In the *Doctrina Addai* (in Pratten's translation, *Syriac Documents*, p. 13) the Apostle is made to say of himself and his colleagues : 'They had received power and authority at the same time that He was received up', and in the *Acts of Peter* (ch. 10) the Apostles are described as 'those upon whom Christ laid His hands'. These early texts show that from about 200 it was possible to take the Ascension as an episcopal consecration, Christ having blessed the Apostles in the Jewish manner by imposing His hands on them. If this event was held to have taken place on the day of Pentecost (as is clearly supposed in *Doctrina Addai*) it may be that a connection was seen between this laying-on of hands and the descent of the Spirit, the two episodes being considered parts of the same sacrament. At the Council of Trent (*Acta*, 9:7) this view was defended by Salmeron and after him (*Acta*, 9:35) by Adamans, an Augustinian from Florence. Suarez (*Opera*, 12:282-4) considered it to be '*verisimilior*'. The quenching of the debate at Trent on whether the powers of bishops came direct from God or through the Pope may have led to its falling out of the orbit of what theologians are wont to discuss.

It is clear from Cassian's work against Nestorianism (*contra Nestorium* 7:22 ; CSEL 380) that in the 5th cent. one reason for making much of the feast of the Ascension was the denial by Nestorians that the humanity of Christ could have risen above the heavens without the aid of the Holy Ghost. According to Cassian they even changed the reading of Ac 1:2, making the verse read that 'He was taken up by the aid of the Holy Ghost'. Cyril of Alexandria (*adversus Nestorium*, 4:3 ; PG 76:185) has much the same argument as Cassian, but does not bring the accusation about altering the text of Acts.

Christ's language in Jn 6:63 seems to imply that the mystery of the Ascension is greater than that of the Eucharist, and that when the disciples see the Ascension happening their faith in the Eucharist will be proportionally strengthened. As the Scripture Commentary states (CCS 795g), 'The Ascension will perhaps surprise the recalcitrants more, but it will eliminate their chief difficulty about eating the flesh of One who in celestial glory takes his place where he was from eternity.' Here and in 3:13 John shows that though he gives no account of the Ascension himself, he was familiar with its place in the scheme of Christ's work of salvation, and in his allusions to the 'exaltation' of the Son of Man he seems to be playing upon the double sense of the word, applying it both to the Crucifixion and to the Ascension (cf. O. Cullmann, *Der johanneische Gebrauch doppeldeutiger Ausdrücke* in *Theologische Zeitschrift* 4 (1948) 360–71).

---

[1] Ad sedem propriam Deus exule morte resurgit,
Ut vitam doceat credentibus esse futuram.

Bibliography. The principal work on the Ascension in modern times is V. Larranaga's *L'Ascension de Notre Seigneur dans le Nouveau Testament* (Rome 1938). See also U. Holzmeister SJ, *Der Tag der Himmelfahrt des Herrn* ZKT 55 (1931) 44–82 ; P. Benoît OP, *L'Ascension* RB 56 (1949) 161–203 ; *E. T. Dewal, 'The Iconography of the Ascension', *American Journal of Archaeology* (1915) 277–319 ; H. Gutberlet, *Die Himmelfahrt Christi in der bildenden Kunst* (Strasburg 1934) ; S. Salaville, 'Ascension et Pentecote', in *Echos d'Orient* 28 (1929) 257–71 ; and for the latest literature on the feast see *Archiv für Liturgiewissenschaft* 3 (1954) 408–9. J. H. C.

ASCETICISM might be described provisionally as the practice of self-discipline for the restraint of the passions and advance in virtue to prepare for union with God by love. Ascetic theories and practices are found (if ritual is included) in almost all religions and philosophies. Here only Christian asceticism can be dealt with, but cf. DSp. *Ascèse* ; *HDB *Asceticism*. After indicating (I) what it is not, an account of (II) OT and (III) NT asceticism will be followed by (IV) a brief history and (V) concluding remarks.

I False Asceticism comes from wrong notions about God and man, especially dualism and contempt for the body. That God made all things good (Gen 1:31) and gave them to man to be enjoyed with thanksgiving (1 Tim 4:1–5) finds confirmation in the Christian beliefs that 'The Word was made flesh' (Jn 1:14) and that our bodies will rise again (1 Cor 15). The God-given nature of marriage was re-affirmed by Jesus (Gen 1:27 f. ; Mt 19:4 ff. ; Mk 10:6–9) and defended by St Paul against the scrupulous and heretical (1 Cor 7 ; 1 Tim 4:3). Jesus also insisted that what goes into the mouth does not defile a man (Mt 15:11–20 ; Mk 7:15–23), and the revelation to Peter (Ac 10:15) showed that Jewish food distinctions were abolished. 'The kingdom of God is not a matter of eating this or that' Rom 14:17, Kn ; cf. Col 2:16, 23.

II The OT's insistence on the service of God by keeping his Commandments involved renouncement in mastering the passions. The ideal was given in the precept : 'Be ye holy because I the Lord your God am holy' (Lev 19:2). The prophets inculcated the vital importance of interior dispositions. Judaism had the fundamental ascetic practices—beautifully exemplified in the Book of Tobias—of almsgiving, prayer and fasting. Though the Law prescribed fasting only for the Day of Atonement (Lev 16:29) its mention, especially for a purpose, is frequent (e.g. 2 Kg 12:16 ; Ps 35 (34):13 ; Dan 9:3 ; Lk 18:12). Taking these practices for granted, Jesus set them in the context of true religion and safeguarded them from hypocrisy (Mt 6:1–18 ; CCS 686f–j). Many Jews lived austerely, the purifying value of God-sent trials was recognized, the Nazarite vow involved asceticism (Num 6:1–21 ; CCS 198i–m) and the Qumran discoveries have confirmed that the Essenes practised celibacy and community of goods. Nevertheless, the tendency of Judaism was to disapprove of asceticism and to favour 'the just mean' (J. Bonsirven SJ, *Judaïsme palestinien* ii, 280–91).

III The New Testament. Christ made all things new (2 Cor 5:17), including asceticism. When the Apostles rejoiced to have been found worthy to suffer for Jesus' name (Ac 5:41), they were not behaving like a Job or a Jeremias. What had happened ?

Although Jesus preluded His mission by a fast, He would not set His new wine in old bottles and came as the Beloved Bridegroom, eating and drinking like other men. But He said that when He was taken away, His friends would fast (Mt 9:14–17 ; Mk 2:18–22 ; Lk 5:33–39). And indeed He proved to be the Suffering Servant who came 'to serve and to give his life a ransom for many' (Is 53 ; Mt 20:28 ; Mk 10:45 ; CCS 644e). The Good Shepherd embraced suffering and death, not for their own sakes, but out of love for his Father and for men (Mt 26:39–44, 53 f. ; Jn 10:14–18 ; 15:10–13). So by suffering many things, He entered into His glory (Mt 16:21 ; Lk 24:26). Christian asceticism meditates and shares a divine love which issues in joy.

But of its demands Christ left no doubt. 'If any man will come after me, let him deny himself and take up his cross (daily, Lk) and follow me. For whosoever wishes to save his life shall lose it ; and whosoever loses his life for my sake, shall find it' (Mt :1612–25 ; Mk 8:31–35 ; Lk 9:22 ff.) The aggressive force of the formula, the circumstances of its utterance, the frequency of its echoes (e.g. Mt 10:37 ff. ; Lk 14:25 ff.) mark its importance and the impression it made. Yet it is a loving invitation ('if') from a Leader who first treads the way Himself. To 'deny' someone (as Peter did, Mt 26:34) is absolutely to reject Him (cf. Lk 12:9). To deny 'oneself' is a requirement going far beyond those of ancient (and modern) philosophers with whom bodily austerities or Stoic, 'existentialist', resignation leave a stronghold of pride in the self. 'Minus quippe est abnegare quod habet, valde autem multum est abnegare quod est' (St Gregory the Great, PL 76:1233). 'Losing' or 'hating' life or soul means sacrificing it for a greater love (cf. Jn 12:24 ff.) Self-abnegation for Christ's sake means renouncing one's own will for His and grows into a grace-transforming union with Him : 'I live, now not I ; but Christ liveth in me' (Gal 2:20). The practical examples given by Jesus of renouncing family, riches and self-importance culminate in carrying one's cross after him. This suggests advancing 'daily' along a road. For profound love comes from long patience and only in death can one say : 'It is consummated' (Jn 19:30) ; cf. DSp. *Abnégation* ; RAM 129 (1957) 3, *Analyse de l'abnégation chrétienne*, A. Gaultier-Sageret, SJ.

While calling all to the perfection of love (Mt 5:43–8) Jesus asked some to follow His own dedicated life. He invited those given the grace to choose virginity for the sake of the Kingdom (Mt 19:10 ff. ; CCS 708 f. ; cf. 1 Cor 7). He told the rich young man, if he would be perfect, to give up all and follow Him ; the Apostles had done the same (Mt 19:16-29 ; Mk 10:17-30 ; Lk 18:18-30). The distinction of precept and counsel is based on these examples, and the Sermon on the Mount s full of ideals of perfection for the generous heart.

Christians love a Person who died for them and with whom they are united : ' With Christ I hang on the Cross ' (Gal 2:19). Asceticism is no longer legal observance (though there is a law of Christ, 1 Cor 9:21) nor Stoic ' apatheia ', but the way and wisdom of the Cross (1 Cor 1:17-2:16). We are ' co-heirs with Christ if we suffer with Him that we may also be glorified with Him ' (Rom 8:17 f.).

Baptism is the sacramental starting point, the new birth incorporating us into the death and risen life of Christ (Jn 3 ; Rom 6:3-14 ; CCS 650h-n). Henceforth we are to live not ' by the flesh ' but ' in the Spirit ' (Jn 6:63 ; Eph 4:22-32 ; Col. 3:1-17). This is not the Greek distinction of body and spirit. The flesh is the ' old man ' disordered by sin, the spirit re-creates this same man, CCS 645k, 648c. To live in the spirit involves sharing Christ's sufferings and crucifying our corrupt impulses (Rom 8:4-18 ; Gal 5:13-25 ; Phil 3:10). Since Christ humbled Himself obediently even to the Cross, humility and obedience are of the essence of Christian asceticism. It is not self-absorbed but self-forgetful, for Christ did not please Himself, and whether we live or die, it is for Him (Rom 14:7 f. ; 15:1-3). Paul hammers his body into subjection lest he lose the race for heaven, but it is after Jesus that he runs, carrying Jesus' dying state in him (1 Cor 9:24-7 ; 2 Cor 4:10 ; Phil 3:10-14). Most of his sufferings came in the course of his missionary labours (1 Cor 4:9-13 ; 9:19-23 ; 2 Cor 11:23-12:10). It was for Christ's Body, the Church, that he offered them (Eph 3:1, 13 ; Col 1:24).

Theologically Christian asceticism is based on the cosmic facts of sin and redemption. The devil's sin, followed at his instigation by man's, shattered the union between God and creatures who became centres of disorder. The union was restored by the Second Adam, who offered to His Father the perfect and willing sacrifice by which He is able to save those who come to God through Him (Heb 7:25 ; 10:10). Concupiscence (i.e. disordered love) which remains even in the baptized, is to be overcome by the love that springs from the grace of Christ (Rom 7:18-25). Thus the final purpose of asceticism is the purity of the ordered love of charity. It is the enemy of egoism but not of proper love of self. It seeks to make us what we are : from God and for God, members of the vast company of His creatures and of the Body of Christ. Hence it involves not only renunciation of ' the world ' as opposed to God (1 Jn 2:15 ff.) but positive practice of the good by a moral life as perfect as possible, by self-disciplined development, by the justice and charity required of a functioning member of Christ's Body. In a word, without charity, asceticism is nothing (1 Cor 13:3).

IV The history of Christian asceticism starts from an age of persecution which enforced detach-

ment from ' the world '. Life was seen as preparation for the supreme imitation of Christ's charity by his ' athlete ' the martyr (1 Clem 5:1 ; Ign., *Mag.* 9:1 ; *Rom.* 4:2 ; 5:3 ; Origen, *Exhortatio ad Martyrium*, PG 11:563-637). After martyrdom ranked virginity, positively considered as a voluntary consecration and spiritual marriage to Christ. Virgins lived in the world, where they were a living apologetic for Christianity. They were counselled not only on preserving chastity but also on meditation and the doing of apostolic works (cf. Tertullian, *De virg. velandis* ; PL 2:936-62 ; Cyprian, *De habitu virg.* ; PL 4:473, 4 ; Pseudo-Clem., *Ep. I ad virg.* ; PG 1:379-416 ; Methodius, *Banquet* ; PG 18:27-220). Thus the way was prepared for clerical celibacy.

Asceticism was given a theology by the Alexandrians, Clement and Origen. Though intellectualist, it was genuinely Christian, for the contemplation which was their aim was subordinate to love and came from the Holy Spirit, cf. Clem. Alex., *Stromata* 6:9 ; GCS 15:467 ; on Origen cf. Introduction to *Origène, Homélies sur les nombres (Sources chrétiennes* 29) by A. Méhat. ' Apatheia ', i.e. freedom from passions, had been the Stoic ideal. Christianized and shown as a gift of God, it became classic in oriental spirituality. The western ideal of perfection was more adapted to ordinary conditions. St Thomas (1-2ae:59:5) teaches that passion is not bad in itself but needs directing to virtue (DSp. *Apatheia*).

After the conversion of the Empire, Christianity's essential opposition to worldly standards found expression in the monastic movement. Yet it was no hatred of the world which led monks to leave it, but the desire to give themselves completely to God by following the Gospel counsels, cf. L. Bouyer, *Vie de S. Antoine*, 88. The *Lausiac History* of Palladius shows the humility, spirit of prayer and charity of those who went into the desert to fight the devil and practise total self-abnegation. These were anchorites. The establishment of cenobitic monasteries by St Pachomius brought a Rule and a practical minimum of observance which included work in common. The most important ascetic element became the abnegation of self-will through humility and obedience to a superior. Discretion ruled a life which remained austere and purity of heart summed up the spiritual aim, cf. Cassian, *Conferences* 1, 2. The father of Eastern monachism, St Basil, shows the value of a common life, resembling that of the first Christians, for the exercise of sympathy, humility, patience, concord, correction and fraternal charity in and outside the monastery (PG 31:928-33). During this period the Church opposed various dualist or rigid ascetics such as the Encratists, Montanists and Manichees, and defended virginity against the Priscillianists and Jovinian. Against the proud rigorism of Pelagius, St Augustine emphasized humility and charity as the virtues attaching us most radically to God (RAM 121 (1955) *L'Humilité à l'école de S. Augustin*, P. Adnès sj).

While Celtic and Irish monks continued the

austerities of Egypt and Syria, the *Rule of St Benedict* adapted monastic life to western conditions with discretion and liberty of spirit. A humility which sums up monastic asceticism, and charity in a common life of prayer, spiritual reading and work, form the Christ-centred sanctification of his monks, and this tradition was dominant for centuries (*see* BENEDICT, INFLUENCE OF). The Cistercian reform, with its Doctor of Love, St Bernard, emphasized the cenobitic side ; the Camaldolese and Carthusians added anachoretical elements. Fasting continued to be the principal corporal austerity ; the hair shirt was widely used and the ' discipline ' spread by St Peter Damian.

With the medieval devotion to Christ's humanity, conformity to His life and death became the main ascetic motive of the new orders. Heroic and joyous fidelity to his poverty, humiliations and sufferings marked the reaction to clerical riches of the followers of St Francis and St Dominic ; cf. St Bonaventure, *De Perfectione Evangelica* ; St Thomas gives a balanced and complete exposition of the primacy of charity in asceticism in the *Summa* (2a–2ae:184–9) and his *opuscula* 18–20 on the religious life and vows. The Dominicans brought out the ascetic value of study, the Regular Canons that of the care of souls. The Third Orders organized lay ascetic life. The Church defended asceticism and condemned the false notions of Cathari, Flagellants, etc. An epitome of medieval doctrine on interior life and asceticism, admirable but somewhat sad, is presented by *The Imitation of Christ*.

The new age brought many anti-ascetic influences : neo-pagan elements in the Renaissance, moral corruption among Catholics, the Protestants' doctrine of justification by faith alone and their rejection of the gospel counsels. The Counter-Reformation saints inspired a vigorous reaction, the ideas of reparation and apostolate being dominant in the work of St Teresa of Avila. The Council of Trent proclaimed the possibility of growth in grace and merit, the necessity of free, human co-operation and the value of good works (D 793–843). The Church also condemned the errors of Alumbrados and Quietists among Catholics (D 1221–88). The sombre Jansenist deformations were countered by the spread of devotion to the Sacred Heart of Jesus and by the joyous peaceful asceticism of St Francis of Sales, whose wise, psychological approach, easy over externals, exigent over interior renunciations, guides innumerable souls, cf. *Introduction to the Devout Life*. St Ignatius, another master of discretion, propagated organized meditation and the particular examination of conscience to correct faults (especially by observing motives) and to acquire virtues. With SS Charles Borromeo and Vincent de Paul, he encouraged retreats, for which his *Spiritual Exercises* is a classic. Meanwhile by the spread of printed ascetical books lay folk were at last better provided.

V Conclusions. Modern asceticism has been set on the firm basis of our membership of the Body of Christ. Inspired by the life of the liturgy, it has developed in the Catholic Action movements. Papal encyclicals have shown its positive purpose in the priestly and religious life, in virginity, in marriage and the family, in the apostolate and in reparation. Instead of an imaginary ideal of violent penances which all spiritual writers recognize as dangerous, it aspires to the humble following of Christ crucified in the full context of temperament, circumstances and function. It requires the devoted fulfilment of the duties of one's state and work, and knows that prayer itself can be excellent mortification.

This asceticism goes with sound psychology. It respects the uniqueness and integrity of the person. Its aim is not to crush but to purify nature. ' I come not to destroy but to fulfil . . . that they may have life and have it more abundantly ' (Mt 7:17 ; Jn 10:10). Christ had a perfect human nature, and it was that He offered. Ours too is good but penetrated by egoism which has to be crucified with Christ that it may be penetrable by His charity. Forms of mortification which lead to contemplation and the liberty of a child of God, are good ; those which do not are evil. For asceticism is a facet of love which aims at the absorption of the whole man into Him whose yoke is sweet and whose burden light.

The martyrs are still with us, and the Church does not cease to produce great ascetics whose joyousness proves their Christian inspiration. But it is St Teresa of Lisieux who has shown to ordinary folk, living in an age of ' neurosis ' and unsuited to the practices of ruder and more vigorous natures, a way of heroism in little things which is within the reach of all. God, who knows what is best for us, sends mortifications more searching than those we impose on ourselves. With spiritual progress, asceticism tends to become acceptance. But it is always necessary, for in the Saint's words : ' Love will consume us only in the measure of our self-surrender '.

Bibliography. DSp. *Ascèse* (much used here); cf. *Abandon, Abnégation, Abstinence, Ascétique, Chair, Chasteté, Concupiscence, Conseils évangeliques, Dépouillement, Désintéressement, Désir de la perfection, Désirs, Devoir d'état, Direction spirituelle, Discipline, Discrétion* ; A. Rodríguez SJ, *Practice of perfection* (1929) ; J. Scaramelli SJ, *Directorium Asceticum* (1897) ; P. Pourrat, *Christian Spirituality* (3 vols, 1922–4) ; U. Berlière OSB, *L'Ascèse bénédictine* (1929) ; A. Tanquerey, *The Spiritual Life* (1930) ; R. Garrigou-Lagrange OP, *Christian Perfection and Contemplation* (1937) ; M. Rouët de Journel SJ, *Enchiridion Asceticum* (1938) ; J. Arintero OP, *Mystical Evolution* (2 vols, 1950–1) ; A. Stolz OSB, *L'Ascèse chrétienne* (1948) ; H. Pétitot OP, *St Teresa of Lisieux ; A Spiritual Renaissance* (1927) ; *Christian Asceticism and Modern Man* (Blackfriars, 1955) ; J. Goldbrunner, *Holiness is Wholeness* (1955).   R. R.

ASHES *See* SACRAMENTALS

ASPERGES This note will try to determine what theological ideas underlie the rite that is practised in parish churches every Sunday morning when the priest makes a tour of the church before the principal Mass and blesses his congregation with holy water. Is it a bit of paganism carried over into Christian ritual on the lines of what Ovid tells of Orestes and Pylades being prepared for sacrifice and the priestess of Iphigenia sprinkling them with 'lustral water' in Greek fashion ? [1] Or is it the extension to every Sunday of what was done at Easter from early times when the baptismal water was blessed and thereafter made available to those of the faithful who wished to carry some of it away to their houses ? Or is there some other reason for the rite ?

There is less enthusiasm today for deriving the Christian *Asperges* from pagan practice, since the philologists have given up the once accepted connection of *lustro* with *lavo* and now say that a *lustrum* was a going-round-in-procession but not necessarily a rite of sprinkling ; other sacred objects might be carried around to sanctify the place or the people who were gathered in it. The Greeks used sprinkling with water to prepare animals for sacrifice but that had nothing to do with the Roman *lustrum*. The basins for hand-washing at the entrance to ancient temples were for public convenience but had no real significance in the ritual that was carried out for the worship of pagan gods. The pagan precedent seems then not to provide a clue to the Christian practice.

St Basil (*de Spiritu sancto* 66 ; PG 32:188) says that the blessing of baptismal water was a matter of apostolic tradition. Certainly, something had to be done to prepare what was to ancient minds the hostile element of water before it could be used for a Christian purpose. The earliest prayers over the font (in Greek, Syriac, Coptic, Armenian, Ethiopic) speak of blessing the water and giving it 'the grace of redemption, the blessing of Jordan'. It is then understood to be of use against the Devil and in some of the Eastern rituals the prayer asks, 'that all who draw this water may have it for purifying soul and body, for healing, for blessing their houses and for all uses'. This agrees with what the pilgrim Antonius of Piacenza (CSEL 39:166) saw when he was present at the Epiphany blessing of the waters on the banks of the Jordan in the 6th cent. Alexandrian shipmasters drew some of the blessed water for sprinkling in their ships.[2] The *Liber Pontificalis* which was being edited about the same time attributed to Pope Alexander I in the 2nd cent. the beginning of this use of water for sprinkling in houses,[3] but it cannot be trusted to describe anything save the use of the 6th cent.

The present rite of the *Asperges* goes back to the 9th cent. where it is found in use possibly at Rome (PL 115:679) by Leo IV (before 855) and certainly at Reims (PL 125:774) by Hincmar (before 879). The prayer *Deus qui ad salutem humani generis*, for

blessing the holy water on a Sunday morning before the *Asperges*, now in the Roman *Ritual*, is found together with the exorcism of the water in Celtic sources (the *Stowe Missal* twice and St Gall MS 1395, not later than 800). The *Stowe Missal* has also the prayer said at the completion of the *Asperges*, *Exaudi nos, Domine sancte Pater . . .*, though it is given in the midst of the prayers for baptism. The prayer *Deus qui* and the exorcism of the water are also found together in the *Lanalet Pontifical* where they are used at the beginning of the Dedication of a church. The bishop is to bless water, salt and ashes after he has traced out the alphabet on the floor of the church and then he is to sprinkle the altar seven times while he chants the anthem *Asperges me Domine*, with the psalm, *Miserere*. The anthem has musical signs added in the MS. Here seem to be gathered all the elements of the *Asperges* as we know it today, and it is linked not with Easter and the font but with the dedication of the church. The link may become clearer when one considers the *Exeter Pontifical* of Edmund Lacy (15th cent.) where the bishop is told, as he waits outside the church, to bless holy water *as he does on Sundays* and then to go round the outside of the church with the people sprinkling the water on to the walls. This practice is vouched for in England by 816, when the synod of Chelsea ordered that, 'when a church is built, le t it be consecrated by the bishop of its own diocese ; let the water be blessed and sprinkled by himself and all things accomplished in order, according to the book of this service'. Columbanus (MGH *Scriptores rerum Merovingicarum* IV, 289) seems to have had this same practice. It would seem then that the Sunday *Asperges* is a reminder of the dedication of the church.

The *Lanalet Pontifical*, which is an odd jumble of earlier Celtic and Frankish material, has a singular prayer for the blessing of the wine (*Domine Deus rex . . .*) asking (ungrammatically) that the church may be consecrated, 'the sacred mixture of the blood of Christ (in wine) with water having been made, just as He once allowed His side to be pierced and to give forth blood and water'. Confusedly, this seems to look back to the ideas that are found in one of the *Pascal Homilies* formerly attributed to Hippolytus (the first of those edited by Nautin in 1950, paragraph 25). Explaining the typology of the Pasch the preacher says : 'Blood upon the lintel, as it were upon the Church, and upon the two doorposts as upon the two peoples'. The early Christians do not seem wholly to have passed over the Jewish ideas of sprinkling the people with the blood of the sacrifice, and it may be that in the Dark Ages these ideas were used to suggest a rite which carried out the sprinkling in a mixture of water and ashes (after the manner of Num 19:12-17) to which some extravagantly added the Blood of Christ under the species of wine, just as they used the Blessed Sacrament along with relics for the consecration of altars. Others with more reverence would substitute wine for the consecrated species. These are conjectures, but they have been arrived at only because of the

---

[1] *spargit aqua captos lustrali Graia sacerdos* (*Ep. ex Ponto* 3:2:73).

[2] *faciunt aquam sparsionis in navibus suis.*

[3] *Hic constituit aquam sparsionis cum sale benedici in habitaculis.*

somewhat troublesome facts that emerge from the history of the *Asperges*. The priest who blesses his congregation on a Sunday morning may not be conscious that he is sanctifying them ' as living and chosen stones for the spiritual edifice ' and that he casts upon them the water of expiation, but that is what seems to be happening none the less.

Bibliography. H. Scheidt, *Die Taufwasserweihegebete* (1935) ; *G. H. Doble, *The Lanalet Pontifical* (1937) ; H. Thurston SJ, The Blessed Sacrament and the Consecration of Altars in MN (1908) 351–62 ; the same, The Alphabet and the Consecration of Churches in MN (1910) 621–31 ; F. Cabrol OSB, s.v. *Eau* in DAC.   J. H. C.

ASSUMPTION, THE This article will be treated under the following headings. After briefly stating (I) the meaning of the doctrine, we will treat (II) the immediate basis of the Church's act in defining it. (III) Its relationship to other dogmas will next be considered in general terms, and (IV) the time lag before a dogma of this nature is explicitly accepted. (V) The Scripture foundation of the Assumption is next considered, and (VI) its early appearance in legend. Then after considering (VII) the traces of the doctrine in the early patristic period, and (VIII) the origin of the feast, we go on to (IX) the earliest fully-explicit witnesses to the doctrine. These latter are in the Eastern Church. So we go on to consider (X) the progress of the doctrine in the West. Next we consider (XI) the Assumption and its relation to living Tradition, as it is understood by modern Catholic theologians, giving reasons for the great contrast in this matter between Catholic and Protestant theology. Finally, there is a select bibliography.

I The Meaning of the Doctrine. The *Assumption* has been defined by Pope Pius XII (Munificentissimus Deus, 1 Nov 1950) : ' By the authority of Our Lord Jesus Christ, of the Blessed Apostles Peter and Paul, and by Our own, we proclaim, declare and define it to be a dogma revealed by God that the Immaculate Mother of God, Mary ever Virgin, when the course of her earthly life was finished, was taken up body and soul into the glory of heaven '. (AAS, 42, n. 15, *Irish Messenger* tr. 53.) It should be noted that, while the Pope did say that the faithful ' had no difficulty in accepting the fact that the great Mother of God departed this life as her Only-begotten Son had already done ' (*Irish Messenger* tr. 14), he did not actually define her death. Resurrection from the dead, then, is only implied in the dogma on the supposition that Mary died before her assumption.

II The immediate basis of the Definition. The outstanding reason which was the basis of the Church's conviction that the Assumption is part of the faith handed down through the Apostles is without doubt the fact that for centuries the whole body of the Church had accepted it as such. There had for centuries been no real theological opposition, though at times there had been theologians who queried its definability. Even in the high Middle

Ages, when the great theologians had scruples about the Immaculate Conception, they agreed about the Assumption. Since that time it had been one of the mysteries of the Rosary. Many churches in the Middle Ages were dedicated in its honour. Of course, at all times reasons were given from Scripture. As will be seen, it only came to be accepted because of its seen fittingness and connection with Scripture.

III Relationship of this to other dogmas. Whereas Our Lord's Ascension is part of His *work* of Atonement, our Lady's Assumption can only be part of its *fruits*. For this reason, while Our Lord is depicted in art and literature as rising by His own power, Mary is represented as being carried up (perhaps by angels) through the merits and power of her Son and Redeemer. The Assumption, then, is not part of any co-redemption on Mary's part.

This dogma is not found in full explicitness in any of the original sources, yet is implicit, as will be seen in the sequel, in other basic christological and salvational dogmas.

As to the manner in which it is contained in its sources, it differs greatly from the christological dogmas defined in the early Councils. The latter were no more than an expression in clear, technical terms of something already fairly clear and explicit in the actual, though non-technical, words of Scripture. The Assumption, like the Immaculate Conception, is not explicit in any words of Scripture or early recorded Tradition, but is rather understood to be contained by implication in the revealed doctrine handed down in these. Some modern authors would express the difference technically by saying that the christological dogmas were revealed in the original deposit with *immediate implicitness* (discoverable by a simple resolution of terms), whereas that of the Assumption was only revealed with *mediate implicitness* (discoverable by methods of inference). In the first type, the dogma tends to be seen as underlying the language of the original revelation, and is proclaimed because necessarily involved in that language. In the second type, the dogma often tends to be proclaimed as true, and as part of the original faith handed down, long before the faithful see exactly how it is contained in the original revealed Deposit. In the latter case, the dogma is seen to be involved in the actual facts revealed. Newman would explain it by saying that dogmas of the Assumption type are informally deduced from the original revelation long before one is able scientifically to articulate the actual process of reasoning. The dogma is in such cases sometimes reached by great numbers of the faithful with conviction at a time when many theologians still confess themselves unable to see sufficiently strong arguments leading to it, or while they are still unable to resolve some apparent tension between the doctrine in question and some other. This is the situation regarding both the Immaculate Conception and the Assumption.

The faithful had come to know Mary personally,

as it were, from the Scriptures and Tradition. She was for them a living human being, the privileged member of their own race who had lately brought forth the Saviour, the one who had been revealed to them as graced beyond all other men for this task. Her mission in the struggle against the forces of evil was already depicted in the Scriptures as connected closely with that of her Son. From an early time, Christians repeated together the words of the angel to Mary, and began to ask for her intercession. In meditating on the gospels and the facts taught there they had come to appreciate more and more deeply the greatness of what God had done in her. Their prayer, and their contemplation of this and of God's other works, together with their faith in God's love and fidelity, had led them to see more clearly and deeply hitherto partly-hidden aspects of the world of revelation, long known in its broad principles and central facts. Newman would have described the process by which they had grown in their understanding of what had been revealed as a process of implicit, spontaneous reasoning. This process had been stimulated and cherished by the force of divine love, under the influence of the grace of the Holy Spirit. To a complete outsider the new understandings that came to them in this living, spontaneous way might seem to come from sentiment or feeling or religious experience. The new understanding might even seem to outsiders as a new revelation. In reality any idea of new revelation would be excluded, since the new view would never be accepted by them except as a clearer understanding of what had been originally revealed, of what the Fathers had taught, and of what Christ had handed down. What Christ had once revealed would now be more clearly understood in all its bearings. It was not something added, but something they now saw always to have been there, at least by implication.

Such growth in understanding on the part of the faithful is not infallibly guaranteed until there is evidence that it arose under the influence of the Holy Spirit. We believe that the Holy Spirit dwells in the Church. But we do not know that any particular development has been actually watched over by the Spirit until this fact is guaranteed by some solemn declaration by the Teaching Church that the dogma in question is part of the revealed deposit.

IV The time lag before a dogma is seen explicitly and consciously accepted. In the first type of development, where the definable dogma is reached by a resolution of the actual expressions of Scripture or early Tradition, we do not expect much delay before the dogma comes to be clearly expressed. Such a process is normally hastened by the provocation that comes from the rise of heresy. The well-known christological doctrines were already held quite clearly at the earliest age, but they were first defined in answer to 4th or 5th cent. heresies.

In the second type of development, where the new truth comes from a deeper understanding of facts already revealed, rather than from a resolution of the words first handed down, there is no reason why

there should not be a long time lag before the doctrine is even expressed in any directly clear form at all. The revealed facts are always part of the faith, but the faithful may go on for long periods without meditating on certain aspects of those facts. There is probably some special opportuneness or other psychological factor which turns people's minds at certain periods to concentrate more on certain hitherto neglected aspects of revelation.

In the case of directly mariological doctrines, there were reasons why there should be delay. In the troubled period of the early centuries, the Church's forces were almost entirely consumed in maintaining the purity of the central and vital doctrines of the Redemption, the Incarnation and the Trinity. Until an orthodox doctrine of Trinity and Incarnation made possible a sound doctrine of the Atonement, scant attention would be paid to the manner and fruits of that Atonement. Even then, those aspects of the Atonement immediately affecting man's faith in salvation through Christ would come before doctrines which, however important in themselves, and however intrinsic to the predestined manner and effect of the Incarnation, would not be directly necessary for man's faith in Christ.

So it happened that the first five centuries were christological, and the great directly Marian doctrines begin to be taught explicitly in the 6th cent.
V The Scripture foundation of the Assumption. The universal view of theologians today is that the principal source of the dogma of the Assumption is Scripture. This is, however, usually understood in the sense that the Assumption is involved in the revealed *facts* which Scripture recorded, rather than that it is involved in the *words* of Scripture.

Nevertheless, there are some words which a number of theologians have for long thought to contain the Assumption in a veiled manner, e.g. Apoc 12. In referring to this at the beginning, it is important to stress that no one regards these words alone as the real reason why Christians became convinced of the Assumption. The most we can say is that, to many Christians, they appear to confirm what is known more clearly through the influence of other arguments.

In favour of the Marian and indeed Assumption interpretation of Apoc 12 is the fact that, if any NT writer would be likely to mention the end of Our Lady's life, it would be St John, who, alone, according to a tradition, lived long enough, and who has been popularly associated with Our Lady's later life. Newman was struck by the fact that, both at the beginning and at the end of the Bible, a *Woman* appears, who is closely associated with a *Child Redeemer* and involved, together with her Child, in a struggle with the Devil, ending in the victory of Woman and Child. The tendency of the earliest Fathers is to interpret this chapter in terms of the Church. Gradually it comes to be applied to Mary, either as a secondary interpretation to the Church one, or as the principal meaning. This becomes more and more common from the 5th cent. onwards. A series of articles were written on this in the CBQ in 1949–50 by Dominic Unger (*see* the bibliography), who concludes, 'In view of the arguments from Scripture; from Pope Pius X, from the ancient Christian writers, from theologians and Scripture scholars through the Middle Ages to the present day, we consider it certain that the Blessed Virgin Mary was intended by the Holy Spirit and St John in chap. 12 of the Apocalypse. But it seems certain, too, that Mary as the mother of Christ and Christians is not the only woman the sacred writer had in mind; he is speaking also of the Church.' (CBQ, XII, 405–6.)

By apocalyptic telescoping of events, the Woman appears in triumphant glory in heaven before she is recorded as bringing forth her male child with pain. Because of the mention of pain, which theologians do not associate with Mary's bearing of Christ, it has been suggested that the Woman must be the Church bringing forth Christ in men's hearts. Without necessarily excluding that interpretation, with as much ease the pains can be attributed to Mary by reason of the sword that pierced her soul as a consequence of her motherhood.

The Child is identified as the Messias, since he is spoken of as destined 'to rule all nations with an iron rod', thus recalling the messianic Ps 2:9. The Child's Ascension seems to be recorded in the words, 'her son was taken up to God, and to his throne'. We are then told of the battle in heaven between the Devil and St Michael, and the Devil finally, being cast out of heaven, turning to persecute the 'woman who brought forth the man child'. The Woman, however, escapes, being taken to a place of refuge on the 'two wings of the great eagle' (cf. Deut 32:11 for the eagle as symbol of God). If the Woman is Mary, these last words might refer to the Mother's Assumption, just as the earlier words almost certainly refer to her Son's Ascension. That the Woman is not the Church appears probable from the sequel, where the Devil, now helpless against Christ and His mother, 'went to make war with the rest of her seed, which keep the commandments of God, and have the testimony of Jesus Christ'. 'The rest of her seed' must surely be the Church, Christ's body, but excluding Mary herself.

It will be seen from what follows that the convincing reasons that converged to lead one Father and theologian after another to admit the Assumption were taken from the facts taught in Scripture that Mary was the Mother of God, that she was the Mother of the Redeemer, that she was the pure Virgin-Mother, and that she was the predestined holiest fruit of His redemption.

The proto-evangel (Gen 3:15), whether understood as literally or typologically referring to Mary's part in the redemption together with her Son, came to be seen as also pointing to her common lot with her Son in His resurrection and passage to glory.

The angelic salutation (Lk 1:28) by its hailing of Mary's fullness of grace was seen to imply an overflowing of God's supernatural gifts to her to the extent of saving her body from even temporary corruption, such as belongs to us.

The same salutation, by its words 'Blessed art thou among women', suggests her uniqueness in grace of body and soul above the rest of mankind, and therefore a uniqueness in the manner in which she benefited by the Redemption.

The widespread scriptural and traditional view connecting corruption with sin, led the Fathers, as they saw more clearly Mary's sinlessness, to couple with it her incorruptibility of body.

Further, any passage in Scripture that spoke of, or typified, the purity and holiness of God's dwelling-place came to be regarded as a sign of the Mother of God's holiness of soul in bodily preservation from disintegration (e.g. Ps 131:8).

Add to these arguments that the Scriptures speak much of the part played by Christ's body as the instrument, and our bodies as co-recipients with the soul of the fruits, of the redemption. The 'resurrection of the body' as an article of the creed reflects the emphasis of Christian teaching in being placed before 'life everlasting'. Christ was triumphant not only over death, but also over corruption. To gain this triumph he passed through temporal death, but did not suffer corruption. His Mother, the first-fruits among His redeemed members, was not merely restored as we are from corruption; she was preserved.

VI The appearance of the Assumption in legend. It is probable, though not certain, that the oldest explicit statements of the Assumption were in apocryphal legends of the 5th cent. or earlier. The oldest and basic form of this legend has been perhaps successfully restored by Fr A. Wenger (*see* bibliography, below). It includes an announcement by an angel of Mary's approaching death; Mary's assembling together of her friends; the arrival of St John and later of the other Apostles, including St Paul; the arrival of Jesus; Mary's death, her funeral, an attack on the mourners by Jews who were struck by blindness by angels and healed on believing; the burial; the return of Jesus after three days; the carrying up by angels of the body of Mary to paradise followed by Jesus and the Apostles; the placing of the body under the tree of life and the return to it of the soul; with, finally, the return of the Apostles to earth. It is not established whether the earliest account was written in Syriac or in Greek; but very soon it is found also in Latin, Gaelic, Coptic and Arabic versions. The original narrative can hardly be later than the 5th cent. These legendary accounts have of course no direct historical or theological value, though they do reflect a very high popular idea of Mary and a pious conviction that her death, like her predestination, must have been unique.

These legends acquired a further importance on account of their influence, both positive and negative, on the development of the theological dogma. A careful history of this development shows that their positive influence was doctrinally not important. They did, however, assist in promoting the gradual change of the early liturgical celebration of the Memory of Mary, Mother of God into the feast of the Assumption, Falling Asleep, or Passing Over of Mary. Add to this that they helped the imagination. In the non-speculative atmosphere of early Christianity, a concrete story made it much easier for a doctrine to be contemplated.

The negative influence of the legends was greater. Their existence, together with their recognized unreliability, as obvious to the scholars of antiquity as it is to us today, formed a real hindrance to the progress of the doctrine. At the time of Charlemagne, the feast came near to being suppressed in the West on the sole ground of its connection with these legends. Nearly all the early, and much of the modern, opposition to the doctrine has come from the same source. This opposition has kept on recurring, in spite of the fact that the defenders of the Assumption, even in the earliest time, have not based their acceptance on the legends, and in some cases have actually not accepted them. They have always looked for reasons based on the facts of Scripture.

Closely connected with the apocryphal stories is a curious legend going back, it seems, at least to the 6th cent., associated with the names of Galbios and Candidus, concerning the Blessed Virgin's robe which had been left behind in her tomb when her body was taken up. It is curious, perhaps significant, that, with all the popular interest in Mary, no rival legends seem to have arisen as to the existence of any relics of her body.

VII What traces of the doctrine exist in the earliest patristic period? Before the 6th cent. there is no undisputed and explicit witness to the doctrine. On the other hand there was a great awareness of those Scripture facts and doctrines which are its theological basis. Who can fail, for instance, to see the significance of the following passage in St Ambrose, where he depicts our Lady's wish, while standing at the foot of the cross, to die at the same time as her Son. 'Did she not rather desire to die at the same time as her Son? In this case, she leapt for joy at the thought of rising with Him, being well instructed in the mystery, and knowing that she was the mother of Him who was to rise again. Since she knew also that the death of her Son was a sacrifice for the common good, she was ready to associate herself with him by her death, so as, if need be, to add something to the work of the world's salvation.' (*De Inst. Virg.*, 7:49 ; PL 16:333).

Several doctrines held with deep conviction in the early period tended to point to Mary's incorruption. One of these was that of the connection between bodily corruption and sin. The more clearly they affirmed Mary's sinlessness, the more inevitably they were led to assert her bodily integrity after death.

Their typological manner of interpreting Scripture, joined to their firm belief in Our Lady's bodily integrity through virginity during her earthly life, led them to compare the Ark of the Covenant with Our Lady. This eventually led them to see the incorruptible wood from which the Ark was made as a type of Mary's fleshly incorruptibility. This development from St Hippolytus in the 3rd cent. to the 7th-cent. writer under the name of Modestus has been recently traced by Father J. Crehan SJ (cf. *The Ark of the Covenant*, Clergy Review, 35 (1951) 301–11).

St Epiphanius, though not a witness of the Assumption, found himself unable to assert that Mary died as others die. 'If people search the Scriptures,' he wrote, 'they will find neither the death of Mary, nor whether she died, nor whether she did not die ; nor whether she was buried, nor whether she was not buried.' After quoting the words of Simeon about the sword that would pierce her soul, he referred significantly to Apoc 12, 'she was given the wings of an eagle, and was taken into the desert that the dragon should not take her'. He commented on these words, 'This may have been straightway fulfilled in her. But I do not affirm it, nor do I say that she remained immortal. Nor do I affirm that she died. For Scripture passed over our human intelligence, leaving the matter uncertain, on account of that noble and distinguished vessel, lest anyone should entertain a suspicion of fleshly matters in her regard. Whether then she died, we do not know. And if she was buried, she (at any rate), had never had fleshly relationship. Far from us be the thought !'

An even clearer witness to the view that Mary was spared the usual lot of mortals in death is found in the writings of the priest, Timothy of Jerusalem, where he said that the Virgin 'remains immortal even till now, for He who had dwelt within her has transferred her to the place of His Ascension' (cf. M. Jugie, *op. infra cit.*, p. 72).

Of the two latter texts, that of St Epiphanius can only be fully understood if we remember that Mary's perpetual virginity was considered a basis for bodily incorruption, and that of Timothy seems to extend to Our Lady the words of Our Lord, 'I go to prepare a place for you.'

VIII The Origin of the Feast. The oldest feast of Our Lady, going back to the 5th cent. was a general 'memory of the Mother of God'. This was kept in some places around Christmas time, in others on 18 January, and in many places on 15 August. The latter date was to prevail over the others. Father Wenger has recently found new evidence for the view that it was this general feast of Our Lady which, by the early 6th cent., had come to be referred to not only as the memory of the *Theotokos*, but alternatively as the *Falling Asleep* (or *Dormition*). Fr Wenger (*see* the bibliography) thinks that it was in order to do away with local divergencies in the celebration of this feast that the Emperor Maurice extended the feast of the Dormition to the whole Eastern Empire. He therefore regulated, rather than established, the feast.

It began, then, as a general feast of Our Lady, with special emphasis on her divine motherhood and virginity. As in the course of time specialized feasts developed in connection with the Annunciation, the Nativity, the Presentation and the Conception of Mary, the original general feast came to be associated—like that of other saints—with the end of her earthly life. Gradually, from the distinction and honour of the person whose passing was celebrated, it came to be a celebration of the glorious manner of her passage to eternity. It was never called her death, but her *Passing Over* or *Falling Asleep*, and eventually her *Assumption*. This development was, of course, helped—at least until they became suspect—by the spread of the apocryphal legends touching upon this event.

After a period in which *Dormition* or *Transition* was the usual technical name, it became known universally in East and West as the *Assumption*. Its meaning also gradually grew more fixed and explicit in the sense of the taking up of both body and soul into heaven. Finally, by the high Middle Ages, in both East and West, and even among all the schismatics, it became Our Lady's principal feast. Already in the 6th–7th cent., it was the feast of one who could not be held by the bonds of death (*Gregorian Sacramentary*). In the 8th–9th cent. popes surrounded it with still greater honours. Yet at the same time, in some parts of the West, the feast was at one time on the verge of suppression, owing to the discredit into which the apocryphal legends had fallen since their condemnation by Gelasius.

In most Eastern rites, August is the month of Mary, by reason of this feast. The Assumption, moreover, is usually preceded by a little Lent with fasting. Since the Middle Ages, it has been a holiday of obligation with a Vigil, in the West.

IX The earliest fully-explicit witnesses to the doctrine. In 1955 there was published (*see* the bibliography, under A. Wenger) what seems to be the earliest, and also one of the most explicit, documents witnessing the Assumption, among the sermons of one Theoteknos, bishop of Livias, in Palestine, his *Encomium for the feast of the Assumption*. The early disappearance of the see of Livias suggests strongly an early date. Several other data, including the then uncommon and non-technical title of the feast, the *Assumption*, rather than the *Dormition* or *Transition*, and the brief, undeveloped and somewhat independent presentation of the arguments, have led Fr Wenger to propose as a probable date the second half of the 6th cent. Theoteknos accepted as background the main features of the apocryphal legend, but drew his arguments for the doctrine from Scripture and theology, not from history or supposed direct revelation.

He began very theologically by referring to Our Lord's Resurrection and Ascension, almost as though he wished to show the parallel between Mother and Son. He then stated that any privileges of the saints must even more truly be understood to apply to Our Lord's Mother. This was presumably to prepare the way for his later reference to the Scripture statement that Henoch and Elias were taken from this world body and soul into paradise. But Mary is greater than they, indeed greater than the whole heavenly choir that took her up to heaven. ' For if

the God-bearing body of this holy one knew death, it did not suffer corruption. But it was saved from corruption and kept free from stain, and raised to the heavens, by the holy archangels and powers, together with her pure and immaculate soul, and is now higher than Henoch and Elias, higher than all the prophets and apostles, higher than the heavens, with the exception alone of God, who, in his kindness has disposed all things in view of our salvation.' (*Encomium*, 15)

Theoteknos recalled the contrast between Mary and Eve, and also the words of St Paul (1 Tim 2:15), where the latter says that woman will be saved by her child-bearing. He recalled Ps 44, with its reference to the queen that leaves her people and her house because her Lord, the King, desires her beauty. He recalled Phil 2:10, in order to show how important it is that the holy Mary should see her Son on his throne, while every knee in heaven and on earth bows before Him. He recalled St John 14:2, to show that, if Jesus went to prepare a place for his disciples, he would prepare a still greater place for her.

Mary, he said, had a special relation to the Trinity. ' This holy one pleased God the Father ; this Virgin pleased the subsistent Word ; this Virgin pleased the life-giving Spirit that enlightens all and makes all the citizens of heaven.' (*Encomium*, 12)

Other arguments he took from the fact that Mary was an ambassadress with her Son during her life, from the fact that she was the spiritual ark containing the vessel of manna and the rod of Aaron, and a second time from the fact that she was the second Eve who had found all that the first Eve had lost. Towards the end of his sermon he quoted more than twenty more passages from the OT, and several from the NT, which he understood as typifying in some way or other Mary's graces. She, he said finally, is the earth which has germinated faithfulness, which has brought forth fruit, in which justice and peace have kissed. ' Our earth is Mary, who is our sister and our sovereign. She has given her fruit in its time, the bread which will never fail, Christ who said, " I am the bread of life. He who eats my flesh and drinks my blood has eternal life." . . . Our earth, the Mother of God and ever-virgin, has brought forth her flower.' (*Encomium*, 36)

Before the discovery of Theoteknos's remarkable homily, the encomium attributed to Modestus of Jerusalem has usually been thought to be the earliest straightforward witness. This writer did not know of earlier homilies. He thought he was a pioneer. He expressed surprise that none before him had spoken on the Assumption. People came to hear about the last days of the Mother of God, and he felt he must say something to them. He quite frankly put forward his views on the basis not of history or direct revelation, but on the grounds of what has been revealed concerning the Mother of God and our Redemption. He said that Christ as God chose her and gave her an incorruptible co-body (or twin-body, Greek *sussōmos*) with His. The Falling-Asleep, he said, was blessed because the Saviour born of her preserved her flesh. Her Assumption, he declared, was the great glory of our race, and he seemed to hold that it had a creative and restorative effect upon us. 'The Mother came to the vine which she herself had brought forth that she might gather from it the grapes of incorruptibility and immortality, rejoicing in heaven in the new fruit of her womb.' (*Encom. in dormitionem.* 2 ; PG 86²: 3284-5)

St Germanus, in the 8th cent., is one of the most important early witnesses, in his sermons on Our Lady's Falling-Asleep. He said that Our Lady's passing over to heaven was a matter of great rejoicing, since she passed to a place where she can greatly influence our own salvation. In her our nature is glorified ; in her all the prophecies of the glory and dignity of man are for the first time fulfilled. In Mary the threefold incorruption which we shall one day all receive, of body, soul and spirit, has already appeared. As God invited Mary into heaven, He promised her : 'Thy godly soul will see the glory of my Father. Thy pure body will see the glory of the only-begotten Son. Thy unstained spirit will see the glory of the all-holy Spirit.' (*In Dorm. Mariae*, 3 ; PG 98:361). This implied, said St Germanus, immediate incorruption, 'For how couldst thou, thy flesh dissolving, be reduced to dust and ashes, when thou didst free the human race from the corruption of death, by means of the flesh thy Son took from thee ?' (*In Dorm. Mariae*, 1 ; PG 98:345). St Germanus did not use the expression *sussōmos* or twin-body, but he did recognize a connection between Mary's oneness of flesh with Jesus and her incorruption. Having in mind the passage, 'Dust thou art', he makes God thus address Mary : 'Affliction of the flesh will not destroy thee. Thou wilt go up to a life more living, to a haven of rest, to undisturbed peace, to a life without care, to joy without suffering, to eternal rest and endless enjoyment, to the light that never sets and the day without evening, Myself, the Maker of all things and of thee.' (*In Dorm. Mariae*, 3 ; PG 98:361) The Son tells the Mother that, since He placed His divinity in her womb, she must entrust her body to Him.

The culmination of this early development was in the sermons of St John of Damascus. His arguments were similar to those of his predecessors, and were taken from her all-purity, her perpetual virginity, her sinlessness, and her divine motherhood.

An outstanding witness to the Assumption in a more official document than any mentioned so far is the liturgical prayer in the Sacramentary sent by Hadrian I to Charlemagne, a prayer which goes back to Sergius I, towards the end of the 7th cent. This is the prayer *Veneranda*, quoted by Pius XII in *Munificentissimus Deus* : 'O Lord, today we celebrate the festival in which the holy Mother of God died a temporal death ; but she who bore Thy Divine Son Incarnate, Our Lord, could not be held fast by the bonds of death.' (*Irish Messenger* tr. 18). The significance of this prayer is that in Acts (2:24) almost the same expression (in Knox, 'releasing him from the pangs of death') is used for Our Lord's bodily Resurrection.

X The progress of the doctrine in the West.

Western theology made little progress in matters Mariological during the period following St Augustine until the 8th and 9th cents. Instead of theology, the apocryphal account was being circulated in a Latin version. Though St Gregory of Tours in the 6th cent. seems to accept it, shortly afterwards it began to be regarded with disfavour, both because of its character and as a result of Gelasius's decree condemning such legendary writings.

From the 8th cent., Western writers began to be divided into two schools. There were the mildly agnostic, who confessed that they would like to believe the best about Our Lady, including her bodily assumption, but were doubtful whether there was any sufficiently clear teaching of the Church to justify its acceptance. In addition, they feared lest the doctrine had come in purely on the basis of these legends. On the other side were the enthusiasts, who were unable to doubt the bodily assumption, but who defended themselves on theology, not on legends. The most influential of the first group was undoubtedly Paschasius Radbert, who in recent years has often been called the Pseudo-Jerome, because he produced his work under Jerome's name. He said we should not fear to confess our ignorance, nor be bold to confess doubtful things as certain. On the other hand, he thought the Assumption should be accepted as a pious opinion, and stated without disapproval the view of many learned people that both Mary and those who rose from their tombs after Our Lord's death are now bodily with Christ.

Having stated his difficulty in asserting the Assumption of Mary as certain, Paschasius yielded to none in his praise of Mary as receiving honours far above all others ; and even stated that whatever of curse was poured into the world through Eve was removed by the blessing of Mary. (Among St Jerome's works, cf. PL 30:131) 'This is the day', he wrote 'on which the immaculate mother and virgin proceeds all the way to the highest throne, and sits down in glory next to Christ, being lifted on to the throne of the kingdom. So that everywhere the holy Church of God sings confidently, what it is not lawful to believe about any others of the saints, that she should rightly ascend beyond the dignity of angels and archangels. . . . For this privilege is not of nature but of the grace of the Blessed Virgin Mary, from whom God and Man was born.' (*loc. cit.* 132) Clearly it is misleading to class the Pseudo-Jerome among opponents of the Assumption, as is sometimes done.

Indeed Father Barré (La Croyance à l'Assomption corporelle en occident de 750-1150, in *Assomption*, ii, 63-123) has pointed out that this writer and many others of the same group, such as Gottschalk, Guibert, Ailred, St Bede, St Willibald, Adamnan and Usuard, only differ from the other group in that they are still uncertain whether they dare assert this privilege of Mary, whereas the second group are sure they can.

The greatest of the positive group is a follower of

St Augustine, whom we only know so far as the Pseudo-Augustine. He began by discussing the difficulty that nothing appears to be said about Our Lady in Scripture after the day of Pentecost. There are, however, he said, some truths, of which no mention is made, which are rightly believed to be implied on the grounds of a certain fittingness. He gave as an example Melchisedek's justice, which, though not mentioned in Scripture, is implied in the great praise given him. Again, though nothing is said of it, we take for granted the blessed life of Henoch and Elias after they were lifted up from earth. So, in order to discover what happened to Mary, we must consider by reason what end to her life befits the truth. 'And let the truth itself be the authority.'

Mary, he said, was free from the curse, 'Dust thou art, and unto dust thou shalt return'. Mary's nature had to be given incorruption. 'If it was not fitting for the sake of Mary, it was so for the sake of the Son she bore' (*De Assumptione BVM*, among the works of St Augustine, PL 40:1144). Just as the second Adam was free from the curse of the first Adam, the second Eve was free from the curse of the first Eve.

The Pseudo-Augustine had a quaint way of expressing the argument from Our Lady's virginity. 'He who was born of her without interfering with her virginity, knew how to preserve her from corruption and ashes.' (*loc. cit.* 1145)

Again, just as unity of grace makes all believers one with Christ spiritually, so much the more will unity of bodily nature make Mary one in bodily nature with Christ. 'Mary in glory not only had the Body she bore as her own, but, as long as it is lawful to do so, I hold that she kept the body that bore Him' (abbreviated from *loc. cit.* 1145).

As the Middle Ages progressed, theologians, with one or two exceptions, came more and more to agree with the Pseudo-Augustine that we could accept by faith not only the words of Scripture but everything which formed part of the truth therein revealed. They agreed further that, where words fail, what is involved in the actual truth can be discovered by a logical examination of that truth in its meaning and involvements. They departed from the purely historical method of inquiry of Paschasius Radbert, and recognized that the facts of revelation are to be discovered by the study of revelation, not—like the facts of profane history—by a study of eye-witness accounts. On the same argument, the lack of eye-witness accounts would be no presumption for a lack of revelation. They used, in fact, the kind of arguments popular with 'Modestus', St Germanus, St John of Damascus, and the Pseudo-Augustine. They saw the privileges of Mary that we know from Scripture, her virginity, her divine motherhood, her share in the reversal of the sentence upon Eve, her Son's filial love, as entailing certain other privileges in harmony with her Son. Among these privileges were her bodily incorruption, and her glorification in body and soul in union with her Son.

All the great 13th-cent. doctors, notably St Anthony of Padua and St Bonaventure, agreed in defending this doctrine. When the breviary came to be reformed, the general deep conviction in favour of the Assumption led Pius V to exclude the Marian homilies of the Pseudo-Jerome, in spite of his devotedness to Mary, because of his uncertainty whether this doctrine was of faith.

In post-Reformation times, the staunchest defenders of the doctrine were St Peter Canisius and Suarez. Both stated that it would be temerarious to deny it. Fr Tommaso Bartolomei finds in Suarez a summary of all the reasons brought forward by the Fathers and doctors of the Church, and he sees in Suarez an anticipation of the present Holy Father's Bull, *Munificentissimus Deus* (cf. *Relazione dottrinale tra la Bolla 'Munificentissimus Deus' e il pensiero del Suarez sull' Assunzione corporea di Maria Vergine*, Divus Thomas (Piacenza), LIV (1951) 334–58).

XI The Assumption and the Living Tradition. Confrontation of Catholic and Protestant Theology. A great deal of attention has inevitably been paid at the present day to the doctrines of the Assumption and the Immaculate Conception. To begin with, the fact of the definition of these doctrines and the desire to be able to give a reason for the faith that is in us has been a sufficient occasion and urge to induce theologians to explain the relation of these doctrines to the original deposit. It has seemed especially difficult for Continental Protestantism to understand these developments. Some of them have even suggested that Roman Catholicism is developing into a new religion centred upon Mary in place of Christ. The attitude of English Protestants has been more ambiguous. They have not been so fully under the domination of the Calvinistic and Lutheran version of Christianity which reduces it to 'justification by faith alone' (in the narrow sense of the word 'faith' characteristic of this school of thought). In so far as Protestants cling to that *articulus stantis vel cadentis Ecclesiae* in its original sense, they have been excluded from any possibility of understanding that Christ's grace is powerful enough to bring about a reflected glory in His saints. To the Catholic the full triumph of Christ is seen in His saints; and in honouring them, we honour Him; but in none of them do we honour Him as fully as in Mary.

In England Protestants have not so completely lost the early Christian and medieval view of Christian sanctity. It has then been comparatively easy for certain groups of Anglicans to revive many, sometimes even all, Catholic Marian doctrines and devotions. Even outside of Anglo-Catholics, English Protestants have rarely been scandalized at the paying of honour to the Virgin-Mother, whom all Christians still mention in the Creed and who has so important a place in the Scriptural account of the Nativity.

The attitude of Continental Protestantism is however still that also of some English evangelicals. For the extreme among these, it seems to the Catholic that the Calvinistic interpretation of *Romans* dictates the meaning of all other parts of Scripture, and they would forbid us to understand the words of the angel and Elizabeth to Mary in their obvious sense, just as we are forbidden to entertain the Marian sense of Gen 3 and Apoc 12. Even the very Incarnation itself has been queried or minimized by some who still accept firmly the Calvinistic doctrine of justification.

Grace, as is well known, is for Catholics a new and higher ' life ', the supreme gift that Christ came to bestow as the fruit of His Redemption. Now that this view is becoming more acceptable to Protestants, the way is opened for a greater understanding of Catholic Marian doctrines.

It is a sign of the essentially Catholic atmosphere of Newman's way of thinking long before he entered the Church that Catholic Mariological teaching never caused him the slightest difficulty. He was accused of holding the Immaculate Conception long before he became a Catholic ; and he always accepted the Assumption as an obviously integral part of Catholic faith.

The endeavour to explain the Assumption to those who are outside the Church has done a great service to our own Catholic theology. It has led us to probe more deeply into the nature of Tradition and doctrinal development. One of the reasons why Newman found it so easy to accept these doctrines was that he was the leader in the growth of the modern theology of doctrinal development. As in many other matters, Newman saw this problem of interest to 20th-cent. theologians much more clearly than did his contemporaries. So important was this problem and its solution to Newman that, had he been unable to solve it, not only would he not have become a Catholic but he might not have been able to remain a believer. Development he saw to be a law of the human mind whenever it grasps an important truth in a living way. Further, for truth to be thus grasped, man must be able to understand more than the mere superficial statement enunciated by the words. Underneath every verbal statement there is conveyed a depth of meaning beyond what is outwardly expressed or superficially grasped. No sooner do we make a statement than we offer or invite further explanations of our meaning. Words and sentences are multiplied in an effort to express more clearly what we stated at the beginning.

The discovering of the meaning of revealed words and facts, like all discovery of meaning, comes more easily when one lives and acts in accordance with that revelation. The more a truth is realized in our concrete life, the more it fits into that life, the more we realize what it means in relation to the rest of reality. So we begin to express it in new ways, and thus make its meaning clearer.

In the case of the Christian faith, this discovery of inner meaning is made easier by the virtue of faith and by the gifts of the Holy Spirit. By these gifts the understanding of both the individual Christian and the Christian community is developed.

There has been much stress among recent theologians (e.g. Dillenschneider, in *Le Sens de la foi*) on the part played by the sense of faith that is found among the body of believers in the progress of doctrine. In relation to Marian developments especially, we see now how unsatisfactory are the older attempts to explain the new understandings or new dogmas as mere logical analyses of what was formerly understood explicitly, or even as strict syllogistic deductions from such earlier dogmas. The classical, formal explanation is unrealistic. Though we use syllogisms to defend or check our conclusions, we do not usually use them to reach those conclusions. Personal reasoning, especially in the important personal matters which are to us matters of life and death, takes place in an informal, spontaneous way which is hard to seize and reproduce. It may happen that a number of people will reach the same conclusion in similar circumstances, and yet, if they have reached it independently, each one will express his arguments differently. The reasons given by one man why he believes in God will be rejected as insufficient by another man who also believes in God and who may give other reasons.

It is expected, if Newman is right in his analysis of the way in which men and women, even under the influence of the Holy Spirit, actually argue, that they will express those arguments differently when they put them on paper. It is natural, then, that millions of Catholics through many centuries should agree on the fact of the Assumption, while there is still no general agreement on which arguments are most effective, nor on the most effective way of wording those arguments.

The nature of the arguments given by a Theoteknos, a ' Modestus ', a St Germanus or a Pseudo-Augustine shows that the reasoning process, in so far as they were able to put it down on paper, was one of numbers of converging reasons pointing to one conclusion. One alone of these reasons might not suffice. Two might not suffice. A certain number of them, when they all point to one converging centre, is seen to be adequate ; though most ordinary people would find it difficult to express articulately why they find such a converging accumulation adequate.

Until, of course, the Church under the guidance of the Spirit, sets her seal upon the conclusion reached by the Christian sense of the faithful, it remains no more than a human moral certainty. In judging this moral certainty, the teaching authority acts on the basis of human prudence after full consultation of the bishops and consideration of theologians' arguments. But in the final decision, the teaching Church is guided by the Holy Spirit. The conclusion that is thus reached is not merely that the doctrine, e.g. the Assumption, is true, but that it is part of the original revealed deposit of faith.

Protestants are sometimes worried by the thought that before a definition of this type Catholics who did not accept the doctrine could be saved, whereas it is taught that after the definition its acceptance is necessary for salvation. This is a completely false view of the matter. Catholics who accept the definition merely show thereby their belief in the guidance of the Holy Spirit, safeguarding the teaching Church. Before the doctrine was defined, they had only their own learning and reasoning, together with any evidence they had of the 'mind' of the faithful, to guide them. They may or may not have been convinced that, say, the Assumption was part of the original revealed doctrine. After the definition, they are certain, because they always accepted the doctrine of the Holy Spirit guiding the Church.

This state of things is sometimes caricatured by the statement that the Catholic sacrifices reason and history for the word of the Church. This is only true in the sense that the individual believer accepts the truths of faith not on the basis of reason or on the testimony of history, but on the basis of God's voice. The Church as a whole still has to use the reason and historical studies of individuals, as well as the 'sense of faith' of the body of believers, in order to reach the conviction which eventually is defined. This is the way in which the Holy Spirit co-operates with human effort.

When the Assumption was defined, it may be said that it was by then clearly seen to be part of the Church's living Tradition. This is a living and developing understanding of what was in the original revelation. Some Catholic theologians say that everything in the living Tradition is contained basically in the words of Scripture. Others claim that there is no sufficient reason for asserting this, and that some elements of the original revelation can only be found in an independent oral tradition never committed to the Scriptures. The former view seems to be the more widely held at the present day ; but the Church leaves it an open question between them.

Bibliography. There is a very complete bibliography of all books and articles which appeared from 1950-3 in ' Echi e commenti della proclamazione del domma dell' Assunzione', *Studia Mariana* (Rome 1954).

We add a select bibliography for English-speaking readers :

The main early source-documents are found in Migne, PL and PG. In most cases, references are given to this edition in the article. Most of the relevant literature from the early centuries was collected by M. Jugie AA, *La Mort et l'assomption de la Sainte Vierge*, (Studi e Testi 114) (Vatican, 1944), and later by C. Balic OFM, *Testimonia de assumptione B.V. Mariae*, I (Romae 1948).

Some more recent evidence, notably Theoteknos quoted in the article, has been recently published in A. Wenger AA, *L'Assomption de la T.S. Vierge dans la tradition byzantine du VIe au Xe siècle*, Études et Documents (1955) (Institut français d'Études Byzantines).

The Papal Bull defining the Assumption, *Munificentissimus Deus*, is in AAS 42 (1950) 753-71 ; also in CR 34 (1950) 407-20, and in IER 74 (1950) 547-558 ; in English in an *Irish Messenger* pamphlet (1950).

The Petitions that preceded the Definition have been published in G. Hentrich and R. G. de Moos (ed.) *Petitiones de Assumptione Corporea B.V. Mariae in Caelum Definienda ad Sanctam Scdem Delatae* (1942, 2 vols).

Other books and articles selected : F. M. Abel OP, *The Place of the Assumption*, Thomist 14 (1951) 109-117 ; *Alma Socia Christi*, Acta I Cong. internationalis mariologici (1950) vol. X, *De Assumptione B. Virginis Mariae* (1953) ; C. Balic OFM, *De proclamato assumptionis dogmate prae theologorum doctrinis et Ecclesiae vita*, Antonianum, 26 (1951) 3-29 ; B. Capelle OSB, ' Théologie de l'assomption d'après la bulle *Munificentissimus Deus*', NRT 72 (1950) 1009-27 ; P. F. Ceuppens OP, *De Mariologia Biblica* (1948) ; F. Cavallera SJ, ' Une Somme sur l'assomption', *Bull. de Litt. Eccl.* 48 (1947) 157-65 ; J. B. Carol OFM, The Apostolic Constitution ' *Munificentissimus Deus*' and ' Our Lady's Co-redemption', AER 215 (1951) 255-73 ; C. Cary-Elwes OSB, *The Background of the Definition*, Life of Spirit 5 (1950) 213-19 ; J. H. Crehan SJ, ' The Ark of the Covenant' CR 35 (1951) 301-11 ; H. F. Davis, ' The Assumption of the Blessed Virgin ', Scripture (1950) 287-300 ; C. Dillenschneider CSSR, *Le Sens de la foi et le progrès dogmatique du mystère marial*, Rome (1954) ; C. Dillenschneider CSSR, *Le Principe d'une théologie mariale organique* (1955) ; J. Duhr SJ (tr. J. M. Fraunces SJ), *The Glorious Assumption of the Mother of God* (1950) ; O. Faller SJ, *De Priorum Saeculorum Silentio circa Assumptionem*, Analecta Gregoriana 36 (1946) ; C. J. Fenton, ' Two Solemn Pontifical Definitions ', AER 124 (1951) 52-61 ; T. Gallus SJ, *Ad Argumentum pro Assumptione B. Virginis ex Protoevangelio hauriendum* (Gen 3:15), Verbum Dei 28 (1950) 271-81 ; E. Graf, *The Assumption of Our Lady*, HPR 51 (1951) 522 ff. R. J. Hammell, M.A., *Munificentissimus Deus : The Proclamation of the assumption as a dogma of faith*, IER 75 (1951) 1-16 ; C. Journet, *Après la définition solennelle de l'assomption de la Vierge*, Nova et Vetera (1950) 39-48, 97-105, 195-204 ; C. Journet, *Esquisse du développement du dogme marial* (1954) ; J. McCarthy, ' The Deposit of Faith and the Dogma of the Assumption ', IER 76 (1952) 409-13 ; H. du Manoir SJ, *Maria. Études sur la Sainte Vierge* (1949), tome I ; G. Mitchell, ' The Definition of Our Blessed Lady's Assumption', IER 74 (1950) 481-91 ; M. J. O'Connell, ' Development of Dogma (of the Assumption),' Thought 26 (1951) 513-22 ; G. M. Roschini OSM, *Il domma dell' Assunzione* (1950) ; R. Russell OSB, ' The Assumption and Eternity ', Downside Review, 69 (1951) 265-75 ; F. J. Sheen, ' The Assumption and the Modern World ', Thomist, 14 (1951) 31-40 ; G. D. Smith, ' The Bull *Munificentissimus Deus*, a summary with some notes ', CR 34 (1950) 361-8 ; G. D. Smith, ' The Dogmatic Definition of the Assumption ', CR 34 (1950) 257-61 ; H. St John OP, ' The Assumption of the Blessed Virgin Mary ', Theology 54 (1951) 183, and ' The Assumption of Our Lady : A letter to a recent convert ', Blackfriars 31 (1950) 461-7 ; *H. A. W. Turner, ' The Assumption of the Blessed Virgin Mary ', Theology 54 (1951) 64-70.

With regard to the interpretation of Apoc 12, note especially the following works : D. J. Unger OFM Cap., *Did Saint John see the Virgin Mary in Glory ?* CBQ XI (1949) 248–62, 392–405 ; XII (1950) 75–83, 155–61, 292–300, 405–15 ; D. J. Unger OFM Cap., *Cardinal Newman and Apocalypse XII*, TS 11 (1950) 356–67 ; G. Bissonnette AA, *The twelfth chapter of the Apocalypse and Our Lady's Assumption*, Marian Studies 2 (1951) 170–7 ; M. Jugie AA, *Le Dogme de l'Assomption et le chapitre XII de l'Apocalypse*, Marianum, 14 (1952) 74–80.

H. F. D.

ASTROLOGY AND THEOLOGY It is not the purpose of this article to trace out the whole development of astrology in the Christian centuries but simply to consider its impact on theology. Astrology was really the belief that the stars governed the events of this world, including the acts of men, but with this belief there usually went the contrary persuasion that by a more exact calculation of the influence of certain stars at certain times men could interfere with this predetermined course of events. Thus magic came to build upon what was for it the uncongenial soil of astrology. To both of these arts the Christian theologian had to reply with an expansion of his teaching on the immunity of both soul and body from astral influence. Yet so much of the language and of the thought-moulds of the astrologers was in common use that some of it found lodgment in the Christian edifice and was assimilated, in particular the astrological week. This article therefore will deal with (I) the christianizing of the week, (II) the immunity of the soul from astral influence and (III) the immunity of the body from the same, with finally (IV) a brief notice of the struggle of theology against magic.

I The week of the astrologers, with its days dedicated to sun, moon and other five planets, Mars, Mercury, Jupiter, Venus, Saturn, gradually imposed itself on the Western world in the 2nd cent. In A.D. 238 one finds Censorinus (*de die natali*, 8) laying down the general belief that men accepted from the astrologers : ' The Chaldeans say that our activities and our lives are subject both to the planets and the fixed stars, and that the human race is governed by their varied and intricate courses, but that their motions, constellations and influences are frequently interfered with by the sun.' About the same time the historian Dio Cassius was explaining how the week of the astrologers arose from the idea of dedicating the successive hours of each day to the planets in their accepted order (*historia*, 37:18). Thus the first hour of the first day was dedicated to Saturn, the next to Jupiter, the next to Mars, to the sun, to Venus, to Mercury and to the moon. The eighth hour then becomes Saturn's and the 15th and 22nd, while the first hour of the next day will fall to the sun. On the next day the first hour will be dedicated to the moon, on the next day to Mars, on the next to Mercury. Thus the days of the week fall into their familiar order, if one starts with the planets in the order which they were held by the

astrologers to occupy and applies that order to the 168 hours of the week. A diagram will show what has been set out above :

SATURDAY (hours)

Saturn	1st —	8th—15th—22nd
Jupiter	2nd—	9th—16th—23rd
Mars	3rd—	10th—17th—24th
Sun	4th—	11th—18th
Venus	5th—	12th—19th
Mercury	6th —	13th—20th
Moon	7th —	14th—21st

SUNDAY (hours)

Sun	1st —	8th—15th—22nd
Venus	2nd—	9th—16th—23rd
Mercury	3rd—	10th—17th—24th
Moon	4th—	11th—18th
Saturn	5th—	12th—19th
Jupiter	6th —	13th—20th
Mars	7th —	14th—21st

Each hour was held to be under its controller ($\delta\iota\acute{\epsilon}\pi\omega\nu$) while the whole day was under the regent ($\pi o\lambda\epsilon\acute{\nu}\omega\nu$) which had control of the first hour of that day. When controller and regent were the same, as on the first and eighth hours of Saturday, for instance, the influence of that planet was thought to be paramount, and as Saturn was usually a malevolent planet, misfortune could be expected at those hours. Now while many Christians may have thought no more of these lucky and unlucky times than we do of Friday when it is the 13th day of a month, it is clear that some of them took it all very seriously. Thus Eusebius of Emesa in the 4th cent., as the historian Socrates tells (HE 2:9 ; PG 67:200), was slandered as a practitioner of the astrologer's art and took refuge in flight. If a bishop could be driven to this, what may not many a layman have suffered ?

There were plenty of warnings in the NT against the curious observation of days and times (Gal 4:10 ; Rom 8:38 ; Col 1:16, 2:8, 20) and though these were meant to guard against Jewish superstititions about a lunar calendar, they were often applied in the sermons of the Fathers to the new astrology which had arisen since the close of the 1st cent. The six days of creation, followed in the Jewish story by the day of rest, gave the Fathers grounds for accepting a seven-day period even while they rejected the astrological implications of the planetary week. It cannot be shown that the astrologers were indebted to Jewish ideas in the construction of their week, and up to the present it is held by most historians that the sevenfold nature of each of these two periods is a simple coincidence (there are traces in Jewish syncretism of the assimilation of Jahweh to Jupiter Sabazios but not to Saturn), but some still hanker after the theory of a primitive revelation which would explain the coincidence. It might be argued that the choice of the sun-god imagery for use in the worship of Christ, as evidenced by the tombs below St Peter's in Rome and by such hymns as *Christe qui lux es et dies*, was originally due to the fact that the day of the Lord fell on the day which the astrologers dedicated to the sun-god. Justin (*apol.* 67) speaks of ' the day that is called the sun's day ', but he is writing for pagans and cannot be taken to mean that Christians venerated the sun on that day. Loisy tried to argue that the Christians remodelled the story of Christ's resurrection to make it seem to have happened on a Sunday after they had fallen in with the pagan practice of keeping the day of the sun ; his view depended amongst other things on a mid-2nd-cent. date for the gospels, and need not be further considered. Ignatius (*Magn.* 9) spoke of the Christians ' no longer keeping sabbaths but living by the Lord's day, on which our life also rose up by means of Him '.

Clement of Alexandria (*Strom.* 6:16:143 ; GCS 15:504), towards the close of the 2nd cent., dilates on the importance of the number seven, starting with the seven ' rulers of the angels ' and going on to mention the astrologers' belief about the seven planets, the seven sense-organs (eyes, ears, nostrils and mouth), seven ages of man, seventh-day crises in illness, and so on. In 269 the first evidence is found of a Christian who had the weekday mentioned on his tombstone. The building of the Septizonium by Septimius Severus (*c.* A.D. 203) shows that the week was firmly fixed by then in popular observance, and Constantine took the obvious step for an emperor who was a Christian by legislating (3 July 321) for a day of rest throughout his empire on Sundays (Eusebius, *vita Constantini* 4:18 ; GCS 7:124) to honour the day of the Lord. The Welsh language has preserved the Roman (astrological) names for the days of the week without a change, whereas in Irish and Scottish Gaelic the names for Sunday, Wednesday (' the first fast '), Thursday, and Friday (' the great fast ') show Christianizing influence at work. The inference seems clear that the Britons under Roman rule received the week before they were Christianized, while in Scotland and Ireland Christianity came to them before they had time to be influenced by Roman astrology. In Greek and Slavonic the Christianizing of the names has been more complete still. On a more popular level one can see in the astrological papyri (*Codices astrologicae Graecorum* VII, 179) an attempt to link the days of the week with the seven archangels. The liturgical linking of weekdays with certain devotions, the Trinity, the angels, the Passion, and so on, seems to have begun with Alcuin, but he may have had forerunners in the Celtic past. For an earlier attempt in Gaul to get people to drop the astrological associations of the weekdays, see Caesarius of Arles in his sermon *de Kalendis Ianuariis* (PL 39:2004–2005).

II The immunity of the soul from astrological influence was strongly defended in various patristic treatises on Fate. Gregory of Nyssa (PG 45:145–73) shows how Stoicism helped the astrologers with their philosophy. He puts the ' argument from twins ' forward as a refutation of the astrologers, an argument that Augustine was to use with so much

effect (*Civ. Dei* 5:6 ; CSEL 40:217), asking how twins of opposite sex could be conceived at the same moment ; if the stars made one of them a boy, why not both ? Diodore of Tarsus, founder of the Antiochene school and master of John Chrysostom, wrote an important work *De Fato*, a lengthy summary of which was made by Photius (*bibliotheca* 223 ; PG 103:829–77). He attacked the astrologers on their own ground ; if the stars are truly eternal, why all this talk of their changing from benign to malevolent at certain times ? If races of men are influenced by the stars which preside over the region where they live, how comes it that most races of men have received the Roman ethos even without any uprooting and transplanting, while the Jews when they went into Egypt stubbornly kept their own ethos ? Why also has Christianity spread throughout the world and made the former *apotelesmata* (predictions of nativities) vain ? Firmicus Maternus was a Christian when he wrote a condemnation of paganism *De errore profanarum religionum* (about 345–350), and yet his *Mathesis* or practical guide to astrology cannot be before 355. One may avoid the problem by claiming that he had lapsed from Christianity in the meantime, but his astrological work has some signs of piety about it and many, with Thorndike, consider that he was trying to reconcile astrology and his new faith. He regards the emperors as under the direct care of God and exempt from the working of the stars (this was a prudent step as it saved him from trouble with the authorities under the *lex maiestatis*) and he seems to think that the soul was partially at least free from the same stellar control, if it made an effort. The survival of this work in the Latin-reading Middle Ages meant that the confusion of Firmicus's position was perpetuated.

Leo the Great (*ep.* 15 to Turibius ; PL 54:685), if the letter is his, condemned the Priscillianists as astrologers, ' There is no place in the Catholic Church for those who follow these arts ; one who commits himself to such beliefs has made a complete apostasy from the Body of Christ '.[1] Yet in the Priscillianist treatise (1:15 ; CSEL 18:14) anathema is pronounced on those who say that the stars are gods ; the OT is cited against astrology (Ecclus 17:30, and Ps 90 with its prophecy of Christ trampling on lion and dragon) and the Manichees are condemned for thinking that sun and moon were gods. It may be that this treatise is a justification of the heresy after the death of its originator, but it is hard to see where the truth lies. Orosius in his report on them (CSEL 18:154) certainly says that they linked up the Zodiac and the parts of the body, Aries ruling the head, Taurus the neck, and so on. A little later than Orosius, Claudianus Mamertus in Gaul (*de statu animae* 2:7 ; CSEL 11:124) stresses the free-will of the human soul with arguments drawn from Plato's *Phaedrus* (245 c) : ' We say that the soul is self-moved, though we place the principal support

[1] Ista sectantibus nullus in ecclesia Catholica locus est, quoniam qui se talibus persuasionibus dedit a Christi corpore totus abscessit.

of that motion in God, for motion is in a sense imparted to the soul by God that it should be self-moving '.[1] Orientius of Aquitaine in one of his poems is careful to make the stars sing the praises of God, thereby indicating their subordination : [2] ' The star of day, with his sister the moon, with the Pleiads, Orion, morning and evening star, all these bright leaping flames sing to Thee, and we men say Amen and Alleluia in imitation of their song.'

Church legislation against astrology is chiefly Iberian, from the Council of Toledo in 447 (D 35) and from Braga in 561 (D 239–40), but there are signs (e.g. in the lost work of Nicetas of Remesiana *adversus genethliologiam*) that the attitude was general. For several centuries the Church was able to keep the Western world free of astrology, but the revived interest in the classics caused by the Carolingian Renaissance and the influence of the Arabians on such men as Adelard of Bath and Bernardus Silvestris, as Saxl has shown, led to a renewal of the practice of astrology by Christians. This culminated in the great scare of 1186, when the astrologers predicted disasters because of their calculation that all the planets would meet in one and the same sign of the Zodiac in that year. The archbishop of Canterbury was stampeded into ordering a three-day fast and excitement was general. Something similar happened in 1484, and this time the astrologers pointed to the first outbreak of syphilis as an effect of sidereal disfavour. In the Middle Ages St Thomas is firm in his refusal to allow any influence of the stars on the human mind or will, but not all agreed with him, notably Roger Bacon. St Thomas sets out his arguments in *contra Gentiles* (3:84–5) ; in some of these he depends upon his philosophical position that the intellect has for its object the timeless and universal, thus excluding that it could be subject to the motion of what is after all corporeal, but not all theologians accepted this position of his. His more general line, that the operation of the mind was strictly not a motion, and thus could not be guided by sidereal motions, was more acceptable to them.

III The immunity of the body from the influence of the stars was not defended by St Thomas. He was willing to allow that the body, and therefore the bodily imagination and memory, could be subject to such influence. In earlier times Bardesanes had thus restricted the operation of the stars to bodily effects, and many Christians had agreed with him. Diodore of Tarsus had rejected such a compromise, asking how Christ did His miracles (i.e. how could they be called miracles ?) if the stars had influence over the bodies of men. Such an argument would not do for a non-Christian, and here Diodore was content to rest his case on an appeal to the common

judgment of men. If the stars influence human choices, then it could be said that harlotry was due to fate, whereas all men would join in rejecting that conclusion. Diodore also urged that so many diseases are joint affairs of both soul and body that to compromise and accept stellar influence for the body while denying it for the soul really goes against the view of man as a *compositum* or harmonious unity of soul and body. In St Thomas's orderly scheme of the universe the stars could affect the body (indirectly by causing changes in the weather, and directly by stirring up the humours which were at the base of the passions), the angels could affect the intellect, but only God could touch the human will. Human choices, he argued, are all ultimately directed towards happiness, and this (though often misunderstood) lies only in the conjunction of the mind with God. This conclusion is true as much in philosophy as in the teaching of the faith (*tam secundum sententiam fidei quam secundum philosophorum opiniones*). Now only God can satisfy the human will, and therefore the stars can never operate on the human will as final causes, i.e. from within the will itself. If they operate from without, then they do violence to the will, and human beings have no awareness through introspection that violence is being done to them. It must therefore remain that the stars have no impact on the will of man.

IV The conflict of theology and magic. Pico della Mirandola was the real scourge of the astrologers, all the more deadly in that he had read their works and understood them. He noted how they put themselves under the patronage of St Thomas, and still more of an apocryphal work of his called *De necromanticis imaginibus*. It was his strength that he refused to accept any occult qualities in the stars ; if they exerted any influence on men, it was by way of universal qualities such as heat or cold, dryness or moisture, and not by occult and selective penetration. (It must be remembered that St Thomas, according to the physics of his time, looked on the behaviour of a magnet with iron filings as due to occult influence from the stars.) Pico urged that if stellar influence was universal it could not at the same time be particular. He went further on to the ground of the astrologers. Among his famous 900 propositions were some that were set down to poke fun at them : ' Every soul that shares a Volcanian intellect was begotten under the moon. From the preceding conclusion I explain why all Teutons are of good corpulence and of a fair complexion. From the same conclusion I explain why all Teutons are most reverential to the Holy See.' In many cases the astrologers were little better than this. In his *Disputationes in astrologiam* (3:23) he ridiculed the idea of the astrologers that the stars excited the bile of a prince who then became more eager to avenge or to inflict injury. ' O blessed Italy, that mightest enjoy perpetual peace if thou couldst have princes that are phlegmatic ; a boon that could be cheaply bought by a single ounce of well-chosen drug, shared out among the princes and calculated to draw out

---

[1] A se moveri animam dicimus, cum principalem motionum cardinem in Deo esse dicamus, quoniam idipsum fere a Deo illi est ut sponte moveatur.

[2]   Te solis astrum cum sorore menstrua,
    Vergiliae, Iugula, Vesperugo Lucifer,
    Omnesque guttae praemicantes invocant,
    Et nos imago consonantis cantici
    Amen sonamus ; alleluia dicimus.

their bile.' He relied much more than St Thomas on the principle that whatever influence there might be from the stars was received by men according to their own disposition, which they could change of their own accord without the stars. Pico's work drove out astrology from serious discussion for a century and more.

On the basis of a doctrine of universal sympathy between natural kinds, with the help of a few observed facts (such as the opening and closing of the lotus-flower according to the movement of the sun) and many fables (such as the story of the cock which, endued with power from the sun, put a lion to flight) there was built up over the centuries a whole pseudo-science of precious stones and plants according to which the influence of the planets on the human body could be intensified or diminished. Churchmen were not always exempt from contamination by this lore. Thus Ibas wrote after the Council of Ephesus, ' Cyril caught the ears of all by use of a magical means, making blind the eyes of the wise, and before the archbishop John had arrived they condemned Nestorius.' Later in the same period one finds a subdeacon and two deaconesses copying *ex officio* books of astrology (*Acts* of the Latrocinium of Ephesus, 49 and 83). The verses of bishop Marbod of Rennes (*c.* 1100, printed in PL 171:1713–70) in his *Liber de gemmis* show how far credulity could go. It is against such a background that the work of the Church in keeping pure her doctrine of the Sacraments should be appreciated (*see* SACRAMENTS IN GENERAL). When Marbod says of the sapphire that men believed it could be used to appease God and to make Him listen to prayer,[1] he was on dangerous ground, but it was not until the whole theory of occult qualities had been rejected (by Pico among the first) that the danger to the Church had passed.

The modern age of conflict between science and religion has not been favourable to such pseudo-scientific competition with the Church. Since the 16th cent. there have been occasional figures (as Kenelm Digby) who have combined an interest in Catholicism with the practice of magic, but they have been the exceptions. Perhaps the new studies of cosmic radiation, the sun's magnetic field and the inner structure of the planets will lead to a revival of astrology on a higher plane than it occupied in antiquity.

In the 16th cent. it was the custom for every university professor who claimed to teach a ' scientific astrology' to issue his calendar of predictions for the coming year. St Thomas (*opuscula* 21 and 22 *de iudiciis astrorum* and *de sortibus*) is prepared to admit that stellar influence inclines a man to certain acts and, since reason is master in few, some predictions will be true. Gradually, the growth of genuine astronomical knowledge made these less and less popular, for the existence of stars hitherto unknown was not infrequently established by the astronomers and the question was inevitably put, ' Had these new stars not had some influence along with those hither-

[1] Placatumque Deum reddit precibusque faventem.

to known, and in that case how could predictions based on partial information be sound ? Dean Swift's satire entitled *Prediction for the year 1708* marks the waning of this fashion, and thereafter the ' Almanacs ' were banished to the intellectual slums. For further discussion of magical chemistry under the invocation of the devil, *see* MAGIC.

Bibliography. *F. H. Colson, *The Week* (1926) ; H. de la Ville de Mirmont, *L'Astrologie chez les Gallo-Romains* (1904) ; *F. Saxl, *Lectures* (1957, 2 vols) ; *L. Thorndike, *History of Magic and experimental Science* (1921–58, 7 vols, completing the story down to the end of the 17th cent.) ; J. Bidez and F. Cumont, *Les Mages hellénisés* (1938) ; A. Festugière OP, *La Révélation d'Hermès Trismégiste*, I, *L'Astrologie* (1950[2]) and ' L'Expérience du médecin Thessalos ', in RB 48 (1939) 45–77 ; *H. J. Rose, ' Hephaistion of Thebes and Christianity ', in HTR 33 (1940) 65–68 ; *M. P. Nilsson, ' The Divinity of the heavenly bodies according to the Greeks ', in HTR 33 (1940) 1–8 ; *P. Kocher, *Science and Religion in Elizabethan England* (1953) ; Pico della Mirandola, *Disputationes in astrologiam* (1494) ; *Bullarium Romanum* at dates 5 Jan 1586 and 1 Apr 1631 for decrees against astrology by Sixtus V and Urban VIII.   J. H. C.

ATHEISM This article is arranged as follows: (I) Introduction ; (II) Grades of Significance : (i) A-theism, (ii) Dogmatic Atheism, (iii) Agnostic Atheism, (iv) Critical Atheism ; (III) Atheism : a sophisticated phenomenon ; (IV) Atheism in Classical Philosophy ; (V) Atheism in Britain ; (VI) Atheism in France ; (VII) Atheism in Germany (VIII) some modern variants ; (IX) the refutation of Atheism.

I Introduction. The term is derived from the Greek prefix α and the word Θεός ; its formation is negative and the word has been very loosely employed. It has been levelled by the more orthodox against the less orthodox, by Christians against deists in the 18th cent. and, in theological controversy, by Christian writers against their non-Christian and even Christian opponents. It has at times been applied to those who refuse to accept a religious pattern laid down by State authority. The early Christians were accused of atheism by their pagan contemporaries, and Catholics in England were sometimes charged with a similar offence in the early 17th cent.

II Grades of Significance. (i) *A-theism.* It will be necessary first of all to examine the term ' atheism ' in its strictest sense as the repudiation of *theism*. Theism includes a notion of God that contains the following points : (*a*) There is a supreme Being, substantially distinct and ontologically separate from the world ; this Being is conceived as personal and not merely as a force ; (*b*) this Supreme Being has brought the world into existence and is therefore its Creator ; (*c*) the Supreme Being is responsible not only for the origin of the world but for its ordered maintenance. He conserves, preserves, maintains. There is a divine providence that directs the universe. The world and individual men are dependent upon God (*see* PROVIDENCE). (*d*) God's ontological separateness from the world does not prevent his immanence. He is closely present to and operative in the world, though his substance is ontologically distinct. (*e*) He is also the Lord and Guardian of the moral order to which man is subject. He is the Lawgiver who can proclaim and promulgate His will and impose sanctions with rewards and punishment. He is offended by man's sin and disobedience. (*f*) Man's relationship to God finds outward expression in cult, worship and sacrifice, which acknowledge God's sovereignty and stress man's dependence on God.

Two further points might be added to complete this attitude of theism : (*g*) Theism includes the conviction, at least in its more developed form, that it is possible to prove God's existence from man's experience in the visible world. (*h*) It also includes the possibility of revelation on God's part, whether that possibility be natural or historical. The existence of a Supreme Being, theistically conceived, is proved by various lines of argument : from the design and order evident in the universe to the Supreme Designer ; from moral obligation and responsibility to the Lawgiver and Guardian of the moral order ; from man's natural desire for happiness to the Supreme object that alone can satisfy the desire ; from the general consensus of men that God exists and must be served ; and from metaphysical arguments from movement to a First Mover, from existence to a First Cause, from contingency to necessary Being, as found in the Five Ways of Aquinas. (For a full treatment of these, *see* GOD, EXISTENCE OF).

These various elements deny the name of theist to a number of schools of thought about the Supreme Being. Pantheism and Cosmic Idealism are excluded because they admit no ontological distinction between God and the world. They regard the world as an emanation from God, as the sum total of the forms taken by the evolving divine substance (*see* PANTHEISM). A monistic system, whether Naturalism or Pantheism, cannot be theistic : it does not matter whether you regard God *as* nature or Nature *as* God. Nature, in Giordano Bruno's terms, is the *explicatio Dei* (the unfolding of God), as God Himself is the *complicatio Naturae* (the infolding of Nature). There is no substantial distinction between the *natura naturans* and the *natura naturata* of Spinoza. Idealist systems (such as Hegelianism), are also excluded, in which everything that exists—individuals, institutions, culture, religion, art—is a manifestation of the one developing and universal Spirit (*see* HEGELIANISM). German Idealism, drawing a distinction between individual consciousness (*Bewusstsein*) and a universal consciousness, is *a-theistic* in this sense.

Polytheism is also excluded in so far as it supposes many deities limited in character and action. Animists argue, e.g. Tylor in *Primitive Culture*, that polytheism was a natural stage on the way to monotheism but the evidence is rather in favour of an earlier monotheism that degenerated into polytheism (*see* ANIMISM). In Roman mythology the 'gods' may be interpreted as subject to Jupiter who is therefore supreme among the gods and perhaps, though not in the completely theistic sense, a supreme deity himself. That was the opinion held by Cicero and Seneca. It is less easy to visualize the Greek Olympus as subordinate to Zeus, but here Greek philosophy parted company with the popular religion and in the doctrines of Plato, Aristotle and Plotinus the various elements of theism may be discovered and the theistic arguments are eloquently sustained. Aristotle is not fully *theist*, since his Supreme Being acts only as final, not as efficient cause, and exercises no providential rule over the world. Plotinus and the Neo-Platonists, whose Highest Principle, the One, is so transcendent that he is essentially beyond the realm of Being and knowledge, employ the language of emanation or procession from the One, though they are certainly not pantheists. Greek philosophy in general thought of the world as dependent upon the Supreme Principle, but not originated by Him in time. With this exception, Greek philosophy is for all practical purposes theistic, even though Greek literature remained concretely polytheistic.

DEISM (q.v.) has also to be ruled out. Deism accepted a Supreme Being as the creator without whom the origin and existence of the world would be inexplicable. But that Supreme Being exercised no providence ; he was the necessary starting point and nothing more. Deism became the fashionable philosophy of rationalists in the 18th cent. and there was hot controversy between deists and atheists. In practice, there was little difference between them in their relation to revelation and religion. P. Bonhomme, in *L'Anti-Uranie, ou le déisme comparé au christianisme* (1763), commented : 'A materialist once said to me that a deist was the sort of man who was not weak enough to be a Christian and not strong enough to be an atheist.'

(ii) *Dogmatic Atheism*. The term 'atheism' is more normally employed to denote the denial of God's existence in any form. This is the dogmatic atheism which expresses itself in the two sentences : 'There is no God', and 'There can be no God'. Feuerbach wrote, 'There is no God ; it is clear as the sun and as evident as the day that there is no God, and still more that there can be none'. Sartre has argued that the notion of God—a combination, in Sartre's terminology, of the *Pour-soi* and the *En-soi*—is self-contradictory (*see* EXISTENTIALISM). With the savagery one finds occasionally in atheists which suggests that the fire of belief still smoulders beneath the ashes of denial, Flourens declared, 'Our enemy is God. Hatred of God is the beginning of wisdom. If mankind would make true progress, it must be on the basis of atheism.' Much language of this sort is found in revolutionary and Communist writers.

Dogmatic atheism is not in itself a philosophical system. But it is a logical consequence of materialism. If everything is material, and mind itself is only an epiphenomenon of matter, then there is no spiritual reality either in or outside the material universe. Atheism was usually associated with an atomic theory of the universe which supposed that everything was built up from indivisible material units through highly-diversified processes of combination and separation. There was no creator and no providence ; the material process itself was sufficient. Obvious difficulties—for instance, how the process started, how life arose from inanimate matter or how mind developed—were ignored or explained away in what was, philosophically, a crude and naïve system. The connection between Atomist and Atheist is illustrated in a passage in Lange's *History of Atheism* (I, 225) in which he registers the isolated case of Nicolaus de Ultricuria in the 14th cent., who was compelled in 1348 to recant the doctrine that there is nothing in the processes of Nature except the combination and separation of atoms. ' Here ', Lange writes, ' is a formal Atomist in the very heart of the dominion of the Aristotelian theory of nature. But the same bold spirit ventured also upon a general declaration that we should put Aristotle, and Averroes with him, on one side, and apply ourselves directly to things in themselves.' Atheism is also a logical consequence of all systems which explain reality by a purely material process, whether of bio-physical factors as with many 19th-cent. Evolutionists or of socio-economic elements as in the Historical Materialism of Marx.

Lange's mention of applying ourselves to ' things in themselves ' reveals a certain connection between Atheism and Empiricism. The empiricist is not necessarily an atheist. Scholastic theories of knowledge are empirical in their rejection of innate ideas and their insistence that all knowledge begins with experience. Locke, who became a father-figure for 17th- and 18th-cent. empiricists, stoutly proclaimed God's existence and thought he could prove it by reason, and in his treatise on *Toleration* he would not extend its benefits to atheists. But, for all that, Locke's principles were interpreted on the Continent in a materialistic and atheist way. Positivism is more definitely atheistic when it rejects everything except the positive data, *les faits*, of experience and denies any higher realm of existence. There is certainly a tendency for those who begin with experience to remain imprisoned within experience and to lose the power to transcend experience—a power which is essential if experience is to be given any satisfactory explanation.

Dogmatic atheism is therefore based upon the assumption that sufficient explanation of the universe is to be discovered within the universe, and that there is no sense in looking outside it. Much 19th- and 20th-cent. atheism has arisen from a similar doctrine about man himself. Man, they declare, is self-sufficient ; the only valid account of man must be sought in terms of man. This was the position of the German historical school of Yorke and Dilthey which regarded man as essentially an *historisches Wesen* and therefore only intelligible in terms of

human history ; of Nietzsche, with his gospel of man's self-sufficiency and his final culmination in the Superman ; of much modern Existentialism which sees *temporality* as the very warp and woof of the human pattern.

(iii) *Agnostic Atheism.* Leaving Marxists and Communists to one side, the dogmatic atheist is less common today than the agnostic atheist, whose position may vary from a convinced atheism, which he is too polite or indifferent to proclaim, to one of genuine doubt whether there is a God or not. A practical mind is often, in speculative matters, an agnostic mind ; it is too deeply involved in the present world to bother much about what may lie beyond it, either here-and-now or in the hereafter. It frequently becomes a *pragmatic* mind, content to accept, for instance, the validity of moral principles or God's existence on purely practical grounds, because the hypothesis works better than any other. This is the philosophy of Vaihinger, that of the *Als Ob* (the *As If*): we must live and act on the assumption that certain principles are true, though we cannot possibly prove their truth. English and North American Pragmatism maintains the same position (*see* AGNOSTICISM).

English empirical philosophy has been strongly agnostic. Thomas Hobbes is often charged with atheism, on the grounds that he excluded spiritual reality from the field of reason and declared that we can have no idea of the infinite or the immaterial : ' whatsoever we imagine is finite. Therefore there is no idea or conception of anything we call infinite.' But Hobbes avoids the charge by falling back upon the distinction between ' that ' and ' what ' in God. We can know *that* God exists ; reason can tell us nothing of what God is. Hobbes's agnosticism is made clear in *Leviathan* (I, 12), ' Therefore men that by their own meditation arrive to the acknowledgment of one infinite, omnipotent and eternal God, choose rather to confess that He is incomprehensible, and above their understanding than to define His nature by *spirit incorporeal*, and then confess their definition to be unintelligible : or if they give Him such a title, it is not *dogmatically*, with intention to make the divine nature *understood* ; but *piously*, to honour Him with attributes, of significations, as remote as they can, from the grossness of bodies visible.' Hume, though an irreligious man, was agnostic rather than fully atheist, and Boswell records Hume's statement that, after reading Locke and Clarke, he had never entertained any belief in religion. He is willing to allow the religious hypothesis as possible or even, under strictly limiting conditions, as more likely than any other ; but it is, in any event, a ' useless ' hypothesis. The extent of Hume's agnosticism is seen in a passage, put into the mouth of Philo, a character in the *Dialogues concerning Natural Religion*, but representing Hume's point of view : ' If the whole of natural theology, as some people seem to maintain, resolves itself into one simple, though somewhat ambiguous, at least undefined proposition, *that the cause or causes of order in the universe probably bear some remote analogy to human intelligence* : if this proposition be not capable of extension, variation or more particular explication : if it afford no inference that affects human life or can be the source of any action or forbearance : and if the analogy, imperfect as it is, can be carried no farther than to the human intelligence, and cannot be transferred, with any appearance of probability, to the other qualities of the mind : if this really be the case, what can the most inquisitive, contemplative and religious man do more than give a plain, philosophical assent to the proposition as often as it occurs ; and believe that the arguments on which it is established exceed the objections which lie against it ?' (xii, 227).

The spiritual affinity between some expressions of agnosticism and dogmatic atheism may be instanced from the language of T. H. Huxley (*Methods and Results*, 245 foll.) in which, if my interpretation be just, he is treating the religious problem with contempt : 'The problem of the ultimate cause of existence seems to me hopelessly out of reach of my poor powers. Of all the senseless babble I have ever had occasion to read, the demonstrations of these philosophers who undertake to tell us all about the nature of God would be the worst, if they were not surpassed by the still greater absurdities of the philosophers who try to prove there is no God. . . . Why trouble oneself about matters which are out of reach, when the working of the mechanism itself, which is of infinite practical importance, affords scope for all our energies ?'

(iv) *Critical Atheism.* Catholic teaching insists that experience of the visible world will bring us to recognize the reality of an invisible world. St Paul condemned the pagans for not arriving at that knowledge. 'The invisible things of Him from the creation of the world are clearly seen, being understood by the things that are made' (Rom 1:20). The Church teaches that man *naturali rationis lumine* may reach a knowledge of God's existence. Critical atheism does not deny that God exists nor, from itself, does it call that existence into question. It rejects the rational arguments for God's existence as invalid. It does not repudiate belief. In fact, it may throw a greater emphasis on faith, since it rules out the validity of rational argument in the service of religion. Luther repudiated all natural theology, asserting that our mind was incapable of reaching God. Karl Barth adopts the same attitude towards the use of reason in religion (*see* PROTESTANT THEOLOGY TODAY). If, therefore, a possibility of natural knowledge of God is an element in Theism, this position may be termed 'a-theistic', not that Luther or Barth deny God's existence but because they will not allow us the natural approach of reason.

The philosophy of Kant, whence derives the epithet 'critical', has given a special sanction to this attitude. Knowledge, for Kant, was a process in which the mind impressed its categories upon the material provided for it in sensitive experience so that knowledge was a combination of mind and material, the formal element proceeding from the mind. Our knowledge is limited to phenomena,

that is, the realm of experience. We have no natural knowledge of *noumena*, things in themselves, or of God. Kant rejected the traditional arguments for God's existence, reducing them, improperly, to various forms of the ontological argument. Curiously, Kant considered that by denying to the speculative reason the capacity to argue to God's existence he had rendered a service to religion, by cutting the ground from beneath the atheists' feet. Knowledge of God is therefore, for Kant, a matter of faith (*see* KANT AND THEOLOGY). By curtailing the range of human reason he thought he had brought faith into her own. The Kantian position is common, even normative, in 19th-cent. thought: cf., in England, Sir William Hamilton and Dean Mansel.

It should finally be noted that religious thinkers and writers in the 19th cent. placed less emphasis upon a rational approach to God and religion, stressing affective, emotional or existential factors. Schleiermacher spoke of it in terms of religious experience—the sense or feeling for what is sacred and saintly ; Rudolph Otto interpreted it as an attitude to the Holy ; it was a question, not so much of objective fact as of subjective appreciation of the religious value. Kierkegaard rejected reason as of secondary significance when he made religion consist in the personal approach of the individual to God or, in Christian language, of the sinner to the Lord he had offended. Kierkegaard presents the claims of Christ as a challenge that is unintelligible to human reason and can be met and overcome only through the personal response to and adventure of faith.

Critical atheism is therefore not atheistic in its content, and the term requires careful use. However, it does deny to the human mind the power of reaching the sure conviction that God exists or, in the second instance mentioned above, does seriously lessen the element of reason in man's approach to God.

III Atheism: a Sophisticated Phenomenon. Man is naturally a believing animal. He was created by God, never entirely lost his religious tradition and showed everywhere an awareness of a Supreme Being. This is trenchantly confirmed by the history of ancient civilizations and the study of primitive peoples. Belief in God as creator and lawgiver, as master both of the material and moral order, is universal. This consensus of history and sociology is so decided that it can discover only one case among primitive peoples where apparently there existed no notion of God. The case was that of the Indians in Brazil, named Tupenici or Tupenambi. Jean de Léry, in his *Voyage au Brésil* (1556-8, re-edited 1927) has this to say of them 'They have no knowledge of the one true God . . . they neither acknowledge nor adore gods of heaven or earth, whereas other idolaters, not many miles away, sacrifice to the sun and moon. Consequently, they have no liturgy or assembly-place for ordinary services, and they have no prayer of any kind, public or private. They know nothing of the creation of the world, give no names to the different days and make no distinction between them.' Half a century later, Père Claude d'Abbeville, in his *Histoire des missions des Pères Capucins en l'isle de Maragnan et terres circonvoisins* (1614) wrote, ' I do not believe that there have been any people in the world without some sort of religion with the exception of the Topinambo Indians who have never worshipped a god of heaven or earth, of gold, silver or stone or wood or any kind whatever. Up to the present they have had no religion, no sacrifice and consequently no priests or ministers or altar, no temples and no church. They have never known the meaning of a vow or prayer or offering or of any public or private worship. They reckon the moons but make no distinction between one day and another and have neither feast day nor Sunday. They consider all days equally good and solemn ; they have no cult, exterior or internal.'

Atheism as a fully-developed phenomenon depends upon theism and supposes a sufficiently elaborate theism. Primitive religion would appear to have been markedly social ; it was the religion of tribe or city rather than individual, and it was at times more concerned with external rite than interior conviction. In any case, there is a natural religion in man. Man is naturally religious as he is by nature social. Irreligion was the exception to the rule, and atheism a position adopted deliberately against the general opinion and frequently in defiance of it. It is a sophisticated, not a spontaneous and natural point of view. It is also ' protestant ' in character, an assertion of the individual man against religious teaching and authority.

IV Atheism in Classical Philosophy. It is difficult to speak of atheism in early Greek philosophy as we do not know the attitude of most of its thinkers to the official religion and we can scarcely call materialists men who had not yet made a distinction between matter and mind. Xenophanes denounced popular religion and Heraclitus proposed a system of continual evolution, in which the determining element was fire. God was identified with the *Logos* immanent in this continuous process. The Atomists, Leucippus and Democritus, explained Nature through the association of material particles, which differed from one another only quantitatively, and Atomism has become the favourite philosophy of atheists. The Stoics accepted and enlarged the doctrines of Heraclitus, introducing a closed deterministic system, in which God was the active element of fire within the universe or, at other times, the consciousness of the world. Like Heraclitus, the Stoics could be dubbed Pantheists, but later Stoicism sublimated its physical theories, and thought of God as the Mind or Reason controlling all things. Seneca's writings, for instance, reveal a more personal approach to the deity, now regarded as the heavenly Father under whose providence all men are gathered together as citizens of the one world.

The School of Epicurus is the one definite school of atheism in ancient philosophy. Its aim was practical rather than speculative, that of rescuing man from all fear of the gods and the underworld and establishing his peace of soul. This theme was developed vigorously in Lucretius's *De Rerum Natura*. The Epicureans did not deny that the gods existed but they declared that the gods had no concern with the lives of men ; they were, in any case, inferior specimens of deity, dwelling in the *intermundia*, happy and beautiful with no interests beyond their own existence. In the last resort, they too were material, being composed of atoms. The Epicureans were certainly not theists ; the best among them were humanists whose principal aim was a detached serenity, *ataraxia* ; for them, as for Protagoras, the Sophist, man was the measure of all things, and sufficient unto himself.

V Atheism in Britain. There are traces of atheism shortly after the religious transformation of England in the 16th cent. Giordano Bruno was in England from 1583 to 1585 and numbered Sir Philip Sidney, Sir Fulke Greville, Dyer, Spenser and Temple among his friends. Sidney's biographer, Zouch, admits that Bruno, Sidney and Greville used to discuss philosophical and metaphysical questions ' of a nice and delicate nature with closed doors '. After Bruno's departure from England there were widespread rumours of atheism. Sir Walter Raleigh was made a scapegoat. Fr. Robert Persons SJ, in his *Christian Directory*, published in 1592, speaks of ' Sir Walter Raleigh's school of atheism . . . and of the diligence used to get young gentlemen to this school, wherein both Moses and our Saviour, the Old and New Testaments, are jested at and the scholars taught among other things, to spell God backwards'. The Harleian papers include a manuscript report of the examination of witnesses by Royal Commissioners in Dorset on this point. One witness stated that, according to the report of many, ' Sir Walter Raleigh and his retinue are generally suspected of atheism ' and referred to Allen, Lieutenant of Portland Castle as ' a great blasphemer and light esteemer of religion and thereabout cometh not to Divine service or sermons '. On the accession of James I, Catholics in England presented a petition, begging to be allowed to practise their religion ; in it they declared that there were ' four classes of religionists in England : Protestants who domineered all the late reign ; Puritans who have crept up among them ; Atheists who live on brawls ; and Catholics '. In the 17th cent., atheists did not entirely disappear but they were no longer persecuted. Controversy associated them with Catholics, as in a work, *The Unmasking of the Politique Atheist* (1602), which was a violent attack on Catholicism, and a similar work, published in 1649, *A Perfect Cure for Atheists, Papists, Arminians, etc.*

Free-thought, deistic and atheistic, was a fashionable atmosphere during the 18th cent., influenced by Spinoza's *Tractatus Theologico-politicus* and the writings of Hobbes and Bayle. Anthony Collins, in his *Discourse on Freethinking* (1713), proclaims the existence of an élite of freethinkers who despised religion. Religious people are incapable of thinking for themselves and are impediments to progress. Materialism, adds Collins, ensures the triumph of the spirit. The book includes a calendar of lay saints, ranging from Socrates, Plato and Aristotle to Bacon and Hobbes. John Toland, author of *Christianity not Mysterious* (1696), founded a lay society intended to be a counterblast to the Church. He opposed any form of religion, yet he invented a form of service for this lay society, which is to procure for men security and serenity. This ' Socratic society ' shall meet in secret ; it will have a settled ritual and its own chants, libations and feasts. Its President will recite verses to which the members will sing responses. Hazard in *The European Mind* (1953) p. 265, quotes from these performances :

President : May all happiness attend our meeting !
Members : We institute a Socratic society.
President : May Philosophy flourish !
Members : And the politer arts !
President : Attend with silence. Let this assembly and all that is to be thought, spoke and done there, be consecrated to Truth, Liberty, Health, the triple wish of the wise !
Members : Both now and for evermore.
President : Let us be called Equals and Brothers !
Members : Companions, too, and Friends !

Hazard adds that the very man who was so bent on destroying the Church built a chapel to his own design. We should not forget that the London Grand Lodge of Freemasons was opened in 1717 and that the first French Lodge was founded in 1725.

British atheism in the 19th cent. centred in the Secularist or Rationalist movement. Its forerunners were Deists like Thomas Paine and Richard Carlile ; also Robert Owen, whose views resembled those of Haeckel, and the group of Utilitarians led by Jeremy Bentham. The two protagonists of Secularism were George Jacob Holyoake and Charles Bradlaugh. They accepted matter as a self-existent and eternal principle that required no extrinsic causality. Holyoake tried to invalidate the argument from design in *Paley Refuted* and *The Trial of Theism*, on the grounds that to admit a designer meant there must exist a person ; this person could not have designed the universe without a brain, and there is no evidence that such a brain existed. They employed metaphysical arguments also, claiming that substance signified what needed nothing antecedent to it and therefore could not have been created, and that creation, had it happened, would have added something to God. Associated with the movement were G. J. Romanes, who afterwards changed his opinions, W. H. Clifford, John Tyndall, T. H. Huxley and Herbert Spencer.

VI Atheism in France ran a parallel course with that in England, becoming the outlook of the more extreme among *les philosophes*. It took an Epicurean form in Benoît de Maillet's *Yelliamed ou Entretiens d'un philosophe indien avec un missionnaire français* (1748). By others reason was exalted into the place of faith ; morality was divorced from religion ; a material explanation was offered of the universe. In 1748 La Mettrie published *L'Homme machine*, which made thought a property of organic

matter like electricity ; the study of mind becomes a branch of natural history. La Mettrie was led by his observation of movements of the blood to maintain that all thinking and willing originate in sensation. Forced to leave France, he took refuge with Frederick II of Prussia, and Voltaire spoke of him as ' The King's Atheist in Ordinary '.

In 1770 appeared Baron d'Holbach's *Le Système de la nature* and, in 1772, *Le Bon Sens, ou idées naturelles opposées aux idées surnaturelles*, an abridgment of the former. The author's purpose was to attack religion everywhere and, if possible, to destroy it. Denying God's existence, he attributed religion to fear and ignorance and substituted matter and motion. When the book was published in London in 1859, it had the title of *The Atheist's Text-book*. During the 18th cent. follows a long succession of names : Charles François Dupuis, Boulanger, Naigeon, Sylvain Maréchal, Lalande. Naigeon collected together in his *Recueil philosophique ou Mélange de pièces sur la religion et la morale* (1770) everything that could be used against religion ; it was, says Hazard, a kind of Atheist's breviary. Sylvain Maréchal aspired to become a Lucretius and set his attack upon religion into verse :

Il n'est point de vertu si l'on admet les dieux.

He compiled what he termed a *Dictionnaire des athées*, for which he recruited some extraordinary candidates, including Abélard, Bishop Berkeley and Gregory Nazianzen. He characterized Christianity in the following terms : ' a long-standing and imposing error, which affects everything in existence, which distorts everything, virtue itself included which is a pitfall for the weak, a lever for the strong, and a barrier to genius—the utter destruction of such a gigantic error would change the face of the world ' (*European Thought in the 18th cent.*, Hazard, p. 127).

This dogmatic atheism gradually waned in the 19th cent. to take a milder form in Positivism, brought into prominence by Saint-Simon and Comte. Comte, its founder, even regarded himself as the prophet of a new secular religion, in which Humanity would be the object of veneration in place of the deity. Saint-Simon wanted to replace *déisme* by *physicisme*. Comte rejected metaphysics ; we can have no knowledge of the nature of things or of final causes. All we can know are the data, *les faits*, of experience. There is nothing beyond the realm of phenomena, and within that realm we can speak only of the co-existence and sequence of data. There exist no laws and no causes. ' There is only one absolute law ', wrote Comte, ' and that is that there is nothing absolute.' Comte explained human development by his famous law of three stages. In primitive times, men attributed all events to deities outside the universe ; after the Renaissance they attributed these events to metaphysical principles ; finally the stage of Positivism had been reached, in which everything was explained positively in terms of experience. This was scientific progress and enlightenment. Comte's disciples applied positivist principles to psychology, sociology and even to literature. Taine, for instance, declared that ' man was an animal of a superior kind who produced philosophies and poetry in the same way that silk-worms made cocoons and bees their honeycombs ' : ' virtue and vice are natural products like vitriol and sugar '. Positivism, as a scientific method, proved most valuable and it gave a considerable impetus to specialized studies in 19th-cent. France and else-where ; it played its part in the advance of psychology and sociology. But, as a philosophy, it was inadequate and disastrous and helped to produce the scientific mind of the late 19th cent. which was closed to religious discussion and often narrowly dogmatic in its atheism. With this went a firm but uncritical belief that science would inaugurate a new dawn for humanity when ancient supersitions, among these recognition of a Supreme Deity, would be brushed away. Renan is the major prophet of this belief in the religious mission of science. ' *La science et la science seule peut rendre à l'humanité ce sans quoi elle ne peut vivre, un symbole et une loi* ' : ' *Ma conviction intime est que la religion de l'avenir sera le pur humanisme, c'est-à-dire le culte de tout ce qui est de l'homme, la vie entière sanctifiée et élevée à une valeur morale. Organiser scientifiquement l'humanité, tel est donc le dernier mot de la science moderne, telle est son audacieuse mais légitime prétention* ' (all from *Avenir de la science* (1894)). Elsewhere, in his *Dialogues*, he claimed that ' *la science est la vraie religion, tandis que les religions officielles ont dégénéré en une pure hypocrisie* ', and that ' *ma religion, c'est toujours le progrès de la raison, c'est-à-dire de la science* '.

VII Atheism in Germany. Although certain circles in Germany were affected by French and English atheism in the 18th cent., it was in no sense a dominant movement as Germany was strongly influenced by the thought of Leibniz and Wolff and later by that of Kant and Hegel, to say nothing of the Romantic Movement. There was, however, in the 19th cent. a crude strain of materialism. Ludwig Feuerbach in his *Essence of Christianity* (1841) attempted to show that religion was the reflection of man's economic needs as God was the figure of man reflected back through space upon man's self-consciousness. The crudeness of Feuerbach's opinions is made clear by his play upon two German words, *ist* and *isst* : *man ist was er isst*, ' man *is* what he *eats* ', and he attributed the failure of the workers in the revolution of 1848 to the fact that their diet consisted of potatoes and not beans. Carl Vogt in his *Physiological Letters* (1845–7) developed the ideas of the Frenchman, Cabanis (1798), and argued that thought ' stands in the same relation to the brain as bile to the liver or urine to the kidneys '. Jacob Moleschott's *Kreislauf des Lebens* (1852), contained the theory that all vital phenomena are to be explained as a perpetual circulation of matter from the inorganic to the organic world, and then back from the organic to the inorganic. ' Without phosphorus ', he declared, ' there is no thought ' ; thought is a brain secretion. In *Kraft und Stoff* (1855) Ludwig Büchner claimed that Darwin's discoveries had destroyed the value of the teleological argument.

Life is a combination of matter, spontaneously generated ; there is no God, no substantial soul, no final cause. Haeckel's *Welträtsel* derived everything from an eternal primitive substance which by condensation passed first into aether and by further condensation into the elements of matter. This eternal material substance is God.

German materialism and atheism comes to its peak point in Marxism, which has since been broadened and adapted by a succession of Communist writers (*see* COMMUNISM). Marx accepted the crude materialism of Feuerbach and blended it with his own dialectic, derived from Hegel. Marx stood the Hegelian philosophy on its head and replaced the Hegelian *Geist* with socio-economic factors which represented the relation of man to the means of production. ' With me,' wrote Marx in the introduction to the first volume of *Das Kapital*, ' the ideal is nothing else than the material world reflected by the human mind, translated into terms of thought.' The central reality is socio-economic in a process of continual evolution. Mind is a by-product of matter, and art, religion, culture, in short all spiritual values, are the shadows cast by the process as it unfolds itself. In his *Historical Materialism* Marx distinguished between the *Unterbau*, which is the socio-economic reality, and the *Oberbau*, the principles and institutions reflected and conditioned by the *Unterbau*. Koestler (*Yogi and Commissar*, 70) states that, ' Marxist society has a basement-production and an attic-intellectual-production ; only the stairs and lifts are missing '. The *Oberbau* will represent the interests of the dominant class, so that existing morality and religion are the body of maxims and standards by which that class thinks it desirable that society should be governed. Religion for Marx is a man-made system that serves the purposes of the dominating and exploiting classes and provides an ' opium for the people '. Marxism is essentially anti-Christian, anti-religious and atheistic, as has been abundantly shown through the history of Soviet Russia. There is an element of Messianism in Marx which, reinforced by a similar element in revolutionary Russian thinking, has harnessed religious sentiments to an anti-religious cause and inspired the militant secularism and atheism that belong to Communism.

VIII Some Modern Variants. This short account of atheism has been confined to Western Europe. For atheism in Buddhism, where it was a conspicuous feature, and expressions of atheism in Islam, *see* BUDDHISM AND THE CHURCH and ISLAM AND THEOLOGY.

Three modern variants may be briefly noted. There has been an attempt to explain away religion as the result of the experience of primitive man, e.g. by sociologists like Dürkheim and Lévy-Bruhl. Primitive man in their opinion had different reactions to Nature from those of today ; he peopled the world with spirits and deities, seeing everything in a pattern of mystical relationships, attributing natural events and phenomena to interference from spiritual forces. Moral obligation is a development of man's early sense of dependence upon a community, symbolized in a totem animal or plant, with a rigid set of taboos and ordinances. God was man's projection of himself, a Father-figure, made to man's image and likeness. Religion, therefore, is a primitive state of mind to be rejected in the light of fuller knowledge, and God is to be relegated to the limbo of outworn ideas. Freud's approach to religion is similar.

Nietzsche represented a revolt of the individualist, placing all his emphasis on vital force and energy, on man's physical and biological qualities, rejecting the restraint and moderating influence of reason. His joy in existence, his Dionysiac enthusiasm, were marks of a fundamentally sick man. He repudiated morality, and especially Christian ethics, as an unnatural attempt to control men of natural gifts and greatness in the interests of the average man. ' God is dead ', was Nietzsche's message to the late 19th cent. Man was self-sufficient and eventually would realize his potentialities in the Superman, the crown of human development. Nietzsche threw down a gauntlet to divinity on behalf of what he thought was humanism and humanity.

Finally, there is atheism in a number of modern Existentialists. Sartre, himself an atheist, claims that ' *L'existentialisme athée qui le représente est le plus cohérent* '. Sartre argues from his distinction between *Pour-soi* and *En-soi* that God is a contradiction in terms and necessarily non-existent (*see* EXISTENTIALISM). Heidegger, in the close analysis of human experience which he presents in *Sein und Zeit*, treats man as a being, essentially temporal, whose existence is but a short span between two abysses of nothingness, the abyss from which he was *geworfen* or hurled into existence and the second abyss in which he will certainly be engulfed. In post-war writings Heidegger insists that he has left the question of God open but that it cannot be resolved until man's being becomes open or receptive to the ' holy ' : only on that level can the problem of God be raised. The term ' existence ' is interpreted as ' ex-sistere ' or ' ex-stare '. Man can raise the problem of Being because he *ex-sists* or stands out from the background of Nature and is consequently ' open ' to, or receptive of, Being. This ' openness ' can be obscured and is often so obscured. But this does not alter the fact that man is fundamentally ' open ' to the mystery of Being and therefore, in Heidegger's more recent writings, to the mystery of God. The atheism of these Existentialists differs considerably from that of the 19th-cent. Secularists ; it is neither confident nor proselytizing. The stress upon *Angst* in Heidegger and *angoisse* and *la nausée* in Sartre shows that these writers are oppressed, if not obsessed, with a sense of the contingency of the world ; this should have led to theism, not to its denial.

IX The refutation of atheism properly belongs to the article on GOD, EXISTENCE OF, and it is noticeable that in its catalogue of heresies the Church, while condemning countless specific errors, has in the past seldom (D 2073, 2109) animadverted on atheism as such, and then only to characterize the errors of the Modernist as leading to atheism. The two main lines of refutation are naturally philosophical, by examining two illicit assumptions of the atheist, that the world is a closed system, fully explained or explicable on this account, and that the notion of being is everywhere the same, or univocal, so that predication about God, as practised by Christians, may be required to conform exactly to the rules for human science about things. This second illicit assumption is fully treated under ANALOGY OF BEING. The first held the field from the days of Newton until the early years of this century but is now being abandoned on all sides. Indeed, the change in Heidegger's thought, noted at the end of section VIII, is one sign of this, and the great contribution of the Catholic philosopher, Maurice Blondel, in his many works from 1894 to 1939, was precisely to impress upon non-Christian philosophers, and in particular dogmatic atheists, the need to leave a gap in their systems, and into this gap he inserted his reasonings about the need for a supreme Being outside of all creation. When Newton was thought to have fully divined the secrets of the physical universe and its laws, a great optimism set in and men such as Hume thought it would not be long before they had reduced to a scientific form ethics and politics, thus covering the field of knowledge and closing the gap completely. Contrariwise, when Newtonian physics broke down, there was a philosophical pessimism to the fore and men were ready to abandon all metaphysical thinking.

Bibliography. F. A. Lange, *History of Materialism*, 3 vols. (1877–81) ; *J. M. Robertson, *Short History of Freethought* (1899) ; *W. E. H. Lecky, *History of the Rise and Influence of Rationalism in Europe*, 2 vols (1893) ; *A. W. Benn, *History of English Rationalism in the xixth century*, 2 vols (1906) ; *Fritz Mauthner, *Der Atheismus und seine Geschichte im Abendland*, 4 vols (1922) ; Paul Hazard, *The European Mind* (1953), *European Thought in the 18th century* (1954) ; Henri de Lubac sj, *Drama of atheistic Humanism* (1950) ; F. C. Copleston sj, *History of Philosophy*, vols i and v (1944, 1957).   J. M.

ATONEMENT, THE After (I) an explanation of terms, and (II) the state of the question in general, the article considers (III) the witness of scripture, (IV) that of patristic and medieval theology, and (IV) the state of the question in modern theology.

I An explanation of terms. Two words are in common English theological use to express technically the work by which Christ saved us. *Atonement* is peculiarly English. It has a history as long as the language to signify the act by which one makes amends or satisfaction in order to bring about a reconciliation. *Redemption* is also an old word and corresponds to the word used for Christ's work in all the Latin languages, conveying in general the idea of a price or ransom paid to free someone from some kind of bondage. Redemption is the only word in scripture translations to convey the action of God or Christ on our behalf. Atonement is in most versions confined to the OT, and refers to certain sacrifices and rites of reparation for sin, translating the Hebrew *Kaphar*.

In the OT, redemption commonly translates two Hebrew roots used for God's act of saving or liberating His people from earthly or spiritual bondage. These words are *Padhah*, meaning radically the buying back of the first-born, or of a slave, and *Ga'al*, meaning radically the act of a kinsman acting in various ways as such, including buying his relative back from slavery. It is thought by some that the latter word may connote that God looks upon His people as kinsmen. *Redemption* also translates λυτροῦμαι and derivatives in the NT, chiefly applied to Christ.

In common usage, *redemption* can always replace *atonement*, but not vice versa. *Redemption*, even in the NT, is patient of a much wider meaning, and can be applied to Christ's whole activity throughout the ages, whereby He has not only won, but now applies, the fruits of His work to us (cf. Heb 9:2, everlasting redemption). Redemption is also extended to include the work of those who co-operate towards their salvation or that of others, in and through Christ. Thus co-redemption (cf. MARY) is possible where co-atonement would hardly be acceptable. From etymology, atonement (at-one-ment) is a more Godward word than redemption, which rather suggests God's coming to man's help. Whatever may be true of the early history of the word, it seems question-begging today to confine the word *atonement*, still less *redemption*, to the idea of vicarious satisfaction. Scripture and early tradition do not justify the assumption that this one concept is the only essential one to express the basic reason of our salvation through Christ's activity. To say the least, such a theory would have to be proved. It cannot be assumed as the only possible interpretation of the evidence.

II The State of the Question. The general idea of the atonement has always been part of the Church's common teaching and preaching, and is clearly involved in the creeds. It seems an excellent example of a doctrine taught by the Church's ordinary teaching authority. For its implication in various creeds, refer, e.g., to D 86, also 9, 10, 13, 16, 54. For councils, see its implication in the Council of Orange in 529 (D 194). That Christ's death was a sacrifice on our behalf is taken for granted in the 11th Council of Toledo (D 286), and at Trent, in relation to the Mass (D 938, 940, 950, 951). That his work was meritorious and satisfactory is assumed in the Decree for the Jacobites (D 711) and at Trent (D 871 and 799).

Though certain non-Catholic modernists have seemed to explain the doctrine away, no body of Christians, Catholic or non-Catholic, seem to have denied it as the basic Christian doctrine. Nothing, however, has been defined as between the various theories of redemption, which are put forward as interpretations.

III The Witness of Scripture. We shall here note (1) the Scripture witness to God's eternal love of us in Christ, decreeing to save us through and in Him ; and (2) its insistence on the need of his assumption of a human nature like ours in order to be able to effect our salvation. (3) A difference of emphasis is pointed out between the Pauline and Johannine ways of preaching the atonement, St Paul emphasizing the work, and St John the Person, of Christ. Though no final explanation is offered as to how Christ's death and resurrection achieved our salvation, suggestions are offered that (4) a price was paid, or (5) a sacrifice was offered, or (6) a mystical identity between ourselves and Christ was established. The result of the Atonement is a victory over the powers of evil that had turned men away from God (7), with our consequent complete reconciliation and restoration (8). But this atonement (9) does not save us apart from our liberation from untruth by Christ, the Word, and His teaching.

(1) *God's eternal love and decree to redeem us in and through Christ.* This truth, taught directly in Eph 1, is the eternal mystery, hidden from ages and generations, now made known, a mystery sometimes identified with Christ Himself (Col 1:26-7 ; 1 Cor 2:7 ; Rom 16:25 ; Eph 3:3 ff.). Christ Himself must then share God's eternity. He is ' before all ' (Col 1:17 ; Jn 1:1 ; 8:58), ' the same for ever ' (Heb 13:8). The redemption is also shown as in a sense the work of the whole Trinity. It is a work of the Father's love, sending His only-begotten Son (Jn 3:16 ; 1 Jn 4:9-10 ; Rom 5:8 ; Rom 8:3, 32 ; Eph 1:3 ; 2:4-5). It is attributed to the love of God the Son, delivering Himself for us (1 Jn 3:16 ; Jn 10:15 ; Gal 2:20 ; Eph 5:2, 25). Even the Spirit helps us to pray and intercedes for us (Rom 8:26). Scripture also connects closely God's decree of creation with His decree of redemption. The God who made the world redeemed it when it had fallen ; the Word, through whom it was created, restored it (Col 1:16 with 22 ; 1 Cor 8:6 ; Jn 1:3, with 14-16 ; cf. Eph 1:10). Such passages as these put the Atonement in the setting of the OT, where God is man's Redeemer, saving His people from Egypt as a type of the coming salvation through His Son.

(2) *The true humanity of Him who is to redeem us.* The NT, though at one with the OT in recognizing the eternal divinity of the Redeemer, is far more explicit than the OT about His true humanity. We are to be redeemed by one of our race (1 Cor 15:21 ; Rom 5:15 ; Phil 2:7 ; Heb 2:14), in the likeness of our sinful flesh (Rom 8:3), by a man sharing manhood's weaknesses (Heb 5:1 ff.), who was tempted as we are in all things without sin (Heb 4:15). He brought about our Atonement by an act of supreme love, obedience and humility towards God (Rom 15:3 ; 5:19 ; Phil 2:8 ; Jn 10:15, 17 ; cf. Jn 12:27). It was at the same time an act of supreme love towards men (Eph 5:25 ; 5:2 ; Rom 5:6, 9 ; 1 Thess 5:10 ; Gal 2:20 ; Rom 14:15). It is principally Christ's death that is spoken of as the saving mystery (1 Cor 2:2 ; 15:3 ; 2 Cor 5:15 ; Gal 6:14, and frequently). But once explicitly, and often

implicitly, Christ's resurrection is given an atoning value, along with His death (Rom 4:25).

There is frequently a similar reference to the importance of Christ's sufferings (Lk 24:26, 46 ; Mk 9:12 ; Mt 17:12). The idea of obedience doubtless underlies His saying that He was sent to save sinners (Mt 9:13 ; Lk 19:10). He freely chose that He should not be saved from suffering and death by His heavenly Father (Mt 26:53).

(3) *A difference of emphasis between the Pauline and Johannine ways of preaching the Atonement.* Though one must guard against exaggerating the difference, it has often been pointed out that the Johannine theology preaches salvation through Christ's Person, and the Pauline theology salvation through His work, His sacrifice, His blood. Each would agree that neither the Person without the work, nor the work without the Person would be sufficient. Indeed, St John in some passages speaks of Christ laying down His life, or giving His flesh for the life of the world. Likewise, St Paul often speaks mystically of our salvation by union with Christ, or with His body. Yet it is more typically Johannine to call Our Lord ' the way, the truth and the life ' (Jn 14:6), and to make faith consist in believing ' in the Son of man ' (Jn 9:35), who, when He is 'lifted up ', 'will attract all men to ' Himself (Jn 12:32 ; 3:14, 15). It is more typically Pauline to say we are saved by His blood (Eph 1:7, and frequently), and must have faith in His blood (Rom 3:25). Yet St John speaks of the work given Him to do by His Father (Jn 17:4), and St Paul speaks of Christ as our life (Col 3:4), which shows that there is no more than a difference of emphasis.

(4) *Redemption by the payment of a price or ransom.* While we are given no metaphysical explanation of the manner in which the sufferings and death of Christ bring about our salvation, they are sometimes spoken of as a kind of ransom of price (1 Cor 6:20 ; 1 Tim 2:6 ; Mt 20:28 ; Mk 10:45 ; 1 Pet 1:19 ; Eph 1:7), without any further details, as, for example to whom the price is given. Perhaps the same idea is present in the many references to Christ's blood or Christ's body (Rom 3:25 ; 5:8, 9 ; Eph 1:7 ; 2:13 ; Col 1:20 ; Heb 9:14 ; 10:5, 10 ; 1 Pet 2:24) as being given for us.

(5) *Redemption by sacrifice.* But the reference to our salvation through Christ's body and blood might well have been intended to convey the idea of a sacrifice on our behalf. This is confirmed by the undoubted application to Christ in the NT of chapter 53 of Isaias (Mt 20:28 ; Mk 10:45 ; Lk 24:26, 46 ; 1 Pet 2:22 ; Ac 8:32 ; 1 Jn 3:5 ; probably Mt 26:28 & Mk 14:24 & Rom 5:19). Occasionally Christ's death is referred to directly in Jewish sacrificial terms (ἱλαστήριος and ἱλασμός) (Rom 3:25 ; Heb 9:5 ; 1 Jn 2:2 ; 4:10). He delivered Himself for us for an odour of sweetness (Eph 5:20), delivered Himself for the Church (Eph 5:25), for me (Gal 2:20), for us (Rom 5:8 ; Eph 5:2). He is made sin for us (2 Cor 5:21), a curse for us (Gal 3:13). Sin was condemned in His flesh (Rom 8:3). He is our pasch, who is sacrificed (1 Cor 5:7). He

is the lamb unspotted (1 Pet 1:19), the good shepherd giving His life for His sheep (Jn 10:11).

(6) *A mystical identity between ourselves and Christ.* This is conveyed in general terms in the parable of the vine and branches (Jn 15), and in the analogy of a body and members (1 Cor 12 ; Eph 4 and 5 ; Col 2 ; and elsewhere). It is also implied in the high priesthood of Christ (Heb. *passim*), and His mediatorship (1 Tim 2:5 ; Heb 8:6 ; 9:15 ; 12:24). Mystically it forms the basis of St Paul's baptismal doctrine, according to which we die with Christ mystically, in order to rise with Christ to a new life (cf. Rom 6 ; Col 2:12).

(7) *The result of Christ's work is a victory over the powers of evil, and especially death.* God in the Scriptures is associated with light and life, and the evil forces with darkness and death. Salvation is often spoken of as salvation from death. God's victory is not only spoken of as a victory over sin. It is a victory over the devil, a victory over corruption, and a victory over death. As will be seen, this important element in Scripture doctrine was to impress deeply most of the Fathers. It is an aspect of redemption which is not confined to St Paul, but is found equally in St John and elsewhere in the NT. The ' prince of this world ' is defeated (Jn 12:31 ; 14:30). The works of the devil are destroyed (1 Jn 3:8). The empire of death is destroyed (Heb 2:14 ; Col 1:13). The application of the fruits of the atonement to our souls will only be through a continued struggle with Christ's spirit-enemies (Eph 6:12 ; 1 Pet 5:8 ; Apoc 12:17). We still have to choose between darkness and light (2 Cor 6:14). Some have already chosen Satan (1 Tim 5:15), and are in danger of sharing his condemnation (Mt 25:41).

Frequently the whole work of redemption is expressed as a victory over death, the enemy which will be destroyed last (1 Cor 15:26). Death shall have no more dominion over Him (Rom 6:9), it is swallowed up in victory (1 Cor 15:54). Jesus, through His death, has destroyed the one who had the empire of death (Heb 2:14), and has brought to light life and incorruption (2 Tim 1:10).

(8) *The effect of this is glory to God, deliverance of man from sin, our reconciliation with God and new life.* Our Lord often tells us that the purpose of His life and death is God's glory (Jn 12:28, 13-31 ff., 17:4, 6, 22). It is likewise to save people from their sins (Mt 1:21 ; 26:28 ; Rom 6:6 ; 1 Cor 15:3) ; which it actually achieves (Rom 6:18, 22 ; 8:2, 21 ; Eph 1:7 ; 1 Jn 3:6). The two purposes are related, since God's holiness forces Him to hate and punish sin (Heb 12:29 ; Is 59:2 ; Rom 2:8 ; 2 Thess 2:11). Since, in fact, sin inevitably brings death if it remains (1 Cor 15:21-2), our redemption is often described as a liberation from sin and the law (Rom 7:6 ; Gal 3:23). The law in itself is holy (Rom 7:10, 14), but it cannot save us from our bondage to itself. Our liberation from all our enemies is frequently called our salvation, purchased by Jesus Christ (1 Thess 5:9 ; Tit 2:11 ; 1 Cor 3:15 ; 5:5).

In this way, we who have been sinners are reconciled with God (Rom 5:10 ff. ; 2 Cor 5:18-20 ;

Eph 2:16 ; Col 1:20). We are given a new life in Christ (Col 2:4 ; Jn 6:52, 55 and *passim* ; Jn 10:10), or made alive in the Son of God, out of His great love (Eph 2:4-7 ; Rom 5:10). We thus become members of the 'kingdom of the Son of His love' (Col. 1:13).

(9) *An essential part of Atonement is our liberation from untruth by Christ, the Word and His teaching.* All through St John's Gospel, above all in chapter 8, Christ is revealed to us as the truth, the truth which will set us free (8:33), the way, the truth and the life (14:6). Not only is He God's free gift, and source of grace, but He is God's truth (1:17). St Paul is equally insistent that he has come to teach the truth, and that sinners have changed God's truth into a lie (Rom 1:25). For St Paul, the truth that saves us is the gospel he is preaching (Gal 1:6-9), and in particular the sincere recognition that we are sinners, and can only be saved through Christ (cf. the Epp. to the Romans and Galatians). The Thessalonians are saved, because they believed the truth, and have not consented to evil (2 Thess 2:10).

IV The Witness of patristic and medieval theology. In this section, we note (i) the general attitude of the Fathers ; (ii) St Ignatius of Antioch's fusion of the Johannine and Pauline lines of thought ; (iii) St Irenaeus's understanding of the atonement as a great drama in which God gathers up in His Son the whole of fallen creation, restoring it to its first purpose. (iv) In both St Irenaeus and St Justin, the redemption is seen as a great victory over evil spirits, who had long held the world in the bondage of untruth ; (v) Origen belongs to the same line of thought, but he for the first time expresses the theory of a ransom paid to the devil. In St Athanasius (vi), we reach the culmination of the early patristic tradition, with the atonement firmly integrated with the doctrines of the Trinity and creation. (vii) The later Oriental Fathers understand the atonement in terms of one or more of these early views drawn from Scripture, but they develop the connection between the redemption and the sacraments, above all, the eucharist. (viii) With St Augustine, we pass into a different climate of thought, one which was to become characteristic of the west. It is the same gospel, but expressed more in ethical than in mystical terms. God became man both as an example of humility, and to be the one just man who could make amends for sin. (ix) Of two elements in St Augustine's thought, Abélard emphasizes the subjective aspect of redemption by example to the exclusion of any objective work, while (x) St Anselm emphasizes the objective almost to the exclusion of the subjective aspect. His theory of an infinite satisfaction to show forth God's infinite holiness was to become the standard theory in the west. (xi) St Thomas shows a return to the breadth and richness of the scriptural and patristic views ; and in him the atonement is once more not just one doctrine but total Christianity. (xii) Certain exaggerations on the part of the Reformers, since they appeared to safeguard the central doctrine of the atonement, failed to cause alarm or

to initiate any important developments in counter-Reformation Catholic theology, and the situation at the beginning of the present century was where it was at the close of the Middle Ages.

(i) *The general attitude of the Fathers.* For the Fathers generally, it may be said that the atonement was not so much one doctrine among others as Christianity itself. Any attack on the Incarnation or Trinity tended to be rebutted by a reference to the atonement. If Christ was not God, they would say, or if He were not true man, or if He were not equal with His Father, then we are not saved. He became man, that we might become gods. Christ, by His Incarnation, and the mysteries of His life, death and resurrection, by all that He was and did, and is still doing, has accomplished the salvation of man, which had been decreed by God from eternity. Especially were they unable to separate this doctrine in their minds from either the Trinity, on the one hand, or creation, on the other.

(ii) *St Ignatius of Antioch.* St Ignatius reflected the influence of both the Pauline and the Johannine theologies. He sometimes attributed our salvation to a kind of mystic union with God simply, or with 'our God Jesus Christ'. But he was equally determined that our salvation came through the flesh and blood of Christ who died for us. He was seriously disturbed by the heresy of docetism, denying the reality of Christ's flesh ; for it was only through His flesh that suffered that we are sanctified. In baptism we are sanctified by His passion (*Eph.* 18). His resurrection is the resurrection of our life (*Magn.* 9). By the 'blood of God' we are restored (*Eph.* 1). Our faith then must be in the blood of Christ (*Smyrn.* 6:1), and in the Eucharist we partake of His flesh which suffered for our sins. From another point of view, we are saved by union with Christ according to both 'flesh and spirit' (*Magn.* 1, and elsewhere some forty times). Our actions in the flesh become spiritual through union with Christ (*Eph.* 8:2). To possess His life, we must be ready to share His passion and death (*Magn.* 5:2 ; *Rom.* 6:1 ; *Rom.* 7:2). St Ignatius was conscious that there is still a threat to us from the 'prince of this world' (*Eph.* 19 ; *Rom.* 7:1). The whole Trinity co-operates in leading us back to God. We are to become temples of the Father, saved by the Son's Cross, and lifted up by the Holy Spirit (*Eph.* 9).

(iii) *St Irenaeus saw the atonement as a great drama in which creation is gathered up and re-created.* St Irenaeus, later in the 2nd cent., wished to win Christians back from false Gnostic ideas of the salvation of the élite through esoteric wisdom. Salvation is neither through worldly wisdom, nor is it confined to the perfect or the spiritual. St Irenaeus saw redemption as a great divine drama, involving the whole of world history, having as its central moment the life, death and resurrection of Jesus Christ. Redemption is in short the restoration of creation to what God had intended. St Irenaeus's theology has been expressed in the aphorism : institution, destitution and restitution. The first and third are the fruits of God's loving activity, the second is the creature's attempt to destroy God's work. This latter was ultimately the work of God's adversary, the apostate angel. The work of restitution was called by St Irenaeus the recapitulation (cf. *adv. haer.* III:xvii:6 ; III:xix:6 ; V:xxi:1 H). Sin had divided mankind. Now God is re-uniting all spirit and flesh, Jew and Gentile, and abolishing all division (*adv. haer.* V:xvii:4 ; V:xxi:1 H). It meant that Christ took to Himself flesh to save flesh (*adv. haer.* V:xiv:1 H) and united Himself to all men's ages (*adv. haer.* II:xxxiii:2 H). He rose in His flesh that we might rise (*adv. haer.* III:xx:3 H). Thus mankind, which had fallen away from God by the devil's seduction of Adam and Eve, is gathered together again under the new Adam, Jesus Christ, and with the co-operation of the new Eve, Mary, who, by listening to the good angel, undid the evil caused by the first Eve when she listened to the bad angel (cf. *adv. haer.* V:xix:1 ; III:xxxii:1 ; III:xxx:1 ; V:xxi:1 ; V:i:1 ; III:xix:6 H). The fruit of the atonement was the undoing of all the devil's work. Man is precious once more to the Father (*adv. haer.* V:xvi:2 H), having again the image and likeness of God (*adv. haer.* V:vi:1 ; V:xvi:1 ; V:xxix:2 H), possessing again the Spirit (*adv. haer.* V:vi:1 ; V:xii:2 H), possessing life, for which he was made (*adv. haer.* II:lvi:2 ; III:xxxiii:1 H), with adoption of sons, immortality and incorruption (*adv. haer.* III:xx:1 ; V:ii:3), destined for the vision of God, and communion with Him (*adv. haer.* IV:xxv:2 ; IV:xxxiv:6 H).

(iv) *The atonement, in St Irenaeus and St Justin, as a great victory over evil spirits, who had long held the world in the bonds of untruth.* Like all the early Fathers, St Irenaeus took from the Scriptures the concept of atonement as a great victory of God over the devil. The doctrine is elaborated considerably in his senior contemporary, St Justin. The few passages where St Irenaeus glorified God for the persuasive and just way in which the redemption was planned, in contrast to the violent and unjust way in which the devil had planned the fall (cf. *adv. haer.* V:xxi:2 ; III:xix:6 H) have often been unfairly quoted as the beginning of the so-called ransom-theory of redemption. The only basis for such a conclusion is his statement that God won us back justly and not violently from bondage to the devil. There does not seem any adequate justification for reading into such words the whole later elaborate theory of a ransom being paid to the devil.

For St Justin, the atonement was the sum of activities whereby Jesus Christ saved mankind from the deceits of the evil spirits. Before Christ, the greater part of the world was misled by those spirits. All false pagan philosophies, and all false religions, were inventions of those spirits in order to keep people from Christ. The evil spirits even went so far as to imitate by anticipation Christian doctrines, e.g. the Incarnation, and Christian rites, e.g. baptism, in order to dispose mankind against the true religion (cf. *passim*, both the *Apol.* and the *Dial.*). The Gentiles lived under the tyranny of these evil spirits until the coming of Christ, when

that tyranny was finally destroyed. In their folly, they had even tried to deceive Christ Himself. Since their defeat, they still have some power to mislead. They do this chiefly by raising up heretical teachers within Christianity.

St Justin completed this Johannine doctrine of Christ as the Truth, who came to free men from the spirit of untruth, with the complementary Pauline doctrine that we are saved, and the kingdom of death and evil spirits destroyed, by Christ's suffering and death upon the Cross. This, St Justin tells us, is a doctrine the demons were never able to understand, that the Cross and resurrection conquered death ; that we were paradoxically cured through the sharing of our miseries by the Word of God (cf. *apol.* 55 ; 63:16 ; 32 ; *append.* 6 ; 13:4). St Justin accepted the sacrificial interpretation of Isaias 53 as a reference to Christ's death on our behalf (*dial.* 13 ; 17 ; 111 ; *apol.* 51:5). As in the case of St Irenaeus, Mary is understood as the second Eve, and her faith is contrasted with Eve's unbelief as a condition of the redemption. It will be seen from these last references how far St Justin was from being a mere philosopher with a Christian veneer, as has sometimes been asserted.

(v) *Origen developed the victory-motif, explained it as involving a ransom-theory and united it again to the liberation-by-truth motif.* Like St Justin, Origen saw the world as a battlefield between the forces of good and evil. He pictured the Magi as recognizing, when they saw Christ's star in the East, that here was one greater than the demons. The good angels rejoiced at Christ's birth that here at last was one who would consolidate their struggle with the evil spirits into a final victory for good. In principle, the rule of demons came to an end with Christ's death. When Christ was crucified visibly, and rose triumphantly, the devil with his principalities and powers was at that moment crucified invisibly, and his power destroyed.

Since the fall, man had been under the power of the devil, for he had, by his sin, sold himself. This was the slavery from which Christ freed us. (In Exod 6:9 ; In Rom 3:7). The devil thought he could hold Christ, as he held the rest of mankind (In Mt 13:9), he sought to destroy Him. He was permitted to seize Christ, but found that he could not retain Him, because of Christ's innocence. In fact, when the devil seized Christ, he failed to be able to hold him, and at the same time lost mankind. (For references in Origen, see Daniélou, *Origen*, pp. 269 ff.)

Origen tried to fill in a gap in the argument by agreeing that the price that Christ paid with His precious blood was paid to Satan as a ransom for our souls. (In Mt 16:8 ; In Jn 6:53). Thus arose out of the scripture doctrine of Christ's victory over death and the devil the theory that was later called the ransom-theory, according to which Christ ransomed us from the devil by His blood, the devil was deceived and abused his ' rights ' by attacking the innocent Christ and, as a result, we were redeemed. This general theory, in one or other of its aspects, was afterwards held in the East by St John Chrysostom (In *Rom. hom.* 13), St Gregory of Nyssa (*oratio catechetica magna*, 23 ff.), St John Damascene (*de fide orthodoxa*, 3:27) ; and in the West by St Ambrose (*ep* 72:8), St Jerome (In *Eph.* 1:7) and St Augustine (*de libero arbitrio* 3:10).

Like St Justin, but in a more developed way, and with a certain neo-Platonic slant, Origen saw the redemption also as a process of liberation from untruth and unwisdom. But, in stressing these special aspects of redemption, he was too great a theologian not to use frequently the straightforward categories of sacrifice, such as are found in the Scripture.

(vi) *St Athanasius, the classical expression of the favourite patristic way of understanding the atonement.* He seems best to capture and express the early and Eastern tradition. He closely related the atonement to the first creation. ' God showed special mercy to man, making him according to His own image, giving him a share of the power of His own Word, in order that, possessing as it were certain reflections of the Logos, and becoming *logikoi*, they might be able to continue in happiness, living the true and real life of the saints in paradise.' (*De Incarnatione*, 3:4.)

Among the 2nd-cent. Apologists and in Origen, there had developed a tendency to interpret both creation and redemption principally in terms of the Logos. St Athanasius combined this Word-redemption theory with the restitution theory of St Irenaeus. The greatest gift of God to man, and man's greatest glory, had been his sharing of the Word. In consequence of this, he had received in his first creation (1) knowledge of God ; (2) immortality ; (3) the sharing of God's nature and happiness. But this first creation had been ruined by the fall. Through man's sin, through his listening to the deceits of evil spirits, and especially through his divinizing of men and angels in pagan religion, as well as his yielding in personal private life to passions and pleasures, he had become subject to the law of death, and was rapidly on the way to corruption. Unless God's goodness and wisdom could find a way to liberate man from this state, the whole purpose of creation would have been frustrated ; and man made to share the Word would remain for ever deprived of it (*De Incarnatione*, 13).

God was faced with a dilemma. His faithfulness to the law demanded that the sinner should die ; but his faithfulness to His own original design and His own original love of man demanded that man should be saved. God found a solution by decreeing that the Word should assume human nature. In this way, He would, by reason of His unity with us, be able to pay our debt of death, while at the same time communicating to us through His human nature the divine gifts we had thrown away (*De Incarnatione*, 9). Thus the law of death would be ended, and we should be restored to life.

In this way St Athanasius understood the necessity of the death and resurrection of Christ, as a payment of the debt of universal death in His own body (*De Incarnatione*, 20). His resurrection became in prin-

ciple the resurrection of all. ' He, indeed, assumed humanity that we might become God. He manifested Himself by means of a body in order that we might perceive the Mind of the unseen Father. He endured shame from men that we might inherit immortality. He Himself was unhurt by this, for He is impassible and incorruptible : but by his own impassibility He kept and healed the suffering men on whose account He thus endured. In short, such and so many are the Saviour's achievements that follow from this Incarnation, that to try to number them is like gazing at the open sea and trying to count the waves ' (*De Incarnatione*, 54, from the translation by a Religious of C.S.M.V.).

St Athanasius clearly implied a certain solidarity between mankind and Jesus Christ, following from the fact that He became man for our sakes, that He was given to us by the Father. One might say that he supposed the doctrine of the mystical body, though he did not explicitly introduce it into the argument.

(vii) *The later Oriental Fathers.* From that time onwards, Eastern theology kept very close to the basic line of thought represented in St Athanasius. Its view of the redemption has sometimes been called a *physical* or *mystical* theory of redemption, sometimes an *incarnational* theory. Clearly there is some basis for such terms. The physical aspect of this explanation is clear from the way in which all the early Eastern writers connect the sacraments, and above all the Eucharist, with the redemption. St John Chrysostom, for instance, seemed to take the view that is commonly today understood to be that of St Paul, that Christ's flesh did not acquire the power of being a life-giving flesh until after his death and resurrection. Chrysostom continually spoke of the wonderful power of Christ's body since it rose up triumphant ; and he seemed to understand the Eucharist as owing its life-giving power to that change which had taken place in Christ's body (*hom.* 34:2 in 1 Cor). St Gregory of Nyssa could not conceive of man being saved, if man could not have some part in the Eucharist (*Great Catechism*, 16). Christ in His own body bestows on our nature the principle of resurrection, raising by His power the whole man (*op. cit.* 32).

Yet for all these writers the passion and death had a greater importance than the resurrection. Indeed the resurrection is the fruit of the Cross. Nearly all St Athanasius's Easter sermons are sermons on Christ's sacrifice rather than on His resurrection. It is then clear that, while for these Fathers the resurrection is more important than it often is in the minds of modern Western Christians, yet none of them ever puts forward a theory of redemption by the mere fact of incarnation and resurrection, as has sometimes been asserted. The importance of the resurrection, as they understood it, is perhaps best illustrated by the following words of St Gregory of Nazianzus: ' We needed an Incarnate God, a God put to death, that we might be cleansed ; we rose again with Him because we were put to death with

Him ; we were glorified with Him, because we rose again with Him ' (*Or.* 45:28).

It would be misleading, however, to suggest that the idea of a price or a satisfaction in some form was ever absent from any of these Fathers. They drew their doctrine from the text of the Scriptures, and such an idea was too scriptural to be forgotten (cf. St Basil, *hom. in Psalm* 48:4). St Gregory of Nyssa and St Basil are among those who follow, at least as a part-explanation of the redemption, Origen's theory of a ransom paid to the devil, whereby the devil was deceived and his work frustrated (cf. St Gregory of Nyssa, *Great Catechism*, 23 ; St Basil, *hom. in Psalm* 7:2 ; 48:3). The doctrine was firmly opposed by St Gregory of Nazianzus (*Orat.* 45:22) ; St John Damascene (*de orthodoxa fide*, 3:27) and others, as being unworthy of God and flattering to the devil.

(viii) *St Augustine, founder of the characteristic Western theology. An explanation more in ethical than mystical terms.* One might say in a general way that the earlier Fathers had thought of the atonement as God coming to the rescue of man, while the Western Fathers from St Augustine were increasingly to think of it as an act of reparation made by man in the presence of God.

The difference is not, of course, one of doctrine, but of interpretation and emphasis. For the Eastern and early Fathers, God is the redeemer, but took on our human nature in order to be able to redeem us. For the Western theologian after St Augustine, with a few exceptions, it is the sinner who must make reparation for his sins. Yet the sinner could not himself do it because of his unworthiness. Someone, then, must step into the sinner's place. God solved the problem by becoming man, and making sacrifice in our name, and on our behalf.

St Augustine saw that this offering would be unethical unless we who were being saved by Christ's sacrifice were also changed in heart, and turned away from our sin. He saw the redemption, then, as partly a changing of the heart of the sinner, and partly as a sacrifice made on behalf of the sinner by one of his race. This is expressed in one place succinctly in five words : ' *sanguis iusti et humilitas Dei* ' (*de Trin.* 4:2, 4), the sacrificial shedding of blood by a just man, on the one hand, and the lesson on humility given by God, on the other.

There are thus two phases. God first gives man a lesson which will have the effect of changing man's heart. He next does for man what man is no longer able to do for himself. The lesson God gives is described by St Augustine principally as a lesson of humility and generosity. The pride of man is revealed to us, condemned and healed by the example set before us of God's humility, in taking on the form of a servant (*Enchiridion*, 108). Man's love is aroused by the example of God's generosity in taking on our nothingness, in order to give us His own riches (*Sermo*, 127:9).

As a further illustration of this insistence of St Augustine on the redemptive importance of God's presence and example, St Thomas, in a famous article of the *Summa Theologica*, takes from various works of St Augustine the following reasons for God's becoming man : the strengthening of our faith, the arousing of our hope, the stimulation of our love, the provision of a divine example of how we should live, a lesson of our own dignity to preserve us from listening to evil spirits or giving way to sin, to teach us the sublimity of the destiny God has decreed for us and lastly, a lesson of humility.

But, for St Augustine, it would not have been sufficient for God to teach us by example unless at the same time God had found a way to enable us to make amends for our sin, and thus satisfy His justice and win for us once more the grace of sonship and the complete destruction of injustice within us. St Augustine took from Scripture sometimes the idea of a just man shedding his blood for the community (*de Trin.* 4:2, 4 ; *Enchiridion*, 108) ; at other times, the general idea of a sacrifice for sin (*de Trin.* 4:13,17 ; In Ps 74:12 ; *de civ. Dei*, 10:20). He also used the idea of the innocent Christ assuming our punishment (*supplicium*) in order to remit our guilt, and put an end to our punishment (*contra Faustum*, 14:4).

A criticism sometimes brought against moral theories, i.e. that they would reduce Christ's death to the status of that of a mere innocent man, clearly does not apply to St Augustine, since it is a necessary part of his interpretation that it must be God's example to move us and teach us in a way that no human example could do, precisely because it is the example of God. Without the Incarnation, therefore, St Augustine's interpretation would be meaningless.

In the early Middle Ages, the two aspects of St Augustine's thought were to become divided, only to be joined again in the 13th cent. by St Thomas. The first aspect, that of salvation by the example and teaching of God, was to be stressed by Abélard (*see* ABELARD) to the exclusion of the aspect of any real sacrifice or vicarious death. This led St Bernard to accuse Abélard of denying the very essence of the atonement (cf. St Bernard, letter 190:8 and 9).

The second aspect was almost exclusively defended by St Anselm (*see* ANSELM) in a small work, *Cur Deus Homo*, which was destined to be the most influential book on this subject for most Western thought since the 12th cent. He introduced more explicitly than any previous writer the notion of satisfaction as being the very essence of objective redemption. That sin demands either eternal punishment or an act of adequate satisfaction he regarded as axiomatic. ' According to the measure of the sin, the satisfaction must be ' (*Cur Deus Homo*, 1:20). He also regarded it as clear on examination that nothing we sinful creatures can do could make adequate satisfaction for grave sin, not even our repentance, contrition, humility, abstinence, bodily labours or almsgiving. When we give God these acts, we are only giving Him what we already owe Him ; we are giving nothing to atone for our sin.

Since St Anselm has come in for a great deal of criticism on the part of both Catholics and Protestants, especially by Liberal Protestants, on the grounds that his system is legalistic, medieval and even unethical, it should be remembered that no previous interpretation of the Incarnation was so consciously based on an understanding of the majesty and goodness of God, as contrasted with the heinousness of sin. If you think, he said, that sin can be satisfied for with anything less than an infinite satisfaction, ' you have not yet considered the full gravity of sin' (*op. cit.* 1:21). You have not yet realized the honour and holiness of God. 'Nothing', he wrote, ' is less to be tolerated . . . than that a creature should take away the proper honour from the Creator, and not pay back what he has taken.'

In answer to the objection that it would be unjust on the part of the Father to punish the innocent in place of the guilty, St Anselm insisted on the distinction between satisfaction, which is an act of love and can be done by a friend, and punishment, which is an act of vindictive justice, and can only be inflicted on the guilty. St Anselm shared with St Athanasius a sense that God owed it to Himself to save His creation ; and that the redemption was ultimately for God's own glory and only subordinately for the good of the creature. Many people today would regard it as a weakness in St Anselm's argument that he cannot easily explain (*a*) why it was necessary for Our Lord to die, when His smallest act would have an infinite value on our behalf, or (*b*) how the resurrection and ascension have any redemptive value.

It has been suggested that St Anselm's notion of satisfaction derived either from the Teutonic *Wergild*, or (through Tertullian) from Roman public and private law. It is certain that the idea of satisfaction goes back to the early Church, since it is present in the Church's penitential discipline. This excludes Teutonic origins. Tertullian is equally excluded, as there is considerable evidence for the existence of the notion of penitential satisfaction before his time. Mr McIntyre has recently made an important study of St Anselm that confirms these views. He concludes : ' It is in the description of God's act of salvation in the *Deus-homo* and not in the setting of Roman law or Teutonic *Wergild* that the notion of satisfaction finds its proper place'. (John McIntyre, *St Anselm and His Critics* (1954) 88 : cf. especially pp. 82 ff.)

(xi) *St Thomas. A return to the fullness of early patristic doctrine.* In many respects St Thomas seems to take us back into the atmosphere of the early Fathers, for whom the atonement was total Christianity. All St Thomas has to say about Christ in the third volume of the *Summa* is seen as one or other aspect of the atonement. It never would have occurred to him to write two separate treatises, the Incarnation and the Atonement. In fact, it seems improbable that he would have written a treatise on the Church separate from the atonement. The two phases of thought which had been united

in St Augustine and then separated in Abélard and St Anselm are found re-united in St Thomas. Not only this, but the whole Eastern line of thought of redemption by a mystical union with the God-made-man, a union with His death, resurrection and ascension, is quite naturally an integral part of St Thomas's doctrine. Likewise the doctrine of the mystical body, which is no part of St Anselm's theory, is for the former, together with the doctrine of Christ's priesthood and mediatorship, a necessary complement to the doctrine of sacrifice or merit or satisfaction. As a sign of the great contrast between St Thomas's teaching and that of St Anselm, satisfaction forms only one out of ten reasons for the Incarnation listed by St Thomas in the beginning of the third part of the *Summa*.

(xii) *The Reformation.* The atonement was not one of the direct Reformation issues. Indirectly, the complete loss of the Catholic doctrine of intrinsic justification and sanctifying grace led them unwittingly further than ever from the atmosphere of the early and Eastern patristic thought. It was the Catholic doctrine of sanctifying grace which prevented the Catholic Western Fathers from ever drifting into a purely extrinsic and legalistic explanation of atonement. The result of the atonement, even in the West, was always understood as a sharing in Christ's risen life, which involved a sharing in His divine life. For the Reformers, rejecting all notion of intrinsic justice, the atonement was an act between Christ and the Father, which was in direct effectiveness completely extrinsic to man for whom Christ died. (For further consideration of the notion of extrinsic justification and its condemnation by the Church, *see* GRACE.) The Reformers' view eventually came to this : Christ in our place was condemned and received the full punishment we all deserved for our sins. He was then raised up and all our sins were forgiven and, because of His act, we are all regarded as though we had not sinned (cf. also PROTESTANT THEOLOGY). However, Catholics did not see the implications of the extreme Reformation view of atonement by vicarious punishment, except in so far as it involved extrinsic justification, and so the punishment theory was never condemned. Since that time, the more orthodox tradition in Protestantism has frequently modified the legalism of the early view, especially as a consequence of corresponding modifications in their theory of justification.

V The State of the Question today. Two tendencies in modern Catholic theology have affected its attitude towards the atonement. One is the modern text-book tendency of dividing the whole matter into separate treatises, and the other is the prestige of St Anselm's *Cur Deus Homo*. When the atonement became a separate treatise, it seemed easier to reduce its complexity in the sources to a more assimilable simplicity. The prestige of St Anselm's argument has undoubtedly been greatly fortified by the authority of J. Rivière. Rivière continued writing on the atonement during half a century. He began in conscious opposition to the continental Protestant liberal theology of A. Reville and A. Sabatier. These latter represented a modern version of Abélard. Christ was an exceptional 'divine' man who gave a supreme example of generosity and self-sacrifice, an example which will be the world's salvation in so far as it is followed. A similar doctrine was supported in England by H. Rashdall. Though its defenders did not need to deny Christ's godhead, they held the doctrine in a form which seemed, unlike that of Abélard, to be essentially independent of incarnation in the strict sense. The tendency of Catholic theology in reaction to this modernism was to stress a highly-objective theory of atonement. In the early part of the century, no view appeared so essentially objective as that of St Anselm. Rivière's books became popular among all, whether Catholic or Protestant, who saw in liberalism the great enemy of the pure Christian gospel.

Though Rivière's position appears to many people today a one-sided one, this was not due to his lack of acquaintance with the sources. He wrote, in fact, a classic history of the doctrine. He did, moreover, recognize the great complexity of the patristic interpretation. But it was his conviction that St Anselm had succeeded in expressing in a simple argument all that was essential in the earlier Fathers and theologians. Thus, he knew that many of the Fathers had preferred sacrificial language, but he decided that the sacrificial language about Christ in the sources could be reduced to the 'satisfaction' interpretation of St Anselm.

In his manner of defending St Anselm, Rivière did theology a great service. He made clear how often St Anselm has been misunderstood. Satisfaction must always be distinguished from punishment. Moreover, in satisfaction, it is not the suffering as such which pleases God, but the love and obedience which inform the suffering. He often condemned Catholic popular theology for falling into the Calvinistic error of interpreting Christ's redemptive suffering and death as an assumption of all the punishment due to man's sin !

The first aspect of atonement interpretation that has received increasing attention, as an element not included in the idea of satisfaction, is that of sacrifice. This is, to a great extent, due to the growth of eucharistic theology. L. Hardy, E. J. Scheller and M. de la Taille are among the many modern theologians who have clearly preferred the language of a sacrifice of praise, gratitude, propitiation and impetration to the narrower category of mere satisfaction. (Cf. L. Hardy, *La Doctrine de la rédemption chez saint Thomas*, Paris (1936) ; E. J. Scheller, *Das Priestertum Christi* (1934) ; and De La Taille, *Mysterium Fidei*, Elucid. XIII ; De La Taille, *The Mystery of the Faith*, London (1941) Bk. 1, chap. V.

In the last decades the great increase of interest in patristics and liturgy has led many theologians back to the early patristic views. This is especially noticeable in the writings of Father L. Bouyer and other followers of the so-called mystery-theology. Scripture theologians have contributed to this tendency. Mgr Cerfaux is convinced that St Paul regarded not only Christ's death, but also His resurrection, ascension and exaltation, and even the preaching of gospel through the history of the Church, as all having their part in the salvation which the redeeming God brings to mankind through His Son, Jesus Christ. Father Prat SJ, earlier in the century, was convinced that for Pauline thought all the Trinity should be given a place in the work of our redemption and that, consequently, the glorification of Christ by the Father in the resurrection is part of the work of our redemption, only secondary to the Cross itself. These views have been strengthened by writers like F. X. Durwell who have specialized on the salvific importance of the resurrection. Finally, there is a growing tendency, initiated by Abbot Vonier in his book, *The Victory of Christ*, once again with so many 2nd-cent. Fathers, to see the redemption as a great divine victory, through the Son of God, over all God's and man's enemies. Vonier, like Mgr Cerfaux, sees the continuation of this victorious battle all through the history of the Church. Mention finally ought to be made of M. Lepin who, in the twenties, writing on the eucharist, defended the view that, not only the cross and ascension and resurrection, and life of Christ in glory, but also all the actions of His earthly life, formed part of the sacrifice of Himself whereby we are redeemed.

Bibliography. For the patristic period, a complete bibliography would include most of the works of most of the Fathers. Of special importance are the *Adversus Haereses* of St Irenaeus and the *De Incarnatione* of St Athanasius. (The first is published in English in the Ante-Nicene Library of the Fathers ; the second is published in a translation by *A Religious of C.S.M.V.* (1953).)

For a general bibliography, beginning with the late 11th cent., cf. the article *Rédemption*, by J. Rivière, D.T.C., XIII, 1993 ff. This bibliography has been republished in an expanded form at the front of the volume, *Le Dogme de la rédemption dans la théologie contemporaine*, J. Rivière (1948).

For further reference to the history of the doctrine, see the above-mentioned, and also the following, works of J. Rivière : *The Doctrine of the Atonement*, translated from the early French edition by L. Cappadelta (1909) 2 vols ; *Le Dogme de la rédemption chez saint Augustin*, 3rd ed. (1933) ; *Le Dogme de la r. après S. Augustin au début du moyen âge* (1934) ; *Le Dogme de la r. : Études critiques et documents*, 1e série (1931) ; *John McIntyre, S. Anselm and His Critics* (1954) ; L. Richard, *Le Mystère de la rédemption* (1959).

Other histories : *H. Rashdall, The Idea of the Atonement in Christian Theology* (Liberal), Bampton lectures for 1915 (1919) ; *H. E. W. Turner, The Patristic Doctrine of Redemption* (1952). For St Thomas, cf. Victor White OP, *God the Unknown* (1956) 96 ff.

For modern theories, see R. G. Bandas, *The Master-Idea of St Paul's Epistles*, or *The Redemption* (1925) ; *T. Hywell Hughes, The Atonement :

Modern Theories of the Doctrine (1949) (mostly evangelical Protestant) ; Geoffrey Graystone SM, *Modern Theologies of the Atonement*, in ITQ, 20 (1953) 225 ff. and 366 ff. ; P. Grech, *De Redemptione in Moderna Theologia Anglicana* (1952).

For the Scripture, see : F. Prat SJ, *The Theology of St Paul*, 2 vols (1933) (translation of the 11th French edition) ; R. G. Bandas, the book above mentioned ; L. Cerfaux, *Christ in the theology of St Paul* (1959) ; Joseph Bonsirven, *L'Évangile de Paul* (1946) ; P. Heinisch, *Christus der Erlöser im Alten Testament* (1955) ; A. Kirchgassner, *Erlösung und Sünde im Neuen Testament* (1950) ; Cahiers 'Evangile', *Le Christ notre rédempteur* and *Jésus notre rançon* (1957) ; M. Lepin, *L'Idée du sacrifice de la Messe*, 741–5.

All the usual text-books of theology have a section on the *Redemption*, usually separately from the Incarnation (an exception to this found in the German theologian, M. Schmaus who, in vol. II of his *Katholische Dogmatik*, includes the Incarnation under the Redemption). A large monograph on *Le Geste rédempteur* by H. Bouesse OP, is expected to appear soon as section 3 of *Le Sauveur du monde*, in the collection, *Doctrina Sacra*. The Cambridge Summer School in 1928 published a volume of essays on *The Atonement*. Chapters XIII and XIV of *The Teaching of the Catholic Church*, ed. G. D. Smith, treat this subject. See also Karl Adam, *The Christ of Faith* (1957) (transl. from German), pp. 285 ff.

For the 'Resurrection-Victory-over-evil' theories of Atonement, see A. Vonier, *The Victory of Christ*, London (1934) ; *G. Aulen, *Christus Victor* (1931) (trans. from Swedish) ; *Christus Victor mortis* (papers of 3rd theological meeting, Gregorian University, Rome) (1958) ; *R. Leivestad, *Christ the Conqueror* (1954) ; L. Bouyer, *Le Problème du mal dans le christianisme antique*, in *Dieu vivant*, VI (1947) ; L. Bouyer, *L'Incarnation et l'église-corps du Christ dans la théologie de saint Athanase* (1943) ; L. Bouyer, *The Paschal Mystery* (1949) ; F. X. Durwell, *La Résurrection de Jésus, mystère de salut*, 3rd ed. (1954).

Among the mass of books on this subject by Protestants, besides those already mentioned, should be specially noted : *K. Barth, *Die kirchliche Dogmatik*, vol. IV, parts I and II, *Die Lehre von der Versöhnung* (1953–4), and vol. V, *Die Lehre von der Erlösung* (in the press) ; *E. Brunner, *The Mediator* (1952) and *The Christian Doctrine of Creation and Redemption, Dogmatic II* (1952), both are translations from the German ; *V. Taylor, *Jesus and His Sacrifice* (1937), and *The Atonement in New Testament Teaching* (1940), and *Forgiveness and Reconciliation* (1941) ; *E. C. Mascall, *Christ, the Christian and the Church* (1946), (Anglican) ; *L. Hodgson, *The Doctrine of the Atonement* (1951), (Anglican).

For further bibliography relating to the subject see articles *Christ, His Divinity*, *Christ, His Mission*, *Body, Mystical* and *Grace*.   H. F. D.

ATTRIBUTES OF GOD, THE After showing (I) what is meant by an attribute of God, and (II)

sketching the background on which a theologian considers God's attributes, this article gives (III) an account of the imperfections inherent in our knowledge of God. We have to show that these are due (i) to the fact that, having no experience of Him, we have no proper nor clear idea of God Himself. We then establish the theological foundation on which the doctrine of the divine attributes has to be based, that the being of God is infinitely perfect and absolutely simple. The imperfections in our knowledge of God are also due (ii) to the fact that we can only think of God in the diffuse and complex way distinctive of our human ways of thinking by means of abstract concepts and judgments. This is the philosophical foundation on which the doctrine of the divine attributes has to be grounded since it deals with human knowledge of God. Finally we explain (IV) how theologians have dealt with the problem of the divine attributes on the basis of these two foundations, and show that we could not reasonably be considered capable of having any more perfect or complete knowledge of God, even from the Scriptures, than we have.

I Definition. In the strict sense a divine attribute is a perfection distinctive of God Himself. Some theologians (cf. Van der Meersch, *De Deo Uno et Trino*, 96 ff) define a divine attribute more freely to cover anything which, apart from the divine essence, can be truly affirmed of God. It seems preferable, however, to take the strict definition in order to avoid having to regard terms such as creator and conserver, which refer properly to God by reason of His free activity with regard to created beings, as attributes distinctive of God's own being. A divine attribute is, properly speaking, a perfection which pertains to God's own being by a necessity inherent in the divine being itself, whereas terms such as creator, conserver, justice, mercy and providence are to be affirmed of God by reason of the ways in which He acts towards created things. We can only affirm these terms of God on condition that He freely chooses to create. He does not create by necessity of His being, and He cannot be just, merciful or provident towards Himself. St Thomas distinguished between the attributes of God's being and those of His activity. In the first part of the *Summa Theologica* he treats first of the attributes of God's being (1a:3–13), and then of the perfections proper to the divine activity (1a:14–25), and he distinguishes between what pertains to the activity of God's knowing and loving Himself and what pertains to His activity with regard to creatures : the former activity alone is at the origin of divine attributes in the strict sense of the term, for in God activity and being are identical. (Garrigou-Lagrange, *De Deo Uno*, 132–3). It is customary to call such terms as creator, justice, mercy ' relative ', as distinct from ' absolute ' attributes.

For the theologian a study of the attributes of God is only a section of a much larger treatise on the Nature of God. It is almost entirely speculative in character, being that part of the treatise in which metaphysical and logical questions arising from a consideration of the knowledge we have of God's nature are studied. We find in the Scriptures that many attributes or perfections are affirmed of God, such as goodness (Mt 19:17), life (Jn 5:26; 6:58), love (1 Jn 4:16), knowledge (Jn 14:6; 1 Cor 2:10-11), unicity (Ac 17:24-9), immutability (Jas 1:17), eternity (1 Tim 1:17), etc. (*See* NATURE OF GOD, and cf. Lessius, *De Perfectionibus Moribusque Divinis* for an exhaustive list of the several attributes of God). The question arises, then, as to how we are to understand the Scriptures in thus ascribing many different perfections to God whose being is simple, that is to say, without any sort of multiplicity or composition whatever. How can we meaningfully affirm many attributes of the God whose being cannot contain, nor be composed of many different perfections really distinct from each other? The theologian often approaches the same problem in a more philosophical manner, and, having proved by reason the existence of a necessary and infinite being, he begins to ask what we can know about the nature of this being from reason, and how we are to think of the being who is infinite in perfection, in all perfections, and yet not a composite being. Both these methods of approach lead up to the same problem. In his efforts to decide how we are to understand the Scriptures when they attribute many different perfections to God the theologian has entered upon an intricate question of speculative theology, in the investigation of which he can join hands with the philosopher reflecting on our human ways of thinking about infinite being.

II Background. Certain basic principles must be kept in mind throughout the treatment of the problem of the divine attributes:

(i) We do not know God as He is in Himself: we do not know the real or so-called 'physical' essence of God: 'No man hath seen God at any time' (Jn 1:18), for 'God inhabiteth light inaccessible' (1 Tim 6:16). God is completely intelligible to Himself; there is nothing mysterious to, nor hidden from, Him about His own being. Those who enjoy the beatific vision know God as He is in Himself and, in the view of St Thomas, from this knowledge they derive eternal happiness. We do not know God in Himself because He does not enter into our experience in such a way that we can be aware of, or come to perceive, His being. Hence we cannot possibly know God Himself in a way that even approaches to that in which He has at times made Himself known to certain saints, as St Paul (2 Cor 12:1-4), in extraordinary mystical experiences. If we cannot know God Himself, we can none the less think of Him and come to know a certain amount about Him. We can at least understand the meaning of statements made about God in the Scriptures, and show that they give us as profound a knowledge of God as our limited minds are capable of possessing.

(ii) We have no special faculty or way of thinking to have recourse to when we turn our minds to consider God (cf. St Pius X, *Pascendi*, D 2074). We have nothing but our ordinary human ways of thinking, and the special techniques involved in thinking by the three ways of causality, negation and extrapolation or eminence (*see* ANALOGY) to help us to face the formidable difficulties that thought about God involves for the human mind. God's knowledge of Himself is absolutely perfect: He knows Himself in one simple, completely adequate act by which He understands His own infinite being, this divine act of knowing being really identical with the divine being itself which is known. God's knowledge of Himself is as mysterious to us as is His being. It does not however follow that, because we cannot know God Himself in some suprarational way, we cannot know anything about God that is true of Him as He really is. The theologian has to show that it is possible to have an imperfect knowledge of infinitely perfect being on the same condition that we have imperfect knowledge of finite beings, viz. that the imperfections inherent in our knowledge are merely ones of inadequacy or incompleteness which do not of themselves involve any falsification.

III (i) The Theological Foundation. All our thinking originates in experience and is centred upon, though not restricted to, the beings of this world with which we become acquainted in experience. We have, or can attain, a certain knowledge of God which is purely natural, but this knowledge is not derived directly from God Himself; it is obtained indirectly from the things of this world in the course of reasoning to the existence of God as the cause of the world (Rom 1:21). Our idea of God (such as it is) is not derived from God Himself; it is built up by each person from such perfections as truth, goodness, beauty, unity, life and sanctity, which he finds embodied in various ways in objects we know from experience in this world. We begin to form some kind of idea of God in so far as we understand that, whereas these perfections belong to created things only in various limited, imperfect and changing ways, they are to be found in God in a way which is infinite, perfect and immutable and so beyond our understanding. Thus the idea that we form of God by reasoning is derived from created things; these reflect dimly something of the perfect being of God, but they cannot possibly give us a clear, proper or even summary idea of what God is in His own being. We can obtain some knowledge, but not a clear idea, of an unperceivable thing from its shadow; even so we can obtain some knowledge of God from His creation which shadows forth something of His being to our minds, making it possible for us to think of Him in terms of certain perfections we find present in created things. Thus we find that the Scriptures speak to us of God in terms of perfections we know from creation, but since the Scriptures are as powerless as created things to give us any idea of *how* these perfections are in God, or just are God, we cannot say that they give us a proper, a positive idea of God as He is in Himself. The Scriptures do enable us to think of God as accurately as is humanly possible through the medium of various ideas derived from creatures, but so far from manifesting to us what God is in Himself, they teach us that the being of God is far more mysterious than man had ever discovered for himself by mere reasoning. The best we can do is to come to think of God as the being who, because He is not contingent nor finite, is necessary and infinite, who exists without being dependent in any way on any other being because He exists in His own right, and who is every perfection in the simplicity of His being. In the words of Aquinas God is *ipsum esse subsistens* (cf. *Contra Gentiles*, 1:22). We can show by reason that there must be a necessarily existent, infinite being, but having done this we have not acquired any positive or clear idea of what such being is in itself. As Aquinas says so often, we know, i.e. have a positive idea of what such being is not, rather than what it is. We cannot even show positively that infinite being is intrinsically possible ; the best we can do, and need to do in defending the validity of theistic argument, is to show that it is not evidently impossible ; we can refute those who maintain that the expression ' necessary being ' is meaningless ; we can show that it has a meaning, but we cannot know positively all that it does mean. The proofs for the existence of God make clear to us that there is a being who is uncaused in His being so that He is the adequate reason of His own being. It is from this proof, which each man at least sketches for himself in weighing up the reasons why he believes in the existence of God, that we derive what knowledge we have of the nature of God by reason. A statement about God, such as ' God is infinite in perfection ', makes sense, then, not because we have a positive idea of God Himself derived from God, but because we can think of God through the medium of perfections we know from created things and which we know must exist in an uncreated manner. We can make meaningful statements about God because we can think of Him whom we do not know in Himself in terms of perfections which we do understand, and which we know are in God in a more perfect manner than they are to be found in the things in which we actually find them. We cannot, of course, think of God as possessing *any* quality or characteristic we find amongst creatures, but only the so-called ' pure perfections ' in the connotation of which no sort of limitation or imperfection is necessarily implied. Qualities which of their very nature involve limitation and imperfection of being (such as rationality, materiality, anger, grief) cannot exist in God (cf. *Summa Theologica*, 1a:13:3@1 ; *Contra Gentiles* 1:30 ; St Anselm : *Monologion*, 15).

III (ii) The Philosophical Foundation. To understand the ways in which we think about God it is necessary to understand first of all how we think about the ordinary things of this world, for these are the connatural objects of the human mind.

Because it originates within sense experience and is naturally orientated towards sensible things, all our thinking is rooted in, and intrinsically fashioned by the abstract concepts or ideas by means of which we come to know real things, and since our concepts are abstract the purely intellectual knowledge we have of *any* existent thing is inevitably imperfect because incomplete. We never know things, that is to say, possess them within our minds, just as they are in their own concrete reality, in the full determination and completeness of their individual reality. We do not know anything just as it is in one simple act of the mind (as, for example, God knows Himself). Our knowledge of things comes about (to simplify as much as possible) in two activities of the mind which philosophers regard as two distinct but complementary stages in the human knowing process, the first being that of forming abstract ideas and the second that of making judgments.

Imagine the case of a man who suddenly catches sight of some distant object, of the nature of which he is at first wholly ignorant. From the moment he apprehends it he is certain that the thing he observes is some kind of being or reality, but his understanding of its individual nature is for the time being wholly undetermined. He can only think of it as ' that something over there ' ; because his knowledge is so incomplete and imperfect he does not know what is to be said about its nature. He will begin his investigations into the nature of the object by looking for some qualities within it which characterize its entire reality, and he will look for a number of qualities, knowing that no one of them can be exhaustive of its entire reality. For example, the object he apprehends at first merely as some being may turn out to be an animal, and once he has learnt this he can begin to think of the entire thing before him in a more determinate manner, saying ' that thing over there is an animal '. In so thinking of the object he is thinking of its entire reality, for there is nothing about it which is not animal ; but he has not as yet attained a knowledge which is exhaustive of its entire reality, for there is much about the object which is not knowable merely from the abstract idea of animal. In other words his knowledge of the object is still relatively undetermined, incomplete or abstract, because the idea of ' animal ', by means of which he now thinks of the object, gives some knowledge of the entire object, but it does not give him a full or adequate knowledge of it. He does not as yet know even what kind of animal it is. His statement ' this is an animal ' is true as far as it goes, but not exhaustive of the truth about the creature. It may happen, however, that the man suddenly perceives that the animal he has been watching is a dog, and then later that it is a Labrador, and so he gradually comes to a more determinate, a more complete or less abstract knowledge of the object he knew first of all merely as some being. He can now form two more judgments, ' that is a dog ', ' that is a Labrador ', as he views the animal by means of the different abstract ideas he forms in his mind. There is a problem that arises out of this process of knowing, for, as conceived by the mind, many individually distinct objects appear to the mind to have the same properties and so to be ultimately the same. For the way in which individuality is known, *see* COSMOLOGY; also D. J. B. Hawkins, *Being and Becoming*, London, 1954, ch. 6, on the Identity of Indiscernibles.

Our observer has now attained a knowledge of what the object before him is and he is able to think of it as belonging to some determinate class of thing. In technical terms we say that he has reached a knowledge of the real 'essence' of the object.

All the time he has been watching the dog our observer will probably have noted many things which he will presumably have set aside as not being of its very essence, but which he now realizes are properties it must possess because it is the kind of animal it is, a dog : for example, the dog wags its tail, growls and barks. These are evidently properties that the animal possesses because it is a dog ; all dogs have, or at least it is natural for them to have, these properties. If, as a result of some accident, a dog loses its tail, its growl or bark, it is more or less seriously mutilated. In the measure that we understand the essence of a thing we can see that there is some kind of connection between its essence and its properties, though we may not know precisely what it is. Thus our observer sees that he must think of the creature before him first and foremost as a dog if he is going to think of it at all, and if he does so think of it he can understand that it must inevitably have a tail to wag and be able to bark and growl. To think the other way about, to say for example, that the creature's very essence consists in its capacity to wag a tail, to growl and bark, and therefore that it has the property of being a dog, that its 'doggy' nature is rooted in its growling and barking, is clearly nonsense.

The ideas or concepts which we use in thinking of an object and which enter into all our judgments about things are all universal and abstract. They are universal, that is to say, they tell us something about the object which it has in common with other objects more or less like it. Clearly the predicate in all our judgments is a universal. They are abstract ; that is to say, these concepts tell us something about the object we are interested in, but *only* what it shares with other like objects. An abstract concept gives us no knowledge of the particular way in which the individual we are interested in (this dog, for example) possesses a quality or attribute affirmed of it. Thus the mere statement, 'Prince is a dog', true as it is, does not tell a person who has never seen Prince what breed of dog he is, nor does the statement that he is four-legged tell anyone whether his legs are short or long, of the sprinting Greyhound or the trotting Aberdeen terrier variety. Thus mere intellectual knowedge of an individual thing is necessarily incomplete and inadequate *vis-à-vis* the individual in its concrete, individual reality because it is grounded on ideas which are abstract ; it is none the less true and satisfactory as far as it goes.

The act by which we know things and attain to the truth about them is the judgment, and a judgment is necessarily a composite act : it is the act by which, having first distinguished the one from the other, we affirm (or deny) some quality of a subject. In saying that 'Prince is a dog' the man who is observing Prince has first of all distinguished mentally between this one dog he calls Prince and the essence he affirms to be his, and having made this distinction in beginning to think about the dog he has to identify the two, Prince and dog, in a second act, affirming one or the other in a judgment because the two are identical in reality.

This composite way of thinking is well suited to knowing the kind of beings in our universe, for they too are composite in structure in that each is an individual substance of a determined essence with certain distinctive properties and a number of accidental qualities. In the beings of this world there is a real difference between the individual as such and the qualities it possesses, and there is some kind of distinction (philosophers are not agreed as to what kind) between the individual and its essence. We are therefore compelled to distinguish in our thinking between the subject in which we are interested and whatever we affirm of it in the predicate of our judgments as an attribute. Thus the basic form of the judgment, S is P, reflects differences we find in things. The basic pattern of our thinking processes corresponds to the basic metaphysical structure of the kind of beings which are the connatural objects of the human mind. The judgment fuses together into one composite idea the individual and the quality we affirm of it, and our judgments are true if there is, in the object of which we are thinking, a corresponding composite structure in its being. Thus in its final stage our thinking must take the form of the judgment. Since the connatural object of the human mind is a composite being, we think naturally in a composite way, i.e. in terms of subjects and qualities we predicate of them (cf. A. Forest, *La Structure métaphysique du concret selon saint Thomas d'Aquin*, Paris (1956), ch. 3). Unless we can think of something to affirm and of a being to affirm this of, we cannot think at all, and this law of human thinking holds good in an analogical way when we try to think of God Himself. We cannot think of God without thinking of Him as though He were a composite being. To lament this shortcoming in our thought about God is as senseless as to lament the discursive process inherent in all our thinking.

We have now to show that, though we have to think of God as if He were a composite being, we do not have to attribute any real composition to Him, so that, though imperfect, the knowledge we have of God, from the judgments we make concerning Him, can be true.

IV Our Knowledge of God. The theological foundation on which we are working assures us that there is no real composition or multiplicity of any kind whatever in God, for His being is simple. In the words of the Fourth Lateran Council God is 'one absolutely simple essence, substance or nature' (D 428)[1], and in those of the Vatican Council,

[1] Una essentia, substantia, seu natura simplex omnino.

'one, unique, absolutely simple and unchangeable spiritual substance' (D 1782).[1]

The philosophical foundation which we have had to provide assures us that since we cannot think of Him save as though He were a composite being, we have to think of God as some kind of being possessing numerous qualities, as though distinct from His substance or essence. Furthermore, since we cannot think of any being as just possessing a numerous assortment of qualities without any sort of order existing among them, we must ask first of all what is constitutive of its essence and then try to order its various qualities one with the other by their common reference to this essence as their ultimate origin. When we begin to think about God, then, we must first of all ask what we are to conceive as being the essence of God. Hence we have to think of God as the being (i) who is the subject of whom we intend to think and make statements (judgments), (ii) who is *what* we conceive Him to be by reason of what we must regard as His essence, and (iii) who has other properties, perfections or attributes which belong necessarily to Him in virtue of the essence we regard as constitutive of His divine being. Since God is necessarily what He is there can be no accidental qualities in His being.

(a) *The Metaphysical Essence of God* : we cannot rest satisfied with the position of the agnostic who says that there exists some kind of being not of this world whom we call God, but that we cannot know anything whatever about Him apart from the fact that He exists in the 'unknown beyond'. The proofs for the existence of God establish that there is a being not of this world on whom this world depends for all that it is, but these proofs are not complete unless they establish something about the nature of the being they prove to exist. The Scriptures speak of many different attributes as belonging to God : hence we are naturally led to ask which of all these attributes is so distinctive of God as to be the one we must identify with Him, so that it is to God as an essence. When we think of God some perfection should come immediately to our minds before any other, and we should be able to see that all the other perfections He has, He must have because they are demanded by reason of the primordial perfection He is. What, then, is God ? This is the question known to theologians as that of the 'metaphysical essence of God'.

It is necessary to be perfectly clear as to what exactly we are asking in putting this question to ourselves. We are *not* asking a question about the real or so-called 'physical' essence of God. If we define an essence as that by which a being is the particular kind of being it is, and regard essence as a principle of limitation of being inherent in all created beings, it is obvious that God has no essence. Since His being is unlimited and positively infinite in perfection, God is not a particular kind of being. Applied to God the term 'essence' can only mean

[1] Una singularis, simplex omnino et incommutabilis substantia spiritualis.

'what infinite being is' ; thus to speak of the 'divine essence' is just another way of speaking of the divine being, for they are one and the same, and if the divine being is itself unknowable to us so also is the divine essence. But we have to think of God in the composite way in which we think of created things, so that we have to conceive the divine being as if at its heart there were an essence making God to be God and making it necessary for Him to have, as so many properties, the perfections He has. Thus theologians speak of 'the metaphysical essence of God' to mean, not His real essence, but that which we conceive as the constitutive principle of the divine being and all its attributes. When they say they are trying to decide what is the metaphysical essence of God, theologians do not mean that they are trying to know something in God Himself which is at the root of His being (for nothing in God is at the root of His being), but that they are trying to decide what it is that, because it makes both the infinity of God and of all His perfections meaningful to us, we are to conceive as being to God what an essence really is to a particular thing. The question is not purely arbitrary : it is at least as legitimate as, for example, that of the mathematicians who ask what we are to understand by $\sqrt{2}$ or $\sqrt{-1}$. Our question is, then, what is God so far as we can think of Him ? What in God must we conceive as being at the heart of His being because to our way of thinking it is the source from which we are able to derive in an ordered way all the other perfections we know belong to God ?

St Thomas did not deal explicitly with this question of the metaphysical essence of God : theologians only began to focus attention on it during the 15th cent. However, his celebrated proofs for the existence of God conclude by showing that in God being (or existence) and essence are identical so that God's name, the name we should give Him in preference to all others is, 'He Who is' (*Summa Theologica*, 1a:3:4, 6 & 7c ; 1a:13:11c ; cf. Ex 3:13-15 ; 6:3 which St Thomas accepted as a Scriptural authority for his view.) In making this the conclusion of the proofs he implicitly affirmed that subsistent being is the perfection we must regard as the essence constitutive of all that we understand God to be. For St Thomas God is, and must be, all we know Him to be because He is first and foremost pure being. The majority of theologians belonging to the Thomist school accept this view ; they hold that in thinking of God we must think of Him as being infinitely perfect because He exists and just is being itself in His own right. Because He is pure being of Himself, God possesses necessarily all perfections, or rather He just is all perfections : the attributes we predicate of God are just an expression of what being in itself is. Before the time of Pope Leo XIII many Thomists expressed this view in a less satisfactory because negative manner by saying that we must think of God first and foremost as the uncaused being, i.e. as not caused by any other being. God is, of course, the uncaused being, but it is preferable, on metaphysical and logical grounds, to identify His metaphysical essence with the positive perfection which explains why He must be uncaused, and this is His subsistent being. God is uncaused for the positive reason that He is being itself in His own right. (Toussaint, *Attributs divins*, DTC 1:2229–30.)

A certain number of Thomists, e.g. Billuart, John of Saint-Thomas and the Salmanticenses, have held that we ought to think of God not as pure being, but rather as pure intellect, for pure being is in fact pure spirit and pure intellect. God is all that He is because He is first and foremost pure spirit and intellect. This view is, however, not generally accepted because we must always think of intellect as a manifestation of being, and not of being as a manifestation of intellect. Knowing is the most perfect form of immanent or living activity, but it is not the root of all perfections. It is itself rooted in the more ultimate perfection of being, for it is one amongst many other possible ways of being.

Scotus considered that the metaphysical essence of God must be what he termed 'Radical Infinity', by which he meant the necessity inherent in the infinite being, which is the divine essence itself, of possessing every perfection in an unlimited way, *Opus Oxoniense*, 1:2:3:17; 4:13:1:31 ff., cf. P. Raymond : *Duns Scot*, DTC 4:1875. Outside Scotist circles this view is generally criticised on the ground that infinity is not so much a perfection in its own right (like goodness, life or justice), as the *manner* in which being and all other perfections are to be found in God. In other words God cannot be just infinite being ; infinity must be rooted in some perfection of which it is an attribute. God is infinite in all perfections, but the metaphysical essence of God must be that which necessitates infinity of being in God. It seems that it is the simplicity and purity of His being which accounts for the infinity of each and every perfection in God ; the 'demand' for the infinity of each of the divine perfections cannot account for the simplicity of God's being.

Finally the Nominalists of the late Middle Ages (William of Ockham, Gabriel Biel and Peter d'Ailly) held that God is just the entirety of all His perfections. This view is universally rejected for it is based on a confusion between the real and metaphysical essences of God. God is the entirety of all His perfections in the simplicity of His being but we cannot in this world know God as He is in Himself (cf. Toussaint, *op. cit.* 2228–9).

(*b*) *The Distinction between the Divine Essence and its Attributes* : Theologians speak of real distinctions and of logical distinctions. By a real distinction they mean (i) a difference or otherness between things, or parts of the same thing, (ii) which holds between the things or parts themselves independently of the mind, and (iii) which is merely discovered and acknowledged to exist by the mind. Such, for example, is the difference between twins, between the body and soul in man, and between an individual and its various qualities as described above. A logical distinction, on the other hand, is one made

by the mind between two aspects of one and the same thing. Unfortunately theologians usually write as though there were two different kinds of logical distinction. There is, however, only one entirely genuine kind of logical distinction, and it is the one known as a 'virtual distinction', this is a difference (i) made by the mind, (ii) which does not correspond to any real difference found in the object itself, but (iii) has to be made by the mind on account of its inability to assimilate all it finds in the object in one complete idea. Such, for example, is the distinction made by the mind between rationality and animality when it thinks about a man. These two concepts are distinct from each other ; it is possible to think of one, animality, without thinking of the other, rationality, and there are in fact some animals which are not rational ; such a distinction is called a 'major' or 'complete' virtual distinction ; and it is possible to think of rationality without *explicitly* thinking of animality but since there are no men, i.e. rational beings, who have not animality, the distinction between rationality and animality in man is called a 'minor' or 'incomplete' distinction. In a real man there is no real distinction corresponding to these two concepts (as there is between his body and soul) ; the whole man is a rational-animal. None the less we have to think of each man now under one aspect as rational, and now under the other as animal, because our minds cannot deal with the real rational-animal unity all at once. The reason for making the distinction between the various aspects we find in the object is not purely mental though the distinction itself is purely mental. There is a real foundation for the distinction we make because within the unity of the object itself we find that which corresponds to each of our concepts. We make a genuine logical distinction as often as the object before the mind presents more to the mind as a unity of being than the mind can assimilate in one concept. The mind often has to view an object in different ways from different points of view, so that what is one and the same in reality becomes known by the mind piece by piece through a multiplicity of different concepts. The object is one in itself, but to our minds this unity takes the form of a multiplicity of different perfections which we conceive by means of different concepts. In such a case the object, though really one, is said to be 'virtually' multiple, because for us it is equivalent to one being with a multiplicity of distinct perfections (cf. Van der Meersch, *op. cit.* 101–105 ; L. Billot, *De Deo Uno et Trino*, thesis xvii).

The other distinction which theologians commonly call logical is in fact only a verbal distinction : this consists in the use of different words to denote one and the same idea we have in our minds in speaking of an object. Such a difference is neither demanded, nor occasioned by anything within the object itself, nor even by our mental activity, but merely by considerations of style and euphony. Thus I can speak indifferently of the Prime Minister or of the head of the government, and in these expressions I am only using different words to express one and the same idea in my mind.

What, then, are we to say about the distinctions we make in thinking of God between His essence and His attributes ? In the case of any created being we have explained that many distinctions are discovered in the object and are merely recognized by the mind, and that it is natural for us to think of a composite being in a composite manner. But God is simple being, so what are we to say about the multiplicity of the attributes affirmed of Him by the Scriptures, and of the distinctions we make, and have to make, between them in thinking about God and in proving His existence ?

Two solutions, representing two extreme positions, are set aside by the Church as erroneous :

(i) The Arians and Eunomians of the fourth–fifth centuries, and later the Nominalists of the 14th–15th cent. denied that there can be any kind of distinction, real or logical, between the divine essence and its attributes, or between the divine attributes themselves, no matter how they are considered. The distinctions we make, e.g. between God and His goodness, are purely verbal, and they must be purely verbal, for the simplicity of God is incompatible with any sort of multiplicity. This view is rejected as incompatible with Scripture which does not fictitiously ascribe many perfections to God, but states that many perfections are really in God. Thus it is impossible to hold that the different statements we make about God are only verbally different ways of saying one and the same thing of God, for this is equivalent to saying that they are all meaningless. The philosophical foundation for the Nominalist opinion, according to which our abstract ideas are devoid of any objective validity, has little to commend it even from the purely philosophical point of view ; and there is no justification for the view that the multiplicity of our concepts of God is incompatible with His simplicity, for the diversity of our concepts is not of itself any sign of a lack of identity or simplicity in God Himself. Pope John XXII condemned the same opinion as expounded by Eckhart (D 523). The great adversaries of the Eunomian theory were the Greek Fathers, especially St Basil, who wrote five books *Adversus Eunomium* (PG 29:498 ff.), and St Gregory of Nyssa, who wrote twelve books, *Contra Eunomium* (PG 45:247 ff.). The Greek Fathers constantly use the term *axioma* for a divine attribute as if to denote its origin in our activity of thinking (cf. Toussaint, *op. cit.* 2225).

(ii) At the opposite extreme to the above view is the doctrine of the Ultra-Realist, Gilbert de la Porrée, Bishop of Poitiers, who during the 12th cent. advanced the view that there is a real distinction between the divine essence and each of its attributes, and between each of the divine attributes themselves, for to each distinction of the mind there must correspond a like distinction in the object known. Gilbert considered that the real distinctions he posited within the divine being do not prejudice God's simplicity because each of the

divine attributes is in God in pure act, i.e. is itself simple (cf. M. Chossat, *Dieu*, 1165–7). This view is to be rejected as certainly erroneous for it cannot be held consistently with the Church's teaching about the divine simplicity. The view of Gilbert de la Porrée was examined and condemned at the Council of Rheims in 1148. The fairness, however, of the Council of Rheims's view of Gilbert has been questioned by M. E. Williams in *The Teaching of Gilbert Porreta on the Trinity*, Rome (1951). The Symbol of Faith issued by the Council by authority of Eugenius III states : ' We believe and confess that God is the simple divine nature . . . we believe that God is only wise by that wisdom which is God ; great by that greatness which is God ; eternal by that eternity which is God ; one by that unity which is God ; God by that Divinity which He is : that is, that He is in Himself wise, great, eternal, one God '.[1] The only multiplicity which the Church acknowledges to be real within God is that of the opposite relations which are constitutive of the three Persons of the Trinity (D 703). The Father is not the Son, and neither the Father nor the Son is the Holy Spirit ; none the less each of these Persons is the divine nature (*see* TRINITY). Granted, then, that the only real distinctions in God are those of the opposite relations between the divine Persons, it follows that there is no real distinction in God between the divine nature and its attributes for there is no opposition of relations between them.

Such, then, are the opinions to be set aside as heterodox. Along what lines are we to solve our problems ? The Church insists that we must safeguard both the real simplicity of God's being and the necessity of our having to attribute many perfections to God, and she allows freedom to her theologians to defend two theories which have been discussed ever since they were propounded in the Middle Ages, as neither fails to meet the requirements of the Church's teaching, the one being that of St Thomas and the other that of Scotus.

(1) The vast majority of theologians are agreed that it is necessary to follow the principles outlined by St Thomas in his treatment of questions about the meaning of the many statements we make about God, cf. in particular, *Sentences* 1:2:1:3c ; *Summa Theologica*, 1a:13:4c and 12c, *Quaestiones de Potentia*, 7:6. The simplicity of God's being means that in God all the divine perfections are one identical reality with the divinity itself and so with each other. Thus there cannot be any real distinctions in God apart from those of the three divine

[1] Credimus et confitemur simplicem naturam divinitatis esse Deum, nec aliquo sensu catholico posse negari, quin divinitas sit Deus et Deus divinitas. Si vero dicitur : Deum sapientem sapientia, magnitudine magnum, aeternitate aeternum, unitate unum, divinitate Deum esse, et alia hujusmodi : credimus nonnisi ea sapientia, quae est ipse Deus, sapientem esse ; nonnisi ea magnitudine, quae est ipse Deus, magnum esse ; nonnisi ea aeternitate, quae est ipse Deus, aeternum esse ; nonnisi ea unitate, quae est ipse Deus, unum esse ; nonnisi ea divinitate Deum, quae est ipse : id est, seipso sapientem, magnum, aeternum, unum Deum (D 389).

Persons. The distinctions between the divine attributes which appear so real to us are only logical or virtual distinctions which we are compelled to make because the eminent perfection and infinite fulness of the divine being not only makes it impossible for us to know God Himself, but makes it necessary for us in thinking of Him to use a multiplicity of concepts, and to make many different statements about Him (as the Scriptures do). It has to be remembered that our knowledge of God is derived, not from God Himself, but from created things in which many of the perfections we predicate of God (e.g. sanctity, justice, knowledge) are to be found really distinct from each other ; and granted that there is no real distinction between being and its transcendental properties of unity, truth and goodness, none the less their real identity, so far from being evident to all minds from experience, has to be established by analyses of some complexity (cf. *Quaestiones de Veritate*, 1:1). Thus we naturally think of the perfections we predicate of God as distinct from each other, even when we ascribe them to God. It is possible, however, for the theologian to deduce the divine attributes in a logical sequence from the metaphysical essence of God, for in God there is only a minor logical distinction between them, but the reasoning involved in doing so presupposes considerable metaphysical acumen in the theologian. Furthermore we have explained that our concepts are abstract, so that each concept we form of a perfection that we predicate of God in a judgment tells us something about the being of God, but it does not tell us *how* that perfection is present in God, nor does it express all that there is in God : it expresses merely what it reveals to us, which is but an aspect of God's infinite being. Since God is infinitely more than any concept can possibly reveal to us, we must form numerous concepts, each one expressing something about God which is not expressed to us in any of the other concepts we have used to think of Him in order to know the little we do know about God. But all the perfections which we use in order to think of God, and which as known to us are either really or logically distinct from each other, are one reality in God, so that we affirm them of Him and at the same time deny that in Him there are any of the distinctions which enter into our thinking. As St Thomas says, ' all the perfections of things which exist in things separately and in many ways, pre-exist as one in God '.[1] God is simple in His being, but to our minds (i.e. virtually) He is multiple, for the very infinite fulness (*see* PLEROMA) of the Divinity is such that we can only know the little we do know about Him in a mosaic of perfections conceived as distinct from each other because each one is only known by us in the imperfect, created manner in which we find it expressed in the things of this world.[2]

[1] *Summa Theologica :* 1a:13:5c : omnes rerum perfectiones, quae sunt in rebus creatis divisim et multipliciter, in Deo praeexistunt unite.

[2] Intellectus noster non potest una conceptione diversos modos perfectionis accipere : tum quia ex creaturis cogni-

This necessity for our thinking in this composite manner about God, the absolutely simple being, is due partly to the nature of the human mind, and also to the fact that, having no knowledge of God as He is in Himself, our knowledge of God cannot be derived from His own being. Our knowledge of God is derived from created things, and so we can only think of Him mediately and indirectly, as for example we think of primitive human life with the aid of a few exhibits preserved in a museum. Our thought about God thus reflects to a certain extent the beings of this world from which we have derived what we know of the perfections which are to be found in God. Further, we have to think of God, not only in the mirror of created things, but also in that of created human thought. Our knowledge of God is thus doubly mediate, for God is viewed remotely through the medium of created things and of created ways of thinking. As St Thomas says, in thinking of God we must always make allowance for the fact that ' the meaning of a term is determined by the object, not immediately but only mediately through the mind '.[3] Our knowledge of God is thus imperfect because purely analogical (*see* ANALOGY). It must inevitably lack much desired precision, and certainly lacks the vividness which goes with knowledge by direct vision. Mere thinking about God will not of itself bring happiness to us on earth, as the vision of Him brings to those who see Him in heaven.

In God Himself, in the simplicity of His divine being, there is present that which corresponds to each of the perfections we conceive as a different attribute without the multiplicity which affects solely our concepts of these perfections. Thus the foundation for the distinctions we make is in God, for the perfections denoted by each of our concepts are in God, but they are in Him in a way which is very different from that in which we conceive them. In God justice is goodness, and goodness is truth. From the purely logical point of view, however, we cannot identify justice and goodness, nor goodness and truth, for the special content of each concept is different from that of the others. Thus the distinctions we make in speaking of God only hold in our minds, and we do not predicate any distinction, composition or multiplicity of God despite the fact that they enter into our thinking about God. We know that the perfections are in God without being really distinct in Him ; the statements we make about God are true because we only affirm of God what is in Him, but the knowledge they give us of God is imperfect for we do not see how these different perfections can be one in the simplicity of the divine being.

(ii) The only critics of this, the Thomist theory of the attributes of God, are the theologians of the

tionem accipit, in quibus sunt diversi modi perfectionum secundum diversas formas : tum quia hoc quod in Deo est unum et simplex, plurificatur in intellectu nostro, etiam si immediate a Deo reciperet ; sicut multiplicatur processio suae bonitatis in aliis creaturis (*Sentences*, 1:2:1:3c).

[3] *Quaestiones de Potentia* 7:6 : significatio nominis non immediate refertur ad rem, sed mediante intellectu.

Scotist school. Scotus was not satisfied with St Thomas's doctrine of virtual distinctions; he criticised the Thomist theory of the divine attributes but, like St Thomas, he wished to avoid the extreme positions of Eunomius and of Ultra-Realism. He held that there is a kind of distinction to be placed between the Real and Virtual distinctions of St Thomas which he called a *distinctio formalis ex natura rei*. A real distinction is one which holds between thing and thing, part and part. A virtual distinction, on the other hand, seemed to Scotus to be an arbitrary distinction because it does not correspond to any difference within the object. Between these two Scotus held we must place the cases in which there is a lack of real identity between formality and formality (i.e. aspect and aspect) within a being independently of our thinking (*ex natura rei*), so that one formality or aspect in the object known is not identical with another. (*Opus Oxoniense*, 1:8:4:16 ff; cf. P. Raymond, *op. cit.* 1875-6; F. Copleston: *A History of Philosophy*, II, 529). He held that there is such a formal distinction between the divine essence and each of its attributes, and between the attributes themselves, this distinction being less than a real one, but none the less more than what Aquinas held a virtual distinction to be.

This view of Scotus has never been censured by the Church, and it is universally acknowledged as an opinion that can be freely defended in the Church's schools of theology. The validity of this theory of the divine attributes stands or falls with Scotus's philosophical theory of knowledge which is based on the presupposition that some kind of difference or non-identity must be found in the real order corresponding to every valid distinction made by the mind, for unless there is some such real non-identity a logical distinction is arbitrary. The majority of theologians, however, have not taken to the idea that there can be any kind of non-identity in the simple being of God other than that of the three divine Persons, and to safeguard the theological foundation on which the theory of the divine attributes must be built, they have preferred to take the Thomist theory of distinctions as satisfactory on both theological and philosophical grounds.

Conclusion. In thinking of God, as in thinking of any created thing, we need to have many different ideas of the perfections He possesses. We attain our knowledge of these perfections from created things and not from God Himself, and distinguish between God Himself Who exists, His metaphysical essence and the perfections we conceive Him to have as properties of this essence. But in attributing these perfections to God in our judgments we do not attribute the distinctions we make between them with our minds, as we generally do when we attribute some quality to a created thing, for God has no qualities distinct from Himself. He does not really possess any perfections: He is all His perfections. In God being, essence and properties are one simple reality.

Bibliography. St Thomas Aquinas, *Sentences*

1:2:1:3; *Summa Theologica*, 1a:13:4c and 12c; *Quaestiones de Potentia*, 7:5:@2, 7:6; *Contra Gentiles*, 1:30-35; Billuart, *Commentary on Prima Pars*, dist. 2; Capreolus, *Commentary* on Sentences, 1, dist. 8, qu. 4; John of Saint-Thomas, *Cursus Theologicus*, In 1, qu. 4, art. 6, disp. 4; Lessius, *De Perfectionibus Moribusque Divinis* (Louvain 1619; recent edition Paris, Lethielleux, undated); Scotus, *Opus Oxoniense* or *Commentary on the Sentences*, 1, dist. 2, qu. 2 and 3; dist. 8, qu. 4; Suarez, *Disputationes Metaphysicae*, disp. 30:4; C. Toussaint, 'Attributs divins' in DTC 1:col. 2223-35; X. Le Bachelet SJ, 'Dieu (Sa nature d'après les Pères)' in DTC 4:col. 1083-94; M. Chossat SJ, 'Dieu (Sa nature d'après les Scolastiques)', in DTC 4:col. 1152-1243; P. Raymond OFM Cap., 'Duns Scot', in DTC 4:col. (1874-81); L. Billot, *De Deo Uno et Trino* (Rome 1935); J. Franzelin, *De Deo Uno* (Rome 1870), especially thesis 6 and thesis 13, on the Fathers; R. Garrigou-Lagrange OP, *De Deo Uno* (Paris 1938); J. Van der Meersch, *De Deo Uno et Trino* (Bruges 1928); F. Copleston SJ, *A History of Philosophy*, vol. 2 (London 1950); E. Gilson, *Jean Duns Scot* (Paris 1952); G. D. Smith, 'God One and Indivisible: The Divine Attributes' (Cambridge Summer School Lectures (London 1931) ch. 3); J. Klein, *Der Gottesbegriff des Johann Duns Scotus* (Paderborn 1913).

E. A. S.

ATTRITION This article presupposes and completes the article on CONTRITION (q.v.) so that the ideas of Repentance and Contrition have been there seen, as also the necessity of Contrition for forgiveness and its qualities. The distinction of Perfect and Imperfect Contrition has there been sketched up to Trent. While that article continued to describe Perfect Contrition, this present article will describe Imperfect Contrition or Attrition.

I The notion of Attrition and its goodness.

II That it is sufficient for forgiveness in the sacrament; and whether it requires an element of the love of God.

III The possibility of a valid but fruitless sacrament.

I Its notion and goodness. The Catholic notion of attrition is given by Trent (XIV:4; D 898) as '. . . that imperfect contrition which is called attrition, since it is conceived commonly either from consideration of the foulness of sin or from fear of hell and punishments [and which] if it excludes the will to sin and has the hope of pardon [the council] declares not only does not make a man a hypocrite and a greater sinner, but is a true gift of God and an impulse of the Holy Spirit, not as yet indwelling but only moving, by whose assistance the penitent prepares for himself the way to justice. And though without the sacrament of Penance it cannot of itself lead the sinner to justification, yet it disposes him to obtain [impetrandam] the grace of God in the sacrament of Penance.' The council touches the use of fear in causing repentance and rejects as calumny the Protestant idea that the Church taught justification to be possible without the good dispositions of the receiver of the sacrament of Penance.

This sorrow can be called imperfect for two connected reasons ; in that its motives are less perfect than the motive of charity, and in that its efficacy is less perfect, for it does not of itself reconcile to God. By the motive 'the foulness of sin' the Council means that the sinner sees his act as evil, devoid of good and virtue. By the motive of 'fear' the Council means that the sinner sees his act as evil because it is the cause of the eternal penalty of hell, or of other punishments that follow on sin. In either case there is included a reference to God, either as the norm of goodness or as the one offended who will inflict the penalty. Upon this mental apprehension and evaluation by the sinner there follows sorrow and detestation of sin as evil. If this proceeds, as it can, to an effective detestation which excludes the will to sin and makes a man turn to God with hope of pardon, then a man has that attrition defended by Trent against Protestant attacks.

Luther, who is still followed with reservations by modern Lutherans (cf. Galtier, n. 98), condemned attrition as a forced and purely natural movement of fear, which did not destroy a sinner's love of sin, did not turn him from evil to good and to God. So it was no true conversion. Hence the gibing name 'Gallow's sorrow' and the imputation of hypocrisy. If the idea is understood in that way, he had good reason for criticism ; but that is far from the Catholic notion.

We will give a brief historical sketch of attrition, with special reference to the motive of fear as approved by Scripture and Tradition. Then we will investigate the notion of attrition from fear to see more clearly what it contains and how it can be good (bonum honestum), can exclude all will to sin and be a step to justification.

In Scripture (cf. also texts on Repentance, s.v. CONTRITION) the motive of fear is often set before sinners to keep them from sin or to turn them from sin (cf. Baruch 2:13 ff. ; Ecclus 1:16, 27 ; 2:22 ; 5:5 ; Ps 2:11 ; 84:5 ff. ; Jer 31:18 ff. In the NT : Mt 10:28 ; Lc 3:7 ff. ; 13:3 ff. ; Rom 2:5 ; Phil 2:12). From such texts it seems clear that sorrow from fear is recommended as honest, useful and salutary, provided always that the fear is of the right kind. Similarly the Fathers, while trying to lead sinners to the most perfect repentance of charity, dilate freely on the punishments due to sin as a reason for turning from sin. See Gregory Nyssa, PG 44:765 ; John Chrysostom, PG 49:154 ; St Gregory, PL 79:332 (cf. Doronzo, II, 255 ff.). St Augustine, often cited by Protestants and Jansenists as rejecting sorrow from a motive of fear, is of the same mind. (PL 37:1835 ; 38:857, 880–2 ; cf. Galtier, p. 80 ff. ; Doronzo, II, 256 ff. ; R. Rimml, 'Das Furchtproblem in der Lehre des h. Augustinus', ZKT, 45 (1921), 244–9.) Thus also the Scholastics, repeating the distinctions of various kinds of fear from the Fathers (Doronzo, II, 242 ff.).

Even such a brief exposition serves to show that such attrition can be honest and salutary. Moreover it can effectively exclude the will to sin, cf. Ecclus 7:40 ; Jn 5:14 ; St Ambrose : '. . . for while he fears punishment, he keeps grace' (PL 15:1277).

A consideration of the various distinctions made in fear explains this doctrine. Fear can be an accompaniment of charity (filial fear, chaste fear, reverence) in that one who loves God fears and detests the evil done to a beloved Father by Sin. This fear is not in question here. Then fear can be concerned with punishment, looking to God as a Master who will punish his erring servant (servile fear). Loving oneself, one hates what is evil for oneself, fears it, detests it. Here two attitudes can be distinguished. The first is 'simply servile fear', which, while not explicitly including love of God yet does not exclude it. It simply prescinds from the aspect of sin that it is an offence against a loving God. The second attitude is 'basely servile fear' (timor serviliter servilis), which is exclusively selfish. It sees only one thing as evil, the sinner's punishment, and excludes the evil of offending God, losing God. The distinction is best seen in this that for basely servile fear punishment is the only evil, so much so that if it were not there the sinner would still sin. In other words he still loves sin. In simply servile fear, while punishment is the actually operative motive, it is not considered as the greatest and only evil. It is seen as including the loss of God and thus the sinner sees the ultimate evil of offending and losing God.

Basely servile fear is to be rejected as a sinful attitude. Simply servile fear is defended as useful and salutary, able to exclude all will to sin. It leads to detestation of sin because sin is seen as an offence against God that brings punishment. Hence a choice can be made by which sin is freely detested because, as an offence against God leading to punishment, it is the greatest of evils, to be avoided at all costs and always. In other words the sinner resolves to keep all the commandments of God whose breaking entails eternal punishment. This last point explains why Trent adds 'with hope of pardon'. For unless hope is there, then despair and further sin will result. But the hope of pardon opens the way to release. So, at least implicitly, the detestation of sin contains a self-interested love of God (amor concupiscentiae, desiring God as one's own good), a love also of the state of justice that secures the good and avoids punishment. Then, included in the love of justice, there is an implicit desire to love God in himself, charity. For this is the great commandment and basic element of the life and justice that the sinner desires. All that may seem a great deal to see in what is simply attrition from a motive of fear. But it is such attrition, and not servilely servile fear, that Catholic teaching defends.

The reason for considering it good (apart from its recommendation by Scripture and Tradition) is simply that it is seeking an end that is good (the avoidance of punishment) by a means that is not only good but is also the only means available (the detestation of sin). Such a means was established by God, and by Him joined to that end by the bond or motive of fear ; for it is God who fixed the penalty for the sinner who does not detest his sin. Obviously such a motive for acting is not the perfect one ; but God sets it before us, so it is clearly good.

The argument continues that attrition so described can exclude all will to sin. For the punishment that man fears is attached not simply to external acts but to the sinful will itself. Hence that too must be removed to avoid punishment. It is not like a man still loving his money as he gives it up to save his life. Here you can only save your life by giving up your sin and also your love of sin.

II Sufficiency in the Sacrament. Need for an element of love. The earlier history of this question is given under CONTRITION, showing the distinction of Perfect and Imperfect Contrition until Trent. In Trent itself the two contritions are clearly distinguished, and the sufficiency of attrition arising from fear is asserted. This attrition Trent so describes that it is an act of true conversion or repentance (D 898). Then, describing the preparation for justification generally, the Council used the phrase '. . . and begin to love him as the source of all justice . . .' (D 798). Thus a point for future dispute was raised.

Baius (d. 1589) inclined to Protestant views by demanding perfect contrition for forgiveness in the sacrament (cf. D 1031–3, 1070–1) and by regarding Attrition from fear as evil (D 1016, 1035, 1038). Among Catholics the teaching of the sufficiency of attrition grew, so that Vasquez (d. 1604) and Suarez (d. 1617) defended it as certainly sufficient. They were less certain that it sufficed when known to be only attrition. Jansen (d. 1638) refused to admit attrition as a sincere repentance (*De Gratia Christi Salvatoris*, 1 5, c. 33) and something of his influence was found among some Catholic defenders of the need for at least a lesser degree of charity in the sorrow brought to the sacrament. They and the attritionists broke into violent controversy between 1661 and 1667 (cf. Döllinger and Reusch, *Geschichte der Moralstreitigkeiten in der römischkatholischen Kirche seit dem sechzehnten Jahrhundert* (1889) T 1). A Jesuit catechism in Belgium taught the sufficiency of attrition from fear without love and some Augustinian theologians replied. C. Lupus and F. Farvacques argued the need for initial charity, citing the phrase of Trent and the need for the total conversion. M. le Dent SJ, defended the attritionist side. Such theological bitterness ensued that the matter was taken to Rome. Alexander VII imposed moderation through a decree of the Holy Office, 5 May, 1667. Both parties were ordered to refrain from attaching theological censures to their opponents. The attritionist view was described as that '. . . which today seems more common among the scholastics' (D 1146). Yet many great names of the 16th and 17th cents. favoured the contritionist view (Morinus, Pallavicini, Contenson, Launoy, Bossuet, Juenin, etc.).

By now only the followers of Jansen favoured the pure contritionist thesis, and they were repeatedly condemned : in general in 1690 (D 1300–5) ; Quesnel in 1713 (D 1397–8, 1410–12) ; the Synod of Pistoia in 1794 (D 1523–5). Meanwhile Catholic Contritionism was being modified into a form commonly attributed to Billuart (d. 1757), and still held today. It defends the need for a love of God between charity and love of concupiscence. This is love of benevolence, and is more than concupiscence, as it is a disinterested love of God himself, less than charity, as it is without the reciprocity, or return of love by God that characterizes charity or friendship. Presaged by Henneguier (OP d. 1712), and possibly by St Charles Borromeo (d. 1584), it is held today by many notable Dominicans (Hugon, Garrigou-Lagrange, Prümmer, Hugueney, Perinelle) and by Diekamp. (Thus Doronzo, II, 289. Jussen's recent edition of Diekamp changes ' benevolence' into an 'unselfish imperfect love of complacency.')

The most common view today, and almost universal, is Attritionism. This holds that attrition as above described is sufficient for forgiveness in the sacrament without perfect charity, initial charity or love of benevolence. Thus Scotists, Jesuits and many Thomists. Love of concupiscence is, of course, at least implicit in such contrition. A few (e.g. Tournely, d. 1729) used to demand an explicit love of concupiscence. Others seemed in the height of the controversy (and perhaps today, cf. Zubizzareta, *Theologia Dogmatica*, 5, n 508, 1939) to exclude even love of concupiscence.

The argument for attritionism makes these points : Perfect contrition, or love of charity, cannot always be needed for justification ; for then the *ex opere operato* efficacy of the sacrament would become meaningless. It would be difficult to see any purpose in instituting such a forgiving power. Nor would the Church's practice of demanding pastoral urgency in absolving the dying have any real reason. For it could not help any except those with perfect contrition, and they would already be saved (cf. St Celestine, D 111 ; St Augustine, PL 33:1016 and the general practice to our own day). Nor would such a view square with Trent's description of attrition in the sacrament, opposed to perfect contrition which is able to justify before the sacrament is received.

Secondly, it argues, there is no need for a beginning of love, in the sense of lesser charity or a love of benevolence. For it does not seem possible to distinguish such love from that charity which is not needed. Further, if it were needed, the Church would be wrongfully tolerating a pernicious view and practice, namely attritionism. Then, Trent's words '. . . they begin to love God as the source of all justice' are not to be interpreted of such love (cf. Galtier, n 411). For Trent was not describing what must happen but what does normally happen. The deliberations of the Council seem to show that the phrase is intended to exclude simply the two extremes, charity and basely servile fear. Hence the implicit love of concupiscence (and more remotely the love of justice and the desire of charity) in any sincere conversion is all that can be concluded from Trent. From what has been said it will be seen that any argument from the notion of total conversion does not demand charity as a basic essential, though it is obviously the ideal.

Of recent years the question has been renewed, mainly in the attempt to deepen understanding of the views of St Thomas and Trent, and to find a continuous thread of teaching and practice in the whole process of development, thus drawing the various theories closer together. No agreement has been reached. It seems likely that the substance of St Thomas's position will be accepted as the best statement, with modifications to supplement his use of dispositive causality, and to eliminate the suggestion of the act of attrition becoming an act of perfect contrition (if that is indeed his view).

The line of continuity and reconciliation seems to be the necessity of true repentance, completed by God's justifying act when the sinner is disposed to the best of his ability. This disposition may be charity which implies the desire of the sacrament. It may be attrition, in varying degrees of perfection or imperfection below charity. At its lowest, that sorrow is still true repentance and implies love of God for oneself, the desire of justice, the intention to fulfil all God's commandments, including that of charity. Since this is a state compatible with grace, justice and charity, God through the sacramental absolution can and does infuse grace and the habit of charity. In that sense the sinner can be said to become contrite from being attrite (*ex attrito fit contritus*) without any psychological change or any awareness of change. He is then like many other just men, capable of charity but without a present act of charity, perhaps kept in the state of grace by motives below charity but not sinful. It remains true, however, that the fullest conversion is to be sought. The longer act of contrition, commonly given to be said by penitents, is an apt description of how the Church, now and always, tries to lead the sinner from lower and interested motives of sorrow to the heights of charity.

III Possibility of valid but fruitless sacrament. This is commonly taught for other sacraments, but is disputed for Penance. The dispute is whether it is possible for all the elements that make up the sacramental sign to be present (so that the sacrament exists, and is valid) but for some defect in one of them to prevent grace from being there and then conferred (so that the sacrament is valid but fruitless, *validum sed informe*). One possibility, formerly defended by some theologians (Ledesma, Vega and others), is now derelict, as it was based on the idea that contrition is not intrinsically needed to constitute the sacrament. A second possibility is sought by supposing some defect to exist, not by the absence of contrition but by its imperfection. One view was held by some authors cited by Suarez (Disp. XX, s. 4, n. 1), revived by Billot (*De Poenitentia*, Thesis XVI) and held by some other moderns (Gihr, Van Noort-Verhaar, Vermeersch, Merkel-

bach, cf. Doronzo, II, 169–70). If a man's sorrow were inadvertently not supreme (*appretiative summa*, cf. CONTRITION), it would suffice to make the sacrament valid but not as a disposition for the reception of grace. This view is more commonly rejected, as it defends attrition as a true repentance even if it has no effective will not to sin. It is based by Billot on a false supposition that true interior repentance can be shown to the priest judging, but the quality of 'being supreme' cannot be so shown, and so is not needed for validity. Finally, it is restricted by Billot to a case of inadvertence, whereas it would seem equally to apply in a case of advertence. Thus would follow the incongruous position of a sinful act being a part of the sacrament of Penance.

A second view is held by Suarez, Lugo, St Alphonsus, Lehmkuhl, etc. (cf. Doronzo, II, 166). A man's sorrow is imagined as inadvertently not being universal. It does not extend to some confessed sin because it is motivated by the consideration of one particular fault. The case is a theoretical possibility, but seems impractical, for penitents detest sin for motives that are universal, e.g. charity, hell.

Most authors reject these two opinions, but for opposed reasons. A few follow Vasquez in saying that in the two cases above the sorrow is both sufficient for validity and for grace, since it would in fact be supreme and universal. The majority reject one or both of the views, arguing that they would imply not only fruitlessness but also invalidity. For the qualities supposed to be absent are (cf. Trent and common teaching) qualities needed for true repentance, i.e. for that contrition which is part of the sacrament. So there is either a fruitful sacrament or no sacrament at all (cf. Galtier n. 417 ; Doronzo, p. 153–94).

Bibliography. E. Doronzo, *De Poenitentia*, II (1951) ; P. Galtier, *De Poenitentia* (1950) Vol. II ; P. Anciaux, *La Théologie de la pénitence au XIIᵉ siècle* (1949) ; *id. Le Sacrement de la pénitence* (1957) ; A. Perinelle, *L'Attrition d'après le Concile de Trent et d'après S. Thomas d'Aquin* (1927) ; H. Dondaine, *L'Attrition suffisante* (1943) ; J. de Blic, *Sur l'attrition suffisante. Mélanges Science Religieuse* 2 (1945) 329–366 ; M. Flick, *L' attimo della giustificazione secondo S Tommaso* (1949) ; C. R. Meyer, *The Thomistic Concept of Justifying Contrition* (1949) ; P. de Letter, *Two Concepts of Attrition and Contrition*, TS 11 (1950) 3–33.   J. McD.

AUGUSTINE AND HIS INFLUENCE A biography (I) will touch on the salient points of childhood, the 16th year, Manicheanism, the chair of rhetoric at Milan, conversion and return to Africa, life as monk, priest, bishop. Of his works (II) only the catalogue, his own *retractationes* and the *indiculus* of Possidius, will be discussed and a selection offered from his major works. A doctrinal sketch (III) deals with these points : authority, reason, Platonism, God (One and triune), man (original justice, sin, consequences, redemption, Church, sacraments, grace, predestination). Augustine's influence is proved (IV) by MSS-survival, by reaction of Popes and Councils, medieval manuals, individual doctors, preachers; significance of pseudo-Augustinian literature, the Augustinian Rule.

I Augustine (354–430), saint of the *Confessions*, greatest among the Fathers, one of the Founders of the West to which he gave a theology and philosophy of its own, through his writings both creative and encyclopedic, was one of the main channels of Tradition through whom the ancient treasures of wisdom and piety were passed on to the middle and modern ages; he was born 13 Nov. 354 (cf. A. Casamassa, *Scritti patristici* 2 (1956) 277). His home town was Tagaste, once in Roman Numidia Cirtensis, today only an archaeological site in Algeria; his full name was Aurelius Augustinus (cf. Tillemont, *Life*, 1:1, 3). By the ill-advised custom of the day, A. was not baptized immediately after birth but only enrolled among the catechumens (*conf.* 1:11, 17), who, by policy, were kept in ignorance about the greatest mysteries of Christianity (*see* CATECHU-MENATE). But fragmentary though his religious knowledge as catechumen was bound to be, A. thought of himself as a Catholic (*de util. credendi* 2), and in his worst moments did not forget about God's existence and His interest in the world, about man's eternal responsibilities and his acquaintance with Christ (*conf.* 1:11, 17). Having been once in Monica's home he could never again feel at home in crude paganism: he might very well despise the style of the Scriptures (*conf.* 3:5, 9) but even Cicero could not drown faint Christian echoes; he missed something even in Cicero, he missed the name of Christ (*conf.* 3:4, 7). From Monica and Monica's friends, A. got a fair amount of religious attention. He discovered that some people pray to God, and he learned from them to think, as children do, that God is somebody very great who though invisible and unnoticeable to eye and ear may see us, hear us and help us. Not being a model child he 'needed' God's protection badly against the then rather liberally administered canings in school (*conf.* 1:9, 14). For he rebelled against the drudgery of the three R's (*conf.* 1:13, 20 sq.); he hated Greek with a special hate (*conf.* 1:13, 20), told enough childish lies (*conf.* 1:19, 30), raided the pantry (*conf.* 1:19, 20), preferred ball-playing to schoolwork (*conf.* 1:9, 15) but by ability and ambition was always to the fore (*conf.* 1:16, 26). After primary schooling in Tagaste followed his secondary education at Madaura which laid the foundations of A.'s culture (cf. P. Alfaric, *L'Évolution intellectuelle de saint A.* (1918) 12–23). In his 16th year A. returned home—no longer a boy. His father, until about this time a pagan, was already dreaming of becoming a grandfather, but Monica trembled and tried in vain to give the young man some good moral advice. Intellectual pride made him deaf to this; moral uncertainty made him envious of the immoral exploits of idle companions. As A. cannot accuse himself of anything definite and yet uses condemnatory terms of ominous significance (cf.

conf. 2:3–10), the reader is better advised not to read too much into the lines of A. This much, however, is certain: the idleness of his lost 16th year marked a sharp falling off of his youthful idealism. The reason for the lost year of 369–70 was a prosaic money question: lack of funds for further study. Patritius, his father, was only a minor town official. As he had not enough assets (*vita* 1; *sermo* 356:13), he could only fret until a Maecenas was found for his A. It was Romanianus who helped to send him off to Carthage, to the university one might say. And ever after he acted as foster-father to A. (*contra academ.* 2:2, 3) who at this very moment, about 370, lost his real father (*conf.* 3:4, 7), shortly after he had been gained for Christ by Monica (*conf.* 9:9, 12 sq.) Patritius had been liberal, quick and somewhat rough-hewn as a man; as a father he seems to have had little influence on his son. It was Monica who shaped him, held him by attraction and repulsion, lost him and found him (cf. V. J. Bourke, *A.'s quest of wisdom* (1945) 1–9 ff.). Carthage was a cauldron of sinful loves when A. arrived and quickly 'fell in love with love' (*conf.* 3:1, 1). For in Carthage he fell. He found a sinful companion, and kept faithful to her for 14 years; at the age of 18 A. became father of Adeodatus (*conf.* 9:6, 14). This sin of A.'s has to be evaluated not only on the black-rimmed pages of the *Confessions* but also on the stage of real life. With all his sins in Carthage, A. lived a life of noble aspirations, *elegans et urbanus* (*conf.* 3:1, 1). Others thought highly of him at this very time (*ep.* 93:13, 51); he was the centre of intellectuals who, spurning the rough circus (*conf.* 6:7, 11 sq.), enjoyed the theatre, a higher pursuit certainly even if perhaps more sensual (*conf.* 3:2, 2). He always remained a horrified outsider to the student gangs of *eversores*, was always unable to stomach their devilishly senseless exhibitionism, though he admits having inwardly almost envied their impure prowess (*conf.* 3:3, 6). During his 19th year—two years after he had found the nameless Hagar—he was still spiritually receptive for the uplifting evolution which a chance acquaintance with Cicero's *Hortensius* started within him (*conf.* 3:4, 7 sq). Subconscience, conscience, and fear of hell-fire never let him sink below the level of a fugitive from Christ and Monica. He was a rebel but no crawling worm; he needed the hours of spiritual exaltation which he sought and found in the writing of the *de pulchro et apto* (*conf.* 4: chaps. 14–15), in working over prize poems (*conf.* 4:1, 1; 4:3, 5), in the reading of Aristotle (*conf.* 4:16, 28 sq), in his lecturing and teaching (*conf.* 4:2, 2). A. was such a personality that even in Carthage noble friends and eager students flocked to him, like Romanianus, Alypius, Honoratus, Nebridius, Vindicianus. Romanianus was probably the one to provide the housing for A.'s *ménage* in Carthage (*contra academ.* 2:3, 5) where life cannot have been very domestic if jealousy, fear, anger, and quarrels were their guests (*conf.* 3:1, 1), but the unknown Hagar is to be credited with the redeeming features of a good mother if their son, Adeodatus, grew up to be a wonder-child of grace (*conf.* 9:6, 14).

How else could she have found the courage to make a vow of chastity a few years later (*conf.* 6:15, 25)?

Manicheanism. In the year 373 A. became a Manichean; in consequence thereof Monica intended to close her door to him during a short teaching period in Tagaste, 373–4 (*conf.* 3:11, 19). But in a vision she was told by an angel that, in regard to her son A., she would see one day that *ubi tu, ibi et ille*, where you are he will be. Upon being informed, the proud young professor wanted to turn it into the mockery *ubi ille, ibi et tu*, where he is you will be; but Monica showed herself a quicker logician than he had expected. About this time a bishop was importuned by Monica to go and talk to the proud A. as others upon her request had done, and with disastrous effect. The homespun wisdom of the elderly man was somewhat disconcerting: Leave him alone; pray for him; the young fighting cock cannot yet listen, and must under no circumstances be given easy chances for cheap victories; let himself read deeper and deeper into it—and one day he will be shocked out of it at a sudden sight of all those errors and blasphemies. The bishop underlined his advice with his personal and parallel experiences. But when Monica persisted he curtly gave the famous answer: Leave me, live your life; it cannot be that the son of your tears should perish.—For A. this meant a longer walk deeper and deeper into the night, *volvi et involvi illa caligine* (*conf.* 4:11 and 12). For 9 long years (*conf.* 3:11, 20; *de moribus manich.* 19, 68), from his 19th to his 28th year (*conf.* 4:1, 1) A. wallowed in Manicheanism, mostly because of its tantalizing promise of easy wisdom for young rationalists like A., contemptuous of all authority and inflated with early intellectual triumphs. That Manicheanism also 'solved' the harrowing problem of evil by shifting responsibility and blame conveniently unto the stars, could only recommend the system to A. at this stage; for as self-made philosopher (*conf.* 4:16, 28) he needed his time for becoming disillusioned with gross materialism (*see* MANICHEANISM). He had himself entered as simple *auditor* (firstgrader) of the sect. Misled by neophyte zeal, the young intellectualist enjoyed misleading his friends and others (*conf.* 4:1, 1) and his conquest became so valuable for the Manicheans that they were not to let him go again without bitter feelings (*de utilit. credendi* 1, 3). It was not long before he started asking embarrassing questions no Manichean could solve. Each time he was referred to their oracle, Faustus of Milevis (*conf.* 5:6, 10 sq.), who finally appeared after 9 long years, absolutely failed, and caused A.'s inner, if not yet outward, break with the sect (*conf.* 5:3, 3 sq.). About 383 A. stole away from Monica, who was still praying at the altar of St Cyprian on the seashore when her son had already embarked secretly for Rome (*conf.* 5:8, 14 sq.). His Manichean friend Alypius having preceded him procured him lodgings with a friendly Manichean of Rome (*conf.* 6:10, 19). As soon as he had recovered from a heavy fever he started lecturing at his residence. His Roman students were as disappointing as his North-Africans

had been; they would sign up, pay little attention and less in fees, and switch over to a second professor as soon as the first showed intentions of collecting his dues. In consequence A.'s financial status cannot have been very flourishing; perhaps he was in debt when an unexpected possibility opened at Milan where they needed a city teacher of rhetoric. The zealously pagan prefect of Rome had some voice in the appointing. A. won the professorship of Milan through personal ability, the political influence of his Manichean friends, and also through the pagan sympathies of the prefect Symmachus, who little foresaw the future when he sent A. off on the Imperial stage-coach (*conf.* 5:12, 22 sq.).

At Milan, 384-6, his spiritual crisis came to a head. He met Ambrose (*conf.* 5:13, 23 sq.) whose sermons freed A. more and more from prejudices against the Bible in general, and the OT in particular, because St Ambrose combined attractive use of allegory with a sound historical presentation. A.'s holy mother, whom he thought he had left behind forever, had courageously crossed the sea after her son. She found him established in a house with garden together with the whole clan, his son Adeodatus, the latter's mother, two cousins, Rusticus and Lastidianus, A.'s brother Navigius, A.'s friends Alypius and Nebridius (*conf.* 6:10, 16 sq.). There must have been a certain drama about the meeting of the two women. Monica's prayers stormed heaven; her prestige with St Ambrose (*conf.* 6:2, 2) closed the gap between the two men (*conf.* 6:3, 3), and her perseverance seemed to gain the upper hand with A. himself. God chose as tool of providence even a pompous busy-body (*conf.* 7:9, 13) who one day offered A. some Neo-platonic books (cf. P. Courcelle, 'Litiges sur *Libri Platonicorum*' in *Augustiniana* IV (1954) 225–39). Inwardly A. had ceased to be a Manichean; he was, however, drifting towards scepticism at the very moment when Plato was given a chance of opening A.'s eyes to the vast horizons of spirituality, a chance, too, of pointing out new beacons that might shed light on his old Manichean problem of evil. But A. was still far from port. As legitimate marriage was now seriously contemplated (*conf.* 6:13, 23), the nameless North-African woman returned home, henceforth to live a nobler life dedicated to God by vow (*conf.* 6:15, 25). Bertrand (*Celle qui fut aimée d'A.* (1935) 116–19) has dramatized the self-effacement of the mother of Adeodatus. The boy she left behind was to follow his father to Milan and the baptismal font (*conf.* 9:16, 14), to Ostia and the deathbed of his grandmother, Monica (*conf.* 9:12, 29 sq.), to his own death in Tagaste where the genius of the father was to immortalize the genius of the son with the *de magistro*. After the departure of 'Hagar' the marriage schemes foundered because A. for a second and a sadder time disappeared in the surf of passion. No one suffered more by these ups and downs than Augustine himself, too noble a soul to feel happy with his eyes on the ground. To make his inner pain more acute he heard, about this time, from Simplicianus (*conf.* 8:2, 3 sq.) what other creatures of flesh and blood had done to conquer their instincts. A.'s was a life of pain, prayer and work.

Conversion. One day his friend, Alypius, was with him when a very influential countryman of theirs, Pontitianus, came for a chance visit. He sat down by a small gaming table, noticed a book, opened it : and to his astonishment had St Paul's codex under his eyes where he naturally had expected to find Cicero's. The visitor, a very true and manly Christian, smiled at such a find in such a place. But when he heard of the Christian interests of A. the visitor began to speak about St Anthony and monastic life in the Catholic Church. Noticing the total ignorance of the brilliant A. in matters so patent, he added another story about a monastery at the city gates of Milan. As their astonishment visibly mounted he related personal experiences. Before the city gates of another imperial city, Trier, two of his fellow-officers had chanced upon a monk's cell, had entered, had perused the monk's copy of a biography of St Anthony, and had on the spot decided to stay with the monk. When their young brides had heard of it, they too, in their turn had matched generosity with generosity by becoming brides of Christ themselves (*conf.* 8:6, 13 sq.). When Pontitianus left, A. was shaken to the last fibre of his being, he almost ferociously turned to Alypius, 'Did you hear ? The unlettered rise and conquer heaven, and we with our letters have no heart, no courage, and look where we wallow.' A. needed the solitary company of his beloved St Paul ; he went out into the garden—and was followed by Alypius. Under a fig-tree A. broke down in convulsive tears. But while he prayed and cried for help, a child's singsong 'Tolle lege, tolle lege' reached him, and made him listen. As he knew of no children's game with such a singsong and did not remember of having ever heard it anywhere before he took it as an order from heaven to consult his St Paul. He went where he had left the codex, and reached for it. It opened, or fell open, at a well-thumbed place, at Rom 13:13. He read in silence : with light in his mind, peace in his heart, mysterious strength came, and stayed with him forever. Alypius who once had followed him into Manicheanism now followed him back into their Father's house, taking as a decisive hint the word of Rom 13:14. It all happened on a day in the beginning of August, 386, three weeks before the schools would close on August 23 (cf. Casamassa, *Scritti patristici* 2 (1956) 282). The simple story is found in *conf.* 8:8-12 ; it has not remained a simple story under the scrutiny of the erudite (cf. H. I. Marrou, 'La Querelle autour du *Tolle lege*' in RHE 53 (1958) 47-57). St A., who has been assumed to have said more than he should, or less than he should, is best supposed to have said what he did (cf. Casamassa, *op. cit.* 244-8). It certainly would be contradictory to doubt the sincerity of this conversion. A. was to resign from his professorship, definitely give up all marriage plans, and consecrate himself to God without any reservations. But for the time being his plans were to remain secret (*conf.* 9:2, 2). After 15 Oct. he did resign, alleging reasons of health.

He retired to the farm of a friend of his, Verecundus, at Cassiciacum (cf. F. Meda, 'La controversia sul *Rus Cassiciacum*' in *Miscellanea Agostiniana* 2 (1930) 49-59). To prepare himself for baptism he prayed, did penance, worked with his hands, and did some teaching of literature and philosophy in the form of dialogues. The written lines which were to fix these earliest dialogues of A.'s cannot be expected to report anything but the fruits of this intellectual work ; but echoes of some prayerful moods are not absent (*contra academ.* 2:2, 5 ; 3:20, 43 ; *de ordine* 2:5, 16 ; 1:8, 25 ; 1:10, 29 ; *soliloquia* 1:1, 2 sq.). At the beginning of Lent A. returned to Milan to receive Baptism in the night of April 24-5, 387, together with Alypius and Adeodatus (*conf.* 9:3, 5 sq.). **Their return to Africa** was resolved upon soon afterwards ; but Monica died at Ostia (*conf.* 9:8, 17 sq.). The return was thereby retarded for about one year which A. passed in Rome unmasking the Manicheans (*de moribus manich.* chaps. 19-20) and studying the life of Catholic monasteries and convents, a life he had already opted for as ' *servus dei* ' (*de moribus eccl. cath.* 31, 65 sq.). In Sept. 388 he finally arrived in Carthage, just in time to witness some miracles (cf. Cuypers, *Biography* nos. 145-54) ; before re-entering at Tagaste he also tried to convert a known Manichean (Cuypers, nos. 155-6).

Life as a monk started at Tagaste; he sold his properties, and began a common life in absolute poverty together with Alypius, Evodius, some townsfolk, and Adeodatus, who was to die shortly afterwards (*ep.* 126:7 ; 157:4, 39 ; *vita* 3, 1 and 5, 1 ; *conf.* 9:6, 14 ; 9:12, 29 ; *retract.* 1:12 ; *de mag.* chaps. 1-14). The news of A.'s conversion spread like wildfire ; soon his learned word and holy life enlisted admirers and followers. In 391 when on his way to recruit a monastic candidate from among the Imperial Services he dreamt of founding a second monastery in Hippo. By chance he entered the church just as Bishop Valerius spoke of plans calling for the ordination of an additional priest. At this dramatic moment A. was recognized, and more or less forcefully convinced to have himself ordained a priest (*sermo* 355:1, 2 ; *ep.* 21:2 ; *vita* chaps. 3-4).

As priest he had no intention of abandoning his monastic ideals ; Bishop Valerius upon A.'s request gave him therefore a garden of the church property in which to found a second monastery, or, as it turned out to be, a spiritual seminary for the low and high clergy in Africa (*sermo* 355:1, 2 ; *vita* 5, 1 and 11, 1 sq.). Scarcely had he settled down when the anti-Manichean efforts of his Roman and Tagastan days were resumed, and the Donatists challenged to battle. Against all precedent the presbyter A., assumed the ministry of preaching even in presence of his own and other bishops. One of the first fruits of his eloquence was the extirpation of some cemetery abuses (*retract.* 1:14-22 ; *ep.* 22 ; *ep.* 23 ; *ep.* 29 ; *vita* chapters 5-7). The eyes of the world started to turn towards the priest of Hippo. As he had already sent out some from his monastery to become bishops and as he was liable to become a bishop himself, Valerius, not willing to give him up, made him

Auxiliary of Hippo (*ep.* 28:1 ; *ep.* 31:4 ; *ep.* 71:2 ; *vita* chaps. 7–8). On the eve of his consecration A. had to disentangle some legal difficulties, and to wipe off some venom of calumny (*vita* 8:3–5 ; *contra Cresconium* 3:80, 92 ; 4:64, 79 ; *contra litt. Petil.* 3:16, 19). Friends like Paulinus of Nola or his own people were enthusiastic over this consecration. Its date, however, is not absolutely certain (perhaps at the beginning of 397 ? cf. Casamassa *op. cit.* 285–6).

The years of his episcopacy (397–430) are characterized by a full display of energy and a mature development of thought. He lived at the episcopal residence but had monastic life introduced among his clergy (*sermo* 355:1, 2 ; *s.* 355:4, 6 ; *s.* 356:14). He built only what he had to (cf. Casamassa *op. cit.* 286). The practice of charity was so dear to him that he might sacrifice even the altar vessels (*vita* 24:12 sq.) ; he held an annual clothing campaign for the poor (*ep.* 122:2 ; *sermo* 25:8 ; *Maii sermo* 128:3 ed. Morin : *Misc. Agost.* 1 (1930) 373). He had a personal interest in the defence of the poor, the weak, the accused (*ep.* 247 ; *ep.* 252 ; *ep.* 255 ; *ep.* 154:1 ; *vita*:20, 1 sq.). He worked for peace among families, and among all the petty contendents who by Roman law were entitled to go to a Catholic bishop's court, thousands of hours of A.'s precious time thus being sacrificed to legal contentions of shoemakers, fishmongers and other humble mortals (*vita* 19:1–6). Sometimes twice a day, sometimes three or even ten days in a row, he would preach from his bishop's chair in the apse of his church ; however sick or old he might feel he never became remiss in raising the moral level of his flock, or kindling the light of religious instruction (*vita* 31:3 ; *enarr. in ps.* 88, *sermo* 2 (CCL 39:1233) ; *tract. in Jn* 22:1 (CCL 36:223) ; *in ep. Jn ad Parthos*, prol.). Sweet though his word usually was, when the occasion so required he could be adamant and strict (*ep.* 65). Far from parochialism, his ecclesiastical interests went beyond Hippo, included all Africa, and in the course of time became world-wide : he took an active part in the frequent meetings of African bishops (*vita* 12:1) ; he was at the Councils of Carthage in 397, 401, 407, and 419 ; at Milevis in 416 and 418. His correspondence covered the Empire geographically, and topically all fields of philosophy or moral and dogmatic theology ; its recipients were among the high and the low. Wherever he went he had to preach (*vita* 12:1) ; wherever a grave problem arose, be it Manicheanism, Donatism, or Pelagianism, A. had to intervene in its solution. His anti-Manichean efforts began in Rome in 388, continued until 405, had their echo in 415 against Priscillianism and in 420 against Marcionism. Fortunatus, Faustus, Felix, Adamantus, Secondinus and Manes himself challenged his mind to find an answer to the problem of evil. The anti-Donatist campaign opened with the letter to Maximinus of Siniti near Hippo (*ep.* 23) and closed with the Inter-faith Meeting of June 411 (*vita* 12:2–3). It gave A. a chance to illustrate, for ages to come, among other things, the efficacy of the sacraments,

and the constitution of the Church. Fateful for the history of repressive dealings with later heretics became the dilemma posed by the Circumcelliones (or farm-raiders). From among the Punic-speaking country folk the Donatists recruited their shock-troops. Under monkish trappings they infested the countryside and struck terror into lonely Catholic farmers, unprotected travellers, or country priests. Augustine (*ep.* 88) and Possidius (*vita* chap. 12) give a description. Rivalling with assassins in letting blood, with anabaptists in spilling baptismal waters, they made the country lanes re-echo to their pious Punic slogan ' *Deo laudes* ' (cf. F. Van der Meer, *A. de Zielsorger* (1947) 82 ff., German trans. by N. Greitemann (2nd, 1953) 100 ff.). A. kept the Punic danger from spreading by kindness towards his own Punic-speaking country folk to whom he gave priests of their own language. Though unable to speak to them save through interpreters, he never snubbed them but would use as much Punic as he knew in his sermons to the Latin congregations, explaining Hebrew words by cognate Punic ones, or appealing to the lowly with a homely Punic proverb (cf. W. M. Green, ' A.'s use of Punic ' in *Semitic and oriental studies* (1951) 179–90). He certainly knew more Greek than Punic ; for, though he preferred reading Greek texts in Latin translation, he could if necessary translate them himself, and also say a few courteous words in Greek to his own bishop, Valerius, who was Greek (Tillemont, *Biography* 1:2, 5 ; Cuypers, *Biography* nos. 32–41). When the Donatists showed signs of abandoning the struggle with St A. the Pelagians appeared on the scene. The first anti-Pelagian battle (411–18) ended in May 418 when Pope Zosimus reaffirmed the dogma of original sin and the necessity of grace (cf. M. Mercator, *Commonitorium super nomine Caelestii* 3 (PL 48:90) ; DTC 12 (1933) 700–2). The second great anti-Pelagian battle lasted from 418 to the death of A., whose main opponent this time was Julianus of Eclanum.

Old age—and the desire of dedicating his last days to a rapid conclusion of literary labours under preparation—decided the appointment of A.'s successor (Sept. 426) in the person of Heraclius, whom his faithful did not accept without a rousing ovation for their beloved old bishop *Augustino vita* : Long live Augustine ! (*ep.* 213 ; A. Casamassa, *Scritti patr.* 2 (1956) 256–9). Shortly afterwards, in a daring manœuvre against the Empire, Count Boniface called the Vandals from Spain, who overstaying their welcome drew the sword against both Boniface and Empire and laid siege to the city of Hippo. In August 430 St A. fell ill while a pall of death and destruction hung over Catholic Africa. In preparation for his death St A. asked his own people who had never before been willing to concede him hours of pious leisure, to abstain from visiting him except at mealtime and during doctor's consultation. For ten days, his last on earth, the request was complied with ; St A. got the time to recite his penitential psalms which he had caused to be written in large script and to be stuck up against the opposite wall.

In full possession of all his faculties he closed his eyes on 28 August 430 (*vita* chaps. 28–31). Buried first in the Peace Church of Hippo, then carried to Sardinia by Catholic exiles, he finally found his resting place in S. Pietro in Ciel d' Oro of Pavia (cf. J. Stilting, *Biography* nos. 736–98).

II Works. After having written his autobiography, the *confessiones*, St A. wrote, about 426, a most honest auto-bibliography, the *retractiones*, in two books, book 1 with 27 chapters, book 2 with 67 ; each chapter deals with an Augustinian work in ' book-form '. His works in ' letter-form ' or ' sermon-form ' are not dealt with in the *retract.* What St A. left untold in his autobiography or his auto-bibliography, Possidius, his disciple, told in the short but famous *Vita S. Augustini* (ed. H. T. Weiskotten (1919)) and in his equally famous Augustinian book-catalogue, the *indiculus* or *indiculum* (ed. A. Wilmart in *Miscellanea Agostiniana* 2 (1930) 149–233). Possidius divides A.'s works into two categories : (1) controversial books against Pagans, Jews, Manicheans, Priscillianists, Donatists, Pelagians, Arians, Apollinarists ; (2) works of general interest. In each of the two categories Augustinian works in ' book-form ' or in ' letter-form ' or in ' sermon-form ' are mentioned together so that the catalogue of Possidius is richer in items than the *retract.* but neither is complete. Possidius enumerates 1030 subdivisions in the works of St A., a breathtaking number of *libri, epistulae, sermones,* or *tractatus.* But Possidius left some unnumbered because St A. had left them so (*indic.* Wilmart, 208). This shows that St A. himself had a library catalogue; in fact he says so in another place (*retract.* 2:41(' in *opusculorum meorum indiculo* ')) ; he needed it because his codices were miscellanea with various items bound together (cf. *retract.* 2:41 ; or *ep.* 101:3–4). The purpose of Possidius was to make his master famous, to give his readers the chance of selection from the rich Augustinian treasures ; to have people send in their orders to copyists, either at the Church Library of Hippo, or wherever the Augustinian books should be made available for reproduction . He added a fervent plea to the lucky owners of Augustinian works, they should encourage copying, not begrudge it (*vita* 18:8 sq.).

A full modern list of Augustinian works with easy reference to their printed editions (PL, CSEL, CCL) should be given here but we can only refer to E. Portalié (*Augustin* DTC 1, 2 (1902) 2311–14 Eng. tr. (1960)), H. Pope (*St Augustine* (1937) 368–87), V. J. Bourke (*Aug.'s quest* (1945) 303–8), E. Dekkers (*Clavis patrum lat.* (1951) 50 sq. ; nos. 250–386), A. Casamassa (*Scritti patr.* 2 (1956) 291–320).

Of the immense number of Augustinian works a few can be selected for special presentation. A., the creator of Western theology, developed several new branches of sacred knowledge. With the *de doctrina christiana* homiletics started, with the *de catechizandis rudibus* a better catechesis. He subordinated philosophy to theology and encouraged the Middle Ages to cherish a faith that looks for intellectual light (*fides quaerens intellectum*). He gave speculative

theologians the example of a vast systematic effort with his *de fide et symbolo* and his *enchiridion*, where he laid the foundations for dogmatic and moral theology. His masterpiece *de civitate Dei* is a vindication of faith, a philosophy of history and civilization on a level that only a genius could reach. The one work that outshines all others, is *de Trinitate.* Never superficial or merely practical, A. meets every issue, discusses every scriptural dogmatic and moral problem, considers every point, faces every heresy. The *confessiones* remain the mystical soul of the ages ; and the *sermones* provide spiritual food for those who seek it (cf. M. Grabmann, *Historia de la teología católica*, Spanish trans. with additions by D. Gutiérrez (1946) 22–4).

III Doctrine. The two fountain-heads of A.'s teaching are authority and reason (*contra academ.* 3:20, 43) precedence being sometimes given to authority and sometimes to reason ; ' authority has precedence in time, reason in its inner reality ' (*de ordine* 2:9, 26). Authority appears concretely in Scripture, Tradition and the Church. Each book of the OT and the NT of which A. gives the canonical list in the year 397 (*de doctrina christ.* 2:8, 13), or briefly all Scripture, being inspired by God is infallibly immune from all error; if error there seems to be, ' the manuscript is faulty, or the translator mistaken, or the reader not intelligent ' (*contra Faustum* 2:5 ; cf. *ep.* 82:1, 3 ; cf. D 1952).

Tradition, reaching us through the Creed, through Church practice, through the writings of the Fathers, has—if it be universal and apostolic—the same demonstrative value which Scripture has (*ep.* 54:1 ; *de baptismo* 4:24, 31 ; 5:33, 31 ; *contra Jul.* 2:9 sq. ; 6:5, 13). The Church with its living authority guarantees the Scriptures, ' I would not believe in the Gospel if the authority of the Catholic Church did not tell me ' (*contra ep. manichaei* 5:6) ; the Church preserves Tradition (*de doctrina christ.* 3:2) and interprets both Tradition and Scripture (*de gen. ad litt. imp.* 1:1) because the Church decides all controversies (*de baptismo* 2:4, 5). Reason together with authority plays its full part in A.'s teaching ; for reason has first to tell ' who is to be believed ' (*de vera religione* 24:45 ; 25:46) ; secondly it has to prove the fact of Divine Revelation ; thirdly to give some possible explanation regarding revealed truth ; fourthly to defend revelation against attack. Like other ancient Christian writers A. sympathizes with Platonic philosophy, of course in expurgated form, free from such errors as are in flagrant contradiction with Christianity such as polytheism, emanationism, pre-existence of souls, the negative character of the somatic, the impossibility of a hypostatic union (cf. A. Casamassa, *Scritti patr.* 1 (1955) 180). At first in over-enthusiasm he imagined that he found some lines of St John equally stated in Plato (*conf.* 7:9, 13 sq. ; 7:20, 26 sq. ; *contra academicos* 3:18, 41 ; 3:20, 43). It was in his youth (*de vera religione* 4:7) when he felt that ' but for a few words or sentences ' there would be no difference between Platonists and Christians (*in Joh. tract.* 2:4 ; *retract.* 1:3, 2) ; as he grew older he tempered his Platonic enthusiasms if he did not consider them as outright sinful. 'I have been more enthusiastic than I should have been, about people so impious' (contra acad. 3:17, 37 and retract. 1:1, 4). Some of his Platonic statements were retracted (retract. 1:1, 4 ; 1:3, 2–3 ; 2:4, 2). A.'s thought, as derived from the two sources mentioned above, turns in a kind of elliptic orbit around two focal points, God and man ; the one axis always being faith, the other axis reason, so that in A. philosophy and theology get intertwined, not sacrificed to each other. Casamassa (Scritti patr. 2 (1956) 323) says that the acumen of Aristotle, the enthusiasm of Plato, the daring of Origen and Tertullian, the traditionalism of Irenaeus or Cyprian, merge in A.'s stream of thought. Though creative he fortunately does not try to create something altogether new ; his creativeness is first blended with a humility no reader can overlook or forget, secondly with a reverence and loyalty for the Catholic past, so that his influence throughout the ages is service humbly done to the Church not just a proud title of glory worn by himself ; for he speaks in the name of the age-old Church, not in the name of Augustine (cf. G. Mártil, La tradición en S. Agustín (1943) 226–30). Existence of God is such an obvious conclusion of reasoning that atheism according to A. has to be considered as the folly of a few (sermo 69:3), as corruption of the heart rather than as sincere conviction of the mind (enarr. in ps. 13:2). His proofs for God's existence are known to be eternity and immutability of truth (de div. qq. 83 q. 54 ; de lib. arb. 2:3, 7 sq. ; conf. 7:10, 16), mutability and contingency of the created (conf. 10:6, 8 sq. ; 11:4, 6), finalistic order and beauty in the universe (sermo 141:2), the concordant voices of mankind (in Ioh. tract. 106:4) undaunted by the few discordant ones. God is cause of being, reason of knowing, order of living, i.e. principle, cause, foundation, finality in three distinct orders, the real, the logical and the moral, so that the Platonic division of philosophy is also his, namely, physical, logical, ethical (de civ. Dei 8:4 sq. ; soliloquia 1:1, 2–4). God has fulness of being (de mor. eccl. 1:14, 24 ; enarr. in ps. 134:4), full actuality without any potency whatsoever. True, our feeble mode and way of understanding casts the 'spirit' in the rôle of the 'something' that can stand by itself, and puts the other perfections in the rôle of inherent 'qualities' that need a support (de Trin. 15:5, 8). Yet in reality, in God's real life, the divine qualities are identical among themselves and are to be identified with the divine essence (in Ioh. tract. 48:6 ; de Trin. 6:7[8] ; sermo 341:6, 8). Carried along by a yearning to look into God's heart and handiwork A. scrutinized the trinitarian dogma and studied creation. The dogma of the Father and the Son and the Holy Ghost kept him busy in contemplation for many years. He discovered numerous and astounding trinitarian analogies, in nature generally, and in the human soul in particular (de Trin. books 8–15 ; conf. 13:11, 12). Unlike the Greeks, who as starting point of their trinitarian speculations preferred the fact of the three persons, A. started from the unity of nature and showed the consubstantiality of the three

as well as the real distinction of the Father, and the Son and the Holy Ghost, Arian subordinationism or Sabellian modalism being efficiently brushed aside (de Trin. book 1–7 ; contra sermonem arian. ; collatio cum Maximino, contra Maxim.). The divine persons are constituted by relations that are outside the category of accident (de Trin. 5:5, 6) the Son is begotten by the Father, the Holy Ghost proceeds from Father-Son as from One, 'You have to admit the Father and the Son to be [one] principle of the Holy Ghost not two principles' (de Trin. 5:14, 15), though the Father is at the source (de Trin. 15:17, 29). Difficult indeed it is to fix the exact difference between the generation of the Son and the procession of the Holy Ghost (de Trin. 15:27, 48). All actions external to the Godhead are acted in common by the three persons. Such are the theophanies of the OT (de Trin. 2:17, 32 ; 3:11, 22 sq.) ; such is creation, 'Of each nature God is the creator, i.e., the Trinity, or the Father the Son and the Holy Ghost' (de gen. ad litt. 9:15, 26). Creation, being a production from blank nothingness, necessitates and demands an exclusively divine act of God (de gen. ad litt. 9:15, 26 ; qq. in heptateuchum 2:21). Creation happened in time, or better, with time, but He lived from all eternity even before creation, bearing from all eternity ideas one day to become arch-patterns of things (de gen. ad litt. 5:13, 33), models so to speak of all contingent realities, 'Each one was created and there was each one's rational reason' (de div. qq. 83, q. 46:2). While giving Ecclus 18:1 a sense of simultaneity A. means that God drew the universe from black nothingness, at one and the same time, but not each thing in the same way, one thing being created so as to step right into actuality, another only so far as to remain in potency, potentially or seminally like a seed only, implying that God established in nature some secret principles, 'rational seedgrains', which developing bud forth into different species of things (de gen. ad litt. 4:33, 51 ; 5:4, 11 ; 5:23, 45 ; 6:5, 8 ; 6:6, 10 ; 9:17, 32 ; de Trin. 3:9 [16]). In order to keep harmony among these ideas A. had to give a rather allegorical exegesis of Gen 1:1 sq. (de gen. ad litt. 4:26, 43 ; 5:5, 15 ; de civ. Dei 11:7). Genesis—interpretations flowed often from his pen (de gen. contra manich. 1:22, 33 sq. ; de gen. ad litt. imp. 7:28). The problem of evil which spoils any serene admiration of the created order was attacked by A. in his Antimanichean works. In the refuting of a Manicheanism which had fascinated him for nine years A. proposes a positive solution, which starts from the principle that evil is just a lack of good, a deficiency caused either by imperfection of the thing (physical evil) or by imperfection and abuse of free will (moral evil). However sombre the background of evil may be it blends with the luminous order established by God, 'who thought making good out of evil a greater good than allowing no evil' (enchiridion 27 ; de civ. Dei 11:18 sq. ; 12:3 ; 22:1–2). A.'s thought orbits around a second focus, man, the 'rational substance consisting of body and soul' (de Trin. 15:7, 11). The body is so marvellous in its structure (de civ. Dei 22:24 (CCL

48:849–51) ; *de gen. ad litt.* 7:12, 20 ; *enarr. in ps.* 130:6) that it could never come from the evil principle, either totally deriving from Evil (*contra Faustum manich.* 20:15 ; 20:22) or partially (*de haeresibus* 85) ; the body is an essential component of man, ' anyone trying to divorce body from human nature indulges in folly ' (*de anima et eius origine* 4:23). It is from the soul that the body receives life, subsistence and being (*de immort. animae* 15:24). The soul is demonstrably one and simple, whole in the whole body, and whole in each of its parts (*de immort. animae* 16:25), demonstrably spiritual on account of the spiritual ideas about things outside and the reflexive idea about the soul, within (*de quant. animae* 13:22 ; 17:52 sq. ; *contra ep. manichaei* 20:22), demonstrably also immortal because spiritual and because the seat of truth (*soliloquia* book 2 ; *de imm. animae* 1–16), and in fine demonstrably in control of the lower faculties, and the higher ones : intellective memory, intelligence, and will (*de civ. Dei* 5:11 ; *de Trin.* 14:11, 14 s q.). But on one important point, on the origin of the soul, the great A. remained wavering between generationism and creationism (*de lib. arb.* 3:20, 55 sq. ; *de gen. ad litt.* ; book 10 ; *ep.* 166 (*de anima et eius origine*)). Man's primitive state, man's original sin, the consequences thereof, redemption and means of redemption, were being challenged widely at the time when A. himself started to study them closely. Man, created by God, was raised to a supernatural order enriched with gifts and privileges so extraordinary as to be beyond the fondest expectations of nature, such as the gift of exemption from death (not the immortality of the immortals (cf. *de gen. ad litt.* 6:25, 36)), or the gift of freedom from bodily infirmity and suffering (*de gen. contra manich.* 2:7, 8 ; *de gen. ad litt.* 8:5, 11 ; *de civ. Dei* 14:10 ; 14:26), the gift of infused, unerring knowledge (*de lib. arb.* 3:18, 52 ; *contra Jul. opus imp.* 5:1), the gift of immunity from all concupiscence coupled with absolute control of reason over the senses (*de gen. ad litt.* 9:3, 6 sq. ; 11:1, 3 ; *de civ. Dei* 14:9 sq. ; *de nupt. et concup.* 1:5, 6 sq.), the gift of a supernatural likeness stamped upon the soul by God (*conf.* 13:22, 32 ; *de gen. ad litt.* 3:19, 29 sq. ; 6:26, 37 sq. ; *de Trin.* 14:16, 22 sq. ; *contra Jul. opus imp.* 6:39), the gift of perfect liberty. i.e. the power of choosing between good and evil, with ease and a leaning towards one side, the good— certainly only the ability of avoiding a fall, not yet the inability of falling altogether, which latter belongs to the elect (*de correptione et gratia* 11:29 sq. ; *contra Jul. opus imp.* 5:61 ; 6:5 ; 6:16). Though capable of persevering in the state of grace with divine help which was graciously offered by God so as to be freely acceptable or rejectable, Adam, freely rejecting help, fell, and his fall became a baneful heritage transmitted to each of his descendants. The existence of original sin in each child of Adam is scripturally proved by A. especially from Rom 5:12 (*sermo* 294:15), traditionally from the testimony of Latin and Greek Fathers (*contra Julianum* 1:3, 5 sq. ; 1:5, 15 sq. ; 1:6, 22 sq.), ritually from the baptism of babies (*contra Julianum* 6:5, 13), psychologically

from the mysterious flood of misery no one can escape (*de civ. Dei* 22:22 (CCL 48:842)). It was in consequence of this original sin, which is so easy to state yet so difficult to understand (*de moribus eccl.* 22:40), that Adam and with him all his descendants had to lose their supernatural and divine likeness (*de gen. ad litt.* 6:24, 35), were deprived of the perfect freedom, exercised in paradise, of course not of our personal freedom (*contra duas ep. pelagian.* 1:2, 5), had to submit to the reign of death (*ep.* 166:7, 21), to the tyranny of concupiscence (*de nupt. et concup.* 1:22, 24 ; *contra duas ep. pelagian.* 1:15, 31 sq.), and to the pall of ignorance and error (*de lib. arb.* 3:18, 52). Mankind having once fallen into the misery of sin became a fermenting mass of iniquity, of wrath and perdition (*enchiridion* 26 sq.), with eternal damnation as its due (*de div. qq.* 83 q. 68:3 ; *sermo* 26:12 sq.). Christ came to repair the ravages of original sin. ' The Son of Man would not have come if the tragedy of man had not occurred' (*sermo* 174:2, 2). Christ is the Word of God who graciously assumed human nature, ' Christ in one person, Word and man ' (*enchiridion* 36), heralded by Hebrew prophets (*ep.* 137:4, 13), and also by the oracles of the gentiles (*ep.* 258:5 ; *de civ. Dei* 18:47 ; 19:23), conceived by the Virgin (*ep.* 137:2, 8 ; *sermo* 186:1, 1 ; *contra Jul. opus imp.* 4:122), born on 25 Dec. (*de div. qq.* 83 q. 56 ; *de Trin.* 4:5, 9), in a year unknown by consular chronology (*de doctrina christ.* 2:28, 42), crucified on 25 April in a year doubtfully fixed in the consular chronology (*de civ. Dei* 18:54). His death had the value of a real sacrifice of atonement ; it was offered by Christ for the sins of mankind (*de Trin.* 4:13, 17) and rescued mankind from the slavery of Satan and sin (*de Trin.* 13:12, 16 sq.) so that at the price of His blood redemption was extended to all sins, to all captives (*enarr. in ps.* 129:3), not excluding even infants who die without baptism (*contra Jul. opus imp.* 2:175). There is no effective sharing in the benefits of redemption without the Church and grace. The Augustinian idea of the Church was clarified in the anti-Donatist struggle. He had to stress holiness of the Church though the unholy were scattered among the holy and certainly were not missing in the Church of his day ; he stressed catholicity against the very narrow parochialism of the Donatists ; he did insist upon unity of faith and government symbolized by the garment of Christ which the very soldiers at the crucifixion had left seamless and intact ; not so the Donatists, who tore it asunder. He put no less emphasis on apostolicity, guaranteed by order of the Master through union of particular churches with the Church of Rome, ' to which the first rank among apostolic chairs (*apostolicae cathedrae principatus*) always belongs ' (*ep.* 43:3, 7), where apostolic continuity between St Peter and the reigning pope, Anastasius, could be checked along a series of 36 names (*ep.* 53:2). As the Donatists made the validity of the sacraments dependent on the dignity or indignity of the minister, St A. had to bring into sharp relief that a baptism or an order is valid not because of any moral qualities in minister or subject but solely because of the merits of Christ who once and for all instituted the sacraments and in all cases has them administered vicariously and also administers them personally (*contra Cresconium* 4:16, 19 ; *in Joh. tract.* 5:7 ; 6:7). Donatist brutalities had also a political effect : a sadder but also wiser A. had to appeal to the Emperor, and consequently to change his ideas about separation between state and Church (*contra ep. Parmeniani* 1:9, 15 ; *contra Cresconium* 3:50, 55 ; *retract.* 2:5). The Augustinian idea and ideal of the Church is a majestic one worthy to be summarized in Cyprian's awe-inspiring phrase, ' There is no salvation outside the Church ' (*de bapt.* 4:17, 24). For A. the Church is clad in awe on account of the infallibility of its magisterium, and the indispensability of membership within it. Augustinian ideas on grace have given A. the special name of Doctor of Grace. The chance of developing his ideas on grace was offered to St A. during the anti-Pelagian controversy, from 411 to his death in 430. Sanctifying grace, says A. implies a spiritual rebirth, not only a remission of an original sin, not only the termination of a sinfulness [*reatus*] of concupiscence or other sins which may happen to cast a shadow over a soul. According to St A. grace resurrects the supernatural and divine likeness in the soul, creates in man a new capacity for acting meritoriously on the supernatural level (*de peccatorum mer. et rem.* 1:10, 11 sq. ; 2:8, 10 ; *de gratia et lib. arb.* 27 ; *contra Jul. opus imp.* 2:227 ; 6:15 ; *de Trin.* 14:16, 22 sq.). The real Pelagian problem was not so much sanctifying grace as actual grace, inner help within will-power, willing, and well-doing. St A. proves the necessity of actual grace (*ep.* 217:4, 12) from the first beginning of faith, from the first desire of conversion (*de predestinatione sanct.* 3:7 sq.) to the great gift of final perseverance (*de dono perseverantiae* 1:1). When a semi-Pelagian movement started among the monks of Southern Gaul, he had to defend the absolute gratuity of grace in its first beginning and in the crowning achievement of lasting perseverance. In the relationship of grace and merit A. always put the stress on grace : not as if man, when helped by grace, could not really gain merit but rather because ' God does not crown our merits so much as his own gifts ' (*ep.* 194:5, 19 ; *de gratia et lib. arb.* 6:15). A. is wont to compare the grace given to man in the state of innocence, which made perseverance possible but did not win it (*adiutorium sine quo non*), with that which is given in the present order, by which man not only can but does (freely) choose the good and reaches eventually final perseverance (*adiutorium quo*), as in *de correptione et gratia* 12:34 and 38. ' Freedom ', says A. (ibid. 11:31) ' is sufficient for evil ; for good it is not enough unless it be empowered by the Omnipotent who is good '. It is a travesty of A.'s thought to suggest that he denied freedom or that he reduced it to passivity under the action of grace. The misinterpretation of A.'s distinction above in this sense by Luther and Jansenius is fundamental in their misguided appeal to A. as sponsoring their erroneous systems (cf. also *de gratia et libero arbitrio* 1:1 and 17:33). During the last years of A. the problem of predestination was forced upon his atten-

tion by the Pelagian controversy. Involved was the mystery of divine sovereignty and human freedom, two parallels that must never intersect. In geometry two lines can be kept parallel by definition ; they cannot be drawn with practical means without actual intersecting. Divine sovereignty and human freedom are two such lines ; we know the fact from reason and from faith : we do not see a way of full compatibility, only God does. St A. did not, nor did St Paul. When Pelagius came along with the serpent's flattery, ' You can do everything without God ', only a few people heard what the serpent hissed aside, ' And you must ! No excuses ! No difference between venial and mortal sin ! Between precept and counsel ' (cf. CE 2 (1907) 96). A. did a service to man when he defended the sovereign rights of God by arguing from a most extreme and inescapable position : If all mankind had lost all rights before God, could they complain if He left them to themselves ? A. answers almost cheerfully : No. We must remember that A.'s God is Love whom you can trust, whom A. did trust. The extreme position was meant to eliminate Pelagian quibbling. This is what the fearful Augustinian word *massa damnata* (mass in fermentation, fermenting unto damnation) re-echoes from St Paul (Rom 9:21). A. says that mankind because of original sin becomes a *massa damnata* ; ' even if no one were freed from it, no one could censure God's justice ' (*enchiridion* 99 (25)). By pure graciousness and sovereign mercy God saves enough to fill up the [many] vacancies left by the rebellious angels (*sermo* 111:1 ; *enchiridion* 29 (9) ; *de civ. Dei* 22:1). Predestination is a boundless mystery in whose expanses a curious traveller may get lost unless he reaffirm God's spotless justice by acts of faith and reason ; little man confronted by the greatest mystery must be willing to overcome his limited way of knowing by unlimited trust in God because in Mt 20:13 ' the first and the last ' and in Mt 22:12 ' the saved and the lost ' are called, and are, God's friends, as the 14th cent. knew very well and only the 17th seemed to forget.*

IV Survival in MSS. Books, their quality and their numbers, might be imagined to indicate something like the groundwater level of a civilization. Since the printing presses have kept on flooding the world with books it sounds incredible that over the long-lasting manuscript age there hung an ever-present danger, namely, that by some chain-reaction library after library might disappear, book after book ' die out ' ; for a book's number of copies might shrink critically, the 10 available copies in Europe—let us imagine—might be reduced to 5, then to 3,

* EDITOR'S NOTE.—The problem of God's salvific will towards all men came to the fore late in Augustine's life, but he did not go back on his early declaration (*de Genesi adversus Manichaeos* 1:3:6 ; PL 34:176) that all men can be saved if they wish (cf. *Retract.* 1:10:2 ; PL 32:599). He re-asserted it against the Pelagians : ' It is true ; all men can be saved, but the will is prepared by God.' He did not cease to preach that it lay within the power of any man to change his destiny : ' Choose while there is yet time ', he says (*Enarratio* 1 on Ps 36:PL 36:356, cf. *Tract.* 26:2 on Jn ; PL 35:1607, *serm.* on Ps 67:3 ; PL 38:150).

finally to 1 copy so that all chances of survival would hang upon the fate of this one lonely copy. Many classical and Christian authors were lost in this game of chance : St A. survived. That he survived so gloriously, so incomparably, proves how influential he was. His chances were good from the beginning : he assembled and left a famous library (*vita* 31:8) at Hippo that was to supply the heart-beat for Augustinian survival ; and Roman stenographers, Roman book-dealers and book-lovers were organized better than during the following millennium, which painfully inched its way back to the classical book level. In the Middle Ages there were relatively few places with time or money to spare for more than a shelf-ful of books ; but wherever we discover such an old nest there is usually an Augustine among them (cf. J. W. Thompson, *The medieval library* (1939)). Most medieval parchment-making and writing efforts served first of all the dire needs of school and choir, altar and administration ; rarely was it possible to have a small collection of non-utilitarian books ; but if you find one you may be sure to find A., some of his copies in small, relatively many in larger, libraries of non-utilitarian books. Today, 500 years after Gutenberg, we still have 10 out of a 12-volume *opera-omnia* MS.-collection of St A. (=MS. Troyes 40; cf. J. de Ghellinck, *Patristique et Moyen Age*, III (1948) 342 ; idem, 'Une édition médiévale des opera omnia de s. Aug.' in *Liber Floridus P. Lehmann* (1950) 63–82.) Medieval parchment being expensive had to serve a second time as palimpsest after the book had been thumbed beyond legibility, and aged beyond the acceptable fashions of penmanship. If St A. had had less influence or prestige, we should have today few MSS., going beyond the 12th cent. When Gutenberg started printing his beautiful 'hand', old-fashioned MS. copies were discarded for the new beauty : but not St A., though his printed copies flooded the market. Reverence and prestige kept the MS.-Augustine. E. A. Lowe ('The oldest extant MSS. of St A.' in *Miscell. Agost.* (1930) 235–51) has over 60 items for the earliest, the uncial and half-uncial period, though he excludes Visigothic, Insular, and pre-Caroline. A. Wilmart has done the preparatory work to give us a faint idea on the survival of the Augustinian MSS.; he has collated all the MSS. of four great Augustinian works (*conf.*; *de Trin.*; *de civ. Dei*; *enarr. in ps.*). It is an overwhelming proof of St A.'s prestige and survival, in dead books if you like, but in dead books that prove a lively interest in the living influence of A. throughout the ages. Yet it is to be remembered that Wilmart found only the poor remains of a once great army swallowed up by time, disaster and human obtuseness (cf. A. Wilmart, 'La Tradition des grands ouvrages de saint A.' in *Miscell. Agost.* 2 (1930) 257–315). He has proved (cf. Wilmart, 261) that, apart from Holy Scripture (or the *Moralia* of St Gregory), no other books have been copied, and therefore used, as often as the *Confessions* and the *City of God*. A corresponding guess in regard to the rest of the works of St A. is justified though we do not have very exact figures. But

these are the figures we have in the case of the four major works. For the *confessiones* we have these MSS. surviving :

Of the		we have		Of the		we have	
Of the	6–7th c.	we have	1	Of the	12th c.	we have	52
,,	9th c.	,,	11	,,	13th c.	,,	51
,,	10th c.	,,	8	,,	14th c.	,,	46
,,	11th c.	,,	19	,,	15th c.	,,	70

There is the whole story of St A.'s spiritual influence during the Middle Ages. For the *de Trinitate* we have these MSS. surviving :

Of the	8th c.	we have	2	Of the	12th c.	we have	53
,,	9th c.	,,	12	,,	13th c.	,,	50
,,	10th c.	,,	9	,,	14th c.	,,	54
,,	11th c.	,,	15	,,	15th c.	,,	38

'These figures are the most eloquent proof of the considerable influence which St A.'s thought in its highest soaring expression never ceased to command in medieval Christianity' is the comment of Dom A. Wilmart (*La Tradition* 278). For the *de civ. Dei* we have these MSS. surviving :

Of the	5th c.	we have	1	Of the	11th c.	we have	22
,,	7th c.	,,	2	,,	12th c.	,,	80
,,	8th c.	,,	1	,,	13th c.	,,	40
,,	9th c.	,,	19	,,	14th c.	,,	56
,,	10th c.	,,	20	,,	15th c.	,,	99

Though blind chance might have preserved many copies of the 12th cent., and few of the 13th, the figures seem to give, however, an indication of greater spiritual interest in the *City of God* during the 12th, or Gregorian, cent. and the 14th cent. of the Black Death. Or was it just campaign-literature during the Investiture struggle of the 12th, and the lay spirit of the 14th, cent. ? Dom Wilmart thinks differently (cf. *La Tradition* 279 note 1).—For A.'s bulkiest work which goes under the Erasmian name of *enarrationes in psalmos* we have of course many MSS. with incomplete sets. A. was the first Father to explain the whole psalter (Wilmart, *La Tradition* 295) but the scholastic period had its own numerous compilations or commentaries on the psalms (Wilmart, 310), whose competition would have ostracized a lesser man than St A. He outshone them all, as these numbers show, which with all due regard for Wilmart's caution (Wilmart, 311–12) are still very impressive. For the *enarrationes in psal.* we have these MSS. surviving :

Of the 6–8th c. we have 7 MSS., and 7 fragments.
Of the 9th c. we have 3 complete sets, 15 partial sets.

Of the	10th c.	we have	24	Of the	13th c.	we have	37
,,	11th c.	,,	61	,,	14th c.	,,	29
,,	12th c.	,,	147	,,	15th c.	,,	38

'The abundance (of 147) in the 12th cent. finds an explanation in the soaring development of monastic life especially among the Cistercians' (Wilmart, 311). The number of surviving witnesses for some four major works of St A. allows a proportionate hypothetical appraisal for the rest of St A.'s books ; there must be several thousand Augustinian MSS. These indisputable facts of MS. survival are the steel

skeleton supporting the other proofs for the outstanding influence enjoyed by St A. in the middle
ages and beyond.

Popes and Councils in their most solemn teaching made St A. their mouthpiece, their Doctor of
Grace. Following the venerable precedents of
Celestine I A.D. 431 (D 129) and Hormisdas A.D. 520
(D 3027) : the 2nd Council of Orange A.D. 529
made the Holy Ghost speak with A.'s words (D 174
sq., D 182, D 184-98). Pope Boniface II A.D. 531
(D 3039), and the 3rd Council of Valence A.D. 855
named A. among the great Doctors (D 320, D 322)
and, of course, the Council of Trent (D 799, D 804,
D 809) followed the Doctor of Grace in many things,
though his identification of concupiscence and original sin was discarded. The official Church has kept
free from exaggerating A.'s importance (D 142,
D 1320) because it is great enough as it is and St A.
himself warned against it (*de dono persev.* 21:55
PL 45:1027-8) ; but the Church has also discouraged denigration of him. When various theological
schools advanced claims to his name because it implied so much prestige, the Church, especially in the
17th cent., protected the name of the schools by
protecting the name of St A. (cf. D 1090-9 with
notes). In other fields of teaching the Church
throughout the ages made St A. the mainstay of
tradition. To remove the cancerous growth of the
Pistoia synod Pius VI often called on St A. to speak
for the Catholic Church (D 1519, 1522-5, 1546,
1570, 1597). When Pius VII warned against abuse
of Holy Writ by heretics (D 1604 ; cf. D 1608), he
quoted someone who certainly was not wont to
discourage love of Scripture, Augustine *tr. in Jn.*
18:1 (CCL 36:180 lines 27-8). Pius IX defended
dogmatic terminology (D 1658) with the *de civ. Dei*
10:23 (CCL 47:297 lines 23-5). Leo XIII relied on
St A. to reassure the children of this age about the
ancient wisdom of faith in regard to the difficult
issues of freedom and faith (D 1875), exegesis and
tradition (D 1944), Bible and languages (D 1941),
Bible and sciences (D 1947), Bible and inspiration,
and its absolute immunity from error (D 1952 ; cf.
D 2102). The pattern has always been the same.
At the request of Pope Pelagius II A.D. 585 the anti-
Donatist A. raised his voice again for unity (D 247) ;
in the name of the official Church he worded the
Catholic belief in the virgin birth A.D. 675 (D 282),
and the Catholic tenet of the possibility of baptism
of desire *c.* 1140 (D 388). **Medieval manuals** of the
greatest dogmatic import, like the Breviary, the
Canon Law, the Sentences of Peter Lombard, the
Glossa, teem with ' authorities ' drawn from St A.
Even today the second and third nocturn of the
Roman Breviary has an absolute preponderance of
Augustinian material. If the *lex orandi* is the *lex
credendi* St A. has wielded a very great dogmatic
influence from the choirstalls of friars and monks.
There never was a theological handbook, nor ever
will be, like that of Peter Lombard, who shaped every
theologian from 1200 to 1600. One glance into
Lombardus convinces the reader that the overwhelming majority of patristic quotations, perhaps eight-

tenths, come from St A.—The same is true for Canon
Law, the same for the Glossa material, the medieval
exegetical handbooks. A doubting Thomas or a
Protestant might be tempted to say that St A.
enjoyed too much influence.—To document A.'s
influence upon the individual medieval doctors is
impossible for lack of space. Before the year 1200
St A. was quoted ' innocently ', that is he was simply
incorporated into a page without getting the com-
pliment of explicit quotation. When after 1200 the
more scientific quoting techniques appear sporadic-
ally, St A.'s name is among the first to get acknowledgment in quoting. Among the 3000 quotations
from St A. found in the major works of St Thomas
(cf. Leonine edition, XVI (1948)) many are quoted
exactly. In the 14th cent. a historical or positive
turn of mind forced the development of scientific
quoting ; again St A. is among the first to be so
honoured (cf. D. Trapp, ' Hiltalinger's Augustinian
quotations ' in *Augustiniana* IV (1954) 412-49).
Scientific quoting techniques demanded chapter-
division in the works to be quoted : again St A. is
among the first to get an internationally-accepted
chapter-division, and this in the age of the MS.-
copyist ! After St A. became fashionable, lesser
minds wanted to plume themselves, busy minds
wanted to have a tool for quick reference ; *tabulae*
to St A.'s works were therefore edited, again outstanding among the *tabulae* literature. The Austin
Friars edited an enormous *Milleloquium S. Augustini*
about 1345 (cf. V. A. Fitzpatrick, *Bartholomew of
Urbino : The sermons embraced in his Mill. S. Aug.* ;
Thesis, Cath. U. of A. (1954)). It dominated the
late Middle Ages, was forgotten, was excavated by
Cardinal A. Mai (*Nova PP Bibl.* I (1852) xxiii-xxiv),
was buried again under the quick wit of D. Morin
(*Miscellanea Agostiniana* I (1930) 277). It still
deserves re-examination because caution against unscientific impeaching of supposedly unscientific
medieval methods is to be advocated (cf. M. Grabmann, *Die Geschichte der scholastichen Methode* 2 (1957[2])
82-6). A.'s influence upon doctors of the early
scholastic period has found a masterly description in
the eight volumes of A. M. Landgraf (*Dogmengeschichte der Frühscholastik* (1952-6)) and in the works
of other masters like J. de Ghellinck (*Patristique et
MA* 2-3 (1947-8) and *Le Mouvement théologique du
XIIe siecle* (1948)), O. Lottin (*Psychologie et morale au
XIIe et XIIIe siècle* (1942, 48-9, 54)), C. Spicq
(*Esquisse d'une histoire de l'exégèse au MA* (1944)).—
The picture does not change much in the 13th
cent. One interesting example of A.'s influence
upon trinitarian speculations may be seen in M.
Schmaus, *Liber propugnatorius* (1930) 653-66. Augustinian influence was unchallenged in the 12th
cent., was lessened somewhat by Aristotle in the
13th, to rise again in the 14th, in exact proportion
to the Aristotelian decline. The second rise can be
followed in studies on the 14th cent. like B. M.
Xiberta's (*De scriptoribus s. XIV ex ordine Carmeli-
tarum* (1931)), and in a corresponding study on
Augustinian theology (D. Trapp, ' Augustinian
theology in the 14th cent.' in *Augustiniana* VI (1956)

146–274). A number of devoted editors have given us a chance of watching the trail of A.'s name across edited pages of the 14th cent. : A. Combes by his editions of Johannes de Ripa (*Determinationes* (1957), *Conclusiones* (1957)) ; E. Buytaert by his editions of Aureolus (1953 ff.) ; B. Jansen by his editions of Olivi (*QQ in 2ᵐ librum Sententiarum* (1922–24–26) esp. 3 (1926) 562–94).

Preachers. By order of the Church the medieval theologian, the canonist, the choir monk, the exegete or Bible student were exposed to ideas of St A. at every turn. The same is true for medieval preachers and their listeners, at least before the 12th cent., i.e. as long as abbots and pastors explained Holy Writ only for devotional purposes. While pious exegesis remained in force, it was patristic, and the sermons were patristic, mostly extracts from Gregory and A. When Holy Scripture in the 12th cent. became the object of professional inquiry, the sermon also followed a new method, the *Ars praedicandi* became less pious and less allegorical, and more intellectual and more literal. The influence of St A. on the exegesis of the Middle Ages is dealt with by C. Spicq (cf. *Esquisse d'une histoire de l'exégèse latine au MA* (1944)). One of the last 'Augustinian' preachers of the 12th cent. was Geoffroy du Loroux (cf. J. P. Bonnes, 'Un des plus grands prédicateurs du XIIᵉ siècle, G. du L., dit Geoffroy Babion' in RB LVI (1945–6) 174–215). Geoffroy might also have something to do with the ps.-Augustinian fabrication of the *Sermones ad fratres in eremo* (cf. J. P. Bonnes, *Geoffroy* 177 sq. n. 1) ; because the most obvious beneficiary of a falsification is not always identical with the falsifier. Some other ps.-Augustinian treatises are guiltless of any literary manœuvres of falsification. At first humble anonymous booklets, they were so steeped in Augustinian piety that uncritical medieval readers and copyists added the name of St A. to their title-pages. The name they had never coveted gave those spiritual booklets a short span of notorious popularity among uncritical religious until the critical humanist came to relegate them, not to the limbo of anonymity but to the penitentiary of the falsifiers, namely the appendix of editions of Augustine, where no one reads them any more for reasons other than literary criticism. They do not deserve their fate, but are certainly witnesses to the fact that St A. had great influence upon the spiritual life of the Middle Ages, since the counterfeit proves the popularity of the genuine currency. Through the **Rule**, which to the eyes of the humanists also appears as illegitimate, St A. has influenced wide sections of spiritual life in the Church. It was always the Rule that made thousands kneel before St A. and give him a chance of intervention on a higher level, more direct and more personal. But, since the day when Erasmus first thought of saving St A. from Canons and Friars, both have continued claiming exclusive rights to the saint's name, and the learned have continued denying all connections between him and monasticism. He certainly was no 'founder' because before Cluny there were only independent houses, no centrally-controlled organizations of many houses, or orders in the modern sense. A. did not 'found' the western monks ; he was an outstanding promoter of western monasticism, like Eusebius of Vercelli (CE 5 (1909) 614), or Martin of Tours (CE 9 (1910) 732–3), both bishops, or like John Cassian (CE 3 (1908) 404–5) ; St A. introduced the western monk into Africa, as we learn from someone who knew, the Donatist Petilianus, who blames A. for it (*contra litt. Petil.* 3:40, 48). A. enjoyed reminding his correspondents of his being a monk : ' I, the writer of this letter, have really fallen in love with this perfection (of Mt 19:21). I have taken the step . . . and, as much as I can, I urge others towards this kind of life, and in the name of God I have confrères who, through my intervention, have been talked into it ' (*ep.* 157:39). The two famous sermons (355 and 356) and the *vita* of Possidius show that A. considered at least three monasteries as his own ' foundations ', one in Tagaste, one in the garden of Hippo, one in the bishop's residence there. By the time the life of Fulgentius of Ruspe was written North Africa had about 50 monasteries (cf. G. G. Lapeyre, *Saint Fulgence, essai* (1929) 109–12). No one should expect to find the modern Canon Law (can. 487–681) in operation either at St A.'s time or at St Fulgentius's but on reading the short Latin biography of the latter (G. G. Lapeyre, *Saint Fulgence, vie* (1929)) one has to smile again and again at the many embryonic beginnings of later developments ; even the monastic titles are there (Lapeyre, *vie*, 117) ' Brother so and so '. There were priests and lay monks in A.'s monasteries ; in one of his letters (*ep.* 60:1) he warns a fellow-bishop against the assumption that the bishop could make a good priest out of a bad monk, or vice versa. There was manual work and intellectual work, common prayer, common meals, simple common dress (hardly uniform), absolute poverty and chastity under the obligation of the vow, obedience towards a priestly superior, and a kind of administrator, though hardly under the obligation of a vow. Kindness, moderation and wisdom were Augustinian characteristics. A. did not lord it over his monks ; he wanted to enlist their good will, their inner co-operation. These principles are scattered all over his writings (cf. A. Zumkeller, *Das Mönchtum des hl. Aug.* (1950) 215–360). Of programmatic monastic works there are two : ' On the work of monks ', and the *Rule*. In the former A. writes against some marauding monks who do nothing, who mouth Holy Writ, and swindle a living out of the gullible whom they impress by their fanciful monastic dress and hair-style. In this work, ' On the work of monks ', there are so many allusions to the *Rule* of St A. that the *Rule* must have been written before the work ' On the work of monks ' (*c.* 400). In the olden days St A. was supposed to have written what is usually referred to as his Rule for men (cf. edition in *Jordani de Saxonia Liber Vitae fratrum* ed. R. Arbesmann–W. Hümpfner (1943) appendix 483–504). This Augustinian Rule for men is accredited as Augustinian by a very respectable number of MSS., among them 1 from the 6th–7th cent.; 4 from the 9th cent.; 4 from the 11th cent.; 5 from the 12th cent.; (we omit the 13th cent.). Such MS. testimony weighs heavier than any later theorizing. In the year 1156 appeared the first suggestion that St A. might have first written a rule for women (= our modern *ep.* 211, first observed by women but later on also adopted for men, with the necessary changes of grammatical gender); the same opinion was expressed by the Augustinian Bartholomew of Urbino (*c.* 1345), in what could be called the first Augustinian patrology; repeated by Erasmus, it was to enjoy quasi-dogmatic status in subsequent centuries (cf. *Vitae fratrum* introd. lxxix–lxxx). The Erasmian theory is undoubtedly very beautiful and appealing to a searching mind. But no MSS. before the year 1200 (cf. *above*) accredit the combination of a female rule with objurgation, two elements which our *ep.* 211 combines, at least today, namely a philippic or objurgation (element no. 1) against some rebellious nuns (whom St A. is supposed to have brought back to reason) with a female rule (element no. 2). Already about the year 600, on the other hand, we have definite indications for the existence of another combination : female rule with female ordo (*ordo* here = a kind of monastic and liturgical programme). M. Verheijen has called attention to this combination again (cf. ' La Regula puellarum et la Regula S. Augustini ' in *Augustiniana* IV (1954) 258–68). But what we need in order to give the Erasmian theory solid ground to stand on would be a MS. group dating back to about 600 containing our modern *ep.* 211, i.e. a venerable witness or witnesses for the combination of female rule with objurgation. If this venerable witness, not yet found but always to be hoped for, would also witness to the Augustinian authorship of the combination of female rule with objurgation we should have a proof that our modern *ep.* 211 comes, as an *epistula*, from St A. As yet we have no MSS. for *ep.* 211 before the 12th cent.; neither the *retractationes* nor the *indiculus* (book catalogue) of Possidius mention *ep.* 211, nor a male or female rule. In the meantime we may go along with the MSS. which attest the male rule of St A.: *one* late uncial MS. of *c.* 700 (MS. Paris Nat. lat. 12634, cf. A. Casamassa, *Scritti patr.* 1 (1955) 105–17): *four* MSS. from the 9th cent., MSS. (Laon 328[bis]; clm 28118; Escorial a–1–13 fol. 3–4; and fol. 71–5): *four* MSS. from the 11th cent. (MSS. Vat. Pal. 211; Florence Laurent. Ashb. 24; Montecassino 172; Bamberg Stadtb. B III 10): *five* MSS. from the 12th cent. (MSS. Escorial R–III–10; Escorial I–II–9; clm 7808 (= A.D. 1125); clm 1018; clm 17174), besides an infinite swarm of later manuscripts, which could compete with, but would not defeat *ep.* 211, if that work had a good pedigree. In all these MSS. we find the male Rule attested; but in many of them it is not the male Rule alone we find but a combination of male Rule with male *ordo*. Mandonnet rediscovered why this *male ordo* was *dropped* from the Augustinian Rule (cf. *Vitae fratrum* introd. lxxix). Why this *male ordo* was *added* in the first place, we do not yet know with absolute clarity and certainty. As the

really living St A. is met with in prayer more than elsewhere it is important that the authorship of this old Rule be preserved in order to invigorate the spiritual life of many thousands of religious whom the one Rule unites under the name of Augustine, though habits be different, and historical continuity shorter or longer (cf. F. Roth, ' Cardinal R. Annibaldi ' offprint from *Augustiniana* (1952–4) : appendix I–II).

Conclusion. If the great Augustine is to be pressed into a little synopsis one might define his thought by its ' magnetic declination ' : his thought is closer to God than to creature, closer to soul than to body, closer to practice than to theory, closer to faith than to reason, closer to charity than to speculation (cf. E. Gilson, *Introduction à l'étude de s. Augustin* (1943[2]) 314–23). His thought consciously integrates polarities like freedom-grace. At the same time he sees the relativity of freedom in grace, of reason in faith, the relativity of the light in its source, of the good in its absolute centre. In regard to form, his thought is often expressed with prismatic clearness, but more often there remains a rich iridescence about A.'s word, and this is not the last reason why it stays fresh, fascinating and charming.

Bibliography. A complete Latin ed. of A.'s works is in PL 32–PL 47, a reprint from Maurist edition of 1679–1700. An incomplete Latin edition in CSEL = *Corpus scriptorum eccl. latinorum* [1866 ff.]. The recently begun CCL = *Corpus Christianorum, Series Latina* will print A. in CCL 27 ff.; these have appeared : CCL 36 (in *Jn ev. tr.*), CCL 38–40 (*enarr. in ps.*), CCL 47–8 (*de civ. Dei*). Each work begins with bibliography, general on life of A. and his works in CCL 27; selected in CCL 36 : introduction xvi–xvii; CCL 38 : introduction xx–xxii; CCL 47 : introduction ix*–xx*. English translations are mentioned in bibliography of CCL; for older translations cf. E. Przywara, *An A.-Synthesis* (1945) introduction xv–xvi. Two sets of new translations are being published in U.S.A. : *Ancient Christian Writers*, and *The Fathers of the Church*; the latter has published its 16th volume of Augustine. Przywara, *Synthesis* offers rich English selections from A.'s works under logical headings. For biography of A. cf. P. Burton, *St. A* (1897[3]); L. Bertrand, *Saint A.*, English translation by V. O'Sullivan (1914); G. Papini, *Sant' Agostino*, English translation by M. P. Agnetti (1930); H. Pope, *St. A. of Hippo* (1937); V. J. Bourke, *A.'s quest of wisdom* (1945). Many volumes of *Patristic Studies* (Catholic University of America) deal with A. philologically, two 28 (1930) and 45 (1935) deal with North-African life. Standard works are: O. Rottmanner, *Der Augustinismus* (1892); P. Batiffol, *Le Catholicisme de s. A.* (1920[3]); M. Schmaus, *Die psychologische Trinitätslehre des hl. A.* (1927); J. Mausbach, *Die Ethik des hl. A.* I–II (1929[2]). The two centenaries of 1930 and 1954 have produced a rich crop of A. studies: *A monument to St A.* (1930[1], 1945[2]); M. Grabmann–J. Mausbach, *Aurelius Augustinus*; *Miscellanea Agostiniana* I–II (1930); *S. Augustin parmi nous* (1954). The International

Augustine Congress of Paris, Sept. 1954, has published *Augustinus Magister*, vol. 1–3; it affords quick acquaintance with Augustinian studies today. E. Gilson, *Introduction a l'étude de S. Augustin* (1943²) has rich bibliography on pp. 325–51. Among the best recent works are: S. J. Grabowski, *The all-present God: a study in St. A.* (1954); the same, *The Church; an introduction to the theology of A.* (1957); B. Switalski, *Plotinus and the ethics of St A.* (1946); C. Boyer, *Christianisme et néoplatonisme dans la formation de s. A.* [1953²]; H. Marrou, *S. Augustin et l'augustinisme* (1955), Eng. tr. *St Augustine and his influence* (1957); E. F. Durkin, *The theological distinction of sins in the writings of St A.* (1952); M. Jacquin 'La Question de la prédestination aux ve et vi^e siècles', in RHE 5 (1904), 725–754; J. J. O'Meara, *The young A.: growth of St A.'s mind up to his conversion* (1954); * R. W. Battenhouse, *A companion to the study of St A.* (1955); * G. G. Willis, *St A. and the Donatist controversy* (1950). A.'s asceticism and mysticism are dealt with in E. Hendrikx, *A.'s Verhältnis z. Mystik* (1936); Ph. Platz, *Der Römerbrief in der Gnadenlehre A.'s* (1938); F. Mayr, *Divus A. vitae spir. magister* I–II (1727, 1731, 1895); G. Armas, *La moral de San Agustín* (1954); C. Vaca, *La vida relig. en S. Ag.* I–II (1955²), III (1955¹) (the last three offer good collections of texts); H. Pope, *The teaching of St A. on prayer and the contempl. life* (1935); D. J. Leahy, *St A. on eternal life* (1939); A. Zumkeller, 'Der klösterliche Gehorsam beim hl. A.' in *Augustinus Magister* I, 265–76. D. T.

AUTHENTICITY OF THE VULGATE In 1546 the Council of Trent passed the following disciplinary decree: 'The same holy synod considering that no small advantage may accrue to the Church of God, if out of all the Latin translations of the sacred books in circulation it make known which is to be held as authoritative: determines and declares that this ancient Vulgate translation which is recommended by the long use of so many centuries in the Church, is to be regarded as authoritative in public lectures, disputations, sermons, and expository discourses, and that no one may make bold or presume to reject it on any pretext.'¹ The need for the decree arose from the number of the new versions and the growing uncertainty arising therefrom as to which texts were safe and reliable. And juridical recognition was given to the Vulgate on the ground of its agelong use in the Church, as such use would have been impossible if it had not been free from error in matters of Faith and morals, and if it had not substantially preserved the

¹ Eadem sacrosancta synodus considerans, non parum utilitatis accedere posse ecclesiae Dei, si ex omnibus latinis editionibus, quae circumferuntur sacrorum librorum, quaenam pro authentica habenda sit, innotescat: statuit et declarat, ut haec ipsa vetus et vulgata editio, quae longo tot saeculorum usu in ipsa ecclesia probata est, in publicis lectionibus, disputationibus praedicationibus et expositionibus pro authentica habeatur, et quod nemo illam reiicere quovis praetextu audeat vel praesumat. 'Concilium Tridentinum', editit Societas Goerresiana V (1911), 91.

true content of Scripture. Other Latin translations were not condemned, nor was the Vulgate preferred to any other on intrinsic grounds. The others remained unaffected by the decree except that no one of them could enjoy the dogmatic assurance attaching to the Vulgate, though it was recognized that help could be derived from them for the better understanding of the sacred text. Moreover this dogmatic assurance gives no stamp of approval to the Vulgate version of individual texts except as regards immunity from error in Faith and morals. It does not even guarantee that a doctrinal statement found in the Vulgate faithfully reflects the original text. If it does not, then, though immune from error, its authority is not scriptural but due to Tradition.

Thus the decree deals with the Vulgate as a translation, and it was clearly recognized at the Council that a stream cannot be purer than its source. The juridical preference given to the Vulgate, therefore, implied no superiority to the original Hebrew, Aramaic and Greek texts. On the contrary, where correction is required or doubt exists, recourse must be had to the languages in which the books were written. This principle was laid down by St Jerome (CSEL 55: 249) and St Augustine (PL 34: 46). And it was not overlooked in the Complutensian Polyglot where the Vulgate text printed between the Hebrew and the Septuagint is compared to our Lord hanging on the Cross between two thieves. The comparison here is not between the texts but between the religious bodies taken to be symbolized by them.

A widespread error has been due to the failure to recognize the use of the word *authentica* with the meaning 'authoritative', which it commonly has in medieval writers. In many books it is erroneously understood to mean 'authentic'.

The main source for the occasion and meaning of the decree is the collection of reports and documents published in the Acta of the Council (see Note 1). Exact references to these and other sources may be found in E. F. Sutcliffe, 'The Council of Trent on the *Authentia* of the Vulgate', JTS 49 (1948) 35–42. E. F. S.

AZYMES In 1439 the Council of Florence, with Greeks and Latins in attendance, decreed (D 692) that the Body of Christ was truly confected from wheaten bread, whether unleavened or leavened. This wise compromise on a matter of liturgical history would have removed the question from theological discussion if the Protestant Reformation had not afforded an opportunity for reviving the controversy. It was in truth a pointless debate, as neither side then had the liturgical information available that would have made a solution possible. So much of the argumentation was by means of the argument from silence that the protagonists of those days look very sorry figures in the light of modern knowledge.

It is certain that the Ebionites used azymes or unleavened bread for their Eucharist (Epiphanius *haer.*

30:16 ; GCS 25:353). It is likewise clear that the Armenians and Jacobites used azymes, for they are both accused of this by a certain Meletius whose tract (PG 95:389) is of the 8th cent. and has been included among the works of John Damascene. He says that both groups followed the Jewish rite of unleavened bread and thus showed themselves to be Apollinarists. His point was that Apollinaris had denied that Christ had a human soul and these groups by consecrating unleavened bread (which lacked leaven, the symbol of the vital principle) were carrying out his heresy in action. The Armenians went on with their practice, but the Jacobites seem to have abandoned it. Meletius argues also that Christ did not eat the Pasch with His disciples, thus indicating that one of the reasons invoked by the Armenians must have been their desire for greater conformity with what happened at the Last Supper. There are other signs in Syria that unleavened bread was in use there. A letter of Rabbula (c. 435) to Gemellinus (printed in Overbeck, *Ephraemi opera selecta* 232) complains of some priests who seek to mitigate their fasting by celebrating the Eucharist several times a day : 'They boast that they never eat bread nor drink water, and yet they are found to be gluttons for the sacred Bread and bibbers of the sacred Wine.... They prepare the eucharistic Bread with rich leaven . . ., so that it may be their food and not the sacred sign of the Body of Christ, which is symbolized in the unleavened bread.' This passage is not quite probatory, though it is advanced by Fr Hanssens as most probable ; taken with the other evidence, it may be held to confirm the view that in Syria of the 4th cent. and then in Armenia (which drew much of its liturgy from Syria, *see* ANTIOCH, LITURGY OF) unleavened bread was used by some, if not universally. Desire to take up Jewish rites (a recurrent desire in Eastern churches) may in part be responsible, but there are also two texts which may have helped to the change from leavened to unleavened bread. Origen, explaining the 'leaven of the Pharisees' said (*in Matthaeum* 12 GCS 40:77) ; 'Leaven is used allegorically for teaching . . ., and so leaven is never offered at the altar, for prayers must not be like lessons which have been learnt but a spontaneous petition for good things from God '. Taken out of its context, this phrase could easily explain why some men wanted the change. The other phrase comes from Philo (*de specialibus legibus* 2:159 ; Cohn–Wendland 5:124) and may have been in Origen's mind : 'Unleavened food is a gift of nature, but leavened is the product of human skill'.

The spread of the custom of using unleavened bread follows what has now come to be recognized as a normal route, from Syria to Visigothic Spain, from there to Ireland and thence to Western Europe, ending finally in Rome, near the end of the 10th cent. In 692 the 16th Council of Toledo ordered that the bread for the Eucharist should not be cut from a loaf but should be specially prepared for the altar ; the obleys should be small, and should be such that if the celebrant has to consume what is left

over, his stomach will not be burdened.[1] The Council does not use the word *azyme*, but it had every reason to avoid the suggestion that it was ordering a revival of Jewish usage. The fact that the bread has to be made specially (and not brought by the offerers, as had been customary) and that it could be described as *oblata*, now for the first time, is a sufficient indication of what was being done. Queen Radegund was in the habit of grinding corn and making the *oblata* herself, but privily out of devotion,[2] as her biographer attests (MGH *Scriptores Merovingici* II, 369). If she had made bread with yeast, the biographer would have said so and not spoken about her making *oblationes*. The great variety of ways of dividing the large Mass-bread practised in the Mozarabic liturgy and copied from there by the Irish, could hardly have flourished if it had been necessary to break a leavened cake, whereas the unleavened wafer is easily broken into the desired number of parts. The (Irish) *Stowe Missal* has at the end a tract on the manner of saying Mass which gives this as one of its rules : ' The arrangement of the confraction at Easter and Christmas : 13 particles in the stem of the crosses, 9 in its cross-piece, 20 particles in its circle-wheel, 5 particles in each angle. . . .' No priest could without a knife divide his Mass-bread in the pattern of a Celtic cross if it was baked with leaven. Evidence for the use of a knife in the Western liturgies is lacking, though the Anglo-Saxons did use a knife to cut up the blessed bread that was distributed *after* the Eucharist.

The Irish use of unleavened bread was argued by F. E. Warren, one of his main pieces of evidence being the illustrations of obleys in the Book of Kells (which the artists would date to the later 8th cent.). This evidence was not dealt with by Mr Woolley when he impugned Warren's conclusion, and it must be allowed to stand. Bede, commenting on Lk 22 (PL 92:593) says that Christ commanded us to live upon the azymes of sincerity and truth throughout this present world-period, which can be likened to the seven days of the unleavened bread, being followed by the eighth day of heaven. He is steering carefully round the Jewish usage and does not want to say that it has been taken up just because it was Jewish. The octonary theory of heaven is certainly Celtic. Lower down (PL 92:595) Bede shows how the unleavened bread began when the manna ceased and Josue had led the people into the Promised Land, and therefore Christ consecrated on the altar of the cross the most pure mysteries of His Body and Blood and offered them to the faithful like azymes of the Promised Land.[3] By calling the mysteries ' most pure ' Bede implies the absence of

[1] Panis integer et nitidus, qui ex studio fuerit praeparatus, neque grande aliquid sed modica tantum oblata, cuius reliquiae . . . non ventrem illius qui sumpserit premant.
[2] Iubet sibi molam secretissime deferri, ad quam . . . oblationes etiam suis manibus faciens locis venerabilibus incessabiliter dispensavit.
[3] Mundissima sui corporis et sanguinis mysteria in crucis altari consecrata quasi azyma terrae repromissionis imbuendis fidelibus offerat.

leaven in the bread, for by his time leaven was synonymous with corruption. Jerome had put *corrumpit* for *fermentat* of the Itala at 1 Cor 5:6, and there are in the *Thesaurus linguae Latinae* (VI 525–7) plenty of examples prior to Bede of leaven in a metaphorical sense as an agent of corruption. The Council of Toledo cited above had called for the breads to be *mundos et studio praeparatos*, which might be rendered ' without leaven and made specially for the altar '.

Alcuin (*ep.* 69 ; PL 100:289) gives what even the opponents of the use of azymes admit to be a clear directive : ' The bread which is consecrated into the Body of Christ should be most pure, without the leavening of an alien corruption '. Rabanus Maurus a little later (PL 107:318) says : ' Unleavened bread, and wine mixed with water, should be consecrated in the mystery of the Body and Blood of Christ, for the gospel relates that the Lord cited these very things on His own behalf '.[1] Rabanus goes on to appeal, now quite openly, to the OT and gives the law of Levit 2:11. One can hardly escape the conclusion that unleavened bread was now being ordered because the Celtic missionary movement was bringing its Irish liturgical customs into lands where they had hitherto been unknown.

The first dispute of Rome and Constantinople, in the time of Photius, does not seem to have touched on the question of azymes, for Rome had not yet succumbed to the usage. At the same time it may be guessed that industrious forgers were at work in the 9th cent. providing such ' evidence ' of early use of azymes as the bogus letter of Gregory the Great which misled St Thomas (*Summa* 3a:74:4c) and the similar letter of Isidore to Redemptus. In 1052 Michael Caerularius made the azymes one of

his chief complaints against Rome, for by now the invasion of Rome by ultramontane ceremonies was an accomplished fact. The documents of this dispute are found in PG 120 for the Greek side and PL 143 for the Latin, where Mabillon's dissertation is also printed in full. He was answering not only the Greeks of former times but also Jacques Sirmond, who had ventured to doubt whether azymes had always been used in the West.

After the compromise at Florence the question of azymes became a live issue again with the Reformation. The *First Prayer Book* of Edward VI left the matter alone, but the *Second* allowed leavened bread : ' It shall suffice that the bread be such as is usual to be eaten at the table with other meats '. When Elizabeth took up this *Second Prayer Book* again in 1559 the rubric was left untouched, but the Queen soon issued Injunctions ordering that, ' for the more reverence to be given to these holy mysteries . . . the sacramental bread be made and formed plain . . ., as the heretofore-named singing cakes which served for the use of the private Mass '. This did not please the extreme Reformers and there was much intrigue about it. In some parts, such as Norfolk, the Injunction was disobeyed from the start, and it was quite generally abandoned under the Cromwellian regime of 1645–60, not to be taken up again until the coming of the Tractarians.

Bibliography. J. Mabillon OSB, *Dissertatio de pane eucharistico* (1723) ; B. Leib SJ, ' Due inediti bizantini sugli azimi ', OCP 2 (1924) 135–263 ; ⋆ R. M. Woolley, *The Bread of the Eucharist* (1913) ; T. Spacil SJ, ' Doctrina Orientis de Eucharistia ', OCP 14 (1929) 114–45 ; A. Michel, a note in *Byzantinische Zeitschrift* 36 (1936) 119 ; J. Gill SJ, *The Council of Florence* (1959) ; J. Hanssens SJ, *Institutiones liturgicae de ritibus orientalibus* (1930) ; ⋆ F. E. Warren, *The Liturgy of the Celtic Church* (1881).

J. H. C.

---

[1] Panem infermentatum et vinum aqua mistum in sacramentum corporis et sanguinis Christi sanctificari oportet quia ipsas res de se Dominum testificari evangelium **narrat.**

B

BAIUS (DE BAY), MICHEL, was born at Mélin, Belgium, in 1513, and died on 1 September 1589. This article will give (I) a summary of his life, (II) an account of his doctrine, and (III) a list of the chief (heretical) conclusions it led to.

I Life. Baius began his philosophical studies at Louvain in 1533 and became a Master of Arts in 1535; his theological studies occupied the years 1536–41. He was Rector of the College of Standonc, 1541–4. From 1544–50, he taught philosophy at the university, and during this period received his Licentiate (1545) and Master's degree (1550) in theology. In 1551 he was named Regius Professor of Sacred Scripture. With his friend Hessels he inaugurated new methods in theology, namely, an almost exclusive study of Scripture and of the Fathers, especially of St Augustine but with an almost total neglect of Scholasticism. The new methods were combined with new doctrinal positions. On 27 June 1560, the Sorbonne condemned eighteen theses extracted from notes taken by his students. In 1563, Baius and Hessels were sent as theologians of the King of Spain to the Council of Trent, but did not exercise a prominent rôle. Between 1563 and 1566 Baius published various *opuscula* which contain his essential outlook and system. After a thorough examination of these writings, Pius V on 1 October 1567 condemned seventy-nine theses in the Bull '*Ex omnibus afflictionibus*'. These theses are contained for the most part in Baius's works, but the Bull did not mention him by name. The condemnation concluding the Bull was written without punctuation and proclaimed: '. . . quas quidem sententias stricto coram nobis examine ponderatas quamquam nonnullae aliquo pacto sustineri possent in rigore et proprio verborum sensu ab assertoribus intento haereticas erroneas...damnamus'.[1] According to whether a comma is placed after '*possent*' or after '*intento*', the condemnation would have two quite different meanings (the famous *comma pianum*). Pius V intended the meaning resulting from a comma placed after '*possent*'. Baius at first submitted, but in 1569 he sent a protest to the Pope. After a new hearing, Pius reiterated his first condemnation. Baius was ordered not only to submit, but to express a formal disavowal of all the condemned propositions. In 1575 he became Chancellor of the Univer-

sity. In 1580 Gregory XIII published the Bull '*Provisionis nostrae*' confirming the condemnation of Pius V. This new Papal condemnation was promulgated solemnly at Louvain by Cardinal Toletus 21 March 1580. Baius and the entire Faculty of Louvain submitted. To put an end to any further dispute, the Faculty, at the instigation of the Papal Nuncio, Bonomini, composed a document entitled: *Doctrinae eius (quam certorum articulorum damnatio postulare visa est) brevis et quoad fieri potest ordinata et cohaerens explicatio* (1586); this document exposes the positive doctrine opposed to the condemned propositions, and still remains an excellent means of understanding correctly the exact force of the condemnation. In the last years of Baius's life the controversy between the Jesuits and the Faculty of Louvain arose. It is difficult to establish with certainty whether, or to what extent, Baius contributed to the composition of the censure against Leonard Lessius SJ in 1587, but he certainly had a share in its wide diffusion. Baius died in union with the Church in 1589.

II Doctrine. An accurate understanding of the principal truths of Christianity depends, according to Baius, on a correct answer to two questions: (i) What was the nature of man's original integrity? (ii) What is to be thought of the 'virtues' of sinners and of infidels? For, without exact answers to these two questions, one will neither recognize the corruption of human nature by Original Sin, nor will one be able to evaluate properly the restoration of human nature through Christ (*De prima hominis iustitia. Praefatio*).

Sacred Scripture teaches that the first man was created in the image and likeness of God; he was righteous, wise, and adorned with all virtues (ibid. cc. 1, 2). The integrity of the first man consisted not only in complete knowledge of the divine law and in full submission to his Creator, but also in the fact that the lower powers of man were subject to his higher faculties, and all the members of the body were submissive to his will (ibid. c. 3). Furthermore, man's initial integrity was not an undue (i.e. supernatural) elevation of his nature, but was his natural possession; for, according to Baius, all perfections which pertain to any class of being in their origin are natural. Thus he considers the lack of integrity in man to be an evil; but evil, in his view, is the privation of what is natural. The evils derived from Original Sin in Adam's posterity can be termed natural, but only in a very loose sense, namely, inasmuch as they are transmitted in the generation of a corrupt nature (ibid. cc. 5, 6). Conversely, if the natural endowments, lost in Adam's sin, are restored to fallen human nature through Christ, they can be called supernatural, but only in the sense that one

---

[1] The translation would be, when the comma is placed after *possent*, 'We condemn as heretical and erroneous, in the sense intended by their authors and according to the strict use of the terms employed, the aforesaid opinions after a close scrutiny of them has been conducted in our presence, even though some of them might in one way or another be defended.' If the comma is placed after *intento*, the clause 'in the sense . . . employed' would have to be put at the end of the whole sentence.

may designate as supernatural what is derived from
a special benefit of God (for example, the miraculous
restoration of sight to one who has been blinded),
not, however, in the sense that this restored integrity
is itself supernatural (ibid. cc. 7–10).

Although Baius calls the endowments of man's
original state natural, he does not mean that they
emanate from the nature of man, as intellect and will
from the soul; rather, they are communicated
directly by God. Nevertheless, they belong to man's
nature and are demanded by man's natural constitution of soul and body, in the sense that their lack
would be an evil for nature itself; they are just as
natural to man as his soul, which is not the product
of the generative act of parents, but must be infused
directly by God through creation (ibid. c. 11).

Created in this state of natural integrity, man was
obliged to obey his Creator, and thus to merit eternal
life, i.e. the unending and intuitive vision of God.
Even as God's immutable wisdom established eternal
death as the punishment of human disobedience and
sin, it also established that the first man would have
received eternal life as the natural and just recompense for his obedience to God; and so the reward
of eternal life would have been due solely to man's
natural merit and not to grace. Similarly the good
angels after their trial received eternal life, not as a
grace, but as the just reward of their obedience (*De
meritis operum*, cc. 1–3).

Baius concludes from the preceding that God
could not have created man without endowing him
with integrity; thus Baius maintains that the state
of pure nature, in which man would be ordained to
an end inferior to the direct and immediate vision of
God and would lack the perfection of integrity, is
chimerical and impossible (ibid.).

Adam lost his integrity through sin, and his sin
with its consequences was transmitted to all of his
descendants by a vitiated and disordered act whereby
all men are conceived (*De peccato originali*, cc. 1, 2).
Original Sin consists in the malice of a will which
does not love God and His justice, in the rebellion of
fallen man's lower nature against the spirit, and in
ignorance (ibid. c. 3). Because of Original Sin, all
men, even infants, are subject to the wrath of God
and to eternal death. Even as Adam was created in
God's favour through no merit of his own, so the
new-born infant is the object of God's loathing;
because of Original Sin alone, and not because of any
personal committment, the new-born babe stands
in opposition to God and to His law (ibid. c. 4).

Baius teaches that sin is essentially disobedience to
the command of God; the question whether sin
should be voluntary has nothing to do with its
essence, but only with its origin. Whatever is contrary to the law of God is a sin in whomsoever it
exists, and is justly imputed as sin, merely because it
exists (ibid. c. 7). In the state of integrity, Adam
could have fulfilled the law of God easily and without
difficulty (*De libero arbitrio*, c. 9). By Original Sin
this power was lost completely (ibid. c. 11).

Nothing more deplorable than the moral condition of fallen man in the Baianist system can be
imagined. Even his indeliberate and inoperative
desires, being infringements of the law *non concu-
pisces*, are actual sins (*De peccato originali* c. 2). Each
sin merits an eternity of pain, for all sins are by their
nature mortal sins (*De meritis operum* c. 2). There is
no certainty that God 'will give what He commands'; the opinion that God commands nothing
impossible finds no support in Augustine, but derives
from Pelagius (*De peccato originali* c. 12). The
general conclusion, so well summed up in the words
of the condemned proposition, 'All the works of
unbelievers are sins' (Prop. 25, D 1025) is defended
by Baius in his *De virtutibus impiorum*. There is, he
says, only one end of man, which is the vision of
God, and one way only of loving God which is
charity. Therefore without charity (which presupposes faith) there is only sin (*De virtutibus impiorum* cc. 5, 8).

Christ came to restore to fallen man the spiritual
state which was his due in creation, but which, owing
to sin, is now 'grace'. Just as man is wholly
characterized and determined, before redemption, by
evil concupiscence, so that his every movement is a
sin, so redeemed man lives and merits heaven by
charity. Charity is 'that motion of the soul whereby
we love God and our neighbour (*De charitate*, c. 2)',
and proceeds immediately from the 'touch of God,
who is charity (ibid. c. 3)'.

Justification, in the sense of 'fulfilling all justice',
means no more than 'having charity'; this proceeds from 'actual grace', and may come before
the remission of sins; it bears no intrinsic relation
to formal justification in the sense used by Scholastics (ibid., c. 7). The Scholastic insistence on charity
as a permanent gift was quite mistaken. The origin
of charity is a transitory impulse received from God,
and this is all that matters, because it enables us to
live in perfect justice (ibid., c. 2). Perfect charity is
not to be defined by reference to any sacrament or
habitual 'state' (ibid., c. 9; cf. Prop. 31–3, D
1031–3). Similarly, justification is really a continual
process, wherein man performs more and more good
works under actual grace, and overcomes more and
more sinful desires, i.e. 'makes progress in the remission of sins' (*De iustificatione*, c. 1).

This denial of the importance, if not of the existence, of habitual or sanctifying grace, has an important bearing upon the notion of merit. According
to Baius, man's work, of itself and alone, merits
heaven or hell: heaven, if it proceeds from charity;
hell, if from concupiscence. The Patristic and
Scholastic belief, solemnly defined by the Council
of Trent (D 809), that it is our adoption as sons of
God and members of Christ which enables us to
merit eternal life, seemed to B. entirely erroneous
(*De meritis operum*, c. 2). Consequently, there is no
need for a man to be in the state of grace in order
that his work may be meritorious (ibid.). The
Pharisaism of Baius's doctrine of merit in fallen man
corresponds to the Pelagianism in his description of
innocent man, and reveals that extraordinary singularity which makes it impossible to call his system by
any other name than his own. In endeavouring to

set aside all subsequent tradition, in order to find the pure spirit of St Augustine, he fell into a disastrous eclecticism.

III Conclusions. (i) Baius set up the anti-Pelagian treatises of Augustine, against the whole body of post-Augustinian thought, as the sole repository of orthodox teaching on Grace. (ii) He professed to mistrust any attempt to interpret, develop, or modify the doctrine of Augustine by the use of historical, philosophical or psychological reasoning. (iii) He was not afraid, but rather glad, to arrive at conclusions, in matters of faith and morals, which were in open contradiction with all contemporary Catholic opinion. The most important of these conclusions are the following : (*a*) The state of pure nature is a useless fiction and involves an insoluble contradiction. (*b*) The justice and merits of man in the state of original innocence were natural and did not proceed from Grace. (*c*) Fallen man is determined to evil whenever he is not drawn by charity into holiness. (*d*) God may command man to do the impossible without injustice. (*e*) The motion of actual grace, which is charity, is the only, and infallible source of good works. (*f*) Man is not free under the influence of grace. It was the method of Baius and the conclusions just enumerated which laid the foundations for the much more important heresy of Jansenism.

Bibliography. *Michaelis Baii opera . . . studio A. P. theologi* (Gerberon) (1696) ; J. B. Du Chesne, *Histoire du baianisme* (1731) ; Martínez de Ripalda SJ, ' Adversus Baium et Baianos ' in *De ente supernaturali*, Vols. V and VI (1872) ; Suarez, *De gratia Dei*, prolegomena VI, c. II, in *Opera omnia* (1857) ; M. Scheeben, ' Bajus ' in *Kirchenlexikon*, Wetzer and Welte (1882) ; F. X. Linsenmann, *Michael Baius und die Grundlegung des Jansenismus* (1867) ; M. Scheeben, ' Zur Geschichte des Bajanismus ', in *Der Katholik* (March 1868, 281 ff.) ; X. M. Le Bachelet, ' Baius ' in DTC, II, 281–303 ; F. X. Jansen, *Baius et le baianisme* (1927) ; H. de Lubac, ' Deux Augustiniens fourvoyés, Baius et Jansenius ', RSR 21 (1931) 422–43, 513–40 ; N. Abercrombie, *The Origins of Jansenism* (1936) ; F. Claeys-Bouuaert, ' La Soumission de Baius, fut-elle sincère ? ' ETL 30 (1954) 457–464 ; G. Fourure, *Les Châtiments divins*—a study of the problem of evil in Baius and Jansenius (1959).

P. D.

BÁÑEZ, DOMINIC (spelt also BÁÑES, VÁÑEZ, IBÁÑEZ ; ' Modragonensis ' is a patronymic), Spanish theologian of the Order of Preachers, was probably born at Valladolid (Medina del Campo is also given as his birth-place), 29 February 1528. After his university studies at Salamanca he took the Dominican habit there at St Stephen's convent, 1546. A pupil of several eminent theologians (Melchior Cano, Vincente Barrón, etc.), he began his own distinguished teaching career in 1551 by teaching various philosophical subjects at San Esteban. Afterwards he expounded the *Summa Theologica* to the Dominican students (whose Student-master he was), and also gave occasional lectures in the university. In 1561

he was sent to Ávila to the Dominican college which had recently been granted university status. In 1567 Báñez held the chair of theology at Alcalá, but in 1570 he was back in Salamanca. In 1573 he became Regent of Studies at Valladolid, in 1575 a consultor of the Inquisition, and in 1576 Prior of Torro. At the same time he won in competition the chair of Durandus at Salamanca and, on Medina's death, in 1581, the chief professorship. He retired in 1600 and died at Medina del Campo on 22 October 1604.

A university disputation at Salamanca in 1582 led Báñez to oppose several theses on the subject of grace propounded by Prudentius Montemayor SJ, whose position was defended by the distinguished Augustinian Luís de León. The dispute attracted attention and the teaching of the three protagonists came before the Inquisition. Báñez was cleared of suspicion, de León had to retract some assertions, while Montemayor was forbidden to teach and sixteen of his propositions were censured. When in 1588 Luís Molina SJ published in Lisbon his *Concordia liberi arbitrii cum gratiae donis*, which was attacked as containing Montemayor's teaching, Báñez was consulted and identified six of the censured propositions, besides making a general criticism of the book. Molina published a reply in an appendix, and the controversy soon grew in intensity and in extent. Eventually, the nuncio in Madrid had to silence everyone and the matter was submitted to Rome. In 1598 Clement VIII authorized both sides to continue their teaching in conformity with the Church's doctrine (*see* GRACE). This ended Báñez's personal participation in the affair but the dispute continued in Rome in the ' *Congregatio de auxiliis* '. In contrast to his opponent's conception of the simultaneous working of grace and the human will, Báñez insisted on the priority of God's initiative. He qualified the influence of grace as ' physical ' in opposition to the concept of ' moral ' causality—hence the phrase ' *praemotio physica* '.

Báñez was confessor and director to St Teresa of Ávila from the beginning of her reform till her death (1562–82). His sound theological learning sheltered her from the danger of illusions, and his teaching probably finds echoes in the saint's writings. Báñez also helped St Teresa by prudent advice in practical affairs ; he championed her enterprise against attacks and moderated her zeal for corporate poverty.

As theologian Báñez aimed at being no more than a faithful commentator of St Thomas, and his Commentaries on the Summa are his chief work, though he wrote several smaller treatises.

Bibliography. A full list of the works of Báñez is given in LTK (1957) I, 1219 by Beltran de Heredia OP, who published a whole series of studies in *Ciencia Tomista*, on Actuación de Báñez en Salamanca 25 (1922) 67–73, 208–40 ; 26 (1922) 63–73, 199–223 ; 27 (1923) 40–51, 361–74 ; on his dealings with the Inquisition, 37 (1928) 289–318 ; 38 (1929) 35–58, 171–186 ; on his position as a theologian 39 (1929) 60–81 ; 40 (1929) 312–22 ; 47 (1933) 27–39, 162–177 ; A. Lépée, *Báñez et S. Thérèse* (1947) ; F. Reusch, *Luís de León und die spanische Inquisition*

(1873) ; T. de Régnon SJ, *Báñez et Molina* (1883) ;
the articles Báñez (by P. Mandonnet) and Moli-
nisme (by F. van Steenberghen) in DTC, and the
standard histories of the *de auxiliis* controversy by
J. Serry OP and L. de Meyer SJ in the 18th cent.
with G. Schneemann SJ, *Controversiarum de . . . concordia initia et progressus* (1881).   C. V.

BAPTISM This first sacrament and gateway of
the Church is treated first of all historically and then
systematically. (I) The baptism of John and (II)
Christ's command to baptize are examined, and
some attempt is made to evaluate (III) the early
Christian understanding of the sacrament from what
it is called in the NT and in early writers and from
its OT types and prefigurations. The systematic
treatment begins with (IV) the form of baptism,
where the relation between formula and interrogations is discussed. (V) The matter of baptism is
briefly examined and (VI) the manner of its being
carried out. (VII) The theological teaching about
the minister includes a survey of the rebaptism
controversy in which the status of heretical
ministers was in question. (VIII) What baptism
effects or produces is treated under the heads of
incorporation into Christ, the conferring of sanctifying grace and the infusion of virtues and gifts.
Short notes are added here on (IX) problematic
baptisms where either *simulatio* or a defective
formula casts some doubt on validity. (X) The
character conferred by baptism is then studied, and
(XI) the necessity of the sacrament for salvation
made clear. Special baptisms which receive separate
treatment are (XII) baptism of blood, (XIII) baptism
for the dead and (XIV) infant baptism. The article
closes with (XV) a brief account of the development
of the Roman ritual for baptism.

I The Baptism of John. Josephus (*Antiquitates
Iudaicae* 18:117) describes John the Baptist as a good
man who urged the Jews to live righteously and 'to
come together for baptism ; for immersion, he said,
would really appear acceptable to God only if
practised not as an expiation for specific offences,
but for the purification of the body, when the soul
had been already thoroughly cleansed by justice.'
This evidence is not in conflict with the well-known
account of John in the gospels (Mt 3:1–12 ; Mk
1:1–8 ; Lk 3:1–17 ; Jn 1:19–28 ; 3:22–30). Josephus is only saying in his own way that John did
not encourage people to think that by washing in
water their sins could be forgiven ; what he wanted
them to do was to repent first and then come to be
dipped. The Messianic purport of his baptism,
brought out by Paul (Ac 19:4), was not mentioned
by Josephus, to whom in his state of apostasy from
the Jewish faith the very idea of the Messias would
have been quite alien.

It cannot be said that John was dependent on a
Jewish rite of proselyte baptism already in use in
his day, for it is not probable that proselyte baptism
is so early in date (Crehan, *Early Christian Baptism
and the Creed*, 1–6). Strack-Billerbeck (*Kommentar
zum NT aus Talmud und Midrasch* i:112) consider the

two rites wholly different from each other. John did
the dipping of his penitents himself ; the proselyte
dipped himself in the presence of witnesses. John's
baptism looked forward to a better baptism that was
to come ; the proselyte was told (Talmud, *Gerim* 1:5)
that he had united himself with One who by His
word had created the world. The Jews were familiar
with their prophets carrying out acted parables, and
John's use of water was therefore easily to be understood, even if it had not a precursor in the rite of
proselyte baptism.

The Early Fathers believed that the baptism conferred by the disciples of Christ (Jn 4:1–3) was John's
baptism. It was Augustine (*ep.* 44:5 ; 265:5) who
began the reaction in favour of calling that act
Christian baptism (*see* Crehan, *op. cit.* 17, 73).

II The Command to Baptize. The command to
baptize, given by Christ to His apostles (Mt 28:19),
is even yet, though quite unreasonably, considered
to be of doubtful authenticity (*Flemington, *The
NT Doctrine of Baptism*, 106–8), the attack upon it
taking three lines, textual criticism, literary parallels
with the other gospels, and the historical circumstances of the time. The text is not omitted by
any known MS. of the gospels or by any version,
though the earliest Syriac version is defective in this
gospel. The words μαθητεύσατε πάντα τὰ ἔθνη
copied from Mt 28:19 appear in *Ascension of Isaiah*
3:18 where they refer to the twelve apostles of the
risen Christ. As this Christian part of the *Ascension*
antedates the *Rest of the Words of Baruch*, it must be
attributed to the first part of the 2nd cent. at
the latest (its editors, Charles and Tisserant, prefer
A.D. 88–100), and therefore the passage in Mt 28:19
must be older still. It is copied in full by the *Didache*
(7:1), but this work cannot be dated with any
certainty between the years 100 and 170. Justin
(*apol.* 61:9) appears to appeal to this command
when he says that the Christians have authority from
the apostles for their practice of baptizing with the
invocation of the triune name. The silence of Luke
about such a command is in no way significant,
since his gospel professes to be an account for
Theophilus of how salvation had made its way to
himself, and need not enter into an account of
baptism itself. The main historical difficulty, which
lies in the apparent opposition between the practice
recorded in the Acts of baptizing ' in the name of
Jesus ' and this trinitarian command, can be met by
showing (*see* Crehan, *op. cit.* 7–26) that the meaning
of the term in Acts is that the candidate invoked or
confessed the Name and was then baptized for the
sake and worship of Jesus but with a trinitarian
formula. The difficulties arising from the silence
of the Council of Jerusalem (Ac 15) about this
command and from Paul's practice of not baptizing
(1 Cor 1:17) are only apparent, for the Council was
not debating about how to baptize pagans but
whether they needed circumcision before baptism,
and Paul was expressing a preference for the work
of preaching, in the absolute Jewish way of speaking,
and not rejecting the work of baptizing completely
(Crehan, *op. cit.* 72–8).

The Christians seem to have taken the word μαθητεύω from this passage in Mt 28:19 for use in a meaning which it did not naturally bear. In Plutarch (*De vit. X orat.* 832c, 837c, 840f) and even in Mt 27:57 it meant 'to go to school to X', 'to be X's disciple', but in Mt and in Christian usage it means 'to make a disciple of someone'. The frequency of this special Christian usage (four times in Ignatius and five times in Justin) shows that the command to baptize was taken for granted in the 2nd cent. The process of making a disciple 'unto the name of Christ' (Justin, *dial.* 39:2) or 'unto the divine teachings' (Justin, *append.* 4:3) was understood to be carried out by his baptism and by its preliminary catechesis.

The whole pattern of Mt's gospel, with its clearly implied comparison of Christ with Moses (according to the prophecy of Deut 18:15) seems to require that the gospel should end with Christ sending forth his apostles, as Moses sent his, across the river of baptism into a Promised Land.

III Early Christian Understanding of the Sacrament.

(*a*) One of the earliest names was φωτισμός or enlightening; this was a natural development from the language of John (12:35) and Paul (Eph 5:8; Heb 6:4 and 1 Thess 5:5) about the sons of Light. Justin (*apol.* 61:12) is the first to give the word as a technical term, but it seems already implied in the hymn cited by Paul (Eph 5:14) and in Heb 6:9. It is notable that while the early Fathers use the term 'initiation' when speaking of the mystery religions, they never use it to describe baptism. What seems to have been the earliest symbolism to be attached to the rite of baptism is that of the entry into the Promised Land. This is attested in the *Odes of Solomon* (*od.* 39), Justin, Tertullian, Origen and Hippolytus, who compare the waters of baptism to the crossing of Jordan (Crehan, *op. cit.* 55, 171–2). From this symbolic interpretation arose the custom of giving the newly baptized cups of milk and honey, a custom existing for some time when Hippolytus wrote his *Traditio apostolica*. The English use of bringing water from Jordan for the baptism of members of the royal house probably belongs to the same circle of ideas. Gradually, but not before the third century, the Promised Land was turned into Paradise and then the nakedness of the candidates could be compared to that of Adam, and the theology of Adam's gifts and their restoration could be developed. The substitution of the crossing of the Red Sea for that of Jordan does not make its appearance until the 3rd cent., even though there is a foundation for it in 1 Cor 10:2 and Justin (*dial.* 138:3). No painting of the escape of Moses and his people across the Red Sea is found in the Catacombs, and when the subject appears on sarcophagi (DAC xi: 478–93) it is a symbol of the passage from this world to the next, in the spirit of the prayer: *Libera Domine animam eius, sicut liberasti Moysen de manu Pharaonis*. The first baptismal use of the image is in Chrysostom (PG 61:191) and in the contemporary mosaics of St Mary Major. Gregory of Nyssa (PG 46:420) in his homily on those who defer baptism speaks of the Jordan throughout and never alludes to the Red Sea.

(*b*) From Jn 3:5 it was natural that there should develop an image of baptism as a new birth. Justin (*apol.* 61) is full of the language of this idea and in the *Odes of Solomon* (*od.* 36:3) one reads: 'The Spirit brought me forth before the face of the Lord, and although a son of man, I was named the illuminated one, the son of God.' The notion of the Church as a mother or even of the baptismal water as a spiritual womb is thereafter quite general, and from this may come the symbolism of the Blessing of the baptismal water on Easter eve. Ephrem and Basil (on Gen 1:2) speak of the Spirit brooding over the waters and gendering children to God (Ephrem, *Opera Syriaca* i:118; Basil, PG 29:44). This image does not import a phallic worship into Christianity, as some moderns have supposed, for the action of the Spirit is thought of as that of the bird brooding over her nest and giving form and feature to the new life that it contains.

(*c*) Another image for baptism is that of the rescue of the family of Noah in the Ark; they were launched upon the waters and thus found salvation, just as the new Christian finds it when committed to the font. This image has the advantage of apostolic patronage, for it is expounded by St Peter (1 Pet 3:21) and may even have been suggested to him by his vision at Joppa (Ac 10:11–12). Clement of Rome repeats the idea (*I Clem.* 7:6 and 9:4) and in Justin (*dial.* 138:2) it is so far elaborated as to give us the claim that the eight souls who were in the Ark foretell the Resurrection on the eighth day. The 24th *Ode of Solomon* links the Flood with the dove that appeared at the baptism of Christ, while Hippolytus goes as far as to say, 'As in the Ark of Noah the love of God towards man is signified by the dove, so also now the Spirit, descending in the form of a dove . . . rested on Him to whom the witness was borne. For what reason? That the faithfulness of the Father's voice might be made known and that the prophetic utterance of a long time past might be ratified. And what utterance is this? The voice of the Lord upon the waters . . . The Lord upon many waters.' (*Theophaneia* 7; GCS Hippol. I:ii:261).

The same passage in Peter's First Epistle (3:19) speaks of the Descent of Christ to Hades, and, whatever his audience there, it is clear that this Descent is already being likened to the act of baptism, when one goes down into the water and comes up again in the newness of life. Thus the ground was being prepared for the practice of baptizing on Easter eve, when Christ's Descent was being commemorated. Hermas (*Similitudo* ix:16) describes how those who are in limbo receive the seal, and then adds, with seeming irrelevance, 'The seal is the water. They go down into the water dead men and come up alive.' Irenaeus, too (*adv. haer.* H III, xxxii:1, 4; xlii:3) has Christ regenerating the patriarchs in limbo, while as late as 633 the Fourth Council of Toledo explains that the descent into the waters of baptism is as it were a descent into Hades (can. 6). It is easy to see how the triple immersion, when this came in, would be interpreted as a reminder of the three days Christ spent between death and resurrection.

(*d*) The prophecy of the clean water in Ezechiel 36:25 is alluded to in the *Epistle of Barnabas* (6:14) and may account for the statement of Ignatius (*Eph.* 18-2) that by His passion Christ cleansed the water. To the Eastern mind the cleansing of water would be a more vivid metaphor than it is to us, and this text, with its reference to the pouring of the water upon the faithful, seems to have early been arrogated to the service of 'clinical' baptism for the sick, who were not strong enough to face the immersion on Easter eve but waited until Pentecost for milder treatment at a later season. Tertullian (*Adversus Iudaeos* 8), who is followed by Cyril of Jerusalem (*Catecheses* 3:11), considered that it was the contact of Christ's body with the Jordan at His baptism which sanctified and cleansed the water, and in this idea he is supported by many of the Fathers, but it is hard to say that the notion of consecration by contact was really primitive.

The later passage in Ezechiel (47:1, 7, 12) about the stream flowing from the Temple has given us our chant of *Vidi aquam* for Paschaltide, but long before this, in Ode 6 of the *Odes of Solomon*, in *Barnabas* (11:10) and in Melito (fragment in Routh, *Reliquiae Sacrae* I:124), the Fathers had used it as a figure of baptismal water controlled by the Church, and even the position of many ancient baptisteries, *a latere dextro*, may be due to this text. For the parallel between baptism and circumcision *see* CIRCUMCISION, and for a discussion on the relevance here of Col 2:11 *see* Crehan, *op. cit.* 47.

IV The Form of Baptism. (*a*) It is often argued (e.g. by de Puniet in the past (DAC II, i:313-14, 341-3) and most recently by Mgr Andrieu and Dr Quasten) that the primitive Form was simply the threefold question and reply which is described in Ambrose (*De sacramentis* 2:7). It is true that Ambrose often claims to be following in all things the example of the Roman church, but in this work he is speaking to those who have been baptized and is explaining to them what it was that they did in the rite. He is not giving a complete account of the whole rite, and the argument from his silence about the use of a formula by the baptizer is not of much weight. Theodore of Mopsuestia in his *Catechesis on Baptism* (*Woodbrooke Studies* VI, 59) gives a full account of the rite as practised in Syria in his day (*c.* 390), and points out that the baptizand was not allowed to speak at the actual moment of baptism but that the baptizer pronounced the formula in three instalments as he immersed the candidate three times. Theodore explains, 'The priest says, "In the name of the Father and of the Son and of the Holy Spirit," as if he were saying, "In the call upon the Father, the Son and the Holy Spirit." The prophet Isaias said this, "Beside Thee we know no other Lord. We are called by Thy name."' This explanation, with its appeal to Is 27:13, shows clearly that the calling upon the Trinity

was understood to be the act of the baptizer, not that of the baptizand. Theodore is not unaware of the credal questions and answers, for at an earlier point in his account of the rite (*op. cit.* 37) he tells how the candidate had to say, 'I engage myself and believe and am baptized in the name of the Father and of the Son and of the Holy Spirit.' He adds, 'The deacons who at that time draw nigh unto you prepare you to recite those words.' Thus at Antioch, in the same epoch as that of Ambrose at Milan, the rite included both the baptizand's profession of faith and the invocation of the names by the baptizer. One may allow that in the West, where a contractual notion of baptism would have more influence owing to the more legalistic outlook of theologians, the profession of faith may have assumed the larger rôle in the whole rite, but one cannot make of Ambrose's silence a reason for rejecting the use of the formula entirely.

(*b*) It is sometimes said that the Western liturgical texts show the absence of a formula, for the *Gelasian Sacramentary* in its earliest MS has the interrogations with the rubric, *Deinde per singulas vices mergis eum tertio in aqua.* This rubric seems to mean, 'Then, after the interrogations, for each candidate you perform the threefold dipping.' *Tertio* must mean three times and not 'for the third time', as the first and second time are not mentioned, and as the later Latin use of the word more commonly makes it serve as an adverbial numeral. One could hardly expect nine dippings in all. The earlier rubric *Baptizas unumquemque in ordine suo sub has interrogationes* does not direct that the interrogations be used as a formula but that the baptism is to follow close upon (*sub* with the accusative) these interrogations. A more difficult liturgical text was first published in 1949, the *Sacramentary of Prague*, which gives the interrogations (p. 62) and then adds the rubric *aut si volueris* followed by the baptismal formula with three intercalated dippings. This text may have arisen from a conflation of a Sacramentary in the tradition of the *Gelasianum* (with interrogations) with some other text which gave the formula for the baptizer as it is found in many of the Celtic MSS such as the *Bobbio Missal*, the *Missale Gothicum* and the *Gallicanum Vetus*. In *Bobbio* the direction runs, *Baptizas eum et dicis* : *Baptizo te in nomine Patris et Filii et Spiritus sancti unam abentem substancia ut abias vitam aeternam partem cum sanctis.* This family of Celtic and Gallican liturgies has as good a pedigree as the *Gelasianum* and the presence in their formulae of clauses designed to combat Arianism shows that they descend from models that were in use when Arianism was a danger. If the scribe of the *Prague Sacramentary*, a monk in a South German monastery, put together what he found in one of these with the simple text of the *Gelasianum*, he would have produced very much what we actually find in his book. The Armenian ritual, which can also boast a considerable antiquity, gives interrogations before the blessing of the font and then at the moment of baptism the priest 'shall say as follows: N or M shall be baptized in the name of the Father and of the

Son and of the Holy Spirit, redeemed by the blood of Christ from the slavery of sin, receiving the freedom of adoption as son of the heavenly Father, having become a co-heir with Christ and a temple of the Holy Spirit, now and for ever. This he shall three times repeat and three times plunge the novice in the water, thereby signifying the three days' burial of Christ.' (Conybeare, 96). The narrative form used here (' X is baptized . . .') is common throughout the Eastern liturgies, and the first instance of the assertory form (' I baptize . . .') in the East is in the commentary of Ammonius upon Acts (PG 85:1574) which dates from *c.* 458. In the West the *Gregorian Sacramentary* has *baptizo te* . . ., but the Celtic-Gallican liturgies are most probably earlier in date and also represent a much earlier tradition. The first Latin writer to cite the formula is the pseudo-Vigilius (PL 62:284). He was writing in the 4th cent. against the Arians. The *Sacramentary of Gellone* (Martene, 176) has the *baptizo* form split up into three parts by the dippings.

(*c*) The small tract of Martin of Braga, *De trina mersione* (edited by Barlow, 1951), throws considerable light on the doctrinal import of different ritual practices about the use of multiple immersions. He maintains that the intercalation of three dippings with three interrogations is an Arian practice. This may well be true if the Arians used the Ambrosian practice to point out a way in which the inferiority of the Son to the Father was expressed in the liturgy. To have one dipping and one naming (a practice some Spanish bishops adopted to avoid Arian implications) lends colour to the views of the Sabellians, and thus the only safe way—and traditional—is to have one continuous naming with three dips. The *Canons of Hippolytus*, representing a Syrian use of *c.* 500, have for good measure a threefold use of the formula by the priest, once after each interrogation and dipping. It is easy to see how this completing of the act of baptism for each Person of the Trinity could be used to show that the Son was not equal to the Father. The Celtic-Gallican formulae with their emphasis on the *homoousios* guard against such danger in a way different to what Martin of Braga suggests. Further echoes of the Spanish trouble are found in Gregory, *Registrum epistularum* 1:41, MGH 57.

(*d*) The development of the Creed out of the interrogations is discussed by Crehan (*op. cit.* 117-130), and depends very much on what is made of the liturgy of baptism given by Hippolytus in the many versions and imitations of his *Traditio apostolica*, but the status of that work is so much open to question that little in the way of firm conclusions can be based upon it. What is certain is that in Africa in Cyprian's day one of the baptismal interrogations ran, *Credis in vitam aeternam et remissionem peccatorum per sanctam ecclesiam ?* and this has no mention of any Person of the Trinity. An overschematic reconstruction, such as that of Quasten, does not leave room for the diversity of such phenomena, and for the present it is best to disregard attempts to derive the baptismal formula out

of three Trinitarian interrogations and to adhere to the statement in the (quite orthodox) *Didascalia apostolorum* (p. 147) that while a deaconess should anoint the women who are being baptized, ' Let a man pronounce over them the invocation of the divine Names in the water.' This does not sound like an exchange of question and answer.

V The Matter of Baptism. There has never been any doubt in the Church that water was the proper matter for baptism. Some Christian-Gnostic writings such as the *Acts of Thomas* (*Acta Thomae* 27) describe baptisms in oil, but these are perversions of Christian practice. In the Middle Ages it was twice necessary for papal directions (D 412 and 447) to be sent to the Archbishop of Trondheim in Norway forbidding the use of saliva or of beer as the matter for baptizing. The Councils of Florence (D 696) and of Trent (D 858) also dealt with the question authoritatively. It seems never to have been seriously proposed by any Catholic that there should be a baptism of fire to carry out the promise of Mt 3:11 and Lk 3:16 ; the tongues of fire at Pentecost have been generally accepted as sufficient fulfilment of that. It is, however, to be noted that the *Codex Vercellensis* at Mt 3:17 and several apocryphal gospels allege that fire was seen upon the Jordan at Christ's baptism. Justin (*dial.* 88:3) asserts this as a fact, and it may be that the original significance of the ceremony of plunging the paschal candle into the font on Easter eve is a memorial of such a supposed happening. The prayer for this ceremony reads in the old *Gelasianum* : *Qui hanc aquam regenerandis hominibus praeparatam arcanà sui luminis admixtione fecundet* (who dost make fruitful this water, prepared for the regeneration of men, by the mingling of thy light). No doubt, to a Jewish Christian there was a particular consolation in believing that the religion of Christ provided a counterpart to the pillars of fire and of cloud which had been commemorated in the daily worship of the Temple. The main practitioners, however, of baptism by fire were the Gnostics, who were no longer held in control by the sobriety of the Church.

VI The Manner of Baptism. As already noted, the practice of affusion was brought in, alongside that of immersion, for the sick from an early date. The seashore is still thought of as being a suitable place for baptism by the writer of the *Acts of Paul* (*c.* 150), but within little more than a decade, and in the same region, Melito of Sardis in his *Homily on baptism* (TU 45:422) implies that Christians already had places called baptisteries, for he speaks in a metaphor of the stars in their courses, ' bathing themselves in the baptistery of the sun as goodly disciples.' *Didache* 7:3 and Cyprian (*ep.* 69:12) are generally cited as the earliest evidence (Ac 16:33 being inadequate to prove affusion) for the allowance of affusion instead of full immersion, but the two practices are not entirely distinct, for the ordinary Greek bath would generally be too shallow to allow of entire immersion, while it would often be provided with a jet of water, flowing from a lion's mouth or other spout, under which the bather could place his body. The supposed tank found in the Christian chapel at Dura-Europos (Princeton expedition, Preliminary to Fifth Report, 1934) measured 1·70 m. × 0·95 m. (length and breadth) × 0·945 m. (depth), with which one may compare a baptistery at Dar Kila in Syria of A.D. 515 which measures 1·86 m. × 0·93 m. × 1·26 m. As this chapel at Dura ceased to be used by 256, it provides strong support for the idea that baptism as then practised was a combination of immersion and affusion. Baptism by sprinkling is admitted by the present discipline of the Church as valid, but is not encouraged (can. 758), and has no ancient warrant. St Thomas speaks of immersion as still the more common practice in his day (3a:66:7c), and some of the fonts in medieval English churches show that this practice prevailed in England at that time.

VII The Minister of Baptism. (*a*) St Thomas (3a:67:6c) argues that there must be only one minister of the sacrament, as the minister represents Christ, and Christ is not divided. As he also points out, there would arise a problem about the intentions of the two or more who might attempt a baptism were the practice of having a team of ministers allowed, for if these intentions were not formed simultaneously, one minister would be intending to baptize someone who was already baptized, and thus would be falling into the heresy of rebaptism. The Fourth Lateran Council (D430) accepted anyone at all as the minister of the sacrament (*a quocunque rite collatum*), and questions about the intention required in the minister (D860) were in part settled by Trent. (*See further* INTENTION)

(*b*) THE REBAPTISM CONTROVERSY between Rome and the African bishops led by Cyprian was really a dispute about the distinction between sacraments that are valid and lawful, and sacraments that are merely valid but not lawful and therefore not fruitful. The early development of the contractual idea of baptism (*see* Crehan, 96–110) made it hard for the Africans to see that where the candidate's faith was not rightly expressed there could be a valid baptism. 'We baptize the faith of the believers' said Clarus of Mascula, one of Cyprian's suffragans (Cyprian, CSEL III:i:459), when he meant that what one baptized was the believer who showed the right faith. The dispute began in North Africa, for the practice of the province of Mauretania in accepting heretical baptisms was reprobated by the bishops of Africa Proconsularis and Numidia. Agrippinus of Carthage seems to have issued some judgment (Cypr. *ep.* 71:4) on the point as early as 220, possibly under the influence of the rigorism of Tertullian (*de bapt.* 15). In 255 was held the council of thirty bishops at Carthage whose letter is extant (Cypr. *ep.* 70). This council seems to have covered Africa Proconsularis alone. Another council was held in spring 256, which included the Numidian bishops, and the resolution of this council not to accept converts from heresy without rebaptism was communicated to Pope Stephen (Cypr. *ep.* 72). The Pope's reply can be gathered from the brief citations in Cypr. *ep.* 74 (D 46) which is

a letter of indignant protest to Pompeius on the receipt of Stephen's rescript. But before (or, as some think, after) this reply arrived, a third council had been held at Carthage on 1 September 256 (its *Acta* are in Cypr. CSEL III:i:435). Some time previously (*c.* 230) a synod had been held at Iconium (Cypr. *ep.* 75:7) which had come to the same decision as the African bishops, and now Cyprian hastened to secure the adherence of Firmilian of Cappadocia to his cause against Stephen. This synod of Iconium along with one at Synnada (Eusebius *HE* 7:7:5) had been exercising Denis of Alexandria for some time, and he wrote to Pope Stephen (the most complete text of this letter is in the Armenian version, printed in EHR, (xxv 1910, 112) saying, 'If then it was from the apostles that this custom took its beginning, we must adjust ourselves thereto, whatsoever may have been their reasons and the grounds on which they acted, to the end that we too may observe the same in accordance with their practice. For as to the things which were written afterwards and which are still found until now, they are ignored by us and let them be ignored.' It is impossible to date this letter exactly, but it must be closely connected with Stephen's rescript to Africa with its declaration : 'Let nothing be changed but as tradition directs —let hands be imposed upon all those who come from what heresy soever . . .' Alexandria was either strengthening the hand of Rome or acquiescing in the decision of Rome. Stephen died 2 August 257 and Cyprian was martyred in September 258. Pope Xystus, who followed Stephen, was thus addressed by Denis of Alexandria (EHR 1910, xxv 113), 'Inasmuch as you have written thus, setting forth the pious legislation, which we continually read and now have in remembrance—namely that it shall suffice only to lay hands on those who shall have made profession in baptism, whether in pretence or in truth, of God almighty and of Christ and of the Holy Spirit ; but those over whom there has not been invoked the name either of Father or of Son or of the Holy Spirit, these we must baptize but not rebaptize—this is the sure and immovable teaching and tradition, begun by Christ.'

(*c*) The onset of persecution and the deaths of the chief contending parties led to the sudden dying-down of the dispute, but in the Council of Arles (in 314 ; can. 8) and at Nicaea (can. 19) the results of the action of Stephen can be seen. At Arles the orthodox African bishops were now anxious to follow the Roman usage, and it was those with Donatist leanings who urged the continuance of Cyprian's practice, but the Council decided that if anyone came from heresy to the Church he should be asked his Creed, and if it was found that he had been baptized in the name of the Father and of the Son and of the Holy Ghost, then it was not to be required of him that he be rebaptized, but hands were to be laid upon him for penance. If his creed showed that this was not so, then he should be baptized. At Nicaea it was specifically decreed that the followers of Paul of Samosata did not baptize in a way that could be accepted as valid. Athanasius (PG 26:237) says that they used the Three Names, but Innocent I (D 97) says they did not. Probably they kept to the actual names but meant something quite different by them (HL I:i:615). The outcome was that the Church now had a clearer notion of a valid sacrament unlawfully conferred by a heretic and therefore the discussion now moved on to the next point, that of the intention required in the minister. (See INTENTION)

VIII The Effects of Baptism. (a) Baptism incorporates its subject into the Body of Christ (1 Cor 12:13), and this incorporation is by an assimilation to the likeness of His death (Rom 6:3–8). These Pauline texts are completed by Gal 3:27, which states that those who have been baptized have 'put on' Christ. Nowhere in this primitive teaching is there any suspicion that baptism might be no more than a cognitive experience of salvation—as Barth wants to hold, in conformity to a dictum of Calvin. On the contrary the effect of baptism is represented as something entirely objective, and is therefore capable of being imparted to infants as well as to adults. This incorporation was pictured by some early writers as a manumission ceremony (Crehan, 99–100), in which the former slave was now adopted into the sonship of God. Where the Roman law was supreme, such a connection of liberty and adoption of sons would seem apt enough, but with the northern peoples it is rather the physical analogies, of grafting and of resurrection, which find most favour. (See D 712 and also ADOPTION OF SONS.) The burial of the 'old Adam' involves the removal of original sin (D 792) and also the actual sins of the adult recipient (Col 2:13), though for this last besides the intention of receiving baptism some movement of attrition is needed (D 410 and St Thomas 3a:68:6c and 3a:87:1c), otherwise the sacrament remains valid but unfruitful. Not only the guilt but also the temporal punishment of sin is remitted by baptism (D 464).

(b) Next in order to the incorporation into Christ, though not later in time, comes the conferring of sanctifying grace (D 792) (see GRACE) and the infusion of the virtues of faith, hope and charity (D 800), which in the case of infants lie dormant until the advent of reason makes them able to put forth their power (see LIMBO). Concupiscence (q.v.) is not removed by baptism (D 792) but remains to be overcome by the baptized himself, being a relic of sin and an inclination to sin, but not sin itself. The child born to two baptized Catholics was thought by Pelagius not to need the water of baptism, according to his interpretation of 1 Cor 7:14. Certainly the practice of the Jews was not to require that the children born to two converts after their conversion should undergo proselyte baptism (Strack-Billerbeck, i:110), but it is doubtful whether this Jewish practice of proselyte baptism was in use at the time of 1 Corinthians. St Augustine (De remissione peccatorum 3:5, 21 ; Maurist edition, tom. x: cols. 73, 82) was troubled about the text, but

held stoutly that whatever it meant it did not imply that parents could by procreation so sanctify their children as to make them Christians ; it might refer to the general atmosphere in which the children were brought up, or to the manner of their begetting.

(c) The seven gifts of the Holy Ghost are also imparted to the soul in baptism (D 799, 904), but the sacrament of Confirmation is meant to bring them out fully (see CONFIRMATION). In fact, as baptism is a new birth, there have to be new powers and qualities to fit the soul for life on a new plane. When St Paul says (Tit 3:4–7) that Christ has saved us 'with the bath of regeneration and with renewal by the Holy Spirit', he is ascribing to baptism the work of a new creation on which he enlarges elsewhere (2 Cor 5:17 ; Gal 6:15 and Eph 4:24). Baptism is therefore not a moral conversion—though it involves that for an adult—but a new life. This life is not something for the individual alone, but it is a corporate life in the Body of Christ. Baptism, says Eph 5:26, is for the Church as such : she has been cleansed by her Spouse, Christ, 'in the bath of water by means of a word.' The 'word' here spoken of may be the confession of faith by the baptizand (see Crehan, 18–19). Hippolytus (in Dan I:16 and 33 ; GCS I:i:26 and 44) allegorizes the story of Susanna in terms of Christ and the Church, and finds a figure of baptism in the washing of the bride of Joakim ; it cannot be said with certainty that Paul has the same thought here, but the use of the Susanna story in the liturgy of Lent, in preparation for baptism on Easter eve, shows that the early Church took the same view as Hippolytus. In the East Syrian liturgy this figure of the bridal bath was very often used, and when the Syrian influence at Rome was strong (680–740) it found its way into the Antiphons for Epiphany, 'Hodie caelesti sponso iuncta est ecclesia, quoniam in Iordane lavit Christus eius crimina.' (Today is the Church joined to her heavenly Spouse, for Christ in the Jordan has washed away her sins.) (See Engberding, 14–20)

IX. (a) The various possibilities of **Simulation** (fictio) in the adult recipient of baptism that were canvassed in the early days of Scholasticism led to lengthy discussions on the way in which the effects of baptism might be held up, wholly or in part, until the right disposition was achieved. These debates have now been studied by Landgraf (87–181), who shows from a very wide survey of texts and MSS that a considerable evolution had taken place before it was possible for St Thomas (3a:69:9c and 10c) to decide so assuredly that there were four kinds of fictio, the lack of faith, the lack of due esteem for the sacrament, the lack of the proper rite and a lack of devotion, and that the fictus receives the character of the sacrament but not its proper effect which is the remission of sins ; these have to be done away by subsequent penance, which does not avail to remove all the temporal punishment due to them as baptism would have done. The importance of this discussion is to show the clear distinction between the working of the sacrament according to Catholic belief and a magical transaction according to the beliefs of its practitioners. They attach value to the act itself, regardless of the co-operation of the subject ; here the idea that the subject must not put an obstacle to the sacrament, and if capable of doing so he must accept the sacrament with his will, for it to have its proper effect, is quite opposed to such views. The debate also helped to elaborate the distinction between attrition and contrition (*see* ATTRITION), for it was the former which was finally held to be sufficient to make the impeded baptism ' come alive '.

(*b*) In later ages, when the origins of the Christian liturgy of baptism had grown obscure, there were several discussions about the validity of baptism in the name of Jesus, on the assumption that this meant using the name of Jesus as the sole formula of baptizing. Pope Nicholas I in his reply to the Bulgarians (PL 119:1014) is dealing with such a dispute, and Paulinus of Aquileia at the Council of Friuli in 791 (Mansi xiii:838) held that the Apostles had a special revelation of the Holy Ghost to tell them to use the one name. This latter view descended to St Thomas (3a:66:6@1), and it was only with Bellarmine that a reaction in favour of a more strictly historical treatment of the question began (*see* Crehan, 178–9). During the early Middle Ages the Scholastics were much given to arguing whether it was needed for validity to express in words the act of baptizing, by using the formula *ego te baptizo*, or whether *In nomine Patris* etc. would suffice by itself. Landgraf (47–86) has made a thorough examination of the opinions put forward and comes to the conclusion that the proposition (D1317) condemned as at least *male sonans* by Alexander VIII, ' *Valuit aliquando baptismus sub hac forma collatus* : *In nomine Patris* etc.', was undoubtedly advanced by some of the medieval Scholastics, and that in parts of France in the 12th cent. the shorter form was actually in use for cases of urgency. The general opinion was to regard the three words as necessary to baptism not by absolute or natural necessity but by necessity of precept, owing to the command of the Church. The upshot was that much greater care was exercised in the administration of the sacrament and the power of the Church to determine what is substantial in the sacraments was more clearly shown.

X The Character. (*a*) It is in this sacrament that the doctrine of the character conferred by certain sacraments was first developed, although in itself the discussion of the character, which is a certain sharing in the priesthood of Christ (*see* ORDINATION), belongs more properly to the sacrament of Order. The use of marking soldiers with the initial letters of the emperor's name (Vegetius, I:8 and II:5, *c.* A.D. 390) came in with the later Empire and almost at once Ambrose (*De obitu Valentiniani*, PL 16:1437) in 392 alluded to this fact in illustration of this effect of baptism : *Charactere domini inscribuntur et servuli, et nomine imperatoris signantur milites*. (Slaves are branded with their owner's name and soldiers are

signed with the name of the Emperor.) The frequency of desertion among those who served the *Soldatenkaiser* called for such a measure as this in the army, and the Christians at once saw how aptly it illustrated the truth that once baptized one could not be a deserter from Christ so as to escape notice for ever, at least before God. The initiation into Christianity made such a change in a man's status in regard to God that it could not be undone. Thereafter two Catholics who entered on a contract of marriage with each other, however sinful they might be and remote from the practice of their faith, would do something which was entirely different in the eyes of God from a contract between two pagans. The removal of the catechumens at the Christian liturgy again emphasized the privileged status of one who was baptized ; he had the right to say proudly when asked by the doorkeepers : ' *Catholicus* ', and pass into the church to join the faithful, while the catechumens gathered near the door.

(*b*) Prior to the use of the term ' character ' this feature of baptism had been designated under the term *seal*. The metaphors connected with this word are many, and it is hard to judge which one is uppermost in the mind of the Early Fathers who use it. To add to the confusion, it was also the practice (e.g. in Ambrose, *De sacramentis* 2:2 ; *De mysteriis* 7:41-2) to refer to Confirmation as the seal, rather in the sense of what perfects and completes the baptismal initiation (the metaphor here being that of the seal or cork which keeps the Spirit in the vessel of the human soul, or sometimes the seal on the door of the temple of the Holy Spirit. The nearness of this last to the sealing of the doorposts with blood at the Passover adds still more to the confusion.). Lampe has discussed the seal without sufficiently distinguishing these two uses of the term *seal* and without keeping them apart from the third use which referred to what is now called the sign of the cross. Anyone could use this seal, but the seal of confirmation was an episcopal act (*see* CONFIRMATION), while the seal of baptism was also conferred publicly by the Church. Hermas (see above, IIIc), who says that the water is the seal, is one of the first to apply the term to baptism ; he also replies to the obvious question as to what is to happen if the seal is broken. Then, he says, there is a second seal, Penance. It is clear that seal can mean many things to these early writers. It is not by the examination of this metaphor that one can hope to find the differences, if any, between baptism and confirmation, but from the consideration of other ideas. For the use of the term in Irenacus and Hippolytus, *see* TS xiv (1953), 273–8, and for the evidence of Justin, Thornton, 45–51. The idea of the gradual reception of the Spirit in trickling increments is implicit in several passages of St Paul where he speaks of the Spirit as the earnest (*arrabon*) or part payment that has been made over to us by God at the contract of our baptism (e.g. 2 Cor 1:21-2 ; 2 Cor 5:5 ; Rom 8:11 [in one reading] and 8:23). If the first reception of the Spirit is a sealing, then so is the second, when the next instalment is paid, whether that act be carried out in quick succession to baptism, at a week's interval (as in *Sacramentarium Pragense*), or much later.

XI The Necessity of Baptism. (*a*) The teaching of the Church on the absolute necessity of baptism is based on Jn 3:5 that all who wish to enter the kingdom of God must be born again of water and the Holy Ghost. Trent (D 858) defined that this text must be taken to refer to natural water and not to anything metaphorical. Clement of Alexandria claimed that the idea of a second birth and therefore of something necessary was familiar to the Greek philosophers (*Strom.* V:2:15 ; GCS ii:335) citing for this Plato (*Symp.* 206c) but not offering any Jewish parallels from the OT. Circumcision was looked on as a new beginning (*see* Crehan, *op. cit.* 2–4), but hardly as a new birth. Not all Jewish teachers held it to be necessary for males (*see* Crehan, *op. cit.* 4). In explaining the incidence of this necessity Trent (D 796) says, again citing Jn 3:5, that no one, since the promulgation of the gospel, can pass from a state of original sin to a state of grace and adoptive sonship of God without baptism or its *votum*. The qualification introduced, *post evangelium promulgatum*, was not the subject of any debate at Trent (Acta V, 693) ; its purpose was simply to exclude from consideration the ages before the coming of Christ. The actual words first occur in Seripando's draft of the decree (Acta V, 511), though the text from Jn was cited in the earlier formulation (Acta V, 422, due to Richard Wauchop of Armagh and three others). It is only in recent times that theories have been advanced which would suggest that this promulgation is not everywhere complete even yet (*see* SALVATION OF NON-CATHOLICS).

(*b*) The *votum baptismi* mentioned by Trent, which is rendered in English 'baptism of desire' and which differs from a mere desire of baptism by the fact that it must also be an act of perfect (charity or) love of God, was given a place in the decree because by then it had become the general teaching of theologians. Abelard had refused to admit any such idea as baptism of desire (*in Rom* 2:4 ; PL 178:845), but St Thomas (3a:68:2c) had the vast majority with him in so interpreting the patristic treatment of such catechumens as Valentinian that salvation without the actual water of baptism was considered in similar circumstances possible. The case of the pagan who has never heard of baptism does not seem to have much troubled the Scholastics, but the question took on a new aspect after the discovery of America in 1492, and theories of an implicit *votum* were elaborated (*see* AMERICA). For modern discussions on the fate of the unbaptized *see* LIMBO.

(*c*) The chief opponents of the necessity of baptism among Christians are the Quakers. In Robert Barclay's theological theses the seventh proposition runs, ' As many as resist not this light, but receive the same, in them is produced a holy, pure and spiritual birth, bringing forth holiness, righteousness, purity and all these other blessed fruits which are acceptable to God ; by which holy birth, to wit, Jesus Christ formed within us and working his works in us, are we sanctified . . .' This spiritualizing of the words in Jn 3:5 had already been ruled out by Trent a century before its being put forward by Barclay. He did not handle the arguments of Trent, but confined himself to an attack on the Catholic doctrine of indulgences and then passed on to show that Protestant divines, if they were consistent, would stake all upon the inner justification and let go the external washing with water (Barclay, 196, 409–45). He made much use of Calvin's comment on 1 Pet 3:21 that this text sets aside physical washing altogether in favour of an inner happening in the conscience, but neither he nor Calvin adverted to the Hebrew usage of stating in absolute terms what was really meant as a comparative judgment. Lacking comparative adjectives in their language they had to say : Not this . . . but that . . ., when they meant rather this than that. Peter did not deny that water was to be used in baptism but stressed the greater importance for the candidate of his profession of faith (*see* Crehan, *op. cit.* 10–12).

XII The Baptism of Blood. So completely was the absolute necessity of baptism understood in the early Church that a special problem quickly arose about the status of those who joined themselves to persecuted Christians and suffered along with them without having been baptized (see the story of the soldier who shared the martyrdom of James in Eusebius, *Historia Ecclesiastica* ii:9:2), or who were martyred while still in the catechumenate. The earliest plain acknowledgment that martyrdom was regarded as equivalent to baptism is made by Melito of Sardis (frag. 4, in Routh, *Reliquiae Sacrae* i:124), who says : Two things there are which provide remission of sins, martyrdom for Christ and baptism. These words are so early in date that one is justified in looking on this as an apostolic tradition which is nowhere recorded in Scripture but which was committed by Christ to the Church orally. Later Fathers discussed the case of the Good Thief, some thinking that he suffered martyrdom, others claiming him as the prototype of baptism of desire. The idea that there was an (invisible) unction for martyrs appears in the ancient prayer for the blessing of oil *Unde unxisti sacerdotes, reges, et prophetas et martyres*, as the *Gelasianum* says. On this anointing of martyrs *see* MARTYRDOM. That the second century was firmly in possession of the truth that baptism was necessary may be deduced from the fact that much debate was then going on about the baptism of the apostles. Tertullian (*de bapt.* 12:1–8) recalls some of this debate, giving various arguments but not coming to any definite conclusion on the fact himself. His final comment that if they were not baptized it will go hard with us seems to show that the subject had talked itself out by his time. Later apocrypha make Peter baptize the rest after he has been baptized by Christ, while St John baptizes Our Lady.

XIII Baptism for the Dead. The desire of recently

converted Christians to have their deceased relatives brought into the Church by some vicarious baptism seems to be first encountered at Corinth (1 Cor 15:29) ; this is a common interpretation of a difficult text, and if true would show great concern about the necessity of baptism at a very early stage of Christian development. Foschini, however, in a detailed study has argued strongly for the idea that ' baptism for the dead' means ' baptism for the purpose of joining the dead ', i.e. a useless act, if there be no resurrection of the dead. He urges that Paul would not appeal to such a practice in his argument for the truth of the resurrection of the dead if it was a reprehensible practice, but Paul had something of the Rabbi in his mentality and was eager to seize every advantage. Many of the Fathers seem to accept the idea of vicarious baptism as being what Paul refers to here, but they do not suggest its adoption by Christians ; indeed Chrysostom has a very curious and cautionary tale about the Marcionites carrying this out (PG 61:347), and Tertullian (de resurrectione 48 and adv. Marc. 5:10) and Ambrosiaster (PL 17:280) are anxious to exculpate Paul from any suggestion that such vicarious baptism ought to be practised. Such a misuse of the text has been made in more recent times by the Mormons (see Joseph Smith's Doctrine and Covenants, 1948, 234). Actual baptizing of a corpse was forbidden by the Third Council of Carthage (can. 6, Mansi, Concilia iii:719), a practice which may be put down to yet another interpretation of this troublesome text.

XIV Baptism of Infants. This perennial debate among the Protestant churches has flared up again in recent years with the insistence by Barth that the old Lutheran view be restored wherein faith is so much emphasized in the baptismal act that one is compelled to deny that an infant can be fit for baptism. Scriptural proofs are not quite conclusive, though Cullmann has urged against Barth that the episodes in the gospels of Christ blessing the children (Mt 19:13 ; Mk 10:13 ; Lk 18:15) would not have found their way into the gospels had not the early Church been familiar with the practice of child baptism. But what is lacking to both sides in the dispute is an adequate notion of Tradition, to which appeal must finally be made to settle the question. It is not merely a question of a liturgical usage but of a definite dogmatic tradition, for the point at issue is one that touches the very centre of the act. Polycarp (Martyrium Polycarpi 9) claimed at his death to have been a slave of Christ for 86 years, and this carries back the date of his baptism to the year 70, when he can scarcely have been more than an infant, and what is more, he received his baptism from the apostles (Iren. adv. haer. III:iii:4 H). Justin (Apol. 15:6) can also tell of some who at the time of his writing were 60 or 70 years old and who had been baptized in childhood, an assertion which again brings the practice back to the decade 70–80. Irenaeus is quite explicit, saying (op. cit. II:xxxiii:2), ' Christ came to save all through Himself, i.e. all who by His means are born again

to God, infants, children, boys, youths and old men.' In the Traditio apostolica of Hippolytus (c. xxi:9, Dix) directions are given for the sponsors to answer the interrogations in the case where children or the dumb are being baptized. Tertullian shows that the logic of Roman law was already coming up against this Christian practice which ran counter to it. Inelegans visum est ab heredis persona incipere obligationem runs the sentence in Gaius (3:100), i.e. it is not logical for an heir to inherit an obligation which he did not himself contract for, and infant baptism seemed thus to be a delayed-action obligation, which began to press upon its subject only years after it had been incurred for him. Where is the need, asks Tertullian (de bapt. 18:4), if it be not absolutely necessary, for the sponsors to be put in peril, for they may fail in their undertaking by death, or they may themselves be cheated by the growth of an evil disposition in the child. . . . Civil affairs are managed more cautiously. It is clear that the lawyer's mind was irked by this delayed obligation, and so have been many others since his day. Erasmus proposed that those baptized in infancy should be asked when they came to maturer years if they accepted the obligations of their baptism, and if they refused, they should be left unmolested by the Church. (Trent, Acta V:837:15.) This opinion figures in a list of errors condemned by Trent (D 870). Pope Pius XI in his teaching on education (D 2213) has clearly rejected this idea that a child should be left to grow up naturally, in the fashion of Emile, and then confronted with the fact of his baptism, to accept or reject it, when mature.

XV The Roman Ritual of Baptism. (a) Pope Siricius (10 February 385) laid it down that baptism was to be conferred publicly at Easter and Pentecost alone (PL 56:556), and that those who wished to be baptized must be prepared for forty days or more preceding their baptism. Leo the Great speaks of their being exorcismis scrutandi during this period, and the term scrutinium for the threefold examination of the candidates is well established by 500, for in the letter about that time of a Roman deacon, John, to Senarius of Ravenna (Wilmart, Analecta Reginensia 170–9) it is explained that the term is customary and that the three scrutinies deal with the memorizing of the Christian prayers (Pater and Creed), with knowledge of the grace of Christ the Redeemer, and with faith in God the Father. Mansi (III:1137) gives the decree of a Roman council of uncertain date (perhaps under Siricius or Innocent) where three scrutinies are ordered. Traces of this arrangement of three scrutinies can be found in the Gelasian Sacramentary by H. A. Wilson (the three masses are given at pp. 34, 38, 42) where a notification of scrutinies to be held, rubrics for holding them and prayers to be used thereat are all inserted in one piece just before Palm Sunday (Wilson, 45–60). In the Ordo Romanus XI (of Andrieu's edition, formerly Ordo VII) seven scrutinies are arranged for, but the reason given, that the candidates are to receive the seven gifts, does not really explain why they were needed.

(b) The *Ordo baptismi* of *Ordo XI* is dependent on the Gelasian, starting with the *Ephtheta* and the *Redditio symboli* and going on to the blessing of the candle and the font. It omits the renunciation of Satan, which is ancient and which comes before the *Redditio* in *Gelasianum*. Andrieu, who holds that *Gelasianum* is dependent upon *Ordo XI* throughout, has not explained this omission in *Ordo XI* satisfactorily; to appeal to the rite in Hippolytus is of no avail, for there the place of the renunciation is, as in the *Gelasianum*, near the start. The renunciation is also present in the *Sacramentary of Gellone*, which Andrieu supposes to be dependent on *Ordo XI*, and in the *Capitulare ecclesiastici ordinis*, which Andrieu prints as his *Ordo XV* and which he considers to be dependent on *Ordo XI* and *Gellone*. *Ordo XI* does not give the act of baptizing in any detail, but simply directs that the bishop baptize one or two, or as many as he please, and then leave the rest to the deacon whom he appoints (Andrieu II:445). Both here and in the *Gelasianum* confirmation follows at once, but *Ordo XV* (Andrieu III:120) anticipates some difficulty in having a bishop always at hand on Easter eve, and directs that the baptized should be confirmed as soon as possible. In the *Sacramentary of Prague*, the confirmation is put down as happening after eight days.

(c) Unlike other Western documents *Ordo XV* has a baptism service on Epiphany in the Eastern manner. This is unparalleled in the West except for a brief postscript to the *Ordo baptismi* in the *Sacramentary of Gellone* (Martène 102), which says that everything is then carried out as on Pentecost, save for the singing of the canticle *Deo laudamus* on the way to the font. *Ordo XV* has this direction also, and in addition it has here a direction that the clergy who baptize take off their shoes and enter into the font. They put on for the task clean or white garments, which the pseudo-Germanus (PL 72:97) says are to recall the act of John the Baptist baptizing Our Lord. It may be that this devotion to John the Baptist is Gallican, but that the custom of baptizing on Epiphany was Gallican does not appear to be proved. Given the importance of the Epiphany in the early IRISH LITURGY (q.v.) it could equally well be said that this choice of Epiphany for baptism was one of the many Syrian borrowings which somehow made their way to Ireland between 450 and 600.

(d) The epiclesis or blessing of the font presents many problems as well as throwing some light on the general question of the EPIKLESIS (q.v.); these problems have been studied by Atchley and again in complete independence by Stommel, who has made probable the explanation of the mysterious Ψ sign made over the font as a symbol of the Holy Ghost, in the form of parted tongues, as at Pentecost. The *Exultet* seems to go back in one form or another to the time of Jerome, who in his letter to Praesidius (RB 1891:20-7 1892:392-7) declines to compose for him a *laus cerei*. Ambrose has been suggested as a possible author of the *Exultet*, though it has undoubtedly been enlarged in the course of centuries.

Bibliography. A. D'Alès SJ, *De Baptismo et Confirmatione* (1927); Doronzo, *De Baptismo et Confirmatione* (1947); *W. F. Flemington, *The NT Doctrine of Baptism* (1948); J. Tyciak, *Der siebenfältige Strom aus der Gnadenwelt der Sakramente* (1954²); W. De Vries SJ, *Sakramententheologie bei den Syrischen Monophysiten* = OCA 125 (1940); J. H. Crehan SJ, *Early Christian Baptism and the Creed* (1950); *O. Cullmann, *Le Baptême des enfants* (1948); *F. J. Leenhardt, *Le Baptême chrétien* (1946); *K. Barth, *The Teaching of the Church regarding Baptism* (Eng. trans. E. Payne) (1948); N. Adler, *Taufe und Handauflegung* (1951); R. Schnackenburg, *Das Heilsgeschehen bei der Taufe nach Paulus* (1950); *J. Jeremias, *Hat die Urkirche die Kindertaufe geübt?* (1949²); *H. H. Rowley, *Jewish Proselyte Baptism*, HUCA XV (1940) 313-34; J. Quasten, 'Baptismal Creed and Baptismal Act in St Ambrose', in *Mélanges de Ghellinck*, I (1951) 223-34; H. Engberding OSB, *Die Kirche als Braut in der ostsyrischen Liturgie*, OCP 3 (1937) 5-48; A. M. Landgraf, *Dogmengeschichte der Frühscholastik* III, ii (1955); B. M. Foschini, *Those who are baptized for the dead*, CBQ XII (1950) 260-76 and 379-88, XIII (1951) 46-78, 172-98, 276-83; *R. Barclay, *An Apology for the true Christian Divinity* (1701); E. Martène OSB, *De antiquis Ecclesiae Ritibus* I (1700); M. Andrieu, *Les Ordines Romani du haut Moyen Âge* I (1931); II (1948); III (1951); *E. G. Atchley, *On the Epiclesis of the eucharistic Liturgy and in the Consecration of the Font* (1935); E. Stommel, *Studien zur Epiklese der römischen Taufwasserweihe*; *Strack-Billerbeck, *Kommentar zum NT aus Talmud und Midrasch*; *L. S. Thornton, *Confirmation, its place in the baptismal Mystery* (1954); *G. W. Lampe, *The Seal of the Spirit* (1951); J. Quasten, *The painting of the Good Shepherd at Dura*, Med. St. IX (1947) 1-18; N. Haring, *St Augustine's use of the word Character*, Med. St. XIV (1952) 79-97; Margaret Pepperdene, *Baptism in the early British and Irish Churches*, ITQ XXII (1955) 110-23; J. H. Crehan SJ, 'Ten Years' work on Baptism and Confirmation', in TS XVII (1956) 494-515.

J. H. C.

BARDESANES or BARDAISAN (son of the river Daisan), was born at Edessa in 155 and died in 223. He is perhaps the most obscure character in that obscure period, for Eusebius (*HE* 4:30) says that he began in the school of Valentinus and afterwards turned to Christianity, though he did not completely wash away the heretical stain from himself; Epiphanius (*Haer.* 56; GCS 31:340) makes out that his development was in the opposite direction and that after being a Christian and teaching Christian doctrine he fell away to the heresy of Valentinus and denied the resurrection of the body. It is far more probable that Epiphanius is right. The school founded by Bardesanes continued until the time of James of Edessa, who died in 708, and Ephrem's *Refutations against Bardaisan* (first published from a British Museum palimpsest in 1921) show that his heresy was formidable. 'Not a little loss is it that has entered through Bardaisan, that inexperienced folk who have heard have suffered loss of the merchandise of their lives.' Ephrem also shows that one of Bardaisan's objections to Catholic doctrine concerned the punishment of Adam's sin. If Abel died before Adam, how could Catholics maintain that death came into the world with Adam and because of his sin? 'Free-will,' replies Ephrem 'in its audacity made an assault on Abel in its envy, and brought in killing before death; by the sentence from the Judge Adam died first, but by that killing from man Abel was killed first.' One might be assisting at a scholastic disputation, so developed is this 3rd-century argument.

Bardesanes expounded a cosmology in which there were four pure Entities, light, wind, fire and water, set at the four points of the compass, with a foul Entity, darkness, below them and with God above. God is not the Creator but merely the arranger of this system and space is regarded as a seventh Entity, for Ephrem has to argue against Bardesanes that space is a notion and not a corporeal reality. It is from this cosmology that the Manichean system is descended (*see* MANICHEES). Perception was explained by a sexual analogy, light being masculine in Aramaic and the eye feminine, so that Bardaisan could say, 'Light sows perception in the eye'. Ephrem ridicules this on the ground that in Greek the genders are the same, and from this it would appear that Bardaisan did not know Greek well, or at least did not work in the language. The charge that he mixed up Stoicism and Platonism may therefore be true.

Like Valentinus his master, Bardesanes composed a set of 150 Psalms and Ephrem credits him with having brought in measures (i.e. metre) into Syriac. Porphyry says that he made acquaintance with the envoys who had been sent from India to Caesar (probably to Marcus Aurelius), and he may thus be a link between Christianity and Buddhism, though there is no sign in Bardesanes of the strong asceticism which would make marriage an evil. He cannot be connected with the *Acts of Thomas* or the *Hymn of the Soul* which is there quoted. Ephrem's own fifty-six *Hymns against the heretics* (some of which deal with Bardesanes) were inspired by the success of the heretical Psalms. The *Book of the Laws of Countries* (printed with a Latin version in *Patrologia Syriaca* I:ii:490–658) is a dialogue in which Bardesanes is the principal speaker. It may have been composed about the time of his death by disciples who wished to present their master as Plato presented Socrates; a passing allusion refers to the Roman conquest of Arabia as having happened 'only yesterday', and this may point to the conquest by Septimius Severus in 195–6. The work argues against an astrological fatalism, one of the arguments being that different peoples have laws that are disparate even though they may be in the same astrological region; the Britons are cited in this connection for their acceptance of polyandry as lawful.

The dialogue *de recta in Deum fide* (GCS 4) has a character named Marinus who defends the views of Bardesanes. He says that these differ from orthodoxy only in the denial of the resurrection of the body, of the birth of Christ from the Virgin, and of the creation of the devil by God. The second of these errors could easily flow from the first, as any disparagement of the body might lead to the idea that Christ could not have assumed what was so unworthy of His divine nature, and it is also on record that Valentinus had said that Christ passed through Mary as water through a pipe (Epiphanius, *Haer*. 31:4; GCS 25:388). The origin of the devil by some process of self-engendering would not be alien from the thought of one who denied that God had created the seven Entities. Marinus is not prepared to be a thorough dualist and is made to say that only God is indestructible; in this, too, he may have been following a tradition of the school of Bardesanes, but we cannot be sure. Ultimately, a belief that the body, as distinct from the soul, is under the influence of the stars and does evil because of this, while it removes from the will of man (in his spiritual part) all taint of evil and side-steps the difficulty that God is good and yet made the soul of man free to choose between good and evil, must lead to dualism of the Manichean kind. Bardesanes had written against Marcion and held the law of the OT to be good and not evil; it may have been this opposition which kept him from being as thorough-paced a dualist as Mani was to become.

Bibliography. Hort's article 'Bardaisan', in DCB, is still the most complete life, though it lacks some of the recent findings; ★ C. W. Mitchell, *Ephrem's Prose Refutations of Mani, Marcion and Bardesanes* (ed. F. C. Burkitt, 2 vols., 1912, 1921); Ephrem's *Hymns against the heretics*, CSCO, vols. 76, 77; F. Nau, *Bardesane : le livre des lois des pays* (1931); ★ R. M. Grant, *Gnosticism and Early Christianity* (1959).   J. H. C.

BAROQUE, the name of the style of art which prevailed during the 17th cent.; or, as some would prefer, during the longer period 1590–1750. Its importance for this Dictionary lies in a mutual influence supposed, with some justification, to exist between baroque art and the religion and culture of the Counter-reformation. After (I) the term 'baroque' has been explained, and (II) the place of art in the Counter-reformation considered, (III) baroque art will be analysed, (IV) its effect on literature noted, and (V) its theological presuppositions examined.

I History of the term. The word 'baroque' is derived from It. *baroco*, a Scholastic mnemonic term signifying a syllogism of the fourth mode of the second figure. At the time when the word first approximated to its present meaning, the Scholastic logic was thought to have decayed: it thus had a pejorative signification and connoted a sophistic use, or even total absence of logic and measure. (The OED derivation from Sp. *barrueco*, 'a pearl of irregular shape', now meets with little acceptance.) In the 18th cent. baroque commonly implied 'extravagant', 'bizarre': such an implication is by no means absent from all present-day usage, as many a modern encyclopedia article betrays. (Croce was perhaps the last important *critic* to employ baroque in this sense.) To Winckelmann the word suggested the 'playfully free', the 'decorative'. Jacob Burckhardt stabilized the meaning of the term for art history; but he used it merely to signify the decadence of Italian High Renaissance. His example led others to speak of baroque in a broader sense as a decadent phase in the history of any style: thus Wilamowitz-Moellendorff wrote of 'ancient baroque', i.e., Hellenistic art. Though primarily interested in architecture and painting, Heinrich Wölfflin was the first to suggest that the term might be used for the discussion of similar phenomena in literature. Recently the term has come to be so broadly applied to so many tendencies and periods as to have become almost empty of meaning. (Wellek, 'The Concept of Baroque in Literary Scholarship' provides the best survey of its changing use, and cites numerous modern employments, some of them fantastic.) It is best restricted to its earliest function of describing a particular period in the history of art; and when used of other periods and in other fields, it ought to be recognized as applying only in the loosest analogical sense.

II Art and the Counter-reformation. The virtual paganism of the arts in the Renaissance was apparent to none more than to the Fathers of Trent. In the chapter *De invocatione, veneratione et Reliquiis Sanctorum et sacris imaginibus* (Sessio XXV) opportunity was taken to admonish and, if necessary, correct the excesses of artists. The abundance of nude figures and the treatment of useless and profane subjects were especially censured. Many artists were directly touched by the Tridentine provisions: in 1573 Paolo Veronese had a passage of arms with the Holy Office. (An account of his trial is given by Elizabeth G. Holt, *A Documentary History of Art*, vol. II (1958) 66–70.) On the other hand, there appeared numerous ecclesiastically-inspired guides for the proper execution of sacred art, such as those of da Fabriano, *Dialogo degli errori dei pittori* (1564), which seeks to determine the moral value of Michelangelo's Vatican frescoes; van der Meulen, *De picturis et imaginibus sacris* (1570), widely circulated and concerned with theological questions; and Romano Alberti, *Trattato della nobiltà della pittura* (1585), published under the auspices of the Accademia di San Luca. Federigo Borromeo (brother of the Cardinal and Saint) in his *Symbolae Litterariae Opuscula* (not printed until 1752) considers the veneration of images and speaks of the moral influence that an artist can exert, e.g., through his refusal to paint an objectionable picture. One work of the next century is of particular interest, the *Trattato della pittura e scultura* (Florence 1652): because of the personality of its authors, the Jesuit Ottonelli and the painter and architect Pietro da Cortona, it may be thought to convey perhaps best the point of view from which both the Church and the artists regarded their common artistic problem. (Weibel, *op. cit.* 14 ff., supplies these and other titles. The *Iconologia* of Cesare Ripa (1603) is considered especially important by E. Mâle.)

The reforming zeal of the great prelates by no means excluded their continued patronage of the arts. Gregory XIII, indeed, declared that to erect buildings was a duty in Christian piety, a public testimony of love; he was not thinking only of churches. More, probably, than such sentiments as these, family pride played its part; its extreme was reached under Urban VIII (Barberini) and its most fruitful issue in that pontiff's patronage of Bernini. The Accademia di San Luca, already mentioned, founded by Gregory XIII in 1577, did much, not only to assist in the purging of heathen elements in the work of contemporary painters, but also to give them a corporate stimulus, as did also the earlier establishment (1543) of the *Virtuosi al Pantheon*.

III Character of baroque art. (*a*) *The fine arts*. The seeds of the baroque style in architecture may be discerned in Michelangelo's work on St Peter's, which, despite the still dominant central plan of the High Renaissance, displays the gigantism and coordination of masses that were to be so remarkable in the work of the next generation. It is in the plan of S Maria dei Monti that the baroque preference for a broad, open nave and diminutive side-aisles and chapels is first seen; still more in the church of the Gesù (Vignola, begun 1568), which was widely imitated, even at St Peter's itself, when Carlo Maderna in 1607–16 extended Michelangelo's Greek cross plan into a Latin cross and added the façade, which, according to correct baroque canons, conceals Michelangelo's dome from view. As the baroque developed, the curve became more prominent; the ellipse provided greater effectiveness of perspective than the oblong, and this curvilinear predilection in the plan was reflected in the concave-convex contour of the façades. These were designed to be viewed from close at hand—often, because of narrow streets, necessarily at a sharp angle; and without reference to the buildings they mask. Unlike Renaissance façades, where columns, niches, windows and pediments were all designed as self-sufficient units combining in a harmony of diversity, the baroque façade fused all elements (clustered columns and pilasters, broken pediments, deeply shadowed niches) into a massive and dramatic whole in which movement is emphasized and sharp outlines merge into a dynamic imbalance (Plate 5b). The spacious interiors, in which all the lines converged into an apse containing the high altar (Plates 7, 8), were enlarged, as the period proceeded, not so much by increasing the dimensions of the building (many baroque churches, such as Borromini's S Carlo alle Quattro Fontane, are quite small) as by the clever use of perspective lines and receding ranks of columns, and by painting which blended into the architecture and in which an endless stretching into infinity was suggested.

In the baroque, as in no previous style, there was close fusion of sculpture, painting and architecture (Plate 5a). Renaissance sculpture was designed to stand free and apart from its architectural setting, to be viewed 'in the round'; baroque sculpture is closely wedded to its architectural framework. Often the lighting, dramatically calculated from openings behind and above, is indispensable for total effect ; so is, frequently, a profuse accompaniment of clouds and rays. The movement of the drapery, swirling and violent, is often in direct contrast to that of the figure which it clothes. There is an effort to capture the climactic moment—of concentrated effort, of ecstasy (Plate 6a), of martyrdom. It should be added that the technical proficiency of baroque sculptors was of a high order.

Though perhaps less important than baroque architecture or sculpture, painting has had more meticulous analysis. In minutely differentiating between 'linear' and 'painterly' technique, between flatness and depth, closed form and open form, multiplicity and unity, clarity and indistinctness, Wölfflin (in his classic *Kunstegeschichtliche Grundbegriffe*) has put his finger on the difference between Renaissance and baroque style. A pervading naturalism (Plate 6b) in baroque painting should be emphasized, though only in the work of Caravaggio ('Entombment of Christ' in the Vatican) did it reach the surface.

The main features of baroque art may now be summarized (as suggested by Martin) : There is a wide choice of subjects, especially those with strong psychological interest ; a tendency to allegory, the abstract idea being conveyed in the most immediate and concrete terms possible ; a delight in the portrayal of extremes : the excessively heroic, the ascetic, the gruesome, the mystic (always by an act of objective experience, such as the vision). The recurrent themes of vision and ecstasy, of death and martyrdom, are always presented at the moment of highest dramatic and emotional tension. There is the sense of the infinite, most apparent in exaggerated architectural perspective and illusionist ceiling painting (Pozzo in S Ignazio, Rome) ; the sense of space, the presentation of the receding landscape ; a feeling for the effective use of light as an external agency capable of dissolving the limited confines of immediate pictorial space ; a preoccupation with time, usually expressed allegorically (Reni's 'Aurora') and reflected nostalgically in the depiction of ruins. There is even humour, in the caricatures of Bernini.

(*b*) *Music*. The classic polyphony of Palestrina (1525–94), constructed of interdependent, yet at the same time virtually autonomous, vocal lines, seems to place him firmly among the artists of the Renaissance, despite his late date and the explicit response of his music to Tridentine requirements. The operas of Monteverdi (1567–1634 ; *Orfeo* 1607), with their painful conflicts resolved in a pleasurable issue, and the madrigals of Gesualdo (1560–1613), with their unsubtle, direct presentation of emotion and their freedom of harmonic activity, seem more spiritually akin to contemporary baroque production in the other arts.

To consider the almost universal, though in the writer's opinion, questionable, application of the term 'baroque' by musicologists to the period of Bach and Handel would fall outside the scope of this article.

IV Literature: allegory and emblem. The greatest poem of the period when the reform movement was at its height, Tasso's 'Gerusalemme liberata' (1581, 1593), is not only constructed on a religious premise, but deals, in courtly and allegorical terms, with an actual religious question of the day, the struggle with the Turks. Tasso himself was deeply concerned that his work should deal with moral themes correctly and effectively ; he was scrupulous over the inclusion of erotic and magic episodes. His friend and mentor, Cardinal Antoniano, wished that he had included fewer courtly gallants and more divines and nuns. Such desires were fulfilled in other works to the verge of sentimentality ; Petrarch and Ariosto, the liberal humanists of an earlier day, were spiritualized, and even the *Decameron* was so transformed as to become an edifying discourse. Nevertheless, a certain ambivalence remains—for example, in what is probably the typical poem of the epoch, Marini's 'Adone' (1623). As in painting and sculpture, so here, the fleshly and erotic is inextricably interwoven with the pious.

The work having the largest influence on the emerging baroque idiom was unquestionably the *Exercitia Spiritualia* (first extant edition 1541) of St Ignatius. The circumstances of its compilation and breadth of its diffusion by the Society in which it originated ensured its full power alike to form and to reflect the spirit of the age. It authorized the 'application of the senses' to the themes of religion. In its successive meditations on sin and hell, on the sufferings, crucifixion, death, resurrection, and ascension of Christ, the imagination is first invited to see, hear, smell, taste and feel the outward lineaments of what it contemplates. The well-known 'composition of place' enlists all the senses and faculties for a reconstruction of the physical scene—a reconstruction remarkably similar in its results to the productions of the painters and sculptors. The step from the application of sight, the chief of the senses, to the devising of symbols is easy, and by such devising even abstract concepts could be made concrete and meaningful. This process was helped by the Renaissance devices of the emblem and the *impresa*. The former, which alone concerns us here, attempted to sum up, in a simple pictorial device, an abstract and often highly complex truth, usually theological ; its origin can be traced ultimately to such symbolic objects in Scripture as the burning bush and Gedeon's fleece. Innumerable collections of emblems appeared, usually accompanied by some form of epigrammatic elucidation. In a typical emblem the heart would be depicted as undergoing all manner of transformation—as being ploughed, tilled, and seeded ; as being forced by the refractory soul (often a cherub) to fit a round world, etc. The English convert, Richard Crashaw (1612?–49), best carries out this emblematic technique in poetry. The hearts, piercing arrows, sighs, tears and raptures of *The Flaming Heart* (his poem on St Theresa) were but the verbal counterparts of Bernini's graphic presentation of the same theme in the Cornaro

Plate 5a

S. Maria dell' Orto :
detail of the sanctuary (Longhi)
Photo : Alinari

Plate 5b

S. Maria in Campitelli :
façade (Rainaldi)
Photo : Anderson

Plate 6a
St Peter's : St Longinus (Bernini)
Photo : Anderson

Plate 6b
S. Maria del Popolo :
Conversion of St Paul (Caravaggio)
Photo : Anderson

Plate 7   S. Ignazio, Rome : the nave (Grassi)   *Photo : Alinari*

Chapel, in the church of Santa Maria della Vittoria, Rome (cf. Warren, *op. cit.* 67–74).

Quite another aspect of the baroque sensibility appears in the ' devout humanism ' of St Francis de Sales, especially in his *Introduction à la vie dévote* (1609). Here, too, there is the harnessing of the natural faculties, of the appetites and the senses, to a supernatural aim ; but instead of the tortured, turbulent world of the emblems, all is tranquil and optimistic. There is question here of a peculiarly French variant of the human ideal of the Counter-reformation ; it is significant that French writers have never acknowledged the presence of the baroque in their country. Deliberation, wit, sagacity, reason governed the life of the emotions in a way unknown to Italy and Spain. Not far behind are the delicate play of the rococo and the academic precision of neo-classicism.

V Theological considerations. The baroque is occasionally called the Jesuit style. There is some justification for this. By putting forward the human consideration of a human Lord, by first enlisting the senses and then bending them to a right direction, the Jesuits made possible such later flights of mystic contemplation as find their record on the pages of Bremond ; and in their full enlistment of man's sensitive, appetitive, and intellectual powers, they provided a retreat to which this contemplation could always return when it became dry and sluggish. For the first time, largely under their aegis, art attempts to express the physical manifestations of ecstasy—the ecstasy toward the divine as opposed to the ecstasy of secular knowledge, power and luxury. ' Against the ecstasy of passion the ecstasy of charity reacted by employing the imagery and language of the earthly lover to express its intenser passion ' (Watkin, *op. cit.* 105). It provided a sublimation of man's passionate energy in an ecstatic love of God (Bernini, Crashaw).

Externally the baroque age was faced by the open revolt of Protestants and the covert revolt alike of Catholic absolute rulers and secular humanism. In the face of these challenges, the generation succeeding the counter-reformation, with the active co-operation of its artists, proposed the magnificent, the overawing—the only sort of counter-challenge likely to have any success in an age of externals. Even by an insistence on the power of the papacy only, God's glory could be asserted. Such an insistence is given striking expression in Bernini's baldachin and ' Cathedra Petri ' in St Peter's, which, though designed and executed some years apart, embody a single magnificent symbolic conception. Dominating all is the glory, centred in the dove ; this counterbalances the Chair, supported by the Doctors of the Church ; both, in turn, look toward and embrace the canopy sheltering the central Act of the Church's life, and both may be clearly divined through the twisted columns of this canopy. Almost a panoramic tableau, the complex at Cathedra and baldachin conveys a mighty impression of the Holy Ghost, ever actively directing and governing the Church.

Everywhere the human was sanctified. Humanism was met by the divine humanity of God Incarnate and the deified humanity of His members : it becomes a Christian humanism. The cultus of the saint sanctified the cult of the hero. Passionate love for the human Jesus and His Mother sanctified erotic passion. In the cultus of the Sacred Heart can be seen a prime example of baroque power to make an abstract concept living and concrete—and the culmination of the emblem. The reaction of many against what they mistakenly regard as sentimentalism and anthropocentrism is due, in fact, simply to a misunderstanding of the nature of emblem. They fail to realize what, indeed, has often been observed : that the baroque age, with its emblems, embodied the last manifestation of a distinctly Christian culture. ' The art of the Counter-reformation, which is rooted in the baroque, was the last in which the Christian world of ideas found unified, universal, and impressive expression ' (Weisbach, *op. cit.* 39).

Bibliography. Of chief interest and importance from the point of view of this article : W. Weisbach, *Der Barock als Kunst der Gegenreformation* (1921) ; E. Mâle, *L'Art religieux après le Concile de Trent* (1932) ; E. I. Watkin, ' Autumn : the Age of Baroque ' in *Catholic Art and Culture* (1941) (rev. ed. with illustrations, 1947). The key works on the genesis and evolution of the baroque in its place of origin, Rome, are H. Wölfflin, *Renaissance und Barock* (1888) (ed. H. Rose, 1926[4]), and T. H. Fokker, *Roman Baroque Art*, 2 vols, (1938). Of innumerable other books and articles, the following deserve mention : A. Blunt, *Artistic Theory in Italy 1450–1600*, especially ch. VIII ' The Council of Trent and religious art ' (1940) ; W. Weibel, *Jesuitismus und Barockskulptur in Rom* (1909) (largely devoted to Bernini) ; A. Warren, *Richard Crashaw : A Study in Baroque Sensibility* (1939) ; R. Wellek, ' The Concept of Baroque in Literary Scholarship ', *Journal of Aesthetics and Art Criticism* V (1946), with an excellent bibliography ; the articles of Hatzfeld, Martin and Stechow in a special ' baroque number ' of this *Journal* (XIV (1955–6)). The influence of St Philip Neri and the Oratorians on the art of Caravaggio is cited by W. Friedlaender in his *Caravaggio Studies* (1955) ; cf. in this connection Ponnelle and Bordet, *St Philip Neri and the Roman Society of his Time* (tr. R. F. Kerr (1932)). For a modern German view of baroque, see *Kirche und Volksfrömmigkeit im Zeitalter des Barock*, by L. A. Veit and L. Lenhart (1956).

A. B.

BARTHIANISM *See* PROTESTANT THEOLOGY

BASIL, LITURGY OF ST A Mass formula which is used on ten days a year by many of the Eastern rites is ascribed to St Basil and is of considerable theological interest. In discussing this, it is necessary (I) to try to decide how much of the formula goes back to Basil and (II) what light this text may throw on his theology.

I The authentic text of the liturgy of St Basil is a matter of dispute. A statement by the pseudo-Proclus

(PG 65:849) says that when men's piety grew cold Basil shortened the pre-existing liturgy (of Clement and James), thus producing a text which went under his name. Peter the deacon (PL 62:90) in the year 520 cites a passage from this liturgy of Basil, part of which can be recognized in the surviving Greek text, and says that this 'prayer of Basil' was much used by almost the whole of the East.[1] It is not clear whether he meant a single prayer or a complete Mass-text, or whether he is speaking of the Orient or simply of Egypt (which was called *Oriens* by the Africans whom he was addressing). Soon after this, in 531, Leontius of Byzantium (PG 86:1368) says that Nestorius did not accept the 'anaphora of Basil', which certainly means a Mass-text. In view of the praise given to Basil by Gregory Nazianzen in his funeral panegyric (PG 36:341) for 'arrangement of prayers', it is safe to conclude that Basil did compose a liturgy, which then was handed down to the churches. The care taken in Basil's own day to preserve unaltered the liturgy compiled by one of the pioneers is shown by his remarks (*de Spiritu sancto* 74 ; PG 32:205) about Gregory Thaumaturgus. It was in the Dark Ages, of the 8th and 9th cents., that interpolation and farcing of liturgical texts went on apace. H. Engberding has argued that of the extant texts of the liturgy of Basil it is the Alexandrian which gives the truest picture of what Basil wrote. Extant in the Coptic version (supported by the Greek and the Ethiopic), this Alexandrian recension is shorter than what survives under the name of Basil in the Byzantine Greek, Armenian and Syriac versions. (One early fragment of the Armenian version is cited by Faustus of Byzantium in his *Historia nationis Armenae* 5:28 of *c.* A.D. 420). The liturgist Goar settled the problem to his own satisfaction by supposing that Basil composed two liturgies. Since Goar's *Euchologion* (1647) many attempts have been made to find a solution and not everyone is happy with the attempt of Engberding, who tries to improve on Goar. In his favour is the argument that if Basil had written the longer version himself it is hard to see who would have dared to curtail it. It may also be urged that there would be every reason for Alexandria to welcome a newly-composed liturgy from Cappadocia at a time when Arianism was just beginning to lose its hold ; the existing liturgies (of Mark and of James) may have lent themselves more easily to Arian propaganda than Basil's, if this last was arranged to counter Arianism (for which point see (II) below). Against Engberding may be brought what might be described as the 'Gresham's Law' of liturgy, that shorter texts tend to drive out the longer ones ; thus the liturgy of Chrysostom (which is shorter) almost succeeded in driving out Basil altogether. May not the same have happened between the two versions of Basil ? Further, it is not easy to accept Engberding's idea that prayers which are heavily enriched with Scriptural phrasing are later than those which are not. The judgment of Fr Hanssens (in OCP 26,

[1] oratio Basliii . . . quam paene universus frequentat Oriens.

1932, 220–2) on Engberding's theory seems the afest, that while it is most probable that the shorter form of Basil's liturgy is the earliest, it by no means follows that he produced the longer one in his old age by adding scriptural matter to the shorter one.

In 1960 there appeared an incomplete Coptic MS. of the liturgy of Basil in the shorter form. Its editors ascribe it to the 7th cent., since it names as still alive ' Benjamin the archbishop and his fellow-minister Colluthos '. Benjamin was the Monophysite patriarch in Egypt (622–62) and the writings of Colluthos were condemned as Monothelite at the Lateran council (649). The new MS. shows signs of Monophysite preoccupations, not stressing the voluntary character of Christ's death. Its *epiklesis* is addressed to the Father, but the *post-Sanctus*, unlike some other versions of this *anaphora*, is not. The fraction-prayer (which is preserved in PO 28:388) is here turned into a preamble to the *Pater noster*.

II The theological interest of the liturgy of Basil is extensive. The *anaphora* of Basil starts with the dialogue before the Preface, and it is not certain that the preliminary prayers (for incense, for the Kiss of peace, for the Church and so on) are his. He knew of a system of grading the public penitents into four classes, weepers, listeners, kneelers and the erect (*ep.* 217:75 ; PG 32:804), but the texts of his liturgy do not preserve a parallel series of prayers to be said as the first three of these were successively dismissed. After the *Sanctus* Basil gives a prayer which runs rapidly through the history of salvation : ' Holy art Thou, God our Creator, who didst place us in the gardens of pleasure, and when we sinned and (in very deed) broke Thy law through the seduction of the serpent, and cut ourselves off from eternal life and went forth from the garden, Thou didst not abandon us for ever but didst visit us by Thy holy prophets and in these last times didst appear to us as we sat in darkness and the shadow of death and didst make to shine on us the light of Thy only Son, who became man through the holy Spirit and the virgin Mary and brought us the way of life . . . and made us a gathered folk and purified us by the Spirit ; for He loved His own that were in the world and gave Himself (of His own free will) to death . . .' The phrases within brackets indicate points that are added in the Ethiopic version but are absent from the Coptic. Thus the stress on the reality of original sin is probably anti-Pelagian, while the emphasis of the voluntary character of Christ's sacrifice might come from the time when there was controversy about the two wills in Christ or it may be anti-Arian. The original text is remarkable for its non-Jewish character ; the prophets are mentioned but not the patriarchs, nor the long list of God's favours to the Jews, which was the mark of some early thanksgiving prayers used in the liturgy. Noticeable too is the freedom with which Basil allows that it is Christ who sends the Spirit on His work of purification ; the Coptic quite explicitly speaks of ' His Spirit '. In the *epiklesis* it is (according to the Coptic) Christ who is asked to send the Spirit, while the Ethiopic, in some copies, has the same sense. If these texts really go back to Basil, they are of very great importance (*see* EPIKLESIS).

The words of Institution (if we may trust later MSS., for here the great Barberini codex fails us) have been made symmetrical by the addition of ' for the forgiveness of sins ' and ' This do in commemoration of Me ' to the words over the bread. The introduction to the words over the chalice speaks of Christ ' mixing ' the chalice before He blessed it, thus giving warrant for the addition of the drops of water. Just before the words over the bread, the priest says that Christ took bread in His hands and *consecrated* it to God His Father. The word used (ἀναδεικνύναι) means normally ' to appoint to an office ', or (as in Hab 3:2 LXX) it may mean ' to reveal ', but it certainly had a sacral use, as Peterson has proved from Greek inscriptions. The word is used again by Basil to designate what the Spirit is being asked to do in the *epiklesis*. Basil thus seems to hold that what Christ did at the Supper is effected by the Spirit at the liturgy, but he does not seem to have asked himself if Christ still operates in the Mass, sending the Spirit now as He did then.

The *Pater noster* in Basil's liturgy came after the Fraction and was introduced by a prelude in which God was asked to ' grant that we may dare with full freedom and without condemnation to call upon Thee as Father . . .' The Greek civic custom of asking for ἄδεια, or immunity from the penalties that were often attached to the making of outrageous proposals in the legislatures, quite naturally explains a similar concern when God was being addressed as Father. A passage in a sermon by Gregory of Nyssa (PG 44:1140–1) on the *Our Father* has some clear echoes of this prayer in Basil. The place of the *Pater*, as a preparation for communion, was due no doubt to the petition for ' daily bread '.

The famous episode in Basil's life when he withstood the emperor Valens, at Epiphany 372, tells us something about his liturgy, but it has been misunderstood by Brightman and others. The story is told by Gregory Nazianzen (*serm.* 43:52 ; PG 36:561). Valens, though an Arian, came into the church where Basil was celebrating the liturgy. He was at once struck by the thunderous waves of psalmody and by the good order observed, at the *bema* and round about it. This *bema* was a raised structure in the centre of the nave, as found in Syria (*see* ANTIOCH, LITURGY OF). Basil himself was on the *bema*, where his throne was, and the seats for the clergy were round him on a somewhat lower level. After Basil's sermon, when the time came for the procession of the gifts, and no one moved forward to take the emperor's, he almost swooned away and would have fallen had not someone reached out from the *bema* and upheld him. The procession formed up and went forward to the altar. The emperor joined it and went up, ' as if sharing membership with us, thrusting himself within the veil ' and then Basil spoke a few words to him, ' words of God indeed ', says Gregory, ' that were heard by us as we were going in with the bishop '. If it be

supposed (as by Brightman) that the *bema* was itself the altar, then the whole incident becomes incoherent. If it be supposed that Valens was at *the altar* when he swooned, it is hard to see how he later went *towards* the altar. The writer in DCB (s.v. Basil) supposed this happened next day.

In 877 the liturgy of Basil was performed at Ravenna in the presence of Charles the Bald, who shared the liturgical interests of his family (cf. Mabillon, *de liturgia Gallicana*, preface). A Latin version was made by Nicholas of Otranto in 1185, and at least two others about the same period. It was printed in Greek at Rome in 1526, and a copy of this print was lent by Stokesley to St John Fisher (see his *de veritate corporis Christi*, 87a, 64a) so that he could use it in controversy with the Lutherans.

The older MSS of Basil's liturgy carry hardly any rubrics, and it is most unsafe to base arguments about what Basil taught in his liturgy on these rubrics as they stand in printed editions. The writer on the Mass among the Greeks in DTC (s.v. *Messe*) tried to make out that the rubrics between the words of institution and the *epiklesis* indicated a belief that transsubstantiation had already taken place, but such a line of argument is not to be trusted. It was once planned that Cardinal Mercati and Edmund Bishop should edit the great Barberini codex of the 8th–9th cents. which contains both Basil's liturgy and Chrysostom's but these plans came to nothing, and though the codex has again been surveyed by Fr Strittmatter OSB the definitive edition has not yet appeared. The text in C. Swainson's *Greek Liturgies* (1884) must still serve.

Bibliography. * P. Trempelas, *The Three Liturgies* (text and commentary in Greek) (1935) ; S. Euringer, ' Die aethiopische Anaphora des heiligen Basilius ', OCP 36 (1934) 138–223 ; A. Strittmatter OSB, ' The Barberini of S. Marco ', *Eph. Lit.* 47 (1933) 329–367, and ' Missa Graecorum ', *Eph. Lit.* 55 (1941) 1–47, and also in *Traditio* 1 (1943) 79–137 ; H. Engberding, *Das eucharistische Hochgebet der Basiliusliturgie* (1931), with the review in OCP 26 (1932) 220–2 ; E. Peterson, 'ἀναδεῖξαι in der Basiliusliturgie ', in *Festgabe für Adolf Deissmann* (1927) ; A. Gelsinger, ' The epiklesis of St Basil ', *Eastern Churches Quarterly* (1954) 243–8 ; J. Doresse, with E. Lanne and B. Capelle OSB, *Un Témoin archaïque de la liturgie copte de s. Basile* (1960).   J. H. C.

BASILIDES, whether a native of Egypt or not, certainly taught his Gnosticism there during the reign of Hadrian (117–38) and into the days of Antoninus Pius (138–61). Eusebius (HE 4:7), who had at his disposal the Catholic reply to Basilides by Agrippa Castor which is now lost, speaks of his founding a school at Alexandria, which must have been prior to the famous catechetical school there. He laid claim to possessing secret Christian traditions coming to him from one Glaucias, a disciple of Peter (Clement, *Stromata* 7:108 ; GCS 17:75), an attempt to rival St Mark in what must already have been his own city. Origen (*hom.* in Lk 1 ; GCS 49:5) says that he ' dared to write a gospel according to Basilides'. Nothing with this title has survived, but among the many apocryphal gospels there are three which were principally used by the Gnostics, those of Thomas (now known from a Coptic version), of Mathias and of Philip. It is curious that Origen in his comment on Luke's opening words about 'those who tried to write gospels' mentions Mathias and Thomas along with Basilides, but not Philip. This might suggest that the gospel of Philip (also extant in Coptic but not yet published) was known to him as that of Basilides. The editors of these new discoveries tell us that the gospel of Philip ' is concerned with the development of the race of the Perfect and the passing from the condition of a Hebrew to that of a Christian', while Irenaeus in his account of Basilides (*adv. haer.* I:xix:3 H) says that he and his followers spoke of themselves as being no longer Jews but not yet become Christians.

Basilides wrote 24 books of *Exegetica* on his gospel, and, if the Jewish manner of commenting practised in those times as seen in the Habacuc commentary and in Akiba was followed, it would not be necessary for him to go outside the framework of his gospel while conveying the whole of his system. There is great dispute about the character of this system, for Irenaeus (*loc. cit.*) has one view of it and Hippolytus (ref. *haer.* 7:20–27; GCS 26:199 ff.) has another. Irenaeus has the common Gnostic emanation scheme: at the beginning of all things an unbegotten Father, from whom is born Nous; from Nous, Logos, and from Logos, Phronesis, and so on down to the 365 angels for an equal number of spheres. Hippolytus holds that Basilides denied all emanation and presented a purely evolutionary system out of an Aristotelian *materia prima* or mustard-seed, which was itself the creation of a non-existent God. (If he meant a super-existent God, he was on the line of thought which led to Plotinus, but we cannot be certain that he did.) Judgment about the value of these two opposed reports on Basilides from antiquity must be reserved until the new Gnostic works are all published. In the meantime one may note that the Gospel of Thomas (in Saying 50 or 51) has a passage which seems to favour the Hippolytean version of Basilides: 'Jesus said, "If they ask you Whence have you come? say to them, We came from the light, the place where the light came into existence through itself alone"'. If light was self-creative, perhaps matter, or the seed-mass, could be also. In the Hippolytean version a three-fold Sonship (described as *consubstantial* with the godhead) emerges from the seed-mass; the first of these, being of refined quality (*leptomeres*) goes quickly to the heavenly spheres, the second, being more dense (*pachymeres*), goes more slowly, and the third (which is ourselves) remains below, needing purgation. The saying of Rom 8:19 that all creation awaits the revelation of the sons of God was used here in a twisted way, and it must be admitted that other bits of exegesis from Basilides are on a par with this. Thus his deduction that St Paul had been a sheep or a bird in a previous existence, from the words of Rom 7:9, was just about as valid (Origen,

Commentary on Rom; PG 14:1015; also *Commentary on Mt* 24:7–8; GCS 38:73). Clement (*Excerpta ex Theodoto* 28; GCS 17:116) adds that he used Deut 5:9 also to prove transmigration of souls.

The catacombs of the Viale Manzoni in Rome (*see* ART AND THE CHURCH, §IV) give some idea of Gnostic habits, particularly of their intermingling of Christian and classical stories. Basilides practised this, for he said that man was like the Trojan horse, being as full of diverse passions as that was of men, and that these passions were appendages and not part of the man himself (Clement, *Strom.* 2:113; GCS 15:174). He also said that the Holy Spirit was like wings attached to the soul, in the manner of Plato's Phaedrus (246a), or like a scented oil that flowed down from the head (Hippolytus *ref. haer.* 7:22; GCS 26:199). It may be inferred from the last passage that Basilides knew some form of confirmation. Baptism was made much of, and the sect kept the feast of Our Lord's baptism on 6 January with an all-night vigil and the readings of Lessons (Clement, *Strom.* 1:145; GCS 15:90). Epiphany baptisms were the rule in some parts of the Church (e.g. Ethiopia), and it need not be assumed that Basilides was a pioneer in this; rather that he was probably following Egyptian church-practice of the time. Baptism was held to forgive only those sins that were indeliberate or due to ignorance (Clement, *Strom.* 4:153; GCS 15:316). Epiphanius (who in his youth had known some of the sect in Egypt) ascribes to them the most revolting practices at the Eucharist, and the same are ascribed to the Manichees by an Egyptian bishop in a pastoral letter (Rylands papyrus 469) of some fifty years earlier. It may be that the Basilidan sect had become assimilated to the Manichees in the course of time and that the practice was not started by Basilides himself. It is reprobated in the Gnostic *Pistis Sophia* (147; GCS 45:251). The words quoted by Epiphanius from their Eucharist may well be traditional in the sect : ' We offer Thee this gift, the Body of Christ, and this is the Pasch by which our bodies have their passion and are compelled to confess the passion of Christ'. The derivation of Pasch from the Greek verb ' to suffer' was accepted in the 2nd cent. by Melito (*hom. on the Pasch*, 46). The sect kept the anniversary of the Passion in March or April, and hence it is hard to believe that Basilides really taught, as some allege, that in the Passion Simon of Cyrene was substituted for Our Lord. This strange idea may be due to some of his followers who wished to rationalize their own unwillingness to face martyrdom for Christian beliefs; if Christ had avoided it in this fashion, so could they.

The chief disciple of Basilides was his son, Isidore, who wrote a book of *Ethics*, thus probably following in his father's Aristotelian line. Clement (*Strom.* 3:1; GCS 15:195) cites this work for its teaching on marriage: ' If your thanksgiving (i.e. eucharist) turns to a beseeching, and you petition for the future, not indeed to go straight but only not to slip away, then marry. But a young man who is poor or depressed may not wish to marry in accordance with this reasoning (or, according to the gospel-word), then let him not separate from his brother. Let him say : " I have come to the holy things ; nothing can befall me." But if he have a suspicion, let him say : " Brother, lay thy hand on me to prevent me sinning ", and he will receive help, spiritual and perceptible.' Many inferences might be drawn from this extract about the liturgy and the spiritual life of the sect. It does not seem to have lasted for long in its primitive state, and the followers whom Epiphanius met in 4th-cent. Egypt were but a degenerate survival.

Bibliography. The article by * F. J. Hort in DCB (s.v. Basilides) is still the best ; new material is briefly described in J. Doresse, *Secret Books of the Egyptian Gnostics* (1960) ; * R. M. Wilson, *The Gnostic Problem* (1958) ; J. Carcopino, *De Pythagore aux apôtres* (1957). J. H. C.

BASLE, COUNCIL OF This Council was in session from 1431 ot 1449, but it is only its early years that have theological significance. It divided its attention between the topics of faith, peace and re-form, for which three Deputations were set up (23 February 1432) soon after the start of its proceedings, while a fourth Deputation *pro communibus* (for day-to-day business) was in reality a vigilance committee to see that the measures of Pope Eugene IV against the Council were held in check. Of these topics, the second, the promotion of peace among Christian rulers, concerns the history of the Church rather than theology, and so the subjects for consideration here will be two, (I) the reduction of heresy, and (II) the attempt to reform the Church by providing it with a federal, instead of a monarchical, constitution.

I The reduction of heresy was the first task of the Council, which received under safe conduct an embassy from the Hussites of Bohemia at the end of 1432 and allowed their representatives (including Peter Payne, the Wycliffite refugee from Oxford) to argue for four months (till 14 April 1433) on their four demands (that the Eucharist be adminis-tered under both kinds (*see* UTRAQUISTS), that public penance be restarted for grave sins, that preaching should be without previous licence, and that the possession of material goods be denied to the secular clergy, who might, however, retain the use of them). Underlying these questions of discipline was the Wycliffite idea that it was the grace of predestination (D 647) which bound the members of the Church to each other and to Christ its Head. If the clergy were habitual sinners, it was, so Peter Payne claimed, the proper thing that the secular arm should deprive them of their possessions. If a priest was excom-municate, that did not take from him (D 644) his right to preach, which came with ordination and which depended on this predestinatory linkage with Christ. Part of the reply to the Hussite envoys took the form of the reading to them by the papal Legate of the Wycliffian articles (D 581–625) which had been drawn up and condemned at Constance in 1418. It was not without significance for the later religious developments in England that Peter Payne, replying to the papal Legate, said that he had been exempted from the anti-Wycliffite oath by King Henry V in England. A theology which gave the Crown the right to despoil the Church would not want for royal protection.

The Hussite envoys returned home with nothing agreed, but they were accompanied by certain repre-sentatives of the Council who managed to win agree-ment for the Compacts of Prague, a set of compro-mise articles which conceded the chalice to the laity but which did not go far enough to suit the extrem-ists in Bohemia. It was the victory in the battle of Lipany (30 May 1434), where the extremist party of the Taborites and Orphans was overcome and its leader, Prokop, killed, rather than any theological compromise, which reduced the Hussite heresy to manageable proportions. This success with the Hussites impressed the Christian princes in favour of the Council but seems to have gone to the heads of those assembled at Basle, for, when Isidore of Kiev and other representatives of the Eastern Church came before them, they were horrified to be told by the Council that they would be treated as heretics. This rebuff was probably a deciding factor in the Greek decision to negotiate with Pope Eugene rather than with the Council.

The other two points of doctrine which occupied the Council, apart from the major struggle with the Papacy, were the Immaculate Conception and the human knowledge of Christ. A treatise by Tor-quemada was presented to the Council in 1437 which attacked the belief in the Immaculate Conception. This treatise was republished by Dr Pusey in 1869 as a reply to Newman. The Council rejected it, deciding that the feast of the Immaculate Conception should be kept as a holiday of obligation, and declar-ing (15 Sept. 1438) that the doctrine that Our Lady, ' at least from the beginning of the infusion of her soul into her body ', was free from original sin was a pious belief that was in accord with Scripture, the faith, reason and the liturgy.

The human knowledge of Christ had been pres-ented by Augustinus Romanus as being almost equal to divine knowledge. His proposition that ' the soul of Christ sees the Godhead as clearly as God sees Himself' was condemned by the Council (15 October 1435) and the Christology of the work where it was found (*De sacramento unitatis Christi et ecclesiae*) seems to have been irregular. Little account has been taken of this decision in subsequent discus-sions on the problem of Christ's knowledge.

II The attempted reform of the Church involved the Council in a direct conflict with the Pope. The calling of the Council had been due to the decision of Constance that Councils should be held at least every seven years. Pope Martin V before his death had agreed to the meeting at Basle and had named Cardinal Giulio Cesarini as his Legate (1 Feb. 1431), dying some twenty days later. The new Pope, Eugene IV, agreed with this act, but just after the Council had at last gathered a reasonable *quorum* and had held its first solemn session (7 Dec. 1431) the

Pope issued (18 Dec. 1431) at Rome a Bull transferring the Council to Bologna, where the Greeks might also be expected to attend. The Council replied by decreeing in its second session (15 Feb. 1432) its own superiority over the Pope, in terms which recalled the pronouncement at Constance. After the Council's success with the Hussites, and under political pressure from the princes, Eugene withdrew (15 Dec. 1433) his many Bulls against the Council (without, however, accepting its decree of conciliar supremacy) and there was harmony for a short time (about fifteen months). Just as he withdrew, Convocation in England decided after long debate (27 Nov. 1433) that Eugene's dissolution of the Council was valid.

The Council had organized itself on a strange plan. It was open to all comers and not merely to bishops. Any ecclesiastic who would take the oath and 'incorporate himself' in the Council might do so, much as one did in the universities of the time. Placemen and fortune-hunters therefore abounded at Basle, and this proclaimed democracy did not please the princes. Henry VI wrote from England (17 July 1433) to express surprise that his envoys had been (in March 1433) asked to take an oath—quite against ordinary usage and canon law—the terms of which they could not fully control. He had hoped that now Christ would awake from sleep and put out a saving hand to Peter's bark, but he was shocked by the intemperate language the Council had been using about the Pope. If they went on as they were doing, the result would be another schism, and that (with the characteristic English understatement) he thought would not increase the fame of the Council. (This letter to the Council is in the letter-books of Thomas Bekynton, later bishop of Bath and Wells, who was then the king's secretary.)

The plan of dividing the members of the Council into deputations cut across the practice of Constance, where the division had been according to nations. In his next set of instructions for his envoys (31 May 1434) Henry VI tells them they are to press for business to be done by national groups (*procedere per nationes*), and here the envoys did their best, putting forward the Joseph of Arimathea legend as a ground for the antiquity of the English nation in Christendom, alongside the four nations already accepted at the Council (i.e. Italian, French, German, Spanish). The English claim for a fifth place was not openly rejected by the Council but does not seem to have been much resorted to in practice ; the Germans (in whose 'nation' the Scots were included) and the Italians favoured the English claim, but the French and Spanish delegates opposed it. This was natural, as Henry VI sent a special embassy to represent him in his rôle of King of France.

In spite of these political cross-currents there was a genuine spirit of reform among the members of the Council. Men like Nicholas of Cusa and Capranica were idealists, and there was manifest a general devotion to the mystical Body of Christ. The theories that moved the men of Basle to devise a new form of government for the Church are in their

origins obscure. It may have been a desire to give the Church the best possible constitution (which according to the political ideas of Aristotle was a mixed régime) ; it may have been an application to Church government of ideas borrowed from the Roman civil lawyers' theory of a corporation, or more immediately it may have been an attempt to reproduce for the government of the Church the machinery of a medieval university. In any case the principle was that of federation. The Deputations (which foreshadow the Roman Congregations of a later century) were rather like the faculties of a university, and they were meant to be in constant session, transacting the business of the Church as it came to them. The Council did not view itself as met for a short period in order to settle disputed points of doctrine. Apart from such legislation (of which there was not much, and that mostly antipapal) the Council acted as executive, sending out Visitors and diverting to itself the streams of papal taxation, and also as judiciary, stopping appeals to the Pope and finally (25 Feb. 1439) declaring Eugene deposed, for heresy.

When Henry VI sent out his envoys a second time to the Council, he (or more probably Chichele, the archbishop of Canterbury) foresaw this possibility of schism and told the envoys that if there was already an anti-Pope when they reached Basle, they were to come straight home ; if they found a majority at the Council bent on such a schism, they were to work for peace and the unity of the Church. This was on 31 May 1434 (Bekynton, *Letters* II, 260) ; two days before that, the Pope had been chased out of Rome by the populace (who declared a republic) and escaped to Florence after hiding under sacking in an open boat as he was rowed down the Tiber. The escape of the Pope to Florence and his continued residence there meant that the Greeks, who were averse to a journey to Rome, could approach the Pope directly without trouble, and this they very soon did. The assembling of the reunion Council with the Greeks at Ferrara, and later at Florence, was due to the acceptance by the Greek emperor and patriarch of the papal invitation and the papal ships, while those hired by the Council from the Genoese had to sail away from Constantinople with their invitation to a meeting at Avignon rejected. Thus, paradoxically, it was the schismatic Greeks who saved the position of the Pope in regard to his rival, the Council of Basle. Even before the failure of the conciliar mission to Constantinople, the *sanior pars* (Cesarini, Capranica, Cusanus and others) had left Basle (between May 1437 and the end of that year), and Henry VI writing to Basle in November 1437 told the Council in plain terms : 'What the Vicar of Christ is joining together, you are seeking to tear apart'. (Bekynton, *Letters* II, 39). In the same month he wrote to the Pope and in his letter spoke of 'the Fathers and those others who are left at Basle', as if not wishing to call this remnant a Council (ibid. 46). In feudal fashion the Council had challenged the Pope to prove his claim by ordeal and he had done so. The majority of Europe soon acquiesced in this result, much as the English and Scots might have done had the bishop of Candida Casa carried through his challenge to the bishop of Norwich to fight him for a decision which was the rightful Pope, during the Western schism in 1389.

The outcome of the Council of Basle has been described as the triumph of Latin ideals of law over Teutonic, but theologically it would be more exact to say that it cleared the ground for the development of the infallibility doctrine. It was now established that, in the words of a papal champion at the Council, 'For a clear and reasonable cause the Pope can change a statute of the universal Church'.[1] The Church was a monarchy, not a federal state. The federal idea might be taken up elsewhere in the Church (e.g. in the balanced constitution chosen by St Ignatius for the new Jesuit order in the next century) but it did not fit the Church as a whole. Only now did the question become insistent that was posed about the guidance imparted by God to that monarchy.

The ecumenicity of the Council of Basle is much debated by canonists. Some hold that it should be accepted up to its 16th Session (5 Feb. 1434), others up to and including Session 25 (7 May 1437), when fighting broke out between the two parties and the minority (which favoured Eugene's plan for the Greeks) finished reading the decree they had supported and burst into a *Te Deum* before the majority party (whose decree was more lengthy) had finished theirs. In any case there was no formal approval by the Pope of the Acts of the Council, for it dragged on until finally (7 April 1449) it passed a decree 'electing' the reigning Pope, Nicholas V, who had by then been Pope for two years.

Bibliography. The *Acts* of the Council are in Mansi, vol. XXIX, and a collection of diaries and other material relating to the Council has been published in eight volumes by J. Haller and others (*Concilium Basiliense: Studien und Quellen* (1896–1936) ; Basle is dealt with in HL VII, where the supplementary material to Hefele's work comes largely from N. Valois, *Le Pape et le Concile 1418–1450* (1909) ; the first volume of Pastor's *History of the Popes* also covers Basle ; H. Jedin, *History of the Council of Trent* I (1957) has much to say on the effects of Basle, and in particular on the attempt to restart it made in 1482 by a Dominican from the Balkans who alleged that the Pope had become a heretic through his forbidding the veneration of the stigmata of St Catherine of Siena ; J. Gill sj, *The Council of Florence* (1959), narrates the story of the rival negotiations of Pope and Council with the Greeks ; V. Martin, *Les Origines du gallicanisme* (1939) ; * E. F. Jacob, *Essays in the Conciliar Epoch* (1952[2]) ; A. Zellfelder, *England und das Basler Konzil* (1913) ; *The Letters of Thomas Bekynton* were edited by G. Williams in the *Rolls Series* (2 vols, 1875) ; the Scottish participation in the Council of Basle is plentifully illustrated by some of the documents collected by J. H. Baxter in *Copiale Prioratus Sancti Andreae* (or The Letterbook

[1] Dominus noster ex certa et rationabili causa potest statutum universalis ecclesiae mutare (*Acts* of Basle, II, 366).

of James Haldenstone) 1930, where a list is given of some forty-two Scots who were incorporated in the Council. One of these, Thomas Livingston, played a large part in the proceedings to depose Eugene IV and to elect an anti-Pope. The federal idea seems to have been popular with the Scots. The *Register of Henry Chichele* (Canterbury and York Society, 1945) vol. III, 245–50 and 262–3 has a report of the proceedings of Convocation in the matter of the Council.   J. H. C.

BEATIFICATION First (I) a brief history will be given of the practice of the Church in proposing certain of her members for veneration because of their noteworthy holiness. (For the theological explanation of this practice, *see* SAINTS, VENERATION OF). Secondly (II) the procedure of Beatification will be described in outline. Then (III) an examination must be made of the precise nature of the decree of Beatification and its relationship with that of Canonization. Finally (IV) the question of the infallibility of the decree of Beatification will be considered.

I Historical Introduction. To understand what is now called Beatification, one must examine the development of the Church's practice of giving some degree of recognition after their death to those of her members who either died as martyrs for the faith or were noted for their virtue. It is the action of the Church which is the critical point. Individual members of the Church from private devotion have always honoured sanctity of life, but it is not mere private veneration which is of interest. How did the Church herself give official recognition to the holiness of her deceased members ?

In the earliest centuries those who first attracted veneration were the martyrs, who included not only those who had died for the faith, but also those who had confessed it by suffering torture or imprisonment without being put to death. Often the veneration was due to popular enthusiasm and, perhaps because of this, by the 4th cent. in at least the African Church, need was felt for careful examination by the bishops of alleged martyrdoms to ensure that honour was not being paid to one who had died for heretical beliefs. If the decision were favourable the veneration acquired a degree of official standing, but normally this would be locally restricted since the liturgical celebrations in honour of the martyr would be held at the site of martyrdom or place of burial. It is true that sometimes a martyr gained a wider veneration, as happened with St Polycarp (d. *c.* 156) and St Cyprian (d. 258), but there does not seem to be evidence that, apart from NT saints, any martyr was formally held in veneration by the whole Church. Apart from the martyrs, from the 4th cent. others also were honoured—bishops who had led lives of great holiness, like Martin of Tours (d. 397), famous monks, such as Antony of Egypt (d. 356). Local bishops, acting individually or in council, gave the official recognition to the veneration of these new types of confessors. In many instances their verdict was expressed by authorization of the translation of the body of the saintly person from a cemetery to a church or, if already buried in church, from a grave to a more honourable position in or above an altar.

One point apparent with the early 'saints' is that there is no difference of title to mark any diversity of recognition given to them. Such terms as *sanctus* and *beatus* were interchangeable, a fact still evidenced in the liturgy, e.g. the 'Confiteor'. It would be meaningless, then, to adopt at this stage the defined terminology of recent centuries, expressive of different degrees of recognition of sanctity. However, it is important to note what led up to the formation of these differences, and in this connection should be mentioned the first clear example of a formal and solemn decision made by a Roman Pontiff. Near the close of the 10th cent. John XV in a council at the Lateran (993) ordered that the memory of Ulric, bishop of Augsburg, should be held in veneration (D 342). From this time it appears that the Holy See is to play a more considerable part in the granting of official approval to the venerating of persons whose sanctity was being discussed. There was need for this, both because of varying practice in deciding who were worthy of veneration and because of undesirable methods of rendering them honour, particularly in the use of their relics. It is in this context that there appeared the declaration of Alexander III (d. 1181), who raised to the altars Edward the Confessor and Thomas of Canterbury, stating that it would not be lawful for a person to be publicly venerated as a saint without the authority of the Roman Church. Whether this declaration is an official reservation of this matter to the Holy See or is a simple statement about a growing practice, is not clear. It is found in a letter to a Swedish king which covers many topics over and above the veneration of saints and, consequently, it cannot be considered a formal declaration, although it does indicate the authoritative concern of the Holy See. After this time some bishops still issued decrees allowing veneration of persons whose holiness had attracted attention. However, in 1634 the definite ruling was made by Urban VIII (d. 1644) that the causes of saints were reserved to the Holy See. And from about the same period the distinction is clearly made between a preliminary stage in the investigations of a cause, a stage culminating in the act of Beatification which allows a person to be called 'Blessed', and a further stage of the same investigations which can terminate in the decisive act of Canonization (*see* CANONIZATION) in which the *beatus* is pronounced a saint.

II Modern Beatification. The present law of the Church repeats the rule of Urban VIII that the causes of saints are reserved to the Holy See (cf. *Codex Iuris Canonici* can. 1999:1), the Sacred Congregation of Rites being in charge of them (CIC canons 253:3 ; 1999:2). This rule does not make diocesan authority completely inoperative. Much of the investigation necessary before Beatification must be conducted under the supervision of the bishop, although at no stage in the proceedings does he on his own authority issue a formal verdict about the sanctity of the person whose cause is being examined. He will see that all this person's writings, published or otherwise, are collected, but they are sent to the Holy See for the verdict about their orthodoxy. He will examine witnesses who can testify to the holiness of the candidate, or to the fact of martyrdom for the faith, or to the reception of favours in the form of miracles due to the intercession of the holy person. Again the evidence is sent to the Holy See. Next, in the normal procedure, it must be ascertained whether or no any of the official forms of veneration reserved for 'beati' or saints has been unlawfully and prematurely shown, for this would be an unwarranted anticipation of the verdict of the Church. In this instance the bishop does pass judgment, but it is subject to confirmation by the Congregation of Rites (cf. CIC canons 2038–86).

The critical stages of the process of Beatification are handled by the Holy See (cf. CIC canons 2065–2124). It decides whether the preliminary procedure has been properly carried out and whether the candidate has a genuine reputation for sanctity. It examines in detail whether the person, if a confessor, possessed in heroic degree the virtues of the Christian life, especially the theological virtues of faith, hope and charity, and the cardinal virtues of prudence, justice, fortitude and temperance. If the cause is for a martyr, it is the reality of the martyrdom which must be established, that is, whether the death was for the faith or the cause of virtue and in fact offered for such a purpose. A favourable verdict allows for the title 'Venerable' to be given, but no form of public veneration may yet be shown. After this comes the detailed examination of the miracles proposed for the cause, unless the requirement of miracles has been dispensed with, as may happen in the case of a martyr. If they are accepted, the way is open for the decree of Beatification.

There are exceptional instances when the whole of the above procedure is not adopted because it is the cause of a person whose veneration had been to a degree officially tolerated in the period between the pontificates of Alexander III and Urban VIII. But there is an examination of the virtues, miracles, or fact of martyrdom, and of the persistence of the veneration (cf. CIC canons 2125–35). If the result is favourable, then the person is considered to be equivalently beatified and may receive the veneration allowed to the ordinary *beatus*.

III The Nature and Force of the Decree of Beatification. The decree of Beatification is a permission from the Holy See for the public veneration of the person whose cause has been considered, and it allows to him or to her the title 'Blessed'. The problem in connection with this decree is the establishing of the precise element which makes it different from Canonization. It might be claimed that a Beatification is not directed, as Canonization is, to the universal Church, the veneration allowed to a *beatus* being very restricted, above all in locality, e.g. for a particular country or diocese (cf. CIC canons 1277:2). Yet it is said by R. Naz (in the 'Dictionnaire de droit canonique', Tome 3ᵉ (1942) col. 10 ' *Causes de béatification et canonisation* ') that the veneration of a *beatus* could be allowed to the whole Church. The difference might be sought, then, in the fact that the veneration of a canonized saint is imposed by the Church, whereas the honouring of the beatified person is something permitted but not ordered. But against this it is maintained that even in the case of a *beatus* veneration can be imposed by the Church—cf. F. Wernz-P. Vidal sj, ' *Ius Canonicum* ', Tomus 4, ' *De Rebus* ', Vol. 1 (1934) section 459.

The solution of the problem must be found, it would seem, in the relationship between Beatification and Canonization within the context of the whole procedure of the cause of a saint. Beatification is essentially no more than the close of the extended preparatory part of the procedure. It is true that it is an official recognition of sanctity ; that the honour to be paid to the *beatus* no longer need be private veneration. But the cause remains incomplete and, in consequence, the decree of Beatification cannot be considered a definitive verdict. Such a verdict will be given only if the cause is completed by being taken through its final stages and these result in a decree of Canonization. The precise element, therefore, constituting the difference between the two is that Beatification lacks the definitive nature which solely belongs to Canonization. For this reason while it is true that the veneration of a *beatus* might be ordered, yet it will not be imposed on the universal Church, because that would imply that the Church had completely committed herself to the recognition of this person's sanctity. And a regulation governing the art-representations of saints and *beati* illustrates the point just established. Whereas the head of the saint may be represented as crowned, or surrounded by the nimbus of glory, that of the beatified person may be surrounded only by separate rays, a symbol of lesser significance.

IV Infallibility. The final matter to be raised is whether the decree of Beatification can be regarded as infallible. Recalling that bishops, on their own or in local councils, used to issue decrees of Beatification, infallibility would not be expected, since bishops do not enjoy the prerogative of infallibility other than when teaching as a united body under the authority of the Pope. However, as Beatification has been reserved to the Holy See, it still remains possible that a papal decree might be regarded as infallible, as is the papal decree of Canonization. But even here distinctions are made. Before 1912 the process for equivalent Beatification concentrated on the historical fact of the veneration paid to the popularly recognized *beatus*. The papal decree did little more than recognize this fact and had much less import than a formal decree of Beatification and, in consequence, it does not merit to be ranked among even possible infallible decisions. But the formal decree, with which can be associated that of the present equivalent process, is issued by the apostolic authority of the Pope and is drawn up in a language of some solemnity. The infallibility of this decree can be considered a possibility.

To settle this point, note must be taken of the character of an infallible decree (*see* INFALLIBILITY OF THE CHURCH and INFALLIBILITY OF THE POPE). It is expressed in terms indicating the plenitude of authority and also indicating the definitive nature of what is being given to the faithful as something imposed on the whole Church. All this is lacking in a decree of Beatification. It is not formulated as from the plenitude of papal authority ; it is not definitive, since it is only the decree of Canonization which contains the definitive verdict about a person's sanctity ; nor is it a decree imposed on the universal Church. The conclusion, then, would seem to be that a decree of Beatification is not infallible. This is the view adopted by Pope Benedict XIV in his work on Beatification and Canonization, ' Although from the preceding remarks it could be deduced that a person daring to say that the Roman Pontiff had erred in a particular formal Beatification, or claiming that in the locality where the Pope permitted it veneration should not be given to a ' *beatus* ', has said something temerarious or deserving of more serious theological censure, yet it cannot be laid down with certainty that the decision in a formal Beatification is infallible or that it is a matter of faith '.[1] Some confirmation is given to the view from the fact that at one period, until the time of Clement IX (d. 1669), the process of Canonization involved a complete re-examination of what had been studied for the cause of Beatification, an unlikely and unnecessary procedure if the latter had been infallible.

It would follow from what has been said that there is the possibility of error in a decree of Beatification. That no error has in fact happened must be accepted when Beatification is followed by Canonization. That error is unlikely may be maintained for those causes which have been subjected to the thorough examination used by the Holy See, though it must be recognized that a later discovery of unfavourable data may create the necessity for revising a decision which is in no way considered to be final and irrevocable. Where Beatification has come about by other ways, such as those found in the earlier periods of its history, there is scope for a prudent reserve over the reliability of the historical foundations of some of them, although the occurrence of mistaken Beatifications may safely be considered a rare event owing to the general protection of God for His Church.

Bibliography. Apart from the works referred to above, the following also treat of Beatification : T. Ortolan, ' *Béatification* ', DTC 2:493–6 ; A. Smith CRL, ' *The Processes of Beatification and Canonization* ', pp. 43–76 in ' *The English Martyrs* ' ed. by

[1] Sed, quamvis ex hoc inferri possit, temeritatis, aut gravioris theologicae censurae nota esse afficiendum, qui auderet asserere Romanum Pontificem in hac vel illa formali Beatificatione errasse ; aut contenderet, non esse Beato exhibendum cultum eo in loco, in quo Papa indulget, ut exhiberi queat : concludi tamen certo non potest, vel ipsum formalis Beatificationis judicium esse infallibile, aut ad Fidem pertinere . . . ' *De Servorum Dei Beatificatione et Beatorum Canonizatione.*' (1766) 1:42:10.

B. Camm OSB (1929) ; * E. W. Kemp, ' *Canoniza-tion and Authority in the Western Church* ' (1948).

D. F.

BEATIFIC VISION or the Intuitive Vision of God. In this treatment (I) The Beatific Vision is described ; (II) the supernatural character of the Vision is considered ; (III) its possibility is established ; (IV) the necessity of the Light of Glory is indicated ; (V) the object and extent of the Beatific Vision are examined, and finally (VI) some consequences of this privilege are pointed out.

I By **Beatific Vision** we understand that knowledge of God which will constitute our eternal happiness in heaven. Then we shall see no longer as ' through a glass darkly, but face to face ' (1 Cor 13:12). The term ' Vision ', derived from corporeal vision is used to denote the clarity and distinction of this knowledge. God Himself becomes the immediate object of our perception. No longer is this object merely an idea of God derived from things other than God ; God Himself in his essence takes the place of the idea in the mind. Nothing, therefore, intervenes between the mind and God. God Himself is in the mind, being present to our understanding as He is to His own understanding. Thus we know Him as He knows Himself.

II Supernatural character. While there are those who have maintained that the Beatific Vision is, in some sense, natural or due to human nature (*see* BAIUS and JANSENISM), Sacred Scripture and Tradition and, indeed, reason, indicate otherwise. For, to see God as He is not only is shown to be the reward or consequence of what is not due to nature, but it is explicitly indicated that this manner of knowledge is proper to God Himself. 1 Jn 3:1 shows the connection between vision and the adoption of Sons ; Jn 17:3, in conjunction with Rom 6:23 ; 8:13, shows that eternal life, which consists in the knowledge of God, is by grace. The essential preparation for glory is grace and the essential part of glory is the beatific vision. The beatific vision therefore comes by grace, and if by grace, then it is not due to nature.

But further, since it is shown that this manner of knowledge is proper to God Himself, God being beyond the sight of any creature, dwelling in ' inaccessible light ' (1 Tim 6:16), ' whom no man has seen at any time ' (Jn 1:18), the direct vision of God must be said to be beyond the capacity of any creature and therefore absolutely supernatural. Mt 11:27 (Lk 10:22), Jn 1:18 ; 6:46 ; 1 Cor 2:11 indicate that this knowledge belongs properly only to the Father, Son and Holy Ghost. We cannot therefore approve the teaching of Ripalda who, agreeing that the beatific vision is beyond the capacity of existing creatures, nevertheless thought it possible for God to create a creature to whom such vision would be natural. St John Chrysostom speaks for all the Fathers when he says, '. . . but what God really is, not only have not the Prophets seen, but not even angels, nor archangels . . . But the Son only beholds Him, and the Holy Ghost. How can any

created nature even see the Uncreated ? ' (*hom. in Jn 15*).

The reasoning of the Schoolmen, following the well-known principle, ' the manner of acting does not exceed the manner of being ', is clear. The manner of being in the creature is potential and finite ; therefore the manner of knowing natural to the creature is potential and finite. But the intuitive vision is knowledge whereby God is known according to the manner of being proper to God, which is not potential and finite. Therefore it is not natural to any creature. Some difficulty is found in the fact that St Thomas seems to teach that there is a natural desire in man of the beatific vision. It is argued that man cannot have a truly innate natural desire for something beyond his nature, so that the presence of this desire in man would indicate that he has a natural capacity for the intuitive vision. On the other hand, St Thomas certainly teaches explicitly that the beatific vision is supernatural. Interpreters are not agreed as to how St Thomas's doctrine of desire is to be understood, but it seems clear that it cannot be such as would indicate that the beatific vision is not entirely supernatural (*see* DESIRE OF GOD).

The supernatural character of the beatific vision, at least as regards existing creatures, was defined by the Council of Vienne in 1311 (D 474).

III Possibility of the Beatific Vision. That the Blessed in heaven do, in fact, enjoy the beatific vision was defined by Benedict XII in the Constitution *Benedictus Deus* (D 530). This teaching was confirmed by the Council of Florence in the Decree for the Greeks (D 693). Therefore we know that what is not possible naturally to the creature is made possible by gift of God.

This future privilege of the Just is described by St Paul (1 Cor 13:9ss) contrasting present imperfection with future perfection. 1 Jn 3:2 is possibly to be understood merely as vision of the Humanity of Christ, but it is difficult to believe that that is all the Apostle meant and, in fact, the text is commonly understood to refer to the direct vision of God. Moreover, '. . . their angels in heaven always see the face of My Father ' (Mt 18:10).

Some of the Fathers, e.g. St Cyril of Jerusalem and St John Chrysostom, appear to deny the possibility of the beatific vision, but it must be understood what they had in mind ; either to deny the corporal vision of God, or the beatific vision in this life ; or else to deny the comprehensive vision of God as it was taught by the Eunomians.

Total comprehension of God is not possible to the creature, who, being raised to the beatific vision, does not thereby become infinite. To comprehend totally the infinite act requires infinite power, which cannot be conferred on a creature. ' Therefore he who sees God's essence sees in Him that He exists infinitely and is infinitely knowable ; nevertheless this infinite mode does not extend to enable the knower to know infinitely ; as, for instance, a person can have a probable opinion that a proposition is demonstrable although he himself does not know how it is demonstrated.' (St Thomas, *Summa* 1a:2:3:@7.)

Theologians admit that the beatific vision was enjoyed in this life by Christ in his human nature. Christ apart, there is no certain evidence that anyone has enjoyed this grace on earth, and its enjoyment would seem to involve consequences that it would be difficult to admit. Thus the experience of St Paul (2 Cor 12:2ss) was something beyond just another ecstasy. Yet it is not suggested that St Paul had a foretaste of the beatific vision (CCS *ad. loc.*). For if this experience is beatific, then it is final. True beatitude cannot be for a time, but must be permanent. St Paul's suggestion is that, having been caught up to the third heaven, he returned to earth again. Had he been caught up to the highest heaven we must say that there could be no question of return but he must remain there. St Thomas held that it is quite impossible to enjoy the vision in this life. Origen (*hom. in Isai* 1:5 ; GCS 33:247) says that Isaias was put to death by the Jews because his claim to have seen God (Is 6:5) was contrary to the teaching of Ex 33:20.

IV The Light of Glory. Anything other than a true vital act of the created intellect is not the beatific vision as Catholic theology understands it. To conceive it as the uncreated act by which God knows Himself and which in some mysterious way is communicated—were that possible—to the creature, or as a created act but produced by God and infused into the intellect, would be to misunderstand it. The act of the beatific vision is the created intellect's own act, an act of which it is incapable naturally but of which it is made capable supernaturally. Therefore we understand that the light of glory, which is simply the God-given capability of the intellect whereby itself knows God in God's own way, is essential to the beatific vision. 'Since the natural power of the created intellect does not avail to enable it to see the essence of God . . ., it is necessary that the power of understanding be added by ' Divine grace'. (*Summa* 1a:12:5). This is also clear from the relationship between grace in this life and glory in the next life. The supernatural acts of this life are deployed towards the supreme supernatural act— the beatific vision—hereafter : sanctifying grace, whereby present supernatural acts are possible, is deployed towards the light of glory. ' For the light of glory is merely the sequel of sanctifying grace ; it is the same entity, the same spiritual reality ; the difference between sanctifying grace and the light of glory, if there be any, would be merely the difference between youth and mature age in the same individual ' (Vonier, *The Human Soul*).

V Object and Degrees of Vision. It is constant Catholic teaching, derived from Sacred Scripture, the Fathers and the Councils, that the Beatific Vision is not equal in all men. The same will be clear from the relationship between grace and the light of glory, in that a greater degree of the one will involve a greater degree of the other, and the greater degree of the light of glory signifies a greater capacity to see God. There is a difficulty here. The

beatific vision signifies knowledge of the whole being of God, of His existence which is His essence. All therefore see the whole being of God and all with direct clarity. Yet a greater degree of the light of glory gives a greater capacity to see the whole being of God, or to know Him more intensively.

To find some explanation of the degrees of the beatific vision we must make a distinction between its primary object—God Himself as He is—and the secondary object—things other than God, which are seen in God. Whoever sees God totally or comprehensively sees also in God whatever is founded in the Divine essence or, as St Thomas puts it, knows whatever God does or can do. Thus God knows Himself. The creature who sees God but sees Him less than totally will not know all that God can do but only so far as the intensity of his knowledge of God allows him to see what God can do. The greater the intensity of the vision of the essence of God, the greater the extent of the truths seen in God. ' It is clear that the more perfectly a cause is seen, the more of its effects can be seen in it. For whoever has his intellect sufficiently uplifted by one demonstrative principle, can receive at once from it the knowledge of many conclusions. But this is beyond the power of a weaker intellect needing things to be explained to it separately. And so that intellect, which knows the cause wholly, can know all the effects of the cause in the cause itself. No created intellect in seeing God can know all that God does or can do ; for this would be to comprehend His power ; but of what God does or can do any intellect can know, the more perfectly it sees God ' (*Summa* 1a:2:8).

VI Consequences of the Vision. ' Beatitude is not of the nature of the creature, but is its end ' (*Summa* 1a:62:4). In the Beatific Vision man is presented with a final end which exceeds his nature ; the only final end, in fact, which is proposed for him. It follows that human nature can be properly judged, in fact, only in relation to this supernatural end. Human nature can only properly fulfil its destiny in striving after what is, in fact, beyond its natural capacity. God's grace enables it to do this. Moral conduct based merely on the dictates of natural reason is not sufficient. Moral philosophy betrays its insufficiency in having to judge human nature in relation to a non-existent natural end. The man of natural philosophy is not a complete man because he is not seen in relation to his true final end. The complete ethic is only that which is perfected by revelation. The complete man is only he who is perfected by grace which leads to glory.

Bibliography. L. Billot SJ, *De Deo uno* (1935) ; J. B. Franzelin SJ, *De Deo uno* (1883) ; G. H. Joyce SJ, *Principles of Natural Theology* (1924) ; B. Lavaud OP, Moïse et S. Paul, ont-ils eu la vision de Dieu dès ici-bas ?, in RT 35 (1930) 75-83 ; H. Lennerz SJ, *De Deo uno* (1940) ; J. O'Mahony, *Desire of God in the Philosophy of St Thomas* (1928) ; A. Vonier OSB, *The Human Soul* (1913) ; H. Pope OP, *The Beatific Vision*, in Cambridge Summer School volume entitled *God*

(1931) ; A. Van der Meersch, 'De intuitiva Dei visione', ETL 7 (1930).　　　　　　K.

BEAUTY, IN THEOLOGY. *See* IMAGO DEI, and EXISTENCE OF GOD.

BEDE THE VENERABLE, INFLUENCE OF St Bede the Venerable (673–735) is an outstanding example of that Christian humanism which was not by any means the least important contribution to civilization made by the monasteries in Europe in the period preceding the descent of what are called the Dark Ages. Since the second century there had been evolving, though not without a great deal of misgiving on all sides, an ideal blending of classical learning and theology, enriched by liturgical and personal prayer, which found its home and flourished in the monasteries. The philosophical aspects of this culture, especially the neo-Platonism then prevalent, had, however, less of an appeal for Bede than for others. He is more in the tradition of Basil or Ambrose than of Augustine or Boethius. It is not surprising, therefore, that this period, also one of vigorous growth for the Church in England, gave us the only one of the English nation to be honoured with the title of Doctor of the Church.

Although there have been a number of first-rate studies on Bede within recent years, we are still not yet in a position to assess fully his place in the history of theology. The reason for this lies mainly in the fact that only a fraction of his commentaries on scripture have appeared in modern critical editions with the sources he used clearly indicated. Even so, some tentative conclusions may be drawn. These are best summed up in the words of Laistner : 'Bede's importance lies not in his original ideas, but in the selfless devotion with which he digested much of the learning and doctrine of the Fathers and passed it on in a simpler and more intelligible form to his own people and to later generations. The manner in which, in a comment of moderate length on a scriptural passage, he will fuse into an organic whole quotations and adaptations from several authorities together with some observations of his own proves him a clear thinker and an admirable teacher . . . In selecting and adapting so much of the teaching of the great Church Fathers for his own pupils and for those that followed after, Bede performed a service of immense value to mediaeval students of theology.' Hence, far from considering Bede as no more than a felicitous compiler of information from earlier sources, we must regard him as a strategic link between the earlier and later Middle Ages.

It is also interesting to note the growth of Bede's own mind. In comparing the *Commentary on the Acts of the Apostles* with the later *Retractation* covering the same book, Laistner observes : ' All through [the *Retractation*] there appears to be much more of Bede's own thought and far greater independence of authorities than in his other exegetical works.' The same progress may be noted by contrasting his earlier commentaries on Mark and Luke with the fifty extant homilies on the Gospels. The commentaries on the two Gospels are, for the most part, a mosaic of passages from Ambrose, Augustine, Jerome and Gregory the Great, as Bede himself readily admits. But the homilies are quite different. While including often similar scriptural passages, they mark their author as a mature thinker. Bede had read more widely in his later years, as the more extensive use of sources in the homilies shows. His *Ecclesiastical History of the English People*, continued down to the year 731, stands out among the chronicle-histories of that age and makes him indeed the father of English history.

From the period immediately following Bede's death, when Boniface was writing from Germany back to England to have copies of Bede's works sent to him, until the 13th cent., when Thomas Aquinas used Bede fairly extensively in compiling his *Summa*, the English Doctor was regarded as highly as any other ecclesiastical writer. If from this time on his works were less frequently used, so were those of the rest of the Fathers. A new type of learning had captivated men's minds ; theology no longer held the lead as the primary subject of human investigation. Today, however, biblical theology has again gained popularity, and with the renewed interest in the writings of the earlier Fathers, Bede too has been brought back into favour. Together with Jerome's exposition of the Gospel of St Matthew, Ambrose's of St Luke and Augustine's of St John, Bede's commentary on the Gospel of St Mark constitutes about as excellent an interpretation of the Gospels as has ever been produced.

Though he roundly condemned the extremes of Origen and of his followers, Bede, whether he realized it fully or not, was a follower of Origen in adopting the allegorical or spiritual interpretation of the scriptures. He used it with greater restraint and moderation, and there is always a severely practical turn to all of his exegesis. Like Origen, he saw the Christian message as a unified whole. The complete message of God to man, the Old Testament with the New, the Church's tradition and practices, especially as found in her liturgical worship, all were explored by Bede to gain an insight into the fullest implications of revealed truth for mankind.

No-one agrees precisely when the patristic age closed—did it end with Isidore, Bede or Bernard ? And both Boethius and the Carthusian Bruno, in widely separated centuries, have been called the ' father of scholasticism '. The truth of the matter is that, while the manner of exposition may differ from time to time and the emphasis may be placed now on this, now on that question, the continuity in the unfolding and presentation of the Church's traditional teaching is remarkably gradual and close-knit, and Bede's place in this development is one of prime importance.

Bibliography. A. H. Thompson (ed.), *Bede, His Life, Times, and Writings* (Oxford 1935) ; G. F. Browne, *The Venerable Bede, His Life and Writings* (London

1930); B. Capelle, 'Le Rôle théologique de Bède le Vénérable', *Studia Anselmiana* vi (1936) 1–40 ; R. W. Chambers, ' Bede ', *The Proceedings of the British Academy* xxii (1936) 129–56 ; R. Davis, ' Bede's Early Reading ', *Speculum* viii (1933) 179–95 ; M. L. W. Laistner, *A Hand-List of Bede MSS* (Ithaca, N.Y. 1943), *Thought and Letters in Western Europe, A.D. 500 to 900* (London 1931) 121–9, ' Bede as a Classical and a Patristic Scholar ', *Trans. of the Royal Hist. Soc.* xvi (1933) 69–94 ; W. Stubbs, *s.v.* Beda, DCB i:300–4. Of Bede's scriptural commentaries, only the *Commentary on the Acts of the Apostles* and *Retractation* (edited by Laistner, Cambridge, Mass. 1939) and the *Homilies* (CCS 122, *Opera homiletica et rhythmica*) are available in annotated critical editions. The following are being prepared for the *Corpus Christianorum* series : *Commentary on Genesis (Hexameron)*, *Commentary on the Prayer of Habakkuk*, *Commentary on St Mark*, *Commentary on St Luke*, *Collectaneum on the Pauline Epistles*, *Commentary on the Catholic Epistles*. For the other works, one still depends on Giles's edition of the *Opera omnia* (London 1844), which was used by Migne PL 90–5 in 1850, while for the historical works there is Plummer's edition (Oxford 1896). C. W. Jones has edited the *Opera de Temporibus* (Cambridge, Mass. 1943). D. H.

BEING. *See* ANALOGY

BELIEF. *See* APOLOGETICS

BELLARMINE, INFLUENCE OF This article is concerned simply with the importance of St Robert Bellarmine as a theologian, and therefore does not deal with his many activities—as archbishop of Capua, in his dealings with Galileo and Giordano Bruno, or in his work on the Vulgate—which do not strictly affect his theological position. After a short statement of the essential biographical facts (I), there will be exposed (II) the debit side of the account (for Bellarmine is today sometimes blamed for mis-directing theological thought), and after this (III) his personal contributions to the progress of theology will be briefly described.

I Robert Bellarmine was born at Montepulciano in Tuscany, 4 Oct. 1542, and became a Jesuit in 1560 in Rome. After noviceship and philosophical studies there and a short period of teaching at Genoa he began his theology at Padua (1567), where he tells us that he listened to the lectures of Fr Claudio Pharaon, who expounded the theory of predestination *post praevisa merita*, while the young Bellarmine wrote in his notebooks Augustine's theory of gratuitous predestination. He went to Louvain soon after starting his theological studies, travelling in the company of Cardinal Allen, and was ordained there. Ruard Tapper was then chancellor of the university and one of his professors was Ravesteyn, who attacked Baius. In old age Bellarmine said that, under God, he owed his learning, such as it was, to his seven years' stay at Louvain. He began to lecture there (17 October 1570), compiling for

his own use the *de scriptoribus ecclesiasticis* (afterwards published) which betokened a wide reading of the Fathers. Nicholas Sander was at Louvain at the time, but Stapleton was probably all that time at Douay, so that the two may not have met. Bellarmine's great success at Louvain led to his being brought back to Rome, where he began to deliver his lectures on the *Controversies*, 26 Nov. 1576. The book was first published in 1586 and was put on the Index in 1590 by Sixtus V (along with the works of Francis de Vitoria) on account of its maintaining that the Pope was not the temporal lord of the whole world. The Pope who followed Sixtus reigned for no more than twelve days, but he managed to remove this stigma from Bellarmine's work, brief though the ban had been.

In 1597 Bellarmine became theological adviser to Pope Clement VIII and in 1599 was made Cardinal. In 1604–5 there took place his controversy with James I of England, and he was afterwards much concerned in the matter of the oath of loyalty which James, with the connivance of the lapsed Jesuit, Christopher Perkins (Dean of Carlisle), sought to impose on his Catholic subjects. This led Bellarmine into more controversy with Fr Thomas Preston OSB (*alias* Roger Widdrington), who published a book against Bellarmine. The answer which Bellarmine composed is still lying unpublished in the Vatican library, but it has been quite fully used by F. X. Arnold in his study *Die Staatslehre des Kardinal Bellarmin* (1934). It is in this unpublished work, and under the stress of controversy, that Bellarmine elaborated his views on the indirect power of the papacy in temporal affairs. Bellarmine died on 17 Sept. 1621.

II Bellarmine as a theologian has been attacked in recent times for having had a large share deflecting the trend of theological thought into blind alleys, deviations or worse. One of these charges, made by Geiselmann, rests on the assumption that Bellarmine had only the text of the decrees of Trent to go upon and no knowledge of what had taken place in the debates which led up to those decrees. In consequence he (along with Canisius) is supposed to have misled posterity about the true import of the Tridentine decree on Scripture and Tradition and to have pioneered a misleading division of the Word of God into what is written (in Scripture) and what is handed on (in Tradition), as if these were two separate entities. This view is alleged to have prevented him and his readers from allowing that the whole of the revelation is somehow contained in Scripture and from giving to the Scriptures their proper reverence. Geiselmann's view has been under fire in Germany and he has admitted that he had overlooked the part played by Melchior Cano in expounding the decrees of Trent, a man whose work Bellarmine had used and who stood so much nearer to the Council and its debates. It is true that Bellarmine cites among his authorities the *Catechism* of Canisius, but he also used Pedro de Soto's work, and it must be recalled that Soto had been at the Council and had afterwards been in England with Cardinal

Pole, being assigned the task of combating Protestant theology at Oxford, a task in which he was, by the admission of Bishop Jewel, quite successful. Bellarmine had other links with the Council. The Jesuit, Jay, had taken part in the debates about Tradition and had proposed some emendations to the draft, which were accepted. Now Jay was joined by Canisius after he had been for a year at the Council, and the two men together acted as theologians to the Cardinal of Augsburg. In view of the fact that very soon Calvin brought out a tract in which he attacked the early proceedings of the Council, it is very improbable that Canisius simply took over the decree of Trent without getting some kind of gloss on it from Jay, and Bellarmine could have had this from Canisius. Equally he might have had information from the entourage of his uncle Marcello Cervini, one of the papal Legates, or from the English exiles he met at Louvain in 1570. In any case, those who accept Geiselmann's view have to prove the negative, that he did not receive such explanations. For the dogmatic point itself, that Trent had altered the draft (which said that revelation was contained *partly* in Scripture and *partly* in Tradition) in favour of a neutral wording which said merely that it was contained in Scripture *and* Tradition, there is no substance in it. The whole decree is at pains to say that one must accept Scripture and Tradition *with equal reverence*, and this quite clearly treats the two sources as independent factors in the transmission of revelation. It was this phrase which excited far more comment than the other, and yet this one was retained by a large majority-vote. It would seem then that this charge against Bellarmine is groundless.

Another charge against him is that he sent into circulation a theology of the notes of the Church which has proved to be a block to the development of the doctrine of the Church. One can admit that some of Bellarmine's fifteen *notes* were sketchy and provocative, as when he suggests that temporal happiness attends on the defenders of the true Church and that its enemies die miserably. Interminable arguments about the comparative prosperity of Catholic and Protestant countries derive from such a claim, and it may be said that here Bellarmine was indulging his baroque fondness for profusion and for overwhelming the adversary by abundance of argument, for these are at the end of his list. His main attack, on the lines of the Nicene creed (with its four adjectives for the Church), was an effective reply to Luther's selection of notes, which would identify the Church by the true preaching of the gospel, a vernacular liturgy and tribulations within and without, along with one or two more ill-assorted features.

The plain fact is that Bellarmine found this kind of argument forced upon him and he conducted his side of it so effectively that theologians in later times have been spared much of the trouble that the Reformation would otherwise have caused them. Arius and Nestorius were equally troublesome in their times, and it would be wiser to look for development in theology arising out of these controversies

of the Reformation rather than to lament the lack of it because of them. It may be that the present time is still too close to that age for the development to be clearly visible, but one may hazard the idea that the order chosen by Bellarmine for his work (the Word of God, Christ, the Pope, the Church), while it had practical advantages for the moment, in concentrating the debate on the papal authority, made it inevitable that the Church should one day have to define what that authority was, and also drew away attention from possible dogmatizing about the position of bishops in the Church. Similarly the fact that Bellarmine had to insist on the visible character of the Church meant that he gave less attention to the way in which its members are linked by grace, and thus the modern developments in the theology of the Mystical Body owe very little to him. (Dean Colet, just before the Reformation, wrote at length on the Mystical Body, but it would be hard to find another great theologian who did, until the time of Scheeben.)

III On the credit side one may point out that the doctrine of marriage as a permanent sacrament, enunciated by Pius XI (D 2238 and AAS 22 (1930) 583), owed much of its development to the theological insight of Bellarmine. The idea is adumbrated in Augustine, at a time when the theology of the sacraments was rudimentary, and it was Bellarmine who made the comparison between marriage and the Eucharist, both sacraments having an event as their ' becoming ' and a state of permanence as their being. From him the idea was taken by Sanchez, and, though repudiated even in modern times (e.g. by such authors as Pohle-Preuss), it has been largely used since its adoption by Pius XI.

Another merit of Bellarmine's work is the defence he undertook of the liturgy against Calvinist iconoclasm. At the end of his *Controversy* on the worship of the saints (*de ecclesia triumphante*, III) he added a short tract on the dedication of churches, on feasts and fasts and the distinction of days (Rom 14:5) which is still useful and which in an age that saw but the beginnings of liturgical scholarship was remarkable. Internal worship belongs to the New Testament, he lays down, while external belonged to the Old. ' We say that fear was the property of the Law and love of the Gospel, and yet God required the Jews to love Him with their whole heart. The patriarchs and prophets did so and thus belonged to the New dispensation, for they were able to do this, not from the letter of the Law but from the spirit of grace. In a similar way we maintain that external worship is proper to the Law, though it cannot be pleasing to God without internal, while internal worship is proper to the Gospel, though without external it cannot exist.' (ibid. ch. IV). It was a long time before theologians generally turned their attention to the liturgy, and in the meantime this balanced view of Bellarmine's was drawn upon very widely. Even in the liturgical encyclical of Pius XII (AAS 39 (1947) 530–1) the relation of internal to external worship is not put more clearly than by Bellarmine. Bellarmine was perforce very explicit in his teaching on the working of the sacraments 'of themselves' (*ex opere operato*), as distinct from the efforts of the recipient, and his two chapters (VIII and XI in book II, Of the sacraments in general) of reasoning on this theological question are a notable development, where he showed his personal quality as a theologian. Here, too, he was indebted to the Tridentine decrees for his starting point, but no one has accused him of misunderstanding them this time. So many manuals and popularizing works have drawn upon his ideas in the course of the last three centuries that his work has here become a part of the tradition.

On the indirect power of the Pope in temporal affairs Bellarmine was for long the accepted authority. In his own day he was heavily involved in controversy with James I of England about it and he was also attacked by some Catholics, who are sometimes styled 'hierarchs' from their desire to defend the thesis (rejected by Francis de Vitoria and by Bellarmine) that the Pope was the *dominus orbis* or Lord of the world. For Bellarmine the power of the Pope is spiritual in itself and is to be extended to the temporal order only on occasion (*casu*). This occasion arises owing to some serious reason, a matter of faith, the salvation of souls, or some necessity of the Church. (He does not use the words *ratione peccati*, by reason of sin, which are so often attributed to him.) Judgment about this occasion rests with the Pope, but he may not 'at his pleasure falsely devise necessities', and he must always act in view of a spiritual end. When he does intervene in the temporal order he should either give positive guidance or reprove. He cannot ordinarily assume civil jurisdiction, but, when two kings are in conflict and there is no one to decide, or when those who should give judgment are unwilling to do so, he may act.

In theorizing about the power of the Pope with regard to States Bellarmine was not at a very high level of abstraction. He sometimes speaks of the Church when he means the commonwealth of Christians as it had existed in the Middle Ages, and his vision of the future may well have been of a condition where that commonwealth would exist again. (He once said that he thought the world could not go on much longer, as it was so wicked.) He was hampered in his thought by some of the metaphors dear to the medieval canonist (such as that of soul and body as representing the relation of the two powers) and his examples were mainly drawn from the dealings of the papacy with the Holy Roman Empire. Had he been more familiar with the common-law countries and with the contractual theories behind the English coronation oath, he might have brought his theory more into relation with the world that was to come after the Peace of Westphalia (*see* CHURCH AND STATE).

After the appearance of Bellarmine's *Controversies* the Roman College of the Jesuits had no need of a Professor of Controversies until 1660; that is the measure of Bellarmine's importance for his own day. St Francis of Sales in his conversion of the Chablais took with him no other books but the Bible and Bellarmine; many lesser men were in like case.

John Williams, archbishop of York under James I and Lord Keeper, gained his doctorate in divinity at Cambridge in 1617 by defending the propositions that the supreme ruler of the state cannot be excommunicated and that the taking away of the chalice (from the laity) is a mutilation of the sacrament of the Eucharist; here, too, Bellarmine was in the foreground of the debate. Even as late as the Vatican Council passages from Bellarmine were used to annotate the *schema* proposed for consideration on papal infallibility, and Bellarmine was frequently appealed to by the speakers, though at the end it was from Cardinal Pole that the ideas were drawn which Cardinal Cullen put into the revised formula which won general acceptance. Bellarmine's debt to Stapleton and the English exiles at Louvain has never been estimated, but it must have been considerable. He himself allowed that he had taken his idea of congruism from the Louvain theologian, Ruard Tapper, and he held to this through all the controversy about grace (*see* CONGRUISM). It may well be that other theological ideas were absorbed at that formative stage in his development which he afterwards expounded so valuably for the whole Church. His fair-mindedness in giving all the arguments of his adversaries before he demolished them was noted in his own day, and his complete candour can be appreciated now, when so much more of the inner history of that age can be read. Thus it was that he incurred rustication to Capua for speaking frankly to Pope Clement VIII on the controversy about grace and for telling him that he might damp down the fires of dispute, or call a general council, but that he could not issue a definition, as the question was still far too complex and unclear. With such qualities of fairness and fearlessness his scholarship was beyond reproach.

Bibliography. J. Brodrick SJ, *Blessed Robert Bellarmine* (1928) 2 vols, revised ed. in 1 vol.; E. A. Ryan SJ, *The historical scholarship of St Bellarmine* (1936); S. Merkle, Grundsätzliche Erörterungen zur Bellarminforschung, ZKG 45 (1926) 26–73; Y. de Montcheuil SJ, 'La Place de Bellarmin dans la théologie', *Mélanges théologiques* (1945); J. Beumer SJ, 'Schrift und Tradition bei Robert Bellarmin', *Scholastik* 34 (1959) 1–22; (replying to J. Geiselmann) *Die mündliche Überlieferung* (1957); F. X. Arnold, *Die Staatslehre des Kardinal Bellarmin* (1934); J. Courtney Murray SJ, 'Bellarmine on the indirect power', TS 9 (1948) 491–535.   J. H. C.

BENEDICT, ST, INFLUENCE OF The article, after giving (I) the outline of his life, examines (II) the character of the Rule, discusses (III) its sources and the debated matter of the *Regula magistri*, and finally (IV) considers the abiding influence which it had, and has, on society.

I. St Benedict was born in central Italy towards the end of the 5th cent. and flourished in the first half of the 6th. His monastic career started at Subiaco about A.D. 500 and culminated at Monte Cassino, where he died before A.D. 550. Neither of these places is far from Rome, where Benedict had studied as a boy and with which he maintained contact as a monk. His life was lived very near to the centre of Church authority, which authority he obviously accepted with unquestioning obedience. It has even been suggested that his Rule was commissioned by the Holy See, in an effort to bring some order into the chaotic medley of current western monachism (Abbot Chapman, *St Benedict and the Sixth Century*, ch. xi). However that may be, Monte Cassino and its founder were well-known in Rome, and towards the end of the 6th cent. this circumstance brought Benedict posthumous publicity of an effective character. No less a person than Pope St Gregory the Great devoted the whole second book of his *Dialogues* to his life and works. It is true that St Gregory is chiefly interested in the miraculous and provides only a small amount of ordinary historical detail; yet without his record we should have known nothing of the person of St Benedict, and should have lacked also St Gregory's valuable testimony regarding his Rule. This is what he says to Peter, his interlocutor: 'I would not have you ignorant of this, that Benedict was eminent not only for his many miracles but also for his teaching. In fact, he wrote a Rule for Monks of singular discretion and great lucidity'. St Gregory's correspondence shows him regularly promoting the use of the Rule; but this passage in the very popular book of his *Dialogues* was his most effective commendation and cannot but have helped its propagation very greatly.

Any account of St Benedict's influence must concern itself chiefly with his Rule. It is to be noted that St Benedict did not found a religious Order with a central authority that should control its constituent monasteries. Although he expected his Rule to be used in other monasteries, he conceived these monasteries as autonomous units and did not seek to unite them by any constitutional bonds. As a consequence the early history of St Benedict's institute is not a history of Benedictine 'foundations', but the history of the gradual diffusion of the Rule. It is considered probable that it was first observed in Rome by St Gregory's monastery of St Andrew on the Coelian Hill. When Monte Cassino was sacked by the Lombards (c. 580) the fugitive community was provided with a monastery in Rome and must have brought the Rule with them. From St Andrew's it may have travelled across Gaul with St Augustine and his companions, on their way to evangelize the English. This was right at the end of the 6th cent. In the 7th cent. we find the Rule being observed in Gaul by the monasteries of St Columbanus, in association with their original rule. The trail is not easy to follow, because of the lack of precise records. However, the Rule continued its progress and gradually won its way to an unquestioned pre-eminence, so that before the end of the 8th cent. it had come to be accepted as the standard code of western monachism. The five centuries from the 8th to the 13th are the 'Benedictine centuries'.

II Character of the Rule. Although it has a Prologue and 73 chapters, the Rule is not a lengthy document. It contains approximately twelve thousand words and would occupy about ten pages of the present book. The prologue and the first seven chapters lay down basic principles and provide some spiritual instruction; there follow thirteen chapters devoted to the Divine Office and prayer in general; apart from eight chapters dealing with faults and their punishment (23–30) and the final chapter (73) which is in the nature of an epilogue, the remainder of the Rule deals with a variety of monastic regulations, assembled in no very strict order. St Gregory commended the Rule for its discretion and lucidity. On the first count, although the monastic ideal is fully maintained, it is noticeably a more lenient document than the older monastic rules, and we find St Benedict himself apologizing for the relative moderation of his requirements. He arranges for the psalter to be said in the course of a week, 'although our forefathers said the whole of it each day'. He approaches the topic of food and drink with much tact, allowing that men differ greatly in this region, so that 'it is with some misgiving that we determine how much others should eat and drink'. It had been said that wine was no drink for monks; but (says the Rule) 'since nowadays monks cannot be persuaded of this, let us agree to use it temperately'. These are examples of the moderation which characterizes the Rule. In the epilogue it is called 'this little beginning of a Rule', and for perfection the monks are referred to Cassian, St Basil and the *Vitae Patrum*. As regards the 'lucidity' which St Gregory commends, the Rule has never been charged with obscurity. Its latinity is of a simple and straightforward character. There are, it is true, some Late Latin constructions, but these are not such as to cause much difficulty to the reader.

III Sources of the Rule. Apart from the Bible, St Benedict shows himself acquainted with the writings of the Latin Fathers, e.g. St Leo and St Augustine. It was natural that he should take a special interest in monastic writings, and the Rule has traces of such items of this literature as were available in Latin. It owes most to the monastic writings of Cassian. But, in mentioning these sources, we do not mean to imply that St Benedict borrowed much of the substance of his Rule from them. He was essentially a traditionalist and took over the best teaching of the ancients; but in taking it over he made it his own and was far from being an unoriginal copyist. However, we must at this point report that recent times have seen the birth of a hypothesis which would make St Benedict a large-scale plagiarist.

The Master's Rule. This is the current title of an anonymous Latin rule (*Regula Magistri*), of uncertain date and place of origin, which is about three times the length of St Benedict's Rule and differs from it greatly in character. It cannot be commended either for moderation or for lucidity. The author commands an exotic vocabulary and uses a complicated syntax. And his regulations are sometimes extravagant or even fantastic. But, the important point for our present purpose is this, that there exists between the Master's Rule and St Benedict's a considerable amount of textual agreement. When two texts exhibit this sort of parallelism, it is always the question, Which is the prior text ? Before the year 1938 this question was answered unanimously in favour of St Benedict's Rule and the other was dismissed as no better than a crude paraphrase. Such, for example, is the position adopted by the Maurist, Dom Hugh Ménard. He is severe on the Master's Rule, castigating it for verbosity, obscurity, and imperfect latinity. He calls attention to the striking contrast between the style of the pieces ' borrowed ' from St Benedict and the ' rude and scabrous style ' of the remainder. All this is very true, and, in consideration of its substance, it is difficult to believe that the Master's Rule was ever actually observed in a monastery. Certainly the paucity of extant manuscripts (two and some fragments) does not suggest any wide vogue. However, despite these adverse considerations, the year 1938 saw the appearance of the revolutionary hypothesis that the Master's Rule was prior to St Benedict's and that the latter had borrowed extensively from it. This position was a reversal of all previous opinion and constituted a paradox of the first magnitude. But the paradox proved a specially attractive one, and a debate was started which has continued for more than twenty years and has produced a great many review articles as well as an elaborate edition of the Master's Rule. During the course of the debate there has been very great variety of view regarding the date and authorship of this Rule, and there is as yet no sign that the argument has ended. However, we detect the appearance of a lull in the debate ; this may mean that the hypothesis of 1938 must remain ' Not proven '. And now there appears opportunely (1960) a new edition of St Benedict's Rule, in the Vienna CSEL, by an Austrian scholar, Professor Rudolf Hanslik, who has made, for his edition, a complete collation of three hundred MSS of the Rule. The Introduction will deal with the question of the Master's Rule, but he declares that ' on the basis of the MS. evidence I have no doubt that it is the Master who has used St Benedict '. [EDITORIAL NOTE : The author of this article, Abbot Justin McCann, died before he could see Hanslik's edition of the Rule. In his preface (xliv) Hanslik states that he cannot believe that Benedict copied the *Regula Magistri*. At the same time he admits that the liturgical regulations of the Master are more ancient than Benedict's ; this he puts down to the Master having used earlier sources. He also considers that Benedict was indebted to the monastic regulations of Lérins.]

IV Substance and Influence of the Rule. St Benedict expects his monks to be ' seeking God ' and gives them no other objective. Summoning them to a life of obedience ' under a rule and an abbot ', he provides three chief occupations : (i) The chanting of the Divine Office, which he calls the *Opus Dei* ; (ii) Devout study (*Lectio Divina*) ; (iii) Manual work (*Opera manuum*). The precise

regulation of the Divine Office occupies several chapters in the Rule and St Benedict evidently regarded this occupation as of primary importance. But he does not fail to stress the other two, introducing them with the principle that ' Idleness is the enemy of the soul '. His *lectio divina* was designed to instruct his monks and to help them with their prayer and the other duties of their vocation. His manual work was exercised normally in the monastery and within its precincts ; but he envisages circumstances when the monks would have to work in the fields. This bare summary sketches the content of the ordered life which soon spread over western Europe and not only exercised an apostolic influence but also constituted a powerful civilizing force.

It is now more than fourteen centuries since the Rule started on its beneficent career. In the medieval period it was observed in England by over two hundred monasteries. Numbers were greater still on the Continent—in Italy, Germany, France, Spain, etc. For the early centuries the Rule had the field to itself and was a major influence in all these countries. In Germany and elsewhere the monks had had much to do with the work of evangelization. That having been achieved, they were everywhere a valuable influence in the maintenance of the Christian faith. We have said that St Benedict made use of the work of his monastic predecessors, but have said little about another chief characteristic of the Rule—its profound and essential Christianity. This appears in its ordinary instructions, but is marked especially by the abundance of the citations from the NT. This was the Rule by which those countless monasteries lived. They could not help but be a powerful religious influence among the people who surrounded them. And so also of their influence in promoting the arts of civilization, from agriculture to learning ; their influence was greater at some periods than at others. And the monasteries of the Rule have been subject to many vicissitudes : they have been suppressed and despoiled ; they have declined in fervour and have needed reform. But, despite all this, if not so numerous as formerly, they have spread to East and West, and have introduced the Rule to countries that were unknown to St Benedict.

Bibliography. St Benedict's Rule has been printed times without number. Modern critical editions, e.g. Abbot Cuthbert Butler's *Editio critico-practica* (1912, 1927, etc.), and the purely critical edition of Dom Benno Linderbauer (1928) are based on the work of Ludwig Traube in his *Textgeschichte der Regula S. Benedicti* (1898). It would seem likely that the edition of Professor Hanslik (1960) will supersede these. For English readers there is a Latin-English edition by the present writer in the Orchard Series (1952). The fullest modern commentary on the Rule is Abbot Delatte's, which has been published in an English translation. For a general account of St Benedict's teaching and Benedictine practice Abbot Cuthbert Butler's *Benedictine Monachism* still has no rival.

As regards the history of Benedictinism, this is an

intractable subject, involving as it does the individual histories of countless monasteries. But something has been done by way of general surveys. We shall mention only two such modern histories : (1) Dom David Knowles, *The Monastic Order in England*, and his succeeding volumes ; (2) Dom Philibert Schmitz, *Histoire générale de l'ordre de saint Benoît*, in 6 vols.

J. McC.

BENEDICTION: ITS THEOLOGY

The theology of Benediction might be put in a few lines. It is a service of the Church wherein adoration is paid to the Blessed Sacrament and a blessing of the congregation with the Sacrament takes place, this blessing being a sacramental. As a sacramental, the blessing gives grace, not *ex opere operato* (by the mere act of blessing), but *ex opere operantis ecclesiae* (by the work of the praying Church), and this distinction is treated under SACRAMENTAL. For the present, some account must be given of (I) how the Church came to practise adoration of the Blessed Sacrament, and (II) why a blessing was associated with this adoration.

I The adoration of the Sacrament was traced back by Fr Thurston to the 15th cent. when monstrances for the exposition of the Blessed Sacrament were commonly made. Since 1936 it has been possible to add the testimony of Margery Kempe, the English mystic of those times, who on her journey from Wilsnak in Prussia to Aachen (probably in 1434) told how they came to a place during the Octave of Corpus Christi where the Blessed Sacrament was exposed on the altar of a church : ' It stood open in a crystal, that men might see It if they would '. She adds that she wept full sore, and seems to have been struck by the novelty of the devotion. More recently Mgr Andrieu has chronicled a number of monstrances of earlier date (Paris 1379), Carpentras (1322), Hasselt (1286), but it is of course quite uncertain whether these were used for exposition on an altar or simply for carrying the Sacrament in the procession on Corpus Christi, a feast which had been kept by the whole Western Church since 1264.

A notable advance in the history of this adoration was made a few years ago by A. A. Barb in a study of the Holy Grail legend. He noted how the archaeological and artistic evidence pointed to the Grail being ' originally and fundamentally the table of the Last Supper, seen in the characteristic shape of certain early Christian circular altar-slabs '. John the Baptist was associated with the Eucharist, for he proclaimed the Lamb of God, and his head, on a dish, was venerated in one artistic form or another, all over Christian Europe ' as a prefiguration of the Eucharistic sacrifice '. Just as Herodias and Antipas had the head of John at their banquet, so the Christians at the eucharistic feast had a representation of the head of John. The liturgy spoke of it : ' It is right and just . . . that at this sacramental feast the head of Thy martyr should be joined with the gospel memory of the Supper and that we should offer on the table of Thy mercy just as on a dish of sparkling

metal '.[1] So the *Missale Gothicum* in a Preface for the feast of John's beheading. The post-communion in the Gelasian Sacramentary for the same feast is equally plain : ' May this solemnity of St John the Baptist give us two things : that we may venerate this great Sacrament (which we have received) in its prefiguring and may rejoice that we now have what is so much more, its realization '.[2] In case there was any doubt the Sarum Missal added the words *patribus nostris* (to our fathers) just before *significata*. The head of John, in an image if not in reality, might be put on the altar like a relic during Mass ; why not have the Sacrament set out on the altar for all to see ? Such seems to have been the line of argument. It is a confirmation of this research to find, though A. A. Barb does not notice it, that some of the earliest monstrances were in the form of a statue of John the Baptist holding up the crystal in which the Sacrament was to be placed. Thus Andrieu reports the Paris monstrance of 1379 at the church of St Sépulchre : ' An image of John the Baptist holding a little vessel where there is an *Agnus Dei* opening at the back for the insertion of relics, and again another vessel with two crystals, for carrying *Corpus Domini* on the day of the holy sacrament, which can be placed in the hand of the image just like the vessel with relics '. Other monstrances of this type from Bourges (1404) and Dijon (1519) are included in his report. Andrieu was inclined to connect the veneration of the Sacrament with that of relics placed on the altar during Mass, but did not see the more precise link through St John the Baptist.

The feast of the Beheading of John the Baptist arrived in the West from Emesa in Phoenicia (thus the entry in the *Martyrology of Tallaght* : ' in Emisma civitate Foeniciae ') and was kept on 27 February. Later it is transferred to August and is assigned by the Paris *Comes* (B.N. Lat. 9451) to a day between the first and second Sundays after St Laurence's day. Later still it is fixed on 29 August. Thus from Syria in the days of Ephrem to Ireland of the 7th cent. there is evidence of the spread of the cult of the Beheading. These dates and places fix an upper limit for the possibility of associating the head of John with the cult of the Blessed Sacrament. It is generally agreed that the date of the *Missale Gothicum*, cited above, falls within the 7th cent. ; thus the beginning of sacramental devotions in the West can be safely set at a date later than this. The obscure history of the rise of the Grail legends cannot be discussed here, but they may have much to do with the early cult of the Blessed Sacrament.

Two English bishops, Philip Repingdon and John Fisher, give some reasons for this external adoration of the Sacrament. In 1419 Repingdon, when he was bishop of Lincoln, issued instructions that the townsfolk were to turn out for the Corpus Christi

[1] Dignum et iustum est . . . inter has sacramentorum epulas martyris Tui caput cum evangelica recordatione misceri, et velut in disco metalli radiantis ita super mensam Tuae propitiationis offerre.

[2] Conferat nobis, Domine, sancti Iohannis utrumque solemnitas, ut magnifica sacramenta quae sumpsimus significata veneremur et in nobis potius edita gaudeamus.

procession, ' that by the frequent sight of this sacrament the devotion of the people may be increased and they may more easily obtain pardon for their sins.' (Wilkins, *Concilia* III, 396), while John Fisher, with Yorkshire common sense, added (*de Veritate Corporis* 1:22) that, if the nobles were conspicuous in the honour they paid to the Sacrament, the unlettered people would the more easily be drawn to devotion. These ideas derive from the common medieval notion that there was some great efficacy (almost *ex opere operato*) in looking at the Sacrament, but Fisher at least is clear that the *opus operantis* was also required. The act of looking at the Sacrament can be traced back to the reaction of the faithful to the heresy of Peter Cantor at the end of the 12th cent., if not to earlier causes.

The medieval Catholic was not left in confusion of mind by the theologians about the difference between seeing the Body of Christ and receiving It in communion. From William of Auxerre to Gabriel Biel they all point out the distinction between seeing, which is allowed to the sinner and is indeed good for him, and eating, which is for those who are in the grace of God (cf. St Thomas, *Summa* 3a:80:4:@4). A few theologians of the early 13th cent. did indeed try to draw from a sentence of Augustine an argument for regarding the sight of the Sacrament as itself a spiritual nutrition and a cause of sanctifying grace. They claimed that (in *Enarratio in Ps.* 90 ; PL 37:1170) Augustine had laid it down that our whole reward in heaven was the vision of God, and that therefore by analogy the vision of the Sacrament on earth was the beginning of this spiritual refection. William of Milton, the continuator of Alexander of Hales (*Summa* 4a:51:5) soon disposed of this claim, and it does not seem to have been raised again. At Trent (D 878, 888) the adoration of the Sacrament was upheld as being according to Scripture (Heb 1:6) and tradition.

II The blessing given with the Sacrament is traced back by Fr Thurston to that given when communion has been taken to the sick, and the priest on regaining the church turns round and blesses those who have accompanied the Sacrament, before he replaces the pyx or ciborium in the tabernacle. A similar blessing is given in the sickroom itself, after communion has been given. Warrant for this can be found as early as the Irish liturgies, the *Stowe Missal*, the *Book of Dimma* and the *Book of Mulling*. In *Stowe* the priest has to say after communion to the sick man, ' May the Lord bless and keep thee, and may the Lord show His face to thee and have mercy on thee ; may He turn His countenance to thee and give thee peace '. In *Mulling* this formula is given the title *Benedictio hominis* and is placed before the anointing and the communion, while in *Dimma* it is placed at the end of the communion with the rubric *tunc signas et dicis* (then you bless the man and say). These Irish blessings of the sick do not speak of the Sacrament being used in the act of blessing, but, given the habitual practice of Irish missionaries (who carried the Sacrament with them on their wanderings, in a *chrismal* slung round the neck), and

given the emphatic wording (show His face, turn His countenance) of the prayer, it does not seem unlikely that, even if the Sacrament was not used for the blessing in the time of the *Stowe Missal*, the custom of such use came in naturally not long afterwards. In early blessings with the monstrance the words used were : *Ille vos benedicat qui sine fine vivit et regnat.*

One might be tempted to think that the rite of giving communion, with the showing of the Sacrament to the faithful (when the *Ecce Agnus Dei* is said) and the blessing of each one with the Host before reception, was in itself the nucleus of the Benediction ritual as we know it. But nothing could be more deceptive. Nothing of the *Ecce Agnus Dei* can be found in the *Sacerdotale* of Alberto Castellani OP, of the first half of the 16th cent., where the rite of communion outside Mass is described. (It should be noticed that communion was always given *after* and not *during* Mass in those times, and so the rite did not find mention in the Missals.) Castellani says : ' The priest shows the Sacrament to all, saying : ' Repeat, all of you, what I say : *Domine non sum dignus* ', and he then says the same words a second and a third time in the vernacular '. This showing of the Sacrament was probably copied from what was done at the time of the consecration.

It seems clear that in the days when the Sacrament was placed in the hands of the communicants there could have been none of this ritual of showing and blessing. The formula in very early times was an act of faith, the priest saying *Corpus Christi* and the recipient answering *Amen*, i.e. ' I do believe it '. The earliest formulae of blessing with the Host, of the type now in use, came in about the 8th cent., just at the time when the practice of giving the Sacrament into the hand was dying out (cf. Bede HE 4:24 ; PL 95:214), and it is significant that Jungmann (*Missarum sollemnia* III, 3:13) goes to the *Book of Dimma* for the earliest instance of a blessing-formula : *Corpus Domini . . . conservet animam tuam in vitam perpetuam.* Decrees of local Councils about this time (at Cordova, 839, and Rouen, 878) show that the Sacrament was no longer being placed in the hands of the faithful. When they were given the Sacrament in their hands, it was their duty to bless their senses, eyes and lips, with the sacred *species* ; when this usage died out, it was not altogether surprising that another form of blessing should be introduced, particularly for a sick man, who in any case could not help himself.

In the days when exaggerated views were held about the value of looking upon the Sacrament, an abuse came in whereby the priest took the Sacrament to show It to a dying man who was judged incapable of swallowing the Host, and this abuse was forbidden by the *Rituale* of Paul V. Another abuse grew out of the many medieval tales of Hosts from which drops of blood had been seen to fall ; this subject was thoroughly examined by Fr Thurston (in his *Life of St Hugh of Lincoln*, 505-10), but it is quite certain that such popular marvels had little if anything to do with the growth of the theology of

Benediction. The stories of miraculous happenings in the Host at Mass which were (c. 830) collected by Paschasius Radbertus (PL 120:1316) include one from the life of Basil and another which is recounted of Gregory the Great by his first biographer, the monk of Whitby, c. 713. These stories antedate the medieval phenomena of bleeding Hosts, and, while some of them may have received the embroideries of superstition, they do in their general pattern stand out as proof of a lively belief in the doctrine of transsubstantiation at that epoch. The abuses of the 17th and 18th cents. were in the opposite direction, for the Jansenists tried to apply here the adage *Assueta vilescunt* (Custom will stale devotion) and wanted to restrict Exposition and Benediction to the feast of Corpus Christi, but their efforts failed against the rising devotion to the Sacred Heart (*see* HEART).

Bibliography. The basic history of the rite of Benediction was worked out by H. Thurston SJ, in four articles in Mn 97 (1901) 587–97; 98 (1901) 58–69; 186–93; 264–76; and in 'The Blessed Sacrament and the Holy Grail' Mn 110 (1907) 617–632; the article *Sacrement* in DAC is drawn from these; M. Andrieu, 'Reliquaires et monstrances eucharistiques' in AB 68 (1950) 397–418; A. A. Barb, 'The Round Table and the Holy Grail', in *Journal of the Warburg and Courtauld Institutes* 19 (1956) 40–67; E. Dumoutet, *Le Désir de voir l'Hostie* (1926), with Fr Thurston's review Mn (1926) 254–8; P. Browe SJ, *Die Verehrung der Eucharistie im Mittelalter* (1933); V. L. Kennedy, 'The Moment of Consecration and the Elevation', in Med St 6 (1944) 121–50 and 8 (1946) 87–96.

J. H. C.

BERKELEY AND CATHOLICISM As one would expect of a Protestant bishop, Berkeley disapproved of Catholicism as a religious system. In his Primary Visitation Charge (*Works*, edited by A. A. Luce and T. E. Jessop, VII, 161–7) he discussed the best means by which his clergy could convert Irish Catholics to Anglicanism. In 1741 he addressed a long letter to Sir John James (*Works*, 143–55) to dissuade him from joining the Roman church. Berkeley expressed the opinion that the true Catholic church is invisible, and that the term 'Roman Catholic' is as illogical as the term 'particular universal'.

But Berkeley was too charitable a man to be a fanatical bigot. He was sincerely concerned with the material betterment of the people of Ireland, irrespective of religion. And in his *Word to the Wise* (*Works*, VI (1749) 235–49) he wrote in sympathetic terms to the Catholic clergy of Ireland, urging them to co-operate in this work and assuring them that he was their 'sincere well-wisher', who desired no other contest with them than a pious rivalry in carrying out the precepts of Christ. He remarks that some people think that the Catholic religion is the cause of the idleness to be found in the country, but that the examples of France, Flanders and northern Italy show that this idea is void of foundation.

In 1745 Berkeley addressed a short *Letter to the Roman Catholics of the Diocese of Cloyne* (*Works*, VI, 229–30), urging them not to lend their support to the Jacobite rising. This advice was in accordance with the doctrine expressed in his *Passive Obedience* (*Works*, VI (1712) 15–46); but in the *Letter* Berkeley appealed to motives of prudence and expediency rather than to his moral doctrine of non-resistance to the civil ruler.

Berkeley noted the implications of his denial of material substance for the Catholic doctrine of transsubstantiation. But he had an evident esteem for the leading Scholastic thinkers, in so far as he was acquainted with them. When discussing the problem of analogy in connection with the terms predicated of God, he refers to the views of St Thomas Aquinas, Suárez and Cajetan (cf. *Alciphron*, Dial. 4, 20–2; *Works*, III, 168–70); and he makes it quite clear that he is in fundamental agreement with them about the need for a theory of analogy. True, there is a formal apology for mentioning 'such unpolished and unfashionable writers as the Schoolmen'; but this is simply a concession to the general prejudice against the Scholastics which had found expression from the Renaissance onwards. In the notes which are known as *Philosophical Commentaries* (*Works*, I) Berkeley observes more than once that the Schoolmen dealt with noble and important subjects, even if their manner of treating them left much to be desired.

The degree to which Berkeley was influenced by Malebranche is a matter for dispute. Berkely himself emphasized the differences between their views and denied that they were similar. But his reasons were philosophical and had nothing to do with the Oratorian's Catholicism.

F. C. C.

BERNARD OF CLAIRVAUX, ST (1090–1153) The article will be divided into three sections, (I) his life, (II) his controversies and (III) his theological influence.

I His Life. Saint Bernard of Clairvaux was born at Fontaines lès Dijon in Burgundy during the year 1090 and he died sixty-three years later in his monastery at Clairvaux. His life was thus cast during the peak of the high Middle Ages, the best qualities of which he was at once both the embodiment and, as much as any one man could be, the creator.

He was one of seven children born of Tescelin, Lord of Fontaines, and Aleth the daughter of the noble Bernard of Montbard. Beyond the fact that he was a comely and highly-intelligent youth, albeit shy and retiring in the presence of strangers, we know little for certain of Bernard's early years. He was sent to school at Châtillon, a small town some fifty miles N. of Dijon, where he studied under the Canons of St Vorles whose small church may still be seen at Châtillon, not greatly changed since the days of Bernard. There is, however, one story amidst a mass of legend, told of him at this time of life that is so well in keeping with all we know of him in later years that it may well be true. Like many highly strung and sensitive people Bernard suffered acutely from what we should call nowadays 'megrims'. During one of these attacks, while his mother was absent, some attendants called in the services of the local wise-woman ; but Bernard, as soon as the witch approached his bed, leapt up and drove her from the house. Of such material was the future Abbot of Clairvaux !

Both Bernard's parents were devout Christians and it seemed to them that the high intelligence, devout disposition, as well perhaps as the rather un-robust constitution of their son indicated for him a career in the Church ; as a monk of Cluny or some other great Benedictine monastery he might have risen high in the councils of the State and Church. At this time Bernard had literary ambitions and there is no doubt that the prospect of a studious life of devout leisure appealed to him ; but, after a stern struggle with himself, he finally decided to devote himself to God's service not in one of the grand Benedictine monasteries but in the poor and obscure house at Cîteaux some fifteen miles S. of Dijon. This house had been founded on 21 March 1098 by three monks, St Robert of Molesme, St Alberic, St Stephen Harding the Englishman, and about nine-teen disciples, in order to escape from the pompous traditionalism of the old Benedictines back to the simplicity of St Benedict's Holy Rule. But the foundation had not prospered, St Robert after a few months had returned to his Abbey at Molesme, and St Alberic after a short time as Abbot had died leaving the burden to St Stephen ; young men had come to try their vocation, but few had persevered ; the life was too hard, the food too scanty, and the situation too unhealthy.

Bernard's decision dismayed his family ; it seemed improbable that he would be physically strong enough to endure the hard life of Cîteaux and it ap-peared a wicked waste of his gifts for him to embrace a way of life that would provide little scope for their use because, although they held studies in high esteem, the monks of Cîteaux lived largely by the work of their hands. But, after what appears to have been some hesitation, very natural under the circum-stances, Bernard remained faithful to his high resolve and leaving all worldly prospects behind him entered Cîteaux in the year 1113, having persuaded about thirty other young men of his age, including his uncle and all his brothers, in fact the flower of the local nobility, to follow him.

A new era started for Cîteaux with the arrival of Bernard and his companions. In the very year of their coming a band of twelve with their abbot was sent out to make a foundation at La Ferté-sur-Grone and a year later yet another followed at Pontigny with one of Bernard's companions, Hugh of Mâcon, as their abbot. In 1115 Bernard's time came ; he was sent by Abbot Stephen to found a monastery on the property of one Josbert de la Ferté, about seventy miles N. of the mother house and not far from Bar-sur-Aube. A valley was chosen for the new house known at the time as the Valley of Wormwood, but soon to become famous throughout the world and in history not any longer as the Valley of Wormwood but as Clairvaux or the Valley of Light.

The life of every new monastic foundation is apt to be hard, even nowadays, but the difficulties which beset Clairvaux were especially severe. The venture was kept alive only by Bernard's strength of character and sanctity ; when things were at their worst and everything seemed on the point of collapse he is said to have been encouraged by a vision of Clairvaux's future glory, but no man can live on visions alone, bread is also necessary and in those early days there was hardly any bread at all at Clairvaux. Finally Bernard himself fell ill with some gastric complaint that was to trouble him for the rest of his life and he was only saved by his friend, William of Champeaux, Bishop of Châlons-sur-Marne, obtaining from the General Chapter of Cîteaux authority to insist on Bernard taking a year of complete rest. A small cell was built for him apart from the main monastery and here Bernard remained for a year slowly recover-ing his health. During this time he was visited by William, a monk of St-Nicasius of Rheims, who afterwards became Abbot of St-Thierry and later, rather against Bernard's wishes, who thought the life might be too hard for him, a Cistercian monk at Signy. The lifelong friendship that grew up be-tween Bernard and William from this visit was not without its effect on the lives of both men. William was not so dynamic a character as Bernard, but he was a profound thinker and a spiritual writer of dis-tinction. Although he was influenced by Bernard he knew how to keep his originality and never became a mere echo of his friend. In 1125 Bernard made another important friend in Theobald Count of Blois and under the patronage of this benevolent nobleman the material difficulties of Clairvaux came to an end. But despite the hard times and despite his illness Bernard's fame had been growing all these ten years. Bishops and statesmen had begun to look to him for help and advice.

II His controversies. When they were still struggling for existence the Cistercians were regarded with a certain benevolence by the older Benedictines and Clairvaux itself had been helped on at least one occasion by the Benedictines of Clémentinpré. But as the prosperity and fame of the new Order began to swell under the increasing prestige of Bernard and the organizing genius of Stephen Harding, Abbot of Cîteaux, the spirit of mutual benevolence gave place to one of unworthy rivalry. It was natural that this should have happened, since even monks remain human beings ; but it was nevertheless unfortunate. Nor were things made any easier when the Grand Prior of Cluny, Bernard de Brancion, descended on Clairvaux during one of Bernard's absences, and in-veigled away a young monk called Robert, a kins-man of Bernard, under the pretext that he had been offered when still a child as an Oblate to Cluny. No one could have regretted this state of affairs more than Bernard and the best spirits amongst the Bene-dictines ; indeed Peter the Venerable, the Abbot of Cluny, and Bernard remained fast friends through-out their lives, but neither could calm the storming emotions of their monks and Bernard was made the butt of the opposing party. Finally things came to such a pass that Bernard, under the influence of the monk William, at that time still a Benedictine himself, launched upon the world his *Apologia*. Beginning with an expression of his admiration for the Benedictine way of life and his distress at the rivalry that had grown up between his own monks and the Benedictines, he then went on to indict in brilliantly satirical terms not their way of life as it should be but the abuses that had seeped into it and deformed it. The effect of this work was dramatic, it exploded like a bomb in the Benedictine cloisters causing an outcry of indignation but also much fruitful searching of hearts amongst the better spirits in the opposing camp and providing Peter the Venerable, far too big a man to take offence at criticism, with an occasion for introducing many necessary reforms. It also had the effect of converting the great Abbot Suger of St-Denys in Paris to a more austere way of life so that he gave up his proud equipages and left his princely ' Abbot's Lodging ' for a room so mean and small that ' men were amazed '.

Hardly had the dust from this controversy subsided than Bernard was caught up in a storm so great that it seemed to threaten the very existence of the Church. In 1130 the Cardinals in Rome surpassed themselves by electing on one and the same day two rival popes who threatened to pull the whole Church to pieces in their lust for power. They were Peter Leon, Cardinal Priest of SS. Cosmas and Damian, who took the name of Anacletus, and Gregory, Cardinal Deacon of S. Angelo, who took the name of Innocent. In this terrible catastrophe all men looked to Bernard for guidance and help. The whole affair is too complicated to unravel at this distance of time but Bernard had no hesitation in giving his support to Pope Innocent on the grounds that his election was the first, that he had been elected by the *sanior pars* of the Cardinals, and that his character was the more worthy of the two. For eight years the Church was rent by the schism and when at last Innocent triumphed it was largely thanks to Bernard that he did so. It was Bernard who swayed France and England to his side, it was Bernard who won the support of the Emperor Lothair, and it was Bernard who kept the peace between his allies.

Even after the schism Bernard was denied the peace he longed for. Peace was the sole thing his contemporaries were not prepared to allow him. He was involved in various disputes and controversies; everyone in any difficulty appealed to him; his correspondence alone was enormous for the time, and so also was his literary output. He was in touch with every notable person—with popes, kings and philosophers, and also with the ordinary men and women of his age. He kept many secretaries busy and prided himself on answering every letter as we should say ' by return of post '. No one who came to him was sent empty away. If a king wanted advice he turned to Bernard, and if a poor man lost his pigs he too turned to Bernard. He was involved in theological controversies with Peter Abélard, with Arnold of

Brescia, and with Gilbert de la Porrée, but the most famous of all was his controversy with ABELARD (q.v.). There can be no doubt at all about Abélard's brilliance and charm, but he had something of the bumptiousness of the clever undergraduate about him; he appeared lacking in emotional stability and modesty, certainly in modesty. Although not wittingly unorthodox, many of his opinions although brilliantly defended were certainly hazardous. In him we see the new spirit of scholasticism staggering on to its feet, as yet uncertain of its balance, and in Bernard we have the old-fashioned spirit and mentality of the Fathers of the Church. It was inevitable that these two giants should come into conflict and they did so. Peter Abélard in 1140 challenged Bernard to a dispute at Sens before the King of France and most of the Bishops, but when Bernard faced him before the assembled multitude he seemed to lose his courage and appealed to Rome, and Rome despite the support of his friends amongst the Cardinals condemned many of his propositions and sentenced him to spend the rest of his days at Cluny in silence and prayer. Here two years later he died a holy death but not before he had been reconciled to Bernard.

When one of his own Cistercian monks, Bernard Paganelli, was elected Pope under the title of Eugenius III, Bernard's influence reached its apogee, so that it is not extraordinary that when the King of France asked for a crusade to save the Holy Places of Palestine from the infidel, the duty of preaching it should have been given to Bernard. He preached the opening sermon at Vézelay on 31 March 1146 and then began an immense campaign throughout France and Germany calling men to the defence of the Holy Places. Everywhere his personality and sanctity stirred enthusiasm; men rushed to receive the cross of a Crusader from his hands, and his words were supported by miracles that added to the wild excitement of the people. The miracles of Bernard at this time are some of the best attested in ancient history, they are vouched for by the witness of his two companions who were present at the time, men of undoubted integrity and intelligence, and Bernard himself refers to them in the first chapter of the second book of his treatise on Consideration. Yet for all this the Second Crusade ended in disaster and, naturally, men blamed Bernard for this because he had preached it and because he had seemed to promise success. But the disaster was not Bernard's fault, its cause lay in the rivalry and petty jealousy of the leaders ; as soon as they were away from the magic of Bernard's personality they began to quarrel amongst themselves, nor had they the slightest idea of the rôle of Byzantium in maintaining peace and civilization in the East ; furthermore the whole affair was planned on too vast a scale for the technical equipment of the age. Bernard never seemed quite to recover his influence and popularity after the crusade and he died in 1153, just five years later, under the shadow of failure.

III His theological influence. St Bernard has been well called ' The Last of the Fathers ', ' *Ultimus*

inter patres sed primis certe non impar' as Mabillon has aptly said, because his whole attitude and mentality was patristic. He is sometimes spoken of as an opponent of studies, at any rate for monks, but the contents of the library at Clairvaux in his day, and even the most superficial acquaintance with his writings, should be enough to prove the contrary. Bernard was no opponent of learning but he did hold very strongly that learning should be fruitful in piety, and that the quest for truth, if it did not lead to the contemplation of Truth, was rather futile.

In his treatises on *Grace and Free will*, on *Precept and Dispensation*, and on *The Errors of Abélard*, he brilliantly interpreted the doctrine of the Fathers of the Church, especially of St Ambrose, St Augustine and St Gregory, but beyond the beauty of his style he did not add to them ; he adorned every subject he touched but he contributed little in the realm of Theology.

Although he was forced by circumstances to take a leading part in the great affairs of his time, although he can be said to have carried his whole age on his shoulders, yet he remained before all else a monk and a man of prayer, and it is in the sphere of mysticism and the monastic life that he made his chief contribution to posterity.

He denied the doctrine of the Immaculate Conception because 'conception' meant for him the act of carnal intercourse and he did not see how an action inspired by concupiscence could be without the stain of original sin. He believed that Mary was purified in the womb like St John the Baptist. Our own doctrine, as defined in the last century by Pius IX, does not seem to have occurred to him. But his tender and loving devotion to Our Blessed Lady and to the humanity of Christ has been the inspiration of all subsequent ages ; even the Courtly Love of the Troubadours bears the signs of Bernard's influence although in a debased form, and the *Imitation of Christ* has the impress of his doctrine so deeply marked that at one time men attributed the authorship to him. But it is in mystical doctrine that the power and depth of Bernard's thought is most apparent. In his *Sermons on the Song of Songs*, in his *Treatises on The Love of God, Consideration*, and *The Degrees of Humility and Pride*, his doctrine reaches heights of mystical insight that have never been surpassed and it has placed all posterity in his debt.

Bibliography. J. Pidier, *Bibliographie critique* (1952) ; *Vitae Sancti Bernardi Abbatis* (auctore Gulielmo olim S. Theoderici, Ernaldo Abbate Bonae-Vallis, Gaufrido monacho quondam Clarae-Vallensi, Alano quondam episcopo Autisiodorensi, Joanne Eremita) PL 185 ; Classical Ed. of *Opera* J. Mabillon (1667) PL 182-5 ; Josephus Canivez, *Statuta Capitulorum Generalium Ordinis Cisterciensis* (1933) ; *The Letters of Saint Bernard of Clairvaux*, trans. by Bruno Scott-James (1953) ; Bruno Scott-James, *The Life of Saint Bernard of Clairvaux* (1957) ; E. Vacandard, *Vie de saint Bernard, abbé de Clairvaux*, 2 vols (1895) ; *G. G. Coulton, *Five Centuries of Religion, Vol. I* (S. Bernard, his predecessors and successors : 1000-

1200) (1923) ; *Watkin Williams, *Saint Bernard of Clairvaux* 2nd ed. (1952) ; Joseph Calmette et Henri David, *Saint Bernard* (1953) ; *Bernard de Clairvaux*, (Commission d'Histoire de l'Ordre de Cîteaux) (1953) ; *J. C. Morrison, *St Bernard* (1863) ; Archdale King, *Cîteaux and her Elder Daughters* (1950) ; *Mélanges St Bernard*, (XXIV Congrès de l'Association Bourgnignonne de Sociétés Savantes, Dijon, (1953)) ; D. Jean Leclercq, 'Études sur st Bernard et le texte de ses écrits', *Analecta Sacri Ordinis Cisterciensis, IX* (1953) ; E. Gilson, *Mystical Theology of St Bernard* 2nd ed. (1955) ; E. Butler, *Western Mysticism* 2nd ed. (1929) ; Joannis Salisburensis, *Historia Pontificalis* (ed. with trans. by M. Chibnall (1956)) ; Louis Bouyer, *La Spiritualité de Cîteaux* (1954).   B. S.-J.

BÉRULLE, INFLUENCE OF   Pierre de Bérulle (1575-1629), though in many ways a controversial figure, was one of the great exponents of affective theology of modern times. After a brief account of (I) his life, (II) his teaching about the Incarnation will be considered, (III) his notion of the 'states' of Jesus Christ and (IV) his ideas on sacrifice. Finally an attempt will be made to give (V) an estimate of his influence.

I Bérulle, the descendant of a race of soldiers and parliamentarians, was educated in the humanism and in the Platonic philosophy of his time at the college of Clermont until 1595, when, on the expulsion of the Jesuits from Paris, he had perforce to complete his studies of theology at the Sorbonne. He was ordained in 1599, and during the next year he made a retreat at Verdun under the direction of Fr Lorenzo Maggio sj, from whom Bérulle seems to have received knowledge of the *Breve Compendio*, a treatise on the mystical life written by a devout lady of Milan, Isabella Bellinzaga. Bérulle produced his own *Bref Discours sur l'abnégation intérieure* as a translation and adaptation of this Italian work. In 1603 and thereafter he was concerned with the introduction of the Teresian Carmelites into France and was for some time their ecclesiastical superior, a position which involved him in polemics which have not yet come to an end. In 1611 he founded the French Oratory, a Congregation which was to have great influence on the religious revival in France during the 17th cent.

Bérulle came to England as one of the chaplains of Queen Henrietta Maria in June 1625. The Bishop of Mende, who was the chief ecclesiastic in her train, claimed in Jan. 1626 the right to crown the Queen, but this was refused and the Queen was not crowned at all, but 'stood in a window at Sir Abraham Williams to see the show', while Charles I was being crowned on 2 Feb. 1626. In July of that year she went from the palace barefoot on pilgrimage to Tyburn, to venerate the place where so many English martyrs had suffered. Great popular indignation was aroused by this act and Buckingham turned it to his own advantage by getting the King to send home all the French chaplains and officials who had come over with the Queen. Thus Bérulle returned to France in August 1626, and, though his mission had failed, he was made Cardinal at the request of the French king in 1627. His last years were clouded by the hostility of Richelieu, which he had somehow incurred, and he died with no external success to his credit save the foundation of the Oratory.

Some six years before this foundation he had been brought to a very vivid realization of the great mystery of the Incarnation. His earlier studies had somewhat enamoured him of 'Denis the Areopagite', of neo-Platonism and of a somewhat Monophysite view of God which goes with both those studies ; it was therefore with all the more emphasis that the mystery of the two natures in Christ came home to him in his spiritual meditations (though the suddenness of his conversion is disputed) and in his devotion to this mystery he never wavered.

II The Incarnation for Bérulle was a mystery of exinanition (*anéantissement*), for the Son of God had in taking a human nature deprived it of a human personality. This state of deprivation was obviously different from any single act of self-abasement which Christ may have practised when on earth ; what was not brought forward by Bérulle about it was that it depends on a particular view of the theology of the Incarnation, a view that may be described as Suarezian. To Suarez human personality is a mode of being (*see* INCARNATION), a positive reality and not something negative as it is in Scotist theory. One can only speak of Christ being in a state of servitude (*Œuvres de piété*, 131, 3, 998), a violent, renunciatory condition, if one also regards human personality as a positive reality. Bérulle in other places shows his debt to Suarez, but this point seems to be one of the more considerable.

Bérulle devised for his Oratory a 'feast of Jesus' which was kept each year on 28 Jan. and for which he composed the Office and Mass. The purpose was to adore the man-God abased through love of the Church in the mystery of the Incarnation. The collect runs : ' God who hast willed Thy only-begotten, who was God from eternity with Thee, to be man for eternity on our behalf, grant we beseech Thee that we may for ever celebrate this mystery of the divine life of the Word in human nature and of human nature in the Word of life, that we may be quickened by His spirit while on earth and enjoy the vision of Him in heaven who is our life and glory and who reigns with Thee . . .'[1] This collect, and the whole Office, manages to keep attention on the metaphysical position of Christ, with no turning aside to any act or event. The double mention of eternity shows that Bérulle, though in his moments of enthusiasm he speaks of the Incarnation as eternal, did not mean that it was from all eternity in the past (or *a parte ante*, as theologians say) but only that it endures for ever. There are times, however, when

[1] Deus qui unigenitum Tuum apud Te ab aeterno Deum, pro nobis in aeternum hominem esse voluisti, fac nos quaesumus hanc ineffabilem et divinissimam vitam Verbi in humanitate et humanitatis in Verbo vitae iugiter celebrari, ut Eius Spiritu animemur in terris et Eius aspectu perfruamur in caelis, qui nostra vita est et gloria et Tecum vivit et regnat . . . (*Office de Jésus pour sa feste* . . . [1673]).

he seems to want to apply his favourite text (Heb. 10:7) to a backward eternity also.

The *Secreta* for the feast applies the theology of the Incarnation to our own sanctification : ' God who hast willed to unite Thy only-begotten to human nature in the unity of a Person, and in Him hast made us a new creation for Thyself, guard this work of mercy and purge it from the stains of time, that by the help of Thy grace we may come to be in the pattern of Him in whom our substance is with Thee.'[2] The adaptation here of a collect from the *Leonine Sacramentary*, by relating our union of grace with Christ to the hypostatic union itself, expresses one of Bérulle's favourite conclusions from the doctrine of the Incarnation. As he prayed elsewhere : ' Just as the Father brings out and imprints in You His own substance, so do You imprint in my soul and my life Your life, interior and exterior '. This was to deduce the doctrine of the Mystical Body from that of the Trinity (cf. *Œuvres de piété* 143, 666) and to make of the exemplar causality which the Leonine prayer spoke of (*in Illius inveniamur forma*) an almost formal causality.

Bérulle is recognized today as one who made the doctrine of the Mystical Body much more at home in the West than it had been for centuries. It may be conceded that the outbreak of Protestantism had led to a neglect of that doctrine which was thought of as likely to encourage loose talk about the invisible church in the manner dear to the reformers. Bérulle went back to the Greek Fathers, chiefly to Cyril of Alexandria. The gospel to be read on his new feast was Jn 17, and for the third nocturn of the Office he chose passages from Cyril on that chapter (PG 74:557–64) to be read on the 7th day of the Octave and on the Octave day. Other lessons were drawn from Augustine's tracts on John (*tr.* 104, 106, 110, 111) and from the letters of Leo (to Julian of Cos, PL 54:805) and the sermons (*serm.* 3 *in Passione* ; PL 54:319 ; *serm.* 8 et 10 *de Nativitate* PL 54:223 and 232). The first Thursday of each month (outside Lent and Advent) was to be kept by the use of a Votive Office of this feast. One sees how all this was to point the way for the later cult of the Sacred Heart.

The two births of Christ (spoken of by the Council of Lyons, D 462) were augmented by Bérulle, who enumerated three, the eternal generation by the Father, the birth from Mary, and a birth into newness of life in the tomb at Easter. Using Jn 1:18, he claimed that the life of the Son with the Father was a continued existence ' au sein du Père, comme au lieu de sa naissance, auquel il est conçu et formé par le Père qui l'engendre en soi-même '. Although this seems to be an abuse of the Greek κόλπος in the text, Bérulle extended the idea to the Church, which was said by him to keep her children in the womb, heretics being the only ones to force a way out by

[2] Deus qui unigenitum Tuum naturae humanae in unitate personae coadunare voluisti et in Eo novam creaturam nos Tibi esse fecisti, custodi opera misericordiae et a maculis vetustatis emunda, ut per auxilium gratiae Tuae in Illius inveniamur forma in quo Tecum est nostra substantia . . .

their violence.[1] Fr Bruno has made suggestions about the psychological constitution of Bérulle which have been ill-received, but there does seem to be something rather abnormal about such a mode of thought. It is closely connected with his ideas on the ' states of Christ '.

III The States of Jesus, interior rather than exterior, are distinct from His acts and the events of His earthly life. They are described, now as dispositions, now as the very constituents of His being. Earlier theologians had spoken of the *status declivior* of Christ in the Eucharist and it may be from here that the Bérullian idea comes. Of any particular mystery he says that the disposition in which Jesus carried it out is something that endures for ever. Again, the eternal existence of the Son with the Father is looked upon as a state and is compared to the seemingly static nine-month life in the womb of the Virgin. Bérulle wished at all costs to exorcise the time-spirit and to provide a firm basis for his spirituality ; he succeeds at times, as when he speaks of the wounding of the side of Christ as ' the symbol of the true and eternal wound of His Heart ', but he can also produce confusion, as when he prays to imitate the eternal Procession of the Son from the Father. If that Procession is, according to the teaching of the Church, *per modum intellectus* (as the thought from the mind), it is hard to see how adoptive sonship, which is all that men have, could make imitation possible of that aspect of the inner life of the Trinity (cf. the propositions of Eckhart, D 511, 522). Bérulle did not so concentrate on the states of Jesus as to encourage a passive Quietist spirituality which, having rejected consideration of the acts of Christ, came to reject all activity on the part of the individual follower of Christ. He looked for a *redundantia*, an overflow, of the imitation of the states of Christ into the spiritual life of the subject. His sense of the perpetuity of the dispositions of Christ does not quite come near the *Mysteriengegenwart* in the spirituality of Casel and of some modern Germans, but it had a great success in its own day and it was peculiarly adapted to the theory of the eternal sacrifice of Christ.

IV The sacrifice of Christ in the Mass was recognized by Bérulle as being an exception to his schematization of the mysteries of Christ, where past actions were distinct from the perpetual and enduring disposition, for here the act was itself enduring and the sacrifice is continually offered by Christ on earth. Taking from Vasquez and Lessius the idea of a purely mystical (and not a real) immolation in the Mass, he made the sacrifice consist in the, ' presenting before God of the victim of the human race, under the appearances of bread and wine, that the Body given for us, this the Blood shed for us '. The theory of Origen, of Clement and of Cyril at Alexandria, and of Thomassin among the disciples of Bérulle, seems to have been held, if only in an undeveloped way, by

Bérulle himself. This theory made the offering of the sacrifice come from Christ *as God*. ' Offering is made to God by means of God ', says Origen in the *Dialektos*, and Bérulle makes the singular excellence of the Christian religion consist in the serving of God by means of God. ' All is divine in this state ; the object adored is God and the means by which Christians adore is so too.' The common teaching of Catholic theologians makes the sacrifice come from Christ who by *His manhood* is our high-priest ; this is one of the cases where the exchange of properties (*see* COMMUNICATIO IDIOMATUM) between godhead and manhood in Christ should not be made. If the Son of God who sits in heaven is not one with the one who sheds His blood in sacrifice on earth, there is no redemption, as Cyril of Alexandria urged (PG 76:1398) but in that same passage he could see and proclaim that Christ exercised His priesthood in His humanity (λειτουργῶν ἀνθρωπίνως), while elsewhere he followed Origen (who had himself learnt from Philo) into the confusion noted above (PG 68:625). Bérulle went on to regard Christ as exercising His priesthood in heaven by sending His Spirit (and therefore acting through His godhead) upon the faithful in baptism so that He could associate them with His sacrifice in the Church. It may be that, when the problem of the *Epiklesis* in the Mass is taken up by the theologians, they may come to see in each Mass a sending (or *Missio*) of the Spirit by Christ and to affirm that after all it is the one Person of the god-man who offers the sacrifice, but the problem of the right to attribute this sacrifice indifferently to the humanity or divinity will remain. When Christ sent the Spirit upon His apostles to give them the power to forgive sins, and this by His humanity. May not the same be said of heaven ?

V The influence of Bérulle on the theology of the heavenly sacrifice is most marked in the writings of his immediate successor as head of the Oratory, Père de Condren. M. Olier, founder of S. Sulpice, took from him the idea of basing the spiritual life on an understanding of the ' states of Jesus ' and St John Eudes drew from his Office for the feast of Jesus many of the notions that would appear again in the devotion to the Sacred Heart as it was preached by the Eudists. With that same Office there was included a Litany of the Holy Childhood, the collect for which gives another aspect of Bérulle's theology, showing how much of modern French spirituality is due to him : ' Lord Jesus, who hast deigned to empty out for us the glory of Thy incarnate divinity and of Thy most divine humanity to the lowly state of infancy and childhood, grant us to recognize Thy divine wisdom in Thy infancy, Thy power in Thy weakness, Thy majesty in Thy lowly state, that we may adore Thee a babe upon earth and look upon Thee almighty in the heavens '.[2] This was not the

---

[1] L'Église . . . engendre et conserve toujours en son sein ses enfants sans les pousser dehors, lesquels aussi . . . vivent de la substance de leur mère. Et si quelques-uns, comme les hérétiques, sortent hors du sein de leur mère . . . ce ne sont plus enfants mais ce sont comme monstres . . . qui déchirent le ventre . . . comme vipères. *Grandeurs*, X:1.

[2] Domine Jesu, qui sublimitatem incarnatae divinitatis Tuae et humanitatis Tuae divinissimae usque ad humillimum nativitatis et infantiae statum pro nobis exinanire dignatus es, da nobis ut divinam in infantia sapientiam, in debilitate potentiam, in exilitate maiestatem agnoscentes Te parvulum adoremus in terris, Te magnum intueamur in caelis.

medieval enthusiasm of a Franciscan for the Christmas crib, just as Bérulle's whole devotion to Christ was not a singling out of the sacred humanity alone; he wanted all the time to keep a balance of the two natures. He was in this sense Christocentric (a much abused word), and that most of all by way of reaction against the air-borne exaggerations of the Dionysians. 'Denis's hid divinity' still counted for much, and if it no longer does so, that may be put down in no small measure to Bérulle.

Bibliography. The *Opera* of Bérulle were published in 1644 and reprinted by Migne in 1856; his *Correspondance* in three volumes was edited by J. Dagens (1937-9); his *Opuscula* by G. Rotureau in 1944; a life, *Le Cardinal de Bérulle* (2 vols) was produced by A. Molien in 1947; J. Dagens has studied the formative period of Bérulle's life in *Bérulle et les origines de la restauration catholique* (1952). The controversy between Bremond and others about the debt of Bérulle to Isabella Bellinzaga and her *Breve Compendio* was summed up in D Sp I (s.v. Breve Compendio) in 1936, but later material has been published by P. Pirri sj, in *La dama milanese, Archivum historicum Societatis Iesu* 14 (1945) 1-72 and 40 (1951) 231-53; other influences can be found treated in J. Zöbelein, *Die Beziehungen Franz von Sales zu Kardinal Bérulle* (1956); Fr Bruno ODC, *La Belle Acarie* (1942); B. Kiesler, *Die Struktur des Theozentrismus bei Bérulle und de Condren* (1934); L. Cognet, *Post-reformation spirituality* (1959). The doctrines of Bérulle are discussed by E. A. Walsh, *The priesthood in the writings of the French School* (1949); J. Galy, *Le Sacrifice dans l'école française* (1951); M. Nicolas OP, 'La Doctrine mariale du cardinal Bérulle', in RT 43 (1937) 81-100; E. Mersch sj, *The Whole Christ* (1938) 531-55.

J. H. C.

BIBLE, USE OF, IN THEOLOGY The word 'Bible' is derived from the late Latin *Biblia*, corresponding to the Greek *ta biblia* 'the books', used specifically of the canonical books of Scripture. Its use here includes, as ordinarily, both the OT and NT.

There are, by accepted reckoning, 73 books in all, of which 46 make up the OT and 27 the NT. All these are received by the Church as divinely inspired and as making up her official Canon of sacred writings (*see* CANON). This divine library may be considered under two aspects in particular: (I) as one of the two sources of God's revelation to men, and (II) as one of the two main sources of theological learning. Under (I), it is emphasized that the Bible is the Church's book; under (II) that the Bible is used in theological study for the proof and establishment of doctrine, whether this doctrine forms part of the dogmas established by papal or conciliar definition or is taught by the Church's ordinary *magisterium*.

I The Bible is one of the two sources of God's revelation to men. Contrary to the teaching of the reformers, who claimed that Scripture alone was the unique source of revelation, the Council of Trent in its fourth session proclaimed that all truths concerning salvation and the rule of right living are contained in written books and unwritten traditions; both of these sources are received by the Church with equal veneration and respect (D 783). This decree of Trent was confirmed by the Vatican Council in its third session (D 1783), which added that the books of Scripture are held to be sacred and canonical not as though they had been written in an ordinary human fashion and subsequently approved by the Church, nor because they contain revelation without error, but 'because, having been written under the inspiration of the Holy Spirit they have God for their author, and as such have been handed down to the Church'.

It is to be noted, in the first place, that Scripture is not the *sole source of revelation*, since, side by side with it, the Church recognizes also divine and apostolic traditions (*see* TRADITION). Whereas William of Ockam had associated with Scripture as the rule of faith the doctrine of the universal Church, the reformers rejected the doctrine of the Church and held that Scripture was the sole infallible rule of faith. The Council of Trent was at pains to correct this heretical aberration.

Further, the Bible is not the *first source of revelation* either in order of time or in the logical order. For (i) in order of time, divine revelation preceded the Scriptures, which did not exist from the beginning. Knowledge of Scripture was not necessary for the acceptance of divine revelation, since God had spoken to men and made known His will to them. So Tertullian in his *Adversus Hermogenem* (PL 2:220-1) decides that, in order of time, the natural knowledge of God antedated the Scriptures, which were added later, much as in the Christian era the apostles' teaching preceded the NT writings (cf. Irenaeus, *adv. haer.* III:i:1). The preaching of the Gospel was made known to the Gentiles without the use of a written NT, and the Christian faith existed for several generations *without the instruction of the Scriptures* (cf. Irenaeus, *op. cit.* IV:xxxviii:2H). One may conclude from this that the reading of the Scriptures was not necessary for the faithful, who received by oral preaching the truths of the supernatural revelation contained in Holy Writ. (ii) In the logical order it was the authority of the Church that determined which books formed part of the canon of Scripture and has full claim to establish the dogmatic and moral teaching revealed by God. The unique criterion of the Scriptures' divine authority is the explicit declaration of the infallible Church.

Again, Scripture, as one of the sources of revelation, is not *superior to the divine and apostolic traditions*, which are no less revealed by God than are the Scriptures. Hence the Council of Trent (D 783) receives both sources of revelation with equal veneration and respect, since both contain materially the word of God, though Scripture, by reason of its inspired character is formally the word of God in a manner not shared by apostolic traditions.

Again, Scripture is *not the total and complete source*

of revelation, since, side by side with it, there is another source, Tradition. It may, in fact, be claimed that Tradition is wider in its ambit than Scripture, since all divinely revealed truths are contained in Tradition, a part of those which are embodied in Scripture having been handed down orally before being written, and all of them having been preserved in the Church and by the Church, even though the Church does not possess the complete deposit of revelation apart from Scripture, of which it is the guardian and the interpreter. Yet, it should be added, the Council of Trent did not pronounce upon the question whether Tradition contains more of divine truth than does Scripture and does not reckon formally as traditions the divine truths contained in the Bible.

How far are all truths necessary for salvation contained in Scripture ? Some theologians have held that all dogmas which must be believed for salvation are therein contained. But the more common teaching of theologians is that the Scriptures do not contain, at least explicitly, all dogmas.

Does the whole of Scripture pertain in some manner to divine revelation ? St Thomas taught that all that is in Scripture pertains to the faith, but he distinguishes between those truths which pertain principally and of themselves to the faith, such as the Trinity and the Incarnation, and those which pertain to it indirectly and secondarily, such as the fact that Abraham had two sons or that, at the touch of Eliseus' bones, the dead man was restored to life (Summa 1:32:4c ; 2–2ae :1:6@1 ; 2:5c). It would follow that all the formal statements of Scripture (i.e. everything that God teaches therein through the human authors) even though not directly revealed to the sacred authors, belong, at least indirectly, to the deposit of revelation, even though not all are the object of divine faith.

Finally, Scripture as a source of revelation is *not sufficient in itself*. It is in itself a dead letter, which is in need of a living interpreter ; it contains doctrine, but this needs to be extracted from it ; in itself it concludes no discussion and is not the final judge in matters of controversy. It is, as experience shows, all too easy to falsify it and to falsify its interpretation. The sole judge in controverted matters is the living apostolic tradition, as it is embodied in the teaching of the apostles' lawful successors. Although the Church is the supreme judge in matters of faith and morals, she is not the *absolute mistress of the Scriptures*. It is her task to keep and defend the treasure of Holy Writ ; she may not neglect it or deviate from it. The rightful authority of the Scriptures is not diminished by their dependence for their interpretation upon the Church's teaching authority.

II The Bible is one of the two sources of theological teaching. The Church, in receiving the truths divinely revealed, looks to Holy Scripture as to the chief source from which theologians derive arguments or proofs in support of theological conclusions. It is for this reason that Pope Leo XIII in *Providentissimus Deus* declares that it is ' most desirable and essential that the whole teaching of theology

should be pervaded and animated by the use of the divine word of God ' (*EnchB* 114).

Scripture, then, since it derives from an authority founded upon divine revelation, is the chief source of proof in theological discussion. Because the divine authority is the weightiest of all, it follows that the argument from Scripture, when it is based upon the deposit of revelation, is firm and beyond dispute. If, however, the proof passages pertain only probably to divine revelation, only probable arguments can be based upon them.

Rules for the use of Scripture in theology. The sacred books of the OT and NT being those recognized by the Church as sacred and canonical, proof-passages from Scripture must be based upon the books forming part of the Church's canon. Further, since all the declarations of Scripture which come from the hands of the inspired writers are part of the deposit of revelation, all are capable of being used as scriptural sources of theological teaching. But, for this purpose, they must be read in the context of the inspired writings with due regard to ' the literary modes adopted by the sacred writer ' (*EnchB* 560) and ' the special character of each one, and, as it were, his personal traits'. (*EnchB* 556). Both quotations are from the Encyclical *Divino Afflante Spiritu*, the latter being taken from *Spiritus Paraclitus*. Those declarations of the sacred writings that contain explicitly articles of faith are absolutely certain and infallible scriptural proofs of theological teaching. If, however, such declarations express truths pertaining only indirectly and secondarily to faith they are to be regarded as scriptural proofs of theological teaching only in so far as they are certainly contained in the deposit of faith (cf. St Thomas, Summa 1–2ae 2:5c). Normally, teaching that is certainly made known by Scripture should be proposed by the Church as revealed and, as such, is something that we are obliged to accept as of faith. This condition is absent in many of the affirmations of Scripture that pertain only incidentally to our supernatural end, and are not, as such, proposed by the Church for our belief. When the Church defines that such and such a scriptural text contains revealed dogma, the exact sense of this being determined, it is a strict duty for Catholic exegetes to accept an infallible definition of this kind. Such is the formal teaching of the Council of Trent (Sess. IV, D 786), the Vatican Council (Sess. III, cap. ii, D 1788), the encyclical *Providentissimus Deus* (D 1942) and the decree *Lamentabili sane exitu* of 3 July 1907, propositions 2–4 (D 2002–4). It is possible, apart from formal definition, to deduce from Scripture an article of faith which is contained therein implicitly. Such a deduction, if it is evident, may be accepted, even before any formal definition by the Church, as a certain source of theological teaching.

From the point of view of *interpretation*, the declarations of Scripture, of which the *explicit* literal sense is certain, provide of themselves, and antecedently to the Church's definition, certain theological proofs and efficacious arguments. The *implicit* literal sense is of itself capable of providing theologians with certain arguments, but, since the passage from the implicit to the explicit sense involves an explanation of terms, a truth contained implicitly in Scripture is not the equivalent of a principle of faith antecedently to the Church's definition. When the literal sense, whether explicit or implicit, is not certain, it can provide only probable theological arguments. When the Church has defined the literal sense, whether this be explicit or implicit, this sense becomes a principle of faith, not to be denied without lapse into heresy, and a certain and infallible theological argument.

When the Church makes use of passages from the Bible without defining that the literal or typical sense which is attributed to them is the true sense, this use provides a certain theological proof but not an infallible one, and it would be temerarious but not heretical to deny this. In matters of faith and morals the sense adopted by the unanimous consent of the Fathers constitutes a sure but not infallible argument in favour of a doctrine. Again, where the Fathers, even when they are unanimous, or the doctors and theologians, use a biblical text in proof of a dogma, not in the name of the Church but on their own authority, their interpretation constitutes a certain but not an infallible proof in support of a dogma. The *typical* or *spiritual* sense of Scripture intended by the Holy Spirit is, in itself, a certain argument, but it is only valid where the existence of such a spiritual sense of Scripture is wholly established. This sense is held to be present, whether certainly or probably, when it is attested certainly or probably by one of the sacred writers or by the unanimous consent of the Fathers.

The so-called *consequent* sense of Scripture, which is deduced by a process of reasoning from a biblical text, has for the theologian sure authority. If the deduction is made from the certain or defined literal sense of a text, it would be an error to contradict it. If, however, it results from the comparison of two texts or from a syllogism in which one member is scriptural and the other from human reason, this has the value of a theological conclusion of the same order. The sense of any scriptural proposition that contradicts the *analogy of faith* is always false, but the sense that is positively in harmony with the analogy is not always necessarily the true one, and it only constitutes a scriptural argument in theological questions if it is otherwise established. The *accommodative* sense can never be of direct service as an argument from Holy Scripture.

As regards the texts of Scripture to be used, a theologian may derive sure arguments from texts in use in the universal Church, such as the Septuagint Greek and the Greek New Testament. Texts in use only in particular churches, such as the Syriac, the Coptic and the Armenian, have slightly less value for the purpose of proof. The Vulgate as the version officially approved by the Council of Trent, has the value of the original texts in matters of faith and morals, and all the texts which it comprises constitute, in this respect, sure theological proofs, equal to those derived from the original Hebrew, Aramaic or Greek texts. Various editions of the original texts and of the ancient versions made by non-Catholics are not to be employed if they are designed for the propagation of heretical teaching. Their use, provided that they are faithful and complete texts, is permitted to students of theology and Holy Scripture. One may mention among others the various editions of R. Kittel's *Biblia Hebraica*, Nestle's *Novum Testamentum Graece et Latine*, Wordsworth and White's ed. of the Vulgate New Testament (now completed by Professor H. D. Sparks), Walton's Polyglot Bible, and H. B. Swete's edition of the Septuagint Greek Old Testament.

Bibliography. Considerable use has been made of E. Mangenot's authoritative article 'Écriture sainte' in DTC, 2092–2101, as also of E. Mangenot and J. Rivière, 'Interprétation de l'écriture', DTC, VII, 2290–2343. See also A. Durand sj, 'Critique biblique' and 'Exégèse', DAFC, I, 760–819 and 1811–1841. A fundamental work is Cardinal Franzelin, *De divina traditione et Scriptura* (3rd ed., 1882). See also Dom H. Höpfl osb, *Introductio Generalis in Sacram Scripturam* (ed. B. Gut, 5th ed., 1950); and the *Institutiones Biblicae scholis accommodatae* (6th ed. 1951) published by the Biblical Institute, Rome.

J. M. T. B.

BILLOT, LOUIS (1846–1931), Jesuit theologian and cardinal. Here are considered (I) his life and writings; (II) his theological aims and method; (III) his influence.

I Life and Writings. Billot was born at Sierck (Moselle), France, 12 Jan. 1846. He was educated at colleges in Metz and Bordeaux and at the Grand Séminaire of Blois, where he was ordained priest in 1869. The same year he entered the Society of Jesus, and after his novitiate lectured on Sacred Scripture at Laval from 1871 to 1875. He spent the next four years as a preacher, first at Paris for three years, and then at Laval. He was professor of dogmatic theology at the Catholic Faculty of Angers from 1879 to 1882, and from 1882 to 1885 at the Jesuit house of studies in Jersey. In 1885 he was selected as professor of dogmatic theology at the Gregorian University, Rome, by Pope Leo XIII. As a remedy for the errors and false philosophy of the day, Pope Leo had in his encyclical *Aeterni Patris* (1879) prescribed a return to scholastic philosophy, and in particular to the doctrine of St Thomas Aquinas, in ecclesiastical education. In pursuance of this policy he reserved to himself the appointment of professors for the principal ecclesiastical colleges in Rome. After one year in Rome Billot returned to Paris, but was recalled by the Pope in 1887. From that year until 1910 he was occupied uninterruptedly in teaching dogmatic theology at the Gregorian University.

As a professor Billot was exceptionally successful. He left an ineffaceable impression, in which admiration and affection were mingled with religious respect, on thousands of students from all parts of the world who over the years followed his lectures at the old Gregorian in the Via del Seminario. He was remarkable for the lucidity with which he handled the most abstract themes, and for the warmth, earnestness and eloquence of his delivery. From 1892 onwards his courses were published at frequent intervals. The qualities which commended his oral teaching are clearly discernible in his books. These raise them well above the level of the average manual of theology. They are vivid, lucid, well-balanced, somewhat rhetorical in style, abounding in bold affirmation and negation, touched at times with irony and sarcasm. In the most abstract realms of theological speculation the author moves with the effortless ease of a master.

The following list gives the titles, date of first edition, date and number of the latest edition of Billot's theological courses : *De Verbo Incarnato*, 1892 (1949[9]) ; *De Ecclesiae Sacramentis*, I, 1894 ; II, 1895 (I & II, 1931[7]) ; *De Peccato Personali*, 1894 ; *De Peccato Originali*, 1912 (combined as *De Personali et Originali Peccato*, 1931[6]) ; *De Deo Uno et Trino*, 1895 (1957[8]) ; *De Ecclesia Christi*, I, 1898 (1927[5]) ; *De Ecclesia Christi*, II, 1910 (1929[3]) ; *De Virtutibus Infusis*, 1901 (1928[4]) ; *Quaestiones de Novissimis*, 1902 (1946[8]) ; *De Inspiratione Sacrae Scripturae*, 1903 (1928[4]) ; *De Sacra Traditione*, 1904 (later title *De Immutabilitate Traditionis contra novam haeresim modernismi* (1929[4])) ; *De Gratia Christi*, 1912 (1954[5]).

In 1909 Billot was nominated a Consultor of the Holy Office. His services were much in demand in this capacity, and his counsel was often at the service of Pope St Pius X during the doctrinal crises of his reign. His services to the Church were recognized in 1911 when he was created Cardinal. Henceforward he occupied himself largely with his work on the Roman congregations and in preparing fresh editions of his books. To *Études*, the journal of the French Jesuits, he contributed between 1917 and 1919 a series of ten articles entitled *La Parousie*, in which he controverted the Modernist eschatology ; and between 1919 and 1923 he dealt in a further ten articles in the same review with the problem of the salvation of souls not reached by the preaching of the Gospel. They appeared under the title, *La Providence de Dieu et le nombre infini d'hommes en dehors de la voie normale du salut*. He also contributed a few articles to *Gregorianum*, the theological review of the Gregorian University.

Billot's conviction that the atheistic philosophy behind the French Revolution was the source of most of the errors of his day, and his fervent adhesion to the hierarchical principle in society, make more intelligible the sympathy he felt with the *Action française* before the doctrinal deviations of that movement brought down on it a formal condemnation by Pope Pius XI early in 1927. The refusal of submission by a number of its adherents, and their attempts to justify their contumacy by alleging his support, were a source of great pain to Billot. He himself urged and practised complete submission, as is clear from a letter written by him to Père Henri du Passage, in March 1928, and printed by the latter in *Études*, CCX (1932) 491 f. Shortly after the condemnation in 1927 Billot was authorized by the Pope to renounce his dignity of the cardinalate,

and retired to the Jesuit novitiate at Galloro near Rome, where he died, 18 Dec. 1931.

II Theological aims and method. In his theological teaching and writing Billot set himself two complementary objectives : the restoration of the scholastic theology of the 13th cent., account being taken of course of genuine progress in later times, and the destruction of Modernism and Liberalism in religion. It was the doctrine and method of St Thomas and his great contemporaries that Billot sought to re-establish, not that of 16th and 17th cent. commentators, whether Dominican or Jesuit. For him these were but relatively modern writers, the ' *recentiores* ', who are to be judged in the light of the great masters of the School, the ' *veteres scholae principes* '. Billot was encouraged to take St Thomas Aquinas for his master not only by the directives of Pope Leo XIII, but also by the Constitutions and *Ratio Studiorum* of the Society of Jesus and the recent 23rd General Congregation of the Society of Jesus held in 1883. Like his colleague Mattiussi, Billot interpreted these directives to signify the adoption in full of the twenty-four theses of the Thomistic philosophy, which were later, in 1914, approved by the Congregation of Seminaries, but never imposed in their entirety. Among them were some which Billot expounded and applied with luminous skill, notably those of the analogy of the concept of being (*see* ANALOGY), its division into act and potency (*see* ACT AND POTENCY), the real distinction between essence and existence in created being, and their real identity in God alone. This last thesis Billot considered the most fundamental in metaphysical theology.

Against the Modernist doctrine of vital immanence (*see* MODERNISM) Billot in his treatise on faith (*De Virtutibus Infusis*, thesis XVII) insisted on the necessity of a rational basis of the judgment of credibility. In his *De Sacra Traditione* he refuted the Modernist conception of the evolution of dogma, with special reference to the theories of Loisy. In his *De Inspiratione Sacrae Scripturae* he attacked their notion of a relative truth in Scripture, and their treatment of literary forms in the Bible. In his *De Sacramentis* he takes issue with the Modernist doctrine of the sacraments as mere signs of human institution.

In Liberalism Billot saw a complexus of heresies, based on the atheistic philosophy of the French Revolution. In his *De Ecclesia*, II, he distinguishes and refutes three forms in which it is found : absolute Liberalism, which advocates the subordination of the Church to the State ; moderate Liberalism, which proclaims as a matter of principle their separation and independence ; Liberal Catholicism, which also advocated their separation, but only as a matter of expediency.

Billot's chosen theological method was that of speculative dogmatic theology. In this he excelled. He has been criticized for his relative neglect of biblical and positive theology. There is some substance in the charge, but it has been exaggerated. In his personal studies he did not neglect positive theology. His books represent the lectures which he gave to beginners in theology. Billot's aim was to form men with a good theological judgment, not *savants*. Certainly a foundation based on the sources of revelation is necessary for this purpose, and Billot did not neglect it ; even if his theological proofs are not copious, they are usually adequate. He was aware, too, that his students received courses on exegesis and historical theology from his colleagues. His method was the speculative dogmatic method, which seeks not so much to prove the data of revelation as to penetrate and interrelate its various parts and aspects, and to demonstrate that it is not intrinsically incoherent and self-contradictory. Billot held, correctly enough, that training in this type of theology is the best for the formation of beginners. He realized too that despite the great progress made by Catholics in positive theology during the 19th cent., the threat to religion from rationalism on the one hand and pietism on the other had not yet been averted. What was needed, he judged, was not so much additional information as sounder principles of criticism and judgment.

III Billot's influence. Through his books, lectures and theological consultations Billot played an important part in the defeat of Modernism. More permanent was the effect of his speculative method on subsequent theology. He showed the importance of laying an adequate philosophical basis of dogmatic speculation. A notable example is the consideration he gives in his *De Verbo Incarnato* to the question of the distinction of essence and existence, before propounding and developing his theory of the hypostatic union. More striking still is the masterly treatment of the concept of relation in his *De Deo Trino*, his theological masterpiece which has been called a ' poem in the metaphysic of relation '. Similarly in his *De Gratia* he first analyses the mode of divine concurrence in created activity, and especially in the actions of free agents. He then develops a theory of physical premotion, without physical predetermination of free-will, on which he builds a doctrine of the nature of actual grace which is intermediate between that of most Molinists and that of Bañez and his followers (*see* GRACE). In his *De Sacramentis* he analyses acutely the concepts of cause and sign before establishing his theory of a sacramental causality which is instrumental and dispositive in the intentional order. His skilful method was such that certain theses which he defended became associated with his name, even though their fundamental idea was taken from some earlier writer. We may mention, for example, his explanation of the hypostatic union, which goes back to Capreolus. Even where in points of detail his solutions have been abandoned they often continue to exercise their influence. In the theology of the sacraments in general, for example, it was he who restored to theology a conception of dispositive causality which had been abandoned since the late Middle Ages. The theory is still in favour, although not quite in the form in which it was developed by Billot. In the theology of the Eucharist he dealt a death blow to certain post-Reformation destruc-

tionist and abasement theories of the nature of the Eucharistic sacrifice by his theory of a mystical immolation in the order of symbolic reality. He thus took the first step in leading theology back to the patristic and medieval conception of a sacramental sacrifice. Here, too, his work has had further and important developments in recent years.

Certain others of his ideas have declined in favour. Among them may be mentioned his advocacy of the possibility of intrinsically supernatural acts on the part of one who has only a natural knowledge of God. The singular theory which he expounded in his articles in *Études*, 1919–23, of the existence of multitudes of men who throughout their lives never arrive at a sufficiently clear notion of God to make them morally responsible for their actions never found acceptance.

Billot was undoubtedly the most brilliant Catholic theologian of his day. As a positive theologian he was not the equal of Franzelin, his predecessor at the Gregorian, but he surpassed him in speculative genius, and it is as a speculative theologian that his influence is still operative.

Bibliography. H. Le Floch, *Le Cardinal Billot* (1947) ; J. Lebreton, ' S.É. Le Cardinal Billot ', *Études* CXXIX (1911) 514–25 ; J. Bittremieux, ' Le R.P. Louis Billot ', *ETL* 9 (1932) 292–5 ; H. Du Passage, 'Réponse à une calomnie', *Études* CCX (1932) 491 f. ; E. Hocedez, *Histoire de la théologie au XIXᵉ siècle* III (1947) ; *Catholicisme*, II, 61–3 ; *LTK²* II, 477.   F. C.

BIOLOGY : IMPACT UPON THEOLOGY

This science has made rapid progress in the last half-century and many of its theories have implications for the theologian. Most of these are in the field of moral, rather than in that of dogmatic, theology ; nevertheless there remain such questions as the origin of man (*see* EVOLUTION), the birth of Christ (*see* VIRGIN BIRTH), and various others. This article will deal with (I) the Incarnation ; (II) Cell Theory and the Mystical Body, and (III) the Resurrection of the Body.

I Biology and the Incarnation. Christ was conceived by the power of the Holy Ghost in the womb of the Virgin Mary. The question arises as to just what was involved in the miraculous conception. In what, in other words, did the miracle consist ? The modern biologist tends to look upon the process of fertilization as being a twofold one. The male seed penetrates the female egg and thus stimulates its division and development. In the higher animals, man included, this development will not take place normally until after the fusion of the male and female nuclei, which are contained within the seed and egg respectively. It is to this second stage that the biologist tends to reserve the term conception. It will be seen that the male seed has then a twofold purpose. It stimulates the egg to undergo growth and development, and also supplies via its nucleus the male parent's contribution to the inheritance of the offspring. In this process the male seed is the active element seeking out and linking with the female egg. In many of the lower animals the egg is stimulated to develop, and does so, without the fusion of a male and female nucleus. This development is called parthenogenetic. Such a mode of development in mammals is not known to date, though its theoretical possibility is not denied. Spontaneous parthenogenesis in mammals would seem to run into difficulties that are largely genetic and, as far as one can see, if it were to occur, the offspring would of necessity have to be female. This on genetic grounds.

In mammalian development, therefore, the two-fold process always seems to take place ; that is, the stimulation of the egg to develop and the fusion of the male and female nuclei.

It would seem, therefore, that we cannot say that the birth of Our Lord was a truly parthenogenetic one, using this term in its strictly technical sense. The action of the Holy Spirit was one which supplied both the stimulation to the egg to develop in its normal way and also supplied what would normally be supplied by the male element by way of the physical basis of the offspring's inheritance. For this point of view one can quote St Thomas in *Commentary on the Sentences* (III:3:2:1c) : ' The divine power did everything that in other conceptions is done by the seed from the father ; and therefore St John Damascene speaks of the divine power as the divine seed '.[1]

On our Blessed Lady's part was supplied what a mother normally contributes towards the conception of a child and this according to the normal laws of nature. She was truly the Mother in that He grew from her flesh. St Thomas again supports this in *Commentary on the Sentences* (III:3:2:2c) : ' The matter which the Virgin supplied was that from which naturally a human body could be formed, but the active power starting the development was divine . . . because of this Christ was the natural son of the Virgin, since the natural material for His conception was prepared within her '.[2]

Since, then, the Holy Spirit supplied what the father would normally supply, we have grounds for a belief that Our Lord could have looked physically like Joseph, and it might be possible to add this to the normal interpretation of the Gospel passage : ' Why, they said, is not this the son of Joseph ? ' (Lk 4: 22 Kn).

II Cell Theory and the Mystical Body. That the Church is a body is frequently asserted in the Sacred Scriptures. ' He too ', says the Apostle, ' is that head whose body is the Church ' (Col 1:18 Kn). Now a body or an organism, as we generally understand it, is composed of many members which are linked together in such a way as to assist each other within the organism of which they form part. So too in the Church the individual members do not live for themselves alone, but all work in mutual collaboration and for the more perfect building up of the whole body which is the Church.

Modern biological theory can help us to get a clearer understanding of St Paul's notion, but we must remember that, this being knowledge by way of analogy, there will be many differences as well.

The term ' cell ' was originally applied to the smallest units of plants and animals that could be seen. This is now no longer the case, as the ' cell ' is known to be a complex consisting of a number of well-defined structures. As a result, in these days the cell is not looked upon as the ultimate structural unit of an organism, but it is a physiological unit. In other words, it is not because for the most part it is bounded by a wall separating it from its neighbouring cells that it is looked upon as a unit, but because of its chemical activities. Within the cell itself the most obvious features are the nucleus and the cytoplasm. The nucleus has a primary rôle in inheritance and embryonic development. The cytoplasm is principally concerned with everyday activity, e.g. respiration of the cell ; secretion ; differentiation, etc. The cytoplasm and nucleus are in intimate contact, physically and physiologically. The nucleus appears to co-ordinate and control the cytoplasmic activities. Neither the nucleus nor the cytoplasm can be looked upon as being structurally simple nor single, but together they form the physiological unit that the biologist calls a ' cell '.

Multicellular organisms are usually derived from a single cell, the fertilized egg in the case of the higher animals. Now the striking feature about these ' organized communities ' is the fact of unity. From one generalized cell we get the myriad of different specialized cells that make up the organism, e.g. a human body, yet that organism is one thing and not just a collection of cells. Each cell behaves as if it knew what was expected of it and as if it knew what all the other cells were up to. This is because communication exists both within a cell and also between cells. This form of intercellular communication is usually chemical. Biology is only just beginning to explore these problems and the process and control of this differentiation from one cell to the multicellular organism is one of the great questions of modern biological research. The process of differentiation has always seemed particularly mysterious, because there is no easy parallel in the non-living world that might give us a clue as to how it takes place. In the inanimate realm we do not come across a situation in which parts of a single mass of material gradually diverge from one another and become completely different in character, whilst at the same time the organism which they form has a unity of a higher order. Yet in all living things this process of differentiation, which is not haphazard but controlled, seems to be a basic law of nature. In the arising organism many of the cells become atrophied, or in dying leave products, which are themselves non-living. These atrophied cells and these products are part of the organism.

[1] Virtus autem divina fecit totum quod fit in aliis conceptionibus per virtutem seminis quod est a patre ; et ideo Damascenus divinam virtutem dicit quasi divinum semen.

[2] Materia enim quam Virgo ministravit fuit materia ex qua naturaliter corpus hominis formari potuit ; sed virtus formans fuit divina . . . et propter hoc dicitur Christus naturalis filius Virginis, quia naturalem materiam ad conceptum praeparavit.

Now just as in a natural body the origin is from a single cell, so too with the Church its origin is from one, Christ. And, as in nature a body is not the result of a haphazard process but is made up of organs, that is, of members that do not all have the same function but are arranged in an order, so too in the Church we find this organic structure of united parts and this grouping of reciprocally dependent members. It is thus that the Apostle describes the Church : ' Each of us has one body, with many different parts, and not all these parts have the same function ; just so we, though many in number, form one body in Christ, and each acts as the counterpart of another ' (Rom 12:4–5 Kn).

In a natural organism we see too that not all the cells are necessarily alive and active but may be atrophied ; so also we see that the Mystical Body of Christ may have members that are far from active and may indeed be atrophied without ceasing to be members of that body.

Just as the natural body arises by a process of growth and differentiation from a single source, so too the Mystical Body arose from Christ and by a process akin to differentiation and growth the Church has grown and will continue to grow. There are, however, many differences which should be noted. In a natural body the parts are united in such a way that in a true sense each lacks its own individual subsistence, but in the Mystical Body the mutual union, though intrinsic, links the members by a bond which leaves to each the complete enjoyment of his own personality. Furthermore, in every physical body the cells forming it and making up its organs are ultimately destined to the good of the whole alone, while in every moral association of men it is to the advancement of all in general, and each single member in particular, for they are persons, that we must look. But, if we compare the Mystical Body with a moral body, there are still further considerable differences to be noted. In the Mystical Body the collaboration between members is supplemented by another internal principle, which is vastly superior to whatever bonds of union may be found in a physical or in a moral body. This is something not of the natural but of the supernatural order ; indeed, it is something in itself infinite, uncreated : the Spirit of God.

III The Resurrection of the Body. From the time that the Sadducees, men who denied the resurrection of the body, put their question to Our Lord, to our own day attacks have been made on this teaching of Christ and His Church. The resurrection of the body is a defined article of faith, but what is meant by saying that we will all rise with the same body which we now have ?

Here in particular we will examine the question of the sexual determination of the human body. The modern biologist tends to look upon the determination of sex as being very largely a quantitative and not so much a qualitative matter. From both parents are handed on to the offspring a number of chromosomes, the physical basis of inheritance, one set from each parent. The father has two different sets to hand on. If he hands on in his seed a set of chromosomes carrying the so-called X-chromosome together with the other (or autosomal) chromosomes, these link with the mother's X- and autosomal chromosomes to produce a female offspring. If, on the other hand, he hands on a Y-chromosome together with the autosomal ones, then these link with the mother's X- and autosomal chromosomes to produce a male offspring. However, the older theory of sex-determination being due to the possession of XX-chromosomes or XY-chromosomes is now held to be not entirely true. The so-called autosomal chromosomes apparently carry factors making for maleness whilst those factors on the X-chromosome carry what is necessary to bring about femaleness. It takes, however, a double dose of these X-chromosome factors to outweigh the effect of the autosomal chromosomes. That is what biologists mean when they say that the sex-determining mechanism is largely quantitative.

Occasionally the offspring is not thrown definitely one way or the other, precisely because the mechanism is a quantitative one, and intersexes arise, though the whole problem is not fully understood.

Normally the exterior determination of sex has been a simple matter of anatomic observation. In cases of doubt, testing of the gonadal tissues was sufficient to indicate the sex of a child. There is, however, a sex difference in the nuclear morphology of cells in the form of a chromatin mass which is found much more frequently in cells from anatomical females than from males. There is no doubt that this chromatin test will prove helpful, but one curious aspect is that anatomically normal males at times have shown a chromatin pattern which is that of female nuclear or genetic sex. In an article in *The Lancet* (7066: 31 Jan. 1959, 217–9) there is a report on 1911 anatomically male infants, of which 5 had sex-chromatin patterns typical of the female. This is something that one would expect to happen if sex-determination is a quantitative matter. From the biological point of view it raises questions as to which is ultimate, anatomy or nuclear structure of the tissues, and since sex-determination appears to be a quantitative thing, is there a clear line of distinction between male and female ? Further, is maleness and femaleness a basic thing at all ?

When theologians have discussed the problem of the resurrection of the body they have often held divergent views about the manner of this. Some, like Billot, have held that the soul alone gives us our identity in the resurrection, and the matter which the soul will acquire at the last day will not be the body we had on earth. This will not be necessary for our personal resurrection. Generally speaking, the official definitions of the Church do not favour this idea, and indeed it is hard to see how one can then talk about the resurrection of the body at all. Christ's resurrection is normally taken as the model of our own and most theologians hold that He rose with the same body He had in His mortal life ; therefore, so shall we. Hence most hold also that we shall rise male and female as we are here on earth.

Perhaps in the end all we can say is that the thing, whatever it is, which expresses itself now in terms of anatomy or nuclear structure of the cells making up that anatomy will persist, although it may be expressed in quite different terms, in that order of creation, whatever it be, which will succeed when, after the last day and the resurrection of the dead, material creation itself has passed away.

Bibliography. A. Mitterer, *Dogma und Biologie* (1952) ; *R. A. Beatty, *Parthenogenesis and Polyploidy in Mammalian Development* (1957) ; The Encyclical : *Mystici Corporis Christi*, 29 June 1943 ; an article by *C. H. Waddington in *The Physics and Chemistry of Life* (1957) ; John R. Connery SJ, in TS 20 (1959) 619.   K. O'C.

BISHOP This article will try to reduce to some kind of order a very intractable topic with many ramifications. (I) The apostolic origin of the office of episcopacy turns upon its adequate distinction from that of the presbyter. (II) Reasons must then be assigned for the confusion of the two terms in the NT. (III) The earliest ordination prayers give some idea of the meaning of episcopacy in early times. (IV) The claim of presbyters to equality with bishops in Jerome and others is noticed, and (V) the tract *de septem ordinibus* with its primitive theology of Orders. (VI) The special case of Alexandria is discussed by itself. (VII) The legacy of Jerome in the Middle Ages helped to obscure the true nature of episcopacy. (VIII) St Thomas and the later Scholastics, and (IX) the Tridentine definition redress the balance. Thereafter in the 17th and 18th cents. (X) political theory minimized the importance of hierarchy in the Church and had to be checked at the Vatican Council. (XI) The present century has seen a return to the idea of the episcopate as the perfection of priesthood and the consequent relations of the two.

I The apostolic origin of episcopacy can now be studied in a clearer light since the existence of a parallel organization in the Dead Sea community has become known. The *Manual of Discipline* and the *Zadokite Work* witness to the existence of an ' overseer ' (*mebaqqer*) of the community whose duties were pastoral and judicial. He was in charge of all admissions to the group ; he had to preach and teach and to ' loose all bonds ', and to him charitable gifts were handed over. He had ten judges under him, who helped to distribute alms, and he was to be appealed to by the priests who led the groups of ten members. It is not therefore necessary with Dibelius and other German critics to appeal to the activities of Syrian building-commissioners (or to the by-name of Anubis, in Pap. Paris 2317) as the first parallel to the function of episcopacy in early times. One does not need to say that the Church copied the Dead Sea sect, but from the parallel it is clear that a religious organization with distribution and sub-ordination of functions was not an impossibility in the fourth decade of the 1st cent. One does not have to suppose that Christ's followers managed to subsist by force of a vague acknowledgment of the

outstanding qualities of some of their number until such time as contact with the efficient organization of the Roman empire caused them to try to imitate it. If other compact and differentiated religious bodies were in existence, or just about to start, why should not theirs also ?

The only attempt so far (1959) to evaluate the Qumran evidence from an evangelical viewpoint is that made by A. Adam (*Religion in Geschichte und Gegenwart* s.v. Bischof), who accepts the parallel of Christian bishop and *Mebaqqer*. He grants that the name of *episcopos* was primitive in Christianity since it occurs as a loanword in Syriac, Latin, Coptic and Ethiopic, and that the ' angels ' of Apoc 2 may have been the guardian spirits of local bishops in Asia. He tries to weaken the force of the parallel with *Mebaqqer* by using TB *Ketuboth* 106 a and Philo (*de specialibus legibus*, I, 166) to argue that Jewish *mebaqqer* were temple officials charged with inspecting animal offerings, a task for which, as Philo says, the most important priests were chosen. Christian *mebaqqer* would then be certain presbyters charged with special liturgical functions. But the Talmud qualifies these *mebaqqer* as ' inspectors of blemishes ' (*Mebaqqer momim*), so that ' inspectors simple ' would be of still greater position. There is more to be gathered about the Christian idea of inspection from a study of the use made in sub-apostolic times of the pastoral passage in Ez 34:11–12 and of similar passages in the apocryphal Ezechiel, which seems to have been a Christian enlargement dealing chiefly with the search for the lost sheep.

The laying on of hands which is several times mentioned in the NT was a Jewish act, first carried out by Moses (Num 27:18 and 23 ; Dt 34:9) when he caused Josue to be filled with the spirit of wisdom, and was a leaning upon the man (*semikah*) not a mere touching (*shith*) with the finger-tips. It was thus distinct from the touching of men for the purpose of healing them, as Professor Daube has made clear. In 1 Tim 4:14 the act of Paul is ' a leaning upon, for the purpose of making elders ', and the text is no warrant for the claim sometimes based upon it that the elders or presbyters themselves are to lay on hands. ' Presbyterate ' is there used as the abstract term and not as a collective. In Ac 9:10 Ananias touches Paul, but does not lean hands on him, and in Ac 13:3 there is a touch and no more. In Ac 6:6 it is the Apostles who lay on hands, as the *codex Bezae*, by correcting a somewhat ambiguous form of words, has been at pains to make clear.

The Jews used *semikah* as a ceremony of authorization whereby one Rabbi passed on his teaching authority to a pupil. The first recorded instance is the act of Johanan ben Zakkai, who thus ' ordained ' Rabbi Eliezer and R. Joshua before A.D. 80. In the time of the 2nd revolt (132) the Roman government forbade it, and R. Jehuda was put to death for having ordained five pupils of the rebel Aqiba in order to carry on the rabbinical tradition at a moment when the revolt was failing. It is of importance to notice that this Jewish evidence comes from the period (62–132) when rivalry and debate is going on between Christians and Jews, and some copying by the Jews of a Christian practice cannot be ruled out. The Talmud (*Sanhedrin* 13b) says that three Rabbis were required to perform *semikah*, both hands were used (*Menahoth* 93a) and it could not be done for women (*Chagigah* 16b), slaves, the deaf and dumb, minors or non-Jews. It was *not* practised for the initiation of a priest, who had a ritual bath, a clothing, anointing and attendance at a sacrifice as his rite. According to *Sanhedrin* 30b, *semikah* could not be undone. When in the later part of the 2nd cent. the Jews have a patriarch, no *semikah* is to be done without his consent. All these details will find an echo in the mind of one who knows early Christian practice about episcopal ordinations and it is reasonable to suppose that Jews and Christians were each aware of what the other was doing.

That the Apostles had bishops as successors in their teaching authority has been shown (*see* APOSTOLIC SUCCESSION), and if the act of *semikah* is an apostolic function in the NT, it would follow that the exercise of this power was from the first reserved to bishops and was not for presbyters to use in isolation. Christ was presented (in Mt and in Jn) as the prophet like unto, and greater than, Moses, and, even if there had been no record in the NT of the practice of *semikah*, it would have been natural to suppose it. 1 Pet 2:25 shows Christ in the rôle of bishop or, one might say, proto-bishop. That the term is *nicht technisch gemeint*, as von Campenhausen claims, would need to be proved, for the pastoral office of apostle and bishop is clear in the NT. His attempt to explain Christian origins by supposing that Jewish Christian communities have presbyters while Gentile groups have bishops and deacons, and that the full ministry comes with a fusion of the two, is not according to the facts.

The idea of a sacrificing priesthood is not present in the practice of *semikah* and the handing on of teaching authority, but since Christ was king-Messias and priest, it was possible to derive from his other function the idea of priesthood in the strict sense. Hippolytus (*in Dan.* 4:30 ; GCS 1:266) says, 'The perfect king and priest arrived, who alone did the will of the Father, as it is written in the book of Kings (citing 1 Sam 2:35) ... The Holy of holy ones is none other than the Son of God, who came and showed Himself to be the one anointed by the Father and sent into the world.' In 1 Pet 2:5 and 9 the 'spiritual sacrifices' which are mentioned as a part of the priest's function are closely linked in the text with Christ's atoning work and the liturgical word *anaferein* is used ; one cannot say that the plural 'sacrifices' shows that the apostle cannot mean the eucharist, for it is obvious that the eucharist can be repeated, thus justifying the plural, and one need not go searching for other sacrifices which Christians could have associated with the one great offering. Episcopal control of the eucharist is evidenced in Ignatius (*Smyrn.* 8:1). Athenagoras stressed the bloodless nature of the Christian sacrifice (*Legatio* 13) and Origen (*hom. in Lev.* 9:1 ; GCS 29:418) saw in it the chief spiritual sacrifice of praise. That all the

faithful are associated by Peter in the one sacrifice is not surprising except to one who has presupposed a laity entirely sundered from the ministerial class in the Church. 'Priest' in Jewish language was so closely linked with animal sacrifice that the Christians seem to have avoided the word until it had shaken off its old associations. St Paul (2 Cor 5:18) preferred the term 'ministry of reconciliation' and the word recurs in a eucharistic context many times, e.g. in the ordination prayer of Serapion of Thmuis.

II Presbyters and bishops are not always easy to differentiate in the NT and in apostolic times. The threefold ministry of bishop, priest and deacon is clear in the epistles of Ignatius ; that is agreed by all, but there are differences of opinion about what went on before his time. There are some texts which have been used to inject prejudice into the question and which can be cleared away at the outset, such as the passage already cited from 1 Tim 4:14, which was often used as if it showed that presbyters were just as important as bishops in the imposing of hands. Another passage (in Hermas *Vis.* 3:1:8 ; GCS 48:8) has been used as evidence that in the church at Rome presbyters had the chief position at the end of the 1st cent. What Hermas there says is not that 'the presbyters are to sit down first' but simply 'elders first' ; he is being polite to the old lady of his vision, who is alone with him and who is his senior, and no presbyters are considered to be present at their conversation. This ambiguity of the word *presbuteros*, which means either an oldish man, an official of the Church, or even (in 2 and 3 Jn) 'the Elder' (a title of honour given to John like the title Hillel the Elder), makes it hard to see what exactly is the drift of some passages. Papias, for instance, in a celebrated text (Eusebius HE 3:39 ; GCS 9:286) is probably talking about 'the generation before me'. Irenaeus has the same use of the word, but by his day time has moved on and his *presbuteroi* are not the same people as those whom Papias had so described.

It has been urged that although it is not easy to decide when the words *presbuteros* and *episkopos* are used as titles of office and when they are simply terms describing functions that do not imply a permanent office, there are signs that presbyterian government was the earlier condition of the Church, arising out of Jewish precedents, while bishops came in later as a somewhat Gentile intrusion. In the light of what is now known about the *mebaqqer* and his ten judges in the Qumran sect, as well as the obvious parallel between Jewish high-priests, sanhedrin and people and the ordinary Mediterranean pattern of archons, *boulê* and *demos*, it is quite impossible now to maintain that government by elders who were all equal among themselves was the Jewish groundwork of the Christian Church. Ac 15 (and 21:18) shows the church at Jerusalem acting very much as any Greek or Jewish community would act in those times. The Ebionites, says Epiphanius (*haer.* 30:18 ; GCS 25:357), had presbyters and synagogue-chiefs and called their churches synagogues ; this Jewish-Christian evidence opens up two possibilities; either the presbyters were administrative heads (like the *mebaqqer*) and the synagogue-chiefs cult-officials subject to them, or the synagogue-chiefs were the leaders and the presbyters their council of elders. In either case it is clear that there was a hierarchy of control, with two levels, above the body of layfolk. The evidence as a whole fits in with what Trent declared (D 966), that one must admit that the hierarchy in the Church is of divine institution i.e. the work of Christ Himself. The description of the hierarchy as bishops, priests and deacons was not proposed under pain of anathema as being of equally divine origin, though some of the Spanish bishops had called for this to be defined.

When presbyter is used as a title of office in these early times, it can lead to misunderstanding, for though it is clear that among the Jews synagogue-chiefs were not the same thing as elders, there is an inscription from before 70 where a synagogue-chief is called a presbyter (*Supplementum epigraphicum graecum* VIII, 170:9). Among the churches of Syria and Asia it seems safe to hold that all bishops were presbyters, but not vice versa. Thus when the opening words of Philippians (1:1) speak of 'bishops and helpers', with no express word for presbyters, it is not to be supposed that this was a new form of organization where presbyters were excluded, but that the bishops who would gather, one from each Macedonian town, to hear Paul's letter when it arrived at Philippi (Ac 16:12) might in another context be described as presbyters, as is the case with Ac 14:23. Indeed, the grouping of small-town bishops round the outstanding leader in a larger centre (as happens in Asia Minor after John is released from Patmos) would naturally suggest that the many bishops were the advisers—or council of elders—to the one. The system of metropolitans did not arise yet awhile, but its roots were there from the beginning. Irenaeus (*adv. haer.* III:xiv:2 H), who was a native of Asia Minor, takes Ac 20:17 as a mustering of bishops from around Ephesus.

The argument that has been drawn from Tit 1:5-7, where Paul instructs him to appoint presbyters in Crete, and then dilates upon the qualities needed in a bishop, does not necessarily prove that bishop and presbyter were all one to him. Rabbinical argument, of which Paul was fond, often took the form of an *a fortiori* : ' Get good presbyters ; if these are the qualities a bishop needs, then you must look for the same in your candidates, out of whom future bishops will come.' As Farrer has noted, the definite article is used with the word ' bishop' in this passage, betraying the fact that Paul thought in terms of a mon-episcopate. The OT typology must have been a source of confusion to minds like Paul's. Moses, the prototype of Christ as bishop-in-chief, appointed men who are termed presbyters, yet these men were the prototypes of the apostles and after them of the Christian bishops. Here was justification for calling such bishops presbyters, while in another situation it would be the group of lesser officials who sat with the bishop who would be styled his presbyters. Teaching, liturgy and administration were the functions of the bishop, and while he can easily depute and reassume part of the work of teaching and administration, he must either be present in person at the liturgy each time or allow a presbyter to do *all* that he does there ; cf. Ignatius (*Smyrn.* 8:1). On this difference seems to be based the later distinction between power of order (*potestas ordinis*) and power of jurisdiction (*potestas iurisdictionis*) : the former might be common to both ranks from the outset, while the latter would remain in the hands of the bishop.

The evidence of I Clement is a battleground from which most recognizable features have been obliterated. He uses a text from Is 60:17 (*I Clem* 42:4) because it refers to ' bishops and helpers '. This is not according to the wording of the LXX, but, as Qumran has shown, there was another recension, if not another version, in use among the sectaries which fits in with the version known to Justin. It may be that Clement is here using that version, or that he had adapted his text to fit in with Phil 1:1 ; no one can be sure, but the Old Latin version of Clement— which is of great antiquity—has here *episcopos et ministros*. In 44:5 he has the term *presbyters* in the sense of ' men older than myself', while in 1:3 and 21:6 he indicates that ' leaders ' (ἡγούμενοι) are greater than presbyters, thus showing that he had the idea of an hierarchy, even though in his concluding passages (54:2 and 57:1) he calls for obedience to presbyters. If they should receive it, much more should they receive their leaders, one might argue, but as we do not know what precisely the trouble was at Corinth, we cannot make much of this exhortation. The ' distinguished men' of 44:1 have been made the subject of the most elaborate hypotheses, which they are clearly unable to support.

Early in the 3rd cent. Hippolytus (*Ref. haer.* preface 6 : GCS 26:3) describes himself and others who are in the apostolic succession as men ' who share in the high-priesthood and teaching and are reputed guardians of the Church ' ; he does not call them ' bishops' in so many words, but he clearly means them to be taken for bishops and presents what must have been the accepted tradition of the 2nd cent. His evidence is supported by the *Didascalia* and by the liturgical documents that go under his own name.

The *Didascalia* envisages some five functions for the bishop. He is ' your levite and high-priest. He is the minister of the word and mediator, but to you a teacher and your father after God, who begot you through the water . . . and he is your mighty king ' (Connolly, 86). To this pastoral authority is added the work of sacrifice, ' Keep the command through him who is bishop and priest and *thy mediator* with the Lord God ' (ibid. 98). He is the judge of sinners and is told how to act with them, ' Weigh his conduct and if he is found blameworthy, do according to the teaching of Our Lord which is written in the gospel, " reprove him between thyself and him, and save him when he repenteth "' (ibid. 102). A bishop is said to ' appoint him presbyters as counsellors and assessors' (ibid. 96) indicating some administration of property or graveyards. Finally ' to you bishops was it said, " All that ye shall bind on earth, it shall be bound in heaven, and all that ye shall loose on earth, it shall be loosed in heaven " ' (ibid. 55). In this duty the bishop is exhorted (ibid. 116) to show mercy, according to Is 58:6. Pastoral, sacrificial, judicial, financial and legislative : all five categories are given to the bishop. It is interesting that the need of presbyters to assist the bishop is seen chiefly in the fourth category, though in forgiving sins he might have to ' take with him one or two'.

III The earliest ordination prayers are found in the *Traditio apostolica* of Hippolytus, but one can never be certain that the versions now extant of that work in Latin, Coptic, Ethiopic and Arabic have not suffered interpolation at some time after its origin *c.* 220. The formula for consecrating a bishop empowers him to be shepherd and high-priest, to do propitiation and offering, to remit sins, to appoint lots and to loose bonds. It thus covers the five functions of the *Didascalia*. This prayer survives in the original Greek, by a fortunate chance, and also in the Ethiopic and Latin versions of the *Traditio*. The derivative *Canons of Hippolytus* have left out the fourth function entirely. The rubric for the deacon's ordination reads (in the Ethiopic) ' He was not ordained to acquire the great spirit of which the presbyters partake, but to occupy himself with that which is proper, that the bishop may trust him and that he may acquaint the bishop with what is fitting.' The Latin has bungled the version of this : *non accipiens communem presbyterii spiritum eum cuius participes presbyteri sunt, sed id quod sub potestate episcopi est creditum*. This shows signs of wanting to enhance the value of presbyters at the expense of the bishop. The deacon is given power, ' to offer in thy holy of holies that which is offered to Thee by thine ordained chief-priests to the glory of Thy Name.' Here it is clear that the deacon is made only a part-offerer with the bishop.

The priest's ordination prayer in the *Canons of Hippolytus* (IV, 31) is ordered to be the same as that for a bishop save for the word ' bishop '. A rubric is added which says, ' A bishop is in all things the equivalent of a presbyter save for the name of his Chair and the laying-on of hands, i.e. the power of doing this is not given to him.' [1] This later work has undergone some transformation. What the *Traditio* laid down (in the Ethiopic version) was, ' In the form which we said before he shall pray ', or in the Arabic, ' according to the pattern which we have said concerning the bishop'. What was required was an ordination-prayer for the priest which followed the model of the bishop's prayer. What the *mutanda* would be, the text did not say, but later writers using the work wrote in their own conjectures. Priests joined with the bishop in laying hands upon a priest at his ordination, ' for it is one

[1] Episcopus in omnibus rebus aequiparetur presbytero excepto nomine cathedrae et ordinatione, quia potestas ordinandi ipsi non tribuitur.

and the same Spirit that descends on him'. The Latin has turned this into an argument for equality of priest with bishop in the act : ' Presbyters lay on hands because of the common and similar Spirit of clerisy ' (*propter communem et similem cleri spiritum*). For the priests' part in the liturgy *see* CONCELEBRATION. In the canon of the Hippolytean mass the bishop prays ' that we may stand before Thee and do Thee Service as priests ' (ἱερατεύειν in the Greek of the Apostolic Constitutions). The Latin version (*et Tibi ministrare*) has failed to preserve this close linking of episcopal office and priestly service in the liturgy, but as long as *sacerdos* and ἱερεύς were kept as words to be used for bishops alone, there could be little danger of confusion arising.

IV The claim of presbyters to equality with bishops, as just hinted, may have been provoked by ambiguities of language. In Syriac the abstract word for ' priesthood ' denoted the ministry in all its grades, though in Arabic *usquf* (bishop) differed from *qass* (priest). The heresy of Aerius (*c.* 300–375), who held that there was one and the same rank and honour for bishop and priest (Epiphanius *haer.* 75:3:1 ; GCS 37:334), helped on the confusion. Replying to him Epiphanius says that sometimes, if there is no great number of Christians in a place, there will be a bishop and no presbyters to assist him, while if there be none worthy among the presbyters there may be a group of them in a place with no bishop. Aerius had appealed to the Pauline epistles, in which (he claimed) Paul was addressing presbyters and deacons, not bishops. It is probable that his way of taking these passages in the epistles was inherited by Ambrosiaster and others in the West. God's dealing with Moses and Aaron (Exod 4:12–17) was brought up by Epiphanius (*haer.* 75:5 ; GCS 37:336) as a type of the earliest stage in the Church, when some looseness of organization had prevailed, as it did before Moses set up the orderly rites of the Tabernacle for the Jews.

The fact (evident from Cyprian's letters) that the presbyters were in control of a church *sede vacante* was also taken as a sign that they could remain so indefinitely. The Liberian Catalogue (MGH. *Auctores* IX, 75) noted as an unusual circumstance that presbyters were in charge at Rome from the consulship of Tuscus and Bassus (258) until 21 July of 259. In a moment of fatal weakness, Jerome wrote his letter (*ep.* 146 ; CSEL 56:308) to bolster up the position of presbyter against the growing assertiveness of deacons. Trying to put things on a scriptural basis he said roundly, ' When the apostle openly teaches that presbyter and bishop are the same, what is a server of tables and helper of widows doing by haughtily setting himself up over those at whose prayer the Body and Blood of Christ is made present ? ' Then comes the remark which echoed through the Middle Ages, ' What does a bishop do that a priest does not ? ' He cites the case of Alexandria and its curious episcopacy and the way in which soldiers make an emperor. When he came to comment on the epistles to Timothy and Titus he had found a reason for the differentiation between bishop and presbyter ; it was sin. 'Before the prompting of the devil produced feuds in the Church, each church was governed by the common counsel of the presbyters, but when each of them had begun to regard his neophytes not as the children of Christ but as his own, it was decided throughout the Church that one of the presbyters should be chosen and set over the others and that all the care of the church should be his, so that the occasion of schisms might be removed.' (PL 26:562). Augustine did not like the theory and wrote to Jerome (*ep.* 82 ; CSEL 34:ii:385) that bishops differed from presbyters '*secundum honorem*', in dignity or rank. Meanwhile Ambrosiaster was applying this 'levelling' exegesis to the relevant passages in St Paul (1 Tim 3:8 and Eph 4:11 ; PL 17:470 and 387). 'Why does Paul put the setting up of deacons after that of bishops, save that bishop and presbyter have a single status (*ordinatio*) ? Each is a priest but the bishop is prior, every bishop being a presbyter but not vice versa.' Isidore (*de off.* 2:7 ; PL 83:787) repeats Jerome and Ambrosiaster, and the same ideas are propagated by Rabanus Maurus (PL 112:479 and 603). The West seems thoroughly convinced that there is really no difference save dignity between the two, though Isidore (PL 83:782) does add a warning note, to the effect that some of the lawyers say that episcopacy is the name of a function not of an honour (*nomen operis, non honoris*).

Origen in *c. Cels* 3:30 (GCS 1:227) had drawn a parallel between the government of a city, with archon, boule and demos, and that of the Church, with bishop, presbyters and laity. The election of a bishop by all the people, their choice being approved by the assembled bishops and presbyters (as described in Hippolytus' *Traditio apostolica*), may have led to the notion that the difference between the ranks was merely one of convention. This popular element in the appointment is not always so much emphasized as in Hippolytus ; Cyprian (*ep.* 67:5) simply says : Let the bishop be chosen in the presence of the people (*praesente populo*), as if they are to be no more than witnesses. The Council of Laodicea (canon 13) says *c.* A.D. 360 that the election of presbyters is not to be entrusted to the multitude. On the other hand a Council of Ancyra (in 314) has a canon to deal with the situation when a bishop has been appointed whose people refuse to have him, thus recognizing some kind of popular veto. The acclamations (*see* ACCLAMATIONS) which were given by the people at an election are probably the reflex of this veto. Athanasius (*apologia contra Arianos* 6 ; PG 25:260) claims that he was elected by the assembled bishops of Egypt and Libya, in the sight of, and with the acclamations of, the people. Where the popular element was very prominent, it would be easy to advance the theory that bishop and presbyter alike, both popularly elected, were equal in power, especially as the presbyter gradually came to act on his own in the liturgy, in dealing with sinners and in baptizing. The very fact that *paroecia* originally meant a bishop's territory and now means the parish of a priest shows that this evolution took place, but it is not easy to say when exactly the word changed its meaning.

V The beginning of a theology of Orders may be seen in the anonymous tract *de septem ordinibus ecclesiae* which was for long attributed to Jerome. A critical edition of it was produced by Kalff in 1938 and since then there have been various attempts to locate its author. He uses an argument from the liturgy, urging that if on occasion (e.g. when sick) the bishop receives Communion from the hands of a priest, there must be a basic equality between them.[1] Yet he is willing to allow (ibid. 59) that one should see Christ in the bishop and the apostles in the presbyters. He has the argument from Tit 1:5–7 that presbyters are there called bishops (ibid. 53), and explains that ordination is reserved to the bishop for disciplinary reasons.[2] A priest is allowed to consecrate chrism because he has the power to consecrate the Body of Christ. Christ was anointed upon His Body, and the priest who has power over His Body has therefore power over anointing. 'Since also the eucharist is greater than Mary the Mother of God, a simple priest can bless virgins, for Mary is the sister of virgins.'[3] The author is very pleased with this kind of liturgical argument ; he is prepared (ibid. 39) to say that the rite whereby the deacon handed the chalice to the bishop for his Communion was meant to check the presumption of bishops.[4] This would not matter if the work was not followed blindly by Isidore (de off 2:8 PL 83:789) and by the Irish collection of canons (III, 5).

Priests are said (ibid. 45) to be *consortes cum episcopis* (sharers with the bishops) and this Roman idea of *consortium* was particularly open to misunderstanding as the proper understanding of Roman institutions gradually perished from the world. Leo the Great was in the habit of using the idea to indicate the distance between the Roman primate and the other bishops (PL 54:671 and 620) ; they were called to share in the burden he carried not in the fullness of power.[5] They were *consortes imperii* in the same way as Roman emperors had taken up younger men who were to assist them as subordinate partners (as Augustus took Tiberius and Nerva took Trajan, etc.). Cyprian (*de unitate* 4) had used the word (in the Received text of that passage). It went

[1] Hi presbyteri in benedictione cum episcopis consortes mysteriorum sunt ac nulla in conficiendo corpore Christi et sanguine inter eos et episcopos credenda distantia est, quia et eucharistiam iampridem per presbyteros benedictam, si necessitas exegerit, episcopus accipere debet et se Christo ac plenitudini Eius communicare cognoscat (Kalff, p. 39).
[2] Cum . . . sola propter auctoritatem summo sacerdoti clericorum ordinatio et consecratio reservata sit, ne a multis disciplina ecclesiae vindicata concordiam sacerdotum solveret, scandala generaret (ibid. 48).
[3] Maria mater Christi soror est virginum, et eucharistia Christi minor est Maria (ibid. 51).
[4] Ipsis sacerdotibus propter praesumptionem non licet de mensa Domini tollere calicem nisi eis traditus fuerit a diacono, ut praecedente ministerio sanctitatis humiliatos se paulisper post consecrationem dum ministro Dei debent reverentiam, recognoscant.
[5] . . . Ut in partem sis vocatus sollicitudinis, non in plenitudinem potestatis.

from Leo into the False Decretals and thence to Gratian and St Thomas (*IV Sent.* 20:1:4:3).

VI The special case of Alexandria has been very closely scrutinized during the recent debates about episcopacy. Dix in *The Apostolic Ministry* made light of it, saying that the evidence for presbyters appointing the bishop of Alexandria (who was the only bishop in Egypt during the first two centuries of Christianity) was from Jerome in the 4th cent. and from Eutychius (patriarch of Alexandria in the 10th), and that it was not concordant in details, while Clement and Origen are quite silent about such a peculiarity. This view passed over the explicit testimony of Severus of Antioch (*Select Letters* VI, 213) : ' The bishop also of the city of the Alexandrines, renowned for its orthodox faith, was in old times appointed by presbyters. But in modern times, in accordance with the canon [of Nicaea] which has prevailed everywhere, the solemn institution of their bishop is performed by bishops ; and no one makes light of the accurate practice which prevails in the holy churches and recurs to the earlier condition of things which has given way to the later clear accurate and deliberate injunctions.' In the *Apophthegmata patrum* (T&S VI i 213) there is a story about the abbot Poemen. When some heretics came to him disparaging the archbishop of Alexandria (Athanasius) as having been ordained by presbyters, he would make no reply. The charge can hardly have been true, for Athanasius had the heretic Ischyras reduced to lay status in 339 for having accepted ordination by the presbyter Colluthus (*apologia contra Arianos* 12 ; PG 25:269), but the practice may have been known in the preceding century, and this would account for the possibility of such a calumny.

It is to be noted that the civil administration of Egypt was peculiar, for Alexandria was the only *civitas* with full civic institutions in the whole prefecture of Egypt until A.D. 202. The other centres of habitation were merely *nomes*. It may have been true that in the early days the church in Egypt was limited to the one bishopric in conformity with the civic pattern ; in that case there would obviously have been a difficulty about the succession of a new man when the bishop was dead. The curious tale (cf. Liberatus, PL 68:1036) that the newly-elect had to keep vigil by the dead bishop's body and had to take the dead man's hand and place it upon his own head may be due to a feeling that the manner of succession would otherwise be irregular.

The church of Carthage was quite content to go for 24 years without a bishop, for when Hunneric in 480 issued an edict (Victor Vitensis 2:3 ; CSEL 7:25) trying to bargain a free election for the Catholics against freedom of preaching and a vernacular liturgy for the Arians in the East, the Catholics replied that Christ had been their bishop for so long and He would continue. It must have been that ordinations to the priesthood went on in other parts of Africa whence Carthage obtained recruits, but the lack of episcopal government for so long without any feeling of distress shows a mentality different

from the present day. It may have been this passage of Victor which influenced some English Catholics in the days of Elizabeth, as they made frequent appeals to his work for analogies with their own time of persecution.

Severus of Antioch (*Select Letters* VI, 223) in discussing the case of Flavian of Antioch, relates how, ' Siricius, who was then archbishop at Rome, decided that after the discussion at Capua the task of making a more careful investigation of the actual facts should be transferred to the East (Caesarea).' He cites the decree of the bishops assembled at Caesarea : ' We have read the letter written by the bishops at Capua . . . and that of the religious Siricius, bishop of Rome, to the effect that before all things we must look to this, not to disturb the canon of Nicaea which lays down that it is not permissible for the ordination of a bishop to be performed by one only . . . With joy therefore we received the accurate teaching of the bishop Siricius concerning the church canons, and following this letter we have decreed these things ratified.'

To sum up : one can see that after Nicaea there is no wavering in the position that a new bishop must be consecrated by bishops, in Egypt as elsewhere. In an earlier time the bishop of Alexandria does seem to have been consecrated (and not merely elected) by his college of twelve city-presbyters (though not by all the presbyters of Egypt). Some theologians (after Batiffol) say that these twelve were really bishops and had been so from the beginning ; others would rely on the power of a priest, under delegation, to consecrate in virtue of the common sacrament of Orders, some of whose powers require delegation to bring them out.

VII The legacy of Jerome passes down to Sedulius Scotus, Claudius of Turin, Rabanus Maurus and Alcuin, while other levelling comments of Pelagius in his commentary on St Paul are repeated by the pseudo-Primasius. In the early Middle Ages Hervaeus of Bourg-Dieu, Gilbert Porreta and Gratian all say that the difference of priest from bishop is merely ' administrative ' and arose from the need to check schism. Hugh of St Victor (PL 176:423) said of the priesthood, ' This degree has diverse positions of dignity within the same Order.' Master Simon (*c.* 1160), however, claimed that prelacy crowned and consecrated all the lesser degrees of Order and was a sacrament by itself. Stephen Langton denied this for the reason that a bishop could not do anything greater than what the priest did in consecrating the Eucharist. One might wonder what he would have said to the reply that it was a much greater thing to empower others to consecrate the Eucharist than to do it oneself. Peter Lombard (PL 192:223) on Phil 1:1 claimed that there, presbyters were called bishops, since there could not be more than one bishop in each place ; on 1 Tim 3:4 he remarked that episcopacy was a name of function not of rank (*nomen operis, non honoris*), while elsewhere (IV *Sent. dist.* 24) he said that the title of presbyter was a name of dignity not a designation of age. Thus his view amounted to saying that in early times it was the function that predominated in the title of bishop while that of presbyter was more like a title of honour. This view is still held by some Catholics. More extreme was the opinion of Sicard of Cremona (*c.* 1180) who said, ' Whatever sacraments were administered by Peter, those can be given by any priest.' This maxim was repeated by many canonists, but time brought a reaction.

VIII The opinion of St Thomas marked the beginning of this reaction. He held that the character of this sacrament of Order was imparted at the moment of the ' investiture ' with the chalice in priestly ordination, but admitted (*Summa*, supplement 38:2:@2 and 40:5:@2) that a bishop received at consecration something that was indelible, even though this could not strictly be called a sacramental character, since it had to do with the members of the mystical Body and did not bring the subject into direct relation with God. He noticed, too, that (ibid. 37:1:@1) while other sacraments were instituted in order that men might *receive* from God, this was one instituted principally in order to empower men to *act*, and thus there was a difference which prevented facile generalizations between sacrament and sacrament. It was a composite sacrament (ibid. 37:1:@2 and 40:4:@3) which was not a manifold whose parts could be summed, but rather was its unity that of a developing series ; the final term of priesthood was the fullness of the sacrament and the preceding lesser orders were partial developments of this that led up to it. It is to be noted that he made priesthood the term, and not episcopacy, and that he did not think of minor orders as states of life which a man could remain in for ever. A breath of Aristotle is wafted over the doctrine when St Thomas says (ibid. 38:1:c) that as it belongs to the *politikos* (*Eth. Nic.* 1094 b 1) to decide what sciences there shall be in the city, who shall learn them and how far, so it belongs to the bishop to place others in the divine ministry. He would thus seem to regard the ministry as complete at the priestly level with episcopacy thrown in as a regulative principle of another kind. The chief priestly act is the consecration of the Eucharist, and so the investiture with this power is the main thing in the sacrament for St Thomas. An accessory power is the forgiving of sins, and the investiture with that power is an accessory part of the sacrament ; the receiving of the power (by a newly-consecrated bishop) to hold such investitures is not looked upon as one of the essential acts of this sacrament.

Later Scholastics such as Biel, Petrus a Palude, Durandus (IV *Sent.* 24:6:8), held that episcopacy was a sacrament and not merely a sacramental. Scotus began this change by maintaining that the principal feature of the sacrament of Orders was the initial imposition of hands (common to priesthood and episcopate) and not the investiture with the chalice. He was thus able to claim (*Reportata* 4:9) that episcopacy was ' a special degree and Order in the Church whose task it is to confer all other Orders'.

Nothing is here said about the power over the eucharistic body of Christ being the principal thing ; rather has Scotus taken the admission of St Thomas (*Summa*, supplement 40:4:@3) that perfection in representing what Christ did is what counts most in Orders, only changing the emphasis to say now that it is not the imitating (in the Eucharist) what Christ did on Calvary that is principal but the imitating Him in His rôle of spouse of the Church (and that is the bishop's task).

Bellarmine developed the idea of episcopate as a sacrament. He admitted (*de sacramento ordinis* 5) that power over the Eucharist was the chief thing involved in Orders, but said that the bishop's right to suspend a priest from saying Mass and to hand on to others the power to say Mass made his possession of this power over the Eucharist greater than a priest's, though the difference was only one of degree. The consecration of a bishop conferred a character which was different from that received in priestly ordination *extensive* (in respect of the powers it carried with it) but not *intensive* (in respect of the power which constituted it). But meanwhile the definitions of Trent had given a new direction to theological speculation.

IX The Tridentine definition about episcopacy came in the 23rd session on 15 July 1563. In the autumn of the preceding year the question was hotly debated, starting from the draft proposal (which had been drawn up in the days of Julius III) that episcopacy was an institute of divine origin and that by the same divine right bishops were superior to priests. The Archbishop of Granada, who led the Spanish group and who championed the view that bishops received power of order and power of jurisdiction direct from God and not mediately through the Pope, cited Basil (PG 31:1409) and Ambrose (really the pseudo-Ambrose *de dignitate sacerdotali*, PL 17:570) for his case and claimed that in the time of Julius the Council had already committed itself. This was denied by the Legates, while others took the view, after Torquemada, that power of order was direct from God while jurisdiction came through the Pope. Medieval canonists had fought about this with the theologians of the time, holding that, as the Pope assigned a territory to a bishop, it was impossible to maintain that his jurisdiction was direct from God, for without his territory his jurisdiction was a shadow. Cases were cited where the chapter of a diocese had the right to elect the successor to a deceased bishop without reference to Rome. Cyprian was brought in with his dictum (*ep.* 3:3) that ' God chooses bishops'. His other dictum about bishops being liable *singuli in solidum* was put forward as applying to power of order rather than power of jurisdiction. Jerome was brought up for the view that bishop and priest were originally the same, and the pseudo-Jerome (*breviarium in psalmos* PL 26:960) was cited as being a change of mind on Jerome's part. The bishop of Ilerda claimed that the condemnation of Marsiglio of Padua (D 498) already settled the matter and that the Council should not allow a single witness,

Jerome, to stand in the way of truth. The Archbishop of Nîmes cited John Fisher, Pole and Contarini, 'who were none of them flatterers of the Pope', as holding that all episcopal jurisdiction came through the Pope. The bishop of Lugo, citing Vitoria, said that if communications should be interrupted at the present time with the Far East, the churches there could set up valid bishops. The Irish bishop, Eugene O'Hart OP, of Achonry, caused a deep impression by pointing out that in Elizabethan England, 'the sovereign makes the bishops; they are consecrated by three, and say that they are true bishops because they are of God; and this we deny because they are not created by means of the Pope, and rightly so'. The diarist adds at this point the comment, 'His statement was approved by all,' a comment that is not found after the other speeches. The Cardinal of Lorraine, who had come to Trent with a crowd of French bishops once this debate had begun, proposed a compromise formula; this and other alternatives were dispatched to Rome for the Pope's opinion while the Council went on in January 1563 to consider abuses connected with the sacrament of Orders. In the summer the emended articles on Orders were brought up again (D 956a–968), and though the Spanish bloc did not succeed with its amendments, it did secure the insertion of the words *divina ordinatione institutam* in canon 6 which asserted the existence of hierarchy in the Church. The Spanish Jesuit Lainez argued with much power against the common opinion of his fellow-countrymen and for the papal position, but the controversy was shelved by the final decree and neither side had the victory.

The first three chapters of the conciliar decree are concerned with the simple priesthood (*see* PRIESTHOOD) and in ch. 4 the existence of an hierarchy is argued from 1 Cor 12:29 and Eph 4:11, and it is inferred from Ac 20:28 that bishops are part of that hierarchy. Three canons (6–8) deal with episcopacy. Canon 6 has been discussed above. Canon 7 asserts —but without the qualification that this is of divine right—the superiority of bishops to priests. The anathema of this canon falls on those who assert that the power of ordaining and confirming which bishops have is common to priests also, that the orders conferred by them need the approval of the laity or of the civil authority, or that men can become ministers of the Word of God and the sacraments without due canonical ordination. Canon 8 condemned those who said that the bishops who had been 'taken up' (the word used, *assumuntur*, is notable for its reticence on the debatable matter of the derivation of jurisdiction) by the Pope of Rome were not real and true bishops but of human devisal. This was directed against a Calvinist statement, just as canon 7 dealt with the position Cranmer had taken up when he said that what mattered in the conferring of orders was not consecration but appointment.

Nothing was laid down at Trent about the claim that episcopacy was a sacrament in its own right. Salmeron (*Conc. Trid. Acta* IX:7) had urged that the blessing given by Christ when He extended His hands upon His apostles at the Ascension was in patristic times taken to be the institution of a sacrament of episcopacy, but this was not put into the decree (*see* ASCENSION). The third chapter of the decree said that in the sacrament of orders grace was conferred by words and signs, but did not specify these (the terms 'matter and form' stood in the draft, but they were rejected in favour of 'words and signs'). One or two of the speakers in the debate argued from the analogy of the sacrament of matrimony that, just as the married state existed for the procreation of children and was blessed by a sacrament, so the bishop who procreated spiritual children was sacramentally instituted (*Acta* III:449). Such an idea might be in keeping with the original pattern of baptism, where the bishop presided and confirmed the neophytes as they came out of the water, but to consider that the ordination of priests was a spiritual procreation—as the speaker did—was to promote confusion.

X The 17th and 18th cents. were the great age of political theorizing, and this activity was reflected in theology. In 1786 Pius VI had to condemn Febronius (D 1500) for claiming that the Church had a republican constitution, that all bishops were equal, the Pope being no more than an emergency primate who had to put things right when unity was threatened and negligence was damaging the Church, but that all his other so-called powers were really usurpations of episcopal rights. It is to be noted that while condemning these errors Pius did not add any new point of positive teaching. When he condemned the Jansenist Synod of Pistoia in 1794 (D 1506–08) he was content to say that the asserted autonomy of bishops, if it meant that they could *exercise* episcopal powers in independence of the Pope, was an error in doctrine, but the *nature* and *origin* of these powers was not stated.

In the succession-states of the great Protestant heresy it had become by the 19th cent. a common idea that religion was but a department of state—often controlled by a minister for cults—and hence Pius IX in 1864 (D 1698) condemned the idea that ecclesiastical authority was not really independent of civil; as the last Prince-bishops were dying out, it had to be affirmed that bishops were not state-functionaries and the exercise of their pastoral office was not just a matter of sufferance on the part of the civil power. Austria and France were at the time rivalling each other in their attempts to mould the temporal power of the Pope to their own pattern, and in their plans the spiritual authority in the Church took second place. Thus it was fitting that the Vatican Council, in the preamble to the dogmatic constitution on the Church (D 1821), should reiterate that Christ had intended pastors and teachers to continue in His Church to the end of time; the episcopate is one and undivided, and the principle of its unity is the papal primacy (*see* PRIMACY). Without defining anything about the origin of episcopal power the Council gave a new direction to theological thought on the structure of the Church, returning to ideas which were implicit in the early Christian typology of Moses. Christ had been the second Moses, apostles and bishops being the elders to whom He imparted the Spirit. Yet Peter was soon exhibited as the counterpart of Moses receiving the Law from Christ and himself laying hands upon elders : ' Peter, towards whose person the power of every bishop has regard.' [1]

The 3rd chapter of this constitution (D 1827) affirmed that the bishops severally and collectively had a duty of hierarchical subordination and obedience to the Pope ; this did not hinder them in their ordinary jurisdiction, for Gregory the great (PL 77:933) had shown that the rights of bishops were the more secure when the papacy was strong to uphold them. Leo XIII had to return to this topic (D 1961) and to issue an interpretation of the Vatican decree. ' No new opinion was canonized by it, nor was it to be regarded as a source of confusion that Catholics should be subject to two authorities, papal and episcopal, for the wisdom of God had ordered things in this way. Papal jurisdiction was supreme, universal and independent ; episcopal was subordinate and confined to a distinct area.' In saying this, Leo was professedly staying within the bounds of Trent and was therefore not undertaking to decide the controversy about the origin of episcopal jurisdiction.

XI In the present century a change has come over the theology of the episcopate. To Italian Modernists, of the type of Romolo Murri, chafing under the *non expedit* that prevented the start of a Catholic party in politics, it seemed a plausible argument that the Church ought to favour democracy in politics since she was really one herself. In the condemnation of Modernism (D 2091) the monarchical structure of the Church was re-asserted, but thereafter the attention of theologians turned from considering the jurisdiction of bishops to examine afresh the power of Order which they possess. New attempts were made, in the light of the priesthood of Christ (now better understood), to see how the episcopate contained the fullness of the priesthood. Confirmation is in patristic sources often called ' the perfecting of baptism ', just as episcopate is the perfecting of priesthood, but, if the two relationships were exactly alike, that would result in a total of eight sacraments instead of seven. The priesthood that is derived from Christ has therefore to be understood in such a way as to allow for two levels, yet not to involve two sacraments. Another reason for examining the power of Order afresh was the new evidence brought to light (*see* ABBOT, ORDINATION BY) which seemed to show a breach of the monopoly that bishops had in the laying on of hands. Of course, at every ordination of priests the assembled body of priests takes part in the laying on of hands, but it had been accepted for centuries that within the power of Order there was an hierarchical structure, just as there was for the power of jurisdiction. If now it was found that by papal com-

mission simple priests had ordained (for abbots are not bishops), was not that hierarchy upset ?

The new concern with the power of order led in some cases to a revival of the view that episcopacy was a sacrament. Attempts had then to be made to show that the sacrament of orders could exist at two levels or alternatively, that priests were really in possession of this sacrament, even though their use of it might be impeded in some way. The old Tridentine controversy was not far below the surface here, for if episcopacy is but a sacramental (effective *ex opere orantis ecclesiae* and not *ex opere operato*), then there can hardly be a case for saying that bishop's jurisdiction comes directly from God ; on the other hand, the new tendency to revive the view that episcopacy is a sacrament would make it easy to claim that with the institution of such a sacrament their jurisdiction had a divine origin immediately from Christ.

The liturgical movement has in the recent past brought back interest to the priesthood of Christ as operative in the Mass, and some modern speculation (chiefly in France) has settled on the twofold anointing of the humanity of Christ (once at the Incarnation and again by John at the baptism), seeing in it a means of approving a distinction between simple priesthood and episcopacy. But while there is plenty of patristic evidence for the twofold anointing (e.g. in Cyril of Alexandria, PG 74:549 and 961 ; Hippolytus on Dan 4:32 ; GCS 1:270 ; and in the *Quaestiones VT et NT* 49:1 ; CSEL 50:96), St Thomas uses it (3a:72:1:@4) to argue that there should be a sacrament of confirmation distinct from baptism, and it would be going too far to suggest that Christ was a simple priest all His earthly life but became a bishop at His baptism in Jordan.

A more fruitful line of speculation (which has been developed chiefly by Père Lecuyer in France) takes the events of the Ascension and Pentecost—which were in early times treated as one complex, *see* ASCENSION—as the consecration of the apostles as bishops. They had been made priests at the Last Supper and now Christ placed His hands over them in blessing before He left them, and the Spirit came down upon them. This idea can be found in the ritual for the consecration of a bishop, where it is the practice to place the open gospel-book on the head of the newly-elect to symbolize the parted tongues of fire which the Spirit brought. The practice is found in the *Apostolic Constitutions* (8:4:6) in the *Statuta ecclesiae antiqua* (canon 90) and in the *Missale Francorum*. Between Syria of the 4th cent. and Poitiers of the 7th there are many other traces of this usage. Severianus of Gabala (in a fragment of a homily on Acts, Cramer's *Catena*, 22) explains that the apostles were then ordained as teachers of the whole world : ' when one puts the book on his head, it symbolizes a tongue, for the preaching of the gospel, and a tongue of fire, after that saying : " I came to cast fire upon the earth ".' A purple-dyed scroll when unrolled in the hands of the two deacons (or assistant bishops) might not seem unlike

---

[1] Petrus, in cuius personam potestas omnium convenit sacerdotum (*dialogus Zacchariae et Apollonii*, 18).

a tongue of fire. Athanasius (on Ps 132 ; PG 27:524), while not alluding to the unfolded book, sees in the events of Pentecost an ordination ceremony, the horn of unction being poured out upon the head and thence the life-giving dew of the Spirit being transmitted to the whole body of the Church (*see also* Irenaeus *adv. haer.* III:xviii:2 H). One might build up a catena of passages in the same sense from many partistic commentaries on that psalm. The pseudo-Chrysostom's homily on the one legislator of OT and NT (PG 56:404) elaborates the idea of the book placed on the head of the bishop by citing 1 Cor 11:10 and saying that now he has come under the power of the gospel. A Greek consecration prayer (Goar, *Euchologion* 250) asks ' that this man may be strengthened to undergo the yoke of the gospel and the high-priestly dignity '.

That a bishop's first duty is to preach is still the burden of the service in the Pontifical, and St Thomas (3a:67:2:@1) stresses this. Although he seems to pass over the link between Ascension and Pentecost, he says (3a:72:2:@1) that the apostles were filled with the Holy Spirit at Pentecost *ut fidei doctores* (as teachers of the faith). Francis Torres at Trent (*Acta* IX:24) claimed St Thomas for the view that at Pentecost the apostles were made bishops *consummate* (in a perfect manner) even though on Easter day they may have been made so *dispositive et designative* (by promise and designation). The Pontifical has kept the emphasis on the work of teaching as principal for a bishop, though what has tended to obscure this in many parts of the ritual and in the minds of theologians is the return of the idea that the Aaronic priesthood is somehow a type of the Christian. The idea is found in Justin (*dial.* 86:4) and the Christian interpolation in the *Testament of Levi* (8:4) is full of it. One has to recall that in the Middle Ages Grosseteste made a Latin version of this *Testament* from a 10th cent. MS. now at Cambridge and that therefore the influence of that work on Irish and Anglo-Saxon scribes who copied service-books in the formative period of Western Christendom must have been considerable. The wavering that can be noticed in the lists of what I have elsewhere (TS 19 (1958) 81–93) called the seven orders of Christ shows that there were many factors at work to obscure the original idea that the teaching office was principal for a bishop. What seems to be the primitive form of the list makes Christ sanctify the order of episcopacy ' when He taught the people in the Temple about the kingdom of God '. The *Egbert Ordo* and the Irish *Canons* make Him do this when He blessed (i.e. consecrated) the apostles at the Ascension. If one supplies the link of Pentecost to Ascension (missing in Western liturgies) the two views become complementary : Christ consecrates His apostles as bishops and then gives them the power to teach as He had taught.

The Apostolic Constitution of Pius XII (AAS 40 (1948) 6) decided that for the future the matter of episcopal consecration was to be the imposition of hands by the chief consecrator and the form to be the words of the *Praefatio* spoken at that time, of

which these were to be essential : *Comple in sacerdote tuo ministerii tui summam, et ornamentis totius glorificationis instructum coelestis unguenti rore sanctifica.* (Bring this thy priest to the crown of his ministry and sanctify him, that is now adorned with the array of Thy full worship, with Thy gentle anointing from heaven.) It is to be noted that the decision did not deal with past history or past controversies, and in fact the wording chosen differs in two points (*ministerii* for *mysterii* and *rore* for *flore* or *fluore*) from the earliest texts of this prayer. If *mysterii* had been retained, that would have lent more aid to those who consider the episcopate to be somehow a sacrament in its own right. The term *flos unguenti* (which is found long before anointing with oil was in use), though good classical Latin (cf. Lucretius 3:221 *flos vini*, and *flos nardi* 2:84), was obviously not understood by the Merovingians, but it must go back to a time when the Pentecostal descent of the Spirit was well understood to have its place at this rite and the Spirit was thought to come down ' like anointing upon the head of Aaron, which droppeth down . . . even to the hem of his garment '.

Doubts have been expressed whether the episcopal status can be a fit object of desire as 1 Tim 3:1 seems to say it is. Fr Holzmeister (Bi 12 (1931) 41–69) thought that as the Fathers were not unanimous in referring this text to bishops, it would be better to hold that it sanctioned a desire of the priesthood. But Chrysostom (*ad loc.* PG 62:547) gives a reasonable distinction ; a man can desire the work but should not covet the honour or the relaxation (*timê* and *anapausis*) of the post. *Non recuso laborem* (I shirk not the toil) has been the device of many Western bishops since St Martin. If preaching the faith—either personally or through others—is the primary work of a bishop (as the rituals seem to show), that is in itself a reasonable object of desire, in the spirit of Isai 6:5–8. The idea that a bishop is wedded to his see, an idea symbolized in his ring, is probably of Celtic origin. In the Ireland of pre-Christian times a king was thus betrothed to his people, and it is notable that the use of a ring for bishops, which in Isidore (PL 83:784) is no more than a sign of honour or else an indication that he must keep close his secrets (*propter signum pontificalis honoris vel signaculum secretorum*), is in the Anglo-Saxon pontificals such as the *Leofric Missal* turned into a wedding-ring, for the elect is told to be mindful of his ecclesiastical betrothal and therefore to take this ring. The nuptial idea was taken up by the clerical side in the Investiture controversy (cf. Rangerius of Lucca in MGH *Libelli de lite* II:527) and found its way to St Thomas (*Supplement* 26:1:c). This nuptial idea would suggest that the episcopate was a suitable object of desire, just as much as a happy marriage could be.

Bibliography. Two collective volumes, *Episcopus* (Festschrift für Kardinal Faulhaber (1949)) and *Études sur le sacrement de l'Ordre* (Lex orandi 22) (1957); *K. E. Kirk and others, *The Apostolic ministry* (1946) ; *J. B. Lightfoot, appendix to *Phillippians* (1892) ; *Pseudo-Hieronymi de septem ordinibus*, edited by W. Kalff OSB (1938) ; M. Michaelis, *Das Ältestenamt der christlichen Gemeinde* (1953) ; A. M. Landgraf, *Dogmengeschichte der Frühscholastik* III/2, ' Die Lehre von Episkopat als Ordo ' (1956) ; *W. Telfer, *Episcopal Succession in Egypt*, JEH 3 (1952) 1–13 ; *E. Kemp, *Bishops and Presbyters at Alexandria*, JEH 6 (1955) 125–42 ; C. Baisi, *Il ministro straordinario degli ordini sacramentali* (1935) ; J. Rivière, *In partem sollicitudinis*, in RevSR 5 (1925) 210–31 ; E. Seiterich, *Ist der Episkopat ein Sakrament ?*, in Scholastik 18 (1943) 200–19 ; V. Martin, *Le Choix des évêques dans l'Église latine*, in RevSR 4 (1924) 221–64 ; J. Lecuyer C.S.Sp., *Aux origines de la théologie thomiste de l'épiscopat*, in Gregorianum 35 (1954) 56–89 ; H. Bouesse, *Épiscopat et sacerdoce*, in RevSR 28 (1954) 240–57 ; J. Colson, *L'Évêque dans les communautés primitives* (1951) ; J. Lecuyer C.S.Sp., *La Grâce de la consécration épiscopale*, in RSPT 36 (1952) 389–417 ; *H. Chadwick, *The Silence of Bishops in Ignatius*, HTR 43 (1950) 169–72 ; *D. Daube, *NT and Rabbinic Judaism* (1956) ; F. Ganshof, *L'Élection des évêques dans l'empire romain*, in Revue internationale des droits de l'antiquité 4 (1950) 467–95 ; F. Gillmann, *Zur Lehre der Scholastik vom Spender der Firmung und des Weihesakraments* (1920) ; J. B. Brosnan, *Episcopacy and Priesthood in St Thomas*, in AER 121 (1949) 125–35 ; G. E. Dolan, *Episcopacy and Presbyterate according to St Thomas* (1950) ; U. Holzmeister SJ, *Si quis episcopatum desiderat*, in Bi 12 (1931) 41–69 ; *Bo Reicke, *The constitution of the primitive church in the light of Jewish documents*, in *The Scrolls and the NT* (1958).   J. H. C.

BODY, MYSTICAL In this article we treat (I) the origin and meaning of the term, (II) the teaching of the Magisterium, (III) the doctrine in the Synoptics and St John, (IV) in St Paul, (V) in the Early and the Greek Fathers, (VI) in St Augustine, (VII) in St Thomas Aquinas, (VIII) in St Robert Bellarmine, (IX) in the Post-Reformation period, (X) in the 20th cent., (XI) in the Encyclical, *Mystici Corporis Christi*, (XII) reactions to the Pope's Encyclical, (XIII) other aspects discussed in modern theology.

I The Origin and Meaning of the Term. The term ' mystical ' appears to have been first attached to the scriptural expression ' body of Christ ' about the 9th cent. It was first used of the Eucharist (cf. H. de Lubac, *Corpus Mysticum* (1948)). The Church at that time was either simply ' the body of Christ ' or the *corpus verum* of Christ. The heated medieval controversy over the real presence gradually led to the avoidance of the term *corpus mysticum* for the Eucharist in favour of *verum corpus* or its equivalent. By the time of St Thomas *corpus mysticum* is the normal term for the Church, and apparently unknown as an expression for the Eucharist. St Thomas himself uses it in a number of places for the Church. At that time it had not yet become forgotten that the Eucharist is the special mysterious means whereby Christ's vivifying body, which died and rose on our behalf, effects a deep spiritual unity between ourselves in Christ which we now call the ' mystical body '. In the succeeding centuries the term came to be so exclusively applied to the Church that there was danger of the latter's relationship to the *mysterium* of the Eucharist being forgotten. The term was used for the Church in the *Schema* drawn up by the Fathers of the Vatican Council, by Leo XIII in *Divinum Illud Munus*, and recently in the supremely authoritative encyclical of Pius XII. It serves, we are there told, ' to distinguish the social Body of the Church, of which Christ is the Head and ruler, from His physical Body, which, born of the Virgin Mother of God, is now seated at the right hand of the Father, and lies hidden beneath the Eucharistic veils. Furthermore, and this is of great importance because of modern errors, we are enabled thereby to differentiate it from any body of the natural order, whether physical or moral.'

II The Teaching of the Magisterium. At no time has there been a definition by the Church directly on the subject of the mystical Body. It was proposed to define at the Vatican Council that ' the Church is the mystical Body of Christ ' (cf. *Schema 1 Constitutionis de Ecclesia*, Mansi, 51:539). In the Annotations to this *Schema*, there was pointed out (1) that this term for the Church is more frequent, accurate and clear than any other ; (2) that it describes the inner essence of the Church as something divine ; and (3) that it has the advantage of excluding at the outset the wrong notion that for Catholics the Church is confined to the external and visible order (cf. Mansi, 51:553).

The only fully authoritative document dealing with this doctrine is the encyclical of Pius XII, *Mystici Corporis*, 1943. A fuller account of this encyclical in its setting will be given in section XI of this article. In brief, this encyclical sees this doctrine as that of the corporate redemption of man in Christ. It explains the fittingness of the term ' Body ' to express the Church's unity and visibility, together with the organic relationship between members. It defines three conditions of membership, baptism, true faith, and non-severance from the Church's ruling authority. It points out the titles on which Christ is the Head, i.e. as Founder, as pre-eminent in perfection, as Ruler, as our like in nature, as deigning to need the co-operation of members, and lastly as the one whose influence alone enlightens, vivifies and sanctifies. He is also the continual upholder of His Body, animating it by His Spirit. The term mystical is explained and defended. The many bonds between Head and members are explained. Warning is given against the two extreme errors of exaggerating or of minimizing the union between Head and members.

Both *Mystici Corporis* and later *Humani Generis* (1950) insist on the identity and common extension of the terms mystical Body and Roman Catholic Church.

III In the Synoptics and St John. In the Synoptics one can only say that some sort of mystical identity between Christ and His Kingdom, i.e. Christ and His followers, whereby His blessings can flow out to them, is implied.

In St John's Gospel, salvation is clearly shown as

dependent upon a deep and intimate union between Christ and mankind. This appears in His sacramental doctrine, especially in his doctrine of the Eucharist, with its insistence on the need for eating the Flesh and drinking the Blood of Christ in order to become one with Christ and share His eternal life (cf. Jn 6:48 ff.). The Greek Fathers clearly understood St John as teaching the need of an assimilation between Christ's being and ours by means of some physical instrumentality of His humanity. The sacraments were the great means of man's divinization. Where St John speaks of the Spirit, not the flesh, which gives life (6:63), these Fathers understand the Spirit as divinizing through the Flesh ; or, if you prefer, the Flesh in the sacrament as saving us in so far as it is the means of conveying to us the Spirit.

The same doctrine of salvation through intimate and almost physical unity with Christ's humanity is seen in the parable of vine and branches. L. Bouyer (*Le Quatrième Évangile* (1955) 204) points out that Christ is not the trunk, but the vine. If we are then the branches, we form a part of a great whole which in some way is identified with Christ (cf. 15:1-9). Many other passages in John confirm this doctrine that we are called to the closest of unions. We have all received of His fullness, grace for grace (1:16). We are called to be one with each other and with Him, as He with the Father (17:11, 22). In fact, the whole Gospel with its emphasis on Christ as the Way, the Truth, the Life and Light of men harmonizes perfectly with the idea of the Mystical Body as a close intimate bond between Christ's human nature and ourselves.

IV St Paul. Paul is of course the chief witness to the doctrine. L. Cerfaux has, however, pointed out that Paul referred to the Church first as the true People of God, the People of whom the OT people were the type. This new Israel was to bind together Jew and Gentile in a higher unity by their faith in Christ, their common Redeemer. Paul first used the expression *Body* or *Body of Christ* (in the early epistles, without an article) to convey the unity of Christians that was effected through their sharing in the natural Body of Christ in the Eucharist. All who shared the bread were one, and the bread they shared was Christ's Body. 'Is not the bread we break a participation in Christ's Body ? The one bread makes us one body, though we are many in number.' (1 Cor 10:16, 17) 'Saint Paul begins,' writes L. Cerfaux, 'with the identity of the bread and the body, and then goes beyond the usual theme by connecting the notion of unity with the word "body"' (L. Cerfaux, *The Church in the Theology of St Paul* (1959) 265). At this early stage, as is convincingly argued by Cerfaux, St Paul had no notion yet of a collective 'body'. Such a notion would, in any case, have been an impossible one to be contained in the Greek word σῶμα (body).

Once St Paul had connected the notion of unity with Christ's natural body, it occurred to him as helpful to use the metaphor of a body to bring home the nature of unity in Christ to the disturbed Cor-

inthian community. In 1 Cor 12, as later in Rom 12, St Paul tells Christians that their unity should be like that of a body, now that they are all one in Christ. ' Each of us has one body, with many different parts, and not all these parts have the same function ; just so we, though many in number, form one body in Christ, and each acts as the counterpart of another' (Rom 12:4, 5 ; cf. 1 Cor 12:11). The image of a body, besides showing how Christians are united with one another as members of a body, enables St Paul to remind them that, in their unity with Christ, they are in a certain sense identified with His natural Body (cf. 1 Cor 12:27). To be identified with Christ's Body meant, in Hebrew usage, to be identified with Christ Himself.

The older, more traditional, interpretation of these passages is that St Paul is already teaching that Christ has a wider ' mystical' body, including ourselves as His members. Members and Head, on this view, form together what St Augustine was to call the *Christus totus*. One passage forms the exclusive direct textual evidence supposed to be available for this view, i.e. 1 Cor 12:12 : ' A man's body is all one, though it has a number of different organs ; and all this multitude of organs goes to make up one body ; so it is with Christ.' The latter words are taken to mean : ' So it is with the mystical Christ, or the *Christus Totus*.' Mersch, Allo and the majority of ancient and modern Catholic Scripture scholars understand the text that way. Huby and Cerfaux object that there are no grounds in St Paul for ever taking the word ' Christ ' in such a collective way. Further, they claim that the term ' body of Christ ', at least in the early epistles, always refers to Christ's natural Body, or, in the Hebrew way of thinking, to His whole Person. Consequently, he prefers Huby's explanation : ' We think that the phrase, " Thus also Christ ", is to be taken as an expression of his work as a unifying principle, and not as the expression of a mode of his being.' (Huby, *Première Épître aux Corinthiens*, 286 f. ; Cerfaux, *op. cit.* 269).

Those who support the ' mystical Christ ' interpretation usually claim that in some passages of St Paul the phrase ' in Christ ' may refer to the collective ' Christ'. It is also claimed by these that verse 13 of 1 Cor 12, with its mention of ' a body ' supports their view. ' We too, all of us, have been baptized into a single body by the power of a single Spirit.' Cerfaux, however, claims that baptism in the New Testament is always into a person (e.g. into Moses, into Christ) ; and so, even here, ' a single body ' could mean the Body of Christ, i.e. Christ Himself. He admits, of course, that, in the following verses, St Paul does carry over the analogy of the body and its members to include Christians as members of Christ. He even admits that St Paul allows the argument to carry him forward to stating in verse 27 that Christians are ' a body of Christ ' (σῶμα Χριστοῦ, without any article). This is, he argues, parallel to Romans (12:5) ; we ' form one body in Christ '. In all these cases, according to Cerfaux, ' body ' is related to the natural Body of

Christ, which we receive in the Eucharist, and with which we become mystically identified, so as to be, as it were, members of that Body. In conclusion, it seems that, according to this interpretation St Paul has not in mind in these early epistles a collective Christ, which he calls Christ's body, but rather that he thinks of all Christians being joined to, and saved by, Christ's natural Body and so becoming, as it were in a mystical way, new members of that natural Body, which in the Hebrew mode of speech is Christ's own Person. We become members of His Person, receiving His Body in the Eucharist, and made by Him into a unity analogous to the unity between a body and its members.

This interpretation, though different from the traditional one, fits in remarkably well with the whole early Christian understanding of the Eucharist, and with the manner in which they understand the Eucharist as the instrument of our salvation. For at all times the early Church insisted on the saving, sanctifying, divinizing function of Christ's Body and Blood through our contact with them in the Sacrament. It fits in also remarkably well with the use of 'mystical body' in the early Middle Ages for the Eucharist, to be later transposed to the Church.

Defenders of the new interpretation have to allow a development in St Paul's thought between these early Epistles and the Captivity Epistles. In the latter, St Paul does without question refer to the Church as the body of Christ. It is not only His body, but also His fullness or completion (Eph 1:23). By now, St Paul uses 'body' not exactly to signify a collectivity, but rather an outward visible expression of Christ. Just as the Son of God was manifested through His human body on earth, so He is now manifested by this body, the Church, which acknowledges Him as its Head. His natural Body was the 'fullness' through which all the grace and glory of His deity shone forth. The whole Church is now joined to Him as a body, through which the grace and glory of His divinity and humanity flow forth. This would be the meaning of the words, 'In Christ the whole plenitude of Deity is embodied, and dwells in him, and it is in him that you find your completion : he is the fountain head from which all dominion and power proceed.'

Huby's and Cerfaux's view agrees with the traditional one in seeing in St Paul the doctrine of an intimate salvific bond between Christians and Christ, their Head, which is the foundation of an intimate organic bond with one another. Both therefore agree against those minimist interpretations which would understand the Church as a mere moral unity, called metaphorically the body of Christ, but not involving any close physical or mystical relationship with Christ.

V The Early and the Greek Fathers. There is nothing in the way of a systematic teaching concerning the nature of the Church. In order to understand the place of the mystical body in their theology, we must look at their teaching on the Incarnation, Redemption and Sacraments. In the Apostolic Fathers we note their emphasis on the unity of the Church, their view of the necessity for our redemption of a real Incarnation, their sacramental doctrine, and their Christ-centred 'mysticism'. For St Ignatius, we can only attain to God through Christ. Both Ignatius and Irenaeus insist that our salvation in general, and our resurrection in particular, depend upon our partaking of the real flesh and blood of Christ. Both insist that, unless Christ had been made one with us by sharing our flesh and blood, we should not have been saved. Their theology supposes a degree of solidarity between Christ and mankind, such as is implied in the doctrine of the mystical body. Explicit statement of a special corporate unity between Christ and His baptized members in the Church was to come gradually. In the early stages the solidarity was assumed rather than stated.

For Irenaeus our salvation is a restoration. God's glory is attained by man's being moulded 'in conformity and correspondence with His own Son' (*adv. haer.*, V:6:1, H). Man has to be 'blended also with that flesh, which is moulded according to the Image of God' (*loc. cit.*). In the Preface to Book V, he says that the Word of God, Jesus Christ our Lord, 'for His immense love's sake was made that which we are, in order that He might perfect us to be what He is'. It is because Christ's members are fed with the Eucharist that their bodies have the power to rise again with Christ : 'How do they say that flesh is not capable of the gift of God which is eternal life, when fed on the body and blood of the Lord, and made His member ?' (*op. cit.* V:2:2, H).

The idea of unity between Christ and His members, and the likeness of redeemed mankind to Christ, through contact with Christ's flesh, also underlies Athanasius's theology of divinization through the Logos made flesh. It is not merely that man needs *the Word* to remake him according to God's Image. Man needs *the Word made flesh*. Christ did not sanctify Himself for His own sake. Nor did He raise Himself for His own sake. The mysteries of His life, death and resurrection were on our behalf (*Oratio contra Arianos* 1:41 ; PG 26:97). 'If it is accepted that all men were lost by the transgression of Adam, then the flesh of Adam was the first to be saved and delivered, for it became the body of the Word Himself. In the second place we also, becoming concorporeal (σύσσωμοι), have been saved by that same body' (*Oratio contra Arianos*, 2:61; PG 26:277). This appears to mean that the Word's being made man was a necessary condition of our redemption ; and that in turn appears to imply the need of our unity with Christ by grace in the mystical body. The effects of this unity with Christ apply to our body as well as to our soul. 'For the solidarity of mankind is such that, by virtue of the Word's Indwelling in a single human body, the corruption which goes with death has lost its power over all.' (*De Incarnatione*, 9, tr. by a Religious of C.S.M.V. (1944) ; cf. L. Bouyer, *L'Incarnation et l'Église-Corps du Christ*).

It is sometimes stated that Athanasius, in his early writings, attributed man's deification to the Word, and later to the Holy Spirit. A passage in his

Oratio contra Arianos, however, suggests that, to his mind, whether early or later, deification comes about through the Incarnate Word sending His Spirit into our hearts. ' Whence, just as we become sons and gods on account of the Word which we have in us, and so we are in the Son and in the Father, we are judged to be one in them, for the reason that the Spirit who is in the Word is in us, for the Word Himself is in the Father ' (*Oratio contra Arianos*, 3:24 ; PG 26:373).

The same doctrine of likeness to Christ and union with Christ as a result of the redemption and the sacraments is found in the theology of the Cappadocians. It is thought by Jules Gross (*La Divinisation du chrétien d'après les pères grecs* (1938)) that Gregory of Nyssa understands the sharing of human nature in the divinity to apply to that nature as a concrete universal. This would interpret his doctrine of the redemption after the manner of a Christian Platonist. Gregory of Nyssa could not then be called an upholder of the theory of salvation by membership of a ' mystical body of Christ ', which one joins by Baptism. Against this interpretation, however, is the general Cappadocian teaching that deification and incorruption come to soul and body through the sacraments of Baptism and Eucharist ; and so would not automatically involve universal mankind, but only the mystical Body. Perhaps the Cappadocians were anticipating our modern theological distinction between objective and subjective redemption. Objectively all mankind are saved by Christ's title to universal headship of the human race and His death for all. Subjectively His grace joins men as living members to Himself through the sacraments. The mystical Body would then extend in principle to all mankind, but in fact only to the Church.

In all this eastern theology of the redemption, the mystical bond between Christ and His members is caused by the physical instrumentality of His humanity, principally acting through the sacraments. This line of thought reaches its most developed patristic expression in the writings of Cyril of Alexandria. One aspect of the latter's anathemas against Nestorius was this desire to defend the life-giving power of Christ's flesh. ' If anyone does not confess that the flesh of the Lord is life-giving and is the proper flesh of the Word of God the Father, but [regards it] as belonging to another joined by dignity to the Word as though to one who is indwelt by God, and not, as we said, as life-giving, having been made the proper flesh of the Word who has power to bring life to all things, let him be anathema ' (Canon 11 ; Cyril's anathemas against Nestorius, D 123).

Cyril teaches that our salvation is both a forming of Christ within us and a reforming of our nature by Christ. ' Christ is formed in us, by the Holy Spirit placing within us a certain divine form through sanctification and justice ' (*In Isaiam*, 4:2 ; PG 70:936). The same passage speaks later of our being formed ' in Christ '. This latter aspect of the mystical body is frequently referred to in Cyril's commentary on St John. ' For I live Myself, he says, for I am Life by Nature, and have shown the Temple of My own Body alive ; but when ye also yourselves, albeit ye are of a corruptible nature, shall behold yourselves living in like manner as I do, then indeed ye shall know exceeding clearly that I being life by nature did knit you through Myself into God the Father, Who is also Himself by nature life, making you partakers as it were and sharers in His Incorruption ' (*In. Jn.* 9:14 ; *Library of the Fathers* trans., II, 321). In this connection also Cyril represents the common Greek doctrine, founded on John, that resurrection of the flesh comes about through our having been blended with Christ in the Eucharist ... ' since Christ is in us through His Own Flesh, we shall surely rise. For it were incredible, yea rather impossible, that Life should not make alive those in whom it is ' (*In Jn* 6:54 ; English trans. I, 421). Commenting on the following verse of St John, Cyril explicitly refers this to the mystical body. ' For it is not the Blood of any chance man, but of the Very Life that is by Nature. Wherefore we are entitled both the Body and the members of Christ, as receiving through the Blessing the Son Himself in ourselves ' (*In Jn* 6:55 ; English tr. I, 422). The analogy of the vine and branches gives Cyril a further opportunity of expressing our union with Christ in a physical way : ' For, as if one entwineth wax with other wax and melteth them by the fire, there resulteth one, so through the participation of the Body of Christ and of His precious Blood, He in us and we again in Him are co-united.'

This view of Christ's action upon us in the mystical Body through the instrumentality of His humanity was to become characteristic of all Eastern theology, and is found in the last great representative of the patristic period, St John Damascene. It is in this way that the latter understands ' the spirit which gives life ' of John 6:63. ' For the Lord's flesh is life-giving spirit because it was conceived of the life-giving Spirit. For what is born of the Spirit is spirit. But I do not say this to take away the nature of the body, but I wish to make clear its life-giving and divine power.' And he concludes, ' Participation is spoken of ; for through it we partake of the divinity of Jesus. Communion, too, is spoken of, and it is an actual communion, because through it we have communion with Christ and share in His flesh and His divinity : yea, we have communion and are united with one another through it. For since we partake of one bread, we all become one body of Christ and one blood, and members one of another, being of one body with Christ.' (*De fide Orthodoxa*, 4:13 ; PG 94:1153). This last passage is most important for the understanding of Greek theology of the mystical body. Not only are we one body of Christ, but we are also one blood. Clearly ' body ' is not taken as a group term ; but to indicate our physical oneness in the Church with the Body and Blood that redeemed us, and that we received in the Eucharist. This is not far from the early theology of St Paul, if we accept the interpretation of Cerfaux (cf. section IV, above).

VI St Augustine. There is much more about the mystical body in the writings of St Augustine than in any other of the Fathers. Yet his approach is completely different from that of the Greek Fathers we have been considering (cf. ' L'Influence du Christ-Chef sur son Corps mystique, suivant saint Augustin ', by Gerard Philips, in *Augustinus Magister*, II, 805–15). He has very little to say of any physical or organic influence of Christ as Head upon His members. Most of what he has to say on the subject is influenced by St Paul rather than St John, and chiefly by its moral aspect in St Paul. For, if L. Cerfaux is right (cf. IV above), St Paul also insists on a relationship with Christ's flesh and blood.

It is of course a matter of emphasis more than of opposition. Many passages could be quoted from St Augustine giving the typical Greek view of salvation by deification. ' He who was God was made man, in order to make those who were men gods.' (*Sermo* 192, 1 ; cf. Capánaga, ' La deificación en la soteriología agostiniana ', in *Augustinus Magister*, II, 745–54. This article gives many similar passages where St Augustine admits in a general way that the purpose of the Incarnation was man's deification.)

While it is then true that St Augustine admits divinizing grace as well as healing grace, he appears to think differently from the Greeks regarding the manner in which Christ's humanity is the means of ourd ivinization. It would appear that, for the Greeks, this is brought about in the mystical body in so far as the Body of Christ, or the Body and Blood of Christ (St John Chrysostom and St John Damascene), is a physical instrument causing this transformation in our souls and bodies. St Gregory of Nyssa cannot conceive how our bodies could receive the fruits of incorruption except by participating in immortality through sacramental reception of Christ's body (cf. St Gregory of Nyssa, *Orat. Catech.* 37 ; PG 45:93). St Augustine never appears to think of any such union of physical influence between Christ's Body and ours.

Yet it must be admitted that St Augustine is more ready to admit an identity between ourselves and Christ in the mystical body than any other of the Fathers. Continually he states that Head and members make one Christ, *totus Christus*, the *Whole Christ*. For him this identity is rather in a collective ' Person of Christ.'

As illustration of this line of thought let the following passages suffice, given in the English translation of E. Przywara's *Augustine Synthesis* (referred to below as A.S.) : ' All mankind is in Christ one man, and the unity of Christians is one Man ' (*In Ps* 29:2, 5 ; A.S., 217). ' Christ is therefore one man, the Head and the Body '' (*In Ps* 127, 1:3 ; A.S., 216). ' For Christ is not simply in the head and not in the body, but Christ whole is in the head and in the body.' (*In Jn*, 28:1 ; A.S., 215). ' We are all in Him both Christ's and Christ, since in some manner the whole Christ is the Head and the body ' (*In Ps* 26, 2:2 ; A.S., 213).

St Augustine is indeed the great defender of the usual collective *Christus totus* interpretation of St Paul, and he would understand St Paul as using the word ' Christ ' in some passages in this collective sense. Yet what he has in mind is some sort of mystical identification. All St Augustine's explanations seem to suggest that this means a kind of moral, rather than any sort of physical, bond. Christ as Head merits, governs, counsels, teaches, but St Augustine never speaks of Christ's humanity as a physical instrument of grace, after the manner of St Cyril or St John Damascene. The grace to live as a member of Christ and receive the adoption of sons and even deification is understood by St Augustine to come through the power of the Holy Spirit, but he says nothing of any physical rôle in its imparting played by Christ's Body and Blood. It is the Holy Spirit who divinizes Christ's members, because of Christ's merits. But the Spirit is not said to do it through Christ's flesh and blood. ' The faithful know the Body of Christ, if they do not neglect to be the Body of Christ. Let them become Christ's Body, if they wish to live by the Spirit of Christ. None lives by the Spirit of Christ, except Christ's Body. . . . Do you also then wish to live by the Spirit of Christ ? Then be in Christ's Body. Does my body live by your spirit. The Body of Christ can only live by the Spirit of Christ. Whence the Apostle says, expounding for us this bread : One bread, one body many of us are. O sacrament of piety ! O sacrament of unity ! O bond of charity ! He who wishes to live has here the source of life. Let him approach, believe and be incorporated, in order that he may live ' (*In Jn* 26:13 ; PL 35:1613). ' The charity of God is shed over our hearts by the Holy Spirit who is given to us. It is then the Spirit who gives life. For the Spirit makes living members. Nor does it make living members unless it finds them in the body which the Spirit nourishes ' (*In Jn* 27:6 ; PL 35:1618). ' What our spirit, that is our soul, is to our members, the Holy Spirit is to the body of Christ which is the Church ' (*Sermo* 268, 2 ; PL 38:1232).

It is quite clear that St Augustine sees the living member of Christ as spiritually nourished and kept alive by the Indwelling Spirit of Christ ; but in no way is the flesh of Christ explicitly made an instrument of this activity. However, in whatever way St Augustine understands the bond between ourselves and Christ, it is to him the very centre of his theology of the Redemption. It is essential to God's scheme of salvation that we should recognize ourselves as all being one body. This recognition, together with the love of God and one another that it involves, is the ground of our Christian hope, and is an essential aspect of the saving faith in Christ which enables the sacraments to be effective. If you wish to receive the Body of Christ worthily, you must be part of the body. As long as we are united to Christ in the body, our sufferings become to us a healing remedy (*In Ps* 61:4 ; A.S., 286).

Closely connected with this mystical bond with Christ which enables us to share in His redemption is the unity of the body for all the world to see.

This unity is something which even the disciples did not see, and is the great Christian privilege and duty. 'This the disciples did not yet see, namely, the Church throughout all nations, beginning at Jerusalem. They saw the Head and they believed the Head in the matter of the Body. By this which they saw they believed that which they did not see. What do we see which they did not ? The Church throughout all nations. What is it we do not see, which they saw ? Christ present in the flesh. As they saw Him and believed concerning the Body, so do we see the Body ; let us believe concerning the Head ' (*Serm.* 116:6 ; A.S., 223). It is only by clinging to the Church, by remaining one with her, and one with one another, throughout the Church Catholic, that we can be saved. The mystical Body is then for St Augustine the necessary condition for us to receive the benefits of Christ's salvation. If we are one with Christ in the body, we are saved. But it is Christ's spirit who makes us one, and who gives us the love to enable us to be one spiritually. Even the Eucharist itself, as we have seen, benefits us only as long as we remain thus one body in Christ. ' He willed that we should belong to Him, and consecrated the mystery of our peace and of our unity on His table ' (*Serm.* 272 ; A.S., 235).

This 'mystical' approach to the doctrine of our unity with Christ in the Body is analogous to St Augustine's symbolic approach to the Eucharist. It is well known, that, although St Augustine shows clearly from some passages that He accepts the realistic understanding of Christ's presence, together with the rest of the Catholic Church, yet he is not normally interested in this aspect. What really interests him is Eucharistic symbolism. It is this that distinguishes him from the Greeks. The latter, apart from the early Alexandrian School, combine an almost exaggerated realism in Eucharistic doctrine with a strong sense of the instrumentality of Christ's Body and Blood as the basis of the mystical body. For St Augustine, the mystical body seems to have been understood as a collective personality. For the Greeks it was a common relationship to the real Body.

VII St Thomas Aquinas. As in other questions, there was some development in Thomistic teaching regarding the mystical body. In his early works, St Thomas looks for Christ's qualities of headship rather more in His divine nature than in His humanity. Just at the time that he was writing the third part of the *Summa*, St Thomas made the discovery of the works of St Cyril of Alexandria and St John Damascene. This had a most important influence on his doctrine of the Incarnation and the Sacraments. It resulted in his uniting the special emphasis of the Greek Fathers on the instrumental causality of the sacred humanity with that of the Latins on the moral and mystical identity between Christ and His members, as seen by Augustine.

By the time St Thomas came to treat of this subject in the *Summa Theologica*, Christ's Headship over the Church was understood of Our Lord as man, rather than as God. It was closely bound up with his treatment of Christ's personal sanctifying grace. Because of His relationship to us, His personal grace was given Him ultimately for our sakes. This means that His personal grace was at the same time grace of headship (or capital grace). It was the grace whereby He, as God, gifted Himself, as man, with created holiness, in order to be the instrument of passing on created holiness to us, His members.

In so far as the human Christ was filled with this grace, His relationship to us bore an analogy to that of a head towards the other members of a body. A head, St Thomas reminds us (*Summa* 3a:8:1), is superior to the body in its order or dignity, in its perfection, and in its directive power. In dignity, Christ has through His created grace a nearness to God and a priority over us which gives Him the supreme dignity. In perfection He possesses the fullness of grace and truth, and so exceeds the rest of mankind (Jn 1:14). In directive power, He is the instrumental cause of grace in us, for ' of His fullness we have all received ' (Jn 1:16).

St Thomas, following patristic and especially Greek theology, gives Christ a headship both over our bodies and over our souls. This headship extends on principle to all mankind, although the effects of it are applied at different times according to God's plan, and in different measure corresponding to people's dispositions. Not only does Our Lord's actual headship include all Christians, but also all just men from the beginning of the world ; further, not only is Christ as man Head of all mankind, but also of the angels.

This headship is exercised both interiorly and exteriorly. He acts interiorly by being the instrumental cause of grace in our souls. This activity is proper to Christ, and is shared by none other, except in so far as He acts through His ministers in the sacraments. Exteriorly he rules His body by directing men's activities externally. In the exterior exercise of His headship He uses subordinate members. In this external way, He Himself is the universal governor of His Church, while he allows men to govern under Him and in His name, either universally over the Church on earth (i.e. the Pope), or locally (the bishops). None of these rule except by His authority. They share the headship in a secondary, or subordinate, way.

All that St Thomas writes on the Redemption reflects his doctrine of the manner in which Christ is Head over His Mystical Body. That Christ is first in dignity and perfection forms the background. For without His superior dignity and perfections He would not have been able to redeem us. But the characteristic way in which St Thomas combines the Greek and Augustinian traditions leads to his very rich doctrine of the manifold way in which Christ is the cause of grace and spiritual life in His members. His life, passion, death and resurrection bring about our salvation in many ways. The special Augustinian tradition is reflected where he says that Christ saves us by way of merit, by way of satisfaction and by way of sacrifice. The special

Greek tradition is reflected where he says that Christ saves us by way of efficient causality, i.e. by being the instrumental cause of grace in our souls. Finally, the early and enduring tradition of salvation by a victory won by the Head of our race over its spiritual enemies is reflected in his doctrine that Christ saved us by way of ransom.

VIII St Robert Bellarmine. Written at a time of crisis, St Robert Bellarmine's contribution concerns the possibility and degree of membership in Christ's mystical body for heretics, schismatics and sinners. He took from St Augustine, and developed, a special way of understanding the soul and body of the Church. He understood by the term *body* the external visible organization which Christ gave to the Church. The *soul* he defined as that group of gifts, virtues and graces of supernatural life, by which the individual members of the faithful are joined to God and Christ (cf. St Robert Bellarmine, *De Ecclesia Militante*, 3:2). The soul he understood as having a wider meaning than body. Not all who are in the body are in it to the same degree. Not all who live by the soul of the Church, live by it to the same degree. It is absolutely necessary for salvation to belong to the soul of the Church, but only necessary by precept to belong to the body. All who die in a state of faith and charity are saved through their relationship to the soul of the Church, even though they may never have been part of its body.

So it is that Catholics in a state of grace are in both soul and body, and are in the fullest sense members of Christ. Catholics no longer in a state of grace belong to the body of the Church, but, since they do not belong to the soul, they are not truly members of Christ. Applying the biological analogy, Bellarmine says that such people are to be compared with the hairs, which, while not truly members of our natural bodies, are yet attached to it. Finally, catechumens and those who are not visibly members of the Church, who yet have faith and charity, belong to the soul of the Church, though not to its body.

Bellarmine's explanation seems to pose two problems. First, it seems to deny membership of the Church to those, even the hierarchy, who happen to be in a state of grave sin. Secondly, there is the problem of reconciling Bellarmine's belief in the salvation of all who are in the soul, even though not in the body, of the Church with the Church's doctrine of the necessity of belonging to the Church for salvation. Could those who are merely in the soul of the Church be said to be within the Church?

The first problem Bellarmine solves by distinguishing between *living* membership, for which one has to be in a state of grace, and *instrumental* membership, which is at all times possessed by the hierarchy. The second problem is resolved by use of the Thomistic distinction between *res* and *votum*. Those who are in the soul, but not in the body, of the Church are members of the Church *voto*. Those who are in both body and soul are members *re et voto*. There still remains unsolved the problem

of those who are visibly within the Church, but who have lost the state of grace and are not members of the hierarchy. This problem is to be later solved by Pius XII by calling them *true* members, but *sick*.

IX Post-Reformation Period. In the period following the Reformation until the present century exclusively, ecclesiology was very little studied under the aspect of the Mystical Body. Most that appeared on the Church was either polemic or apologetic. The Catholic concept of the Church had to be defended, or other concepts attacked. Inevitably this approach kept the attention of theologians almost exclusively on the external visible aspects of the Church, rather than on its inner relationship with its Head.

The most important exceptions were probably Scheeben in Germany and Newman in England. Scheeben has a more patristic outlook than most of his contemporaries, and this guides him to an incarnational understanding of Christianity similar to that of St John of Damascus. Salvation is brought about by the Incarnation of the Word in the midst of the human race. Since Christ's presence and mediatorship influences all the life of His Church, He is called its supersubstantial Head (cf. M. Scheeben, *Dogmatik*, III, 144). He takes up from Irenaeus the idea of recapitulation, and says that Christ by this method is in the process of taking hold of all creation to hand it back to its Creator. Newman sees Christ as the leaven of the New Creation, who came to sum up in Himself and transform all that is good in human nature. ' Christ came for this very purpose, to gather together in one all the elements of good dispersed throughout the world, to make them His own, to illuminate them with Himself, to reform and refashion them into Himself. He came to make a new and better beginning of all things than Adam had been, and to be a fountain-head from which all good henceforth might flow.' (*Lectures on Justification* (1892) 193 : this view of the Mystical Body as an extension of the Incarnation to include and baptize all that is good in man and his culture underlies all these *Lectures*, and also underlies Newman's *Idea of a University*.) Both Scheeben and Newman recognize the great importance of the Holy Spirit as the vivifying principle of the Church's Body.

X The Twentieth Century. Several factors have tended to make this pre-eminently the century of the Mystical Body. The development of the theology of the Eucharist and, in general, of the sacraments, the liturgical revival, the oecumenical movement—all these characteristic movements of our age have fostered the development of the theology of the Mystical Body. From a scriptural point of view the first great studies of the century were F. Prat's *The Theology of St Paul* and E. Mersch's *The Whole Christ*. These writers saw this doctrine as the basis of all St Paul's teaching. E. Mersch saw the same doctrine as the basis of both Synoptic and Johannine teaching. For all NT writers, according to F. Prat, the doctrine of the Body of Christ is the mystery hidden from the beginning of the world, and now revealed in Christ (Eph 1 & 3). ' The mystery *par excellence* is the design conceived by God from all eternity, but revealed only in the Gospel, to save all men without distinction of race, identifying them with his well-beloved Son in the unity of the mystical body. This idea is now so familiar to us that we can hardly conceive how it could have been the most characteristic feature in St Paul's teaching, even to the point of being called his Gospel ; but this idea, so simple in itself, swept away all privileges and put an end to the claims which Israel had made for centuries' (F. Prat, *The Theology of St Paul*, English trans. (1933) 308).

Following upon the rediscovery of the importance of the Scripture doctrine, there appeared in the first quarter of the century a series of important theology monographs on various aspects of this doctrine, which prepared the way for the encyclical *Mystici Corporis*. Because of their historical importance in the development of the doctrine, it will be useful to pick out especially Karl Adam and E. Mersch.

Karl Adam showed the great theological extension of the doctrine in *Das Wesen des Katholizismus* (English trans. (1929), *The Spirit of Catholicism*). He saw the secret of Catholicism as the continued presence of Christ among men until the end of the world by the drawing successively of individuals into union with Himself through Baptism. The Church begins with the Incarnation. The Incarnation continues in the Church. We join both, as it were, by putting on Christ. Without ceasing to be ourselves, we are grafted on to Him. From this follows the paradox of the Church, which is divine and spotless, and yet has sinful members. By means of the Church, Christ is continually transforming His members into His own likeness. A consequence of this is that the whole Church is of a personal nature. It is not something which Christ instituted, but rather Christ Himself within His people. The sacraments are not mere rites, they are the ' visible guarantee, authenticated by the word of Jesus and the usage of the Apostles, that Jesus is working in the midst of us ' (*The Spirit of Catholicism*, 21). ' They are . . . the truest expression of that original and central Christian belief that the Christian should be inseparably united with Christ and should live in Christ ' (*op. cit.* 23). Because of this aspect of the Church, the Catholic still, in a world which chafes at authority, loves and respects her authority, for it takes his eyes from himself and the world below, and directs ' his gaze to Christ and Christ alone ' (*op. cit.* 26).

Karl Adam sees the Church's sense of unity and community as a direct result of this realization of Christ's presence and action in His Church. Christ became man, ' to reunite to God mankind as a unity, as a whole, not this or that individual man '. (*op. cit.* 38). In fact, it is only in the community that the Spirit of Christ is realized. In this world there cannot be a community without external structure ; and the purpose of the papacy in the mystical body is for the protection of the Church.

The Church's outward structure is but the frame-work within which the personal faith of each Christian is incorporated in the living Church. The Church was built on the living faith of a community, not primarily on written records. Those who reduce Christianity to the Bible alone, or who try to enclose the wide flow of the Church's life within catch-phrases such as the Fatherhood of God, the expectation of a Second Coming, or Justification by Faith alone, fail to understand it. It is necessary to recognize the Church's intimate organic unity, which ' in all stages of its unfolding is a unity and a whole, the Christianity of Christ ' (*op. cit.* 71). The Church is then the still living body of Christ, embracing the whole of human life, sanctifying all its heights and depths. K. Adam developed the same doctrine in his work *Christ our Brother*, which appeared in English in 1931. This was all directed against the view of the Church as a mere organization or hierarchy. ' The vital fact is not that God dwelt bodily among us and that we can see the glory of God in the face of Christ Jesus, but that God is our brother, that He is of one blood with us, that He is the Head of our body ' (*Christ our Brother*, 62). In this the author takes us back to the eucharistic doctrine of St Thomas and St Augustine, reminding us that it is a community sacrament, not a private communion between the individual soul and Jesus Christ. ' Do we Catholics really feel and realize that holy unity and sacred fellowship whose Head is Christ, or are we not isolated and separated from one another, forming all too often no more than an external organisation ? I see but one road to renewal, and that is the road which both dogma and liturgy point out to us, and of which we ourselves shall be daily reminded as often as we pray ' through Christ our Lord ' (*op. cit.* 76).

The second great name in the modern presentation of the doctrine of the Mystical Body is that of Émile Mersch (cf. Mersch-Kelly, *The Whole Christ* (1938), trans. from *Le Corps mystique du Christ*, (1932)). It was for him a consuming life-interest. sees in this doctrine a safeguard against all heresies. It is the especial antidote against the heresy of our age, Modernism, with its false immanentism confining each man within his own experience. It is the antidote to the modern exaggerations of nationalism and liberalism. Mersch is convinced that it is this doctrine which the Fathers used against Arianism, Apollinarianism, Nestorianism, Donatism, Pelagianism and, in modern times, Protestantism and naturalism. For all heresies arise from the break-up or neglect of the true unity (*a*) of the Christian with Christ, and (*b*) of Christians with one another.

As to the theological explanation of this unity, Mersch leaves theological freedom between the view (*a*) that it is a mere moral unity, and (*b*) that it is in some way ontological. He confesses that he favours the latter view, and he is convinced it is the view of the Fathers. He realizes already what is to be openly expressed in the Encyclical *Mystici Corporis* that there is a danger in exaggerating either point of view. The one extreme can lead to pantheism, the other to a denial of any Mystical Body at all.

In his later works, Mersch applies the doctrine of the mystical body to our spiritual lives. Through our union with Christ in that body, we share his life. In so far as we are His members, we act with His life. So Mersch goes back to the Greek emphasis on divinization through Christ. But he argues further that only in Christ can we become perfectly human; so our divinization is at the same time true humanization. He adopts a similar line to Newman in his incarnationalism, wherein he insists that the whole of human activity is meant to be raised up in and through Christ.

Lastly, it is for Mersch through our union with Christ in the mystical body that we become personally related to Father and Holy Spirit. Thus our redemption and sanctification are brought about by our mystical identification with the Second Person. 'Redemption is not a concept or abstract theory. It is someone, someone intensely living, living in the activity in which his life is most intense. It is the immense personal constraint with which God draws sinful humanity to His heart, saving it from itself and its evil in spite of itself, in His Incarnate Son. All the divinity is here giving itself utterly, all humanity utterly purified from its sin, all Christ pouring Himself into His own, and sacrificing Himself entirely. Who could hope to include these totalities, these avalanches of totalities in one concept or even in a group of concepts, since concepts are only partial human knowledge that express part of heaven?'

Grace, Mersch maintains, is not just a sharing of the divine nature; it must have a reference to the Son, whose adoptive brethren it makes us. Just as Christ's own grace was both *personal* and *capital*, i.e. it belonged to Him both as individual and as our Head, so our grace is both *individual* and *social*. From the latter point of view (and here we see grace in an unexpected light), 'it is divinization, not of an isolated man, but of humanity. There is no isolated man. Grace does not enter into man without uniting him to all. Christ only is the full divinization of the race; Christ only, but not alone.'

In our personal relation with our Head, grace gives us a share in the unity that Christ has with His Father. Through grace we share in God's presence in the depths of Christ's humanity. The Son is our link with God. This gives us a special relationship of adoptive sonship to the Father, and a second special relationship to the Holy Spirit. Not that these Divine Persons have any separate action upon us; but at least we know them in a special personal way, depending on their relations with the Son. This is the view of Scheeben, Waffelaert, de Régnon and a number of modern theologians, including de La Taille. It is quite different from the view, condemned by Pius XII in *Mystici Corporis*, of a distinction between the Divine Persons in external activity. It was Mersch's object, as it was Karl Adam's, to personalize all the dogmas of our faith, to enable us to see them all as aspects of Christ living within us.

Ernest Mura (*Le Corps mystique de Christ, sa nature et sa vie d'après s. Paul et la théologie* (1934)) produced a scholastic *summa* on the question. He attempted to show, on theological principles, the intimate nature of the organism of the Church as Christ's mystical body. He outlined the principles that underlie its unity, i.e. juridical unity, moral unity through charity, unity of life through the Holy Spirit, unity of efficient causality through Christ's humanity and the Eucharist, and obvious unity of exemplary and final causality. Regarding the nature of this unity, Mura holds that it is more than a moral one, yet less than a substantial one. It was more than the union between husband and wife. We must call it a union *sui generis*, best termed by the traditional word, *mystical*. He thinks it right to call this mystical union physical, since there are many ontological bonds. Most of the seven principles of unity mentioned above imply some ontological bond between Head and members.

On the whole question of the nature of this union *see also* the article BIOLOGY, section II.

XI Mystici Corporis Christi. This has already been briefly summarized. The treatment here has the purpose of locating the encyclical in its context as an important stage in the development of this key doctrine.

The immediate occasion of the encyclical was twofold. On the one hand Catholics were having more contacts with non-Catholics, and there was need for restating the Catholic position in relation to other Christians. Secondly the great up-surge of interest in this doctrine had inevitably led to exaggerations, which needed to be corrected. It would be mistaken, however, to suggest that its purpose was primarily polemical or restrictive. The theological interest which had grown up in the previous quarter of a century demanded a positive statement on what was now one of the most important recoveries of modern theology.

The first Catholic exaggeration that was condemned was the 'extreme right' view that our union with Christ in the mystical body was a kind of 'accidental hypostatic union'. According to the defenders of this view, we share Christ's divinity, but Christ shares our human weaknesses and sins. This view endangered or denied the proper distinction between creature and Creator. The second, an extreme left, view denied any supernatural reality whatever to the mystical Body.

In his positive treatment of the mystical Body, the Pope took three concepts, that of Body, that of Christ and that of 'mystical'. It was an important departure from traditional theology to begin by considering the Church in its social aspect of body. Usually both Catholics and Protestants had been in the habit of starting from the relationship of each individual soul to Christ, with the result of occasionally never arriving at the idea of a real community at all. The Church is clearly a community into which members are incorporated. The Pope developed the Pauline metaphor of a body. A body is one, undivided, visible, possessed of various members, yet forming one organism with its own life. It has its own means of fostering its life, health and growth and that of its members. So the Church has its own social life, its own visible bonds and its own visible unity. Sick members are not excluded until they are cut off from it.

As the Body *of Christ*, the Pope considers the many ways in which it is related to Christ. As in the case of a body with its head, this relationship is not purely internal. In fact, some bonds are purely external. From another point of view, Christ is related to His Church as Founder, Head, Upholder and Saviour. He is the Founder on the Cross and at Pentecost. As Head, he is the pre-eminent member, ruling both interiorly and exteriorly, directly in the interior heart and exteriorly through the hierarchy. Something new in the Pope's encyclical is his stress on the fact that Christ not only gives, He also receives from His members. Members of Christ by His grace have a contribution to make to the body. Christ as Head is alike in nature to His members, but pre-eminent in all perfections. Interiorly, Christ is the source of light and holiness. All this interior work is done through His Holy Spirit, who can be called the soul of the Church.

The nature of the union between Christ and His members is not physical in the strict sense, as that word is used of natural bodies. Nor is it moral in the natural sense. We should rather call it a singular union, of which no analogy can be found and which is therefore best called mystical. In this matter two errors must be avoided : (*a*) that which would make it a purely external institution ; and (*b*) that which would make it a purely internal bond with no external or juridical unity (cf. M. Bévenot, in CR 24 (1944) 145–50). One aspect of the juridical unity of the Church concerns the Church's authority. 'Hence there can be no real opposition or incompatibility between the invisible mission of the Holy Spirit and the juridical office which Pastors and Teachers have received from Christ. Like body and soul in us, the two realities are complementary and perfect each other.' The words just quoted have led to a distrust among theologians of the Augustine-Bellarmine distinction between the body and soul, in the sense that one can belong to the soul without belonging to the body.

Regarding the Church's position over against non-Catholics, the encyclical does two things : (*a*) it gives three conditions for membership of the mystical body ; (*b*) it gives some recognition to sincere Christians out of communion with the Church. The three conditions are baptism, profession of the true faith, and that members should not be cut off either by their own action or by excommunication from the visible structure of the Body. Sinners who fulfil these conditions, but are out of a state of grace, remain in the Church as sick members. With regard to non-Catholics, two sentences are of special interest : (1) 'We invite them all, each and every one, to yield their free consent to the inner stirrings of God's grace and to strive to extricate themselves from a state in which

they cannot be secure of their own eternal salvation ; for though they may be related to the mystical Body of the Redeemer by some unconscious yearning and desire, yet they are deprived of those many great heavenly gifts and aids which can be enjoyed only in the Catholic Church.' (2) 'We await them, not as strangers, but as those who are coming to their own Father's house' (*Mystici Corporis*, CTS trans., 102).

XII Reactions to the Pope's Encyclical. The problem of the relationship of the Church to sincere Christians outside visible membership with it, is one of the most discussed questions in 20th cent. theology. This is due to the interest in oecumenism, and the many bonds of sympathy that have grown up between Christians in the face of many common enemies.

In 1948, A. Chavasse made a special study of the phrase 'related to the mystical Body' (NRT, 70 (1948) 703 ff.). He concluded that the Pope purposely avoided the term 'members', in order to preclude misunderstanding. Those who are not in visible communion cannot be called members in any normal sense. He discussed the meaning of their 'unconscious desire', together with the term 'related' ; and came to the conclusion that the words of the Holy Father could refer not only to non-Catholics in good faith, but also to non-Catholics in bad faith, in so far as they could, by Baptism or in any other way, be said to be related to the Church. This would not mean that they can be saved while in bad faith ; but that they can be said to have a relation to the Church. We cannot be certain that such is the meaning of the Pope's words ; Fr. Chavasse merely argues that it could be. Perhaps the Pope wished to leave it to theologians to specify in detail in what ways such a relation could be verified.

T. Zapalena agrees that such an explanation, even to the extent of including everyone outside the Church, whether in good or bad faith, could be read into the word 'ordinari'. (T. Zapalena, *De Ecclesia Christi*, II (1954) 378.) But he thinks that the further words, 'by some unconscious yearning and desire', imply that there is some sort of subjective wish, in addition to the objective relation involved, say, in God's universal salvific will. Clearly it need not be a conscious wish to enter the Church. It could, he suggests, mean either : (*a*) a desire of which they are not reflectively aware, though really elicited ; or (*b*) a desire for something else which virtually includes such a wish.

The words 'coming to their own father's house' have given rise to the distinction between *re et actu perfecto* (perfectly and fully) and *non re sed voto* (as by a hidden tendency). (Thus Charles Journet, *L'Église du Verbe Incarné*, II (1951) 1078.) Some see in the words of Pius XII a form of St Robert Bellarmine's distinction between *re* and *voto*. Schismatics retain something of the sacraments, faith, or Catholic life of the Catholic Church, some more than others. They must be presumed to be in good faith. If they are truly baptized, accept the

Creed, and are not conscious of having willingly broken off from communion with the true Church, they have much which justifies the statement that they are on their way to their Father's house.

It has been generally agreed that no one can be saved unless through the mystical Body. In order to meet some of the difficulties aroused by the oecumenical outlook, a few theologians after the encyclical *Mystici Corporis* put forward the theory that the mystical Body might be wider than the Roman Catholic Church, and include some outside its limits. Pius XII corrected this view in *Humani Generis*, 1950, and reaffirmed the identity between the two realities. The more common recent way of explaining the possibility of salvation for non-Catholics is to distinguish between visible and invisible membership of the one true visible Church. People have the duty of being visibly united. But invincible ignorance might make it possible for those who are baptized and have the essentials of the faith to belong to that one true Church, but without their realizing it, and without their communion with it being visible before men.

XIII Other aspects discussed in modern theology. In modern theology various suggestions have been put forward as to the *soul* of the mystical Body. Everyone today agrees that in a wide sense the Holy Spirit can be called by this name. Yet it has to be admitted that the Holy Spirit could not act as a form of the Church, in any sense really analogous to the soul's function of form of the body. The Holy Spirit must be a kind of efficient, rather than formal, cause. If we must discover some internal bond analogous to a 'soul', we might accept C. Journet's suggestion that it is charity, or A. Sauras's suggestion that it is 'Christian grace as such'. The latter suggestion makes it easier to explain how sinners without charity can still be in the Church. Though they have lost charity, they still have certain Christian graces, e.g. faith and hope. C. Journet thinks that tradition, with the use of the term *agape* in the early centuries, so strongly favours charity that it must be retained as the Church's inner form of unity. Sinners, thinks Journet, come under the unifying influence of the charity of the whole body. T. Zapalena is opposed to the whole idea of a created 'soul'. Neither charity nor grace, he says, forms an ontological bond, since each person's charity and grace is individual to himself.

Another question discussed today is that of the extension of the term 'mystical Body'. Does it include the Church in heaven and purgatory, or is it confined to the Church on earth? Does it include the fathers of the OT as well as those of the New? The encyclical *Mystici Corporis* and most of what St Paul wrote seem to restrict the Mystical Body to the Church on earth. St Augustine and St Thomas are for the wider interpretation in both cases. It is clear that the question is an open one, since it is mainly one of terminology.

In all this article it will be clear that the mystical Body has an interior life of its own, under the inspiration and guidance of the Holy Spirit, and is more rightly compared to an organism than to an organization (*see* BIOLOGY, section II).

Bibliography. K. Adam, *The Spirit of Catholicism* (1929); *Christ our Brother* (1931); J. Anger, *The Doctrine of the Mystical Body* (1932); E. Mura, *Le Corps mystique du Christ* (1934); K. Feckes, *Das Mysterium der heiligen Kirche* (1951)²; A. Vonier, *The Spirit and the Bride* (1935); Fulton J. Sheen, *The Mystical Body of Christ* (1935); A. Wikenhauser, *Die Kirche als der mystische Leib Christi nach dem Apostel Paulus* (1937); E. Mersch SJ, *The Whole Christ* (1938); S. Tromp SJ, *De Spiritu sancto anima Corporis Mystici testimonia selecta*, 2 vols (1932 and 1948); L. Bouyer, *L'Incarnation et l'Église corps du Christ dans la théologie de s. Athanase* (1943); E. Mersch, *La Théologie du Corps mystique*, 2 vols (1946) (English trans., *The Theology of the Mystical Body*, 1954); G. Dejaifve SJ, *La Théologie du Corps mystique de P. Mersch*, NRT 67 (1945) 408; M. Scheeben, *The Mysteries of Christianity* (English trans. by Vollert, 1947); A. M. Landgraf, *Die Lehre vom geheimnisvollen Leib Christi . . . in der Frühscholastik*, in *Divus Thomas* 24 (1946) 393–428; 25 (1947) 365–94; 26 (1948) 160–80, 291–323, 395–434; Pius XII, Encyclical *Mystici Corporis Christi* (English trans., 1947); A. Chavasse, *Ordonnés au Corps mystique*, in NRT 70 (1948) 690–702; A. Liégé, *L'Appartenance à l'Église et l'encyclique Mystici Corporis*, in RSPT 32 (1948) 351–357; H. de Lubac SJ, *Corpus Mysticum* (1949)²; K. Feckes, *Die Kirche als Herrenleib* (1949); T. Soiron, *Die Kirche als der Leib Christi nach der Lehre des hl. Paulus* (1951); C. Journet, *The Church of the Word Incarnate*, I (1955); C. Journet, *L'Église du Verbe Incarné*, I (1955²), II (1951); Stanislas Jakí OSB, *Les Tendances nouvelles de l'ecclésiologie* (1957); F. Prat SJ, *The Theology of St Paul* (one-volume edition, 1957); L. Cerfaux, *The Church in the Theology of St Paul* (1959); L. Cerfaux, *Christ in the Theology of St Paul* (1959); A. Sauras OP, *El Cuerpo místico de Christo* (1952); J. M. Bover SJ, *Teologia de San Paolo* (1946). Two notable Protestant books on this doctrine are John A. T. Robinson, *The Body* (1952) and E. Best, *One Body in Christ* (1954). There is a survey of fifty years' work on this subject in J. Bluett SJ, *The Mystical Body of Christ*, 1890–1940, in TS 3 (1942) 261–89. For the influence of the doctrine on spirituality, see D Sp., s.v. *Corps mystique et spiritualité*, by E. Mersch and R. Brunet.   H. F. D.

BOETHIUS, INFLUENCE OF. After a brief summary of the life of Boethius (I), and an account of his works (II), his character as a Christian and a Martyr will be examined (III). The final section (IV) will consider his thought and influence.

I Anicius Manlius Severinus Boethius was born in Rome about the year A.D. 480. He came of a noble family and appears to have received an excellent education. His knowledge of Greek was remarkable and Cassiodorus speaks of him as *peritissimus orator* in that language as well as in Latin. He was also well versed in music and mathematics.

His gifts attracted the attention and the favour of Theodoric and we find Boethius sole consul in A.D. 510 and, towards the end of his life, *magister officiorum*. He had married the daughter of Symmachus and his two sons were joint consuls in 522. The occupations of public life never caused him to interrupt his studies and writing which he regarded as a form of public service (cf. PL 64:201 B). But he appears to have made enemies, and was convicted of treason in circumstances that remain somewhat obscure. He was confined in prison at or near Pavia for about a year, during which period he wrote the *De Consolatione Philosophiae* wherein he eloquently protests his innocence. He was finally executed, the date of this event being most probably A.D. 524.

II His literary works. Boethius wrote profusely. We cannot here discuss the full extent of his writings, several of which have perished. For further details the reader may be referred to the article on Boethius by M. Cappuyns in the *Dictionnaire d'Histoire et de Géographie Ecclésiastiques*. We possess two works on the *Quadrivium*, the *Institutio de Arithmetica* and the *Institutio de Musica* (both in PL 63). He also wrote on geometry, translating and no doubt commenting on Euclid, but the works on this subject attributed to him in Migne are of a later date, though they may embody something of Boethius himself. These works are not original, but are free translations of earlier authorities with some personal additions by way of commentary.

In the field of logic and philosophy, Boethius had hoped to translate all the works of Aristotle and Plato into Latin with commentaries, a plan which was only very partially realized. In fact nothing of Plato was translated. As regards Aristotle, Boethius translated and commented on the *De Interpretatione*, the *Topics* and the *Prior Analytics* and *Posterior Analytics*, and probably some other works as well: all that we have with certainty are the translations and commentaries on the *Categories* and the *De Interpretatione* and the translation of the *Prior Analytics*. The rest is lost. In addition, Boethius translated and commented on the *Isagoge* of Porphyrius (he also used here the translation of Marius Victorinus). He also composed some short treatises on various questions of Logic.

We have five treatises—known as the *opuscula sacra*—on theological questions. Two of these are on the Trinity, one is of a more philosophical character (it deals with the problem: *quomodo substantiae in eo quod sint bonae sint cum non sint substantialia bona* and was known to the Middle Ages as the *De hebdomadibus*), the fourth consists of a brief exposition of the Catholic faith, the fifth is the *Liber contra Eutychen et Nestorium*. His final and best-known work was the *De Consolatione Philosophiae* written in prison.

III Boethius as Christian and Martyr. That Boethius was by external profession a Christian seems beyond doubt, but doubts have been cast on the depth and sincerity of his faith. The main reason for such doubts lies in the nature of his final and greatest work, the *De Consolatione Philosophiae*. This work, written at the time when the author must have been aware of the possibility, if not the probability, of his execution, contains no explicit mention of any specifically Christian tenets and might indeed be regarded as the production of a noble pagan, an *anima naturaliter Christiana* maybe, but one unaware of the deep supernatural consolations of the faith. This consideration led certain authors to question the authenticity of the theological tractates: their authenticity, however, was clearly demonstrated by H. Usener in his *Anecdoton Holderi* (1877). The problem remains, and various explanations have been attempted. Cappuyns (*art. cit.*), while conceding Boethius's sincerity as a Christian, remarks on the lack of an inner conversion in many educated Christians of the time, ' the Church's doctrine had difficulty in penetrating the inmost recesses of their souls'. Hence Boethius would naturally in a moment of trial turn to those purely philosophical truths learnt in youth and not of themselves incompatible with the faith.

While not entirely denying the value of this explanation, we believe there is more to be said. Boethius was reluctant to write publicly about theological and religious truth: he appears, especially towards the end of his life, to have reached pessimistic conclusions concerning the abilities of the ordinary reader to apprehend it. His theological treatises (which, it should be noted, were written as letters) contain several remarks to this effect. It is, accordingly, not unreasonable to suppose that Boethius, writing a work which he foresaw might attain more general publication, should have deliberately abstained from explicitly Christian allusions: the more so as he would be aware that an educated and sensitive Christian reader would recognize and interpret the symbolism used. M. T. d'Alverny has shown (cf. Bodleian Library Record (1956)) that this symbolism (e.g. the Noble Lady as representing Wisdom, or the Word of God) was widely employed by Christians. Even such a detail as the ladder joining the letters Π and Θ on the Lady's robe was ' un des motifs les plus typiques du symbolisme chrétien'. Such considerations greatly reduce the difficulties that have been raised in this matter : the problem, such as it is, has some analogy to that raised by the apparently pagan mosaics and bas-reliefs found on Christian tombs of the early centuries.

In the Middle Ages a cult of Boethius (under the name of St Severinus) arose in Pavia and its neighbourhood, and this local cultus was approved by the Sacred Congregation of Rites in 1883. Leaving to one side questions about the origin and development of this cult, it may be asked whether the circumstances of Boethius's death justify the appellation of Martyr. An early chronicle (PL 123:1076) of the 9th cent. says *pro Catholica pietate idem Theodoricus occidit :* no earlier mention of Boethius as a martyr can be found. Historically, nothing very definite can be put forward on this matter: it is reasonable to suppose that Boethius's known anti-

Arian views counted against him at the end, nor would it be the first time that political and religious motives have been intermingled. It should be noted that Boethius himself, writing in the *De Consolatione Philosophiae* of the accusations made against him, makes no mention of any religious issue ; but this could be accounted for on the general lines mentioned earlier.

IV Thought and Influence. Boethius was not an original thinker : his theology (on the Trinity and Incarnation) largely derives from Augustine, his philosophy may not unfairly be described as eclectic, primarily Platonist in inspiration. He was essentially, and would not perhaps himself have claimed to be more than, a transmitter. His originality lies above all in his method and presentation, and is best seen when we consider his influence.

The medieval teaching of the *Quadrivium* owes more to him directly than to any other : in music and mathematics his works were regarded as the standard text-books, so to speak. In the field of logic, his works diffused a certain degree of knowledge of the Aristotelian logic. Though the West had to wait several centuries for a fuller knowledge of Aristotle's philosophical system (*see* ARISTOTLE, PLACE OF), it must not be thought that Boethius's influence in this matter was limited to the realm of pure logic : he introduced concepts and set problems that led beyond the merely logical. The best-known example of this is to be found in the impulse given to the development of the controversy on Universals by a passage from his Commentary on the *Isagoge* of Porphyrius (CSEL 48:158 seq.) : here the problem is put forward, the views of Plato and Aristotle briefly stated, and the Aristotelian position favoured (more because the *Isagoge* is an introduction to Aristotle's *Categories* than because of any settled philosophical conviction on the part of Boethius himself). An example of a more purely metaphysical discussion is to be found in the work known as the *De hebdomadibus* : here a distinction is proposed between *esse* and *id quod est*, in which some authors have erroneously seen an adumbration of the real distinction between essence and existence. *Esse* for Boethius is, however, rather to be identified with substantial form than with existence (cf. on this the chapter on Boethius in Roland-Gosselin's edition of the *De ente et essentia* of St Thomas (1926)). Boethius does, however, raise the central metaphysical question of the participation of being, and despite the incompleteness of his solution, he provided the great scholastics with the logical and terminological equipment whereby a more satisfactory solution could be reached. St Thomas, commenting on Boethius, uses his terminology to explain the distinction between essence and existence, and indeed interprets Boethius in this sense. Similar remarks could be made about Boethius's contribution to the scholastic treatment of the theological doctrines of the Trinity and Incarnation, though here we must not neglect the terminological contributions of previous Latin writers, especially Marius

Victorinus and Augustine, both familiar to Boethius. Gilson claims that the *De Trinitate* of Boethius dominated the 12th cent. schools of Chartres.

It may then be stated that Boethius's influence was pre-eminently one of terminology and method (apart from his rôle in the transmission of earlier thought). He introduced certain definitions (those of eternity and person are celebrated) and made use of categories (primarily Aristotelian) and distinctions which became the common stock-in-trade of the scholastics. Above all, he taught method : the Middle Ages learnt from him how to present and organize their thought. The method of the commentary owes much of its widespread popularity to the example of Boethius, and his own works on the Trinity and the *De hebdomadibus* were themselves expounded in this manner. Nor is it any exaggeration to say that he taught his successors how to think a theological doctrine philosophically. He was not the first to do so himself, but he had a clear conception, and conveyed a clear conception, of the necessity and manner of so doing. His exhortation to John the Deacon, ' *Fidem, si poteris, rationemque conjunge* ' (PL 64:1302), lays down the programme to be followed by the great scholastics.

No account of the influence of Boethius would be complete without some mention of the enormous popularity enjoyed by the *De Consolatione Philosophiae* in the Middle Ages and beyond. Some conception of this popularity may be deduced from the number and eminence of the translators of this work, which includes King Alfred, Notker of St Gall, Jean de Meun and Chaucer. Its appeal lies largely in its style and in the perennial nature of the main problem treated, the question of destiny, of the reconciliation between human liberty and divine foreknowledge. It is one of the few works of late Roman antiquity that has enduring literary value.

Bibliography. The works of Boethius are contained in PL 63 and 64. The commentaries on the *Isagoge* of Porphyrius and the *De Consolatione Philosophiae* appear in the CSEL, volumes 48 and 67 respectively. The Theological Tractates or *opuscula sacra* and the *De Consolatione Philosophiae* have been edited with translation in the Loeb Classical Library by H. F. Stewart and E. K. Rand (1946). M. Cappuyns's article on Boethius in the *Dictionnaire d'Histoire et de Géographie Ecclésiastiques* deals exhaustively with his life, works and influence and contains a full bibliography up to about 1934. There is a good account of his thought in Gilson, *History of Christian Philosophy in the Middle Ages*, English trans. (1955). On his Trinitarian theology De Régnon, *Études de théologie positive sur la Sainte Trinité*, vol. 1 (1892) may be consulted. An excellent general account of Boethius may be found in E. K. Rand's *Founders of the Middle Ages* (1941), and Gerald Vann's *The Wisdom of Boethius* (Aquinas Paper no. 20) (1952) may also be consulted for a general view. A. J. Macdonald's *Authority and Reason in the Early Middle Ages* (1933) is useful for this particular question. The discovery of Boethius's version of the *Prior Analytics* is due to Dr L. Minio-Paluello, who published his findings in *Journal of Hellenic Studies* 77 (1958) 93–102.   P. R.

BOGOMILS Bogomil—'dear to God'—a village priest of Bulgaria in the time of Tsar Peter, 927–969, taught a form of dualism which, deriving ultimately from Manichaeism (*see* MANICHEES), was essentially a synthesis of the doctrines of the Massalians and the Paulicians. The Massalians, who flourished in Mesopotamia and elsewhere from the 4th cent., taught that all men were from birth infused with an evil spirit which could only be expelled by prayer, the one necessary and sufficient means of salvation. The Paulicians, who originated in Armenia in the 7th cent., attempted to reconcile Manichaeism with Christianity. They retained a belief in two first principles, of good and evil, but rejected much of the cosmology of the Massalians and introduced an extreme form of asceticism allegedly derived from St Paul. The Paulicians, together with many other sectaries, entered Bulgaria during the period of conversion to Christianity in the 9th cent. The national opposition to the growing influence of the Eastern Empire and the contest between Rome and Constantinople for ecclesiastical control of the country favoured the propaganda of the heretical sects, and it was this situation which was successfully exploited by Bogomil. He taught a mitigated dualism in which the Devil is ultimately dependent on God. The material world is evil, the creation of Satanael, the fallen son of God and the elder brother of Christ. Only the souls of men are spiritual, being infused by God the Father into the bodies of men made by Satanael. Salvation comes through prayer and mortification. Bogomil taught a form of Docetism, rejecting the Incarnation and Redemption, the hierarchical Church and the sacraments, marriage, the eating of flesh and the drinking of wine.

The introduction of Bogomilism to Constantinople after the conquest of Bulgaria by Boris II in 1018 led to a schism and the emergence of a new Bogomil sect, the *Ecclesia Dugunthiae*, or church of the Dragovitsans (from Dragovitsa in Thrace) who taught a radical dualism as opposed to the mitigated dualism of the *Ecclesia Bulgariae*, or Old Bogomils. Persecution of the sectaries under Alexius I (1081–1118), and Manuel (1143–80) led to exile and an active missionary movement which introduced the doctrines of both Bogomil churches to the Western empire. A form of this teaching had already penetrated to the West early in the 11th cent. In the 12th cent. a widespread heretical movement, antisacramental in character but lacking a coherent system of doctrine, first came under the influence of Old Bogomil missionaries, and the Cathari, who first appear under this name at Cologne in 1163, already held their distinctive doctrines. In 1167 Nicetas, the Bogomil bishop of Constantinople, appeared in Lombardy and there converted a deacon of the Old Bogomil church to the doctrines of the radical sect. Shortly after the two embarked on a new missionary enterprise in the south of France where they were successful in converting the Catharists to their creed. The heretics of Languedoc (*see* ALBIGENSES) thus received their system of doctrine from the reformed sect of the Bogomils.

Bibliography. D. Obolensky, *The Bogomils. A Study in Balkan Neo-Manichaeism* (1948) ; A. Borst, *Die Katharer* (1953).   G. C.

BONAVENTURE, INFLUENCE OF. St Bonaventure was an altogether outstanding figure at his time in the world of theology ; and his time was the greatest period in the history of theology. Even the great figure of St Thomas, his contemporary, did not assume its true proportion until later years. The century was one of great and rapid development in the world of thought in which Bonaventure was a dominating figure ; and that in spite of the fact that, in a sense, he did not contribute anything new. This article will deal with (I) his life, (II) his period, (III) his school, (IV) his doctrine and (V) his influence.

I His life. St Bonaventure was born in the year 1221 at Bagnorea near Viterbo in Tuscany. Little is known of his early life and even the date and place of his entry into the Franciscan Order are matters of dispute. At all events it was round about the year 1240 that Bonaventure became a friar and he was most likely studying in Paris before the death of Alexander of Hales in 1245. It was in that year that Bonaventure received his licentiate, after which he was himself engaged in teaching until 1255. It was during this ten-year period that the greater part of his works was written. Owing to the prevailing opposition to the mendicants in the University, St Bonaventure, together with St Thomas, was denied his doctorate until 1257, during which year he was also made General of his Order, thus being compelled into the paths of administration to the loss of his academic career. In 1273 he was created Cardinal Bishop of Albano, having already refused the Archbishopric of York in 1265. He died in 1274 while attending the Council of Lyons.

II The man and the period. The traditional theology of the Schools was largely Augustinian in inspiration, and the philosophic mould in which the theology was cast was likewise derived chiefly from St Augustine, who himself owed much to the Neo-platonists. We speak in general terms, for St Augustine was not primarily a philosopher, so that his system, if we can call it such, became inadequate to deal with the development that was taking place in theology. The mould was discovered to be too small and so there was a borrowing of philosophic ideas from other sources. St Augustine's inspiration was largely Platonic, but we later find the introduction of other philosophers, especially Aristotle. The earlier medieval theologians knew little of Aristotle, but the greater part of the great philosopher's works was introduced to the thought of Europe through the Arabians in the 13th cent. Together with the Arabian commentaries these made a great impact upon the Schools and the new ideas were adopted with more or less enthusiasm. St Bonaventure himself was among those who received them ; yet while he was not averse from adopting that which would complete what was lacking in the traditional modes of thought, he likewise recognized the danger to the Faith in an uncritical acceptance of much that was new. On the other hand, there were many in the University of Paris who unhesitatingly adopted much, if not all, of the interpretation of Aristotle given by such men as the Arabian Averroes, even where this was in contradiction to traditional and sound doctrine. St Bonaventure became the first to attack the new development in his Commentary on the Sentences of Peter Lombard. ' This is his greatest work which contains virtually or actually, all the ultimate lines on which his thought was to develop' (Gilson, *Philosophy of St Bonaventure*, 35). He made it quite clear just where he stood ; alongside Augustine with Gregory, Anselm, Denis, Bernard and the Victorines. This is the Christian tradition which has nothing to learn in theology from any pagan philosopher however great. Their authority is never to be quoted in opposition to the great doctors. St Bonaventure put philosophy quite surely and firmly in its place, as merely the servant of theology but by itself always incomplete and necessarily prone to error unless corrected by Faith. Study was for him simply a step to piety, and speculation for its own sake was abhorrent to his mind. His professed intention was to hand down what he himself had received : ' I have lectured on the common opinion of the Masters, especially on those of my lector and father Alexander. I will continue in his footsteps, for it is not my intention to teach new doctrines' (*II Sent*. Praelocutio). His presentation was, however, masterly, and though his Commentary is often a reproduction of the *Summa* of Alexander, he far surpasses Alexander in style, expression and illustration. Alexander had been a giant among masters but he was outstripped by his pupil. The list of those who studied under Bonaventure is a galaxy of famous names : Matthew of Aquasparta, John Peckham, William de la Mare, Peter John Olivi, Richard Middleton and others ; those who later were to battle fiercely under his inspiration against the slowly rising tide of the new Scholastic Aristotelianism championed by Albert the Great and Thomas Aquinas.

III The Franciscan School. Alexander of Hales must be regarded as the real founder of the Franciscan School but Bonaventure evidently emerges as its principal proponent, who provided the charter for its continuance and development. This is not the place to go into the disputes within the Order on the question of studies. It is sufficient to say that St Bonaventure had no doubts on the score but regarded study as eminently conformable with the Franciscan vocation. His mind was made clear before he became General when he defended the position of the mendicants at the University against the attacks of William of St Amour. His attitude is more than adequately justified in his *Quaestiones*

Disputatae de Perfectione Evangelica. The conflict in the University was finally decided in favour of the mendicants. St Bonaventure and St Thomas were admitted as doctors in 1257 and the religious obtained a secure standing in the faculty. The result was that the fate of Scholasticism was practically committed to teachers who belonged to the Franciscan and Dominican Orders. Thus when St Bonaventure in his position as General of the Friars Minor positively encouraged studies in the Order, the ground was already prepared for the growth of two distinct modes of thought. The weight of his authority would keep the Friars Minor true to the traditional modes and in opposition to the newer Thomism.

IV Teaching. In the realm of actual dogma there is little difference between the two schools, and on all the major points St Bonaventure teaches substantially the same doctrine as St Thomas. The difference lies rather in the approach and in a turn of mind. St Thomas is the intellectual, striving for an adequate reasonable basis for the Faith. St Bonaventure is the practical man who already knows the way to God by Faith and will not be held back by a philosophical difficulty. He will, therefore, argue from Faith to reason rather than from reason to Faith and will always seek to see the deficiencies of reason completed by Faith. His theory of knowledge must therefore be sought in conjunction with his mystical tendency which he develops in his works : *Itinerarium mentis in Deum* and *De reductione artium ad Theologiam*. All knowledge is by Divine illumination, but this does not mean that our knowledge of all things is innate, only that the objective light by which things are known to us is innate. Thus he accepts the distinction between the active and passive intellect but rejects the Aristotelian implications of this distinction. Similarly, in the realm of metaphysics St Bonaventure adopts the Aristotelian hylomorphism but not exactly in the manner of Aristotle as adopted by St Thomas. All finite being is composed of matter and form but the form is not necessarily one in each being. There are, besides the substantial form, other subordinate forms which are the principles of ulterior perfections. St Bonaventure was faithful to the doctrine of seminal reasons received from St Augustine. At the very centre of his philosophy is the doctrine of Divine Exemplarism. Most of these teachings became characteristic of the Franciscan School. In his dogmatic teaching, chiefly contained in the *Commentary on the Sentences* and in that gem of medieval theology the *Breviloquium*, St Bonaventure is characterized by a courteous diffidence. He adopts the view which has the weight of tradition behind it and, when forced to proffer his own, it will be that which is most consonant with tradition. His aim is not to oppose the opinions of others but to teach sound doctrine and he will often seek to reconcile conflicting views. The existence of God is a truth which does not require demonstration in the true sense. He adopts the ontological argument of St Anselm but it would be a gross perversion of his teaching to make him an Ontologist. His teaching on the Trinity owes much to the influence of Dionysius and the Victorines, perhaps more than to St Augustine on this point. With St Thomas, St Bonaventure teaches that the Redemption is the main purpose of the Incarnation but there is evidence that he would have liked to affirm that God intended the Incarnation for its own intrinsic perfection. He bowed to tradition on the point but we find in him many traces of that doctrine of the Absolute Primacy of Christ that was later to be so admirably developed by Scotus. Similarly, though he could not grant that Our Lady was conceived Immaculate he noted the opposite view, coming close to an understanding of the true doctrine and paving the way for the great exposition of the true doctrine by Scotus. His sacramental theology is practical. The sacraments are true causes of grace but he sees the causality as moral rather than physical, and this position the Franciscans have generally adopted. Grace and the gifts of the Holy Ghost are finally operative in the soul when it reaches the heights of contemplation. At the summit is the union of love. In the Beatific Vision it is the will which takes possession of God, for there is true peace where the object of the will is finally attained. St Bonaventure shows himself to be a voluntarist rather than an intellectualist. There are those who would make a clear distinction between the earlier and the later Franciscan School, and it is true that Scotus introduced a fuller peripateticism and abandoned the position of Bonaventure in several respects. Yet the influence of Bonaventure is still evidently there. He provided the approach which Scotus turned in the direction of his own genius.

Scotus too was a voluntarist and it is that fact rather than any other which explains his opposition to St Thomas.

V Influence and works. The authority of St Bonaventure has always been recognized in the Church at large. It was in a great measure due to his influence that the Greeks accepted the union at the Council of Lyons in 1274. The Councils of Vienne (1311), Constance (1417), Basle (1431), Florence (1438) bear witness to the authority of his writings which also had an influence on some of the decisions of the Council of Trent (1546). His teaching on the authority of the Supreme Pontiff was invoked at the Council of the Vatican (1870) and sentences from his writings were embodied in the decrees on papal supremacy and infallibility. Commentaries on his works have been many, chiefly from the pens of succeeding generations of Friars Minor who have always looked upon St Bonaventure as one of the greatest of the Doctors. Sixtus V, who granted to St Bonaventure the same ecclesiastical honours as Pius V had accorded to St Thomas, founded a special chair in Rome for the study of the Franciscan doctor and such chairs existed at several universities. After a period of neglect in which the influence of Bonaventure was overshadowed by that of Scotus, there has been a revival of interest in the works of the Seraphic

Doctor in recent years. The title ' Seraphic Doctor ' which the centuries have conferred on him is an indication of the esteem in which St Bonaventure has ever been held as an exponent of Mystical Theology. Though his mystical writings are comparatively few, yet the whole of his works is pervaded with this spirit to the extent that even when Bonaventure the philosopher or Bonaventure the dogmatic theologian has been ignored, Bonaventure the mystic has been regarded as, in the words of Leo XIII, ' *facile princeps* in that field '. His *Opuscula Mystica* were always popular within the Franciscan Order. ' Indeed, they formed the models of many beautiful treatises which, in turn, exercised a great influence. Bonaventure determined the direction taken by later spiritual writings emanating from Franciscan sources ' (D. Dobbins OFM Cap., *Franciscan Mysticism* (1927) 196). The debt owed by Gerson to Bonaventure is well known and freely acknowledged by Gerson himself : ' If you ask me which teacher is to be preferred, I answer, Master Bonaventure. For his doctrine is sound, safe, just, pious and fervent. While trying to illuminate the intellect, he employs everything to elevate the spirit and arouse devotion. Hence many scholastics who are devoid of piety neglect him, though no teaching is more sublime, more divine, more salutary, more pleasing ' (cf. Bonaventure, *Opera Omnia*, Quaracchi Edition, X, 34). ' Some of the English mystics such as Rolle and Hilton are indebted to the Treatises of Bonaventure and it has been asserted that the author of the *Imitation of Christ* was inspired by him to a great extent ' (Dobbins, *op. cit.* ibid.). The works of St Bonaventure are very numerous. They include exegetical and theological works, several treatises on spirituality, various sermons and works concerning the religious life in general and the Franciscan Order in particular. A mark of his reputation is found in the number of spurious works that have been attributed to him. Fifteen editions of his works were published in the 15th cent. Sixtus V commissioned a new edition which was published at Rome (1588–96). It was contained in seven folio volumes and was reprinted four times, the last time being at Paris in 1864. The last and critical edition is that published by the Friars Minor of Quaracchi near Florence (1882–1902). This is contained in ten volumes and supersedes all previous editions. It contains all the genuine works of the Saint that have come down to us.

Bibliography. S. Bonaventure, *Opera Omnia* (1882–1902) ; L. de Carvalho e Castro, *Saint Bonaventure* (1923) ; F. Cayré, *Manual of Patrology* (1910) II ; F. Copleston, *A History of Philosophy* (1950) 2 ; J. d'Albi, *St Bonaventure et les luttes doctrinales de 1207–1277* (1923) ; D. Dobbins, ' Franciscan Mysticism ', *Franciscan Studies*, No. 6 (1927) ; Fliche-Martin, *Histoire de l'Église* 13, ' Le Mouvement doctrinal du x au xiv siècle ' (1954) ; É. Gilson, *The Philosophy of St Bonaventure* (1940), *History of Christian Philosophy in the Middle Ages* (1955) ; S. Grünewald, *Franziskanische Mystik. Versuch zu einer Darstellung mit besonderer Berücksichtigung des* *hl. Bonaventura* (1932) ; F. Imle, *Die Theologie des hl. Bonaventura* (1932) ; A. M. Landgraf, *Dogmengeschichte der Frühscholastik*, IV (1956) ; L. Lemmens, *S. Bonaventure* (1921) ; E. Longpré, *Dictionnaire d'Histoire et de Géographie Ecclésiastique*, Art. ' Bonaventure ' IX (1937) ; P. Robinson, CE. Art. ' Bonaventure ' (1907) ; E. de Saint-Béat, *St Bonaventura, Scholae Franciscanae Magister Praecellens* (1888) ; G. H. Tavard, *Transiency and Permanence* : The Nature of Theology according to St Bonaventure (1954) ; Various, ' Basic Trends of the Franciscan School ', *Franciscan Studies*, new series Vol. 2, No. 4 (1942) ; L. Veuthy, *S. Bonaventurae Philosophia Christiana* (1943) ; B. Vogt, ' Origin and Development of the Franciscan School ', *Franciscan Studies* No. 3 (1925) ; L. Wegener, ' St Bonaventure, the Seraphic Doctor, *Franciscan Studies* No. 2 (1925).

K.

BOSCOVICH, SYSTEM OF. The article has four parts : (I) the theory of matter, space and time, (II) inertia and *vis viva*, (III) the law of forces, and (IV) its application to the Eucharist.

Roger Joseph Boscovich, astronomer, mathematician, philosopher and poet, was born at Ragusa, now Dubrovnik, 18 May 1711, entered the Society of Jesus at Rome 31 Oct. 1725, was ordained priest 30 Oct. 1740 and solemnly professed 15 Aug. 1744. He was professor of mathematics at the Roman College (1740–59), at Pavia (1764–70), professor of astronomy and optics at Milan and director (1770–2) of the observatory of Brera, which he built. He was elected corresponding member of the Academy of Sciences of Paris in 1748 and Fellow of the Royal Society in 1761. After the suppression of the Society of Jesus in 1773 he was invited to Paris where the post of Director of Optics to the French navy was created for him. He returned to Italy in 1782 and died at Milan 13 Feb. 1787. Despite his many contributions to mathematics, astronomy and optics he will be remembered chiefly for his theory of matter, a theory which led St Venant to call him the most consistent of Newtonians, and Russell to declare the true Leibnizian monadology to be that of Boscovich.

I Matter, Space and Time. According to Boscovich the material universe is composed of points of matter (*puncta materiae*) which are unextended and indivisible. Any two points are always a finite distance apart : contact is impossible. Their movement is governed by a single law which is capable of explaining a surprising number of physical phenomena. The statement of this law requires a preliminary account of Boscovich's ideas of space and time and of the terminology of his mechanics.

He holds that neither the view of Newton that empty space is real, nor that of Leibniz, who identifies space with order, can explain why a body is where it is : on either theory there is need of a real mode of being in virtue of which the body is where it is. Granted this local mode, the difficulties both theories involve can be avoided by defining real space as the set of all such modes existing at a given instant. The number of points of matter being finite, so is the number of local modes ; thus real space consists of finitely many real points of place (*puncta loci realia*). It is similarly necessary to admit the existence of a real temporal mode in virtue of which a body exists when it does. This mode is a real point of time, or an instant. The set of all temporal modes is real time.

These modes found the real relations of distance in space and interval in time. Local modes which, were they to exist simultaneously, would induce between their subjects the relation of zero distance are to be considered identical. Similarly for temporal modes. The set of all possible local modes is empty (or imaginary) space. As the distance between two points of matter cannot be zero, it is always possible to insert between any two a third coincident with neither : then between either of the resulting pairs it is possible to insert another point of matter, and so on. Thus we come to conceive imaginary space as infinitely divisible, continuous and infinite in extent. Similar remarks apply to imaginary time. Lines, surfaces and solids belong to imaginary space. A line is not a set of points : it is generated by the continuous movement of a point, surfaces by the continuous movement of lines, solids by the continuous movement of planes. All are constructs and do not exist in nature. The idea that extension, weight, inertia, impenetrability and the other primary qualities of Locke are on a different footing from the secondary qualities is prejudice, due probably to the fact that in his mother's womb man can use no other sense than touch, and so his first experience is one of sensibly continuous resistance. Had he, during these months, no other sense but sight, he would consider colours as primary qualities and would explain all others in terms of colour.

Having stated that each material point unites a temporal and a local mode, Boscovich goes on to examine the ways in which points and modes may be linked. He asks, Can the same point of matter be (i) in the same place at two different times ? (ii) in the same place over a continuous interval of time ? (iii) in two places at the same time ? (iv) in every point of a continuous region at the same time ? Can two or more points of matter (v) be each in a different place at the same time ? (vi) be each in the same place at different times ? (vii) be both (or all) in the same place at the same time ? (viii) neither be at different times in the same place, nor exist at the same time in different places ? He answers no to each question except the fifth, thus excluding absolute rest (ii), replication, or multilocation (iii), virtual extension (iv), and compenetration (vii). He is speaking of what is naturally possible. It has often been said that he held compenetration to be possible. The mistake (first made by Priestley) may have arisen from Boscovich's saying that, were two points of matter to touch, they would coincide. That Boscovich did not think compenetration possible will also be clear from his law of motion. To enunciate this it is necessary to explain what Boscovich meant by *vis*, a word commonly, but in this context wrongly, translated by *force*.

II *Vis inertiae* and *vis viva*. It was generally agreed that all material bodies obeyed Newton's first law, i.e. they possessed what was called *vis inertiae* and was thought of as a tendency to persevere in a state of rest or uniform rectilinear motion. Boscovich was not certain whether this was more than a prejudice of contemporary philosophy. Since, he argued, it was impossible to detect absolute motion, Newton's first law could at most be established for motion relative to a space imagined by us to be at rest : whether that space were really at rest, or were moving, would not affect our observations. Nor could it (as Euler imagined) be proved that a single body, in otherwise empty space, would possess inertia. Nevertheless the success of this law in saving the phenomena justified its retention provided that it was understood to mean that, prescinding from the tendency which points of matter have to move away from, or towards, one another, they also have a tendency to continue in their state of rest or uniform rectilinear motion. This latter tendency is *vis inertiae*. It is not a force. Neither is the tendency of material points to approach one another, or to separate, to be regarded as a force or due to a force. Boscovich calls this tendency *vis viva*. The term had already been used by Leibniz to denote twice the kinetic energy of a body : as such it was commonly conceived as a physical reality and the quantity of *vis viva* in the universe was assumed to be constant. The *vis viva* of a moving body was also considered to be the proper measure of the force which it could exert.

These views were opposed by the Newtonians who held the proper measure of that force to be the momentum of the body. The dispute was also connected with the theory of collisions. For Newton, atoms were perfectly rigid and therefore inelastic. When such atoms collide there is a loss of kinetic energy and a sudden change of velocity. The former violates the principle of conservation of energy, the latter the principle of continuity. Maclaurin and Maupertuis therefore denied both principles. To save the principle of continuity Boscovich denied the possibility of contact, and hence of impact. He derived the usual laws of impact by assuming that, when atoms were near enough to one another they behaved as though they repelled one another. The same assumption explained resistance to compression. Hard extended atoms were no longer necessary. Newton's own rules now demanded that atoms should be regarded as unextended.

Boscovich also refuses to admit that there is anything in nature corresponding to the *vis viva* of Leibniz. The concept of energy is constructed by us. Further, to say that a body whose motion is not uniform has a velocity at an instant is meaningless. Uniform velocity is the ratio of distance traversed to the time taken. As both can be measured, velocity is, in this case, observable. When, on the other hand, the motion is not uniform, we cannot thus measure velocity at an instant : we may say that the body has a certain potential velocity, i.e. a tendency to move with a certain velocity. It is to this tendency, regarded as a further determination of the *vis inertiae*, that Boscovich gives the name of *vis viva*. When therefore he calls the exposition of his system *Theoria philosophiae naturalis redacta ad unicam legem virium in natura existentium*, he has in mind, not a law of force, but a law which states how one point of matter will tend to move in the presence of another.

III The *lex virium* states that, at the smallest distances, points of matter behave as though they repelled one another, the repulsion increasing without limit as the distance diminishes. As the distance increases the repulsion decreases, giving place to an attraction which, after further decrease of distance, changes again to a repulsion. After an unspecified number of alterations between repulsion and attraction, the 'force' is ultimately one of attraction according to the inverse square law, as for gravitation. This single law of nature was represented by the famous Boscovich curve (cf. Gill, *op. cit.* 10–12). The law has been stated, according to custom, in terms of attractions and repulsions : but it must be emphasized that it is a law of virtual velocities, not a law of force ; it intends to do no more than describe how points of matter will move. The question of what causes them to move is left open, indeed Boscovich considers it, in principle, unanswerable from the standpoint of natural philosophy. The theory is thus kinematical not dynamical. On one point Boscovich is definite : nothing passes from one point of matter to another, nor does one point act on another. The presence of a material point at a certain distance from another is the occasion of that other's being determined to possess a certain potential velocity. We cannot know the cause of this determination. It may result from some essential property of material points, or from some accidental property, or God may impose on points of matter some freely chosen law. The emphasis on God's freedom seems to stem from a desire to avoid suspicion of sympathy with the Optimism of Leibniz.

Boscovich does not discuss in detail the cause of the behaviour he describes. In view of the obscurity of the little he has to say on this subject, it is not surprising that critics have objected that his theory necessitates recourse either to (i) the pre-established harmony of Leibniz, or (ii) action at a distance, or (iii) occasionalism. Boscovich expressly rejects (i) (cf. Stay, *op. cit.* I, 335). As for (ii) Boscovich says that he cannot understand the prejudice which disallows action for every value of the distance except zero, yet allows action at zero distance. However, on his theory there is no action of one point on another. A useful discussion of these difficulties is given by J. B. Horvath (*Institutiones logicae et metaphysicae* (1781[5]) 217–21).

IV The influence of the system on the theology of the Eucharist was mainly indirect in that the idea of an atom as a point centre of force, taken over from Boscovich, inspired many later scientific theories which, in turn, stimulated efforts such as those of Tongiorgi, Palmieri and Bayma to reconcile Eucharistic theology with contemporary science. Boscovich does not discuss the relation of his theory to the theology of the Real Presence. Horvath (*op. cit.* 144, note a) writes : [1] ' In Latin *species* is really the same thing as appearance ; the appearances therefore remain, but whether those appearances are to be attributed to the persistence of absolute accidents in the Aristotelian sense, or whether they are to be explained otherwise, is a purely philosophical question. Nowadays philosophers consider them to arise from the fact that Christ, present in the Eucharist, deigns by His supernatural action to make on our senses the same impressions that bread and wine would naturally produce were they present.' This opinion, common at the time, might be interpreted as foreshadowing that of Franzelin, but it seems too close to the theory of ' apparences eucharistiques ' of Maignan and others to be satisfactory.

J. Bayma (*Molecular Mechanics* (1866)) developed a theory differing from that of Boscovich chiefly in admitting action at a distance and attributing attraction and repulsion to two different types of material points. His very original attempt to reconcile this system with the permanence of the Eucharistic species, perhaps because it was misrepresented, met with the disapproval of the Holy Office (D 1843–6).

Bibliography. R. J. Boscovich : *Theoria philosophiae naturalis etc.* with English translation by J. M. Child (1922). B. Stay : *Philosophiae recentioris versibus traditae libri XX cum adnotationibus et supplementis P. R. J. Boscovich*, Vol. I (1755), II (1760). For other works of Boscovich, earlier studies and biographies see C. Sommervogel sj, *Bibliothèque de la Compagnie de Jésus*, I (1890) col. 1828–48. For criticism from standpoint of scholasticism see A. Maier : *Philosophia corpuscularis R. I. B. proposita atque examinata* (1928) and J. Fejer : *Theoriae corpusculares typicae in universitatibus Societatis Jesu Saec. XVIII et Monadologia Kantiana* (1951). For the relation of the system to modern science see H. V. Gill sj, *Roger Boscovich S.J.* (1941) and L. L. Whyte, *R. J. Boscovich, S.J., F.R.S.* in *Notes and records of the Royal Society* XIII, 1 (1958) 38–48. G. V. Schiaparelli, *Sull' attività di Boscovich quale astronomo in Milano* (1938). The latest researches on the life and work of Boscovich are to be found in *Rad Jugoslavenske Akademije Znanosti i Umjetnosti* CLXXXI (1910), CLXXXV (1911), CCXXV (1921), CCXXX (1924). (An English translation of this long critical review of the 1922 edition of the Theoria appeared

in the *Bulletin des travaux de la classe des sciences mathématiques et naturelles* of the same Academy. XIX–XX (1924) 45–102) CCXXXII and CCXXXIV (1926) and also in Ž. Marković : *Graođa za život i rad Rudžera Boškovića*, I (1950) and II (1957).

F. K.

BREVIARY, THEOLOGICAL AUTHORITY OF THE Since the Breviary contains so much that is drawn from Scripture, and this element has a special authority (*see* BIBLE), the problem of deciding what theological authority belongs to the Breviary resolves itself into that of evaluating the Lessons of the Second and Third Nocturns of Matins, where lives of saints and accounts of the origin of feasts may be found, along with much that is to be classified as patristic literature. These lives and festal readings belong to what one may call ' second-class matter ', edifying writings which may be read in church but which the Church does not reverence as she does Scripture. The category existed from very early days. The Muratori fragment in the 2nd cent. speaking of the *Shepherd of Hermas* says that it should indeed be read, but should not be made public to the people in church among the Old or New Testament Scriptures.[2] Reading in those times meant reading aloud and the distinction made is therefore one between Scripture readings and other readings (almost what we should now call liturgical readings and those which take place at a nonliturgical meeting, such as that of a confraternity), and not between reading out loud in church and reading privately at home. Athanasius (*Festal Letter* 39 ; PG 26:1176) has the same distinction between books read as Scripture to the faithful and other books which ' were prescribed to be read to those newly come to the faith and desirous of being catechized in the way of piety'. He mentions *Hermas* and the *Didache* along with some of the deutero-canonical books as examples. The affair of Serapion of Antioch and the church at Rhossus (Eusebius, HE 6:12) shows the same practice being observed. Serapion finds the people of Rhossus reading in their services the *Gospel of Peter*. He tells them it is not canonical and they show disappointment. He then says they can go on reading it (but presumably as second-class matter ; he could not have let them keep it in the Canon), but after his departure he finds out much more about its heretical contents and writes to them to stay proceedings until he comes to them again.

The practice of having second-class matter to read at functions distinct from the public liturgy easily explains how the monks came to use at Matins extracts from a *Passionale* or collection of lives and martyrdoms of holy men and women. If, again, these writings were highly coloured in the details of their narratives and more concerned with edification than sober history, that can be attributed to a praiseworthy desire to make the readings lively and

[1] Species reapse latinis idem est ac apparentia ; remanent ergo apparentiae panis. . . . At num apparentiae illae remanentibus absolutis accidentibus, sensu peripateticorum acceptis, attribui debeant an aliter explicandae sint quaestio mere philosophica est. Censent autem hodierni philosophi, eas inde proficisci, quod Christus in Eucharistia praesens easdem dignetur actione supernaturali facere in organa nostra impressiones, quas panis et vinum naturaliter facerent si adessent.

[2] Legi eum quidem oportet, se publicare vero in ecclesia populo neque inter prophetas completo numero neque inter apostolos . . . potest.

calculated to keep awake even a sleepy monk at his night-office. With the passage of centuries and the disappearance of so much historical writing, these Lessons came to have a much greater importance than was ever intended for them at the outset. They were preserved, and copied as they were needed for the Office, while other writings perished. This was the problem that faced the Renaissance humanists among the Churchmen.

The Council of Trent in 1561 (cf. Martène : *Scriptorum amplissima collectio*, VIII, 1426) received a petition from the Emperor Ferdinand asking that everything save Scripture should be expunged from the Breviary, but this was not acted upon. In 1568 the new Breviary which was brought into use by Pius V was in substance the Franciscan office from the Middle Ages. In 1588 Sixtus V set up the Sacred Congregation of Rites, but the Bull of institution (*Immensa*, of 22 Jan. 1588) speaks rather vaguely of the Congregation's duty to examine the Offices of patron saints and approve them after consultation with the Pope. This seems to envisage some gradual regulation of the many local devotions but no general revision of the calendar of saints. None the less, the efforts of Bellarmine, Stapleton (whose objections, with replies, still lie unpublished in a Vatican MS.) and others led to some omissions and corrections. Even here it was possible for Spanish influence to have the cautious words of Bellarmine (*traditio est*) removed from before the statement that St James visited Spain, so that it became once more an asserted fact.

Benedict XIV tried to revise the Lessons once more, but admitted to a friend that it cost him more trouble to bring into order the Commission of Cardinals appointed for the work than to restore order in the Breviary itself. He did, however, succeed in having some of the more suspect narratives corrected, often by the simple expedient of omitting the feast from the calendar. At the Vatican Council the German bishops submitted a request that, as the Roman Breviary in some places contains things which cannot be reconciled with sound history or a reasonable interpretation of Scripture, it should be revised.[1] The French bishops also stated (ibid. 844) in a long list of requests that the Breviary lessons were not sufficiently cleared of apocryphal stories.

Leo XIII, who slowly worked through many of the requests left over at the abrupt ending of the Vatican Council, came in 1902 to set up a historical and liturgical Commission to prepare this revision. The members were Mgr Duchesne, Mgr Wilpert, Fr Ehrle SJ, Fr Roberti OFM, and Mgr Benigni ; Mgr Mercati was later added as secretary. It was this Commission which consulted Edmund Bishop soon after it started work, but its first task was to arrange for the redistribution of the psalms in the Breviary so that the whole Psalter would be read through in the course of the week. When this task was finished in 1912 Pope Pius X issued orders (AAS 4 (1912) 376 and 538) that in each diocese the historical Lessons of local saints should be scrutinized and where it was found that the text deviated from the oldest and most reliable MSS and from solidly based tradition it was to be corrected.[2] It is plain that a Commission of six which counted among its members the two chief protagonists in the Modernist affair, Duchesne and Benigni, could not work very harmoniously and some devolution was needed, but this assignment to local authorities did not touch the problems arising out of the inclusion of saints or feasts with doubtful pedigree in the Roman Breviary. The instruction added that there was no need for haste and that thirty years was the estimate then taken of the time needed for a thorough-going reform.

It should be obvious from this brief historical survey that any theological argument which is based on what is found in the non-Scriptural parts of the Breviary has no other value than that of the sources on which the Breviary itself has drawn. The introduction of the Office of St Gregory VII (Hildebrand) was once resisted in France as an attempt to exalt Ultramontanism by a use of the *lex credendi, lex orandi* principle, but that principle cannot rightly be invoked as a preface to the use of statements in Breviary lessons in theological argument. The Commission of 1742 removed the reference to *Pope St Hippolytus* and was unanimous for the suppression of the feast of the Apparition of St Michael on May 8, but until a complete reform of the Lessons has been completed, their authority cannot be more than provisional. The reforms promulgated on 26 July 1960 included the suppression of this feast of St Michael, along with those of Anacletus, Leo II, Vitalis and St John before the Latin Gate. The reduction of several other feasts to mere commemorations automatically excluded their Lessons from the Breviary.

Bibliography. S. Bäumer OSB, *Geschichte des Breviers* (1895), French translation in 1905 in 2 vols (at least 80 pages of this work were written by Edmund Bishop) ; N. Abercrombie, 'Edmund Bishop and the Roman Breviary', in CR 38 (1953) 75–86 and 129–139 ; A. Baumstark, *Nocturna Laus* (1957) ; H. Delehaye SJ, *Étude sur le légendier romain* (1936).   J. H. C.

BROWNSON IN THE THEOLOGICAL FIELD As one of the famous journalists of the 19th cent., Orestes A. Brownson covered an uncommonly wide range of subjects with remarkable competence, including the field of theology. Immediately after his conversion to the Church, 1844, he was given a systematic course in theology by Bishop J. B. Fitzpatrick of Boston, specializing in Billuart's Commentary on the *Summa Theologica*, the *Summa* itself,

[1] Breviarium Romanum nonnullis locis quaedam continet quae cum historia certa fide digna et sana Scripturae sacrae exegesi non omnino convenire videntur. . . . (*Collectio Lacensis*, VII, 874.)

[2] Lectiones historicas ad trutinam revocare operae pretium erit ; . . . si reppererint historias contra fidem codicum . . . et solidae traditionis in aliam formam degenerasse, adlaborent ut vera narratio restituatur.

and some of St Augustine's works. (In later years Brownson asserted that he had never met ' an abler and sounder theologian ' than Bishop Fitzpatrick.) Although Brownson saw an imperishable miracle in every article of the *Summa* of St Thomas, like Newman, he preferred the Early Fathers to the scholastic theologians. As a theologian, he identified himself with the Augustinian school, and wrote upon practically every aspect of Catholic theology from the doctrine of the Blessed Trinity down to the simplest popular devotions of the Church. In his *Problems of the Age*, Fr A. F. Hewitt CSP remarked that, ' in modern times, Bossuet, Lacordaire, and Dr Brownson have reasoned profoundly on the rational evidence of the Trinity '. Much of his powerful rhetoric was directed on the one hand against Calvinism, Jansenism and the other theological -isms of the modern world, and on the other hand mainly against Pelagianism, Gallicanism, Liberalism, naturalism and rationalism. What he admired particularly in Catholicism ' is its ineffable harmony between nature and grace '. His son, Henry, summed up well the general nature of his father's writings when he said in his introduction to his father's *Works* (Vol. I, p. xi) that ' the essays of Dr Brownson on theology, politics, and morals, are all based on his philosophy, according to which nature and grace, reason and revelation, the order of reality and that of science are brought into harmony which for three hundred years had been the aim of thinking men '.

One of the first instances in which Brownson showed his skill as a theologian after his conversion was in his notice and close examination of Newman's theory of the Development of Christian Doctrine. In spite of the sharpness of Brownson's attack on him, Newman invited his opponent to become a visiting lecturer at the Irish university (see the account with documentation in F. McGrath, *Newman's Irish University* (1951)). [Later, on reading *Loss and Gain*, Brownson was moved to withdraw much of what he had said against the theory of Development. (Editors' note.)] While W. G. Ward was the upholder and defender of that theory at the time, Brownson feared a wrong trend or application of the theory, and spoke out against the danger. In the ensuing controversy Brownson ' displayed genuine theological erudition wedded to argumentative ability of the first order ', said Fr Edwin Ryan (AER, April 1915). ' There are probably few laymen today (1915) ', he added, ' so well read in the post-Tridentine theologians.' Fr E. Ryan expressed the wish that some genuine theologian would give Brownson's treatises on the subject a close examination and evaluate their theological importance.

But there are two great battles in particular that Brownson fought in the theological field that are worthy of special notice, to wit : his heroic battle against a false interpretation of the dogma, *Nulla Salus extra Ecclesiam*, and his equally heroic battle for a recognition and practical acceptance of the great papal prerogatives of Supremacy and Infallibility, particularly that of the Supremacy of the Holy Father. In his encyclical, *Humani Generis*, the late Holy Father, Pope Pius XII, complained of those who were reducing the Church's claim of exclusive salvation to ' a meaningless formula '. That is precisely what Brownson was opposing so persistently over a hundred years ago. Protests, strong and emphatic, are scattered all through his writings of over thirty years, as he encounters author after author who whittles down this dogma to ' a meaningless formula '. In spite of all the badgering he had to take, his zeal in the matter did not abate one jot. ' There is no more fatal mistake ', he said, ' than to soften, liberalize, or latitudinize this terrible dogma, " Out of the Church there is no salvation ", or to give a man an opportunity to persuade himself that he belongs to the soul of the Church, though an alien from the body ' (his *Works*, xx, p. 414). He was greatly fearful of allowing those outside any false hopes in the matter, and hence his unremitting efforts to put down the latitudinarian interpretation of this dogma so rampant already in his day. Although some modern theologians might be quoted as seeming to favour the theory that one might attain salvation through belonging to ' the soul of the church', in the sense that the soul extends beyond the visible body, Brownson was theologian enough to know that such a theory is altogether untenable. He insisted in his elaborate expositions of this dogma on the very point Pope Pius XII determined once for all in his encyclical, *Mystici Corporis*, namely, that to be joined to the soul of the Church one must be joined to the visible body of the Church, in some sense at least, for the soul of the Church does not extend beyond the visible body of the Church.

In discussing the qualities of soul through which any outside the Church can be joined to the Church invisibly, namely, supernatural faith and perfect charity, supposing invincible ignorance in each case, Brownson was a little too strict in arguing that an act of faith cannot be made outside the Church. (As Fr Healy of Maynooth remarked in 1884, ' if he erred at all, it was on the safe side ' (cf. the encyclical of Pius IX, *Quanto conficiamur moerore*, 10 Aug. 1863.) Neither did he think that perfect charity is easily to be supposed in those outside the Church. He was wont to quote St Augustine to the effect that ' the bond of Christian charity cannot be kept out of the unity of the Church ' (*De Unitate Ecclesiae* 15). Nor could he agree with Catholics in supposing so liberally the good faith of those outside the Church. When the eminent Roman theologian, Fr Perrone SJ, sent him his *Il protestantesimo e la regola de fede* for review, while praising it highly, Brownson could not agree with the author in supposing the good faith of Protestants so generally. ' He has never been a Protestant ', he said, ' and lends to them more of the qualities of his own Catholic heart than we believe them entitled to . . . We have, with the few exceptions of individuals on their way to the Church, seldom found them either earnestly seeking for the truth, or prepared to embrace it when presented. . . . Their ignorance is crass and supine rather than invincible' (his *Review* (1854) p. 129). Brownson had himself been a Protestant minister for almost twenty years, although not always a practising one.

But Brownson's battle for the recognition of the papal powers of Supremacy and Infallibility well-nigh twenty years before the solemn definitions of the Vatican Council was still more remarkable. He was so far ahead of his time in an atmosphere tainted with Gallicanism that there was scarcely a Catholic of real culture in his entire native land to uphold him. The controversy stirred up such a storm of abuse that, yielding to the suasion of friends, he suspended his fight after a few years for the sake of peace in the Church, but with unaltered convictions. He had brought up the question, he said, merely because he knew no other way possible by which to meet and vanquish, if possible, that gangrene that has eaten its way so deeply into the vitals of modern nations, namely, political atheism. The capital evil of Gallicanism, as he understood it, is not its denial of papal Infallibility, but rather its denial of papal Supremacy, i.e. that the judicial authority of the Holy Father extends over the secular order as well as over the spiritual. Such a denial means the emancipation of the political order from the over-sight of the spiritual order as represented by the Vicar of Christ, therefore from the law and sovereignty of God. He took issue in particular with M. Gosselin, Director of the Seminary of St Sulpice, Paris, in his work, *The Power of the Popes in the Middle Ages* (1853). Gosselin and his school held that the popes of the Middle Ages exercised their power of deposing tyrannical sovereigns merely by the *Jus Publicum* of the time, that is, *jure humano*. Brownson did not of course deny that the medieval popes held and exercised such a right, but he objected to the Gosselin theory inasmuch as it denied that they held that same right also by virtue of the power of the keys, *jure divino*. No one can deny, he said, that the Vicar of Christ has plenary authority to judge the morality of all human actions whether of states or of individuals. So much Pope Innocent III asserted very distinctly in his letter to Philip Augustus, king of France. 'We do not intend', he said, 'to judge of the fee ; that belongs to the king of France. But we do have the right to judge of the sin, and it is our duty to exercise it against the offender, be he who he may' [1] (Brownson's *Works*, II, 258).

Yet this power which the popes have by virtue of the keys is only an indirect power over the temporal order, Brownson explained, in so far as the secular order itself has a spiritual end, and the power in question is merely judicial or declarative in nature. But whether drawing his arguments from the Decretal, *Novit*, of Innocent III, or the *Unam Sanctam* of Boniface VIII, or any other source, his arguments defending the popes of the Middle Ages were masterful and powerful. Writing in the

Irish Ecclesiastical Record, January 1884, Fr J. Healy, Professor of theology in Maynooth and later arch-bishop of Tuam, asserted that Brownson ' seems to have gone quite as far as, if not further than Bellar-mine ' in defending the medieval popes who ' pro-nounced the deposition of outrageously tyrannical kings, who [had] violated their coronation oath, broke the constitutional pact, and raged like lions against the Church'. In fact, it would probably be impossible to find any one using the English language who was ever such a staunch and uniform vindicator of the authority of the Holy See, or of the immense significance to society at large of the Papacy. It is in no way surprising that Cardinal Manning, another great protagonist of the papal powers, wrote Brown-son in 1873 to say, ' You see as I see, and your discernment confirms mine. You have so long and so powerfully maintained the authority of the Holy See in the midst of indifference, liberalism, and half-truths that we all owe you a debt of gratitude ; and the Church in America will bear the marks of your testimony to the highest conviction of Catholic Truth. We have one point in common. You, I believe, have always had a special devotion to the Holy Ghost. It was this that brought me out of darkness into light. And it is this that has made the prerogatives of the Vicar of Christ the first axioms of my faith ' (Brownson's *Life* by his son, Henry, III, 274).

Bibliography. Brownson's *Quarterly Review*, 1844–1855, Boston ; 1856–64, 1873, 1875, New York. Brownson's *Works* (collected and arranged by Henry F. Brownson), 20 vols (1882–7), Detroit ; *Life of Brownson, Early, Middle*, and *Later* (3 vols), by his son, Henry (1898–1900) Detroit ; Arthur M. Schlesinger, Jr., ' Life of Brownson ', *Orestes A. Brownson, A Pilgrim's Progress* (1939) ; Sidney A. Raemers, *America's Foremost Philosopher* (1931) ; Augustine F. Hewitt CP, *Problems of the Age* (1858) ; Edwin Ryan, ' Brownson and Newman ', in AER, 53 (1915) 406 ; Fr John Healy, ' Brownson's Works ', in IER, 5 (1884) 13–21 ; Papal Encyclicals : *Mystici Corporis*, Pius XII, 29 June 1943 ; *Humani Generis*, Pius XII, 12 Aug. 1950 ; *Quanto Con-ficiamur Moerore*, Pius IX, 10 Aug. 1863.

T. R. R.

BUDDHISM This article will treat briefly of (I) the origins of Buddhism, and then more at length of its teaching as a way of life (II), its theology or the lack of it (III), and finally (IV) touch upon its relations with Christianity.

I The origins of Buddhism are normally associated with a sage of the 6th cent. BC., but unlike Christi-anity Buddhism does not set great store upon historical beginnings and shows absolute unconcern about the times before the appearance on this earth of Sākyamuni. This is the title (sage of the Sākya clan) given to a young man of Nepal, born of a royal family and so affected by the vanity of life that he abandoned parents, wife and child, and fled to the forest, seeking a spiritual guide. The guides he finds cannot take him far enough, and he turns

---

[1] Non intendimus judicare de feudo, . . . sed decernere de peccato, cujus ad nos pertinet sine dubitatione censura, quam in quemlibet exercere possumus, et debemus. (Cited by Suarez, *De Primatu Summi Pontificis*, Cap. XXIII, 172.)

alone and unguided to the practice of severe austerities. These proving fruitless, he remembers that as a boy he had once experienced a condition of mindful happiness and so resolves to place himself in this condition again and if possible to progress from there. In this he succeeds, and, going from stage to stage, he reaches the end of his quest and knows that he is a *buddha*, an enlightened one. He gains followers and leads them along his own way, until at last an organized order is set up. He dies at the age of eighty, passing into a condition of *nirvāna* for which his enlightenment had qualified him.

Legend has considerably embellished this simple history, some of the details of which may be inaccurate since Buddhists from their belief that Sākyamuni was but one in a series of buddhas did not keep to anything like a 'gospel tradition'. Sites connected with the life, such as the 'tree of enlightenment' at Bodhgaya and the shrine at Kusinagara where he died, help to authenticate some of the details.

The Singhalese canon, which is written in Pāli, an ancient Indian language, comprises a set of works concerned with monastic discipline (*vinaya*), a set of 'discourses' (*sūtra*) attributed to Sākyamuni, and a third section on philosophical definition (*abhidharma*). It was not committed to writing until the 1st cent. B.C., but certainly contains a great deal of very early material especially in the first two sections. In northern India Sanskrit soon became the recognized medium for Buddhist scriptures (as it already was for Brahmanical ones), and although Buddhism was all but completely effaced from the land of its origin in the 13th cent. A.D., large quantities of these Sanskrit Buddhist manuscripts have been preserved in Nepal and Tibet. It was this vast Sanskrit Buddhist literature which in translation provided the material for the later Chinese and Tibetan canons. Thus everything is preserved in these translations. It was only in the course of last century that Western scholars began to study them closely.

The canonical texts of these northern Buddhist countries, apart from the texts on monastic discipline (*vinaya*), fall into two main categories, *sūtras* and *tantras*. Both these terms mean 'thread of discourse', but while *sūtras* are mainly doctrinal in character, *tantras* are more concerned with the theory and practice of ritual. The earlier *sūtras*, like those which appear in the Singhalese Canon, are historical or quasi-historical in character and represent Sākyamuni giving instruction to his followers at Rajgir or Banaras or some other place of his abode. The later *sūtras* present with little serious attempt at historicity a transcendent form of the sage expounding new philosophical theories and commending the career of *bodhisattva* (a being set upon buddhahood). Both types of *sūtra* have the same practical aim, to promote morality, concentration and wisdom, but they differ somewhat in ascetical temper.

The *tantras* make no claim whatever to historicity.

They are revealed by the transcendent Buddha, and differ from the *sūtras* in that they tell of means whereby buddhahood can be obtained in this present life and not (as formerly believed) by passing through the cycle of existences. These practices involve complicated forms of ritual and the use of magical spells. The transcendent Buddha who is held to have revealed them is not conceived as a person once human who had passed to another life but as an Olympian : ' He has the colour of saffron and is like the rising sun. He holds a great wheel which is turning. He is like a great king with his crown and ornaments ; his lower garment is of fine cloth and his upper garment of many colours. He is bewreathed and handsome, adorned with strands and garlands. He smells a wreath of flowers held in the right hand. . . .' Attributes such as sovereignty, light and power belonged to this transcendent being and easily led to the production of a whole pantheon of buddhas, not thought of as following one another in time but as manifesting themselves spontaneously from an undifferentiated absolute.

II Buddhism as a practical way of life does not differ enormously between Tibet, China, Japan or Ceylon ; there are the four truths and the eightfold path. The truths are (1) the existence of misery, (2) the cause of misery, which is desire, (3) the end of misery, which is the uprooting of desire and (4) the way to end misery, which is the eightfold path. This path can be summarized as enjoining good morals, mental concentration and wisdom. Morals are covered by the ten prohibitions, not to take life, not to steal, to avoid unchastity, not to lie, not to slander, not to insult, not to chatter, not to covet, not to give way to anger, not to doubt. For monks the last six precepts are somewhat different ; not to drink intoxicants, not to use garlands or scents, not to join in dancing and so on. Buddhahood, that timeless actualization of essential reality, realizable by man through his own striving in time, is not to be achieved by morally right conduct alone ; that is but a preliminary condition. There must be added right concentration and right-mindedness or wisdom.

Concentration is to be sought by techniques of meditation, withdrawing the mind from sense-objects and from conceptual thought. It is obvious that the end-state of wisdom governs to a great extent the choice of meditation-techniques. Fr Desideri SJ, who at the beginning of the 18th cent. spent some years in Tibet studying its religion, writes of the purpose of this meditation : ' They say that all passions can be traced to lust and wrath, which originate solely in the natural tendency of man to look on some things as pleasing and on others as painful and unpleasant. Having ascertained this, they proceed to search for the roots of lust and wrath, and assert that they arise from man's innate conception that some things are pleasant while others are painful. Investigating the cause of such a conception they declare that it arises from the illusion that all beings and things are endowed with a self. Having reached thus far, they determine that all this must be extirpated from our hearts. To destroy lust and wrath, they say, we must banish from our imagination the differences attributed to things pleasant and unpleasant, opportune and in-opportune, and even the consciousness of self and of any other thing. Having attained to this, as a cause which no longer exists cannot yield any effect, it is impossible for such a being to be exposed to any evil or trouble ; he will therefore remain free from everything worldly, variable or temporal, and will then attain to impassibility and immortality and arrive at buddhahood.'

Buddhist enlightenment is held to consist of wisdom (or sublime contemplation) and the practice of compassion. Desideri says of this wisdom : ' They pretend that man disappears even to himself, and that to a cleansed and purified mind all things vanish and that nothing exists. This supreme grade of contemplation is very much on a par with our Christian idea of leading others and ourselves to higher thoughts ; but how different are the methods adopted. . . . Their method is to emancipate the will from all affections and from all fear of any object, so that it may be absolutely neutral and even suspended. Our method is far surer (as far as any-thing on earth can be) ; to place our will in God's hands, to trust in Him and to be, in a manner, in-corporated with Him so that all other love and other objects fade away, as a man in mid-ocean loses sight of land ' (see ABANDONMENT).

Traditionally Sākyamuni's enlightenment was ex-plained as a threefold knowledge, viz. knowledge of his previous births, a knowledge of all beings dying and being reborn, and a knowledge of his own release. Some of the earlier followers (whose tradi-tions are now represented primarily by the Sing-halese canon) conceived of the Buddha as a lord and master far above themselves. But in the later Indian traditions, which were afterwards worked over by the Chinese and the Tibetans, and later still by the Japanese and the Mongolians, the whole scope of the Buddhist ideal was infinitely extended. It was no longer a matter of experiencing a form of impersonal tranquillity, but of striving to become in turn a universal saviour, and thus to save all beings in the process of one's own perfecting. (They called their way the Great Way, Mahāyāna, and the ideal of the earlier practisers was castigated as a Lesser Way, Hīnayāna). But the Buddhist scheme is centrifugal as well as centripetal. If men, as bodhi-sattvas, can advance towards buddhahood, buddhas, manifesting themselves as divine bodhisattvas, can come to man's assistance. Thus the whole concep-tion of divine beings who are worthy of worship finds its way into Buddhism.

III The theology of Buddhism grew out of the disputes about the Great Way. Buddhism had no idea of a Creator, as Desideri showed, but, as he said, though they deny the existence of a Divinity theoretically and speculatively, they admit an object worthy of adoration and invocation, and so in practice and implicitly do admit some kind of Divinity. They accept rewards and punishments for good and bad deeds (though they think these pass on through the transmigration of souls to another existence) but do not seem to have the con-cept of a Rewarder. Desideri noted that the worship paid to those who had attained to buddhahood did not imply that they were regarded as gods but as ' human beings, brute beasts or damned beings, who have by their own exertions attained to eternal happiness after cleansing themselves of all sins and passions '. Thus they would count as no higher than Catholic saints, but would exist in a Pelagian heaven of their own making, for no divine grace entered into their story ; they may have received compassion from successful predecessors, but this was not the gift of God. Where human personality is obscurely understood owing to a theory of transmigration, it must follow that divine personality will be too, for this has to be approached with the help of analogy (see ANALOGY) and in the light of the fundamental Christian revelation of the Trinity. The first Jesuit missionary to make contact with the Tibetan Buddhists thought that they too had a Trinity, for they agreed with him in praising the Three-in-one, but this was a misunderstanding ; the Buddhist triad of Buddha, Dharma (the word or doctrine) and Sangha (or congregation) are clearly not equals.

Other accretions which Buddhism acquired were the feminine partners of the bodhisattvas (with whom came in from the subsoil of Indian religiosity a whole ritual and metaphysic of sexual union), and also a considerable daemonic mythology with its attendant rites of propitiation. The first image of the Buddha has been traced by the late Sir W. Tarn to a coin of one of the Greek Bactrian rulers of c. 70 B.C. ; the Buddha is shown on the reverse of the coin (the divine side) and is enthroned as a ruler rather than as a teacher. The Greek-inspired Gandhara sculptures follow soon after this, whereas the purely Indian statues from Mathura (1st and 2nd cent. A.D.) are a native reaction away from the Apollo-type to something more spiritual.

Desideri rightly took the doctrine of transmigra-tion as the root-error of Buddhism, for if there have to be innumerable existences gone through before the arrival at final bliss, how is one sure that it will be one's own bliss ? Desideri compiled four volumes of a refutation of Buddhism (in Tibetan) which still await a student in the Roman archives. Buddhists may urge that there is continuity between tree and fruit, between the child and the man, and that they suppose something like this between the series of existences which form as it were a harmonic progression. But always there remains the difficulty which Plato formulated in the Phaedo : If the human soul is a harmony, what is it the harmony of ? Fr Taymans SJ, a modern student of Buddhism in Ceylon, tried to westernize the Buddhist philo-sophy by suggesting that it could be taken as a metaphysic of action ; action should be thought of just as action, without its qualification as good or bad. Action as such comes from a will that is perfectly detached and that is beyond good and evil ; but, if it has somehow incorporated into itself the residue of former acts, it must thereby be qualified, and, if it has not, how is it part of the series ? It is true that St Thomas (in his commentary on the *Ethics* of Aristotle) envisages unending action as the final *natural* end of man, but this is far from Buddhist ideas, even those of the Theravadin of Ceylon, who stand apart from the followers of the Great Way.

The *stūpa* or Buddhist shrine, conical in shape and domed, of which the earliest examples were believed to contain relics of Sākyamuni, is a sign of the presence in early Buddhism of some external worship. Clement of Alexandria (*Strom.* 3:6:60 ; GCS 15:225), citing Alexander Polyhistor, knows of these *stūpas* and calls them 'pyramids'. 'They venerate some kind of pyramid beneath which they deem the bones of some god to be buried.' Elsewhere Clement says expressly that the Buddhists worship Buddha as a god. (*Strom.* 1:15:71 ; GCS 15:46.) Sacrifices are part of Tibetan Buddhist ritual, but not holocausts, only libations and partial offerings.

IV Contacts with Christianity. The earliest explicit Christian mention of Buddhism occurs in the passages just cited from Clement of Alexandria. In his day the library at Alexandria contained information gathered by travellers in the East (particularly in the period after A.D. 60, when the use of the monsoon for sailing to India had been exploited for the first time and there was a great expansion of commerce between the Roman empire and India through Egypt). In view of this definite contact, it becomes somewhat more probable that elements of Buddhist asceticism may have been absorbed by some of the later Gnostic sects ; as for Plotinus, so for them borrowing cannot be ruled out. The *Hymn to the Soul* (edited by A. Bevan in T & S 5) seems to have some possible echoes, but these may be due to Bardesanes (*see* BARDESANES).

In the Middle Ages Buddhism suddenly became a subject of interest to Christians. In Fr John of Plano Carpini's mission to the Mongols (1247) the Kitayans (Chinese) are described as pagans who 'have an Old and a New Testament (perhaps *sūtras* and *tantras*) ; they say they have some saints ; they worship one god and honour Our Lord Jesus Christ ; they give much in alms and seem most affable . . .'. Nestorian missionaries had already reached China and the readiness of Buddhists to absorb any or every element of local worship might account for the honour paid to the name of Christ. The next mission (of Fr William of Rubruc) led to a debate before the Great Khan, Mongka, at Karakorum in 1254, between the Christian friar and some Buddhists. At one point there was produced a boy, 'who, judging by his size, was not yet three years old but whose reasoning powers were fully developed and who said that he had had three reincarnations already'. Fr William seems to have countered this with an insistence on the oneness of God, which led the debate on to other ground.

Only by a little did the opportunity of a large-scale dogmatic approach to Buddhism fail to be realized at this time. The Tartars were enemies of the Saracen, and a working agreement between Tartar and Frank in Palestine to the disadvantage of the Moslem was in being for some years (PO 12:372). Had the fortunes of war been different, a great *Summa contra Orientales* might have been produced in the heyday of Scholasticism alongside St Thomas's work against the Moslems.

Buddhism had vanished from India when the first Jesuit missions began there, but it was encountered in Ceylon, Nepal and finally (by Fr de Andrade in 1624) in Tibet. What St Francis Xavier found in Japan was the fragmentation of Buddhism (he himself distinguished nine varieties of it), and it was some time before the missionaries came to realize that there was any link between the paganism they met in Japan and that of Ceylon or of Nepal. Francis at the end of his life regarded Sākyamuni as a daemonic myth with no historic existence. St Francis admitted that he found some men of wisdom and great asceticism among the Japanese Buddhists, alongside many who were vicious, and the problem of the bestowal of grace outside Christianity was to be brought up by the Jansenists against the Jesuit missioners (hence the condemned proposition [D 1379] that 'no grace is given outside the Church'). Some of the ramifications of this problem are still under discussion.

The influence of Christianity on Buddhism in the 3rd cent. by way of Manicheism has been little attended to but seems quite clear. The *Acta Archelai* (63 ; GCS 16:91) tell of one Terebinthus, a precursor of Mani, who travelled far into Baluchistan and had himself proclaimed as a Buddha, with the addition that he was of a virgin birth and had been brought up in the mountains by an angel. Epiphanius (*haer.* 66:1 ; GCS 37:16) has the same story, and there is some likelihood that Mani was recognized as a Buddha by the king of Mekran. The Manichean frescoes from Turfan are very like Buddhist paintings and the *bema*-ceremony of the Manichees seems to resemble the Buddhist 'general confession' or reading of the 258 rules. The hybrid work known as *Barlaam and Joasaph* (PG 96:859–1240), said to have come to Jerusalem from 'Ethiopia' and incorporating Buddhist legends and the Christian *Apology* of Aristides, came from a similar circle. A Georgian version found at Jerusalem and prior to the Greek (which was made from it) was published at Tiflis in 1957 (*see* D. M. Lang, *The Wisdom of Balahvar*, 1957).

Bibliography. The first contacts of Christianity with Buddhism can be studied in G. Messina SJ, *Cristianesimo, buddhismo, manicheismo nell'Asia antica* (1947), and in the medieval narratives gathered in *The Mongol Mission* (ed. by C. Dawson, 1955) ; Fr Desideri's narrative *An Account of Tibet* was edited for the *Broadway Travellers* series by F. de Filippi (1932) ; C. Wessels SJ, *Early Jesuit Travellers in Central Asia* (1924), gives details of Desideri's unpublished Tibetan work on Buddhism ; Fr de

Andrade SJ, *O descobrimento do Tibet* (1624) was published at Coimbra in 1921 ; the evidence of Greek influence on Buddhism is in W. W. Tarn, *The Greeks in Bactria and India* (1951) ; modern doctrinal expositions of Buddhism are sometimes unreliable as they set out to propagate some derivative form of the doctrine with more or less assimilation to Western ideas ; the following are recommended : D. L. Snellgrove, *Buddhist Himalaya* (1957) used in this article with permission ; F. Taymans d'Eypernon SJ, *Les Paradoxes du bouddhisme* (1947) ; D. L. Snellgrove, 'Buddhist Morality', in *The Springs of Morality*, edited by J. Todd (1956) ; *E. J. Thomas, *The Life of Buddha as legend and history* (1927) ; *E. Conze, *Buddhism, its essence and development* (1951).

BYZANTINE ART This article has four parts, (I) the idea of the function of a religious image, (II) the veneration of images, (III) the schematism of the Byzantine church and (IV) the quality of Byzantine art.

The Byzantine Empire may be held to have begun on 11 May 330 when the Emperor Constantine placed his capital in the Greek city of Byzantium which was later to be known as Constantinople. But Byzantine Art is not fully formed until the reign of the Emperor Justinian from 527 to 565 when Byzantium had at last succeeded Antioch and Alexandria as well as Rome as the cultural centre of the Christian world. It was to have a continuous history for nine hundred years until Constantinople was stormed by the Turks on 29 May 1453 and it was to exercise vital influences throughout the west.

I The conception of the function of the religious image was the most important of these for the theologian. This is first certainly apparent in the 6th cent. Immemorially by then it had been the custom to decorate the walls and sometimes the roof and floor of Christian churches, baptisteries and funerary chambers. But the purpose of these wall paintings or mosaics had been conceived as primarily decorative or didactic. The Christian could be taught the mysteries of the Faith, or be reminded of them, either through narrative scenes or by the use of symbols. There is no evidence for the existence of cult images. It used to be asserted that their gradual emergence in the 5th and 6th cents. was due to the influence of pagan religious feeling which had been brought into Christianity through mass conversions. This has never been substantiated. It is of course very possible that this was a factor in the devotions of the illiterate, particularly among the proletariat of the great eastern cities. But the Christian episcopate and priesthood and educated laity seem to have been singularly immune from direct pagan religious influences ; behind them lay centuries of bitter anti-pagan polemic. In contrast they were very ready to receive secular influences from the non-Christian Graeco-Roman world. Two such secular influences directly stimulated the new development in Christian art. They were the veneration of the Imperial Image and the use of funerary portraits.

It had been held from the beginning of the Empire that there was a special relationship between the Emperor and his Image. It is not that they were ever confused together. But its presence signified his presence, any honour or insult paid to it was paid to him. When the Emperor Justinian and his wife the Empress Theodora were portrayed in mosaics in the church of San Vitale at Ravenna they were shown bearing their offerings for the Eucharist. To their contemporaries this signified that they were present perpetually at each offertory in the church they had founded. By a natural association the presence of angels and saints sharing in the liturgy was signified by their representation upon walls, as they hovered above the altar or moved processionally towards it. Increasingly Christ was shown in the apse to signify that He presided at the altar beneath Him. Honour paid to the image passed to the imaged.

There was a parallel development in the 6th cent. in the use of portable panel paintings, most frequently of saints. These were kept in private houses or placed at cross-roads or in wayside shrines. The earliest that are still extant belong to the late 5th or early 6th cents. and are preserved in the monastery of St Catherine on Mount Sinai. They are wooden tablets. The heads painted on them in wax colours, full-faced, motionless and conventionalized, are obviously directly derived from the secular funerary portraits of the non-Christian period, of which so many examples have survived from Roman Egypt. Yet there is much evidence that they were used in private devotion and that some were reputed to work miracles and became the object of pilgrimage. Still it should be noted that all the 'Wonder-Working Images' of this period belonged to two categories. Some were held to be of directly miraculous origin 'not made with hands', others were representations of Stylite Saints and contained 'Sacred Dust' scraped from the Stylite's body. It would seem therefore that they were held to work miracles not as images but as relics. Certainly the miraculous power was held to be conferred through contact ; the ikon had to be touched as well as prayed before. It is becoming increasingly clear that the veneration of relics and the veneration of images are closely interwoven in their origins.

II The veneration of images would seem to have reached its height in the 7th cent. in the eastern sea-ports and in the shrines of the great abbeys. There was an inevitable reaction. In 730 the Emperor Leo III the Iconoclast issued an edict that decreed the destruction of all images in human form of Christ and of His Mother and of His saints and angels. This was the beginning of the struggle between Iconoclasts and Iconodules—Image Destroyers and Image Worshippers—which divided Eastern Christianity for a hundred and thirteen years.

The origins and the character of Iconoclasm are still frequently misrepresenetd. It is still sometimes ascribed to Muslim influence. But the Iconoclast Emperors were munificent patrons of art who delighted in graven images. It has been described as 'puritanical', but the Iconoclasts luxuriously embellished their churches; the Cross that represented Christ, like the peacocks for immortality and the trees for Paradise, was placed against backgrounds of gold mosaic and interspersed with purely decorative compositions. It has been attributed to the personal convictions of Leo III, but it would seem that he was hesitantly following a movement begun by a group of bishops in Asia Minor and it is improbable that he would have done so if it had not been supported by his army, mainly recruited from the conservative Christian peasantry of the Asia Minor uplands.

The central tenet of Iconoclasm was that all corporeal sacred images must be removed from places of worship since their presence there led to idolatry. Between 741 and 775 during the reign of the second Iconoclast Emperor Constantine V the movement also came to be supported by all those who wished that the monks of each diocese should be under the effective control of their bishops and by all those who wished the Church to be under the effective supervision of Emperors. It therefore came to be supported by the mass of the episcopate and by many of the civil service. In 754 three hundred and thirty-eight Eastern bishops declared for Iconoclasm at the Council of Hiereia. In contrast and perhaps partly in consequence the Iconodule opposition was supported by the great majority of the monks and by all those who, like St Theodore the Studite, cared deeply for the freedom of the Church. It is thus easy to understand that Iconoclasm was supported by some very moderate Iconoclasts and Image Worship by some very moderate Iconodules.

A temporary alliance between the moderates on both sides brought back peace at the Seventh Œcumenical Council held at Nicaea from 23 September until 13 October 787. A Definition was passed at its seventh session and promulgated at Constantinople on 22 October. It decreed that pictorial representations of Christ, of His Mother, of His Angels and of His Saints were to be displayed in churches, in houses and on the roads in order to 'arouse those who behold them to remember and to desire the prototypes'. It was licit to 'give them greeting and worship of honour but not the true worship of our faith which befits only the Divine Nature'. It was licit to light candles before them and offer incense, but only in the same fashion as the gospel books were incensed.

Papal legates had been present at the Council which had been convoked, at least partly, on the initiative of Pope Hadrian I. In spite of the opposition of Charlemagne and of the Synod of Frankfurt (both probably from political motives) the Decree came to be given œcumenical authority throughout the West. It is possible that in the East it satisfied neither party. The Emperor Michael I was an extreme Iconodule, and his defeat and death in 813 led to an Iconoclast reaction under the Emperor Leo V. The controversy was only finally settled at the Council of Constantinople in 843. This

marked the final victory of the Iconodules. Not only was the Decree of Nicaea recognized as of œcumenical authority but it was interpreted in the light of the teaching of the two Iconodule controversialists St John Damascene and St Theodore the Studite, and their doctrine on Sacred Images became the official doctrine of the Byzantine provinces of the Church. It is quite untrue, though it is fashionable, to say that this doctrine presupposed a 'magical identity' between the Image and the Imaged. Both St John and St Theodore emphasize that the Image and its Prototype differ in essence. They are no more of the same substance than a man's shadow is of the same substance as the man, but they are as closely related.

The first effect of the Decree was to authorize the conception of the Wonder-working Image; standing beneath it the believer could be healed as the Saint's shadow fell upon him. Again, just as man's presence can be argued from his shadow, so the presence of the God-Bearer and the Saint is shown by that of the image. This led to localized cults, notably of the Mother of God, and created the classic scheme of Byzantine church decoration. (*See also* ICONOCLASTS.)

III The schematism of a Byzantine church. Byzantine architecture was perpetually evolving new forms from the ground plans of the great 5th cent. basilicas and cruciform 'Martyria'; the high domed rectangle of Haghia Sophia, the domed radiate shrine of San Vitale, the domed basilica, the five-domed cruciform 'cathedral' like St Mark's at Venice, the single-domed cruciform village church. Behind all there was an underlying symbolism. The Eucharist was at the heart of the church, like the Passion at the heart of the world. The church was therefore a microcosm of the world representing all earth and sky. Christ, His Mother and the Angels were present through their images in the dome and the high vaults and the conch of the apse; the 'sky' of the Church, the Kingdom of Heaven. Saints were placed on the lower half of the walls, moving among the church militant on earth. The intermediate sphere was seen as a counterpart of the Holy Land and therefore of the gospel narrative, the link between the Kingdom of Heaven and man's life on earth. Scenes from the NT, and at times from the NT Apocrypha, were present here in the mosaics and paintings that shadowed them. The scheme had evolved gradually; its roots can be traced into the 5th cent., it became obligatory after the Iconoclast controversy. It was never to be forgotten, though it became obscured in the late medieval period when wooden panels of Christ and His Mother were placed beneath their 'sky' representations to reflect them and to be touched by the faithful. The steady replacement of mosaic by wall painting, the desire to represent many saints and Feasts, turned the late Byzantine church into a single great Icon.

Praying before the Holy Images men prayed through them and so reached their prototypes. It became customary therefore to present them frontally so that they could be gazed at eye to eye. The necessity of making the identity of each saint clear led both to the use of inscriptions and to an elaborate iconography which was inherited by the West. Meditating on the Twelve or sometimes Fifteen Mysteries, that began with the Annunciation and ended with the close of the Virgin's life on earth, the believer could feel himself in some sense present in turn at each and this led to their strictly chronological order. The Iconodule theory of the image thus provided the framework for all later evolutions in Byzantine art.

IV The quality of Byzantine art. Byzantine art was never static. Until quite recently works that commonly passed as Byzantine art were in fact re-paintings from the late 17th cent. to the middle of the 19th cent., stiff and conventionalized and dead. The masterpieces at Constantinople were hidden under Turkish plaster. Mosaics and wall paintings are being uncovered at Constantinople and at Salonika. Panel paintings are being uncovered at the Byzantine Institute at Athens and Venice and at the central Restoration Workshop at Moscow. There are new detailed studies in textiles, metal work and ivories. It is becoming possible to date any Byzantine art object within fifty years, at least after the end of the Iconoclast controversy. The balanced rhythm, the carefully centralized composition, the strongly classical reminiscences of the 9th and 10th cents. are replaced in the early 11th cent. by a new, sometimes crude, vigour derived from provincial monastic art. The details of the gospel narrative are rendered dramatically. There are persistent attempts to convey emotional tension. A new phase begins about 1120; figures are treated monumentally; often a single figure is predominant, the emphasis is on majesty and serenity. Sometime about 1300 fresh tendencies become dominant. There are new rhythms in the elaborate flowing composition of small figures; there are fresh combinations in colour. Mosaic is being replaced everywhere by painting, and perhaps painting is conceived as a form of music. Certainly the later ballet is being perpetually foreshadowed. At first there is an obvious delight in an exact rendering of detail but this vanishes through new experiments in varieties of perspective. This experimentalism survived for a century in Crete after the Turks had taken Constantinople and was brought to the West by El Greco. But through all these changes the unaltering conception of the Image gave Byzantine art its unity.

Bibliography. For the use of images before the Iconoclast controversy : Ernst Kitzinger, ' The Cult of Images in the Age before Iconoclasm ' in *Dumbarton Oaks Papers* VIII, pp. 85–108 (1954); ★Paul Alexander, *The Patriarch Nicephorus of Constantinople* (1958) pp. 1–53 ; André Grabar, *Martyrium*, 2 vols (1943, 1945).

For the Iconoclast controversy : ★Paul Alexander, *The Patriarch Nicephorus of Constantinople* (1958) pp. 52–262 ; Louis Bréhier, *La Querelle des images* (1907) ; ★Georg Ostrogorsky, ' Les Débuts

de la querelle des images ' in *Mélanges Charles Diehl* (1930) pp. 230–55 ; *Vita Theodori Studitae*, PG 99:113–28.

For Iconoclast theory : ★Milton Anastos, ' The Ethical Theory of Images ', in *Dumbarton Oaks Papers* VIII, pp. 151–60 (1954).

For the Iconodule theory of Images : St John Damascene, *Orationes tres adversus eos qui sacras imagines impugnant*, PG 94:1231–420 ; St Theodore the Studite, *Parva Catechesis* (ed. Auvray, 1891) ; St Theodore the Studite, *Epistulae*, PG 99:903–1679.

For the Decrees of the Seventh Œcumenical Council : Mansi, XIII:377.d. seq. Cf. HL III, ii:741–804.

For Byzantine Art after the Iconoclast controversy : Otto Demus, *Byzantine Mosaic Decoration* (1948) ; ★Thomas Whittemore, *The Mosaics of St. Sophia* (1933–52) ; André Grabar, *Byzantine Painting* (1953). G. M.

BYZANTINE LITURGY Leontius of Byzantium, writing against Nestorius in 531–5, says that the heretic Theodore of Mopsuestia made up an *anaphora* of his own, ' not reverencing that of the Apostles, nor considering as worth a straw that of the great Basil, which was written in the same spirit ' (PG 86:1368). This remark, coming from a Byzantine, has been the beginning of all speculation about the character of the liturgy in use at Byzantium. As it does not mention the liturgy of St John Chrysostom, various theories have been put forward to account for this silence in the 6th cent., whereas it is admitted by all that it was the so-called liturgy of Chrysostom that was mainly employed at Constantinople from the 11th cent. onwards.

First of all comment will be made upon : (I) the possible alternative theories ; then (II) the material drawn from Chrysostom himself ; finally (III) the theological character of the liturgy of Chrysostom, as it was later called.

I The possible alternative theories are three. Either the liturgy of the Apostles was later turned into what we know as that of Chrysostom, or the liturgy of Basil (*see* BASIL, LITURGY OF) was so used, or else the liturgy of Chrysostom (so-called) must be pronounced to be a product of some period after the middle of the 6th cent. and quite unconnected with the saint himself. Lebrun suggested that there was some likeness between the Syriac liturgy of the XII Apostles and that called after Chrysostom, and recently his suggestion has been taken up and given very powerful support, first by H. Engberding in 1938 and more recently by A. Raes, the editor of the Syriac *anaphorae*, in 1958. A comparison of the order and wording of the prayers of offertory, preface, institution, *epiklesis*, intercessions, fraction and thanksgiving shows that the two liturgies, as represented (for the Syriac liturgy of the XII Apostles) by a 10th-cent. Syriac codex (B.M. Add 14493), and by the famous Barberini codex, written in 788–97 (for the Greek of ' Chrysostom '), have quite considerable tracts in common. On the other hand, some have pressed the fact that in the Barberini codex it is only two prayers (of the catechumens and of the *proskomide*) which are labelled ' of Chrysostom ', while the liturgy as a whole is without a name, even though the liturgy of Basil (which precedes it in the MS.) is given its full title. Probst argued long ago that Chrysostom had shortened the original liturgy of Basil and that every place where our present liturgy of Chrysostom was longer than Basil was a later interpolation. Grancolas in his turn took the third alternative and held that it was another John, namely John II of Constantinople, who was the author about the year 518. This would not get over the difficulty about the silence of Leontius, but there are many later Johns who could be put into the breach instead of John II.

The first alternative seems much the most likely, but it is always well to remember that the basis of our knowledge of Chrysostom's liturgy is conjectural. A study of the liturgical odyssey of Dr Baumstark during some fifty years of theorizing, an odyssey which ended more or less where it began (see his final recantation in *Comparative Liturgy*, p. 55), would show how weak the basis can be. It may turn out that, when the Barberini codex is finally printed in a critical edition, new light will be shed on some of the assumptions hitherto made about it by liturgists. The fact that in the MS. the liturgy of Basil is numbered into sections (I to XIV) and that the liturgy which follows is numbered XV to XXIII, and not numbered afresh from I, might argue that it was felt to be a mere supplement to the principal liturgy in use at the end of the 8th cent. On the other hand there are some leaves in Old Slavonic at St Catherine's Convent on Mt Sinai which give the opening prayer, the *epiklesis* and intercessions of our ' Chrysostom ' but they are headed with the title, ' Prayer of Basil '. The leaves themselves date from about 1100, but from the character of the wording they must represent a text that is much older still. They are found in PO 25:608-9.

II The life of Chrysostom gives one valuable indication about the liturgy he used at the end of his days. The *Dialogue* of Palladius (edited by Coleman-Norton, 68 and 45) about Chrysostom's life tells that before his death, ' he put on his finest vestments and partook of the Lord's sacrament, speaking thereafter the usual prayer, " Praise be to God for all things "'. Now this prayer of postcommunion is not found in ' Basil ' or in ' Chrysostom ', but it *is* found in the liturgy of the Presanctified which follows after ' Chrysostom ' in the Barberini codex. It would be quite normal for such a liturgy to be performed to give viaticum to the dying Chrysostom, if the day of his death (Sept. 16) was in fact aliturgical. The evidence of Palladius thus points to the authenticity of the liturgy of the Pre-sanctified, which is found immediately after that of ' Chrysostom ' in the Barberini codex, and which is usually ascribed to him.

Another fact about Chrysostom's liturgy which Palladius vouches for is that he introduced the custom of the faithful taking a drink of water after com-munion (or even a pastille), for he was accused of this by two deacons whom he had penanced. The practice of giving the ablutions to the laity (*see* ABLUTIONS) after communion cannot then have been known in Constantinople, even though something like it is ordered in the *Traditio apostolica*, a document which does not seem to have much connection with Constantinople. Perhaps Chrysostom was here importing the Antiochene custom into his episcopal city. The motive in any case was greater reverence for the sacred elements, a motive which many have recognised as being operative in the prayers of the liturgy of ' Chrysostom ' as distinct from that of Basil.

The commentary·on Acts which Chrysostom delivered at Constantinople is quite without help for the liturgist at the points where one might expect this to be given and is in general a rather summary production. The homilies on Hebrews, which someone copied or wrote up after his death from the notes that he had left, have one valuable insight into what he thought about the Eucharist as a sacrifice. Commenting on Heb 13:15 (PG 63:229) he says, ' The Jews offered sheep and oxen ; we offer nothing like this but instead the Eucharist and the copying in all things, as far as possible, of what Christ did. That is the fruit of our lips. . . . Let us offer such a sacrifice to Him that He may offer it to the Father. Not otherwise is offering made save through the Son ; yes, and also through a heart that is contrite.' It would be reasonable to look for signs of this association of the contrite heart with the *mimesis* of Christ's action in any liturgy which claimed to be Chrysostom's. In *hom*. 17 on Heb (PG 63:133) Chrysostom compares the proclamation of the *Sancta sanctis* before communion to what happened at the Olympic games, when a herald came forward to warn off the competitors who were not properly qualified. He says that the priest raised his hand high in the air. This seems to have been an Elevation of the Host, for such an Elevation is found in the liturgy of the Armenians at this point, a liturgy which was reorganized by St John Mantaguni in the 5th cent. on the basis (according to tradition) of the liturgy of Chrysostom. Still stressing the sinfulness of the worshipper, Chrysostom comments on Heb 9:28 (PG 63:129) that at the Eucharist we say, ' Whether we have sinned deliberately or without deliberation, give us pardon '. These words are not found in the liturgy of Chrysostom just as they stand, but there is a phrase in the *proskomide* (ascribed in the Barberini codex to Chrysostom himself) where pardon is asked ' for our sins and for the ignorant deeds of the people '.

III The theological interest of the liturgy of Chrysostom was said by Edmund Bishop (in a note attached to Connolly's edition of the *Liturgical Homilies of Narsai*) to be that he changed the emphasis at the Eucharist from a motif of thanksgiving and praise to one of fear and dread. Bishop claimed that there was no trace of fear and dread in Serapion or the Cappadocians and that it came in through Chrysostom and through Antioch, being a religious trait of West Syria. This was an over-simplification, for it did not notice that the keynote of Serapion is that of reconciliation (expressed in the great cry that comes between the two con-secrations, in the post-communion and in the prayer for ordaining priests), while in the liturgy of Basil there is a petition before the *Pater noster*, 'that we may dare, with full freedom and without con-demnation, to say . . .', and the six-winged Seraphim who cover their faces are commemorated at the *Sanctus*. The change is only that Chrysostom has found a word (φρικώδης) which sums up and makes explicit what was implied in earlier works. Long before any of these writers there is in the *Traditio apostolica* a direction about showing care for the consecrated elements, while the purpose of Christ's death is said to be, 'that He might set free from their passion those that believe in Thee'.

One great difference between 'Chrysostom' and Basil is at the *Epiklesis*, Basil asking that the Spirit 'may bless, hallow and consecrate', while 'Chryso-stom' says directly, 'make this the Body of Christ, transforming it by the Spirit', and the same is repeated for the chalice. This is at once much more downright and at the same time much more like the language of transubstantiation. 'Chrysostom' does not give the Lord's command, 'Do this in com-memoration of Me' after the words of institution, but starts the *anamnesis* with the phrase, 'Being mindful therefore of Thy salvific command and of all that was done for us, Thy death and burial . . .', while Basil gave the command and then continued, 'Mindful of Thy salvific passion and death . . .'. It would seem that 'Chrysostom' is here a shorten-ing of Basil. Again, at the end of the *anamnesis*, the elaborate phrase that is devoted to the Second Coming in Basil has disappeared in 'Chrysostom', which goes to show that not all the fearsome con-siderations are the invention of the later liturgist.

'Chrysostom' has two mentions of the Blessed Virgin, an *ekphonesis* in the Intercessions and a second mention in the post-communion. For the purpose of comparison the liturgy of Basil cannot in the first of these instances be used with any con-fidence, for at that point the Barberini codex has a gap which cannot be filled by any other MS. of comparable age. In the post-communion, where comparison is possible, the liturgy of Basil has no mention of Our Lady, and thus the phrase in 'Chrysostom' (from which is derived the familiar Latin prayer *Precibus et meritis beatae Mariae semper virginis* . . .) may with some hesitation be claimed as perhaps the first instance of a Mariological prayer in the Eucharist.

Our curious fact has been noted about the Syriac liturgy of the XII Apostles (from which 'Chryso-stom' is thought by many to have been derived) ; at the consecration of the chalice it speaks of Christ mixing wine and water and tasting of it before He gave to the disciples. This is omitted in 'Chryso-stom', but James of Edessa attributes to Chrysostom the words, 'He drank from His blood which He gave to the disciples to drink'. In this Syriac liturgy, for which we have MSS going back to the 10th cent., it is notable that the *epiklesis* asks at great length that the Eucharist may be to those who receive it a means of confidence before the dread judgment-seat of Christ. All of this is omitted in 'Chrysostom' (another sign of his not being pre-occupied by fear and dread) and in general the omissions practised are such as one might expect from an orator who was accustomed to listen for the balance of a sentence and the rhythm of a paragraph. One cannot be sure that John Chryso-stom *did* make this liturgy out of the anaphora of the *XII Apostles* which he had known in Antioch, but if he did, it would not be surprising, nor would the later popularity of this simple and harmonious liturgy be any the more difficult to understand.

Bibliography. For the text of the liturgy of Chrysostom : *C. Swainson, *Greek Liturgies* (1884) has still to be used, pending the publication of a critical edition of the Barberini codex ; the recon-struction by Brightman in *Liturgies Eastern and Western* (1896) is at some points unsatisfactory. H. Engberding OSB, 'Die syrische Anaphora der zwölf Apostel', in *Oriens christianus* 34 (1937) 213-247 ; A. Raes SJ, 'L'Authenticité de la liturgie byzantine de s. Jean Chrysostome', in OCP 24 (1958) 5-16 ; I. Rahmani, *Les Liturgies orientales et occidentales* (1929) ; P. de Meester OSB, in DAC VI (s.v. GRECQUES, LITURGIES) and in a commemorative volume for the centenary of Chrysostom issued in Rome in 1908 entitled Χρυσοστομικά (but work done so long ago is now somewhat antiquated, save for the article on the Armenian liturgy) ; *F. Bright-man, 'The Historia Mystagogica and the Byzantine Liturgy' in JTS 9 (1908) 248-67, 387-97 ; H. Codrington, *The Liturgy of St Peter* (1936).

J. H. C.

C

CAELESTIUS. *See* PELAGIUS.

CAJETAN, INFLUENCE OF Thomas de Vio was born at Gaieta (whence his name ' Caietanus ') in the kingdom of Naples in 1469. He became a Dominican in 1484, studied at Bologna and Padua, lectured at the latter as Bachelor in 1493, and wrote there his treatise *De Ente et Essentia*. He held a chair of theology at Pavia in 1497 (*De Nominum Analogia* (1498)) and Milan, 1499. Going to Rome as Procurator General of his Order in 1501, he was elected Master General in 1508, was created Cardinal of Saint Sixtus in 1517, and given the see of Gaeta in 1519. He died in 1534 and was buried in the precincts of the Minerva at Rome.

Cajetan's administrative career was diversified by various missions in the service of the Church, but his theological writing was never more intently and voluminously carried on than when he was busiest with more immediately practical matters. In 1511–1512 he was occupied, in different ways, with the pseudo-council of Pisa and the fifth council of the Lateran, the former occasioning two works on papal authority. In 1518 he was charged to summon Luther before him at Augsburg, an event followed by a series of treatises relevant to the reformer's doctrines. Meanwhile the years 1507–22 saw also the writing of the commentary on St Thomas's *Summa Theologica*. As the Leonine Edition of this contains also Cajetan's work, included at the instance of Leo XIII, it will be well to say something of its scope and method.

Noting that the text of St Thomas is found even by his followers to have an appearance of ease which is deceptive, and on the other hand that many celebrated theologians, and chiefly Scotus, have concentrated on attacking particularly the *Prima Pars*, Cajetan determines not to be content with straightforward exposition, but on occasion to raise doubtful points and to defend what he considers to be the truth. In so doing he does not intend to complicate with subtleties a work designed for beginners ; he means rather to purify and improve the tradition of interpretation, and gain recruits to St Thomas's teaching by clarifying it. ' Doctrina haec in Italia satis dormit, et tamen opportuna est valde ' (Prologue to 1–2ae). Additions are to be ' not what is greater but what is later ' (Prologue to I). The result is acknowledged to be a major enrichment of the Thomist tradition, always careful and thorough, extremely well ordered, often dry—' a rose in Cajetan ' has become proverbial—but at times rising to passages of great power and insight.

Fruitful commentary on the moral part of the *Summa* needs further gifts, and Cajetan's practical knowledge of the springs of human action stands him in good stead here. Yet the same grasp of principle beneath the letter, for which he repeatedly pleads against formalism, is dominant in the *Secunda Pars* as elsewhere. These were the qualities which enabled Cajetan, more than any other, to transmit Thomism as a living way of thought to the new age. The commentaries on Scripture to which he chiefly devoted the last twelve years of his life have also had their influence, though the strong impress of the critical methods and views of Erasmus render them more easily appreciated nowadays than in his own time.

Bibliography. P. Mandonnet, Cajétan, DTC col. 1313–29 ; *Revue Thomiste*, N.S. XVII (1934–5) : Cajétan (commemorative number containing especially : P. Congar : Bio-bibliographie, pp. 3–49) ; also a commemorative number of the *Rivista di Filosofia Neo-scolastica* (Milan 1935) ; recent editions from the Collegium Angelicum, Rome, are : *De comparatione auctoritatis Papae et Concilii* (1930) ; *De Nominum Analogia* (1952) ; *Opuscula Oeconomico-Socialia* (1934) ; *Comm. in Porphyrii Isagogen* (1934) ; *Comm. in De Anima* Vol. I–II (1938) ; *Comm. in Praedicamenta* (1939) ; V. Pollet : *De Caietani scripto ' Ad septemdecim quesita responsiones '*. Angelicum 14 (1937) 538–59. I. T.

CALVINISM is the theological system inspired by the Reformer John Calvin (1509–64). This article comprises (I) the life of Calvin, (II) the origins of Calvinism, (III) the meaning of theology (IV) and mystery in that system, (V) its relation to Lutheranism, (VI) its treatment of salvation, (VII) predestination, (VIII) sanctification and (IX) tradition. (X) Contrasts with Catholicism are seen in the Calvinist treatment of the Person of Christ, (XI) the idea of revelation and (XII) of the Church.

I John Calvin. Calvin was the second son of Gérard Cauvin (the family name was latinized as Calvinus, and then turned into French as Calvin), a notary and ecclesiastical lawyer of Noyon in Picardy. John was born at Noyon on 10 July 1509, twenty-five years junior to Luther. In May 1521, he received the tonsure and was granted a modest benefice in the cathedral of Noyon. He never proceeded to Orders. His early schooling was received in the household of the noble family of Hangest de Montmor, and in the Collège des Capettes at Noyon.

He went to Paris with his patron's children in Aug. 1523. He attended first the Collège de la Marche, where he had as master his future disciple, Mathurin Cordier. In 1526 he moved to the Collège de Montaigu, where Erasmus had studied.

In the same year the famous Scottish theologian, John Major, returned to Paris and to the Collège de Montaigu. In Sept. 1527, Calvin was given the benefice of St Martin de Marteville.

He left Paris for Orleans and the study of law on 29 Jan. 1528, four days before a mature student, Inigo de Loyola, enrolled in the College he had just left. At Orleans Calvin had a relative, Pierre Robert, known as Olivétan, who was to translate the OT into French. He also came under the influence of the Lutheran Melchior Wolmar, who introduced him to the Greek of the NT. In July 1529, he exchanged his benefice for that of Pont-l'Évêque near Noyon, where his father had been born. In the autumn he moved to Bourges to continue his study of the law under Andrea Alciati. At Bourges he found a Lutheranizing circle of scholars.

His father died in May 1531, excommunicate as a result of quarrels with the chapter of Noyon. John Calvin's brother, an ex-priest, was to die similarly excommunicate in 1537. In the year of his father's death Calvin moved to Paris and lodged in the Collège Fortet. Here he continued the study of Greek under Pierre Danès and began Hebrew under François Vatable. In the following year he published a commentary on Seneca's *De Clementia*. He returned for a space to Orleans, and then after a visit to Noyon retraced his steps to Paris, in 1533. It was about this time that he made the acquaintance of the aged Catholic humanist, Jacques Lefèvre d'Étaples (Faber Stapulensis), the translator of the Bible into French (NT 1523, OT 1528), and Gérard Roussel.

As a result of a heresy-hunt occasioned by an oration of his friend Nicholas Cop, Rector of the University of Paris, he retired to Noyon but soon returned to Paris. In the new year he was the guest of Louis du Tillet, canon of Angoulême, and spent what was probably a formative period among his books. During this time he paid a visit to Nérac, where Lefèvre (who never joined the Reform) was living under the patronage of Queen Margaret of Navarre, a key figure in the spread of Lutheran ideas.

On 4 May 1534 he resigned his chaplaincy at Noyon and his benefice at Pont-l'Évêque, thereby marking formally his break with Rome. Towards the end of the month he was arrested and suffered two short terms of imprisonment, but the charges against him were dropped. He returned for a time to Paris, where there occurred on 17–18 Oct. the 'affaire des Placards', which provoked anti-Lutheran reprisals under royal patronage. After some journeyings he finally set out with du Tillet for Basle and safety.

In March 1536 appeared the first edition of his masterpiece, *Christianae religionis Institutio*, with a prefatory letter to Francis I dated 23 Aug. 1535. This edition was a brief manual of Christian doctrine in six chapters. From its first appearance it was continually being revised, until by 1559 it had grown to eighty chapters in four books in its final Latin edition.

In April 1536, Calvin paid a short visit to the court of Renée, Duchess of Ferrara, cousin of Queen Margaret of Navarre. On his way back, finding himself unable to reach Strassburg because of the war between Francis I and Charles V, he made his way to Lyons and so to Geneva, making for Basle. At Geneva he was importuned by Guillaume Farel to settle there. Geneva was by then wholly under the influence of Reform. His decision to stay was epoch-making.

In 1538, as a result of a dispute over the liturgical use of leavened bread, he was banished along with Farel. After a visit to Berne and Zürich, Calvin settled in Strassburg, where he met Martin Bucer. In 1540 he married Idelette de Bure, who died nine years later.

He finally returned to Geneva on 13 Sept. 1541. Here he established a theocracy, fully equipped with a thorough-going inquisition with a grim record of executions and banishments. It was here that he died, on 27 May 1564.

II Origins of Calvinism. The origin and development of Calvin's system before his break with Rome still remain obscure. It would seem that, like Lefèvre and many others, he was in favour of a spiritual reformation without a decisive break. But the break, when it did come, could not have been unheralded. He himself wrote of a ' sudden conversion ', but it was more probably a rapid fusion of ideas after prolonged deliberation. This explanation harmonizes with the very multiplicity of theories advanced by specialists in their search for a dominant principle underlying his development.

The study of theology in the ivory tower of du Tillet's library might have produced an ineffectual theorist, but in the case of Calvin it may well have been the necessary stimulus for his genius for synthesis. Yet he had had little formal theological training, perhaps less even than Luther. What background he possessed was a threadbare scholasticism. In the twilight of medieval theology he produced his masterpiece.

Had he lived in another age and with a different intellectual background, a new system might have dominated Catholic theology. As it was, his vision of God was cramped only by the context in which it evolved : an effete Nominalism, and reaction against Luther and Zwingli. There were other strands in the texture of his thought—Augustinianism, Scotism, French humanism—but they are more elusive.

III The Meaning of Theology. There has been some confusion in the interpretation of Calvin from a tendency to treat him as a scholastic theologian employing the methods of traditional theology. Calvin's approach to theology is entirely different from that of the systematic theologian. For him theology is not the study of ideas about God. Its object is God Himself.

In this sense he is much more a mystical theologian —or an OT prophet—than a scholastic. At the heart of his system lies the surpassing mystery of God Himself. Even when God reveals Himself it is still as the transcendent, inscrutable God that He is revealed. The whole object of Calvin's theology is not to tell us about God but to allow God to reveal Himself to the individual soul.

IV Mystery. At the heart of his theology is the fascination of mystery. For all the highly articulate structure of his teaching it is built round a profoundly mystical awareness of God. For all its forbidding logic there is a compelling power that logic alone could not explain. For all its cold despair of human effort it makes an eloquent appeal to the human heart in its anguished search for God. His theology glows with a luminous awareness of the transcendent majesty of God.

This element in the evolution of his theology may be traced immediately to the vague mysticism that found expression in Lefèvre and the school of Meaux. This pre-Lutheran French movement of reform may have been the seed-ground in which the ideas of Luther struck firm root and grew up into the sturdy growth of Calvinism. Luther himself owed much to the mystics of the Rhineland, inspired by Eckhart and Tauler.

Whatever its origin, this strain of mysticism is the real key to Calvinism. Without it the twin sources of Calvin's power over men—the systematic manual of instruction and the rigid organization of church discipline—would have commanded respect but inspired no enthusiasm.

The mystical element explains also the power of survival of Calvinism. Much of Calvin's teaching—notably his doctrine of predestination—was later abandoned or modified. What survived owed its continued existence to its mystical appeal. The great contemporary revival of Calvinism, Karl Barth's *The Theology of the Word of God*, owes its vigour to this ' dark vision ' of God. The first principle of neo-Calvinism is the ' otherness ' of a God so transcendent that there exists on man's side no path to His Presence, even by natural religion. Barthianism has led to a fresh examination of Calvin, thrown a flood of light on his theology, and given a new impetus to his teaching. The study of Calvin has been revolutionized by Barth.

V Calvin and Luther. Calvinism is a development within the heart of Lutheranism. In the event it was bitterly opposed to the parent system, chiefly on account of its different ecclesiastical organization, and it made gigantic strides at the expense of the older doctrine. But the main principle of both is the same : the movement to God comes wholly from God.

This is, of course, a Catholic principle, embodying the necessity and sovereignty of grace. With Luther it is interpreted in the context of man's utter incapacity to cooperate with grace. For him God is the exclusive author of salvation.

Calvin adopts Luther's principle, but corrects what he sees as a false emphasis in it. For Luther the main psychological interest is in man and his salvation. With Calvin the centre of interest shifts back to God. Where God does anything for man,

it is really for God's glory. The movement from God goes back wholly to God.

Calvin corrects Luther's *sola gratia, sola fide* (salvation is wholly from God, and faith is its necessary condition) by adding to it his own *soli Deo gloria* (glory is due to God alone). This principle of Calvin's, it may be noted, is incorporated in the teaching of the Vatican Council : God is *rerum omnium principium et finis*, the origin and final cause of all things (D 1785).

VI Salvation. For Calvin as for Luther salvation is essentially a mystery, something surpassing reason and imagination. The anomalies of their teaching are, in consequence, not contradictions but parts of the mystery. In illustration of this we may instance Calvin's doctrine of the Real Presence of Christ in the Eucharist. Reacting strongly against Luther's explanation of the Real Presence by means of the omnipresence of Christ, Calvin preferred to give no explanation of the manner in which the Eucharist communicates to us Christ's Body and Blood, and treated it as a mystery which human understanding cannot pierce. In a similar way the Lutheran and Calvinist doctrine of justification, according to which a sinner is made just and yet remains a sinner, is absorbed into their teaching without embarrassment, a relic of Nominalism.

Calvin takes over Luther's views on the meaning of salvation. Human nature was totally corrupted at the Fall. Original sin is not the loss of supernatural life but the disintegration of something basically natural, a right relation to God. There is no way of restoration save through trust in the saving merits of Christ. These are applied to us through Redemption, but because of our corruption through original sin they cannot effect any inward change in us. Justification (grace) is extrinsic : it is God's favour extended to us because of Christ.

Calvin goes further than Luther in his teaching on the certainty of salvation. Grace once given cannot be lost. To be justified is to be one of the elect. Because it is due to an eternal decree of God, election is irreversible.

VII Predestination. The doctrine of predestination, commonly assumed to be the distinctive teaching of Calvin, is simply a more developed presentation of Luther's teaching. It fits in more logically with Calvin's preoccupation with the transcendence of God. Since God cannot be influenced by any human choice, and since grace is gratuitous, God must decree from all eternity, without reference to the use of free-will, that certain souls shall be saved, and others damned. This doctrine is, of course, completely different from the Catholic view, which upholds man's freedom and responsibility even where it asserts God's omnipotence (*see* GRACE).

VIII Sanctification. Justification in Calvin's system leads on to sanctification. Although good works cannot be in any sense meritorious, the fruit of justification is sanctification, which extends to the whole of life. As faith implies continued obedience to God throughout life, in the same way justification implies continued and life-long sanctification.

Viewed from a psychological standpoint, this doctrine might encourage reckless presumption. If election is certain and cannot be undone, good works are strictly irrelevant to the spiritual condition of the elect. So far, however, from inducing presumption, the notion of election seems to have been in Calvin's mind a guarantee of humility and right conduct.

IX Scripture and Tradition. We turn now to what is distinctive in the teaching of Calvin. The central point of his own contribution to theology is the Person of Christ. Calvin goes behind the Church and the Bible to Christ. This means that for him the written Word is not a source of dogma, which in any case is for him a secondary consideration, but it is a witness to Christ. There is in consequence little room speculatively for a teaching Church. The Word of God is the Person of God the Son. Faith is trust in a Person, not an intellectual assent to truth. Calvin's preoccupation is with Christ, not with the teaching Church, nor with Scripture as a source of dogma. Scripture and Tradition are both subordinate to Christ.

X Christ and History. The mystery of Christ in Calvin's teaching might have proved an enrichment of theology. In fact it is an impoverishment. It has been given a new emphasis in Barthian theology, but there has been no gain in depth. Calvinism and neo-Calvinism alike ignore an essential dimension of the Pauline 'mystery' in repudiating the Church as part of its fullness. For the Calvinist the work of Christ in history is narrowed down to the unique act of Redemption.

The Redemption in this view is an episode only in human history, terminated by the Ascension of Christ. The ascended Lord gathers up His Church as His Body, uniting it to Himself. But He no longer acts in history. Christ in His heavenly life is outside history.

On this view the whole economy of Redemption, the Incarnation itself, is an episode only, having no continuing influence on history. The mystery of Christ is isolated from His Mystical Body, the Church. The reality of the Church is thus removed from this earth and centred wholly in heaven. The saving acts of Christ are no longer active in history, but only through their union with the heavenly life of Christ. The ministry of the Church exists only in what Karl Barth calls the 'new time', the continuity of the new creation in indissoluble union with the eternal God.

There is therefore no real relation between Christ and history apart from His life on earth. There is, it is true, a kind of historical continuity through God's action downwards—an ever-new breaking in of the creative Word by means of the charismatic ministry of the Spirit, not through the continuing ministry of the Apostolic Church. There is no place for the sacramental ministry of the priesthood. There is room only for the prophetical function, a charismatic ministry through the arbitrary and unpredictable intervention of God in history. Reduced

to its last analysis, this view of God's action in history is in fact a denial of any abiding Covenant between God and man.

XI Calvin and the 'Mystery' Theologians. In spite of profound differences in other directions, there is a surprising affinity between Calvin's central 'insight' and the modern Catholic theological movement associated with the late Dom Odo Casel, 'theologian of the Mystery'. It will be useful at this point to summarize Catholic teaching on the mystery of Christ.

For the Catholic the mystery of Christ is one global mystery comprising Revelation and Redemption. Revelation was given once and for all in Christ the Word of God. Redemption was achieved once and for all in Christ the Redeemer. Everything has been done on the part of Christ, the one Mediator between God and man, except in so far as He has chosen to associate His Church with Him as the instrumental means of communicating Redemption. The central and surpassing mystery of Christ comprises also the 'extension' of the Incarnation which is the Church.

The ultimate aim of Revelation and Redemption is the glorification of God in Christ as the Head of His Church. There is therefore a continuing process of Redemption through the Church. Hence the true meaning of eschatology is not limited, as it has been limited by Protestant scholars, to final judgment, but is that of a beginning of a climactic process which will culminate in the final glorification of Christ in His Church. The Church is Christ's Body, working in and through history, and destined to share His triumph as the Kingdom of glory (*see* BODY, MYSTICAL).

Revelation and Redemption have to be communicated. Seen in the mind of God, both are vital and continuing processes, not static and unique events. They are communicated through the Word (Revelation) and through the sacraments (Redemption), through faith (the response to Revelation) and through justification (a real communication of the divine life).

Calvinism, as Protestantism generally, stresses the one-way character of Redemption : those who are redeemed are enfolded in the Mystery of Christ without really sharing in the Mystery. Thus it limits the Mystery to the Cross and the historical events of Christ's life ; in a word, it by-passes the Church. The meaning of Revelation as a function of the Church loses in depth : it is scaled down to mean little more than the sermon, instead of the whole activity of the Church's witness to Christ's Gospel.

XII Calvin's Doctrine of the Church. In spite of this central weakness Calvin's doctrine of the Church retains a good deal of Catholic teaching. It might even be that some rapprochement between Calvinism and Catholic doctrine might begin with the theology of the 'Mystery'. The neo-Calvinist Karl Barth is more susceptible of a Catholic interpretation than is generally realized.

For Calvin, as for the Catholic, the Church is a

visible society. There is but one Church, the true Church, and it is visible. Outside the Church there is no salvation : God has so decreed it. The Church in a fuller sense is also the assembly of the Elect People, so that as known to God the Church is the total number of the elect.

Christ alone is Lord of the Church, a Catholic doctrine that issues in Calvinism with an undertone of the rejection of Papal authority. But in its primary affirmation the statement is wholly Catholic: the Church is the steward of the Gospel and may not exploit it for its own ends.

For Calvin it is not the visible Church that is spotless. He rejects fiercely the idea of a sinless Church. False brethren may exist in it. This is partly Catholic doctrine in so far as the Church embraces both saints and sinners. But in regard to the purity of the Church's teaching, the Catholic view is that in its proclamation of the Word entrusted to it the Church cannot err. For Calvin the Church may err in doctrine, though he did attempt to specify the points of fundamental doctrine that are necessary for salvation, and on which presumably the Church is infallible.

Since there is only one true Church, there is needed a criterion for discovering it and differentiating it from the spurious Church, the harlot. Calvin rejects as inadequate certain criteria. The Church for him is not identified merely by size : even in the Roman Church there existed a ' body ' of Christians ; nor by piety, for the Church is the means of grace, not constituted by grace. His positive criterion is the due preaching of the Word and the proper administration of the sacraments.

Is this an ultimate criterion or does it require further specification ? In order to ascertain what is true doctrine and what are true sacraments, one has to invoke some other norm. Traditionally, it has been the Vincentian canon, the appeal to tradition, to the belief of the universal Church. An absolute norm becomes especially urgent in the case not of heresy but of schism. Two Churches may agree in doctrine and yet be cut off from each other's communion. Calvin would agree that schism is sinful : the only justification for it in his eyes would be the complete disintegration of doctrine in the other Church : in other words, heresy.

But what would be the norm for discerning the true Church where the only division is schism ? A Catholic would appeal to the principle of visible unity in adhering to the successor of St Peter. Calvin would be unable to resolve the dilemma. Even in the case of heresy Calvin's criterion is scarcely satisfactory. For him tradition has no value. The only norm is Scripture, or rather Christ. But such a norm tends ultimately to be subjective if one subordinates the authority of the Church to one's own interpretation of Scripture or of the mind of Christ.

Bibliography. *H. Beveridge (tr.): *Institutes* (1845, reissued 1949) ; *Calvin's Tracts and Treatises* (ed. *T. F. Torrance), 1958 (in progress) ; *D. W. and T. F. Torrance (tr.) : *Calvin's Commentaries*, 1959 (in progress) ; *W. Niesel, *The Theory of Calvin* (tr. H. Knight) (1956) ; *T. H. L. Parker, *The Doctrine of the Knowledge of God* (A Study in the Theology of John Calvin) (1952) ; *T. F. Torrance, *Calvin's Doctrine of Man* (1949) ; *R. S. Wallace, *Calvin's Doctrine of the Word and Sacraments* (1953); *Calvin's Doctrine of the Christian Life* (1959) ; *H. Quistorp, *Calvin's Doctrine of the Last Things* (1955); L. Bouyer, *The Spirit and Forms of Protestantism* (tr. A. V. Littledale) (1956).   J. Q.

CANDLEMAS This article is an attempt to extract some theology out of the unpromising material of the ritual of the blessing of candles on the feast of the Purification, 2 Feb. After a short section (I) on the supposed pagan antecedents of the feast, there will be (II) an account of its history, followed by (III) some theological conclusions, and ending with a brief survey (IV) of the patristic sermons for the occasion.

I. It is often said that the Christians began this feast as a counter to the Roman *Lupercalia*, which were held on 15 Feb. As the feast seems to have started in the East and not to have been known in the West at any time when paganism was a menace, this claim is hard to substantiate. The Eastern date of the feast was indeed 15 Feb., but the Lupercal was not kept in the East, and, by the time the feast reached the West, its date was, as now, 2 Feb. Another view, put forward in a 10th-cent. sermon, was that the *Amburbale* (which was held at Rome every five years at the beginning of Feb.) had to be countered by a Christian feast. Dom de Bruyne, who found and published this document, was inclined to accept it as true, but it really cannot be much more than a bit of reconstruction—of which there was a good deal during the Carolingian Renaissance—based on no more than scraps of surviving classical learning imperfectly understood. The gap between an annual and a quinquennial feast is hard to bridge. Augustine (*Civ. Dei* 7:7 ; CSEL 40:312) speaks of a ' a sacred cleansing which they call *Februus* ', but that was at the Terminalia, which fell at the end of the month. More plausible is it to say that the Celtic quarter-day which came between Samhain (1 Nov.) and Beltane (1 May) affected the feast when it was kept in the far West.

II The feast of the Presentation of Our Lord in the Temple was kept at Jerusalem on 14 or 15 Feb. in the 4th cent. This appears from the evidence of the Armenian *Lectionary* (published by Conybeare in 1905, *Rituale Armenorum*, 518) and from the narrative of the pilgrim Etheria. She says, ' The fortieth day after the Epiphany is celebrated here with the very highest honour ; on that day there is a procession, in which all take part, at the Anastasis ; everything is carried out in order and with immense joy as if it was Easter. In addition, all the priests hold forth and then the bishop, treating of that passage in the gospel where Joseph and Mary took the Lord on the fortieth day to the Temple . . . and after everything that is customary has been completed, the sacred mysteries are performed and there is the dismissal.' In the Armenian *Lectionary*, 'the fortieth day from the birth of Our Lord', which the two MSS assign to 14 and 15 Feb. respectively, is said to have as its scripture-portions Gal 3:24–9 and Lk 2:22–40. Elsewhere in the *Lectionary* the portions given (for Lent) are the same as those used by Cyril in his *Catecheses* and must therefore go back to the middle of the 4th cent. Etheria (the Spanish nun) made her pilgrimage at an uncertain date near the end of the 4th cent.

The sense of this festival seems (particularly if one regards the choice of the lesson to be read) to have been a celebration of the official taking over of the Temple by Christ on His first approach to it ; up to now, Moses and the prophets, henceforth grace and truth through Jesus Christ. The day is chosen because of the Levitical law of purification but there is no suggestion that the feast is kept in honour of the Purification of Our Lady. The Introit psalm used was Ps 97 (Vulgate numbering) with the refrain : ' All the ends of the earth have seen the salvation of our God '. The concluding verses of this psalm : ' Rejoice before the face of the Lord, for He is coming to judge the earth ', may not have been without significance in giving the feast a note of looking-forward to the Parousia, a note which will be encountered in the later evolution of the feast.

It must be quite clear that when the Church in various places takes up the practice of celebrating the birth of Christ on 25 Dec., the date of this feast of the Presentation would automatically be moved forward to 2 (or 3) Feb. Now, if it be said that the purpose of introducing the feast in the West was to combat the pagan influence of the Lupercalia (15 Feb.) or of the Parentalia (13 Feb.), as Baumstark and others argued, it is obvious that this introduction must have been made before the West started to keep Christmas on 25 Dec. Forty days on from 25 Dec. brings us to 2 Feb., on which day there was no annual counter-attraction in Roman paganism. The birthday of Hercules on 1 Feb. does not seem to have excited much interest even in the heyday of paganism, let alone in the decline. Now while there are various opinions about the date of the change in the West from 6 Jan. to 25 Dec. for the birthday of Our Lord, it seems safe to say that 336 is the last possible year in which the change could have taken place (*see* CHRISTMAS). Absolutely speaking, it could be held that a feast on 2 Feb. would be a check to Catholics joining in pagan rites on 15 Feb., but very strong reasons would have to be produced to make one think this true ; usually (as in the example of the recent feast of St Joseph on 1 May) the same day has to be chosen or a day immediately before or after. It is to be noted further that the main incidence of the temptation to forsake Christian for pagan rites was after the middle of the 4th cent., when in the face of a Church divided by Arianism a pagan revival was staged on the senatorial level in Rome.

Evidence for the spread of the feast from Jeru-

salem is scanty and hard to evaluate. Early in the 6th cent. Severus of Antioch says that it had not been taken up at Antioch (*hom.* 125), though it had at Constantinople. A decree of Justinian of 542 purports to fix its celebration there for 2 Feb., but there is clear evidence that in 602 the feast was still being kept on 14 or 15 Feb. A chronicler (Theophylact Simocatta) happens to record that in 602 the emperor was walking barefoot in the *Hypapante* procession at night when the mob began to throw stones and to riot, but the emperor was able to complete the litany and go into the church of Our Lady (Blachernae) for Mass without interruption. The report shows that the feast had acquired a certain penitential aspect now, which will reappear in Rome, showing that Rome was most probably indebted to Constantinople for the feast. The Roman evidence is this curious entry in the *Liber pontificalis* for the reign of Sergius I (687–701) : ' He laid it down that on the Annunciation of Our Lord, the Dormition and Birthday of the ever-virgin Mary, mother of God, and on the birthday of St Simeon—which is called *Hypapanti* by the Greeks—the processional litany should start from the church of St Hadrian and the people should gather at St Mary Major '.[1] This ruling may be taken to do no more than order a procession on four days in the year (whereas there had previously been a procession on one of them, i.e. on 2 Feb., as Batiffol argued), or it may be held to report the introduction of four new feasts. No one knows. It is perhaps significant for the diffusion of the feast in the West that in the *Gradual* of Monza, the *Sacramentaries* of Gellone, Angoulême, St Gall and Zürich it is styled *Natale S. Symeonis*, as in Rome, while the old Gelasian (*Vat. Reg.* 316) calls it *Purificatio S. Mariae*, and the gospel-book of Würzburg (from about 650) has portions assigned for *die II Februarii* but does not use any title for the day.

Candles are commonly thought to have been introduced into the rite for the feast by a lady named Ikelia who came to live in Palestine in the middle of the 5th cent. and of whom Cyril of Scythopolis wrote, ' The blessed Ikelia, being versed in every practice of piety, first showed how the Hypapante of Our Saviour could be kept with wax-lights ' (TU 49:ii:236). The words used ($\mu\epsilon\tau\grave{\alpha}$ $\kappa\eta\rho\acute{\iota}\omega\nu$) and the run of the sentence imply that Ikelia did no more than bring about the use of candles (by all ? by the laity ?) in a procession of lights which had formerly been confined to lamps carried by official bearers. The nature of a $\acute{\upsilon}\pi\alpha\pi\acute{\alpha}\nu\tau\eta\sigma\iota\varsigma$ or $\acute{\alpha}\pi\acute{\alpha}\nu\tau\eta\sigma\iota\varsigma$ (an official reception of a dignitary) has been investigated by E. Peterson, who showed that the Christians were but taking over a practice used for the emperor or his representative on great occasions ; a procession would advance from the town to meet him, bearing lights and torches ; flowers would be

[1] Constituit autem ut diebus Adnuntiationis Domini, Dormitionis et Nativitatis sanctae Dei genetricis semperque virginis Mariae ac sancti Symeonis, quod Ypapanti Greci appellant, letania exeat a sancto Hadriano et ad sanctam Mariam populus occurrat.

thrown and there would be official rejoicing (cf. Theodoret, HE 5:34:6 ; GCS 44:335). How all this was suited to the Christian feast of Christ's Presentation at the Temple is a theological matter which must now be examined.

III The theology of the feast starts from the words of Malachy (3:1), ' Straightway there shall come to His temple the Lord whom you seek and the messenger of the covenant whom you desire '. The immediacy of Christ's advent to His temple, on the fortieth day after His birth, needed no emphasis for early Christians, and the joyous celebration of this event (noticed by Etheria) was fully justified. The doctrine of the double Advent of Christ (*see* ADVENT) wrought a change of emphasis in the celebration of this going-out-to-meet Christ coming to His temple. Now He was the bridegroom of the Church coming a second time at the end of all things in all His majesty. This time He would come straightway to His Church, and it was fitting for all its members to be ready with lamps in their hands to go out to meet Him. This ὑπαπάντησις (cf. Mt 8:34 ; 25: 1 ; Jn 12:13) was an annual dress rehearsal for the actual event. This idea is well expressed in the prayer of the *Lanalet Pontifical* on this day : ' Grant us, almighty God . . . that, when the Spouse, Thy only-begotten Son, shall come, our lamps may be alight and we may give Him worthy escort '.[1] In *Lanalet* this prayer is followed by the anthem *Adorna thalamum tuum, Sion*, which thus is taken to mean that Christ, the bridegroom, is coming for His bride, the Church. Dom H. Peillon, in his study of this anthem, has shown that one MS., going back to a Roman original of *c.* 750, has the words in Greek and Latin, the Greek being written out in Latin letters as if for singers who knew no Greek but who had to sing in that language.

The same idea of the faithful awaiting the Second Coming is made more emphatic in later French Pontificals of Narbonne and Arles (in Martène, *De antiquis ecclesiae ritibus*, IV:15) where, after the candles are blessed, there is a blessing of new fire and then the deacon has to chant *suppressa voce*, ' *Venite et accendite* ' (' Come and light your candles '), to which the choir answer with the refrain from the parable of the foolish virgins, ' *Aptate vestras lampades : Ecce sponsus venit ; exite obviam Ei* ' (' Trim your lamps. Lo, the bridegroom cometh ; go forth to meet Him '). This is sung three times, on a higher note each time and then the anthems *Lumen ad revelationem* and *Adorna thalamum* follow. Martène dated the *Narbonne Pontifical* about 1100, and he also reported a prayer for blessing candles found in the *Sacramentary* of St Thierry (of *c.* 850), where the prospective aspect of the feast was emphasized. ' Whosoever in this holy temple of Thy glory are decked with the brightness of the lights they hold before them, may all these, when they are cleansed from all stain of

sin, deserve to be presented to Thee in the temple of Thy heavenly dwelling with the fruit of their good works.'[2] The words about ' the holy temple of Thy glory ' survive in modern liturgies, but they have lost their counterpart.

The *ordo Romanus antiquus* printed by Hittorp gives what is clearly a compound service for the blessing of candles, some of the prayers being borrowed from those for the Paschal candle, while the rest are found in the very early set of *Benedictiones* of the *Lanalet Pontifical*, which *Pontifical* has, however, the notable singularity that it gives the prayer cited above which speaks of the Second Coming and the *occursus Domini*. This prayer is not found elsewhere (save in the later English *Missal* of Jumièges) and may be a product of the British Isles. When one examines the attempts made to adapt in various ways a Nativity-Preface to make it serve for Candlemas, attempts that can be followed through the fragments of several *Sacramentaries* of 750–850, most of them in Insular script, it does seem that the feast was being propagated widely at that time in the Celtic and Anglo-Saxon missions. As all trace of the feast is lacking in Spanish sources, it may be thought that it was a local British or Irish foreboding about the Second Coming (for which *see* ADVENT) which elaborated the theology of this feast (cf. also Bede, in PL 90:351 for the same idea).

The Preface for the feast in its Irish form (JTS 9 (1908) 414) speaks of Christ as, ' consummator of the mystery, at the same time the one who made the Law and saw that it was kept. He gave the command and obeyed it Himself ; He was born unto the likeness of our miseries, rich in His own nature but poor in ours. He, the owner of heaven and earth, scarce contrived to present for the offering the pair of turtles or the two young pigeons. To-day was He carried in the feeble arms of aged Simeon, and there was given to Him the prophetic utterance of the widow who acclaimed Him and bore witness, it being most fit that both sexes should proclaim Him since He was the saviour of both.'[3] As consummator of the mystery of His Presentation Christ would come again to His Church as the first act of His Second Coming, but meanwhile both sexes should praise Him for His lowliness. The part of Our Lady in the mystery is scarcely noticed in this Preface, in any of its forms.

The idea of purification seems to come from the application of the OT rules of the segregation of women after childbirth to Christian lands. The Church has from time to time been beset with waves of what can only be called Judaizing influence,

---

[1] Quaesumus, omnipotens Deus, . . . ut venienti Sponso Filio tuo unigenito accensis lampadibus nostris dignum praestemus occursum : per Dominum.

[2] Quicunque in templo sancto gloriae Tuae praesentium luminum adornantur lucernis, omnium vitiorum contagiis expiati, in templo caelestis habitationis Tuae cum fructu bonorum operum Tibi valeant praesentari.

[3] . . . consummatorque mysterii, idem legislator et custos, praecipiens et obediens ; qui natus est in similitudinem passionum nostrarum, dives in suo, pauper in nostro ; par turturum vel duos pullos columbarum sacrificio vix sufficit caeli et terrae possessor ; hodie grandaevi Symeonis invalidis gestatur in manibus ; accedit confitentis et testificantis oraculum viduae, quoniam deccebat ut ab utroque annuntiaretur sexu utriusque salvator.

attempts being made to bring back this or that part of the ceremonial law which was abrogated by the coming of Christ. Denis of Alexandria provides an early example of trouble being caused by the OT ideas about uncleanness (*Works*, edited by Feltoe, 103). The Pastoral Letter of an Egyptian bishop (dating from before 300) has been found recently on papyrus (*Papyrus Rylands* III, 469), which warns Christians against certain Manichean rites. Gregory the Great wrote to Augustine of Canterbury on the point (in Bede, HE 1:27) saying that if a mother came into the church to give thanks in the very hour when she had given birth, she was not incurring any stain of sin thereby. This papal response was frequently appealed to, by St Boniface, by Nicholas I and Innocent III, when zeal for the OT law showed signs of reappearing. The Church survived such anticipations of Puritanism, but they left their mark on this feast. The lessons at Matins in the Breviary (in the 1st Nocturn), where Leviticus and not Malachy is read, are a sign of this. The penitential element in the feast (witnessed by the Pope going barefoot and in black vestments (hence our modern violet ones) in the Procession, according to the 9th cent. *Ordo S. Amandi*) may have come from the same influence. It can be found at Constantinople in 602 (where the emperor walked barefoot) in a *milieu* which was receptive of OT ideas, but it is in complete contrast with the gladness of the original feast as reported by Etheria. It may also be suspected that the term *Quadragesima natalis Domini*, originally a simple statement of fact that this was the fortieth day from the birth, was after the introduction of Lent (also called *Quadragesima*) understood to imply that the day was one of penance. For the penetration of these Greek ideas into Anglo-Saxon England one has to look to Naples. The marble calendar of Naples calls 2 Feb. the Purification (the entry reads : PURIF . SCE MARIE SUMEO) and one can see how the early English calendars gradually abandon the term *Ypapanti* for *Purificatio* after the end of the 10th cent. With the change of name went a greater interest in the Mariological aspect of the feast.

IV The many sermons on the Purification found among the works of the Fathers contain much that is theologically important, but they are seldom used because of the difficulty of knowing which are authentic. The line starts with Origen, whose *Homilies on Luke* deal with the gospel story of the Presentation in the Temple. These homilies survive in a Latin version (copies of which seem to have been plentiful in Anglo-Saxon England) with some Greek fragments. In one of these (*frag.* 66 ; GCS 49:255) he comments on the word glory used in Simeon's canticle and says, ' It is glory for those who are on the watch to go out to meet the one they are expecting '. The word used (ἀπάντησις) may have suggested the name for the feast, Hypapante. Elsewhere (*hom.* 14 ; GCS 49:86) he cites the prophet Zacharias (3:3), ' Josue [i.e. Jesus, in the Gk version] was clothed in dirty garments ', and proceeds to apply the text to the Incarnation, at

which Christ took on Him the uncleanness, as distinct from the sin, of humanity, and because of this was obedient to the Law of Moses. Here the ideas of the Preface cited above (*natus est in similitudinem passionum nostrarum*) can be found expressed. The suggestion of homily 15 (GCS 49:93) that we should copy Simeon by taking Jesus in our arms and bearing Him with us joyfully whithersoever we go may have been seen in the Dark Ages as a justification for the missionary carrying the Blessed Sacrament with him in a chrismal on his journeys. The words are quite explicit, ' Let him take Jesus in his hands, put his arms about Him and hold Him to his breast ; and then he may go joyfully where he would '.[1]

The sermon by Cyril of Alexandria (PG 77:1040) is authentic and has an apt use of Is 62:1 for the occasion (My salvation will be kindled as a lamp). This seems to require the presence at Cyril's feast of a procession of *Lampadephoroi*, even if the whole multitude did not carry tapers. As Cyril was speaking before the days of Ikelia it does not seem right to reject as spurious the parallel sermon of Gregory of Nyssa (PG 46:1151–82) on the ground that it speaks (1157) of a lighted procession and therefore cannot be earlier than the time of Ikelia. Gregory of Nazianzen, preaching to the newly baptized (PG 36:425) told them that the candles they now held lighted were a pre-figuring of those they would have when they went out to meet the Bridegroom at His Coming ; it may be that such words as these led to the spread of ideas that linked the Hypapante with the Second Coming.

The sermon ascribed to Methodius (PG 18:348) has been by some transferred to a later namesake who was patriarch of Constantinople in the 9th cent., but it may be that it belongs to a mysterious Methodius of Patara in the 5th, about whom nothing is known. It speaks of how ' the ark of God, having moved from its station at Bethlehem, found rest on the mountains of Sion ' (PG 18:356) ; such language is quite fitted to the 5th cent. A genuine sermon from the same period is that of Abraham of Ephesus (PO 16:448), which confines itself to a simple exegesis of the gospel. The pseudo-Cyril (PG 33:1189), who preached a sermon at Jerusalem about the same time, has, however, an appeal to the daughters of Jerusalem, ' Come out to meet Him. Kindle your lamps brightly from the true Light. Put in good array the garments of your soul for Christ, the Bridegroom. With Sion let us peoples of the Gentiles go forth with lamps in our hands for His *Hypapante*.' Here beyond a doubt are the ideas that reappear in England of the 8th and 9th cents.

The sermon attributed to Fulgentius of Ruspe (PL 65:838–42) was probably the work of Ambrose Autpert in the 8th cent. We are all Simeons, he says, awaiting the Coming of Christ with sobriety and then engulfed with sudden joy. In a chance

---

1 . . . sumat Iesum in manibus suis et circumdet Eum brachiis suis ; totum habeat in sinu suo, et tunc exsultans ire poterit quo desiderat.

remark he shows the development of doctrine which was taking place. 'It is plain to all the faithful that the mother of the Redeemer could not have contracted a stain from the act of giving Him birth.' [1] From this to the medieval arguments about the retrospective value of that maternity for the soul of Mary was but a step.

Bibliography. A summary of the history of the feast, as available in 1930, will be found in Thurston-Butler, *Lives of the Saints : February* (1930) ; more recent studies are : E. Bickersteth, 'John Chrysostom and the early history of the Hypapante', in *Studi bizantini* 8 (1951) 401–4 ; E. Peterson, 'Die Einholung des Kyrios', in *Zeitschrift für systematische Theologie* 7 (1930) 682–702 ; M. Higgins, 'Note on the Purification at Constantinople', in *Archiv für Liturgie* 2 (1952) 81–3 ; *E. Kantorowicz, 'The King's Advent', in *Art Bulletin* 26 (1944) 207–31 ; D. de Bruyne OSB, 'Les Processions de la Chandeleur', in R Ben 34 (1922) 14–26 ; H. Peillon OSB, 'L'Antiphonaire de Pamelius', in R Ben 29 (1912) 411–37 ; E. de Moreau SJ, 'L'Orient et Rome dans la fête du 2 février', in NRT 62 (1935) 5–20 ; A. Dold OSB, 'Ein kostbares Sakramentarfragment', in *Scriptorium* 6 (1952) 260–73.   J. H. C.

CANON OF THE MASS About the time (350–400) that the canon of Scripture was finally promulgated, a semi-fixed text of the Mass in Latin was produced at Rome, called Canon or *Canon actionis*. St Justin's *Apologia prima* (65, 67), supposes free formulation; Hippolytus about 225 wrote a text in Greek as a help for one hard put at improvising (*Traditio Apostolica* 10:5). It is not known when Latin supplanted Greek as the liturgical language at Rome : Bardy held that this took place about 350–60 ; others link it with St Damasus (366–84).

St Ambrose at Milan, 390, cites passages of *Quam oblationem* and *Qui pridie* with consecration forms, and shorter parts of *Unde et, Supra quae* and *Supplices* (*De Sacramentis* 5, 6). This provisional canon of around 400 was altered, it seems, by Innocent I (402–17), Leo the Great (440–61), Gelasius I (492–6), and possibly others. Gregory I (590–604) polished and revised it. It then began : *Vere dignum*, now *Te igitur*, and ended : *omnis honor et gloria : Amen*. The oldest extant copy is probably Bobbio Missal, *c.* 700.

Gregory's version, sent to Charlemagne for general use, was edited by Alcuin, 789. Save for intruded *Amen's*, it has withstood permanent change. But if textually the same, it was strangely transformed as the result of a Frankish practice later adopted by Rome. In this way the Canon, formerly sung or said aloud, came thenceforth to be said secretly, Preface and ending excepted.

Vere dignum, this specifically *eucharistic* element, was mistakenly considered to be the approach to the Canon itself, and detached as Preface. *Te igitur* insists that it is through Jesus Christ, God's Son, that we beg God's acceptance of the sacrificial gifts

[1] Cunctis fidelibus! iquet nequaquam Redemptoris matrem ex Eius nativitate maculam contraxisse.

for Church, pope, bishop, people. A letter of Innocent I to Decentius indirectly witnesses to *Memento, Domine* (*Ep.* 25 ; PL20:553). The 5th-cent. compilation, *Communicantes*, disturbs the structure of the prayer. *Hanc igitur* crystallizes former variant intentions. That the gifts become for us the Body and Blood of Christ is the prayer of *Quam oblationem*.

Qui pridie, Simili modo, the symmetry, richness and gravity of these forms by which transubstantiation is effected, have won universal admiration. That we are mindful of Christ's death, resurrection and ascension, as we await the fruits of the Eucharist, is attested by *Unde et memores*. St Leo I retouched the older *Supra quae* (*Lib. Pont.*, ed. Duchesne, I, 239). An older *Supplices* is also rephrased, the reference to angels being made singular and applied to Christ. The *Memento etiam*, formerly used for *Requiems*, seems to have been inserted by Alcuin. *Nobis quoque* eloquently begs for part and fellowship with God's saints, men and women. *Per quem* was formerly used to bless alms and other objects offered at Mass, which were here hallowed by association with the Eucharist. The final, grand doxology, *Per ipsum*, is closely linked with the 3rd-cent. form Hippolytus wrote in Greek. That the response *Amen* be said by all is recalled by *Mediator Dei* (104).

Bibliography. G. Bardy, *La Question des langues dans l'Église ancienne* (1948) I, 164 ; E. Bishop, 'The Roman Canon', *Liturgica Historica* (1918) 77–115 ; E. Botte, *Le Canon de la messe romain* (1935) ; L. Eizenhöfer, *Canon Missae Romanae* (1954) ; G. Ellard, 'Interpolated Amen's', TS 6 (1945) 380–91 ; J. A. Jungmann, *Missarum Sollemnia* (1952³) I, 63–77 ; II, 127–340 ; J. A. Jungmann, *The Eucharistic Prayer* (1956) ; V. L. Kennedy, *The Saints of the Canon of the Mass* (1938) ; B. Opfermann, 'Die Erforschung d. röm. Messkanons', *Theologie und Glaube*, 44 (1954) 263–79 ; *E. C. Ratcliffe, *The Institution narrative of the Roman 'Canon Missae'* (TU 64, 5 (1957) 64–82).   G. E.

CANON OF THE SCRIPTURES This article will not recapitulate the details of the acceptance by the Church of each book of the canonical Scriptures nor of the rejection of the more promising Apocrypha, as these questions have been dealt with in CCS 11a–18f. It will deal with the theological problem of the Canon, which arises out of the fact that (I) the Canon is a part of revelation, while on the other hand (II) the signs of its early acceptance before the death of the last apostle are not abundant, though they are clearer than is sometimes thought. (III) The manner in which development of this doctrine may be thought to have taken place is variously explained, and some of the theories will be examined.

I The revealed character of the Canon follows from the practice of the Church in requiring its acceptance in a profession of faith (D 995), and from the anathematizing by Trent (D 784) of those who did not accept it. The Church would not be justified in these two acts if the inspiration of the individual books listed in the Canon were not a truth that has been revealed. It is not enough to accept the books by a historical judgment as having been used by the Church as Scripture from the earliest times. Such a historical judgment was, on a low view of the Thirty-nine Articles, held to satisfy Article VI, which called for the acceptance of 'those books of which there never was doubt in the Church'. Thus Harold Browne in his classic work on the Articles, but in more recent times High Church theologians have attempted to interpret the article as equivalent to the Tridentine decree on the Bible.

To an inquirer the Church may present the Gospels and other NT works as historical documents, out of which he may be able to gather for himself something about Christ and His Church (see CHRIST, MISSION OF), but this use is quite another thing from the use of the Scripture within the Church as a God-given source of doctrine. Pagan writings (e.g. those of Tacitus and Pliny) are of use to the inquirer in the same way as the Gospels are, for what they say about Christ, but when once he has accepted (see APOLOGETICS) the credibility of Christ's claims and has bowed his intellect in an act of faith in Christ and His Church, then the Church shows him the Scriptures in a new light which marks them off from all other writings.

II The acceptance by the Church of certain Christian writings alongside and on an equality with the OT, so that thereby a NT canon was formed, is commonly held to have come about as a reaction against Marcion after A.D. 144. Harnack was the protagonist of this view, having fought down (too vehemently, as he himself admitted) the opposing view of Zahn that the Catholic Canon was earlier. Now while it is true that Harnack's championship of Marcion (who rejected the OT) is today regarded as an aberration (for it made him into the spiritual Father of the Nazi intellectuals), his claims about Marcion's Canon are often accepted. There is a general readiness to see that the NT is 'the Church's book' and that 'the recognition of the Canon is an act of the Church', but still a heretic is allowed to be the prime mover in the affair, because Harnack held that he was. Some of Harnack's presuppositions (such as the idea that the Spirit - bearers, whether apostles, prophets or teachers, in the earliest times decided for themselves what was Scripture, 'and they could not but be obeyed') will hardly bear examination now, when the origins of the Church from a primitive welter of chaotically inspired individuals is so clearly disproved. It was, however, ideas like this which made Harnack neglect some of the evidence which was before him. Since his day there has piled up much more evidence, much of it telling against his view.

Valentinus fell into heresy at Rome about the time of Marcion's arrival there, but Valentinus did not, according to Tertullian (de praescript. haer. 38; PL 2:52), reject the Catholic NT. 'Even if Valentinus seems to make use of all our documents, he has not for all that shown less skill than Marcion in violating the truth. Marcion in open and violent fashion used a dagger rather than a pen and carved up the Scriptures to suit his theology. Valentinus showed restraint, for he excogitated his theology to fit the Scriptures rather than make the Scriptures fit his theology; and yet he suppressed more of the truth and added more to it, for he even destroyed the technical meaning of certain terms and added ideas for which there was no foundation in fact.' [1] Since the discovery of the *Gospel of Truth* (1956) it has been possible to see how right Tertullian was in his judgment, for this new-found Valentinian work combines NT phrases in such a fashion as to turn primitive Christian theology into Gnosticism, while managing to quote from most of the NT books except the Pastoral Epistles. Hebrews and Apocalypse are certainly used.

If Tertullian has been supported by recent discoveries about Valentinus, it must be with greater respect that one takes up his evidence about Marcion. Here he uses the metaphor of the tug-of-war. Marcion appeals to his own Canon, the Catholics to theirs; what is to decide except the pull of antiquity. Whose Canon is older? Marcion has one Gospel and ten epistles of Paul; the implication must be that the Catholics have more than this and were earlier in the field. How, indeed, could Marcion carve up the Scriptures (the NT must be meant, for he rejected the OT out of hand) if there was no torso to carve up? Tertullian is ready for Marcion's challenge. 'I say mine is true, Marcion his. Who or what shall decide between us except a comparison of dates allowing by prescription authority to whichever shall be found to be older?' (adv. Marc. 4:4; CSEL 47:428). Prescription in Roman law was a matter of ten years *inter praesentes*, or of twenty *inter absentes*, as here.

It is no use arguing, said Tertullian,[2] that the apostles wrote nothing but that their disciples did, for how could they be disciples if they did not inherit doctrines from their masters? It is these that Marcion should have laid hands on, either to change them or to accept them, for they have been with the Churches continuously and were 'initiated' at the same time as the Churches themselves (adv. Marc. 4:5; CSEL 47:431). His picture is one of each of the apostolic churches having so many books which it accepted as Scripture from early times. The work known as II Clement cites a gospel

1 Neque enim, si Valentinus integro instrumento uti videtur, non callidiore ingenio quam Marcion manus intulit veritati. Marcion enim exerte et palam machaera non stylo usus est, quoniam ad materiam suam caedem scripturarum confecit: Valentinus autem pepercit, quoniam non ad materiam scripturas sed materiam ad scripturas excogitavit. Et tamen plus abstulit et plus adiecit, auferens proprietates singulorum quoque verborum et adiciens dispositiones non comparentium rerum.
2 Ceterum quale est si nihil apostoli ediderunt, ut discipuli potius ediderint, qui nec discipuli existere potuissent sine ulla doctrina magistrorum? Igitur dum constet haec quoque apud ecclesias fuisse, cum ipsis ecclesiis dedicata, cur non haec quoque Marcion attigit aut emendanda . . . aut agnoscenda?

text as Scripture, but has not yet a unified concept of the Bible as having the NT alongside the OT, for it speaks of 'the Bible and the Apostles'. Lightfoot dated this work as 120–40, though Harnack put it later to fit it into *his* picture.

That the four Gospels were authenticated and put into the stream of tradition at Ephesus before the death of John the Apostle can be established with some assurance, as I have argued elsewhere (TU 73 (1957) 3–13), and the Pauline epistles are generally admitted to have been gathered into a *corpus* by the last decade of the 1st cent. (with the possible exception of the Pastorals). There thus remains the problem of what came to be called the Catholic epistles. That term is perhaps the key to the problem. Clement (*Strom.* 4:97 ; GCS 15:291) calls the letter of the Council at Jerusalem in Ac 15 'the Catholic epistle of all the Apostles' and in his commentary on the Catholic epistles (preserved in a Latin version) he calls 1 Pet and Jude *catholicas*. At an earlier date Denis of Corinth is said by Eusebius (HE 4:23) to have made himself useful to all and to have written several 'Catholic epistles'. The term thus seems to mean 'what is of general interest', or 'what is of general application'. The new papyrus of 1 and 2 Peter (P 72) has headings inserted in the margin 'about God the creator', 'about false teachers', etc., which may indicate that such letters were still in the early 3rd cent. used for the sake of their general teaching. That Apocalypse was classed with the Catholic epistles would be natural if one took account chiefly of its opening chapters with the letters to the seven churches. About its canonicity in very early times there can be no doubt ; Justin (*dial.* 81:4) and Papias are sufficient guarantee of that. If doubts developed in the East at a later time, they are the doubts of learned critics, not of the guardians of tradition. The use of the word *catholica* in the Muratori fragment (Jude and two letters of John, ' *in catholica habentur* ') may be taken as another case of the same term being applied. The two short letters of John (2 and 3 Jn) and Jude would not naturally seem to be 'of general application', and so the fragmentist has to say that they are ; he had mentioned the longer letter of John earlier in his work.

A difficulty that arises is that if Denis of Corinth can write Catholic epistles, how are these to be excluded from the Canon ? The answer comes from a consideration of the two classes of reading-matter used by the Church. The Jews had Scripture and Targum or Pesher and made a sharp distinction between the two ; Scripture 'defiled the hands', but Targum did not, and it was the practice to allow Targum to be copied in a variety of wordings (as Professor Kahle has so well shown), simply in order that it might not be put on a level with the stereotyped sacred text. That the Christians took over this classification may be argued from many signs. The opening words of the homily of Melito on the Passion speak of a διασάφησις which has followed the reading of Exodus. The Syriac and Old Latin versions of the NT seem to have the same looseness

of wording as Jewish *Targumim*, and probably for the same reason. The Muratori fragment says of Hermas that it *should be read* but not given to the public as Scripture of OT or NT. Cyril of Jerusalem in his *Catecheses* (4:35 ; PG 33:497) has the distinction explicitly. It may be suggested that the purpose of Marcion's *Antitheses*, and even of Valentinus's *Gospel of Truth*, was to act as para-Scriptural readings of the second class. The behaviour of Serapion of Antioch when he finds (HE 6:12) the church of Rhossos reading the apocryphal *Gospel of Peter* is at first to allow them to continue to use it, even while pointing out that it is not canonical, but, when he reads it himself and finds it is heretical, he forbids it at once. His first reaction must have been to remove it from class I readings and to put it in class II, to avoid disheartening the people. Given this use of two kinds of reading matter the early emergence of a Canon seems much more natural. From Qumran we now know how discursive a *Pesher* could become ; Christian second-class matter was widened to include the acts of a martyrdom or the letter of a great man like Denis or Clement of Rome.

III The modern theories which have been formulated to account for the passage from implicit to explicit in the acceptance of the Canon depend in part upon the size of the gap that is supposed to intervene between the death of the last apostle and the setting up of the explicit Canon, and in part on the manner of development of doctrine in general which the theologian is prepared to admit. Thus Lagrange, though he does not discuss this last point, seems to have had in mind a syllogistic development of doctrine whereby the major proposition (held already in the 1st cent.) that all apostolic writings are canonical Scripture (or equivalent to the OT), was able in the 2nd cent., when there was added to it the minor premiss that this or that writing was apostolic, to lead to the formation of a complete Canon. Since his day the idea of development of doctrine by syllogism has fallen into disfavour.

Recently Fr Karl Rahner has put forward a new theory. He thinks the gap in time is quite large, and though he does not want to be too precise about the dating of the death of the last apostle (and pleads for an extension of perhaps twenty years after 100 on the strength of a distinction between real and apparent death), he is prepared to bridge the gap by a claim that NT Scripture was all an expression of the nature of the Church, and that, 'the Spirit-filled Church by a connatural process comprehended as within the Canon writings which were expressive of her own nature'. The wider extension of his theory to the OT (which he takes as acceptable to the Church only as the prehistory of Christ and His redemption) shows up one of its weaknesses, for if a book (such as Esther, Job or Proverbs) had no passage where a typical sense might surely be detected, it would be hard on this theory to account for its acceptance as canonical by the Church. It would be hard to suppose that when after the Resurrection Christ expounded to the disciples (Lk 24:27, 44) 'the things that concerned Himself' in the OT, He expounded the whole text of that work.

The appeal to connatural knowledge for the expansion of doctrine is somewhat more in fashion now, but needs to be carefully handled (D 2324). When one speaks of the Church 'reflecting upon her treasures', one is either making an appeal to distinct acts of early bishops who approved this book or that as 'first-class matter', or else making use of that very difficult hypostasis, 'the mind of the Church'. (By rights, the Holy Spirit is the mind of the Church, and to appeal to a created mind involves one in the responsibility of deciding in what body this created mind inheres.) When Ignatius of Antioch (in Eusebius, HE 3:36) taught that for the safety of apostolic tradition it must be put down in writing also, he seems to have been bringing into play a motive which Fr Rahner thinks was the chief operative force in the making of the NT. It is strange, in that case, that Ignatius did not realize that the work was already done. Fr Rahner claims that by making a distinction between the basic revelation of the fact that a book is inspired and the reflex comprehension and expression of that revelation he has left room for the slow elaboration of the Canon until the time of the full conciliar statements (of Laodicea in the East and of Carthage and Innocent I in the West, D 92 and 96). He accounts for the first stage (the basic revelation) by suppressing the distinction between content and act of inspiration, so that what the primitive Church becomes conscious of as her own is at once inspired. This seems a difficult notion, which puts too much weight on the 'mind of the Church'.

An alternative theory has to say, as Fr Rahner rightly maintains, that there was a period of clarity early in the 2nd cent. about the Canon and that uncertainties began after that. He denies that there is any evidence for this early clarity and dismisses it as an *a priori* supposition. This is a pity, for the evidence given above about Apocalypse is precisely of that nature ; first an acceptance without scruple, later learned doubts, and then final agreement all round. That Hebrews went through the same process can be argued from its unquestioned acceptance as Pauline and Scriptural by Pantaenus (in Eusebius, HE 6:14), Denis of Alexandria, the Council of Antioch in 268, by Eusebius himself, and finally by its place (between Rom and 1 Cor) in the Chester-Beatty codex. Origen had heard of doubts about it in the West (perhaps from Hippolytus) and though he accepted it himself, he took these into consideration. The Western position, however, was probably a reaction against the seemingly harsh doctrine of Hebr 6:1-4 on penance, combined with some learned perplexity about the Greek translator or secretary who gave it so different a style from that usual with Paul. It contrasts sharply with the spontaneous acceptance shown in Clement of Rome, who without calling the epistle Pauline or scriptural cites it some twenty times and borrows many of its ideas.

The existence of two categories of matter for reading in church helps to make plausible the idea that primitive clarity was followed by some uncertainties, for individual bishops could promote or 'demote' a book in their own church without much check, particularly at the daily instruction. This, according to Hippolytus (*Trad. apost.* 27), was a reading and expounding of the Scriptures and was distinct from the weekly Eucharist ; second-class matter would have been much in demand for this. When the anti-Montanist (in Eusebius, HE 5:16) says that for one who has chosen to live according to the gospel it is impossible either to add to or to take away from 'the word of the New Covenant of the gospel', he shows awareness of the command in Apoc 22:18-19 (which the Montanists were disobeying by adding their prophecies to the NT) and also some understanding of the Canon as an apostolic fixture. The Muratori fragment has much the same understanding, for when it enumerates the Pauline epistles, it says of Romans that it is 'about the arranging of the Scriptures and how Christ is their main theme'. This singular opinion must be due to what is said in Rom 15, a chapter which Marcion suppressed and which is still missing in some NT MSS, but, whatever its value as a summary of Romans, it indicates a sturdy belief that it was for the Apostles to fix the Canon. Just at the beginning of the 2nd cent. the words κανών and κανονικά were coming to be used in the papyri for 'assessment' or 'tax-quota' ; when adopted by the Church for a set of books, they would have in the popular mind the connotation of 'books committed to the Church', which would be required of her 'without addition or subtraction' at the Second Coming. It is rather by patient gathering of the evidence than by rapid metaphysical theories that the mysteries of the Canon are likely to be made more acceptable.

Bibliography. Many of the earlier works have been cited by Fr Foster in CCS 11a. In addition one may name : K. Rahner SJ, *Ueber die Schriftinspiration* (Quaestiones disputatae I (1959)) ; *G. Ostborn, *Cult and Canon* (1950) on the OT mainly ; *F. Filson, *Which books belong in the Bible ?* (1957) ; J. Ruwet SJ, 'Lecture liturgique et livres saints', in Bi 21 (1940) 378-405, where, however, the place of second-class matter is not made clear ; *E. Blackman, *Marcion and his influence* (1950) ; *O. Cullmann, *La Tradition* (1953) ; *P. Kahle, *The Cairo Geniza* (1959²) ; *L. Wenger, *Canon in den Rechtsquellen* (1942) ; *H. F. D. Sparks, *The Formation of the New Testament* (1952) ; *J. Finegan, 'The original form of the Pauline collection', in HTR 49 (1956) 85-104.   J. H. C.

CANONICAL COLLECTIONS The general principles of the Church's constitution and a few isolated precepts are contained in the NT and tradition, but otherwise the Church has had to create her laws. Canon Law therefore, unlike dogma, necessarily has a history of continuous growth and change. Until 1918 there was no unified codification of law—only private or semi-official collections of laws. Since Canon Law is essentially a practical science, an out-of-date law-book is no use to an ecclesiastical judge or administrator, and so history shows us a long series of discarded compilations, terminating with Gratian (who wrote *c.* 1141) ; his work, with later supplements of papal decretals, formed the *Corpus Iuris Canonici* which was accepted universally until 1918. The centuries before Gratian are the period of the Canonical Collections.

I From the beginning until the end of the 5th cent. In the first three centuries the need for law was met more by local customs than by written decrees. With the end of the persecutions regional councils were held in Spain, Gaul and Asia Minor, at which common policies were worked out, e.g. on reconciling those who had lapsed under persecution. The first General Council was held at Nicaea in 325. The decrees of the General Councils are binding everywhere and every bishop would have a copy of them. But there were also private collections containing both general and local councils, for each bishop legislating in his own diocese would naturally be guided by the wise legislation of other regions and other times. The first collection of canons seems to have been the *Syntagma Canonum* compiled privately, probably at Antioch about 380 : in spite of a warning by Innocent I (PG 67:1588) about its orthodoxy, it seems to have been widely accepted. The decrees of these early councils were circulating in Latin translation in Italy and Spain in the 4th cent., and they form the core of nearly all subsequent collections in both East and West. By 440 there were also collections of Papal decretals, e.g. the *Canones Urbicani* and the *Epistolae Decretales*. From the 5th cent. onwards the common pattern was for each diocese or region to have its own book of canons—a miscellany of ancient councils, Papal decretals and its own local decrees—e.g. the *Statuta Ecclesiae Antiqua* in France or Italy about 450. In Rome between 496–523 Dionysius Exiguus made new accurate translations of the ancient councils and added selected decretals to form the *Dionysiana* (PL 67) which was adopted by the Roman church ; it was the first important attempt to provide western Europe with a uniform system of canon law, but it was in chronological order and unwieldy.

II From the 6th until the mid-9th cent. The *Dionysiana* was widespread with many variations, especially in Italy, but this did not prevent an abundant crop of other collections. In Africa two attempts were made to arrange canons in systematic order, by *Ferrandus* (*c.* 546—PL 67) and *Cresconius* (*c.* 600–700—PL 88). In Spain the *Hispana* or *Isidoriana* (PL 84) was compiled in chronological order about 633, possibly under the influence of Isidore of Seville. In the British Isles the *Dionysiana* was in use, and also the discipline of the *Penitentials*. The *Hibernensis*, compiled about 700 in Ireland, was arranged systematically, and was the first to supplement the canons with extracts from Scripture and the Fathers. In France Charlemagne promulgated the *Dionysiana-Hadriana*, an augmented edition of the *Dionysiana* sent to him by Pope Hadrian I. In Germany *Rabanus Maurus* compiled (*c.* 830–7) two penitentials based on the *Dionysiana* and *Hispana* (PL 110, PL 112). Between 845–52 the *False Decretals* appeared in France, the *Capitula Angilramni* (PL 96), the *Capitularia Benedicti Levitae* (PL 97) and *Pseudo-Isidore* (PL 130). See FALSE DECRETALS, INFLUENCE OF.

III From the mid-9th cent. to the Decree of Gratian. The endless variety of private collections arranged in unwieldy chronological order, like scrap-books, yields in this period to the systematic collections of the 11th cent. Reform, and culminates in the work of Gratian, which outmoded them all. In Italy there was the *Collectio Anselmo Dedicata* (*c.* 882–96) ; in Germany the collection of *Regino of Prüm* (*c.* 906) ; and later the influential Decretum of *Burchard of Worms* (*c.* 1012—PL 140), compiled in systematic order from the Dionysiana-Hadriana, Pseudo-Isidore and local decrees. The Reform as initiated in Germany was indulgent to some abuses, and the Papacy under Leo IX and Gregory VII, aiming at a rigorous suppression of the abuses of simony and a married clergy, rejected local traditions and variations : in the Gregorian collections only those canons were admitted which had been guaranteed authentic by papal approval : so *Anselm of Lucca* (*c.* 1083—PL 149), *Cardinal Deusdedit* (*c.* 1087) and *Bonizo of Sutri* (*c.* 1089). The abuses were deeply rooted and there was a vigorous reaction, particularly in the north, and under Urban II the first attempts were made to temper the strictness of the law by prudent interpretation—so *Bernold of Constance* (*c.* 1100), *Alger of Liège* (*c.* 1106 —PL 180) and *Ivo of Chartres* (*c.* 1116—PL 161). These attempts were taken up in Bologna by Gratian, who was trained in the Roman Law principles of interpretation ; he selected some 3,800 passages from the earlier collections and so arranged them systematically as to produce the first complete treatise of Canon Law—and the last of the collections—his *Concordia Discordantium Canonum*, commonly called the *Decree of Gratian* (*c.* 1141).

Bibliography. See the standard commentaries on Canon Law, particularly A. Van Hove, *Prolegomena* (1945[2]), and A. Cicognani, *Canon Law* (1949[2]) ; also B. Kurtscheid, *Historia Iuris Canonici* (1943–51) ; P. Fournier-G. Le Bras, *Histoire des collections canoniques en Occident* (1930–1) ; G. Le Bras in *Legacy of the Middle Ages* (1926) 321–61 ; *H. D. Hazeltine in *Cambridge Medieval History*, vol. 5, 697–764 ; *Report on *The Canon Law of the Church of England* (1947) 3–42 ; W. Ullmann, *The Growth of Papal Government in the Middle Ages* (1955).

D. S.

CANONISATION This article on Canonisation is necessarily a continuation of the one on BEATIFICATION, since both these acts are different stages in the cause of a saint. (I) The term ' Canonisation ' will first be explained and then its relationship to Beatification recalled. (II) An outline of the procedure of Canonisation will be given. (III) In a third section the infallibility of this act will be discussed. (IV) Finally, it will be decided who it is the Church is empowered to canonise, and following on this a general conclusion will be drawn.

I The Meaning of 'Canonisation'. There seems to be a great measure of doubt about the etymological history of the word 'Canonisation'. Its connection with the making of saints may be derived from the fact that the names of some saints were placed in the Canon of the Mass, or from the placing of the names of saints in general lists or canons (Martyrologies), or because persons were declared saints *canonice*, that is, by an act governed by the rules of the sacred canons. But whatever the doubts about the antecedents of the word, its present meaning is clear. Canonisation is a solemn and definitive act by the Pope in which it is infallibly decreed that a person is in heaven and should be given the public veneration due to the saints of God. The essential elements of this definition will be explained in the course of the article. What must be recollected here is that the process of Canonisation, as specially distinctive, is the final stage in the cause of a saint, taking place after the procedure of Beatification. The exactness of this distinction has been obvious only in comparatively recent centuries. The Church had to evolve her method for examining the sanctity of her members, and a definition of Canonisation is feasible now because this evolution has progressed beyond the less precise procedure of the periods before the 17th cent. (*See* Historical Introduction in BEATIFICATION.)

II Modern Canonisation. The final stages of the cause of a saint are almost entirely the work of the Holy See, the sole division of labour being when a diocesan tribunal investigates the miracles attributed to the *beatus*. For the Canonisation procedure to commence, it must be officially and authentically established that the person has been beatified (cf. *Codex Iuris Canonici*, canons 2136–7). Then it is required that miracles have been performed after the Beatification through the intercession of the beatified person, two miracles in the case of one who was formally beatified and three in the case of one declared a *beatus* by the 'equivalent process' of Beatification. The miracles are examined in full detail under the same rules as in the process of Beatification (cf. CIC. canons 2138–9). If these miracles are approved, the way is open for the Supreme Pontiff to sign the decree *de tuto* which states that it is safe to proceed to the solemn Canonisation of the *beatus* (cf. CIC. canon 2140), though this decree is not signed until several papal consistories have been held. After the decree all that remains to take place is the elaborate and magnificent ceremony in which the actual Canonisation of the new saint is performed by the Supreme Pontiff. The act of Canonisation is expressed in a formula which has been practically unchanged through several centuries, and as it clearly expresses the authoritative and decisive verdict of the Church in this matter, the following example of one is given, taken from

the *acta* of the Canonisation of Pope Pius X by Pope Pius XII :

'In honour of the holy and undivided Trinity, to the glory of the Catholic faith and the increase of Christian religion, by the authority of Our Lord Jesus Christ, the holy apostles Peter and Paul, and by our own authority, after mature deliberation and frequent invocation of the divine assistance, and by the counsel of our venerable brethren the Cardinals of the holy Roman Church and of the Patriarchs, archbishops and bishops resident in Rome, we inscribe in the catalogue of the saints the blessed Pius X, Pope and confessor, and we define and declare him to be a saint, appointing that his memory be devoutly kept annually on 20 August, his birthday into heaven.'[1]

Once a person has become a canonised saint not only is the honour to be paid to him or to her universally of obligation, but new saints also have a special status in the public worship of the whole Church. Churches, chapels and altars may be everywhere dedicated to them (cf. CIC. canons 1168 ; 1191 ; 1201). They may be constituted the patrons of countries, dioceses, religious institutions and other ecclesiastical organisations (cf. CIC. canon 1278). Feast days can be instituted in their honour on which will be said their Mass and Office. It is in these various ways that they receive the public veneration which, as was stated in the definition of Canonisation, is due to them because they are the saints of God.

III The Infallibility of Canonisation. In the report from a commission appointed by the Archbishop of Canterbury to discuss the question of the recognition of saints in the Anglican communion, exception is taken to the claim—'that the Church on earth can through the agency of the Pope pronounce with certainty that some particular persons belong to the second glorious category' (that is, of the saints who have already attained their goal in heaven). (*The Commemoration of Saints and Heroes of the Faith in the Anglican Communion* (1957) 10–11.) The commission is decidedly in favour of some veneration being given by their Church to those who have led lives of heroic holiness. But inevitably one must face the question as to how far one is entitled to be certain that a person is a saint, or could not there be in some instance a wholly mistaken impression about a person's sanctity ? Already it has been remarked (cf. BEATIFICATION) that there is the possibility of error in a decree of Beatification and, in consequence, it cannot be excluded that in a

[1] 'Ad honorem Sanctae et Individuae Trinitatis, ad exaltationem Fidei Catholicae et Christianae Religionis augmentum, auctoritate Domini Nostri Jesu Christi, Beatorum Apostolorum Petri et Pauli ac Nostra ; matura deliberatione praehabita et divina ope saepius implorata, ac de Venerabilium Fratrum Nostrorum, Sanctae Romanae Ecclesiae Cardinalium, Patriarcharum, Archiepiscoporum et Episcoporum in Urbe exsistentium consilio ; Beatum Pium Papam Decimum, Confessorem, Sanctum esse decernimus et definimus, ac Sanctorum catalogo adscribimus : statuentes illius memoriam quolibet anno die eius natali, vigesima nempe augusti, pia devotione recoli debere.' (AAS 46 (1954) 306.)

particular instance one could be dubious about the genuine holiness of some *beatus*. However, in regard to Canonisation, it must be said that the act is infallible and, consequently, never can there be cause for doubt about the status of the canonised saint.

The above assertion is not surprising. A person who is canonised as a saint is being placed before the whole Church as a concrete example or model of the Christian life in its highest moral perfection. In other words, the supreme teaching authority of the Church is here being officially and definitively exercised in a matter of moral doctrine—not, it is true, in the sphere of moral principle, but quite certainly in the sphere of moral instruction. From the Vatican Council it is known that in exercising a function such as this, the Pope is infallible (D 1839). Again, looking at the assertion from another angle, it could be said that if a decree of Canonisation can be completely erroneous, it would be because the canonised saint was in fact in hell. In itself this would be no more than an unfortunate mistake, if the papal decree of Canonisation were merely a tentative proposal of restricted importance. Instead, the decree vitally concerns the entire Church which is being wholly committed to a papal decision to give public honour and worship to one who is perhaps damned for eternity in hell. Such a situation could reasonably be described as one where the gates of hell have prevailed, contrary to the promise of the divine founder of the Church (cf. Mt 16:18). To rule out such a possibility, it would seem necessary to claim that the act of Canonisation is infallible.

To decide conclusively whether a decree of Canonisation is infallible, one must examine how the Pope expresses himself in that decree. Given the infallibility of the Supreme Pontiff, for this prerogative to be of practical value he must know when he has to speak infallibly and so express himself that this may be apparent in his pronouncement. Inspection of the formula used by the Popes in canonising (cited in §II) makes it quite evident that an infallible decision is being given. The formula is couched in terms indicating the plenitude of authority; it expresses the definitive nature of the decree in respect of the sanctity of the new saint; it indicates that the decree is being imposed on the whole Church. The conjunction of these characteristics shows that the Pope is speaking infallibly, hence the insertion in the definition of Canonisation that it is 'an act . . . whereby it is infallibly decreed that a person is in heaven'. But it must be noted that this conclusion is not defined teaching. Rather should it be described as a doctrine which is theologically certain (cf. H. Dieckmann SJ, *De Ecclesia*, II (1925) section 852).

Accepting, then, that a decree of Canonisation is infallible, it must next be decided whether everything contained in the decree is covered by this infallibility. Usually, as published, it contains not merely the formula of Canonisation, but also the life of the saint and an account of the miracles

examined in the cause (cf. AAS. 43 (1951) 413–26—the decree of Canonisation of St Mary Ann of Jesus). The answer to this is that infallibility is found solely in what is defined by the Pope, namely, that the person whose cause has been considered possessed heroic holiness; is, therefore, in heaven as a saint; and has to be honoured as such. No more than this is defined; no more than this is covered by infallibility, which protects only what is defined. Therefore it does not extend over the historical incidents related about the life of the saint. Nor does it operate to guarantee the miracles used in the process of Canonisation, although owing to the care with which these are examined little doubt can be raised about their genuineness. Thus it is that in the approach to the formal judgment of Canonisation the Church uses fallible though reliable means, and then, when these are favourable, with the assistance of the Holy Spirit the Supreme Pontiff makes his infallible decision (cf. C. Pesch SJ, *Praelectiones Dogmaticae*, I; ed. 5 (1915) section 552). Consequently, one cannot exclude the possibility of incidental error in the general data of a process, a possibility which is confirmed by strong evidence of confusion in the details of the cause of St John Nepomucene who was canonised in 1729. Instead of dying in 1383 as a martyr for the seal of confession as was claimed, it seems that in fact he died in 1393 in defence of the rights of the Church in connection with the appointment of an abbot to a religious house, though the confessional issue may have some part in the story. One might experience dissatisfaction at discovering such discrepancies, but it cannot be said that thereby the decree of Canonisation is substantially rendered inaccurate (cf. T. Zapelena SJ, *De Ecclesia Christi*, II; ed. 2 (1954) 249–52).

A final point to add is that when a Canonisation has taken place, it must be accepted by all the faithful. Their motive for accepting it is the infallible teaching authority of the Pope and not the details of the life and miracles of the saint which may be contained in the decree. Therefore, the assent of the faithful is an act of faith, but not an act of divine faith, since nowhere is it in any way revealed that a canonized saint must be considered to be in heaven.

IV The Act of Canonisation as a Papal Prerogative. It was pointed out when discussing Beatification that the causes of saints are now reserved to the Holy See. But in the case of Beatification, which is not an infallible act, there is no intrinsic reason why it should not be performed by individual bishops, as often did happen in the past. With the further stage of Canonisation, as defined above, it is not merely the extrinsic factor of the reservation of the causes of saints to the Holy See which has to be borne in mind, but also the intrinsic element of its infallibility. Infallible acts proceed from two sources in the Church—from the Pope or from a General Council. Consequently, from these two sources alone can be expected decrees of Canonisation. Of these two, only the Pope now canonises, although in the past councils of the Church have dealt with the causes of saints. This is because the matter is reserved to the Holy See, under which name the General Council is not included (cf. CIC canon 7). For these reasons, then, one must assert that Canonisation is a prerogative of the Supreme Pontiff.

It is because of this assertion that the problem of non-papal Canonisations arises from the history of the causes of saints. It has two aspects, of which the first is to decide whether in the past lesser authorities in the Church, such as individual bishops, have in fact canonised. The second aspect of the problem is whether the Pope could delegate to another ecclesiastic the power to canonise. A negative answer to the first would not exclude the possibility of the second happening ; but if one is compelled to reject the second, then it follows that individual bishops have never canonized saints. It is current Protestant opinion both that bishops on their own authority did canonise and that the Pope could delegate to others the power to canonize.[1] What must immediately be pointed out about this view is that it does not cite any cases of non-papal Canonisation after the 13th cent.

The solution of this problem must be derived from our present knowledge of the nature of Canonisation, a knowledge which was certainly lacking in the centuries previous to the 17th cent. In other words, the practices of the past must be interpreted according to the more exact knowledge of the present and not by the obscurity of earlier imprecise notions and terminology. Such must be the rule of interpretation wherever there is organic development of practice and doctrine. For instance, from a later and more exact knowledge of sacramental theology it can be said that the liturgical rite of the washing of the feet on Maundy Thursday was never a source of grace *ex opere operato*, although the rite was once thought by some to be a sacrament. Similarly, then, as Canonisation must be an infallible act, it can be performed only by the Pope or by a General Council held under the presidency of the Pope. In no way could the Pope delegate to other prelates the authority to canonise because, apart from the functioning of a General Council under the Pope, an act involving infallibility of its nature must be restricted to the very person of the one who possesses the plenitude of authority in the Church, namely, the Supreme Pontiff. Just as he cannot delegate to another the plenitude of his authority, neither can the Pope delegate to another the power to make an infallible decision. Canonisation, therefore, in the sense in which it has been defined, cannot ever have been performed by other ecclesiastics, except in General Council, whether they might be considered as using their own powers or as acting by a delegated authority.

What then of the historical evidence that bishops

[1] That bishops have canonized is claimed by E. W. Kemp in his *Canonization and Authority in the Western Church*, 55 ; 79–81 ; 169–70. The same view is expressed in the report of the commission set up by the Archbishop of Canterbury, 19 ; 72. Papal delegation to canonize is instanced by Kemp, *op. cit.* 67–8, 95, 163–7.

have canonised saints ? The answer is that it has yet to be proved that the title ' saint ' and the term ' Canonisation ' have always meant in the past exactly what they mean in recent centuries. Sufficiently has it been stressed that it was not until well after the Middle Ages that clear distinctions came to be made between the *beatus* and the saint, between Beatification and Canonisation. Consequently, from our present knowledge it must be categorically stated that if in the past bishops formally declared persons to be saints, they could have done no more than what is done in modern Beatification. Even when the words ' Canonisation ' and ' saint ' are used of papal acts in these earlier centuries, one cannot be certain that they must always mean more than what is understood by a modern Beatification. If instances can be given of episcopal action connected with a real Canonisation, then this action would have to be interpreted as a preliminary procedure to a papal decision, or as a promulgation of a papal decision, or, in the last resort, as a futile attempt on the part of a bishop to do what was beyond his power. As was stated in the definition of Canonization, it is an act performed by the Pope.

Concluding this study of Canonisation, it should be remarked that it is an act of the Church on earth which has a special link with the Church Triumphant in heaven. The elaborate juridical procedure which must take its protracted course before a saint is canonized is directed to establishing more firmly a vital relationship within the Communion of Saints. However, it should be evident from what has been said that a decree of Canonisation is not a decision from the Holy See whereby a person is transferred from the pain of Purgatory to the glory of Heaven, as though the Church controlled the actual passage of souls from the one place to the other. Rather is Canonization a declaration of what has already happened within the Communion of Saints, namely, that God has welcomed one of his heroic servants into the Kingdom of Heaven and, in consequence, it is decreed for the Church on earth that this person must be given the veneration due to the saints of God.

Bibliography. Apart from the literature referred to in the article on Beatification and in the course of the present article, the following should be noted : T. Ortolan, ' Canonisation dans l'Église romaine ', DTC 2 (1905) 1626–59 ; J. Bois, ' Canonisation dans l'Église russe ', *op. cit.* 1659–72 ; P. Séjourné, ' Saints (Culte des) ', DTC 14 (1939) 870–978 ; H. Leclercq, ' Saint ', DAC 15 (1950) ; L. Hertling, ' Canonisation ', *Dictionnaire de spiritualité*, II (1953) 77 85 ; A. Crnica OFM, ' De canonizatione aequipollenti ', in *Monitor Ecclesiasticus* 2 (1961) 268–80.

D. F.

CAPHARNAITES This term is used for those who took a carnal view of the Eucharist, but it can be, and was, variously applied according as one looks on this or that view as carnal. In English the word has been traced to Ridley, who in 1549 claimed that ' they who teach transsubstantiation are right sacramentaries and Capharnaites '. This was simply theological abuse, and the normal use of the term would be to designate those whose eucharistic theology approximated to the ideas of the people of Capharnaum, who in Jn 6:52, after hearing Our Lord's discourse on His flesh and blood, took His words in too literal a way, implying cannibalism on the part of the recipients of the ' meat and drink ' which He offered. When Augustine was developing the doctrine of signs (de doctrina christiana 3:9 ; PL 34:71) he said, ' The Lord Himself and apostolic teaching have handed on certain signs, easy to produce, most sublime in meaning and most holy to use, such as the sacred sign of baptism and the frequenting of the Body and Blood of the Lord. Each one who receives these knows—if he be baptized—what their import is, and he venerates them not with the slavery of the flesh but rather with the freedom of the spirit.' [1] The slavery of the flesh did not mean for Augustine all theories of the Eucharist which involved the bodily presence of Christ in the sacrament (for in de baptismo contra Donatistas 5:8 ; CSEL 51:270, he clearly says that the unworthy receive Christ in the Eucharist) but in an age when food-offerings were commonly set out by pagans for their dead and when the Manichees had a very carnal idea of the presence of Mani at their annual Bema-festival, the danger of Christians holding a cannibalistic view of the Eucharist was not remote. Calumnies on this subject had been current in the early days of the Church, and they most probably originated in the tales told to the government authorities (such as Pliny) by apostates. The imposition of a rule of secrecy (Disciplina arcani) by the Church in the 3rd and 4th cents. checked these tales, for by it no candidate for baptism was instructed about the Eucharist until (after his baptism) he heard the Easter-week catecheses.

In the 9th cent. Charles the Bald put to Ratramnus the question, whether what the faithful at church receive in their mouths is made the Body and Blood of Christ in a mystery or in truth, i.e. whether it holds some secret element which is perceived by the eyes of faith alone, or whether without any cloak of secrecy the bodily eye sees from without the same thing that the mental vision perceives within.[2] The reply of Ratramnus (see RATRAMNUS) gave a subtle answer to a subtle question and generated great confusion throughout the Middle Ages, his speculations being guided by the pseudo-Augustine categoriae (PL 32:1439, which he cites in his reply, 13), a Latin adaptation of Aristotle which did not fit in

with the speculations of Augustine himself on body and spirit, which were Neo-platonic. Trent (D 874) put an end to these disputes by declaring that the sacramental presence of the bodily substance of Christ was a manner of existence which could scarcely be put into words but that the mind enlightened by faith could and should believe that it was possible to God.

A consequence of Capharnaitic views was the belief that there was in the Eucharist a substance which the human body of the recipient broke down in the ordinary process of metabolism. The Armenians (D 546) are apparently guilty of holding such erroneous views, for they were made to renounce them on reunion. The term Stercoranistae was used by Cardinal Humbert in 1054 to designate similar views of Nicetas Pectoratus, and it was often used in the East-West debate of those times. Not that all the supporters of such theories were to be found in the East ; Rabanus Maurus in a letter to Heribald (MGH Epistulae V, 513) seems to have begun this line of speculation by propounding the question why a special miracle should be postulated to safeguard the eucharistic species from ordinary metabolism.[3] The question did not arise for earlier theologians since, according to the biology of the time, it was considered that the nobler and purer foodstuffs did not leave any residue in the body (cf. Chrysostom, PG 49:345). Paschasius Radbertus (PL 120:1331) dismissed the whole debate as frivolous, and it is clear that it arose from somewhat Capharnaitic views of the Eucharist. St Thomas (Summa 3a:77:6) gives what may be considered to be the normal medieval view of such discussions. **Bibliography.** Alban Langdale, Catholica confutatio D. Ridley (1556) ; St John Fisher, De veritate Corporis Domini (1527) ; Ratramnus, critical edition of his De corpore et sanguine Domini by J. Bakhuizen van den Brink (1954) ; A. Landgraf, Dogmengeschichte der Frühscholastik III. 2, 207–22, ' Quid sumit mus ? ' ; J. Geiselmann, Die Eucharistielehre der Vorscholastik (1926). There is no good work in English on this matter.   J. H. C.

CARDINALS, COLLEGE OF

CARDINALS, COLLEGE OF The cardinals of the Holy Roman Church constitute, as their name implies, the official clergy of the church and city of Rome. The word ' cardinal ' derived from the Latin cardo, a hinge, signifies a cleric who is permanently incardinated in the ranks of the ministers of a given church. It was formerly used in various parts of the world, and there are still two cardinal minor canons at St Paul's Cathedral, London. There is mention of cardinals in the Acts of the synod said to have been held at Rome by St Sylvester in 324, but really dating from about 500, or perhaps somewhat earlier.

Like every other local or ' particular ' church, the Apostolic See of Rome had its complement of bishop, deacons and priests, the latter forming the

---

[1] Signa . . . factu facillima et intellectu augustissima et observatione castissima ipse Dominus et apostolica tradidit disciplina ; sicuti est baptismi sacramentum et celebratio Corporis et Sanguinis Domini. Quae unusquisque cum percipit, quo referantur imbutus agnoscit, ut ea non carnali servitute sed spirituali potius libertate veneretur.

[2] Quod in ecclesia ore fidelium sumitur, corpus et sanguis Christi in mysterio fiat an in veritate ; id est, utrum aliquid secreti contineat quod oculis fidei solummodo pateat an sine cuiuscunque velatione mysterii hoc aspectus intueatur corporis exterius quod mentis visus inspiciat interius ?

[3] Quae est ratio ut hoc quod stomacho digeritur et in secessum emittitur iterum in statum pristinum redeat, cum nullus hoc unquam fieri asseruerit ?

senate of the chief pastor. For administrative purposes Rome was divided by St Fabian in 238 into seven regions, each of which was served by one of the seven deacons instituted in 101 by St Evarist. Seven other sub-deacons were entrusted with the compilation of the acts of the martyrs, and eventually each had his own church, so that there were fourteen deaconries.

The presbyteral titles, originally twenty-five in number (though the same one might be held by more than one cardinal), were definitely limited by Sixtus V to fifty in 1586. The present pope, John XXIII, has, however, increased the number. They were originally the parish churches of the city and the cardinals were the parish priests. Finally the bishops of the seven dioceses immediately surrounding Rome, the suburbicarian sees, were called in, in a way in which suffragan bishops of a metropolitan see would not have been, to help in the administration of the ecclesiastical affairs of the capital of the Empire. They were also required to take it in turn to act as *hebdomadarii* in the services at the patriarchal basilica of St John Lateran, just as the cardinal priests did in the other patriarchal basilicas. They were almost what we should call *auxiliary* bishops in the see of Rome.

A cathedral chapter, or 'presbytery', which forms the bishop's 'crown' seated around his throne in the centre of the church's apse, has three principal functions : the advising of the bishop in his administration ; the carrying on of his government in his absence or after his death ; and the choosing of his successor. All these functions are performed by the College of Cardinals, whom Dante compares to the oarsmen in the bark of Peter. They give the pope their counsel in the consistories (D 387), and, since the time of Sixtus V, they preside over the various Congregations, which govern the Church ; they *supply* for the pope in his absence (as they did for St Martin during his captivity in 653), or after his death, though they do not *succeed* to his prerogatives ; finally they elect his successor. The pope was originally elected by the clergy and people of Rome, later on by the principal clerics and, since 1179, by the cardinals alone. They do not confer jurisdiction on the man they choose, for that comes directly from God, and, once their choice is made, no one can annul it. Wyclif's challenge to this manner of election was condemned (D 620).

As things are today, with cardinals appointed from nearly every country, it may be said that the pope is elected by representatives of the whole Catholic world. Cardinals are styled Princes of the Church and take precedence over all other prelates. The development of their external dignity is studied by Fr Thurston in the article cited below.

Bibliography. M. Andrieu, 'L'Origine du titre de cardinal', *Miscellanea Mercati* 5 (*Studi e Testi*, vol. 125 (1946) 113–44) ; S. Kuttner, *Cardinalis*, the origin of a canonical concept, in *Traditio* 3 (1945) 129–214 ; H. Thurston sj, 'The Cardinal's Hat and its History', in MN 119 (1912) 1–16 ; J. B.

Sägmuller, 'Zur Tätigkeit und Stellung der Kardinale bis Bonifaz VIII', in TQ 80 (1898) 596–608 ; 83 (1901) 45–60 ; 88 (1906) 595–609.   R. P.

CASUISTRY The method of solving problems of right and wrong in human conduct by the systematic application of ethical or moral principles to concrete cases is known as casuistry. It will be dealt with here (I) in its theological usage. This requires (II) a brief historical summary and (III) a consideration of its relevance to contemporary Catholic Moral Theology.

I As a specific method, casuistry is a dialectic process for determining, in a concrete situation, one's moral liberty or obligation regarding a particular act, as well as the guilt, or freedom from guilt, to be attached to the deliberate performance or omission of that act. Its norms are drawn from the natural ethical law, from positive divine precepts contained in Sacred Scripture and Tradition, from the canons and decisions of the Church, as well as from the opinions of approved theologians. Casuistry in the theological sense should not be confused with the popular notion of equivocation or specious reasoning. Since it is the systematic use of a reasoning process in search of right decisions in the realm of moral conduct, casuistry is to be distinguished from the virtue of prudence, although it cannot be practised safely without that virtue. It is rather a method of forming the conscience beforehand, or of solving cases of conscience after the performance or omission of particular acts. Although it is used to solve problems in canon law, liturgy, the administration of the sacraments, spiritual counselling and asceticism, many moral theologians maintain that the term casuistry should be reserved strictly for the discussion of cases of freedom or obligation in moral conduct.

II The history of Casuistry. Strictly speaking, both the name 'casuistry' and the process of solving problems according to the 'case method' come into prominence in Moral Theology only in the 16th cent. Though not characteristic of the OT Hebrew religion, a very detailed casuistry developed in the Rabbinical schools as it is reflected in the Mishna and the Talmud. It is employed by Christ in dealing with the Pharisees (Mt 12:9–14 ; Mk 10:2–12) although its abuse (Pharisaism) is explicitly condemned (Mk 7:1–13). Instances of casuistic argumentation are found in St Paul's epistles (e.g. Rom 13–14 ; 1 Cor 12 ; Phm) and in St Peter (1 Pet 2:11–25) although they are always associated with a kerygmatic or hortatory element. It is in this latter form that casuistic reasoning is found in the early Patristic writings, though with Tertullian and Cyprian in the West, and Clement of Alexandria and Origen in the East, explicit treatises are devoted to discussing the principles of divine and natural law that bear on the Christian's conduct in regard, for example, to attending the *Spectacles* and the *Adornment of Women* (Tert), the *Salvation of a Rich Man* and the elements of *Christian Perfection* (Clement of Alexandria). St Ambrose makes the first explicit attempt to Christianize the stoic ethical procedures in his adaptation of Cicero's *De officiis* as a textbook for his priests. St Augustine lays the true foundations for the development of a casuistic Moral Theology.

Meanwhile the discipline of penance, the first monastic rules, and the development of ecclesiastical laws provide further elements for a casuistic treatment of moral problems. During the pre-scholastic period, along with much copying and collating of the Fathers, various collections of Canons as well as the Penitential Books originating in England and Ireland (6th to 9th cents.) stimulated the systematic application of rational norms to the solution of practical cases of conscience arising out of conflicting principles and regulations. With St Anselm (d. 1109), the Aristotelian dialectic becomes a recognized tool in dealing with moral as well as doctrinal difficulties. Hugh of St Victor (d. 1141), Abelard (d. 1142), and particularly, Peter Lombard (d. *c.* 1160) in his *Sententiae*, devote specific sections of their Scripture Commentaries to the treatment of moral problems. With St Thomas Aquinas and St Albert the Great stress is laid on the metaphysical, objective and intellectual aspect of moral obligations (God's being and the nature of things as the norms for good and evil) ; with St Bonaventure, Duns Scotus and Henry of Ghent, the direction is more towards the affective, voluntaristic aspects (the will of God, and man's intention). Though illustrated with frequent casuistic examples, their writings are still speculative theological treatises in the framework of Scripture Commentaries.

The explicit rise of casuistic doctrine and practice is to be found in the contemporary writings known as the *Summae de poenitentia*, beginning with Robert of Flamesbury's *Poenitentiale* (*c.* 1210) and the *Summa de poenitentia et matrimonio* of St Raymond of Peñafort (d. *c.* 1275). The spread of Nominalism (William of Occam, Gabriel Biel) introduced a rapid decline in practical as well as speculative theology despite the abundant production of casuistic, moral treatises such as the *Summa moralis theologiae* of St Antoninus (1389–1459), who was the first true casuist in the modern theological sense. His *Summa* is a systematic body of moral teachings in which he applies speculative principles to concrete social and economic elements of daily life.

The golden age of casuistic practice begins with the Council of Trent (1545–63). It runs on to the decadence of the 17th cent. The period sparkles with great names from De Vitoria, Melchior Cano, and Cardinal Cajetan to Bañez, Bonacina and Suarez. The final decadence is brought about by moralists who gradually abandon speculative principles for legalistic norms and truisms in dealing with every conceivable kind of practical case. It is brought up short by the great debate over the use of probabilism to form one's conscience and to solve casuistic difficulties. Pascal in his *Lettres provinciales* dramatically features the Jesuits as alleged exponents of a laxist morality based on sheer casuistry. The Jansenist controversy serves further to discredit the casuistic method in treating problems of conscience. Balance is restored to Catholic Moral Theology mainly through the efforts of St Alphonsus Liguori (1696–1787) (*see* ALPHONSUS, INFLUENCE OF). In many of his writings, and particularly in his major work on moral theology, Alphonsus applies the casuistic method to the whole field of human conduct. He justifies the use of casuistry as necessary to equip moralists and confessors with the practical knowledge, the sensitive perception, and the appropriate technique requisite in handling the complex problems that arise in every aspect of human life.

In the 19th cent. the controversy over the use of casuistic methods continued. Alongside the production of almost countless manuals of Moral Theology based on the casuistic system, a number of German theologians in particular tended to move away from the method. Characteristic of a similar effort today are the Moral Theologies of F. Tillmann (*Handbuch der katholischen Sittenlehre*, III[2], 'Die Idee der Nachfolge Christi' (1939) and IV, 1 and 2 (1935–6)), and J. Leclercq (*L'Enseignement de la morale chrétienne* (1949)).

III Two contemporary schools of thought divide Catholic Moral Theologians generally. One decries the use of the casuistic method as necessarily conducive to a 'minimal morality', that is, an ethos in which principal consideration is given to drawing the line between what is licit and what is forbidden in human conduct under the aegis of divine and human law. Casuistry, they say, has become once more the instrument of a sterile legalism or a practical laxism wherein attention is turned from the love of God and concentrated on the avoidance of sin. These critics advocate a Moral Theology concerned primarily with the attainment of personal holiness. They deny the utility of discussing a multitude of cases in the formation of a confessor or a moralist. They insist upon the sufficiency of the virtue of prudence in guiding properly formed Christian consciences towards the solution of moral problems no matter what their complexity.

The supporters of the casuistic method, on the other hand, consider these critics as unrealistic. They accuse them of underestimating the complexities to be met with in most moral problems. They attribute the abuses connected with the use of casuistic methods to causes that have no necessary connection with casuistry ; but that arise rather from a de-orientation of moral and ascetical ideals. They insist equally on the love of God as the only true motivation for a Christian's conduct ; nor can they see how the employment of casuistry in itself deviates from such motivation. Only by giving the Christian a clear notion of what is right and wrong in particular instances, they maintain, can he be guided to the realization of his ideals in striving for the love of God. Such precision requires an adequate familiarity with the casuistic method on the part of confessors and moralists.

These concerns have been given particular pertinence by the current discussion of 'Situation Ethics'

—a movement in which such stress is placed upon the subjective reaction to the circumstances involved in an ethical obligation as to eliminate, for all practical purposes, the objective principles of morality, and all thought of the employment of casuistry. Full reliance, instead, is placed on the rightness of one's personal reaction to an ethical problem.

The dangers envisaged by each group of Catholic Moralists are real. The solution would seem to lie in giving due stress to what is valuable in each position. What is essential is an integrated training in the exercise of the virtue of prudence through the medium of a well-ordered casuistry. Only thus will the Christian faced with the complexities of modern living be able to accommodate his thoughts and actions to the striving for holiness that is his vocation in keeping with the law and the love of God.

Bibliography. GENERAL : E. Dublanchy, 'Casuistique', in DTC 2 (1909) 1859–77; J. Klein, 'Kasuistik', in *Religion in Geschichte und Gegenwart* III³ (1959) 1166–77. For the HISTORY : L. Vereeke's survey in B. Häring, *La Loi du Christ* I (Fr. transl. of *Das Gesetz Christi* (1958)). On the problem today : M. Labourdette, 'Theologie Morale', in RT 58 (1950) 215–30 ; F. Clark, 'The Challenge to Moral Theology', CR 38 (1953) 214–23 ; J. Ford and G. Kelly, *Contemporary Moral Theology* (1959).

F. X. M.